Bob Swart, Ma
Paul Gustavso
Jarrod Hollingworth

Borland C++Builder 6 Developer's Guide

SAMS

201 West 103rd Street, Indianapolis, Indiana 46290

Borland C++Builder 6 Developer's Guide

International Standard Book Number: 0-672-32480-6

Library of Congress Catalog Card Number: 2002109779

Printed in the United States of America

First Printing: December 2002

05   04   03   4   3   2

Trademarks

Warning and Disclaimer

Associate Publisher
Michael Stephens

Acquisitions Editor
Carol Ackerman

Development Editor
Songlin Qiu

Managing Editor
Charlotte Clapp

Project Editor
Matthew Purcell

Copy Editor
Chip Gardner

Indexer
Erika Millen

Proofreaders
Leslie Joseph
Suzanne Thomas

Technical Editor
Paul Qualls

Team Coordinator
Lynne Williams

Multimedia Developer
Dan Scherf

Interior Designer
Gary Adair

Cover Designer
Alan Clements

Page Layout
Juli Cook

Graphics
Steve Adams
Tammy Graham
Oliver Jackson
Laura Robbins

Contents at a Glance

Table of Contents

About the Author

Jarrod Hollingworth

Jarrod has been professionally programming since 1993. He is now running his own business, Backslash (http://www.backslash.com.au), developing software applications for the Internet and key business sectors and working as a software development consultant. He has a solid background in C/C++ programming in the telecommunications industry and assisted in the development of the world's first live operator–answered GSM (digital mobile) short-messaging system.

Starting in 1985 as a self-taught hobbyist programmer in BASIC and Assembly, he moved to Pascal and C/C++ through completion of a bachelor of science degree in computing at Deakin University in Australia. His professional roles in software development have ranged from programmer to software department manager.

With several years of experience in C++Builder and Delphi and having worked on project teams using Microsoft Visual C++, he believes that with few exceptions C++Builder is the best tool for developing Windows applications.

Jarrod lives in Melbourne, Australia, with his wife, Linda. His other major interests include traveling and cycling. Jarrod can be contacted at jarrod@backslash.com.au.

Bob Swart

Bob Swart (also known as "Dr.Bob"—http://www.drbob42.com) is author, trainer, consultant, and webmaster for his own company Bob Swart Training & Consultancy (eBob42) in Helmond, The Netherlands. Bob is a technical author for *The Delphi Magazine, Harcore Delphi, C++Builder Developer's Journal, Der Entwickler, SDGN Magazine, UK-BUG Developer's Magazine,* has written for the Web sites of DevX, TechRepublic/CNET, the IBM and Borland protal, and has spoken at (Borland) conferences all over the world since 1994. Bob is coauthor of *The Revolutionary Guide to Delphi 2, Delphi 4 Unleashed, C++Builder 4 Unleashed, C++Builder 5 Developer's Guide, Kylix Developer's Guide,* and *Delphi 6 Developer's Guide.*

Bob is married to Yvonne and they have two internet-aware children: Erik Mark Pascal (8.5 years) and Natasha Louise Delphine (6 years).

Mark Cashman

Mark Cashman is a Senior Architect for Hartford Technology Services Company, from which he provides consulting on strategic and tactical architecture for a variety of application and technical areas at The Hartford. He has previously served in a variety of roles, including Manager of Information Systems, and Director of Software Development, and has worked for firms in manufacturing, software development, distribution, and financial services. He is also a long-standing member of Borland's TeamB for C++Builder, and has written extensively on C++ and C++ Builder. He maintains a Web site at http://www.temporaldoorway.com for his efforts in digital art, writing, music and programming advice (including C++ Builder), and a second Web site at http://www.newenglandtrailreview.com to indulge his love of the outdoors.

Paul Gustavson

Paul has over 14 years of computer engineering experience supporting a wide variety of modeling and simulation, software development, and Web technology efforts. Paul is a co-founder of SimVentions, Inc, a software development company that develops and leverages existing technologies and techniques to create innovative applications and solutions. He has written and presented numerous publications on simulation interoperability, is a contributing author of the "C++Builder 5 Developer's Guide," and the technical editor for "SAMS Teach Yourself UML (2nd Edition)." Paul is also the chief architect for PhotoVisor, a multimedia slide show creation tool, and XML SkinGen, a developer's tool for creating skin-able Delphi and C++Builder apps. Paul lives in Virginia with his wife and two boys.

Dedication

Jarrod Hollingworth
I dedicate this book to my wife, Linda.

Bob Swart
For Yvonne, Erik, and Natasha.

Mark Cashman
My efforts in this book are dedicated to my friends on TeamB and around the world in the Borland newsgroups, who have helped me learn enough to be ready to contribute to books like this. And, of course, to my wife, daughter, and other friends, who have put up with the nights taken from them to work on it.

Paul Gustavson
I'd like to dedicate this book to those that have shown their dedication and commitment to me while I've squirreled away on this book. To my wife Barbara, my two boys Michael and Ryan, my Mom and Dad, and to the God of all creation whose mercies are never ending.

Acknowledgments

Jarrod Hollingworth

This book has opened my eyes to the fact that the publishing process is very involved indeed. As the acquisitions editor, Carol Ackerman took the book onboard and managed the manuscript submissions and the overall schedule. Songlin Qiu was the development editor for this book. Her eagle eye for quality and content-related issues ensured that the book as a whole is more than the sum of its parts. It was a pleasure working with both Carol and Songlin. I'd also like to thank technical editor Paul Qualls for his attention to detail, copy editor Chip Gardner (who, with his superior knowledge of English, improved the grammar in just about every paragraph), project editor Matt Purcell, and all other staff at Sams.

Finally I'd like to thank each and every author in this book, but in particular Bob Swart and Paul Gustavson, who showed exceptional commitment and enthusiasm. With such a large breadth of experience, each author has donated a piece of his knowledge to make this book an invaluable resource for C++Builder developers.

Bob Swart

I need to thank Yvonne for putting up with me writing yet another set of chapters. The phrase "almost done" has lost all meaning to her.

Mark Cashman

My thanks go to my editors, my technical editor, and my copy editor at Sams, all of whom have worked hard to make this an excellent book and who have been very kind to me during the process.

Paul Gustavson

There are so many people to thank for their efforts in helping make this book possible. Let me start off on the home front. If it was not for the love and encouragement demonstrated by my wife, Barbara, this past year through my knee surgery, various work efforts, and the book writing, I'd be limping through life. As proud as you are of me for what I've done Barb, it is nothing compared to what you've done for me and the boys. I cherish you! To my two boys Michael and Ryan who give me such joy and pleasure. Whether it's playing PlayStation, throwing a baseball, or wrestling on the floor with the dog, you guys know how to keep me real. To my Mom and Dad and everyone else in my family (Don, Peggie, Kurt, Kathy, Angi, Jim) who have prayed for me while I've burned the candle at both ends. It's your prayers that have sustained me. To my business partners Larry and Steve, who have never let our dreams die. Thanks for keeping it alive guys, here's to 2003! To those I work with at ACS Defense (formerly known as Synetics) who have encouraged and backed me on this project. That includes you George, Nick, Buddy, Mike, Brian, Jane, Steve, and Neal (and anyone else I missed). You guys are a joy to work with. Special thanks to my co-authors: Dr. Bob, Mark, and Jarrod. It's been a real privilege to have worked with you guys in putting together such a great book. Let's hook up at the next BorCon. To the folks at Borland who have provided me their guidance: Mark Edington, Trevor Strudley, Rebecca Martinez, "JT" Thomas, and John Kaster. It's you guys that have created something that we enjoy writing about. Special big thanks to the crew at SAMs who made all this possible: Carol Ackerman, Songlin Qiu, Matt Purcell, Chip Gardner, Paul Qualls. Without you guys, where would we be? Finally, I'd like to give my thanks to God who never gives up on me and gives me strength. Despite my busyness and forgetfulness, Lord, thank you for never being too busy or forgetting me!

We Want to Hear from You!

As the reader of this book, *you* are our most important critic and commentator. We value your opinion and want to know what we're doing right, what we could do better, what areas you'd like to see us publish in, and any other words of wisdom you're willing to pass our way.

As an associate publisher for Sams, I welcome your comments. You can email or write me directly to let me know what you did or didn't like about this book—as well as what we can do to make our books better.

Please note that I cannot help you with technical problems related to the *topic* of this book. We do have a User Services group, however, where I will forward specific technical questions related to the book.

When you write, please be sure to include this book's title and author as well as your name, email address, and phone number. I will carefully review your comments and share them with the author and editors who worked on the book.

Email: feedback@samspublishing.com

Mail: Michael Stephens
             Sams Publishing
             201 West 103rd Street
             Indianapolis, IN 46290 USA

For more information about this book or another Sams title, visit our Web site at www.samspublishing.com. Type the ISBN (excluding hyphens) or the title of a book in the Search field to find the page you're looking for.

Introduction

Welcome to *Borland C++Builder 6 Developer's Guide*. Our goal for this book was to put forth the most informative and practical reference on C++Builder to date. Building on the success of *C++Builder 5 Developer's Guide*, we have concentrated on the essential elements and capabilities of C++Builder, including the very latest features provided by C++Builder 6.

Topics in this edition include fresh material on XML, SOAP, the Windows API, COM, DLLs, VCL, CLX component development, database development, plus much more including a look at mobile application development. We've gone to great lengths to provide practical examples and discussions to common issues, and explore topics not previously covered. As you read through this book, we encourage you to leverage the concepts and techniques that are presented. Our hope is that you'll find the material to be an invaluable guide in helping you build and deploy cutting-edge C++Builder applications.

Who Should Read This Book?

This book is intended for current and potential users of C++Builder. What you hold in your hand is designed to help expand your current C++Builder skills. It is not a C++ primer, nor a tutorial in helping you navigate within the C++Builder environment. Rather, it's a guide to help developers in the following ways:

- Maximize use and knowledge of C++Builder and related technologies.

- Examine the latest features provided in C++Builder 6.

- Facilitate the development of efficient and robust software such as components, cross-platform applications, and distributed client/server environments.

If you already have experience developing applications with C++Builder, are looking to upgrade to version 6, or simply want to build on your current knowledge, this book will provide an excellent reference. Although this book will largely draw the interest of intermediate and advanced users, the organization is laid out so there is a natural progression through most of the chapters and through the book as a whole allowing it to be also useful to C++Builder neophytes.

How This Book Is Organized

This book is organized into several parts and is arranged to accommodate the wide breadth of topics that are considered essential for mastering C++Builder development:

- **Part I: "C++Builder Essentials"**—This part, consisting of Chapters 1–5, contains everything you need to know to make the best use of C++Builder when developing applications. It starts with an introduction to C++Builder, and its Integrated Development Environment (IDE). It then covers best practices in programming with C++Builder. Finally, it moves on to the advanced topics of creating custom components, their editors and their property editors.

- **Part II: "Database Programming"**—Chapters 6–13 cover this key topic in C++Builder programming. These chapters include information on the use of Borland's database engine (the BDE); the important topic of client datasets, which are used for multitier and client/server programming; and a variety of specialized component sets including dbGo (formerly known as ADOExpress) and dbExpress (a new component set newly offered in C++Builder 6, which is specifically designed as a lightweight replacement for the BDE in client/server scenarios). This part of the book closes with coverage of XML and the XMLMapper, which can be used to make your applications work with XML.

- **Part III: "Windows Programming"**—A frequent topic of discussion among C++Builder programmers is the use of the Windows API. Part III covers this in detail within Chapters 14–17. This includes a breakdown of the API's functional areas, techniques for graphics and multimedia programming, how to program and utilize DLLs, and how to create and use COM objects.

- **Part IV: "Distributed Computing"**—Chapters 18–22 cover the important topic of distributed computing. C++Builder offers many tools to help programmers devise systems whose components are distributed across multiple computers and networks. These chapters cover standards such as DCOM and SOAP, Borland tools such as DataSnap (formerly known as Midas), WebSnap, and how to create Web Services using XML and Borland's BizSnap.

- **Part V: "Open Tools API"**—Chapter 23 covers the Tools API, which consists of Borland's Open Tools API and the Native Tools API, for extending the capabilities of the C++Builder and Delphi IDEs. As an example, this chapter progresses through the development of a practical wizard that can be added to the environment for supporting performance assessments of applications you develop using C++Builder.

- **Part VI: "Appendixes"**—The appendixes offer a variety of extras, including a look at the Borland examples provided by the C++Builder installation CD, developing mobile applications using the C++ Mobile Edition, some important information resources for C++Builder, and how to enable Borland's TXMLDocument control for Professional users.

The Companion CD-ROM

A companion CD-ROM has been provided that contains the example code and C++Builder projects highlighted within this book. The code is organized by chapter and can be accessed from the start-up application provided on the CD-ROM. Also provided on the CD-ROM as an added reference, is the full electronic version of the *C++Builder 5 Developer's Guide*.

C++Builder System Requirements

Several segments of the *Borland C++Builder 6 Developer's Guide* are intended for users of C++Builder 6 Professional and Enterprise; nevertheless, the majority of text and example code is applicable to previous versions of C++Builder. We anticipate the material provided in the book and on the companion CD-ROM will be applicable to future versions of C++Builder as well.

However, the project files found on the CD-ROM strictly adhere to the C++Builder version 6 format. This format is incompatible with previous versions of C++Builder. Therefore, it will be necessary for users of older versions of C++Builder to create new projects consisting of the code and forms provided on the companion CD-ROM.

NOTE

Despite our best efforts, it is inevitable that there will be the occasional error in the text and accompanying program code. In light of this, a list of errata will be provided on the Sam Publishing Web site at http://www.samspublishing.com.

Conventions Used in This Book

This section describes the important typographic conventions and terminology used in this book. Features in this book include the following:

NOTE

Notes give you comments and asides about the topic at hand, as well as full explanations of certain topics.

TIP

Tips identify shortcuts and hints on how to use C++Builder more effectively.

CAUTION

These warn you of pitfalls that might be encountered during programming.

Also look for the occasional *side notes* within several chapters of this book which provide greater insight into specific sub-topics.

In addition, you'll find various typeface conventions throughout this book:

- Code lines, commands, variables, directories, and files appear in text in a `monospaced` font.

- Placeholders in syntax descriptions appear in a `monospaced italic` typeface. Replace the placeholder with the actual filename, parameter, or other element that it represents.

- New terms and keywords are typically identified using an *italic* typeface.

- Functions are indicated by open and close parenthesis after the function name. This helps to differentiate functions from properties, variables, and types.

PART I

C++Builder Essentials

IN THIS PART

1

Introduction to C++Builder

This chapter will introduce you to Borland C++Builder, one of the leading development environments for creating Internet, desktop, client/server, and distributed applications. C++Builder combines the ease of a RAD environment with the power and performance of ANSI C++.

The C++Builder Integrated Development Environment (IDE) is where most of your work is done. Have a look at Figure 1.1 to see the user interface of the C++Builder IDE.

C++ remains the most widely used language for developing applications, which range from sophisticated multitier business systems to high performance data visualization and hard, real-time systems. C++Builder is an excellent choice for implementing any application.

NOTE

For more information on the features and benefits of C++Builder, see the Features & Benefits and New C++Builder Users links on the C++Builder Web site at http://www.borland.com/bcppbuilder/.

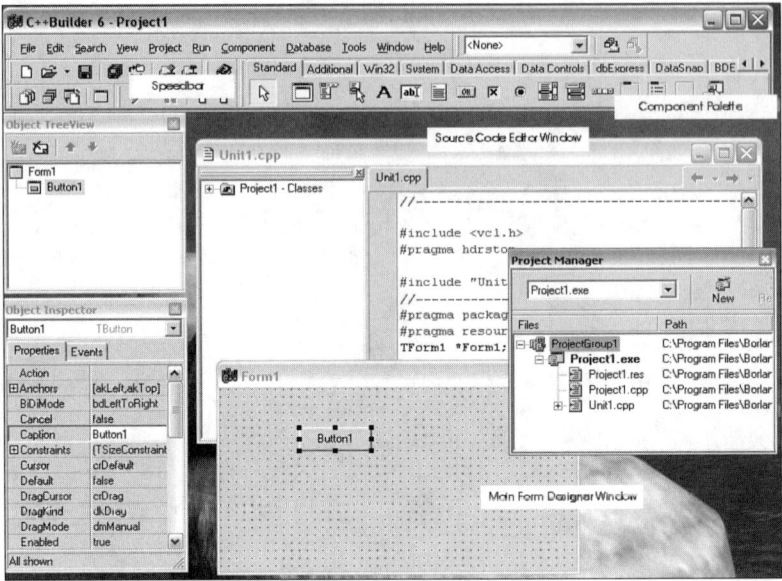

FIGURE 1.1   The C++Builder IDE.

C++ Language

The C++ language is at the core of C++Builder. C++Builder offers a high level of support for this standardized programming language.

ANSI Compliance

The C++ language was the next step in the development of the Bell Labs C language. And, like C, C++ gained widespread acceptance.

Widespread acceptance is a good thing because it leads to competition among vendors of compilers and development environments. But, as those vendors struggle for technological dominance, they often produce unique language features, which, although useful, mean that programs written for one compiler might not be able to be compiled by another.

The American National Standards Institute (ANSI) was founded in 1918, and is a private, nonprofit organization that coordinates the definition and publication of voluntary industry standards in a variety of fields. As such, they are the perfect organization to take on the problem of standardizing both the C and C++ languages.

NOTE

The document available at their Web site (`http://webstore.ansi.org/ansidocstore/product.asp?sku=ISO%2FIEC+14882%3A1998`) is the result of this effort, which was completed in 1998.

In the 21st century, "ANSI compliance" is a critical factor sought by developers who want to have the freedom to develop and compile using several different development systems, or who need to target more than one operating system or CPU instruction set.

Borland offers a powerful set of proprietary extensions to C++ so that they can provide the component-oriented features of the Visual Component Library class framework. But, they also provide what might be the highest level of ANSI compliance in the industry. You can force the compiler to only accept ANSI-compliant programs by clicking a check box in the development environment (pick the menu entry Project, Options; in the dialog box, click the Advanced Compiler tab; and under Language compliance, choose ANSI), as shown in Figure 1.2.

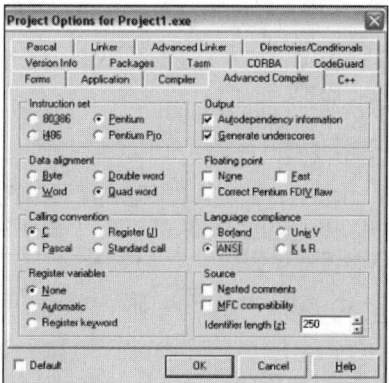

FIGURE 1.2   Project Options showing the ANSI Compliance option set.

To be safe, under Source, make sure to leave Nested comments and MFC compatibility unchecked.

Keep in mind that choosing ANSI compliance means that you cannot develop Windows programs because there are many features of the Windows operating system that cannot compile under ANSI compliance. You also cannot use Borland's Visual Component Library (VCL). You can, however, create programs that use streams for input and output, which are usually referred to as console programs.

Microsoft Compatibility

When a program is compiled without ANSI compatibility (for instance, with the Borland compatibility option selected), it will compile programs using Windows features. This is the basic level of Microsoft compatibility.

But, some programs won't compile.

For instance, programs that use the older Microsoft Foundation Classes (MFC) will not compile without using the MFC compatibility check box on the Advanced Compiler page.

This relaxes numerous rules in the compiler, including

- Not allowing spurious semicolons in a class scope

- Not allowing anonymous structs

- Not using the old-style scoping resolution for loops

- Not allowing methods to be declared with a calling convention, where the declaration leaves off the calling convention in the definition

- Not trying the operator new if it cannot resolve a call to the operator new

- Not letting you omit the operator and on member functions

- Not allowing a const class that is passed by value to be treated as a trivial conversion, not as a user conversion

- Not allowing you to use a cast to a member pointer as a selector for overload resolution when the qualifying type of the member pointer is not derived from the class in which the member function is declared

- Not accepting declarations with duplicate storage in a class

- Not accepting and ignoring `#pragma comment(linker, ",")` directives

In addition to this, you need to link your program with the `nafxcw.lib` MFC compatibility library that comes with C++Builder. This occurs automatically as a result of selecting MFC compatibility when compiling with the C++Builder-development environment, but requires a special flag if compiling and linking from the command line (the VF option).

Using MFC with the VCL has proven to be somewhat more difficult, in that specific header file changes have typically needed to be made to avoid conflicts between the names used by the MFC and by the VCL. These are documented at http://www. temporaldoorway.com/programming/cbuilder/otherlibrary/usingvclandmfc.htm for C++Builder versions through 4.

Another level of Microsoft compatibility lies in the capability to import a Microsoft Visual C++ project directly into the C++Builder development environment. Just open it and compile it.

To permanently convert the project, you can use the VCTOBPR utility, which will turn Visual C++ project and workspace files into their C++Builder equivalents.

Recommended Language References

Learning about C++ can be difficult, but the right books and online materials can make things easier.

- For reference, of course, the ANSI standard document is the definitive source of "language law," along with the documents available via the Web site (http://www.research.att.com/~bs/C++.html) of C++ originator Bjarne Stroustrup (though Stroustrup is a more enjoyable writer than the boards who compose standards).

- You can also get his newly revised book at sites such as Amazon.com (http://www.amazon.com/exec/obidos/ASIN/0201700735/104-5455331-5996736).

For less formal material, Sams publishes several excellent language instruction books, including

- *Sams Teach Yourself C++ in 10 Minutes* (recently revised), which breaks up C++ into manageable, easily understood lessons; great for getting a rapid, yet comprehensive exposure to the C++ language.

- *Sams Teach Yourself C++ in 21 Days* (recently revised), which gives three weeks of detailed instructional material on every aspect of C++.

Borland Language Extensions and Standard Objects

Borland's C++Builder integrates the Delphi Visual Component Library into its use of the C++ language. The problem is that Delphi is a Pascal-based language, whereas C++ is a C-based language. So, Borland used the ANSI-approved method of creating vendor-specific extensions, and added features to C++.

Properties

Object-oriented languages provide member variables to retain the state of the object during its lifetime. But when those member variables are directly exposed beyond the object, other parts of the program can disrupt the object by setting values that are inconsistent.

To overcome this problem, many object-oriented developers create member functions, called getter and setter functions, and hide access to the member variables within these member functions. This enables the programmer to be able to edit values that will be assigned to the member variable and generate an exception or other error condition when an incorrect value is provided. It also enables the programmer to hide the type of the internal variable, and even to provide a variety of hidden implementations for the member variable's storage (such as a file, a database, or even a complex computation).

A variety of problems exist with getters and setters, one of which is that they look a lot different from member variables in calculations.

For instance

```
int Something =
    SomeObject.GetMember() +
    SomeOtherObject.GetMember();
```

Another is that you don't really assign to a getter function—you pass a variable or expression as an argument to the function, which is equivalent to assignment.

```
SomeObject.SetSomeMember
(
    SomeObject.GetMember() +
    SomeOtherObject.GetMember()
);
```

When Borland created the Delphi language, they provided properties as a way to offer getters and setters as an implicit part of a class—giving the advantages of getters and setters combined with the expressiveness of member variable use.

In a C++Builder class, a property usually consists of a member variable declaration (private), a getter and setter function (protected), and a property declaration (public).

```
class aClassWithAProperty
{
    private:
        int myMemberVariable;
    protected:
        int __fastcall GetMemberVariable(void)
        {
            return myMemberVariable;
        };
        void __fastcall SetMemberVariable(int theMemberVariable)
        {
            myMemberVariable = theMemberVariable;
        };
    public:
```

```
    __property int MemberVariable =
    {
        read=GetMemberVariable,
        write=SetMemberVariable
    };
```

Of course, you can use an instance of this class and its property as shown below:

```
AClassWithAProperty ClassWithAProperty;
ClassWithAProperty.MemberVariable = 2;
int Something = ClassWithAProperty.MemberVariable;
```

Any code is allowed in the getter and setter.

Properties are most often used in C++Builder components. To help support the visual environment provided by C++Builder, Borland has created a special section for the class (identified by __published), just like public and private. If a property is in the __published section, it will appear in the C++Builder object inspector where it can be modified. In addition, when a project is saved, the values of component properties that are in the __published section of the component class are also saved for every instance of the component class.

The following is the earlier class, changed into a component (note the __published section, which now contains the __property declaration):

```
class aClassWithAProperty: public TComponent
{
    private:
        int myMemberVariable;
    protected:
        int __fastcall GetMemberVariable(void)
        {
            return myMemberVariable;
        };
        void __fastcall SetMemberVariable(int theMemberVariable)
        {
            myMemberVariable = theMemberVariable;
        };
    __published:
        __property int MemberVariable =
        {
            read=GetMemberVariable,
            write=SetMemberVariable
        };
};
```

Delphi-Style Default Properties

The Delphi language supports a property that is the default property for the class when you use the subscript operator. In earlier versions of C++Builder, you needed to use awkward constructs like

```
StringListVariable->Strings[Index]
```

Now you can simply use

```
(*StringListVariable)[Index]
```

try/finally

The Delphi language introduced a feature to exception handling that was later adopted in Java. The C++Builder extensions to C++ include this extension.

Called __finally (the two leading underscores are required by the ANSI standard to indicate an extension), this extension marks the part of an exception-handling block that will be executed regardless of whether an exception occurs. It is particularly useful for cleaning up dynamically allocated storage.

```
TStringList *List = new TStringList;

try
{
   // Do something
}
__finally
{
   delete List;
};
```

The code in the __finally block is executed when the try block is completed, or when an exception occurs.

This sort of statement can be inside or outside of exception handling code, but is usually inside so that resources can be released before an exception is handled.

The VCL, Forms, and Components

The Visual Component Library (VCL) is the source of many of the components used to create C++Builder applications (there are cross-platform components in a similar library called CLX). A component is an object, often visual, such as a check box, a drive combo box, or a graphical image. Components can also be nonvisual, such as database connections or sockets for distributed system communication.

Components are chosen from the component palette of the IDE by left-clicking and placing them in your work area. See the section "The Component Palette," later in this chapter, and Figure 1.1, which shows the windows of the IDE.

You can also add or write your own components, as discussed in upcoming chapters. Whether you are creating new components or using existing ones, the components that make up the VCL remove most of the hard work for you.

All components have properties, whose values can be modified at design time in the development environment. You can modify the properties of a component with the Object Inspector (refer to Figure 1.1 to see the window). You can also change property settings in code, but this should be avoided wherever possible.

The Object Inspector has an Events tab, where you can attach code to events that occur during user interaction with the component. These event handlers make up the bulk of the code in a C++Builder program.

The Form

A form is a visible window that is part of the user interface of your application. When you create a new application in C++Builder, a blank main form is created automatically. To build your user interface, simply add visual components to the form, then position and size them accordingly. You can also add nonvisual components to a form, such as timers. These appear as a simple component icon at design time, but are not visible at runtime. You can create specialized forms for tool windows or dialogs.

By default, when a user runs your application the main form will be displayed where you placed it on the screen in the IDE. You can alter the initial position of the form and other settings by changing the form properties in the Object Inspector.

The Component Palette

The Component Palette, located under the main menu, is an inventory of all the components in the VCL. These components are grouped by categories named on the tabs above the components. To pick a component, click it with your left mouse button, then click again on the form to place the component where you want it. As indicated previously, you can modify the component's properties with the Object Inspector. You can also change visual components by dragging their edges to resize them, or dragging the component to reposition it.

Events and Event Handlers

As a first lesson on using C++Builder, you can place a simple button on the form, set an event for the button, and run the program.

You see buttons on almost every Windows application. It is a simple object that enables a user to trigger an event handler in the program.

The Button component is located under the Standard tab of the Component Palette. Its icon looks like a standard button with OK in the middle. To place a Button component on the form, left-click the icon one time, then left-click again on the center of the form. Figure 1.3 shows the form with the button.

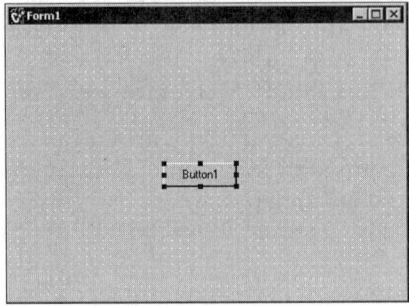

FIGURE 1.3   A Button component added to the form.

C++Builder has now created an instance of a button as part of your program. At the moment the button isn't very useful because it doesn't do anything. If you were to compile and run the application, nothing would happen as a result of a click of the button. Typically though, the event handler will perform some action, such as saving information the user has entered, displaying a message, or any one of thousands of other possibilities.

When the button is clicked at runtime, an event is generated. For your application to respond to this event you need to have coded an event handler. An event handler is a function that is automatically called when its event occurs. C++Builder creates the outline for the OnClick event handler, the event that occurs when the user clicks the button, when you double-click the Button component at design time. You can do the same thing by selecting the Button, and then double-clicking in the OnClick field on the Events tab in the Object Inspector. After the outline for the event handler is created, you can then add code to perform the necessary action that should occur when the button is clicked.

The outline for an OnClick event handler is shown in the following code.

```
void __fastcall TForm1::Button1Click(TObject *Sender)
{
}
```

If you right-click with the mouse in the Code Editor and choose Open Source/Header File, you will see the following code:

```
//----------------------------------------------------------------------
#ifndef Unit1
#define Unit1
//----------------------------------------------------------------------
#include <Classes.hpp>
#include <Controls.hpp>
#include <StdCtrls.hpp>
#include <Forms.hpp>
//----------------------------------------------------------------------
class TForm1 : public TForm
{
__published:    // IDE-managed Components
        TButton *Button1;
        void __fastcall Button1Click(TObject *Sender);
private:    // User declarations
public:         // User declarations
        __fastcall TForm1(TComponent* Owner);
};
//----------------------------------------------------------------------
extern PACKAGE TForm1 *Form1;
//----------------------------------------------------------------------
#endif
```

This code is generated automatically within C++Builder. I put it here to show you what C++Builder can do for you automatically.

Now, we'll add code to display a message when the button is clicked, that the program is going to end, and then we'll terminate the program. In the code editor, click Unit1.cpp to move back to the Button component's event. Type the following code inside the event that you just created:

```
void __fastcall TForm1::Button1Click(TObject *Sender)
{
    ShowMessage("Hello world! This is a test application! Press OK");
    Close();
}
```

Even a beginner can probably understand this code. When the program runs, the user clicks the button and an event is triggered. Your OnClick event handler will display a dialog box with your friendly message. When the user closes the dialog box our program then terminates because of the Close() call made to the form.

Testing the Program

From the IDE toolbar, click the green arrow that looks like the Play button of a tape player—this is the Run button. When you press this button, C++Builder will start to compile and execute the program. It then waits until you press the button. When you do so, the dialog box appears revealing the message. The program exits when you press OK.

After viewing your program, from the main menu, choose File, New Application. C++Builder will ask if you want to save the application project you were working on; answer No. Next will be your chance to write a real program that can do something.

Creating Your First Real Program

Here's the chance to create a program with a purpose. It will let you load and display an image from disk.

Choose File, New Application from the main menu. C++Builder will create a new project and generate code to create an empty form. Now the VCL will help you create an application with only a tiny amount of code.

On the Component Palette, select the Additional tab, and then click the Image component. If you aren't sure, its icon has the sky, a hill, and water at the foot of the hill. If you hold your mouse pointer over each icon, a ToolTip will display to tell you what it is.

After selecting the Image component by clicking it, move your mouse to the form and click time to place the component on the form. You will not see much, but a square outline will appear. This component displays graphical images.

Under the Properties tab in the Object Inspector, go to the stretch attribute and select True.

From the Component Palette, go to the Dialogs tab and choose the OpenDialog component. If necessary, scroll through the Component Palette with the left and right arrows. The OpenDialog component looks like an open yellow folder. Select it with your left mouse button and place it anywhere in the top right corner of the form. The component now is part of your form and is used for displaying a dialog box in which you can choose files.

Now we want to set an attribute to this component. Go to the Object Inspector and look for the attribute named Filter, located under the Properties tab. Enter the following text into the edit box for that attribute:

```
BMP files|*.bmp
```

From the Standard tab of the Component Palette, select two Button components. Instead of placing one Button component at a time, you can place multiple Button components by holding down the Shift key and pressing the Button icon from the Component Palette.

Click the form and a Button component appears. Click the form again and another Button component appears.

Click one time on the Button1 component on the form. This selects the button. Now you can change the properties of the button. In the Object Inspector, click inside the Caption property value (currently reading Button1) and replace the existing text with the words Get Picture. This will change the label on the button.

Go to the Win32 tab in the Component Palette and select the status bar. It looks like a gray bar with a grip. Hold your mouse over each component a couple of seconds to see the hint; it will read StatusBar. A status bar is often located at the bottom of most Windows applications to display the status of an application.

Place this on the form. You will see that the component automatically repositions to the bottom of the form.

Now double-click the Button component on the form (Object Inspector will display Button1) to set its OnClick event. Enter the code inside the braces:

```
void __fastcall TForm1::Button1Click(TObject *Sender)
{
    if(OpenDialog1->Execute())
    Image1->Picture->LoadFromFile(OpenDialog1->FileName);
    StatusBar1->SimpleText = OpenDialog1->FileName;
}
```

The window into which you just entered your code is called the Source Code Editor.

Now go back to the form. You can use the Speedbar tool button that shows the hint Toggle Form/Unit. It looks like a form and a piece of paper with arrows pointing toward the form on both sides. If you hold your cursor over this button, it will display Toggle Form/Unit (F12). This tells you that another way to toggle between forms and code is with the F12 key. Press F12 now to set focus on the form.

Click one time on Button2 (Object Inspector will display Button2) on the form and set the caption to Close. Double-click that button and enter the code between the braces:

```
void __fastcall TForm1::Button2Click(TObject *Sender)
{
    Close();
}
```

Now focus on your form again by moving the source code editor out of the way and clicking your form. Doesn't look like much, does it? Soon you will see how much C++Builder has done for you with just a little bit of code!

NOTE

Before running this application, it is a good idea to arrange your buttons and other components nicely to give a clean look. Use the white arrow selector on the left side of the Component Palette or the Object Tree View Window to select any component. You will not be able to move the StatusBar component at the bottom of the form, so leave it alone.

Press the green Run arrow or choose Run from the Project menu. C++Builder should compile the program successfully if you do not have any errors (otherwise, you'll have to fix anything you typed wrong). Your program should appear with the form displaying the two buttons with the captions Get Picture and Close. Choose the Get Picture button.

An Open dialog box will appear asking for a file with the .BMP extension. Go to your Windows directory under your C: drive and select SETUP.BMP or another file that has a .BMP extension.

After selecting the file, press OK. You should see a picture of the Windows Setup bitmap. At the bottom of the form, the name of the file will be in the status bar. You have written your first application that really works, and with as little code as possible!

First you placed a TImage component on the form. This component enables you to display .BMP files within your program, requiring no programming on your part.

If you want to change the filter settings at design time, on Form1 click on the TOpenDialog component to select it. Then, press F11 to go to the Object Inspector. In the Filter property, double-click within the text area and a table will come up that lets you change the filter.

Now you can write a completely different program using different components. This will give you a second example of RAD technology within C++Builder.

NOTE

Go ahead and close the project. You do not have to save it. Choose File, Close All from the main menu and answer No.

However, if you choose to save the project, you will be prompted to save the main form (Unit1.cpp) and the project (Project1.bpr) in separate dialogs.

You might want to save the project and main form for each project together, using a separate directory for each project. This can be easily done using the standard Windows dialogs; simply navigate to where you want the new project's directory to be located; on the dialog toolbar click the new directory button and give the directory a name. Then double-click into the directory and save the main form, and then when the next dialog (for the project) appears, if it is not already positioned on the new directory, navigate there and save the project file.

From the main menu, select File, New Application. A new project will be created. Let's save this project by selecting File, Save Project As from the main menu.

Give the form's source code a name. Change the default `Unit1.cpp` to `Mainform.cpp`.

After saving the form's source code, the project source code will appear. By default, it is `Project1.bpr`; name it `Project2.bpr`.

Place two `ListBox` components on the form. The list boxes are in the Standard tab in the Component Palette. Don't worry about placing them in a specified location, but do align them next to each other. C++Builder creates them as `ListBox1` and `ListBox2`.

Drop an `EditBox` and two `Buttons` below the list boxes. They are also located in the Standard tab in the Component Palette. Align them any way you want. C++Builder creates the buttons as `Button1` and `Button2`. It also creates an `Editbox` named `Edit1`.

Select `Button1`. In the Object Inspector, select the `Caption` property. Change the caption to **ADD**.

Select `Button2`. In the Object Inspector, select the `Caption` property. Change the caption to **REMOVE**.

Select `Edit1`. In the Object Inspector, select the `Text` property. Remove the string within the `Text` property.

Drop a `Label` component under the `Edit1` edit box. In the Object Inspector, select the `Caption` property. Enter **Friends' Names**.

To select the form itself, click anywhere on the form, but not on any component. You can also do this inside the Object Inspector by selecting `Form1` in the drop-down box. Next, select the Events tab in the Object Inspector and look for the `OnShow` event. Double-click inside the property setting for this event. C++Builder will now create the following code for the event handler:

```
void __fastcall TForm1::FormShow(TObject *Sender)
{
}
```

This event is triggered when the form is shown at runtime. This means that when you run this program, Windows will create the form and execute any code within the event. Type the code in the braces inside the event handler:

```
void __fastcall TForm1::FormShow(TObject *Sender)
{
    ListBox1->Items->Add("David Sexton");
    ListBox1->Items->Add("Randy Kelly");
    ListBox1->Items->Add("John Kirksey");
    ListBox1->Items->Add("Bob Martling");
}
```

Switch back to the form and double-click Button1. This is the button with the Add caption. An OnClick event will be created. Type the code in the braces into the event handler:

```
void __fastcall TForm1::Button1Click(TObject *Sender)
{
    String GetListItem = ListBox1->Items->Strings[ListBox1->ItemIndex];
    ListBox2->Items->Add(GetListItem);
}
```

Switch back to the form, and double-click Button2. This is the button with the Remove caption. C++Builder will create an event handler. Type the code in the braces into the event handler:

```
void __fastcall TForm1::Button2Click(TObject *Sender)
{
    ListBox2->Items->Delete(ListBox2->ItemIndex);
}
```

Switch back to the form and select the Edit1 edit box. From the Object Inspector, choose the Events tab. Find the OnKeyPress event. Double-click in the empty area for this event, and C++Builder will create the event handler. Type the code in the braces into the event handler:

```
void __fastcall TForm1::Edit1KeyPress(TObject *Sender, char &Key)
{
    if (Key==13)
    {
        ListBox2->Items->Add(Edit1->Text);
        ListBox1->Items->Add(Edit1->Text);
    }
}
```

Now save the project. Remember to always save your work! Select File, Save All from the main menu. After saving the project, make the project. Press Ctrl+F9 or choose Project, Make. This will create the executable. If there are any errors, check for typos.

Press the green arrow to run it and see what happens. You can also choose Run from the Project menu as well. I will explain how the code works in a minute.

The application will appear as a regular window with two list boxes displaying names. There should also be two buttons on the form.

The edit box (which is our Edit1 component) will have the cursor in it ready for us to type. Enter your friends' names.

As soon as you press Enter, each name will be added not only to the first list box but also to the second list box.

Select one of the names and press the Add button. The name you selected will appear in the next list box beside it. If you press Remove, the name will disappear only from the second list box. Select the names and add them to the other list box; then remove the names.

You added an event handler for FormShow. This executes after the form's creation, but before it is shown. In that event handler you will see that there are some strings to be added inside ListBox1. The strings are added to the Items property of the list box.

The next event is under Button1. You created a string from the String class named GetListItem, which equals the item that was selected by the user. How did this event know that the item was selected? It didn't. It read the item's index. If there was no selection, it would be null. The next line adds the string from the index of ListBox1.

Button2's event is smaller than the first. It gets the index of the item inside ListBox2 and deletes it.

For our third event, you used an OnKeyPress for the Edit1 edit box. When someone enters data and presses a key, the event is triggered, executing the code inside it. This particular event scans for the Enter key, which is equal to 13. You could also have used the VK_ENTER value that C++Builder defines as the Enter key. In any case, the if statement checks the passed parameter of Key to see if this is true. If it is, the code inside the if statement executes and adds the string within the edit box to both list boxes.

You created three event handlers, and the code is pretty small. You also put several components on the form without any code at all. Thus, you have a working program with minimal code.

This took just a few minutes of effort. After you get used to the Component Palette, the Object Inspector, and the IDE, you'll be able to do this with much larger and more complex programs. If you compare the time required to develop applications using other environments, such as Visual C++ or Microsoft Foundation Classes (MFC), you will see that C++Builder is far superior to the others.

Explore the menu items under C++Builder. The online help can also guide you through the menu items, Object Inspector, and some of the other important options within the IDE.

Commonly Asked Questions

This section gives the answers to some commonly asked questions about the C++Builder compiler.

- How do I look at a project's source code and other source code for each form?

  You can do this by using the Project Manager or the Project menu item in the main menu. Project, View Source will display the main entry source for the starting application. If you want to view source files from other forms, includes, or resource files, use the Project Manager. To open the Project Manager, select View, Project Manager or press Ctrl+Alt+F11.

- How do I change properties on a component?

  You can do this with the Object Inspector. To bring it up, press F11 or choose View, Object Inspector. In the Object Inspector, select your component and the properties will be loaded within the Object Inspector. From there you can set events and change properties.

- I am trying to arrange my components precisely, but I am having difficulty. Can I have more control over the alignment?

  To move a component to the exact location you want, press Control and use the arrow keys to move it. This will give you the exact pixel alignment you need within C++Builder. However, it is better to use the Align and Anchor properties to produce user interfaces that are independent of window size.

- I just compiled and ran my application, but now it seems to be locked up. A bunch of weird windows popped up and I don't know what to do. How can I stop this madness?

  You can get C++Builder to reset the program. Press Ctrl+F2 or select Run, Program Reset. This will kill your program completely and take away those nasty whatever-they-are-windows, and you'll be back to your code.

- I compiled my first program, but I want to create my own icon and include it in my program. How do I do this?

  First, use the Image Editor. Open it by selecting Tools, Image Editor in the main menu. Simply create a new icon from there and save it. Then, select Project, Options. The Project Options dialog will appear. Select the Application tab and press the Load Icon button. Locate your icon and press OK. Then, you will have to rebuild your project; simply compiling or making your project will not do it. You will have to rebuild all by choosing Project, Build All Projects from the main menu. After that, your application will contain your new icon.

- Every time I compile an application, my form has the name Form1. How do I change this?

  Remember the Object Inspector? We talked about this for setting properties for components. You can also use it to set properties for your forms. Use the Caption property attribute to change a form's title. Try experimenting with the Object Inspector for different results!

- I am tired of choosing the menu items for something simple. Isn't there an easier way?

  Yes—it's called the Speedbar, and it is located right above the Object Inspector (by default). If you want, for example, to create a new application object, press the button with the image of a white piece of paper. If you do not know what those buttons are, hold your cursor over one for a couple of seconds and a helper will appear to tell you what the button is.

- I have all my components in place and do not want to move them. But, some- times I accidentally move them by mistake. Is there a way I can keep these components still?

  Yes, you can do this by choosing Edit, Lock Controls from the main menu. This will lock all controls on the form.

What's New in C++Builder 6?

As with the staggered releases of new versions of Borland C++Builder and Borland Delphi in the past, C++Builder 6 introduces new features first seen in Delphi 6 and then adds some more. There are many new features and enhancements in the areas of Web programming, distributed application development, database application development, and developer productivity, among others. Most of the new features and enhancements are covered in more detail throughout this book.

C++Builder 6 is available in three versions: Standard (Std), Professional (Pro), and Enterprise (Ent). Standard has the fewest features, but is still a powerful development environment for Windows programming and includes more than 85 components for RAD programming, the award-winning compiler, advanced debugger, and more. The Professional version has more than 150 components and adds features including the CodeGuard™ tool, multiprocess debugging, and standard database functionality. The Enterprise version has more than 200 components, including Internet Express,

CORBA development, Microsoft SQL Server and Oracle support, distributed development, a full suite of internationalization tools, TeamSource version control manager, and more.

Missing from C++Builder 6 is Merant (formerly Intersolv) PVCS Version Control.

NOTE

The full-feature matrix, which highlights all the new features in each version (Standard, Professional, Enterprise) of C++Builder 6, is available from the Feature List link on the C++Builder Web site at `http://www.borland.com/cbuilder/`.

You can also see information on the new features in the "What's New" section of the C++Builder online help.

The features listed in the following sections are available in the Professional and Enterprise versions of C++Builder and not in the Standard version, except where noted. In the remainder of the book, we will not designate which versions of C++Builder the new features apply to. Consult the full-feature matrix if necessary.

Compatibility with Previous Releases—Projects

When you load a package from an earlier version of C++ Builder, if possible, it will be converted to the C++Builder current version format. Because of the many changes in a typical major release, this doesn't always work for complex projects, so, in the event you have problems compiling, running, or debugging your prior version project, be prepared to create a new project to incorporate your code. It is recommended that you create a backup of your project and its directories before converting it to the current version.

Also note that prior version symbol files are generally not compatible with the current version—thus, you should rebuild your project immediately after converting.

In an effort to simplify future project conversions, it looks like Borland has decided to remove version numbers from their package names, so vcl50.bpi will for release 6 and the future be just plain vcl.bpi; however, runtime packages still have version numbers to enforce compatibility.

Compatibility with Previous Releases—Standard C++ Library

Prior versions of C++ used the Rogue Wave implementation of the C++ standard template library (STL). In version 6, Borland has switched to the STLport implementation. This implementation is an open-source product produced by a company that is also called STLport. Borland suggests that there might be some changes in the way code using this library operates, but that you can expect your STL code to compile without difficulty.

Compatibility with Previous Releases—Database Program Changes

Some changes in the new version affect your database programs (this does not, of course, affect owners of the Standard Edition, but only the Professional and Enterprise Edition).

One of the most important changes is that Borland has changed the way `LoginPrompt` works with your `Tdatabase`- or `Tconnection`-based component. There is now no default login dialog box: you need to `#include DBLogDlg.hpp` or your program will not prompt for the username.

Compatibility with Previous Releases—`DsgnIntf` Renamed and Split Up

Some advanced packages contain references to `dsgnintf.hpp`, which is the header file needed for creating property and component editors.

For whatever reason, Borland has now renamed that package, adding a few vowels: now you must reference `designintf.hpp`. You might also need the new packages `DesignEditors.hpp`, `VCLEditors.hpp`, and `RTLConsts.hpp`.

Other New Features

- Support for WebServices (Professional and Enterprise Editions only)

- Improved Web page generation from Web modules (Professional and Enterprise Editions only)—for more information, see Chapter 22, "Web Server Programming with WebSnap."

- SOAP support for multitier database applications (Enterprise Edition only)—for more information, see Chapter 19, "SOAP and Web Services with BizSnap," and Chapter 20, "Distributed Applications with DataSnap."

- A non-BDE database component set called dbExpress, which allows for easy deployment of client server database applications (Interbase, DB2, Oracle, MySQL, Informix)—for more information, see Chapter 12, "Data Access with dbExpress."

- Enhancements to Actions—for more information, see Chapter 3, "Programming with C++Builder."

- Enhancements to the IDE—for more information, see Chapter 2, "C++Builder Projects and More on the IDE."

Linux, Kylix, CLX, EJB, and C++Builder

C++Builder now offers several features to support cross-platform development activities—you can develop on Windows and deploy to Linux (a variant of the popular Unix operating system) or develop on Linux and deploy to Windows.

C++Builder is primarily focused on Windows development. But any program you produce in C++Builder, so long as it only uses the CLX components, can be compiled on Linux using Borland's Kylix (currently at version 3). So, your company can have copies of C++Builder on Windows, use those for creating and testing programs, and then recompile those programs on one or more Linux computers, using Kylix, for deployment.

What's the catch? You need to limit your use of the rapid application development features of C++Builder to controls that are part of the Borland CLX cross-platform component set. Fortunately, this isn't much of a burden because most of the standard UI, data, and Web components are part of CLX.

CLX Overview

Deep details about CLX can be found in *Sams Kylix Developer's Guide*, but here are the highlights:

- CLX is not VCL and VCL is not CLX, but both are rooted at `TComponent`.

- CLX wraps the Qt class library, a cross-platform library from TrollTech, which works on both Windows and Linux.

- Why not do this with the VCL? Simply because the VCL exposes certain Windows-based data structures that need to be hidden for cross-platform applications.

- Unlike VCL, CLX completely hides the idea of user interface messages. Instead, it provides a comprehensive set of event handlers for anything you might have used messages for. There is no message loop, no message dispatcher, and no capability to redirect messages with `BEGIN_MESSAGE_MAP` / `END_MESSAGE_MAP`.

- Qt is a least common denominator class library—it surfaces the features common to Windows and Linux. It is up to Borland and third-party developers to reimplement those features that might be specific to each platform, or even beyond the platforms.

- There's no CLX tab on the component palette. How do you know which components are CLX? Well, first of all, all the dbExpress components are, whereas the ADO and BDE components aren't. So, if you want to access databases on both platforms, dbExpress is the way to go. As for user interfaces, data aware user interfaces are done with conventional TDB controls such as `TDBGrid` and TDBEdit. Dialogs such as TOpenDialog are part of CLX. None of the ActiveX or OLE controls are usable within CLX. The FastNet controls are also not usable for cross-platform Internet work: the Internet components you can use in CLX are those on the WebSnap, Internet, and Indy tabs.

Your ultimate resource for cross-platform components is the help file that comes with C++Builder—look at the section "CLX Component Reference" for a complete and up-to-date list.

Cross-Platform Help System Integration

Cross-platform systems need to be able to provide cross-platform help. CLX (and VCL) both provide access to help viewers without locking you into a platform—help viewers are provided by classes that implement the ICustomHelpViewer interface; for Windows, this is TWinHelpViewer. On Linux, it might well be another class provided by your help viewer vendor or implemented by you to provided that capability.

An application must register itself with the global HelpManager so that its help requests can be passed to the correct viewer; this is done automatically by TApplication. And, of course, the help viewers/help systems must register themselves and the help they provide with the Help Manager so they can get and handle the requests.

The biggest problem is the help context, which the help viewer uses to determine what help the user wants displayed. Most Linux help viewers will not understand the numeric help contexts that are common in WinHelp files. This implies that you will need to hide the nature of your help contexts and use numeric contexts under Windows, and non-numeric contexts under Linux (using a conditional compilation to control what is generated).

Simplified IDL, IIOP, and EJB

The Borland Enterprise Server (and its ancestor, Borland Application Server), implemented communication between Java programs and Enterprise Java Beans (EJB) using IIOP (Internet Inter-ORB Protocol), a standard devised for communication between CORBA (Common Object Request Broker Architecture) objects.

Why does this matter to a C++ programmer? Well, there are more and more EJB-style interfaces being made available by various software package vendors, and, perhaps, even by a programmer down the hall from you. It would be nice if you could easily leverage their facilities from your C++Builder programs, and you might even be able to avoid bringing yet another language (Java) into your shop.

The process is conceptually simple: If you use JBuilder, create the IDL for your EJB through the IDE for JBuilder (right-click the project, pick Options, then from the dialog pick Build, and click Generate IDL in the Java2IDL Settings; the next compile will generate the IDL you need).

If you are not using JBuilder, or don't have the Java source, create the IDL with the Borland Enterprise Server Visibroker java2idl command-line utility.

Either method produces a file that describes the interface to the EJB in language-independent terms.

In C++Builder, use File, New, CORBA Client and provide the name of the IDL file as requested by the wizard.

At this point you now have a client that can call the EJB. All you need to do is to have the EJB in an appropriate application server (one which, like Borland Enterprise Server, implements EJB and application server communication with IIOP).

The C++ Standard Library

In addition to the VCL and CLX, C++Builder offers one other important library: The C++ Standard Library (formerly known as the Standard Template Library [STL]). Like CLX, in C++Builder 6, this is a cross-platform library with the capability to be used both in Windows and Linux programs.

This is a complex and powerful library, and not all its features can be covered in this short presentation. Instead, here is a look at some of its most important capabilities.

Containers

The template in STL refers to its use of C++ templates to help make sure the classes in the library can create typesafe instances. Nowhere is this more important than when considering container classes.

Containers include

- `vector`—a list of items kept in the sequence in which they were added. This is most efficient for adding to the end of the container.

- `list`—A list of items kept in the sequence in which they were added, but equally efficient inserting items anywhere.

- `deque`—A list of items that can be used as a double-ended stack.

- `set`—An ordered collection, with no duplicates allowed.

- `multiset`—An ordered collection that allows duplicates.

- `bitset`—Contains a set of unique bits.

- `map`—Contains unique keys associated with values, providing access to values by keys.

- multimap—A map where there can be multiple keys with the same value.

- string—A special character container with string-oriented functions.

The library also includes adaptors that force certain access patterns on the containers: stack (insert and remove only from the top); queue (insert from one end, remove from the other); and priority queue (same as a queue, but each entry has a priority, and items are ordered by sequence within priority).

Selecting a container can be more complex than you might expect, but you can also use the containers intuitively and attain good results. The help file offers guidance on the more complex aspects of selecting a container.

Using containers is fairly simple as you can see in this example. It uses a vector to store two integers and then copies those integers out to the lines of a VCL memo:

```
 1:    vector<int> IntegerVector;
 2:
 3:    IntegerVector.push_back(1);
 4:    IntegerVector.push_back(2);
 5:
 6:    vector<int>::iterator First = IntegerVector.begin();
 7:    vector<int>::iterator Last = IntegerVector.end();
 8:
 9:    CollectionMemo->Lines->Clear();
10:
11:    while (First != Last)
12:    {
13:        CollectionMemo->Lines->Add(String(*First));
14:        ++First;
15:    };
```

Line 1 declares the vector as storing integers. Lines 3 and 4 add elements to the vector. Lines 6 and 7 create and initialize iterators that can be used to go from the beginning to the end of the vector. Line 9 clears a TMemo object that is used to display the content of the vector. Line 11 tests the iterators for equality. When they are equal, the iterator has gone past the end of the vector. Line 13 dereferences the iterator, which, thanks to C++ operator overloading, returns the content the iterator has reached; it then converts the integer to a string and puts it in the memo. Line 14 completes the loop by advancing the iterator to the next element of the vector.

Note that this example requires you to #include <vector> and <iterator>.

There are many more features of containers, which can be found in any one of the various books on the STL.

Memory Management

One of the most powerful aspects of using the container classes lies in the memory management they provide for the objects they contain.

When you add an object (rather than a primitive type) to a container, the container uses the copy constructor to create a copy of the object. However, if what is being added is a pointer, it is assumed that the instance is shared with something else, and it is left to the programmer to manage the memory.

The library offers yet another tool for managing memory, and this is a tool that can be especially useful: smart pointers.

Smart pointers are objects that live on the stack, and which will be deallocated when the object passes out of scope. When you allocate an object with new, of course, it lives beyond the scope in which it was allocated. To constrain the scope of memory allocations usually requires the use of a delete that follows the new. For instance, the try/__finally, extension of C++Builder's C++ language is often used to ensure resources allocated from the heap are released.

auto_ptr is the class used for this purpose.

Here's the example:

```
auto_ptr<TStringList> ListHolder(new TStringList);
ListHolder->Add("String");
```

Note that if you have added objects to the Objects property of a TStringList, you will still be responsible for releasing the memory for those objects manually.

When the ListHolder goes out of scope, whether through normal completion of the function, or through an exception being thrown, the TStringList instance is also destroyed.

Summary

This chapter has discussed C++Builder and some of its important features, with a particular focus on those features new in C++Builder 6.

The basic features of language-standard compliance, capability to use Microsoft projects and code styles, cross-platform capabilities, and a simple C++Builder project have all been examined. In upcoming chapters, these features, core and new, will be examined in depth.

C++Builder Projects and More on the IDE

In Chapter 1, "Introduction to C++Builder," you were exposed to the C++ Builder implementation of the C++ language, the VCL and CLX class libraries, the IDE, and projects—all integral parts of C++Builder. This chapter builds on that experience to take you through the advanced features of the IDE, how to use projects and packages, how to debug, and how to speed up compilation.

C++Builder IDE Features

C++Builder offers a powerful environment with many options. This section covers its core features and some of the newest, most advanced features.

Main Window and Toolbars

The main window of the IDE fits to the upper section of your desktop. It contains various toolbars, including the menu bar, all of which can be moved. You can add or remove buttons by picking Customize from the pop-up menu on any of the toolbars. You can drag and drop from any of the commands listed under the dialog Commmands tab onto any of the toolbars. Unfortunately, you have to piggyback on the existing toolbars—you cannot create your own.

You can also remove buttons while customizing by dragging them off the toolbar that holds them.

Project Manager

The Project Manager is not displayed in the default window configuration, but is usually important to have available. Pick Project Manager from the View menu to show the manager for the current project.

As you've seen, the project manager displays the current project files. You can control the build order for those files by rearranging them in the Project Manager window. You can also set local options and perform a variety of other tasks by using the pop-up menu available for each file or project.

The Project Manager will be covered in more detail later in this chapter.

Arranging Windows in the IDE

Many of the IDE windows can be docked to each other. This enables you to customize the user interface layout to your own needs.

If it weren't for the need to have separate form windows, you might dock all the windows into a tiled user interface. However, some experimentation will show you what works best docked while still allowing access to the form.

As you drag windows onto each other for docking, you will see the outline that tells where the docked window will go. Figure 2.1 shows an example of the Object Tree View at the bottom of the Object Inspector Window, before starting docking. Figure 2.2 shows the outline that indicates where the dragged window will fall, and Figure 2.3 shows the window after.

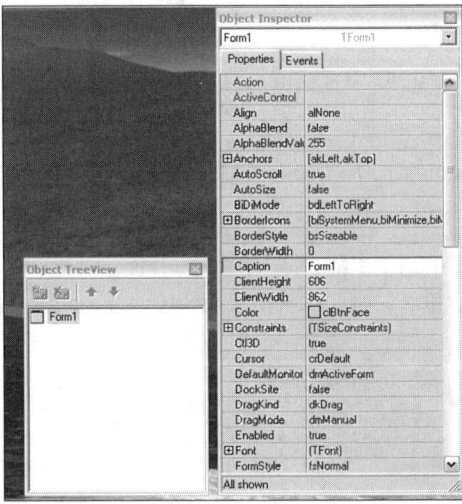

FIGURE 2.1   The two windows to participate in the drag and drop.

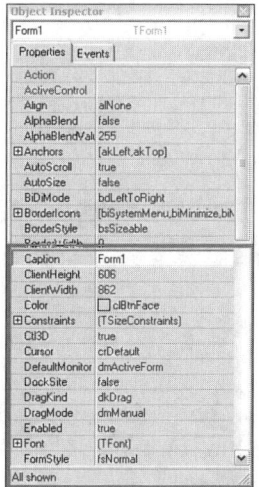

FIGURE 2.2   The drop outline on the Object Inspector window shows where the dropped window will go.

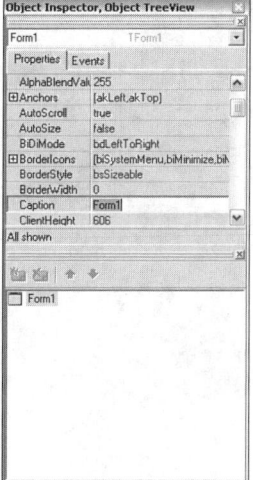

FIGURE 2.3   The window after the drop has occurred.

There are several places you can dock a window (called dock sites), though not every window supports every dock site possibility.

- Bottom, Top, Left, Right—Fills the bottom, top, left, or right of the destination window with the dropped window.

- Center—Adds the newly dropped window as a tabbed page to the drop-site window.

One of the most useful arrangements is to dock the Project Manager, the Object Inspector, and the Object Tree View window into a single window.

After windows are docked, you can resize the proportion of each using the flat part of the bar that separates them. Look for the cursor to turn into a double-headed arrow when it's over the splitter bar.

Object Inspector

As you've seen, the Object Inspector displays the properties for the currently selected component or form. You can also use the instance drop-down list at the top of the Object Inspector to pick a specific component.

Figure 2.4 shows the Object Inspector window.

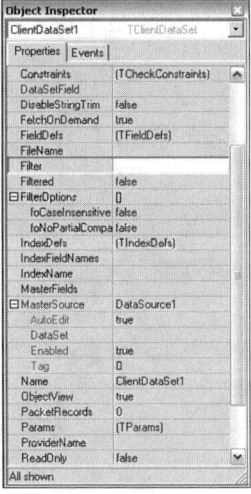

FIGURE 2.4   Object Inspector.

This view of the Object Inspector shows its features. In this case, the properties are for a TclientDataSet component, but similar properties exist for every class of component.

You can see that some properties have a plus sign (+) next to them. Some of those are enumerated properties with true/false flags next to each enumeration, such as FilterOptions. Others, such as MasterSource, are references to another component on the form, and the Object Inspector displays the properties of that component when the + has been clicked.

In addition to the plus sign, the Object Inspector uses color to show the nature of the property. Red property names indicate references to other components. Green property names indicate the properties of those referenced components brought over into the current object's inspector for convenience (making it easy to change related components' properties).

Finally, the plus sign can also be used for instances that are contained within the current instance being examined. Font is an example of this type of property.

The colors for various elements of the Object Inspector can be set from the Object Inspector tab of the IDE Tools, Environment dialog.

Property Categories in the Object Inspector

In Chapter 1 we described how the IDE's Object Inspector can be used to display and edit component properties and event handler functions. C++Builder 5 introduced the idea of property categories. All properties (including events that are also properties) can be arranged by category in the Object Inspector, as well as the normal alphabetical listing. The purpose of categories is to allow the logical grouping of related properties. A property might belong to more than one category, if appropriate. Additionally, it is possible to hide a property from the Object Inspector by hiding its category. This is referred to as *filtering*.

Filtering works on properties in the Object Inspector window, and also applies to the entries on the Events tab.

Using Property Categories

By default the Object Inspector displays properties alphabetically. To view by category, right-click the working area of the Object Inspector and select Arrange, By Category from the pop-up menu. The property categories will now be displayed in the Object Inspector. These can be expanded or collapsed by clicking the + (expand) or – (collapse) icon (by default they are initially collapsed). If a category is expanded and the properties are viewed by name before viewing them again by category, the category remains expanded. If another component is selected and it has properties in the same category, those will also be shown expanded.

To filter which property categories are displayed in the Object Inspector, right-click again and select View. A category is checked or unchecked: Unchecked categories are hidden.

Selecting View, All automatically checks all categories, selecting View, None unchecks all categories (and therefore hides them), and selecting View, Toggle toggles the state of the categories. That is, checked categories become unchecked and vice versa. It doesn't matter which category is visible when you change a property that is a member of multiple categories—you are changing the underlying value, not a separate entry in each category.

Using the Predefined Property Categories

There are 13 predefined property (and event) categories, 12 of which are used by the VCL in C++Builder. These are described in Table 2.1, with the kind of property contained in each category and example properties.

TABLE 2.1 Property Categories in C++Builder

Category Name	Category Specification
Action	Contains properties that are managed by actions and whose behavior is related to runtime functionality. The Hint and Checked properties of TMenuItem are in this category.
Data	Contains properties that manage the data shown by a component. This category is not currently used by the VCL. It was originally used for the Text, EditMask, and Tag properties, but these can now be found in the Localizable, and Miscellaneous categories, respectively.
Database	Contains properties whose behavior is related to database operations. The DatabaseName, MasterSource, and OnCalcFields properties of TTable are in this category.
Drag, Drop, and Docking	Contains properties that arerelated to drag and drop or docking operations. The OnDragOver and DockSite properties of TForm are in this category.
Help and Hints	Contains properties (and events) that are related to help, hint, or assistance operations. The OnHint and HelpContext properties of TStatusBar are in this category.
Input	Contains properties that are related to controlling input to the component. The OnKeyPress, OnClick, and Enabled properties of TForm are in this category.
Layout	Contains properties that are related to the layout and visual display of a control at design time. The OnResize and Width properties of TForm are in this category.
Legacy	Contains properties that are now obsolete. The Ctl3D and OldCreateOrder properties of TForm are in this category.
Linkage	Contains properties that are related to the linking of one component to another. The PopupMenu property of TForm and the DataSource property of TDBGrid are in this category.
Locale	Contains properties that are related to international locales or compliance with international locale operating systems. The BiDiMode and ParentBiDiMode properties of TForm are in this category.
Localizable	Contains properties that are subject to possible change, depending on where the application is deployed. The BiDiMode, Hint, and Font properties of TForm are in this category.
Miscellaneous	Contains properties that have not been categorized, do not fit into any category, or do not require categorization. The Tag and Name properties of TForm are in this category.

TABLE 2.1 Continued

Category Name	Category Specification
Visual	Contains properties that are related to the layout and visual display of the control at runtime. The `BorderStyle`, `Color`, and `Width` properties of `TForm` are in this category.

The Object Tree View

The Object Tree View is an important adjunct to the Object Inspector. For one thing, the Object Inspector drop-down list can become unwieldy when there are more than ten or twenty items. The Object Tree View window, shown in Figure 2.5, shows the objects in their parent/child relationships, and, of course, is scrollable. This is especially valuable in situations where a child component completely fills or covers its parent, and thus cannot be clicked with the mouse on the form.

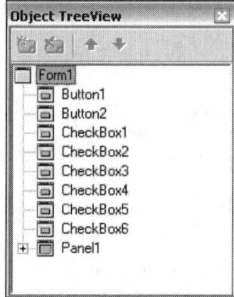

FIGURE 2.5 Object Tree View.

Entries in the Object Tree View have a pop-up menu. The most important feature of this menu is its capability to Edit (Copy, Cut, Paste), which enables you to create copies of the selected item.

Source Code Editor

The source code editor window is a window with tabs for each file currently opened. Figure 2.6 shows the Source Code Editor and the docked Class Explorer.

This is used to show and edit a variety of file types, including

- C++ header and implementation files (.cpp, .h, and .hpp, which are Delphi interface sections translated into C++)

- Delphi files (.pas)

- Text files (.txt or any other extension)

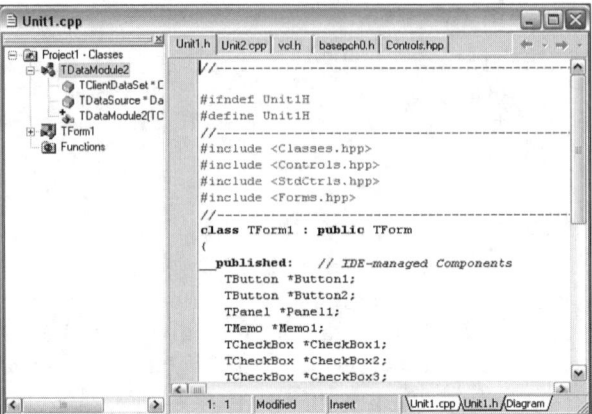

FIGURE 2.6   Source Code Editor.

- Text format of a form, data module, project makefile, and so on
- SQL statements from the Tquery, and other similar database components

The tabs across the top of the source code editor show the name of the file; these tabs can be reordered by drag and drop. The title bar shows the path to the file being edited, unless it is in the current directory. If it is in the current directory, only the name will be shown.

Each file has at least one tab at the bottom. A .cpp file has a tab for the .cpp file and the .h file, as well as a diagram.

The editor also allows for custom surface designers, which are used to provide the diagram editor and the special editors for Professional and Enterprise Edition WebSnap applications.

The Diagram Tab

This tab reveals a diagram editor you can use to help document the component.

Figure 2.7 shows the diagram editor in use.

The Diagram tab is only present for top-level components such as forms and data modules. When you click the tab, the Object Tree View switches to show the correct top-level component and its children. You can then drag components from the Object Tree View to the diagram editor. The diagram editor will automatically connect the components if they have a relationship such as parent/child.

You can also add notes to the diagram to indicate the function of specific components or design rationales, or other similar information.

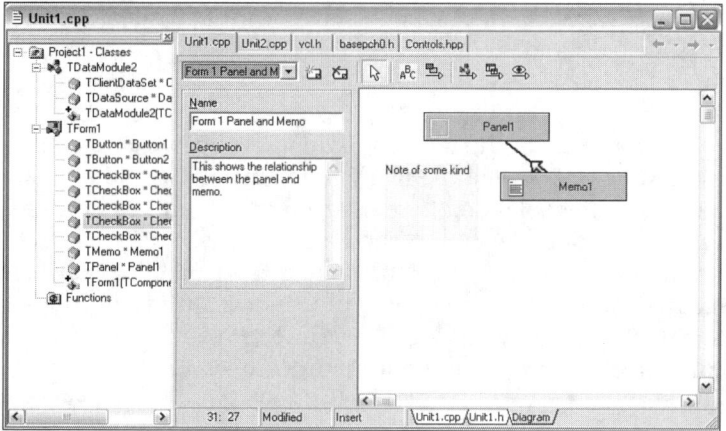

FIGURE 2.7   Source Code Diagram Editor.

The components in the diagram are live in the sense that deleting them from the form or Object Tree View will delete them from the diagram. The reverse, however, is not true—the component can be deleted from the diagram without affecting the actual instance of that component in your project.

On the other hand, if you click the component in the diagram you select the component on the form and the Object Tree View. This suggests the most important use of diagrams—clustering components into meaningful groups that are separate from the parent/child or positioning relationships. This is helped by the ability to have multiple diagrams for each top-level component.

The toolbar allows, from left to right:

- Selection of the diagram to edit
- Creation of a new diagram, deletion of the current diagram
- Selection of a diagram element
- Adding a sticky note
- Drawing a relationship line between two components
- Drawing a property navigation line between two components (though this is performed automatically for most components that refer to each other)
- Drawing a master detail relationship between two data sets
- Drawing a lookup relationship between two data sets

Each diagram must have a name and can have a description.

When the project is saved, the diagram is saved with it, apparently in the .bpr (project) file.

Code Insight

The Code Insight feature of the IDE is an important one. A difficult challenge for a developer is getting to know all the many functions of class libraries and their parameters. Code Insight enables you to see these methods and parameters as you type in the Source Code Editor. Figure 2.8 shows Code Insight offering a set of possible methods for the object to the left of the pointer to member operator. As you type a possible method name, the number of entries shown shrinks to those whose initial characters match what you've typed so far. Functions with void return are displayed in teal (bluish green) and functions with return values are dark blue.

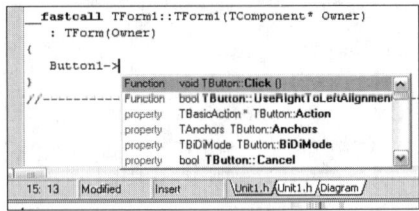

FIGURE 2.8   Code Insight offers a function definition.

Figure 2.9 shows Code Insight offering two possible argument lists because there are two separate overloaded functions for the PaintTo capability.

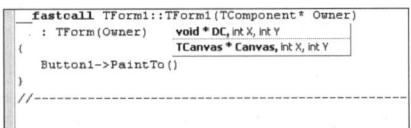

FIGURE 2.9   Code Insight offers an argument list.

The OpenTools API enables you to create custom code completion managers. See Chapter 23, "Open Tools API," for more information.

If you Ctrl-click any entry in the list, the Source Code Editor retrieves the header file that contains the declaration of the function, positioned right on the function.

You can also resize the code completion pop-up window, and that size is remembered across sessions.

If you have the Professional or Enterprise Edition, you also get code completion for HTML documents.

Forms—Save As Text

This feature saves forms as text rather than in binary form and is the default.

Right-click any project form to get the context menu. The Text DFM option is checked by default.

When the form unit or project is saved, the form will be stored as plain text in its DFM file. An example text DFM file is shown in Listing 2.1.

LISTING 2.1   An Example DFM File Saved as Text

```
object Form1: TForm1
  Left = 192
  Top = 107
  Width = 311
  Height = 158
  Caption = 'Text Form'
  Color = clBtnFace
  Font.Charset = DEFAULT_CHARSET
  Font.Color = clWindowText
  Font.Height = -11
  Font.Name = 'MS Sans Serif'
  Font.Style = []
  OldCreateOrder = False
  PixelsPerInch = 96
  TextHeight = 13
  object Label1: TLabel
    Left = 13
    Top = 24
    Width = 277
    Height = 20
    Caption = 'This form is saved as text (default)'
    Font.Charset = DEFAULT_CHARSET
    Font.Color = clWindowText
    Font.Height = -16
    Font.Name = 'MS Sans Serif'
    Font.Style = [fsBold]
    ParentFont = False
  end
  object Button1: TButton
    Left = 114
    Top = 72
    Width = 75
    Height = 25
```

LISTING 2.1   Continued

```
    Caption = 'OK'
    TabOrder = 0
    OnClick = Button1Click
  end
end
```

Unchecking the Text DFM option of a form will cause the form to be saved as binary. You can make this the default for all new forms by unchecking the New Forms as Text option on the Preferences tab of the Environment Options dialog box, shown in Figure 2.10. This is reached by selecting Tools, Environment Options from the main C++Builder menu.

Note, however, that the text version of a form is much less likely to be incompatible with prior or following versions than the binary version.

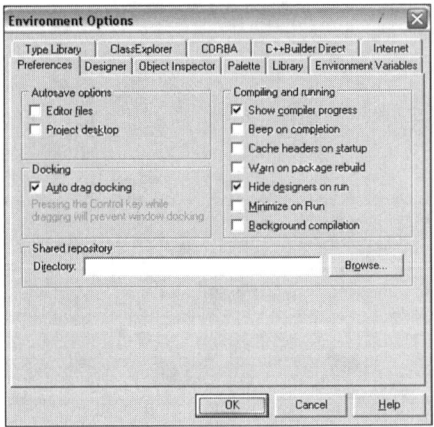

FIGURE 2.10   The Preferences tab of the Environment Options dialog box.

Understanding C++Builder Projects

The IDE provides two-way development by integrating a graphical Form Designer and a text-oriented Source Code Editor, enabling you to develop applications from two angles. Using the ClassExplorer, Code Insight, and standard features of the Form Designer, C++Builder can even generate quite a bit of code!

You can use C++Builder to develop applications of many types, including those in the following list:

- Windows or console applications

- Client/server applications

- Dynamic link libraries (DLLs)

- Custom components and Packages

- Component Object Model (COM) and ActiveX controls

All these applications are created using projects. A *project* is a collection of C++ source files, form files, and other file types that together define the application. C++Builder uses a special project file to store the structure of the project and to remember various project options that change the way the application is built.

Files Used in C++Builder Projects

C++Builder projects consist of many different types of files. C++Builder creates some files automatically; when a new project is started or when new items are added to an existing project, for instance. The developer creates other files, and there are still other files that are created when the application is compiled. Project files, no matter how they are created, can be categorized as follows:

- Main project files

- Form files

- Package files

- The desktop layout file

- Backup files

Main Project Files

When you create most projects, three main files are automatically created. They are shown in the following list:

- C++Builder project file *ProjectName*.bpr

- Main project source file *ProjectName*.cpp

- Main project resource file *ProjectName*.res

The files are initially created internally for you to start using. The files will not be created on disk until you save the project.

By default your project is named Project1. You can change the name of the project when you first save it by renaming the Project1.bpr file in the Save Project As dialog that appears. You should be careful naming the various files in your project. It's a good idea to name each form file the name of the form followed by Unit or Module (for instance, Form1Unit.cpp).

The C++Builder Project File The project file is a text file that contains the project options settings and the rules to build the project. This file has changed somewhat through the different versions of C++Builder. In C++Builder 1 through 4, the file was in a Makefile format. In C++Builder 1 the project file actually had the extension .mak to signify this. In C++Builder 5 the file changed to the Extensible Markup Language (XML) format.

The Main Project Source File This file contains the application entry (startup) code, and little else. C++Builder automatically maintains the file throughout development.

In a standard Windows application, the main project source file contains the WinMain() function as the application entry point. In other types of applications, this function might be named DllEntryPoint() or simply main(). Unlike most other auto-generated source files, this file has no corresponding header (.h) file. You'll seldom need to change the main project source file except to execute a function as the application starts, such as displaying a splash screen while the application is initializing.

NOTE

The IDE will regenerate this function when you add, remove, or reorder the forms in your project. Any code you change within the WinMain function will be removed, so be prepared to replace it.

In a VCL or non-VCL console application, this function is the standard main() function, and it will not be changed by C++Builder, so you can add your own code as needed.

The Project Resource File This file contains the application's icon, the application version number, and other information. Not all application types have a project resource file.

Resource files in general store images, icons, and cursors for your project. To create these items, you typically use a tool such as the Image Editor provided by C++Builder. Resource files can also contain strings and other objects. For a more in-depth look at storing images in a resource file, see "Using Predefined Images in Custom Property and Component Editors" in Chapter 5, "Creating Property and Component Editors."

Form Files

For each Form you create, C++Builder generates the following files:

- The Form layout file *UnitName*.dfm

- The Form source file *UnitName*.cpp

- The Form header file *UnitName*.h

By default the unit name is Unit1 for the first Form created, Unit2 for the second, and so on. You can rename the Form files when saving the project. The extension .dfm stands for Delphi Form, a reminder that C++Builder is based partially on Borland's Delphi product. The .dfm file contains values that represent the graphical part of the Form, such as component locations, font styles, and so on.

In C++Builder versions 1 through 4, the .dfm file is saved in a binary format. It can be viewed as text in these versions by right-clicking the Form, and then selecting View As Text. In C++Builder 5, the .dfm file is saved in a text format by default, but it can be saved in binary format if required. For more information see the "Forms—Save as Text" section in this chapter. You can edit the .dfm Form files if you want, but you rarely need to do so.

The .cpp file and its associated .h header file are created with the .dfm file each time you create a new Form. The .h file contains the C++ class definition for the Form. The .cpp file contains the event handler functions for the Form and for the components that you add to the Form. In simple applications, most of the code that you write will be placed in the Form's .cpp file.

To view the .cpp and .h files, do the following:

1. If your project is not open, select File, Open.

2. Select View, Units, and then choose the unit file of your Form and click OK or press Enter. The .cpp file for the Form will be displayed in the Code Editor.

3. To view the header file, right-click in the Form's .cpp file displayed in the Code Editor and choose Open Source/Header File, or click the tab for the .h file at the bottom of the editor window.

NOTE

Everything mentioned previously for Form files is also true for the DataModule forms that are used to contain nonvisual components. Those are discussed in Chapter 7, " Database Programming."

The Package Project Files

Packages are simply dynamic link libraries (DLLs) that can be shared among many C++Builder applications. They enable you to share classes, components, and data between applications. For example, the most frequently used C++Builder components reside in a Package called VCL. Most applications created in C++Builder share some common code from this package, provided in the Package file vcl60.bpl.

When you create your own components or libraries, you will need to create a package project.

The following are specific Package files:

- The Package Project Options (.bpk) file.

  Consider this file to be like a .bpr project file, but applicable only for packages. This file is created if you choose File | New | Package from the IDE menu.

- The Borland Package Library (.bpl) file.

  This is the runtime library generated by C++Builder for the package. It is like a DLL, except that it contains C++Builder-specific features. Its base name matches the Package source base name.

- The Borland Package Import Library (.bpi) file.

  Each time you compile the package source file, a .bpi file will be created. Again, its base name matches the package source base name.

The Desktop Layout

The window layout for a project stores the arrangement of the various windows open in the IDE and the files open in the Source Code Editor. The next time the project is opened, these settings will be restored.

The Desktop options used to be stored in a file whose name had the format *ProjectName*.dsk and in the same folder as the project. As of C++Builder 6, these values are stored in the project file.

The IDE can be set to save the layout automatically when you close the project. From the menu, select Tools, Environment Options. This will take you to the Environment Options dialog. Select the Preferences tab and check AutoSave Options, Project Desktop.

Backup Files

C++Builder will create a backup file for each of your project's .bpr, .dfm, .cpp, and .h files each time you save your project, except for the first save. All backup file extensions are prefixed with the ~ symbol; thus, the .bpr file extension will become .~bp, .cpp will become .~cp, and so on.

Project Manager

The Project Manager displays the file structure of a project or project group. The Project Manager can be viewed by selecting View, Project Manager from the C++Builder menu. Figure 2.11 shows an example of the Project Manager window.

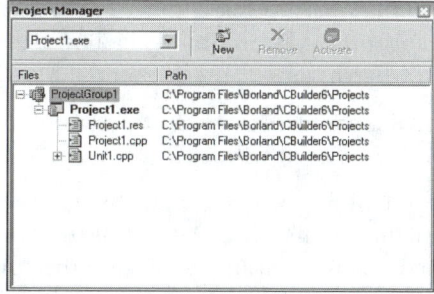

FIGURE 2.11   The Project Manager window for C++Builder.

A project group is a collection of projects. Sometimes you need to create more than one project for an application. For example, an application could have a VCL project, a DLL project, and a console project. The information about the project group is stored in a project group file in the same folder as the project. It has the filename *ProjectName*.bpg.

The following are many of the things you can do in the project Manager:

- Create a project group to hold one or more projects.
- Add or remove projects in a project group.
- Add or remove units from a project.
- Reorder projects within a project group or units within a project using drag and drop.
- Select a project for further operations.
- Compile or build one or more of your projects.

Most of the operations (except for those using drag and drop) can be done using pop-up menus associated with the project group, project, or unit.

Different Builds for Different Files

C++Builder offers a wide variety of options for you to use in controlling the build of your application. Those options generally apply to the project as a whole and are set at that level using the Project, Options menu entry, or Options from the project manager window pop-up for each project in a project group.

These options include a variety of important elements such as the interpretation of C++ language statements as pure ANSI or allowing VCL or MFC extensions; controlling the default data structure element alignment (default is quad word, but a particular program might require byte or word alignment); or what will happen to stack data when an exception is thrown.

You might want to have these settings be different in some compilation units. For instance, you might want some platform independent sections of the code to be compiled as pure ANSI, whereas a user interface should be able to use the VCL.

In many cases, you can and should deal with these option differences by creating and linking separate packages, each with their own options.

But in other cases, you might be able to restrict these option changes to a single or small number of compilation units, with the rest of the project using a standard set of options. This can be done fairly easily by clicking the compilation unit and picking Local Options from its pop-up menu. The resulting dialog offers a variety of options that are generally a subset of the options available for the project (for instance, linker options are not available for compilation units, but are available for the entire project).

Options for C++ units include language options, compiler options, directory search paths for include files, output paths for object files, and many others.

Not all units have local options. Delphi units, for example, do not enable you to override the Pascal options set for the project.

Custom Build Tools

You might not only want to set specific project options for a compilation unit, but you might want a specific build tool as well (for instance, another compiler) for a specific compilation unit. C++ Builder allows this for some types of compilation units.

Tools, Build Tools enables you to create a new entry in the list of build tools and to associate that tool with one or more file extensions. Figure 2.12 shows the dialog to edit or add a tool.

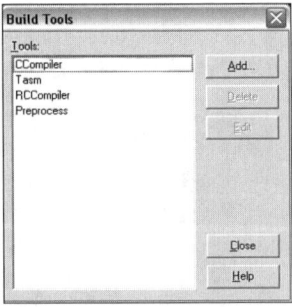

FIGURE 2.12   Dialog to pick or add a Build Tool.

Editing an existing tool such as the CCompiler or Preprocessor produces the dialog in Figure 2.13:

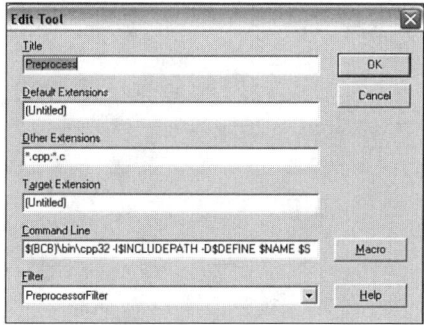

FIGURE 2.13   Build Tool configuration dialog.

This dialog enables you to identify a variety of important elements that control the use of your build tool.

For instance, you can specify the file extensions this tool should automatically be applied to at build or make time (Default Extensions). You can specify the file extensions for which the tool will be available in the Program Manager pop-up menu. The final extension you can specify is the extension of the output from the tool. Although the documentation is silent on this, it is possible that a match of target extension to default extension is used to help order the sequence of executing the tools.

Command Line specifies the command line that will be executed when the time comes to use the tool in the build sequence. A variety of build macros can be supplied to the command line, which expands as follows:

- $DEFINE—any Project Options level #defines in effect.

- $EXT—The extension of the current file.

- $INCLUDEPATH—The directory path for #include files, drawn from the project or local options.

- $NAME—The name and extension of the current file.

- $PATH—The directory where the file exists.

- $TARGETNAME—The name of the target to be produced (usually the same as $NAME without the extension; can be used by the tool to help produce target files).

You can create your own command-line tool quite easily. For instance, the simple program (a VCL console application) in Listing 2.2 is the one shown running in

Figure 2.14. It displays its command line (captured by the IDE and displayed in the message window), which includes expanded versions of the previous macros. Here is the command line from the Build Tool dialog:

```
F:\Mark\Development\CBuilder6\CommandLineTool\MacroLineTool $NAME $EXT $PATH
$INCLUDEPATH $DEFINE $SAVE $TARGETNAME $LOCALCOMMAND
```

LISTING 2.2   A Sample Build Tool

```
//-------------------------------------------.

#include <vcl.h>
#pragma hdrstop

#include <iostream>


//-------------------------------------------.

#pragma argsused
int main(int argc, char* argv[])
{
    for (int Index = 0; Index < argc; Index++)
    {
       std::cout << argv[Index] << "\n";
    };

    return 0;
}
//-------------------------------------------.
```

Obviously, you might get such a tool from a tool vendor, as well as writing one yourself. What kind of things could these tools do? Well, they could produce documentation, generate code, update program information databases, upload the latest build to the deployment machine, anything you can imagine. Build tools are not limited to processing source code—they can process .obj files, or .res files, or anything else you need.

Drag and Drop within Tree to Reorder Compilation

The make process uses the interdependencies between compilation units to decide what to compile first, what to compile next and what to compile last.

In the normal course of events, you don't really care how the make process decides to compile a project, as long as it makes sense. When you have a problem with a specific unit, you can simply compile it by itself.

FIGURE 2.14 A build tool run on itself, displaying all the macros allowed on the command line, expanded, one on each output line.

But sometimes it makes sense to have infrequently changing modules compile following those that change frequently, which can shorten make times.

Understanding and Using Packages

This section discusses packages and how they are used both in applications and by the IDE. The term package refers specifically to a source module with the .bpk extension (Borland Package) and more generally to a Borland Package Library (BPL) file (.bpl extension) that is created when the Package is built. A BPL file is very similar to a dynamic link library (DLL) and is used for the same purpose, to dynamically link executable code to an application.

A package can be one of three types: *design time-only*, *runtime-only*, or dual *design time/runtime*. Essentially, the only difference between these packages is that a design time package can be installed into the IDE, whereas a runtime package cannot. Runtime packages can be used only at runtime. The dual package can be used in either situation and is often used for convenience when initially developing components.

A package consists of two sections: a Contains section and a Requires section. Files that appear in the Contains section are those that the package contains and are compiled and linked when the package itself is compiled and linked. These files are part of the package.

Import files appearing in the Requires section are references to runtime packages that this package must access to function correctly. This mechanism will be explained more clearly later in this section. When a package is built, all the files in the Contains section, where appropriate, are compiled and linked, and object files for each are created.

In addition, a BPL file is generated, as are a Borland Package Import (BPI) file (.bpi extension) and a static library (LIB) file (.lib extension). To not generate a BPI file, select the Linker tab in the Project, Options dialog, and uncheck the Generate Import Library option in the Linking group. To not generate a LIB file, uncheck the Generate .lib File option.

You always need to generate a BPI file, which is used by the IDE during linking, so that the executable can use the respective BPL file at runtime. This is true except in a design time–only Package. Therefore, the same types of files are produced for all Package types. The difference is only apparent in their use. Figure 2.15 shows the structure of a Package in the Project Manager.

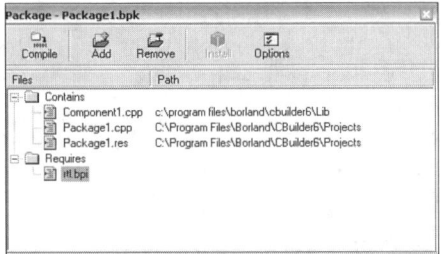

FIGURE 2.15   The structure and output of a package.

Note that in Figure 2.15, the contained units are implied to be C++ translation units. Hence, for each translation unit, an object file is produced when the package is compiled and linked successfully. Other files can also be added to a package's Contains section, most notably resource files and object files. These files are commonly needed when a Package is used to Package components.

The Requires section in Figure 2.15 includes the import file rtl.bpi. This indicates that the Package *requires* executable code contained in rtl.bpl (the runtime library BPL). Placing the .bpi file in the package's Requires section enables the linker to resolve any external references to the runtime library.

Three files are produced when a package is built. One is the BPL file. The nature of the BPL file depends on whether the package is a design time package or a runtime package. If it is a dual package, the functionality of both package types is available. With design time packages, the BPL file is used to install the package into the IDE. You do this by selecting Install Packages from the Components menu and browsing for the design time package .bpl file. With runtime packages, the BPL file is used specifically to allow applications to link dynamically to the functions and data that the package contains at runtime.

For an application to link dynamically to a .bpl file, the linker must be able to resolve references to the functions and data contained by the .bpl file during linking. Such a reference is referred to as an *external reference* because it refers to something external to the current application. To resolve an external reference, the linker searches for an *import record* for the function called by the application. The import record is contained in the corresponding Borland Package Import (BPI) file (.bpi extension) for the package.

For every function that is *exported* from the package (basically any function that is declared in a unit contained by the package), there is an entry that states the internal name of the function and the name of the module that contains the function. In this case, that is the name of the package's BPL file (more information than this is presented, but it is not relevant to this discussion). The linker to the application's executable file copies this information. This creates a dynamic link to the function that will be resolved by Windows each time the application is executed. It does this by searching all the files on the system path (for example, files in the Windows system directory) for the file named by the import record when the application is loaded into memory. If it finds the required BPL file, that also is loaded into memory. The external reference is then referenced to the correct location within the BPL file. If the required BPL is already loaded into memory, all the better. The overhead for this operation is not incurred, and the BPL is shared by the applications using it. The function or data can then be used by the application.

It should be clear that the BPL and BPI files produced by a runtime package are used to support dynamic linking of the code that the package exports. The LIB file is used to support static linking of the code that the package exports. Essentially, the LIB file contains the OBJ files of the units contained by the package itself and is in fact an *object library*. When a function is required from the package, the appropriate OBJ from the LIB file is copied to the target executable. Each such executable, therefore, has its own copy.

Table 2.2 summarizes the purpose of the files produced by a package when it is successfully built.

TABLE 2.2   Package Files Created on a Successful Build

Extension	Description	Type	Purpose
.bpl	Borland Package Library (BPL)	Dynamically linkable library	Contains executable code of the package and exports the functions and data of the package. A runtime library accessed by applications that are dynamically linked to it. A design time library that can be installed into the IDE to make new components or editors available at design time.
.bpi	Borland Import Library (BPI)	Import library	Contains import records for the functions and data exported by the corresponding BPL file required for dynamic linking to the BPL file.
.lib	Static Library File (LIB)	Object library	A static library containing the object files of the units contained by the package. Used to statically link exported functions and data to a target application.

Table 2.2 shows that, in order to use a runtime BPL, the corresponding BPI file must be available at link time for the external references to the BPL to be resolved.

When you compile and link a project, you can choose whether the project is dynamically linked or statically linked to the packages it requires. By default, dynamic linking is used. To change this setting for the project, uncheck the Build with Runtime Packages option on the Project, Options, Packages page.

It is also possible to choose units from a package that you want to be statically linked to a given unit within a project. To do this, add the `#pragma link "unitname"` directive, generally near the top of the unit, where *unitname* is the name of the unit that you want to be statically linked to the unit within your project. This results in the linker copying the required object file from the package's .lib file.

Considerations When Using Packages

For a class to be properly imported and exported from a package, the PACKAGE macro must be used after the class keyword in the class definition, as shown in the following code:

```
class PACKAGE TMyComponent : public TComponent
{
    // Component class definition here.
};
```

The PACKAGE macro must also be given in the declaration of the Register() function for the component. This is shown in the following code:

```
namespace Newcomponent
{
    void __fastcall PACKAGE Register()
    {
        TComponentClass classes[1] = {__classid(TMyComponent)};
        RegisterComponents("Samples", classes, 0);
    }
}
```

Of course, this applies to component class definitions. If you use the Component Wizard (Component, New Component) to create the component, C++Builder will insert the PACKAGE macro for you.

To ensure that functions and data are properly imported and exported from a unit contained in a package, the #pragma package(smart_init) directive should be placed in the unit's source file, typically after any #include statements, but before any source code. Failing to do so will not prevent the unit from compiling, but it will prevent the package from statically linking. The purpose of the directive is to ensure that the packaged units are initialized in the order determined by their dependencies.

The #pragma package(smart_init,weak) directive is also available. This is used when you do not want a particular unit to be contained in the BPL file. Instead, the unit is placed in the BPI file. When the unit is required, it is copied from the BPI file and statically linked to the target application. Such a unit is said to be *weakly packaged* and is used to eliminate conflicts among packages that might depend on the same external library.

Using the C++Builder Interactive Debugger

C++Builder's interactive debugger contains many advanced features, including expression evaluation, data setting, object inspection, complex breakpoints, a machine code disassembly view, an FPU and MMX register view, cross-process debugging, remote debugging, attaching to a running process, watching expression results, call stack viewing, the capability to single-step through code, and more. During development you will spend a lot of time using it, or at least you probably will need to!

The debugger is not just for finding bugs; it is also a general development tool that can give you great insight into how your application works at a low level.

To use the debugger effectively, you must first disable compiler optimizations. When compiler optimizations are enabled, the optimizer will do everything in its power to speed up or reduce the size of your code, including removing, rearranging, and grouping sections of machine code generated from your source. This makes it very difficult to step through your code and to match up source code with machine code in the CPU view. If you set a breakpoint on a line, and it is not hit when you are confident that the line was executed, it is probably because you have optimizations enabled.

Screen real estate becomes a problem with the many debug views that you're likely to need during a debugging session. You can make use of the desktop settings to create a layout appropriate for programming and a separate layout for debugging.

A typical desktop layout for debugging is shown in Figure 2.16. You can see at the bottom the docked windows, now tabbed pages, for the call stack and the watch list. To the right is the Debug Inspector, which is much like the Object Inspector, except it shows runtime values (this window is not dockable). Docked to the right of the Source Code Editor are the Breakpoint List Window and the Local Variable Window (which shows the current values of the local variables for the current breakpoint function).

For the remainder of this section, it is assumed that you understand the basics of debuggers. Such basics include using source breakpoints with expression and pass-count conditions, stepping over and into code, and using ToolTip expression evaluation (holding the mouse pointer over an expression while the application is paused in the debugger).

Multithreaded Application Debugging

If you are writing multithreaded applications, you can name your thread. Simply select File, New, and pick Thread Object from the Dialog. This creates a compilation unit whose class is based on TThread. The dialog shown in Figure 2.17 enables you to specify a name for the thread. Why does this matter? Well, the debug window for threads will use that name and make it much easier for you to see what's happening in your multithreaded application.

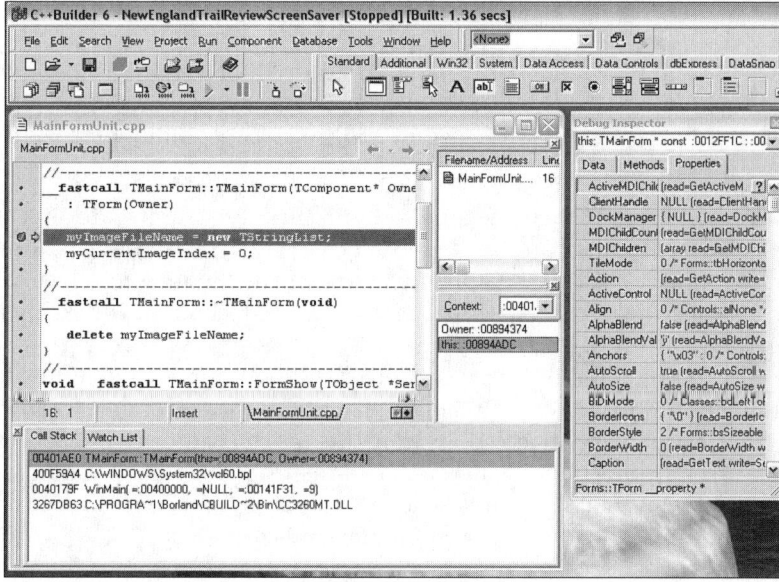

FIGURE 2.16   An example debugging window layout.

FIGURE 2.17   Task Object dialog.

After you have created your thread object and set up your program to run it, you can open the thread debugging window (which is done by picking View|Debug Windows|Thread). Figure 2.18 shows this dialog:

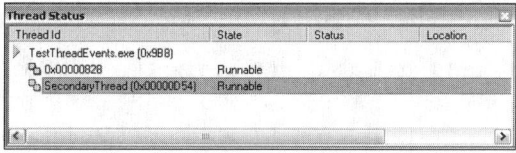

FIGURE 2.18   The Thread debug window shows the name of the named thread.

Advanced Breakpoints

Apart from the standard source breakpoints that simply halt execution when the selected source or assembly line is reached, there are more advanced breakpoints that can be used in particular debugging cases.

Module load breakpoints are particularly useful when debugging DLLs and packages. You can pause execution when a specified module is loaded, providing a perfect entry point into the DLL or package for debugging. To set a module load breakpoint, you have two options.

The first option applies when the application is already running within the IDE. First, display the Modules window by selecting View, Debug Windows, Modules. Next, in the modules list in the upper-left pane of the Modules window, locate the module for which you want to set the module load breakpoint. If the module is not in the modules list, it has not yet been loaded by the application. In that case, you will need to add the module to the modules list by selecting Add Module from the context menu, then name or browse to the module, and select OK. Finally, select the module in the modules list, and then select Break On Load from the context menu. This is shown in Figure 2.19. If the module has already been loaded by the application, the breakpoint will work only when the module is loaded again, either after being dynamically unloaded or when the system is restarted.

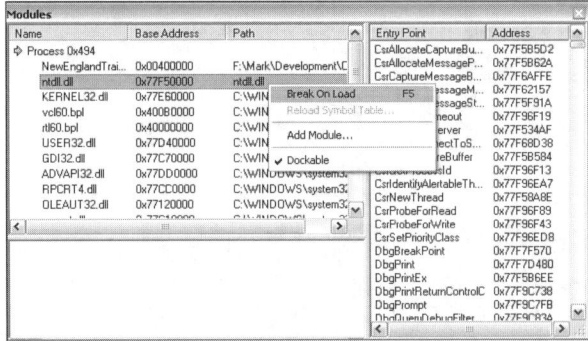

FIGURE 2.19   Setting a module load breakpoint from the Modules view.

The second option applies when the application is not yet running within the IDE. Select Run, Add Breakpoint, Module Load Breakpoint, then enter the module name or browse to it and select OK. Finally, run the application.

Address breakpoints and Data breakpoints provide a way to pause the application when a particular code address is reached or data at a particular address is modified. They can only be added when the application is running or paused.

Address breakpoints work in the same manner as source breakpoints, but instead of adding the breakpoint to a particular line of source code, you add the breakpoint to the memory address for a particular machine code instruction. When the machine code is executed, the breakpoint action is taken. If you set an address breakpoint for a machine code instruction that is related to a line of source code, the breakpoint is set as a normal source breakpoint on that line of source code. Address breakpoints are typically used when debugging external modules on a low level using the CPU view. The CPU view is explained in the section "The CPU View," later in this chapter.

You can also set an address breakpoint. In the `Breakpoints` folder on the CD-ROM that accompanies this book, you will find the `BreakpointProj.bpr` project file. Load it with C++Builder, and then compile and run the application by selecting Run, Run. When the form is displayed, pause the application by selecting Run, Program Pause from the C++Builder main menu. The CPU view, which we will use in a moment, will be displayed.

Next, select View, Units, then select `BreakpointForm` from the units list and select OK. The unit will be displayed in the Code Editor. Scroll down to the `AddressBreakpoint` `ButtonClick()` function. Right-click the `Label2->Caption = "New Caption"` statement in the function and select Debug, View CPU from the context menu. The CPU view is again displayed, this time at the memory address where the machine code for the C++ statement is located.

In the upper-left pane in the CPU view, note the hexadecimal number on the far left of the line containing the machine code statement `lea eax,[ebp-0x04]`. On my system at present, this number is `004016ED`, but it is likely to be different on yours. This is the address at which we will set the address breakpoint.

To add an address breakpoint for this address, select Run, Add Breakpoint, Address Breakpoint. Then, in the Address field, enter the address that you previously noted. Hexadecimal numbers, such as the address displayed in the CPU view that you noted, must be entered with a leading `0x`; in my case I would specify the address as `0x004016ED`.

To test the address breakpoint, continue the program by selecting Run, Run. Select the application from the Windows taskbar and click the Address Breakpoint button. The address breakpoint that was previously set will cause the application to pause. The CPU view will be displayed with the current execution point, marked by a green arrow, set on the address breakpoint line of machine code. You can continue the application by selecting Run, Run.

If, in the CPU view, you display the line of machine code at the address you want to place an address breakpoint, you can set an address breakpoint simply by clicking in the gutter of the machine code line, as you would in source code for a source breakpoint.

Data breakpoints can be invaluable in helping to track bugs, by locating where in the code a particular variable or memory location is being set. As an example, load the BreakpointProj.bpr project file from the previous demonstration. Run and then pause the application. Select Run, Add Breakpoint, Data Breakpoint. In the Address field, enter Form1->FClickCount and click OK. This private data member of the form counts the number of times that the form's DataBreakpointButton button is clicked. Setting this data breakpoint will cause the application to break whenever the count is modified.

As you can see, any valid data address expression can be entered, not just a memory address. Alternatively, to obtain the address, we can select Run, Inspect, enter Form1->FClickCount in the expression, and obtain the address from the top of the Debug Inspector window. This hexadecimal address could then be entered (with a leading 0x) in the data breakpoint Address field.

To test the data breakpoint, continue the program by selecting Run, Run. Select the application from the Windows taskbar and click the Data Breakpoint button. The previously set data breakpoint will cause the application to pause at the location where the data was modified. If this is on a source line, the Code Editor will be displayed; otherwise the CPU view will be displayed. You can continue the application by selecting Run, Run.

TIP

Adding a data breakpoint is much trickier for a property such as the Caption of a label or the Text of an edit box. These properties are not direct memory locations that are written to when the property is modified. Instead, the properties use Set functions to change their values. To break when the property is changed, it is easiest to add an address breakpoint for the Set function of the property, rather than finding the memory address where the data is actually stored and adding a data breakpoint. I'll explain this method using the Caption property of ClickCountLabel on the form of the previous demonstration project.

With the application paused, select Run, Inspect. In the Expression field enter Form1->Click CountLabel. Select the Properties tab in the Debug Inspector window and scroll down to the Caption property. The write method for this property is specified as SetText. Click the Methods tab and scroll down to the SetText method. The address of this method will be displayed on the right. Select Run, Add Breakpoint, Address Breakpoint and enter the address of the SetText method, prefixing it with 0x and leaving out the colon; then click OK. Continue the application by selecting Run, Run. Now, whenever the label caption is modified, the breakpoint will pause the application.

For a standard AnsiString variable without a Set method to control its modification, such as the FSomeString private data member of the form in the demonstration project, you can set a data breakpoint on the .Data variable of the AnsiString class that contains the underlying string data. For the demonstration project, the data breakpoint would be set on Form1->FSomeString.Data.

When adding a data breakpoint, the Length field in the Add Data Breakpoint window should be specified for nonsingular data types such as structures or arrays. The breakpoint will pause the application when any memory location within this length from the data address is modified. Data breakpoints can also be added by selecting Break when Changed from the context menu in the View, Debug Windows, Watches view.

NOTE

Address and data breakpoints are valid only for the current application being run. You must set them for each new run because the machine code instruction and data addresses can change each time.

Advanced Breakpoint Features

Breakpoints can be organized into groups and have actions. With breakpoint actions, you can enable and disable groups of actions, enable and disable exception handling, log a message to the event log, and log the evaluation of an expression to the event log.

Using these features, you can set up complex breakpoint interaction to break only in specific program circumstances. For example, you can cause a set of breakpoints to be enabled only when a specific section of code is executed.

By disabling and enabling exceptions, you can control error handling in known problem areas of code. Message logging helps automate variable inspection and execution tracing.

Breakpoint action and group information are available in the breakpoint ToolTip in the Code Editor and in the Breakpoint List Window.

C++Builder Debugging Views

The debugger can be used to display many types of information that are helpful with debugging an application, such as local variables, a list of all breakpoints, the call stack, a list of the loaded modules, thread status, machine code, data and register status, an application event log, and more.

The Floating-Point Unit (FPU) view shows the current state of the floating point and MMX registers. All debugging views are accessible from the View, Debug Windows menu option, or by pressing the appropriate shortcut key. In the following sections we'll look at some of the advanced views, and how you can use them in debugging your application.

The CPU View

The CPU View displays your application at the machine code level. The machine code and disassembled assembly code that make up your application are displayed along with the CPU registers and flags, the machine stack, and a memory dump. The CPU view has five panes, as depicted in Figure 2.20.

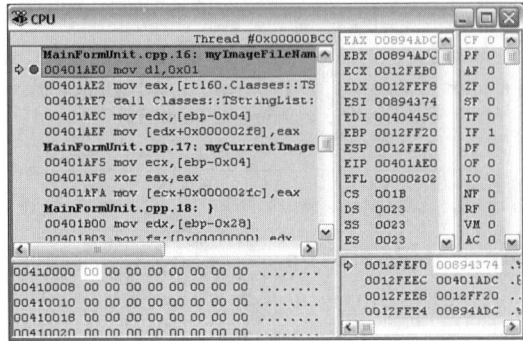

FIGURE 2.20 The CPU view in action.

The large pane on the left is the disassembly pane. It displays the disassembled machine code instructions, also known as assembly code, that make up your application. The instruction address is in the left column, followed by the machine code data and the equivalent assembly code. Displayed above the disassembly pane are the effective address of the expression in the currently selected line of machine code, the value stored at that address, and the thread ID.

If you enabled the Debug Information option on the Compiler tab of the project options before compiling your application, the disassembly pane shows your C++ source code lines above the corresponding assembly code instructions. Some C++ source code lines can be seen in Figure 2.20.

In the disassembly pane, you can step through the machine code one instruction at a time, much like you step through one source code line at a time in the source code editor. The green arrow shows the current instruction that is about to be executed. You can set breakpoints and use other features similar to debugging in the source code editor. Several options, such as changing threads, searching through memory for data, and changing the current execution point are available in the context menu.

The CPU registers pane is to the right of the disassembly pane. It shows the current value of each of the CPU registers. When a register changes, it is shown in red. You can modify the value of the registers via the context menu.

On the far right is the CPU flags pane. This is an expanded view of the EFL (32-bit flags) register in the CPU register pane. You can toggle the value of a flag through the context menu. Consult the online help for a description of each of the flags.

Below the disassembly pane is the memory dump pane. It can be used to display the content of any memory location in your application's address space. On the left is the memory address, followed by a hexadecimal dump of the memory at that address and an ASCII view of the memory. You can change how this data is displayed from the context menu, and also go to a specified address or search for particular data.

The final pane is the machine stack pane, located at the bottom right of the CPU window. It displays the content of the application's current stack, pointed to by the ESP (stack pointer) CPU register. It is similar to the memory dump pane and offers similar context menu options.

The CPU view is a good tool for getting to know how your application works at a very low level. If you come to understand your application at this level, you will have a better understanding of pointers and arrays; you'll know more about execution speed (helpful when optimizing your application); and you'll find it easier to debug your application because you will know what's going on in the background.

The best reference for the x86 machine code instruction set and detailed information on the Pentium processor range is the Intel Architecture Software Developer's Manual. This three-volume set tells you just about everything you want to know about the Pentium processors. It is available for download on Intel's Web site (http://developer.intel.com/design/processor) from the appropriate processor's Manuals section.

Assembly language programming is a black art these days. It is extremely complex and is usually reserved only for writing small sections of very efficient, speed-critical code.

The Call Stack View

A call stack is the path of functions that lead directly to the current point of execution. Only functions that have been previously called and have not yet returned are in the call stack.

The Call Stack view displays the call stack with the most recently entered function at the top of the list. Used in conjunction with conditional breakpoints, the Call Stack view provides useful information as to how the function containing the breakpoint was reached. This is particularly useful if the function is called from many places throughout the application.

You can double-click a function listed in the Call Stack view to display it in the Code Editor. If there is no source code for the function—for example, if the function is located in an external module—the disassembled machine code of the function is displayed in the CPU view. In either case, the next statement or instruction to be executed at that level in the call stack is selected.

You can display the Local Variables view for a particular function on the call stack by selecting View Locals from the context menu.

The Threads View

Debugging multiprocess and multithreaded applications can be very difficult. Threads, in particular, usually execute asynchronously. Often the threads in the application communicate with each other using the Win32 API PostThreadMessage() function or use a mutex object to gain access to a shared resource.

When debugging a multithreaded application, you can pause an individual thread. One thread might hit a breakpoint and another might not. The problems occur when another thread is still running and is relying on interthread communication, or the stopped thread has an open mutex for which another thread is waiting.

Even the fact that the application runs more slowly under the debugger can cause timing problems if the application is multithreaded. In general, it is bad programming practice not to allow for reasonable timing fluctuations because you cannot control the environment in which the application is run.

The Threads view helps to alleviate some of these difficulties by giving you a snapshot of the current status of all processes and threads in the application. Each process has a main thread, and might have additional threads. The Threads view displays the threads in a hierarchical way, such that all threads of a process are grouped together. The first process and the main thread are listed first. The process name and process ID are shown for each process, and the thread ID, state, status, and location are shown for each thread. Figure 2.18 shows an example of the Threads view.

For secondary processes the process state is Spawned, Attached, or Cross-Process Attach. The process state is Runnable, Stopped, Blocked, or None. The thread location is the current source position for the thread. If the source is not available, the current execution address is shown.

When debugging multiprocess or multithreaded applications, there is always a single-current thread. The process that the thread belongs to is the current process. The current process and current thread are denoted in the Threads view by a green arrow, which can be seen in Figure 2.18. Most debugger views and actions relate to the current thread. The current process and current thread can be changed by selecting a process or thread in the Threads view and selecting Make Current from the context menu, from which you can also terminate a process. For information on additional settings and commands in the Threads view, see "Thread status box" in the Index of the C++Builder online help.

The Modules View

The Modules view lists all DLLs and packages that have been loaded with the currently running application or modules that have a module load breakpoint set when the application is not running. It is very useful when debugging DLLs and packages, as discussed in the "Advanced Breakpoints" section earlier in this chapter. Figure 2.19 shows a typical Modules view.

The Modules view has three panes. The upper-left pane contains the list of modules, their base addresses, and the full paths to their locations. Note that the base address is the address at which the module was actually loaded, not necessarily the base address specified on the Linker tab of the project options when developing the module. By selecting a module, you can set a module load breakpoint from the context menu.

The lower-left pane contains a tree view of the source files that were used to build the module. You can select a source file and view it in the Code Editor by selecting View Source from the context menu.

The right pane lists the entry points for the module and the addresses of the entry points. From the context menu, you can go to the entry point. If there is source available for the entry point, it will be displayed in the Code Editor. If there is no source, the entry point will be displayed in the CPU view.

The FPU View

The Floating-Point Unit (FPU) view enables you to view the state of the floating-point unit or MMX information when debugging your application.

The FPU view has three panes. The left pane displays the floating-point register stack (ST0 to ST7 registers), the control word, status word, and tag words of the FPU. For the floating-point register stack, the register status and value are shown. The status is either Empty, Zero, Valid, or Spec (special), depending on the register stack's contents.

When a stack register's status is not Empty, its value is also displayed. You can toggle the formatting of the value from long double to words by selecting the appropriate option under Display As in the context menu. You can also zero, empty, or set a value for a particular stack register, and zero or set a value for the control word, status word, and tag word from the context menu.

The middle pane contains the FPU single and multibit control flags, which change as floating-point instructions are executed. Their values can be toggled or cycled via the context menu.

The right pane contains the FPU status flags. It is an expanded view of the status word in the FPU registers pane, listing each status flag individually. Their values can be toggled or cycled via the context menu.

When a value changes, it is displayed in red in all panes. You can see this effect best by performing single steps through floating-point instructions in the CPU view.

Watches, Evaluating, and Modifying

A watch is simply a means of viewing the contents of an expression throughout the debugging process. An expression can be a simple variable name or a complex expression involving pointers, arrays, functions, values, and variables. The Watches view displays the expressions and their results in the watch list. You can display the Watches view by selecting View, Debug Windows, Watches. The Watches view is automatically displayed when a new watch expression is added.

You can add expressions to the watch list using one of three methods. The first method is from the Add Watch item of the context menu in the Watches view. The second method is by selecting Run, Add Watch. The third method is by right-clicking the appropriate expression in the Code Editor and selecting Debug, Add Watch at Cursor from the context menu. This last method automatically enters the expression for you.

Watches can be edited, disabled, or enabled via the context menu. Watches can be deleted by selecting the appropriate expression and pressing the Delete key or by selecting Delete Watch from the context menu. If the expression cannot be evaluated because one or more of the parts of the expression is not in scope, an undefined symbol message appears instead of the evaluated result.

On the other hand, evaluating and modifying expressions enables you to more readily change the expression, view the subsequent result, and modify variables at runtime. With Evaluate/Modify, you can perform detailed live testing that is difficult to perform by other means.

To use Evaluate/Modify, your application must be paused. There are two ways to use it. One is to simply select Run, Evaluate/Modify, and enter the expression to evaluate. Perhaps the easiest method is to invoke Evaluate/Modify from the Code Editor.

When the application is paused in the debugger, you can evaluate expressions in the source code simply by placing the mouse pointer over them. Evaluate/Modify enables you to change the expression at will. You can invoke it by right-clicking the expression and selecting Debug, Evaluate/Modify. In the Evaluate/Modify window, you will see the expression and its result. The Modify field enables you to change the expression value if it is a simple data type. If you need to modify a structure or an array, you will have to modify each field or item individually.

Function calls can be included in the expression. Be aware, though, that evaluating an expression produces the same result as if your application executed that expression. If the expression contains side effects, they will be reflected in the running state of your application when you continue to step through or run.

Unlike the Watches view, the Evaluate/Modify dialog box doesn't update the result of the expression automatically when you step through your code. You must click the Evaluate button to see the current result. The expression result can also be formatted using a format modifier at the end of the expression. See the online help for more information.

Typical uses for Evaluate/Modify include testing error conditions and tracking down bugs. To test an error condition, simply set a breakpoint at or just before the error check or step through the code to reach it, and then force an error by setting the appropriate error value using Modify. Use Single Step or Run to verify that the error is handled correctly.

If you suspect that a certain section of code contains a bug and sets incorrect data, set a breakpoint just after the suspected code, fix the data manually, and then continue execution to verify that the bad data is producing the bug's symptoms. Trace backward through code until you locate the bug, or use a data breakpoint to find out when the data is modified.

The Debug Inspector

The Debug Inspector is like a runtime object inspector. It can be used to display the data, methods, and properties of classes, structures, arrays, functions, and simple data types at runtime, thus providing a convenient all-in-one watch/modifier.

With the application paused in the debugger, you can start the Debug Inspector by selecting Run, Inspect, and entering the element to inspect as an expression, or by right-clicking an element expression in the Code Editor and selecting Debug, Inspect from the context menu. The element expression in the second method is automatically entered into the inspector.

The title of the Debug Inspector window contains the thread ID. In the top of the window are the name, type, and memory address of the element. There are up to three tabs, depending on the element type, that display the name and contents or address of each data member, method, or property. The Property tab is shown only for classes derived from the VCL. At the bottom of the window, the type of the currently selected item is shown.

The values of simple types can be modified. If the item can be modified, an ellipsis will be shown in the value cell. Click the ellipsis and enter the new value.

The Debug Inspector can be used to walk down and back up the class and data hierarchy. To inspect one of the data members, methods, or properties in the current inspector window simply select it, and then choose Inspect from the context menu. You can also hide or show inherited items.

There are four Debug Inspector options that can be set from Tools, Debugger Options: Inspectors Stay On Top, Show Inherited, Sort By Name, and Show Fully

Qualified Names. Show Inherited switches the view in the Data, Methods, and Properties tabs between two modes, one that shows all intrinsic and inherited data members or properties of a class and one that shows only those declared in the class. Sort By Name switches between sorting the items listed by name or by declaration order. Show Fully Qualified Names shows inherited members using their fully qualified names and is displayed only if Show Inherited is also enabled. All three new options can be set via the context menu in the Debug Inspector.

The Debug Inspector is a commonly used tool during a debugging session because it displays so many items at once. It also enables you to walk up and down the class and data hierarchy.

Advanced Debugging

As mentioned previously, debugging is an advanced topic in itself. However, there are several specific issues and cases that are beyond the basic debugging techniques presented in the first section of this chapter.

For any serious application development and debugging, I thoroughly recommend that you use the Windows NT (WinNT), Windows 2000 (Win2K, which is based on Windows NT), or Windows XP Professional operating systems, and not the Windows 95 or Windows 98 (Win9x) operating systems. The newer versions provide a much more stable environment, particularly with buggy applications.

WinNT-based operating systems handle application stopping and crashes much better than Win9x. On a Win9x system, it is much easier to crash C++Builder or even the whole system when debugging or stopping an application midstream. Use Run, Program Reset sparingly, and stop the application through normal user means if possible.

Note that on any system it might be possible for database applications to hang the BDE as a result of a Program Reset.

When your application performs an illegal operation or access violation while running within the C++Builder IDE, an error occurs, and you are presented with an error dialog box. On a Win9x system you should reset your application using Run, Program Reset before closing the dialog box. This usually recovers more reliably than when closing the dialog box first.

For really serious debugging, particularly of Windows system applications, you can obtain a debug version of the Windows operating system, called a debug binary for Win9x and checked/debug build for WinNT/2K/XP. The checked build provides error checking, argument verification, and system debugging code for the Windows operating system code and Win32 API functions, mostly in the form of assertions that are not present in the retail version. This checking imposes a performance penalty.

These special builds of Windows operating systems are provided with some Microsoft Developer Network (MSDN) subscriptions (see http://msdn.microsoft.com for more information).

Sometimes it is useful to know if your application is running in the context of the debugger. The Win32 API function IsDebuggerPresent() returns true if it is. You can use this fact to alter the behavior of the application at runtime; for example, outputting additional debug information to make the application easier to debug.

Now let's look at several more advanced debugging tasks.

Locating the Source of Access Violations

Earlier in this chapter we examined some basic techniques for locating bugs. Access violations (AVs) are sometimes more difficult to locate than general program bugs. Other application errors are similar to AVs, and the techniques described here apply to those also.

Access violations can be caused by access to memory that is not within the application's memory space. If at all possible, you should use CodeGuard to check your application at runtime. CodeGuard can detect many errors that would normally result in an AV and pinpoint the exact line of source code that produced the error. If you can't use CodeGuard for your application, or CodeGuard does not detect the error that caused the AV, there are other things you can do to track down the error.

When an AV occurs, a dialog box is presented with the message Access violation at address YYYYYYYY. Read of address ZZZZZZZZ. Application errors can present a different message, such as The instruction at 0xYYYYYYYY referenced memory at 0xZZZZZZZZ. In these cases, the YYYYYYYY address is the machine code that caused the error, and address ZZZZZZZZ is the invalid memory address that it attempted to access.

It is possible to locate where some access violations occurred by implementing a global exception handler. Alternatively, you can run your application within C++Builder and wait for the AV to occur.

If you can't reproduce the AV when running within C++Builder, simply pause your application using Run, Pause or by setting and hitting a breakpoint, open the CPU view and select Goto Address from the context menu. This is not foolproof, but it often works. Enter the code address given in the AV dialog box in hexadecimal as 0xYYYYYYYY. The code around this address might give you some clue as to where in your source code the AV occurred, particularly if the application was compiled with debug information.

When the memory address ZZZZZZZZ is close to zero, for instance 00000089, the cause is often an uninitialized pointer that has been accessed. The following code would produce an AV with this memory address because the MyButton object was never created with new.

```
TButton *MyButton;
MyButton->Height = 10;
```

What is actually happening is that when MyButton is declared it is initialized with a value of zero. The address 00000089 is actually the address of the Height property within the TButton object if it were located at address zero.

As a general rule, you should explicitly initialize pointers to some recognizable value before the memory or object is allocated, and back to that value once it has been freed. If you get an AV that lists this value, you know an uninitialized pointer caused it.

Sometimes an AV can occur in a multithreaded application in which concurrent access to objects and data is not controlled. These can be very difficult to find. Use data breakpoints and the outputting debug information techniques described earlier in this chapter if you suspect concurrency problems.

Attaching to a Running Process

When a process is running outside the C++Builder IDE, you can still debug it using the integrated debugger by attaching to it while it is running. This feature can be handy during testing. When you detect the occurrence of a bug in the application, you can attach to the application process and track down the bug. The only drawback is that Windows does not provide a method for detaching from the process without terminating it.

To attach to a running process, select Run, Attach to Process. The Attach To Process window is displayed with a list of running processes on the local machine. Select the appropriate process from the list and click the Attach button. The C++Builder debugger will then attach to the process. The process will be paused, and the CPU view will be displayed at the current execution point. You can step through the code, set breakpoints, load the source code, if available, using View Source from the context menu, inspect values, and so on.

Attach To Process is even more useful for remote debugging. In the Attach To Process window, you can view and attach to processes on another machine that is running the remote debug server. This is covered in the "Using Remote Debugging" section, later in this chapter.

In the window you can also view system processes by checking Show System Processes.

You should be very careful about attaching to any old process; you can cause Windows to crash or hang by attaching to system processes. Stick to attaching to your own processes.

Using Just-In-Time Debugging

Just-in-time (JIT) debugging is a feature of the Windows NT and higher operating systems that enables you to debug a process at the time that it fails; for instance, when an access violation is caused. JIT debugging might not be available on Windows 9x machines.

If you've used Windows NT or Windows 2000 before, you've no doubt heard of Dr. Watson. This is a JIT debugging tool provided with Windows to help identify the cause of a program failure. The selected JIT debugging tool can be changed. The current JIT debugging tool is usually set via a Registry entry; however, the Borland debugger launcher, BORDBG*.EXE (the * refers to the current version number), can be called instead of Dr. Watson. Then, with each JIT debugging instance, you can select which debugger to use from the debugger launcher, such as the C++Builder debugger, Delphi debugger, Dr. Watson, or even the Borland Turbo Debugger.

Prior to C++Builder 5, the call to Dr. Watson could be replaced with a call directly to the C++Builder debugger; no debugger selection was available. If only one debugger is configured in the list, it is automatically launched. See "Just in time debuggers," in the C++Builder online help for instructions on how to configure the JIT debuggers to list in the debugger launcher.

After configured, JIT debugging is easy to use. When the application crashes, Windows will run the debugger launcher. Select the appropriate debugger from the list, BCB (C++Builder) in this case, and click OK. At this point, C++Builder will start if it is not already running, and the application will be paused as if it were attached while running. You can then use any of the techniques described earlier in this chapter to locate the source of the bug.

Remote Debugging

Remote debugging is the capability to debug an application running on another machine using the C++Builder interactive debugger running on your local machine. It is beneficial for applications running on remote machines that would be inconvenient to access physically, and it does not require C++Builder to be installed on the remote machine.

Remote debugging is very useful for debugging distributed applications, such as those that use DCOM or CORBA. Debugging should be performed locally whenever possible because of the reduced performance when debugging across a network.

Remote debugging is supported for executables, DLLs, and packages. The application must have been compiled with debugging information, and the debugging symbol's .tds file must be available with the application on the remote machine. The easiest way to achieve this is to load the application's project into C++Builder on the local machine. Then, specify the Final output path in the Directories/Conditionals tab of the project options to be the shared network folder on the remote machine where the application will run. And, finally, compile the application with debug information.

Remotely debugging an application is virtually seamless. After the remote debug session is connected, you work just as you would when debugging a local application.

Configuring Remote Debugging

Remote debugging works by running the Borland debug server on the remote machine. You might notice that the Borland debug server is the same program as the Borland debug launcher, described previously in the "Using Remote Debugging" section. It can perform either of these functions depending on the command-line options used to start it. The debug server requires additional DLLs to be installed. The local C++Builder debugger communicates with the debug server.

On remote Windows NT and higher machines, the debug server is usually installed as a service. It will show as Borland Remote Debugging Service in the Services applet of the Control Panel. The debug server service can be started or stopped from the applet and can be set to start automatically when the system boots. Use the -install and -remove command-line options to install and remove the service.

On remote Windows 9x machines, the debug server is a standalone process. This is also an option for WinNT and up machines. In any case, the remote debug server must be running before remote debugging can commence.

You can install the debug server with associated DLLs required from the C++Builder installation CD using the standard install dialog or by running SETUP.EXE in the RDEBUG folder of the CD. Remote debugging uses TCP/IP for communication between the local C++Builder IDE and the remote debug server. You must have TCP/IP networking configured correctly on both machines.

To start the debug server manually, run BORDBG*.EXE -listen. You will need administration or debugging rights to run the debug server.

Using Remote Debugging

When the debug server has been installed on the remote machine and it is already running, you can start debugging remotely. From the local C++Builder IDE, open the project for the remote application that you will be debugging. Select Run, Parameters, click the Remote tab, and set Remote Path to the remote application's full path and application filename as you would use locally on that machine, such as C:\Temp\MyProj.exe. If you are debugging a DLL on the remote machine, enter the path and name of the remote application that will host the DLL. Enter any command-line parameters for the application in the Parameters field. Set Remote Host to the hostname or IP address of the remote machine.

To start debugging immediately, or when you don't have the application project loaded in C++Builder, just click the Load button. If you have the application project loaded, you can check Debug Project On Remote Machine and click OK. When you perform any debug command on the application within C++Builder, the debugging connection to the remote application will be established. You can then debug the application just as if it were running on the local machine.

If you get the error `Unable to connect to remote host`, check that the debug server service or process is running, Remote Host is set correctly, and that you have connectivity to the remote host using `ping.exe` or another network tool. If you get the error `Could not find program 'program'`, check that Remote Path is correct and that the application is actually located there.

Another feature of remote debugging is an extension of Attach To Running Process. Select Run, Attach To Process, enter the name of the remote machine in the Remote Machine field, and press Enter. The processes on the remote machine are listed; select one and click Attach to debug it. To use remote process attachment, the remote machine must be running the debug server. Remember that when attaching to a running process, there is no way to detach without terminating it.

Debugging DLLs

Debugging a DLL is very similar to debugging any normal executable application except that a host application is required to load it. You can create the host application that uses the DLL, but in most cases you will be using an existing host, such as an application written in another language that uses the DLL that you have developed.

Load the DLL project into C++Builder and set any breakpoints in the DLL source code as necessary. Specify the host application that will load the DLL by entering the full path and name of the host application in the Host Application field on the Local tab from the Run, Parameters dialog. Enter any command-line parameters for the application in the Parameters field if necessary.

When the host application is specified, either select Load to run the host application and begin debugging, or simply press OK and run the host application at a later time with Run, Run. You might do this after setting additional breakpoints or setting up watches, for example.

That's all there is to it. When the breakpoint in the DLL code is hit, you can step through the source code and use the Debug Inspector, watches, or any other technique during the debug process. You can use this technique for debugging COM objects and ActiveX components, but for separate processes you can do this only on Windows NT and Windows 2000 systems that allow cross-process debugging.

Speeding Up Compile Times

The C++Builder compiler is fast! It compiles C++ code almost twice as fast as the GNU C++ compiler and is comparable in speed to the Microsoft Visual C++ compiler. If you've used Delphi before, and you think that the C++Builder compiler takes much longer to compile a similar size application, you're right. The relatively slow compilation speed of C++ when compared to Delphi's Object Pascal is because of several reasons:

- C++ allows for header (include) files, whereas Object Pascal does not. Header files can be nested, and this can set up a lot of complex code to be processed. A simple 10-line program can be several hundred thousand lines long because of header file nesting, which takes up most of the compile time.

- C++ has macros, whereas Object Pascal does not. Macros require a preprocessor to parse and expand them.

- C++ has templates, whereas Object Pascal does not. Templates are very complex to analyze.

- C++ semantics must conform to the ANSI standard. The "grammar" of C++ is somewhat more complex than that of Delphi, which is based on Pascal, but developed to Borland's standard.

In general, C++ provides more flexibility in program design than Delphi's Object Pascal. However, this comes at the expense of compile time and in some cases code readability. There are several simple methods you can employ to speed up your C++Builder compile times. The most dramatic improvement can be achieved by using precompiled headers. This and other methods are described in the following sections.

Precompiled Headers

Precompiled headers are presented as a set of options on the Compiler tab of the Project Options dialog. When enabled by checking either Use Precompiled Headers or Cache Precompiled Headers, the compiler stores a compiled binary image of header files included in the various units in a disk-based file (`vcl50.csm` in the C++Builder `lib` directory by default). Subsequent use of the same sequence of header files in another unit dramatically speeds up that unit's compile time by using the header files previously compiled. Selecting Cache Pre-Compiled Headers causes the compiler to load the precompiled headers in memory to further speed up the compile process.

The `#pragma hdrstop` directive in a unit causes the compiler to stop generating precompiled headers at that point. It is important to note that the order of the header files before the `#pragma hdrstop` directive in each unit is significant. Changing the order of the header files in two separate units can change the code resulting from those header files in each unit. Therefore, this requires both lists of header files to be compiled and stored separately as precompiled header groups.

Header files after the `#pragma hdrstop` directive are processed each time the unit is compiled. Typically, you should include header files common to two or more units before this directive so that they are compiled once only. Include all header files specific to each unit after the directive. By doing this, we are trying to get the most common match between header file lists in each unit to obtain the maximum benefit from this option.

The IDE automatically inserts the `#pragma hdrstop` directive in new units and places VCL header files included before the directive and unit-specific header files after the directive. A good example of header file grouping and order is shown in the top section of the fictional units `LoadPage.cpp` and `ViewOptions.cpp` in Listings 2.3 and 2.4.

LISTING 2.3 Precompiled Header File Group in `LoadPage.cpp`

```
//-------------------
// LoadPage.cpp

#include <vcl.h>
#include <System.hpp>
#include <Windows.hpp>
#include "SearchMain.h"
#pragma hdrstop

#include "LoadPage.h"
#include "CacheClass.h"
//-------------------

// Code here...
```

LISTING 2.4 Precompiled Header File Group in `ViewOptions.cpp`listing

```
//-------------------
// ViewOptions.cpp

#include <vcl.h>
#include <System.hpp>
#include <Windows.hpp>
#include "SearchMain.h"
#pragma hdrstop

#include <Graphics.hpp>
#include "ViewOptions.h"
//-------------------

// Code here...
```

By effectively grouping header files included in each unit and using precompiled headers, you can often see compile speeds increase up to 10 times!

> **NOTE**
>
> For information on speeding up compile times even further using precompiled headers, there is an excellent article on the BCBDEV Web site at `http://www.bcbdev.com/` under the Articles link.

Other Techniques for Speeding Up Compile Times

Other techniques can be used to speed up compile times. They aren't as effective as using correctly grouped precompiled headers, but they are worth considering if compile speed is very important, particularly on large projects.

You should be careful about which header files are included in your units. Compiling unnecessary code is a waste of precious compile time, so in general you should not include unused header files. However, if you have included an unused header file in a unit to preserve header grouping when using precompiled headers, leave it in. Also, avoid changing header files too often. Each time you change a header file, the precompiled header groups that use this header file must be regenerated.

Use Make instead of Build. When Make is selected, the compiler attempts to detect and compile only the source files that have been modified since they were last compiled. Build, on the other hand, will recompile every source file in the project. Obviously, Build will take more time than Make, but there are times where Build is required.

Build is recommended after changing project options and when files are checked out or updated from a version control system. You should also use Build when compiling a release version of your application. This could be a debug or beta build going to testers or the final version to ship.

You should uncheck the Don't Generate State Files option on the Linker tab of Project Options. This will speed up subsequent compiles (particularly the first compile when reopening the project and when working with multiple projects in the IDE) as the linker saves state information in a file.

If you are not in a debugging phase for the project, disable all debugging options by selecting the Release button on the Compiler tab of Project Options and uncheck Use Debug Libraries on the Linker tab. If you do not yet need to compile a release version of the application, set Code Optimization on the Compiler tab of Project Options to None and uncheck Optimization in the Code Generation section on the Pascal tab.

It is important to look at the application structure and consider using packages or DLLs for modular parts, particularly in large projects. Both Make and Build will be considerably faster.

If you are not using floating-point math in your applications, checking None in the Floating Point group of the Advanced Compiler tab will speed up the link time slightly because the floating-point libraries will not be linked with your application.

These are things you can do within C++Builder and your code to minimize compile times. However, an important consideration is the computer hardware you are using. A software development system such as C++Builder requires higher-than-average system specs for CPU speed, RAM, and disk speed. Increasing these will yield a faster compile. In general, you should place slower IDE peripherals (such as an older CD-ROM drive) on a separate IDE controller from the hard drive. Defragmenting your hard drive might also slightly improve the compile time.

On multiprocessor (SMP) machines you can take advantage of all processors by invoking compilation of several modules simultaneously. The Borland MAKE utility provided does not support this directly, but you can write a script to run individual MAKEs of separate modules simultaneously. Alternatively, you can use the free GNU Make with the -j [jobs] command-line switch for parallel execution. You can get GNU Make for Windows from http://sourceware.cygnus.com/cygwin/.

Download the full Cygwin distribution, or at least the cygwin1.dll and make.exe files. For documentation, see http://www.gnu.org/software/make. To use GNU Make in C++Builder 5 and above, you'll need to export a makefile, either from the Project menu in the IDE or using the BPR2MAK.EXE command-line utility, because the project file is now stored in XML format. See BPR2MAK.EXE in the online help index for more information.

Finally, it probably doesn't need to be said that you should close other applications when working with C++Builder, particularly those that are memory or CPU intensive. If you're getting low on memory, things will certainly slow down considerably. I've also found that development on Windows NT and above is more responsive than Windows 95/98 (and provides a better debugging environment).

Summary

In this chapter you have looked at C++Builder projects in detail, learned how to reuse projects and other program elements using the Object Repository, and gained an understanding of what packages are and how they can be used. You also saw several of the new IDE features in C++Builder's current release.

3

Programming in C++Builder

by Mark Cashman

C++Builder influences programming on many levels, and this chapter helps you to see how. This chapter assumes your basic understanding of the C++ language and the C++Builder IDE as described in previous chapters.

This chapter begins with the programming practices that form the basis of C++ Builder programming. Some of these differ from those used in pure C++ programming, but they add to your productivity by leveraging the key advantages of the C++Builder environment.

This is followed by an overview of the VCL (Visual Component Library) that provides the rapid application development capability unique to C++Builder among C++ development environments.

Next comes a quick trip through the most useful components on the component palette.

One of the core advantages of C++Builder is the visual development environment that you can use to build user interfaces. You will get a trip through all the important features, including screen layout techniques to create interfaces that work well as the user changes the window's size, and how to use Actions to simplify user interface implementation.

Then, a brief discussion of the use of nonvisual components in C++Builder leads to an in-depth discussion of multithreading to wrap up this trip through key C++Builder programming practices.

Better Programming Practices in C++Builder

This section looks at some ways to improve how you write C++ code in C++Builder. Entire books are devoted to better C++ programming, and you are encouraged to read such texts to deepen your understanding of C++. The topics discussed here are those that have particular relevance to C++Builder, and those that are often misunderstood or misused by those new to C++Builder.

Use a String Class Instead of char*

Say goodbye to char* for string manipulation. Use either the string class provided by the C++ Standard Library or the VCL's native string class AnsiString (which has been conveniently typedefed to String). You can even use both. Access the C++ Standard Library's string class by including the statement

```
#include <string>
```

at the top of your code. If portability across operating systems is a goal, you cannot use the VCL, so this is the string class to use. Otherwise, use AnsiString, which has the advantage that it is the string representation used throughout the VCL and, thus, allows your code to work seamlessly with the VCL. For circumstances in which an old-style char* string is required, such as to pass a parameter to a Win32 API call, both string classes offer the c_str() member function, which returns such a string. In addition, the AnsiString class also offers the popular old-style sprintf() and printf() functions (for concatenating strings) as member functions. It offers two varieties of each: a standard version and a cat_ version. The versions differ in that the cat_ version adds the concatenated string to the existing AnsiString, and the standard version replaces any existing contents of the AnsiString. The difference between the sprintf() and printf() member functions is that sprintf() returns a reference to the AnsiString, and printf() returns the length of the final formatted string (or the length of the appended string, in the case of cat_printf). The function declarations are

```
int __cdecl printf(const char* format, ...);
int __cdecl cat_printf(const char* format, ...);
AnsiString& __cdecl sprintf(const char* format, ...);
AnsiString& __cdecl cat_sprintf(const char* format, ...);
```

These member functions ultimately call vprintf() and cat_vprintf() in their implementation. These member functions take a va_list as their second parameter as opposed to a variable argument list. This requires the addition of the #include <stdarg.h> statement in your code. The function declarations are

```
int __cdecl vprintf(const char* format, va_list paramList);
int __cdecl cat_vprintf(const char* format, va_list paramList);
```

The respective `printf()` and `sprintf()` functions perform the same task, differing only in their return types. As a result, this is the only criterion that is required when deciding which of the two to use.

WARNING

Note that the `printf()` and `sprintf()` AnsiString member functions in C++Builder version 4 are the same as the `cat_printf()` and `cat_sprintf()` functions in version 5, *not* the `printf()` and `sprintf()` AnsiString member functions. Care should be taken when converting code between those two versions.

Understand References and Use Them Where Appropriate

References are often misunderstood and, therefore, are not used as often as they should be. Often, it is possible to replace pointers with references, making the code more intuitive and easier to maintain. This section looks at some of the features of references and when they are most appropriately used.

The reason for the abundance of pointer parameters in the VCL in C++Builder is often a key point of controversy among C++ programmers moving to C++Builder.

A reference always refers to only one object, its *referent*, and it cannot be rebound to refer to a different object (object in this context includes all types). A reference must be initialized on creation; a reference cannot refer to nothing (NULL). Pointers, on the other hand, can point to nothing (NULL), can be re-bound, and do not require initialization on creation. A reference should be considered an alternative name for an object, whereas a pointer should be considered an object in itself. Anything that is done to a reference is also done to its referent and vice versa. This is because a reference is just an alternative name for the referent; they are the same. You can see, therefore, that references, unlike pointers, are implicitly dereferenced.

The following code shows how a reference can be declared:

```
int X = 12; // Declare and initialize int X to 12

int& Y = X; // Declare a reference to an int, i.e. Y, and
            // initialize it to refer to X
```

If you change the value of Y or X, you also change the value of X or Y, respectively, because X and Y are two names for the same thing. Another example of declaring a reference to a dynamically allocated variable is

```
TBook* Book1 = new TBook(); // Declare and create a TBook object

TBook& Book2 = *Book1;      // Declare a TBook reference,
```

```
                              // i.e. Book2, and initialize it
                              // to refer to the object pointed
                              // by Book1
The object pointed to by Book1 is the referent of the reference Book2.
```

One of the most important uses for references is the passing of user-defined types as parameters to functions. A parameter to a function can be passed by reference by making the parameter a reference and calling the function as if it were passed by value. For example, the following function is the typical swap function for two ints:

```
void swap(int& X, int& Y)
{
    int temp;
    temp = X;
    X = Y;
    Y = temp;
}
```

This function would be called as follows:

```
int Number1 = 12;
int Number2 = 68;

Swap(Number1, Number2);

// Number1 == 68 and Number2 == 12
```

Number1 and Number2 are passed by reference to swap, and, therefore, X and Y become alternative names for Number1 and Number2, respectively, within the function. What happens to X also happens to Number1 and what happens to Y also happens to Number2. A predefined type such as an int should be passed by reference only when the purpose is to change its value; otherwise, it is generally more efficient to pass by value. The same cannot be said for user-defined types (classes, structs, and so on). Rather than pass such types to functions by value, it is more efficient to pass such types by const reference or, if the type is to be changed, by non-const reference or pointer. However,

```
void DisplayMessage(const AnsiString& message)
{
    //Display message.
    // message is an alias for the AnsiString argument passed
    // to the function. No copy is made and the const qualifier
    // states that the function will not (cannot) modify message
}
```

is not really better than:

```
void DisplayMessage(AnsiString message)
{
    //Display message.
    // message is a copy of the AnsiString argument passed
}
```

This is because AnsiString itself implements a copy-on-write, shared string model, and thus only a very small object is passed from caller to function.

But for non-VCL classes (because VCL classes other than AnsiString are usually passed as const pointers) the first format is better for two reasons. First, the parameter is passed by reference. This means that when the function is called, the object used as the calling argument is used directly, rather than being copied. The copy constructor of AnsiString does not need to be invoked (as it would be on entering the second function), and neither does the destructor, as it would be at the end of the second function when message goes out of scope. Second, the const keyword is used in the first function to signify that the function will not modify message through message. Both functions are called in the same way:

```
AnsiString Message = "Hello!";

DisplayMessage(Message);
```

Functions can also return references, which has the side effect of the function becoming an *lvalue* (a value that can appear on the left side of an expression) for the referent. This also enables operators to be written that appear on the left side of an expression, such as the subscript operator. For example, given the Book class, an ArrayOfBooks class can be defined as follows:

```
class Book
{
    public:
            Book();
            int NumberOfPages;
};

class ArrayOfBooks
{
    private:
            static const unsigned NumberOfBooks = 100;
    public:
            Book&  operator[] (unsigned i);
};
```

In this case, an instance of `ArrayOfBooks` can be used just like a normal array. Elements accessed using the subscript operator can be assigned to and read from, similar in the following:

```
ArrayOfBooks ShelfOfBooks;
unsigned PageCount = 0;

ShelfOfBooks[0].NumberOfPages = 45;            // A short book!
PageCount += ShelfOfBooks[0].NumberOfPages; //PageCount = 45
```

This is possible because the value returned by the operator is the actual referent, not a copy of the referent.

Generally, you can say that references are preferred to pointers because they are safer (they can't be re-bound and don't require testing for `NULL` because they must refer to something). Also, they don't require explicit dereferencing, making code more intuitive.

But what about the pointers used in C++Builder's VCL?

The extensive use of pointers in the VCL is caused by the fact that the VCL is written in, and must remain compatible with Delphi (Delphi), which uses Delphi-style references. A Delphi-style reference is closer to a C++ pointer than a C++ reference. This has the side effect that, when the VCL is used with C++, pointers have to be used as replacements for Delphi references. This is because a Delphi reference (unlike a C++ reference) *can* be set to `NULL` and *can* be re-bound. In some cases it is possible to use reference parameters instead of pointer parameters, but because all VCL-based objects are dynamically allocated on free store and, therefore, are referred to through pointers, the pointers must be dereferenced first. Because the VCL relies on some of the features of Delphi references, pointers are used for object parameter passing and returning. Remember that a pointer parameter is passed by value, so the passed pointer will not be affected by the function. You can prevent modification of the object pointed to by using the `const` modifier.

Avoid Using Global Variables

Unless it is absolutely necessary, don't use global variables in your code. Apart from polluting the global namespace (and increasing the chance of a name collision), it increases the dependencies between translation units that use the variables. This makes code difficult to maintain and minimizes the ease with which translation units can be used in other programs. The fact that variables are declared elsewhere also makes code difficult to understand.

One of the first things any astute C++Builder programmer will notice is the global form pointers present in every form unit. This might give the impression that using global variables is OK; after all, C++Builder does it. However, C++Builder does this for a reason, which we will discuss at the end of this section. For now, we will examine some of the alternatives to declaring global variables.

Let's assume that global variables are a must. How can we use global variables without incurring some of the side effects that they produce? The answer is that we use something that *acts* like a global variable, but is not one. We use a class with a member function that returns a value of, or reference to (whichever is appropriate), a static variable that represents our global variable. Depending on the purpose of our global variables (for example, global to a program or global to a library), we may or may not need access to the variables through static member functions. In other words, it might be possible to instantiate an object of the class that contains the static variables when they are required. We consider first the case where we do require access to the static variables (representing our global variables) through static member functions. We commonly refer to this kind of class as a *module*.

With a module of global variables, you improve your representation of the variables by placing them into a class, making them private static variables, and using static getters and setters to access them (for more information, see *Large-Scale C++ Software Design* by Lakos, 1996, p. 69). This prevents pollution of the global namespace and gives a certain degree of control over how the global variables are accessed. Typically, the class would be named Global. Hence, two global variables declared as

```
int Number;
double Average;
```

could be replaced by

```
class Global
{
 private:
    static int Number;
    static double Average;

    //PRIVATE CONSTRUCTOR
    Global(); //not implemented, instantiation not possible

  public:
  // SETTERS
    static void setNumber(int NewNumber) { Number = NewNumber; }
    static void setAverage(double NewAverage) { Average = NewAverage; }

  // GETTERS
    static int getNumber() { return Number; }
```

```
        static double getAverage() { return Average; }
};
```

Accessing Number is now done through Global::getNumber() and Global::setNumber(). Average is accessed similarly. The class Global is effectively a module that can be accessed throughout the program and does not need to be instantiated (because the member data and functions are static).

Often such an implementation is not required, and it is possible to create a class with a global point of access that is constructed only when first accessed. This has the benefit of allowing control over the order of initialization of the variables (objects must be constructed before first use). The method used is to place the required variables inside a class that cannot be directly instantiated, but accessed only through a static member function that returns a reference to the class. This ensures that the class containing the variables is constructed on first use and is constructed only once.

This approach is often referred to as the *Singleton pattern* (for more information, see *Design Patterns: Elements of Reusable Object-Oriented Software* by Gamma *et al.*, 1995, p. 127). Patterns are a way of representing recurring problems and their solutions in object-based programs. For more on patterns, see Chapter 4, " Creating Custom Components."

The basic code required to create a Singleton (as such a class is commonly referred to) is as follows:

```
class Singleton
{
    public:
            static Singleton& Instance();

protected:
            Singleton(); // Not Implemented, Instantiation not possible
};
```

An implementation of Instance is

```
Singleton& Singleton::Instance()
{
    static Singleton* NewSingleton = new Singleton();
    return *NewSingleton;
}
```

The initial call to Instance will create a new Singleton and return a reference to it. Subsequent calls will simply return a reference. However, the destructor of the Singleton will not be called; the object is simply abandoned on free store. If there is important processing that must be executed in the destructor, the following implementation will ensure that the Singleton is destructed:

```
Singleton& Singleton::Instance()
{
    static Singleton NewSingleton;
    return NewSingleton;
}
```

This implementation causes its own problem. It is possible for another static object to access the Singleton after it has been destroyed. One solution to this problem is the *nifty counter technique* (for more information, see *C++ FAQs Second Edition*, Cline *et al.*, 1999, p. 235, and *Large-Scale C++ Software Design*, Lakos, 1996, p. 537), in which a static counter is used to control when each object is created and destroyed. If you find the need for this technique, perhaps a rethink of the code would also be helpful. It might be that a slight redesign could remove the dependency.

It should now be clear that static variables are like global variables and can almost always be used in place of global variables. Remember, though, that ultimately global variables should be avoided.

Understand How C++Builder Uses Global Variables

What then of the global form pointer variables in C++Builder? Essentially, global form pointer variables are present to enable the use of nonmodal forms. Nonmodal forms are conventional windows that last for long periods of time and enable you to work with the rest of the application, even while they are open. Modal forms are dialogs, which block interaction with the rest of the application.

Nonmodal forms require a global point of access for as long as the form exists, and it is convenient for the IDE to automatically create one when the form is made. The default operation of the IDE is to add newly created forms to the autocreate list, which adds the line

```
Application->CreateForm(__classid(TFormX), &FormX);
```

(where *X* is a number) to the WinMain function in the project .cpp file. Modal forms do not require this because the ShowModal() method returns *after* the forms are closed, making it possible to delete them in the same scope as they were created. General guidelines on the use of forms can, therefore, be given.

First, determine if a form is to be a modal form or a nonmodal form.

If the form is modal, it is possible to create and destroy the form in the same scope. This being the case, the global form pointer variable is not required, and the form should not be autocreated. Remove the `Application->CreateForm` entry from `WinMain` either by deleting it or by removing it from the autocreate list on the forms page in the Project, Options menu. Next, either delete or comment out the form pointer variable from the .h and .cpp files, and state explicitly in the header file that the form is modal and should be used only with the `ShowModal()` method. That is, in the .cpp file remove

```
TFormX* FormX;
```

and from the .h file, remove

```
extern PACKAGE TFormX* FormX;
```

Add a comment such as the following:

```
// This form is MODAL and should only called with the ShowModal() method.
```

To use the form, simply write

```
TFormX* FormX = new TFormX(0);
try
{
    FormX->ShowModal();
}
__finally
{
    delete FormX;
}
```

Because you most likely do not want the form pointer to point elsewhere, you could declare the pointer as `const`:

```
TFormX* const FormX = new TFormX(0);
try
```

```
{
   FormX->ShowModal();
}
__finally
{
   delete FormX;
}
TFormX(this);
FormX->ShowModal();
delete FormX;
```

The use of a try/__finally block ensures that the code is exception-safe. An alternative to these examples is to use the Standard Library's auto_ptr class template:

```
auto_ptr<TFormX> FormX(new TFormX(0));
FormX->ShowModal();
```

> **NOTE**
>
> You might need to reference the std namespace to create an auto_ptr; this is done either by using a namespace std or by prefixing auto_ptr with std::.

Whichever technique you use, you are guaranteed that if the code terminates prematurely because an exception is thrown, FormX will be automatically destroyed. With the first technique this happens in the __finally block; with the second it occurs when auto_ptr goes out of scope. The second technique can be further enhanced by making the auto_ptr const because generally it is not required that the auto_ptr lose ownership of the pointer, as in the following code. (For more information, see *Exceptional C++: 47 Engineering Puzzles, Programming Problems, and Solutions* by Sutter, 2000, p. 158.)

```
const auto_ptr<TFormX> FormX(new TFormX(0));
FormX->ShowModal();
```

Of particular note in the code snippets is that 0 (NULL) is passed as the argument to the AOwner parameter of FormX. This is because we handle the destruction of the form ourselves.

> **TIP**
>
> Using auto_ptr is an effective way of managing the memory of VCL-based objects. It is exception-safe and easy to use. For a VCL object that takes an owner parameter in its constructor, you can simply pass 0 because you know that the object will be deleted when the auto_ptr goes out of scope.

If the form is non-modal, you must only decide whether you want it autocreated. If you don't, you must ensure that it is removed from WinMain. When you want it created later, you can use the form's global pointer and the new operator. Show the form using the Show() method. Remember that you cannot delete modal forms because Show() returns when the form is shown, not when it is closed. Therefore, it might still be in use. For example, if the form is autocreated, write

```
FormX->Show();
```

Otherwise, create and show it this way:

```
FormX = new TFormX(this);
FormX->Show();
```

As an aside to this topic, the practice of declaring variables or functions as static so that they have scope only within the translation unit in which they are declared is deprecated. Instead, such variables and functions should be placed in an *unnamed* namespace. (For more information, see *ANSI/ISO C++ Professional Programmer's Handbook: The Complete Language* by Kalev, 1999, p. 157.)

Understand and Use const in Your Code

The const keyword should be used as a matter of course, not as an optional extra. Declaring a variable const enables attempted changes to the variable to be detected at compile time (resulting in an error) and also indicates the programmer's intention not to modify the given variable. Moreover, not using the const keyword indicates the programmer's intention to modify a given variable. The const keyword can be used in a variety of ways.

First, it can be used to declare a variable as a constant:

```
const double PI = 3.141592654;
```

This is the C++ way to declare constant variables. Do not use #define statements. Note that const variables must be initialized. The following shows the possible permutations for declaring const variables. Pointer and reference declarations are read from right to left, as the following examples show:

```
int Y = 12;
const int X = Y;        // X equals Y which equals 12, therefore X = 12
                        // X cannot be changed, but Y can


// In the next declaration the pointer itself is constant

int* const P = &Y;      // The int pointed to by P, i.e. Y can be
                        // changed through P but P itself cannot change
```

```
// The next two declarations are the same:

const int* P = &Y;      // The int pointed to by P, i.e.
int const* P = &Y;      // Y cannot be changed through P


// The next two declarations are the same:

const int* const P = &Y;    // Neither P, nor what it points to, P
int const* const P = &Y;    // i.e. Y can be changed through P

// The next two declarations are the same:

const int& R = Y            // The int referred to by R, i.e. R
int const& R = Y            // Y cannot be changed through R
```

After reviewing the previous examples, it is helpful to reiterate how const is used with pointer declarations. As stated previously, a pointer declaration is read from right to left so that in int * const the const refers to the *. Hence, the pointer is constant, but the int it points to can be changed. With int const * the const refers to the int. In this case, the int itself is constant, though the pointer to it is not. Finally, with int const * const, both the int and the * are constant. Also remember that int const and const int are the same, so const int * const is the same as int cosnt * const.

If you want to declare a literal string of chars, declare it as one of the following:

```
const char* const LiteralString = "Hello World";
char const * const LiteralString = "Hello World";
```

Both of the previous strings and the pointers to them are constant.

Function parameters should be declared as const in this fashion when it is appropriate, such as when the intention of the function is not to modify the argument that is passed to the function. For example, the following function states that it will not modify the arguments passed to it:

```
double GetAverage(const double* ArrayOfDouble, int LengthOfArray)
{
   double Sum = 0;

   for(int i=0; i<LengthOfArray; ++i)
   {
```

```
        Sum += ArrayOfDouble[i];
    }

    double Average = Sum/LengthOfArray;
    return Average;
}
```

Another way of thinking about this is to assume that if the const keyword is not used for a parameter, it must be the intention of the function to modify that parameter's argument, unless the parameter is pass-by-value (a copy of the parameter is used, not the parameter itself). Notice that declaring int LengthOfArray as a const is inappropriate because this is pass-by-value. LengthOfArray is a copy, and declaring it as a const has no effect on the argument passed to the function. Similarly, ArrayOfDouble is declared as follows:

```
const double* ArrayOfDouble
```

not

```
const double* const ArrayOfDouble
```

Because the pointer itself is a copy, only the data that it points to needs to be made const.

The return type of a function can also be const. Generally, it is not appropriate to declare types returned by value as const, except in the case of requiring the call of a const-overloaded member function. Reference and pointer return types are suitable for returning as consts.

Member functions can be declared const. A const member function is one that does not modify the this object (*this). Hence, it can call other member functions inside its function body only if they are also const. To declare a member function const, place the const keyword at the end of the function declaration and in the function definition at the same place. Generally, all getter member functions should be const because they do not modify *this. For example

```
class Book
{
    private:
            int NumberOfPages;
    public:
            Book();
            int GetNumberOfPages() const;
};
```

The definition of GetNumberOfPages() could be

```
int Book::GetNumberOfPages() const
{
    return NumberOfPages;
}
```

The final area in which const is commonly encountered is when operators are overloaded by a class and access to both const and non-const variables is required. For example, if a class ArrayOfBooks is created to contain Book objects, it is sensible to assume that the [] operator will be overloaded (so that the class acts like an array). However, the question of whether the [] operator will be used with const or non-const objects must be considered. The solution is to const-overload the operator, as the following code indicates:

```
class ArrayOfBooks
{
    public:
            Book&       operator[] (unsigned i);
            const Book& operator[] (unsigned i) const;
};
```

The ArrayOfBooks class can use the [] operator on both const and non-const Books. For example, if an ArrayOfBooks object is passed to a function by reference to const, it would be illegal for the array to be assigned to using the [] operator. This is because the value indexed by i would be a const reference, and the const state of the passed array would be preserved.

Remember, know what const is and use it whenever you can.

Be Familiar with the Principles of Exceptions

Exceptions offer a mechanism for handling runtime errors in a program. Several approaches can be taken to handling runtime errors, such as returning error codes, setting global error flags, and exiting the program. But, in most circumstances, an exception is the only appropriate method. (For more information, see *ANSI/ISO C++ Professional Programmer's Handbook: The Complete Language* by Kalev, 1999, p. 113.)

Exceptions will commonly be encountered in two forms in C++Builder programs: C++ exceptions and VCL exceptions. Generally, the principles involved with both are the same, but there are some differences.

C++ uses three keywords to support exceptions: try, catch, and throw. C++Builder extends its exception support to include the __finally keyword.

The try, catch, and __finally keywords are used as headers to blocks of code (that is, code that is enclosed between braces). Also, for every try block there must *always* be one or more catch blocks *or* a single __finally block.

The try **Keyword**

The try keyword is used in one of two possible ways. The first and simplest is as a simple block header, to create a try block within a function. The second is as a function block header, to create a *function* try block, either by placing the try keyword in front of the function's first opening brace or, in the case of constructors, in front of the colon that signifies the start of the initializer list.

> **NOTE**
>
> C++Builder does not currently support function try blocks. However, because it makes a real difference only with constructors, and even then has little impact on their use, it is unlikely that its omission will have any effect. For those who are interested, it will be supported in version 6 of the compiler.

The catch **Keyword**

Normally, at least one catch block will immediately follow any try block (or function try block). A catch block will always appear as the catch keyword followed by parentheses containing a single exception type specification with an optional variable name. Such a catch block (commonly referred to as an *exception handler*) can catch only an exception whose type *exactly* matches the exception type specified by the catch block. However, a catch block can be specified to catch *all* exceptions by using the *catch all* ellipses exception type specifier, catch(...).

A typical try/catch scenario is as follows:

```
try
{
    // Code that may throw an exception
}
catch(exception1& e)
{
    // Handler code for exception1 type exceptions
}
catch(exception2& e)
{
    // Handler code for exception2 type exceptions
}
catch(...)
{
```

```
    // Handler code for any exception not already caught
}
```

The __finally Keyword

The last of these, __finally, has been added to allow the possibility of performing cleanup operations or ensuring certain code is executed regardless of whether an exception is thrown. This works because code placed inside a __finally block will always execute, even when an exception is thrown in the corresponding try block. This allows code to be written that is exception-safe and will work properly in the presence of exceptions. A typical try/__finally scenario is

```
try
{
    // Code that may throw an exception
}
__finally
{
    // Code here is always executed, even if
    // an exception is thrown in the preceding
    // try block
}
```

It should be noted that try/catch and try/__finally constructs can be nested inside other try/catch and try/__finally constructs.

The throw Keyword

The throw keyword is used in one of two ways. The first is to throw (or rethrow) an exception, and the second is to allow the specification of the type of exceptions that a function might throw. In the first case (to throw or rethrow an exception), the throw keyword is followed optionally by parentheses containing a single exception variable (often an object) or simply the single exception variable after a space, similar to a return statement. When no such exception variable is used, the throw keyword stands on its own. Then, its behavior depends on its placement. When placed inside a catch block, the throw statement rethrows the exception currently being handled. When placed elsewhere, such as when there is no exception to rethrow, it causes terminate() to be called, ultimately ending the program. It is not possible to use throw to rethrow an exception in VCL code. The second use of the throw keyword is to allow the specification of the exceptions that a function might throw. The syntax for the keyword is

```
throw(<exception_type_list>)
```

The *exception_type_list* is optional and, when excluded, indicates that the function will not throw any exceptions. When included, it takes the form of one or more exception types separated by commas. The exception types listed are the only exceptions the function can throw.

Unhandled and Unexpected Exceptions

In addition to the three keywords described, C++ offers mechanisms to deal with thrown exceptions that are not handled by the program and exceptions that are thrown, but are not expected. This might include an exception that is thrown inside a function with an incompatible exception specification.

When an exception is thrown, but not handled, terminate() is called. This calls the default terminate handler function, which by default calls abort(). This default behavior should be avoided because abort() does not ensure that local object destructors are called. To prevent terminate() being called as a result of an uncaught exception, the entire program can be wrapped inside a try/catch(...) block in WinMain() (or main() for command-line programs). This ensures that any exception will eventually be caught. If terminate() is called, you can modify its default behavior by specifying your own terminate handler function. Simply pass the name of your terminate handler function as an argument to the std::set_terminate() function. The <stdexcept> header file must be included. For example, given a function declared as

```
void TerminateHandler();
```

The code required to ensure that this handler is called in place of the basic terminate() handler is

```
#include <stdexcept>

std::set_terminate(TerminateHandler);
```

When an exception is thrown that is not expected, unexpected() is called. Its default behavior is to call terminate(). Again, the opportunity exists to define your own function to handle this occurrence. To do so, call std::set_unexpected(), passing the function handler name as an argument. The <stdexcept> header file must be included.

Using Exceptions

This brings the discussion to consideration of the exceptions that can and should be thrown by a function and where such exceptions should be caught. This should be decided when you are designing your code, not after it has already been written. To this end, you must consider several things when you write a piece of code. Some of the topics are very complex, and it is beyond the scope of this book to cover all the issues involved.

You must consider if the code you have written could throw one or more exceptions. If so, you must then consider if it is appropriate to catch one or more of the exceptions in the current scope or let one or more of them propagate to an exception handler outside the current scope. If you do not want one or more of the exceptions to propagate outside the current scope, you must place the code in a try block and follow it with the one or more appropriate catch blocks to catch any desired exceptions (or all exceptions, using a catch-all block). To this end, you should be aware of the exceptions built into the language itself, the C++ Standard Library, and the VCL, and be aware of when they can be thrown. For example, if new fails to allocate enough memory, std::bad_alloc is thrown.

Throw an exception in a function only when it is appropriate to do so, when the function cannot meet its promise. (For more information, see *C++ FAQs*, Second Edition, Cline *et al.*, 1999, p. 137.)

You should catch an exception only when you know what to do with it, and you should always catch an exception by reference. (For more information, see *More Effective C++: 35 New Ways to Improve Your Programs and Designs* by Meyers, 1996, p. 68.) VCL exceptions *cannot* be caught by value. Also, it might not be possible to fully recover from an exception, in which case, the handler should perform any possible cleanup, and then rethrow the exception.

You should understand when and how to use exception specifications for functions and be wary of the possibility of writing an incorrect specification. This will result in unexpected() being called if an unspecified exception is thrown inside a function and it is not handled within that function.

You should ensure that you write exception-safe code that works properly in the presence of exceptions. For example, simple code such as this is not exception safe:

```
TFormX* const FormX = new TFormX(0);
FormX->ShowModal();
delete FormX;
```

If an exception is thrown between the creation and deletion of the form, it will never be deleted, so the code does not work properly in the presence of exceptions. For an exception-safe alternative, see the section "Avoid Using Global Variables," earlier in this chapter.

If you are writing library or container classes, endeavor to write code that is *exception-neutral*—code that propagates all exceptions to the caller of the function that contains the code. (For more information, see *Exceptional C++: 47 Engineering Puzzles, Programming Problems, and Solutions* by Sutter, 2000, p. 25.)

Never throw an exception from a destructor because the destructor might have been called as a result of stack unwinding after a previous exception was called. This calls terminate(). Destructors should have an exception specification of throw().

A Final Note on Exceptions

Finally, you should appreciate the differences between VCL and C++ exceptions. VCL exceptions allow operating system exceptions to be handled as well as exceptions generated from within the program. Such exceptions must be caught by reference. VCL exceptions generated from within the program cannot be caught by value. An advantage of VCL exceptions is that they can be thrown and caught within the IDE.

Use new and delete to Manage Memory

The VCL requires that all classes that inherit from TObject be created dynamically from free store. Free store is often referred to as the heap, but free store is the correct term when applied to memory allocated and deallocated by new and delete. The term *heap* should be reserved for the memory allocated and deallocated by malloc() and free(). (For more information, see *Exceptional C++: 47 Engineering Puzzles, Programming Problems, and Solutions* by Sutter, 2000, p. 142.) This means a lot of calls to new and delete in C++Builder programs, so it is important to understand a few things about how new and delete work.

> **WARNING**
>
> A Non-Plain Old Data (Non-POD) object is essentially all but the most trivial of classes. Such objects must have their memory allocated by using new; the C equivalent malloc() will not suffice (its behavior is undefined) and be subsequently deallocated with delete, not free(). The new and delete operators ensure that, in addition to the allocation/deallocation of memory, the object's constructor and destructor, respectively, are called.
>
> The new operator also returns a pointer that is suitable to the object created; not merely a void pointer that must be cast to the required type. new and delete call operator new/operator delete, respectively, to allocate/deallocate memory, and these can be overloaded for specific classes. This enables the customization of memory allocation/deallocation behavior. This is not possible with malloc() and free().
>
> (For more information, see *ANSI/ISO C++ Professional Programmer's Handbook: The Complete Language* by Kalev, 1999, p. 221.)

A successful call to new allocates sufficient memory in free store (using operator new) calls the object's constructor and returns a pointer of the type pointer-to-the-object-type-created. A correctly initialized object is the result. Subsequently, calling delete calls the object's destructor and deallocates the memory obtained previously by calling new.

> **WARNING**
>
> Never call a VCL object's Free() method to destroy a VCL object. Always use delete. This ensures that the object's destructor is called and that the memory allocated previously with new is freed. Free() does not guarantee this, and it is bad practice to use it.

If the call to new is unsuccessful, a std::bad_alloc exception is thrown. Note that the bad_alloc exception is defined in the standard library file <new>. Hence, you must include #include <new> in your program, and it is in the std namespace. It does not return NULL. Therefore, you should not check the return pointer for equality with NULL. The program should be prepared to catch the std::bad_alloc exception and, if the function that calls new does not catch the exception, it should pass the exception outside the function so that calling code has the opportunity to catch it. Either of the following would be appropriate:

```
void CreateObject(TMyObject* MyObject) throw()
{
    try
    {
        MyObject = new TMyObject();
    }
    catch(std::bad_alloc)
    {
        //Print a message "Not enough memory for MyObject";
        // Deal with the problem
        // or exit gracefully
    }
}
```

or

```
void CreateObject(TMyObject* MyObject) throw(std::bad_alloc)
{
    MyObject = new TMyObject();
}
```

The use of exceptions enables the code that handles the error to be centralized, which leads to safer code that is more intuitive. The throw keyword added to the function header is called an *exception specification*. The effect of its inclusion in the function header is to specify which exceptions the function can throw. For more explanation refer to the section "Be Familiar with the Principles of Exceptions," earlier in this chapter. In the case of the first CreateObject() function, a throw() exception specifier is used to indicate that no exception will be thrown by the function. This is acceptable because the only exception that can be thrown, std::bad_alloc, is caught and dealt with by the function itself. In the case of the second implementation of CreateObject(), the exception specifier throw(std::bad_alloc) is used to indicate that the only exception that the function can throw is std::bad_alloc. This should be caught and handled by one of the calling routines.

There is also the possibility of writing your own out-of-memory function handler to deal with failed memory allocation. To set a function as a handler for out-of-memory conditions when using new, call the set_new_handler() function (also defined in <new>), passing as a parameter the name of the function you will use as the out-of-memory handler. For example, if you write a function (nonmember or static member) called OutOfMemory to handle such occurrences, the necessary code is

```
#include <new>

void OutOfMemory()
{
    // Try to free some memory
    // if there is now enough memory then this
    // function will NOT be called next time
    // else either install a new handler or throw an exception
}

// Somewhere in the main code, near the start write:
std::set_new_handler(OutOfMemory);
```

This code requires some explanation, because the sequence of events that occurs when new fails dictates how the OutOfMemory function should be written. If new fails to allocate enough memory, OutOfMemory is called. OutOfMemory tries to free some memory (how this is done will be discussed later); new will then try again to allocate the required memory. If it is successful, you are finished. If it is unsuccessful, the process just described will be repeated. In fact, it will repeat infinitely until either enough memory is allocated or the OutOfMemory function terminates the process.

To terminate the process, the OutOfMemory function can do several things. It can throw an exception (such as std::bad_alloc()), it can install a different memory handler that can then try to make more memory available, it can assign NULL to set_new_handler (std::set_new_handler(0)), or it can exit the program (not recommended). If a new handler is installed, then this series of events will occur for the new handler (which is called on the subsequent failed attempt). If the handler is set to NULL (0), then no handler will be called, and the exception std::bad_alloc() will be thrown.

Making more memory available is dependent on the design of the program and where the memory shortage arises. If the program keeps a lot of memory tied up for performance reasons but does not always require it to be available at all times, then such memory can be freed if a shortage occurs. Identifying such memory is the difficult part. If there is no such memory usage in the program, the shortage will be a result of factors external to the program such as other memory-intensive software or physical limitations. There is nothing that can be done about physical limitations, but it is possible to warn the user of a memory shortage so that memory-intensive software can be shut down, thereby freeing additional memory.

The trick is to give an advance warning before all the memory is used. One approach is to preallocate a quantity of memory at the beginning of the program. If new fails to allocate enough memory, the memory successfully allocated can be freed. The user is warned that memory is low and told to try to free more memory for the application. Assuming that the preallocated block was large enough, the program should be able to continue operating as normal if the user has freed additional memory. This preemptive approach is simple to implement and reasonably effective.

It is important to note that if you want to allocate raw memory only, operator new and operator delete should be used instead of the new and delete operators. (For more information, see *More Effective C++: 35 New Ways to Improve Your Programs and Designs* by Meyers, 1996, p. 38.) This is useful for situations in which, for example, a structure needs to be allocated dynamically, and the size of the structure is determined through a function call before the dynamic allocation. This is a common occurrence in Win32 API programming:

```
DWORD StructureSize = APIFunctionToGetSize(SomeParameter);

WIN32STRUCTURE* PointerToStructure;
PointerToStructure = static_cast<WIN32STRUCTURE*>(operator new(StructureSize));
// Do something with the structure
operator delete(PointerToStructure);
```

It is clear that the use of malloc() and free() should not be required.

Finally, we will discuss the use of new and delete in dynamically allocating and deallocating arrays. Arrays are allocated and deallocated using operator new[] and operator delete[], respectively. They are separate operators from operator new and operator delete. When new is used to create an array of objects, it first allocates the memory for the objects (using operator new[]), and then calls its default constructor to initialize each object. Deleting an array with delete performs the opposite task: It calls the destructor for each object, and then deallocates the memory (using operator delete[]) for the array. So delete knows to call operator delete[] instead of operator delete, a [] is placed between the delete keyword and the pointer to the array to be deleted:

```
delete [] SomeArray;
```

Allocating a single-dimensional array is straightforward. The following format is used:

```
TBook* ArrayOfBooks = new TBook[NumberOfBooks];
```

Deleting such an array is also straightforward. However, remember that the correct form of delete must be used—delete []. For example

```
delete [] ArrayOfBooks;
```

Remember that [] tells the compiler that the pointer is to an array, as opposed to simply a pointer to a single element of a given type. If an array is to be deleted, it is essential that delete [] be used, not delete. If delete is used erroneously, at best only the first element of the array will be deleted. You know that when an array of objects is created, the default constructor is used. This means that you will want to ensure that you have defined the default constructor to suit your needs. Remember that a compiler-generated default constructor does not initialize the classes's data members. Also, you will probably want to overload the assignment operator (=) so that you can safely assign object values to the array objects. A two-dimensional array can be created using code such as the following:

```
TBook** ShelvesOfBooks = new TBook*[NumberOfShelves];

for(int i=0; i<NumberOfShelves; ++i)
{
    ShelvesOfBooks[i] = new TBook[NumberOfBooks];
}
```

To delete such an array use the following:

```
for(int i=0; i<NumberofShelves; ++i)
{
    delete [] ShelvesOfBooks[i];
}

delete [] ShelvesOfBooks;
```

One thing remains unsaid: If you want to have an array of objects, a better approach is to create a vector of objects using the vector template from the STL. It enables any constructor to be used and also handles memory allocation and deallocation automatically. It will also reallocate memory if there is a memory shortage. This means that the use of the C library function realloc() is no longer required.

Placement new (allocation at a predetermined memory location) and nothrow new (does not throw an exception on failure, it returns NULL instead) have not been discussed because they are beyond the scope of this section.

Understand and Use C++-Style Casts

The four C++ casts are outlined in Table 3.1.

TABLE 3.1   C++-Style Casts

Cast	General Purpose
static_cast<T>(*exp*)	Used to perform casts such as an int to a double. T and *exp* can be pointers, references, arithmetic types (such as int), or enum types. You cannot cast from one type to another; for example, from a pointer to an arithmetic.
dynamic_cast<T>(*exp*)	Used to perform casting down or across an inheritance hierarchy. For example, if class X inherits from class O, a pointer to class O can be cast to a pointer to class X, provided the conversion is valid. T can be a pointer or a reference to a defined class type or void*. *exp* can be a pointer or a reference. For a conversion from a base class to a derived class to be possible, the base class must contain at least one virtual function; in other words, it must be polymorphic. One important feature of dynamic_cast is that if a conversion between pointers is not possible, a NULL pointer is returned; if a conversion between references is not possible, a std::bad_cast exception is thrown (include the header file <typeinfo>). As a result, the conversion can be checked for success.
const_cast<T>(*exp*)	This is the only cast that can affect the const or volatile nature of an expression. It can be either cast off or cast on. This is the only thing const_cast is used for. For example, if you want to pass a pointer to const data to a function that only takes a pointer to non-const data, and you know the data will not be modified, you could pass the pointer by const_casting it. T and *exp* must be of the same type except for their const or volatile factors.
reinterpret_cast<T>(*exp*)	Used to perform unsafe or implementation-dependent casts. This cast should be used only when nothing else will do. This is because it enables you to reinterpret the expression as a completely different type, such as to cast a float* to an int*. It is commonly used to cast between function pointers. If you find yourself needing to use reinterpret_cast, decide carefully if the approach you are taking is the right one, and remember to document clearly your intention (and possibly your reasons for this approach). T must be a pointer, a reference, an arithmetic type, a pointer to a function, or a pointer to a member function. A pointer can be cast to an integral type and vice versa.

The casts most likely to be of use are static_cast (for trivial type conversions such as int to double) and dynamic_cast.

An example of using static_cast can be found in the last line of the following code:

```
int Sum = 0;
int* Numbers = new int[20];

for(int i=0; i<20; ++i)
{
    Numbers[i] = i*i;
    Sum += Numbers[i];
}


double Average = static_cast<double>(Sum)/20;
```

One of the times when dynamic_cast is commonly used in C++Builder is to dynamic_cast TObject* Sender or TComponent* Owner, to ensure that Sender or Owner is of a desired class, such as TForm. For example, if a component is placed on a form, it can be necessary to distinguish if it was placed directly or was perhaps placed on a Panel component. To carry out such a test, the following code is required:

```
TForm* OwnerForm = dynamic_cast<TForm*>(Owner);
if(OwnerForm)
{
    //Perform processing since OwnerForm != NULL, i.e. 0
}
```

First a pointer of the required type is declared, and then it is set equal to the result of the dynamic_cast. If the cast is unsuccessful, the pointer will point to the required type and can be used for accessing that type. If it fails, it will point to NULL and, hence, can be used to evaluate a Boolean expression. Sender can be similarly used. The situations that require such casting are many and varied. What is important is to understand what it is that you want to achieve and make your intention and reasoning clear.

Each of the C++ casts performs a specific task and should be restricted for use only where appropriate. The C++ casts are also easily seen in code, making it more readable.

Know When to Use the Preprocessor

It is not appropriate to use the preprocessor for defining constants or for creating function macros. Instead, you should use const variables or enum types for constants and use an `inline` function (or `inline` template function) to replace a function macro. Consider also that a function macro might not be appropriate anyway (in which case the `inline` equivalent would not be required).

For example, the constant π can be defined as

```
const double PI = 3.141592654;
```

If you wanted to place this inside a class definition, you would write

```
class Circle
{
  public:
        static const double PI; // This is only a declaration
};
```

In the implementation (`*.cpp`) file, you would define and initialize the constant by writing

```
const double Circle::PI = 3.141592654;
// This is the constant definition
// and initialization
```

Note that the class constant is made `static` so that only one copy of the constant exists for the class. Also notice that the constant is initialized in the implementation file (typically after the `include` directive for the header file that contains the class definition). The exception to this is the initialization of integral types, `char`, `short`, `long`, `unsigned`, and `int`. These can be initialized directly in the class definition. When a group of related constants is required, an `enum` is a sensible choice:

```
enum LanguagesSupported { English, Chinese, Japanese, French };
```

Sometimes an `enum` is used to declare an integer constant on its own:

```
enum { LENGTH = 255 };
```

Such declarations are sometimes seen inside class definitions. A `static const` variable declaration (like that for `PI`) is a more correct approach.

Replacing a function macro is also easily achieved. Given the macro

```
#define cubeX(x) ( (x)*(x)*(x) )
```

the following `inline` function equivalent can be written:

```
inline double cubeX(double x) { return x*x*x; }
```

Notice that this function takes a `double` as an argument. If an `int` were passed as a parameter, it would have to be cast to a `double`. Because you want the behavior of the function to be similar to that of the macro, you should avoid this necessity. This can be achieved in one of two ways: Either overload the function or make it a function template. In this case, overloading the function is the better of the two choices because a function template would imply that the function could be used for classes as well, which would most likely be inappropriate. Therefore, an `int` version of the inline function could be written as

```
inline int cubeX(int x) { return x*x*x; }
```

Generally, you want to avoid using `#define` for constants and function macros. `#define` should be used when writing include guards. Remember that include guards are written in the header file to ensure that a header already included is not included again. For example, a typical header file in C++Builder will look like this:

```
#ifndef Unit1H  // Is Unit1H not already defined?
#define Unit1H  // If not then you reach this line and define it

// Header file code placed here...

#endif          // End of if Unit1H not defined
```

This code ensures that the code between `#ifndef` and `#endif` will be included only once. It is a good idea to follow some convention when choosing suitable defines for header files. C++Builder uses an uppercase `H` after the header filename. If you write your own translation units, you should follow this convention. Of course, you can use a different naming convention, such as prepending `INCLUDED_` to the header filename, but you should be consistent throughout a project. Using include guards prevents a header file from being included more than once, but it must still be processed to see if it is to be included.

> **TIP**
>
> When you follow the IDE naming convention for include guards (appending an 'H' to the end of the header filename), the IDE treats the translation unit as a set, and it will appear as such in the Project Manager. If you do not want your `.cpp` and `.h` files to be treated in this way, do not use IDE-style include guards.

It has been shown that for very large projects (or more generally, projects with large, dense include graphs), this can have a significant effect on compile times. (For more information, see *Large-Scale C++ Software Design* by Lakos, 1996, p. 82.) Therefore, it is worth wrapping all include statements in an include guard to prevent the unnecessary inclusion of a file that has been defined already. For example, if `Unit1` from the previous code snippet also included ModalUnit1, ModalUnit2, and ModalUnit3, which are dialog forms used by other parts of the program, their include statements could be wrapped inside an include guard as follows:

```
#ifndef Unit1H   // Is Unit1H not already defined?
#define Unit1H   // If not then you reach this line and define it

#ifndef ModalUnit1H      // Is ModalUnit1H not already defined?
#include "ModalUnit1.h"  // No then include it
#endif                   // End of if Unit1H not defined

#ifndef ModalUnit2H
#include "ModalUnit2.h"
#endif

#ifndef ModalUnit3H
#include "ModalUnit3.h"
#endif


// Header file code placed here...

#endif          // End of if Unit1H not defined
```

This is not pretty, but it is effective. Remember that you must ensure that the names you define for include guards must not match any name that appears elsewhere in your program. The define statement will ensure that it is replaced with nothing, which could cause havoc. That is why a naming convention must be agreed on and adhered to.

TIP

Note that the Project Manager in C++Builder 5 was improved to include an expandable list of header file dependencies for each source file included in a project. Simply click the node beside the source filename to either expand or collapse the list. Note that the header file dependency lists are based on the source file's .obj file, hence the file must be compiled at least once to use this feature. Also note that the list could be out of date if changes are made without recompilation.

In C++Builder 6, the relationship between .h and .cpp is extended to automatically loading both into the Source Code Editor and providing tabs at the bottom of the editor window, so you can easily switch from header to implementation and back.

Know when using the preprocessor will benefit the program, and when it won't. Use it carefully and only when necessary.

Learn About and Use the C++ Standard Library

The C++ Standard Library, including the Standard Template Library (STL), is a constituent part of ANSI/ISO C++, just as the definition for bool is. You can save a lot of unnecessary coding by learning to use its features in your programs. The Standard Library has an advantage over homegrown code in that it has been thoroughly tested and is fast, and it *is* the standard, so portability is a big bonus. Standard Library features are summarized in the following list:

- Exceptions, such as bad_alloc, bad_cast, bad_typeid, and bad_exception

- Utilities, such as min(), max(), auto_ptr<T>, and numeric_limits<T>

- Input and output streams, such as istream and ostream

- Containers, such as vector<T>

- Algorithms, such as sort()

- Function objects (functors), such as equal_to<T>()

- Iterators

- Strings, such as string

- Numerics, such as complex<T>

- Special containers, such as queue<T> and stack<T>

- Internationalization support

Nearly everything in the Standard Library is a template, and most of the library consists of the STL, so it is very flexible. For example, the vector template class can be used to store any kind of data of the same type. As a result, it is a direct replacement for arrays in C++ and should be used in preference to arrays whenever possible.

In C++Builder 6, Borland introduced the STLPort open source C++ Standard Library, which should compile and operate in the same fashion as the old Rogue Wave implementation. STLPort will run both under Windows and Linux, so it is compatible with CLX programs.

VCL Overview

Supplied with C++Builder is a chart that schematically represents the Visual Component Library (VCL) object hierarchy. Not surprisingly, this chart has expanded with each new version of C++Builder. What you can't see, however, is the true complexity of the VCL. The explanation is simple: The VCL is much more than objects descending from other objects.

The VCL is based on what is known as the PME model, including properties, methods, and events. This architecture is joined with the Component Palette, Object Inspector, and IDE, giving developers a rapid approach to building applications known as Rapid Application Development (RAD). A developer can drop components onto a form and have a working Windows application almost without writing a single line of code. Obviously, writing code is required to make the application fully functional, but the VCL handles most of the work for you, making application development very expedient and more enjoyable. You can spend more time building the working blocks of your application rather than having to spend repetitive time with the framework of each Windows application you develop.

The remainder of this topic will take a very brief look at the hierarchy of VCL objects in general.

It All Starts at TObject

The VCL is fundamentally a group of objects that descend from the abstract class TObject. This class provides the capability to respond to the creation and destruction of objects, supports message handling, and contains class type and Runtime Type Information (RTTI) of its published properties.

RTTI enables you to determine the type of an object at runtime even when the code uses a pointer or reference to that object. As an example, C++Builder passes a TObject pointer to each of its events. This might be a mouse-click event or an object obtaining focus. Through the use of RTTI it is possible to perform a cast (dynamic_cast) to either use the object or determine the object type. The RTTI mechanism also enables testing an object type by using the typeid operator. The dynamic_cast operator is demonstrated later in this chapter. The C++Builder Language Guide online help provides additional information on this topic.

Descending from TObject are many simple nonpersistent data classes, wrappers, and streams, such as TList, TStack, TPrinter, TRegistry, and TStream, to name a few.

Persistent data, in terms of the VCL, refers to the mechanism of storing property values. The simplest example is the caption of a button or label. At design time you enter the caption in the Object Inspector. This caption is maintained between programming sessions and is available at runtime. The data is persistent. *Nonpersistent classes*, therefore, refers to simple classes designed to perform particular functions, but unable to save their state between sessions.

A *wrapper* can be described as a means of placing an envelope around the more complex Windows API. Wrappers allow for the creation of objects or components that are easier to use and can be used across multiple projects. Components, and other objects to some extent, shield you from the API and at the same time provide the convenience of using its powerful features in an easy-to-use fashion. Later chapters will provide additional information on these topics.

Another commonly used descendant of TObject is the Exception class, which provides many built-in exception classes for handling conditions such as, divide-by-zero and stream errors. With very minimal work this class can also be used to create custom classes for use in your own applications.

The other major branches of TObject include TPersistent, TComponent, TControl, TGraphicControl, and TWinControl.

TPersistent adds methods to TObject that enable the object to save its state prior to destruction, and reload that state when it is created again. This class is important in the creation of components that contain custom classes as properties. If the property needs to be streamed, it must descend from TPersistent rather than TObject. This branch includes many types of classes with the most common being TCanvas, TClipboard, TGraphic, TGraphicsObject, and TStrings. TPersistent descends to provide TComponent, the common base for all VCL components.

Property streaming refers to the mechanism by which the object's property values are written to the form's file. When the project is reopened, the property values are streamed (or read) back, thereby restoring their previous values.

TComponent objects provide the foundation for building C++Builder applications. Components have the capability to appear on the Component Palette, become parents for other components, control other components, and perform streaming operations.

There are two types of components—visual and nonvisual. Nonvisual components require no visual interface and are, therefore, derived directly from TComponent. Visual components are required to have the capability to been seen and interact with the user at runtime. TControl adds the drawing routines and window events required for defining a visual component. These visual components are divided into two groups: windowed (TWinControl) and nonwindowed (TGraphicControl).

TGraphicControl components are responsible for drawing themselves, but never receive focus. Examples include TImage, TLabel, TBevel, and TShape.

TWinControl components are similar to TGraphicControl except that they can receive focus, allowing for user interaction. These components are known as *windowed controls*, have a window handle, and can contain (or be the parent of) other controls.

Building on Existing Objects

The C++Builder object-oriented architecture means faster application development through reuse of existing objects and supporting classes. Giving the component objects the capability to present their published properties to the developer via the Object Inspector provides the extra dimension that further improves the development cycle.

But, the Object Inspector does more than simply present the component's published properties for review or editing. In Figure 3.1 you can see the Object Inspector showing the common properties of TLabel, TEdit, TButton, and TCheckBox controls. Looking at the hierarchy of these controls, you can see that TLabel descends from TGraphicControl, and the remainder descend from TWinControl. The common ancestor for all four controls is therefore TControl (because TGraphicControl and TWinControl descend from TControl).

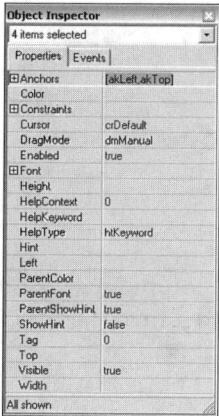

FIGURE 3.1   Common properties of multiple selected components.

Figure 3.1 is, therefore, displaying all the common properties the components have inherited from TControl. If you change one of these properties while they are all selected, this change will be reflected in all the controls simultaneously.

Building objects from existing classes or objects enables you to develop additional functionality into the descendants while at the same time enabling the base classes to remain available for new descendants that require a common base with some additional unique features. Some developers might argue that this additional class and the associated RTTI contained within the hierarchy are only adding to the overhead of the application. This overhead is well worth the benefits this object model provides. Each of the objects and components provided with C++Builder can appear quite differently, but share common features that are inherited from ancestor objects, making the development process more streamlined.

Using the VCL

It is important to understand how the VCL differs from regular classes and objects. The VCL originates from Delphi. As a result, all VCL objects are created on the free store and referenced as pointers rather than static objects. Only VCL objects need to be created and used in this fashion. All standard C/C++ objects can be used in either fashion.

An example will illustrate this. The following code first shows how a standard C++ class can be created on the stack, and then on the heap. Then, it shows how VCL objects *must* be created.

The C++ class code is as follows:

```
class MyClass
{
private:
    int MyVar;
public:
    MyClass(void);
};
```

Creating an instance of this class on the stack is shown next. When the class goes out of scope, the memory allocated for the object is released automatically.

```
MyClass Tmp;
Tmp.MyVar = 10;
// do something
```

Next, you look at creating an instance of this class on the heap. It is the responsibility of the creator to destroy the object before it goes out of scope. Otherwise, the memory is not released, resulting in a memory leak.

```
MyClass *Tmp;
Tmp = new MyClass;
Tmp->MyVar = 10;
// do something
delete Tmp;
```

VCL objects are like the second example, created on the heap. If you attempt to create a VCL object on the stack, the compiler will complain with the error message, `VCL style classes must be constructed using operator new.`

C++Builder has also made provisions for automatic destruction of objects that have owners. Let's assume you create a `TLabel` object dynamically and pass this as the owner:

```
TLabel *MyLabel = new TLabel(this);
```

When MyLabel goes out of scope, you at first assume a memory leak has occurred. Objects of this nature don't have to worry about freeing themselves explicitly because the VCL has a built-in mechanism to free all child objects before an owner object is destroyed. The term *parent object* was carefully avoided. This will be explained further.

Nonvisual components have owners, whereas visual components have owners and parents. The easiest way to distinguish the two terms is to think of the owner as the creator and the parent as the container allowing the component to exist. Suppose you have a TPanel component on a form, and on this component are three label components. There are two possible scenarios, depending on who created the labels.

In the first scenario, you have the labels being dropped onto the panel at design time. In this case, the panel is the parent for each of the labels, but the application is the owner. When the application is closed, the VCL ensures that each of the child objects (the panel and the three labels) are all destroyed before the application itself is destroyed.

In another case, you might drop an aggregate component (a component made up of many components) onto a form. For this example you assume it is a panel with three labels on it. The component creates the panel, and then creates three labels to sit on that panel. The panel is still the parent of the labels, but now the owner of the panel and the three labels is the component that was dropped onto the form. If the component is destroyed, the panel and labels also will be automatically destroyed.

This is a great feature for design time objects, but if you create objects at runtime, you should delete them explicitly. You won't have any memory leaks if you don't, but it makes the code more readable and documents the intention of the code. The following code demonstrates creating these objects at runtime.

```
TPanel *Panel1;
TLabel *Label1, *Label2, *Label3;
Panel1 = new TPanel(this);
Panel1->Parent = Form1;
Label1 = new TLabel(this);
Label1->Parent = Panel1;
Label2 = new TLabel(this);
Label2->Parent = Panel1;
Label3 = new TLabel(this);
Label3->Parent = Panel1;
// set other properties such as caption, position, etc
// do something
delete Label1;
delete Label2;
delete Label3;
delete Panel1;
```

The panel is created with the application as the owner and the form as the parent. The labels are then created similarly, with the difference being that the panel is made the parent of the labels. You could move the labels to another panel just by changing the Parent property. It is possible to delete the panel so that the labels would be deleted automatically, but I prefer to delete everything explicitly. This becomes more important when dealing with real-world applications in which global pointers are shared. It is also good practice to set the pointers to NULL (or zero) after they have been deleted (unless they are about to go out of scope). If another part of your application tries to delete the object after it has been destroyed, and you haven't nulled the pointer, an access violation is certain.

As mentioned earlier, the use of std::auto_ptr offers a mechanism for exception safe, class, and function local allocation of VCL objects.

The C++ Extensions

C++Builder has added extensions to the C++ language to make it a powerful product capable of utilizing the VCL and fitting seamlessly into the PME model. Some programmers consider the issue of C++ extensions controversial, but they can be useful, so long as they make the product powerful, maintain compatibility with ANSI standards, and provide for a shorter development cycle. In all cases, C++Builder manages this very well.

The extensions are listed next with a brief description. Please note that each of the extensions is prefixed with two underscores.

The __automated Class Extension

Object linking and embedding (OLE) does not provide type information in a type library. The automated section of a class that is derived from TAutoObject or a descendant of TAutoObject is used by applications supporting OLE automation. The required OLE automation information is generated for member functions and properties declared in this section.

```
class TMyAutoClass : public TAutoObject
{
public:
    virtual __fastcall TMyAutoClass(void);

__automated:
    AnsiString __fastcall GetClassName(void) { return("MyAutoClass"); }
};
```

The last point to make is that the declared method is of type __fastcall (described a little later). This is required for automated functions and causes the compiler to attempt to pass the parameters in the registers rather than on the stack.

The `__classid(class)` Class Extension

The `__classid` extension is used to bridge the gap between the VCL, RTTI functions, and the C++ language. It is used when an RTTI function requires class information as a parameter.

As an example, the `RegisterComponentEditor()` method enables you to create and register a custom editor for your components. My business produces a security component package (MJFSecurity) specifically for C++Builder. This package includes a number of custom components designed for protecting applications from piracy. One of these components is called `TAppLock`, and it uses a custom editor called `TAppLockEditor`. As part of the `Register()` method of the package, the editor is registered using the following code:

```
namespace Applock
{
    void __fastcall PACKAGE Register()
    {
        // ... code omitted from here
        RegisterComponentEditor(__classid(TAppLock), __classid(TAppLockEditor));
    }
}
```

The `RegisterComponentEditor()` method takes two parameters as pointers to `TMetaClass` (C++Builder's representation of the Delphi class-reference type). The `TMetaClass` for a given class can be acquired by using the `__classid` operator. The compiler uses the `__classid` operator to generate a pointer to the `vtable` (virtual table) for the given class name.

For further information on MJFSecurity, go to `http://www.mjfreelancing.com/`.

The `__closure` Class Extension

Standard C++ enables you to assign a derived class instance to a base class pointer, but does not enable you to assign a derived class's member function to a base class member function pointer. Listing 3.1 demonstrates this problem.

LISTING 3.1   Illegal Assignment of a Derived Class Member Function

```
enum HandTypes {htHour, htMinute, htSecond};

class TWatch
{
public:
    void MoveHand(HandTypes HandType);
};
```

LISTING 3.1   Continued

```
class TWatchBrand : public TWatch
{
public:
    void NewFeature(bool Start);
};

void (TWatch::*Wptr)(bool);          // declare a base class member
                                     // function pointer
Wptr = &TWatchBrand::NewFeature;     // illegal assignment of derived
                                     // class member function
```

C++Builder includes the __closure keyword to permit the previous situation.
Listing 3.2 uses the classes from Listing 3.1 to demonstrate how this is done.

LISTING 3.2   Assigning a Derived Class Member Function to a Base Member Function
Pointer by Using __closure

```
TWatchBrand *WObj = new TWatchBrand;  // create the object
void (__closure *Wptr)(bool);         // define a closure pointer
Wptr = WObj->NewFeature;              // set it to the NewFeature member function
Wptr(false);                          // call the function, passing false
Wptr = 0;                             // set the pointer to NULL
delete WObj;                          // delete the object
```

Note that you can also assign closure pointers to the base class member functions, as
Listing 3.3 shows.

LISTING 3.3   Assigning Closure Pointers to Base Class Member Functions

```
void (__closure *Wptr2)(HandTypes);
Wptr2 = WObj->MoveHand;
Wptr2(htSecond);
```

The __closure keyword is predominantly used for events in C++Builder.

The __declspec **Class Extension**
VCL classes have the following restrictions imposed on them:

- No virtual base classes are allowed.

- No multiple inheritance is allowed.

- They must be dynamically allocated on the heap by using the global new
  operator.

- They must have a destructor.

- Copy constructors and assignment operators are not compiler generated for VCL-derived classes.

The __declspec keyword is provided for language support with the VCL to overcome the previously mentioned items. The sysmac.h file provides macros that you should use if you need to use this keyword. The __declspec variations are discussed next.

__declspec(delphiclass, package)
sysmac.h defines the macro DELPHICLASS as __declspec(delphiclass, package). The delphiclass argument is used for the declaration of classes derived from TObject. If a class is translated from Delphi, the compiler needs to know that the class is derived from TObject. Hence, this modifier is used.

Similarly, if you create a new class that is to be used as a property type in a component, and you need to forward declare the class, you need to use the __declspec (delphiclass, package) keyword for the compiler to understand. Listing 3.4 shows an example of forward declaring a class where a new component has a pointer to that class type.

LISTING 3.4   Forward Declaring a Class to Use as a Member of Another Class

```
class TMyObject;

class TMyClass : public TComponent
{
private:
    TMyObject *FMyNewObject;

public:
    __fastcall TMyClass(TComponent *Owner) : TComponent(Owner){}
    __fastcall ~TMyClass(void);

};

class TMyObject : public TPersistent
{
public:
    __fastcall TMyObject(void){}
    __fastcall ~TMyObject(void);
};
```

Listing 3.4 will compile because the compiler only has a reference to the TMyObject class. If you need to include a property of type TMyObject, you need to tell the compiler the class is derived from a descendant of TObject. The modified code is shown in Listing 3.5.

LISTING 3.5   Using DELPHICLASS to Forward Declare a Class Required as a Property of Another Class

```
class  DELPHICLASS TMyObject;

class TMyObject;

class TMyClass : public TComponent
{
private:
  TMyObject *FMyNewObject;

public:
   __fastcall TMyClass(TComponent *Owner) : TComponent(Owner){}
   __fastcall ~TMyClass(void);

__published:
   __property TMyObject *NewObject = {read = FMyNewObject};
};

class TMyObject : public TPersistent
{
public:
   __fastcall TMyObject(void){}
   __fastcall ~TMyObject(void);
};
```

sysmac.h also defines a closely related macro RTL_DELPHICLASS as __declspec (delphiclass). This macro is used when nonpackaged RTL (runtime library) functionality is required in a class. Because components are created in design time packages or runtime/design time packages, you will find the DELPHICLASS macro used.

```
__declspec(delphireturn, package)
```
sysmac.h defines the macro DELPHIRETURN as __declspec(delphireturn, package).

The delphireturn parameter is used internally by C++Builder to enable classes created with C++Builder to support Delphi's built-in data types and language constructs. Examples include Currency, AnsiString, Variant, TDateTime, and Set.

Similar to __declspec(delphiclass), there is also a macro defined for __declspec(delphireturn). This macro, RTL_DELPHIRETURN, is used when Delphi's semantics are required in nonpackaged classes.

__declspec(dynamic)

sysmac.h defines the macro DYNAMIC as __declspec(dynamic). The dynamic argument is used for dynamic functions and is valid only for classes derived from TObject. These are similar to virtual functions except that the vtable information is stored only in the object that created the functions. If you call a dynamic function that doesn't exist, the ancestor vtables are searched until the function is found. Dynamic functions effectively reduce the size of the vtables at the expense of a short delay to look up the ancestor tables.

Dynamic functions cannot be redeclared as virtual and vice versa.

__declspec(hidesbase)

sysmac.h defines the macro HIDESBASE as __declspec(hidesbase). The hidesbase parameter is used to preserve Delphi semantics. Imagine a class called C1; derived from it is another class called C2. If both classes contain a function called foo, C++ interprets C2::foo() as a replacement for C1::foo(). In Delphi, C2::foo() is a different function to C1::foo(). To preserve this in C++ classes, you use the HIDESBASE macro. Listing 3.6 demonstrates its use.

LISTING 3.6   Using HIDESBASE to Override Class Methods in Descendant Classes

```
class TMyObject : public TPersistent
{
public:
  __fastcall TMyObject(void){}
  __fastcall ~TMyObject(void);
    void __fastcall Func(void){}
};


class TMyObject2 : public TMyObject·
{
public:
  __fastcall TMyObject2(void){}
  __fastcall ~TMyObject2(void);
    HIDESBASE void __fastcall Func(void){}
};
```

__declspec(hidesbase, dynamic)

sysmac.h defines the macro HIDESBASEDYNAMIC as __declspec(hidesbase, dynamic). This is used when Delphi's semantics need to be preserved for dynamic functions. The HIDESBASE macro is used when you need to preserve the way Pascal overrides methods in descendant classes. The HIDESBASEDYNAMIC macro does the same for dynamic methods.

`__declspec(package)`

`sysmac.h` defines the macro PACKAGE as `__declspec(package)`. The package argument in `__declspec(package)` indicates that the code defining the class can be compiled in a package. This enables classes to be imported and exported from the resulting BPL file.

`__declspec(pascalimplementation)`

`sysmac.h` defines the macro PASCALIMPLEMENTATION as `__declspec(pascalimplementation)`. The pascalimplementation argument indicates that the code defining the class was implemented in Delphi. This modifier appears in a Delphi portability header file with an `.hpp` extension.

The `__fastcall` Keyword

The `__fastcall` keyword is used to declare functions that expect parameters to be passed in registers. If the parameter is a floating-point or struct type, the registers are not used.

In general, use the `__fastcall` keyword only when declaring VCL class member functions. Using this modifier in all other cases will, more often than not, result in reduced performance. Typical examples of its use are found in all form class and component member functions. You should also note that the `__fastcall` modifier is used in name mangling.

The `__property` Keyword

The `__property` keyword is used to declare properties in classes, even non-VCL classes. Properties are data members, with the following additional features:

- They have associated read and write methods.

- They can indicate default values.

- They can be streamed to and from a form file.

- They can extend a property defined in a base class.

- They can make the data member read-only or write-only.

Refer to Chapter 4, "Creating Custom Components," for a more detailed look at properties.

The `__published` Keyword

The `__published` keyword is permitted only in classes descendant from TObject. Visibility rules for the `__published` section of a VCL class are the same as the public section, with the addition of RTTI being generated for data members and properties declared. RTTI enables you to query the data members, properties, and member functions of a class.

This RTTI is useful in event handlers. All standard events have a parameter passed of type TObject*. This parameter can be queried when the type of sender is unknown.

The following example shows how this is done when the OnButtonClick event is called from either a button click or a manual call such as Button1Click(NULL). Note that you can also do a manual call, passing the pointer of another button such as Button1Click(Button2). Listing 3.7 shows how this can be implemented.

LISTING 3.7   Using RTTI to Query an Object Type

```
void __fastcall TForm1::Button1Click(TObect *Sender)
{
TButton *Button = dynamic_cast<TButton *>(Sender);
if (Button)
    {
    // do something if a button was pressed.
    }
else
    {
    // do something when a call was made
    // passing a NULL value for  *Sender)
    }
}
```

VCL and CLX

Although the underpinnings of VCL and CLX are very different (which is why VCL is not portable across platforms), from a usage perspective they are almost identical, providing largely the same components in the same hierarchy with the same methods and properties. Look in the help to see if a component is VCL, CLX, or both.

NOTE

If you create a new CLX Application or new CLX MDI Application, you get a project that only supplies CLX components on the component palette. These projects are available from the File, New menu, or from the dialog that is presented when you pick File, New, Other (CLX Application is on the New page and CLX MDI Application is on the Projects page).

Review of the Component Palette

The VCL provides a large and mature family of interactive and noninteractive components for use in your application. These can be found on the IDE component palette.

To make that easier, the component palette is broken into pages, each containing a variety of components. Also, some components only exist on the component palette for specific editions.

- The Personal Edition contains the core VCL components.

- The Professional Edition adds the CLX components, the database components (excluding support for Oracle 8i special features), Quick Reports, TeeCharts (graphs), ActionLists and Actions, Office and other OLE Automation Server components, a WebBrowser component, and the Indy Internet components.

- The Enterprise Edition adds special component features for Oracle, DataSnap components for access to remote data module applications, SOAP, COM, and CORBA-oriented distributed system connection components for use with remote data modules, and Internet Express components to easily use XML with remote data modules.

The pages of the component palette conveniently arrange these more than three hundred components into something manageable.

Figure 3.2 shows the component palette properties dialog, which is produced when you pick Properties from the pop-up menu you get with a right-button press over the component palette.

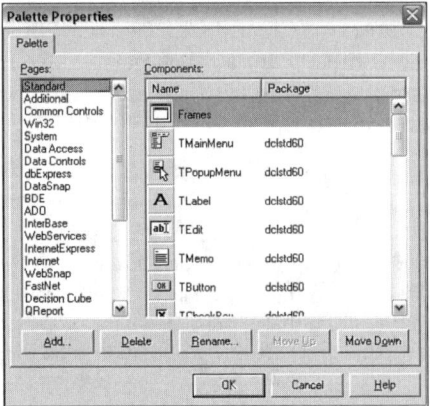

FIGURE 3.2 Component palette properties dialog.

The pages contain components as follows (you can see the name of the component in a hint if you hover over the component image on the palette):

- Standard: Basic user interface components, such as TMainMenu, TPanel, TLabel, TEdit, TMemo, and TButton. These are typically standard Windows/Linux user interface elements.

- Additional: More user-interface components, offering specialized features not available from standard operating system components. These include special buttons such as TBitBtn and TSpeedButton (extending TButton with images); TMaskEdit (extending TEdit with the capability to enforce a format for input); TDrawGrid and TStringGrid (which provide a scrollable spreadsheet-such as interface object for images and strings, respectively); TImage and TShape, which can be used as graphical elements, and the special Action components.

- Common Controls and Win32: There are many useful controls here. They include the TpageControl, which enables you to create multipage user interfaces; TProgressBar, which you can use to show the progress of some noninteractive processing; TimageList, which can contain a set of indexable images for sequential display or use with controls such as TBitBtn. Note that the Common Controls page is for CLX applications only and Win32 for Windows VCL applications only.

- System: A Windows only page, this contains a variety of specialized Windows controls, including TPaintBox, TMediaPlayer, OLE, and DDE controls.

- Data Access: This now contains only a relatively small set of components that are used for data access. These include TdataSource, which is used to connect database components to the data-aware controls on the DataControls page); TClientDataSet, which is used when working with client-server database queries, and a set of XML transformation components.

- Data Controls: These are data-aware versions of standard user interface controls. They can be hooked to a data source that makes the controls capable of displaying data set rows or fields. Controls such as TDBGrid, TDBText (a label-displaying field content), TDBEdit (allowing editing of the content of a field), TDBImage (displaying an image stored in a BLOB field) makes it very easy to connect your application to databases regardless of how they are implemented.

The next four pages offer components that provide similar interfaces, but which use very different methods of accessing data in databases. At one time, C++Builder provided only one type of database access component—the components now on the BDE page. Now there are several different component sets for database access—which means more choices. Fortunately, all those components link to the same data aware controls using the TDataSource component on the Data Access page.

- dbExpress: These are a set of components to interface with the new lightweight client-server database drivers from Borland. Those drivers can work with enterprise databases such as Oracle.

- DataSnap: These components connect to Remote Data Modules (RDM). RDM are used to form the provider tier of a multitier system. TDCOMConnection enables you to use DCOM to connect to the RDM, and pass data back and forth from the components of the RDM as if they were on the local system. Other types of connection are also provided. DataSnap is discussed in Chapter 21, "DataSnap Multitier Connections."

- BDE: These are a set of components to interface with Borland Database Engine drivers, which allow access to databases both directly through the BDE and indirectly through ODBC. Note that the BDE is currently stable—which means it will not see much if any further development.

- ADO: This set of components only applies to Windows, where it connects to databases through ActiveX Data Objects.

- Interbase: This set of components connects to the Borland open source Interbase client-server database.

Multitier applications other than pure database applications are also easy to program using components. The next few pages are dedicated to those sorts of distributed programs:

- WebServices: These components are used to provide or work with WebServices-enabled applications, which are covered in Chapter 19, "SOAP and Web Services with BizSnap."

- InternetExpress, Internet, WebSnap, FastNet: These components work with HTML, HTTP, and other Web protocols.

- Decision Cube: This powerful database component set enables you to provide fairly high-end analytical capabilities to your users.

Creating User Interfaces

As you saw in Chapter 1, it is easy to create a user interface in C++Builder by combining forms with components. You can put application code in event handlers on the controls so they can react to mouse and keyboard actions.

But, as your user interfaces become more complex, controls piled on forms are not enough to make your programs manageable. In this section, you explore the next-level techniques required to deal with complex user interfaces.

Component Templates and Frames

As you develop your applications, you might develop a style of components for your user interfaces. For instance, your database user interfaces might typically have a TDBGrid to its right, a splitter to its left, and a TDBRecordView to the left of that.

C++Builder offers three ways to solve this problem, any of which is better than repeatedly dropping the same configuration of components on a form.

- Use Component Templates—these are combinations of components that you select, set properties for, and put on the component palette as a group for later reuse. The reused components are independent of the template after they have been dropped on the form.

- Use Frames—these are combinations of components placed on a form-like object, which are considered a cohesive whole. You can set properties and event handlers for these components and for the frame as a whole. Frames can be placed on the component palette in which case they can be dropped onto other user interfaces (forms or frames). They can also be placed in the Object Repository, which enables them to also be used as the basis for inheritance. Such frames can be used to extend an already created frame, and then changes to the original frame will also affect the descendant frame.

- Create your own combined component by programming the creation of subcomponents into a new component. Component creation is covered in Chapter 4, "Creating Custom Components."

Component Templates

You can see a pair of components about to be turned into a component template in Figure 3.3:

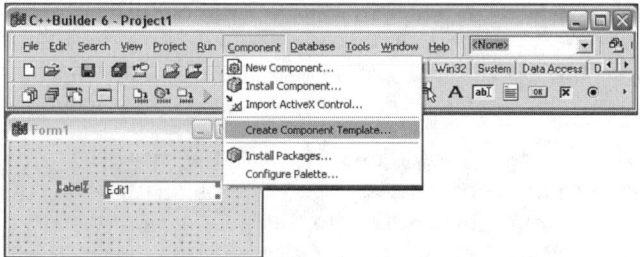

FIGURE 3.3 Creating a component template from a pair of components.

Figure 3.4 shows the form from which the template was derived, after the template was dropped on the form. You can see the component on the template, where it shows the icon of the first of the two components selected to make the template; the hint shows that the component is called TEchoedEdit, demonstrating that you can set a desired name for this new component. You can also see in the editor window that the dropped component template has inserted a copy of the original event handler, with the referenced component names changed.

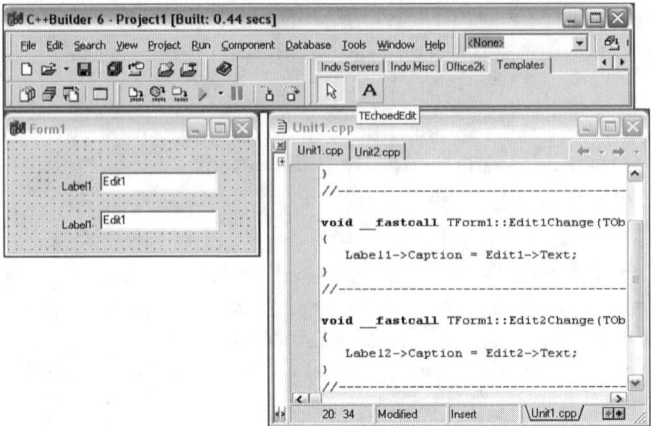

FIGURE 3.4   Template on the form.

What happens when the event handler refers to a component outside the template? That name is not changed. Of course, that will cause a compilation problem if you drop the template on a form that does not include the named external component.

So, component templates are useful, but they should be constructed carefully if they are to be successfully reused.

Frames

The word *Frame* is used to describe an object of the TFrame class or one of its descendants. Conceptually, a Frame can be thought of as a child Form, although in reality, a Frame is more closely related to a ScrollBox. Let's examine this argument more closely.

The TFrame class is a direct descendant of the TCustomFrame class, serving only to publish selected properties of TCustomFrame; no implementation code is added. The TCustomFrame class, in turn, descends from the TScrollingWinControl class. Both the TCustomForm and TScrollBox classes are also descendants of the TScrollingWinControl class.

The TScrollingWinControl class, a direct descendant of the TWinControl class, extends its parent class by providing support for horizontal and vertical scrollbars and management of the controls that it contains. The TCustomForm class extends the TScrollingWinControl class by providing support for aspects specific to top-level windows. The TScrollBox class extends the TScrollingWinControl class only via the BorderStyle property. However, the TCustomFrame class presents no additional properties or member functions to its parent class.

In short, a Frame is little more than a TScrollingWinControl object—a child window with scrolling support. At design time, a Frame most closely resembles a TForm object. At runtime, a Frame most closely resembles a TScrollBox object with its BorderStyle property set to bsNone.

The TCustomFrame Class

Because the TFrame class is a descendant of the TCustomFrame class and serves only to publish selected properties of its parent class, it is worth examining the TCustomFrame class in $(BCB)\Source\VCL\Forms.hpp.

Within the TCustomFrame constructor, the Width property is assigned a value of 320 and the Height property is specified as 240. Also from within the constructor, the following state flags are added to the ControlState property: csSetCaption, csAcceptsControls, csCaptureMouse, csClickEvents, and csDoubleClicks. In fact, apart from the csAcceptsControls flag, the other state flags are automatically set for all TControl descendants. It is the csAcceptsControls state flag that makes the Frame object a container control. In addition, similar to the case when working with a Form (or a Data Module) at design time, the TCustomFrame class can also contain nonvisual components. Because these nonvisual components should be streamed to the .DFM file with the Frame object, the TCustomFrame class extends (by overriding) the DYNAMIC GetChildren() member function in which a direct call to the supplied TGetChildProc-type callback function is made for each owned nonvisual component. Note that this is the same technique performed by the TCustomForm and TDataModule classes.

ActionLists are supported in the TCustomFrame class via the private AddActionList() and RemoveActionList() member functions. These functions serve to append and delete any ActionList objects (contained within the TFrame descendant class) to and from the internal ActionList array of the parent Form, respectively. As such, each of these member functions is called appropriately from within the overridden SetParent() (when the parent Form changes) and Notification() (when an ActionList is added/removed) member functions.

Working with Frames at Design Time

When a new TFrame descendant class is added to a project at design time, the IDE presents an instance of this class contained inside a Form Designer (a TWinControlForm object). You can then work with this class just like a form. For example, you can change aspects of the TFrame descendant class by changing any of its published properties. In fact, except for the TScrollBox::BorderStyle property, the properties (including event types) of the default TFrame descendant are identical to those of the TScrollBox class.

Manipulation of a TFrame descendant class within its own Form Designer makes changes to the class itself. This is identical to what happens with a TForm descendant class in its Form Designer. For example, when you drop a new component on a Form at design time, the header file of the TForm descendant class is updated to reflect this change. Similarly, when you change a property of a TFrame descendant class in its Form Designer, the changes affect either the class header file or the corresponding .DFM file. This is in contrast to working with most other components, where design time manipulation only affects a particular instance of the component class. For example, when you drop a TPanel component on a Form at design time, and then change the Color property of this Panel, you are only altering a single instance of the TPanel class, not the class itself. When utilizing components you expect that: In many situations, the creation of a custom component class for each instance of a particular component is not warranted. There's no need to create, for example, a TRedPanel class just to use a red-colored TPanel variation.

Of course, the C++Builder IDE supports the design time manipulation of a particular instance of a TFrame descendant class. For example, you can select the Frames icon from the Standard page of the Component Palette to add an instance of any TFrame descendant class to another container control, such as a Form, a Panel, or even another Frame, and then modify it. Or, you can add a TFrame descendant class to the Component Palette by picking Add To Palette from the pop-up menu that appears when the Frame is right-clicked in its Form Designer, from which you can reuse it elsewhere.

The values set in properties of any TFrame descendant class or its components are considered defaults for the frame's instances and descendants. If you do not set those properties in an instance or descendant, changes to the ancestor will take immediate effect in the descendant or instance.

For example, imagine you have a button in your frame class that has the value Big Button as the default for its caption. Drop an instance of this frame on your form. Then, change the caption of the button in the class to Former Big Button. The instance you dropped on the form will change to match. However, if you change the caption on the button in the instance of the frame on your form to X, and then change the caption of that same button in the class to Y, the instance will retain the caption X.

Working with Frames at Runtime

There is nothing special about working with a TFrame descendant class instance at runtime—it is just another type of TWinControl descendant. Indeed, a Frame most closely resembles a ScrollBox at runtime. Without the design time enhancements presented by the IDE and TCustomFrame class, there would be little advantage to using a Frame over a ScrollBox.

However, frames have more sophisticated resource management than most other controls. For example, if you place a TImage component on a Form, load the TImage component with a 1MB bitmap file, and then make a dozen copies of this TImage component, the result would be a significant increase in the size of your application. On the other hand, if you add a new Frame to your project, drop a TImage component on the Frame in its Form Designer (in other words, modify the TFrame descendant class), load the TImage component with a 1MB bitmap file, and then use a dozen instances of this Frame instead of the individual TImage objects, you would not see a significant increase in application size. This results from the fact that each Frame instance will share only one copy of the compiled bitmap resource. This is in contrast to using a dozen TImage instances, where a dozen copies of the bitmap would be compiled into your application's resources.

Creating a TFrame Descendant Class

As you have seen, creating a TFrame descendant class is simplified by the visual editing features of the IDE. This is in contrast to creating, for example, a TScrollBox descendant, which requires programming. You are also not required to package and register the component class when working with frames.

Practical Example: Using Frames to Create a Pop-Up Window

Many of the latest applications present temporary pop-up windows that contain different types of controls. For example, many of the toolbar buttons in Microsoft Office 2000 present what appear to be standard pop-up menus, but are actually custom topmost, captionless windows. Another common example of such a window is the drop-down list portion of a combo box control.

You can create your own version of a pop-up window via a TCustomFrame descendant class (see Figure 3.5). The interface for this class is provided in Listing 3.8.

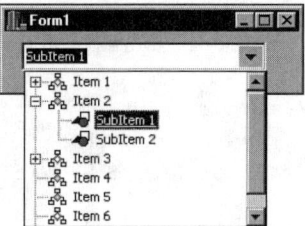

FIGURE 3.5   Using a Frame as a pop-up window containing a TreeView control.

LISTING 3.8   TPopupFrame.h, a TFrame Descendant Class

```
//--------------------------------------------------------------------------//
#ifndef PopupFrameUnitH
#define PopupFrameUnitH
//--------------------------------------------------------------------------//
```

LISTING 3.8   Continued

```cpp
#include <Classes.hpp>
#include <Controls.hpp>
#include <ComCtrls.hpp>
//------------------------------------------------------------------//

class TPopupFrame : public TFrame
{
__published:
    TTreeView *TreeView1;
    void __fastcall TreeView1MouseMove(TObject *Sender, TShiftState Shift,
        int X, int Y);
    void __fastcall TreeView1MouseUp(TObject *Sender, TMouseButton Button,
        TShiftState Shift, int X, int Y);

private:
    TNotifyEvent OnCloseUp_;
    MESSAGE void __fastcall CMMouseEnter(TMessage& AMsg)
    {
        ReleaseCapture();
    }
    MESSAGE void __fastcall CMMouseLeave(TMessage& AMsg)
    {
        if (Visible) SetCapture(TreeView1->Handle);
    }

protected:
    virtual void __fastcall CreateParams(TCreateParams& AParams)
    {
        TFrame::CreateParams(AParams);
        AParams.Style = AParams.Style | WS_BORDER;
        AParams.ExStyle = AParams.ExStyle | WS_EX_PALETTEWINDOW;
    }
    virtual void __fastcall CreateWnd()
    {
        TFrame::CreateWnd();
        ::SetParent(Handle, GetDesktopWindow());
        SNDMSG(TreeView1->Handle, WM_SETFOCUS, 0, 0);
    }
    DYNAMIC void __fastcall VisibleChanging()
    {
        TFrame::VisibleChanging();
```

LISTING 3.8   Continued

```
      if (Visible) ReleaseCapture();
      else SetCapture(TreeView1->Handle);
   }

public:
BEGIN_MESSAGE_MAP
   VCL_MESSAGE_HANDLER(CM_MOUSEENTER, TMessage, CMMouseEnter)
   VCL_MESSAGE_HANDLER(CM_MOUSELEAVE, TMessage, CMMouseLeave)
END_MESSAGE_MAP(TFrame)

public:
   __fastcall TPopupFrame(TComponent* AOwner);
   __property TNotifyEvent OnCloseUp = {read = OnCloseUp_, write = OnCloseUp_};
};
//------------------------------------------------------------------------//
extern PACKAGE TPopupFrame *PopupFrame;
//------------------------------------------------------------------------//
#endif
```

A pop-up window is actually a child of the desktop window (the WS_CHILD style bit is set) that is created with a combination of the WS_EX_TOOLWINDOW and WS_EX_TOPMOST extended style bits (represented by WS_EX_PALETTEWINDOW). The WS_CHILD bit prevents your Form from losing activation when the pop-up window itself is activated. The WS_EX_PALETTEWINDOW bit prevents the pop-up window from being obscured by other windows (WS_EX_TOPMOST) and from appearing in the dialog that's displayed when the end user presses the Alt+Tab keystroke combination (WS_EX_TOOLWINDOW).

To realize the style bit manipulation, you override the virtual CreateParams() member function:

```
   virtual void __fastcall CreateParams(TCreateParams& AParams)
   {
      TFrame::CreateParams(AParams);
      AParams.Style = AParams.Style | WS_BORDER;
      AParams.ExStyle = AParams.ExStyle | WS_EX_PALETTEWINDOW;
   }
```

First, you call the CreateParams() member function of the parent class so that (up the heirarchy ladder) the TWinControl can add the WS_CHILD bit, among others. Next, you add the WS_BORDER bit to the Style data member, and the WS_EX_PALETTEWINDOW bit to the ExStyle data member of the TCreateParams-type argument.

To change the parent of the pop-up window to the desktop window, you override the virtual CreateWnd() member function:

```
virtual void __fastcall CreateWnd()
{
   TFrame::CreateWnd();
   ::SetParent(Handle, GetDesktopWindow());
   SNDMSG(TreeView1->Handle, WM_SETFOCUS, 0, 0);
}
```

First, you call the CreateWnd() member function of the parent class so that (up the heirarchy ladder) the TWinControl class can register the class with Windows and create the window via CreateWindowHandle() member function. Next, you use the SetParent() API function along with the GetDesktopWindow() API function to change the parent of the pop-up window to the desktop window. This manipulation ensures that the contents of the pop-up window are not clipped to the bounds of its usual parent (a Form). You also send the child TreeView control the WM_SETFOCUS message to fool it into thinking it has keyboard focus.

In addition to manipulating the style and parent of the pop-up window, you also need to manage its mouse-related events—specifically, those that should trigger the pop-up window to close. To this end, you make use of the VCL CM_MOUSENTER and CM_MOUSELEAVE messages and extend the virtual VisibleChanging() member function. You also make use of the readily available TTreeView::OnMouseMove and TTreeView::OnMouseUp events. Mouse capture is accordingly granted/removed from the TreeView control so that its OnMouseUp event handler will fire, even when a mouse button is released when the cursor is beyond the bounds of your pop-up window. Specifically, unless your pop-up window has captured the mouse, the WM_*BUTTONUP messages will not be sent when the cursor is located outside the client area of your pop-up window.

In fact, every step that you performed to create your pop-up window class could just as well have been performed without the use of Frames. However, the goal of this example was to demonstrate that the use of Frames can significantly simplify the process of implementing such a class. For example, you did not have to manually declare, and then assign the appropriate member functions to the TreeView's OnMouseMove and OnMouseUp events. Such a task can quickly become cumbersome when a component contains several different child components, each with a vast number of event handlers. For a slightly more complex example of a TFrame descendant class, examine the TMCIWndFrame class included in the companion CD-ROM as part of the Proj_VideoDemo.bpr project in the VideoDemo folder.

Finally, note that the redefinition of any virtual or dynamic member function applies only at runtime. In this case, your redefined version will not be called at design time. This would not be the case if you are going to place your component in a design time package and register it with the IDE. Indeed, when a `TFrame` descendant class is registered as a design time component, use of the `csDesigning` `ComponentState` flag might be needed.

Inheriting from a `TFrame` Descendant Class

Descendants of a `TFrame` descendant class can also be visually manipulated at design time. For example, if you create a descendant of your `TPopupFrame` class, it too will open in its own Form Designer and reflect the attributes of its parent class. The aforementioned rules of inheritance apply here as well—subsequent design time changes made to the parent class will be reflected in the descendant, but not vice versa.

It seems, however, that the IDE is not well-suited to handle visual Frame inheritance. That is, the procedure, although straightforward, is not entirely user friendly. The following steps are required to create a descendant of a `TFrame` descendant class that can be visually designed:

1. Add the parent `TFrame` descendant class to the project (for example, `TFrame2`).

2. Choose File, New Frame to add a new `TFrame` descendant class to the project (for example `TFrame3`).

3. Edit the header and source files of the new `TFrame` descendant class (`Unit3.h`, `Unit3.cpp`), replacing all occurrences of the original parent class (`TFrame`) with the name of the new parent class (for example, `TFrame2`).

4. Edit the `.DFM` file of the new descendant class, changing the keyword `object` with the keyword `inherited`.

Reusing Frames

Like forms, frames can be added to the Object Repository for use in subsequent projects. Frames can also be distributed to other developers by simply supplying the source code (interface and implementation) and the `.DFM` file. Moreover, as previously mentioned, a `TFrame` descendant class can be placed in a design time package and registered with the IDE much like any other custom component class. For example, to register a new `TFrame` descendant class `TMyFrame`, you simply use the `PACKAGE` macro where necessary, and then define the familiar `ValidCtrCheck()` and `Register()` functions in the class source file:

```
static inline void ValidCtrCheck(TMyFrame*)
{
    new TMyFrame(NULL);
}
```

```
namespace Myframeunit
{
    void __fastcall PACKAGE Register()
    {
        TComponentClass classes[1] = {__classid(TMyFrame)};
        RegisterComponents("Samples", classes, 0);
    }
}
```

However, there are some caveats when working with a Frame in a package at design time. First, when utilizing with the Package Editor, the IDE insists on opening the .DFM file of a TFrame descendant class as if it was a standard Form object. Consequently, the entries of the .DFM file are changed to reflect those of a TForm descendant class. For example, a normal default TFrame descendant class will exhibit the following entries:

```
object Frame2: TFrame2
  Left = 0
  Top = 0
  Width = 320
  Height = 240
  TabOrder = 0
end
```

On the other hand, the .DFM file for the same TFrame descendant class that has been mangled by the IDE will appear as follows:

```
object Frame2: TFrame2
  Left = 0
  Top = 0
  Width = 320
  Height = 240
  Color = clBtnFace
  Font.Charset = DEFAULT_CHARSET
  Font.Color = clWindowText
  Font.Height = -11
  Font.Name = 'MS Sans Serif'
  Font.Style = []
  OldCreateOrder = True
  PixelsPerInch = 96
  TextHeight = 13
end
```

Aside from the removal of the entry for the TabOrder property, the IDE appends entries that apply to descendants of the TForm class, but not to TFrame descendants (OldCreateOrder, for example). Moreover, after a TFrame descendant class is registered, subsequent attempts to open its source file (and thus, its .DFM file) will result in the aforementioned mangling (regardless of whether the Package Editor is in use). Note that if a .DFM should become inadvertently changed, you can simply append an entry for the TabOrder property, and then remove all nonapplicable entries.

Another side effect of registering a TFrame descendant class is that its contained components cannot automatically be manipulated at design time. For example, when included as a component template or simply added to a project, the contained components of a TFrame descendant class instance can be individually manipulated at design time. However, when working with a design-time instance of a registered TFrame descendant class, these contained components are no longer accessible; instead, other measures must be implemented (for example, individual property editors).

Closing Remarks on Frames

Admittedly, the design-time functionality presented by Frames is far from that necessary for true visual component development. At this stage, Frames are perhaps more useful for simply managing groups of controls rather than for creating complex components. Indeed, when system resources are an issue, the use of a TFrame descendant class might not be the most robust approach. Recall that the TFrame class is a TWinControl descendant, and thus each instance consumes a window handle. Still, frames are a step in the right direction, and the concept is sound. Undoubtedly, you can expect to see an increased level of sophistication in subsequent versions of C++Builder.

Coping with Different Screen Conditions

Another important issue in user interface design is managing windows as they are resized so that their components continue to occupy an optimal arrangement in the space available.

Fortunately, C++Builder provides a variety of mechanisms for allocating the window real estate:

- Alignment—controls the location of visual components by specifying the relative space they should occupy to the left, right, top, bottom, and client (remainder) of the parent.

- Anchor—controls the specific positioning of a visual component by anchoring one or more corners of the component.

In addition to these properties, two components are especially important in managing window layouts:

- TScrollbox—a panel that forms scrollbars when it gets too small to show all the components it contains.

- TSplitter—a panel that enables you to change the size of aligned controls it separates by dragging the splitter.

Alignment

TPanel and many other controls support alignment through the Align property.

Figure 3.6 shows the variations in alignment of a TPanel on a form.

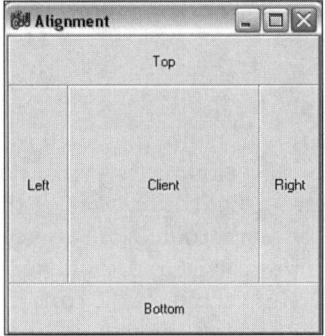

FIGURE 3.6   Alignment of panels on a form.

Figure 3.7 shows how the panels adjust in size as the window changes shape.

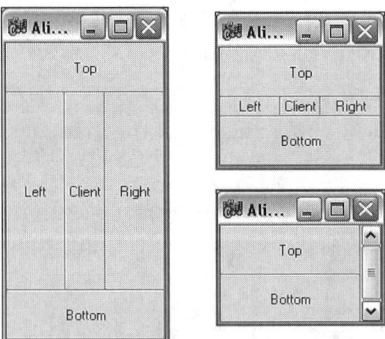

FIGURE 3.7   Panels on a form change shape when aligned.

Figure 3.8 shows a fully aligned user interface with many aligned elements: grids, panels, tabbed pages. Each panel is separated by splitters allowing their relative sizes to be changed.

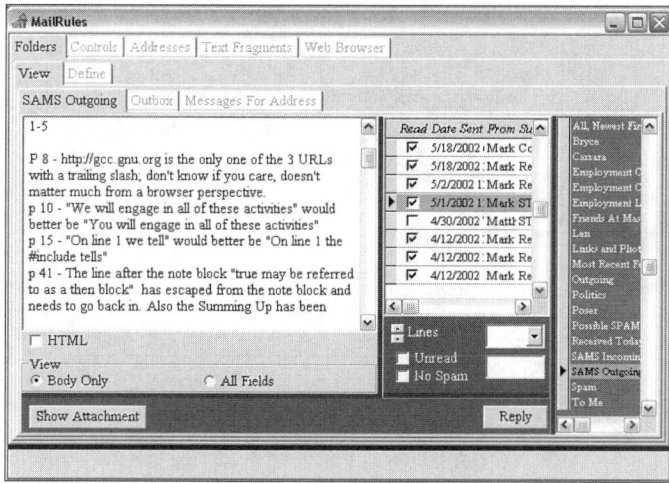

FIGURE 3.8   A user interface with many aligned elements.

Anchors
This figure also shows some anchored elements—TButton, TEdit, TUpDown components. Such components do not offer the Align property, but they do offer the Anchor property.

Figure 3.9 shows what happens to buttons anchored in a variety of ways as their parent changes shape and size.

Notice that, unlike alignment, anchoring does not prevent elements from overlapping. Under alignment, a component can shrink to invisibility.

Alignment, Anchors, Splitters, and Scroll Boxes
As you can see in Figure 3.10, the TSplitter components work with alignment to allow user flexibility in changing the shape and size of portions of the user interface.

By moving the splitters (the dark vertical lines at the right edge of the Left panel and on the left edge of the Right panel), the proportion of the form given to each of the aligned components can be changed at runtime. Notice how the shapes and sizes of the anchored components also change—within limits. When the limits are transgressed, such components disappear over the edge of their parent panel and are unreachable.

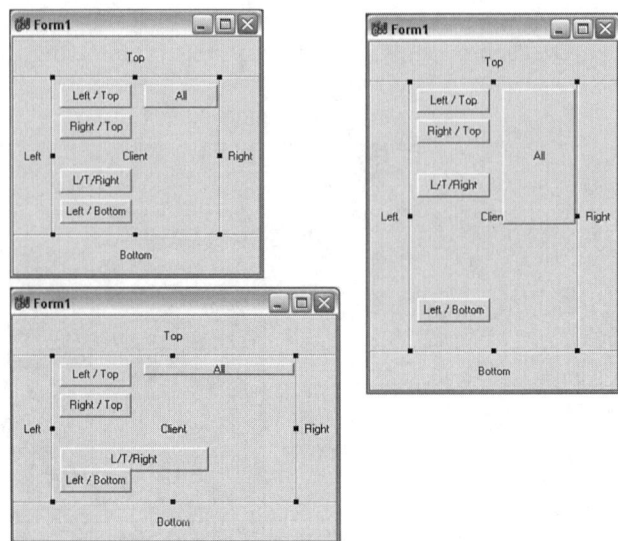

FIGURE 3.9   The behavior of anchored buttons.

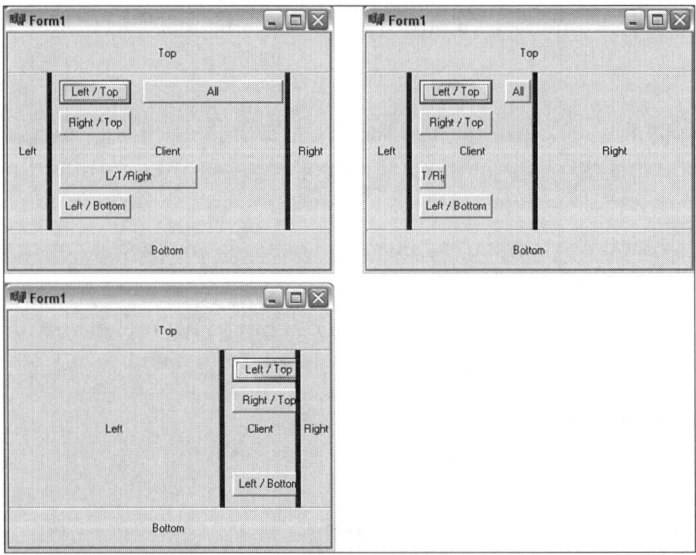

FIGURE 3.10   The behavior of aligned panels and anchored buttons as TSplitters are moved.

The TSplitter component needs to be a sibling of, and aligned the same as, the component it controls. Thus, the left splitter, which controls the left pattern, has its alignment set to alLeft; the right splitter is aligned alRight.

Because splitters and alignment can cause unanchored and anchored components alike to become unreachable, it is a good idea to use the TScrollBox for panels where that can occur.

In Figure 3.10, for instance, the top and bottom panels cannot be affected by either resizing or by the splitters. But the left, right and client panels can be. In Figure 3.11, you can see the effect of replacing the client-aligned panel with a client-aligned TScrollBox.

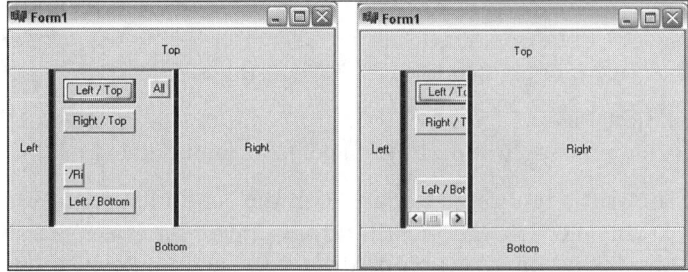

FIGURE 3.11   The behavior of a TScrollBox as TSplitters are moved.

Although the anchors can squeeze some of the controls out of existence, those not affected by the size of the TScrollBox are still able to be reached even when the scroll-box starts to cut them off, simply by using the scrollbar.

Coping with Complexity in the Implementation of the User Interface

Although much of the complexity of the user interface resides in the layout and behavior of visual components, most of the real work of the application is done in the component event handlers.

Unfortunately, this can lead to various problems, especially when it is desired to share the actions of the user interface with several different visual representations. For instance, a typical application might reveal a particular feature as a menu entry, a toolbar icon, and a control in a dialog. For even more controllability, it might offer a macro language that enables control from external applications, perhaps through a COM interface.

C++Builder does allow event handlers to be shared. The event handlers can interrogate the Sender argument to determine the source of their invocation. This offers some ability to reduce the complexity of the user interface implementation.

There is another element of such user interfaces that presents a problem. Sometimes a feature might be disabled or an option can be checked off. Managing this in conventional event handlers usually results in the event handler having code that sets the appearance of every user interface element that represents the feature. That adds complexity to the event handler, and can lead to errors in the behavior of the user interface.

To ease the implementation of user interfaces, Borland introduced the TAction classes. These actions, are components that can respond to control events. Unlike event handlers, which are attached to components, components attach to actions. This reversal of direction helps to ensure that any number of components can share and be affected by the state of the action—for instance, whether it is enabled or checked.

Action instances can be organized into lists, represented by the TActionList class. Usually a given form or application will have a single action list.

One of the easiest ways to see a TActionList in action is to create an MDI (Multiple Document Interface) Application in the File, New menu dialog tab Projects.

Figure 3.12 shows the resulting interface with the action list open, and its File category selected. The File New action within that category is selected, and the Object Inspector is displaying the event properties for the action. Below all that is the Source Code Editor showing the default code automatically created for the event handler on the action.

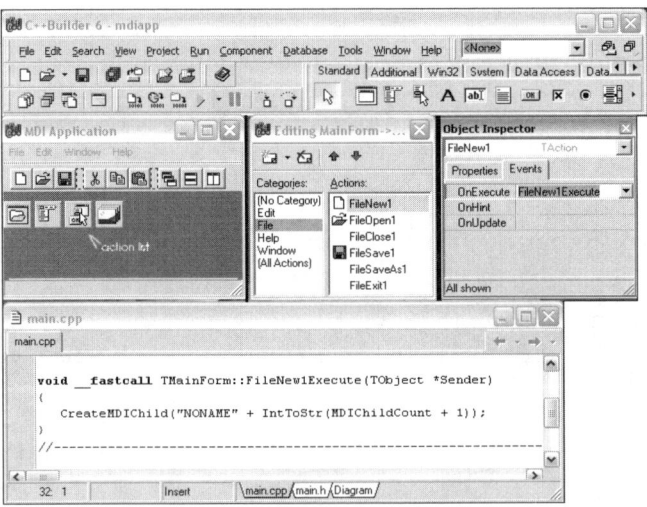

FIGURE 3.12 Editing an action event handler.

Naturally, you could add any additional code you might need to the event handler. Also of interest is that the application's menu entry for File, New and the toolbar icon for creating a new file (the white sheet of paper icon) both share the action and, through it, the event handler.

It is simple to create your own action list with actions, and associate each action with a user interface element like a menu entry or button.

Figure 3.13 shows a simple program with two actions and an action list.

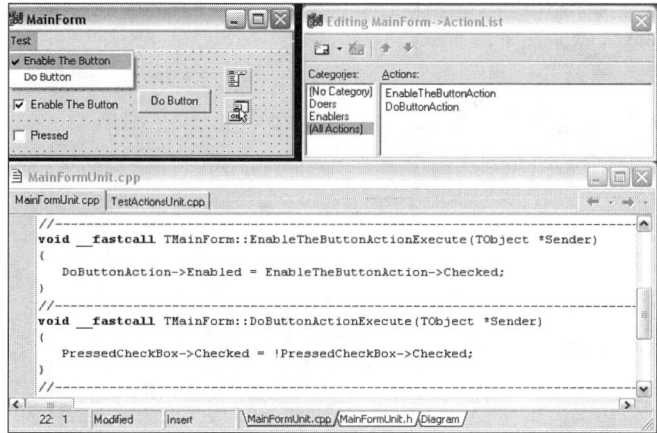

FIGURE 3.13   A simple Action List Program.

This example shows how the action contributes the caption to the menu and the check box label. If you change the caption on the action, all the controls displaying that text change to match the text you provided.

You can also see from the event handler for the EnableTheButtonAction that it sets the action for the button to be enabled or disabled based on its Checked state. When the action is disabled, both the button and the menu item will be disabled—and vice versa.

Action Manager

C++Builder 6 introduced the Action Manager and Action Bands. Action Bands enable you to create user interfaces by dragging and dropping actions onto special visual components: the TActionMainMenuBar and the TActionToolBar.

NOTE

TActionManager, TactionMainMenuBar, and TActionToolBar are not allowed in CLX programs at this time.

Figure 3.14 shows a design session with an Action Manager–oriented program. You can see the Action Manager window, which is displaying the list of actions and action categories. These actions are no different from those you create for an ActionList–oriented program.

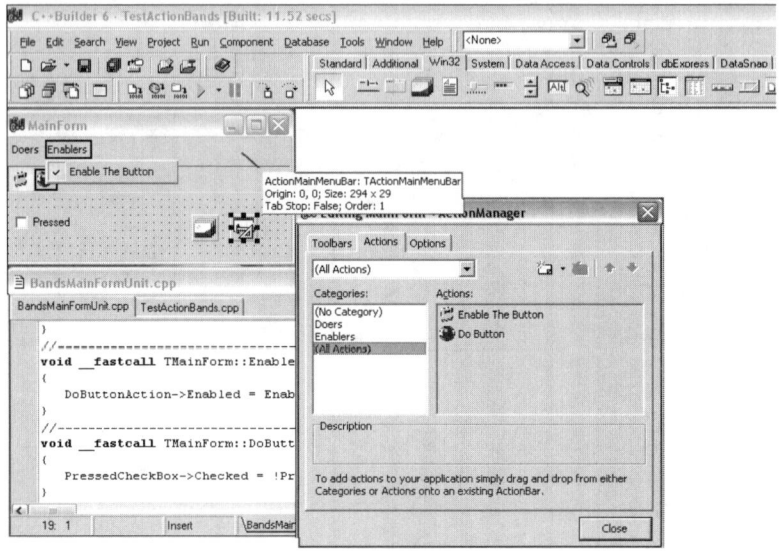

FIGURE 3.14　A session with the Action Manager.

What is different is the use of TActionMainMenuBar and TActionToolBar. Actions from Action Manager have been dragged and dropped onto the TActionToolBar, automatically forming buttons (the images are from the image list and are attached to the action so that they are consistent across the application. The categories have been dropped on the menu bar to form menu headings with items underneath them.

A number of properties affect the appearance and behavior of the menus, menu items, and the buttons. For instance, the Action Window contains Caption Options that control whether buttons on the toolbar show captions, and if captions are shown, whether they are always shown or if showing captions is selective.

Action Manager–driven menus and toolbars offer the same features present in many modern applications such as Microsoft office—including the capability to order menu items based on the usage during the session.

Another feature of the Action Manager is the capability to present the Action Manager to the user at runtime so that they can customize the tool bars and menu bars. Adding the Customize Action Bars standard action to the Action Manager and dragging and dropping it on the menu or tool bar are all you need to do.

Standard Actions

C++Builder offers a wide variety of standard actions such as Copy, Paste, File Open, and File Save As.

Some of these actions can be very useful either as everything you need, or as building blocks for enhancement. Here are some of the more interesting types:

Format actions—These actions affect the active TRichEdit on the form (if there is one) and alter the attributes of its selected text. They are attached to the button or menu item that causes the action.

- TRichEditBold
- TRichEditItalic
- TRichEditUnderline
- TRichEditStrikeOut
- TRichEditBullets
- TRichEditAlignLeft
- TRichEditAlignRight
- TRichEditAlignCenter

Help Actions

- THelpContextAction—If this action is assigned to the Action List, the currently selected control's HelpContext property is forwarded to the Help Manager so that the appropriate help can be displayed. Note that this is not assigned to a control, but to the list, and that it operates with all the controls on the form.

File Actions

- TFileOpen—Attach this to a control or menu item and put appropriate code in the OnAccept and OnCancel event of the action to make sure that the right things happen after the dialog is presented. The action's Dialog property can be used to find information about the file to be opened, and, at design or runtime, you can also use this to set the various properties that pertain to which files will be displayed.

- TFileSaveAs—This is much like FileOpen, with an OnAccept and OnCancel event to be filled in with what you need to have done.

- TFilePrintSetup—This action, like the other file actions, presents a dialog, which, in this case sets up the printer. Because the dialog reaches directly into the printer parameters, there is no need for additional processing.

- TFileRun—This runs the specified application or file.

- TFileExit—This closes the main form.

Search actions—Like the formatting actions, the search actions pertain to the active control, assuming it can accept search and/or replace operations. The dialogs automatically move the selection appropriately.

- TSearchFind

- TSearchFindFirst

- TSearchReplace

- TSearchFindNext

Tab (page control) Actions—These operate on the currently active tab or page control

- TPreviousTab

- TNextTab

List actions—These operate on the currently selected list control.

- TListControlCopySelection

- TListControlDeleteSelection

- TListControlSelectAll

- TListControlClearSelection

- TListControlMoveSelection

- TStaticListAction—This action supplies items to the target control or controls. On a TActionToolBar, it provides a drop-down list.

- TVirtualListAction—This is similar to the TStaticListAction, except that it uses the OnGetItem event handler as its way of supplying items. This means it can get the items from other controls or from a database or some other source.

Dialog Actions—These actions provide the specified dialog, and offer the appropriate events to enable you to process the selection.

- TOpenPicture

- TSavePicture

- TColorSelect

- TFontEdit

- TPrintDlg

Internet Actions

- TBrowseURL—Launches the system default browser on the specified URL.

- TDownLoadURL—This causes the specified URL to be downloaded to a local file. A periodic event occurs to report progress, and you can write code to do things like update a progress bar.

- TSendMail—This enables the user to send a MAPI email message made from the material in the Text property.

Tools Actions

- TCustomizeActionBars—Provides an Action Manager–based customization dialog so that the user can rearrange the content of the TActionMainMenuBar and the TActionToolBar.

Enhancing Usability by Allowing Customization of the User Interface

A good way to improve the usability of your interface is to enable the user to customize its appearance. This can be as simple as changing the color of different elements of the interface, or it can be as complex as allowing the user to undock parts of the interface or rearrange others. The ability to resize an interface is important, as is the ability to make only certain parts of the interface visible at any given time. Of all these, using color is probably the simplest. All you need to do is give the user access to the Color properties of the controls you use to create the interface. In some cases this might not be appropriate; for instance, when the interface is highly graphical because there might only be small areas of the interface suitable for such customization. A good way to meet the user's expectations in terms of color is to use the system colors when possible. The system colors are shown in Table 3.2 along with a brief description of what they are for.

TABLE 3.2 System Colors

System Color	Description
clBackground	Current background color of the Windows desktop
clActiveCaption	Current color of the title bar of the active window
clInactiveCaption	Current color of the title bar of inactive windows
clMenu	Current background color of menus
clWindow	Current background color of windows
clWindowFrame	Current color of window frames

TABLE 3.2 Continued

System Color	Description
clMenuText	Current color of text on menus
clWindowText	Current color of text in windows
clCaptionText	Current color of the text on the title bar of the active window
clActiveBorder	Current border color of the active window
clInactiveBorder	Current border color of inactive windows
clAppWorkSpace	Current color of the application workspace
clHighlight	Current background color of selected text
clHighlightText	Current color of selected text
clBtnFace	Current color of a button face
clBtnShadow	Current color of a shadow cast by a button
clBtnShadow	Current color of text that is dimmed
clBtnText	Current color of text on a button
clInactiveCaptionText	Current color of the text on the title bar of an inactive window
clBtnHighlight	Current color of the highlighting on a button
cl3DDkShadow	Dark shadow for three-dimensional display elements
cl3DLight	Light color for three-dimensional display elements (for edges facing the light source)
clInfoText	Text color for ToolTip controls
clInfoBk	Background color for ToolTip controls

For example, when displaying text in a window, use the clWindowText color. If the text is highlighted, use clHighlightText. These colors will already be specified to the user's preference and should, therefore, be a good choice for the interface. This section concentrates on the resizing, aligning, visibility, and docking capabilities of a user interface. The MiniCalculator provides all these features, so it is used as an example. The remainder of this section is broken into subsections, each giving an example of a particular technique.

Docking

In the some programs, the portions of the display can be undocked from the rest of the interface, and then positioned and resized independently. To make it possible to undock a panel from the main form, you must do three things:

1. Set DragKind to dkDock.

2. Set DragMode to dmAutomatic.

3. Set DockSite to true.

You can do all this at design time using the Object Inspector.

This is enough to make a panel dockable, but to make it really do the job, a little more work is required.

Consider what changes, if any, you need to make when the panel is undocked from the form. A first thought might be to write a handler for the form's OnUnDock event. However, this might not be suitable if you are using a version of C++Builder that has the bug in the VCL that results in OnUnDock not being fired the first time a control is undocked. If you require any resizing, clearly it will not work as you expect. A better approach is to write a handler for panel's OnDockEnd event and check the value of the Floating property of the panel. If Floating is true and this is the first call to OnDockEnd, the control has been undocked. This event occurs at the same time as the OnUnDock event, so there is no perceptible difference to the user. The only additional requirement of using this method is that you must use a variable to indicate whether the call to OnEndDock is the first call in the docking action. This is because OnEndDock is called at the end of every move made by a docking control. You can use a bool variable, for instance FirstPanelEndDock, to indicate if the OnEndDock event is the first in the current docking sequence. This requires you to add the line

```
bool FirstPanelEndDock;
```

to the form's class definition and initialize it to true in the constructor:

```
FirstPanelEndDock = true;
```

The code required in the panel's OnEndDock event is shown in Listing 3.9.

LISTING 3.9 Implementation of OnEndDock

```
void __fastcall TMainForm::PanelEndDock(TObject *Sender,
                                        TObject *Target,
                                        int X,
                                        int Y)
{
   if(Panel->Floating)
   {
      SetFocus();
   }
   if(FirstPanelEndDock)
   {
      if(Panel->Floating) FirstPanelEndDock = false;
      Height = Height - Panel->Height;
   }
}
```

If this is the first time that Panel's OnEndDock event is fired in the current docking sequence (that is, Panel has just been undocked and FirstPanelEndDock is true), you resize the form by subtracting the Height of Panel from The form's current Height. You do this even if the control is not floating because you add the Height of Panel back to the form in the form's OnDockDrop event, which will be fired if Panel is not loating. This can occur the first time you try to undock Panel where it is possible to undock and dock Panel in the same docking action.

You can now undock Panel, and the form will be automatically resized appropriately. Notice that before you resize the form you first reset the FirstPanelEndDock to false, but only if Panel is Floating. Again, this is because the first time you undock the panel it is possible to undock and dock in the same action. Panel might not be Floating, and setting FirstPanelUnDock to false would mean that this code would not be executed the next time the panel is actually undocked.

Note that every time PanelEndDock() is called and Panel->Floating is true, you call SetFocus() for the form. This ensures that the form never loses input focus from the keyboard.

Docking Panel back onto the form is a bit more complicated than undocking it. First you must implement the form's OnGetSiteInfo event handler. This event passes a TRect parameter, InfluenceRect, by reference. This TRect specifies where on the form docking will be activated if a dockable control is released over it. This enables you to specify docking regions on a control for specific controls. You can specify a dockable region equal to the Height of Panel and the ClientWidth of the form starting at the top of the main form. The event handler is shown in Listing 3.10.

LISTING 3.10   Implementation of the form ->OnGetSiteInfo

```
void __fastcall TMainForm::FormGetSiteInfo(TObject* Sender,
                                           TControl* DockClient,
                                           TRect& InfluenceRect,
                                           TPoint& MousePos,
                                           bool& CanDock)
{
    if(DockClient->Name == "Panel")
    {
        InfluenceRect.Left   = ClientOrigin.x;
        InfluenceRect.Top    = ClientOrigin.y;
        InfluenceRect.Right  = ClientOrigin.x + ClientWidth;
        InfluenceRect.Bottom = ClientOrigin.y + DockClient->Height;
    }
}
```

The first thing you do inside FormGetSiteInfo() is check to see if the DockClient—the TControl pointer to the object that caused the event to be fired—is Panel. If it is, you define the docking site above which Panel can be dropped by specifying suitable values for the InfluenceRect parameter. You do not use the remaining parameters: MousePos and CanDock. MousePos is a reference to the current cursor position, and CanDock is used to determine if the dock is allowed. With CanDock set to false, the DockClient cannot dock.

You must now implement the form's OnDockOver event. This event enables you to provide visual feedback to the user as to where the control will be docked if the control is currently over a dock site (the mouse is inside InfluenceRect) and the control is dockable (CanDock == true). You use the DockRect property of the Source parameter, a TDragDropObject pointer, to define the docking rectangle that appears to the user. The implementation of OnDockOver is shown in Listing 3.11.

LISTING 3.11   Implementation of OnDockOver

```
void __fastcall TMainForm::FormDockOver(TObject* Sender,
                                        TDragDockObject* Source,
                                        int X,
                                        int Y,
                                        TDragState State,
                                        bool& Accept)
{
    if(Source->Control->Name == "Panel")
    {
        TRect DockingRect( ClientOrigin.x,
                           ClientOrigin.y,
                           ClientOrigin.x + ClientWidth,
                           ClientOrigin.y + Source->Control->Height );

        Source->DockRect = DockingRect;
    }
}
```

When the docking control moves over its InfluenceRect (as defined in OnGetSiteInfo), the outline rectangle that signifies the control's position is snapped to the Source->DockRect defined in OnDockOver. This gives the user visual confirmation of where the docking control will be docked if the control is released. In this case, Source->DockRect is set equal to the Height of the control and the ClientWidth of the main form, with TRect starting at ClientOrigin. In fact, this is the same as the InfluenceRect specified in OnGetsiteInfo.

The remaining parameters are not used: X, the horizontal cursor position; Y, the vertical cursor position; State, of type TDragState, the movement state of the mouse in relation to the control; and Accept. Setting Accept to false prevents the control from docking.

Finally, you implement OnDockDrop. This event enables you to resize the control to fit the DockRect specified in the OnDockOver handler. It also enables you to perform any other processing that is needed, such as resizing the form or resetting the Anchors or Align property. The implementation for FormDockDrop is shown in Listing 3.12.

LISTING 3.12   Implementation of the form ->OnDockDrop

```
void __fastcall TMainForm::FormDockDrop(TObject* Sender,
                                        TDragDockObject* Source,
                                        int X,
                                        int Y)
{
    if(Source->Control->Name == "Panel")
    {
        Source->Control->Top = 0;
        Source->Control->Left = 0;
        Source->Control->Width = ClientWidth;

        // Allow space...
        Height = Height + Source->Control->Height;

        // Must reset the Align of Panel
        Source->Control->Align = alTop;

        // Reset the FirstPanelEndDock flag
        FirstPanelEndDock = true;
    }
}
```

The implementation of FormDockDrop() as shown in Listing 3.12 is not as simple as it first appears. First you resize Panel to fit the top of the form. Then, you allow space for the docked panel by increasing the Height of the form by the Height of Panel. Next reset Panel->Align to alTop. You must do this as the Align property is set to alNone when Panel is undocked. Finally, you reset FirstPanelEndDock to true in readiness for the next time Panel is undocked.

Note that you must adjust the Height of the form *before* you reset the Align property of Panel to alTop. If Panel->Align is set to alTop before the form's Height is adjusted, the form's Height might be adjusted twice. This is because the form will be automatically resized to accommodate Panel if Panel->Align is alTop and there is not sufficient room. Subsequently, changing the form's Height manually results in twice as much extra height as was needed. Changing the Height of the form first circumvents this problem because there will always be enough room for Panel. When its Align property is set to alTop, no automatic resizing is required.

In many ways, the docking capabilities of this example are small, but they are sufficient. For a more involved example of docking in C++Builder, you should study the example project dockex.bpr in the $(BCB)\Examples\Docking folder of your C++Builder 5 or above installation.

Controlling Visibility

Offering users the ability to show or hide parts of the interface is a relatively easy way to allow user customization. By simply changing the Visible property of a control, you can control whether the control appears in the interface. This enables you to provide functionality that some users want, but that others might find a nuisance. Those that need the functionality can make the required controls visible, and those that don't want it can hide the controls. The main consideration with showing and hiding controls is that you must ensure that the appearance of the interface remains acceptable. In other words, hiding a control should not leave a large gap in the interface, and showing a control should not affect the current layout any more than necessary.

Customizing the Client Area of an MDI Parent Form

Allowing the user to customize the background of an MDI parent form, typically by adding an image to it, is not as easy as it first appears and, therefore, deserves a special mention. To do this, you must subclass the window procedure of the client window of the parent form. This is because the client window of the parent form is the background for the MDI child windows. You must draw on the client window, not the form itself. For more information about this, refer to the Win32 SDK online help under "Frame, Client, and Child Windows." To access the client window, use the form's ClientHandle property. To draw on the client window, you must respond to the WM_ERASEBKGND message. The image can be centered, tiled, or stretched. You should draw onto an offscreen bitmap, and then you use either the WinAPI BitBlt() or StretchBlt() function to draw the image onto the client window. This minimizes flicker. Second, you use the Draw() method to draw your image onto the Canvas of the offscreen bitmap. You do this rather than use BitBlt() because you want to support JPEG images. TJPEGImage derives from TGraphic and so implements the Draw() method, but TJPEGImage does not have a Canvas and so cannot be used with BitBlt().

Working with Drag and Drop

One of the very early features on Microsoft's Windows operating system was drag and drop. The nature of the mouse makes dragging and dropping things on the screen seem a very natural extension of human behavior. It is one of the very first things that new Windows users grasp and, as such, should be implemented in all your applications whenever it makes sense to do so. Fortunately the concept is pretty simple and C++Builder makes the implementation very easy.

The Solution

To enable drag-and-drop in your application, you must first inform the operating system that your application is ready to receive dropped files. You do this by calling the DragAcceptFiles() method from the Win32 API. You then need to handle the events that are created by the drop action. You do this by creating a message map and an event handler for the WM_DROPFILES message that will read the name of the dropped file and act accordingly.

The Code

To illustrate this concept, you can build an application that closely resembles the System Configuration Editor that ships with Windows. To see it in action, click your Start button, select Run, type Sysedit in the Run dialog box, and click OK. If you play with it a little bit, you will notice that the Sysedit application does not handle dropped files, but yours will. However, in the interest of brevity, that little application will not handle most of the other functionality of the Sysedit application, including allowing you to save edited files. That functionality is simple enough for you to implement yourself if you want. Notice in Figure 3.15 the DragDrop application displaying some of the readme files that come with C++Builder.

WARNING

Do not edit the contents of any of the child windows in the System Configuration Editor unless you know what you're doing. Depending on your version of Windows, these files tell the operating system how to start up properly. Making any mistakes in these files or entering improper values can result in a long night.

If you opened up the System Configuration Editor to look at it, close it now and let's go to work. Follow the instructions to create the DragDrop application, or you can just load it from the CD-ROM that accompanies this book.

1. Start C++Builder and create a new application.

2. Change Form1's name to MainForm.

3. Create a new form called `ChildForm`. Set its `ClientHeight` and `ClientWidth` properties to about `250` and `350`, respectively.

4. Add a `TRichEdit` component from the Component Palette's Win32 tab to `ChildForm`, and set its `Align` property to `alClient`.

5. Save the application by clicking the floppy disk stack on the C++Builder toolbar. Save the main form's unit as `MainUnit.cpp`, the `ChildForm`'s unit as `ChildUnit.cpp`, and the project file as `DragDrop.bpr`.

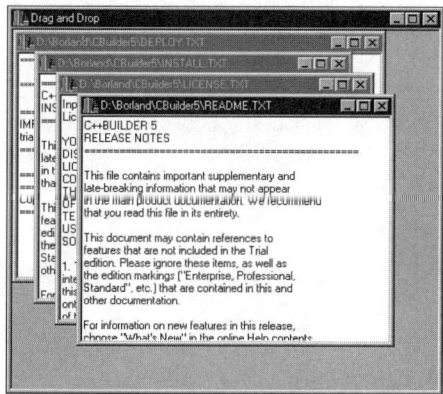

FIGURE 3.15 `DragDrop` at runtime.

Now that your form is done, it's time to add the code to the event handlers.

To inform the operating system that you want to accept dropped files, you need to call the `DragAcceptFiles()` method. The best place to do this is in the constructor for the main form. Select the `MainForm` from the tabs on the Source Code Editor and put the following line in its constructor:

```
DragAcceptFiles(Handle, True);
```

To create an event handler for the `DragDrop` event, open the header file for the main form by right-clicking the `MainUnit.cpp` tab in the code editor and select Open Header, Source File from the pop-up menu. Insert the following code in the public section of the `TMainForm` class declaration:

```
class TMainForm : public Tform
{
__published:     // IDE-managed Components
    void __fastcall FormCreate(TObject *Sender);
private:          // User declarations
    void virtual __fastcall WMDropFiles(TWMDropFiles &message);
```

```
public:            // User declarations
    __fastcall TMainForm(TComponent* Owner);
    BEGIN_MESSAGE_MAP
    MESSAGE_HANDLER(WM_DROPFILES, TWMDropFiles, WMDropFiles)
    END_MESSAGE_MAP(TForm);
};
```

Now switch back to the MainUnit.cpp file and add the code from Listing 3.13 to the end. You can leave out all the comments if you want.

LISTING 3.13   WMDropFiles Event Handler

```
// fires an event when a file, or files are dropped onto the application.
void __fastcall TMainForm::WMDropFiles(TWMDropFiles &message)
{
    AnsiString FileName;
    FileName.SetLength(MAX_PATH);

    int Count = DragQueryFile((HDROP)message.Drop, 0xFFFFFFFF, NULL, MAX_PATH);

    // index through the files and query the OS for each file name...
    for (int index = 0; index < Count; ++index)
    {
        // the following code gets the FileName of the dropped file.  it
        // looks cryptic but that's only because it is.  Hey, Why do you think
        // Delphi and C++Builder are so popular anyway? Look up DragQueryFile
        // the Win32.hlp Windows API help file.
        FileName.SetLength(DragQueryFile((HDROP)message.Drop, index,FileName.c_
➥str(), MAX_PATH));

        // examine the filename's extension.
        // If it's a text or Rich Text file then ...
        if (UpperCase(ExtractFileExt(FileName)) == ".TXT" || UpperCase
➥(ExtractFileExt(FileName)) == ".RTF")
        {
            // create a new child form...
            TChildForm *Viewer = new TChildForm(Application);
            // display the file...
            Viewer->Caption = FileName;
            Viewer->RichEdit1->Lines->LoadFromFile(FileName);
            Viewer->Show();
        }
```

LISTING 3.13   Continued

```
    }
    // tell the OS that you're finished...
    DragFinish((HDROP)  message.Drop);
}
```

To prevent the application from leaking memory, you need to ensure that the memory is properly freed when each viewer is closed. Select the ChildForm in the Object Inspector. Switch to the Events tab and double-click the OnClose event to create the OnClose event handler. Insert the following code into the event handler:

```
Action = caFree;
```

Open MainForm.cpp in the code editor, select File, Include Unit Header and select the child form. This makes MainForm aware of the ChildForm so that the compiler knows what you are talking about when you refer to the child form.

Compile and execute the application. When you drag a plain text or rich text file into the application, it will open a simple text viewer in its client area.

How Does It Work?

When the application initializes and creates the MainForm, it calls the Win32 API method DragAcceptFiles(), passing the application's handle and the value true indicating to the OS that the application is ready to accept dropped files. Passing false to the OS will disable drag and drop in your application.

If drag and drop is enabled in your application, the application will receive a WM_DROPFILES message from Windows for each file it receives. For the application to properly handle these messages, you must define a MESSAGE_HANDLER macro, which is a structure that associates a particular Windows message with one of the application's custom message handlers. The DragDrop application's message map associates the WM_DROPFILES message with the WMDropFiles message handler.

Inside the WMDropFiles message handler, the DragQueryFile() method will query the OS for information about the dropped files. The following is Microsoft's definition of the DragQueryFile() method. It can be found in Win32.hlp.

> The DragQueryFile() function retrieves the filenames of dropped files.
>
> ```
> UINT DragQueryFile(
>     HDROP hDrop,      // handle to structure for dropped files
>     UINT iFile,     // index of file to query
>     LPTSTR lpszFile,     // buffer for returned filename
>     UINT cch     // size of buffer for filename
>     );
> ```

Parameters:

hDrop

Identifies the structure containing the filenames of the dropped files.

iFile

Specifies the index of the file to query. If the value of the iFile parameter is 0xFFFFFFFF, DragQueryFile() returns a count of the files dropped. If the value of the iFile parameter is between zero and the total number of files dropped, DragQueryFile() copies the filename with the corresponding value to the buffer pointed to by the lpszFile parameter.

lpszFile

Points to a buffer to receive the filename of a dropped file when the function returns. This filename is a null-terminated string. If this parameter is NULL, DragQueryFile() returns the required size, in characters, of the buffer.

cch

Specifies the size, in characters, of the lpszFile buffer.

Return Values:

When the function copies a filename to the buffer, the return value is a count of the characters copied, not including the terminating null character.

If the index value is 0xFFFFFFFF, the return value is a count of the dropped files.

If the index value is between zero and the total number of dropped files and the lpszFile buffer address is NULL, the return value is the required size, in characters, of the buffer, not including the terminating null character.

When the DragDrop application receives a dropped file, it fires the WMDropFiles() method, which uses the Message handle to query the operating system for the number of files dropped. It then iterates through the file list, examining each file's extension looking for a .txt or .rtf extension. If the file has one of those extensions, the application creates an instance of ChildForm and loads the file into the TRichText component for display to the user. As each ChildWindow is closed, it calls the caFree action, which releases the memory associated with the ChildForm's instance.

Wrapping Up Drag and Drop

Although there's no default VCL wrapper for drag and drop, C++Builder makes it pretty easy to implement it in your applications. If you have neglected adding this capability because you thought it would be too hard, you've just been empowered.

Nonvisual Components and Programming

C++Builder components are not just edits and panels and grids. There are a variety of nonvisual components, including the database components covered in Chapters 6 through 12.

Other than the database components, there are components such as Ttimer, which enables you to one-time or repeatedly trigger an event after a certain elapsed time.

The entire WebSnap and BizSnap component sets are also nonvisual (see Chapter 19 "SOAP and Web Services with BizSnap," and Chapter 22 "Web Server Programming with WebSnap").

Actions, ActionLists, and ActionManager are also nonvisual.

In short, you don't have to see a component for it to be useful. And in Chapter 4, "Creating Custom Components," you will see that creating a nonvisual component can be a great way for you to solve important programming problems.

Creating Multithreaded Applications

For Scrabble players, "multitasking" and "multithreading" might be a great opportunity to earn points. For developers, these terms are often sources of confusion and unnecessary headaches. I should emphasize *unnecessary* here because, when explained, they become part of the obvious programming concepts.

Understanding Multitasking

To put it simply, multitasking is the capability of the operating system to run multiple programs at the same time. Unconsciously, you've been using this capability while switching from your Microsoft Word document to Windows Explorer. Although multitasking might seem characteristic of graphical operating systems such as Windows or Linux, earlier computers also used multitasking to some extent. For example, Unix enables you to run multiple programs in the background.

Under Windows 3.x, applications used cooperative multitasking. *Cooperative* means that a program has control over the CPU and, before switching to another application, this program must finish processing data. This type of multitasking has a serious drawback: If an application stops responding, the entire operating system will hang. 32-bit versions of Windows solved this problem by introducing preemptive multitasking. A simple dictionary definition will help you understand its meaning:

> preemptive: done before somebody else has had an opportunity to act.

In other words, to allow task-switching, 32-bit versions of Windows suspend the current application, whether it is ready to lose control or not.

NOTE

Cooperative multitasking is also called "nonpreemptive multitasking" for obvious reasons. Unlike preemptive multitasking, the operating system is unable to suspend an application that has stopped responding.

Understanding Multithreading

Multithreading is the capability of a program to run multiple tasks (threads) at the same time. Most Windows applications use only one thread, the *primary* thread. A primary thread takes care of child windows creation and message processing. All secondary threads are used to perform background operations: loading large files, looking for information, performing mathematical calculations.

WARNING

Throughout their learning process, young children tend to repeat words they have overheard here and there, simply to prove their knowledge or to resemble "big people." A similar situation occurs with programmers. Some developers tend to overuse programming techniques they've learned.

Do not use separate threads in your application unless you're dealing with lengthy background operations. Sometimes, with small code readjustments, you can simply avoid the use of threads. Why complicate your work? That said, multithreaded applications offer advantages, as you'll see later in this chapter.

Creating a Thread Using API Calls

You can create a new thread from another one by calling the CreateThread() API function. The CreateThread() parameters specify, among other things, the security attributes, the creation flags, and the thread function:

```
HANDLE CreateThread(
    LPSECURITY_ATTRIBUTES lpThreadAttributes,
    DWORD dwStackSize,
    LPTHREAD_START_ROUTINE lpStartAddress,
    LPVOID lpParameter,
    DWORD dwCreationFlags,
    LPDWORD lpThreadId
    );
```

The SECURITY_ATTRIBUTES structure determines whether other processes can modify the object and whether a child process can inherit a handle to this object. If lpThreadAttributes is NULL, the thread gets the default security descriptor.

The dwCreationFlags parameter specifies the thread creation flags. If its value is CREATE_SUSPENDED, the thread will not run until you call the ResumeThread() function. Set this value to 0 to run the thread immediately after creation.

The lpThreadId parameter points to an empty DWORD that will receive the thread identifier. Under Windows NT/2000, if this parameter is NULL, the thread identifier is simply not returned. Windows 9x requires a DWORD variable. To ensure complete compatibility with the current operating system, do not use the NULL value.

The most crucial parameter is the starting function, also known as *thread function*. lpStartAddress is the address of the function that accepts one parameter and returns a DWORD exit code:

```
DWORD WINAPI ThreadFunc(LPVOID);
```

> **TIP**
>
> In a sense, the starting function can be compared to the main() or WinMain() function in a C++ program. ThreadFunc() is the main entry point for your thread.

Finally, dwStackSize and lpParameter specify the size of the stack (in bytes) and the parameter passed to the thread, respectively.

> **TIP**
>
> CreateThread(), as many other API calls, contains a large list of arguments more or less complex. In the beginning, understanding all aspects of this function can be disorienting.
>
> A simple trick to overcome this problem is to first look at the arguments that can be zeroed. For example, in almost all parameters of CreateThread() except for lpStartAddress and lpThreadId, you can safely specify 0. After you fully understand these two arguments, you can always go back and further explore the CreateThread() function.

With the previous explanations and a little help from the Win32 Programmer's Reference help file, you should now be able to write a simple multithreaded application. Your example project should contain two buttons: Start and Stop. When the user clicks the Start button, this resumes the newly created thread. The thread should draw random ellipses and rectangles on the form. By clicking the Stop button, the user should be able to suspend the thread. Take a look at Listing 3.14. Don't forget that you can find the complete source code in the ThreadAPI folder of the companion CD-ROM.

LISTING 3.14   ThreadFormUnit.cpp

```cpp
#include <vcl.h>
#pragma hdrstop

#include "ThreadFormUnit.h"
#pragma package(smart_init)
#pragma resource "*.dfm"

TThreadForm *ThreadForm;
HANDLE Thread;

DWORD WINAPI ThreadFunc(LPVOID Param)
{
    HANDLE MainWnd(Param);

    RECT R;
    GetClientRect(MainWnd, &R);

    const MaxWidth = R.right - R.left;
    const MaxHeight = R.bottom - R.top;
    int X1, Y1, X2, Y2, R1, G1, B1;
    bool IsEllipse;

    while(true)
    {
        HDC DC = GetDC(MainWnd);

        X1 = rand() % MaxWidth;
        Y1 = rand() % MaxHeight;
        X2 = rand() % MaxWidth;
        Y2 = rand() % MaxHeight;

        R1 = rand() & 255;
        G1 = rand() & 255;
        B1 = rand() & 255;

        IsEllipse = rand() & 1;

        HBRUSH Brush = CreateSolidBrush(
            RGB(R1, G1, B1));
        SelectObject(DC, Brush);
```

LISTING 3.14 Continued

```
    if(IsEllipse)
        Ellipse(DC, X1, Y1, X2, Y2);
    else
        Rectangle(DC, X1, Y1, X2, Y2);

    ReleaseDC(MainWnd, DC);
    DeleteObject(Brush);
    }
}


__fastcall TThreadForm::TThreadForm(TComponent* Owner)
    : TForm(Owner)
{
    randomize();

    DWORD Id;
    Thread = CreateThread(0, 0, ThreadFunc,
        ThreadForm->Handle, CREATE_SUSPENDED, &Id);

    if(!Thread)
    {
        ShowMessage("Error! Cannot create thread.");
        Application->Terminate();
    }
}


void __fastcall TThreadForm::StartClick(TObject *)
{
    ResumeThread(Thread);
    Start->Enabled = false;
    Stop->Enabled = true;
}


void __fastcall TThreadForm::StopClick(TObject *)
{
    SuspendThread(Thread);
    Stop->Enabled = false;
    Start->Enabled = true;
}
```

NOTE

As you can see in Listing 3.14, the code uses API functions almost exclusively. One of the reasons is that you must avoid accessing VCL properties and methods from secondary threads. I will describe why and provide a solution in the next section.

In the form constructor, you create a suspended thread using the `CreateThread()` function and check whether the new thread is valid or not. The Start and Stop buttons use the `ResumeThread()` and `SuspendThread()` API functions to modify the thread state. Finally, the thread function draws random shapes on the form's canvas. (Notice how the window handle is passed to `ThreadFunc()`.) Figure 3.16 shows the project.

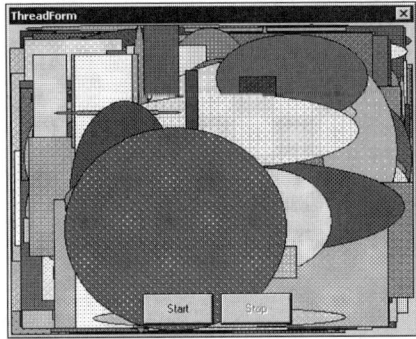

FIGURE 3.16   The ThreadAPI project.

NOTE

Another efficient way to start a new thread is the `_beginthread()` routine defined in `process.h` (you can find `process.h` in the C++Builder installation `Include` folder):

```
unsigned long _beginthread(void (_USERENTRY *__start)(void *),
    unsigned __stksize, void *__arg);
```

Because it requires fewer parameters, this function is commonly used in multithreaded applications.

Understanding the TThread Object

C++Builder encapsulates Windows thread objects into the `TThread` object. Creating a new thread is basically a matter of creating a new instance of a `TThread` descendant. Listing 3.15 contains the definition of the `TThread` abstract class.

LISTING 3.15   TThread Class

```
class DELPHICLASS TThread;
class PASCALIMPLEMENTATION TThread : public System::TObject
{
    typedef System::TObject inherited;

private:
    unsigned FHandle;
    unsigned FThreadID;
    bool FTerminated;
    bool FSuspended;
    bool FFreeOnTerminate;
    bool FFinished;
    int FReturnValue;
    TNotifyEvent FOnTerminate;
    TThreadMethod FMethod;
    System::TObject* FSynchronizeException;
    void __fastcall CallOnTerminate(void);
    TThreadPriority __fastcall GetPriority(void);
    void __fastcall SetPriority(TThreadPriority Value);
    void __fastcall SetSuspended(bool Value);

protected:
    virtual void __fastcall DoTerminate(void);
    virtual void __fastcall Execute(void) = 0 ;
    void __fastcall Synchronize(TThreadMethod Method);
    __property int ReturnValue = {read=FReturnValue, write=FReturnValue,
        nodefault};
    __property bool Terminated = {read=FTerminated, nodefault};

public:
    __fastcall TThread(bool CreateSuspended);
    __fastcall virtual ~TThread(void);
    void __fastcall Resume(void);
    void __fastcall Suspend(void);
    void __fastcall Terminate(void);
    unsigned __fastcall WaitFor(void);
    __property bool FreeOnTerminate = {read=FFreeOnTerminate, write=
        FFreeOnTerminate, nodefault};
    __property unsigned Handle = {read=FHandle, nodefault};
    __property TThreadPriority Priority = {read=GetPriority, write=
        SetPriority, nodefault};
```

LISTING 3.15   Continued

```
    __property bool Suspended = {read=FSuspended, write=SetSuspended,
        nodefault};
    __property unsigned ThreadID = {read=FThreadID, nodefault};
    __property TNotifyEvent OnTerminate = {read=FOnTerminate, write=
        FOnTerminate};
};
```

If you're wondering how to create a TThread descendant, the answer is simple. Open the File, New dialog and select Thread Object from the Object Repository. C++Builder will prompt you for the class name of the new descendant. Enter TRandomThread and click OK.

C++Builder will create automatically a new source file containing the TRandomThread object:

```
#include <vcl.h>
#pragma hdrstop

#include "Unit2.h"
#pragma package(smart_init)

__fastcall TRandomThread::TRandomThread(bool CreateSuspended)
    : TThread(CreateSuspended)
{
}

void __fastcall TRandomThread::Execute()
{

}
```

The Execute() method contains the code that will be executed when the thread runs. In other words, Execute() replaces your thread function. Also notice that the constructor of your object contains a CreateSuspended parameter. Just like the CREATE_SUSPENDED flag, when CreateSuspended is true, you must first call the Resume() method; otherwise, Execute() won't be called.

Tables 3.3 and 3.4 summarize the most common properties and methods of the TThread class.

TABLE 3.3   TThread Properties

Property	Description
FreeOnTerminate	Determines whether the thread object is automatically destroyed when the thread terminates.
Handle	Provides access to the thread's handle. Use this value when calling API functions.
Priority	Specifies the thread's scheduling priority. Set this priority to a higher or lower value when needed.
ReturnValue	Determines the value returned to other threads when the current thread object finishes.
Suspended	Specifies whether the thread is suspended or not.
Terminated	Determines whether the thread is about to be terminated.
ThreadID	Determines the thread's identifier.

TABLE 3.4   TThread Methods

Method	Description
DoTerminate()	Calls the OnTerminate event handler without terminating the thread.
Execute()	Contains the code to be executed when the thread runs.
Resume()	Resumes a suspended thread.
Suspend()	Pauses a running thread.
Synchronize()	Executes a call within the VCL primary thread.
Terminate()	Signals the thread to terminate.
WaitFor()	Waits for a thread to terminate.

Now it's time to try to use VCL objects exclusively.

You've already created a TRandomThread object, so use this object as the secondary thread of your application. The first step is to add the main unit's include file to the new thread unit. Select File, Include Unit Hdr and then select ThreadFormUnit.

There's not much to put in the TRandomThread constructor, except for the random numbers generator:

```
__fastcall TRandomThread::TRandomThread(bool
  CreateSuspended) : TThread(CreateSuspended)
{
  randomize();
}
```

Now take care of the core part of your thread: the Execute() method. You no longer need to determine the form size using the GetClientRect() API function. You can simply read the ClientWidth and ClientHeight properties:

```
const MaxWidth = ThreadForm->ClientWidth;
const MaxHeight = ThreadForm->ClientHeight;
int X1, Y1, X2, Y2, R1, G1, B1;
bool IsEllipse;
```

The TCanvas object, with which you're probably familiar, can greatly simplify the drawing process. There is a small problem: The VCL does not allow multiple threads to access the same graphic object simultaneously. Therefore, you must use the Lock() and Unlock() methods to make sure that other threads do not access the TCanvas while you're drawing:

```
while(true)
{
    ThreadForm->Canvas->Lock();

    X1 = rand() % MaxWidth;
    Y1 = rand() % MaxHeight;
    X2 = rand() % MaxWidth;
    Y2 = rand() % MaxHeight;

    R1 = rand() & 255;
    G1 = rand() & 255;
    B1 = rand() & 255;

    IsEllipse = rand() & 1;

    ThreadForm->Canvas->Brush->Color =
        TColor(RGB(R1, G1, B1));

    if(IsEllipse)
        ThreadForm->Canvas->Ellipse(X1, Y1,
            X2, Y2);
    else
        ThreadForm->Canvas->Rectangle(X1, Y1,
            X2, Y2);

    ThreadForm->Canvas->Unlock();
}
```

This puts an end to the thread object code. Take a look now at the main unit. In the form constructor, you create a new instance of TRandomThread:

```
TRandomThread* Thread;

__fastcall TThreadForm::TThreadForm(TComponent* )
   : TForm(Owner)
{
   Thread = new TRandomThread(true);
   if(!Thread)
   {
      ShowMessage("Error! Cannot create thread.");
      Application->Terminate();
   }
}
```

The Start button calls the Resume() method:

```
void __fastcall TThreadForm::StartClick(TObject *)
{
   Thread->Resume();
   Start->Enabled = false;
   Stop->Enabled = true;
}
```

The Stop button calls the Suspend() method:

```
void __fastcall TThreadForm::StopClick(TObject *)
{
   Thread->Suspend();
   Stop->Enabled = false;
   Start->Enabled = true;
}
```

TIP

The C++Builder IDE provides a Threads debug window containing the list of available threads: their ID, state, location, and status. To display this window, choose View, Debug Windows, Threads from the C++Builder menu or press Ctrl+Alt+T.

The thread is automatically terminated when the Execute() function finishes executing or when the application is closed. To ensure that memory occupied by your thread object is freed on termination, always insert the following in the Execute() method:

```
FreeOnTerminate = true;
```

Sometimes, however, you might need to terminate a thread by code. To do so, you could use the `Terminate()` method. `Terminate()` tells the thread to terminate by setting the `Terminated` property to `true`.

It is important to understand that `Terminate()` does not exit the thread by itself. You must periodically check in the `Execute()` method whether `Terminated` is `true`. For example, to terminate your `TRandomThread` object, add the following line:

```
while(true)
{
    if(Terminated) break;
```

`Terminate()` has the advantage of enabling you to do the cleaning by yourself, thus giving you more control over the thread termination. Unfortunately, if the thread stops responding, calling `Terminate()` will be useless.

The `TerminateThread()` API function is a more radical way to cause a thread to exit. `TerminateThread()` instantly closes the current thread without freeing memory occupied by the thread object. You should use this function only in extreme cases, when no other options are left. The `TerminateThread()` syntax is simple. Here is an example:

```
TerminateThread((HANDLE)Thread->Handle, false);
```

Understanding the Main VCL Thread

Properties and methods of VCL objects are not necessarily thread safe. This means that when accessing properties and methods, you can use memory that is not protected from other threads. Therefore, the main VCL thread should be the only thread to have control over the VCL.

> **NOTE**
>
> The main VCL thread is the primary thread of your application. It handles and processes Windows messages received by VCL controls.

> **NOTE**
>
> Graphic objects are exceptions to the thread-safe rule. By using the `Lock()` and `Unlock()` methods, other threads can be prevented from drawing on the canvas.

To allow threads to access VCL objects, `TThread` provides the `Synchronize()` method. `Synchronize()` performs actions contained in a routine as if they were executed from the main VCL thread:

```
void __fastcall Synchronize(TThreadMethod &Method);
```

Consider the example of a thread displaying increasing values in a Label component. Obviously, you'll use a for loop in the Execute() method. But, how will you change the Label's caption? By synchronizing with the VCL. Listing 3.16 contains the source code of the TLabelThread object, and Figure 3.17 shows the results.

LISTING 3.16   TLabelThread Thread Object

```cpp
#include <vcl.h>
#pragma hdrstop

#include "ThreadFormUnit.h"
#pragma package(smart_init)

#include <Classes.hpp>

class TLabelThread : public TThread
{
private:
protected:
    int Num;
    void __fastcall Execute();
    void __fastcall DisplayLabel();
public:
    __fastcall TLabelThread(bool CreateSuspended);
};
//------------------------------------------------
__fastcall TLabelThread::TLabelThread(bool
    CreateSuspended) : TThread(CreateSuspended)
{
}

void __fastcall TLabelThread::DisplayLabel()
{
    ThreadForm->Label->Caption = Num;
}

void __fastcall TLabelThread::Execute()
{
    FreeOnTerminate = true;
    for(Num = 0; Num <= 1000; Num++)
    {
```

LISTING 3.16 Continued

```
    if(Terminated) break;
    Synchronize (DisplayLabel);
  }
}
```

TIP

As opposed to the TRandomThread example, where you had an endless loop, in this project the thread is terminated when the value of 1000 is reached. By handling the OnTerminate event of TLabelThread, you can determine when the thread is about to exit:

```
void __fastcall TThreadForm::bStartClick(TObject *)
{
   Thread = new TLabelThread(false);
   Thread->OnTerminate = OnTerminate;
   bStart->Enabled = false;
}

void __fastcall TThreadForm::OnTerminate(TObject *)
{
   bStart->Enabled = true;
}
```

In fact, you can use OnTerminate as a replacement for the Synchronize() method. If your thread has actions to perform before exiting, OnTerminate will enable you to access VCL properties and methods from within the main unit.

Consider the previous example where you enabled the bStart button in the OnTerminate event handler. To accomplish the same thing directly from the thread object, you would have written a far more complex code:

```
// void __fastcall EnableButton();

void __fastcall TLabelThread::EnableButton()
{
   ThreadForm->bStart->Enabled = true;
}

void __fastcall TLabelThread::Execute()
{
  // ...
      if(Terminated)
      {
```

```
        Synchronize(EnableButton);
    // ...
  }
```

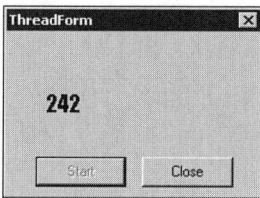

FIGURE 3.17   The `LabelThread` project.

Establishing Priorities

In an application using multiple threads, it is important to know which threads will have a higher priority and run first. Table 3.5 describes all possible priority levels.

TABLE 3.5   Thread Priorities

Priority Level	Description
THREAD_PRIORITY_TIME_CRITICAL	15 points above normal
THREAD_PRIORITY_HIGHEST	2 points above normal
THREAD_PRIORITY_ABOVE_NORMAL	1 point above normal
THREAD_PRIORITY_NORMAL	Normal
THREAD_PRIORITY_BELOW_NORMAL	1 point below normal
THREAD_PRIORITY_LOWEST	2 points below normal
THREAD_PRIORITY_IDLE	15 points below normal

All threads are created using the THREAD_PRIORITY_NORMAL. After a thread has been created, you can adjust the priority level higher or lower using the SetThreadPriority() function. A general rule is that a thread dealing with the user interface should have a higher priority to make sure that the application remains responsive to the user's actions. Background threads are usually set to THREAD_PRIORITY_BELOW_NORMAL or THREAD_PRIORITY_LOWEST so that they can be terminated when necessary.

NOTE

Priority levels are commonly called *relative scheduling priorities* because they are relative to other threads in the same process.

The TThread object provides a Priority property, which determines the thread priority level. Its possible values are

```
tpTimeCritical
tpHighest
tpHigher
tpNormal
tpLower
tpLowest
tpIdle
```

As you can see, they closely match the priority levels you previously described.

If you're still not convinced of the importance of thread priorities, take a look at the following example. Start a new application and add two progress bars (Max property set to 5000) and a Start button. You will try to increment the position of the progress bars using threads of different priorities. Listing 3.17 contains the source code of the TPriorityThread thread object.

LISTING 3.17   TPriorityThread Thread Object

```cpp
#include <vcl.h>
#pragma hdrstop

#include "PriorityThreadUnit.h"
#include "ThreadFormUnit.h"
#pragma package(smart_init)

__fastcall TPriorityThread::TPriorityThread(bool
    Temp) : TThread(false)
{
    First = Temp;
}

void __fastcall TPriorityThread::DisplayProgress()
{
    if(First)
        ThreadForm->ProgressBar1->Position++;
    else
        ThreadForm->ProgressBar2->Position++;
}
```

LISTING 3.17 Continued

```
void __fastcall TPriorityThread::Execute()
{
   FreeOnTerminate = true;
   for(Num = 0; Num <= 5000; Num++)
   {
      if(Terminated) break;
      Synchronize (DisplayProgress);
   }
}
```

Notice that I slightly modified the TPriorityThread constructor. The Temp boolean variable (which replaces CreateSuspended) will indicate which progress bar should be accessed.

The main unit contains only the code for the Start button OnClick handler:

```
void __fastcall TThreadForm::bStartClick(TObject *)
{
   TPriorityThread *First;
   First = new TPriorityThread (true);
   First->Priority = tpLowest;

   TPriorityThread *Second;
   Second = new TPriorityThread(false);
   Second->Priority = tpLowest;

   bStart->Enabled = false;
}
```

Run the program and click the Start button. Both progress bars should reach the end at approximately the same time, as shown in Figure 3.18. Now, set the priority of the first thread to tpLower. Any difference? See the result in Figure 3.19.

Timing Threads

Sometimes when developing it is useful to time sections of code. The basic principle is to record the system time before and after the code and subtract the start time from the end time to calculate the elapsed time. For general applications this can be done with the Win32 API function GetTickCount(). This is illustrated in Listing 3.18.

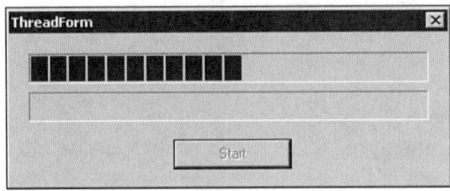

FIGURE 3.18   Threads with same priority.

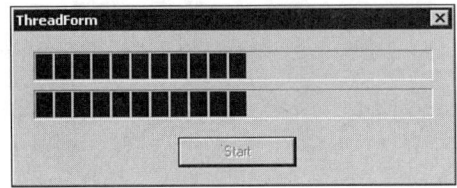

FIGURE 3.19   Threads with different priorities.

LISTING 3.18   Timing Code with `GetTickCount()`

```
int Start = GetTickCount();

// ...
Form1->Canvas->Lock();
for(int x = 0; x <= 100000; x++)
    Form1->Canvas->TextOut(10, 10, x);
Form1->Canvas->Unlock();
// ...

int Total = GetTickCount() - Start;
ShowMessage(FloatToStr(Total / 1000.0) + " sec");
```

A similar example could be created using the `clock()` instead of `GetTickCount()`. There are also other functions that can be used to time code.

Unfortunately, because of the preemptive behavior of Windows, threads are often interrupted. For this reason, you can't rely on `GetTickCount()` to retrieve the thread execution time. However, Windows provides the `GetThreadTimes()` API function, which helps you time your threads:

```
BOOL GetThreadTimes(
    HANDLE hThread,
    LPFILETIME lpCreationTime,
    LPFILETIME lpExitTime,
```

```
   LPFILETIME lpKernelTime,
   LPFILETIME lpUserTime
);
```

WARNING

GetThreadTimes() is available only with Windows NT/2000.

As you can see, GetThreadTimes() uses the FILETIME structure. Before performing arithmetic operations, you must first store the user time information in a LARGE_INTEGER. Then, by subtraction of the 64-bit QuadPart members of the LARGE_INTEGER structure, you could obtain the number of 100 nanoseconds that your code takes to execute. Listing 3.19 illustrates this.

LISTING 3.19 GetThreadTimes() Example

```
FILETIME CreationTime, ExitTime, KernelTime;
union {
   LARGE_INTEGER iUT;
   FILETIME fUT;
} UserTimeS, UserTimeE;

GetThreadTimes((HANDLE)Handle, &CreationTime,
   &ExitTime, &KernelTime, &UserTimeS.fUT);

// ...
Form1->Canvas->Lock();
for(int x = 0; x <= 100000; x++)
   Form1->Canvas->TextOut(10, 10, x);
Form1->Canvas->Unlock();
// ...

GetThreadTimes((HANDLE)Handle, &CreationTime,
   &ExitTime, &KernelTime, &UserTimeE.fUT);

float Total = UserTimeE.iUT.QuadPart - UserTimeS.
   iUT.QuadPart;
Total /= 10 * 1000 * 1000; // Converts to seconds

OutputDebugString(FloatToStr(Total).c_str());
```

TIP

OutputDebugString() is a useful API function that sends a string to the Event Log debug window. Under normal circumstances, I have the tendency to use message boxes or to change the window caption, but in multithreaded applications these actions can sometimes be disastrous without considerable coding. OutputDebugString() is, therefore, a perfect alternative.

The OutputDebugString() function is covered in more detail in win32.hlp, which is part of the C++Builder installation in the Borland Shared\MSHelp directory.

Synchronizing Threads

Probably the greatest disadvantage of using threads is the difficulty in organizing them. Let's say your application is simultaneously running two threads, which modify some global data. What will happen if they try to access the same data at the same time? Or, what if the second thread has to wait for the first thread to process this data, and then execute? To coordinate threads, Windows offers various methods of synchronization.

Critical Sections

To illustrate two threads accessing the same global data, you'll create a sample application using the TCriticalThread object (see Listing 3.20).

LISTING 3.20   CriticalThreadUnit.cpp: TCriticalThread Thread Object

```
#include <vcl.h>
#pragma hdrstop

#include "CriticalThreadUnit.h"
#include "ThreadFormUnit.h"

#pragma package(smart_init)

__fastcall TCriticalThread::TCriticalThread(bool CreateSuspended)
    : TThread(CreateSuspended)
{
}

void __fastcall TCriticalThread::DisplayList()
{
    ThreadForm->ListBox->Items->Add(Text);
}
```

LISTING 3.20   Continued

```cpp
void __fastcall TCriticalThread::Execute()
{
    FreeOnTerminate = true;

    for(int x = 0; x <= 50; x++)
    {
        if(Terminated) break;

        // EnterCriticalSection(&ThreadForm->CS);
        Sleep(50);
        ThreadForm->ListText.Insert("=====", 1);
        Text = ThreadForm->ListText;
        Synchronize(DisplayList);
        ThreadForm->ListText.SetLength(ThreadForm->
            ListText.Length() - 5),
        // LeaveCriticalSection(&ThreadForm->CS);
    }
}
```

And in your main unit, you'll create two instances of this object (see Listing 3.21).

LISTING 3.21   ThreadFormUnit.cpp

```cpp
#include <vcl.h>
#pragma hdrstop

#include "ThreadFormUnit.h"
#include "CriticalThreadUnit.h"

#pragma package(smart_init)
#pragma resource "*.dfm"

TThreadForm *ThreadForm;

__fastcall TThreadForm::TThreadForm(TComponent* Owner)
    : TForm(Owner)
{
    ListText = "=====";
    // InitializeCriticalSection(&CS);
}
```

LISTING 3.21   Continued

```
void __fastcall TThreadForm::StartClick(TObject *Sender)
{
   TCriticalThread *FirstThread;
   FirstThread = new TCriticalThread(false);

   TCriticalThread *SecondThread;
   SecondThread = new TCriticalThread(false);
}

void __fastcall TThreadForm::FormClose(TObject *,
      TCloseAction &Action)
{
   // DeleteCriticalSection(&CS);
}
```

Your code is both simple and useless, but it will demonstrate the importance of thread synchronization. First, the TCriticalThread object adds to the global ListText variable five equals (=) characters. Then, it adds the value of ListText to a ListBox. Finally, TCriticalThread() truncates five characters, thus setting ListText to the value it initially had. Logically, all ListBox items should display ==========, but as Figure 3.20 shows, that's not always the case. Why? Because the second thread also accesses the same global variable.

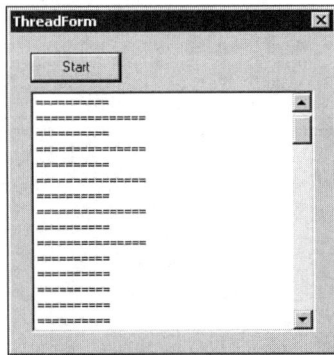

FIGURE 3.20   The CriticalThread project without critical sections.

Critical sections are an easy and efficient way to temporarily block other threads from accessing data (similar to the Lock() and Unlock() methods for graphic objects). To define a critical section, you'll use four basic API functions:

```
VOID InitializeCriticalSection(
    LPCRITICAL_SECTION lpCriticalSection
    );

VOID EnterCriticalSection(
    LPCRITICAL_SECTION lpCriticalSection
    );

VOID LeaveCriticalSection(
    LPCRITICAL_SECTION lpCriticalSection
    );

VOID DeleteCriticalSection(
    LPCRITICAL_SECTION lpCriticalSection
    );
```

It's not so difficult to guess how to use these functions. First, you declare a variable of type CRITICAL_SECTION. You initialize this variable at program startup (InitializeCriticalSection()) and delete it when the program closes (DeleteCriticalSection()). When your thread starts processing data, you block access to other threads with EnterCriticalSection() and, when it finishes, you exit the critical section (LeaveCriticalSection()).

Go back to Listings 3.20 and 3.21, and comment out the four lines, which call the critical section functions I described. Then, open the header file of your main unit and add the following line:

```
CRITICAL_SECTION CS;
```

As shown on Figure 3.21, all ListBox items now contain the same string.

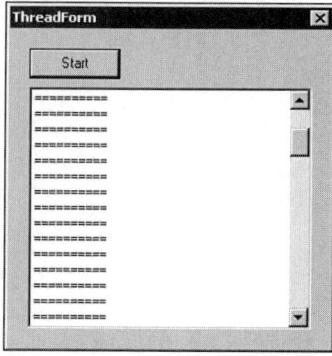

FIGURE 3.21   The CriticalThread project with critical sections.

Mutexes

Mutexes offer the functionality of critical sections, while adding other interesting features.

TIP

Although featureless, critical sections are slightly faster then mutexes and semaphores. If time is an important factor in your application, consider using critical sections.

Mutex objects are created using the `CreateMutex()` API function:

```
HANDLE CreateMutex(
    LPSECURITY_ATTRIBUTES lpMutexAttributes,
    BOOL bInitialOwner,
    LPCTSTR lpName
);
```

After you have the handle of the newly created mutex object, you must use the `WaitForSingleObject()` function. This API call will request ownership for the mutex object, wait until this object becomes available, and use the mutex until `ReleaseMutex()` is called:

```
HANDLE Mutex;
Mutex = CreateMutex(NULL, false, NULL);
if(Mutex == NULL)
{
    ShowMessage("Cannot create mutex!");
    return;
}

// ...

if(WaitForSingleObject(Mutex, INFINITE) ==
    WAIT_OBJECT_0)
{
    // ...
}

ReleaseMutex (Mutex);
```

NOTE

Unlike critical sections, two or more processes can use the same mutex.

> **NOTE**
> ---
> If a thread doesn't release its ownership of a mutex object, this mutex is considered to be abandoned. Therefore, `WaitForSingleObject()` will return `WAIT_ABANDONED`. Although it's not perfectly safe, you can always acquire ownership of an abandoned mutex.
> ---

Others

Other synchronization objects such as semaphores and timers are also available. By familiarizing yourself with critical sections and mutexes, you'll already be one step ahead into mastering thread synchronization.

Summary

This chapter has covered the major building blocks of programming with C++Builder, ranging from the basics of the VCL to the complexities of user interfaces and thread management.

4

Creating Custom Components

by Mark Cashman

This chapter deals with creating and distributing custom components. The components that you use in C++Builder are often the beginning of your applications, but even when you are the only developer on a project, you will probably find situations where creating components based on the components you already have can, in the long run, save time and money. When you are a developer on a large project, or when you want to make a capability available to the wider development community (either as a package of components for sale or simply as freeware or shareware) the creation of custom components is a major focus of your effort.

Creating, Compiling, and Installing Packages

Three types of packages can be generated to create custom components: design time only, runtime only, and dual design time/runtime packages. When you distribute components, you should endeavor to always distribute a design time only and runtime only package pair—two packages. When you are still developing a component or components, the dual package is a reasonable and convenient choice.

In addition to deciding how to structure your packages, you must adopt a sensible naming convention for both the units inside your package and the components themselves. You must also decide if you want your components to be usable in different versions of the compiler.

Packaging Components

Getting ready to create a component or components requires you to have a package within which they will be compiled. You need to start with a project group to hold your package because any package you create will be within the current project group, and you usually do not want a package to be part of the application project group you are currently using. Creating a project group is accomplished by picking File, New from the IDE menu, and then, from the New tab of the resulting dialog, picking Project Group. Next, pick File, New from the IDE menu and pick Package from the New tab of the dialog.

The New tab of the File, New dialog is shown in Figure 4.1.

FIGURE 4.1   View of the items in the File | New Dialog.

Next, you need to identify the type of package you are creating. Pick Options from the pop-up menu on the package window, as shown in Figure 4.2.

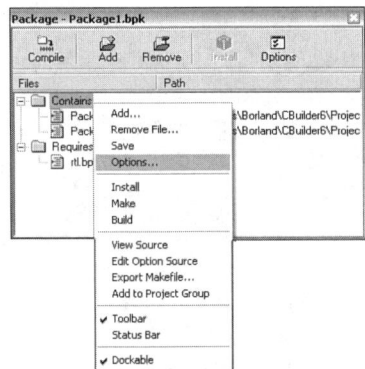

FIGURE 4.2   Getting ready to edit the package type.

This produces a dialog where you can specify the type of package, as shown in Figure 4.3.

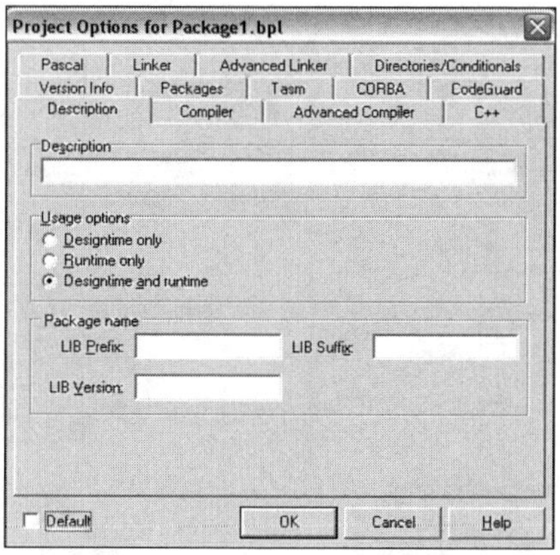

FIGURE 4.3 Setting the package type.

For most package development, it is convenient to create a dual design time, runtime package. However, later, when preparing your package for distribution, you might want to put your code into separate design time and runtime packages. This will be the case when you have special property editors or other facilities that you need to provide to those using the component (see the following section on component distribution and Chapter 5, "Creating Property and Component Editors").

When you are satisfied that your components are working properly, you should make sure that they are packaged correctly. The most correct approach involves separating the design time and runtime code. The correct way to do this using packages involves creating a minimum of two packages: a runtime-only package and a design time-only package—a runtime-only/design time-only package pair. This requires two steps:

1. Create a runtime-only package containing *only* the source of your component(s). Do not include any code to register the component(s) or any code for the design time interface of the component(s) (such as code for property and component editors).

2. Create a design time-only package containing *only* the registration code and optionally any design time interface code for your component(s). Do not include any source code for your component(s). Instead, add the import library (the `.bpi` file) of the component(s) run time-only package to the package's Requires list.

The design time package is the package installed into the IDE. Figure 4.4 illustrates the relationship between the two packages.

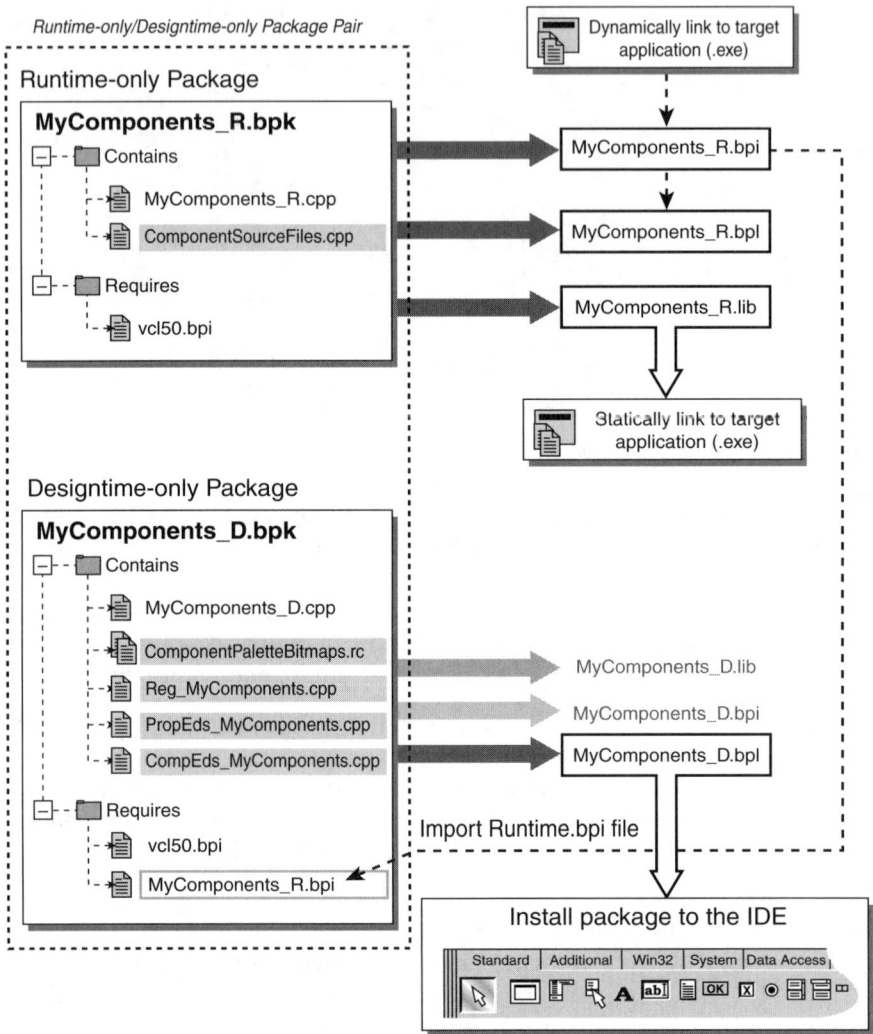

FIGURE 4.4   A runtime-only/design time-only package pair.

It can be seen in Figure 4.4 that the design time package is only used to create a `.bpl` file for installation into the IDE. The runtime package is used to create the files that will actually be used by an application. In reality, one or more runtime-only packages could be used in conjunction with a single design time-only package (in other words, appear in the Requires section of the design time-only package). All code, save registration code, can be removed from the design time-only package, effectively making the design time-only package a registration package.

For comparison, a dual design time/runtime package is shown in Figure 4.5.

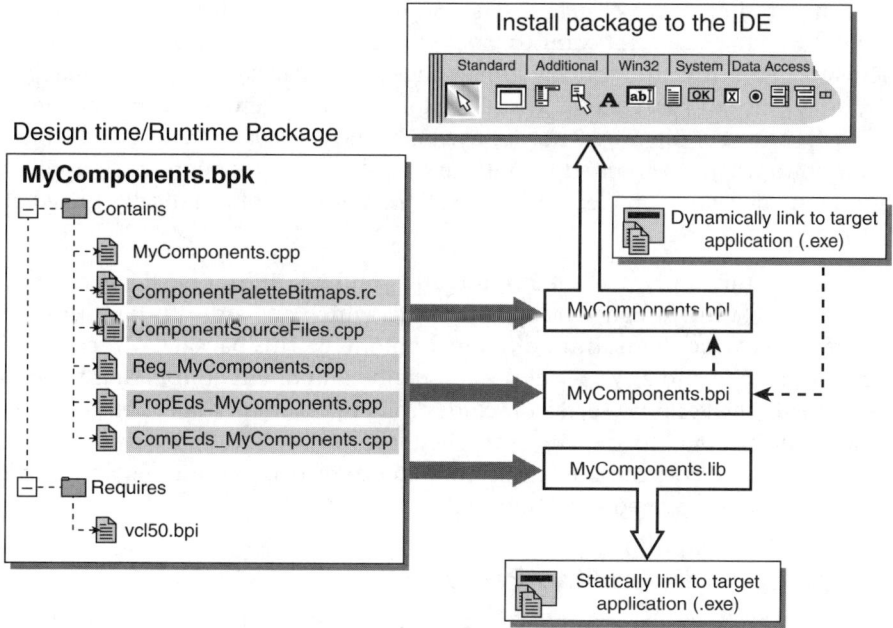

FIGURE 4.5   A dual design time/runtime package.

The code required for registration and for property and component editors will be unnecessarily included in any applications that use a dual package such as that shown in Figure 4.5. For simple packages with no property or component editors, this might be acceptable. Testing a component or set of components using a dual package is also generally more convenient, however, you can simplify the effort by including both design time and runtime packages in the same program group. Don't forget to save the program group and the package projects—generally into the directory where you are keeping the code for the components they contain.

Dual packages add some development complexity. Here are the considerations you need to keep in mind.

The runtime-only package will be the first package created. To specify that a package is a runtime-only package, check the Runtime Only option on the Description page of the package's Options dialog box. This package should contain only the source for the component(s).

Any import libraries (`.bpi` files) required by the component(s) should be added to the `Requires` list for this package project. Care should be taken to only add those import libraries that are necessary for a successful build. Remember, packages that are referenced in the `Requires` list are linked during compile time to any future application that uses this package and one or more units from the `Required` package.

After the runtime-only package is successfully built, you will have three files (unless you indicated you did not want to create a `.lib` file by having unchecked the Generate `.lib` File option on the Linker page of the package's Options dialog): a `.bpl` file, a `.bpi` file, and a `.lib` file. Make sure all three are present because all are required. The `.lib` file might not always be needed, but it should be available for those times when it is desired to statically link your components to an application (and many developers prefer the distribution simplicity of a statically linked application).

After the runtime-only package is built, and you have an import file available, you can now create the design time-only package, which depends on the runtime package to provide the features of your component. This package will contain your registration code and any special property and component editors that your components need. The `Requires` section includes the import library of the runtime-only package. If there are no special component or property editors for this package, you are only required to write the registration code. (Property editor and component editor creation is covered in Chapter 5.)

Compiling and Installing Packages

Package projects can be compiled in the normal fashion and produce the normal compiler and linker output. Packages are essentially fancy DLLs under Windows and fall into a similar category under Linux.

The package can be installed into the IDE in either of two ways. The first way is to compile the package with the Install entry on the package project's pop-up menu. The second way is to compile the package normally, and then pick Install from that menu, in which case, Install will simply add the package without recompiling.

A third way also exists, which is the one typically used by the recipients of your package—that is, picking Install Packages from the IDE Components menu.

The Visual Component Library (VCL) is an extremely powerful tool, and putting together an application is very easy using the many stock components, classes, and methods that C++Builder provides. However, in some situations you might find that a component doesn't quite provide the capabilities you need. The ability to write and modify components gives you a distinct advantage over other programming languages and is one reason why C++Builder is the tool of choice for many programmers around the world. Creating custom components will give you an insight into how the VCL works and increase your productivity with C++Builder. Judging by the number of commercial component sites on the Internet, it can be a profitable exercise as well.

Creating Custom Components

The task of creating components can be quite daunting at first. After reading several articles and tutorials on the topic, it is quite easy to find yourself wondering where to start. The easiest approach is to start with a component that already exists and build on its features and capabilities.

As trivial as this might seem, you might just find yourself customizing or extending a number of the standard VCL components to suit the design and style of your real-world applications. While building a database application, you might drop a TDBGrid onto your form and change several properties to the same value. Similarly, while developing some in-house utilities, you always drop a TStatusBar onto your form, add some panels, and remove the size grip. Instead of doing this for every project, it would make sense to create your own custom component and have these properties set for you automatically. Not only does this make each new application faster to create, but you also have confidence that they are all bug free. Additionally, should you discover a new bug, all you have to do is correct the code in the component and recompile your package projects. They will all inherit the changes without any additional reprogramming.

Understanding Component Writing

There are different types of components; therefore, the ancestor of your own components will be determined by the very nature of that component.

Nonvisual components are derived from TComponent. TComponent is the minimal descendant that can be used for the creation of a component because it is the lowest-level component to offer the capability to be integrated into the IDE and have its properties streamed.

A nonvisual component is one that is simply a wrapper for other complex code in which there is no visual representation provided to the user. An example is a component that receives error log information and automatically sends it to a linked edit control, such as a TMemo or TrichEdit, and appends it to a file on disk. The component itself is invisible to the user of the application, but it continues to function in the background, providing the functionality required by the application.

Windowed components are derived from TWinControl. These objects appear to the user at runtime and can be interacted with (such as selecting a file from a list). Although it is possible to create your own components from TWinControl, C++Builder provides the TCustomControl component to make this task easier.

Graphic components are similar to windowed components with the main difference being that they don't have a window handle and, therefore, do not interact with the user. The absence of a handle also means fewer resources are being consumed. Although these components do not interact with the user, it is possible to have these components react to window messages such as those from mouse events. These components are derived from TGraphicControl.

Why Build on an Existing Component?

The biggest advantage you will find from building on existing components is the reduced development time of projects. It is also worthwhile to know that all the components used in your projects are bug free.

Take TLabel as an example, of which every project has more than one. If every project you created needed to maintain a particular design style, you could find yourself adding multiple label components and changing their properties to the same values for each new application. By creating a custom component descending from TLabel, you can add several of these new labels to a form and be left with only the task of setting their captions and positions.

To demonstrate how easy this can be, we can create a component in about a minute and have to type only three lines of code. From C++Builder's menu, choose Component, New Component. After the New Component dialog opens, select TLabel for the new component's Ancestor Type, and for the Class Name, type TStyleLabel. For a component that you will be installing into C++Builder's Component Palette and using in applications, you will probably want to choose a more descriptive class name. For this example, you could leave the other options with their default values and simply click the OK button. C++Builder will create the unit files for you; all that is needed is to add the lines of code that will set the label's properties. After you've made the necessary changes, save the file and from C++Builder's menu choose Component, Install Component. If you have the file open in C++Builder's IDE, the Unit File Name edit box will reflect the component's file. Click the OK button to install the component in the Component Palette. Listings 4.1 and 4.2 show the complete code.

LISTING 4.1   The TStyleLabel Header File, StyleLabel.h

```
//------------------------------------------------------------------
#include <SysUtils.hpp>
#include <Controls.hpp>
#include <Classes.hpp>
#include <Forms.hpp>
#include <StdCtrls.hpp>
//------------------------------------------------------------------
class PACKAGE TStyleLabel : public TLabel
```

LISTING 4.1   Continued

```
{
private:
protected:
public:
    __fastcall TStyleLabel(TComponent* Owner);
__published:
};
//------------------------------------------------------------------------
#endif
```

LISTING 4.2   The TStyleLabel Code File, StyleLabel.cpp

```
//------------------------------------------------------------------------
#include <vcl.h>
#pragma hdrstop

#include "StyleLabel.h"
#pragma package(smart_init)
//------------------------------------------------------------------------
// ValidCtrCheck is used to assure that the components created do not have
// any pure virtual functions.
//

static inline void ValidCtrCheck(TStyleLabel *)
{
    new TStyleLabel(NULL);
}
//------------------------------------------------------------------------
__fastcall TStyleLabel::TStyleLabel(TComponent* Owner)
  : TLabel(Owner)
{
    Font->Name = "Verdana";
    Font->Size = 12;
    Font->Style = Font->Style << fsBold;
}
//------------------------------------------------------------------------
namespace Stylelabel
{
    void __fastcall PACKAGE Register()
    {
```

LISTING 4.2   Continued

```
        TComponentClass classes[1] = {__classid(TStyleLabel)};
        RegisterComponents("TestPack", classes, 0);
    }
}
//------------------------------------------------------------------
```

Another advantage to building on existing components is the ability to create a base class with all the functionality it requires, while leaving the properties unpublished. An example of this would be a specific TListBox type of component that doesn't have the Items property published to the user. By descending this component from TCustomListBox, it is possible to publish the properties you want the user to have access to (at design time), while making the others available (such as the Items property) only at runtime.

Finally, the properties and events you add to an existing component means writing far less code than if you create the component from scratch.

Designing Custom Components

Although it might seem trivial, the same rules apply to component design as per-application development when creating a custom component from an existing one. It is important to think about the possible future direction your components might take. The previously mentioned components that provide a list of database information don't just descend from TListBox. Instead, we decided to create a custom version of TCustomListBox that would contain the additional properties common to each descendant we wanted to create. Each new component was then built on this custom version, eliminating the need for three different versions of the same code. The final version of each component contained nothing more than the code (properties, methods, and events) that made it unique compared to its relatives.

Using the VCL Chart

To gain an appreciation for C++Builder's VCL architecture, take some time to review the VCL chart that ships with the product. This resource gives you a quick visual overview of not only what components are available, but also what they are derived from.

During your learning phase of component design and creation, you should endeavor to model your own components in this same object-oriented fashion, by creating strong, versatile base classes from which to create custom components. Although the source code for the C++Builder components are written in Pascal, it is a worthwhile exercise to look at each of the base classes for a particular component and see for yourself how they all come together. You will soon observe how components sharing the same properties are all derived from the same base class, or a descendant of one.

Finally, the chart shows what base classes are available for your own custom component requirements. In combination with the VCL help files, you can quickly determine the most suitable class from which to derive your components. As mentioned previously, the minimum base class will be `TComponent`, `TWinControl`, or `TGraphicControl`, depending on the type of component you will be creating.

Writing Nonvisual Components

The world of components is built on three main entities: properties, events, and methods. This section looks at each of these, with the aim of giving you a greater understanding of what makes up a component and how components work together to provide the building blocks of your C++Builder applications.

Properties

Properties come in two flavors: published and nonpublished. *Published* properties are available in the C++Builder Integrated Development Environment (IDE) at design time (they are also available at runtime). *Nonpublished* properties are used at runtime by your application. We will look at nonpublished properties first.

NonPublished Properties   A component is a packaged class with some additional functionality. Take a look at the sample class in Listing 4.3.

LISTING 4.3   Getting and Setting Private Variables

```
class LengthClass
{
private:
    int FLength;

public:
    LengthClass(void){}
    ~LengthClass(void){}
    int GetLength(void);
    void SetLength(int pLength);
    void LengthFunction (void);
}
```

Listing 4.3 shows a private variable used internally by the class and the methods used by the application to read and write its value. This can easily lead to messy code. Take a look at Listing 4.4 for another example.

LISTING 4.4   Using Set and Get Methods

```
LengthClass Rope;
Rope.SetLength(15);
// do something
int NewLength = Rope.GetLength();
```

The code in Listing 4.4 isn't complex by any means, but it can quickly become difficult to read in a complex application. Wouldn't it be better if we could refer to Length as a property of the class? This is what C++Builder enables you to do. In C++Builder, the class could be written as shown in Listing 4.5.

LISTING 4.5   Using a Property to Get and Set Private Variables

```
class LengthClass2
{
private:
    int FLength;

public:
    LengthClass2(void){}
    ~LengthClass2(void){}
    void LengthFunction(void);
    __property int Length = {read = FLength, write = FLength};
}
```

The sample code in Listing 4.4 would be changed when using properties as shown in Listing 4.6.

LISTING 4.6   Setting and Getting with a Property

```
LengthClass Rope;
Rope.Length = 15;
// do something
int NewLength = Rope.Length;
```

The class declaration has now been altered to use a __property (an extension to the C++ language in C++Builder). This property has read and write keywords defined. In Listing 4.6, when you read the Length property, you are returned the value of FLength; when you set the Length property, you are setting the value of FLength.

Why go to all this trouble when you could just make the FLength variable public? Properties enable you to do the following:

- You can make the Length property read-only by not using the write keyword.

- You can provide an application public access to private information of the class without affecting the implementation of the class. This is more relevant when the property value is derived or some action needs to be taken when the value of the property changes.

- You can cause side effects when the value is assigned to the property. These side effects can be used to maintain a consistent internal state for the object, to write information to a persistent store, or prepare other property values to be requested by a caller (eager evaluation).

- You can compute a value when it is asked for (lazy evaluation). This is especially nice for things such as infinite sequences of numbers (such as prime numbers), or complex calculations that you might want to avoid performing if nothing ever requests the value.

Listing 4.7 shows a slight variation on the previous example.

LISTING 4.7   Combining Set and Get Methods with Properties

```
class LengthClass3
{
private:
    int FLength;
    int GetLength(void);
    void SetLength(int pLength);

public:
    LengthClass3(void){}
    ~LengthClass3(void){}
    void LengthFunction(void);
    __property int Length = {read = GetLength, write = SetLength};
}
```

The example in Listing 4.7 is starting to show how properties can become quite powerful. The property declaration shows that the value is returned by the GetLength() method when Length is read. The SetLength() method is called when Length needs to be set.

The GetLength() method might perform some calculations based on other private members of the class. The SetLength() method might perform some validation, and then continue to perform some additional tasks before finally setting the value of FLength.

In C++Builder, an example of this is the connection to a database source when the name of an alias is changed. As a developer, you change the name of the alias. In the background, the component is disconnecting from the current database (if there is one) before attempting to connect to the new source. The implementation is hidden from the user, but it is made available by the use of properties.

Types of Properties   Properties can be of any type, whether it is a simple data type such as int, bool, short, and so on, or a custom class. There are two considerations when using custom classes as property types. The first is that the class must be derived from TPersistent (at a minimum) if it is to be streamed to the form. The second is that, if you need to forward declare the class, you need to use the __declspec(delphiclass) keyword.

The code in Listing 4.8 will compile using typical forward declaration. Note that we haven't yet defined a property.

LISTING 4.8   Forward Declaration

```
class MyClass;
class PACKAGE MyComponent : public TComponent
{
private:
    MyClass *FMyClass;
// …
};

class MyClass : public TPeristent
{
public:
        __fastcall MyClass (void){}
};
```

The PACKAGE keyword between the class name and class keyword is a macro that expands to code that enables the component to be exported from a package library (.BPL—Borland Package Library). A package library is a special kind of DLL that allows code to be shared between applications. For more information about package libraries and the PACKAGE macro, see "PACKAGE macro" and "Creating packages and DLLs" in the C++Builder online help.

But, if we want to add a property of type MyClass, we need to modify the forward declaration as shown in Listing 4.9.

LISTING 4.9 Custom Class Property

```
class __declspec(delphiclass) MyClass;

class PACKAGE MyComponent : public TComponent
{
private:
    MyClass *FMyClass;
// …

__published:
    __property MyClass *Class1 = {read = FMyClass, write = FMyClass};
};

class MyClass : public TPeristent
{
public:
    __fastcall MyClass (void){}
};
```

Published Properties   Publishing properties provides users with access to the properties of the component within the C++Builder IDE at design time. The properties are displayed in the Object Inspector, enabling the user to see or change the current value of those properties. The properties are also available at runtime, but their main purpose is to provide the user a quick method of setting up the component settings without the need to write a single line of code. Additionally, published properties are streamed to the form, so their values become persistent. This means the values are restored each time the project is opened and when the executable is launched.

Published properties are defined the same as all other properties, but they are defined in the __published area of the class declaration. Listing 4.10 shows an example.

LISTING 4.10 Publishing a Property

```
class PACKAGE LengthClass : public TComponent
{
private:
    int FLength;
    int GetLength(void);
    void SetLength(int pLength);

public:
```

LISTING 4.10   Continued

```
    __fastcall LengthClass(TObject *Owner) : TComponent(Owner) {}
    __fastcall ~LengthClass(void){}
    void LengthFunction(void);


__published:
    __property int Length = {read = Getlength, write = Setlength};
}
```

The previous class is the same as in Listing 4.9 except that the Length property has been moved to the __published section. Published properties shown in the Object Inspector are readable and writeable, but it is possible to make a property read-only and still visible in the IDE by creating a dummy write method. Listing 4.11 shows how to add a published property in the previous component that shows the current version of the component.

LISTING 4.11   A Version Property

```
const int MajorVersion = 1;
const int MinorVersion = 0;

class PACKAGE LengthClass : public TComponent
{
private:
    AnsiString FVersion;
    int FLength;
    int GetLength(void);
    void SetLength(int pLength);
    void SetVersion(AnsiString /* pVersion */ )
      {FVersion = AnsiString(MajorVersion) + "." +
      AnsiString(MinorVersion);}

public:
    __fastcall LengthClass(TObject *Owner) : TComponent(Owner)
          {SetVersion("");}
    __fastcall ~LengthClass(void){}
    void LengthFunction(void);

__published:
    __property int Length = {read = Getlength, write = Setlength};
    __property AnsiString Version = {read = FVersion, write = SetVersion};
}
```

We have defined a private variable FVersion, which has its value set in the class constructor. We have then added the Version property to the __published section and assigned the read and write keywords. The read keyword returns the value of Fversion, and the write method sets the value back to the original value. The variable name in the parameter list of SetVersion() has been commented out to prevent compiler warnings that the variable is declared, but not used. Because the property is of type AnsiString, the SetVersion() method by design must have an AnsiString parameter in the declaration.

Array Properties   Some properties are arrays, rather than simple data types such as bool, int, and AnsiString. This is not greatly documented for the user. An example of an array property is the Lines property of the TMemo component. This property enables the user to access the individual lines of the Memo component.

Array properties are declared the same as other properties, but with two main differences: The declaration includes the appropriate indexes with required types, and these indexes are not limited to being integers. Listings 4.12 through 4.15 illustrate the use of two properties. One takes a string as an index, and the other takes an integer value as an index.

LISTING 4.12   Using a String as an Index

```
class PACKAGE TStringAliasComponent : public TComponent
{
private:
    TStringList RealList;
    TStringList AliasList;
    __AnsiString __fastcall GetStringAlias(AnsiString RawString);
    AnsiString __fastcall GetRealString(int Index);
    void __fastcall SetRealString(int Index, AnsiString Value);
public:
    __property AnsiString AliasString[AnsiString RawString] =
        {read = GetStringAlias};
    __property AnsiString RealString[int Index] = {read=GetRealString,
        write=SetRealString};
}
```

The previous example could be part of a component that internally stores a list of strings and another list of alias strings. The AliasString property takes the RawString value and returns the alias via the GetStringAlias() method. The one thing many component writers are confused about when they first start using array properties is that the declaration uses index notation (that is, [ ]), yet in code you use the same notation as when calling another method. Look at the RealString property, and notice that not only does it have an AnsiString return type, but it also takes an integer as an index. The GetRealString() method would be called when retrieving a particular string from the list based on the index, as in Listing 4.13.

LISTING 4.13   Array Property Read Method

```
AnsiString __fastcall TStringAliasComponent::GetRealString(int Index)
{
    if(Index > (RealList->Count -1))
        return "";
    return RealList->Strings[Index];
}
```

In code, the property would look like this:

```
AnsiString str = StringAlias1->RealString[0];
```

Now take a look at the SetRealString() method. This method might look a bit odd if you are unfamiliar with using arrays as properties. It takes as its first parameter an integer value as its index and an AnsiString value. The RealList TStringList variable will insert the AnsiString in the list at the position specified by the index parameter. Listing 4.14 shows the definition of the SetRealString() method.

LISTING 4.14   Array Property Write Method

```
void __fastcall TStringAliasComponent::SetRealString(int Index,
  AnsiString Value)
{
    if((RealList->Count - 1) < Index)
        RealList->Add(Value);
    else
        RealList->Insert(Index, Value);
}
```

In Listing 4.14, the value of the Index parameter is checked against the number of strings already in the list. If Index is greater, the string specified by Value is simply added to the end of the list. Otherwise, the Insert() method of TStringList is called to insert the string at the position specified by Index. Now you can assign a string to the list like this:

```
StringAlias1->RealString[1] = "Some String";
```

Now here is the fun part. The GetStringAlias() method is the read method for the AliasString property, which takes a string as an index. You know that the string lists are arrays of strings, so every string has an index, or a position within the list. You can use the IndexOf() method of TStringList to compare the string passed as the index against the strings contained in the list. This method returns an integer value that is the index of the string within the list, or it returns -1 if the string is not present. Now all you have to do is return the string with the index returned from the call to IndexOf() from the list of aliases. This is demonstrated in Listing 4.15.

LISTING 4.15   The GetStringAlias() Method

```
AnsiString __fastcall TStringAliasComponent::GetStringAlias(
  AnsiString RawString)
{
    int Index;
    Index = RealList->IndexOf(RawString);
    if((Index == -1) || (Index > (AliasList->Count-1)))
        return RawString;

    return AliasList->Strings [Index];
}
```

To use the property, you would do something like this:

```
AnsiString MyAliasString = StringAlias1->AliasString("The Raw String");
```

Beyond Read and Write   The code examples in Listings 4.5 through 4.15 have shown properties using read and write keywords as part of the declaration. C++Builder also provides three more options: default, nodefault, and stored.

The default keyword does not set the default value for the property. Instead, it tells C++Builder what default value will be assigned to this property (by the developer) in the component constructor. The IDE then uses this information to determine whether the value of the property needs to be streamed to the form. If the property is assigned a value equivalent to the default, the value of this property will not be saved as part of the form. For example

```
__property int IntegerProperty = {read = Finteger, write = Finteger,
  default = 10};
```

The nodefault keyword tells the IDE that this property has no default value associated with it. When a property is declared for the first time, there is no need to include the nodefault keyword because the absence of a default means there is no default. The nodefault keyword is mainly used when you need to change the definition of the inherited property. For example

```
__property int DescendantInteger = {read = Finteger, write = Finteger,
  nodefault};
```

Be aware that the value of a property with the nodefault keyword in its declaration will be streamed only if a value is assigned to the property or underlying member variable, either in one of its methods, or via the Object Inspector.

The stored keyword is used to control the storing of properties. All published properties are stored by default. You can change this behavior by setting the stored keyword to true or false or by giving the name of a function that returns a Boolean result. The code in Listing 4.16 shows an example of the stored keyword in use.

LISTING 4.16   Using the stored Keyword

```
class PACKAGE LengthClass : public TComponent
{
protected:
    int FProp;
    bool StoreProperty(void);

__published:
    __property int AlwaysStore = {read = FProp, write = FProp, stored = true};
    __property int NeverStore = {read = FProp, write = FProp, stored = false};
    __property int SimetimesStore = {read = FProp, write = FProp,
      stored = StoreProperty};
}
```

Order of Creation   If your component has properties that depend on the values of other properties during the streaming phase, you can control the order in which they load (and hence initialize) by declaring them in the required order in the class header. For example, the code in Listing 4.17 loads the properties in the order PropA, PropB, PropC.

LISTING 4.17   Property Dependencies

```
class PACKAGE SampleComponent : public TComponent
{
private:
    int FPropA;
    bool FPropB;
    String FProC;
    void __fastcall SetPropB(bool pPropB);
    void __fastcall SetPropC(String pPropC);
```

LISTING 4.17   Continued

```
public:
    __property int PropA = {read = FPropA, write = FPropA};
    __property bool PropB = {read = FPropB, write = SetPropB};
    __property String PropC = {read = FPropC, write = SetPropC};
}
```

If you have properties with dependencies and are having trouble getting them to initialize correctly, ensure that the order of the property declarations in the class is correct.

Events

An event in a component is the call of an optional method in response to another incident. The incident could be a hook for the user to perform a task before the component continues the catching of an exception or the trapping of a Windows message.

As a simple example, let's assume we have a component that traverses directories from a given root location. If this component were designed to notify the user when the current directory has changed, this would be referred to as an *event*. When the event occurs, the component determines if the user has provided an event handler (a method attached to the event) and calls the respective method. If this all sounds confusing, take a look at Listing 4.18.

LISTING 4.18   Declaring an Event Property

```
class PACKAGE TTraverseDir : public TComponent
{
private:
    AnsiString FCurrentDir;
    TNotifyEvent *FOnDirChanged;

public:
    __fastcall TTraverseDir(TObject *Owner) : TComponent(Owner){
      FOnDirChanged = 0;}
    __fastcall ~TTraverseDir(void){}
    __fastcall Execute();

__published:
    __property AnsiString CurrentDir = {read = FCurrentDir};
    __property TNotifyEvent OnDirChanged = {read = FOnDirChanged,
      write = FOnDirChanged};
}
```

Listing 4.18 shows the relevant sections of code to describe the declaration of a read-only property and a standard event. When this component is executed, there will be instances when the current directory is changed. Let's have a look at some example code:

```
void __fastcall TTraverseDir::Execute(void)
{
// perform the traversing of a directory

// This is where the directory has changed,
// call the DirChanged event if there is one.

if(FOnDirChanged)
    FOnDirChanged(this);

// remainder of component code here
}
```

The variable FOnDirChanged in the previous example is a pointer to a TNotifyEvent, which is declared as

```
typedef void __fastcall (__closure *TNotifyEvent)(System::TObject* Sender)
```

As you can see, the declaration indicates that a single parameter of type TObject* is expected. When the event is created (by double-clicking the event in the Object Inspector), the IDE creates the following code:

```
void __fastcall TTraverseDir::Traverse1DirChanged(TObject *Sender)
{
}
```

Within this code, the user can now add code to be performed when this event is called. In this case, the event is a standard event that simply passes a pointer of the object that generated the event. This pointer enables you to distinguish between multiple components of the same type within the project.

```
void __fastcall TTraverseDir::Traverse1DirChanged(TObject *Sender)
{
if(Sender == Traverse1)
    // perform this code for the component called Traverse1
else
    // handle the alternative here
}
```

How to Create an Event That Contains Additional Parameters You will recall that the standard event is defined as shown in the following code:

```
typedef void __fastcall (__closure *TNotifyEvent)(System::TObject* Sender)
```

The following code shows how to define a custom event:

```
typedef void __fastcall (__closure *TDirChangedEvent)
   (System::TObject* Sender, bool &Abort)
```

We have done two things in the previous code:

- Created a unique typedef. TNotifyEvent is now TDirChangedEvent.

- Added the required parameters to the parameter list.

We can now modify our class declaration. The changes are shown in Listing 4.19.

LISTING 4.19 Custom Event Properties

```
typedef void __fastcall (__closure *TDirChangedEvent)(
  System::TObject* Sender, bool &Abort)

class PACKAGE TTraverseDir : public TComponent
{
private:
    TDirChangedEvent *FOnDirChanged;

__published:
    __property TDirChangedEvent OnDirChanged = {read = FOnDirChanged,
      write = FOnDirChanged};
}
```

Now when the user creates the event, the IDE will add the following code:

```
void __fastcall TTraverseDir::Traverse1DirChanged(TObject *Sender, bool &Abort)
{
}
```

There is only one more change to make: the source code that calls the event, as shown in Listing 4.20.

LISTING 4.20   Calling the Event

```
void __fastcall TTraverseDir::Execute(void)
{
// perform the traversing of a directory

bool &Abort = false;

// This is where the directory has changed,
// call the DirChanged event if there is one.

if(FOnDirChanged)
    FOnDirChanged(this, Abort);

if(Abort)
    // handle the abort process

// remainder of component code here
}
```

The component has been sufficiently modified to enable the user to abort the process if required.

Methods

Methods of a component are supporting routines developed to carry out the various tasks required; they are no different than the methods defined for a typical class. In writing components, the goal is to minimize the number of methods the application needs to call. Here are some simple rules to follow when designing your components:

- The user must not be required to call any methods to make the component behave the way he expects. For example, the component must take care of all initializations.

- There must be no dependencies on the order in which given methods must be called. You must design your component to allow for any combination of events to take place. For example, if a user calls a routine that is state dependent (such as trying to query a database when there is no active connection), the component must handle the situation. Whether the component should attempt to connect or should throw an exception is up to the developer based on the component's function.

- The user must not be able to call a method that would change the state of a component while it is performing another task.

- The method should not generally be used to set or get values from the component because that is the role of the property.

Write your methods so that they check the current component state. If all of the requirements are not met, the component should attempt to correct the problem. The components should throw an exception if the component state cannot be corrected. Where appropriate, create custom exceptions so that the user can check for component-specific exception types.

Try to create properties rather than methods. Properties enable you to hide an active implementation from the user and, hence, make the component easier to understand.

Methods you write for components will typically be public or protected. Private methods should be written when they are hiding a specific implementation for that component, to the point that even derived components should not call them.

Public Methods   *Public* methods are those that the user needs to make the component perform as required.

When you have a method that runs for a long time, consider creating an event that can be used by the developer to inform the user of any processing activity taking place. Providing an opportunity for the user to abort the processing, for instance, through a return value from the event is another possibility.

Imagine a component that searches a tree of directories for a given file. Depending on the system being searched, this could take a great deal of processing time. Rather than leaving the user wondering if the application has ceased functioning, it is better to create an event that is called within the method. This event can then provide feedback, such as displaying the name of the current directory being traversed.

Protected Methods   If your components have methods that must not be called by the application developer, but need to be called from derived components, these methods are declared as *protected*. This ensures that the method is not called at the wrong time. It is safer to create public methods for the user that call protected methods when all requirements are established first.

When a method is created for the implementation of properties, it should be declared as a *virtual protected* method. This enables descendant components to enhance or replace the implementation used.

An example of a virtual protected method is the Loaded() method of components. When a component is completely loaded (streamed from the form), the Loaded() method is called.

In some cases, a descendant component needs to know when the component is loaded after all properties have been read so that it can perform some additional tasks. An example is a component that performs validation in a property setter, but cannot perform the validation until all properties have been read. In such a case, create a private variable called IsLoaded and set this to false in the constructor. (Although this is done by default, doing it this way makes the code more readable.) Then, overload the Loaded() method and set IsLoaded to true. This variable can then be used in the property-implementation methods to perform validation as required.

Listings 4.21 and 4.22 are from the custom TAliasComboBox component. TAliasComboBox is part of the free MJFPack package, which can be downloaded from http://www.mjfreelancing.com. The package contains other components that can be linked together in this fashion.

LISTING 4.21   The TAliasComboBox Header File

```
class PACKAGE TAliasComboBox : public TSmartComboBox
{
private:
    bool IsLoaded;

protected:
    virtual void __fastcall Loaded(void);
}
```

LISTING 4.22   The TAliasComboBox Source File

```
void __fastcall TAliasComboBox: :Loaded(void)
{
TComponent::Loaded();

if(!ComponentState.Contains(csDesigning))
    {
    IsLoaded = true;
    GetAliases();
    }
}
```

In this code, you can see that the Loaded() method has been overloaded in the class declaration. In the .CPP file, start by calling the ancestor Loaded() method, and then your additional code. Listing 4.22 shows the component verifying that it is not in design mode before it retrieves available alias information. Because the state of certain properties might depend on other properties, additional methods for this component check the IsLoaded variable before performing any processing that might require the value of those properties to be set. Essentially, most of the processing by this component is performed only at runtime.

Creating Component Exceptions

Sometimes it is possible to rethrow an exception that you have caught in your component, which enables the user to deal with the situation. You have more than likely performed a number of steps in your component that need to be cleaned up when an exception occurs. After you have performed the cleanup process, you need to do one of two things.

First, you can rethrow the exception. This would be the standard approach for an error such as Divide By Zero. However, there are situations in which it would be better to convert the exception into an event. This provides very clean handling methods for your users. Don't make the mistake of converting all exceptions to events because this can sometimes make it harder for your users to develop their applications.

An example might help to make this clearer. Imagine a component performing a number of sequential database queries. This component would be made up of a TStrings property that contains all the queries and an Execute() method that performs them. How does the user want to use this component? Something such as the following would be the most desirable.

```
MultiQuery->Queries->Assign(Memo1->Lines);
MultiQuery1->Execute();
```

This is very simple code for the user to implement, but what about a possible exception? Should the user be required to handle any exceptions himself? This might not be the best approach during one of the queries. A better approach would be to build an event that is called when an exception occurs. Within the event, the user should have the opportunity to abort the process.

Let's create a custom exception that will be called if the user attempts to execute an individual query when it is outside the available index range. For the moment, assume that there is another method called ExecuteItem() that takes an index to the list of available queries.

First, we need to create the exception in the header file. This is as simple as creating a new exception class derived from the Exception class, as shown in Listing 4.23.

LISTING 4.23   A Custom Exception Class

```
class EMultiQueryIndexOutOfBounds : public Exception
{
public:
```

LISTING 4.23   Continued

```
    __fastcall EMultiQueryIndexOutOfBounds(const AnsiString Msg) :
    Exception(Msg){}
};
```

That's it. Now if the user tries to execute a query (by index), and the index provided is outside the available range, we can throw our unique exception.

The code for throwing this exception is shown in Listing 4.24.

LISTING 4.24   Throwing the Custom Exception

```
void __fastcall TMultiQuery::ExecuteItem(int Index)
{
if(Index < 0 || Index > Queries->Count)
    throw EmultiQueryIndexOutOfBounds;

// … perform the query here
}
```

As you can see from Listings 4.23 and 4.24, a custom exception is very easy to create and implement. If this component is to perform the query at design time, you need to provide the user with a message (rather than have an exception thrown within the IDE). You should modify the code as shown in Listing 4.25.

LISTING 4.25   Throwing an Exception at Design Time

```
void __fastcall TMultiQuery::ExecuteItem(int Index)
{
if(Index < 0 || Index > Queries->Count)
    {
    if(ComponentState.Contains(csDesigning))
        throw EmultiQueryIndexOutOfBounds("The Query index is out of range");
    else
        throw EmultiQueryIndexOutOfBounds;
    }

// … perform the query here
}
```

The namespace

As you develop your components and name them, there might be other developers who, by coincidence, use the same names. This will cause conflicts when using both components in the same project. This is overcome with the namespace keyword.

When a component is created using the New Component Wizard, the IDE creates code similar to that shown in Listing 4.26.

LISTING 4.26   namespace Code

```
namespace Aliascombobox
{
    void __fastcall PACKAGE Register()
    {
        TComponentClass classes[1] = {__classid(TAliasComboBox)};
        RegisterComponents("MJF Pack", classes,  0);
    }
}
```

The namespace keyword ensures that the component is created in its own subsystem. Let's look at a case where namespace needs to be used even further within a package.

Suppose that two developers build a clock component, and they both happen to create a const variable to indicate the default time mode. If both clocks are used in an application, the compiler will complain because of the duplication.

```
// From the first developer
const bool Mode12;    // 12 hour mode by default
class PACKAGE TClock1 : public TComponent
  {
  }
// From the second developer
const bool Mode12;    // 12 hour mode by default
class PACKAGE TClock2 : public TComponent
  {
  }
```

As you can see, it is important to develop your component packages with this possibility in mind. To get around this issue, use the namespace keyword. After all the #include statements in your header file, surround the code as shown in Listing 4.27.

LISTING 4.27   Surrounding Your Code

```
namespace NClock1
{
class PACKAGE TClock1 : public
  }
}
```

Develop a convention for all your components. For example, you could start your namespace identifiers with a capital *N*, followed by the component name. If it is possible that the same name has already been used, come up with something unique, such as prefixing with your company's initials. Using namespaces in this fashion ensures that your packages will integrate smoothly with others.

Responding to Messages

The VCL does a fantastic job of handling almost all of the window messages you will ever require. There are times, however, when a need arises to respond to an additional message to further enhance your project.

> **NOTE**
>
> Keep in mind that the explicit use of Windows messages will prevent porting your component to other operating systems. CLX components you create should never use Windows messages directly.

An example of such a requirement is to support filename drag and drop from Windows Explorer onto a string Grid component. We can create such a component, called TSuperStringGrid, that is nothing more than a descendant of TStringGrid with some additional functionality.

The drag-and-drop operation is handled by the API message WM_DROPFILES. The information needed to carry out the operation is stored in the TWMDropFiles structure.

The interception of window messages in components is the same as for other areas of your projects. The only difference is that we are working with a component and not with the form of a project. Hence, we set up a message map, as shown in Listing 4.28.

LISTING 4.28   Trapping Messages

```
BEGIN_MESSAGE_MAP
    MESSAGE_HANDLER(WM_DROPFILES, TWMDropFiles, WmDropFiles)
END_MESSAGE_MAP(TStringGrid)
```

NOTE

No trailing semicolons are used in declaring the message map. This is because BEGIN_MESSAGE_MAP, MESSAGE_HANDLER, and END_MESSAGE_MAP are macros that expand to code during compilation. The macros contain the necessary semicolons.

The code in Listing 4.28 creates a message map for the component (note TStringGrid in the END_MESSAGE_MAP macro). The message handler will pass all intercepts of the WM_DROPFILES messages to the WmDropFiles() method (which will be created shortly). The information is passed to this method in the TWMDropFiles structure as defined by Windows.

Now we need to create the method that will handle the message. In the protected section of the component we define the method as shown in the following code:

```
protected:
    void __fastcall WmDropFiles(TWMDropFiles &Message);
```

You'll notice we have provided a reference to the required structure as a parameter of the method.

Before this component will work, we need to register the component with Windows, telling it that the string grid is allowed to accept the dropped filenames. This is performed when the component is loaded via the DragAcceptFiles() command.

```
DragAcceptFiles(Handle, FCanDropFiles);
```

In the previous code, the FCanDropFiles variable is used by the component to indicate whether it is allowed to accept the filenames as part of a drag-and-drop operation.

Now the method accepts the filenames when the component intercepts the Windows message. The code in Listing 4.29 is stripped slightly from the full version.

LISTING 4.29 Accepting Dropped Files

```
void __fastcall TSuperStringGrid::WmDropFiles(TWMDropFiles &Message)
{
char buff[MAX_PATH];
HDROP hDrop = (HDROP)Message.Drop;
POINT Point;
int NumFiles = DragQueryFile(hDrop, -1, NULL, NULL);
TStringList *DFiles = new TStringList;
```

LISTING 4.29   Continued

```
DFiles->Clear();
DragQueryPoint(hDrop, &Point);
for(int you = 0; you < NumFiles; i++)
    {
    DragQueryFile(hDrop, i, buff, sizeof(buff));
    DFiles->Add(buff);
    }
DragFinish(hDrop);

// do what you want with the list of files now stored in DFiles

delete DFiles;
}
```

An explanation of this code is beyond the scope of this chapter. The help files supplied with C++Builder provide a good overview of what each function performs.

As you can see, intercepting messages is not hard after you understand how to set them up, although some understanding of the Windows API is required. Refer to the messages.hpp file that comes with your C++Builder installation for a list of the message structures available.

Design Time Versus Runtime

We've already made some references to the operation of a component at design time compared to runtime. *Design time* operation refers to how the component behaves while the user is creating the project in the IDE. *Runtime* operation refers to what the component does when the application is executed.

The TComponent object has a property (a Set) called ComponentState that is made up of the following constants: csAncestor, csDesigning, csDesignInstance, csDestroying, csFixups, csFreeNotification, csInline, csLoading, csReading, csWriting, and csUpdating. Table 4.1 lists these ComponentState flags and gives the purpose of each.

TABLE 4.1   The ComponentState Flags

Flag	Purpose
csAncestor	Indicates that the component was introduced in an ancestor form. Set only if csDesigning is also set. Set or cleared in the TComponent::SetAncestor() method.
csDesigning	Indicates that the component is being manipulated at design time. Used to distinguish design time and runtime manipulation. Set or cleared in the TComponent::SetDesigning() method.

TABLE 4.1 Continued

Flag	Purpose
csDesignInstance	Indicates that the component is the root object in a designer. For example, it is set for a frame when you are designing it, but not on a frame that acts like a component. This flag always appears with csDesigning. Set or cleared in the TComponent::SetDesignInstance() method.
csDestroying	Indicates that the component is being destroyed. Set in the TComponent::Destroying() method.
csFixups	Indicates that the component is linked to a component in another form that has not yet been loaded. This flag is cleared when all pending fixups are resolved. Cleared in the GlobalFixupReferences() global function.
csFreeNotification	Indicates that the component has sent a notification to other forms that it is being destroyed, but has not yet been destroyed. Set in the TComponent::FreeNotification() method.
csInline	Indicates that the component is a top-level component that can be modified at design time and also embedded in a form. This flag is used to identify nested frames while loading and saving. Set or cleared in the component's SetInline() method. Also set in the TReader::ReadComponent() method
csLoading	Indicates that a filer object is currently loading the component. This flag is set when the component is first created and not cleared until the component and all its children are fully loaded (when the Loaded() method is called). Set in the TReader::ReadComponent() and TReader::ReadRootComponent() methods. Cleared in the TComponent::Loaded() method. (For more information on filer objects, see "TFiler" in the C++Builder online help index.)
csReading	Indicates that the component is reading its property values from a stream. Note that the csLoading flag is always set when csReading is set. That is, csReading is set for the period of time that a component is reading in property values when the component is loading. Set and cleared in the TReader::ReadComponent() and TReader::ReadRootComponent() methods.
csWriting	Indicates that the component is writing its property values to a stream. Set and cleared in the TWriter::WriteComponent() method.

TABLE 4.1   Continued

Flag	Purpose
csUpdating	Indicates that the component is being updated to reflect changes in an ancestor form. Set only if csAncestor is also set. Set in the TComponent::Updating() method and cleared in the TComponent::Updated() method.

The Set member we are most interested in is csDesigning. As long as the component exists in the IDE (as part of a developing project), the component will contain this constant as part of the Set to indicate that it is being used at design time. To determine if a component is being used at design time, use the following code:

```
if(ComponentState.Contains(csDesigning))
    // carry out the designtime code here
else
    // carry out the runtime code here
```

Why would you need to run certain code at runtime only? This is required in many instances, such as the following:

- To specifically validate a property that has dependencies available only at runtime.

- To display a warning message to the user if he sets an inappropriate property value.

- To display a selection dialog or a property editor if an invalid property value is given.

Many component writers don't go to the trouble of providing the user with these types of warnings and dialogs. However, it is these extra features that make a component more intuitive and user friendly.

Linking Components

Linking components refers to giving a component the capability to reference or alter another component in the same project. An example in C++Builder is the TDriveComboBox component. This component has a property called DirList that enables the developer to select a TDirectoryListBox component available on the same form. This type of link gives the developer a quick and easy method to update the directory listing automatically every time the selected drive is changed. Creating a project to display a list of directories and filenames doesn't get any easier than dropping three components (TDriveComboBox, TdirectoryListBox, and TFileListBox) onto a form and setting two properties. Of course, you still need to assign code to the event handlers to actually make the project perform something useful, but up to that point there isn't a single line of code to be written.

Providing a link to other components starts by creating a property of the required type. If you create a property of type TLabel, the Object Inspector will show all available components on the form that are of type TLabel. To show how this works for descendant components, we are going to create a simple component that can link to a TMemo or a TRichEdit component. To do this, you need to realize that both components descend from TCustomMemo.

Let's start by creating a component descending from TComponent that has a property called LinkedEdit, as shown in Listing 4.30.

LISTING 4.30   Linked Components

```
class PACKAGE TMsgLog : public TComponent
{
private:
    TCustomMemo *FLinkedEdit;
➥// can be TMemo or TRichEdit or any other derived component

public:
    __fastcall TMsgLog(TComponent* Owner);
    __fastcall ~TMsgLog(void);

    void __fastcall OutputMsg(const AnsiString Message);

protected:
    virtual void __fastcall Notification(TComponent *AComponent,
      TOperation Operation);

__published:
    __property TCustomMemo *LinkedEdit = {read = FLinkedEdit,
      write = FLinkedEdit};
};
```

The code in Listing 4.30 creates the component with a single property, called LinkedEdit. There are two more things to take care of. First, we need to output the messages to the linked Memo or RichEdit component (if there is one). We also need to take care of the possibility that the user might delete the linked edit control. The OutputMsg() method is used to pass the text message to the linked edit control, and the Notification() method is used to detect if it has been deleted.

The following provides the output:

```
void __fastcall TMsgLog::OutputMsg(const AnsiString Message)
{
if(FLinkedEdit)
    FLinkedEdit->Lines->Add(Message);
}
```

Because both TMemo and TRichEdit components have a Lines property, there is no need to perform any casting. If you need to perform a task that is component specific (or handled differently), use the code shown in Listing 4.31.

LISTING 4.31   The OutputMsg() Method

```
void __fastcall TMsgLog::OutputMsg(const AnsiString Message)
{
TMemo *LinkedMemo = 0;
TRichEdit *LinkedRichEdit = 0;

LinkedMemo = dynamic_cast<TMemo *>(FLinkedEdit);
LinkedRichEdit = dynamic_cast<TRichEdit *>(FLinkedEdit);

if(FLinkedMemo)
    FLinkedMemo->Lines->Add(Message);
else
    {
    FLinkedRichEdit->Font->Color = clRed;
    FLinkedRichEdit->Lines->Add(Message);
    }
}
```

The final check is to detect the linked edit control being deleted. This is done by overloading the Notification() method of Tcomponent, as shown in Listing 4.32.

LISTING 4.32   The Notification() Method

```
void __fastcall TMsgLog::Notification(TComponent *AComponent,
  TOperation Operation)
{
// We don't care about controls being added.
if(Operation != opRemove)
    return ;
```

LISTING 4.32   Continued

```
// We have to check each one in case the user did something
// like have the same label attached to multiple properties.
if(AComponent == FLinkedEdit)
    FLinkedEdit = 0;
}
```

The code in Listing 4.32 shows how to handle code resulting from another component being deleted. The first two lines are to show the purpose of the Operation parameter.

The most important code is the last two lines, which compare the pointer AComponent to the LinkedEdit property (a pointer to a component descending from TCustomMemo). If the pointers match, we NULL the LinkedEdit pointer. This removes the reference from the Object Inspector and ensures that our code is no longer pointing to a memory address that is about to be lost (when the edit component is actually deleted). Note that LinkedEdit = 0 is the same as LinkedEdit = NULL.

One final point is that if you link your component to another that has dependencies (such as TDBDataSet descendants that require a database connection), it is up to you to ensure that these dependencies are checked and handled appropriately. Good component design is recognized when the user has the least amount of work to do to get the component to behave as expected.

Linking Events Between Components

We've looked at how components can be linked together via properties. Our discussion so far has been about how a property of TMsgLog can be linked to another component so that messaging can be provided automatically without the user having to write the associated code.

What we are going to look at now is how to link events between components. Continuing with the previous examples, we're going to show how we intercept the OnExit event for the linked edit control (note that TMemo and TRichEdit both have an OnExit event and are of type TNotifyEvent) so that we can perform some additional processing after the user's code has executed. Let's assume the linked edit control is not read-only. This means the user could enter something into the log; this change needs to be recorded as a user-edited entry. We will demonstrate how to perform the intercept and leave the functionality up to you.

Component events can be implemented differently according to the nature of the event itself. If the component is looping through a process, the code might simply have a call to execute the event handler if one exists. Take a look at the following example:

```
// start of loop
if(FOnExit)
    FOnExit(this);
endif;
// …
// end of loop
```

Other events could result from a message. Listing 4.26 showed the message map macro for accepting files dropped onto a control from Windows Explorer as follows:

```
BEGIN_MESSAGE_MAP
    MESSAGE_HANDLER(WM_DROPFILES, TWMDropFiles, WmDropFiles)
END_MESSAGE_MAP(TStringGrid)
```

If our component has an OnDrop event, we can write our implementation as shown in the following code:

```
void __fastcall TSuperStringGrid::WmDropFiles(TWMDropFiles &Message)
{
if(FOnDrop)
    FOnDrop(this);
endif;

// … remainder of code here
}
```

What you should have noticed by now is that the components maintain a pointer to the event handler, such as FOnExit and FOnDrop in the previous example. This makes it very easy to create our own pointer to note where the user's handler resides, and then redirect the user's event so that it calls an internal method instead. This internal method will execute the user's original code, followed by the component's code (or vice versa).

The only other consideration to make is when you redirect the pointers. The logical place to do this is in the component's Loaded() method. This is called when the entire component is streamed from the form, and, hence, all of the user's event handlers have been assigned.

Define the Loaded() method and a pointer to a standard event in your class. (The event is the same type as the one we are going to intercept—in our case it is the OnExit event, which is of type TNotifyEvent.) We also need an internal method with the same declaration as the event that we are intercepting. In our class, we create a method called MsgLogOnExit. This is the method that will be called before the OnExit event of the linked edit control. In Listing 4.33, we include a typedef of type

TComponent called `Inherited`. The reason will become obvious when we get to the source code.

LISTING 4.33   The TMsgLog Class Header File

```
class PACKAGE TMsgLog : public TComponent
{
typedef TComponent Inherited;

private:
    TNotifyEvent *FOnUsersExit;
    void __fastcall MsgLogOnExit(TObject *Sender);

protected:
    virtual void __fastcall Loaded(void);

// … remainder of code not shown
}
```

In the source code, you might have something such as Listing 4.34.

LISTING 4.34   The TMsgLog Class Source File

```
void __fastcall TMsgLog::TMsgLog(TComponent *Owner)
{
FOnUsersExit = 0;
}

void __fastcall TMsgLog::Loaded(void)
{
Inherited::Loaded();

if(!ComponentState.Contains(csDesigning))
    {
    if(FlinkedEdit)
        {
        if(FlinkedEdit->OnExit)
            FOnUsersExit = FlinkedEdit->OnExit;

        FlinkedEdit->OnExit = MsgLogOnExit;
        }
    }
}
```

LISTING 4.10 Continued

```
void __fastcall TMsgLog::MsgLogOnExit(TObject *Sender)
{
if(FOnUsersExit)
    FOnUsersExit(this);

// … and now perform the additional code we want to do
}
```

When the component is first created, the constructor initializes FOnUsersExit to NULL. When the form is completely streamed, the component's OnLoaded event is called. This starts by calling the inherited method first (the typedef simply helps to make the code easy to read). Next, we make sure the component is not in design mode. If the application is in runtime mode, we see if the component has a linked edit control. If so, we find out if the user has assigned a method to the OnExit event of that control. If these tests are true, we set our internal pointer FOnUsersExit to the address of the user's event handler. Finally, we reassign the edit control's event handler to our internal method MsgLogOnExit(). This results in the MsgLogOnExit() method being called every time the cursor exits the edit control, even if the user did not assign an event handler.

The MsgLogOnExit() method starts by determining if the user assigned an event handler; if so, it is executed. We then continue to perform the additional processing tasks we want to implement. The decision to call the user's event before or after our own code is executed depends on the nature of the event, such as data encryption or validation.

Writing Visual Components

As you've seen, components can be any part of a program that the developer can interact with. Components can be nonvisual (TOpenDialog or TTable) or visual (TListBox or TButton). The most obvious difference between them is that visual components have the same visual characteristics during design time as they do during runtime. As the properties of the component that determine its visual appearance are changed in the Object Inspector, the component must be redrawn or repainted to reflect those changes. Windowed controls are wrappers for Windows Common Controls, and Windows will take care of redrawing the control more often than not. In some situations, such as with a component that is not related to any existing control, redrawing the component is up to you. In either case, it is helpful to know some of the useful classes that C++Builder provides for drawing onscreen.

Where to Begin

One of the most important considerations when writing components is determining the parent class from which to inherit. You should review the help files and the VCL source code if you have it. This is time well spent; there is nothing more frustrating than having worked on a component for hours or days just to discover that it doesn't have the capabilities you need. If you are writing a windowed component (one that can receive input focus and has a window handle), derive it from `TCustomControl` or `TWinControl`. If your component is purely graphical, such as a `TSpeedButton`, derive from `TGraphicControl`. Very few if any limitations exist when it comes to writing visual components, and there is a wealth of freeware and shareware components and source code on the Internet from which to get ideas. `http://www.torry.net/` is one of the most comprehensive sources; others can be found on the C++Builder Programmer's Webring, which starts on `http://www.temporaldoorway.com/programming/cbuilder/index.htm`.

TCanvas

The `TCanvas` object is C++Builder's wrapper for the Device Context. It encapsulates various tools for drawing complex shapes and graphics onscreen. `TCanvas` can be accessed through the `Canvas` property of most components, although Windows draws some windowed controls and, therefore, those windowed controls do not provide a `Canvas` property. There are ways around this, and we'll discuss them shortly. `TCanvas` also provides several methods to draw lines, shapes, and complex graphics onscreen.

Listing 4.35 is an example of how to draw a line diagonally from the upper-left corner to the bottom-right corner of the canvas. The `LineTo()` method draws a line from the current pen position to the coordinates specified in the X and Y variables. First, set the start position of the line by calling the `MoveTo()` method.

LISTING 4.35   Drawing a Line Using `MoveTo()`

```
Canvas->MoveTo(0, 0);
int X = ClientRect.Right;
int Y = ClientRect.Bottom;
Canvas->LineTo (X, Y);
```

Listing 4.36 uses the `Frame3D()` method to draw a frame around a canvas, giving the control a button appearance.

LISTING 4.36   Creating a Button Appearance

```
int PenWidth = 2;
TColor Top = clBtnHighlight;
TColor Bottom = clBtnShadow;
Frame3D(Canvas, ClientRect, Top, Bottom, PenWidth);
```

It is also very common to use API drawing routines with the TCanvas object to accomplish certain effects. Some API drawing methods use the DeviceContext of the control, although it isn't always necessary to get the HDC of the control to call an API that requires it. To get the HDC of a control, use the GetDC() API.

NOTE

HDC is the data type returned by the call to GetDC(). It is simply the handle of the DeviceContext and is synonymous with the Handle property of TCanvas.

Listing 4.37 uses a form with TPaintBox (we'll use TPaintBox because its Canvas property is published) and calls the RoundRect() API to draw an ellipse within the TPaintBox. The TPaintBox can be placed anywhere on the form. The code would be placed in the OnPaint event handler for the TPaintBox. The full project can be found in the PaintBox1 folder on the CD-ROM that accompanies this book. The project filename is Project1.bpr.

LISTING 4.37   Using API Drawing Methods

```
void __fastcall TForm1::PaintBox1Paint(TObject *Sender)
{
    // We'll use a TRect structure to save on typing
    TRect Rect;
    int nLeftRect, nTopRect, nRightRect, nBottomRect, nWidth, nHeight;

    Rect = PaintBox1->ClientRect;
    nLeftRect = Rect.Left;
    nTopRect = Rect.Top;
    nRightRect = Rect.Right;
    nBottomRect = Rect.Bottom;
    nWidth = Rect.Right - Rect.Left;
    nHeight = Rect.Bottom - Rect.Top;

    if(RoundRect(
        PaintBox1->Canvas->Handle, // handle of device context
        nLeftRect,  // x-coord. of bounding rect's upper-left        corner
        nTopRect,     // y-coord. of bounding rect's upper-left corner
        nRightRect,   // x-coord. of bounding rect's lower-right corner
        nBottomRect,  // y-coord. of bounding rect's lower-right corner
        nWidth,  // width of ellipse used to draw rounded corners
        nHeight  // height of ellipse used to draw rounded corners
        ) == 0)
        ShowMessage("RoundRect failed...");
}
```

Try changing the values of the nWidth and nHeight variables. Start with zero; the rectangle will have sharp corners. As you increase the value of these two variables, the corners of the rectangle will become more rounded. This method and other similar drawing routines can be used to create buttons or other controls that are rounded or elliptical. Some examples will be shown later. See "Painting and Drawing Functions" in the Win32 help files (win32.hlp, specifically) that ship with C++Builder for more information.

Using Graphics in Components

Graphics are becoming more commonplace in components. Some familiar examples are TSpeedButton and TBitButton, and there are several freeware, shareware, and commercial components available that use graphics of some sort. Graphics add more visual appeal to components and, fortunately, C++Builder provides several classes to handle bitmaps, icons, JPEGs, and GIFs. The norm for drawing components is to use an offscreen bitmap to do the drawing, and then copy the bitmap to the onscreen canvas. This reduces screen flicker because the canvas is painted only once. This is very useful if the image you are working with contains complex shapes or images. The TBitmap class has a Canvas property, which is a TCanvas object and, thus, enables you to draw shapes and graphics off the screen.

The following example uses a form with a TPaintBox component. A TBitmap object is created and used to draw an image similar to a TSpeedButton with its Flat property set to true. The TBitmap is then copied to the screen in one action. In this example we add a TButton, which will change the appearance of the image from raised to lowered. The full project can be found in the PaintBox2 folder on the CD-ROM that accompanies this book. The project filename is Project1.bpr. First, take a look at the header file in Listing 4.38.

LISTING 4.38   Creating a Raised or Lowered Appearance

```
class TForm1 : public TForm
{
__published:  // IDE-managed Components
    TPaintBox *PaintBox1;
    TButton *Button1;
private:       // User declarations
    bool IsUp;
public:                 // User declarations
    __fastcall TForm1(TComponent* Owner);
};
```

We declare a Boolean variable IsUp, which we'll use to swap the highlight and shadow colors and to change the caption of the button. If IsUp is true, the image is in its up state; if the value of IsUp is false, the image is in its down state. Because IsUp is a member variable, it will be initialized to false when the form is created. The Caption property of Button1 can be set to Up via the Object Inspector.

The OnClick event of the button is quite simple. It changes the value of the IsUp variable, changes the Caption property of the button based on the new value, and calls the TPaintBox's Repaint() method to redraw the image. This is shown Listing 4.39.

LISTING 4.39   The Button1Click() Method

```
void __fastcall TForm1::Button1Click(TObject *Sender)
{
    IsUp = !IsUp;
    Button1->Caption = (IsUp) ? "Down" : "Up";
    PaintBox1->Repaint ();
}
```

A private method, SwapColors(), is declared and will change the highlight and shadow colors based on the value of the IsUp variable, which is shown in Listing 4.40.

LISTING 4.40   The SwapColors() Method

```
void __fastcall TForm1::SwapColors(TColor &Top, TColor &Bottom)
{
    Top = (IsUp) ? clBtnHighlight : clBtnShadow;
    Bottom = (IsUp) ? clBtnShadow :  clBtnHighlight;
}
```

The final step is to create an event handler for the OnPaint event of the TPaintBox. This is shown in Listing 4.41.

LISTING 4.41   Painting the Button

```
void __fastcall TForm1::PaintBox1Paint(TObject *Sender)
{
    TColor TopColor, BottomColor;
    TRect Rect;

    Rect = PaintBox1->ClientRect;

    Graphics::TBitmap *bit = new Graphics::TBitmap;
    bit->Width = PaintBox1->Width;
```

LISTING 4.41   Continued

```
    bit->Height = PaintBox1->Height;
    bit->Canvas->Brush->Color = clBtnFace;
    bit->Canvas->FillRect(Rect);
    SwapColors(TopColor, BottomColor);
    Frame3D(bit->Canvas, Rect, TopColor, BottomColor, 2);
    PaintBox1->Canvas->Draw(0, 0, bit);
    delete bit;
}
```

Listing 4.42 will go one step further and demonstrate how to use bitmap files as well as drawing lines on a canvas. Most button components, for example, contain not only lines and borders that give it shape, but also icons, bitmaps, and text. This can become a bit more complicated because it requires a second TBitmap to load the graphics file, the position of the graphic must be calculated and copied to the first bitmap, and the final result must be copied to the onscreen canvas. The full project can be found in the PaintBox3 folder on the CD-ROM that accompanies this book. The project filename is Project1.bpr.

LISTING 4.42   Using Bitmaps and Lines

```
void __fastcall TForm1::PaintBox1Paint(TObject *Sender)
{
    TColor TopColor, BottomColor;
    TRect Rect, gRect;

    Rect = PaintBox1->ClientRect;

    Graphics::TBitmap *bit = new Graphics::TBitmap;
    Graphics::TBitmap *bitFile = new Graphics::TBitmap;

    bitFile->LoadFromFile("geom1b.bmp");
    // size the off-screen bitmap to size of on-screen canvas
    bit->Width = PaintBox1->Width;
    bit->Height = PaintBox1->Height;

    // fill the canvas with the brush's color
    bit->Canvas->Brush->Color = clBtnFace;
    bit->Canvas->FillRect(Rect);

    // position the second TRect structure centered h/v within Rect
    gRect.Left = ((Rect.Right - Rect.Left) / 2) - (bitFile->Width / 2);
```

LISTING 4.42   Continued

```
    gRect.Top = ((Rect.Bottom - Rect.Top) / 2) - (bitFile->Height / 2);

    // move the inner rect up and over by 1 pixel to give the appearance of
    // the panel moving up and down
    gRect.Top += (IsUp) ? 0 : 1;
    gRect.Left += (IsUp) ? 0 : 1;

    gRect.Right = bitFile->Width + gRect.Left;;
    gRect.Bottom = bitFile->Height + gRect.Top;

    // copy the bitmap to the off-screen bitmap object using transparency
    bit->Canvas->BrushCopy(gRect, bitFile,
      TRect(0,0,bitFile->Width, bitFile->Height), bitFile->TransparentColor);

    // draw the borders
    SwapColors(TopColor, BottomColor);
    Frame3D(bit->Canvas, Rect, TopColor, BottomColor, 2);

    // copy the off-screen bitmap to the on-screen canvas
    BitBlt(PaintBox1->Canvas->Handle, 0, 0,    PaintBox1->ClientWidth,
      PaintBox1->ClientHeight, bit->Canvas->Handle,    0, 0,    SRCCOPY);

    delete bitFile;
    delete bit;
}
```

Responding to Mouse Messages

Graphical components are normally derived from TGraphicControl, which provides a canvas to draw on and handles WM_PAINT messages. Remember that nonwindowed components do not need to receive input focus and do not have or need a window handle. Although these types of components cannot receive input focus, the VCL provides custom messages for mouse events that can be trapped.

For example, when the Flat property of a TSpeedButton is set to true, the button pops up to show its borders when the user moves the mouse cursor over it, and it returns to a flat appearance when the mouse is moved away from the button. This effect is accomplished by responding to two messages—CM_MOUSEENTER and CM_MOUSELEAVE, respectively. These messages are shown in Listing 4.43.

LISTING 4.43   The `CM_MOUSEENTER` and `CM_MOUSELEAVE` Messages

```
void __fastcall CMMouseEnter(TMessage &Msg);  // CM_MOUSEENTER
void __fastcall CMMouseLeave(TMessage &Msg);  // CM_MOUSELEAVE

BEGIN_MESSAGE_MAP
  MESSAGE_HANDLER(CM_MOUSEENTER, TMessage, CMMouseEnter)
  MESSAGE_HANDLER(CM_MOUSELEAVE, TMessage, CMMouseLeave)
END_MESSAGE_MAP(TBaseComponentName)
```

Another important message to consider is the `CM_ENABLEDCHANGED` message. The `Enabled` property of `TGraphicControl` is declared as public, and the setter method simply sends the control the `CM_ENABLECHANGED` message so that the necessary action can be taken; for example, showing text or graphics as grayed or not firing an event. If you want to give your component the capability to be enabled or disabled, you would rede-clare this property as published in your component's header file and declare the method and message handler. Without it, users will still be able to assign a `true` or `false` value to the `Enabled` property at runtime, but it will have no effect. The `CM_ENABLECHANGED` message is shown in Listing 4.44.

LISTING 4.44   The `CM_ENABLEDCHANGED` Message

```
void __fastcall CMEnabledChanged(TMessage &Msg);
__published:
    __property Enabled ;

BEGIN_MESSAGE_MAP
  MESSAGE_HANDLER(CM_ENABLEDCHANGED, TMessage, CMEnabledChanged)
END_MESSAGE_MAP(TYourComponentName)
```

Other mouse events such as `OnMouseUp`, `OnMouseDown`, and `OnMouseOver` are conveniently declared in the protected section of `TControl`, so all that is necessary is to override the methods to which you want to respond. If you want derivatives of your component to have the capability to override these events, remember to declare them in the protected section of the component's header file. This is shown in Listing 4.45.

LISTING 4.45   Overriding `TControl`'s Mouse Events

```
private:
    TMmouseEvent FOnMouseUp;
    TMouseEvent FOnMouseDown;
    TMouseMoveEvent FOnMouseMove;

protected:
```

LISTING 4.45   Continued

```
    void __fastcall MouseDown(TMouseButton Button, TShiftState Shift, int X,
      int Y);
    void __fastcall MouseMove(TshiftState Shift, int X, int Y);
    void __fastcall MouseUp(TMouseButton Button, TShiftState Shift, int X,
      int Y);

__published:
    __property TMouseEvent OnMouseUp = {read=FOnMouseUp, write=FOnMouseUp};
    __property TMouseEvent OnMouseDown = {read=FOnMouseDown,
      write=FOnMouseDown};
    __property TMouseMoveEvent OnMouseMove = {read=FOnMouseMove,
      write=FOnMouseMove};
```

In the example projects shown previously, an event handler was created for the
OnPaint() event of TPaintBox. This event is fired when the control receives the
WM_PAINT message. TGraphicControl traps this message and provides a virtual Paint()
method that can be overridden in descendant components to draw the control
onscreen or, as TPaintBox does, provide an OnPaint() event.

These messages and others are defined in messages.hpp. If you have the VCL source
code, take time to find out which messages or events are available and which
methods can be overridden.

Putting It All Together

This section will cover putting all the previous techniques into a basic component
that you can expand and enhance. This component is not complete, although it
could be installed onto C++Builder's Component Palette and used in an application.
As a component writer, you should never leave things to chance; the easier your
component is to use, the more likely it will be used. The example shown in Listings
4.46 and 4.47 will be a type of Button component that responds like a TSpeedButton
and has a bitmap and text. The source code is shown in Listings 4.46 and 4.47, and
then we'll look at some of the obvious enhancements that could be made. The
source code is also provided in the ExampleButton folder on the CD-ROM that accompanies this book.

LISTING 4.46   The TExampleButton Header File, ExampleButton.h

```
//---------------------------------------------------------------------
#ifndef ExampleButtonH
#define ExampleButtonH
//---------------------------------------------------------------------
#include <SysUtils.hpp>
```

LISTING 4.46 Continued

```cpp
#include <Controls.hpp>
#include <Classes.hpp>
#include <Forms.hpp>
//--------------------------------------------------------------------

enum TExButtonState {esUp, esDown, esFlat, esDisabled};

class PACKAGE TExampleButton : public TGraphicControl
{
private:

    Graphics::TBitmap *FGlyph;
    AnsiString FCaption;
    TImageList *FImage;
    TExButtonState FState;
    bool FMouseInControl;
    TNotifyEvent FOnClick;
    void __fastcall SetGlyph(Graphics::TBitmap *Value);
    void __fastcall SetCaption(AnsiString Value);
    void __fastcall BeforeDestruction(void);
    void __fastcall SwapColors(TColor &Top, TColor &Bottom);
    void __fastcall CalcGlyphLayout(TRect &r);
    void __fastcall CalcTextLayout(TRect &r);
    MESSAGE void __fastcall CMMouseEnter(TMessage &Msg);
    MESSAGE void __fastcall CMMouseLeave(TMessage &Msg);
    MESSAGE void __fastcall CMEnabledChanged(TMessage &Msg);
protected:

    void __fastcall Paint(void);
    void __fastcall MouseDown(TMouseButton Button, TShiftState Shift,
                             int X, int Y);
    void __fastcall MouseUp(TMouseButton Button, TShiftState Shift,
                             int X, int Y);
public:

    __fastcall TExampleButton(TComponent* Owner);

__published:

    __property AnsiString Caption = {read=FCaption, write=SetCaption};
    __property Graphics::TBitmap * Glyph = {read=FGlyph, write=SetGlyph};
```

LISTING 4.46 Continued

```
    __property TNotifyEvent OnClick = {read=FOnClick, write=FOnClick};

BEGIN_MESSAGE_MAP
  MESSAGE_HANDLER(CM_MOUSEENTER, TMessage, CMMouseEnter)
  MESSAGE_HANDLER(CM_MOUSELEAVE, TMessage, CMMouseLeave)
  MESSAGE_HANDLER(CM_ENABLEDCHANGED, TMessage, CMEnabledChanged)
END_MESSAGE_MAP(TGraphicControl)
};
//--------------------------------------------------------------------------
#endif
```

LISTING 4.47 The TExampleButton Source File, ExampleButton.cpp

```
//--------------------------------------------------------------------------
#include <vcl.h>
#pragma hdrstop

#include "ExampleButton.h"
#pragma package(smart_init)
//--------------------------------------------------------------------------
// ValidCtrCheck is used to assure that the components created do not have
// any pure virtual functions.
//

static inline void ValidCtrCheck(TExampleButton *)
{
    new TExampleButton(NULL);
}
//--------------------------------------------------------------------------
__fastcall TExampleButton::TExampleButton(TComponent* Owner)
  : TGraphicControl(Owner)
{
    SetBounds(0,0,50,50);
    ControlStyle = ControlStyle << csReplicatable;
    FState = esFlat;
}
//--------------------------------------------------------------------------

namespace Examplebutton
{
    void __fastcall PACKAGE Register()
```

LISTING 4.47   Continued

```
    {
        TComponentClass classes[1] = {__classid(TExampleButton)};
        RegisterComponents("Samples", classes, 0);
    }
}
// --------------------------------------------------------------------------
void __fastcall TExampleButton::CMMouseEnter(TMessage &Msg)
{
    if(Enabled)
        {
        FState = esUp;
        FMouseInControl = true;
        Invalidate();
        }
}
// --------------------------------------------------------------------------
void __fastcall TExampleButton::CMMouseLeave(TMessage &Msg)
{
    if(Enabled)
        {
        FState = esFlat;
        FMouseInControl = false;
        Invalidate();
        }
}
// --------------------------------------------------------------------------
void __fastcall TExampleButton::CMEnabledChanged(TMessage &Msg)
{
    FState = (Enabled) ? esFlat : esDisabled;
    Invalidate();
}


// --------------------------------------------------------------------------
void __fastcall TExampleButton::MouseDown(TMouseButton Button, TShiftState
  Shift, int X, int Y)
{
    if(Button == mbLeft)
        {
        if(Enabled && FMouseInControl)
            {
            FState = esDown;
```

LISTING 4.47   Continued

```
            Invalidate();
        }
    }
}
// --------------------------------------------------------------------------
void __fastcall TExampleButton::MouseUp(TMouseButton Button, TShiftState
  Shift, int X, int Y)
{
    if(Button == mbLeft)
        {
        if(Enabled && FMouseInControl)
            {
            FState = esUp;
            Invalidate();
            if(FOnClick)
                FOnClick(this);
            }
        }
}
// --------------------------------------------------------------------------
void __fastcall TExampleButton::SetGlyph(Graphics::TBitmap * Value)
{
    if(Value == NULL)
        return;

    if(!FGlyph)
        FGlyph = new Graphics::TBitmap;
    FGlyph->Assign(Value);
    Invalidate();
}


// --------------------------------------------------------------------------
void __fastcall TExampleButton::SetCaption(AnsiString Value)
{
    FCaption = Value;
    Invalidate();
}
// --------------------------------------------------------------------------
void __fastcall TExampleButton::SwapColors(TColor &Top, TColor &Bottom)
{
    if(ComponentState.Contains(csDesigning))
```

LISTING 4.47   Continued

```
        {
        FState = esUp;
        }

    Top = (FState == esUp) ? clBtnHighlight : clBtnShadow;
    Bottom = (FState == esDown) ? clBtnHighlight : clBtnShadow;
}
// -------------------------------------------------------------------
void __fastcall TExampleButton::BeforeDestruction(void)
{
    if(FImage)
        delete FImage;

    if(FGlyph)
        delete FGlyph;
}
// -------------------------------------------------------------------
void __fastcall TExampleButton::Paint(void)
{
    TRect cRect, tRect, gRect;
    TColor TopColor, BottomColor;

    Canvas->Brush->Color = clBtnFace;
    Canvas->FillRect(ClientRect);
    cRect = ClientRect;
    Graphics::TBitmap *bit = new Graphics::TBitmap;
    bit->Width = ClientWidth;
    bit->Height = ClientHeight;
    bit->Canvas->Brush->Color = clBtnFace;
    bit->Canvas->FillRect(cRect);

    if(FGlyph)
        if(!FGlyph->Empty)
            {
            CalcGlyphLayout(gRect);
            bit->Canvas->BrushCopy(gRect, FGlyph,
                Rect(0,0,FGlyph->Width,FGlyph->Height),
                  FGlyph->TransparentColor);
            }
    if(!FCaption.IsEmpty())
        {
```

LISTING 4.47   Continued

```
        CalcTextLayout(tRect);
        bit->Canvas->TextRect(tRect, tRect.Left,tRect.Top, FCaption);
        }

    if(FState == esUp || FState == esDown)
        {
        SwapColors(TopColor, BottomColor);
        Frame3D(bit->Canvas, cRect, TopColor, BottomColor, 1);
        }

    BitBlt(Canvas->Handle, 0, 0, ClientWidth, ClientHeight,
      bit->Canvas->Handle, 0, 0, SRCCOPY);

    delete bit;
}
// --------------------------------------------------------------------
void __fastcall TExampleButton::CalcGlyphLayout(TRect &r)
{
    int TotalHeight=0;
    int TextHeight=0;

    if(!FCaption.IsEmpty())
        TextHeight = Canvas->TextHeight(FCaption);

    // the added 5 could be a 'Spacing' property but for simplicity we just
    // added the 5.
    TotalHeight = FGlyph->Height + TextHeight + 5;

    r = Rect((ClientWidth/2)-(FGlyph->Width/2),
            ((ClientHeight/2)-(TotalHeight/2)), FGlyph->Width +
            (ClientWidth/2)-(FGlyph->Width/2), FGlyph->Height +
            ((ClientHeight/2)-(TotalHeight/2)));
}
// --------------------------------------------------------------------
void __fastcall TExampleButton::CalcTextLayout(TRect &r)
{
    int TotalHeight=0;
    int TextHeight=0;
    int TextWidth=0;
    TRect temp;
```

LISTING 4.47 Continued

```
    if(FGlyph)
        TotalHeight = FGlyph->Height;

    TextHeight = Canvas->TextHeight(FCaption);
    TextWidth = Canvas->TextWidth(FCaption);

    TotalHeight += TextHeight + 5;

    temp.Left = 0;
    temp.Top = (ClientHeight/2)-(TotalHeight/2);
    temp.Bottom = temp.Top + TotalHeight;
    temp.Right = ClientWidth;

    r = Rect(((ClientWidth/2) - (TextWidth/2)), temp.Bottom-TextHeight,
        ((ClientWidth/2)-(TextWidth/2))+TextWidth,  temp.Bottom);
}
```

Here only the OnClick event is published. In a real component you would more than likely publish the OnMouseUp, OnMouseDown, and OnMouseMove events as well. The two properties Caption and Glyph are published, but you should have a Font property to enable users to change the font of the caption.

It would probably be a good idea to catch the CM_FONTCHANGED message so that the positions of the button glyph and caption can be redrawn accordingly. In calculating the position of the image and the text, we use a value of five pixels as the spacing between the two. It would also be a good idea to create a property that enables the user to specify this value.

In Listing 4.47, take a look at the write method for the Glyph property, SetGlyph(). If a NULL pointer is assigned to the Glyph property, the method simply returns without doing anything. This might seem like typical behavior for this type of property, but after you have assigned an image there is no way to get rid of it. In other words, you cannot show only the caption without deleting the component and creating a new one.

The last thing we will look at is the Boolean FMouseInControl FMouseInControl>variable. Because the control is responding to mouse events, it is wise to keep track of it. This variable is used to track whether the mouse cursor is over the control. Without this variable in place, certain member functions would be called inappropriately because the component will still receive mouse events even though the action did not begin over the control. For example, if a user clicked and held the mouse button, and then moved the mouse over the component and released the button, the CMMouseUp() method would be called without the component knowing that the mouse is actually over the control. This in effect would cause the component to redraw itself in its Up state and would not redraw unless you moved the mouse away, and then back again or clicked the button. The FMouseInControl variable prevents this.

In Listing 4.47, the shape of the button is drawn using the Frame3D() method. By including the Buttons.hpp header file in your source file, you can gain access to another method for drawing button shapes, DrawButtonFace(), shown in Listing 4.48.

LISTING 4.48   The DrawButtonFace() Method

```
TRect DrawButtonFace(TCanvas *Canvas, const TRect Client,
  int BevelWidth, TButtonStyle Style, bool IsRounded, bool IsDown,
  bool IsFocused);
```

The DrawButtonFace() method will draw a button shape the size of Client on the Canvas specified. Some of the parameters are effective according to the value of the others. For example, the BevelWidth and IsRounded parameters seem to have an effect only when Style is bsWin31. IsFocused has no apparent effect.

The DrawButtonFace() method uses the DrawEdge() API (see the Win32 online help included with C++Builder). This can also be used in your own drawing routines.

Modifying Windowed Components

As stated previously, windowed components are wrappers for the standard Windows controls. These components already know how to draw themselves, so you don't have to worry about that. In modifying windowed controls, you most likely will want to change what the component actually does rather than its look. Fortunately, the VCL provides protected methods in these components that can be overridden to do just that.

In this last example we'll use some of the techniques shown in this chapter to create a more familiar and robust replacement for the TFileListBox component that comes standard with C++Builder. Before we write any code, it's a good idea to get an overview of what we want to accomplish. Remember that we want to make this component as easy to use as possible and relieve the user from the task of writing code that is common when using a component that lists filenames. The following lists the changes we'll make in our component:

- Display the correct icon for each file.

- Give the user the ability to launch an application or open a document when the item is double-clicked.

- Allow the user the option to add a particular item to the list box.

- Allow an item to be selected when right-clicked.

- Show a horizontal scrollbar when an item is longer than the width of the list box.

- Maintain compatibility with TDirectoryListBox.

Now that we know what our component should do, we must decide from which base class to derive it. As stated previously, C++Builder provides custom classes from which to derive new components, which is currently not the case in our component. TDirectoryListBox and TFileListBox are linked together through the FileList property of TDirectoryListBox. This property is declared as a pointer to a TFileListBox, so a component derived from TCustomListBox or TListBox will not be visible to the property. To maintain compatibility with TDirectoryListBox, we will have to derive our component from TFileListBox. Fortunately, the methods it uses to read the filenames are protected, so all we have to do is override them in our new component.

Next, we'll consider the changes we want to make to this component and declare some new properties, methods, and events. First we want to allow the user to launch an application or open a document by double-clicking an item. We can declare a Boolean property that will allow the user to turn this option on or off, as shown in the following code.

```
__property bool CanLaunch = {read=FCanLaunch, write=FCanLaunch, default=true};
```

When a user double-clicks the list box, it is sent a WM_LBUTTONDBLCLK message. TCustomListBox conveniently provides a protected method that is called in response to this message. Listing 4.49 shows how we can override the DblClick() method to launch an application or open a document.

LISTING 4.49 The DblClick() Method

```
void __fastcall TSHFileListBox::DblClick(void)
{
  if(FCanLaunch)
    {
    int ii=0;
    // go through the list and find which item is selected
    for(ii=0; ii < Items->Count; ii++)
      {
      if(Selected[ii])
        {
        AnsiString str = Items->Strings[ii];
        ShellExecute(Handle, "open",  str.c_str(), 0, 0, SW_SHOWDEFAULT);
```

LISTING 4.49   Continued

```
        }
      }
    }
  // fire the OnDblClick event
  if(FOnDblClick)
    FOnDblClick(this);
}
```

It the FCanLaunch variable is true, we must first find which item is selected, and then use the ShellExecute() API to launch the application. This method also fires an OnDblClick event, which is declared as shown in the following code.

```
private:
  TNotifyEvent FOnDblClick;

__published:
  __property TNotifyEvent OnDblClick = {read=FOnDblClick, write=FOnDblClick};
```

The OnDblClick event does not really need to provide any information, so we can declare it as a TNotifyEvent variable. This behavior can certainly be changed if the need arises, but for now this will suffice. Now let's tackle the problem of allowing an item to be selected when right-clicked. First, we need to declare a new property as shown in the following code.

```
__property bool RightBtnClick = {read=FRightBtnSelect, write=FRightBtnSelect,
  default=true};
```

Notice that the property is referencing a member variable, and there is no read or write method. This is because we'll use the member variable in the MouseUp() event to determine whether to select the item. Listing 4.50 shows the code for the MouseUp() method.

LISTING 4.50   The MouseUp() Method

```
//-----------------------------------------------------------------------
void __fastcall TSHFileListBox::MouseUp(TMouseButton Button, TShiftState Shift,
  int X, int Y)
{
  if(!FRightBtnSel)
    return;

  TPoint ItemPos = Point(X,Y);
```

LISTING 4.50   Continued

```
  // is there an item under the mouse ?
  int Index = ItemAtPos(ItemPos, true);
  // if not just return
  if(Index == -1)
    return;
  // else select the item
  Perform(LB_SETCURSEL,  (WPARAM)Index, 0);
}
```

The code in Listing 4.50 is fairly simple. First we check the FRightBtnSel variable to see if we can select the item. Next, we need to convert the mouse coordinates to a TPoint structure. To find which item is under the mouse, we use the ItemAtPos() method of TcustomListBox, which takes the TPoint structure we created and a Boolean value that determines if the return value should be -1 or one more than the last item in the list box if the coordinate contained in the TPoint structure is beyond the last item. Here the parameter is true and, if the return value is -1, the method simply returns. You could change this value to false and remove the if() statement that checks the return value. Finally, we use the Perform() method to force the control to act as if it has received a window message. The first parameter to the Perform() method is the actual message we want to simulate. LB_SETCURSEL tells the list box that the mouse has changed the selection. The second parameter is the index of the item we want to select; the third parameter is not used, so it is zero.

Next, we want to enable the user the option to add a particular item. TFileListBox has a Mask property that enables you to specify file extensions that can be added to the list box. It is possible to redeclare the Mask property and provide a read and write method that filters the filenames according to the value of the Mask property. You took the easy way out and chose to provide an event that enables the user to apply his own algorithm for filtering the filenames. You could keep this event in place and still cater to the Mask property to provide even more functionality.

First, let's declare our new event.

```
typedef void __fastcall (__closure *TAddItemEvent)(TObject *Sender, AnsiString
  Item, bool &CanAdd);
```

As you can see, the event provides three parameters. Sender is the list box, Item is an AnsiString value that contains the filename, and CanAdd is a Boolean value that determines if the item can be added. Notice that the CanAdd parameter is passed by reference so that a user can change this value to false in the event handler to prevent Item from being added to the items in the list box.

Before we look at how to get the filenames and add them to the list box, let's look at Listing 4.51 and see how we can use the same icons as Windows Explorer.

LISTING 4.51   Getting the System Image List

```
SHFILEINFO shfi;
DWORD iHnd;
TImageList *Images;
Images = new TImageList(this);
Images->ShareImages = true;
iHnd = SHGetFileInfo("", 0, &shfi, sizeof(shfi), SHGFI_SYSICONINDEX |
                                 SHGFI_SHELLICONSIZE | SHGFI_SMALLICON);
if(iHnd != 0)
    Images->Handle = iHnd;
```

Notice in Listing 4.51 that the ShareImages property of FImages is set to true. This is very important. It informs the image list that it should not destroy its handle when the component is destroyed. The handle of the system image list belongs to the system, and if your component destroys it, Windows will not be able to display any of its icons for menus and shortcuts. This isn't permanent; you would just have to reboot your system so that Windows could get the handle of the system images again.

At this point we can override the ReadFileNames() method of TFileListBox to retrieve the filenames in a slightly different manner. Our version will use the shell to get the filenames using COM interfaces. Because walking an itemid list can look a bit messy and is beyond the scope of this chapter, we will not go into detail. We will create a new method, AddItem(), shown in Listing 4.52. It will retrieve the display name of the file and its icon index in the system image list and fire the OnAddItem event we created previously.

> **NOTE**
>
> An *itemid* is another name for an item identifier or identifier list. You can find more information about "Item Identifiers and Identifier Lists" in the Win32 help files that ship with C++Builder.

LISTING 4.52   The AddItem() Method

```
int __fastcall TSHFileListBox::AddItem(LPITEMIDLIST pidl)
{
  SHFILEINFO shfi;
  int Index;
```

LISTING 4.52   Continued

```
SHGetFileInfo((char*)pidl, 0, &shfi, sizeof(shfi), SHGFI_PIDL |
➥SHGFI_SYSICONINDEX |
  SHGFI_SMALLICON | SHGFI_DISPLAYNAME | SHGFI_USEFILEATTRIBUTES);

  // fire the OnAddItem event to allow the user the choice to add the
  // file name or not
  bool FCanAdd = true;
  if(FOnAddItem)
    FOnAddItem(this, AnsiString(shfi.szDisplayName), FCanAdd);

  if(FCanAdd)
    {
    TShellFileListItem *ShellInfo = new TShellFileListItem(pidl, shfi.iIcon);
    Index = Items->AddObject(AnsiString(shfi.szDisplayName),
➥(TObject*)ShellInfo);
    // return the length of the file name
    return Canvas->TextWidth(Items->Strings[Index]);
    }
  // return zero as the length as the file has not been added
  return 0;
}
```

The AddItem() method takes an itemid as its only parameter and returns an integer value. In Listing 4.52 we use the SHGetFileInfo() API to retrieve the display name of the file and its icon index. After we have the file's display name, we create a Boolean variable named CanAdd to determine if the item can be added, and then fire the OnAddItem event. We can then check the value of CanAdd and, if it is true, we go ahead and add the new item to the list box. After the item is added, we use the TextWidth() method of TCanvas to get its width in pixels. This value is the return value of the method, if the item was added, or zero if not. You will see the reason for this shortly.

One thing that we haven't discussed yet is the TShellFileListItem class. Because we need to do the actual drawing of the icons and text in the list box, we need some way of keeping track of each item's icon index. For each item that is added to the list box, we create an instance of TShellFileListItem and assign it to the Object property of the list box's Items property. This way we can retrieve it later when we need to draw the item's icon. TShellFileListItem also holds a copy of the item's itemid. This is for possible future enhancements; for example, you could create a descendant of TSHFileListBox and override the MouseUp() method to display the context menu for the file.

One thing to remember about using the `Object` property in this way is that the memory being used to hold the `TShellFileListItem` instance must be freed when the item is deleted from the list box. We do this by overriding the `DeleteString()` method, as shown in Listing 4.55.

As stated previously, the return value from the `AddItem()` method is the length in pixels of the item that has just been added to the list box. This value is used to determine the longest item and to display a horizontal scrollbar if the longest item is longer than the width of the list box. Take a look at the following code:

```
while(Fetched > 0)
        {
        // add the item to the listbox
        int l = AddItem(rgelt);
        if(l > hExtent)
          hExtent = l;
        ppenumIDList->Next(celt, &rgelt, &Fetched);
        }
```

This is a snippet from the `ReadFileNames()` method. It loops through a folder's `itemid` list and retrieves an `itemid` for each file. The `AddItem()` method returns the item's length and compares it to the previous item. If it is longer, the variable l is assigned the new length and the process is repeated until no more files remain. At the end of this loop, l holds the length of the longest item. Then, the `DoHorizontalScrollBar()` method can be called to determine if the horizontal scrollbar needs to be displayed.

The `DoHorizontalScrollBars()` method, shown in Listing 4.53, takes an integer value as its parameter. This is the length in pixels of an item just added to the list. The value is increased by two pixels for the left margin and, if the `ShowGlyphs` property is true, 18 pixels more is added to compensate for the width of the image and spacing between the image and text. Finally, the `Perform()` method is called to set the horizontal extent of the items in the list box, which in effect will show the scrollbar if the value of `WPARAM` is greater than the width of the control.

LISTING 4.53   Adding a Horizontal Scrollbar

```
void __fastcall TSHFileListBox::DoHorizontalScrollBar(int he)
{
    he += 2;
    if(ShowGlyphs)
        he += 18;

    Perform(LB_SETHORIZONTALEXTENT,  he, 0);
}
```

Listings 4.54 and 4.55 are the full source code for the TSHFileListBox component, which can be found in the SHFileListBox folder on the CD-ROM that accompanies this book.

LISTING 4.54   The TSHFileListBox Header File, SHFileListBox.h

```cpp
//--------------------------------------------------------------------------
#ifndef SHFileListBoxH
#define SHFileListBoxH
//--------------------------------------------------------------------------
#include <SysUtils.hpp>
#include <Controls.hpp>
#include <Classes.hpp>
#include <Forms.hpp>
#include <FileCtrl.hpp>
#include <StdCtrls.hpp>
#include "ShlObj.h"


//--------------------------------------------------------------------------

class TShellFileListItem : public TObject
{
private:
  LPITEMIDLIST Fpidl;
  int FImageIndex;
public:
  __fastcall TShellFileListItem(LPITEMIDLIST lpidl, int Index);
  __fastcall ~TShellFileListItem(void);
  __property LPITEMIDLIST pidl = {read=Fpidl};
  __property int ImageIndex = {read=FImageIndex};
};

typedef void __fastcall (__closure *TAddItemEvent)(TObject *Sender, AnsiString
  Item, bool &CanAdd);

class PACKAGE TSHFileListBox : public TFileListBox
{
private:
  TImageList *FImages;
  TNotifyEvent FOnDblClick;
  bool FCanLaunch;
  bool FRightBtnSel;
  TAddItemEvent FOnAddItem;
```

LISTING 4.54   Continued

```
 int __fastcall AddItem(LPITEMIDLIST pidl);
 void __fastcall GetSysImages(void);
protected:
 void __fastcall DblClick(void);
 void __fastcall ReadFileNames(void);
 void __fastcall MouseUp(TMouseButton Button, TShiftState Shift, int X,
   int Y);
 void __fastcall DrawItem(int Index, const TRect &Rect,
   TOwnerDrawState State);
 void __fastcall DoHorizontalScrollBar(int he);
 void __fastcall DeleteString(int Index);

public:
  __fastcall TSHFileListBox(TComponent* Owner);
  __fastcall ~TSHFileListBox(void);
__published:
  __property bool CanLaunch = {read=FCanLaunch, write=FCanLaunch,
    default=true};
  __property bool RightBtnSel = {read=FRightBtnSel, write=FRightBtnSel,
    default=true};
  __property TNotifyEvent OnDblClick = {read=FOnDblClick, write=FOnDblClick};
  __property TAddItemEvent OnAddItem = {read=FOnAddItem, write=FOnAddItem};
};
#endif
```

LISTING 4.55   The TSHFileListBox Source File, SHFileListBox.cpp

```
//---------------------------------------------------------------------------
#include <vcl.h>
#pragma hdrstop

#include "SHFileListBox.h"
#pragma package(smart_init)
//---------------------------------------------------------------------------
__fastcall TShellFileListItem::TShellFileListItem(LPITEMIDLIST lpidl,
  int Index)
  : TObject()
{
  // store a copy of the file's pidl
  Fpidl = CopyPIDL(lpidl);
  // and save its icon index
```

LISTING 4.55 Continued

```
  FImageIndex = Index;
}
//-----------------------------------------------------------------------
__fastcall TShellFileListItem::~TShellFileListItem(void)
{
  LPMALLOC lpMalloc=NULL;
  if(SUCCEEDED(SHGetMalloc(&lpMalloc)))
    {
    // free the memory associated with the pidl
    lpMalloc->Free(Fpidl);
    lpMalloc->Release();
    }
}


//-----------------------------------------------------------------------
__fastcall TSHFileListBox::TSHFileListBox(TComponent* Owner)
  : TFileListBox(Owner)
{
  ItemHeight = 18;
  ShowGlyphs = true;
  FCanLaunch = true;
  FRightBtnSel = true;
}
//-----------------------------------------------------------------------
__fastcall TSHFileListBox::~TSHFileListBox(void)
{
  // free the images
  if(FImages)
    delete FImages;
  FImages = NULL;
}
//-----------------------------------------------------------------------
void __fastcall TSHFileListBox::DeleteString(int Index)
{
  // This method is called in response to the LB_DELETESTRING messeage
  // First delete the TShellFileListItem pointed to by the string's
  // Object property
  TShellFileListItem *ShellItem = reinterpret_cast<TShellFileListItem*>
    (Items->Objects[Index]);
  delete ShellItem;
  ShellItem = NULL;
```

LISTING 4.55   Continued

```
  // now delete the item
  Items->Delete(Index);
}
//--------------------------------------------------------------------------
namespace Shfilelistbox
{
  void __fastcall PACKAGE Register()
  {
     TComponentClass classes[1] = {__classid(TSHFileListBox)};
     RegisterComponents("Samples", classes, 0);
  }
}
//--------------------------------------------------------------------------
void __fastcall TSHFileListBox::ReadFileNames(void)
{

  LPMALLOC g_pMalloc;
  LPSHELLFOLDER pisf;
  LPSHELLFOLDER sfChild;
  LPITEMIDLIST pidlDirectory;
  LPITEMIDLIST rgelt;
  LPENUMIDLIST ppenumIDList;
  int hExtent;

  try
    {
    try
      {
      if(HandleAllocated())
        {
        GetSysImages();
        // prohibit screen updates
        Items->BeginUpdate();
        // delete the items already in the list
        Items->Clear();
        // get the shell's global allocator
        if(SHGetMalloc(&g_pMalloc) != NOERROR)
          {
          return;
          }
        // get the desktop's IShellFolder interface
```

LISTING 4.55 Continued

```
    if(SHGetDesktopFolder(&pisf) != NOERROR)
      {
      return;
      }

    // convert folder string to WideChar
    WideChar oleStr[MAX_PATH];
    FDirectory.WideChar(oleStr, MAX_PATH);
    unsigned long pchEaten;
    unsigned long pdwAttributes;
    // get pidl of current folder
    pisf->ParseDisplayName(Handle, 0, oleStr, &pchEaten,
            &pidlDirectory, &pdwAttributes);

    // get an IShellFolder interface for the current folder
    if(pisf->BindToObject(pidlDirectory,NULL,
        IID_IShellFolder, (void**)&sfChild) != NOERROR)
      {
      return;
      }
    // enumerate the objects withing the folder
    sfChild->EnumObjects(Handle, SHCONTF_NONFOLDERS |
      SHCONTF_INCLUDEHIDDEN, &ppenumIDList);

    // walk through the enumlist
    ULONG celt = 1;
    ULONG Fetched = 0;
    ppenumIDList->Next(celt, &rgelt, &Fetched);
    hExtent = 0;
    while(Fetched > 0)
      {
      // add the item to the listbox
      int l = AddItem(rgelt);
      if(l > hExtent)
        hExtent = l;
      ppenumIDList->Next(celt, &rgelt, &Fetched);
      }

    }
  }
catch(Exception &E)
```

LISTING 4.55   Continued

```
      {
      throw(E); // re-throw any exceptions
      }
    }
  __finally
    { // make sure we do this reguardless
    g_pMalloc->Free(rgelt);
    g_pMalloc->Free(ppenumIDList);
    g_pMalloc->Free(pidlDirectory);
    pisf->Release();
    sfChild->Release();
    g_pMalloc->Release();
    Items->EndUpdate();
    }
  // Show the horizontal scrollbar if necessary
  DoHorizontalScrollBar(hExtent);
}
// -------------------------------------------------------------------
void __fastcall TSHFileListBox::DoHorizontalScrollBar(int he)
{
  // add a little space for the margins
  he += 2;
  // if we're showing the images make room for it plus a bit more
  // for the space between the image and the text
  if(ShowGlyphs)
    he += 18;

  Perform(LB_SETHORIZONTALEXTENT, he, 0);
}


// -------------------------------------------------------------------
void __fastcall TSHFileListBox::GetSysImages(void)
{
  SHFILEINFO shfi;
  DWORD iHnd;
  if(!FImages)
    {
    FImages = new TImageList(this);
    FImages->ShareImages = true;
    FImages->Height = 16;
    FImages->Width = 16;
```

LISTING 4.55 Continued

```cpp
    iHnd = SHGetFileInfo("", 0, &shfi, sizeof(shfi), SHGFI_SYSICONINDEX |
      SHGFI_SHELLICONSIZE | SHGFI_SMALLICON);
    if(iHnd != 0)
      FImages->Handle = iHnd;
    }
}
// -----------------------------------------------------------------------
int __fastcall TSHFileListBox::AddItem(LPITEMIDLIST pidl)
{
  SHFILEINFO shfi;
  int Index;

  SHGetFileInfo((char*)pidl, 0, &shfi, sizeof(shfi), SHGFI_PIDL |
    SHGFI_SYSICONINDEX |
    SHGFI_SMALLICON | SHGFI_DISPLAYNAME | SHGFI_USEFILEATTRIBUTES);

  // fire the OnAddItem event to allow the user the choice to add the
  // file name or not
  bool FCanAdd = true;
  if(FOnAddItem)
    FOnAddItem(this, AnsiString(shfi.szDisplayName), FCanAdd);

  if(FCanAdd)
    {
    TShellFileListItem *ShellInfo = new TShellFileListItem(pidl, shfi.iIcon);
    Index = Items->AddObject(AnsiString(shfi.szDisplayName),
      (TObject*)ShellInfo);
    // return the length of the file name
    return Canvas->TextWidth(Items->Strings[Index]);
    }
  // return zero as the length as the file has not been added
  return 0;
}
// -----------------------------------------------------------------------
void __fastcall TSHFileListBox::DrawItem(int Index, const TRect &Rect,
  TOwnerDrawState State)
{
  int Offset;

  Canvas->FillRect(Rect);
  Offset = 2;
```

LISTING 4.55   Continued

```cpp
  if(ShowGlyphs)
    {
    TShellFileListItem *ShellItem = reinterpret_cast<TShellFileListItem*>
      (Items->Objects[Index]);
    // draw the file's icon in the listbox
    FImages->Draw(Canvas, Rect.Left+2, Rect.Top+2, ShellItem->ImageIndex,
      true);
    Offset += 18;
    }
  int Texty = Canvas->TextHeight(Items->Strings[Index]);
  Texty = ((ItemHeight - Texty) / 2) + 1;
  // now draw the text
  Canvas->TextOut(Rect.Left + Offset, Rect.Top + Texty,  Items->Strings[Index]);
}
//--------------------------------------------------------------------------
void __fastcall TSHFileListBox::DblClick(void)
{
  if(FCanLaunch)
    {
    int ii=0;
    // go through the list and find which item is selected
    for(ii=0; ii < Items->Count; ii++)
      {
      if(Selected[ii])
        {
        AnsiString str = Items->Strings[ii];
        ShellExecute(Handle, "open",  str.c_str(), 0, 0, SW_SHOWDEFAULT);
        }
      }
    }
  // fire the OnDblClick event
  if(FOnDblClick)
    FOnDblClick(this);
}
//--------------------------------------------------------------------------
void __fastcall TSHFileListBox::MouseUp(TMouseButton Button, TShiftState Shift,
  int X, int Y)
{
  if(!FRightBtnSel)
    return;
```

LISTING 4.55   Continued

```
  TPoint ItemPos = Point(X,Y);
  // is there an item under the mouse ?
  int Index = ItemAtPos(ItemPos, true);
  // if not just return
  if(Index == -1)
    return;
  // else select the item
  Perform(LB_SETCURSEL, (WPARAM)Index, 0);
}
//------------------------------------------------------------------------
// ValidCtrCheck is used to assure that the components created do not have
// any pure virtual functions.
//
static inline void ValidCtrCheck(TSHFileListBox *)
{
  new TSHFileListBox (NULL);
}
```

Creating Custom Data-Aware Components

Just as with any other custom component, it is important to decide from the start which ancestor will be used for the creation of a data-aware component. In this section, we are going to look at extending the TMaskEdit edit component so that it will read data from a datasource and display it in the masked format provided. This type of control is known as a *data-browsing control*. We will then extend this control further to make it a data-aware control, meaning that changes to the field or database will be reflected in both directions.

Making the Control Read-Only

The control we are going to create already has ReadOnly, a read-only property, so we don't have to create it. If your component doesn't, create the property as you would for any other component.

If our component did not already have the ReadOnly property, we would create it as shown in Listing 4.56 (note that this code is not required for this component).

LISTING 4.56   Creating a Read-Only Property

```
class PACKAGE TDBMaskEdit : public TMaskEdit
{
private:
    bool FReadOnly;
```

LISTING 4.56   Continued

```
protected:
public:
    __fastcall TDBMaskEdit(TComponent* Owner);
__published:
    __property ReadOnly = {read = FReadOnly, write = FReadOnly,
    default = true};
};
```

In the constructor we would set the default value of the property.

```
__fastcall TDBMaskEdit::TDBMaskEdit(TComponent* Owner)
  : TMaskEdit(Owner)
{
    FReadOnly = true;
}
```

Finally, we need to ensure that the component acts as a read-only control. You need to override the method normally associated with the user accessing the control. If we were creating a data-aware grid, it would be the SelectCell() method in which you would check the value of the ReadOnly property and act accordingly. If the value of ReadOnly is false, you call the inherited method, otherwise, just return.

If the TMaskEdit control had a SelectEdit() method, the code would look like this:

```
bool __fastcall TDBMaskEdit::SelectEdit(void)
{
    if(FReadOnly)
        return(false);
    else
        return(TMaskEdit::SelectEdit());
}
```

In this case, we don't have to worry about the ReadOnly property. TMaskEdit already has one.

Establishing the Link
For our control to become data aware, we need to provide it the data link required to communicate with a data member of a database. This data link class is called TFieldDataLink.

A data-aware control owns its data link class. It is the control's responsibility to create, initialize, and destroy the data link.

Establishing the link requires three steps:

1. Declare the data link class as a member of the control

2. Declare the read and write access properties as appropriate

3. Initialize the data link

Declare the Data Link   The data link is a class of type `TFieldDataLink` and requires `DBCTRLS.HPP` to be included in the header file.

```
#include <DBCtrls.hpp>

class PACKAGE TDBMaskEdit : public TMaskEdit
{
private:
    TFieldDataLink *FDataLink;
  ...
};
```

Our data-aware component now requires `DataSource` and `DataField` properties (just like all other data-aware controls). These properties use pass-through methods to access properties of the data link class. This enables the control and its data link to share the same datasource and field.

Declare `read` and `write` Access   The access you allow your control is governed by the declaration of the properties themselves. We are going to give our component full access. It has a `ReadOnly` property that will automatically take care of the read-only option because the user will be unable to edit the control. Note that this will not stop the developer from writing code to write directly to the linked field of the database via this control. If you require read-only access, simply leave out the `write` option.

The code in Listings 4.57 and 4.58 shows the declaration of the properties and their corresponding `read` and `write` implementation methods.

LISTING 4.57   The `TDBMaskEdit` Class Declaration from the Header File

```
class PACKAGE TDBMaskEdit : public TMaskEdit
{
private:
    ...
    AnsiString __fastcall GetDataField(void);
    TDataSource* __fastcall GetDataSource(void);
    void __fastcall SetDataField(AnsiString pDataField);
    void __fastcall SetDataSource(TDataSource *pDataSource);
```

LISTING 4.57   Continued

```
    . . .
__published:
    __property AnsiString DataField = {read = GetDataField,
      write = SetDataField, nodefault};
    __property TDataSource *DataSource = {read = GetDataSource,
      write = SetDataSource,  nodefault};
};
```

LISTING 4.58   The TDBMaskEdit Methods from the Source File

```
AnsiString __fastcall TDBMaskEdit::GetDataField(void)
{
    return(FDataLink->FieldName);
}


TDataSource * __fastcall TDBMaskEdit::GetDataSource(void)
{
    return(FDataLink->DataSource);
}


void __fastcall TDBMaskEdit::SetDataField(AnsiString pDataField)
{
    FDataLink->FieldName = pDataField;
}


void __fastcall TDBMaskEdit::SetDataSource(TDataSource *pDataSource)
{
    if(pDataSource != NULL)
        pDataSource->FreeNotification(this);

    FDataLink->DataSource = pDataSource;
}
```

The only code here that requires additional explanation is the FreeNotification()
method of pDataSource. C++Builder maintains an internal list of objects so that all
other objects can be notified when the object is about to be destroyed. The
FreeNotification() method is called automatically for components on the same
form, but in this case there is a chance that a component on another form (such as a
data module) has references to it. As a result, we need to call FreeNotification() so
that the object can be added to the internal list for all other forms.

Initialize the Data Link   You might think everything that needs to be done *has* been done. If you attempt to compile this component and add it to a form, you will find access violations reported in the Object Inspector for the DataField and DataSource properties. The reason is that the internal FieldDataLink object has not been instantiated.

Add the following declaration to the public section of the class's header file:

```
__fastcall ~TDBMaskEdit(void);
```

Add the following code to the component's constructor and destructor:

```
__fastcall TDBMaskEdit::TDBMaskEdit(TComponent* Owner)
  : TMaskEdit(Owner)
{
    FDataLink = new TFieldDataLink();
    FDataLink->Control = this;
}


__fastcall TDBMaskEdit::~TDBMaskEdit(void)
{
    if(FDataLink)
        {
        FDataLink->Control = 0;
        FDataLink->OnUpdateData = 0;
        delete FDataLink;
    }
}
```

The Control property of FDataLink is of type TComponent. This property must be set to the component that uses the TFieldDataLink object to manage its link to a TField object. We need to set the Control property to this to indicate that this component is responsible for the link.

Accessing the TObject is achieved by adding a read-only property. Add the property to the public section of the class definition.

```
__property TField *Field = {read = GetField};
```

Add the GetField declaration to the private section:

```
TField * __fastcall GetField(void);
```

Add the following code to the source file:

```
TField * __fastcall TDBMaskEdit::GetField(void)
```

```
{
    return(FDataLink->Field);
}
```

Using the OnDataChange **Event**

So far we have created a component that can link to a datasource, but doesn't yet respond to data changes. We are now going to add code that enables the control to respond to changes in the field, such as moving to a new record.

Data link classes have an OnDataChange event that is called when the datasource indicates a change to the data. To give our component the capability to respond to these changes, we add a method and assign it to the OnDataChange event.

> **NOTE**
>
> TDataLink is a helper class used by data-aware objects. Look in the online help files that ship with C++Builder for a listing of its properties, methods, and events.

The OnDataChange event is of type TNotifyEvent, so we need to add our method with the same prototype. Add the following line of code to the private section of the component header.

```
class PACKAGE TDBMaskEdit : public TMaskEdit
{
private:
    // …
    void __fastcall DataChange(TObject *Sender);
}
```

We need to assign the DataChange() method to the OnDataChange event in the constructor. We also remove this assignment in the component destructor.

```
__fastcall TDBMaskEdit::TDBMaskEdit(TComponent* Owner)
    : TMaskEdit(Owner)
{
    FDataLink = new TFieldDataLink();
    FDataLink->Control = this;
    FDataLink->OnDataChange = DataChange;
}

__fastcall TDBMaskEdit::~TDBMaskEdit(void)
{
    if(FDataLink)
```

```
    {
    FDataLink->Control = 0;
    FDataLink->OnUpdateData = 0;
    FDataLink->OnDataChange = 0;
    delete FDataLink;
    }
}
```

Finally, define the DataChange() method as shown in the following code:

```
void __fastcall TDBMaskEdit::DataChange(TObject *Sender)
{
    if(!FDataLink->Field)
        {
        if(ComponentState.Contains(csDesigning))
            Text = Name;
        else
            Text = "";
        }
    else
        Text = FDataLink->Field->AsString;
}
```

The DataChange() method first checks to see if the data link is pointing to a datasource (and field). If there is no valid pointer, the Text property (a member of the inherited component) is set to an empty string (at runtime) or the control name (at design time). If a valid field is set, the Text property is set to the value of the field's content via the AsString property of the TField object.

You now have a data-browsing control, so-called because it is capable only of displaying data changes in a datasource. It's now time to turn this component into a data-editing control.

Changing to a Data-Editing Control

Turning a data-browsing control into a data-editing control requires additional code to respond to key and mouse events. This enables any changes made to the control to be reflected in the underlying field of the linked database.

The ReadOnly Property   When a user places a data-editing control into his project, he expects the control *not* to be read-only. The default value for the ReadOnly property of TMaskEdit (the inherited class) is false, so we have nothing further to do. If you create a component that has a custom ReadOnly property added, be sure to set the default value to false.

Keyboard and Mouse Events   If you refer to the controls.hpp file, you will find protected methods of TMaskEdit called KeyDown() and MouseDown(). These methods respond to the corresponding window messages (WM_KEYDOWN, WM_LBUTTONDOWN, WM_MBUTTONDOWN, and WM_RBUTTONDOWN) and call the appropriate event if the user defines one.

To override these methods, add the KeyDown() and MouseDown() methods to the TDBMaskEdit class. Take the declarations from the controls.hpp file.

```
virtual void __fastcall MouseDown(TMouseButton, TShiftState Shift, int X,
  int Y);
virtual void __fastcall KeyDown(unsigned short &Key, TShiftState Shift);
```

Refer to the controls.hpp file in your C++ Builder installation (or the help file) to see the original declaration.

Next we add the source code, shown in Listing 4.59.

LISTING 4.59   The MouseDown() and KeyDown() Methods

```
void __fastcall TDBMaskEdit::MouseDown(TMouseButton Button, TShiftState Shift,
  int X, int Y)
{
    if(!ReadOnly && FDataLink->Edit())
        TMaskEdit::MouseDown(Button, Shift, X, Y);
    else
        {
        if(OnMouseDown)
            OnMouseDown(this, Button, Shift, X , Y);
        }
}


void __fastcall TDBMaskEdit::KeyDown(unsigned short &Key, TShiftState Shift)
{
    Set<unsigned short, VK_PRIOR, VK_DOWN> Keys;
    Keys = Keys << VK_PRIOR << VK_NEXT << VK_END << VK_HOME << VK_LEFT
       << VK_UP << VK_RIGHT << VK_DOWN;

    if(!ReadOnly && (Keys.Contains(Key)) && FDataLink->Edit())
        TMaskEdit::KeyDown(Key, Shift);
    else
        {
        if(OnKeyDown)
            OnKeyDown(this,  Key, Shift);
        }
}
```

In both cases, we check to make sure the component is not read-only and the FieldDataLink is in edit mode. The KeyDown() method also checks for any cursor control keys (defined in winuser.h). If all checks pass, the field can be edited, so the inherited method is called. This method will automatically call the associated user event if one is defined. If the field cannot be edited, the user event is executed (if one exists).

Working Toward a Dataset Update

If the user modifies the contents of the data-aware control, the change must be reflected in the field. Similarly, if the field value is altered, the data-aware control will require a corresponding update.

The TDBMaskEdit control already has a DataChange() method that is called by the TFieldDataLink OnDataChange event. This method reflects the change of the field value in the TDBMaskEdit control. This takes care of the first scenario.

Now we need to update the field value when the user modifies the contents of the control. The TFieldDataLink class has an OnUpdateData event where the data-aware control can write any pending edits to the record in the dataset. We can now create an UpdateData() method for TDBMaskEdit and assign this method to the OnUpdateData event of the TFieldDataLink class.

Add the declaration for our UpdateData() method to the TDBMaskEdit control, as shown in the following code:

```
void __fastcall UpdateData(TObject *Sender);
```

Assign this method to the TFieldDataLink OnUpdateData event in the constructor:

```
__fastcall TDBMaskEdit::TDBMaskEdit(TComponent* Owner)
  : TMaskEdit(Owner)
{
    FDataLink = new TFieldDataLink();
    FDataLink->Control = this;
    FDataLink->OnUpdateData = UpdateData;
    FDataLink->OnDataChange = DataChange;
}
```

Set the field value to the current contents of the TDBMaskEdit control:

```
void __fastcall TDBMaskEdit::UpdateData(TObject *Sender)
{
    if(FDataLink->CanModify)
        FDataLink->Field->AsString = Text;
}
```

The TDBMaskEdit control is a descendant of TMaskEdit, which happens to be a descendant of the TCustomEdit class. This class has a protected Change() method that is triggered by Windows events. This method then triggers the OnChange event.

We are going to override the Change() method so that it updates the dataset before calling the inherited method. In the protected section of the TDBMaskEdit class, add the following method:

```
DYNAMIC void __fastcall Change(void);
```

Add the Change() method in Listing 4.60 to the source code.

LISTING 4.60   The Change() Method

```
void __fastcall TDBMaskEdit::Change(void)
{
    if(FDataLink)
        {
        // we need to see if the datasource is in edit mode
        // if not then we need to save the current value because
        // placing the datasource into edit mode will change the
        // current value to that already present in the table

        AnsiString ChangedValue = Text;

        // get cursor position too
        int CursorPosition = SelStart;

        // need to be in edit mode
        if(FDataLink->CanModify && FDataLink->Edit())
            {
            Text = ChangedValue;        // just in case we were not in edit mode
            SelStart = CursorPosition;
            FDataLink->Modified();      // posting a change (the datasource
                                        // is not put back into edit mode)

            }
        }

    TMaskEdit::Change ();
}
```

This change notifies the TFieldDataLink class that modifications have been made and finishes up by calling the inherited Change() method.

The final step is to provide for when focus is moved away from the control. The TWinControl class responds to the CM_EXIT message by generating an OnExit event.

We can also respond to this message as a method of updating the record of the linked dataset. Creating a message map in the TDBMaskEdit class does this. Add the following code to the private section:

```
void __fastcall CMExit(TWMNoParams Message);


BEGIN_MESSAGE_MAP
  MESSAGE_HANDLER(CM_EXIT, TWMNoParams, CMExit)
END_MESSAGE_MAP(TMaskEdit)
```

This message map indicates that the CMExit() method will be called in response to a CM_EXIT message with the relevant information passed in the TWMNoParams structure.

The CMExit() method is added to the source file.

```
void __fastcall TDBMaskEdit::CMExit(void)
{
    try
        {
        ValidateEdit();
        if(FDataLink && FDataLink->CanModify)
            FDataLink->UpdateRecord();
        }

    catch(...)
        {
        SetFocus();
        throw;
        }
}
```

This attempts to validate the contents of the field against the defined mask. If the datasource can be modified, the record is updated in the dataset. If an exception is raised, the cursor is positioned back in the control that caused the problem, and the exception is raised again so the application can handle it.

Adding a Final Message
C++Builder has a component called TDBCtrlGrid. This control displays records from a datasource in a free-form layout. When this component updates its datasource, it sends out the message CM_GETDATALINK. If you perform a search for this in the C++Builder header files, you'll find a message map defined in all of the database

controls. Following this with the corresponding .pas file, you will find message handlers such as the following:

```
procedure TDBEdit.CMGetDataLink(var Message: TMessage);
begin
  Message.Result := Integer(FDataLink);
end;
```

We can add this support to our component by adding the message map, declaring the method, and implementing the message handler.

In the private section

```
void __fastcall CMGetDataLink(TMessage Message);
```

In the public section, modify the message map to look like the following:

```
BEGIN_MESSAGE_MAP
  MESSAGE_HANDLER(CM_EXIT, TWMNoParams, CMExit)
  MESSAGE_HANDLER(CM_GETDATALINK, TMessage, CMGetDataLink)
END_MESSAGE_MAP(TMaskEdit)
```

Finally, implement the method in the source file:

```
void __fastcall TDBMaskEdit::CMGetDataLink(TMessage Message)
{
    Message.Result = (int)FDataLink;
}
```

And that's it. We now have a complete data-aware control that behaves just like any other data control.

Registering Components

Registering components is a straightforward, multistage procedure. The first stage is simple. You must ensure that any component you want to install onto the Component Palette does not contain any pure virtual (or pure DYNAMIC) functions—in other words, functions of the following form:

```
virtual ReturnType __fastcall FunctionName(ParameterList) = 0;
```

Note that the __fastcall keyword is not a requirement of pure virtual functions, but it will be present in component member functions. This is why it is shown.

You can check for pure virtual functions manually by examining the class definition for the component, or you can call the function ValidCtrCheck(), passing a pointer to your component as an argument. The `ValidCtrCheck()` function is placed anywhere in the implementation file. For a component called TcustomComponent, it is of the form

```
static inline void ValidCtrCheck(TCustomComponent *)
{
    new TCustomComponent(NULL);
}
```

All this function does is try to create an instance of TCustomComponent. Because you cannot create an instance of a class with a pure virtual function, the compiler will give the following compilation errors:

```
E2352 Cannot create instance of abstract class 'TCustomComponent'
E2353 Class 'TCustomComponent' is abstract because of 'function'
```

The second error will identify the pure virtual function. Both errors refer to this line:

```
new TCustomComponent(NULL);
```

Using this function is often not necessary because it is not likely you will create a pure virtual function by accident. However, when you use the IDE to create a new component, this function is automatically added to the implementation file. Then, you might as well leave it there just in case.

After you have determined that your component is not an abstract base class and that it can be instantiated from, you can now write the code to perform the actual registration. To do this, you must write a `Register()` function. The `Register()` function *must* be enclosed in a namespace that is the same as the name of the file in which it is contained. There is one proviso that must be met. The first letter of the name-space *must* be in uppercase, and the remaining letters *must* be in lowercase. Hence, the `Register()` function must appear in your code in the following format:

```
namespace Thenameofthefilethisisin
{
    void __fastcall PACKAGE Register()
    {
        // Registration code goes here
    }
}
```

You must not forget the PACKAGE macro in front of the `Register()` function. Now that the `Register()` function is in place, it requires only that the component (or components) that we want to register is registered. To do this, use the `RegisterComponents()` function. This is declared in `$(BCB)\Include\Vcl\Classes.hpp` as

```
extern PACKAGE void __fastcall RegisterComponents(const AnsiString Page,
                                    TMetaClass* const * ComponentClasses,
                                    const int ComponentClasses_Size);
```

RegisterComponents() expects two things to be passed to it: an AnsiString representing the name of the palette page onto which the component is to be installed, and an open array of TMetaClass pointers to the components to be installed. If the AnsiString value for Page does not match one of the palette pages already present in the Component Palette, a new page is created with the name of the AnsiString passed. The value of this argument can be obtained from a string resource if required, allowing different strings to be used for different locales.

The TMetaClass* open array requires more thought. There are essentially two ways of doing this: Use the OPENARRAY macro or create the array by hand. Let's look at an example that illustrates both approaches.

Consider that we want to register three components: TCustomComponent1, TCustomComponent2, and TCustomComponent3. We want to register these onto a new palette page, MyCustomComponents. First, we must obtain the TMetaClass* for each of the three components. We do this by using the __classid operator, for example:

```
__classid(TCustomComponent1)
```

Using the OPENARRAY macro, we can write the RegisterComponents() function as follows:

```
RegisterComponents("MyCustomComponents",
                OPENARRAY( TMetaClass*,
                        ( __classid(TCustomComponent1),
                          __classid(TCustomComponent2),
                          __classid(TCustomComponent3) ) ) );
```

We could use TComponentClass instead of TMetaClass* because it is a typedef for TMetaClass*, declared in $(BCB)\Include\Vcl\Classes.hpp as

```
typedef TMetaClass* TComponentClass;
```

Note that you are restricted to registering a maximum of 19 arguments (components) in any single RegisterComponents call because limitations of the OPENARRAY macro. Normally this is not a problem.

The other approach is to declare and initialize an array of TMetaClass* (or TComponentClass) by hand:

```
TMetaClass Components[3] = { __classid(TCustomComponent1),
                            __classid(TCustomComponent2),
                            __classid(TCustomComponent3) };
```

We then pass this to the `RegisterComponents()` function as before, but this time we must also pass the value of the last valid index for the array, in this case 2:

```
RegisterComponents("MyCustomComponents", Components, 2);
```

The final function call is simpler, but there is a greater chance of error in passing an incorrect value for the last parameter.

We can now see what a complete `Register()` function looks like:

```
namespace Thenameofthefilethisisin
{
    void __fastcall PACKAGE Register()
    {
        RegisterComponents("MyCustomComponents",
                            OPENARRAY( TMetaClass*,
                                      ( __classid(TCustomComponent1),
                                        __classid(TCustomComponent2),
                                        __classid(TCustomComponent3) ) ) );
    }
}
```

Remember that you can have as many `RegisterComponents()` functions in the `Register()` function as required. You can also include other registrations such as those for property and component editors. This is the subject of the next chapter. You can place the component registration in the implementation file of the component, but typically the registration code should be isolated from the component implementation.

The Streaming Mechanism

C++Builder is referred to as a Rapid Application Development (RAD) environment. This is partly because of the GUI interface to the developer and the object-orientated nature of the language itself. In addition, C++Builder uses a streaming (read and write) mechanism to maintain property settings.

During design time, you set various properties of components. The IDE stores these settings (described in more detail later) as part of the form on which these components belong. The forms are saved as part of the project in a file with a .dfm extension. What is stored in the form's file is loaded again at runtime. In other words, the properties are persistent.

The __published area is used to define properties that will be persisted. Such "storable" properties are written to the form file at design time save.

When a component is created, the developer gives it a set of default values for its published properties. These defaults are assigned in the constructor of the component. At runtime, the user modifies these properties via the Object Inspector. In fact, every property shown in the Object Inspector is a `published` property. Properties can be declared in the `public` section of a component's definition (the class), but these will be available only at runtime.

Not all properties that are published are required to be stored, however. Imagine two properties, one with a default value of 10 and the other defined not to be stored.

```
__property int SomeProperty1 = {read=FProp1, write=FProp1, default=10};
__property AnsiString SomeProperty2 = {read=FProp2, stored=false};
```

The declaration of `SomeProperty1` does not set its value to 10. This is always done in the constructor. The `default` keyword is used to tell the IDE to store the value of this property in the form file only if it has a value other than 10.

The second property, `SomeProperty2`, is declared to not store its value in the form file. An example of this might be a property to indicate the current version for the component. Because the version number will not change, it does not need to be stored in the form.

When the component is saved, the property information that differs from the default is written to the form file. When a project is opened again, an instance of each component is created, the component properties are set to their defined defaults, and the stored, nondefault values are read and assigned.

Component construction and the associated property-streaming processes are something that the programmer often doesn't have to worry about.

Advanced Streaming Requirements

Component properties can be numerical, character, strings, enumerated types (including Boolean), sets, or more complex objects such as custom-defined structs and classes. C++Builder has built-in handling for the streaming of simple data types. Support for streaming custom objects, such as class properties, is provided if that class is derived from `TPersistent`.

`TPersistent` provides the capability to assign objects to other objects and enable the reading and writing of their properties to and from a stream. Additional information can be found in the index of the online help under the topic "TPersistent."

Some property types, such as arrays, require their own property editor. Without an editor, the Object Inspector is unable to provide the programmer an interface to edit the contents of the property. Refer to Chapter 5, for more information on property editors.

Streaming Unpublished Properties

So far we have learned that the Object Inspector provides the programmer a design-time interface to the published properties of a component. This is the default behavior of components, but we are not limited to this. We have also discovered that properties derived from TPersistent have the capability to stream to and from a form file. This means we have the ability to create persistent properties that do not appear in the Object Inspector. Additionally, we can create streaming methods for properties that C++Builder does not know how to read or write.

Saving an unpublished property is achieved by adding code to tell C++Builder how to read and write the property's value. This is accomplished in a two-step process.

- Override the DefineProperties() method. The previously defined methods are passed to what is known as a *filer object*.

- Create methods to read and write the property value.

We have already ascertained that published properties are automatically streamed to the form file. Using read and write methods defined for the various property types handles this. The property names and the methods used to perform the streaming are defined by the DefineProperties() method. When you want to stream a nonpublished property, you need to tell C++Builder. This is done by overriding the DefineProperties() method.

Listing 4.61 provides an example component, TSampleComp, which has three unpublished properties. The component is capable of streaming the properties by the methods provided. It creates an instance of a second component called TComp at runtime and is referenced via the property Comp3. Because this component is not dropped onto a form by the developer, the properties for it are not automatically streamed to the form file. We will provide our component with the code it requires to stream this information as well.

LISTING 4.61   A Component to Stream Unpublished Properties

```
// A minimum class declaration to get the example to compile
class TComp : public TComponent
{
public:
   __fastcall TComp::TComp(TComponent *Owner) : TComponent(OWner) {}
};


class TSampleComp : public TComponent
{
private:
```

LISTING 4.61   Continued

```
    int FProp1;
    AnsiString FProp2;
    TComp *FComp3;

    void __fastcall ReadProp1(TReader *Reader);
    void __fastcall WriteProp1(TWriter *Writer);
    void __fastcall ReadProp2(TReader *Reader);
    void __fastcall WriteProp2(TWriter *Writer);
    void __fastcall ReadComp3(TReader *Reader);
    void __fastcall WriteComp3(TWriter *Writer);

protected:
    void __fastcall DefineProperties(TFiler *Filer);

public:

    __fastcall TSampleComp(TComponent* Owner);
    __fastcall ~TSampleComp(void);

    __property int Prop1 = {read = FProp1, write = FProp1, default = 10};
    __property AnsiString Prop2 = {read = FProp2, write = FProp2, nodefault};
    __property TComp *Comp3 = {read = FComp3, write = FComp3};
};

void __fastcall TSampleComp::TSampleComp(TComponent* Owner) :   TComponent(Owner)
{
FProp1 = 10;                    // The default
FComp3 = new TComp(NULL); // we will need to stream this
}

void __fastcall TSampleComp::~TSampleComp (void)
{
if(FComp3)
    delete FComp3;
}

void __fastcall TSampleComp::DefineProperties(TFiler *Filer)
{
// Call the base method first
TComponent::DefineProperties(Filer);
```

LISTING 4.61   Continued

```
Filer->DefineProperty("Prop1", ReadProp1, WriteProp1, (FProp1 != 10));
Filer->DefineProperty("Prop2", ReadProp2, WriteProp2, (FProp2 != ""));

// need to determine if the properties for Comp3 need to be written

bool WriteValue;
if(Filer->Ancestor) // check for inherited value
  {
  TSampleComp *FilerComp = dynamic_cast<TSampleComp *>(Filer->Ancestor);

  if(FilerComp->Comp3 == NULL)
    WriteValue = (Comp3 != NULL);
  else
    {
    if((Comp3 == NULL) || (FilerComp->Comp3->Name != Comp3->Name))
      WriteValue = true;
    else
      WriteValue = false;
    }
  }
else     // no inherited value, write property if not null
  WriteValue = (Comp3 != NULL);

Filer->DefineProperty("Comp3", ReadComp3, WriteComp3, WriteValue);
}

void __fastcall TSampleComp::ReadProp1(TReader *Reader)
{
Prop1 = Reader->ReadInteger();
}

void __fastcall TSampleComp::WriteProp1(TWriter *Writer)
{
Writer->WriteInteger(FProp1);
}

void __fastcall TSampleComp::ReadProp2(TReader *Reader)
{
FProp2 = Reader->ReadString();
}
```

LISTING 4.61   Continued

```
void __fastcall TSampleComp::WriteProp2(TWriter *Writer)
{
Writer->WriteString(FProp2);
}


void __fastcall TSampleComp::ReadComp3(TReader *Reader)
{
if(Reader->ReadBoolean())
    FComp3 = (TComp *)Reader->ReadComponent(NULL);
}


void __fastcall TSampleComp::WriteComp3(TWriter *Writer)
{
if(FComp3)
  {
  Writer->WriteBoolean(true);
  Writer->WriteComponent(Comp3);
  }
else
  Writer->WriteBoolean (false);
}
```

The DefineProperties() method contains these two lines of code to register the first two properties:

```
Filer->DefineProperty("Prop1", ReadProp1, WriteProp1, (FProp1 != 10));
Filer->DefineProperty("Prop2", ReadProp2, WriteProp2, (FProp2 != ""));
```

This tells C++Builder to use the read-and-write methods provided when streaming these properties. The last parameter is a flag to indicate if we have data to store. Prop1 and Prop2 need to be stored only if their values differ from the default value.

The Comp3 property is different and will require some additional explanation. This property is different from other properties because it is a component (instantiated by the class at runtime) rather than a data type. Listing 4.62 presents the section of code responsible for determining if this property requires streaming.

LISTING 4.62 Determining If a Property That Is a Component Requires Streaming

```
bool WriteValue;
if(Filer->Ancestor) // check for inherited value
  {
  TSampleComp *FilerComp = dynamic_cast<TSampleComp *>(Filer->Ancestor);

  if(FilerComp->Comp3 == NULL)
    WriteValue = (Comp3 != NULL);
  else
    {
    if((Comp3 == NULL) || (FilerComp->Comp3->Name != Comp3->Name))
      WriteValue = true;
    else
      WriteValue = false;
    }
  }
else    // no inherited value, write property if not null
  WriteValue = (Comp3 != NULL);

Filer->DefineProperty("Comp3", ReadComp3, WriteComp3, WriteValue);
```

This property represents a component instantiated at runtime. Because the component is not dropped onto a form, the default mechanism of streaming the properties is not performed. This implementation of the `DefineProperties()` method will take care of that for us.

First we need to determine if the filer's `Ancestor` property is `true` to avoid saving a property value in inherited forms. If there is no inherited value, we will stream the property (which is a component) if `Comp3` is not `NULL`.

If the filer's `Ancestor` property is `true`, we need to look at the `Comp3` property of the ancestor next. If this property is `NULL`, we stream our property (`TSampleComp->Comp3`) if it is not `NULL`. If the filer's `Ancestor Comp3` property is not `NULL`, we perform two final checks. If our property (`TsampleComp->Comp3`) is `NULL` or the name of our `Comp3` property is different than the ancestor's, we will stream the property (a component).

Finally, we define our property, using `DefineProperty()` as previously explained.

We have seen the uses of the `DefineProperty()` method, which deals with data types such as integers, strings, chars, Booleans, and enumerated types. There is another method, `DefineBinaryProperty()`, that is designed to be used for the streaming of binary information such as graphics and sound files. Refer to the "DefineBinaryProperty" section of "TWriter" in the online help index for additional information on this.

Distributing Components

When considering distribution of your components, the file of most interest to you is the `.bpl` file. This is the package library that the IDE will use to make the components available at design time.

WARNING

Whenever you build your packages, be sure to check the Option source (Edit, Option, Source) of the package and remove any unnecessary library file entries in the `<LIBRARIES>` and `<SPARELIBS>` sections. If this is not done, you might find that you have many frustrated users looking for a `.lib` file that your package references, but that they don't have. However, because your package references the `.lib` file, they will not be able to use the package without it, even though it is not required for the correct operation of the package.

The files that must be distributed for each package to be useable are shown in Figure 4.6.

As can be seen from Figure 4.6, in addition to the `.bpl`, `.bpi`, and `.lib` files previously mentioned, the header (`.h`) files for each unit appearing in the runtime-only package's `Contains` section must also be distributed. You should also distribute the header files of the units used in the design time-only package; the exception to this is the header file for the registration unit itself—this is normally empty and is of no use. Typically, though, you would distribute the source for the registration unit so that the users of your components can see what changes your package will make to the IDE. Note that `.rc` files are shown as the resource files to store the Component Palette bitmaps for the components. There are alternatives to this: `.res` files or `.dcr` files can be used. This is discussed in the "Creating Component Palette Bitmaps" section later in this chapter. Consider also that if you do ship custom property and component editors, it should be possible for the user to derive new editors from them.

Remember from the "Understanding and Using Packages" section in Chapter 2, "C++Builder Projects and More on the IDE," that the `.lib` file for a package is effectively a collection of the package unit's `.obj` files. Distributing either the `.lib` file for the runtime-only package (that containing the source for the component(s)) or the `.obj` files for the component(s) will enable the components to be statically linked to the application, if the user so desires. The `.lib` file has the advantage that all the components' `.obj` files are contained in a single file, making file maintenance easier.

Where Distributed Files Should Be Placed

Where your distribution files are placed on the target computer can affect how easy they are to use. Using the default directories that C++Builder uses, shown in Figure 4.7, effectively guarantees that the user will not have to edit his project's directory settings. Most people prefer that third-party components not be placed in to these directories. However, an appreciation of the structure that C++Builder uses is useful.

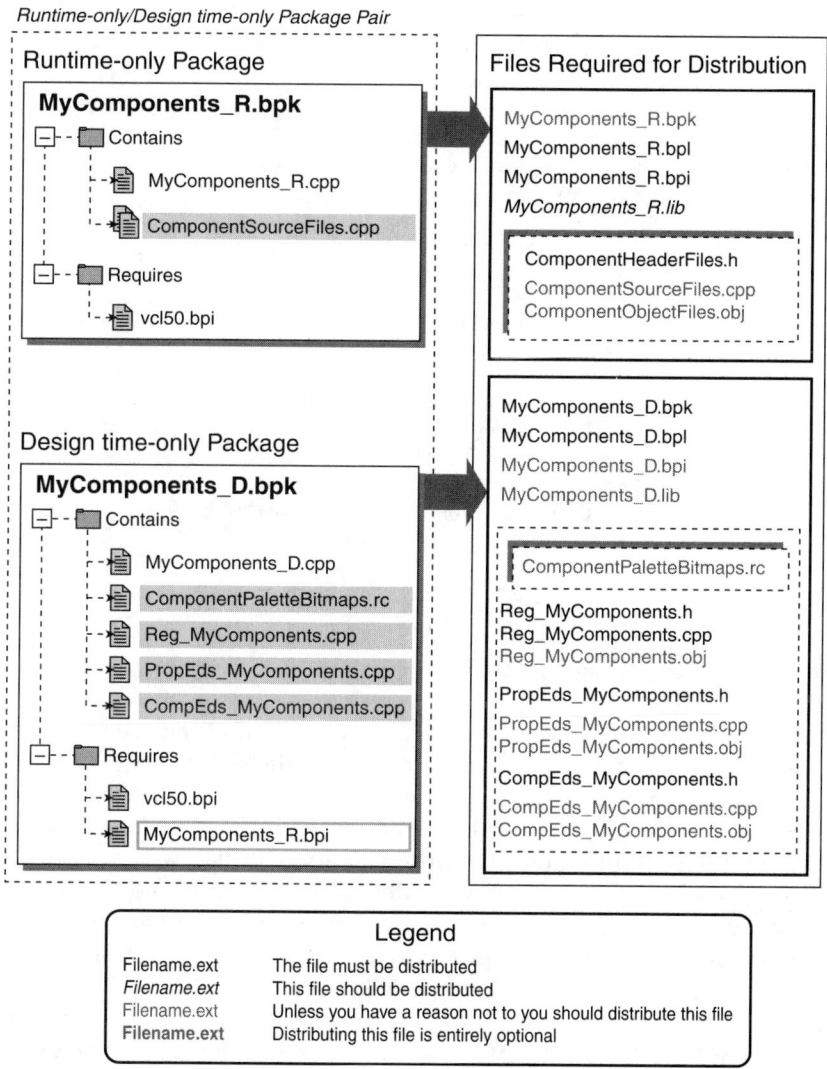

FIGURE 4.6   Files required for package distribution.

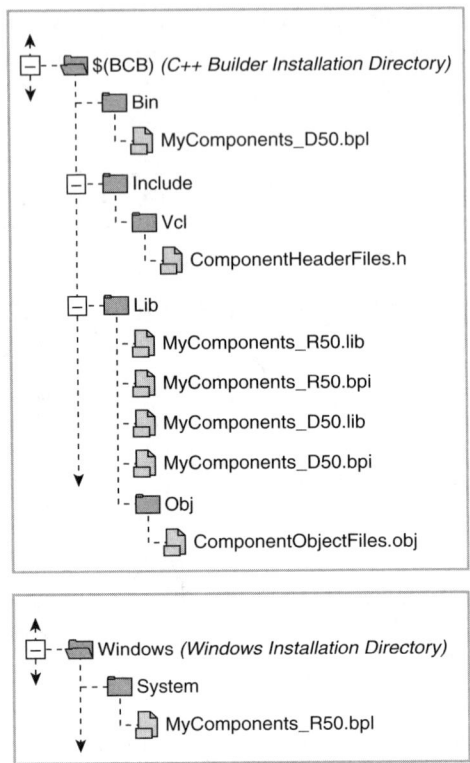

FIGURE 4.7   Default package directories.

Note that the naming convention shown in Figure 4.7 has been used for consistency. Also, source modules have not been shown because their placement is only of concern when compiling the package. The simplest alternative to using the default directories of Figure 4.7 is to place all the files belonging to a package into a single directory, with the exception of the runtime library .bpl files, which should be placed in Windows\System or an equivalent directory. This makes adding paths to a project's directory settings easier. For linking, the linker must be able to find the .bpi and .lib files of the runtime package (assuming a runtime/design time pair), so the directory that contains these should be added to the global Library Path setting (Tools, Environment Options, Library). This can also be modified by editing the Registry key HKEY_CURRENT_USER\Software\Borland\C++Builder\6.0\Library\Search Path, where 6.0 is the version number of C++Builder (it could be 1.0, 3.0, or 5.0). Remember that if the directory (or directories) that contain your components is off the main C++Builder installation directory, you can use the $(BCB) string to represent the installation directory in any pathnames required.

Naming Packages and Package Units

The naming of packages and package units is of crucial importance when preparing components for distribution. Assuming that a runtime-only/design time-only package pair (or similar model) is adopted for packaging the components, we must name the runtime-only package (or packages) so that it can be distinguished from the design time-only registration package. Typically, an _R or _RTP is appended to runtime-only package names and _D or _DTP is appended to design time-only package names. An underscore is entirely optional.

Another consideration is that you should include a number that represents the version of the VCL that was used in the creation of the package. In the case of packages made for C++Builder 6, this would be 60 (the version number of the VCL in C++Builder 6). This makes it immediately obvious for which version of C++Builder the package is intended. For example, runtime-only packages could have _R60 appended to their names and design time-only packages could have _D60 appended to their names (again the underscore is optional). As long as this information is presented in some obvious way, the exact approach taken is immaterial. For example, the convention used for the VCL packages is to replace the V of VCL with a D (making DCL) when the package is a design time-only package. The version number is appended to the end of the package name in both cases. For example, the package names for data access and data control components are VCLDB50.bpl and DCLDB50.bpl for the runtime-only and design time-only packages, respectively.

In addition to the naming of packages to reflect how the package should be used (design time or runtime), and the version of the VCL for which they are designed, the names must also be unique. It is not possible to install or use a package whose name clashes with an existing package in the same application.

The naming of units inside a package is equally as important as that of the package itself. Before we consider the possibilities, we must be aware that units exported from a package *must be unique* for any application that uses them (it is not possible to have units of the same name in more than one package if those packages are used simultaneously by the same application), and this includes the IDE.

Two cases must be considered. The first is the naming of units that would normally only be found in a design time-only package (units containing registration code and units containing property and component editors). The second is the naming of units normally found only in a runtime-only package (the units that contain the source for components).

When naming units in the design time-only package, you should include the package name in the unit name. This ensures that the unit name will be unique. For example, the unit containing the registration code could be called Registration_PackageName.cpp. Changing the word order, replacing Registration with

Reg (and so on), and using underscores are all matters of personal choice; the essential thing is to keep the purpose of the unit clear and the name unique. Because the package must be unique, including this in the unit name helps ensure that it too will be unique. Therefore, for a design time-only package called NewComponentsD60, the following are all suitable names for the registration unit of the package:

```
Reg_NewComponentsD60
RegNewComponentsD60
Registration_NewComponentsD60
RegistrationNewComponentsD60
```

Many more possibilities abound, but basically you simply need to adopt an approach and use it. The requirement for unit names to be unique precludes obvious choices for the names of units containing property and component editors. This means PropertyEditors.cpp and ComponentEditors.cpp are not good choices. The easiest way to ensure a unique name is as demonstrated earlier; append the package name to the unit name. However, there is an alternative to uniquely naming the units used to contain property and components editors. It is possible to use the #pragma package(smart_init,weak) directive in place of the normal #pragma package(smart_init) directive for these units. This results in these units being weakly packaged to the design time-only package. Effectively, the name of the unit becomes irrelevant because the unit itself is not added to the design time-only package; instead, the code from the unit is directly accessed when it is required. Everything will be fine as long as the property and component editor class names are unique.

The second case that should be considered when naming units is that of the units for the runtime-only package (or packages). If each unit is used to contain an individual component, it is sensible to use the component's name as the name of the unit, omitting the initial T. Because the component name must be unique (see the next section), following this convention will almost certainly guarantee that the unit name is unique. For units that contain several components, a sensible naming convention to follow is to choose a name that reflects the components contained within the package, and then append the package name to this name—similar to the method presented for naming design time-only packages. If these guidelines are followed, the chances of name clash are small.

Naming Components

Choosing a suitable component name is very important. There are two considerations: First, the component name must be unique, and second, it must accurately represent the component's purpose.

Making sure the component name is unique is not as easy as it sounds. It is surprising how many components are made to accomplish the same task, such as encapsulating the serial port on a computer. There are only so many sensible variations of

`TComport` that you can have. Because of this, developers serious about distributing their components normally assign a signature to the component name in the form of initials placed after the `T` and before the component name. Making such initials either all lowercase or all uppercase makes them easy to ignore. Some might find all-uppercase initials easier to ignore than all-lowercase letters because of the more symbolic nature of uppercase letters. The use of initials is similar to the approach taken when naming enumerations used by component properties. The choice of initials could be arbitrary or it could be the initials of your company. Assuming a company is called *Components for Builder*, the initials `cfb` could be used. Using our `TComport` example, the component's name becomes `TcfbComport`. It might not be pretty but, when the user has no access to the source of the component, it can be quite necessary. The likelihood of another component vendor using the same name *and* the same initials is slim. We mentioned user access to the source of a component. If the user has the full source for the component, the name of the component is not as important because the user can change it if he wants.

Choosing a name that adequately reflects the component's purpose can sometimes require careful thought. It is important to adhere to conventional names as often as possible and be aware of implied meanings for any names that you choose. For example, avoid choosing a name such as TCOM for a component that encapsulates the serial port because this obviously implies that the component offers functionality related to COM programming. This is a rather silly example, but it illustrates the point. If you are having difficulty choosing a suitable name for a component, it might be a symptom of poor design. Perhaps a rethink of the component is necessary.

Distributing Only a Design Time-Only Package

So far we have looked at distributing components as a set of packages—a design time-only package with one or more runtime packages required by the design time-only package. In this section, we will look briefly at the distribution of components using a design time-only package model. If this is done, the user will be forced to statically link the object (`.obj`) files of your components directly to any application that uses them. This might appear to add complexity to the user's use of the components, but this is not the case. When a non-VCL component is added to a form in an application, the IDE does two things: It includes the header file of the unit that contains the component's definition, and it adds a `#pragma link "unitname"` statement to the form's implementation file (where `unitname` is the name of the unit that implements the component). This has the effect of requesting that the linker statically link the component to the application. The user need not write any additional code for this to be done. Assuming the linker can find the necessary `.obj` files, everything will be fine. Figure 4.8 shows the structure of a design time-only distribution. Files that must be distributed when using this technique are also shown.

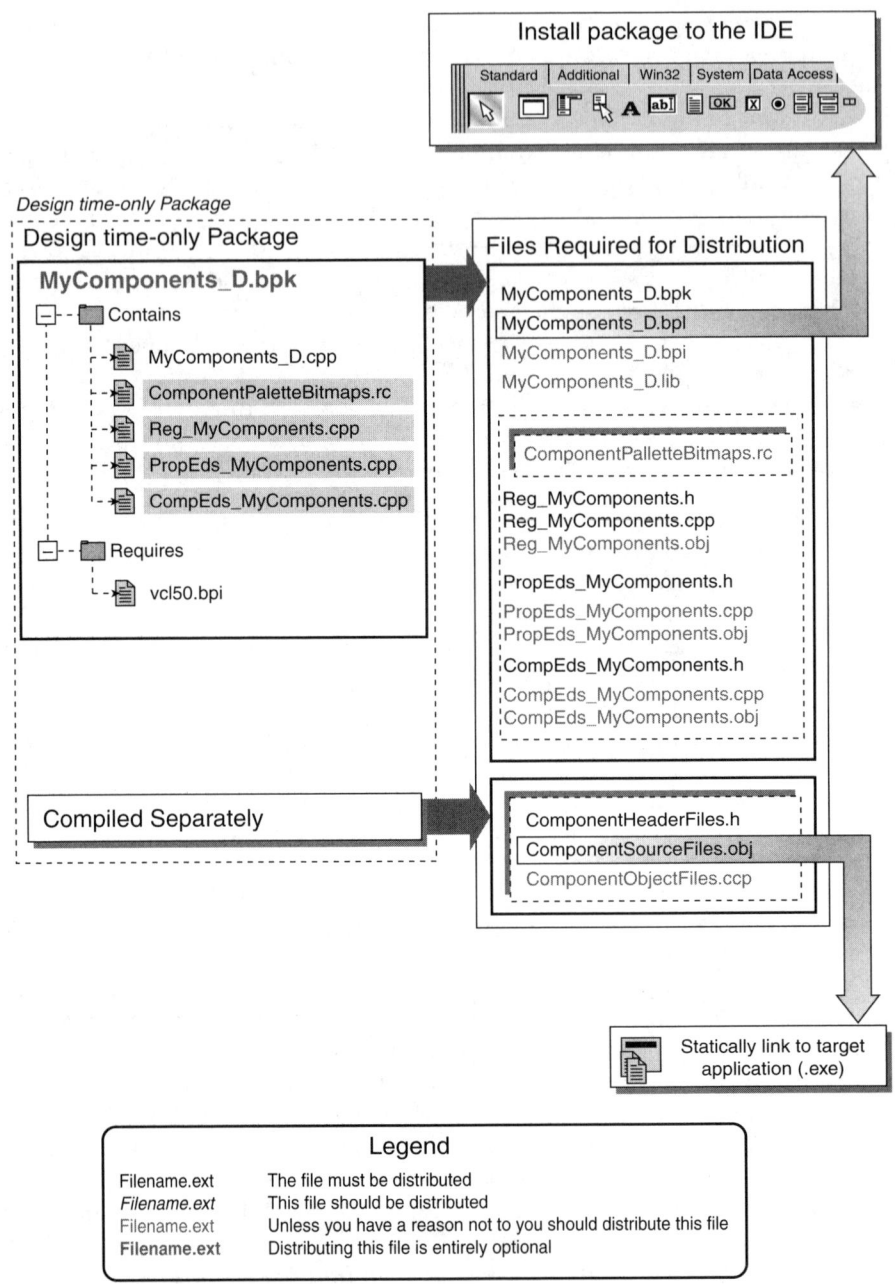

FIGURE 4.8   The design time-only package model.

One thing that is worth noting about this technique is that you can distribute a static library (.lib) file containing the object files of the components, rather than distribute the .obj files themselves. This can be achieved in one of two ways. You could create a runtime-only package containing only the components. When built, the .lib file will contain the necessary .obj files of the components. The remaining package files, the .bpl and .bpi files, are not required. This .lib file can be distributed instead of separate .obj files. Another possibility is to add the .obj files directly to the design time-only package using the USEOBJ macro. You can then distribute the design time-only package's .lib file. In either case, if the linker does not find the necessary .lib file, the project's Option source must be edited and the name of the static library added to the <SPARELIBS> line, as shown in the following:

```
<SPARELIBS value="VCL50.lib MyStaticLibrary.lib"/>
```

As long as this file is on one of the library file paths as specified in the project options, it will link successfully.

The thing to note about using this single design time-only package approach is that only one package needs to be maintained. When creating a package for different versions of C++Builder (the subject of the next section), this could possibly make life easier. The object files of the components can be generated simply by compiling the components in the different versions of C++Builder that are required, assuming of course that the code is structured so that it will compile on each version. You might also want to use this packaging model if you don't want to distribute a runtime library for dynamic linking (for whatever reason). On the whole, though, the runtime-only/design time-only package pair approach is superior and should be used in preference to this one.

Distributing Components for Different Versions of C++Builder

In cases where you want to distribute components as a component vendor, you will want to provide versions of your components that can be used on as many versions of C++Builder as possible (currently five versions exist: 1, 3, 4, 5, and 6). Of course, it might not be possible to do this in some cases because your components might rely on a feature or extend a feature that is only available in certain versions of the compiler. However, if we assume that it is possible to make the components available for more than one version of C++Builder (the majority of cases), more than one version of components must be produced. Distributing your components to different versions of C++Builder requires that you compile your code for each version to which you want to distribute. You must also create a package for components to be installed into versions 3, 4, 5, and 6 of the compiler (in the first version of C++Builder components are installed directly into CMPLIB32.CCL, and packages are not used). For this, the considerations presented previously are appropriate. The appropriate import libraries for each version of C++Builder are used and the package is built as before. This will be fine, assuming that the component source will compile on each version of the compiler. This is unlikely and, hence, this is the area that causes the most problems when trying to distribute to different versions. It is often not practical to maintain separate source listings for each version of the compiler for which the components are to be available, so an alternative approach is used. This alternative approach uses the same units for the components for each version of C++Builder. To allow for differences in compiler versions, the version of the compiler is detected and the preprocessor is used to select which code is to be used for which compiler. This and other topics relevant to the compiler version are listed in the following sections.

Detecting the Compiler Version at Compile Time

Each version of C++Builder defines a specific version number. By checking the value of this number, it is possible to selectively compile different sections of code. Listing 4.63 shows a method of setting a #defines for the different versions of C++Builder.

LISTING 4.63   Setting #defines for C++Builder Versions

```
#ifndef VERSION_DEFINES
#define VERSION_DEFINES

    #if(__TURBOC__ == 0x550) // C++Builder 5
    #define CPPBUILDER_VERSION_5
    #endif

    #if(__TURBOC__ == 0x540) // C++Builder 4
    #define CPPBUILDER_VERSION_4
    #endif

    #if(__TURBOC__ == 0x530) // C++Builder 3
    #define CPPBUILDER_VERSION_3
    #endif

    #if(__TURBOC__ == 0x520) // C++Builder 1
    #define CPPBUILDER_VERSION_1
    #endif

#endif
```

Including the code shown above in the header file of your component's unit, or indirectly by placing it in another header file on its own and including that header file, allows code such as the following to be written:

```
#ifdef CPPBUILDER_VERSION_5
// Register Property Filters as only version 5 supports this
#endif
```

By using #ifdef/#endif and #ifndef/#endif, you can selectively remove sections of code for different versions of the C++Builder. In Chapter 3, it was advised that you avoid using the preprocessor unless absolutely necessary. This is one of those times when the preprocessor is your friend, and using it can save a lot of trouble.

Using the ValidCtrCheck() Function

This function is used to determine if any of the components that you want to install contain pure virtual functions. It detects this condition at compile time. Components containing pure virtual functions cannot be installed to the IDE. The function used for this is different in version 1 of C++Builder. The following ValidCtrCheck() function is used:

```
static inline TComponentName *ValidCtrCheck()
{
    return new TComponentName(NULL);
}
```

For versions 3, 4, 5, and 6 of C++Builder, the following ValidCtrCheck() function is appropriate:

```
static inline void ValidCtrCheck(TComponentName *)
{
    new TComponentName(NULL);
}
```

The Use of Packages and C++Builder Version 1

Version 1 of the compiler does not use packages, so the PACKAGE macro should not be used after the class keyword in the component's definition, and it should not appear before Register() in the registration function. Also, the #pragma package(smart_init) directive should not be found by the compiler in the component source files.

Because packages are not used in version 1 of the compiler, only the component's header and object files need to be distributed, optionally with a separate registration unit.

Using Sets in Components

The following discussion relates to the implementation of Sets in the different versions of C++Builder. Essentially, the use of Sets in versions 1 and 3 of the compiler is different than that in versions 4 up of the compiler. The following discussion explains this more fully.

In Malcolm Smith's MJFSecurity package for C++Builder 3 (available at http:\\www.mjfreelancing.com), the following code appears in the header file:

```
#include <sysdefs.h>

enum TFailedShareRegKey { fsrNone, fsrInstalledDate,
                          fsrRegUser, fsrRegOrgn,
                          fsrRegCode, fsrRunCount,
                          fsrUserDefined };


typedef Set<TFailedShareRegKey, fsrNone, fsrUserDefined> TFailedShareRegKeys;


typedef void __fastcall (__closure *TLoadErrorEvent) (TObject *Sender,
                            TFailedShareRegKeys FailedKeys, bool &Terminate);
```

In the implementation file, code similar to that shown in Listing 4.64 is used.

LISTING 4.64   Source Code Illustrating the Use of a Set

```
TFailedShareRegKeys FailedKeys;
FailedKeys << fsrNone;

// ... some sample code while reading the registry:

if(MyReg->ValueExists(KeyNames->InstalledDate))
    FInstalledDate = MyReg->ReadDate(KeyNames->InstalledDate);
else
{
   FailedKeys >> fsrNone;
   FailedKeys << fsrInstalledDate;
}

if(MyReg->ValueExists(KeyNames->Username))
    FRegisteredName = MyReg->ReadString(KeyNames->Username);
else
{
   FailedKeys >> fsrNone;
   FailedKeys << fsrRegUser;
}

// ... and many more
// ... and then later in the code that calls the event:
```

LISTING 4.64 Continued

```
if(FOnLoadError)
{
   bool Terminate = TerminateOnLoadError;
   FOnLoadError(this, FailedKeys, Terminate);
}
```

The code above should allow the component to construct a Set defining all possible causes for the application's failure to load. This Set is passed as a parameter to the OnLoadError event, where the user can examine the information and act accordingly.

This code will work fine in versions 4 and 5 of C++Builder, but not in version 1 and 3. In version 1 and 3, the following declaration is required:

```
template class TFailedShareRegKeys;
```

This explicit declaration forces the compiler to compile all methods of the Set class.

C++Builder 4 and 5 already contain an explicit declaration for Set in $(BCB)\Include\Vcl\Sysmac.h included indirectly through the line #include <system.hpp>. This is shown here:

```
template<class T, unsigned char minEl, unsigned char maxEl>
   class RTL_DELPHIRETURN Set;
```

By wrapping the line

```
template class TFailedShareRegKeys;
```

in preprocessor directives it can be selectively compiled for versions 1 and 3 and ignored for versions 4 and 5.

Creating Component Palette Bitmaps

Throughout this discussion of packages, the Component Palette bitmaps have been referred to as .rc (resource script) files. The reason for this is that using resource script files (or a single resource script file with entries for all palette bitmaps—the preferred method) enables greater flexibility over palette bitmap creation. Essentially, creating your Component Palette bitmaps using a more powerful graphics tool and manually adding them through a resource script file allows custom palettes to be used effectively. This can greatly enhance the appearance of your component bitmaps on the Component Palette.

Using Guidelines in the Design of Components for Distribution

Writing components for yourself or for in-house use is not the same as writing components for outside use by unknown parties. The main reason is that you have no idea how an outside party might want to use your component. To this end, you should design your component with the following considerations in mind:

- Don't hide functionality from the user that he *probably* won't need. If making a feature available does not compromise the component design, make it available. There will always be someone who does need that functionality.

- When adding events to components, be sure to fire events for each possible event that the user might want to handle. Failing to allow the user to respond to certain events because they have been omitted severely limits the usefulness of your component.

- Don't force the user to rely on component linking as a method of achieving certain functionality by linking several of your components together. For example, if you write a component that allows input from a sound card to be captured and a component that displays this data, it makes sense to allow them to be linked together and the process controlled by the components. However, if that is the only way you can use the components, they can be virtually useless—for example, the data that the sound card component captures should always be accessible for display or manipulation by any other means that a components user might require.

- Try to keep the interface of your component intuitive, particularly at design time; this will be most users' first experience of your component. Where appropriate, make intelligent use of property and component editors. Sensible use of property filters (property Categories) can also make a component with many properties much easier to navigate.

- Finally, you might want to create an abstract base class version of your component, such as the TCustom components in C++Builder. This might not always be appropriate, but it can prove very useful for users of your component.

Taking a Look at Other Distribution Issues

Other issues regarding distributing components include customizing the component's component editors so that a hyperlink is available to your Web site, your company logo is displayed, or other information is given (the component's version, for example).

Other things to consider are whether you want your component to be freeware or shareware. Do you want to include source or not? Should you pack your components so that they must be installed from an installation program that requires a license agreement to be accepted? And so on. These issues are beyond the scope of this section. However, it is important to be aware of them before you start to distribute your components to others.

A final consideration is that for all but the most trivial of components, you should always distribute accompanying documentation. You can do this in the form of help files, an actual electronic document, or even extensive instruction and comments in the header files of the components themselves. The general preference is for both help files and some printable electronic document. No matter how good a component is, it is virtually useless if no proper documentation is available for it. On a similar note, you should endeavor to ship example code and possibly a demo application(s) that shows your component being used.

Summary

This chapter has shown the important issues involved with component development, including the best ways to make and deploy packages of components and how to create components of various types.

5

Creating Property and Component Editors

Components are the building blocks of C++Builder. They are the essential elements of every C++Builder program. Developers spend much of their time working with components, learning about their features, and trying to make the best use of the facilities that they offer. To that end, improving the design-time interface of a component is one of the single most powerful ways to improve a component's usefulness. Developers often spend great effort on improving their application's user interface for their customers. Component writers should also consider the interface that they present to their customers—the developers.

This chapter covers the techniques required to successfully implement property editors and component editors. Some of the biggest changes to C++Builder's IDE have been to allow improved property and component interfaces at design time to help improve the productivity of developers. All the new features added in C++Builder are covered in depth, and definitive guidelines are presented as to their proper use.

All the code of the property editors and component editors discussed in this chapter is contained on the accompanying CD-ROM. By examining the source to these editors, it should be possible to develop a good understanding of the issues involved in creating custom editors for components. The code shown in the listings throughout the chapter is contained in two packages: the EnhancedEditors package (EnhancedEditors.bpk, a design time–only package), and the NewAdditionalComponents design time and runtime packages.

The design-time package, called NewAdditionalComponentsDTP.bpk, contains property and component editor code as well as registration code. The runtime package, called NewAdditionalComponentsRTP.bpk, contains code for components.

It would probably be helpful to install these packages into your installation of C++Builder before reading this chapter. That way you can see the effect that the property and component editors have while you are reading the chapter. Before you install either package, first copy the folder called Chapter5Packages to your hard drive. It contains the files you require. Feel free to give the folder a more imaginative name. Then, copy both files in the System folder to a folder on the system path, for example, Windows\System on Windows 9x machines or WINNT\System32 on Windows NT and Windows 2000 machines. These files are runtime packages required by the two design-time packages you will install shortly. Both of those design-time packages require the TNonVCLTypeInfoPackage.bpl runtime-only file, and the NewAdditionalComponentsDTP.bpl design time–only package also requires the NewAdditionalComponentsRTP.bpl runtime-only package.

There are several additional directories that should also be copied to some location where you keep your development source code files:

- NonVCLTypeInfoPackage—provides runtime type information for types not based on Tobject.

- NewAddtionalComponents (Contains NewAddtionalComponentsRTP and NewAdditionalComponentsDTP for the runtime and design-time packages respectively—provides various components to use the property and component editors.

- EnhancedEditors—provides special component and property editors for use with the "new additional components".

Each of these contains source code and projects needed to demonstrate the content of this chapter.

To install the EnhancedEditors package, run C++Builder and click Install Packages in the Component menu. Click the Add button in the Design packages group and browse to where you have copied the EnhancedEditors\BPL directory and select the EnhancedEditors.bpl file. When you click Open, the Add Design Package dialog will close and the package will appear in the Design packages list as Enhanced Property and Component Editors. Click OK to finish. Table 5.1 lists the property and component editors contained in the EnhancedEditors package and indicates whether they are registered (in other words, installed) with the IDE when the package is installed.

TABLE 5.1   Property and Component Editors Registered by the EnhancedEditors Package

Editors	Registered
TShapeTypePropertyEditor	Yes
TImageListPropertyEditor	Yes
TImageIndexProperty	No—An Abstract Base Class
TPersistentDerivedImageIndexProperty	Yes
TComponentDerivedImageIndexProperty	Yes
TMenuItemImageIndexProperty	Yes
TTabSheetImageIndexProperty	Not required
TToolButtonImageIndexProperty	Yes
TCoolBandImageIndexProperty	Not required
TListColumnImageIndexProperty	Yes
TCustomActionImageIndexProperty	Not required
THeaderSectionImageIndexProperty	Not required
TDisplayCursorProperty	Yes
TDisplayFontNameProperty	Yes
TUnsignedProperty	Yes
TCharPropertyEditor	Yes
TSignedCharProperty	Yes
TUnsignedCharProperty	Yes
TImageComponentEditor	Yes

The method for installing the NewAdditionalComponents package is the same as for the EnhancedEditors package. Click Install Packages on the Component menu. Click the Add button in the Design packages group and browse into the NewAdditional Components\NewAdditionalComponentsDTP\BPL directory for the NewAdditional ComponentsDTP.bpl file. When you click Open, the Add Design Package dialog will close, and the package will appear in the Design packages list as New Components for the Additional Palette Page. Click OK to finish. The following components are registered with the IDE by this package:

- TEnhancedImage

- TFilterEdit

The TImageIndexPropertyEditor property editor is also registered by this package. Additionally, the TNonVCLTypeInfoPackage runtime-only package (TNonVCLTypeInfoPackage.bpk) is included. This contains code referred to in Listings 5.7 and 5.8 in the section "Obtaining a TTypeInfo* (PTypeInfo) from an Existing Property and Class for a Non-VCL Type," later in this chapter. Both the EnhancedEditors.bpk and the NewAdditionalComponentsDTP.bpk package require this package for their registration code. Therefore, if you want to recompile either package, the header files (*.h) and import file (.bpi) of this package must be found by the IDE when it is compiling and linking the packages.

Creating Custom Property Editors

One of the best ways to improve a component's design-time interface is to ensure that property editors are easy to use and intuitive. This section looks at the main principles involved in creating your own property editors. All custom property editors descend ultimately from TPropertyEditor, which provides the basic function-ality required for the editor to function within the IDE. Listing 5.1 shows the the class definition for TPropertyEditor (in C++ Builder 5 and earlier, this is from $(BCB)\Include\Vcl\VCLEditors.hpp, where $(BCB) is the C++Builder installation direc-tory. In C++Builder 6, this has been moved to $(BCB)\Include\VCL\VCLEditors.hpp or $(BCB)\Include\VCL\CLXEditors.hpp depending on whether you are constructing editors for Windows alone or for CLX compatibility).

LISTING 5.1   TPropertyEditor Class Definition

```
class DELPHICLASS TPropertyEditor;
class PASCALIMPLEMENTATION TPropertyEditor : public Designintf::TBasePropertyEditor
{
    typedef Designintf::TBasePropertyEditor inherited;

private:
    Designintf::_di_IDesigner FDesigner;
    TInstProp *FPropList;
    int FPropCount;
    AnsiString __fastcall GetPrivateDirectory();

protected:
    virtual void __fastcall SetPropEntry(int Index, Classes::TPersistent*
    ➥AInstance, Typinfo::PPropInfo APropInfo);
    Extended __fastcall GetFloatValue(void);
    Extended __fastcall GetFloatValueAt(int Index);
    __int64 __fastcall GetInt64Value(void);
    __int64 __fastcall GetInt64ValueAt(int Index);
    System::TMethod __fastcall GetMethodValue();
    System::TMethod __fastcall GetMethodValueAt(int Index);
    int __fastcall GetOrdValue(void);
    int __fastcall GetOrdValueAt(int Index);
    AnsiString __fastcall GetStrValue();
    AnsiString __fastcall GetStrValueAt(int Index);
    Variant __fastcall GetVarValue();
```

LISTING 5.1   Continued

```cpp
    Variant __fastcall GetVarValueAt(int Index);
    System::_di_IInterface __fastcall GetIntfValue();
    System::_di_IInterface __fastcall GetIntfValueAt(int Index);
    void __fastcall Modified(void);
    void __fastcall SetFloatValue(Extended Value);
    void __fastcall SetMethodValue(const System::TMethod &Value);
    void __fastcall SetInt64Value(__int64 Value);
    void __fastcall SetOrdValue(int Value);
    void __fastcall SetStrValue(const AnsiString Value);
    void __fastcall SetVarValue(const Variant &Value);
    void __fastcall SetIntfValue(const System::_di_IInterface Value);
    bool __fastcall GetEditValue(/* out */ AnsiString &Value);
    bool __fastcall HasInstance(Classes::TPersistent* Instance);

public:
    __fastcall virtual TPropertyEditor(const Designintf::_di_IDesigner ADesigner,
    ➥int APropCount);
    __fastcall virtual ~TPropertyEditor(void);
    virtual void __fastcall Activate(void);
    virtual bool __fastcall AllEqual(void);
    virtual bool __fastcall AutoFill(void);
    virtual void __fastcall Edit(void);
    virtual Designintf::TPropertyAttributes __fastcall GetAttributes(void);
    Classes::TPersistent* __fastcall GetComponent(int Index);
    virtual int __fastcall GetEditLimit(void);
    virtual AnsiString __fastcall GetName();
    virtual void __fastcall GetProperties(Designintf::TGetPropProc Proc);
    virtual Typinfo::PPropInfo __fastcall GetPropInfo(void);
    Typinfo::PTypeInfo __fastcall GetPropType(void);
    virtual AnsiString __fastcall GetValue();
    AnsiString __fastcall GetVisualValue();
    virtual void __fastcall GetValues(Classes::TGetStrProc Proc);
    virtual void __fastcall Initialize(void);
    void __fastcall Revert(void);
    virtual void __fastcall SetValue(const AnsiString Value);
    bool __fastcall ValueAvailable(void);
    __property Designintf::_di_IDesigner Designer = {read=FDesigner};
    __property AnsiString PrivateDirectory = {read=GetPrivateDirectory};
    __property int PropCount = {read=FPropCount, nodefault};
    __property AnsiString Value = {read=GetValue, write=SetValue};
private:
```

LISTING 5.1   Continued

```
    void *__IProperty;        /* Designintf::IProperty */

public:
    operator IProperty*(void) { return (IProperty*)&__IProperty; }


};
```

To customize the editor's behavior, one or more TPropertyEditor virtual (or DYNAMIC) functions must be overridden. You can save a lot of coding by deriving your custom property editor from the most appropriate property editor class. The hierarchy of TPropertyEditor descendants is shown in Figure 5.1. Descendants in shaded boxes are those that override the custom rendering functionality of TPropertyEditor.

The hierarchy shown in Figure 5.1 is useful when deciding which property editor to inherit from. The purpose of each property editor is fairly self-explanatory, with the exception of one or two of the more specialized. For your convenience, brief descriptions of the more commonly encountered property editors are given in Table 5.2.

TABLE 5.2   Common Property Editor Classes and Their Uses

Property Editor Class	Use
TCaptionProperty	The editor for all Caption and Text named AnsiString properties. The Caption property of TForm and the Text property of TEdit are examples. The difference between this property editor and the TStringProperty from which it derives is that the component being edited is continually updated as the property is edited. With TStringProperty the updating occurs after the edit has finished.
TCharProperty	The default editor for all char properties and subtypes of char. Displays either the character of the property's value or the value itself preceded by the # character. The PasswordChar (char) property of TMaskEdit is an example.
TClassProperty	The default editor for TPersistent-derived class properties. Published properties of the class are displayed as subproperties when the + image before the property name is clicked. The Constraints (TSizeConstraints*) property of TForm is an example.
TColorProperty	The default editor for TColor type properties. Displays the color as a cl*XXX* value if one exists, otherwise displays the value as hexadecimal (in BGR format; 0x00*BBGGRR*). The value can be entered as either a cl*XXX* value or as a number. Also allows the cl*XXX* value to be picked from a list. When the property is double-clicked, the Color dialog is displayed. The Color (TColor) property of TForm is an example.

TABLE 5.2   Continued

Property Editor Class	Use
TComponentProperty	The default editor for pointers to TComponent-derived objects. The editor displays a drop-down list of type-compatible objects that appear in the same form as the component being edited. The Images (TCustomImageList*) property of TToolBar is an example.
TCursorProperty	For TCursor properties. Allows a cursor to be selected from a list that gives each cursor's name and its corresponding image. The Cursor (TCursor) property of TForm is an example.
TEnumProperty	The default editor for all enum-based properties. A drop-down list displays the possible values the property can take. The Align (TAlign) and BorderStyle (TFormBorderStyle) properties of TForm are examples.
TFloatProperty	The default editor for all floating-point–based properties, namely double, long double, and float. The PrintLeftMargin (double) and PrintRightMargin (double) properties of TF1Book are examples.
TFontProperty	For TFont properties. The editor allows the font settings to be edited either through the Font dialog (by clicking the ellipses button) or by editing an expandable list of subproperties. The Font (TFont) property of TForm is an example.
TIntegerProperty	The default editor for all int properties. The Height (int) and Width (int) properties of TForm are examples.
TMethodProperty	The default editor for pointer-to-method (member function) properties; that is, events. The editor displays a drop-down list of event handlers for the event type matching that of the property. The OnClick and OnClose events of TForm are examples.
TOrdinalProperty	All ordinal-based (that is integral) property editors ultimately descend from this class, such as TIntegerProperty, TCharProperty, TenumProperty, and TSetProperty.
TPropertyEditor	The class from which all property editors are descended.
TSetElementProperty	This editor is used to edit the individual elements of a Set. The property can be set to true to indicate that the element is contained in the Set and false to indicate that it is not.
TSetProperty	The default editor for all Set properties. Each element of the Set is displayed as a subproperty of the Set property allowing each element to be removed from or added to the Set as desired. The Anchors (TAnchors) and BorderIcons (TBorderIcons) properties of TForm are examples.
TStringProperty	The default editor for AnsiString properties. The Hint and Name properties of TForm are examples.

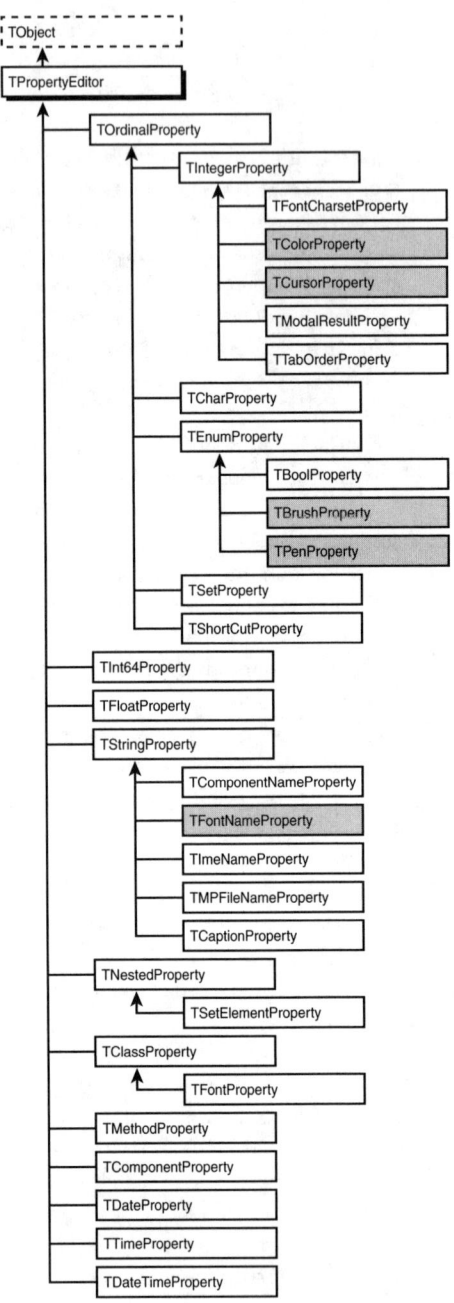

FIGURE 5.1   The TPropertyEditor inheritance hierarchy.

Choosing the right property editor to inherit from is linked inextricably with the requirements specification of the property editor. In fact, the hardest part of creating a custom property editor is deciding exactly what behavior is required. This is an issue that will come up later in this section.

The stages of developing a new property editor are summarized in the following list:

1. Decide exactly how you want the editor to behave. Property editors often are developed to offer a bounded choice that ensures proper component operation and an intuitive interface. The nature of bounding, such as to restrict the user to a choice of some discrete predefined values, must be decided.

2. Decide whether a custom property editor is even required. By slightly changing how a property is used, it might be that no custom property editor is necessary. To this end, it is important to know which property editors are registered for which property types; Table 5.2 can be used as a guide. Because this section is about creating custom property editors, that alternative will not be explored further. Needless to say, you cannot know too much about the existing property editors and how they work. A good source of information is the `$(BCB)\Source\ToolsApi\VCLEditors.pas` file.

3. Choose carefully the property editor from which your custom property editor descends. A careful choice can save a lot of unnecessary coding.

4. Decide which property attributes are applicable to your property editor.

5. Determine which functions of the parent property editor need to be overridden and which do not.

6. Finally, write the necessary code and try it out.

After it has been decided that a custom property editor is required and the parent property editor class has been chosen, the next step is to decide which property attributes are suitable. Every property editor has a method called `GetAttributes()` that returns a `TPropertyAttributes` Set. This tells the Object Inspector how the property is to be used. For example, if the property displays a drop-down list of values, you must ensure that `paValueList` is contained by the `TPropertyAttributes` Set returned by the property editor's `GetAttributes()` method. Unless the property attributes of the parent property editor class exactly match those required in the custom property editor, the `GetAttributes()` method must be overridden. Table 5.3 shows the different values that can be contained by the `TPropertyAttributes` Set. Methods that might require overridding as a result of the property editor having a particular attribute are also shown.

TABLE 5.3   `TPropertyAttributes` Set Values

Value	Purpose
`paAutoUpdate`	Properties whose editors have this attribute are updated automatically because they are changed in the Object Inspector, such as the `Caption` property of `TLabel`. Normally, a property will not be updated until the Return key is pressed or focus leaves the property. `SetValue()` is called to convert the `AnsiString` representation to the proper format and ensure the value is valid. Overriding `SetValue()` is probably necessary. Override: `SetValue(const AnsiString Value)`
`paDialog`	Properties with this attribute display an ellipsis button (...) on the right side of the property value region. When clicked, this displays a form to allow the property to be edited. When the ellipses button is pressed, the `Edit()` method of the property editor is invoked. This must, therefore, be overridden for properties with this attribute. Override: `Edit()`
`paFullWidthName`	Properties with this attribute do not display a value region in the Object Inspector. Rather, the property name extends to the full width of the Object Inspector.
`paMultiSelect`	Properties whose editors have this attribute can be edited when more than one component is selected on a form. For example, the property editor for the `Caption` property of `TLabel` and `TButton` has this attribute. When several `TLabel` and `TButton` components are placed on a form and selected, the `Caption` properties can be edited simultaneously. The Object Inspector displays all properties whose editors have the `paMultiSelect` attribute *and* whose property names and types are exactly the same.
`paReadOnly`	Properties whose editors have this attribute cannot be edited in the Object Inspector.
`paRevertable`	Properties whose editors have this attribute enable the Revert to Inherited menu item in the Object Inspector's context menu, allowing the property editor to revert the current property value to some default value.
`paSortList`	Properties with this attribute have their value lists sorted by the Object Inspector.
`paSubProperties`	Properties with this attribute tell the Object Inspector that the property editor has subproperties that can be edited. A + symbol is placed in front of the property name. The `TFont` property editor is an example of this. To tell the Object Inspector which subproperties to display, `GetProperties()` must be overridden. Override: `GetProperties(TGetPropEditProc Proc)`

TABLE 5.3 Continued

Value	Purpose
paValueList	Properties whose editors have this attribute display a drop-down list of possible values that the property can take. A value can still be entered manually in the editable property value region. For example, TColor properties behave this way. To provide a list of values for the Object Inspector to display, you must override the GetValues() method. Override: GetValues(Classes::TGetStrProc Proc)

After the attributes of the property editor have been decided, it is easy to see which methods of the parent property editor must be overridden. Other methods can also require overriding; this will depend on the specifications of the property editor. Table 5.4 lists the virtual and DYNAMIC methods of TPropertyEditor. The methods are grouped and ordered according to their use; they are not listed alphabetically.

TABLE 5.4 The virtual and DYNAMIC Methods of TPropertyEditor

Method	Declaration and Purpose
GetAttributes()	virtual TPropertyAttributes __fastcall GetAttributes(void); Returns a TPropertyAttributes Set. Invoked to set the property editor attributes.
GetValue()	virtual AnsiString __fastcall GetValue(); Returns an AnsiString that represents the property's value. By default (that is, in TPropertyEditor) it returns (unknown). Therefore, if you derive directly from TPropertyEditor, you *must* override this method to return the correct value.
SetValue()	virtual void __fastcall SetValue(const AnsiString Value); Called to set the value of a property. SetValue() must convert the AnsiString representation of the property's value to a suitable format. If an invalid value is entered, SetValue() should throw an exception that describes the error. Note that SetValue() takes a const AnsiString as its parameter and returns void. An exception, therefore, is the only appropriate method of dealing with invalid values.
Edit()	virtual void __fastcall Edit(void); Invoked when the ellipses button is pressed or the property is double-clicked (GetAttributes() should return paDialog). Normally used to display a form to allow more intuitive editing of the property value. Edit() can call GetValue() and SetValue(), or it can read and write the property value directly. If this is the case, input validation should be carried out. If an invalid value is entered, an exception describing the error should be thrown.

TABLE 5.4   Continued

Method	Declaration and Purpose
GetValues()	`virtual void __fastcall GetValues(Classes::TGetStrProc Proc);` Only called when paValueList is returned by GetAttributes(). The single parameter Proc is of type TGetStrProc, a __closure (pointer to an instance member function), declared in $(BCB)\Include\Vcl\Classes.hpp as: `typedef void __fastcall (__closure *TGetStrProc)(const AnsiString S).` The Proc parameter is in fact the address of a method with a const AnsiString called S as its single parameter, which adds the AnsiString passed to the property editor's drop-down list. Call Proc(const AnsiString S) once for every value that should be displayed in the property value's drop-down list, for example: `Proc(value1); //value1 is an AnsiString,` `Proc(value2); //value2 is an AnsiString,` and so on.
Activate()	`virtual void __fastcall Activate(void);` Invoked when the property is selected in the Object Inspector. Enables the property editor attributes to be determined only when the property becomes selected (with the exception of paSubProperties and paMultiSelect).
AllEqual()	`virtual bool __fastcall AllEqual(void);` Returns a bool value. Called only when paMultiSelect is one of the property editor's attributes (when it is returned by GetAttributes()). It determines if all properties of the same name and type for which that editor is registered are equal when more than one is selected at once (it returns true). If this is the case (they are equal), GetValue() is called to display the value; otherwise the value region is blanked.
AutoFill()	`virtual bool __fastcall AutoFill(void);` Returns a bool value. Called only when paValueList is returned by GetAttributes(), it determines whether or not (returns true or false) the values returned by GetValues() can be selected incrementally in the Object Inspector. By default it returns true.
GetEditLimit()	`virtual int __fastcall GetEditLimit(void);` Returns an int representing the maximum number of input characters allowed in the Object Inspector for this property. Overriding this method allows this number to be changed. The default value for the Object Inspector is 255.

TABLE 5.4   Continued

Method	Declaration and Purpose
`GetName()`	`virtual AnsiString __fastcall GetName();` Returns an `AnsiString` that is used by the Object Inspector to display the property name. This should be overridden only when the name determined from the property's type information is not the name that you want to appear in the Object Inspector.

`GetProperties()`	`virtual void __fastcall`
	`GetProperties(TGetPropEditProc Proc);`
	If it is required that subproperties be displayed, you must override this method. The single parameter `Proc` is of type `TGetPropEditProc`, a `__closure` declared in `$(BCB)\Include\Vcl\VCLEditors.hpp` as
	`typedef void __fastcall (__closure`
	`*TGetPropEditProc)(TPropertyEditor* Prop);`
	`Proc` is, therefore, the address of a method with a pointer to a `TPropertyEditor`-derived editor called `Prop` as its single parameter. Call `Proc(TPropertyEditor* Prop)` once for each subproperty, passing a pointer to a `TPropertyEditor`-derived editor as an argument. For example, `TSetProperty` overrides this method and passes a `TSetElementProperty` pointer for each element in its `Set`. `TClassProperty` also overrides the `GetProperties()` method, displaying a subproperty for each of the class's published properties.

`Initialize()`	`virtual void __fastcall Initialize(void);` This is invoked when the Object Inspector is going to use the property editor. `Initialize()` is called after the property editor has been constructed, but before it is used. When several components are selected at once, property editors are constructed, but are often discarded because they will not be used. This method allows the possibility of postponing certain operations until it is certain that they will be required.

The following are methods inherited from the interface IcustomPropertyEditor. If you want to implement these, you must add ICustomPropertyEditor to the inheritance list for your property editor—it doesn't come automatically when you inherit from other property editors. Note that inheriting interfaces is the only exception to the rule that prevents multiple inheritance in VCL classes.

`ListMeasureWidth()`	`virtual void __fastcall ListMeasureWidth(const AnsiString Value, Graphics::TCanvas* ACanvas, int& AWidth);`

This is called during the width calculation phase of the property's drop-down list. If images are to be placed alongside text in the drop-down list, this method should be overridden to ensure the list is wide enough.

ListMeasureHeight()

```
virtual void __fastcall ListMeasureHeight(const
AnsiString Value, Graphics::TCanvas* ACanvas, int&
AHeight);
```

This is called during the height calculation phase of the property's drop-down list. If an image's height is greater than that of the property value text, this must be overridden to prevent clipping the image.

ListDrawValue()

```
virtual void __fastcall ListDrawValue(const AnsiString
Value, Graphics::TCanvas* ACanvas, const TRect&
ARect, bool ASelected);
```

This is called to render the current list item in the property's drop-down list. If an image is to be rendered, this method must be overridden. The default behavior of this method is to render the text representing the current list value.

PropDrawValue()

```
virtual void __fastcall PropDrawValue(Graphics::TCanvas*
ACanvas, const TRect& ARect, bool ASelected);
```

This is called when the property value itself is to be rendered in the Object Inspector. If an image is to be rendered with the property value, this method must be overridden.

PropDrawName()

```
virtual void __fastcall PropDrawName(Graphics::TCanvas*
ACanvas, const TRect &ARect, bool ASelected);
```

This is called when the property name is to be rendered in the Object Inspector. If an image is to be rendered with the property name, this method must be overridden. However, this is rarely needed.

Now, you should have a reasonable idea of the capabilities that can be implemented for a custom property editor. The next few sections look at some of the most important methods and present basic coding guidelines for their proper use. The last five methods (ListMeasureWidth(), ListMeasureHeight(), ListDrawValue(), PropDrawValue(), and PropDrawName()) are concerned with rendering images in the Object Inspector and are looked at in the section "Using Images in Property Editors," later in this chapter.

The methods that are most often overridden by custom property editors are GetAttributes(), GetValue(), SetValue(), Edit(), and GetValues(), the first five methods in Table 5.4. Listing 5.2 shows a class definition for a custom property editor derived from TPropertyEditor.

TIP

A key point to note in Listing 5.2 is the use of the typedef:

```
typedef TPropertyEditor inherited;
```

This allows inherited to be used as a namespace modifier in place of TPropertyEditor. This is commonly encountered in the VCL and makes it easy to call parent (in this case TPropertyEditor) methods explicitly while retaining code maintainability. If the name of the parent class changes, only this one occurrence needs to be updated.

For example, you can write code such as this in the property editor's GetAttributes() method:

```
return inherited::GetAttributes() << paValueList >> paMultiSelect
```

This calls the property editor's base class GetAttributes() method, returning a TPropertyAttributes Set. paValueList is added to this Set, and paMultiSelect is removed from the Set. The final Set is returned.

LISTING 5.2   Definition Code for a Custom Property Editor

```cpp
class TExamplePropertyEditor : public TPropertyEditor
{
        typedef TPropertyEditor inherited;

public:
    virtual TPropertyAttributes __fastcall GetAttributes(void);
    virtual AnsiString __fastcall GetValue();
    virtual void __fastcall SetValue(const AnsiString Value);
    virtual void __fastcall Edit(void);
    virtual void __fastcall GetValues(Classes::TGetStrProc Proc);

protected:
    #pragma option push -w-inl
    inline __fastcall virtual
      TExamplePropertyEditor(const _DesignIntf::di_IDesigner ADesigner,
                             int APropCount)
                            : TPropertyEditor(ADesigner, APropCount)
    { }
    #pragma option pop
```

LISTING 5.2   Continued

```
public:
    #pragma option push -w-inl
    inline __fastcall virtual ~TCustomProperty(void) { }
    #pragma option pop
};
```

The GetAttributes() Method

The GetAttributes() method is very simple to implement. The only consideration is you should change just the attributes returned by the parent class that have a direct effect on your code. Remaining attributes should be unchanged so that you add only attributes that you definitely need and remove only attributes that you definitely don't want. Be sure to check the attributes of the parent class. You might not need to change them at all. For example, a property editor that derives directly from TPropertyEditor is required to display a drop-down list of values and should not be used when multiple components are selected. Suitable code for the GetAttributes() method is

```
TPropertyAttributes __fastcall TExamplePropertyEditor::GetAttributes(void)
{
    return TPropertyEditor::GetAttributes()
        << paValueList >> paMultiSelect;
}
```

Because TPropertyEditor::GetAttributes() returns paRevertable, the following is the same:

```
TPropertyAttributes __fastcall TExamplePropertyEditor::GetAttributes(void)
{
    return TPropertyAttributes() << paValueList << paRevertable >> paMultiSelect;
}
```

The GetValue() Method

Use the GetValue() method to return an AnsiString representation of the value of the property being edited. To do this, use one of the GetXxxValue() methods from the TPropertyEditor class, where *Xxx* will be one of Float, Int64, Method, Ord, Str, or Var. These are listed in Table 5.5.

TABLE 5.5   TPropertyEditor GetXxxValue() Methods

Method	Description
GetFloatValue()	Returns an Extended value, in other words a long double. Used to retrieve floating-point property values, such as float, double, and long double.
GetInt64Value()	Returns an __int64 value. Used to retrieve Int64 (__int64) property values.

GetMethodValue()	Returns a TMethod structure:
	`struct TMethod`
	`{`
	`    void *Code;`
	`    void *Data;`
	`};`
	Used to retrieve Closure property values, in other words, events.

GetOrdValue()	Returns an int value. Used to retrieve Ordinal property values such as char, signed char, unsigned char, int, unsigned, short, and long. Can also be used to retrieve a pointer value; the int must be cast to the appropriate pointer using reinterpret_cast.
GetStrValue()	Returns an AnsiString value. Used to retrieve string (AnsiString) property values.
GetVarValue()	Returns a Variant by value. Used to retrieve Variant property values. The Variant class models Object Pascal's intrinsic variant type. Refer to the online help for a description of Variants.

The following code shows an implementation of the GetValue() method to retrieve the value of a char-based property by calling the GetOrdValue() method.

```
AnsiString __fastcall TExamplePropertyEditor::GetValue()
{
    char ch = static_cast<char>(GetOrdValue());
    if(ch > 32 && ch < 128) return ch;
    else return AnsiString().sprintf("#%d", ch);

    // Note the '#' character is pre-pended to characters
    // that cannot be displayed directly. This is how the
    // VCL displays non-printable character values, for
    // example #8 is the backspace character (\b).
}
```

Notice the use of static_cast to cast the returned int value as a char. The casting operators are often used when overriding the GetValue() and SetValue() methods of TPropertyEditor. It is essential that their proper use be understood.

The SetValue() Method

Use the SetValue() method to set a property's actual value by converting the AnsiString representation to a suitable format. To do this, use one of the SetXxxValue() methods from TPropertyEditor, where *Xxx* will be one of Float, Int64, Method, Ord, Str, or Var. These are listed in Table 5.6.

TABLE 5.6   TPropertyEditor SetXxxValue() Methods

Method	Sets
SetFloatValue()	Pass an Extended (long double) value as an argument. Used to set floating-point property values, namely float, double, and long double.
SetInt64Value()	Pass an __int64 value as an argument. Used to set Int64 (__int64) property values.
SetMethodValue()	Pass a TMethod structure as an argument. Used to set Closure (event) property values.
SetOrdValue()	Pass an int value as an argument. Used to set Ordinal property values, namely char, signed char, unsigned char, int, unsigned, short, and long. It can also be used to set pointer property values, though the pointer value must first be cast to an int using reinterpret_cast.
SetStrValue()	Pass an AnsiString as an argument. Used to set string (AnsiString) property values.
SetVarValue()	Pass a Variant as an argument. Used for variant (Variant) property values.

SetValue() should ensure that values passed to it are valid before calling one of the SetXxxValue() methods, and it should raise an exception if this is not the case. The EPropertyError exception is sensible to use or serve as a base class from which to derive your own exception class. Sample code for an int property is shown in the following, where a value of less than zero is not allowed:

```
void __fastcall
   TExamplePropertyEditor::SetValue
      (const AnsiString Value)
{
   if(Value.ToInt() < 0)
   {
      throw EPropertyError("The value must be greater than 0");
   }
   else SetOrdValue(Value.ToInt());
}
```

The `Edit()` Method

The `Edit()` method is generally used to offer a better interface to the user. Often this is a form behaving as a dialog. The `Edit()` method can also call `GetValue()` and `SetValue()` or even call the `GetXxxValue()` and `SetXxxValue()` methods. It should be noted at this point that `TPropertyEditor` (and derived classes) has a property called `Value` whose read and write methods are `GetValue()` and `SetValue()`, respectively. Its declaration is

```
__property AnsiString Value = {read=GetValue, write=SetValue};
```

This can be used instead of calling `GetValue()` and `SetValue()` directly. Regardless of how `GetValue()` and `SetValue()` are called, the `Edit()` method should be able to display a suitable form to allow intuitive editing of the property's value.

Two basic approaches can be taken. The first is to allow the form to update the property's value while it is displayed. The second is to use the form as a dialog to retrieve the desired value or values from the user, and then set the property's value when the form returns a modal result of `mrOK` upon closure. Which of the two approaches is taken affects the code that appears in the `Edit()` method.

Now consider the first instance in which the form will continually update the value of the property. There are two basic types of property value: one that represents a single entity, such as an `int`, and one that represents a collection of values, such as the class `TFont` (though the property editor for `TFont` behaves according to the second approach). The difference between the two is in how `Value` is used to update the property. In a class property, `Value` is a pointer. For the form to be able to update the property, it must have the address of `Value` or whatever `Value` points to. For a class property this is simple; the pointer to the class is read from `Value`, and the class's values are edited through that pointer. A convenient way to do this is to declare a property of the same type as the property to be edited. This can then be equated to `Value` before the form is shown, allowing initial values to be displayed and stored.

In a single entity, a reference to `Value` should be passed in the form's constructor. Using a reference to `Value` ensures that each time it is modified the `GetValue()` and `SetValue()` methods are called. The only other consideration for this approach is that it is probably a good idea to store the value or values that the property had when the form was originally shown. This allows the edit operation to be cancelled and any previous value or values restored. Suitable code for these situations is shown in Listings 5.3 and 5.4, for a class property and a single entity property, respectively.

LISTING 5.3   Code for a Custom Form to Be Called from the Edit() Method for a Class Property

```
// First show important code for TMyPropertyForm

// IN THE HEADER FILE
//------------------------------------------------------------------//
#ifndef MyPropertyFormH
#define MyPropertyFormH
//------------------------------------------------------------------//
#include <Classes.hpp>
#include <Controls.hpp>
#include <StdCtrls.hpp>
#include <Forms.hpp>
#include "HeaderDeclaringTPropertyClass"
//------------------------------------------------------------------//
class TMyPropertyForm : public TForm
{
__published:     // IDE-managed Components
private:
    TPropertyClass* FPropertyClass;
    // Other decalrations here for example restore values if 'Cancel'
    // is pressed

protected:
    void __fastcall SetPropertyClass(TPropertyClass* Pointer);
public:
    __fastcall TMyPropertyForm(TComponent* Owner);
    __property TPropertyClass* PropertyClass = {read=FPropertyClass,
                                      write=SetPropertyClass};

    // Other declarations here
};
//------------------------------------------------------------------//
#endif

// THE IMPLEMENTATION FILE
//------------------------------------------------------------------//
#include <vcl.h>
#pragma hdrstop

#include "MyPropertyForm.h"
//------------------------------------------------------------------//
#pragma package(smart_init)
#pragma resource "*.dfm"
//------------------------------------------------------------------//
```

LISTING 5.3   Continued

```
__fastcall TMyPropertyForm::TMyPropertyForm(TComponent* Owner)
        : TForm(Owner)
{
}
//-------------------------------------------------------------------//
void __fastcall TMyPropertyForm::SetPropertyClass(TPropertyClass* Pointer)
{
   FPropertyClass = Pointer;
   if(FPropertyClass != 0)
   {
      // Store current property values
   }
}
//-------------------------------------------------------------------//


// NOW SHOW THE Edit() METHOD

#include "MyPropertyForm.h" // Remember this

void __fastcall TExamplePropertyEditor::Edit(void)
{
   // Create the form
   std::auto_ptr<TMyPropertyForm*>
      MyPropertyForm(new TMyPropertyForm(0));
   // Link the property
   MyPropertyForm->PropertyClass
                  = reinterpret_cast<TPropertyClass*>(GetOrdValue());
   // Show the form. The form does all the work.
   MyPropertyForm->ShowModal();
}
//-------------------------------------------------------------------//
```

Notice the use of reinterpret_cast to convert the ordinal (int) representation of the pointer to the class to an actual pointer to the class. Listing 5.4 is shorter than Listing 5.3 because only the different code is shown.

LISTING 5.4   Code for a Custom Form to Be Called from the Edit() Method for an int Property

```
// First show important code for TMyPropertyForm
//-------------------------------------------------------------------//
// IN THE HEADER FILE CHANGE THE DEFINITION TO:
```

LISTING 5.4   Continued

```cpp
class TMyPropertyForm : public TForm
{
__published:     // IDE-managed Components
private:
  AnsiString& Value;
  int OldValue;
  // Other declarations here

public:
  __fastcall TMyPropertyForm(TComponent* Owner,  AnsiString& PropertyValue);
  // Other declarations here
};
//.........................................................................//
#endif

//.........................................................................//

// IN THE IMPLEMENTATION FILE MODIFY THE CONSTRUCTOR TO:

__fastcall TMyPropertyForm::TMyPropertyForm(TComponent* Owner,
                                            AnsiString& PropertyValue)
      : TForm(Owner),Value(PropertyValue)
{
  // Store the current property value. In this case it is an int
  // so code such as this is required
  OldValue = Value.ToInt();
}
//.........................................................................//

// NOW SHOW THE Edit() METHOD, almost the same...

#include "MyPropertyForm.h" // Remember this

void __fastcall TExamplePropertyEditor::Edit(void)
{
  // Create the form as before, but pass the extra parameter!
  std::auto_ptr<TMyPropertyForm*>
    MyPropertyForm(new TMyPropertyForm(0, Value));
  // Show the form. The form does all the work.
  MyPropertyForm->ShowModal();
}
//.........................................................................//
```

The difference between the second approach and the previous approach is that the value is modified after the modal form returns rather than continually modifying it while the form is displayed. This is the more common way to use a form to edit a property's value. Listing 5.5 shows the basic code required in the Edit() method.

LISTING 5.5   Code for a Custom Form to Be Called from the Edit() Method with No Updating Until Closing

```
#include "MyPropertyDialog.h" // Include the header for the Dialog!
                              // Dialog is TMyPropertyDialog


void __fastcall TExamplePropertyEditor::Edit(void)
{
    // Create the form
    std::auto_ptr<TMyPropertyDialog*>
        MyPropertyDialog(new TMyPropertyDialog(0));

    // Set the current property values in the dialog
    // MyPropertyDialog->value1 = GetValue();
    // MyPropertyDialog->value2 = GetXxxValue();
    // and so on...

    // Show the form and see the result.
    if(MyPropertyDialog->ShowModal() == IDOK)
    {
        // Then set the new property value(s)
    }
}
```

Note that TMyPropertyDialog might not be a dialog itself, but a wrapper for a dialog, similar to the standard dialog components. If this is the case, the dialog is shown by calling the wrapper's Execute() method. For more information on this method of displaying a dialog, refer to the C++Builder online help under "Making a Dialog Box a Component." In this case, such a dialog wrapper need only descend from TObject, not TComponent.

The GetValues() Method

The GetValues() method is used to populate the drop-down list of a property. This is done by successively calling Proc() and passing an AnsiString representation of the value. For example, if a series of values is desired that represents the transmission rate between a computer's communication port and an external modem, assuming the property editor had paValueList as an attribute, the GetValues() method could be written as follows:

```
void __fastcall GetValues(Classes::TGetStrProc Proc)
{
    Proc("300");
    Proc("9600");
    Proc("57600");
    // and so on...
}
```

Using the TPropertyEditor **Properties**

TPropertyEditor has four properties that can be used when writing custom property editors. One of these, Value, we have already discussed in the previous two sections. The remaining three properties are not used very often. They are described in the following list:

- Designer—This property is read-only and returns a pointer to the IDE's Designer interface. This is used to inform the IDE when certain events occur or to request the IDE to perform certain actions. For example, if you write your own implementation for one of the SetXxxValue() methods, you must tell the IDE that you have modified the property. You do this by calling Designer->Modifed();. In fact, you would call TPropertyEditor's Modified() method, which calls the same code. TPropertyEditor's Revert() method also uses this property. You probably will not need to use this property. It is shown for completeness.

- PrivateDirectory—This property is a directory, represented as an AnsiString, as returned by GetPrivateDirectory(), which itself obtains the directory from Designer->GetPrivateDirectory(). Hence, we can see that this directory is specified by the IDE. If your property editor requires a directory to store additional files, it should be the directory specified by this property. This property is read-only.

- PropCount—This property is read-only and returns the number of properties being edited when more than one component is selected. It is only used when GetAttributes() returns paMultiSelect.

Considerations When Choosing a Suitable Property Editor

Consider a property in a component that wraps the Windows communication API and allows different baud rates to be set. The values that can be chosen are predetermined, but a user-defined baud rate may be specified. What is the best way to enter such values?

It would be nice to have a drop-down list of choices. It would also be nice if the values in the drop-down list were numbers, not enumerations. The first thought that springs to mind is a custom property editor that descends from TintegerProperty, but displays a drop-down list of the values that can be set. A user-defined value could be entered in the editing region of the property value in the Object Inspector. This is trivial to implement and will work fine.

Have we really thought about whether this is the best approach? Let's think again. All is well when a value from the drop-down list is chosen, but we must detect when a user-defined value is entered. This is relatively simple, but requires that all values in the list be compared with the value returned by the property. If it is different, it is a user-defined baud rate. The component must then request a user-defined baud rate from the communication API equal to the value entered. Some values might be too big or too small. We must, therefore, perform bounds checking each time a value is entered. Our property editor is simple, but we have to write an increasing amount of maintenance code to support it. Not only that, but all these problems will be revisited by the runtime code.

We could restrict the values allowable to only those in the drop-down list by overriding the SetValue() method, and then creating two separate properties: one to enter a user-defined baud rate, and a Boolean property to indicate which we want to use. It seems that we are doing an awful lot of code writing just to enter a simple integer. Let's go back to the start and look at our original requirements.

We want to be able to enter a value from a given list of possible values, and we want to be able to specify a user-defined value, which may not be acceptable. Our initial thought was probably to use an enumeration for the values, but the convenience of using actual integer values made that option seem more attractive. Let's look at the enumeration route. A set of values is easily generated; we can even ensure that they appear in numerical order in the drop-down list by using underscores between the enumeration initials and the value. For example, given an enum called TBaudRate with the initials br, the baud rates 9600 and 115200 could be represented as br___9600 and br_115200, respectively.

We can even add a brUserDefined value to the enum. When brUserDefined is selected, an int UserDefined property can be read and the value tried. Therefore, we need this property as well. To do all this, we don't need to create a custom property editor at all since TEnumProperty is already defined as an editor for enum-based properties. We have a problem though: Any time we want to set or get a value at runtime, we must use the enumeration, which is often inconvenient. We must make this enumeration available to the component user. In the interest of keeping the global namespace clean, we could wrap the enum in a namespace, but this will make the enum even more of a hassle to use, so we won't do that. In fact, most components don't do this either. That is why initials are used in the enum's values.

So, which is best? It all depends on *exactly* what is required of the property and the component as a whole. Because this is a hypothetical discussion, it is hard to choose which method is better. The one thing to remember is that you must make your components robust and easy to use. Overly complex code should be avoided especially, because it might hide some of the more subtle features of how your component works. The enumeration approach might be a bit of a hassle as you convert to and from int values, but everyone knows what you can and cannot do with them. The time you save on not having to write a custom property editor could be used elsewhere. Remember also that if you need to read a value, you can simply create a read-only property so that, for example, the int value of the baud rate could be stored when it is successfully set by the enum property. This then could be read from an int-based read-only property.

Always think carefully when you are writing property editors and components in general. Consider the big picture and think ahead.

Properties and Exceptions

When a property value is to be changed and there is a possibility that the new value might not be valid, the function obtaining the value should detect the invalid value and throw an exception so that the user can enter a valid value. Where can the property value be changed? It can be requested to change from one of three places: from a property editor dialog, from a property editor, and from the property itself at runtime. The relationship between the three is shown in Figure 5.2. Note that the parameter to the SetValue() method is a const AnsiString even though it is pass-by-value . This only restricts Value from being modified within SetValue(). This is contrary to the normal use of const, where the main purpose of the keyword is to indicate that the argument passed to the function will not be modified. With pass-by-value, the argument is copied so it will not be modified in any way. If an error occurs, throwing an exception is the only appropriate way of informing the user. The other set methods can also be written using this approach, that is, pass-by-value variables declared as const.

From Figure 5.2 it can be seen that the set method for the property, in this case SetColor(), is ultimately called every time (unless an exception is thrown). It can then be tempting to detect only the validity of the property value at this stage and throw an exception from here. Remember that the purpose of throwing the exception is to detect the error and allow the user to enter a new value. By the time an exception is thrown from the property's set method, the user's edit operation is most likely finished. This might mean redisplaying a dialog or other inconveniences. You should throw an exception at the source of the error. Throwing an exception only from the property editor (or property editor dialog) is also no good because the property editor will not be used at runtime, letting invalid values silently cause havoc.

The solution is to throw an exception from the point of error. It might not be the easiest solution to implement, but it is the most robust.

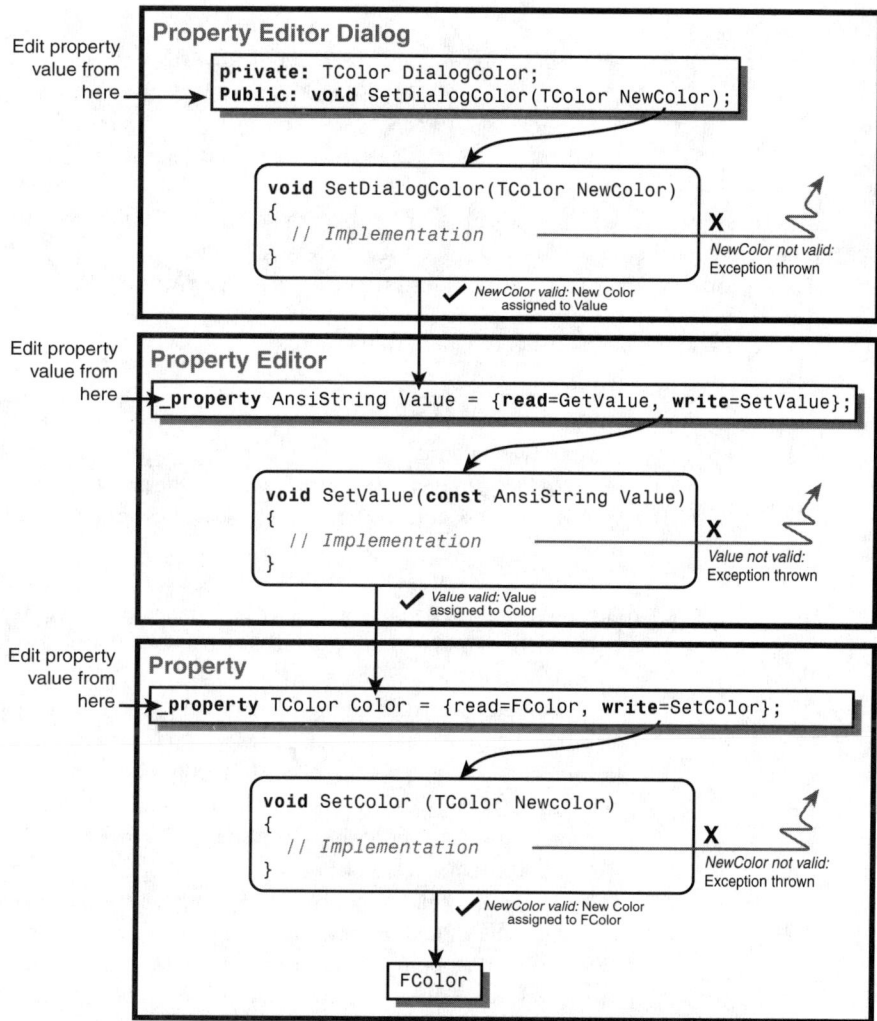

FIGURE 5.2   Exceptions thrown when editing a property.

Registering Custom Property Editors

Registering property editors is almost straightforward. I say *almost* because even though RegisterPropertyEditor() is all that is required, the parameters that need to

be passed are not always so trivial. As with other registration functions, the
RegisterPropertyEditor() function must be placed inside the package's Register()
function. The declaration for the RegisterPropertyEditor() function is

```
extern PACKAGE
    void __fastcall RegisterPropertyEditor(Typinfo::PTypeInfo PropertyType,
                                           TMetaClass* ComponentClass,
                                           const AnsiString PropertyName,
                                           TMetaClass* EditorClass);
```

Each parameter's purpose and an example of its use are shown in Table 5.7. The
PropertyType and PropertyName parameters are used to specify criteria that must be
matched by a property for it to be considered for use with the property editor.

TABLE 5.7   RegisterPropertyEditor() Parameters

Parameter Name	Purpose
PropertyType	This parameter expects a pointer to a TTypeInfo structure that contains type information for the property for which the editor is to be used. This parameter *must* be specified. If the property type is a VCL-derived class, the pointer can be obtained using the __typeinfo macro: __typeinfo(*TVCLClass*) Otherwise, it must be obtained either by examining the typeinfo of a similar existing property or by manually creating it. Both techniques are discussed in this section.
ComponentClass	This parameter is used to specify whether the editor is to be used for all matching properties in all components or only matching properties in components of the type specified. To specify a particular component type, use the __classid operator (which returns TMetaClass* as required) with the component class name: __classid(TComponentClassName) Otherwise, specify all components by passing 0 as the parameter.
PropertyName	This parameter is used to specify a property name, in the form of an AnsiString, that a property must have (in addition to having the same type information). It is used to restrict the property specification. If all properties of matching type information are required, an empty AnsiString is passed (""). If ComponentClass is 0, this parameter is ignored.
EditorClass	This parameter must be specified. It tells the IDE which property editor you want to register. As in the ComponentClass parameter, a TMetaClass pointer is expected. The property editor class name is, therefore, passed wrapped in the __classid operator, such as __classid(TPropertyEditorClassName)

In Table 5.7 you can see that ComponentClass and PropertyName can both be given a value so that they do *not* restrict the property editor to a specific component class or property name, respectively. This is contrary to their normal use. The only parameter that requires any further comment is PropertyType. As was stated before, the __typeinfo macro can be used to retrieve this information if the property type is a VCL-based class (ultimately derived from TObject). The __typeinfo macro is defined in $(BCB)\Include\Vcl\Sysmac.h as

```
#define __typeinfo(type)  (PTypeInfo)TObject::ClassInfo(__classid(type))
```

If the property is not a VCL class, information must be obtained through other means. There are two approaches to this: Either the appropriate PTypeInfo can be obtained from the property's name and the PTypeInfo of the class it belongs to, or the PTypeInfo can be manually generated.

PTypeInfo is a pointer to a TTypeInfo structure:

```
typedef TTypeInfo* PTypeInfo;
```

TTypeInfo is declared in $(BCB)\Include\Vcl\Typinfo.hpp as

```
struct TTypeInfo
{
    TTypeKind Kind;
    System::ShortString Name;
};
```

TTypeKind, declared in the same file, is an enumeration of type kinds. It is declared as

```
enum TTypeKind { tkUnknown, tkInteger, tkChar,
                 tkEnumeration, tkFloat, tkString,
                 tkSet, tkClass, tkMethod,
                 tkWChar, tkLString, tkWString,
                 tkVariant, tkArray, tkRecord,
                 tkInterface, tkInt64, tkDynArray };
```

The Name variable is a string version of the actual type. For example, int is "int", and AnsiString is "AnsiString". The following two sections discuss how a TTypeInfo* pointer can be obtained for non-VCL property types.

Obtaining a TTypeInfo* (PTypeInfo) from an Existing Property and Class for a Non-VCL Type

This approach requires that a VCL class containing the property already be defined and accessible. Then a PTypeInfo for that property type can be obtained using the

GetPropInfo() function declared in $(BCB)\Include\Vcl\Typinfo.hpp. PPropInfo is a typedef for a TPropInfo pointer, as in the following:

```
typedef TPropInfo* PPropInfo;
```

The GetPropInfo() function returns a pointer to a TPropInfo structure (PPropInfo) for a property within a particular class with a given property name, and optionally of a specific TTypeKind. It is available in one of four overloaded versions:

```
extern PACKAGE PPropInfo __fastcall GetPropInfo(PTypeInfo TypeInfo,
                                                const AnsiString PropName);


extern PACKAGE PPropInfo __fastcall GetPropInfo(PTypeInfo TypeInfo,
                                                const AnsiString PropName,
                                                TTypeKinds AKinds);

extern PACKAGE PPropInfo __fastcall GetPropInfo(TMetaClass* AClass,
                                                const AnsiString PropName,
                                                TTypeKinds AKinds);

extern PACKAGE PPropInfo __fastcall GetPropInfo(System::TObject* Instance,
                                                const AnsiString PropName,
                                                TTypeKinds AKinds);
```

These overloaded versions all ultimately call the first overloaded version of the method listed, namely

```
extern PACKAGE PPropInfo __fastcall GetPropInfo(PTypeInfo TypeInfo,
                                                const AnsiString PropName);
```

This is the version we are most interested in. The other versions also allow a Set of type TTypeKinds to be specified. This is a Set of the TTypeKind enumeration and is used to specify a TypeKind or TypeKinds that the property must also match. From the PPropInfo returned, we can obtain a pointer to an appropriate PTypeInfo for the property, which is the PropType field of the TPropInfo structure. TPropInfo is declared in $(BCB)\Include\Vcl\Typinfo.hpp as

```
struct TPropInfo
{
    PTypeInfo* PropType;
    void* GetProc;
    void* SetProc;
    void* StoredProc;
    int Index;
```

```
    int Default;
    short NameIndex;
    System::ShortString Name;
};
```

For example, the PTypeInfo for the Name property of TFont can be obtained by first obtaining a PPropInfo:

```
PPropInfo FontNamePropInfo = Typinfo::GetPropInfo(__typeinfo(TFont),
                                      "Name");
```

Then, obtain the PTypeInfo for the required property:

```
PTypeInfo FontNameTypeInfo = *FontNamePropInfo->PropType;
```

This PTypeInfo value can now be passed to the RegisterPropertyEditor() function. What we have actually obtained from this is a pointer to the TTypeInfo for an AnsiString property. This PTypeInfo could, therefore, be obtained and used as the PTypeInfo parameter anytime the PTypeInfo for an AnsiString is required. Additionally, the PTypeInfo for a custom property for a custom component can be similarly obtained:

```
PPropInfo CustomPropInfo = Typinfo::GetPropInfo(__typeinfo(TCustomComponent),
                                      "CustomPropertyName");

PTypeInfo CustomTypeInfo = *CustomPropInfo->PropType;
```

Note that it is possibly more clear if TTypeInfo* and TPropInfo* are used instead of their respective typedefs (PTypeInfo and PPropInfo). The typedefs have been used here for easy comparison with the GetPropInfo() function declarations.

The intermediate steps shown to obtain the PTypeInfo can be ignored. For example, the following can be used as an argument to RegisterPropertyEditor() for the custom property of a custom component:

```
*(Typinfo::GetPropInfo(__typeinfo(TCustomComponent),
                       "CustomPropertyName"))->PropType
```

This method of obtaining a TTypeInfo* relies on there being a published property of the desired type already in use by the VCL. This might not always be the case. Also, sometimes it might appear that a type already in use matches a type you want to use, but in fact it does not. An example of this is the Interval property of the TTimer component. The type of the Interval property is Cardinal, which is typedefed to unsigned int in the file $(BCB)\Include\Vcl\Sysmac.h. It is reasonable, therefore, to believe that retrieving the TypeInfo* for this property would enable you to register property editors for unsigned int properties. This is not so. You must have a property whose type is unsigned int, and it must appear in a C++–implemented class. There is an important lesson here: The TTypeInfo* for a non-VCL class type is not necessarily the same if the property belongs to an Object Pascal–implemented class and not a C++–implemented class. There is a very simple and effective way around this problem, and that is to create a class containing published properties of the types we desire. We then use the techniques previously discussed to retrieve a suitable TTypeInfo*, which we then use to register our property editor. Listing 5.6 shows such a class.

LISTING 5.6   Non-VCL Property Types in a Single Class

```
class PACKAGE TNonVCLTypesClass : public TObject
{
public:
__published:

    // Fundamental Integer Types
    __property int IntProperty = {};
    __property unsigned int UnsignedIntProperty = {};

    __property short int ShortIntProperty = {};
    __property unsigned short int UnsignedShortIntProperty = {};

    __property long int LongIntProperty = {};
    __property unsigned long int UnsignedLongIntProperty = {};

    __property char CharProperty = {};
    __property unsigned char UnsignedCharProperty = {};
    __property signed char SignedCharProperty = {};

    // Fundamental Floating Point Types
    __property double DoubleProperty = {};
    __property long double LongDoubleProperty = {};
    __property float FloatProperty = {};

    // Fundamental Boolean type
    __property bool BoolProperty = {};

    // The AnsiString class
    __property AnsiString AnsiStringProperty = {};

private:
```

LISTING 5.6   Continued

```
// Private Constructor, class cannot be instantiated from
inline __fastcall TNonVCLTypesClass() : TObject()
{ }

};
```

If you created a component called `TTestComponent` with an unsigned `int` property called `Size`, the following code would allow you to register a custom property editor:

```
RegisterPropertyEditor( *(Typinfo::GetPropInfo
                           (__typeinfo(TNonVCLTypesClass),
                            "UnsignedIntProperty")
                       )->PropType,
                       __classid(TTestComponent),
                       "Size",
                       __classid(TUnsignedProperty) );
```

The first parameter is a bit confusing. It is shown again for clarification:

```
*(Typinfo::GetPropInfo(__typeinfo(TNonVCLTypesClass),
                       "UnsignedIntProperty"))->PropType
```

This is the same as the code we saw earlier in this section. It's not very attractive to look at or easy to write. To help make it easier to use, you can create a class that contains static member functions that return the correct `TTypeInfo*` for each type. The definition for such a class is shown in Listing 5.7.

LISTING 5.7   NonVCLTypeInfo.h

```
//--------------------------------------------------------------------------//
#ifndef NonVCLTypeInfoH
#define NonVCLTypeInfoH
//--------------------------------------------------------------------------//
#ifndef TypInfoHPP
#include <TypInfo.hpp>
#endif
//--------------------------------------------------------------------------//

class PACKAGE TNonVCLTypeInfo : public TObject
{
public:
    // Fundamental Integer Types
```

LISTING 5.7 Continued

```
    static PTypeInfo __fastcall Int();
    static PTypeInfo __fastcall UnsignedInt();

    static PTypeInfo __fastcall ShortInt();
    static PTypeInfo __fastcall UnsignedShortInt();

    static PTypeInfo __fastcall LongInt();
    static PTypeInfo __fastcall UnsignedLongInt();

    static PTypeInfo __fastcall Char();
    static PTypeInfo __fastcall UnsignedChar();
    static PTypeInfo __fastcall SignedChar();

    // Fundamental Floating Point Types
    static PTypeInfo __fastcall Double();
    static PTypeInfo __fastcall LongDouble();
    static PTypeInfo __fastcall Float();

    // Fundamental Boolean type
    static PTypeInfo __fastcall Bool();

    // The AnsiString class
    static PTypeInfo __fastcall AnsiString();

private:
    // Private Constructor, class cannot be instantiated from
    inline __fastcall TNonVCLTypeInfo() : TObject()
    { }

};

// The definition for TNonVCLTypesClass goes here (Listing 5.6)

//--------------------------------------------------------------------------//
#endif
```

The implementation is shown in Listing 5.8.

LISTING 5.8   NonVCLTypeInfo.cpp

```cpp
#include <vcl.h>
#pragma hdrstop

#include "NonVCLTypeInfo.h"
//---------------------------------------------------------------------------//
#pragma package(smart_init)
//---------------------------------------------------------------------------//

PTypeInfo __fastcall TNonVCLTypeInfo::Int()
{
   return *(Typinfo::GetPropInfo(__typeinfo(TNonVCLTypesClass),
                             "IntProperty"))->PropType;
}

PTypeInfo __fastcall TNonVCLTypeInfo::UnsignedInt()
{
   return *(Typinfo::GetPropInfo(__typeinfo(TNonVCLTypesClass),
                             "UnsignedIntProperty"))->PropType;
}
//---------------------------------------------------------------------------//

PTypeInfo __fastcall TNonVCLTypeInfo::ShortInt()
{
   return *(Typinfo::GetPropInfo(__typeinfo(TNonVCLTypesClass),
                             "ShortIntProperty"))->PropType;
}

PTypeInfo __fastcall TNonVCLTypeInfo::UnsignedShortInt()
{
   return *(Typinfo::GetPropInfo(__typeinfo(TNonVCLTypesClass),
                             "UnsignedShortIntProperty"))->PropType;
}
//---------------------------------------------------------------------------//

PTypeInfo __fastcall TNonVCLTypeInfo::LongInt()
{
   return *(Typinfo::GetPropInfo(__typeinfo(TNonVCLTypesClass),
                             "LongIntProperty"))->PropType;
}

PTypeInfo __fastcall TNonVCLTypeInfo::UnsignedLongInt()
```

LISTING 5.8   Continued

```
{
   return *(Typinfo::GetPropInfo(__typeinfo(TNonVCLTypesClass),
                                 "UnsignedLongIntProperty"))->PropType;
}
//--------------------------------------------------------------------------//

PTypeInfo __fastcall TNonVCLTypeInfo::Char()
{
   return *(Typinfo::GetPropInfo(__typeinfo(TNonVCLTypesClass),
                                 "CharProperty"))->PropType;
}

PTypeInfo __fastcall TNonVCLTypeInfo::UnsignedChar()
{
   return *(Typinfo::GetPropInfo(__typeinfo(TNonVCLTypesClass),
                                 "UnsignedCharProperty"))->PropType;
}

PTypeInfo __fastcall TNonVCLTypeInfo::SignedChar()
{
   return *(Typinfo::GetPropInfo(__typeinfo(TNonVCLTypesClass),
                                 "SignedCharProperty"))->PropType;
}
//--------------------------------------------------------------------------//

PTypeInfo __fastcall TNonVCLTypeInfo::Double()
{
   return *(Typinfo::GetPropInfo(__typeinfo(TNonVCLTypesClass),
                                 "DoubleProperty"))->PropType;
}

PTypeInfo __fastcall TNonVCLTypeInfo::LongDouble()
{
   return *(Typinfo::GetPropInfo(__typeinfo(TNonVCLTypesClass),
                                 "LongDoubleProperty"))->PropType;
}

PTypeInfo __fastcall TNonVCLTypeInfo::Float()
{
   return *(Typinfo::GetPropInfo(__typeinfo(TNonVCLTypesClass),
                                 "FloatProperty"))->PropType;
```

LISTING 5.8   Continued

```
}
//--------------------------------------------------------------------//

PTypeInfo __fastcall TNonVCLTypeInfo::Bool()
{
    return *(Typinfo::GetPropInfo(__typeinfo(TNonVCLTypesClass),
                              "BoolProperty"))->PropType;
}
//--------------------------------------------------------------------//

PTypeInfo __fastcall TNonVCLTypeInfo::AnsiString()
{
    return *(Typinfo::GetPropInfo(__typeinfo(TNonVCLTypesClass),
                              "AnsiStringProperty"))->PropType;
}
//--------------------------------------------------------------------//
```

Using our previous example of registering a property editor for an unsigned int property called Size in a component called TTestComponent, the registration function is

```
RegisterPropertyEditor(TNonVCLTypeInfo::UnsignedInt(),
                       __classid(TTestComponent),
                       "Size",
                       __classid(TUnsignedProperty));
```

The previous code is simple, easy to understand, and easy to write. This should be your preferred method of registering property editors for non-VCL based properties.

It was mentioned earlier that determining a TTypeInfo* for a non-VCL property implemented in Object Pascal is not the same as one implemented in C++. An example of this is the PasswordChar property of TMaskEdit. To register a new property editor for all char types requires two registrations: one for Object Pascal–implemented properties and one for C++ implementations. The previous approach (a special class containing the appropriate non-VCL type properties) works fine for C++ implementations, but to get the correct TTypeInfo* for the Object Pascal implementations, the TTypeInfo* pointer must be determined directly from the VCL class, in this case from the PasswordChar property of TMaskEdit. This was the very first way we used to obtain a TTypeInfo*. If we want to register a new char property editor called TCharPropertyEditor for all components and all properties of type char, the registrations required are

```
TPropInfo* VCLCharPropInfo = Typinfo::GetPropInfo(__typeinfo(TMaskEdit),
                                                  "PasswordChar");
// Register the property editor for native VCL (Object Pascal) components

RegisterPropertyEditor(*VCLCharPropInfo->PropType,
                       0,
                       "",
                       __classid(TCharPropertyEditor));


// Register the property editor for C++ implemented components

RegisterPropertyEditor(TNonVCLTypeInfo::Char(),
                       0,
                       "",
                       __classid(TCharPropertyEditor));
```

Obtaining a TTypeInfo* (PTypeInfo) for a Non-VCL Type by Manual Creation

Creating a TTypeInfo* manually is an alternative approach to obtaining a TTypeInfo* from a VCL class for a non-VCL type. It is shown largely for comparison purposes and also because it is a commonly used technique. However, it should generally be avoided in preference to the first method. Manually creating the required PTypeInfo pointer can be done in place before the call to RegisterPropertyEditor(), or the code can be placed in a function that will return the pointer.

There are two ways to write the code to do this. One is to declare a static TTypeInfo structure locally, assign the appropriate values to it, and use a reference to it as the PTypeInfo argument. The other is to allocate a TTypeInfo structure dynamically, assign the appropriate values, and then use the pointer as the PTypeInfo argument. Both methods for generating a suitable PTypeInfo for an AnsiString property are shown in Listing 5.9. Note that this code and other similar functions are found in the GetTypeInfo unit on the CD-ROM.

LISTING 5.9   Manually Creating a TTypeInfo*

```
//----------------------------------------------------------------------//
//                          As Functions                                //
//----------------------------------------------------------------------//
TTypeInfo* AnsiStringTypeInfo(void)
{
    static TTypeInfo TypeInfo;
    TypeInfo.Name = "AnsiString";
```

LISTING 5.9   Continued

```
   TypeInfo.Kind = tkLString;
   return &TypeInfo;
}

// OR

TTypeInfo* AnsiStringTypeInfo(void)
{
   TTypeInfo* TypeInfo = new TTypeInfo;
   TypeInfo->Name = "AnsiString";
   TypeInfo->Kind = tkLString;
   return TypeInfo;
}

//---------------- In the Registration code simply write:-------------------//

RegisterPropertyEditor(AnsiStringTypeInfo(),
                       0 ,
                       "",
                       __classid(TAnsiStringPropertyEditor));


//-------------------------------------------------------------------------//
//            In Place Before RegisterPropertyEditor()                     //
//-------------------------------------------------------------------------//

static TTypeInfo AnsiStringTypeInfo;
TypeInfo.Name = "AnsiString";
TypeInfo.Kind = tkLString;

RegisterPropertyEditor(&AnsiStringTypeInfo,
                       0 ,
                       "",
                       __classid(TAnsiStringPropertyEditor));

// OR

TTypeInfo* AnsiStringTypeInfo = new TTypeInfo;
TypeInfo->Name = "AnsiString";
TypeInfo->Kind = tkLString;
```

LISTING 5.9   Continued

```
RegisterPropertyEditor(AnsiStringTypeInfo,
                        0 ,
                        "",
                        __classid(TAnsiStringPropertyEditor));
```

Notice that when the TTypeInfo structure is dynamically allocated (with new), it is not deleted after the call to RegisterPropertyEditor(). If this is done, the registration will fail. The reason for this is explained in the following section.

How to Obtain a TTypeInfo* for a Non-VCL Type

Which of the two approaches you use to obtain a TTypeInfo* for a non-VCL type—determine it from a VCL class or manually create it—is straightforward. Always use the first method when you can. In particular, you must use the first method if you are writing a property editor to override an existing property editor for which an editor has been specifically registered by the VCL (as opposed to being determined dynamically) or one that has been previously registered using the first approach. In general, the first approach is more robust because you are using the VCL's representation of the TTypeInfo* for the given property. The need to use the first method to override a property editor registered using the first method should be noted. Creating a class with static member functions to return a suitable TTypeInfo* makes the first method just as easy as the manual creation method and should be considered the superior technique.

An important point about using the two approaches is that writing a function to a specific PTypeInfo (the second method) is *not* the same as obtaining the PTypeInfo from the VCL (the first method). The reason for this is that the implementation of TPropertyClassRec, used internally by the RegisterPropertyEditor() function, maintains only a PTypeInfo variable, not the actual values that it points to, namely the Name and Kind of the TTypeInfo. This is why a reference to a locally declared non-static TTypeInfo structure cannot be used and a dynamically allocated TTypeInfo structure must not be deleted (it is simply abandoned on free store).

Registering property editors is then relatively easy. However, care must be taken to ensure that the parameters passed are exact. Often it is possible to compile and install property editors that do not appear to function, only to find later that the registration code is not quite right (such as when the PropertyName parameter has been spelled incorrectly) and that the property editor worked all along.

Rules for Overriding Property Editors

With the knowledge of how to register custom property editors and the realization that it is possible to override any previously installed property editor, the question is this: What are the rules for overriding property editors? The following highlights the two main considerations:

- In general, property editors are used from newest to oldest. In other words, the most recently installed property editor for a given property will be used. The exception to this is noted in the next point.

- A newly registered property editor will override an existing property editor only if the specification used to register it is *at least as specific* as that used to register the existing editor. For example, if a property editor is registered specifically for the Shape property (of type TShapeType) in the TShape component, installing a new editor for properties of type TShapeType for *all* components (ComponentClass == 0) will *not* override the property editor for the Shape property of TShape.

The only other consideration when overriding property editors is the method used to obtain the appropriate PTypeInfo, as previously discussed. Such property overriding can be seen in practice by examining the EnhancedEditors package on the accompanying CD-ROM.

Using Images in Property Editors

This section introduces the techniques required to render images in the Object Inspector for custom property editors. Some property editors already render images in the Object Inspector. For example, a property of type TColor will appear automatically in the Object Inspector as other TColor properties do. However, there are many more types of properties that could benefit from the use of images when editing the property. To facilitate this, you must not only inherit from TpropertyEditor or a descendant, but must also inherit from ICustomPropertyEditor; ICustomPropertyEditor provides six new methods, five of which can be overridden. The declarations for those five functions are as follows:

```
void __fastcall ListMeasureWidth(const AnsiString Value,
                                 Graphics::TCanvas* ACanvas,
                                 int& AWidth);

void __fastcall ListMeasureHeight(const AnsiString Value,
                                  Graphics::TCanvas* ACanvas,
                                  int& AHeight);

void __fastcall ListDrawValue(const AnsiString Value,
                              Graphics::TCanvas* ACanvas,
                              const TRect& ARect,
                              bool ASelected);
```

```
void __fastcall PropDrawValue(Graphics::TCanvas* ACanvas,
                              const TRect& ARect,
                              bool ASelected);

void __fastcall PropDrawName(Graphics::TCanvas* ACanvas,
                             const TRect& ARect,
                             bool ASelected);
```

The remaining method, to be used in conjunction with the *XxxxDrawValue* methods, is declared as

```
AnsiString __fastcall GetVisualValue();
```

These are listed in Table 5.8, along with a description of the purpose of each. Note that you must implement all five of the overridable methods or your class will not link.

TABLE 5.8   New Methods of `ICustomPropertyEditor` to Allow Custom Images

Method	Purpose
ListMeasureWidth()	This is used to allow the default width of an entry in the drop-down list to be modified. As the width of the overall drop-down list is set to that of the widest entry or greater, this is effectively the minimum width of the drop-down list.
ListMeasureHeight()	This is used to allow the default height of each list entry to be modified. Unless a large image is displayed (as is the case with TCursor properties), this method does not generally need to be overridden.
ListDrawValue()	This is called to render each property value in the drop-down list.
PropDrawValue()	This is called to render the selected property value for the property when it does not have focus. When the property has focus, the current property value is shown as an editable AnsiString.
PropDrawName()	This is called to render the property name in the Object Inspector. It is not required often.
GetVisualValue()	This is used to return the displayable value of the property. This method is used in conjunction with the ListDrawValue() and PropDrawValue() methods to render the AnsiString representation of the property value.

Where in the Object Inspector these methods are used is illustrated in Figure 5.3. You can see that the three most important methods to override are `ListMeasureWidth()`, `ListDrawValue()`, and `PropDrawValue()`.

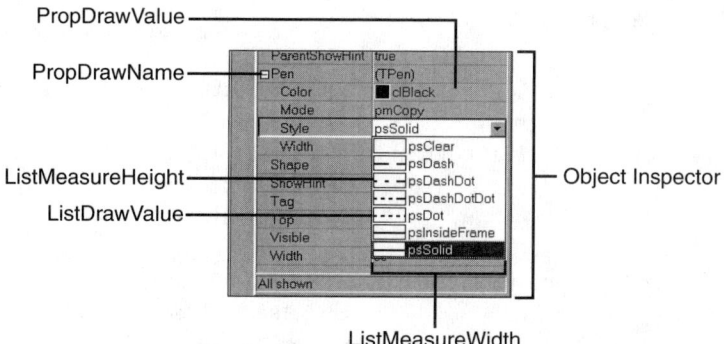

FIGURE 5.3   Areas in the Object Inspector that are affected by the new overridable `TPropertyEditor` methods.

To create your own custom images in the Object Inspector, you must derive a new property editor class from `TPropertyEditor` or from a class derived from `TPropertyEditor`. Which you choose depends on the type of the property that the editor is for. For example, a property of type `int` would descend from `TIntegerProperty`. Refer to the section "Creating Custom Property Editors," earlier in this chapter, for more information. A new property editor class can then be defined according to the format in Listing 5.10. As an example, the editor is derived from `TEnumProperty`.

LISTING 5.10   Definition Code for a Property Editor That Renders Custom Images

```
#include "VCLEditors.hpp"

class TCustomImagePropertyEditor : public TenumProperty,ICustomPropertyEditor
{
    typedef TEnumProperty inherited;

public:
    void __fastcall ListMeasureWidth(const AnsiString Value,
                                     Graphics::TCanvas* ACanvas,
                                     int& AWidth);

    void __fastcall ListMeasureHeight(const AnsiString Value,
                                      Graphics::TCanvas* ACanvas,
                                      int& AHeight);

    void __fastcall ListDrawValue(const AnsiString Value,
                                  Graphics::TCanvas* ACanvas,
```

LISTING 5.10   Continued

```
                                     const TRect& ARect,
                                     bool ASelected);

    void __fastcall PropDrawValue(Graphics::TCanvas* ACanvas,
                                     const TRect& ARect,
                                     bool ASelected);

    void __fastcall PropDrawName(Graphics::TCanvas* ACanvas,
                                     const TRect& ARect,
                                     bool ASelected);

protected:
    #pragma option push -w-inl
    inline __fastcall virtual
        TCustomImagePropertyEditor(const _DesignIntf::di_IDesigner  ADesigner,
                             int APropCount)
                              : TEnumProperty(ADesigner,
                                              APropCount)
    { }
    #pragma option pop

public:
    #pragma option push -w-inl
    inline __fastcall virtual ~TCustomImagePropertyEditor(void)
    { }
    #pragma option pop

};
```

It is assumed that only the drawing behavior of the property editor is to be modified. The remainder of the class is not altered.

The implementation of each of the five functions is discussed in the sections that follow. For each of the methods, comments will indicate the code that should be present in each method. This will be followed by the actual code used to produce the images shown in Figure 5.4, which shows a finished property editor in use.

As an example, a property editor for the TShapeType enumeration from the TShape component will be developed. The class definition for such a property editor is exactly the same as that shown in Listing 5.10. However, the class is called TShapeTypePropertyEditor. The parameters used in the five image-rendering methods are detailed in Table 5.9 so that an overall picture of how they are used can be developed.

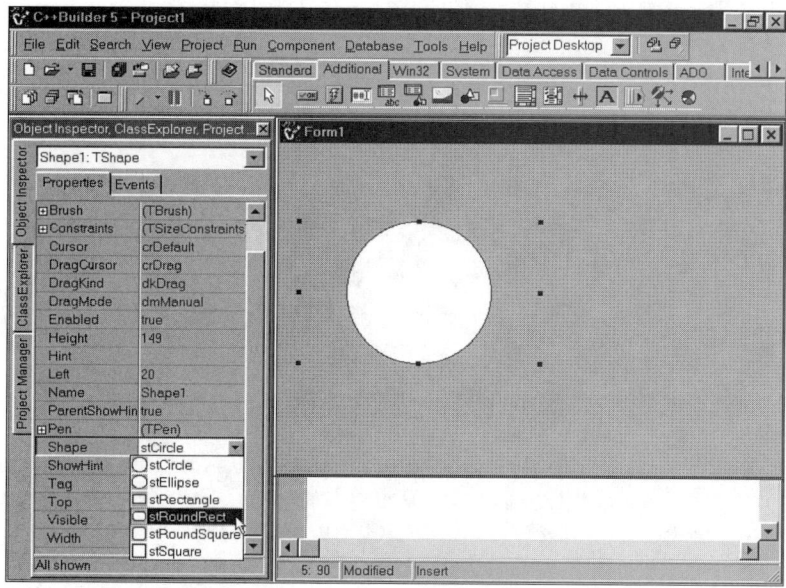

FIGURE 5.4   The `TShapeTypePropertyEditor` in use.

TABLE 5.9   Parameters for Custom Image-Rendering Methods

Method	Purpose
AWidth	This is the current width in pixels of the `AnsiString` representation of the value as it will be displayed in the Object Inspector, including leading and trailing space.
AHeight	This is the default height of the display area for the current item. Typically, this is 2 pixels greater than the height of `ACanvas->TextHeight("Ag")`, where Ag is chosen simply to remind the reader that the actual font height of the current font is returned, that is the ascender height (from A) plus the descender height (from g). Adding 2 pixels allows a 1-pixel border. Remember that the ascender height also includes the internal leading height (used for accents, umlauts, and tildes in non-English character sets), typically 2 to 3 pixels. Refer to Figure 5.5 for clarification.
ACanvas	This encapsulates the device context for the current item in the Object Inspector.
ARect	This represents the client area of the region to be painted.
ASelected	This parameter is `true` when the list item is currently selected in the Object Inspector.

Figure 5.5 shows a diagram illustrating how the height of text is calculated.

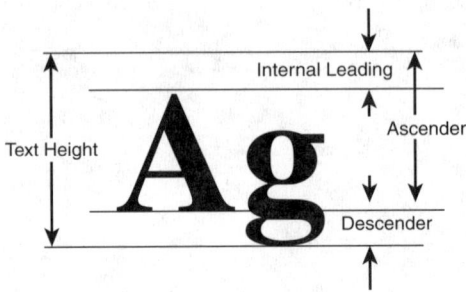

FIGURE 5.5   Calculating text height.

Figure 5.6 shows the relationship between the parameters in Table 5.9 and the actual rendering of an image and text in the Object Inspector. This figure will be referred to throughout the discussion, and additional information is therefore shown.

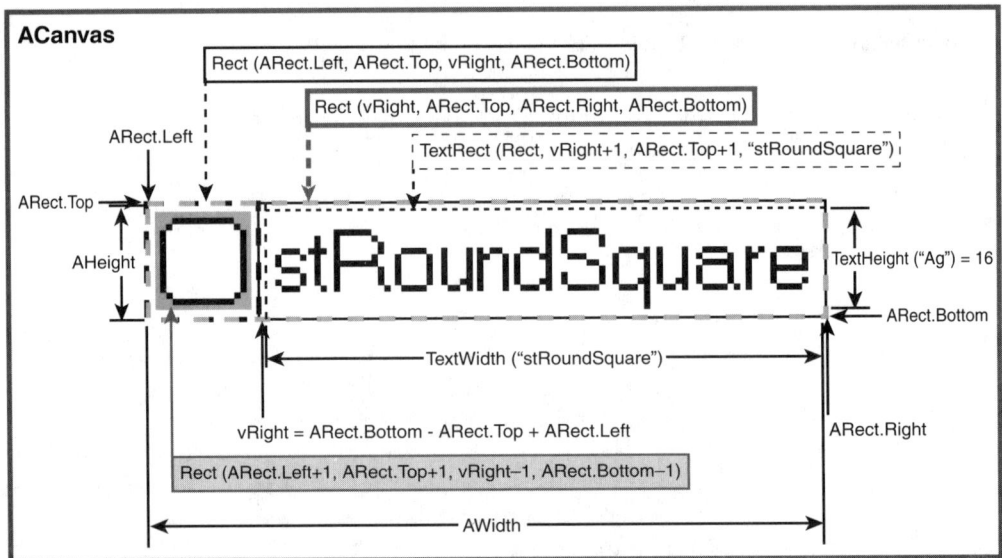

FIGURE 5.6   The relationship between image-rendering parameters and actual display.

The `ListMeasureWidth()` Method

Initially, `AWidth` is equal to the return value of `ACanvas->TextWidth(Value)`. However, if an image is added to the display, the width of the image must be added to `AWidth` to update it. This method, called during the width calculation phase of the drop-down list, enables you to do this. If a square image region is required, AWidth can simply be adjusted by adding ACanvas->TextHeight("Ag")+2 to its current value. This is because this value will equal the default AHeight value, as previously mentioned in Table 5.9. (Also, see Figure 5.6, in which ACanvas->TextHeight("Ag")+2 is 18 (16+2) pixels.) Remember that Ag could be replaced by any characters. If a larger image is required, a multiple of this value can be used or a constant can be added to the width. If the image width is known, this can simply be added to the current AWidth value. The code is shown in Listing 5.11.

LISTING 5.11   Overriding the ListMeasureWidth() Method

```
void __fastcall
    TShapeTypePropertyEditor::ListMeasureWidth(const AnsiString Value,
                                               Graphics::TCanvas* ACanvas,
                                               int& AWidth)
{
    AWidth += (ACanvas->TextHeight("Ag")+2) + 0; // 0 can be replaced
                                                 // by a constant
}
```

The ListMeasureHeight() **Method**

AHeight must not be given a value smaller than ACanvas->TextHeight("Ag")+2 because this would clip the text displayed. Therefore, two choices are available. A constant value can be added to the current AHeight, normally to maintain a constant ratio with the image width, or AHeight can be changed directly. If it is changed directly, the new value must be greater than ACanvas->TextHeight("Ag")+2; otherwise, this value should be used. The code is shown in Listing 5.12.

LISTING 5.12   Overriding the ListMeasureHeight() Method

```
void __fastcall
    TShapeTypePropertyEditor::ListMeasureHeight(const AnsiString Value,
                                                Graphics::TCanvas* ACanvas,
                                                int& AHeight)
{
    AHeight += 0; // 0 could be replaced by a constant value
}
// OR :

void __fastcall
    TShapeTypePropertyEditor::ListMeasureHeight(const AnsiString Value,
```

LISTING 5.12   Continued

```
                                        Graphics::TCanvas* ACanvas,
                                        int& AHeight)
{
   if( (ACanvas->TextHeight("Ag")+2) < ImageHeight )
   {
      AHeight = ImageHeight;
   }
}
```

The ListDrawValue() Method

This method does most of the hard work. It is this method that renders each item in the drop-down list by drawing directly onto the list item's canvas. To write well-behaved code, this method should have the layout in Listing 5.13.

This listing works for the case where you are inheriting from a property editor that implements IcustomPropertyEditor. If you do not inherit from such an editor, it is inappropriate to call the inherited methods, since they have no implementation.

To get an appreciation of what the actual rendering code is doing, refer to Figure 5.6. For the big picture, refer to Figure 5.3.

LISTING 5.13   A Template for Overriding the ListDrawValue() Method

```
void __fastcall
   TCustomImagePropertyEditor::ListDrawValue(const AnsiString Value,
                                        Graphics::TCanvas* ACanvas,
                                        const TRect& ARect,
                                        bool ASelected)
{
   // Declare an int vRight to indicate the right most edge of the image.
   // The v prefix is used to indicate that it is a variable. This used
   // to follow the convention used in VCLEditors.pas.

   try
   {
      // Step 1 - Save ACanvas properties that we are going to change.

      // Step 2 - Frame the area to be modified. This is required so that any
      //          previous rendering on the canvas is overwritten. For example
      //          when the IDE selection rendering is applied, i.e. the
      //          property value is surrounded by a dashed yellow and black
```

LISTING 5.13   Continued

```
    //              line and the AnsiString representation is highlighted in
    //              clNavy, and focus then moves to another list value the
    //              modified parts of ACanvas are cleared, ready for the custom
    //              rendering. If the entire ACanvas is going to be changed then
    //              this operation is not required.

    // Step 3 - Perform any preparation required. For example paint a
    //              background colour and place a highlight box around the image
    //              of the list value if ASelected is true.
    //
    //              To choose a colour to match the current text used by windows
    //              select clWindowText, this is useful as an image border, hence
    //              this is often selected as a suitable ACanvas->Pen colour.
    //
    //              To give the appearance of a clear background, clear border or
    //              both set the ACanvas->Brush and/or ACanvas->Pen colour to
    //              clWindow.
    //
    //              To use a colour the same as the Object Inspector choose
    //              clBtnFace.

    // Step 4 - Determine the value of the current list item.

    // Step 5 - Draw the required image onto ACanvas.

    // Step 6 - Restore modified ACanvas properties to their original values.
}
__finally
{
    // Perform the following operation to render the AnsiString
    // representation of the current item, i.e. Value, onto ACanvas.

    // 1. Either call the parents ListDrawValue method passing vRight as the
    //    l (left) parameter of the Rect variable, i.e.
    //
    //    TEnumProperty::ListDrawValue(Value,
    //                                 ACanvas,
    //                                 Rect(vRight,
    //                                      ARect.Top,
    //                                      ARect.Right,
    //                                      ARect.Bottom),
```

LISTING 5.13 Continued

```
//                                  ASelected);
//    which becomes:
//
//    inherited::ListDrawValue(Value,
//                  ACanvas,
//                  Rect(vRight,
//                      ARect.Top,
//                      ARect.Right,
//                      ARect.Bottom),
//                  ASelected);
//
//    using our typedef which is more maintainable.

// 2. Or perform this operation directly by calling the TextRect() member
//    function directly removing the need to call the parent version of
//    this (ListDrawValue()) virtual function
//    i.e.
//    ACanvas->TextRect( Rect(vRight,
//                      ARect.Top,
//                      ARect.Right,
//                      ARect.Bottom),
//                  vRight+1,
//                  ARect.Top+1,
//                  Value );
  }
}
```

Actual code based on the template in Listing 5.13 is shown in Listing 5.14. The code renders each item in the drop-down list. Each item in the list consists of an image followed by text representing the enum value to which the item refers. Figure 5.4 shows an image of the rendered drop-down list.

Once again, keep in mind that this assumes there is an inherited implementation for the ICustomPropertyEditor member functions. If that is not the case, do not call the inherited member functions.

LISTING 5.14 An Implementation of the ListDrawValue() Method

```
void __fastcall
    TShapeTypePropertyEditor::ListDrawValue(const AnsiString Value,
                                    Graphics::TCanvas* ACanvas,
                                    const TRect& ARect,
```

LISTING 5.14   Continued

```cpp
                                          bool ASelected)
{
    // Declare vRight ('v' stands for variable)
    int vRight = ARect.Bottom - ARect.Top + ARect.Left;

    try
    {
        // Step 1 - Save ACanvas properties that we are going to change

        TColor vOldPenColor = ACanvas->Pen->Color;
        TColor vOldBrushColor = ACanvas->Brush->Color;


        // Step 2 - Frame the area to be modified.

        ACanvas->Pen->Color = ACanvas->Brush->Color;
        ACanvas->Rectangle(ARect.Left, ARect.Top, vRight, ARect.Bottom);


        // Step 3 - Perform any preparation required.

        if(ASelected)                        // Choose a Pen colour
        {                                    // depending on whether
            ACanvas->Pen->Color = clYellow;  // the list value is
        }                                    // selected or not
        else
        {
            ACanvas->Pen->Color = clBtnFace;
        }

        ACanvas->Brush->Color = clBtnFace;   // Choose a background color to
                                             // match the Object Inspector


        ACanvas->Rectangle( ARect.Left + 1,  // Draw the background onto
                            ARect.Top + 1,   // the Canvas using the
                            vRight - 1,      // current Pen and the
                            ARect.Bottom - 1 );  // current Brush :-)
```

LISTING 5.14   Continued

```
// Step 4 - Determine the value of the current list item

TShapeType ShapeType = TShapeType(GetEnumValue(GetPropType(), Value));

// Step 5 - Draw the required image onto ACanvas

ACanvas->Pen->Color = clBlack;
ACanvas->Brush->Color = clWhite;

switch(ShapeType)
{
    case stRectangle   : ACanvas->Rectangle(ARect.Left+2,
                                            ARect.Top+4,
                                            vRight-2,
                                            ARect.Bottom-4);
                         break;
    case stSquare      : ACanvas->Rectangle(ARect.Left+2,
                                            ARect.Top+2,
                                            vRight-2,
                                            ARect.Bottom-2);
                         break;
    case stRoundRect   : ACanvas->RoundRect(ARect.Left+2,
                                            ARect.Top+4,
                                            vRight-2,
                                            ARect.Bottom-4,
                                            (ARect.Bottom-ARect.Top-6)/2,
                                            (ARect.Bottom-ARect.Top-6)/2);
                         break;
    case stRoundSquare : ACanvas->RoundRect(ARect.Left+2,
                                            ARect.Top+2,
                                            vRight-2,
                                            ARect.Bottom-2,
                                            (ARect.Bottom-ARect.Top)/3,
                                            (ARect.Bottom-ARect.Top)/3);
                         break;
    case stEllipse     : ACanvas->Ellipse(ARect.Left+1,
                                          ARect.Top+2,
                                          vRight-1,
                                          ARect.Bottom-2);
                         break;
    case stCircle      : ACanvas->Ellipse(ARect.Left+1,
```

LISTING 5.14   Continued

```
                                       ARect.Top+1,
                                       vRight-1,
                                       ARect.Bottom-1);
                       break;
        default : break;
    }

    // Step 6 - Restore modified ACanvas properties to their original values

    ACanvas->Pen->Color = vOldPenColor;
    ACanvas->Brush->Color = vOldBrushColor;

  }
  __finally
  {
    // Render the AnsiString representation onto ACanvas
    // Use method 1, call the parent method

    inherited::ListDrawValue(Value,
                             ACanvas,
                             Rect(vRight,
                                  ARect.Top,
                                  ARect.Right,
                                  ARect.Bottom),
                             ASelected);
  }
}
```

Step 4 in Listing 5.14 is of crucial importance to the operation of ListDrawValue().
The value of the drop-down list item is determined here. This allows a decision to be
made in Step 5 as to what should be rendered. For enumerations such as TShapeType,
the AnsiString representation of the value must be converted to an actual value. The
code that performs this is

```
TShapeType ShapeType = TShapeType(GetEnumValue(GetPropType(), Value));
```

GetEnumValue() is declared in $(BCB)\Include\Vcl\TypInfo.hpp and returns an int value.
This int value is used to construct a new TShapeType variable called ShapeType. The
function GetPropType() returns a pointer to a TTypeInfo structure containing the
TypeInfo for the property type (in this case TShapeType). This could alternatively have
been obtained using

```
*GetPropInfo()->PropType
```

This is similar to the approach used to obtain type information when registering property editors (see the section "Obtaining a `TTypeInfo*` (`PTypeInfo`) from an Existing Property and Class for a Non-VCL Type," earlier in this chapter, for more details) and can be used more generally. `Value` is the `AnsiString` representation of the current enumeration value. `GetPropType()` and `GetPropInfo()` are both member functions of `TPropertyEditor` and, as such, are declared in `$(BCB)\Include\Vcl\VCLEditors.hpp`. Techniques such as these are indispensable to writing property editors, so it is important to be aware of them.

Each of the images is rendered according to the bounding `ARect` parameter. This means that the code does not need to be modified to enlarge or reduce the rendered images. To do this, simply change the values of `AWidth` and `AHeight`. Changing the constant `0` in the `ListMeasureWidth()` and `ListMeasureHeight()` methods to `10`, for example, will increase the rendered image size in the drop-down list by `10` pixels in each direction. Note that the image in the property value region will not be affected.

The `PropDrawValue()` Method

This method is responsible for rendering the current property value in the Object Inspector. The height of the area to be rendered is fixed (`ARect.Bottom - ARect.Top`) so there is less flexibility over the images that can be rendered compared with images rendered in the drop-down list. The code required for this operation is the same as that required to render the same value in the drop-down list. The only difference is the value of the `ARect` parameter. The rendering can, therefore, be carried out by the `ListDrawValue()` method, passing the `PropDrawValue()` parameters as arguments. The code for this member function is shown in Listing 5.15.

LISTING 5.15   An Implementation of the `PropDrawValue()` Method

```
void __fastcall
    TShapeTypePropertyEditor::PropDrawValue(Graphics::TCanvas* ACanvas,
                                            const TRect& ARect,
                                            bool ASelected)
{
    if( GetVisualValue() != "" )
    {
        ListDrawValue(GetVisualValue(), ACanvas, ARect, ASelected);
    }
    else
    {
        // As in the ListDrawValue method either the parent method can be called
        // or the code required to render the text called directly, i.e.
        //
        // inherited::PropDrawValue(ACanvas, ARect, ASelected);
```

LISTING 5.15   Continued

```
      //
      // or:
      //
      // ACanvas->TextRect( ARect,
      //                      ARect.Left+1,
      //                      ARect.Top+1,
      //                      GetVisualValue() );
      //
      // For comparison the text is rendered directly, i.e.

      ACanvas->TextRect( ARect,
                          ARect.Left+1,
                          ARect.Top+1,
                          GetVisualValue() );
   }
}
```

The `PropDrawName()` Method

This is the last of the overridable methods for custom rendering and the one least often required. It controls the rendering of the property `Name` (see Figure 5.3). As with the `PropDrawValue()` method, the height of the drawing region is fixed. This method has limited use, but it can be used to add symbols to properties that exhibit certain behavior, read-only properties, for instance (such as About properties). Overuse should be avoided because it might confuse rather than help users.

Another possible use is to add an image to `TComponent`-derived properties to indicate the component required. This method is not used in the `TShapeTypePropertyEditor` example, but the required code, should it be needed, is shown in Listing 5.16.

LISTING 5.16   An Implementation of the `PropDrawName()` Method

```
void __fastcall
   TCustomImagePropertyEditor::PropDrawValue(Graphics::TCanvas* ACanvas,
                                             const TRect& ARect,
                                             bool ASelected)
{
   if( GetName() != "" )
   {
      // Write a function to render the desired image, similar to
      // the ListDrawValue() method, i.e.
      //
```

LISTING 5.16   Continued

```
      // PropDrawNameValue(GetName(), ACanvas, ARect, ASelected); // Must be
                                                                // defined

  }
  else
  {
      // As in the PropDrawValue method either the parent method can be called
      // or the code required to render the text called directly, i.e.
      //
      // inherited::PropDrawName(ACanvas, ARect, ASelected);
      //
      // or:
      //
      // ACanvas->TextRect( ARect,
      //                    vRect.Left+1,
      //                    ARect.Top+1,
      //                    GetName() );
      //
      // For comparison the text is rendered directly, i.e.

      ACanvas->TextRect( ARect,
                         ARect.Left+1,
                         ARect.Top+1,
                         GetName() );
  }
}
```

The `TImageListPropertyEditor` from the `EnhancedEditors` package (see Table 5.1) does implement this method to display an icon representing a `TImageList` component for `TCustomImageList*` properties. Listing 5.17 shows its implementation of this method for comparison. Note that `ImageListPropertyImage` is a resource loaded in the property editor's constructor.

LISTING 5.17   An Alternative Implementation of the `PropDrawName()` Method

```
void __fastcall
  TImageListPropertyEditor::PropDrawName (Graphics::TCanvas* ACanvas,
                                          const TRect& ARect,
                                          bool ASelected)
{
  TRect ValueRect = ARect;
```

LISTING 5.17 Continued

```
try
{
    // Clear the canvas using the current pen and brush
    ACanvas->FillRect(ARect);

    if(GetName() != "")
    {
        if(Screen->PixelsPerInch > 96) // If Large fonts
        {
            ACanvas->Draw( ARect.Left + 1,
                           ARect.Top + 2,
                           ImageListPropertyImage );
        }
        else // Otherwise small fonts
        {
            ACanvas->Draw( ARect.Left + 1,
                           ARect.Top,
                           ImageListPropertyImage );
        }

        ValueRect = Rect( ARect.Left + 16 + 2,
                          ARect.Top,
                          ARect.Right,
                          ARect.Bottom );
    }
}
__finally
{
    // Whether or not we successfully draw the image we must draw the text
    inherited::PropDrawName(ACanvas, ValueRect, ASelected);
}
}
```

The code in Listing 5.17 is reasonably straightforward. Of note is the try/__finally block to ensure that the text is always rendered. The code inside the try block is similar to that in Listing 5.16; the only difference is that the ImageListPropertyImage resource is positioned differently, depending on whether the screen is using large or small fonts. After the ImageListPropertyImage resource is rendered, the Rect for rendering the text is offset to allow for the width of the resource, which in this case is 16 pixels.

Creating Custom Component Editors

The previous section discussed property editors for components as a method of allowing a more intuitive and robust interface at design time. Component Editors take this further by allowing custom editors for the whole component to be created. Custom component editors also allow the context menu for each component (shown when the component is right-clicked) to be customized, along with specifying the behavior when a component is double-clicked on a form. This section, like the previous one, presents the background and principles required to create custom component editors. Component editors add the possibility of customizing the default behavior associated with editing a component and also allowing additional behavior to be specified. Two classes are available for creating component editors: TComponentEditor and TDefaultEditor. The relationship between the two is shown in Figure 5.7.

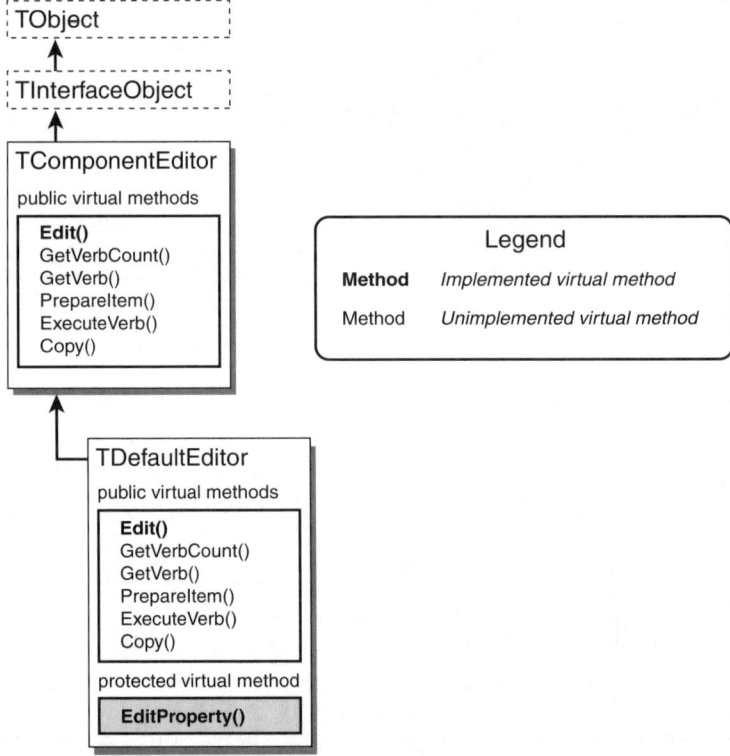

FIGURE 5.7   The TComponentEditor inheritance hierarchy.

Figure 5.7 shows additional information, namely the virtual functions that should be overridden to customize the component editor's behavior. This can be referred to when the virtual functions themselves are discussed later in this section, in Table 5.11 and in subsequent sections with the methods' names.

As was stated initially, creating a custom component editor allows the default behavior that occurs in response to the component being right-clicked or double-clicked in the IDE to be specified. Table 5.10 lists both mouse events and indicates which of the virtual functions are invoked. The default behavior of each of the classes is also stated.

TABLE 5.10   TComponentEditor and TDefaultEditor Mouse Responses

When the component is...	Default Action	virtual Functions Invoked
Right-Clicked	The component's context menu is displayed.	GetVerbCount() is invoked first. This is used to return the number of items to be added to the top of the default context menu. GetVerb() is called next. This allows an AnsiString representing each of the menu items to be returned. PrepareItem() is called before the menu item is shown, allowing it to be customized. ExecuteVerb() is called only if one of the newly added menu items is clicked. Code to execute the desired behavior goes here.
Double-Clicked	The default action depends on the class from which the editor is derived. TComponentEditor: If items have been added to the context menu, the first item is executed. TDefaultEditor: An empty event handler is created	Edit() is invoked. Code to perform the desired action is placed here.

TABLE 5.10   Continued

When the component is...	Default Action	virtual **Functions Invoked**
	for OnChange, OnCreate, or OnClick, whichever appears first in the component's list of event properties. If none of the previous events exist for the component, a handler is created for the first event that appears. If the component has no events, nothing happens.	

In Figure 5.7 we can see that TComponentEditor and TDefaultEditor are essentially the same in that they offer similar functionality. Where they differ (as seen in Table 5.10) is in the implementation of the Edit() method. Choosing which of the two classes to derive your custom component editor from should be based on the following criteria.

If you want the component editor to generate an empty event handler for one of three default events or for a particular event, when the component is double-clicked, you should derive it from TDefaultEditor; otherwise, derive it from TComponentEditor. If you do not create a custom component editor for a component, C++Builder uses TDefaultEditor.

After the decision has been made as to which component editor class to derive from, the appropriate methods should be overridden. Table 5.11 lists the methods from both classes and details the purpose of each.

TABLE 5.11   TComponentEditor and TDefaultEditor virtual Functions

virtual **Function**	Purpose
int GetVerbCount(void)	Returns an int representing the number of menu items (verbs, as in *doing* words) that are going to be added.

TABLE 5.11   Continued

virtual **Function**	**Purpose**
AnsiString GetVerb(int Index)	Returns an AnsiString representing the menu item's name as it will appear in the context menu. The following conventions should be remembered: Use & to designate a hotkey. Append ... to an item that executes a dialog. Use a - to make the menu item a separator bar.
void PrepareItem(int Index, const Menus::TMenuItem* AItem)	PrepareItem() is called for each verb in the context menu, passing the TMenuItem that will be used to represent the verb in the context menu. This allows the menu item to be customized. It can also be used to hide an item by setting its Visible property to false.
void ExecuteVerb(int Index)	ExecuteVerb() is invoked when one of the custom menu items is selected. Index indicates which one.
void Edit(void)	Edit() is invoked when the component is double-clicked. What happens is user defined. The default behavior is listed in Table 5.10.
void EditProperty(TPropertyEditor* PropertyEditor, bool& Continue, bool& FreeEditor) (TDefaultEditor only)	Used to determine which event an empty handler is generated for when the component is double-clicked.
void Copy(void)	Copy() should be invoked when the component is copied to the Clipboard. This needs to be overridden only if a special format needs to be copied to the Clipboard, such as an image from a graphical component.

Suitable class definitions for TComponentEditor- and TDefaultComponent-derived component editors are shown in Listing 5.18 and Listing 5.19, respectively.

LISTING 5.18   Definition Code for a Custom TComponentEditor-Derived Component Editor

```
#include "VCLEditors.hpp"

class TCustomComponentEditor : public TComponentEditor
{
    typedef TComponentEditor inherited;

public:
    // Double-Click
```

LISTING 5.18   Continued

```
   virtual void __fastcall Edit(void);

   // Right-Click
   // CONTEXT MENU - Step 1
   virtual int __fastcall GetVerbCount(void);
   //            - Step 2
   virtual AnsiString __fastcall GetVerb(int Index);
   //            - Step 3 (OPTIONAL)
   virtual void __fastcall PrepareItem(int Index,
                                const Menus::TMenuItem* AItem);
   //            - Step 4
   virtual void __fastcall ExecuteVerb(int Index);

   // Copy to Clipboard
   virtual void __fastcall Copy(void);

public:
   #pragma option push -w-inl
   inline __fastcall virtual
      TCustomComponentEditor(Classes::TComponent* AComponent,
                        _DesignIntf::di_IDesigner  ADesigner)
                        : TComponentEditor(AComponent, ADesigner)
   { }
   #pragma option pop
public:
   #pragma option push -w-inl
   inline __fastcall virtual ~TCustomComponentEditor(void) { }
   #pragma option pop
};
```

LISTING 5.19   Definition Code for a Custom `TDefaultEditor`-Derived Component Editor

```
#include "VCLEditors.hpp"

class TCustomDefaultEditor : public TDefaultEditor
{
   typedef TDefaultEditor inherited;

protected:
   // Double-Click
```

LISTING 5.18   Continued

```
    // CHOOSE EVENT
    virtual void __fastcall EditProperty(TPropertyEditor* PropertyEditor,
                                         bool& Continue,
                                         bool& FreeEditor);
public:
    // Right-Click
    // CONTEXT MENU - Step 1
    virtual int __fastcall GetVerbCount(void);
    //              - Step 2
    virtual AnsiString __fastcall GetVerb(int Index);
    //              - Step 3 (OPTIONAL)
    virtual void __fastcall PrepareItem(int Index,
                                        const Menus::TMenuItem* AItem);
    //              - Step 4
    virtual void __fastcall ExecuteVerb(int Index);

    // Copy to Clipboard
    virtual void __fastcall Copy(void);

public:
    #pragma option push -w-inl
    inline __fastcall virtual
       TCustomDefaultEditor(Classes::TComponent* AComponent,
                            _DesignIntf::di_IDesigner  ADesigner)
                          : TDefaultEditor(AComponent,  ADesigner)
    { }
    #pragma option pop
public:
    #pragma option push -w-inl
    inline __fastcall virtual ~TCustomDefaultEditor(void)  { }
    #pragma option pop
};
```

In Listing 5.18 and Listing 5.19, it can be seen that there is little difference between the definitions of the two kinds of component editor. In fact, the techniques for implementing context menu items are identical. The difference between the classes is that you override the Edit() method for a TComponentEditor-derived class's double-click behavior, whereas you override the EditProperty() method for a TDefaultEditor class's double-click behavior.

The following sections take each of the virtual methods in turn and discuss implementation issues. Information presented for the Edit() method is applicable only to TComponentEditor-derived classes, and information presented for the EditProperty() method is applicable only to TDefaultEditor-derived classes. Note that the example namespace modifiers used in the function implementation headers reflect this. TCustomComponentEditor is a hypothetical TComponentEditor-derived class, TCustomDefaultEditor is a hypothetical TDefaultEditor-derived class, and TMyCustomEditor is a class that could be derived from either.

The Edit() Method

The main purpose of overriding the Edit() method is to display a form to the user to allow easier editing of the component's values. A good example of this is the component editor for the TChart component on the Additional page of the Component Palette. To this end, the code required is similar to that presented for TPropertyEditor's Edit() method in the "Creating Custom Property Editors" section, earlier in this chapter. As before, there are two approaches to implementing such a form. Either the form can update the component as the form itself is modified, or the component can be updated after the form is closed.

There is one extra and very important consideration that must be remembered: Each time the component is updated, the Modified() method of TComponentEditor's Designer property *must* be called. This is so that the IDE knows that the component has been modified. Hence, the following is required after code that modifies the component:

```
if(Designer) Designer->Modified();
```

An if statement is used in the previous code to ensure that a nonzero value is returned from Designer before we try to call Modified(). If zero is returned, there is little we can do because it means the IDE is not accessible. We know that, for the form to be able to change the component's properties, we must somehow link the form to the component in a similar fashion as for property editors previously. This is reasonably straightforward and requires two things. The first is that a public property should be declared in the form's definition that is a pointer to the type of component the component editor is for. Secondly, this must be pointed to the actual instance of the component that is to be edited. The pointer to the current instance of the component is obtained by using TComponentEditor's Component property, as follows:

```
TMyComponent* MyComponent = dynamic_cast<TMyComponent*>(Component);
```

The pointer obtained can be equated to the form's component pointer property. However, we must also make a reference to Designer available from within the form so that the IDE can be notified of changes that are made to the component. This can be passed as a parameter in the form's constructor. The component can then be modified directly through the property in the form. Suitable code for this approach is shown in Listing 5.20. Don't forget to call `Designer->Modified()` after the component is modified by the form.

LISTING 5.20 Code for a Custom Component Editor Form to Be Called from `Edit()` That Allows Continual Updating

```
// First show important code for TComponentEditorForm

// IN THE HEADER FILE
//-----------------------------------------------------------------//
#ifndef MyComponentEditorFormH
#define MyComponentEditorFormH
//-----------------------------------------------------------------//
#include <Classes.hpp>
#include <Controls.hpp>
#include <StdCtrls.hpp>
#include <Forms.hpp>
#include "HeaderDeclaringTComponentClass"
//-----------------------------------------------------------------//
class TMyComponentEditorForm : public TForm
{
__published:     // IDE-managed Components
private:
  TComponentClass* FComponentClass;
  _DesignIntf::di_IDesigner & Designer;
  // Other decalrations here for example restore values if 'Cancel'
  // is pressed

protected:
  void __fastcall SetComponentClass(TComponentClass* Pointer);
public:
  __fastcall TMyComponentEditorForm(TComponent* Owner,
                              _DesignIntf::di_IDesigner & EditorDesigner);

  __property TComponentClass* ComponentClass = {read=FComponentClass,
                                    write=SetComponentClass};
  // Other declarations here
};
//-----------------------------------------------------------------//
#endif
```

LISTING 5.20 Continued

```cpp
// THE IMPLEMENTATION FILE
//-----------------------------------------------------------------//
#include <vcl.h>
#pragma hdrstop

#include "MyComponentEditorForm.h"
//-----------------------------------------------------------------//
#pragma package(smart_init)
#pragma resource "*.dfm"
//-----------------------------------------------------------------//
__fastcall
TMyComponentEditorForm::
   TMyComponentEditorForm(TComponent* Owner,
                          _DesignIntf::di_IDesigner & EditorDesigner)
                       : TForm(Owner), Designer(EditorDesigner)
{
}
//-----------------------------------------------------------------//
void __fastcall TMyPropertyForm::SetComponentClass(TComponentClass* Pointer)
{
   FComponentClass = Pointer;
   if(FComponentClass != 0)
   {
      // Store current component values and display them
   }
}
//-----------------------------------------------------------------//

// NOW SHOW THE Edit() METHOD

#include "MyComponentEditorForm.h" // Remember this

void __fastcall TCustomComponentEditor::Edit(void)
{
   // Create the form
   std::auto_ptr<TMyComponentEditorForm*>
      MyComponentEditorForm(new TMyComponentEditorForm(0));

   // Link the component property
   MyComponentEditorForm->ComponentClass
                       = dynamic_cast<TComponentClass*>(Component);
```

LISTING 5.20 Continued

```
   // Show the form. The form does all the work.
   MyPropertyForm->ShowModal();
}
```

As in the case of custom property editor forms, the component's current property values can be stored when the form's Component property is linked to the component. This allows the operation to be cancelled and the previous values restored. One thing to pay attention to is the possibility of a NULL pointer being returned from dynamic_cast; this should not occur, but if it does the form will not be able to modify any of the component's properties. An exception could be thrown to indicate this to the user.

The second approach to implementing the Edit() method is equally simple. A form is displayed as a dialog and, when it returns, the values entered are assigned to the component. A pointer to the current instance of the component being edited is obtained from TComponentEditor's Component property:

```
TMyComponent* MyComponent = dynamic_cast<TMyComponent*>(Component);
```

The code required in the Edit() method in this approach to its implementation is greater because the component property values must be assigned to the form after it is created, but before it is shown. On closing, the form's values must be assigned to the requisite component properties. The code required for the Edit() method is shown in Listing 5.21.

LISTING 5.21 Code for a Custom Form to Be Called from the Edit() Method with No Updating Until Closing

```
#include "MyComponentEditorDialog.h" // Include the header for the Dialog!
                                     // Dialog is TMyComponentDialog

void __fastcall TCustomComponentEditor::Edit(void)
{
   TMyComponent* MyComponent = dynamic_cast<TMyComponent*>(Component);
   if(MyComponent != 0)
   {
      // Create the form
      std::auto_ptr<TMyComponentDialog*>
         MyComponentDialog(new TMyComponentDialog(0));

      // Set the current property values in the dialog
      // MyComponentDialog->value1 = MyComponent->value1;
```

LISTING 5.21   Continued

```
        // MyComponentDialog->value2 = MyComponent->value2;
        // and so on...

        // Show the form and see the result.
        if(MyPropertyDialog->ShowModal() == IDOK)
        {
            // Then set the new property value(s)
            // MyComponent->value1 = MyComponentDialog->value1;
            // MyComponent->value2 = MyComponentDialog->value2;
            // and so on...
            if(Designer) Designer->Modified(); // DON'T FORGET!
        }
    }
    else
    {
        throw EInvalidPointer
            ("Cannot Edit: A component pointer is not available!");
    }
}
```

In the second approach to implementing the Edit() method shown in Listing 5.21, implementation code for the dialog has not been shown. This is because there are no special considerations specific to this approach that need to be highlighted. Also be aware that a dialog wrapper class could be used instead of calling the dialog directly, in which case the dialog's Execute() method would be called to display the dialog.

The EditProperty() Method

The purpose of overriding the EditProperty() method is to specify a particular event or one of a number of possible events that should have an empty event handler generated for it by the IDE when the component is double-clicked. For example, consider a component for serial communications. Typically, the most commonly used event would be one that signals when data has been received and is available, perhaps named OnDataReceived. For this to be the event for which a handler is generated, EditProperty() needs to be overridden as follows:

```
void __fastcall
    TCustomDefaultEditor::EditProperty(TPropertyEditor* PropertyEditor,
                                       bool& Continue,
                                       bool& FreeEditor)
{
```

```
   if( PropertyEditor->ClassNameIs("TMethodProperty") &&
       (CompareText(PropertyEditor->GetName(), "OnDataReceived") == 0) )
   {
      inherited::EditProperty(PropertyEditor, Continue, FreeEditor);
   }
}
```

The if statement checks two things. First, it checks that the property editor is a TMethodProperty class; in other words, it checks that the property editor is for an event. It then checks to see if the property editor is called OnDataReceived. The CompareText() function is used for this. CompareText() returns 0 when the two AnsiStrings passed to it are equal. Note that CompareText() is not case sensitive. If the property editor matches these criteria, the parent EditProperty() method is called, in this case TDefaultEditor's EditProperty(), which generates the empty event handler for this event. This is called by using the inherited typedef as a namespace modifier, so the previous code could be written as follows:

```
TDefaultEditor::EditProperty(PropertyEditor, Continue, FreeEditor);
```

The reason for using the typedef is that if the name of TDefaultEditor ever changed, the implementation code would not be affected. Only the class definition in the header file would need to be changed.

If a choice of events was to be specified, perhaps because the same component editor was to be registered for a variety of components, the if statement would be replaced by if-else-if statements. For example:

```
if( PropertyEditor->ClassNameIs("TMethodProperty") &&
    (CompareText(PropertyEditor->GetName(), "OnEvent1") == 0) )
{
   inherited::EditProperty(PropertyEditor, Continue, FreeEditor);
}
else if( PropertyEditor->ClassNameIs("TMethodProperty") &&
         (CompareText(PropertyEditor->GetName(), "OnEvent2") == 0) )
{
   inherited::EditProperty(PropertyEditor, Continue, FreeEditor);
}
else if( PropertyEditor->ClassNameIs("TMethodProperty") &&
         (CompareText(PropertyEditor->GetName(), "OnEvent3") == 0) )
{
   inherited::EditProperty(PropertyEditor, Continue, FreeEditor);
}
```

It also could be replaced by a single if that ORs the possible event occurrences:

```
if( (PropertyEditor->ClassNameIs("TMethodProperty") &&
     (CompareText(PropertyEditor->GetName(), "OnEvent1") == 0)
     ||
     (PropertyEditor->ClassNameIs("TMethodProperty") &&
      (CompareText(PropertyEditor->GetName(), "OnEvent1") == 0)
     ||
     (PropertyEditor->ClassNameIs("TMethodProperty") &&
      (CompareText(PropertyEditor->GetName(), "OnEvent1") == 0) )
{
    inherited::EditProperty(PropertyEditor, Continue,  FreeEditor);
}
```

In either case, the first matching occurrence will be used.

The `GetVerbCount()` Method

Few methods are as easy to override as this. Simply return an integer that represents the number of additional menu items that you want to appear in the component's context menu. Don't forget that a separator bar constitutes a menu item. Sample code for three custom menu items would be as follows:

```
int __fastcall TMyCustomEditor::GetVerbCount(void)
{
    return 4;
}
```

The `GetVerb()` Method

Almost as straightforward as the `GetVerbCount()` method, this method requires that the `AnsiString` text for each menu item be returned. Remember that returning a - makes the menu item a separator bar. Sample code is

```
AnsiString __fastcall TMyCustomEditor::GetVerb(int Index)
{
    switch(Index)
    {
        case 0 : return "&Edit Component...";
        case 1 : return "© 2000 Me";
        case 2 : return "-";
        case 3 : return "Do Something Else";
        default : return "";
    }
}
```

If you do not specify an accelerator key (using the & symbol), one is determined automatically by the IDE. In fact, all predefined context menu items' accelerator keys are determined by the IDE at runtime. This will avoid clashes with user-defined accelerator keys. Accelerator key definitions for user-defined menu items take precedence over a predefined context menu item's accelerator key definitions. If a clash occurs, the predefined menu item's accelerator key is reassigned to a different letter. Finally, remember that a separator bar is automatically placed between the custom menu items and the predefined menu items, so it is not necessary to add one as the last item. However, doing so will not make any difference because the context menu's AutoLineReduction property is set to maAutomatic (refer to the C++Builder online help for further details).

The PrepareItem() Method

This method, new to C++Builder, need not be implemented, and in fact it generally isn't. What it offers is the option to customize each menu item further. Most notably, it allows custom rendering of a menu item, the capability to disable the menu item (Enable = false), the capability to hide the menu item (Visible = false), and the capability to add submenu items. This is possible because PrepareItem() has two parameters. The first, Index, serves the same purpose as it does in the preceding context menu functions, namely to indicate which menu item the function call refers to. However, the second parameter is a pointer to the menu item (TMenuItem) that will be used to represent the menu item in the context menu. This gives you access to all the facilities that TMenuItem offers. There is a catch, however: The pointer is to const TMenuItem, so it is not possible to modify the menu item through the pointer passed. Instead, a non-const pointer of type TMenuItem should be pointed to the same menu item and the menu item modified through that pointer. For example, maintaining continuity with our previous examples, to custom render the second menu item (the copyright item), we would write the code in Listing 5.22.

LISTING 5.22   Basic Code for the PrepareItem() Method

```
void __fastcall TMyCustomEditor::PrepareItem
   (int Index, const Menus::TMenuItem* AItem)
{
switch(Index)
   {
      case 0 : break;

      case 1 :
      {
         TMenuItem* MenuItem = const_cast<TMenuItem*>(AItem);
```

LISTING 5.22   Continued

```
            // Now that we have a pointer we can do what we like
            // For example:
            // 1. To Disable the menu item write -
            // MenuItem->Enabled = false;
            // 2. To Hide the menu item write -
            // MenuItem->Visible = false;
            // 3. To add a bitmap to the menu item write -
            // MenuItem->Bitmap->LoadFromResourceName
            //                    (reinterpret_cast<int>(HInstance),
            //                      "BITMAPNAME");
            // or any other stuff, for example assign an event handler
            // or even add menu sub-items...
        }
            break;

    case 2 : break;
    case 3 : break;
    default : break;
    }
}
```

Pay particular attention to this line:

```
TMenuItem* MenuItem = const_cast<TMenuItem*>(AItem);
```

This is where we obtain the pointer with which we can edit the TMenuItem. Also note the third example of adding a bitmap to the menu item:

```
MenuItem->Bitmap->LoadFromResourceName(reinterpret_cast<int>(HInstance),
                                        "BITMAPNAME");
```

This assumes that a resource file has been imported into the package that contains an image called BITMAPNAME. Otherwise, MenuItem will be unable to load the image. Not being able to load the image is quite disastrous: The IDE will crash, so make sure your names are right. Note also that reinterpret_cast is used to cast HInstance of type void* to type int, as expected by the LoadFromResourceName member function.

Adding Custom Event Handlers to Context Menu Items

Adding custom event handlers to custom menu items involves a two-step process.

First, the required event handler must be written as a member function of the component editor class. Its signature must match exactly that of the event it is to handle. Second, when the PrepareItem() function is called and the non-const

MenuItem pointer is obtained, the handler member function can be equated to the appropriate MenuItem event. For example, to create a custom event handler for the menu item's OnAdvancedDrawItem event, declare a function with a name such as AdvancedDrawMenuItem1() (because it refers to MenuItem 1) with the same parameters as OnAdvancedDrawItem in the component editor's class definition. You will probably want to make it protected and virtual, just in case you want to derive another class from this one. The code appearing in the class definition is as follows:

```
protected:    .
    virtual void __fastcall AdvancedDrawMenuItem1(System::TObject* Sender,
                                        Graphics::TCanvas* ACanvas,
                                        const TRect& ARect,
                                        TOwnerDrawState State);
```

The empty implementation for this would be

```
virtual void __fastcall
    TMyCustomEditor::AdvancedDrawMenuItem1(System::TObject* Sender,
                                        Graphics::TCanvas* ACanvas,
                                        const TRect& ARect,
                                        TOwnerDrawState State)
{
    // Custom rendering code here
}
```

The second stage, to ensure that our event handler is called for this menu item, is to set MenuItem's OnAdvancedDrawItem event to this one. Add the following line of code to that shown previously in Listing 5.22 (after MenuItem is obtained):

```
MenuItem->OnAdvancedDrawItem = AdvancedDrawMenuItem1;
```

Now, each time OnAdvancedDrawItem() is called, our custom rendering code will be executed. The remaining TMenuItem events can also be overridden: OnMeasureItem, OnDrawItem, and OnClick; removing the need for code in the ExecuteVerb() method for this item. However, this is not advised because ExecuteVerb() conveniently centralizes the code associated with clicking the context menu. That leaves only the OnMeasureItem and OnDrawItem events. Essentially, OnDrawItem is a simpler (and older) version of OnAdvancedDrawItem. It is called less often and contains less information. Use the OnAdvancedDrawItem instead. However, OnMeasureItem is a useful event that enables the size of the menu item as it appears in the context menu to be modified. The code required in the class definition for this event is as follows:

```
protected:
    virtual void __fastcall MeasureMenuItem1(System::TObject* Sender,
```

```
                                   Graphics::TCanvas* ACanvas,
                                   int& Width,
                                   int& Height);
```

A typical implementation for this would be

```
virtual void __fastcall
    TMyCustomEditor::MeasureMenuItem1(System::TObject* Sender,
                                   Graphics::TCanvas* ACanvas,
                                   int& Width,
                                   int& Height)  .
{
    Width = x - Height; // Where x is the required width subtracting Height
                        // allows for Flip Children's sub-menu arrow
    Height = y;         // Where y is the required height
}
```

Adding the line of code that follows to the PrepareItem() method in Listing 5.22 in the correct section for this item ensures the event will be called:

```
MenuItem->OnMeasureItem = MeasureMenuItem1;
```

One thing to remember is that modifying Width will have an effect on the size of the menu item only if it is bigger than the current context menu width, which is most likely controlled by other context menu items. In other words, the current context menu width will be equal to the width of the widest item. Notice that if a value is assigned to Width, perhaps because an image is going to be drawn inside the menu item, the value that should be assigned will be the desired width *minus* the default height. The reason for this is to allow for the submenu arrow symbol for the IDE's menu item Flip Children. See Figure 5.8.

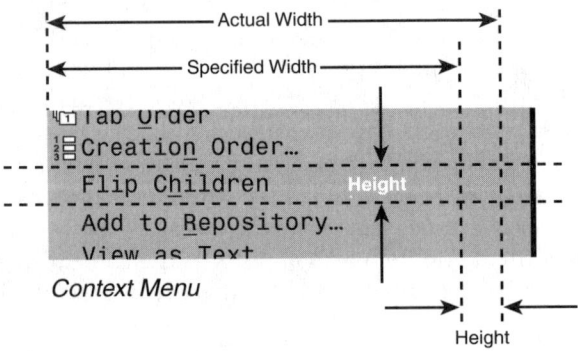

FIGURE 5.8   Cropped view of the TImageComponentEditor context menu, showing height and width.

The width required for the submenu arrow symbol is equal to the default Height of the Flip Children menu item. This value is added to any Width value that you specify, so to prevent having an unpainted strip down the right side of your context menu item, you must account for it by subtracting it from the width that you specify. Modifying the Height parameter will always have an effect on the height of the menu item, and setting it to 0 will make the item disappear.

The motivation behind defining your own custom event handlers for any of the menu items is so that the rendering of the item can be customized. There is increased scope for this with the new OnAdvancedDrawItem event. The TOwnerDrawState Set variable gives a lot of information about the current state of the item. For example, if the menu item is selected, State will contain odSelected, allowing code such as this to be placed in the event handler:

```
if(State.Contains(odSelected))
{
    // Draw the item with a clRed background
}
else
{
    // Draw the item with a clBtnFace background
}
```

Remember when you assign a handler to either OnAdvancedDrawItem or OnDrawItem that you are responsible for the entire rendering process, including displaying the text on the item's canvas. You will need to use the TextRect method of TCanvas to do so. For more information on this, refer to the "Using Images in Property Editors" section earlier in this chapter or to the C++Builder online help. An example custom component editor (TImageComponentEditor) that handles the OnAdvancedDrawItem and OnMeasureItem events for editing the TImage class is shown in Figure 5.9. The component editor also implements both Copy to Clipboard and Paste from Clipboard methods.

The possibilities offered by customizing the menu items using these events are endless. For example, it is possible to place your company logo as an image on one of the menu items or make all your custom menu items appear larger with a nicer background, making them stand out from the IDE-defined items. Incidentally, if you place menu items that perform no function, consider placing them *after* those that do. It can be very irritating after right-clicking a component to have to study the menu for the item needed, especially if it is a common operation. Normally, items used most often should be placed first in the menu.

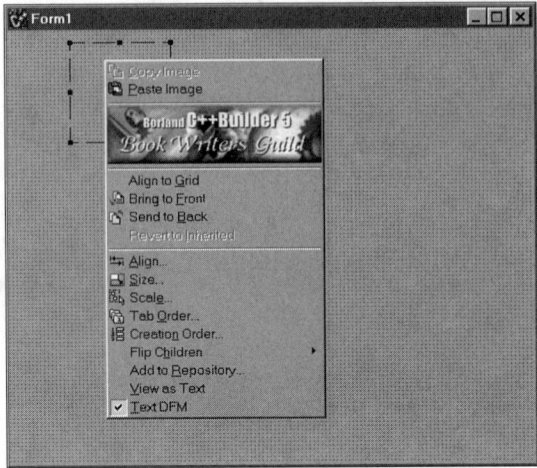

FIGURE 5.9   The context menu for `TImageComponentEditor`.

Adding Submenu Items to Context Menu Items

Adding submenu items (which are `TMenuItems` themselves) to a custom context menu item requires that you create the submenu items that you want to add at runtime. The submenu items are then added to the appropriate menu item using the `Add()` method. Typically, more than one submenu will be added, and the `Add()` method is overloaded to accept an array of `TMenuItems` as well as single `TMenuItems`. Because the added submenu items are also of type `TMenuItem`, they have all the functionality of `MenuItem` and can be similarly customized. As an example, code to add submenu items to the second menu item will be shown (remember that the index is zero-based). The number added is arbitrary; this could be made a `static const` value in the component editor class, for example. A symbolic name, `NoOfSubMenusForItem1`, is used in the code snippets for greater clarity.

First, the submenu items must be declared. If more than one submenu is required (as is the requirement here), it is simplest to declare an array of pointers to `TMenuItems`. We must be able to access the submenu items throughout our component editor class, so we'll declare the pointer array as a `private` variable in the class definition:

```
TMenuItem* SubMenuItemsFor1[NoOfSubMenusForItem1];
```

The submenu items must be constructed. A good place to do this is in the component editor's constructor. Currently, the constructor is empty and inline. It needs to be changed in both the class definition and the class implementation. The code required is

```
// In "MyCustomEditor.h" change the constructor declaration to
// the following and remove the surrounding #pragma option push
// and pop directives

__fastcall virtual TCustomComponentEditor(Classes::TComponent* AComponent,
                                _DesignIntf::di_IDesigner  ADesigner);


// The implementation for the constructor becomes:

__fastcall TCustomComponentEditor::
    TCustomComponentEditor(Classes::TComponent* AComponent,
                     _DesignIntf::di_IDesigner  ADesigner)
                     : TComponentEditor(AComponent, ADesigner)
{
    for(int i=0; i<NoOfSubMenusForItem1; ++i)
    {
        SubMenuItemsFor1[i] = new TMenuItem(Application);
        SubMenuItemsFor1[i]->Caption.sprintf("Sub-Menu %d", i);
        // Other Sub-Menu initialisation
    }
    // Other Sub-Menu initialisation
}
```

If the submenus are created in the component editor's constructor, they should be deleted in the component editor's destructor. It is also currently empty and inline, so it must be changed as the constructor was. The code required is

```
// In "MyCustomEditor.h" change the destructor declaration to
// the following and remove the surrounding #pragma option push
// and pop directives

__fastcall virtual ~TCustomComponentEditor(void);


// The implementation for the destructor becomes:

__fastcall TCustomComponentEditor::~TCustomComponentEditor(void)
{
    for(int i=0; i<NoOfSubMenusForItem1; ++i)
    {
        delete SubMenuItemsFor1[i];
    }
}
```

With the code in place, it is trivial to add the submenus to menu item 1. Looking back to Listing 5.22, an implementation of the `PrepareItem()` method, we simply add the following line of code after the non-const pointer `MenuItem` is obtained:

```
MenuItem->Add(SubMenuItemsFor1, NoOfSubMenuItemsFor1-1);
```

From here the submenus can be used as any other menu items on the context menu.

WARNING

Be careful not to assign code to a menu item with submenus in the `ExecuteVerb()` method. This can have unpredictable results.

The `ExecuteVerb()` Method

The `ExecuteVerb()` method is used to place the code that should be executed when one of the custom context menu items is clicked. The basic structure is the same as that for the `GetVerb()` method; that is, the code is wrapped inside a `switch` statement. Sample code is as follows:

```
void __fastcall TMyCustomEditor::ExecuteVerb(int Index)
{
   switch(Index)
   {
      case 0 : EditComponet();
               break;
      case 1 : break; // Do nothing - copyright info
      case 2 : break; // Do nothing - Separator line
      case 3 : // Do something else ...
               break;
      default : break;
   }
}
```

This shows the basic structure required to implement the `ExecuteVerb()` method. Typically, a menu item will show a dialog when it is clicked, unless the item is there as a line separator or to present textual or graphical information. To that end, the code that should be placed here depends very much on the features of the component being edited. In our example, clicking the first menu item should invoke a form through which to edit the component. This is typical and the most useful for users. The code needed is identical to that shown previously for the `Edit()` method. If the component editor is derived from `TComponentEditor`, and the `Edit()` method already contains the code required to show the component editor form, it makes sense not to repeat that code. The best approach is to place the necessary code in a separate function, in this case `EditComponent()`, and call that function in both the `ExecuteVerb()` and `Edit()` methods. In fact, if the first menu item is used for this function, you need only ensure that the code is called from the `ExecuteVerb()` method. This is because `TComponentEditor` already implements the `Edit()` method to execute the code associated with the first menu item. Consequently, the `Edit()` method need not be overridden. Regardless of whether code is duplicated, if the code required to invoke a dialog is complex, it is better placed in a separate function.

All the necessary information regarding displaying forms has already been presented, and you are referred there for further information. The fourth method has been left undefined. Depending on the component, it could be anything. However, in all probability it will display a form to the user. The code presented previously for the `Edit()` method will also be applicable in this situation.

The `Copy()` Method

The `Copy()` method is used to copy *additional* Clipboard formats to the Clipboard, to allow additional functionality that users might expect or find especially useful. This might be something such as the capability to copy an image in a `TImage` component to the Clipboard so that it can be pasted into a graphics package. The code required to implement this method depends entirely on what data is to be copied, making the implementation of this method highly variable. Therefore, it will not be dwelled on. The principles are shown in the following sample code, which allows an image from a `TImage` component to be copied to the Clipboard.

```
#include "Clipbrd.hpp"

void __fastcall TImageComponentEditor::Copy(void)
{
    // Step 1 : Obtain a suitable pointer to the component
    TImage* Image = dynamic_cast<TImage*>(Component);

    // Step 2 : If successful then proceed
    if(Image)
    {
        // Step 3 : Obtain the required data in a format the
        //          clipboard will recognize

        WORD     AFormat;
        unsigned AData;
        HPALETTE APalette;
```

```
        Image->Picture->SaveToClipboardFormat(AFormat, AData, APalette);

        // Step 4 : Obtain a pointer to the global instance
        //          of the clipboard
        TClipboard* TheClipboard = Clipboard();

        // Step 5 : Copy the data to the clipboard
        TheClipboard->SetAsHandle(AFormat,  AData);
    }
}
```

The first stage is straightforward. A suitable pointer is obtained by dynamic_casting
the TComponent pointer returned by TComponentEditor's Component property. If this
doesn't work, something is wrong. The second stage involves presenting the data in
a way that the Clipboard will recognize. The data formats that the Clipboard
supports are listed in the online help (it is also possible to register custom Clipboard
formats; however, this is beyond the scope of this discussion). After this is done, a
pointer to the global instance of the Clipboard is obtained. Calling the global
Clipboard() function returns this pointer. A new instance of TClipboard should *not* be
created. Finally, the data can be copied to the Clipboard. A simpler implementation
of the function is as follows:

```
void __fastcall TImageComponentEditor::Copy(void)
{
    TImage* Image = dynamic_cast<TImage*>(Component);

    if(Image)
    {
        Clipboard()->Assign(Image->Picture);
    }
}
```

The more complex approach was shown because it is more general, and the techniques are transferable to other copy operations.

It is important to note that this Copy() function does not interfere with the IDE's
copying and pasting of components on forms using the normal menu and key shortcut methods. This function offers additional copying capabilities and must be
invoked manually. It could, therefore, be placed as a menu item on the component's
context menu. It is also perfectly conceivable that a Paste() method be defined and
implemented. The definition for such a method would be

```
virtual void __fastcall Paste(void);
```

The corresponding implementation is

```
void __fastcall TImageComponentEditor::Paste(void)
{
   TImage* Image = dynamic_cast<TImage*>(Component);

   if(Image)
   {
      Image->Picture->Assign(Clipboard());
   }
}
```

Registering Component Editors

Registering component editors uses RegisterComponentEditor() and is straightforward. Its declaration is

```
extern PACKAGE void __fastcall
   RegisterComponentEditor(TMetaClass* ComponentClass,
                           TMetaClass* ComponentEditor);
```

This must be called inside the package's Register() function. Only two parameters are required. Both parameters will be TObject descendants, so the __classid operator can be used to obtain a TMetaClass pointer for each. The first parameter is the component class for which the component editor is to be registered. The second parameter is the component editor class itself. For example, to register a custom TImage component editor called TImageComponentEditor, you would write the following:

```
RegisterComponentEditor(__classid(TImage),
                        __classid(TImageComponentEditor));
```

Component editors are like property editors in that they are used from newest to oldest. As a result, it is possible to override existing component editors in preference to custom component editors offering greater capabilities.

Also as with property editors, it is possible to register component editor packages without components. This has been done with the TImageComponentEditor component editor discussed previously. It is included in the package containing the enhanced property editors developed in the "Using Images in Property Editors" section, earlier in this chapter.

Summary

This chapter's aim was to cover the main concerns and techniques associated with the development of a component's design time interface.

Creating property and component editors can be tricky, and many of the methods required can easily be misunderstood. But, when you understand how to override important methods of `TPropertyEditor` in your custom property editor class, you can create property editors that can handle any level of complexity. These include `GetAttributes()`, `GetValue()`, `SetValue()`, and `Edit()`.

The same is true for `ComponentEditors`, where overriding `GetVerbCount()`, `GetVerb()`, `PrepareItem()`, `ExecuteVerb()`, `Edit()`, `EditProperty()`, and `Copy()` enables you to provide the necessary information to the IDE, so it can support the design time needs of component editing.

The ability to create property and component editors makes it possible for you to create components that are easy to use, even when they are complex.

PART II

Database Programming

IN THIS PART

Borland Database Component Architecture

IN THIS CHAPTER

- Borland Database Component Types Overview
- The Borland Database Engine
- BDE Single-Tier and dbGo
- BDE/SQL Links, IBExpress, dbExpress, and dbGo (Two-Tier)
- DataSnap Distributed Databases (Multitier)

C++Builder and the VCL were specifically designed to make it easy to create elegant and functional database systems of any scale, and to make those systems easily maintainable. In this chapter you'll be introduced to the components available to be used for building database applications with C++Builder.

Borland Database Component Types Overview

This section offers an overview of the component sets offered by Borland for database applications.

Component Sets

Borland provides a variety of component sets for accessing databases.

- BDE—The Borland Database Engine components are the original component set provided for Borland products. It connects programs with the Borland Database Engine and its database drivers. The BDE provides a common abstraction layer across a variety of database management systems (DBMS) (for more information on these components, see Chapter 8, "The Borland Database Engine.")

- Interbase Express (IBExpress)—Components very similar to the BDE component set, which are optimized for Borland's Open Source DBMS—Interbase, and which don't require the BDE to be installed on the client system (for more information on these components, see Chapter 10, "Interbase Express Component Overview.")

- dbExpress—A lightweight component set with lightweight drivers for widely used client-server databases—no BDE required. (for more information on these components, see Chapter 12, "Data Access with dbExpress.")

- dbGo—A component set known as ADO Express prior to C++Builder 6. These components provide an interface to Microsoft's ActiveX Data Objects database drivers (usually referred to as providers). Although dbGo doesn't need the BDE, it also cannot be run under Linux, and, therefore, shouldn't be used in CLX applications. (for more information on these components, see Chapter 11, "ADO Express Components for C++Builder.")

Database components are only as good as their user interface counterparts. Almost every conventional user interface component has a "data aware" counterpart, which can be hooked to a TDataSource. TDataSource components can connect to TDataSet descendants, which, for all of the component sets, are the basic data access components they provide.

Figure 6.1 shows the relationships between these major component subsets in the UML (Unified Modeling Language) notation.

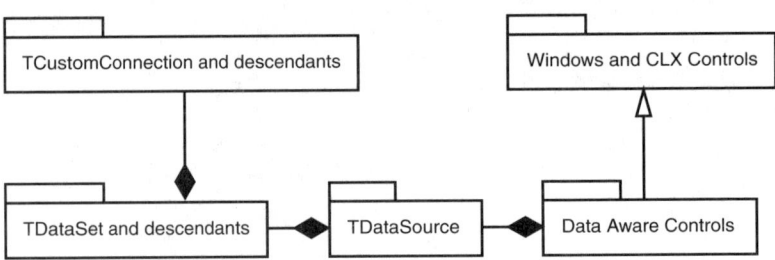

FIGURE 6.1 The major data components and their relationships.

In this diagram, the arrow with the diamond indicates that components at the diamond end reference an instance of a component from the other end. The arrow indicates a group of components that are derived from the group of components at the arrow end.

Figure 6.2 shows the UML notation for how each component set specializes the TCustomConnection class to provide a connection optimized for the database access model provided by each specific component set.

In Figure 6.3 you can see the TDataSet descendants for each component class.

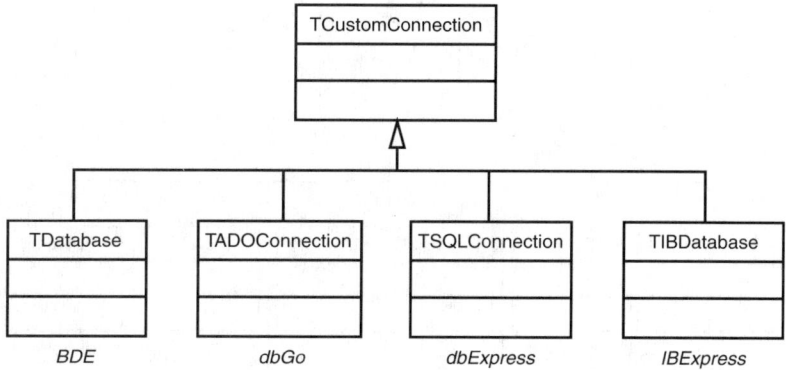

FIGURE 6.2   The connection components and their relationships.

Subsequent chapters will discuss this in some detail, but first, an overview.

The Borland Database Engine

The *Borland Database Engine* (BDE) is a layer directly beneath the VCL. Inprise/Borland created it to allow various database formats to work seamlessly with the VCL. The supported formats are ASCII delimited (text), xBase, Paradox, relational model (also known as SQL/remote databases), and Open Database Connectivity (ODBC). Note that ODBC leaves the door open for any other format (Access, for instance). The first three are handled directly and are, therefore, BDE-native formats. The others are handled through an additional layer.

As you can see, the BDE enables you to use very different database formats without having to purchase and learn new components. In fact, it is often effortless to use different database management systems without changes to the application.

Furthermore, the BDE hides the complexity of many powerful features such as transactions, cached updates, and XML support. The bottom line is that it enables you to concentrate on what data to fetch instead of how to fetch it.

The BDE also abstracts the complexity of connecting to a database by allowing BDE components in the VCL to simply reference an *alias*. The alias is a name established by the developer or installer by using the BDE administration tool (bdeadmin32.exe) to associate the name with a database driver and its settings, including those that identify the location of the database itself.

As can be expected, there is a price to pay. The BDE can be expensive in terms of memory and disk space. However, all C++Builder and Delphi applications share the BDE.

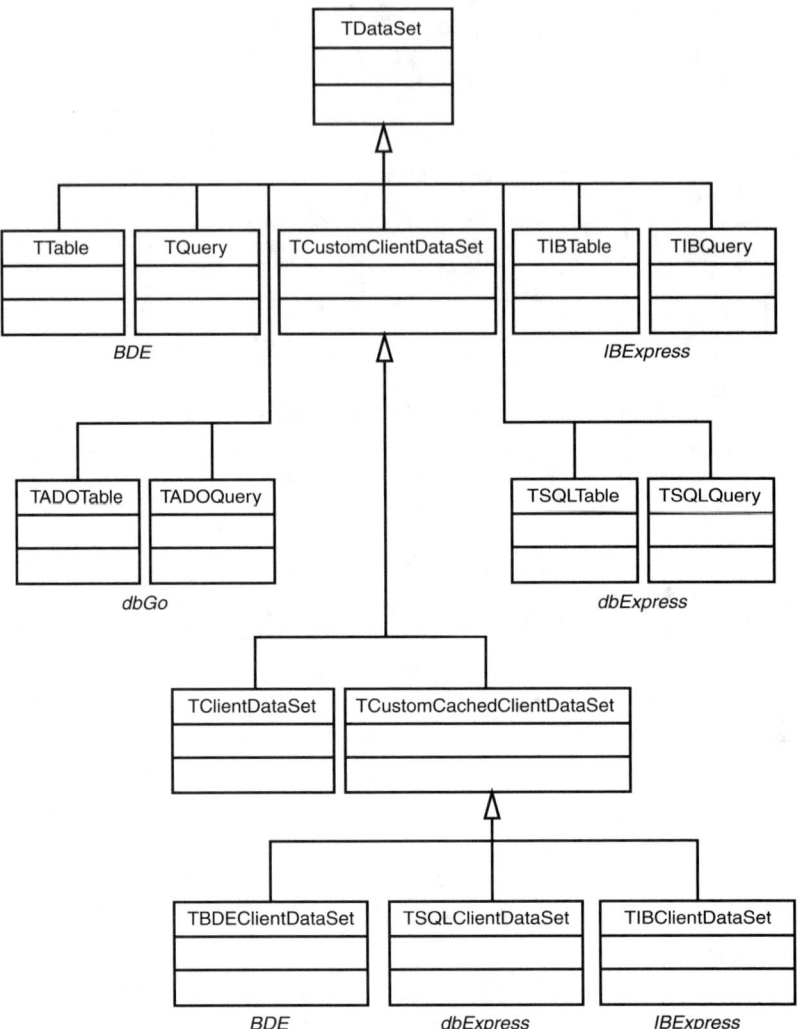

FIGURE 6.3   The TDataSet descendant components and their relationships.

Accessing data through the BDE is standard when using C++Builder. All the database and data-aware components included with the product are designed for it. This is true for single-tier, two-tier, and even multitier architectures.

Note, however, that Borland has essentially frozen the BDE and is planning to phase it out eventually.

BDE Single-Tier and dbGo

Borland has always enjoyed an outstanding reputation for its compilers and has been a leader in providing single-tier database engines for the PC. The BDE integrates many of the database engines Borland owns, so it provides native access to these various formats. They are ASCII delimited (text flat-file), xBase (dBase, Clipper, and FoxPro), as well as Paradox. You can also use a client-only installation of Interbase with the BDE in a single-tier configuration.

dbGo also provides access to these types of databases; usually, through ODBC (Open Database Connectivity) drivers. And, of course, dbGo only works with Windows.

These components and drivers are great for small programs where performance and price are more important than database-engine power or data security and integrity.

BDE/SQL Links, IBExpress, dbExpress, and dbGo (Two-Tier)

The BDE deals with client-server relational databases through an additional layer called *SQL Links.* You can think of it as a translator between the BDE API and the database engine's API (the SQL Links modules are often called drivers). The Enterprise version includes SQL Links for Oracle, SQL Server, DB2, and InterBase. The Professional version includes only SQL Links for InterBase.

This is also called a two-tier architecture, and it is one of the most popular for traditional database applications. It provides the most power, flexibility, and integration for the price without adding the extra complexities of a multitier architecture.

Interbase is usually a client-server database, so the IBExpress components can be used as part of a client-server installation.

This is also true for the dbExpress components, whose drivers provide access to Interbase, DB2, Oracle, MySQL, and Informix.

ADO components in dbGo can also use client-server providers or ODBC drivers for client-server databases.

DataSnap Distributed Databases (Multitier)

Distributed applications are also referred to as *multitier* applications. This means that the program is split in two or more pieces that might reside on separate servers. These pieces communicate using CORBA, DCOM, or HTTP. CORBA is open, multi-platform, and considered easy to use, but it must be purchased separately. DCOM is from Microsoft and is for Windows only. HTTP is open and multiplatform, but it is less powerful and, therefore, has more limited use. DataSnap, formerly called MIDAS, is covered in Chapter 20, "Distributed Databases with DataSnap." DataSnap provides the mechanism for spreading your database applications across multiple servers.

The *standard multitier* model allows an application with a specific task to use other program parts residing on other servers. This is so that the business logic can be encapsulated and shared between any number of applications. As you can imagine, there are many benefits in terms of data integrity, logistics, and maintenance (to name a few).

This is also the architecture of choice if your project requires the *thin-client* model. This is when only the interface part of the program runs on the client computer. All the application logic and business rules are on another server. This is ideal for low-bandwidth networks (such as the Internet), for network computers, when centralized processing is required, or when the interface must run on many different operating systems.

Another model is also supported by the multitier components—it's called *briefcase*. It enables the client part of the application to work even when it is not connected to the network. The trick is that the components can use a cached copy of the data in a local flat file. As a result, users can get the data they need from the server and take it on the road or home with them. In this model, the client-side must also contain the application logic and some business rules. When the mobile user returns, changes can be automatically reconciled between the two separate databases, but such reconciliation sometimes requires someone to identify the appropriate result of contradictory changes.

The Remote Data Modules that Borland provides as part of DataSnap can use BDE components, or any of the other component sets listed here.

NOTE

Sources for More Information on Borland's Database Architectures are

Borland C++Builder 5 Developer's Guide (the manual provided with C++Builder), Inprise Corporation: Chapters 13–15, Chapter 23, and Chapter 25

Calvert, Charlie, *Accessing Databases Using ADO and Delphi*, Borland Community Web site, `http://community.borland.com/soapbox/techvoyage/article/1,1795,10270,00.html`

Cantù, Marco, *Data Access Dilemma*, Borland Community Web site, `http://community.borland.com/article/0,1410,20191,00.html`

Summary

As you have seen, C++Builder offers many features for the database system developer, including

- Support for single-tier, client/server, and multitier architecture.

- Components that offer a range of data access options including BDE, ADO, specialized lightweight drivers, and Interbase-specific options.

- Use of DataSnap to make remote access to multitier data simple and convenient; a briefcase mode is also supported.

The component sets provided with C++Builder make it an ideal platform for large or small database applications, regardless of which architecture you choose.

7

Database Programming

by Mark Cashman

C++Builder Data Modules are the fundamental basis for implementing the nonvisual side of your C++ Builder application. This chapter covers the fundamentals and stylistic elements of using Data Modules in your implementations.

The C++Builder Data Module Designer does for data modules what the Form Designer does for visual forms—it enables you to place, select, modify, delete, and edit components in data modules. But what are data modules, and how are they useful?

What Are Data Modules?

Data modules enable you to separate access to your data (and to nonvisual components) from the user interface presented by your forms. This offers an extremely powerful and visually oriented way to create the nonvisual portions of your systems, especially when coupled with the C++Builder capabilities provided by form inheritance.

A data module is a special kind of form, with its own form designer. Any nonvisual component can be dropped into a data module from the Component Palette. Most often, these are database-oriented components such as TTable, Tquery, and TDataSource, but the data module is not limited to those components. Components such as TTimer and TActionList are also frequently found in data modules.

You can add data modules to the Object Repository, just like forms, and you can copy or inherit from the data modules you put in the repository—also just like forms.

Why Use a Data Module?

For a simple system, and especially when you are just starting with C++Builder, it is sufficient to place nonvisual components, such as timers, queries, and data sources, right on the form. But this clutters the form with components, and, as the system grows, it is more difficult to manage these nonvisual components so that they stay out of the way of the visual components. Data modules enable you to group those components outside the user interface form, in a central location of their own.

In addition, you will notice as you develop new applications around a specific database that you have to duplicate nonvisual database components in each separate application. This fails to take advantage of the ability to reuse, which is such an important feature of object-oriented programming.

Data modules, on the other hand, can be shared with multiple projects, either directly, or through inheritance from the Object Repository; thus, your database logic implementations can be easily reused to provide consistency across applications. Indeed, the same data module can be used in a form application, a DLL, a COM object, a CORBA object, or a Web application, making data modules the ideal home for core program logic.

You might find a need to use databases that are similar to each other, where one database extends another in important ways. When you use data modules, you can use form inheritance to create a data module for the basic features of the database, and then create an extended data module that inherits from the ancestor data module, but adds components, handlers, fields, and extends event handlers from the base data module.

Data modules also offer the ability to encapsulate validation and referential integrity logic outside the database—which can be a good idea even when a DBMS does offer referential integrity support because it offers an extra layer of protection.

And, when used with MIDAS, a special form of data module—the Remote Data Module (RDM)—enables you to use data modules as one or more middle-tiers in a multitier distributed database system.

Finally, data modules can reflect your database design. If you use Entity-Relationship style modeling or similar methods, each data module can be an entity from the diagram. For example, the Order data module in Figure 7.1 (which represents an Order entity) contains a table for the orders (called simply Table), a product table (called Product) for all the valid products that can be associated with an order, and a status table (called Status) for all of the valid status values an order can have.

You can, of course, have as many data modules as you have entities, and you can link the tables within or across data modules in master/detail or other relationships—even regardless of differences in underlying DBMS.

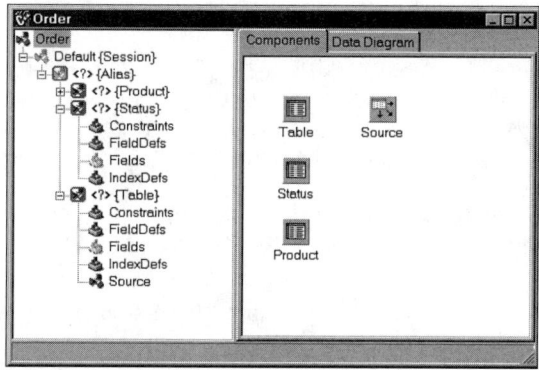

FIGURE 7.1   An Order data module.

This style of data module development allows for easily read notation, such as

```
OrderStatus = Order->Table->FieldByName("Status")->AsString;
```

and also makes it easy to reuse consistent names, as in the following:

```
OrderStatus = Order->Table->FieldByName("Status")->AsString;
AccountStatus = AccountStatus ->Table->FieldByName("Status")->AsString;
```

How to Use a Data Module in Applications, DLLs, and Distributed Objects

Data modules are just like forms in the sense that they are encapsulated in their own
.h and .cpp files, that they have a .dfm file that describes the components in the data
module, and that they can reference other forms or data modules. Data modules can
be autocreated (see the list in Project, Options, or edit the project source using
Project, View Source), or can be created with the new operator (as in SomeDataModule =
new TSomeDataModule(Application)). A data module also has an owner that takes
responsibility for freeing it. This is typically the application, in which case your data
module will be automatically freed by the application when the application terminates. It can also be a form (in which case the form automatically frees the data
module when the form is freed), a component (which will automatically free the
data module when it is freed), or even NULL (in which case you must make sure the
data module is freed by your own code, usually in a destructor because there is no
owner to perform that action automatically).

To use a data module with a form, you typically need only two steps:

- Make sure the data module will be created before any form that uses it (by altering the order of creation in changing the project source or the autocreate list, if needed). Of course, if the form is not autocreated, it can simply be created with new as needed, and deleted as needed.

- Use File, Include Unit Hdr on the form that will use the data module to ensure that the data module is #included in the form .cpp file.

Using a Data Module with a DLL, COM, or CORBA object is actually just as simple.

If you are using a data module with a DLL and need the data module to remain open across calls to the DLL for the duration of time the DLL is loaded, you can open the data module in the DllEntryPoint(). The code in Listing 7.1 shows how this works.

LISTING 7.1   Creating a Data Module in a DLL

```
#include <vcl.h>
#include <windows.h>
#pragma hdrstop

#include <Forms.hpp>
#include <TestDataModuleUnit.h>

#pragma argsused

String InternallyMaintainedResultString;

int WINAPI DllEntryPoint(HINSTANCE hinst, unsigned long reason, void*
➡lpReserved)
{
    // This is called on every process attach,
    // so make sure we need to initialize by checking the global variable...

    if (TestDataModule == NULL)
    {
        Application->Initialize(); // This is essential
        Application->CreateForm(__classid(TTestDataModule),&TestDataModule);
    };

    return 1;
}
```

Similar procedures can be followed for COM (the data module must be instantiated in the DllEntryPoint() function of the generated Active Server Library) and CORBA. In CORBA, the server is itself a data module, so it is very easy to use data module techniques with CORBA.

For more on multitier and distributed programming, see Part IV, "Distributed Computing."

What Goes in a Data Module?

The basic data module is one that is used to contain datasets and data sources. This simple use of the data module enables you to encapsulate database objects, persistent fields, and event handlers for referential integrity, data validation, and the propagation of changes across database tables. The resulting data module can be used with any user interface, as long as there are no references to controls on any specific form. Thus, when committing to the use of data modules, you also must commit to the use of data-aware controls in your user interfaces. In most cases, the existing data-aware controls are sufficient, but you might also need to be prepared to create your own data-aware control classes from nondata-aware control classes, through the use of the TDataLink and related classes.

Data modules also often contain a TCustomConnection descendant for use either by the data components in the data module or by other data module data components.

The next type of data module contains nondatabase controls—controls such as timers, custom nonvisual components, and so on. Developers often create special custom components for things like registry access, access to devices such as the serial and parallel ports, or to hardware modules. All of these components can also be at home in the data module. This enables them to be shared across applications, just like data components.

How to Add Properties to a Data Module?

As with all forms, data modules do not easily allow the addition of published properties. The best method for getting around this problem is to create a special TComponent descendant with published properties that are the ones you would add to the data module if you could. Such a component can then be manipulated, and its property values set at design time or runtime. The component can be accessed by the code in data module event handlers during program operation, or by forms that need to make values (including pointers to controls) available to the data module without having the data module be coupled to a specific form.

Naturally, you can also use public methods, variables, or properties, but then you will be limited to setting values at runtime. This is more error prone and more difficult to verify because you cannot look at the component alone, but must also read the associated C++ statements in the `.cpp` file that uses the component. Nevertheless, such methods have a place. For instance, you can have a user interface that needs to register a control, such as a progress bar, with the data module. This cannot be done at design time without coupling the data module to the form, so it must be done by setting a public variable or property in your C++ code.

How to Use the Data Module Designer

The data module designer consists of two panes. To the left is a tree representation of the components in the data module (such as datasets, data sources, and persistent fields). To the right is a two-page interface. One page is for the components you drop into the data module. The other page is for drawing data diagrams.

The Object Tree View and the Data Module Designer

The Data Module Designer window is where you drop your components. As you work with your data module, spend some time making sure your components line up with each other and are clustered together so that it is clear that they are related to each other.

In versions of C++Builder prior to 6, there is a left pane that shows the components in a tree-structured view. This allowed you to see the dependencies between data components, such as `TSession`, `TDatabase`, `TDataSet`, `TDataSource`, and `TField`. In C++ Builder 6 and above, the Object Tree View, discussed in Chapters 1 and 2, is what provides this capability, for a simple Data Module with a single table, as is shown in Figure 7.2.

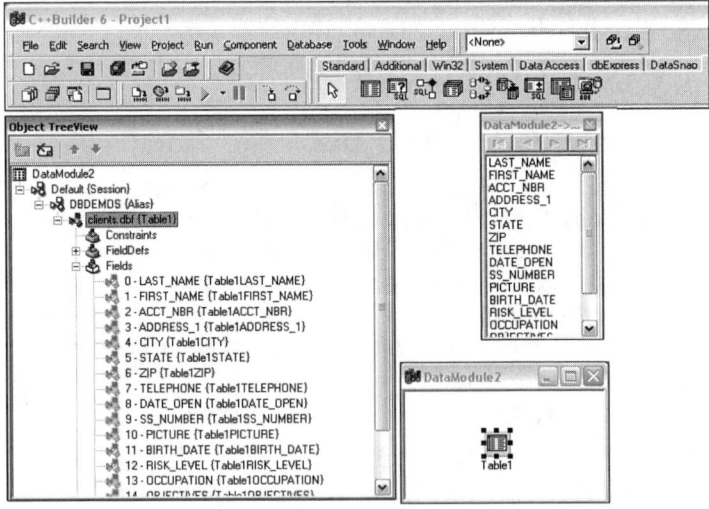

FIGURE 7.2   Component page and tree view.

You can see in the tree view that Table1 uses DBDEMOS as its alias. The persistent fields for Table1 are also visible.

The Data Diagram Editor

Another way to view your data components is to use the Data Diagram page, which is a subpage of the tab for the unit that represents the Data Module in the Source Code Editor. This page is little known because its documentation is squirreled away deep in the help. But a search in the Help index for Data Module Designer, followed by double-clicking it, will give you a set of topics that include the Data Diagram editor.

Figure 7.3 shows a sample diagram in that window.

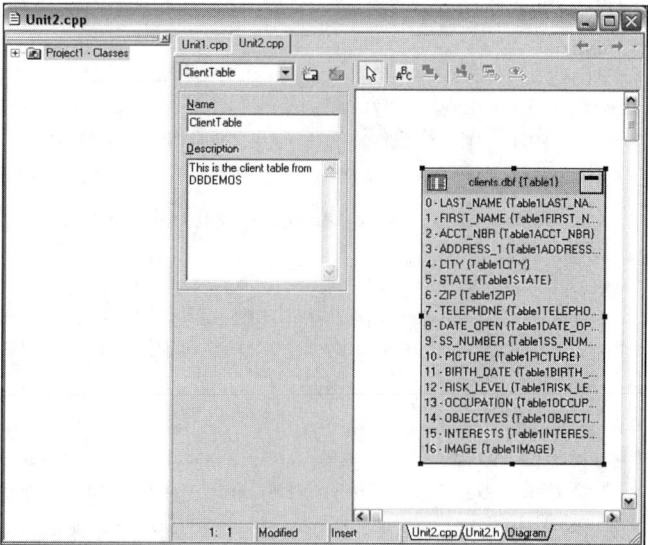

FIGURE 7.3   A data diagram.

This shows the table from the data module (added to the diagram by dragging it from the tree view to the diagram view—note that this is the only way to add components to the diagram), and its persistent fields. With a more complex data module it can show their relationships (for instance, a lookup field and a master/detail relationship are automatically generated in the diagram).

As you change components (adding or removing fields, changing properties, attaching them to new data sources, or even deleting a component), those changes will be reflected in the diagram—at least for the components that have been dragged into the diagram.

Components can be removed from the diagram with Delete, and each object has a pop-up menu that can be used for things like invoking the fields editor on a table or running the SQL Explorer to see details about the table. Connections between components also have a pop-up menu that can, among other things, be used to remove the relationship represented by the connection.

Note that you are not limited to using data components in the diagram—components such as TTimer and your own custom components can be dragged into the diagram.

The Data Diagram editor has several buttons on the top. From left to right, they are

- Select—Enables you to point at and select diagram objects.

- Comment—The yellow comment block enables you attach notes to any diagram components. To edit the comment, simply double-click it and type. Pressing Esc abandons any changes in progress. To complete the editing, just click outside the comment.

- Allude Connector—Allows you to connect the comments to the relevant components in the diagram. Drag between the comment and the component receiving the comment or vice versa. Any number of components can share a comment. A comment can also point to any number of components.

- Property Connector—Enables you to show a link between the property of one component and the component that property references. If you use this between two components not yet connected, the designer determines the intended property assignment and automatically fills in the property with the appropriate link. To use this, click the button and drag from the referencing component to the referenced component.

- Master/Detail Connector—Enables you to connect two data sets in a master/detail relationship. To use this, click the button and drag from the master to the detail data set. The field link editor will appear and allow you to specify the relationship.

- Lookup Connector—Enables you to set up a lookup field between two tables. As with the Master/Detail, drag from the data set that will contain the lookup field to the data set that contains the data to be looked up. The lookup field editor dialog will appear and allow you to specify the lookup field.

Unfortunately, you cannot zoom out of a Data Diagram to see it as a whole. However, you can print it, and you can scroll around in it as needed.

Finally, note that the data diagram does not participate in form inheritance, so when you create a descendant data module, you do not get a copy of the ancestor's diagram. That means you must either recreate the diagram in the descendant or only document the descendant's components.

Advanced Concepts in Data Module Usage

After you get beyond using basic data modules, there are a number of advanced design and development techniques that are available to you. These include the following:

- Using specialized objects and event handlers to encapsulate application logic.

- Keeping data modules and user interfaces separate with data awareness and interface objects.

- Using form inheritance to create trees of related data modules.

- Dealing with special issues of making sure linked components are found by other data modules and forms when they are using a data module that is a form-inheritance descendant, and when they refer to components in the ancestor.

- Using data modules in packages.

Form Inheritance with Data Modules

Form inheritance works with data modules as it does with regular forms. Simply add a data module to the repository, and you can then use File, New to use the data module in a project (Use), create a copy in the current project (Copy), or create a descendant (Inherit) of the data module. Figure 7.4 shows the File, New dialog.

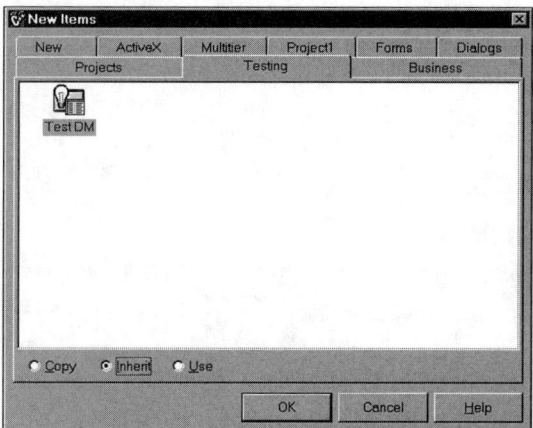

FIGURE 7.4   File, New inheriting from a data module previously added to the repository.

Of the three ways to use data modules from the repository, Inherit is by far the most useful. With it, you can extend the capabilities of a data module by adding components, adding fields, adding or extending event handlers, or changing properties. (Note that you cannot remove a component derived from the ancestor.)

Data Module form inheritance can be used for several different purposes:

- Avoid commitment to a specific set of data set components by creating a base data module with only data sources. Link forms to the data sources in the base data module. Then, add actual data sets to the descendant. You can use this technique to create a data module that supports both ADO and BDE components. Note that you will need to create event handling member functions in the base class that can be called by the descendants to implement the event handling. The descendant data module actual event handlers can then call these functions.

- Add capabilities to a data module to support a variety of product lines. The core product can be supported with the base data module, and the descendants can support capabilities added to that core product, including additional tables, fields, and processing.

- Create lookup and editing descendants of the base data module. The editing descendant can offer event handlers for validation of persistent fields and to perform actions when data is changed. The lookup descendant can have data sets with the same names to satisfy lookup fields and Locate() operations.

Handling Uneven Form Inheritance with Data Modules

When using form inheritance with data modules, there are several important elements to keep in mind. First, if you intend to use a descendant data module with a base class form that refers to the data module ancestor, you need to make it possible for the runtime component lookup system to find the descendant when it is actually looking for the base data module. This can be handled by code similar to Listing 7.2, where the base classes are Base1 and Base2 and the descendant classes are Descendant1 and Descendant2.

LISTING 7.2 Helping C++Builder Find Inherited Data Modules at Runtime

```
TFindGlobalComponent OldFindGlobalComponent;

TComponent* __fastcall FindGlobalComponentExtended
   (const System::AnsiString Name)
{
    if (Name == "Base1") return (TComponent *) (Base1 *) Descendant1;
    if (Name == "Base2") return (TComponent *) (Base2 *) Descendant2;
    return OldFindGlobalComponent(Name);
}
```

LISTING 7.2   Continued

```
WINAPI WinMain(HINSTANCE, HINSTANCE, LPSTR, int)
{
    try
    {
        Application->Initialize();

        OldFindGlobalComponent = FindGlobalComponent;
        FindGlobalComponent = FindGlobalComponentExtended;
```

In addition, each data module's constructor (base or descendant) must set the data module global variable because the automatic initialization of that variable will not occur in the ancestor. For instance, in Base1

```
Base1 = this;
```

and in Descendant1

```
Descendant1 = this;
```

How to Avoid Dependence on Specific User Interfaces

There are two ways to create data modules that avoid dependencies on specific user interfaces. One, the most common and the safest, is to use data-aware controls for that purpose. The second, which should only be used very carefully, involves making available a variable, function, or property in the data module class definition that the user interface can use to register a control with the data module. To safely implement the latter case, the constructor should set that reference to NULL, and every reference to the control should be tested to verify that the pointer is not NULL. This will enable the data module to work properly, even when there is no user interface, or when the user interface does not contain a desired control.

How to Work with Application-Specific and Framework Components in Data Modules

One important design strategy for working with data modules has to do with creating and using specialized generic and application-oriented components and their event handlers to encapsulate application logic.

Most developers simply use the generic components that are part of the VCL or third-party libraries. Event handlers, such as AfterPost(), are then used to enforce application logic, such as forcing the refresh of related data sets when a new record has been written.

But you can also create both generic and application-specific components with their own event handlers and use those components to express complex application logic in the context of a data module. For example, the generic nonvisual component interface in Listing 7.3 offers a framework for undoable actions.

LISTING 7.3   An Application-Oriented, Generic, Nonvisual Component Interface

```
class TUndoableFramework: public TComponent
{
    public:
        void __fastcall (__closure *)
          TExecuteHandler
             (TUndoableFramework *theUndoableFramework);
      void __fastcall (__closure *)
         TRecordUndoHandler
            (TUndoableFramework *theUndoableFramework);
      void __fastcall (__closure *)
         TUndoHandler
            (TUndoableFramework *theUndoableFramework);
      void __fastcall (__closure *)
          TCleanupUndoHandler
             (TUndoableFramework *theUndoableFramework);
    private:
        TExecuteHandler myToExecute;
        TRecordUndoHandler myToRecordUndo;
        TUndoHandler myToUndo;
        TCleanupUndoHandler myToCleanupUndo;
    protected:
      virtual void __fastcall DoExecute(void);
      virtual void __fastcall DoRecordUndo(void);
      virtual void __fastcall DoUndo(void);
      virtual void __fastcall DoCleanupUndo(void);
      public:
          virtual void __fastcall TUndoableFramework(void);
          virtual void __fastcall ~TUndoableFramework(void);
          virtual void __fastcall Execute(void);
             // also invokes ToRecordUndo
          virtual void __fastcall Undo(void);
          virtual void __fastcall CleanupUndo(void);
        __published:
          __property TRecordUndoHandler ToRecordUndo =
             {read=myToRecordUndo,write=myToRecordUndo};
          __property TUndoHandler ToUndo =
```

LISTING 7.3   Continued

```
            {read=myToUndo,write=myToUndo};
    __property TCleanupUndoHandler ToCleanupUndo =
            {read=myToCleanupUndo,write=myToCleanupUndo};
};
```

This shows a component that provides event handlers for performing an action (which invokes an additional handler to record the undo information as a side effect); for undoing that action; and for cleaning up any special remnants of preparation for undo. For example, if undoing a delete actually involved changing the marking on deleted records rather than deleting them, undo cleanup might include performing a final, nonundoable delete of those records. It does not specify how to perform those actions (which are managed by the handlers), only the available actions and, in one case, constrains the order in which they can be performed.

Used in a data module, this component makes it easier to reflect the structure of a system that involves undo. Descendants of the component class can offer specific methods wrapping the calls to the handlers for executing, recording undo, undoing, or cleaning up, or form inheritance can be used with the data module and handlers can be augmented in the data module descendant. A combination of the two techniques can be used—for example, a descendant can offer an event stack for recording events, while descendants of the data module can augment the execution handler to cope with additional requirements.

This is a generic nonvisual component for data module use, but you can also create an application-specific nonvisual component for data module use. For example, the interface to a component (shown in Listing 7.4) handles reservations. (Note that the ... indicates parts of the code not shown to keep the example brief.)

LISTING 7.4   A Completely Application-Specific Nonvisual Component

```
class TReservationDesk: public TComponent
{
    ...
  public:
    void __fastcall MakeReservation
        (TReservation *theReservation);
    void __fastcall UpdateReservation
        (TReservation *theReservation);
    void __fastcall RemoveReservation
        (TReservation *theReservation);
  __published:
    __property TQuery *Reservations =
```

LISTING 7.4   Continued

```
        {read=myReservations,write=myReservations};
    __property TAfterReservationAdded =
        {read=myAfterReservationAdded,write=myAfterReservationAdded};
    __property TBeforeReservationUpdated BeforeReservationUpdated…
    __property TAfterReservationUpdated…
    __property TBeforeReservationRemoved…
    __property TAfterReservationRemoved…
};
```

This component offers the capability to use separate instances of the component for different reservation tables (probably assuming a common field naming scheme), and allows the developer to customize the component behavior with specific event handlers keyed to the available member functions. Of course, such a component can also be further specialized through its own inheritance tree, or its instances can be specialized through the use of form inheritance.

Data Modules in Packages

Data modules, like forms, can be used in packages. However, a common problem arises when you use the package modifier directly in the form class definition—in that case, the data module suddenly looks like a regular form, and all of the data module designer features disappear. This can be easily solved using the following forward and actual definition:

```
class PACKAGE TMyDataModule;
class TMyDataModule…
```

Summary

Data modules are one of the most powerful features in C++Builder, second only to components. A variety of design and implementation techniques can be used to take advantage of data modules.

As you have seen, C++Builder offers database and nonvisual component visual designers—data modules.

You can also use components in data modules to offer design time properties.

And you have seen that there are special data module–oriented patterns that can make your work simpler and easier.

8

The Borland Database Engine

by Mark Cashman

Of all the ways to access data through C++ Builder, the Borland Database Engine (BDE) is one of the most widespread. In addition, the architecture used for its components remains the basis of almost every other component set.

In this chapter you will learn about the capabilities of the BDE and how they are accessed through BDE-based VCL components.

Note that Borland has ceased development on the BDE, and no new features or support for additional databases will be added.

Introduction to the Borland Database Engine (BDE)

The *Borland Database Engine* (BDE) is a language-independent layer directly beneath the VCL. Borland created it to allow various database formats to work seamlessly with their programming tools.

Supported formats include

- Desktop databases: ASCII delimited (text), xBase, Paradox

- Client/server databases: Oracle, Interbase, Sybase, and others.

- Open Database Connectivity (ODBC): Note that ODBC leaves the door open for many other formats (Access, for instance) because, as a Microsoft standard, it has led to the creation of a wide variety of drivers.

As you can see, the BDE enables you to use very different database formats without having to purchase and learn new components. In fact, it is often effortless to use different database engines with the same application. And a special feature of the BDE, heterogeneous joins, enables you to join tables across different database management systems—something still unavailable from any other commonly available technology.

Furthermore, the BDE hides the complexity of many powerful features such as transactions, cached updates, and XML. The bottom line is that it enables you to concentrate on what data to fetch instead of how to fetch it.

The BDE also abstracts the complexity of connecting to a database by allowing BDE components in the VCL to simply reference an *alias*. The alias is a name established by the developer or installer by using the BDE administration tool (bdeadmin32.exe) to associate the name with a database driver and its settings, including those that identify the location of the database itself.

As can be expected, there is a price to pay. The BDE can seem expensive in terms of memory and disk space. These issues might be less compelling, of course, as the power of typical computers increases.

There are many different ways to use the BDE, including desktop (single tier), client/server (two tier).

Single-Tier

This is great for small programs where performance and price are more important than database-engine power or data security and integrity. Shared desktop databases are not robust for multiuser access, but a single-user desktop database can add great flexibility to a program at low cost.

Advantages

- Using any of these formats will yield the best performance while using the VCL.

- Many of these formats are royalty free.

- xBase is a very popular format on PCs and is recognized by most applications that allow importing.

- It is relatively easy to switch formats.

- There is no need to purchase and learn new components/libraries.

Disadvantages

- None of these formats provide good security or internal integrity. Use on a network or in multiuser settings requires great care and is sometimes dangerous because each application updates tables directly, and those updates are, therefore, capable of overwriting each other.

BDE/SQL Links (Client/Server)

This provides the most power, flexibility, and integration for the price without adding the extra complexities of a multitier architecture.

Advantages

- All database engines (DBMS) supported by SQL Links use client/server technology.

- All database engines supported by SQL Links are true relational databases.

- It is relatively easy to switch database engines.

- It performs better than ODBC.

Disadvantages

- Most of these database formats require royalties.

- SQL Links drivers are DBMS-specific and support only Oracle, Sybase, MS SQL Server, Informix, DB2, Access, and InterBase.

- The BDE plus SQL Links puts two layers between the program and the database engine, which can affect performance.

ODBC Using the BDE

Open Database Connectivity (ODBC) is a Microsoft initiative that has become an industry-wide standard. Like SQL Links, you can think of it as a translator for DBMS APIs. The difference is that any vendor can provide a driver for its database format to become an ODBC data source. Thus, virtually all database engines have an ODBC driver today.

ODBC achieves DBMS independence by inserting two layers before the database engine. The first provides a standard API that applications can count on being consistent. It is the ODBC client. The second is the driver that does the translation.

Advantages

- ODBC is an industry-wide standard.

- It can work with the BDE and no program changes are required when switching between native BDE, SQL Links, or ODBC drivers, which offers great flexibility.

- It allows the same application to work with virtually any database, regardless of its format (provided there is an ODBC driver for it).

- It can turn an otherwise single-tier application into a client/server application.

- There will be no need to purchase and learn new components/libraries.

Disadvantages

- The BDE and ODBC combined have large disk and memory requirements, which can reduce performance. Furthermore, there are now three layers between the program and the database engine.

- Some ODBC drivers are not robust. It is important to check the one you intend to use before committing to this architecture.

- Upgrading is an issue. The application, the VCL, the BDE, the ODBC manager/client, the ODBC driver, and the database engine must all be updated independently.

Hedging Your Bets

It is a good idea to immediately create a thin layer between your system and the data components you choose to use. You can do this by creating a descendant or facade for each component you intend to use, and never using the raw components themselves in your system. You can then change the ancestor of the component, or the type of its contained component, either directly or by conditional compilation, and all the uses of the component will, hopefully without change, use the new component set. If you must use specialized methods or properties of the underlying components, try first to hide them in methods or properties of a more general nature in the thin layer. If that cannot be done for some reason, bracket them with #ifdef, #else, #endif commands keyed on a #define that identifies the underlying components in use.

Component Overview

The BDE components form a cooperative framework within the data-aware components of the VCL. And their design, being the first in the VCL, set the standard for the other, subsequent component sets, as you will see in subsequent chapters.

Component Architecture

BDE components fall into several categories:

- Connection components: TSession, TDatabase

- Non-SQL data set component: TTable

- SQL data set component: TQuery

BDE components fit into the VCL through the standard data aware framework—that is, data set components are linked to data sources, which are linked to data-aware controls.

Connection Components

The BDE components connect with the BDE through two linked components—TSession and TDatabase.

TSession is the representation of a database user or connection, and every thread in a multithread program that wants to access a database needs one. Single-threaded programs automatically get a default TSession object called Session, but you can also drop a TSession object into a data module to use with a TDatabase object. Of course, each TSession object typically uses up a database connection, which can be a problem when your DBMS is licensed on a per connection basis.

If you use a TSession component, you must use a TDatabase component. As with TSession, C++Builder automatically provides a default TDatabase object (which uses the default TSession object). The default TDatabase, called Database, is the TDatabase component used by TTable and TQuery objects that do not specify a particular TDatabase object.

However, using a TDatabase component does not require use of a specific TSession (except in a multithreaded program). Unless otherwise specified, TDatabase components use the default TSession.

The TDatabase component typically refers to a DatabaseName or AliasName. The alias is established in the BDE Administrator, which can be run from the Windows Control Panel. A change to the alias can quickly switch from one database to another without any change to your program—one of the particular advantages of the BDE.

To open a TSession, set Active to true or call Open(). To open a TDatabase, set Connected to true. To close the TSession, call Close(). To close the database, set Connected to false.

If the TDatabase is opened, its TSession will be opened. If the TSession is closed, all of its databases will be closed. If the Database is closed, any database components (such as TTable, described below) will be closed.

TTable—**Non-SQL Dataset**

TTable enables you to work with a database without knowing anything about the SQL (Structured Query Language). All you need to do is specify the name of the database alias (or the TDatabase object that represents the database in the program—take your pick), and the name of the table.

You can create persistent field objects for TTable by right clicking the component and picking the fields editor; then from the field editor, right click, and pick Add. Add all the fields or just those you want.

If the table in the database has an index, you can pick that index in the IndexName property of the TTable.

Naturally, a TTable can drive a TDBGrid or any other data-aware control, through a TDataSource component.

TTable can be opened with Open() or by setting Active to true. It is closed with Close() or by setting Active to false.

Adding and Editing Records in a TTable

TTable offers a very simple model for adding and changing records in a database table. To insert a record, use the Append() function followed by setting field values as needed; to edit the current record, use the Edit() function and follow by setting field values as needed.

For either of these activities, the completion of the addition or edit is caused by a call to Post(), which makes the change to the table effective.

For example:

```
Table1->Append();
Table1->FieldByName("Somefield")->AsString = "string of some sort";
Table1->FieldByName(FieldNameInAVariable)->AsInteger = 3;
Table1->Post();
```

Transactions

The BDE supports transactions through the TDatabase component. Transactions have a variety of characteristics, but the most important is that they protect the records involved in a transaction from simultaneous changes, and they hide changes in progress, even across tables, until they are complete.

The TDatabase component offers functions to

- StartTransaction()—Any subsequent Edit() or Append() will participate in this transaction.

- Commit()—Make all the changes permanent and visible, and end the transaction.

- Rollback()—Undo all the changes which occurred under this transaction.

You can also set the degree to which changes made during a transaction are visible to other users of the database, through the TransIsolation property.

One of the powerful aspects of this feature is its capability to use transactions with desktop databases. Normally, transactions are only available for more powerful and expensive client/server databases.

Master/Detail Tables

Many databases contain master/detail tables—for instance, a customer with orders, or orders with a record for each order line. C++Builder makes it very easy to establish such relationships between tables using the BDE.

The master table must have a TDataSource that is linked to it. Then, the detail table must reference that component from its DataSource property. It also needs to specify which field it contains and which fields from the master table need to match. For instance, an order table might have a CUSTOMER_ID field that needs to match the customer table ID field.

Both the master and the detail table linked TDataSource components can also be used to link to TDBGrid or other data-aware components.

TQuery—SQL Dataset

SQL enables you to have much more control over your data set content than TTable. You can select a subset of fields, you can join multiple tables, and you can even join tables across different aliases, which can mean across different databases.

You code your SQL statement into the SQL property of the TQuery. As with TTable, you need to provide a DatabaseName, which can be an alias or the name of a TDatabase component.

Like TTable, TQuery can be opened with Open() or by setting Active to true. It can be closed with Close() or by setting Active to false.

In addition to allowing you to specify a selection from one or more tables in a database, you can use any other valid SQL statement in the SQL property—including INSERT, UPDATE, DELETE, CREATE TABLE, and ALTER TABLE. However, you cannot use Active = true or Open() for those types of SQL—instead, use the ExecSQL() function.

Finally, TQuery components, like TTable components, can participate in transactions.

TQuery **Master/Detail**

As with TTable, TQuery can participate in a master/detail relationship, but setting up that relationship is a little more complex. First you need the normal basis for the relationship—a common field between the two tables. You need to have a TDataSource linked to the master TTable or TQuery (either can be used). But setting up the relationship in a TQuery detail component is a little more complex because you have to craft your SQL with a parameter string whose name matches the name of the field from the master. Typically, this might look as follows:

```
SELECT * FROM ORDER WHERE CUSTOMER_ID = :ID
```

This assumes the master table is the previously mentioned customer table, with an ID field named ID.

The BDE takes care of matching the type of the parameter, so if the ID were a string, you would *not* have to write:

```
SELECT * FROM ORDER WHERE CUSTOMER_ID = ':ID'
```

In fact, if you do, you will experience an error, in the sense that the query will try to find an order with a customer ID containing the string :ID—something that is unlikely to be successful.

Parameters in General

Parameters are a powerful technique for driving TQuery components, and they are not limited to master/detail relationships. You can establish a parameter and set it from within your program. For instance, if you have a TEdit for entering an ID, such as...

```
Query1->ParamByName("ID")->AsInteger = Edit1->Text.ToInt();
```

will set the query to use that as the parameter value.

When you reset a parameter such as this, it automatically closes the query, so you need to follow this by setting Active = true or calling Open().

In this case, of course, you do not need a TDataSource to drive the TQuery.

Parameters are also useful in SQL statements other than SELECT; for instance, field values for an INSERT or UPDATE can be provided.

```
Query1->SQL->Text = "INSERT INTO SOMETABLE(A,B,C) VALUES (:A,:B,:C)";
Query1->ParamByName("A")->AsInteger = 34;
Query1->ParamByName("B")->AsString "Something else";
Query1->ParamByName("C")->AsDouble = 564.32;
Query1->ExecSQL();
```

Constructing a Query in Your Program

Parameters only go so far—they are not a general macro facility. For instance, they cannot appear as an attribute or table name, and cannot be used in any clause other than the WHERE clause. But, because the SQL property is available to your program as a TStringList, you can construct a query using values available in your program. For instance, instead of a parameter for the ID, you might use...

```
Query1->SQL->Text =
   "SELECT * FROM ORDER WHERE CUSTOMER_ID = '" + IDEdit->Text + "'";
```

This can also be used for constructing a query for a variety of tables:

```
Query1->SQL->Text =
   "SELECT * FROM " + TableNameEdit->Text +
   " WHERE CUSTOMER_ID = '" + IDEdit->Text + "'";
```

UpdateSQL and RequestLive

TQuery has one drawback—unlike TTable, it is not a component, where direct updates of rows in the table are generally possible.

If a TQuery contains a simple SQL statement, the BDE can generally allow you to update through the TQuery, just as you would with a TTable. This requires you to set the TQuery property RequestLive to true. Setting RequestLive, however, is as the name suggests, a request and does not guarantee success.

One way to ensure that a query can be updated is to use TUpdateSQL components. A single TUpdateSQL component encapsulates the SQL needed to insert, update, and delete from the underlying tables of an SQL SELECT. That SQL is generated from the TQuery associated with the TUpdateSQL component. A double-click opens the TUpdateSQL editor, as shown in Figure 8.1.

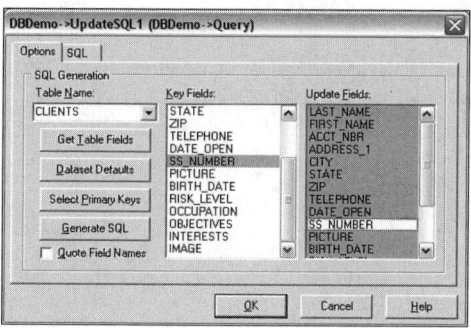

FIGURE 8.1 The TUpdateSQL component editor.

This editor enables you to specify key fields, even from joined tables, but a single TUpdateSQL component only is allowed to update a single table. If a TQuery component represents a SELECT statement that joins several tables, and you need to be able to update them all, you need a TUpdateSQL component for each.

Unfortunately, the TQuery component only has one UpdateObject property that can reference a single TUpdateSQL component. And, although TUpdateSQL has a DataSet property, it isn't available at design time for some reason. The answer is to programmatically assign that property at runtime. A good place to do that is in your Data Module's constructor because its body is executed after all the components have been loaded and their cross references assigned. Here's what the assignment might look like.

```
UpdateQuery1->DataSet = Query1;
```

Cached Updates and TUpdateSQL

The VCL takes care of making sure the TUpdateSQL is called when it is needed. But, there are a couple of things you need to set up, as discussed in the next section.

Making TUpdateSQL work also requires that the TQuery have its CachedUpdates property set to true. Applying the cached updates forces the VCL to invoke the appropriate TUpdateSQL components.

Cached updates are a lot like transactions—they hide the changes made to records until ApplyUpdates() is called. In most cases, however, you want to apply cached updates right away. This is best done in the AfterPost event of the TQuery component. Usually, you also want to follow ApplyUpdates() with CommitUpdates() to clear the various caches.

Heterogeneous Joins

The BDE provides a special feature that can make some very difficult integration projects easier—the capability to join tables across databases.

This can only be done in TQuery, and requires a special notation in your SQL to indicate the alias name of each source table. For instance:

```
SELECT * FROM
:SomeOracleDatabase:ORACLETABLE AS O,
:SomeXBaseDatabase:XBASETABLE AS X
WHERE O.ID = X.ID
```

This notation leverages the BDE alias in the names surrounded by ":". The BDE handles the differences between the DBMS and performs the join in its own way, without relying on the technology of the DBMS.

Summary

The BDE and its component set offer a tremendous package of power and value to every developer and user. Although it is sometimes perceived as a burden to install and upgrade the BDE across your software installation, the capabilities it offers are often key to your application's success.

In addition, understanding the BDE component set is critical to understanding any of the database components in the various component sets in the VCL and available from third parties.

You have seen the various features of the BDE including tables, queries, transactions, and cached updates. Working with these features will help you understand all the implementation alternatives they provide.

9

Client Datasets and Client Dataset Enhancements

by Mark Cashman

Client data sets offer capabilities to improve the performance of your client/server and multitier database. In this chapter you will learn about how client data sets work, and how you can use VCL database components to work with them.

Introduction to Client Dataset Concepts

Typical client/server database applications obtain records from a provider across the network (we usually call this a database server). When the client is data intensive, displaying large numbers of records as you scroll back and forth in a grid or other data-aware control, this can cause large amounts of network traffic. Such network traffic can involve transferring redundant records and can unnecessarily use up network bandwidth. It can also slow application response time below tolerable levels.

The answer to the problem is to provide some sort of buffering that is local to the client. The implementation of that in the VCL is TClientDataSet and its descendants.

Client datasets are write-through caches. A write-through cache acts as a buffer for records retrieved and also intercepts and duplicates changes being sent back to the provider. The application sees the changes immediately when it next reads from the client dataset, without the need to request changed records from the provider, thus, eliminating unnecessary network traffic.

Figure 9.1 shows a diagram describing the relationship between the various elements of the chain from database server to user interface.

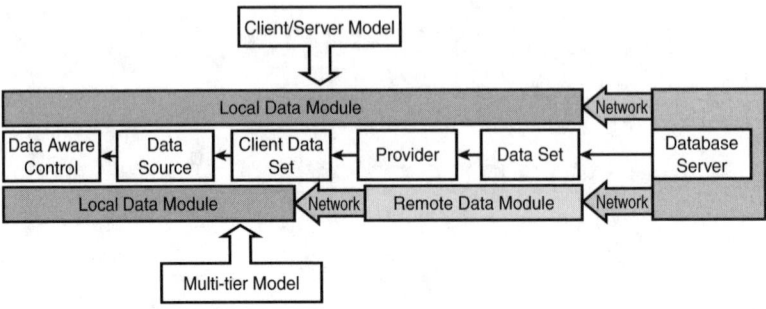

FIGURE 9.1   Client data set and provider in client/server and multitier configurations.

This diagram depicts the relationship between the database server, the datasets, the provider, the client datasets, the data source, and, finally, the data-aware control. It also shows the location of those components in two different models: the client/server model and the multitier model.

In the client/server model, all components reside within a local data module, except for the database server, which exists on its own, separate platform.

In the multitier model, some components reside on a separate platform within a remote data module; others exist within the local data module.

In the case of the client/server model, there is a single transport of information across the network. In the case of the multitier model, information is passed across the network twice: once from the database server to the remote data module and once from the remote data module to local data module. More information on the multitier model can be found later in this chapter.

Generally, client datasets are located in the memory of the client. This optimizes their performance in a way not possible with disk-located client/server buffers.

One other feature of client datasets can be useful. Client datasets enable your application to work in a briefcase mode. Briefcase mode, similar to the briefcase mode on the Windows desktop, enables you to be detached from the network on which the client/server database is located and still work with records from that database. At the time that you reconnect with the home network of the client/server database server, the client/server dataset will attempt to propagate changes back to the server. If errors occur during that resolution process, for instance, if fields have values that were changed by applications during the time the briefcase was separated, exceptions will be thrown or events will be triggered that can enable you to provide alternatives to the user of your application.

Using Basic Client Datasets in the Client/Server Environment

In the client/server environment, client datasets are used as a buffer for records transferred from the provider to client. Typically, you have a `TQuery` or other `TDataSet` descendant issuing SQL to the database server, which responds with the appropriate records. Associated with that `TDataSet` descendant is a `TDataSource`, linked to various data-aware controls, which, in turn, displays records in the client-user interface.

When using `TClientDataSet` the association is changed slightly. The `TClientDataSet` is associated with a `TProvider` component. The `TProvider` connects the `TClientDataSet` with the provider through the `TDataSet` descendant. The `TDataSet` descendant simply retrieves records normally, as requested by the client data set. But the `TClientDataSet` requests records much less frequently than would be the case otherwise.

Figure 9.2 shows a typical `TDataModule` containing such datasets, providers, client datasets, and data sources.

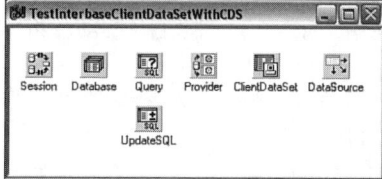

FIGURE 9.2   Typical client data set usage in a client/server data module.

Figure 9.3 shows the user interface for a sample program that uses two `TDataModules`—one with a client data set and one with a normal data set.

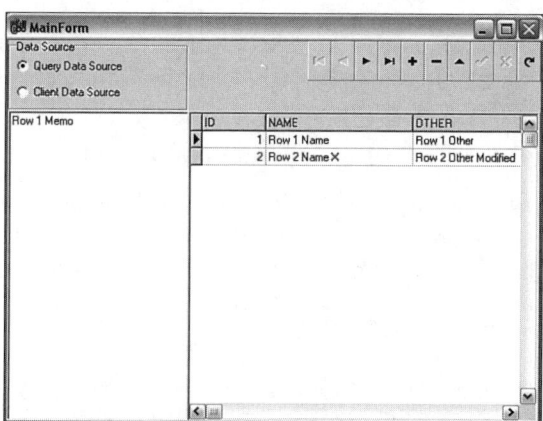

FIGURE 9.3   User interface for a program using the client data set and normal data modules.

The program provides a user interface with a radio group from which you can select whether to see the datasets from the point of view of the TQuery itself, or from that of a TClientDataSet that uses TQuery through a provider.

Unfortunately, even TClientDataSet components cannot solve the problem of multiple applications modifying the same record. But, when you attempt to post from the TClientDataSet to the underlying dataset, the TClientDataSet sees differences and generates an OnReconcileError. Note that this type of error might not be detected when it occurs in a text blob.

Listing 9.1 shows a simple event handler to deal with a reconcile error. However, keep in mind that this does not cover the various possible causes with their appropriate responses, and that significant experimentation would be needed to properly manage these errors.

LISTING 9.1   Event Handler for *OnReconcileError*

```
void __fastcall TTestInterbaseClientDataSetWithCDS::ClientDataSetReconcileError(
    TCustomClientDataSet *DataSet, EReconcileError *E,
    TUpdateKind UpdateKind, TReconcileAction &Action)
{
    ShowMessage(E->Context + " / " + String(E->ErrorCode) + ": " + E->Message);
    Action = raCancel;
}
```

Improving Performance with Client Datasets

Just using a TClientDataSet can improve performance, if your performance throughput is affected by network bandwidth demands. However, you can do more.

There are a variety of options you can use to improve performance with client datasets. Some of those options are available on the TProvider component. Others appear on the TClientDataSet component.

On the TClientDataSet some of the properties that affect performance include

- PacketRecords—This indicates how many records should be passed across the network from the provider. The default used for this is—1, which indicates that as many records as necessary should be passed across the network at any given time. How many records that might be, is controlled by the on demand options of the client datasets.

- FetchOnDemand—This is an overall constraint on how frequently records are fetched from the provider. As the user scrolls through a data-aware grid or uses some other control to conduct a search, when FetchOnDemand is true, records are obtained as needed to fill the visible area of the grid. If false, the application must explicitly fetch records as needed. False is generally not appropriate for interactive applications.

On the `TProvider`, there are other properties that affect performance:

- Options—These include `poFetchBlobsOnDemand` and `poFetchDetailsOnDemand`. If `TClientDataSet`'s `FetchOnDemand` property is true, the client will only request blobs as needed. This means that blobs will not be unnecessarily passed over the network. For instance, if you use a `TDBMemo` control to display text blobs, you will only be displaying a single blob at a time. Your grid might normally request 20 or 30 rows transferred to the network for a given page display, despite only needing to display one. Obviously, this option can significantly improve performance, particularly when your data set contains large blobs.

One other property can be useful in improving performance with client datasets. If your application surfaces its user interface on the Web, it might require an XML representation of its data. If that is the case, the XML data property of the `TClientDataSet`, can be used to provide a copy of the client dataset's local in-memory data as an XML data packet. This can save you from having to assemble the XML yourself programmatically.

Using Client Datasets in a Multitier Environment

Client datasets are useful in a client-server environment as well as in multitier environments. In a multitier environment the client-user interface is separated from the business logic, which is in turn separated from the database server. The relationship between the business logic tier and the database tier is similar to that found in client/server applications. Thus, `TClientDataSet` can play a role.

In multitier, or distributed, environments, `TClientDataSet` does not connect directly with a local `TQuery`, but instead connects with a remote data module. A remote data module is a `TDataModule` that acts as an independent executable running (potentially) on a separate machine. Although the details of remote-data modules are best saved for a later chapter (Chapter 20, "Distributed Applications with DataSnap," and Chapter 21, "DataSnap Multitier Connections"), here is a brief look to identify the basic principles.

Figure 9.4 shows an image of a remote data module that surfaces a `TQuery`.

Figure 9.5 shows the image of the local data module that is used by the client to contact the middle tier.

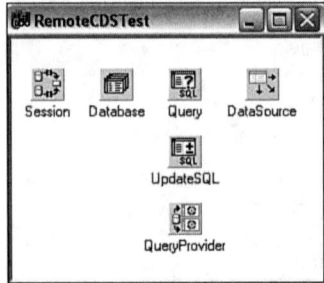

FIGURE 9.4   Remote data module.

FIGURE 9.5   Local data module for a remote data module.

As you can see, the local data module contains a `TClientDataSet` for each `TQuery` in the remote data module; which, in turn, contains a separate provider for each `TQuery` it chooses to surface. The provider is contacted by the client data set on the client side, and packets are exchanged containing data from each `TQuery` in the remote data module, as needed.

Specialized Types of Client Datasets

Although the generic `TClientDataSet` component is usable in a wide variety of situations including client/server and multitier, client/server applications can use specialized descendants of `TClientDataSet` that contain not only client dataset capabilities, but also a default provider. Such specialized `TClientDataSet` descendants include

- `TBDEClientDataSet`—which is usable with BDE components such as `TQuery` and `TTable`.

- `TSQLClientDataSet`—which is usable with the dbExpress components such as `TSQLQuery` and `TSQLTable`.

- `TIBClientDataSet`—which is usable with the IBExpress components such as `TIBQuery` and `TIBTable`.

Of course, these components are only useful in a client/server environment. In a multitier environment, where the client dataset is required to communicate with a remote provider in a remote data module, TClientDataSet is the preferred method. This is because TClientDataSet is provider neutral, and is unaware of the underlying technology of the provider.

Summary

Client datasets offer the capability to easily optimize client/server and multitier dataset performance. In conjunction with data modules and remote data modules they offer the opportunity to share that optimization across multiple applications.

In this chapter you have had an opportunity to see many different ways of using client datasets. You've also had an opportunity to see different parameters and property settings that can impact performance when using client datasets in both the client tier and multitier environment.

10

Interbase Express

by Mark Cashman

The IBExpress components are an extension of the BDE components that support a special and optimized connection to the Interbase DBMS. Because Interbase is a comparatively inexpensive and powerful client/server database, it can be an attractive alternative for commercial software developers needing such a product. This chapter will show you how to use these components in your application.

Introduction to IBExpress Components

This section will introduce the InterBase Relational Database Manager System (RDBMS) and the InterBase Express (IBExpress) components supplied with C++Builder. Although originally designed as a commercial client/server (C/S) database server, InterBase has joined the Open Source movement with the introduction of version 6.0. This development will benefit database application developers around the world; it will combine a fast, powerful RDBMS solution with a freely distributable license.

Starting with the release of C++Builder 5, Borland supplied IBExpress components that enable the creation of powerful C/S applications without having to distribute the BDE. These applications directly access the InterBase client, which in turn handles the communication with the database server.

IBExpress components tend to look almost exactly like their BDE equivalents. There are some changes in the meaning of various properties as a consequence of the specific nature of Interbase. For instance, it is possible, and sometimes necessary, to specify the IP address of the server on which Interbase is running.

To demonstrate IBExpress components in action, we will design and create a simple database application that will incorporate many of them. The application will track a number of programming projects, their revisions, and their known bugs. We will name this application Bug Tracker. You can find the source code for this application in the BugTracker folder on the CD-ROM that accompanies this book. The project filename is BugTracker.bpr.

> **NOTE**
>
> If you have projects requiring C++Builder 4 or earlier that you want to convert to pure InterBase, Jason Wharton's InterBase ObjectsInterBase Objects (http://www.ibobjects.com) is an excellent set of components to consider. This site also offers a replacement for ISQL, called IB-WISQL, which provides many features that make the design and administration of InterBase databases easier.

Setting Up a Schema

Bug Tracker uses three different tables: Program, Revision, and Bugs. As illustrated in Figure 10.1, Program is the master table, and Revision and Bugs are detail tables. The relationship among the tables is that Programs may have Revisions or Bugs. A Revision must belong to a Program. A Bugs *must* belong to a Program and *may* belong to a Revision.

Specifying these relationships in the creation of a database enables InterBase to enforce referential integrity on the server. Listing 10.1 shows the SQL used to create the Bugs table.

LISTING 10.1   SQL Used to Create the Bugs Table

```
/*Bugs Table*/
create table bugs (
    bug_id          integer not null,
    bug_name        varchar (80) not null,
    bug_description varchar (255),
    bug_resolved    smallint not null,
    bug_date        date not null,
    pro_id          integer not null,
    r_id            integer,
primary key (bug_id),
constraint fk_bugs_pro_id foreign key (pro_id) references program (pro_id),
constraint fk_bugs_r_id foreign key (r_id) references revision (r_id));
```

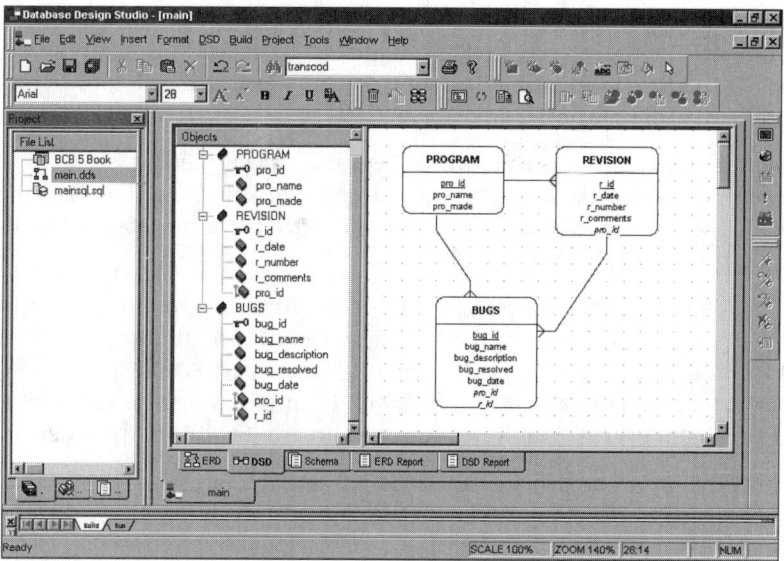

FIGURE 10.1   The tables used in Bug Tracker.

NOTE

At the end of each constraint declaration, the `on update (cascade||set null)` and `on delete (cascade||set null)` statements can be added. These are executed when the selected field in the table being referenced is modified or deleted and saves time by not requiring triggers to make the changes needed to maintain referential integrity.

For example, if we changed to

```
constraint fk_bugs_pro_id foreign key (pro_id) references program
➥(pro_id) on update cascade on delete cascade,
```

when any `Program` table records were deleted, or when any of the `Program` tables `pro_id` values were changed, any `Bugs` record would be deleted or modified automatically.

We can define foreign keys without a name and have InterBase name them, but it is far easier to debug `violation of FOREIGN KEY constraint "FK_BUGS_PRO_ID" on table "BUGS"` than `constraint "INTEG_XX"`. Unfortunately, the table's primary key cannot be assigned a name.

NOTE

The database supplied with the CD-ROM accompanying this book, `BCB5BOOK6.GDB`, was designed under InterBase 6.0 and will not be accessible under any earlier InterBase version.

The `Bugs` table consists of fields that are used to describe the bug and foreign keys. Each field has a name, a type, its length, and an indicator if it must have a value assigned. If the field is identified as not null, InterBase will not allow a record to be posted with that field as null.

Although this is useful, it is the foreign keys that specify referential integrity for InterBase to enforce. The `Bugs` table has two foreign keys: one that identifies a relationship to the `Program` table, and one that specifies a relationship to the `Revision` table.

InterBase automatically enforces specified referential integrity. In our sample program, a `Bug` record can reference a `Program` record. An attempt to delete a `Program` record will return an error message such as `Violation of FOREIGN KEY constraint "FK_BUGS_PRO_ID" on table "BUGS"`. Additionally, an attempt to insert a record into either the `Bugs` or `Revision` table without a valid `pro_id` will return an error message.

As another example, we declared the `r_id` foreign key in the `Revision` table as permitted to hold a null value. Any other value assigned to this key must correspond to a valid revision record or a constraint error message will be returned.

Referential integrity rules protect a database from bad or invalid data sent by client applications. To take full advantage of this protection, it is important to invest time and care in designing and testing the database schema. After a database becomes live, it is extremely difficult to change any of its relationships without deleting data. In a recent application that was developed, one table's primary key had to be changed. The change would have taken a couple of minutes in the development stage, but, because the database was live, it took several hours of programming to create the large SQL script necessary to make the update without affecting any of the existing data.

Database Rules

In addition to referential integrity, InterBase enables you to place server-side rules in the database. This is one of the great strengths of C/S development. Database rules that reside inside the database are enforced, regardless of the client that is accessing the data. An added advantage is that internal rules can often be changed without updating the client applications that are in use. For example, if it is decided that deleting a `Revision` record should set the corresponding bug record's `bug-resolved` field to zero, a trigger can be created or modified to handle the event. This means that for our earlier referential integrity problem (where we are trying to delete a record from the `Program` table), we could create a database rule that will automatically delete any `Bugs` table records that are assigned to that particular program.

There is no universally accepted standard concerning the placement of rules, and there are many differing opinions as to which rule should be on the server and which should be in the client. We would recommend that any rule that involves referential integrity or that operates on a large number of rows in the database should be placed on the server. Other rules can be located on the server or in the client, whichever seems best to you.

In multitier databases, on the other hand, the best place to keep database rules is generally in the programs of the middle tier. The only rules kept in the database tier are referential integrity rules, to ensure that even database administrators cannot damage the integrity of the data. This scheme ensures scalability as the middle tier is replicated, while still protecting the integrity of the underlying data.

Generators, Triggers, and Stored Procedures

Generators, triggers, and stored procedures (sprocs) can be used to create server-side rules in InterBase. They are used in many operations, ranging from the simple implementation of an autoincrement field in a table to complex SQL operations involving several tables and thousands of records. Because they reside in the database with the data, they typically can perform an operation on the database faster than a similar rule residing in the client.

Generators

Generators can be viewed as global integer variables for the database. They are not tied to any table or field, but merely generate numbers in sequence through the use of the GEN_ID() function. Although generators are not often used on their own, they are extensively used for assigning values to unique keys in triggers and sprocs.

The following will create a generator and set its value:

```
CREATE GENERATOR PRO_ID_GEN;
SET GENERATOR  PRO_ID_GEN TO 1;
```

This code creates the generator PRO_ID_GEN and sets its value to 1. We will use this generator to supply the Program table with its unique key values.

It is important to realize that generators are not affected by transactions. For example, if you start a transaction and call the GEN_ID() function, rolling back the transaction will not change back the new value of the generator. The new value will remain the same as if the transaction had been committed and retained.

Triggers

An InterBase trigger is similar to a component event. A trigger can be set to execute a command or commands when a row in a table or view is inserted, deleted, or updated. However, a trigger cannot be called directly.

Triggers have many uses: maintaining referential integrity, validating input information, and creating logs of user activities involving the database. One common use of triggers is the implementation of autoincrement fields. InterBase does not come with an autoincrement field type, but this operation can be duplicated by using a normal integer field, the PRO_ID_GEN generator seen earlier, and the trigger in Listing 10.2.

LISTING 10.2   SQL to Create One of the Program Table's Triggers

```
CREATE TRIGGER SET_PRO_ID FOR PROGRAM
BEFORE INSERT AS
BEGIN
    IF (NEW.PRO_ID IS NULL) THEN
    BEGIN
        NEW.PRO_ID = GEN_ID(PRO_ID_GEN,1);
    END
    IF (NEW.PRO_MADE IS NULL) THEN
    BEGIN
        NEW.PRO_MADE =  'TODAY';
    END
END
```

This trigger is assigned to the Program table to execute before a record is inserted. The NEW variable contains the fields to be inserted. If there is no pro id value supplied, the GEN_ID() function takes the supplied generator, increases it by 1, and returns the new value. This value is then assigned to the new record's pro_id field. If there is no value supplied for the pro_made field, it is assigned the current server date.

The one drawback to assigning the autoincrement field's value in this way is that C++Builder InterBase components don't normally receive notification that the trigger has incremented the field's value. The table must be refreshed, the record must be refreshed, or some other means must be found to make this information viewable to the application. There are several methods of addressing this drawback.

In C++ Builder 6, the new property is provided on the TIBQuery or TIBTable component. The TIBCustomDataset's TIBGeneratorField type of property is GeneratorField. GeneratorField identifies one of the TIBCustomDataset's field objects as a field to be refreshed directly from the table after insert. It is assumed that this field is updated because of the execution of a generator in a stored procedure in the Interbase database.

Prior to C++Builder 6 the only method of accomplishing this was through the use of stored procedures. The following section discusses the method to introduce the concept of stored procedures, and how they can interact with the IBExpress components.

Stored Procedures

A stored procedure (sproc) is a routine that resides in the database. Sprocs can be created to perform operations on the database that return anything from a single value to multiple rows of information. For example, Listing 10.3 shows a procedure that takes the supplied name of a program to be created, generates a new record with that information and the PRO_ID_GEN generator, and returns the program's pro_id field.

LISTING 10.3   SQL to Create the Create_Program Stored Procedure

```
CREATE PROCEDURE CREATE_PROGRAM /*name of procedure*/
(THE_PRO_NAME CHAR(80))/*supplied params*/
RETURNS (THE_PRO_ID INTEGER)/*returned params*/
AS
BEGIN
    THE_PRO_ID = GEN_ID(PRO_ID_GEN,1);/*get the next program id*/
    INSERT INTO PROGRAM(PRO_ID,PRO_NAME,PRO_MADE)
    VALUES(:THE_PRO_ID,:THE_PRO_NAME,'TODAY');/*insert the new record*/
END
```

This procedure is a better solution than the trigger we created previously because it solves the problem of retrieving the newly created record's PRO_ID. Like a trigger, this procedure is stored in the database, and its internal workings can be changed without having to update any of the clients. We will use both triggers and sprocs in Bug Tracker.

NOTE

There might be times when you want to retrieve a generator's value through a normal query statement. To accomplish this, you would use a statement such as

```
SELECT GEN_ID(PRO_ID_GEN,1) NEXT_PRO_ID FROM RDB$DATABASE
```

When this statement is executed in a TIBQuery, it will return the field NEXT_PRO_ID, which will contain the next PRO_ID_GEN generator's value.

Another alternative to using stored procedures with triggers, or the GeneratorField property, is to use the ForcedRefresh property of IBExpress. ForcedRefresh is an easy way to bring back changes made by a trigger. The key to using ForcedRefresh is that the client needs to have knowledge of a secondary key, and the lookup for the WHERE clause of the RefreshSQL should be on the secondary key instead of the generated primary key. This is explored in more detail in the "modify, delete, insert, refresh" section, later in this chapter.

It is generally a good rule of thumb not to allow the client-side to modify primary keys. If the client-side needs to modify a table's primary key, that table is a prime candidate for a generated primary key. The modifiable part should be a secondary key.

Debugging an InterBase Application

In addition to the normal collection of forms and controls that the application might have, this application must work with the InterBase server. This includes providing connection information, starting transactions, executing search requests, and obtaining any other information the client requires.

Many activities are the responsibility of the database server, which can make it difficult to debug them from the C++Builder IDE. To view these activities, IBExpress supplies the TIBSQLMonitor component. This is a component that generates an event for every InterBase activity that occurs. Events of interest should be specified in the TraceFlags property of the TIBDatabase to which the TIBSQLMonitor component is linked. If we take the information supplied in the generated event and add it to a TMemo, we have a powerful tool for determining which InterBase activities occurred and in what order. Although seemingly cryptic at times, this information can help solve problems involving sequential interactions between multiple transactions and queries.

Database Creation and Connection

The TIBDatabase component is used to establish connections to InterBase databases using either the local host, TCP/IP, NetBEUI, or SPX protocol. However, parameters for connecting to a database are different from those used for creating a database. The server and the database to be connected to are specified in the DatabaseName property. C++Builder's help file has information on formatting the DatabaseName property for different protocols. Listing 10.4 shows how to use an enum type and a function to create an appropriate string for each protocol.

LISTING 10.4   The CreateConnectionString Function

```
enum ConnectionType {ctLocal,ctTCPIP,ctNetBEUI,ctSPX};
AnsiString __fastcall TdmMain::CreateConnectionString(AnsiString Server,
➥AnsiString FileName, ConnectionType CType)
{
    AnsiString ConnectionString = "";
    switch (CType)
    {
    case ctLocal : ConnectionString = FileName;break;
```

LISTING 10.4   Continued

```
case ctTCPIP : ConnectionString.sprintf("%s:%s",Server,FileName);break;
case ctNetBEUI : ConnectionString.sprintf("\\%s\%s",Server,FileName);break;
case ctSPX : ConnectionString.sprintf ("%s@%s",Server,FileName);break;
}
return ConnectionString;
}
```

CAUTION

In certain instances, it might be necessary to use a server name in place of an actual IP address when connecting to InterBase using TCP/IP connections. For example, `ibserver:c:\bugger.gdb` will work, but `192.168.0.9:c:\bugger.gdb` sometimes won't, even if the `ibserver` machine's address is `192.168.0.9`. This is frequently seen in machines that have a version of Winsock earlier than version 2.0.

To overcome this anomaly, add an entry in the `hosts` file in Windows 95/98 (located under the `Windows` folder) or the `hosts` file in Windows NT/2000 (located under `%SystemRoot%\System32\Drivers\Etc`).

For example, if you want to connect to a server at `192.168.0.11`, add the following line:

```
192.168.0.11 theserver
```

```
The following hosts file shows how this might look after the addition.
# Copyright (c) 1993-1999 Microsoft Corp.
#
# This is a sample HOSTS file used by Microsoft TCP/IP for Windows.
#
# This file contains the mappings of IP addresses to host names. Each
# entry should be kept on an individual line. The IP address should
# be placed in the first column followed by the corresponding host name.
# The IP address and the host name should be separated by at least one
# space.
#
# Additionally, comments (such as these) may be inserted on individual
# lines or following the machine name denoted by a '#' symbol.
#
# For example:
#
#      102.54.94.97     rhino.acme.com         # source server
#       38.25.63.10     x.acme.com             # x client host
127.0.0.1        localhost
192.168.0.11 theserver
```

After saving the file, either restart the system to effect the changes or run the following command from the DOS prompt:

```
nbtstat -R
```

Note that the -R parameter must be capitalized. We can then access the server at 192.168.0.11 by using theserver:c:\bugger.gdb.

Also, when coding paths in C++ functions don't forget that the \ is an escape character used to indicate other characters and that to show an actual backslash requires two backslashes in a row.

Having assigned the DatabaseName property, we must supply the username and password. This can be done in one of two different ways. The first is to set the LoginPrompt property to true, which will open a window asking the user for the information. The second is to assign the username and password in the Params property. The following code shows a sample set of parameters for logging in:

```
user_name=SYSDBA
password=masterkey
```

Keep in mind that to avoid the login dialog is necessary to set the login prompt property to false. Also, under C++Builder 6 to use the login prompt dialogue you need to include a special unit in your project. The #include is DBLogDlg.hpp, which should appear in your .cpp file. You also need to add DBLogDlg.pas from your C++ Builder installation Source\VCL directory, where project will not successfully link.

After these items are established, setting the Connected property to true will make the connection to the database.

NOTE

If you have problems generating the proper connection string parameters at runtime, the TIBDatabase component has an editor that will generate examples for you to use.

Although InterBase Express can create and drop databases, it does not currently support SQL scripts. Therefore, you are unable to run an SQL script against a newly created database to create the necessary tables, triggers, and so on. An empty database of the correct format normally would be created and shipped and with a product such as this, however, it is possible to repeatedly insert and execute appropriate CREATE TABLE and ALTER TABLE statements through a TIBQuery component using the ExecSQL() function.

Using Transactions

Transactions are an integral part of a client/server database. IBExpress provides the TIBTransaction component to manage transactions. Each TIBTransaction component handles one transaction on the database to which it is assigned.

A TIBTransaction component enables you to specify the properties of a transaction. These are stored in the Params property of the component. TIBTransaction has a built-in editor that enables you to use four predefined transaction settings. In Bug Tracker, we will use the Read Committed setting. InterBase and IBExpress both default to the transaction to Snapshot. Changing to Read Committed is a normal first step when dropping a new TIBTransaction onto a data module or form.

CAUTION

Most problems involving disappearing data or incorrectly updated information can be traced back to an error in implementing a transaction. With the version of IBExpress that we used for this section (version 4.1), we were occasionally surprised by an unexpected commit that occurred on a record post.

This problem was because of a known logic bug in IBExpress wherein a dataset will commit a transaction that it autostarts if there are no other active datasets when it closes. This bug was scheduled for repair in a later update of IBExpress, and might have been fixed in C++ Builder 6. In the meantime, it is a good idea not to allow datasets to autostart transactions, but instead to start them yourself.

If you run across a problem such as this, the TIBSQLMonitor component is invaluable for tracing the transaction events that are occurring.

Accessing Interbase

IBExpress offers many different ways of working with the information in a database. These include TIBTable, TIBQuery, and TIBDataSet. If a TIBTable or TIBQuery is used, the TIBUpdateSQL component can also be used.

TIBUpdateSQL

The TIBUpdateSQL component is designed for use with the TIBTable or TIBQuery component. It provides SQL statements to be executed to perform the actions needed for the four different operations you can perform on the database: deleting, inserting, updating, and refreshing.

The component has an editor (as seen in Figure 10.2) to supply the creation of these statements. The editor can only work when the component has been assigned to a TIBTable or TIBQuery, and the TIBTable or TIBQuery has been set up for a specific table or query. This is because otherwise it will not know the names of the fields involved in the update, insert, or delete operations.

The editor will automatically create a base statement for each of the four operations, but it might be necessary to edit the automatically generated statements to take into account triggers, stored procedures, or other database-specific considerations. To accomplish this, the TIBUpdateSQL component supplies two sets of parameters to the SQL statements. The first of these sets is simply the field names relevant to the underlying table or query (such as :PRO_ID). The second set appends the prefix OLD to the field name (such as :OLD_PRO_ID) and represents the value of a field as it was prior to applying the cached updates.

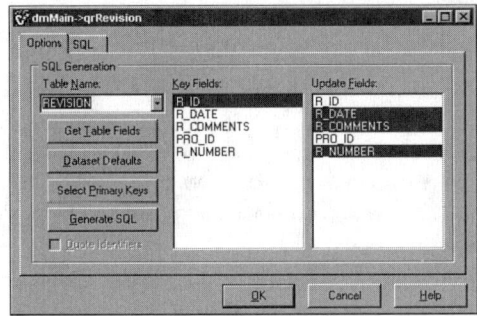

FIGURE 10.2   The TIBUpdateSQL dataset editor.

TIBTable

Just like the standard C++Builder data access components, TIBTable tries to create a live (editable) dataset on a specified table or view. The tables available to the component can include the database's underlying system tables, if they are specified in the TableTypes property.

TIBTable attempts to return a live dataset, but because this is an actual client-server database rather than a desktop database, it might not be possible under certain conditions. This is especially true when referring to views. For these conditions, or when more flexibility is desired, TIBTable can use a TIBUpdateSQL component to enable specific SQL statements to execute the changes to the underlying dataset.

TIBTable is rarely a good component for client/server clients. Because TIBTable polls as much data to the client from the server as possible in a single try, it requires much more network traffic than a similar select * from <table> in a TIBQuery or TIBDataset.

The use of the Insert function of TIBTable is not recommended. Appending data to a specific position in a SQL backend has no real meaning. In a file-based database, such as Paradox, Insert occurs where indicated, but there is no natural meaning to row position in a client/server database such as Interbase, Lulu move because the table rows are spread out across multiple data pages and are rarely contiguous. If you try to use Insert(), InterBase will place the data wherever it wants. Although TIBTable will do a FetchAll and place the new record at the end of the internal record buffer, it is highly inefficient because of the processing required of the client and the network traffic generated.

TIBQuery

TIBQuery returns a read-only dataset based on any InterBase SQL statement. TIBQuery offers a higher degree of control over what data is presented than TIBTable. By using joins, you can specify SQL queries that combine information in several different tables. TIBQuery should be used instead of TIBTable whenever possible.

If the TIBQuery needs to insert, edit, or delete information, a TIBUpdateSQL component must be assigned to it. However, it is typically preferable to use a TIBDataSet, which combines the capabilities of a TIBQuery and TIBUpdateSQL, to accomplish these tasks.

TIBDataSet

TIBDataSet combines the data-selection features of a TIBQuery component with the data-editing features of a TIBUpdateSQL component. One difference between TIBDataset and TIBQuery is that the Params for TIBDataset are not TParams, but TIBExpressSQLDA instead. The TIBExpressSQLDA parameter type is required if you are using InterBase version 6.0 and need Int64 parameters. For the Bug Tracker application, we will make extensive use of TIBDataSets.

TIBSQL and TIBStoredProc

The TIBSQL component offers a fast, low-overhead means of executing InterBase data operations. Descended from the TComponent object, the TIBSQL component does not support any of the data-enabled objects, and, thus, is primarily designed to return a quick value from a database or generator or to be used as a data pump.

TIBStoredProc can work with data-enabled objects, but a TIBQuery or TIBDataSet should be used for stored procedures that return multiple rows or components. Designed to simplify accessing stored procedures, TIBStoredProc enables you to specify the procedure to execute and the parameters for that procedure. Note that any values that are returned by the stored procedure will be accessible through the corresponding parameter.

TIBEvents

Using InterBase and stored procedures or triggers, events can be set up to be generated by the server. An example of a generated event is the command POST_EVENT 'BUG_DELETE', where BUG_DELETE is the name of the event fired.

The TIBEvent component allows the client application to tell the server what events it wants to be notified of, receive that notification, and generate an OnEventAlert() event. Bug Tracker executes a simple ShowMessage() when a bug record is deleted, but more complex functions could easily be included.

Events of this sort are one of the most powerful features of Interbase. It is one of the few DBMS that enables you to register interest in particular internal database events. Such notifications make it much easier to create client/server, or multitier applications. Such applications can register their interest, for instance, in updates or Row insertions that might affect their user interface. This helps to alleviate a problem that often plagues client-server systems with client side user interfaces. Such systems usually do not know when another application or instance of the same application has modified database, and, therefore, they are unable to modify their user interfaces, or refresh their datasets, to display newly inserted or modified records.

Setting Up Bug Tracker

IBExpress components simplify many of the procedures involved in accessing InterBase data, but care must be taken in their use. If the components are set up properly, the end user need not be concerned with referential integrity, supplying all needed fields, transactions, or the like.

Bug Tracker is designed to isolate the user from these issues by presenting a clean, simple interface.

We will begin the setup with the TIBDataSet for the Program table. We start by dropping the component into our data module and assigning it to a connected TIBDatabase and active TIBTransaction (to simplify the setup process). After this is done, we need to specify our select statement. Because the component is attached to a live connection, we can use the CommandText editor to easily create our select statement, which in this case would be select * from PROGRAM.

update, delete, insert, refresh

Having specified the information the component will display, we need to establish what it will do on update, insert, delete, and refresh. As discussed earlier, the TIBUpdateSQL component can create base statements for these events. However, after these statements are created, it's critical that they be checked to ensure that they do not present an opportunity for the user to input incorrect information. The following code shows the IBExpress-provided modify statement.

```
update PROGRAM
set
    PRO_ID = :PRO_ID,
    PRO_NAME = :PRO_NAME,
    PRO_MADE = :PRO_MADE
```

```
where
    PRO_ID = :OLD_PRO_ID
```

There is a problem with this statement in that it theoretically enables the user to change the pro_id field, which is the primary key of the Program table. This should not be allowed, so we will remove the PRO_ID = :PRO_ID statement from the query.

We will also edit the insert statement. Remembering that we assign a new program's pro_id field with a value from pro_id_gen, we can automatically include that value in the insert statement. The following shows a sample of how we can do this:

```
insert into PROGRAM
    (PRO_ID, PRO_NAME, PRO_MADE)
values
    ((select GEN_ID(PRO_ID_GEN,1) FROM RDB$DATABASE), :PRO_NAME,
:PRO_MADE)
```

This statement could also exclude specifying the pro_id field because we have a "before insert" trigger for the Program table that will detect a NULL value for it and assign it the appropriate generator value anyway.

The delete statement is adequate for Bug Tracker, but the following refresh statement is not:

```
select
    PRO_ID,
    PRO_NAME,
    PRO_MADE
from PROGRAM
where
    PRO_ID = :PRO_ID
```

This statement creates a problem because the pro_id is not known on the client-side when a user inserts a record. The pro_id field in the grid would remain blank if we did an insert and refresh using this statement.

Using a secondary key, in this case the pro_name field, can solve this problem. The refresh select statement must return only one row. We can change the refresh statement to match up the pro_name field instead of the pro_id field because there is a constraint on the pro_name field limiting it to a one-row return, and because the pro_name field value is known to the client side. Duplication is prevented by the unique constraint on the pro_name field. Consideration should be given to providing secondary keys for use in refresh statements during the database design phase. For example, in the Revision table, we created the following constraint:

```
add constraint con_rev_pro_id_r_number unique (pro_id,r_number)
```

which enables us to use the following select statement and only return a singleton result set.

```
where
    PRO_ID = :PRO_ID
    AND R_NUMBER = :R_NUMBER
```

Fields

Database fields for IBExpress TDataSet descendants are specified in the same way as normal BDE components. However, we will make two changes to the pro_id field. Set Required to false will enable the user to insert a record without specifying a value for pro_id. Set ReadOnly to true will prevent users from changing the generated value. We will make similar changes to the Revision and Bugs tables.

It is important to make these changes. C++Builder takes no notice that a database has a trigger that will populate a field when it is inserted. If a field is designated as NOT NULL, the user will be forced to supply a value to insert the record, which will cause confusion when that supplied value is replaced.

Cached Updates

InterBase Express components support cached updates through the CachedUpdates property. Cached updates allow changes to the information contained in the dataset without the changes being applied to the actual database. The changed information in the dataset is not under transaction control until it is sent to the server by the ApplyUpdates() method.

For Bug Tracker, we will not use cached updates, but will instead use normal transaction control.

NOTE

As with BDE components, the use of the CachedUpdates property, and the ApplyUpdates(), and CommitUpdates() functions overlaps with transactions, but is essential for the correct use of TIBUpdateSQL components. Generally, it is a good idea to put code to ApplyUpdates() and CommitUpdates() in the AfterPost event handler for the data set.

Transactions and Data-Aware Components

For most simple data forms, the method shown in Listing 10.5, when attached to the TIBUpdateSQL's AfterPost() event, will keep information on the client synchronized with the information that is on the server. This method was created using the

qrProgram component, and it can be used by any TIBUpdateSQL or TIBQuery component. For refreshing after information has been posted, we set the ForcedRefresh
property to true in our datasets.

LISTING 10.5   The qrProgram Component's AfterPost Event

```
void __fastcall TdmMain::qrProgramAfterPost(TDataSet *DataSet)
{
    try
    {
        //commit the changes, and retain the transaction
        trMain->CommitRetaining();
    } catch (Exception &E)//if *any* error happens, we'll rollback and restart
    {
        trMain->RollbackRetaining();
        ShowMessage("Error commiting changes.  "+E.Message);
    }
}
```

There is always an active transaction. When a change is made to the data covered by
a transaction, the updates are applied and the transaction is committed and retained.
The transaction immediately becomes active again, waiting for the next data entry or
change. This helps prevent the possibility of a deadlock caused by two clients editing
the same record. Also, after we change the information in a dataset that is used by
another (for example, the qrBugs dataset uses qrRevision as a lookup), we call the
qrProgramAfterPost() method and then refresh it in that dataset's AfterPost event.
This is shown next. In this case, because grBugs uses grRevision, a change in the
grRevision dataset should initiate a refreshing of grBugs.

```
void __fastcall TdmMain::qrRevisionAfterPost(TDataSet *DataSet)
{
    qrProgramAfterPost(DataSet);
    if (!qrBugs->IsEmpty()){
        qrBugs->Refresh();
    }
}
```

NOTE

InterBase 6 provides another method for handling transactions. The RollbackRetaining()
method enables you to roll back the database, but keep the current transaction context. This
saves overhead in not having to start a new transaction, such as after a normal rollback.

Bug Tracker Wrap Up

As Figure 10.3 shows, we have finished setting up a simple application that connects to an InterBase server, views and edits information in a transaction-safe manner, and maintains referential integrity. Although Bug Tracker is by no means a finished product, it demonstrates how easily a thin InterBase client can be written using familiar Data Control components.

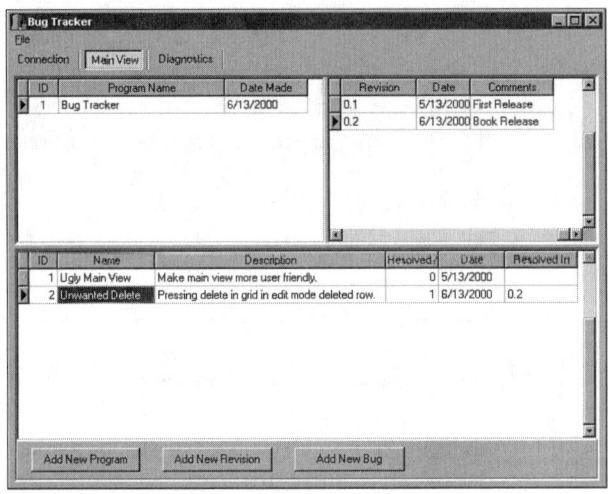

FIGURE 10.3   Bug Tracker in action.

InterBase is an exciting and powerful RDBMS development platform. It enjoys a strong following of users, many of whom are willing to provide assistance or answer questions in public forums or in chat rooms. With the release of the Open Source InterBase 6, many developers will start using InterBase in their applications, and many more will start working on strengthening this excellent RDBMS.

Summary

The Interbase Open Source DBMS is a powerful and inexpensive way for you to offer client/server capabilities to users of your applications. You can use any of the component sets offered by C++Builder, such as the BDE components, dbGo, or the specialized IBExpress, to work with your Interbase database. Of those, the IBExpress components are the most specialized to leverage the capabilities of Interbase. Although this creates a complete dependency on Interbase as your DBMS, there are situations where this is not a problem. If your application requires the use of every feature of Interbase, this component set is Tisch the best alternative to achieve that end.

11

ADO Express Components for C++Builder

by Mark Cashman

ADO stands for ActiveX Database Objects. ADO is Microsoft's replacement for the ODBC (the Open Database Connectivity) standard and earlier data access technologies, such as DAO and RDO.

ADO is a COM (Component Object Model) API (Application Programming Interface) that replaces the C language-based ODBC API and makes it easier to use object-oriented techniques with databases even in low-level programming.

The ADO components hide most of the complexity of dealing with the COM aspects of ADO behind an interface much like that of normal Borland VCL database components. In addition, they allow data from ADO to be used in normal VCL data-aware controls, such as grids, edit boxes, and charts. This is possible because the ADO components descend from TDataSet, and because TDataSource can work with any TDataSet descendant.

ADO can work with any database that has an ODBC driver. In addition, ADO offers support for data stored in nonrelational forms, such as XML (the successor to HTML) or email message stores, so long as there is a data provider that conforms to ADO standards. In theory, you can issue SQL against any ADO data, but there might be specialized forms of SQL needed to access nonrelational data.

ADO is a capable technology that offers complete access to almost every database in use. This chapter shows how the dbGo components provide you with the ability to access every feature of ADO, through an interface similar to the powerful framework Borland established for use with the BDE components.

ADO Versus BDE

There has always been a market for non-BDE components to be used with VCL programs in Delphi and C++Builder. There are a number of reasons for this. First, the BDE, rightly or wrongly, is perceived as being slow for some applications. Second, the memory and disk footprint of the BDE is thought by some to be larger than they prefer. Finally, even with installation programs such as Wise and InstallShield to reduce the complexity of installing the BDE, it has remained complex to ensure a safe BDE installation/upgrade, especially for releases of the BDE occurring between releases of the installer.

Prior to ADO, most component sets targeted either specific DBMS, such as dBase or InterBase, or database technologies, such as ODBC. Others implemented their own replacements for the BDE. However, they all had a problem—their components had a unique interface that was not the same as that offered by the BDE-oriented components. This made it harder to change an application back to the BDE if that was desired. Unfortunately, the ADO components share this drawback.

ADO has several other drawbacks in comparison to the BDE. For one, it requires an explicit connection string that names a provider, server, and database, which makes it more difficult to provide easy retargeting of ADO components to other databases or DBMS without code changes. Secondly, unlike the BDE, SQL in ADO components cannot be used to heterogeneously join tables across databases within the same DBMS or across different DBMS.

One caution with the ADO components is that they do not eliminate the need to worry about revisions of the underlying libraries—in this case, the ADO objects and the facilities needed by the database you are using (such as the Jet database engine required by Access).

Given all this, what are the advantages of the ADO components?

- Much of their supporting software is delivered with the operating system, so you do not have to deploy it.

- With driver development for the BDE somewhat slower than previous versions (though the BDE can use newer ODBC drivers, and those will continue to keep pace with DBMS development for some time), ADO can be your ticket to access unusual or advanced data technologies such as XML.

- The ADO components can ease the transition from Microsoft tools, such as Visual C++ to C++Builder.

- TADOQuery components are always editable without recourse to cached updates, UpdateSQL, or the complex conditions that allow a successful RequestLive. Note that a form of cached update (called *batch update*) is available for ADO components.

- The ADO components allow for SQL to be executed asynchronously and for monitoring the progress of commands through event handlers. This can also be used to provide the highly desirable progress meter to show how much of a query or command operation is complete.

- Unlike the BDE components, it is fairly safe to halt a database program using Program Reset (this usually provokes an out of memory error from the BDE on the next run)—however, when it is not safe, it usually takes your system down with it.

- Finally, though you should conceal as much of the "ADOness" of the ADO components from your programs as you can, familiarity with the concepts of ADO can be useful for future employment or projects where management mandates the use of ADO.

Hedging Your Bets

It is a good idea to immediately create a thin layer between your system and the data components you choose to use. You can do this by creating a descendant or facade for each ADO component you intend to use, and never using the raw components themselves in your system. You can then change the ancestor of the component or the type of its contained component either directly or by conditional compilation, and all the uses of the component will, hopefully without change, use the new component set. If you must use specialized methods or properties of the underlying components, try first to hide them in methods or properties of a more general nature in the thin layer. If that cannot be done for some reason, bracket them with #ifdef, #else, or #endif commands keyed on a #define that identifies the underlying components in use.

Copying Records and Datasets

Unfortunately, TBatchMove will not work with the ADO components. You will have to write your own generic mover to perform copies with these components. Consider a thin layer class to replace TBatchMove.

Component Overview

The following list describes each of the ADOExpress components found on the ADO tab of the Component Palette. It is important to learn about the components in an order that makes sense. In this case, we will cover the components in an order that both eases your transition from the BDE components (by showing the similar components in ADOExpress first), and which also reflects the dependencies between the components. Thus, we will first cover the TADOConnection component (used by all other ADO components), followed by TADOTable and TADOQuery (both similar to their BDE counterparts TTable and TQuery), and only then will we move on to the more unusual components, such as TADODataSet and TADOCommand.

- TADOConnection   Connects to the database, manages transactions; it is essentially equivalent to TDatabase. Note that there is no TSession equivalent for the ADO components. Some TSession capabilities are present in TADOConnection.

- TRDSConnection   Connects to a database in such a way that allows multitier access to an ADO recordset. Only usable with TADODataSet; supports the Microsoft Remote Data Space facility, which enables an ADO recordset to be passed across tiers of a multitier database application. Note that this is not the same as MIDAS support for Remote Data Modules.

- TADOTable   Accesses a single database table name by table name; essentially equivalent to TTable.

- TADOQuery   Accesses one or more tables in a single database using SQL commands. Can perform any SQL including SELECT, INSERT, DELETE, ALTER TABLE, and so on; essentially equivalent to TQuery.

- TADOStoredProc   Executes a stored procedure from a particular database; essentially equivalent to TstoredProc.

- TADODataSet   Essentially the same as TADOQuery, except that you cannot execute SQL that does not return a result set.

- TADOCommand   Essentially the same as TADOQuery. You can execute any SQL with TADOCommand, but to access the resultset, you need to provide a separate TADODataset that will be connected to the command's result set.

How Do They Fit into the VCL?

The inheritance of the ADO components is rooted in TDataSet. However, the immediate descendant of TDataSet is not TADODataSet, which you might expect to provide the root of the rest of the ADO components; instead, the hierarchy has the form shown in Figure 11.1.

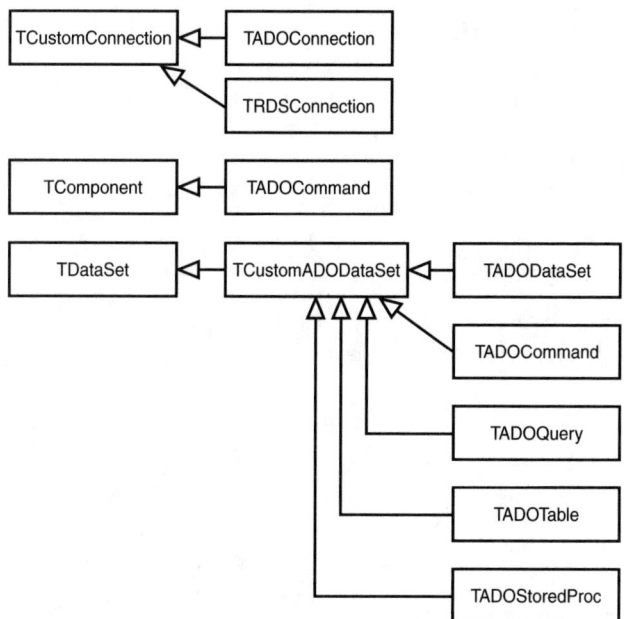

FIGURE 11.1   The ADO component class hierarchy.

Database Connections

Connecting to the database is necessary so that the components can reach out through the driver to the actual database. Until a connection is made, no access to the database is possible.

The TADOConnection Class

This class takes the place of a combination of TSession and TDatabase and is generally used to establish the connection. As with TDatabase, it is not critical that this component be used—each data component has the capability to form its own connection and can contain its own connection string.

The Provider

ADO connects to a database via a Provider, which is a named OLE object that implements an OLE DB (Object Linking and Embedding Database) interface. The provider is contacted by the ADO facility when ADO is given a connection string. Some of the connection string is used by the ADO facility; the rest is passed on to the provider.

The Connection String

The connection string combines the features of a BDE alias and the more complex information that stands behind the alias. It can also be identical to the ODBC connection string, in which case, the standard ODBC data provider will be used. That provider will access the specified installed ODBC driver to perform all operations.

Connection strings can be specific to the provider, but usually look something like the following (an example SQLServer connection string):

```
Provider=SQLOLEDB.1;Persist Security Info=False;
➥User ID=sa;Initial Catalog=mydatabase
```

The connection string has the following components:

- Provider is the name by which the provider COM object can be found in the registry. In practice, you cannot necessarily know this name in advance. You should instead prompt the user for the provider. The only method of determining available providers is to either use the rather complex OLE DB enumerator technology in its raw form (that is, unsupported by components, see http://msdn.microsoft.com/library/default.asp?url=/library/en-us/oledb/htm/oledbroot_enumerator_object.asp) or to use the dialog box provided for constructing connection strings (discussed in a following section).

- User ID and Password can be supplied as is usually done in the Login Prompt property of BDE data components, except that under ODBC, the keywords are usually uppercase, whereas they are proper case in ADO.

- Initial Catalog is the name of the database desired.

The Home of Transactions

The TADOConnection is the place to start, commit, or roll back transactions.

If you don't specify a separate connection object, the documentation implies you can use the Connection property of the TADOTable or TADOQuery object to access an internal connection. This is just as you would use the Database property of a BDE data component to access the default database object of a BDE TSession. Unfortunately, it does not work for ADO components because the Connection property remains NULL in an ADO object that has its own connection string, even once it is opened. Therefore, if you want transactions, you must create a separate TADOConnection object and use that as the connection for the TADOCustomDataSet descendant.

Accepting the Defaults

There are many properties and methods supplied by TADOConnection. In most cases, it is best to accept the defaults. Some instances where it is a good idea to change the defaults are discussed next under topics such as transactions and performance optimization.

Accessing Datasets

After connected to the database, you will want to access individual or joined datasets. This can be done with several of the ADO components.

Accessing a Dataset with TADOTable

To access a dataset with TADOTable, you need to

1. Set a connection so that the database can be accessed.

2. Set a table name so the component knows what table in the database you want.

3. Open the table.

After that, you will often need to connect the TADOTable through a TDataSource to some data-aware components for display or editing.

Setting the Connection for TADOTable

As mentioned, you have two options for establishing a database connection for any ADO object. The object can share a TADOConnection object, which it references by design time or runtime assignment to the Connection property; or it can have one created when it is opened, by providing a connection string. Again, this can be done at design time or runtime. Note, however, that any TADOCustomDataSet descendant must be inactive if you intend to change its Connection or ConnectionString. The same is true for the TADOConnection when you are going to change its ConnectionString.

Setting the Table Name for TADOTable

The next thing to do is establish which table will be opened. This is done using the TableName property. Once again, this can be done at either design time or runtime but, in either case, the TADOTable must be closed when a change is made.

Opening TADOTable

As with BDE tables, you can either set the Active property or call Open() to activate the table.

Using a Data-Source and Data-Aware Controls with TADOTable

TADOTable objects, like all TDataSet descendants, can be used with TDataSource objects and can be referenced from components that have a TDataSet type property. Note that this suggests that your components that may reference an ADO or BDE data set should not be of type TADOTable * or TTable *, but TDataSet *, if you want maximum compatibility.

Iterating Through the TADOTable

Like any TDataSet descendant, the TADOTable can use First(), Eof(), Next(), Prior(), and Last() for navigation through the table.

Adding or Editing Records Through TADOTable

Use Append() or Insert() to create a new record and Edit() to prepare to change field values. FieldByName, Fields->Field[Index], and other properties and methods with the same names as their BDE component counterparts all work as they do with BDE components. See the online help for the specifics.

Locating Specific Records in TADOTable

The same methods that work for BDE tables work for TADOTable and the other TCustomADODataSet descendants. For instance, Locate and Lookup can be used to shift the database cursor to a record and to return values from a record without moving the cursor, respectively.

Using Filters with TADOTable

In general, filters can be used with the ADO components because they are used with the BDE components. Filters are client-side, so records from the underlying table must travel to the client for the filter to decide whether to pass or hide them. If you can't afford this, you will need to use a TADOQuery to include the filter condition in the selection on the server-side (assuming you are using the ADO components to access a client/server database, that is). Of course, this is not an issue for desktop databases, such as dBase, Paradox, or Access.

There are some special considerations when using filters. First, although BDE component filters are tolerant of contact between operators, field names and literal values, the ADO components are not. They require a space on each side of an operator. Thus, SomeField = 'String' is fine, but SomeField='String' is not.

Secondly, the BDE component filters allow for partial comparison of string fields using * as a wildcard in the literal side of the expression. This also works with the equals sign, as in SomeField='String*', which matches any value that starts with 'String'. The ADO components allow this same form, except that you must use LIKE in place of the equals sign. Note that you will receive no error (and no records) if you use the BDE style of a * with the equals sign.

Accessing a Dataset with TADOQuery

A TADOQuery is the same as a TADOTable (or, for that matter, is largely the same as a TQuery) in the properties and methods it offers. But there are a few differences explained in the following list.

- Of course, you must supply explicit SQL. Keep in mind that, unlike the BDE components, the ADO components do not offer a Local SQL to insulate you from differences between provider's SQL dialects, so you must make sure to comply with any special requirements of the driver or DBMS. It is wise to carefully conceal such differences in a central location so that you can easily shift between DBMSs in the future. Also, you cannot use SQL that references other databases or DBMS—it is the BDE Local SQL that supports heterogeneous joins.

- The SQL you supply can, as with TQuery, contain parameters. However, there is a small and annoying difference. Specifically, the parameters for a TADOQuery are supplied through a property called Parameters (not Params), and the type of the elements supplied to Parameters is TParameter, not TParam. Finally, you cannot assign to AsString or AsFloat properties of a TParameter because they do not exist. There is only one accessor property for the value of a TParameter, and that is Value, which takes a Variant.

As with any query, insertions or changes will not be reflected in the query data set until you refresh the query by closing and opening it. There are some special properties you can set to allow for better performance during a refresh—they will be discussed in the "Performance Optimizations" section, later in this chapter.

Running a Stored Procedure with TADOStoredProc

Stored procedures are a staple of client/server database programming. Though not supported by all DBMS (particularly desktop databases such as Access or dBase), these SQL scripts can be useful for performing repeatable functions on the server-side of a client/server connection, with the performance advantages that implies.

Setting Up TADOStoredProc

As with the other ADO components, you need to set up a connection, either through the Connection or ConnectionString property.

You need to set the stored procedure name through the ProcedureName property. Because procedure name restrictions vary, consult your database documentation. Note that the names of procedures in a database can be obtained through a TADOConnection member function call.

Finally, establish any necessary parameters using the TParameter objects in the TParameters class collection represented by the Parameters property. Note that parameters have a direction (input, output, and so on) as well as a type, but that values can only be set with Value (as with TADOQuery).

Executing TADOStoredProc

Use ExecProc if the stored procedure is a command or set of commands, such as UPDATE or DELETE, that do not return results. If the stored procedure returns a result set, such as the results of a query, use Open or set the stored procedure to Active.

Getting Results from TADOStoredProc

A stored procedure can either return a result through the parameters or through a special parameter with direction pdReturnValue. The latter allows the return of a result set—that is, the results of an SQL select. However, the pdReturnValue parameter is not examined; it is automatically linked to any TDataSource that references the TADOStoredProcedure through its DataSet property. This enables you to display the result set in a grid or to use any other data-aware controls.

Executing an Update with TADOCommand

The TADOCommand class is of limited additional utility and is provided primarily for compatibility with ADO. It can be used for any SQL that does not return a result, but because the TADOQuery can be used for such commands and for regular SQL, little advantage comes from using TADOCommand instead.

Setting Up TADOCommand

TADOCommand offers the same properties as the other ADO components, and they are set in the same fashion with the same types of values.

Executing TADOCommand

The Execute() method is used to perform the command. If the command is executed with ExecuteOptions of one of the eoAsync types, the command in progress can be interrupted with Cancel, as long as that call occurs before CommandTimeout passes. Note that the capability to cancel a long-running command is the only advantage offered by TADOCommand over TADOQuery. Though you can have an asynchronous TADOQuery and can receive periodic events while it executes, you cannot interrupt it.

Using `TADOCommand` **for Dataset Access**

A `TADOCommand` can be used to execute SQL that returns a result set. However, to do that, it must be associated with a `TADODataSet`. Executing the command, and then assigning the resulting `Recordset` property to a `TADODataSet` object's `Recordset` property, will accomplish that association. For example

```
ADODataSet1->Recordset = ADOCommand->Execute();
```

The resulting `TADOCommand` can be used with a `TDataSource` and any data-aware controls compatible with it.

Using `TADODataset` **for Dataset Access**

A `TADODataSet` is for use with SQL that produces a result set. Other than the capability to work with the asynchronous and abortable `TADOCommand`, it offers no compelling features. However, it is the component that must be used to work with the Microsoft RDS (Remote Data Space) multitier data access capability. This is accomplished by assigning a `TRDSConnection` object to the `RDSConnection` property. Of course, such a connection is mutually exclusive of the `Connection` property.

Managing Transactions

The `TADOConnection` is used to manage transactions. Other than an annoying variation in the names used from those used with the BDE components, this is relatively straightforward:

- `BeginTrans` equates to the `TDatabase` `StartTransaction`
- `CommitTrans` to commit
- `RollbackTrans` to roll back

Using Component Events

The ADO components offer a variety of events that are specific to their operation. They also support the standard events used by other `TDataSet` descendant components, such as `AfterPost`. Most of the ADO specific events have names that are self-explanatory.

`TADOConnection` **Events**

- `OnWillConnect()`   Notifies the application that the connection has been accepted, but not yet made.

- `OnConnectComplete()`   Notifies the application that the connection has been completed.

- `OnInfoMessage()`   Notifies the application that the provider is offering an informational message; this should occur right after the connection is made.

- `OnBeginTransComplete()`   Notifies the application that the transaction has begun.

- `OnCommitTransComplete()`   Notifies the application that the commit has completed.

- `OnRollbackTransComplete()`   Notifies the application that the rollback has completed.

- `OnWillExecute()`   Notifies the application that the command will be executed, but has not yet started to execute. Note that this is fired for any components that use the connection, as opposed to the same event on the individual component, which only fires when that component is asked to execute a command. Because `TADOCommand` offers no events, this is the only way to handle a `TADOCommand` execution-related event.

- `OnExecuteComplete()`   Notifies the application that the command execution is complete.

- `OnDisconnect()`   Notifies the application that the connection has been closed.

`TADOCommand` **Events**

`TADOCommand` does not have any events.

`TADOCustomDataSet` **Descendant Events**

- `OnEndOfRecordset()`   Notifies the application that the end of the recordset (in other words, EOF) has been reached.

- `OnFetchComplete()`   Notifies the application when an asynchronously executed SQL command has completed the production of a recordset.

- `OnFetchProgress()`   Periodically notifies the application of the progress of an asynchronously executed SQL command.

- `OnFieldChangeComplete()`   Notifies the application that a change to the underlying database field (not the VCL `TField` descendant) has completed.

- `OnMoveComplete()`   Fires when the database cursor movement has completed (similar to the `TDataSource` `OnDataChange()` event).

- `OnRecordChangeComplete()`   Notifies the application that the record change has been completed. This is separate from the completion of changes to the recordset.

- `OnRecordsetChangeComplete()`   Notifies the application that the recordset change is complete.

- `OnWillChangeField()`   Notifies the application that ADO is prepared to perform a field change, but the change has not yet occurred.

- `OnWillChangeRecord()`   Notifies the application that ADO is prepared to perform a record change, but the change has not yet occurred.

- `OnWillChangeRecordset()`   Notifies the application that ADO is prepared to perform a recordset change, but the change has not yet occurred.

- `OnWillMove()`   Notifies the application that ADO is prepared to move the cursor, but the change has not yet occurred.

Creating Generic Database Applications

Many developers have had to deal with a requirement to create programs that work on a database or table specified at runtime. Most of the techniques for doing this with BDE programs are well known and well documented. Not so for the ADO components, but it is fairly simple to do these things after you know where to look.

Getting a Connection String from the User

Because connection strings are so complex and vary greatly between providers, it is fortunate that there is an undocumented function call that can help. This call is `PromptDataSource()`, which can be found in the `ADODB.hpp` include file provided with C++Builder, and it has the following signature:

```
WideString PromptDataSource
          (int theWindowHandle,WideString theOriginalConnectionString);
```

This function presents the same dialog as displayed by the connection string property editor—actually, it is the secondary dialog (from clicking Build) because the first dialog simply displays the string for manual editing. If you provide an original connection string, the dialog sets its controls accordingly so that the user is editing the connection string rather than creating it. Note that this is not a `TADOConnection` member—it is a standalone function.

Getting Table Names

`TADOConnection::GetTableNames()` works essentially the same as
`TSession::GetTableNames()`. It will update a supplied string list (that may, for instance,
be the `Items` property of a `TComboBox` or `TListBox`). Naturally, the connection must be
open for this to work.

Getting Field Names

Field names are obtained in the same fashion as for BDE components—by iterating
through the `TDataSet` descendant's `Fields` property as follows:

```
for (int Index = 0; Index < ADOTable->FieldCount; Index++)
    Field = ADOTable->Fields->Fields[Index]->FieldName;
```

Or, you can get a list of the names into a `TStringList` with the following:

`TADOConnection::GetFieldNames(TStringList *theList).`

Note that you must have previously allocated the list, or you can use a list such as
that from a `TComboBox` or `TListBox`.

Getting Stored Procedure Names

Again, a bit of a secret here—`TADOConnection::GetProcedureNames(TStringList
*theList)` is the method you need to get the list of stored procedure names. Note
that you must have previously allocated the list, or you can use a list, such as that
from a `TComboBox` or `TListBox`.

Performance Optimizations

The ADO components offer a variety of potential performance trade-offs. Obviously,
the success of these optimizations will depend on the nature of your database, such
as whether it is a client/server database or a local desktop database. Therefore, you
are encouraged to try to understand the performance implications of the various
component properties; even those not discussed here.

Query or Table

For client/server work, a query that will be executed on the server is preferable to a
table because a table-based component will typically transfer all the records from the
database server to the client system, consuming network bandwidth and taking extra
time. This is especially important when you intend to filter the records, because a
query can have the server apply the filter before the records are sent to the client.

Cursor Location

A cursor is basically the current state of the dataset—which record is current, the means by which insertions and deletions are performed, and so on.

The ADO components enable you to have a cursor on the client- or the server-side. A client-side cursor can initially be more expensive than a server-side cursor, but if the data set is relatively unchanging, it can be a setting that offers greater throughput in the long run. It will upload a copy of the selected data once to the client machine, and all subsequent operations are performed on that local copy, but then reflected back to the server. In this sense, it is much like the BDE ClientDataSet, except that no special management is required. However, critical to making client-side cursors perform well on inserts and updates is setting MarshalOptions to moMarshalModified Only. The other setting, moMarshalAll, will transmit the entire client-side copy of the data to the server on any change.

But a server-side cursor can be more efficient for a large dynamic dataset, especially when you typically need only a small part of the data on the client side. Although a thousand-row table might be suitable for a client-side cursor, a million-row table is much more likely to perform well with a server-side cursor.

Note that a server-side cursor is more likely to be unidirectional (forward only) than a client-side cursor according to the documentation.

Cursor Types

Cursors can also operate with different restrictions that have performance implications. The performance of various cursor types are described in the following list.

- A ctOpenForwardOnly cursor is very fast because it does not require the extra overhead (whatever that may be, depending on the DBMS) that would enable it to seek backward to an earlier portion of the dataset. Such a cursor must always start from the beginning and move forward. Note that such a cursor is read-only.

- A ctStatic cursor is nearly as fast, but it allows forward and backward movement. Like the forward-only cursor, it is read-only and is isolated from changes made by other users.

- A ctKeyset cursor is a read/write, any position, any direction cursor that remains isolated from changes by other users.

- A ctDynamic cursor adds the capability to see changes from other users.

Buffering

The CacheSize property controls how many records are cached locally. A larger cache can mean better performance, as long as you stay within the bounds of the cached records. But the larger the cache, the more expensive random movement or sequential traversal of the dataset might be because the cache must be refreshed with the new region of the dataset. In addition, this is affected by the choice you make for the location of the cursor. A larger buffer is probably more critical for a server-side cursor than for a client-side cursor because the client-side cursor typically has the entire data set locally anyway.

Error Handling Issues

The trouble with ADO error messages is that they are terrible and nonspecific. It is not unusual to get an exception that says only "Errors occurred" or that claim a problem with the type of a field without saying which field is at issue.

Unlike the `EDBEngineError` that returns detailed BDE error messages in series, `EADOError` is your only source of error information from a thrown exception, and it might be uselessly nonspecific. Be prepared for some frustration when dealing with ADO component errors that are reported by ADO itself.

Note, however, that the `TADOConnection` offers an `Errors` property that can be indexed. Sadly, it seems this seldom offers additional information. However, if you want to try working with it, the following loop can access individual error messages from the `TADOConnection::Errors`:

```
for (int Index = 0; Index < ADOConnection1->Errors->Count; Index++)
{
    String Message = ADOConnection1->Errors->Item[Index]->Description;
};
```

See the file `$(BCB)\source\vcl\ADOInt.pas` (note: `$(BCB)` is the standard environment variable referring to the C++Builder installation directory) for more information on the `Error` properties, such as `Description`, but be aware that source is written in Object Pascal (Delphi), not C++.

Multitier Applications and ADO

ADO can be used with Microsoft's multitier RDS technology. You can use the `TRDSConnection` in conjunction with `TADODataSet` to access RDS. However, a discussion of that topic is beyond the scope of this book; for more information visit `http://msdn.microsoft.com/`.

Borland Remote data modules can use the ADO components as their datasets. No special provisions need to be made to implement a multitier implementation with the ADO components.

You can also use ADO components in data modules to be used by CORBA, MTS, socket-based, ISAPI, or ASP distributed objects.

Summary

ADO Express provides components that offer the closest mapping to Microsoft's ActiveX Data Objects technology. Fortunately, the same components match the VCL component model and, thus, can easily be linked with data aware controls such as TDBGrid and TDBMemo. For applications where a close coupling between ADO-based data providers, and the application is an acceptable alternative, this can be ideal. And for applications that need to use every capability of ADO, the only other alternative is direct API calls to the underlying COM objects.

12

Data Access with dbExpress

by Bob Swart (a.k.a. Dr. Bob)

In this chapter, you will learn about (cross-platform) Data Access with dbExpress in C++Builder.

In this chapter, we will cover database and data access programming using dbExpress, the new cross-platform, data-access layer from Borland for use with Delphi, C++Builder, and Kylix. This chapter will cover all dbExpress components and explain in detail why, how, and where to use them, including some points on migrating to dbExpress from applications using the BDE or SQL Links.

dbExpress

dbExpress is a cross-platform, lightweight, fast, and open database access architecture. A dbExpress driver must implement a number of interfaces to get metadata, execute SQL queries or a stored procedure, and return a unidirectional cursor. We get back to this in a moment.

C++Builder supports both the VCL (Visual Component Library—native to Windows) and CLX (Component Library for Xplatform—both Windows and Linux at this time). Although dbExpress is classified as cross-platform, it can be used in both VCL and CLX applications.

C++Builder 6 (as well as Delphi and Kylix) was released in two major editions: Professional and Enterprise. The Professional edition includes dbExpress drivers for InterBase and MySQL. The Enterprise edition adds drivers for DB2 and Oracle 8i (public betas for Informix and other dbExpress drivers are also available).

NOTE

For a complete list of third-party drivers, check out John Kaster's article on the Borland Community Web site at `http://bdn.borland.com/article/0,1410,28371,00.html`.

Custom dbExpress

And that's not all, because dbExpress was created as an Open Database Architecture, meaning that anyone can write a dbExpress compliant driver—both on Linux for use with Kylix, and on Windows for use with Delphi and C++Builder. A more detailed article about the dbExpress internals by Ramesh Theivendran, the architect of dbExpress, is published on the Borland Community Web site at `http://bdn.borland.com/article/0,1410,22495,00.html`.

dbExpress Components

If you start C++Builder 6 and take a look at the Component Palette, you'll notice a tab called dbExpress (see Figure 12.1). Actually, most of the components are part of DataCLX and wrap the dbExpress functionality.

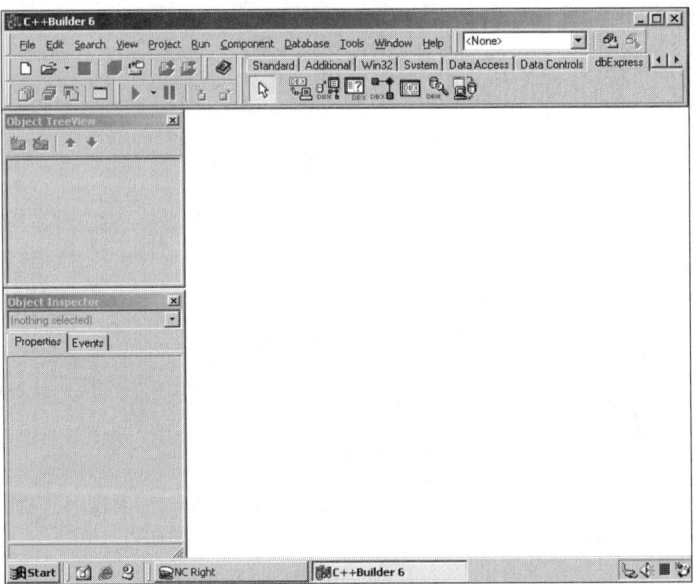

FIGURE 12.1　dbExpress Components in C++Builder 6.

The dbExpress tab contains seven components: TSQLConnection, TSQLDataSet, TSQLQuery, TSQLStoredProcedure, TSQLTable, TSQLMonitor, and TSQLClientDataSet. Now, we'll examine these components in more detail and build a dbExpress example application along the way. Note that the actual steps are repeated at the end of this chapter, when I build a Borland Database Engine (BDE) application and a similar dbExpress application, both connecting to an InterBase database. I'll also discuss how to migrate from the BDE to dbExpress.

TSQLConnection

The TSQLConnection component is literally the connection between the dbExpress drivers and the other DataCLX components. If you drop this component on a C++Builder form or data module, you'll see only 12 properties. The DriverName property shows you the dbExpress drivers that are available in your installation of C++Builder. For instance, on my C++Builder 6 Enterprise machine the DriverName property can be DB2, InterBase, MYSQL, or Oracle. However, instead of using the DriverName property to set up a dbExpress connection, we should look at the ConnectionName property, which points to a predefined connection. Entries for the DriverName property can be found in the dbxDrivers.ini file, and entries for the ConnectionName property can be found in the dbxConnections.ini file (both files are located in the C:\Program Files\Common Files\Borland Shared\dbExpress directory and can be edited manually as well as automatically as we'll see in a moment).

You can open the Params string list editor to edit the values of the parameters. These are also automatically filled in when you select a value for the ConnectionName property. If you do not want this to happen, like when writing some nonvisual code to access databases where you want to provide your own parameter values, you can set the LoadParamsOnConnection property to false.

If you right-click the TSQLConnection component and select the Edit Connection Properties pop-up menu option, you'll see the Connection Settings for the different Connection Names (there might be fewer connection names on your machine, depending on the number of dbExpress drivers installed and connections specified in the dbxConnections.ini file).

Note the Database property, which is set to database.gdb by default, should be set to a real database instead. It is recommended to prefix the location of the actual database with the machine name (or IP address) where the database is located. In my case, that's voyager:d:\data\employee.gdb (which can be seen in Figure 12.2), but it could also be localhost:C:\Program Files\Common Files\Borland Shared\Data\Employee.gdb for the default installation of the InterBase example (and the source code on CD-ROM). Any changes that you make in the Connection Properties editor are saved to the dbxConnections.ini file again, so you only have to make these changes once.

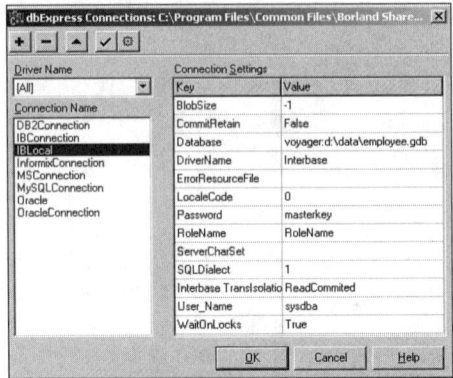

FIGURE 12.2 dbExpress Connections.

When you have specified all required parameters, and have made sure InterBase is actually running, you can set the `Connected` property to true. This will show the Login Prompt for which you must enter **sysdba** as user and **masterkey** as (not so secret) password. To avoid seeing this login prompt, you must set the `LoginPrompt` property to false, but must make sure to enter the `User_Name` and `Password` parameter values in the Connection Properties dialog box.

CAUTION

If you get an error message about an "unavailable database," you must check to make sure InterBase is indeed running and that the database that you point to (in the Connection Properties) actually exists.

TSQLDataSet

When you have a connected `TSQLConnection` component, you can use a number of the other DataCLX components, such as the `TSQLTable`, `TSQLQuery`, `TSQLStored Procedure`, or `TSQLDataSet` (which is the most flexible of these four components). Because a `TSQLDataSet` can actually mimic the behavior of the `TSQLTable`, `TSQLQuery`, and `TSQLStoredProcedure`, I always use a `TSQLDataSet` component and make sure it behaves as required. In fact, the `TSQLQuery`, `TSQLStoredProc`, and `TSQLTable` components can be seen as specialized versions of the `TSQLDataSet` component.

When using `TSQLDataSet`, you should start by specifying the `SQLConnection` property of this component to (one of) the available `TSQLConnection` component(s) on your form or data module. The two most important properties of the `TSQLDataSet` component are the `CommandType` and `CommandText` properties. With these two properties you can determine the specific type and behavior of the component. If you set the value of the CommandType property to ctQuery, the CommandText property is interpreted as SQL query (and the component behaves like a TSQLQuery component). If on the other hand you set the CommandType to ctStoredProc, the CommandText specifies the name of the stored procedure (and the component behaves like a TSQLStoredProcedure component). And finally, if you set CommandType to ctTable, CommandText contains the name of the individual tables (and the component behaves like a TSQLTable component).

I just told you that the TSQLQuery, TSQLTable, and TSQLStoredProducedure are hardly necessary in everyday use (the TSQLDataSet component is flexible enough). But the purpose of these components might be to offer easier migration from existing BDE code to dbExpress (where you can replace a regular BDE TTable component with a new dbExpress TSQLTable component, for example).

In this case, using the general TSQLDataSet component, we can set the CommandType property to ctTable, and the CommandText property to CUSTOMER to select the customer table from the InterBase database. If you set the Active property to true, you get live data at design time. Note, however, that there's no way to see the data just yet (we have only used nonvisual components so far), so in the next section we'll add some data-aware controls and discover how this new dbExpress dataset behaves.

Data-Aware Controls

We can now move to the Data Controls tab of the component palette, and start using some of the data-aware controls to display the data we receive from the active TSQLDataSet component. I should warn you beforehand that we cannot use these components immediately. In fact, this is the biggest difference between the BDE and the dbExpress architecture. TSQLDataSet (and the related TSQLQuery, TSQLStoredProc, and TSQLTable components) returns a unidirectional cursor; meaning that you can move forward, but not backward. This can be a problem if you try to connect a TSQLDataSet component to data-aware components. For example, if you drop a TDataSource and TDBGrid component next to the TSQLDataSet, connect the DataSet property of the TDataSource to the TSQLDataSet component, and try to connect the DataSource property of the TDBGrid to the TDataSource component, you will see exactly what I mean. At that time, you will get an error message (assuming the TSQLDataSet component is still active—otherwise you'll see the error message when you set the Active property of the TSQLDataSet component to true). The message indicates that an Operation is not allowed on a unidirectional dataset—see Figure 12.3 for the exact dialog.

Apparently, the TDBGrid component performs just like an operation (caused by showing more than one record at the same time, expecting the DataSet to buffer these records for it to walk through them). Note that you can get exactly the same error message when using a TDBNavigator component and accidentally clicking the Back or First button.

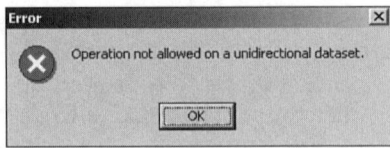

FIGURE 12.3　Unidirectional error message.

In short: It's almost unworkable to connect data-aware controls directly to a TSQLDataSet component because of the unidirectional nature of this dataset.

Why Unidirectional

So, why do we get (or need) a unidirectional cursor in the first place? Well, the obvious advantage is speed. The Borland Database Engine (BDE) has never been our best friend (let's call it a friendly neighbor), but it has helped with the small and simple database needs with the dBASE and Paradox local table formats, and the InterBase connectivity. Unfortunately, the BDE footprint and overhead hasn't been small, and BDE tables have never been known for amazing speed. That's an area where Borland wanted to show some real improvements. The new cross-platform data access architecture called dbExpress is designed with this in mind. Hence, it provides unidirectional cursors as results, with no overhead for buffering data or managing metadata. This, combined with the fact that Borland has announced that development and support of the BDE has been frozen and SQL Links will even be deprecated (in future versions of C++Builder), leads to the conclusion that dbExpress will play an important role for data access with C++Builder.

A unidirectional cursor is especially useful when you really only need to see the results once or need to walk through your resultset from start to finish (again once). For example in a while-loop, processing the results of a query or stored procedure, and converting the contents of the records on-the-fly. Real-world situations where this is useful include reporting and Web server applications that produce dynamic Web pages as output.

But, especially when combined with visual data-aware controls, we realize that the user will want to go back one record, which is not supported directly. So, you need to somehow cache the provided records to be able to show them in a DBGrid and to browse back as well as forward. That's where the TClientDataSet component comes in, which you might remember from the MIDAS chapter of the *C++Builder 5 Developer's Guide.* Chapter 20, "Distributed Applications with DataSnap," of this book addresses this issue as well. Using dbExpress, we can use a TDataSetProvider component (from the Data Access tab of the C++Builder 6 component palette) to hook up with the TSQLDataSet component, and then use a TClientDataSet component to obtain the records from this TDataSetProvider. The result is a local ClientDataSet that gets its records (once) from a unidirectional source: the SQLDataSet. The DataSetProvider is only used as a local transportation means, whereas the ClientDataSet is used to cache the dataset locally (and feed it to TDBGrid and TDBNavigator components without problems), see Figure 12.4 for an example.

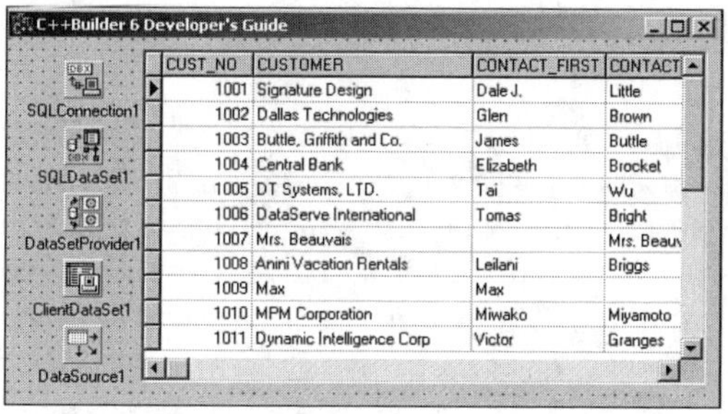

FIGURE 12.4   TSQLDataSet-—TDataSetProvider-—TClientDataSet.

This combination of the three TSQLDataSet, TDataSetProvider, and TClientDataSet components works very well, and in fact, ended up as a single TSQLClientDataSet component in its own right. The only downside of using the integrated TSQLClient DataSet component is that you can no longer access some of the (now hidden) properties of the internal TDataSetProvider and TSQLDataSet components.

TSQLClientDataSet

The TSQLClientDataSet component combines the speed and lightweight nature of the new dbExpress architecture with the caching and speed capabilities of the TClient DataSet component. There is another reason we have to use the TSQLClientDataSet (or the TClientDataSet component) at certain times, namely when it comes to updates. The unidirectional TSQLDataSet (and derived components) have an additional limitation in that they cannot be used to update the data in the dataset. For that, you have to use a TClientDataSet or TSQLClientDataSet component and call the ApplyUpdates method.

As a regular ClientDataSet, all changes that are made locally are cached inside the component. All changes are sent back and resolved to the actual database (via the dbExpress driver) only by calling the ApplyUpdates method. The ApplyUpdates call will use the DataSetProvider to send the so-called Delta dataset packet to the database server, something a lone TSQLDataSet component can't do, but a set of connected TSQLDataSet-TDataSetProvider-TClientDataSet can call ApplyUpdates just fine, just as a single combined TSQLClientDataSet component, of course. To implement an explicit call to ApplyUpdates, we can drop a TButton component, call it btnApplyUpdates, point its Caption property to Apply Updates, and write the following line of code in the OnClick event handler (using the TSQLClientDataSet component to apply the updates):

```
void __fastcall TForm1::btnApplyUpdatesClick(TObject *Sender)
{
  SQLClientDataSet1->ApplyUpdates(0);
}
```

The user of your application might wonder about the need to click this ApplyUpdates button. Suppose the user changes a lot of data, but is surprised that other users don't see his changes because he never clicks the ApplyUpdates method. Clearly, this can be a big problem, and at first sight the ClientDataSet layer seems only to add potential confusion. But fortunately making sure the ApplyUpdates method is called on a frequent or even automatic basis can solve this. In fact, you can easily use the OnAfterPost event handler of the TClientDataSet or TSQLClientDataSet component to call the ApplyUpdates method, which will make sure that the data is immediately sent as an update packet to the database server after every (local) post to the TClientDataSet component.

```
void __fastcall TForm1::ClientDataSet1AfterPost(TDataSet *DataSet)
{
  dynamic_cast<TClientDataSet*>(DataSet)->ApplyUpdates(0);
}
```

Note that because the TSQLClientDataSet is derived from the TClientDataSet, we can actually reuse the OnAfterPost event handler from the TClientDataSet as OnAfterPost event handler for the TSQLClientDataSet.

TSQLMonitor

The TSQLMonitor component is the last component from the dbExpress tab of the C++Builder 6 component palette that we need to cover. It's actually more of a supporting component, and mainly used when tracing or debugging dbExpress applications. As such, TSQLMonitor can be used to literally monitor the SQL statements and trace messages that are sent from the dbExpress application to the SQL DBMS. This can be very helpful when you need to pinpoint problems in your dbExpress application.

The TSQLMonitor component has a number of properties that we must work with. First of all, we should assign a value to the SQLConnection property to specify the TSQLConnection component that we want to monitor. After this, we can set the Active property to true to activate the monitoring and to false to (temporarily) deactivate it again. This toggle feature can be very helpful because you can actually turn the TSQLMonitor on right before things start to go wrong, so you don't have to watch everything going on as the application itself starts and the initial connection is made. The monitor messages will end up in the TraceList property of type TStrings.

Two other related properties are the FileName property and the AutoSave property. If you've set the FileName to a certain logfile and the AutoSave to true, the monitoring messages will be saved in the logfile automatically (if the Active property is also true). You can then view the logfile with the trace messages for details.

If you want to process the trace messages directly, you can also respond to the two event handlers of the TSQLMonitor component, namely OnTrace and OnLogTrace. The OnTrace event handler is called right before a message is added to the TraceList property. Inside this event handler we can change this message or even prevent it from being logged in the TraceList altogether by using the LogTrace argument, as shown in the following code:

```
void __fastcall TForm1::SQLMonitor1Trace(TObject *Sender,
      pSQLTRACEDesc CBInfo, bool &LogTrace)
{
  if (CBInfo->eTraceCat == traceMISC) LogTrace = false;
  else
    LogTrace = true;
}
```

CAUTION

It seems that the dbExpress driver for InterBase doesn't really use the CBInfo->eTraceCat field, so the above code may result in no trace messages at all when using in our example project. For that reason, the code is commented out in the source code on CD-ROM (until a better dbExpress driver is found that uses this field).

Although the OnTrace event handler is called right before, the OnLogTrace event handler is called right after a trace message has been added to the TraceList property. OnLogTrace can be used to display the trace message somewhere else (for example, if you always want to show the last trace message in the statusbar). Some not very efficient C++ code in the OnLogTrace event handler to show the contents of the TraceList property in a TMemo component is as follows:

```
void __fastcall TForm1::SQLMonitor1LogTrace(TObject *Sender,
      pSQLTRACEDesc CBInfo)
{
  Memo1->Lines->Clear();
  Memo1->Lines->Add(SQLMonitor1->TraceList->Text);
  Memo1->Lines = SQLMonitor1->TraceList;
}
```

The problem with this code is that the `OnLogTrace` event handler will be called quite often, and clearing the `TMemo->Lines` property every time is a costly operation that will slow down the overall performance of your application. It would be better to add the individual trace messages in the `OnTrace` event handler. But, there's an even faster approach: directly pointing the `TraceList` property to the `Lines` property of the `TMemo` component—both are of type `TStrings`. This means that updates to the `TraceList` will be shared automatically by the `Lines` property of the `TMemo` component because both point to the same memory space. The code for this is as follows:

```
__fastcall TForm1::TForm1(TComponent* Owner)
        : TForm(Owner)
{
  Memo1->Lines->Clear();
  Memo1->Lines = SQLMonitor1->TraceList; // pointing...
}
```

Finally, we can add a `TCheckBox`, call it `cbTrace`, and in the `OnClick` event handler set the `Active` property of the `TSQLMonitor` component to `true` or `false`, so we can control the trace messages from our own application. The implementation of this last `OnClick` event handler is as follows:

```
void __fastcall TForm1::cbTraceClick(TObject *Sender)
{
  SQLMonitor1->Active = cbTrace->Checked;
}
```

And the final dbExpress application (at design-time) can be seen in Figure 12.5.

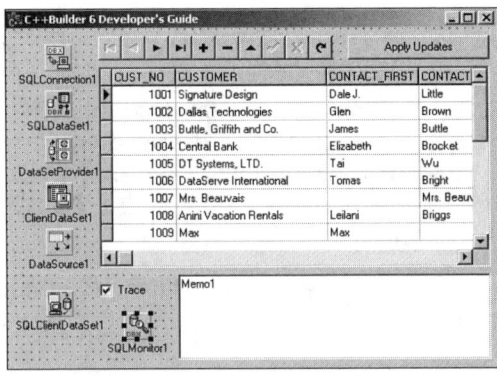

FIGURE 12.5   SQLMonitor at design time.

Running the application will show the log messages inside the Memo control as expected (we can control the appearance of new trace messages with the Trace check box), see Figure 12.6.

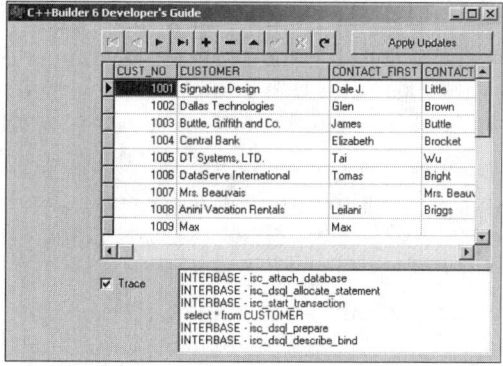

FIGURE 12.6   SQLMonitor at runtime.

Now that we've covered all seven components from the dbExpress tab of the component palette, it's time to focus on the last topic—migrating C++Builder applications from Borland Database Engine (BDE) to dbExpress.

Migrating from Borland Database Engine (BDE)

The first step in moving your BDE applications to dbExpress consists of converting your data from a BDE format to a database format that can be used by dbExpress. The BDE supports dBASE, Paradox, and InterBase, and for dbExpress we have drivers for InterBase, among others. The one format that both share is InterBase, so if you want to migrate existing BDE applications that are not in InterBase format, you might consider moving the data to InterBase in the first place. This will solve half of your migration problem; the rest consists of replacing BDE components with corresponding dbExpress components.

The BDE components that you can migrate are TTable, TQuery, TstoredProc, and TDatabase. The TSession component is only relevant for BDE-specific applications, so it's not needed in a dbExpress application.

The equivalent of the BDE TDatabase component is the dbExpress TSQLConnection component. Both are used to make a connection to the actual database. TSQLConnection has a number of predefined connections that can be found in the drop-down list for the ConnectionName property, such as a DB2Connection, IBLocal, MySQLConnection, or OracleConnection. You can also right-click the TSQLConnection component and pick Edit Connections Properties to see the Connection Settings for the different Connection Names, like we did earlier in this chapter.

The dbExpress TSQLTable, TSQLQuery, and TSQLStoredProcedure will all use a TSQLConnection component to connect to the dbExpress database, just as the BDE TTable, TQuery, and TStoredProc components use a TDatabase component to connect to the BDE database.

The equivalent of the BDE TTable component is the dbExpress TSQLTable component. The main difference is the fact that the TSQLTable component returns a read-only and unidirectional dataset. This means that you can only navigate forward, to be used to walk through once. If you try to move backward, an exception will be raised.

The equivalent of the BDE TQuery component is the dbExpress TSQLQuery component. The main difference is the fact that the TSQLQuery component returns a read-only and unidirectional dataset (just like the difference between the BDE TTable and the dbExpress TSQLTable component).

A unidirectional dataset involves no caching or overhead. This is the main reason why dbExpress data access components are much faster than their BDE equivalents. On the other hand, dbExpress components such as TSQLTable and TSQLQuery turned out to be a bit harder to use on a visual form connecting to a TDBGrid or TDBNavigator component, therefore, we have to add an additional TDataSetProvider and TClientDataSet component.

The equivalent of the BDE TStoredProc component is the dbExpress TSQLStoredProcedure component. However, this is the place where you can possibly encounter a number of problems if you migrate a local BDE application to dbExpress because a stored procedure for use in one DBMS is likely to differ from a stored procedure for use in another DBMS. InterBase, which is supported by both the BDE and dbExpress (and runs on Windows as well as Linux) might be the exception again.

Now that we've mapped four basic BDE dataset components, we still have two dbExpress components left that can still play an important role while migrating BDE applicatons: the TSQLDataSet and TSQLClientDataSet. The TSQLDataSet component is capable of acting like a TSQLTable, TSQLQuery, or TSQLStoredProcedure component all in one, with the CommandType property as main discriminator (the value of CommandType determines how the value of the CommandText property is interpreted).

Finally, the TSQLClientDataSet component is the powerful combination of a TSQLDataSet, a TDataSetProvider, and a TClientDataSet component to produce a bidi-rectional caching dataset (remember that the TSQLTable, TSQLQuery, and TSQLStoredProcedure all return a unidirectional read-only dataset, so if you want to use them in a bidirectional way like the BDE datasets, you need to connect these three components to a TClientDataSet component via a TDataSetProvider compo-nent—or use the TSQLClientDataSet component instead).

Migration Example

As a final example, I will list the steps to create an application that features a TDBGrid and TDBNavigator connecting to a local InterBase table using the BDE first, and then dbExpress. If you compare the steps, you can also see what is needed to remove the BDE components and replace them with dbExpress components (assuming you have migrated the database tables to a dbExpress compatible format as well).

Using BDE to Build an Application

Using the Borland Database Engine, the steps to build an application using the InterBase CUSTOMER table are as follows (assuming we have started a new project):

1. Drop a TDatabase component; point its AliasName property to IBLocal, and its DatabaseName property to IBL (this is just the name that we will use in our application).

2. Drop a TTable component, point its DatabaseName property to IBL (which points to the Database component from the previous step).

3. Open the drop-down combo box for the TableName property and select the CUSTOMER table. This will pop-up the Database Login dialog with username sysdba. The password is masterkey.

4. Drop a TDataSource component; point its DataSet property to the TTable component.

5. Drop a TDBNavigator component; point its DataSource property to the TDataSource component.

6. Drop a TDBGrid component; point its DataSource property to the TDataSource component.

7. Set the Table, Active property to true to see the live data at design time.

Using dbExpress to Build an Application

Using dbExpress instead of the BDE, the steps to build an application using the InterBase CUSTOMER table are as follows (again starting with a new application):

1. Drop a TSQLConnection component, and select IBLocal as the value for its ConnectionName property (edit the Connection Properties to make sure the Database points to a valid InterBase database).

2. Drop a TSQLClientDataSet component, point its DBConnection property to the TSQLConnection component and set CommandType to ctTable (we want to select a tablename).

3. Open the drop-down combo box for the CommandText property and select the CUSTOMER table. This will pop-up the Database Login dialog with username sysdba. The password is masterkey.

4. Drop a TDataSource component; point its DataSet property to the T(SQL)ClientDataSet component.

5. Drop a TDBNavigator component; point its DataSource property to the TDataSource component.

6. Drop a TDBGrid component; point its DataSource property to the TDataSource component.

7. Set the (SQL)ClientDataSet, Active property to true to see the live data at design time.

The second and third steps can be replaced with the following four steps (replacing the TSQLClientDataSet with the TSQLDataSet, TDataSetProvider, and TClientDataSet combination):

1. Drop a TSQLTable component; point its SQLConnection property to the TSQLConnection component.

2. Select a TableName (such as CUSTOMER).

3. Drop a TDataSetProvider component; point its DataSet property to the TSQLTable component.

4. Drop a TClientDataSet component, point its ProviderName property to the TDataSetProvider component.

Summary

In this chapter, we have examined the cross-platform data access layer dbExpress, which consists of new, fast, and unidirectional DataSet components that can be connected to ClientDataSets for caching and bidirectional cursor support. Especially now that development and support of the BDE has been frozen and SQL Links will even be deprecated in future versions of C++Builder, leads to the conclusion that dbExpress will play an important role for data access with C++Builder.

13

XML Document Programming and XML Mapper

by Bob Swart (a.k.a. Dr. Bob)

In this chapter, we will cover XML Document Programming using the TXMLDocument component. The capabilities from the TXMLDocument component will then be enhanced using XML Data Binding and even further using the XML Mapping Tool. All these techniques are part of the BizSnap featureset of C++Builder 6 Enterprise, which also includes support for SOAP and Web Services (see Chapter 19, "SOAP and Web Services with BizSnap," for coverage of those BizSnap features).

XML Document Programming

The place to start the coverage of XML Document Programming in C++Builder 6 is the TXMLDocument component, which can be found on the Internet tab of the Component Palette. But, before we can actually start to use this component, we first need an actual XML document to work with. While writing this chapter for the *C++Builder 6 Developer's Guide*, I decided to write my own XML document, which reflects the structure of this chapter (it also helped me to focus on the topics to write about). The XML document that will be used throughout the entire chapter is stored in BizSnap.xml and defined as follows:rage of XML Document Programming in C++Builder 6 is the

```
<?xml version="1.0" standalone='yes' ?>
<Chapter Title="XML Document Programming and XML Mapper">
 <Section Title="XML Document Programming">
```

```
  <Components>TXMLDocument</Components>
  <Wizards/>
 </Section>
 <Section Title="XML Data Binding">
  <Components>TXMLDocument</Components>
  <Wizards>XML Data Binding Wizard</Wizards>
 </Section>
 <Section Title="XML Mapping Tool">
  <Components>TXMLDocument, TXMLTransform, TXMLTransformProvider, TXMLTransform
➥Client</Components>
  <Wizards>XML Mapper</Wizards>
 </Section>
</Chapter>
```

As you can see, the chapter is divided into three sections. Each section covers certain components as well as, optionally wizards, which are all found in C++Builder 6 Enterprise (although in the appendix we will show how you can use the TXMLDocument component also in the Professional version of C++Builder 6). We are currently in the first section, which introduces XML document programming, using the previous XML document and, as you can see, the TXMLDocument component. This component can be found on the Internet tab of C++Builder 6 Enterprise (or Professional—if you've followed the steps in the appendix). If you drop it on a form, there are a number of important properties to examine.

XML Document Properties

First, we have the DOMVendor property, which is set to MSXML by default, but can also be set to Open XML (at least on my machine). Apart from these two values for DOMVendor, you are free to install and register other DOMs to be used by the TXMLDocument component, such as one found in TurboPower's XML Partner. You can use the global variable DOMVendors for this task (refer to the online help for more information about installing, registering, and using other DOM Vendors).

The FileName property should point to the XML document that we want to work with. If the XML document is not stored in an external file, but rather received directly as a stream of XML data, you can use the XML property (note that these properties are mutually exclusive—if you specify a value for one, the other is cleared). The property editor for the XML property consists of a String list editor where you can type (or paste) the XML directly. For our example, let's use the BizSnap.xml file that is also available on the CD-ROM in the directory for this chapter (or on my Web site at http://www.drbob42.com/books/BizSnap.xml).

> **NOTE**
>
> Note that after you've selected the Filename, the Object Inspector will prepend the path, making it a fully qualified filename. This is nice, but a potential problem if you plan to move your project (or just the .XML document) to another location (for example, when you load the example project from the CD-ROM onto your own machine or deploy the final application to another machine).
>
> Personally, I always modify the `FileName` property to make sure it only holds a relative filename such as `..\xml\BizSnap.xml` or just `BizSnap.xml` (to use an XML document that must be in the same directory as the executable itself). The later (a single filename) will also help to produce a cross-platform application, without worries about slashes and backslashes.

The `NodeIndentStr` property specifies the indentation level of the nodes in the XML tree. Anything between one and eight spaces or a tab can be used. You are free to enter your own indentation string, such as 12 spaces. The value of this property is used if and only if the `doNodeAutoIndent` flag is set in the `Options` property. By default, this property is set to `false`, so the value of `NodeIndentStr` is ignored.

Apart from the `doNodeAutoIndent`, the `Options` property contains flags for `doNodeAutoCreate`, `doAttrNull`, `doAutoPrefix`, `doNamespaceDecl`, and `doAutoSave`. The last flag, which is also set to `false` by default, is used to automatically save the contents of the XML document in the `FileName` or the `XML` property (depending on which one is used), whenever the `TXMLDocument` component is deactivated. If you want to explicitly save the contents of the XML document, you can always call the `SaveToFile()` method, which has an optional `FileName` argument (if you omit this argument, it will use the value of the `FileName` property). Let's set the `doAutoSave` property to `true` in our example.

Next, are the `ParseOption` flags, consisting of `poResolveExternals`, `poValidateOnParse`, `poPreserveWhiteSpace`, and `poAsyncLoad`. All are set to `false` by default, and won't be used in this chapter.

XML Document Interfaces

The `TXMLDocument` component implements two different interfaces, although one is only available through a property. To start with the latter, the `DOMDocument` property of the `TXMLDocument` component implements the `IDOMDocument` Delphi interface (which gets typecast into C++Builder `_di_IDOMDocument` interface), a low-level Document Object Model (DOM) interface definition. The DOM consists of a tree-based API (compared to SAX, which is an event-based API). The Delphi unit `xmldom.pas` contains the definitions for `IDOMDocument`, `IDOMNode`, `IDOMNodeList`, `IDOMAttr`, `IDOMElement`, and `IDOMText` for this purpose. The C++Builder imported header file `xmldom.hpp` contains the typecasts of these interfaces into `_di_IDOMDocument`, `_di_IDOMNode`, `_di_IDOMNodeList`, `_di_IDOMAttr`, `_di_IDOMElement`, and `_di_IDOMText`, respectively.

Apart from the standard DOM interface, the TXMLDocument component also directly implements the Delphi interface IXMLDocument (typecast into _di_IXMLDocument), a more high-level approach to working with XML documents and data. This is still a somewhat DOM-like interface, but a bit more powerful and easier to use, as I'll show in this section. The interfaces IXMLDocument, IXMLNode, IXMLNodeList, and IXMLNode Collection are defined in the XMLIntf.pas unit (and typecast in XMLIntf.hpp to _di_IXMLDocument, _di_IXMLNode, _di_IXMLNodeList, and _di_IXMLNodeCollection).

Although _di_IDOMDocument is also available through the DOMDocument property, the _di_IXMLDocument is an easier and the preferred way (in C++Builder 6) to work with the TXMLDocument component, so let's examine the _di_IXMLDocument interface in some more detail now.

Reading XML Documents

To put the XML document programming theory into practice, let's now build an example application using the TXMLDocument component. Start a new Application, save the main form in the default Unit1, and the project in Project1. Drop a TXMLDocument component next to a TMemo and TButton component. Set the Caption property of the TButton component to XML Doc and its Name to btnXMLDoc (see Figure 13.1).

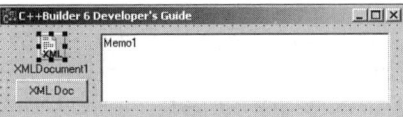

FIGURE 13.1   TXMLDocument component at design time.

Connect the FileName property of the TXMLDocument component to the BizSnap.xml file, and set the doAutoSave flag of the Options property to true. Now, we can open the TXMLDocument by setting the Active property to true as well. After the TXMLDocument is active, we can access the root and traverse through the hierarchy of nodes, reading and writing values, adding nodes, and more. Each node in the hierarchy is of type _di_IXMLNode.

We can traverse through the nodes in this hierarchy and use the TMemo component to display the nodes and their attributes we encounter along the way. First of all, the root node can be obtained using the DocumentElement property. After we have the root, we can get the attributes as well as child nodes. The following code for the OnClick event handler of btnXMLDoc will get the root node, the attribute with name Title, followed by the first child node with attributes Title, and child nodes Components, and Wizards.

```cpp
void __fastcall TForm1::btnXMLDocClick(TObject *Sender)
{
  Memo1->Lines->Clear();
  _di_IXMLNode Chapter = XMLDocument1->DocumentElement;
  Memo1->Lines->Add("Chapter: " + Chapter->Attributes["Title"]);
  _di_IXMLNode Section = Chapter->ChildNodes->GetNode(0);
  Memo1->Lines->Add("Section: " + Section->Attributes["Title"]);
  Memo1->Lines->Add("Components: " +
    Section->ChildNodes->Nodes[
      Section->ChildNodes->IndexOf("Components")]->GetText());
  Memo1->Lines->Add("Wizards: " +
    Section->ChildNodes->Nodes[
      (AnsiString)"Wizards"]->GetText());
}
```

Note that the Nodes property can be indexed with a name or index. If you want to use a name, however, you need to explicitly cast it to an AnsiString first.

The output of clicking the XMLDoc button can be seen in Figure 13.2.

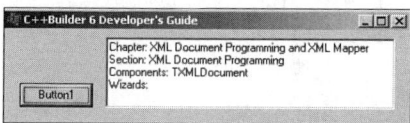

FIGURE 13.2 XMLDocument Component at runtime.

Note that we have to make sure to give the exact names of the attributes and child nodes. If we supply an incorrect name for an attribute, for example, we get an exception of class EVariantTypeCastError telling us that an invalid variant type conversion was attempted. An incorrect name for a child node results in an empty node, and hence, no value for the Text property. In other words, we should be careful not to make accidental typing mistakes.

For each node, we can check the HasChildNodes property to make sure it indeed contains any child nodes. The ChildNodes->Count property contains the number of child nodes, just as the AttributeNodes->Count contains the number of attributes. And finally, each node can return its Text as well as XML representation.

Writing XML Documents

Apart from browsing through an XML document, we can also modify and save the updated XML document. In fact, it's so easy to change the XML Document that sometimes you've already done it without even knowing it. Remember how I told you about the doAutoSave option; this will make sure the contents of the TXMLDocument component is automatically saved whenever we make a change to it. Another option, the doNodeAutoCreate, will make sure that if we try to access a node that doesn't exist yet, it will dutifully create one for us. This flag is set to true by default. But the side-effect of this all is that if you make one typing mistake (for example, in the first listing) and don't search for the ChildNode->Nodes[(AnsiString)"Wizards"], but the ChildNode->Nodes[(AnsiString)"Wizard"] instead, a new (empty) child node with name Wizard will have been added to the XML Document without an error message or warning of any kind.

Apart from changing the XML Document by accident, we can also use the IXMLDocument methods that are made for this, such as AddChild (which will explicitly add a child node) as well as SetAttribute, SetChildValue, SetNodeValue, and SetText. To illustrate this, drop a second TButton component, call it btnNewSection and write the following code in the OnClick() event handler:

```
void __fastcall TForm1::btnNewSectionClick(TObject *Sender)
{
  _di_IXMLNode Chapter = XMLDocument1->DocumentElement;
  Chapter->AddChild("Section");
  _di_IXMLNode NewSection = Chapter->ChildNodes->GetNode(
    Chapter->ChildNodes->Count-1);
  NewSection->SetAttribute("Title", (AnsiString)"New Section Title");
  NewSection->AddChild("Components");
  NewSection->AddChild("Wizards");
  XMLDocument1->SaveToFile();
  AnsiString XML;
  XMLDocument1->SaveToXML(XML);
  ShowMessage(XML);
}
```

Note the last few lines in the btnNewSectionClick() event handler, which were added to illustrate the fact that we can always call the SaveToFile() method of the TXMLDocument component (when called without arguments, it will use the value of the FileName property), and we can also call the SaveToXML() method to save the current contents of the TXMLDocument component as XML string.

Although we've seen some helpful methods, it's always much easier to perform these operations if you have some more design-time support from the C++Builder IDE. Specifically with Code Insight based on the layout or semantics of the underlying XML document, which will be available when using XML Data Binding—the topic of the next section.

XML Data Binding

In the previous section we worked with the _di_IXMLDocument interface as implemented by the TXMLDocument component. And, although it's useful, the downside is that is doesn't offer us semantic support for the XML document. One typing mistake causes you to not find the value of a child node, but accidentally add a new child node to the tree.

Fortunately, C++Builder 6 also contains a way to perform XML Data Binding, whereby an XML Document is used to generate specific interfaces and C++ class definitions and implementations that will help us make fewer mistakes by offering named methods as well as Code Insight support. You'll get the idea when we look at how it works.

The work is done by the XML Data Binding Wizard, which can be found in the Object Repository after you do File, New, Other (see Figure 13.3).

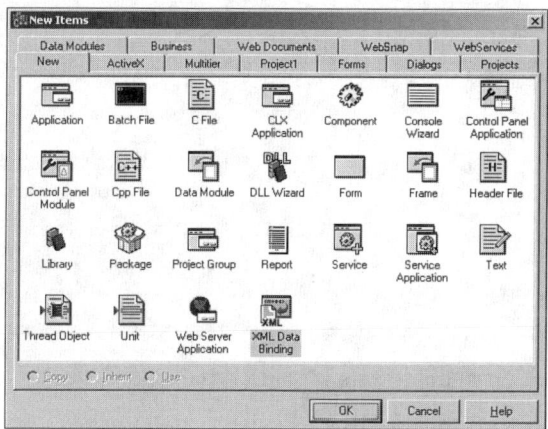

FIGURE 13.3   XML Data Binding icon in Object Repository.

The XML Data Binding Wizard has three pages, although the first page is optional (as I'll explain in a moment). The fist page is used to specify the name of the XML document, which is shown in Figure 13.4. Note that apart from an actual XML data document, we can also specify an XML schema file because it's the structure (and not the actual contents) that counts at this time.

However, instead of starting the XML Data Binding Wizard from the Object Repository, we can also start it by double-clicking the TXMLDocument component. This will make sure the XML Data Binding Wizard is already loaded with the XML Document that was specified by the TXMLDocument component itself, moving us to the second page of the Data Binding Wizard automatically (see Figure 13.5).

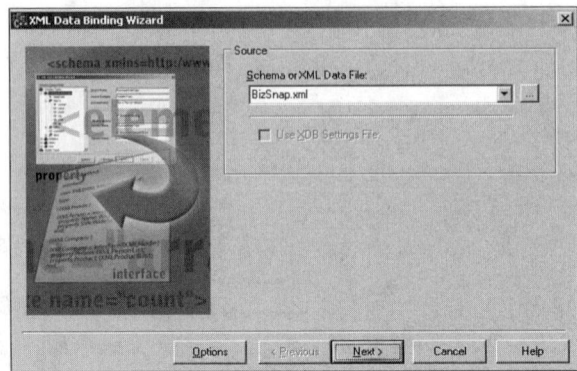

FIGURE 13.4   First page of Data Binding Wizard.

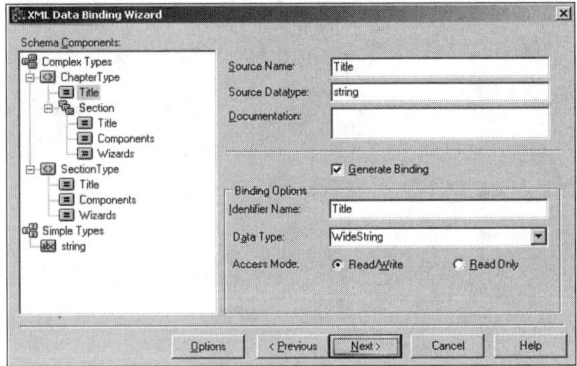

FIGURE 13.5   Second page of Data Binding Wizard.

On this second page of the XML Data Binding Wizard we get an overview that
shows how the Wizard will represent each XML element, and which source code
types or elements will be generated. As you can see in Figure 13.5, there are a
number of complex types (ChapterType, SectionType) as well as simple types (string)
used by our XML document.

A helpful feature of this second page is the fact that we can still modify everything,
including the access mode of attributed and child nodes, which is very useful. By
default set to Read/Write, we can change this to Read-Only, which means an
attribute value can be read, but not accidentally modified.

Before we move on to the last page, let's click the Options button to view the possible
options you might want to change (see Figure 13.6).

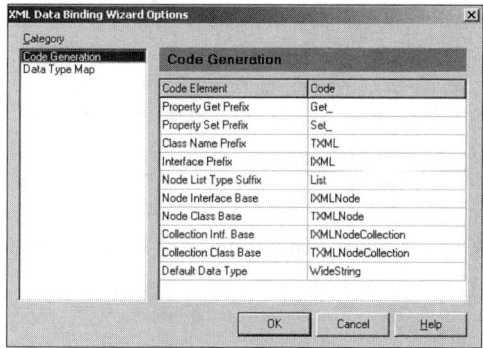

FIGURE 13.6   Options page of Data Binding Wizard.

As you can see in Figure 13.6, we can change some of the code that will be generated, such as the Get_ and Set_ prefixes for the getter and setter routines. The Data Type map is not useful for this example because we only use the String type, but it might be convenient when you want to use custom types at a later time.

When you're ready, close the XML Data Binding Wizard Options dialog, and click the Next button to go to the third and last page of the XML Data Binding Wizard (which can be seen in Figure 13.7).

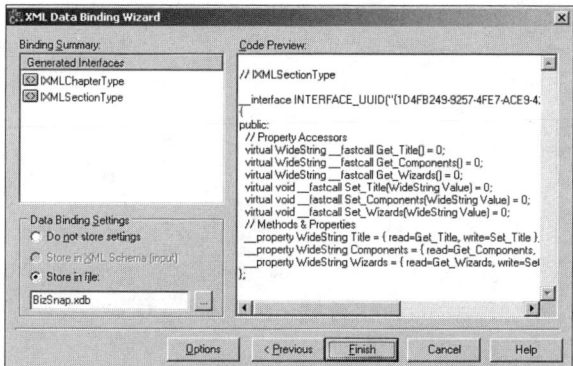

FIGURE 13.7   Third page of Data Binding Wizard.

This third and last page of the XML Data Binding Wizard is only used as information again, and in our case displays two generated interfaces: IXMLChapterType and IXMLSectionType (and the C++Builder editions _di_IXMLChapterType and _di_IXML SectionType). For both types, we can preview the generated interface definition, for which the properties are most interesting. The IXMLChapterType contains a Title as well as Section (array) property to access the Title attribute and the Section child nodes. The IXMLSectionType will contain properties for Title, Components, and Wizards.

We can decide to store the binding settings for later use in the suggested file
BizSnap.xdb (this file can be reused at the first page of the Data Binding Wizard).
When we click the Finish button, the source code for the interfaces will be generated
in a new unit that will be added to the current project. Save this new unit as
BizSnap.cpp, so we know where it belongs. The definitions of the new interfaces and
classes can be read in the BizSnap.h file, and are as shown in Listing 13.1.

LISTING 13.1   XML Data Binding–Generated BizSnap.h

```
// ***************************************** //
//
//            XML Data Binding
//
//        Generated on: 2002-08-04 23:14:19
//       Generated from: BizSnap.xml
//    Settings stored in: BizSnap.xdb
//
// ***************************************** //


#ifndef   BizSnapH
#define   BizSnapH

#include <System.hpp>
#include <xmldom.hpp>
#include <XMLDoc.hpp>
#include <XMLIntf.hpp>
#include <XMLNodeImp.h>


// Forward Decls

__interface IXMLChapterType;
typedef System::DelphiInterface<IXMLChapterType> _di_IXMLChapterType;
__interface IXMLSectionType;
typedef System::DelphiInterface<IXMLSectionType> _di_IXMLSectionType;

// IXMLChapterType

__interface INTERFACE_UUID("{2E7DECFE-0AD3-43BB-BEF7-24FAAF467567}")
IXMLChapterType : public IXMLNodeCollection
{
public:
public:
```

LISTING 13.1   Continued

```cpp
  // Property Accessors
  virtual WideString __fastcall Get_Title() = 0;
  virtual _di_IXMLSectionType __fastcall Get_Section(int Index) = 0;
  virtual void __fastcall Set_Title(WideString Value) = 0;
  // Methods & Properties
  virtual _di_IXMLSectionType __fastcall Add() = 0;
  virtual _di_IXMLSectionType __fastcall Insert(const int Index) = 0;
  __property WideString Title = { read=Get_Title, write=Set_Title };
  __property _di_IXMLSectionType Section[int Index] = { read=Get_Section };
};

// IXMLSectionType

__interface INTERFACE_UUID("{F85BA1A2-DB61-42AC-A95C-74F8710FA90C}")
IXMLSectionType : public IXMLNode
{
public:
  // Property Accessors
  virtual WideString __fastcall Get_Title() = 0;
  virtual WideString __fastcall Get_Components() = 0;
  virtual WideString __fastcall Get_Wizards() = 0;
  virtual void __fastcall Set_Title(WideString Value) = 0;
  virtual void __fastcall Set_Components(WideString Value) = 0;
  virtual void __fastcall Set_Wizards(WideString Value) = 0;
  // Methods & Properties
  __property WideString Title = { read=Get_Title, write=Set_Title };
  __property WideString Components = { read=Get_Components, write=Set_Components };
  __property WideString Wizards = { read=Get_Wizards, write=Set_Wizards };
};

// Forward Decls

class TXMLChapterType;
class TXMLSectionType;

// TXMLChapterType

class TXMLChapterType : public TXMLNodeCollection, public IXMLChapterType
{
  __IXMLNODECOLLECTION_IMPL__
protected:
```

LISTING 13.1   Continued

```
// IXMLChapterType
virtual WideString __fastcall Get_Title();
virtual _di_IXMLSectionType __fastcall Get_Section(int Index);
virtual void __fastcall Set_Title(WideString Value);
virtual _di_IXMLSectionType __fastcall Add();
virtual _di_IXMLSectionType __fastcall Insert(const int Index);
public:
virtual void __fastcall AfterConstruction(void);
};


// TXMLSectionType

class TXMLSectionType : public TXMLNode, public IXMLSectionType
{
    __IXMLNODE_IMPL__
protected:
// IXMLSectionType
virtual WideString __fastcall Get_Title();
virtual WideString __fastcall Get_Components();
virtual WideString __fastcall Get_Wizards();
virtual void __fastcall Set_Title(WideString Value);
virtual void __fastcall Set_Components(WideString Value);
virtual void __fastcall Set_Wizards(WideString Value);
};


// Global Functions

_di_IXMLChapterType __fastcall GetChapter(_di_IXMLDocument Doc);
_di_IXMLChapterType __fastcall GetChapter(TXMLDocument *Doc);
_di_IXMLChapterType __fastcall LoadChapter(const WideString FileName);
_di_IXMLChapterType __fastcall  NewChapter();


#endif
```

As we can see from Listing 13.1, there are two new interface types: IXMLChapterType and IXMLSectionType, which we saw earlier in the last page of the XML Data Binding Wizard, together with their _di_IXMLChapterType and _di_IXMLSectionType C++Builder interface typecasts.

What's even more useful is the fact that the new unit also contains the class definitions (in BizSnap.h) and implementations (in BizSnap.cpp) for TXMLChapterType and
TXMLSectionType. TXMLChapterType is derived from TXMLNodeCollection (it contains child
nodes), and TXMLSectionType is derived from TXMLNode. Both implement their similar-
named interface.

That's not all, because the BizSnap unit also contains three global functions:
GetChapter() (overloaded), LoadChapter(), and NewChapter(). The first can be used to
extract a Chapter from an existing TXMLDocument component or _di_XMLDocument interface. The second can be used to load a Chapter from an existing, compatible XML
file (such as the BizSnap.xml file), and the NewChapter() function can be used to start a
new, empty, Chapter. All three return a _di_IXMLChapterType interface, which can
then be used to work with C++Builder.

As an example, let's use the GetChapter() function to extract the _di_IXMLChapterType
from the TXMLDocument component and work with it using the named methods and
properties. First, we must add the BizSnap header to the includes section of our main
form (in the header file of our main form), so we can use the interface types and
global functions. Then, to use the _di_IXMLChapterType interface during the lifetime of
the form, we can add a variable Chapter of type _di_IXMLChapterType to the form
(place it in the private section). Also, add a private field called CurrentSection of type
int, and a private method called DisplaySection(), as follows:

```cpp
#include <BizSnap.h>
//————————————————————————————————————————
——————-
class TForm1 : public TForm
{
__published:  // IDE-managed Components
        TXMLDocument *XMLDocument1;
        TMemo *Memo1;
        TButton *btnXML;
        TButton *btnFirst;
        TButton *btnPrev;
        TButton *btnNext;
        TButton *btnLast;
        void __fastcall btnXMLClick(TObject *Sender);
private:        // User declarations
        _di_IXMLChapterType Chapter;
        int CurrentSection;
        void DisplaySection(void);
public:         // User declarations
        __fastcall TForm1(TComponent* Owner);
};
```

Now, write the following code for the OnCreate() event handler of the Form, as well as the private method DisplaySection():

```
void __fastcall TForm1::FormCreate(TObject *Sender)
{
  Chapter = GetChapter(XMLDocument1);
  CurrentSection = 0; // First Section
  DisplaySection();
}


void TForm1::DisplaySection(void)
{
  Memo1->Lines->Clear();
  Memo1->Lines->Add("Chapter: " + Chapter->Title);
  Memo1->Lines->Add("Section: " +
    Chapter->Section[CurrentSection]->Title);
  Memo1->Lines->Add("Components: " +
    Chapter->Section[CurrentSection]->Components);
  Memo1->Lines->Add("Wizards: " +
    Chapter->Section[CurrentSection]->Wizards);
}
```

As you'll find out when you type along, the Code Insight features of the C++Builder 6 IDE will now help us when writing code. Specifically, if you type GetChapter(), you will be helped with the argument. When you want to use the Chapter (of type _di_IXMLChapterType), Code Insight will show you a list of available properties and methods. No more accidental typing mistakes resulting in modified XML documents with nonsense child nodes.

Now, let's add four TButton components, called btnFirst, btnPrev, btnNext, and btnLast. Write the following code for their OnClick event handler (to display information from the first, previous, next, and last section).

```
void __fastcall TForm1::btnFirstClick(TObject *Sender)
{
  CurrentSection = 0;
  DisplaySection();
}


void __fastcall TForm1::btnPrevClick(TObject *Sender)
{
  if (CurrentSection)
  {
    CurrentSection-;
```

```
    DisplaySection();
  }
}

void __fastcall TForm1::btnNextClick(TObject *Sender)
{
  if (CurrentSection < Chapter->Count-1)
  {
    CurrentSection++;
    DisplaySection();
  }
}

void __fastcall TForm1::btnLastClick(TObject *Sender)
{
  CurrentSection = Chapter->Count-1;
  DisplaySection();
}
```

We can now view the contents of one item of the XML document inside the TMemo control and use the Next and Prev buttons to navigate through the XML document (see Figure 13.8 for the application in action).

FIGURE 13.8 XML Data Binding in action.

As a final enhancement, we can disable the First/Prev buttons if we are showing the first section, and enable them otherwise. Similarly, we can disable the Last/Next buttons if we are showing the last section, and enable them otherwise. This is done by adding a few lines of code to the private DisplaySection() method.

```
void TForm1::DisplaySection(void)
{
  Memo1->Lines->Clear();
  Memo1->Lines->Add("Chapter: " + Chapter->Title);
  Memo1->Lines->Add("Section: " +
    Chapter->Section[CurrentSection]->Title);
  Memo1->Lines->Add("Components: " +
```

```
    Chapter->Section[CurrentSection]->Components);
  Memo1->Lines->Add("Wizards: " +
    Chapter->Section[CurrentSection]->Wizards);
  // Enable/disable buttons
  btnFirst->Enabled = CurrentSection > 0;
  btnPrev->Enabled = CurrentSection > 0;
  btnNext->Enabled = CurrentSection < Chapter->Count-1;
  btnLast->Enabled = CurrentSection < Chapter->Count-1;
}
```

This concludes the XML Document Programming using Data Binding example. As you might have experienced yourself, the generated interfaces and support classes greatly enhance the functionality of the plain _di_IXMLDocument capabilities.

XML Mapping Tool

The last example in the previous section must have felt a bit like using a dataset and/or data-aware controls, where we could navigate through the items of an XML document. If you liked that, you're in for more enjoyment because we'll now start to use the XML Mapping Tool (or XML Mapper for short). You can find it in the Tools menu of the C++Builder 6 IDE, as well as with a separate icon in the Borland C++Builder 6 Program Group. Whichever way you start it, you can do File, Open to load the BizSnap.xml file, and it will display a treeview with the list of XML nodes.

The XML Mapper is divided into three areas. On the left side we have the XML document, displayed in a treeview. We can also enable the Data View, which will display the actual contents of the XML nodes and switch to the Schema view to see the generated DTD as well as the XML Schema (you can even save the generated XML Schema if you need one).

The right side will show the transformed (generated) DataSet, which we'll see in a moment. In the middle we can set some options, make some modifications, and so on. In Figure 13.9, you can see the Node Options for the Title attribute of the Chapter node. Note the value for Max Length, which is based on the actual values present in the XML Document (in this case only the chapter title "XML Document Programming and XML Mapper," which is indeed 39 characters long). Similarly, the Max Length for the Title of the Section node is 24, and the Max Length for Components and Wizards is 71 and 32, respectively.

After you've loaded an XML document, you need to specify which nodes are required to be transformed into a DataSet. You can do this with a right-click of the mouse. For our example, I've selected all nodes, but there may be situations where only a subset of the nodes are useful; for example, if you only want to work with the section title and components.

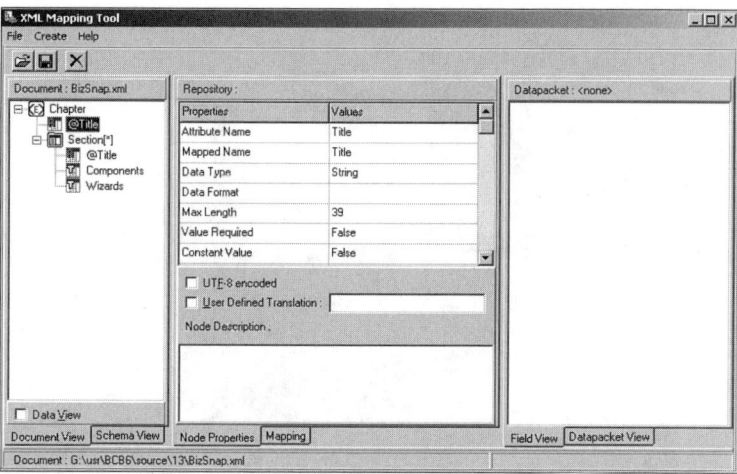

FIGURE 13.9   Loading BizSnap.xml in XML Mapper.

After we've selected one or more nodes, the information in the middle of the XML Mapper changes to display the Selected Nodes, as shown in Figure 13.10.

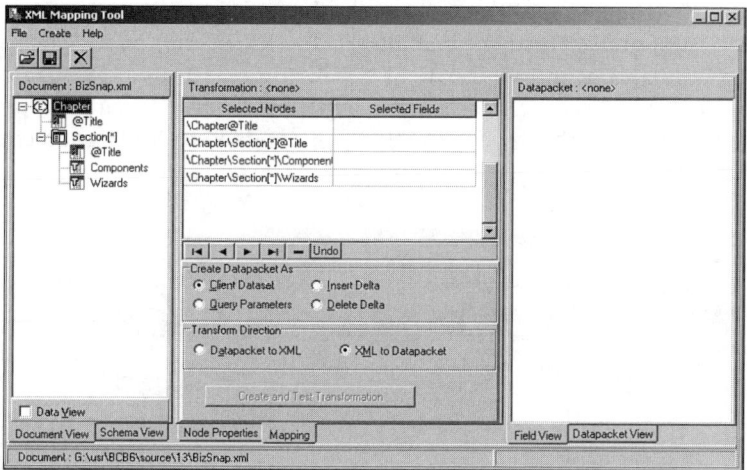

FIGURE 13.10   Selecting All Nodes in XML Mapper.

To actually transform the selected nodes from the XML document into a datapacket, we must right-click the left side and select the Create Datapacket from XML pop-up menu choice (or press Ctrl+D). See Figure 13.11.

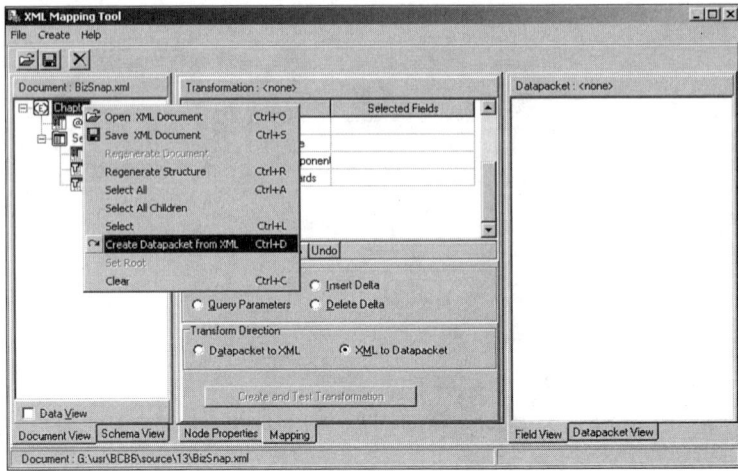

FIGURE 13.11   Create Datapacket from XML.

Figure 13.12 displays datapacket, which will be the result of the transformation. I was surprised to notice a little unexpected discrepancy: The Title field of the nested Section dataset is set to have a Length of 39 (instead of the required 24). This is most likely caused by the fact that the Chapter also has a field with the name Title, which had a Max Length of 39. This is a small bug in the XML Mapper, which should hopefully be fixed in an upcoming update of C++Builder 6. Fortunately, it's not a big problem in our case because the second Length field was originally supposed to be smaller (24 characters) than the value that was assigned to it (39 characters). So we're fine in this case.

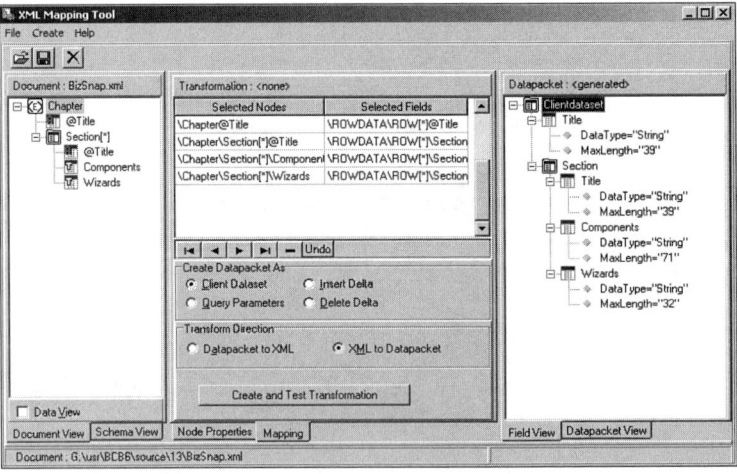

FIGURE 13.12   Title Field with Length of 39.

If the size of the second Length field had to be longer than the first one (that is, if it was clipped from its original length to the new value of 39), we would have a problem. Unfortunately, in that case there is no place to modify the settings for the generated datapacket. Therefore, no other option is available but to return to the Title attribute of the Chapter node on the left side, change the Max Length to the maximum of the two, and re-create the datapacket from XML again. This time, the result will be as required, with both Title fields having a specified Length of the maximum value of their original value. That's okay, at least no field values will be truncated or clipped.

Finally, to create and test the transformation and verify that this time nothing went wrong, we should click the big Create and Test Transformation button. This will show a form with the generated dataset (along with the contents from the XML document inside the dataset). We could have noted from Figure 13.12 that the Section dataset is actually a nested dataset (a field of type TDataSetField). So at first, we only see the Title and Section of the chapter and have to click the ellipsis to get a second form with a grid that shows the three sections from the chapter, see Figure 13.13.

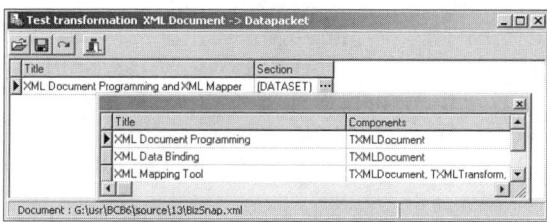

FIGURE 13.13   Create and Test Transformation.

After we've verified that the transformation is okay, we should save the current transformation information in the suggested ToDp.xtr file. Next, if you also want to be able to transform the dataset back to an XML document, you should click the radio button to set the direction from XML to Datapacket to Datapacket to XML. Then, click the Create and Test Transformation button, which will result in an XML document this time, and save the transformation information again, this time in ToXml.xtr. At this time you can close the XML Mapper, because it has performed its task.

Transforming

Armed with the BizSnap.xml file and the two ToDp.xtr and ToXml.xtr transformation information files, we can now convert the XML document to a dataset, make changes to the data inside the dataset, and convert it back to an XML document again.

We can use the same XML Document component: the BizSnap.xml file. Now we should access it using the Transform components from the Data Access tab of the component palette. From left to right, we have the TXMLTransform, TXMLTransformProvider, and TXMLTransformClient components.

The TXMLTransform can be used to transform an XML document into a datapacket or back. The TXMLTransformProvider can be used to transform an XML document into a data packet that is provided to a TClientDataSet (or a TXMLBroker component) component. It can be exported in a DataSnap application, as I'll show in the last section of this chapter. Finally, the TXMLTransformClient component converts the dataset from a TDataSetProvider back into an XML document.

Transformation Demonstration

To demonstrate this transformation process, start a new application and drop a TXMLTransformProvider component from the Data Access tab on the main form. Set the TransformationFile subproperty of the TransformRead property to the ToDp.xtr transformation file, which is used when XML information is read so it can be transformed into a dataset data packet, which will be provided to a receiving TClientDataSet component. If you also want to update the XML document again, we must set the TransformationFile subproperty of the TransformWrite property to the ToXml.xtr transformation file, which is used when the connecting TClientDataSet calls the ApplyUpdates method back through the TXMLTransformProvider all the way to the XML document. Apart from the transformation information, we should make sure to set the XMLDataFile property to the BizSnap.xml document itself. I often use .xtr and .xml files in the same directory as my executable, which means that I can remove the directory information in front of each of these three filenames (leaving only ToDp.xtr, ToXML.xtr, and BizSnap.xml). Therefore, I can easily move the application and accompanying files around and to other machines.

Anyway, after we've specified the external files to use, we can drop a TClientDataSet component on the main form as well, call it cdsChapter and point its ProviderName property to the TXMLTransformProvider component. We can open cdsChapter, which will request data from the XMLTransformProvider, and as a side-effect, start the XML transformation. Right-click the cdsChapter component to start the Fields Editor, right-click again and do Add All Fields to create a persistent Title field as well as the nested dataset Section.

Now, drop another TClientDataSet component, and call it cdsSection. Obviously, this one will be used to connect to the nested dataset Section, so make sure to assign the DataSetField property to the cdsChapterSection field. To see the transformed data, drop two TDataSource components (one for each ClientDataSet), a TDBEdit (for the Title field of cdsChapter) and a DBGrid (for the entire cdsSection).

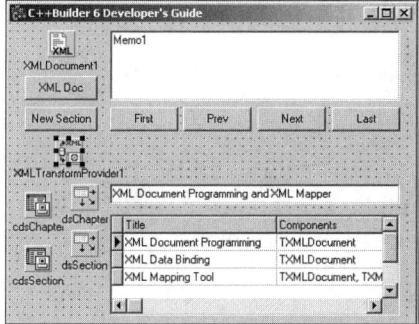

FIGURE 13.14 XMLTransformProvider at design time.

We can now use this application to browse through the grid as if we were indeed browsing through a regular dataset. If we make changes to the data, we can call the ApplyUpdates methods of the (master) ClientDataSet cdsChapter to apply the updates back to the original XML document (via the TXMLTransformProvider component, hence, the need for the transformation back to an XML document).

A good technique is to update the XML document as soon as a change is made in the cdsChapter or the cdsSection dataset, which can be done in the OnAfterPost event handler of these ClientDataSets as follows:

```
void __fastcall TForm1::cdsChapterAfterPost(TDataSet *DataSet)
{
  dynamic_cast<TClientDataSet*>(DataSet)->ApplyUpdates(0);
}

void __fastcall TForm1::cdsSectionAfterPost(TDataSet *DataSet)
{
  cdsChapter->ApplyUpdates(0);
}
```

Note that I'm using two different approaches here: In the OnAfterPost of the cdsChapter, I can take the DataSet argument, whereas in the OnAfterPost of the cdsSection I just take the cdsChapter member of the TForm itself. In both cases, it's the master ClientDataSet that makes the call to ApplyUpdates because the detail is only connected to the DataSetField cdsChapterSection.

Another option is to perform a final check at the FormClose event handler by looking at the ChangeCount property of both the cdsChapter and cdsSection. If the sum of them is bigger than zero (that is, if any change is made in either dataset), calling the ApplyUpdates on the master table.

```
void __fastcall TForm1::FormClose(TObject *Sender, TCloseAction &Action)
{
  if ((cdsChapter->ChangeCount + cdsSection->ChangeCount) > 0)
    cdsChapter->ApplyUpdates(0);
}
```

For more information about DataSetProviders, ClientDataSets, and calling ApplyUpdates, see Chapter 20, "Distributed Applications with DataSnap."

Summary

In this chapter, we have covered XML Document Programming with the TXMLDocument component, as well as the XML Data Binding Wizard and the XML Mapper, which can transform XML documents to data packets (and back).

PART III

Windows Programming

IN THIS PART

by Paul Gustavson

14

Win32 API Functional Areas

The Windows 32-bit (Win32) Application Programming Interface (API) provides a wide set of C-language functions and structures for developing and deploying Windows-compliant applications. API calls often perform various services for a Windows application such as providing a common dialog box for opening and saving files or sending a document to the printer.

In this chapter, we will examine the functional areas of the Win32 API as identified in Figure 14.1. Examining these functional areas provides the necessary insight into understanding the composition and capabilities the API provides developers. For each key functional area, we will also develop some useful examples with C++Builder that demonstrate the application of the Win32 API.

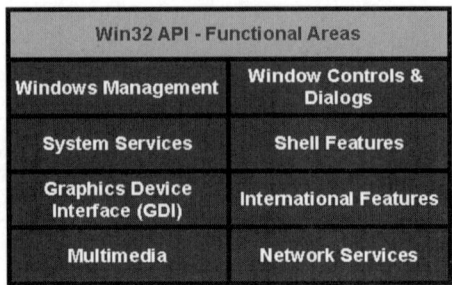

FIGURE 14.1   Functional area block diagram.

Win32 API Background

The Win32 API provides numerous capabilities that are worth exploring. Allegedly, there are over 10,000 API functions available within current versions of Windows that are strewn across dozens of dynamic link libraries (DLLs). These Windows API DLLs can be found in the Windows/System directory under 95, 98, and ME, or the Windows/System32 directory under NT, 2000, and XP. Key DLLs that have been a part of Windows since 95 and NT 3.5 include the Windows kernel library (kernel32.dll), the user library (user32.dll), and the graphical device interface (GDI) library (gdi32.dll).

Also important are some of the extensions and support libraries that have been added by Microsoft as Windows has evolved. Examples include the multimedia system library (mmsystem.dll), the Windows Shell library (shell32.dll), the Windows Internet Extensions library (wininet.dll), Windows Sockets (winsock.dll and wsock32.dll), DirectX libraries, and many more. Many of these extensions and support libraries are not necessarily required for Windows to work, but provide useful features that make programs more robust and powerful.

TIP

The Win32 API functions that are made natively available to the Borland developer reside in an import library called import32.lib. This library is linked into each project that is built. To view the functions contained in this import library use Borland's TLIB command-line tool as follows:

```
TLIB import32.lib, import32.txt
```

This will produce a file called import32.txt that contains a list of the Win32 modules and the functions provided by each of those modules. Although it might appear to be lengthy when you view import32.txt, it's not an exhaustive list of the Win32 API. A number of other Win32 API modules and functions might never make it into the import32.lib, which is produced with each release of C++Builder. To utilize other Win32 API modules, you must locate the DLL that supports the desired feature and either use the implib command-line tool to create a library that can be supported by the Borland compiler and linker, or dynamically load a DLL using the LoadLibary() call.

To discover the list of available functions and services supported by a specific Win32 API library, try using Borland's impdef command-line tool to generate an interface definition (.def) file of the DLL, as shown in the following example:

```
impdef -a user32.def user32.dll
```

When using this command-line utility, or any other one that requires a filename, be sure to supply the full path to the dll file or position your active directory in the folder the dll resides. The .def file, which can be viewed by any text editor, will contain a list of available functions that can be used by application developers. Browsing the windows/system (95, 98, Me) or windows/system32 (NT, 2000, XP) directory will reveal a plethora of DLLs, yet only a small percentage of these DLLs are true Win32 API DLLs. Often, a Win32 DLL will contain a 32 tag embedded within the filename. The Properties feature (see Figure 14.2) within Windows Explorer can be used to reveal more information about the DLL. If it says Microsoft and says API, you can be certain it's a Win32 API module.

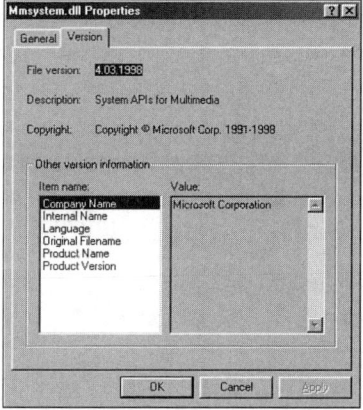

FIGURE 14.2   The DLL Properties dialog.

Alternatively, an example utility called "DLL LIB Util" is included on the book CD-ROM, which automates the steps described previously in displaying information regarding a specified DLL or LIB file (see Figure 14.3). The source code for this program is provided on the CD-ROM and utilizes several Win32 API calls for discovering information regarding Windows files such as a DLL.

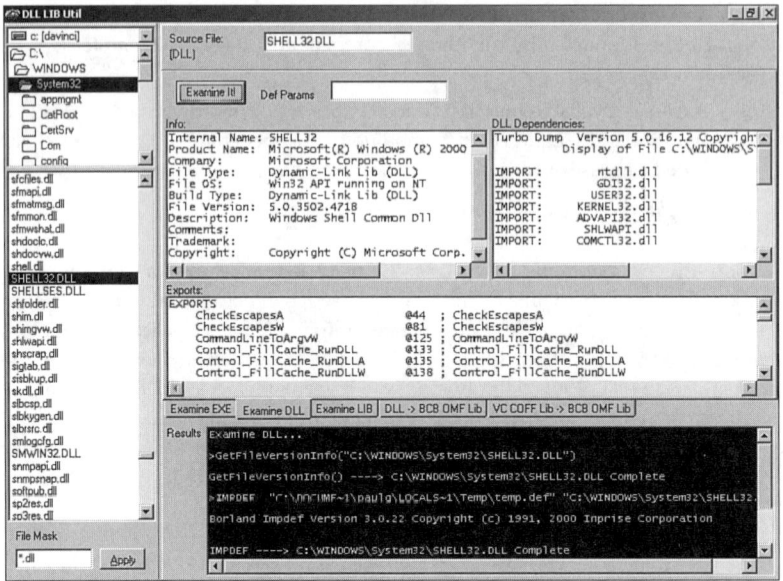

FIGURE 14.3   DLL LIB utility.

Within C++Builder and Delphi, many of the common Win32 API features have been wrapped within the core set of VCL components used to help construct a typical Windows application. VCL Win32 examples include TEdit, TLabel, TMemo, TRichEdit, TImageList, TTreeView, TOpenDialog, Ttimer, and much more. In fact, many of the visual VCL components that are derived from TWinControl are simply wrappers to Microsoft Windows screen objects. In addition, several other non-visual VCL components provide other Win32 API support such as TTimer.

Although the VCL provides an object-oriented–based interface to the Win32 API, it is not all inclusive. Many of the Win32 API functions and features have not made their way into a VCL component. As a result, there are Win32 functions and features that are often untapped by the C++Builder (and Delphi) developer.

Let's explore these capabilities by examining each of the Win32 API functional areas.

Windows Management

Let's start off by examining the Windows Management functional area. Windows applications are created and managed through a majority of the functions provided by the user library (user32.dll). The user library interface includes services for window and menu management, dialogs, messaging, message boxes, mouse and keyboard access, and other built-in controls.

Before we dive any deeper, it's important to first understand the concept of a window. A window acts as the interface between the user and the application. At least one window, called the main window, is created by a Windows application. Applications can create additional windows as well. A window's primary purpose is to display information and receive input from a user.

Windows Management functions are used to control the aspect of the windows created and used by an application. The main window receives mouse and keyboard input through messages. These messages are passed between window resources through Windows Management support. Windows Management functions also provide the capability for an application to display icons, menus, and dialog boxes that receive and display additional user information.

NOTE

Some type of handle identifies all window resources. Examples of entities with handles include modules, processes, threads, frame windows, menus, bitmaps, icons, cursors, and color space. A handle is always represented by a 32-bit unsigned value and is an extremely important aspect of the Win32 API. Handles provide the means and mechanism to control and manipulate objects, such as a window and children processes, and they provide the capability to pass input to other applications through message callbacks. You'll find that a number of the Win32 API examples provided in this chapter make use of handles.

The functions in Table 14.1 provide a sampling of some of the more popular Windows Management API routines used to create and manage windows. These routines are accessed simply by including the windows.h header file or Borland's vcl.h header file within your application's source file.

TABLE 14.1   Common Windows Management Functions

Windows Management Common Functions	Description
CascadeWindows()	Cascades the specified windows or the child windows of the specified parent window.
CloseWindow()	Minimizes, but does not destroy a specified window.
CreateWindow()	Creates an overlapped, pop-up, or child window.
DestroyWindow()	Destroys a window. The system responds by sending a WM_DESTROY message to a specified window.
EnableWindow()	Enables or disables mouse and keyboard input to a specified window or control.
EnumWindows()	Enumerates by looping through each top-level window on the display and passing the handle of each window individually to an application-defined callback function.

TABLE 14.1   Continued

Windows Management Common Functions	Description
EnumWindowsProc()	Used by the EnumWindows() function. This is the application-defined callback function that EnumWindows() uses to pass the handles of top-level windows.
FindWindow()	Retrieves the handle to the top-level window in which the class name and window name match the specified strings.
FindWindowEx()	Retrieves the handles of available active windows. Similar to FindWindow(), but also provides support for locating child windows.
GetWindowRect()	Retrieves the screen coordinates of the specified window.
GetWindowText()	Retrieves the title bar caption of the specified window.
MessageBeep()	Plays a predefined waveform sound asynchronously.
MessageBox()	Creates a small dialog box containing an application-defined title and message.
MoveWindow()	Moves the location and size of a specified window.
PostMessage()	Directs a specified message to another window and returns immediately.
RegisterWindowMessage()	Defines a new windows message that is guaranteed to be unique.
SetWindowText()	Modifies the text of the title bar for the specified window.
SendMessage()	Directs a specified message to another window and waits until the message has been processed.
ShowWindow()	Sets the show state of the specified window. Show states include hiding, maximizing, minimizing, restoring, and activating a window.
TileWindows()	Tiles the specified windows or the child windows of the specified parent window.
WinMain()	Called by the system as the initial entry point for a Win32-based application.

Many other Windows Management routines exist that we have not identified. In fact, there are more than 640 routines provided by the user32.dll within current versions of Windows. Use Borland's impdef command-line tool or the DLL LIB Util utility, described in the Tip section earlier, to view the full list of available functions within user32.dll.

Let's now create an example application in C++Builder that uses some of the Windows Management routines identified in Table 14.1.

Windows Management Example

In the Chapter 14 source directory on the CD-ROM, there is a project called WinManUtil, which is illustrated in Figure 14.4. This project contains a comprehensive sample that utilizes the Windows Management API calls and messages to manage and control other Windows applications.

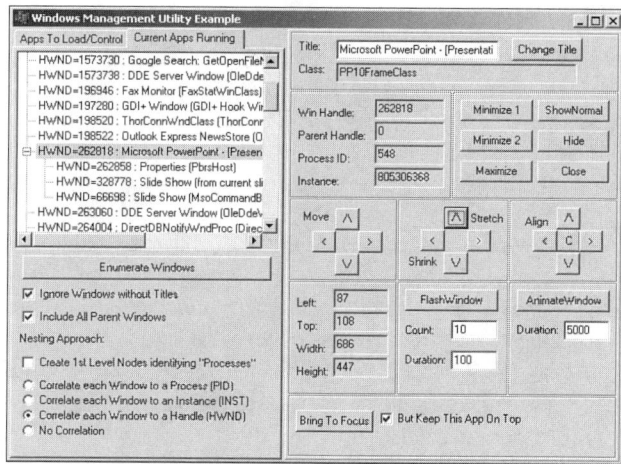

FIGURE 14.4   Windows Management Utility screen shot.

We'll take a look at five different aspects of the program that demonstrate the application of the Windows Management API: Enumerating Windows, Controlling External Windows, Message Handling Support for moving an external window, Flashing a Window for user notification, and Window Animation Effects on open and close.

Enumerating Windows

Listing 14.1 shows some of the source code used to enumerate active windows in the system by using the EnumWindows() call and an application-defined callback function called GetWinHandleAll(). The information gathered by the callback function is displayed to the user within a tree view control.

LISTING 14.1   Windows Management Utility—Enumerating Windows Example

```
void __fastcall TFormWinMan::ButtonEnumWindowsClick(TObject *Sender)
{
    TCursor Save_Cursor = Screen->Cursor;
    Screen->Cursor = crHourGlass;      // hourglass cursor
    try
    {
        TreeView1->Items->Clear();                      // clear tree
        EnumWindows((WNDENUMPROC)GetWinHandleAll,0); // enumerate all windows
        TreeView1->AlphaSort();    // sort tree which contains enum results
```

LISTING 14.1   Continued

```
    }
    __finally
    {
      Screen->Cursor = Save_Cursor; // restore cursor
    }
}

//-------------------------------------------------------------------------

BOOL CALLBACK TFormWinMan::GetWinHandleAll(HWND hwnd, unsigned long hproc)
{
 int correlation = FormWinMan->GetCorrelationChoice();
 FormWinMan->ProcessHandleInformation(hwnd,correlation);

 if (hwnd != NULL) return true;  // keep going (we want them all)
 return false; //stop enumeration
}

//-------------------------------------------------------------------------

TTreeNode* __fastcall TFormWinMan::ProcessHandleInformation(HWND H_Window,
                                        unsigned int correlation_type)
{
    // get the handle of the application instance
    HINSTANCE  hAppInstance = (HINSTANCE)GetWindowLong(H_Window,GWL_HINSTANCE);
    unsigned long dwProcessId = 0;

    // find out who created window
    unsigned long tempID = GetWindowThreadProcessId(
          H_Window,
          &dwProcessId);      // address of variable for process identifier

    int length = GetWindowTextLength(H_Window);    // get the length
    if ((CheckBoxIgnoreWindowsNoTitles->Checked) && (length == 0))
        return NULL;

    char classname[80];
    char windowtitle[80];

    GetWindowText(H_Window, windowtitle, 80);
    GetClassName(H_Window, classname, 80);
```

LISTING 14.1   Continued

```
HWND hwndParent = (HWND)GetWindowLong(H_Window,GWL_HWNDPARENT);

if ((!CheckBoxIncludeParent->Checked) && (hwndParent == 0))
  return NULL;

TAppInfo *appinfo = new TAppInfo();
appinfo->DeviceContext      = GetWindowDC(H_Window);
appinfo->Title              = AnsiString(windowtitle);
appinfo->Class              = AnsiString(classname);
appinfo->WindowHandle       = H_Window;
appinfo->ParentWindowHandle = hwndParent;
appinfo->InstanceHandle     = (int)hAppInstance;
appinfo->ProcessID          = dwProcessId;

TTreeNode* current_node = NULL;

// let's double check to make sure we have a node for the parent.
if ((CheckBoxIncludeParent->Checked) && (appinfo->ParentWindowHandle != 0))
{
    TTreeNode* parent_node = FormWinMan->GetNode_AppInfoValue(
            FormWinMan->TreeView1->Items,
            NULL,
            WINHANDLE,
            (unsigned long)appinfo->ParentWindowHandle);

    if (!parent_node)  // need to create node with parent info
        current_node = ProcessHandleInformation(      // recurse
                    appinfo->ParentWindowHandle,
                    correlation_type);
}

AnsiString treetext;
switch (correlation_type)
{
  case PROCESS :
      current_node =
              FormWinMan->GetNode_AppInfoValue(
                        FormWinMan->TreeView1->Items,
                        NULL,
                        PROCESSID,
                        (unsigned long)appinfo->ProcessID);
```

LISTING 14.1   Continued

```
            treetext = "PID=" + AnsiString(appinfo->ProcessID) + " : ";
            break;
        case INSTANCE :
            current_node =
                    FormWinMan->GetNode_AppInfoValue(
                                FormWinMan->TreeView1->Items,
                                NULL,
                                INSTANCEHANDLE,
                                (unsigned long)appinfo->InstanceHandle);
            treetext = "INST=" + AnsiString(appinfo->InstanceHandle) + " : ";
            break;

        case WINDOW :
            current_node =
                    FormWinMan->GetNode_AppInfoValue(
                                FormWinMan->TreeView1->Items,
                                NULL,
                                WINHANDLE,
                                (unsigned long)appinfo->ParentWindowHandle);
            treetext = "HWND=" + AnsiString((unsigned int)appinfo->WindowHandle) +
                    " : ";
            break;
        default :
                if (CheckBoxProcessRootNode->Checked)
                        current_node = FormWinMan->GetNode_Process(
                                    FormWinMan->TreeView1->Items,
                                    appinfo->ProcessID);
                treetext = "";
    }

    TTreeNode* node = NULL;
    if (CheckBoxProcessRootNode->Checked) // user wants process IDs at 1st level
    {
        TAppInfo *processinfo = new TAppInfo();
        processinfo->ProcessID = appinfo->ProcessID;
        // make sure we have ProcessRootNode for this WindowHandle
        node = FormWinMan->GetNode_Process( FormWinMan->TreeView1->Items,
                                            appinfo->ProcessID);
        if (!node) {
            // need to create Process Node
            AnsiString temptext = "PID=" + AnsiString(appinfo->ProcessID);
```

LISTING 14.1 Continued

```
            node = FormWinMan->TreeView1->Items->AddObject(NULL,
                                                temptext,
                                                processinfo);
            current_node = node;     // reset current_node
        }
    }

    node = FormWinMan->GetNode_AppInfoValue(FormWinMan->TreeView1->Items, NULL,
                                    WINHANDLE,
                                    (unsigned long)appinfo->WindowHandle);
    if (!node)   // make sure we don't already have the WindowHandle
    {
        if (!current_node)  // parent node
        {
            if (FormWinMan->TreeView1->Items->Count > 0)
                    current_node = FormWinMan->TreeView1->Items->Item[0];

            node = FormWinMan->TreeView1->Items->AddObject(current_node,
                        AnsiString(treetext +
                            AnsiString(windowtitle) +  " (" +
                            AnsiString(classname) + ")"),appinfo);
        }
        else // child node
        {
            node = FormWinMan->TreeView1->Items->AddChildObject(
                            current_node,
                            AnsiString(treetext +
                                    AnsiString(windowtitle) + " (" +
                                    AnsiString(classname) + ")"),appinfo);
        }
    }
    return node; // make sure we pass back the node
}

    node = FormWinMan->GetNode_AppInfoValue(FormWinMan->TreeView1->Items, NULL,
                                        WINHANDLE,
                                        (unsigned long)appinfo->
                                        ➥WindowHandle);
    if (!node)   // make sure we don't already have the WindowHandle
    {
        if (!current_node)  // parent node
```

LISTING 14.1   Continued

```
        {
            if (FormWinMan->TreeView1->Items->Count > 0)
                current_node = FormWinMan->TreeView1->Items->Item[0];

        node = FormWinMan->TreeView1->Items->AddObject(current_node,
                    AnsiString(treetext +
                        AnsiString(windowtitle) +  " (" +
                        AnsiString(classname) + ")"),appinfo);
        }
        else // child node
        {
            node = FormWinMan->TreeView1->Items->AddChildObject(
                        current_node,
                        AnsiString(treetext +
                            AnsiString(windowtitle) + " (" +
                            AnsiString(classname) + ")"),appinfo);
        }
    }
    return node; // make sure we pass back the node
}

//-----------------------------------------------------------------------

void __fastcall TFormWinMan::TreeView1Change(TObject *Sender, TTreeNode *Node)
{
    TTreeNode* node  = TreeView1->Selected;

    if ((node->Level == 0) && (CheckBoxProcessRootNode->Checked)) return;

    TAppInfo* info = (TAppInfo*)node->Data;
    winhandle = info->WindowHandle;
    UpdateAppInfo(winhandle);
}
```

Let's examine what's happening in this code. The `ButtonEnumWindowsClick()` method is used to enumerate all the active windows in the system. The actual Win32 API call used to initiate this enumeration is provided by the `EnumWindows()` call. As a parameter to the `EnumWindows()` call, we passed a parameter to a callback function that we've defined called `GetWinHandleAll()`. All callback functions provided to `EnumWindows()` must take on this same form.

The GetWinHandleAll() callback that we've created receives the windows handle to each enumerated window. Calls used to process and display the windows handle information is provided by the ProcessHandleInformation() method defined for this sample. The GetWinHandleAll() also checks for a NULL window handle to determine when all windows have been enumerated, and returns false after this condition is met.

ProcessHandleInformation() examines each window handle using Windows Management API calls and builds a tree of the enumerated data using objects. The specific Win32 API calls used to collect the information for each node object include GetWindowLong() with the parameter GWL_INSTANCE to determine the handle instance of the window; GetWindowThreadProcessID() to determine the Process ID for the window handle; GetWindowText() to determine the caption title of the specified window; and GetClassName() to determine the class used to defined the window. This information is used to organize and label the nodes within our tree view.

TreeView1Change() event handler is triggered when the user clicks or keys any of the nodes within the tree view. When this occurs, the windows handle is retrieved from the node object and additional information is provided to the user through UpdateAppInfo().

Let's take a look, for a moment, at the UpdateAppInfo() function created for this example.

```cpp
void __fastcall TFormWinMan::UpdateAppInfo(HWND winhandle)
{
    EditWHandle->Text = (AnsiString)(int)winhandle;

    int length = GetWindowTextLength(winhandle);
    char * title = new char[length+1];
    title[length] = 0;
    GetWindowText(winhandle,title,length+1);
    EditTitle->Text = AnsiString(title);

    char classname[80];
    GetClassName(winhandle, classname, 80);
    EditClass->Text = AnsiString(classname);

    RECT Rect;
    GetWindowRect(winhandle,&Rect);     // get the size for the current window
    EditLeft->Text = AnsiString((unsigned int)Rect.left);
    EditTop->Text = AnsiString((unsigned int)Rect.top);
    EditWidth->Text = AnsiString((unsigned int)(Rect.right - Rect.left));
    EditHeight->Text = AnsiString((unsigned int)(Rect.bottom - Rect.top));
```

```
unsigned long dwProcessId = 0; //(unsigned long)
⟿GetWindowLong(H_Window,GWL_ID);
// find out who created window
unsigned long tempID = GetWindowThreadProcessId(
        winhandle,
        &dwProcessId);        // address of variable for process identifier
EditProcessID->Text = AnsiString(dwProcessId);

    // get the handle of the application instance
HINSTANCE  hAppInstance = (HINSTANCE)GetWindowLong(winhandle,GWL_HINSTANCE);
EditIHandle->Text = AnsiString((unsigned int)hAppInstance);

HWND ParentWindowHandle= (HWND)GetWindowLong(winhandle,GWL_HWNDPARENT);
EditPWHandle->Text = AnsiString((unsigned int)ParentWindowHandle);
}
```

In this code, we again use several Win32 API calls to obtain and display information regarding the windows handle that was passed in as a parameter.

GetWindowTextLength() and GetWindowText() are used in tandem to retrieve the window text such as a title bar caption. In the next example, we'll use SetWindowText() to modify text of an external window.

GetClassName() is used to retrieve the class name associated to the window. For a C++Builder application you might see TApplication, a TForm descendent, or a class used to represent a subcomponent on the form. It really depends on the level of the window being examined.

GetWindowRect() is then used to retrieve the screen coordinates of the window. Some simple math is performed to determine the width and height of the window. In a short bit, we will demonstrate how to move an external window. The code on the CD-ROM also shows how to resize an external window.

GetWindowThreadProcessID() is used to find out what process is associated with the window we use. Finally, we use GetWindowLong() twice to find out the Instance Handle of the window by using the GWL_HINSTANCE flag, and, if it exists, the Window handle of the parent using the GWL_HWNDPARENT flag.

Controlling External Windows

Let's now take a look at some other code from this sample that uses the Windows Management calls to control the external windows that have been enumerated (see Listing 14.2).

LISTING 14.2 Windows Management Utility—Manipulating External Windows Example

```
void __fastcall TFormWinMan::ButtonChangeTitleClick(TObject *Sender)
{
        SetWindowText(winhandle, EditTitle->Text.c_str());
}

//------------------------------------------------------------------------

void __fastcall TFormWinMan::ButtonBringToFocusClick(TObject *Sender)
{
        SendMessage(winhandle,WM_SYSCOMMAND,SC_RESTORE,0);
        SetForegroundWindow(winhandle);
        if (CheckBoxTop->Checked) SetForegroundWindow(Handle);
}

//------------------------------------------------------------------------

void __fastcall TFormWinMan::ButtonMaximizeClick(TObject *Sender)
{
    SendMessage(winhandle,WM_SYSCOMMAND,SC_MAXIMIZE,0);
}

//------------------------------------------------------------------------

void __fastcall TFormWinMan::ButtonHideClick(TObject *Sender)
{
    ShowWindow(winhandle, SW_HIDE);
}
```

This listing provides just a handful of some of the functions that manipulate other windows through Windows Management API calls. Let's examine some of these calls.

In `ButtonChangeTitleClick()`, the `SetWindowText()` API call is used to alter the text associated to a window handle. This can be used to change the window's title bar or the text of window controls such as a button caption or menu item if we know its window handle.

```
BOOL SetWindowText(
  HWND hWnd,           // handle to window or control
  LPCTSTR lpString     // title or text
);
```

In our example, we simply pass as parameters the active window handle of the window currently being examined, and the text that we want to assign to the control.

There are up to three Windows Management API Calls used in the ButtonBringToFocusClick() event handler. The first call used is SendMessage(), which is used to transmit a synchronous Windows message to a single window handle or to all top-level windows. The message that is being passed in this example is the WM_SYSCOMMAND windows message with the SC_RESTORE parameter as the command being requested. Here we are requesting that the targeted application restore its window to its normal position and size. The ButtonBringToFocusClick() then waits until this message has been processed by the targeted window.

Following the SendMessage() call, ButtonBringToFocusClick() issues a SetForegroundWindow() to activate and raise the targeted window into the foreground. Additionally, if the user has checked the CheckBoxTop control, which indicates that the user wants the WinManUtil app to not be masked by the targeted window, our example app is raised one layer higher than the targeted window by using SetForegroundWindow() again. This time, however, we pass its own windows handle.

NOTE

Windows messages provide the interaction mechanism used to pass input to various objects represented by a handle. The two common API calls used to pass a specified message to a window or windows are SendMessage() and PostMessage(). Although these calls perform a similar action, there are some differences between the two. SendMessage() is used to pass a message synchronously; the call waits until the message has been processed. PostMessage(), however, is used to pass a message asynchronously; it does not bother to wait for the message to be processed and returns immediately. The declaration for the PostMessage() is provided below:

```
LRESULT PostMessage(
    HWND hWnd,      // handle of destination window
    UINT Msg,       // message to send
    WPARAM wParam,     // first message parameter
    LPARAM lParam     // second message parameter
    );
```

Both SendMessage() and PostMessage() require four elements: a window handle indicating the target window, a message identifier that describes the purpose of the message, and two 32-bit message parameters. The message parameters can be used to pass value information or address information to the destination handle. The LRESULT value returned by the SendMessage() or PostMessage() function specifies the result of the message processing. For instance, a return value of nonzero indicates success for PostMessage().

In `ButtonMaximizeClick()` we again use `SendMessage()`, but this time requesting for the target window to Maximize its window by using the `SC_MAXIMIZE` command in connection with the `WM_SYSCOMMAND` message.

In `ButtonHideClick()` we are using another Windows Management routine called `ShowWindow()` to change the state of the targeted window. In this case, we are requesting the window to be hidden and no longer active on the desktop by using the `SW_HIDE` command.

Message Handling Support

Let's take a look at a few more code excerpts from this sample that demonstrates some practical ways of using the Windows Management calls for moving the display location of an external window. Code to support this functionality is provided in Listing 14.3.

LISTING 14.3   Windows Management Utility—Message Handling Support for Moving an External Window

```
__fastcall TFormWinMan::TFormWinMan(TComponent* Owner)
        : TForm(Owner)
{
    // define custom messages
    WM_MOVE_A_WINDOW = RegisterWindowMessage("WM_MOVE_A_WINDOW");
    WM_STRETCH_A_WINDOW = RegisterWindowMessage("WM_STRETCH_A_WINDOW");
    WindowProc = MyWndProc;
}
//-----------------------------------------------------------------------


void __fastcall TFormWinMan::MyWndProc(Messages::TMessage &Message)
{
  // If the window receives a notification message then
  // pass it to the appropriate windows messaging function. Otherwise
  // let the default processing for the message take place.

  if (Message.Msg == WM_MOVE_A_WINDOW)
      wmMoveAWindow(Message);
  else if (Message.Msg == WM_STRETCH_A_WINDOW)
      wmStretchAWindow(Message);
  else
      WndProc(Message) ;
}


//-----------------------------------------------------------------------
```

LISTING 14.3   Continued

```
void __fastcall TFormWinMan::ButtonMoveRightMouseDown(TObject *Sender,
    TMouseButton Button, TShiftState Shift, int X, int Y)
{
    ButtonDown = true;
    PostMessage(Handle, WM_MOVE_A_WINDOW, (unsigned int)winhandle, MOVERIGHT);
}
//-----------------------------------------------------------------------

void __fastcall TFormWinMan::ButtonMoveRightMouseUp(TObject *Sender,
    TMouseButton Button, TShiftState Shift, int X, int Y)
{
    ButtonDown = false;
}


//-----------------------------------------------------------------------

void __fastcall TFormWinMan::wmMoveAWindow(TMessage Msg)
{
    RECT rect;
    HWND wh = HWND(Msg.WParam);
    GetWindowRect(wh, &rect);  // get the size for the current window
    int width  = rect.right  - rect.left;
    int height = rect.bottom - rect.top;
    int direction = Msg.LParam;
    while (ButtonDown)
    {
        switch (direction)
        {
            case MOVEUP    : rect.top--;  break;
            case MOVEDOWN  : rect.top++;  break;
            case MOVELEFT  : rect.left--; break;
            case MOVERIGHT : rect.left++; break;
        }
        MoveWindow(wh, rect.left, rect.top, width, height, true);
        Application->ProcessMessages(); // process other messages
        UpdateAppInfo(winhandle);
    }
}
```

In this example, the effect that is desired is for the user to be able to hold the Move
Right button down, and for the targeted window to continually move horizontally

to the right until the Right button is finally released—that is, the button comes back up. To do this, however, we will need to use a custom windows message that will be handled by our application. The custom windows message of interest is called `WM_MOVE_A_WINDOW`, which has been declared as an integer property for `TFormWinMan`. To set this up, we use the `RegisterWindowMessage()` API call in the constructor for `TFormWinMan`. `RegisterWindowMessage()` will guarantee that the user-defined message `WM_MOVE_A_WINDOW` will be unique throughout the system. The `WindowProc` property of the form, which is inherited from TConrol, is also set to a new windows-handling method called `MyWndProc()`. `MyWndProc()` will now intercept any incoming Windows message calls for our application. If the method receives a specific message such as `WM_MOVE_A_WINDOW`, it passes it to the appropriate windows messaging-handler function. Otherwise, the default processing for the message takes place through a call to the form's standard `WndProc()` method. In this example, after `WM_MOVE_A_WINDOW` is intercepted, a call is made to another routine defined for our application called `wmMoveAWindow()`. In a short bit, we will take a look at `wmMoveAWindow()` and how it is applied to support the task of moving our targeted window. But next, let's examine how we trigger the move event.

The `ButtonMoveRightMouseDown()` function provides the desired processing after the mouse-down event occurs. In our case, the `ButtonDown` property associated to the form is set to `true`, indicating that we have a button down. Then, a `PostMessage()` call is made to itself using our user-defined message `WM_MOVE_A_WINDOW` with parameters identifying what window to move (a handle), and in what direction to move. The code that receives and processes this specific message is contained within the `wmMoveAWindow()` method. Although the Move Right button is down—remember we're keeping track of the status of that button through the `ButtonDown` property—we issue a `MoveWindow()` API call passing the window handle of the target, and the new desired desktop location in the form of a `RECT` structure. We continue to call `MoveWindow()` until `ButtonDown` is false.

You may ask, "Why do you post a windows message to yourself? Why not put the `MoveWindow()` looping code right into the event handler?" The reason why a `PostMessage()` call is made, is because in Borland C++Builder (and in Delphi) the insertion of any type of loop processing directly into a VCL event handler could jeopardize the capability to capture other similar events. In our case, we're looking for two events associated to the same button: a mouse-down event and a mouse-up event. If we put `while` loop type processing directly into the method handling the first event, we risk missing the back-end event, which is the mouse release. If we miss the mouse release, the target window we're moving will keep moving forever. Obviously, that's not the desired effect, so we need some way to provide loop processing for an event and still be able to field other events that might occur. The easiest way to do that, short of threading, is to use the asynchronous `PostMessage()` call with a custom windows message, just as we have done in our example. The handler of that message provides the conditional looping. In our case, this conditional looping is found in the wmMoveAWindow() routine. Notice also the use of the Application->ProcessMessages() routine, which temporarily interrupts the looping that is occurring so that other window message events can be processed and fielded.

The ButtonMoveRightMouseUp() method is simply used to process the mouse-up event associated to the Move Right button by toggling the ButtonDown property to false. After the ButtonDown property is set to false, the loop processing that has been occurring within the wmMoveAWindow() routine finishes because the loop condition, while (ButtonDown), has now failed.

Flashing a Window

Sometimes it's helpful to notify the user that an application has completed its task without being interrupted by an annoying message box. Microsoft has two API calls that provide a nonobtrusive way of signaling a notification to the user: FlashWindow() and FlashWindowEx(). Both of these routines can be used to alert a user that his attention is recommended, but not required. Whereas, a message box, which can be generated by the Windows API MessageBox() call, requires that a user perform the extra step of closing the window alert.

Let's take a look at the code in our sample program that uses FlashWindowEx().

```
void __fastcall TFormWinMan::ButtonFlashClick(TObject *Sender)
{
  FLASHWINFO flash_info;
  flash_info.cbSize    = sizeof(FLASHWINFO);
  flash_info.hwnd      = winhandle;
  flash_info.dwFlags   = FLASHW_TIMER | FLASHW_ALL;
  flash_info.uCount    = EditCount->Text.ToIntDef(10); // # times to flash
  flash_info.dwTimeout = EditDur->Text.ToIntDef(100); // duration for each flash

  FlashWindowEx(&flash_info);
}
```

In this code, FlashWindowEx() simply flashes the title bar of the application, and/or the icon representing the application in the taskbar.

> **NOTE**
>
> You might have noticed the use of FlashWindow() or FlashWindowEx() in popular programs such as America Online's Instant Messenger, Yahoo Pager, and ICQ. This feature is used to alert a user that something in a specific program has occurred and is in need of attention, or to let the user know that that a window is ready to receive focus.

FlashWindowEx() requires a pointer to a structure containing the flash information. The variable to this pointer is defined by FLASHWINFO, which is listed as follows:

```
typedef struct {
  UINT  cbSize;
  HWND  hwnd;
  DWORD dwFlags;
  UINT  uCount;
  DWORD dwTimeout;
} FLASHWINFO, *PFLASHWINFO;
```

The FLASHWINFO structure controls the way the FlashWindowEx() function is going to execute. First, cbSize identifies the size of the FLASHINFO structure using sizeof (FLASHWINFO). Hwnd is used to identify the handle of the window to be flashed. dwFlags identifies how the flashes are going to be carried out. Table 14.2 shows the different flags:

TABLE 14.2   FlashWindowEx() Flags

Flag	Meaning
FLASHW_STOP	Stop flashing. The system restores the window to its original state.
FLASHW_CAPTION	Flash the window caption.
FLASHW_TRAY	Flash the taskbar button.
FLASHW_ALL	Flash both the window caption and taskbar button. This is equivalent to setting the FLASHW_CAPTION and FLASHW_TRAY flags.
FLASHW_TIMER	Flash continuously until the FLASHW_STOP flag is set.
FLASHW_TIMERNOFG	Flash continuously until the window comes to the foreground.

In our example, we used the FLASHW_TIMER to identify that we want to use a timer, and FLASHW_ALL flags to identify that we want both the title bar and taskbar icon to flash. The uCount parameter identifies the number of times we want the window to flash. In our example, we retrieve the flash count from a TEdit control with a default of ten counts. The dwTimeout parameter contains the number of milliseconds the window is to flash. Again, we retrieve a user entry from a TEdit control, this time with a default duration of 100. Using these default values, the target app will flash ten times with one flash every 100 milliseconds for a total duration of flashes at approximately 1,000 milliseconds (or one full second).

CAUTION

FlashWindowEx() is a fairly new Win32 API that is not supported by Windows 95, so use it cautiously. Its older sibling FlashWindow(), however, is supported by Windows 95. The difference is that FlashWindow() does not have the flexibility offered by FlashWindowEx() with such features as a built-in timer and count support.

> If you are developing applications that need to operate under Windows 95, you can mimic `FlashWindowEx()` simply by creating your own function that uses a windows timer, a counter, and `FlashWindow()`. However, be aware that `FlashWindow()` can have varying effects across different versions of Windows, specifically between 9x and NT-based systems. Therefore, if you add this capability, be sure to test your application under various Windows platforms before you deploy your application.

Window Animation Effects

Within C++Builder, you can get some pretty interesting form effects for your apps through the use of `AnimateWindow()`. This is one of the newer features introduced in Windows 98 and Windows 2000. `AnimateWindow()` can be used in place of the standard `ShowWindow()` call used to show or hide a window. It provides window animation effects including slides, blends, center expansions, and contractions of a window. Let's take a look at a short example that uses `AnimateWindows()`.

```
void __fastcall TFormWinMan::Button1Click(TObject *Sender)
{
  // hide it
  AnimateWindow(Handle, 5000, AW_HIDE | AW_SLIDE | AW_VER_POSITIVE);
  // show it
  AnimateWindow(Handle, 5000, AW_ACTIVATE | AW_SLIDE | AW_HOR_POSITIVE);
}
```

In this example, we hide the window represented by the Form's `Handle` property with a five second (5,000 millisecond) animation using a slide effect in the upward vertical direction. Then we reactivate the same window using a slide effect in the right horizontal direction, also in five seconds. It's simple, but can be quite impressive.

`AnimateWindow()` looks quite easy, but if you don't use it correctly, you won't get good results. It has the following parameters:

```
BOOL AnimateWindow(
  HWND hwnd,       // handle to window
  DWORD dwTime,    // duration of animation
  DWORD dwFlags    // animation type
);
```

hwnd is a handle to the window in which you want to animate.

dwTime is the time in milliseconds to perform the animation.

dwFlags represents different flags and types of animation you can perform. Table 14.3 lists the flags from which to choose.

TABLE 14.3 `AnimateWindow()` Flags

Flag	Value
AW_SLIDE	Uses slide animation. By default, roll animation is used. This flag is ignored when used with `AW_CENTER`.
AW_ACTIVATE	Activates the window. Do not use this value with `AW_HIDE`.
AW_BLEND	Uses a fade effect. This flag can be used only if *hwnd* is a top-level window.
AW_HIDE	Hides the window. By default, the window is shown.
AW_CENTER	Makes the window appear to collapse inward if `AW_HIDE` is used. If `AW_HIDE` is not used, the window appears to expand outward.
AW_HOR_POSITIVE	Animates the window from left to right. This flag can be used with roll or slide animation. It is ignored when used with `AW_CENTER` or `AW_BLEND`.
AW_HOR_NEGATIVE	Animates the window from right to left. This flag can be used with roll or slide animation. It is ignored when used with `AW_CENTER` or `AW_BLEND`.
AW_VER_POSITIVE	Animates the window from top to bottom. This flag can be used with roll or slide animation. It is ignored when used with `AW_CENTER` or `AW_BLEND`.
AW_VER_NEGATIVE	Animates the window from bottom to top. This flag can be used with roll or slide animation. It is ignored when used with `AW_CENTER` or `AW_BLEND`.

If `AnimateWindow()` doesn't work, there are typically three reasons why it failed: you are trying to show the window when it is already visible, you are trying to hide the window when it is already hidden, or the thread or process calling `AnimateWindow()` does not own the specified window. In the case of the sample program included on the CD-ROM, the `AnimateWindow()` demo will only work on a window owned by the sample program. If you try it on a window owned by a another process, `AnimateWindow()` will do nothing.

NOTE

Using `AnimateWindow()` might not work for all users because the Animate Windows feature can be disabled within the Windows Control Panel.

Message Identifiers

In our sample program earlier, we used the `RegisterWindowMessage()` API call to dynamically define a unique user-defined Windows message. Our program also issued several different types of predefined Windows Message Identifiers through the

SendMessage() and PostMessage() calls to affect the appearance of other applications. This included WM_CLOSE and WM_SYSCOMMAND.

There are well over 200 predefined Windows Message Identifiers within current versions of Windows that both the Windows system and applications can dispatch. A majority of the predefined Windows Message Identifiers within Windows all begin with the WM_ prefix. Windows Messages are used to signify input, system changes, or direct information passed from one application or windows object to another. In general, Windows Messages are used to perform interrupt handling between applications and/or the operating system. For instance, when a user left clicks the mouse, the system generates a WM_LBUTTONDOWN message to the appropriate application indicating the action that occurred. If a user resizes the active screen, the system generates a WM_SIZE message to the appropriate application indicating the type of resizing and the size values to be applied. The key to making messaging work is to know the *windows handle* for which the message is to be delivered.

Responding to Windows Messages

To respond to specific messages sent either by the SendMessage() or PostMessage() routines, an application needs to have some type of message handling capability. In our sample program, we created our own window message handling procedure, temporarily overriding the form's WndProc method so that it could respond to both user-defined messages, which we created dynamically, and standard Windows Messages.

However, the common way to field Windows Messages that are predefined is to use an event response table. The most popular way to set up an event response table within C++Builder is to declare callback routines and a message map within the protected area of the main form's class declaration. Here is an example:

```
protected:       // User declarations
    void __fastcall Process_wmMoveAWindow(TMessage &);
    void __fastcall Process_wmQuit(TMessage &);
    void __fastcall Process_wmXYZ(TMessage &);
    BEGIN_MESSAGE_MAP
       MESSAGE_HANDLER(WM_PAINT,TMessage,Process_wmPaint);
       MESSAGE_HANDLER(WM_QUIT,TMessage,Process_wmQuit);
       MESSAGE_HANDLER(WM_XYZ,TMessage,Process_wmXYZ);
    END_MESSAGE_MAP(TForm);
```

Within the source code for an application, the callback routine would look something like the following:

```
void __fastcall TForm1::Process_wmXYZ(TMessage Msg)
{
```

```
int fromhandle = LOBYTE(LOWORD(Msg.WParam));
int infoid = Msg.LParam;
AnsiString StatusText =
" Application sent message XYZ\nApplication Handle = " + IntToStr(fromhandle) +
"\nInfo = " + IntToStr(infoid);

MessageBox(Handle,StatusText,"Received Message Callback",MB_OK);
}
```

In this example, Borland's TMessage provides the structure for containing the Windows message information, specifically the 32-bit WParam and LParam values that were passed by the SendMessage() or PostMessage() call. As with most callback routines, in our example we've examined and deciphered the WParam and LParam values.

TIP

Either one of the 32-bit WParam or LParam values passed by SendMessage() or PostMessage() (and contained within the TMessage structure) can also be used to represent a pointer to an accessible address location, but only if the caller resides within the same process as the recipient. In the Win16 days, address space was accessible across multiple processes. Theoretically, you could pass pointers anywhere in the system if you wanted. Win32, however, is much more protected. But the same trick is applicable. If a pointer is passed using WParam or LParam to a DLL resident in the same memory segment or to a local thread, more information than just a 32-bit data value can be shared with other objects. Keep that in mind the next time you need to pass a structure or character string to or from a DLL or thread.

System Services

System service functions allow an application to manage and monitor resources, provide access to files, folders, input and output devices, as well as enable an application to log events and handle errors and exceptions. Furthermore, system services functions provide features that can be used to create other types of applications, such as console applications and driver services.

The Windows kernel library (kernel32.dll) provides a majority of the low-level system service support for the operating environment. This includes file access, interprocess communication (IPC), memory and resource management, and multitasking and multithreading support. All Windows applications use the Windows kernel to operate. For instance, when an application needs memory (both at startup and during execution), it requires the Windows kernel to allocate the necessary memory.

These key aspects of the system services are described in Table 14.4.

TABLE 14.4   Key System Services

Feature	Description
Atoms	Support for sharing strings with applications through 16-bit integer identifiers. Functions include `AddAtom()` and `FindAtom()`.
Clipboard	IPC support for transferring data between applications or within an application. Common functions include `GetClipboardData()` and `SetClipboardData()`. Communication support for communication resources, such as serial ports, parallel ports, modems, and device driver I/O within an application. Functions include `DeviceIoControl()`, `SetupComm()`, and `SetCommState()`.
Console Support	Support of input/output management for character-mode (non-GUI) applications. Involves the use of an input buffer for capturing keyboard and mouse events, and one or more screen buffers for character and color data output. Functions include `AllocConsole()` and `FreeConsole()`.
Debugging	Provides event-driven support for application debugging. Functions such as `DebugActiveProcess()` and `WaitForDebugEvent()` enable an application to debug events, cause breakpoint exceptions, and transfer execution control to the debugger.
Dynamic Data Exchange (DDE)	IPC support for transferring data between applications. DDE functions such as `DdeNameService()` and `DdeConnect()` are provided through the user library (`user32.dll`), but requires access to the DDE Management Library (`ddeml.dll`).
Dynamic Link Library (DLL)	Support for creating and managing libraries that can be loaded by an application at runtime. Functions include `LoadLibrary()` and `FreeLibrary()`.
Error Message	Support for handling messages such as `MessageBeep()` and `FlashWindow()`. Error Message functions are actually supported by the user library (`user32.dll`).
Event Logging	Support for recording application events into a log such as `RegisterEventSource()`.
File Mapping	IPC support for mapping a file's contents to a virtual address location, such as `CreateFileMapping()`.
Files	Support for file input and output of storage media such as `CopyFile()` and `CreateDirectory()`.
Handles and Objects	Support for creating and managing handles and objects that provide an abstract and secure access to Windows system resources, such as `SetHandleInformation()`.

TABLE 14.4   Continued

Feature	Description
Help Support	Support routines used in conjunction with the Windows Help application, such as `WinHelp()`. Help support is actually provided by the user library (`user32.dll`), but Microsoft considers help support to be a facet of system services.
Large Integer Operations	Support for 64-bit integer operations. Functions include `Int32x32To64()`, `UInt32x32To64()`, and `MulDiv()`.
Mailslots	Support for creating and managing one-way IPC (mailslots) over a network. Functions include `CreateMailslot()`, `GetMailslotInfo()`, and `SetMailslotInfo()`.
Memory Management	Support for allocating and using memory. Functions include `GlobalAlloc()`, `FillMemory()`, and `CopyMemory()`.
Pipes	Support for creating, managing, and using pipes. Pipes are IPC communication conduits that enable one process to communicate with another process. Functions include `CreatePipe()` and `GetNamedPipeInfo()`.
Portable Execution (PE) File Manipulation	Support for manipulating or accessing a portable executable (PE) binary image, which is created by a compatible Win32 linker. The `IMAGEHLP` DLL provides PE functions that support image access, modification, integrity checking, plus debugging services. Functions include `BindImage()`, `StackWalk()`, and `SymEnumerateModules()`.
Power Management	Provides functions and messages that reveal the system power status and notify of power management events. Functions include `GetSystemPowerStatus()` and `SetSystemPowerStatus()`.
Process and Thread Management	Support for multitasking, scheduling, creating, and managing multiple threads and child processes within an application. Functions include `CreateProcess()` and `CreateThread()`.
Registry	Support for storing, accessing, and managing the Windows system-defined database with application and system component configuration data. Functions include `RegOpenKey()`, `RegEnumKey()`, and `RegSaveKey()`.
Security	NT support for granting or denying application and user access to an object. Many of the security routines are provided by the Advanced API library (`advapi32.dll`). Functions include `SetFileSecurity()` and `GetFileSecurity()`.
Services	Support for automated services in which an application (or driver) can operate without user intervention (or user knowledge). Support for these types of applications is controlled by the Service Control Manager (SCM). The Advanced API library

TABLE 14.4   Continued

Feature	Description
	(advapi32.dll) provides many of the service routines. Functions include CreateService() and StartService().
String Manipulation	Support for copying, comparing, sorting, formatting, and converting character strings and determining character types. Provides Unicode support. Functions include lstrcat(), CharLower(), and IsCharAlpha().
Structured Exception Handling	Provides compiler support for exception handling and termination. Functions include RaiseException() and GetExceptionCode().
Synchronization	Provides mechanisms that threads can use to synchronize access to a resource. Functions include CreateMutex() and WaitForSingleObject().
System Information	Support for determining and retrieving system information such as computer name, username, environment variables settings, processor type, and system-color information. Functions include GetSystemInfo() and GetSysColor().
System Messages	Support for notifying applications and drivers of device change events. System Message support is provided by the user library (user32.dll). Functions include RegisterWindowMessage(), SendMessage(), and PostMessage(), which are also used to provide Windows Management support.
System Shutdown	Support for logging off the current user or shutting down the system. System Shutdown support is provided by both the user32.dll and advapi32.dll. Functions include ExitWindows() and InititateSystemShutdown().
Tape Backup	Support for enabling backup applications to perform tape read/write and initialization and retrieving tape and drive information. Functions include CreateTapePartition() and GetTapeParameters().
Time	Support for retrieving and setting the date and the time for the system, files, and the local time zone. Functions include GetFileTime() and SetSystemTime().
Window Stations and Desktops	Service support for secured objects (called window stations and desktops) in making USER32 and GDI32 function calls, regardless of the user logon status. Intended for developers of services, not application developers. Functions include CreateWindowStation() and CloseDesktop(), which is provided by the user library (user32.dll).

As you can see, there are vast amounts of system services provided by the Win32 API. In fact, there are more than 750 system service routines alone in the kernel library (kernel32.dll), and more system service support provided by the user library (usr32.dll) and ancillary libraries such as the imagehlp.dll and advapi32.dll. To view the full list of the available functions provided by these libraries, use Borland's impdef command-line tool or the DLL LIB Util utility, described in the Tip earlier.

Let's now look at some example code in C++Builder that uses a few of the System Services routines mentioned in Table 14.4.

System Services Example

In the source code that's provided on the CD-ROM for this chapter is a project called WinSysUtil. This project contains sample code that utilizes several useful System Services API calls for attaining system, memory, disk, and file information. The WinSysUtil application is illustrated in Figure 14.5

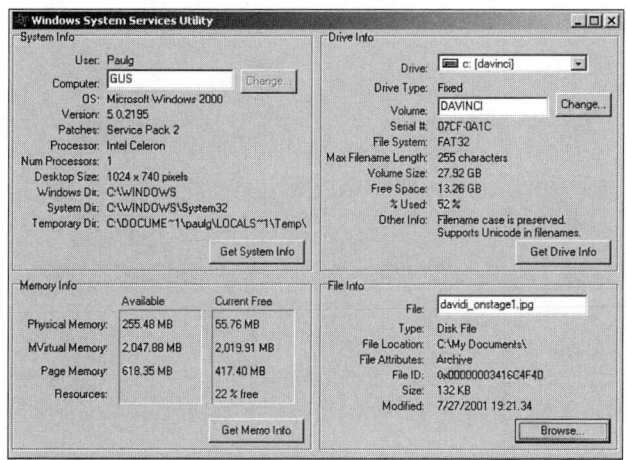

FIGURE 14.5   Windows System Services Utility screen shot.

In this sample, we'll examine four different aspects of the program that demonstrate the application of System Services for retrieving system, memory, disk, and file information.

System Information

System Information includes such things as determining login names, computer names, and the Windows version. Listing 14.4 shows some of the source code used to attain and display system information.

LISTING 14.4   System Service Utility—System Information

```
void __fastcall TFormSystemService::ButtonSystemInfoClick(TObject *Sender)
{
    // get user
    char name[MAX_PATH];
    DWORD size = MAX_PATH;
    GetUserName(name, &size);    // Win32 API call
    LabelUser->Caption = AnsiString(name);

    // get computer name
    char computername[MAX_COMPUTERNAME_LENGTH];
    size = MAX_COMPUTERNAME_LENGTH;
    GetComputerName(computername, &size);    // Win32 API call
    EditComputer->Text = ComputerName();

    // let's get the windows version
    char os[MAX_PATH];
    char version[MAX_PATH];
    char patch[MAX_PATH];
    bool NT = WindowsVersion(os,version,patch);   // Win32 API "wrapper"
    LabelOS->Caption = AnsiString(os);
    LabelVersion->Caption = AnsiString(version);
    LabelOther->Caption = AnsiString(patch);

    // let's get the processor info
    char processor[MAX_PATH];
    LabelNumProcessors->Caption =
                 ProcessorInfo(NT,processor); // Win32 API "wrapper"
    LabelProcessor->Caption = AnsiString(processor);

    LabelScreenSize->Caption = ScreenSize();

    char dir[MAX_PATH];
    dir[0] = '\0';
    GetWindowsDirectory(dir,MAX_PATH);
    LabelWinDir->Caption = AnsiString(dir);

    dir[0] = '\0';
    GetSystemDirectory(dir,MAX_PATH);
    LabelSysDir->Caption = AnsiString(dir);

    dir[0] = '\0';
```

LISTING 14.4   Continued

```
    GetTempPath(MAX_PATH, dir);
    LabelTempDir->Caption = AnsiString(dir);
}


//--------------------------------------------------------------------------


bool __fastcall TFormSystemService::WindowsVersion(char * os, char * version, char
* other)
{
    bool NT = false;

    OSVERSIONINFO version_info;

    version_info.dwOSVersionInfoSize = sizeof(OSVERSIONINFO); // initilize size
    GetVersionEx(&version_info); // now let's get version info - Win32 API call

    if(version_info.dwMajorVersion < 4)  // must be win nt 3.x
    {
        sprintf(os,"Windows NT ");
        sprintf(version,"3.x");
    }
    else
    {
        sprintf(version,"%d.%d.%04d",version_info.dwMajorVersion,
                        version_info.dwMinorVersion,
                        version_info.dwBuildNumber);
    }
    switch (version_info.dwPlatformId)
    {
        case VER_PLATFORM_WIN32s:
            sprintf(os,"%s","Microsoft Win32s");
            break;
        case VER_PLATFORM_WIN32_WINDOWS:
            sprintf(os,"%s","Microsoft Windows 95/98");
            break;
        case VER_PLATFORM_WIN32_NT:
            NT = true;
            switch (version_info.dwMajorVersion)
            {
                case 4: sprintf(os,"%s","Microsoft Windows NT"); break;
                case 5: sprintf(os,"%s","Microsoft Windows 2000"); break;
```

LISTING 14.4   Continued

```
                case 6: sprintf(os,"%s","Microsoft Windows XP"); break;
                default :
                    sprintf(os,"%s","Microsoft Windows ??");
            }
            break;
        default : // unknown
            sprintf(os,"%s","Microsoft Windows ??");
    }
    sprintf(other,"%s",version_info.szCSDVersion);
    return NT;
}


//-------------------------------------------------------------------------

int __fastcall TFormSystemService::ProcessorInfo(bool NT, char* processor)
{
    SYSTEM_INFO sys_info;

    AnsiString Processor;
    AnsiString Level = "";
    GetSystemInfo(&sys_info); // determine processor type - Win32 API call
    int value;
    if (NT)
    {
        switch (sys_info.wProcessorArchitecture)
        {
            case  PROCESSOR_ARCHITECTURE_INTEL :
                Processor = "Intel";
                switch (sys_info.wProcessorLevel)
                {
                    case  3 : Level = "80386"; break;
                    case  4 : Level = "80486"; break;
                    case  5 : Level = "Pentium"; break;
                    case  6 :
                        value = HIBYTE(sys_info.wProcessorRevision);
                        switch (value)
                        {
                          case  1           : Level = "Pentium PRO"; break;
                          case  3,5         : Level = "Pentium 2"; break;
                          case  6           : Level = "Celeron"; break;
                          case  7,8,10,11 : Level = "Pentium 3"; break;
```

LISTING 14.4   Continued

```
                    }
                    break;
                case 15 : Level = "Pentium 4"; break;
                default : Level = "unknown";
            }
            break;
        case  PROCESSOR_ARCHITECTURE_ALPHA :
            Processor = "ALPHA";
            switch (sys_info.wProcessorLevel)
            {
                case  21064 : Level = "21064"; break;
                case  21066 : Level = "21066"; break;
                case  21164 : Level = "21164"; break;
                default :   Level = "unknown";
            }
            break;
        case  PROCESSOR_ARCHITECTURE_MIPS :
            Processor = "MIPS";
            switch (sys_info.wProcessorLevel)
            {
                case  0004 : Level = "R4000"; break;
                default :   Level = "unknown";
            }
            break;
        case  PROCESSOR_ARCHITECTURE_PPC :
            Processor = "PPC";
            switch (sys_info.wProcessorLevel)
            {
                case  1 : Level = "601"; break;
                case  3 : Level = "603"; break;
                case  4 : Level = "604"; break;
                case  6 : Level = "603+"; break;
                case  9 : Level = "604+"; break;
                case 20 : Level = "620"; break;
                default :   Level = "unknown";
            }
            break;
        default :   Processor = "unknown";
        }
    }
}
else  // Win 9x
```

LISTING 14.4   Continued

```
    {
        switch (sys_info.dwProcessorType)
        {
            case  PROCESSOR_INTEL_386     :
                    Processor = "Intel"; Level = "80386"; break;
            case  PROCESSOR_INTEL_486     :
                    Processor = "Intel"; Level = "80486"; break;
            case  PROCESSOR_INTEL_PENTIUM :
                    Processor = "Intel"; Level = "Pentium"; break;
            default:   Processor = "unknown";
        }
    }
    sprintf(processor,"%s %s",Processor.c_str(),Level.c_str());
    return sys_info.dwNumberOfProcessors;
}

//---------------------------------------------------------------------------

AnsiString TFormSystemService::ScreenSize()
{
    AnsiString value;

    RECT screen_coords;
    SystemParametersInfo(SPI_GETWORKAREA,0, &screen_coords, 0); //Win32 API call

    int width  = screen_coords.right - screen_coords.left;
    int height = screen_coords.bottom - screen_coords.top;
/*
   // here's another way, but width and height is obsurced by the tray

    int height = GetSystemMetrics(SM_CYFULLSCREEN);
    int width  = GetSystemMetrics(SM_CXFULLSCREEN);
*/
    value = AnsiString(width) + " x " + AnsiString(height) + " pixels";
    return value;
}

//---------------------------------------------------------------------------

void __fastcall TFormSystemService::ButtonChangeComputerClick(TObject *Sender)
{
```

LISTING 14.4   Continued

```
    SetComputerName(EditComputer->Text.c_str());
    if (MessageBox(Handle,"You must reboot system for change to take affect.",
            "Reboot System?",MB_YESNO) == IDYES)
    {
        bool success = ExitWindowsEx(EWX_REBOOT, 0);
        if (!success)
            MessageBox(Handle,
                "Unable to shutdown system due to a system restriction.",
                "System Restriction",MB_OK);
        else
            Close();
    }
}
```

In this example, the ButtonSystemInfoClick() event handler initiates the system calls in gathering the desired system information when the user clicks Get System Info. The first Win32 API call made is to GetUserName(), which provides the name of the user logged onto the system. A name buffer and the address to the size variable are passed as parameters into the GetUserName() function.

The GetComputerName() API function is used next to retrieve the computer label name identified within the Registry. As you can see in the code listing, GetComputerName() behaves very similar to GetUserName().

Now, we want to retrieve the Windows version information and display it to the user. The Win32 API call used to gain this information is provided by the GetVersionEx(). However, because of the complexities associated to deciphering the Windows version, we've placed the Windows version processing information inside a custom wrapper function called WindowsVersion(). Our ButtonSystemInfoClick() event handler makes a call to this custom function by passing three character strings: os, version, and patch. In return, we will receive the os label, such as Microsoft Windows 2000; the version, such as 5.00.2195; and patch information, such as Service Pack 2. Plus, a boolean result value will be returned indicating if the OS is of the NT genre or not. This information will be important a little later.

Let's take a closer look at the WindowsVersion() method we've created to handle this version processing. As mentioned earlier, the GetVersionEx() call is used to collect the system information. After this call is made within our custom wrapper function, we need to start examining the fields associated to the version_info variable, which is based on the OSVERSIONINFO structure. The version_info variable contains the following fields:

```
DWORD dwOSVersionInfoSize;
DWORD dwMajorVersion;
DWORD dwMinorVersion;
DWORD dwBuildNumber;
DWORD dwPlatformId;
TCHAR szCSDVersion[ 128 ];
```

As shown in the code listing, the WindowsVersion() wrapper function examines the dwMajorVersion and dwPlatformId to determine the Operating System (OS). It then uses dwMajorVersion, dwMinorVersion, and dwBuildNumber to annotate the OS version. And finally, it uses the szCSDVersion character string to identify the latest patch update applied to the OS. If the dwPlatformId value is equal to VER_PLATFORM_WIN32_NT, the function returns a true result to identify that the OS is NT-based.

Let's now step back into the ButtonSystemInfoClick() method and see how we determine the remaining System information. After retrieving the Windows Version information, the next task for our method is to gather and display information regarding the computer's processor. Determining the type of processor is not a trivial task. Over the course of the last decade, an assortment of processors have been introduced, many of which can be supported using current versions of Windows. So, again, we have created a custom method called ProcessorInfo() based on the GetSystemInfo() Win32 API call, which serves as a wrapper for retrieving and dissecting system information and returning a processor type. As one of the inputs, this method needs to know whether the OS is part of the 9x family or if it is NT-based. Fortunately, we determined that piece of information earlier with the WindowsVersion() wrapper. We need it because the application of GetSystemInfo() and the extraction of data from the sys_info variable, which is based on the SYSTEM_INFO structure, varies depending on the OS. Let's take a look at the SYSTEM_INFO structure.

```
typedef struct _SYSTEM_INFO { // sinf
    union {
        DWORD   dwOemId;
        struct {
            WORD wProcessorArchitecture;
            WORD wReserved;
        };
    };
    DWORD   dwPageSize;
    LPVOID  lpMinimumApplicationAddress;
    LPVOID  lpMaximumApplicationAddress;
    DWORD   dwActiveProcessorMask;
    DWORD   dwNumberOfProcessors;
    DWORD   dwProcessorType;
```

```
    DWORD   dwAllocationGranularity;
    WORD    wProcessorLevel;
    WORD    wProcessorRevision;
} SYSTEM_INFO;
```

If the OS is NT-based, the wProcessorArchitecture and wProcessorLevel is used to determine the processor. Otherwise, the dwProcessorType is used for Windows 9x systems. We also use dwNumberOfProcessors to determine the number of processors within the system. If more than one processor exists, we can use the dwActiveProcessorMask to identify the processor we want to examine.

After ButtonSystemInfoClick() receives and displays the processor information, we calculate the available working space (also known as screen size) for the display. Again, we have created a custom function called ScreenSize() that calculates the screen dimensions based on the SystemParametersInfo() Win32 API call. There are other routines, such as GetSystemMetrics() in combination with the SM_CYFULLSCREEN and SM_CXFULLSCREEN flags, that can be used to determine screen space as well. However, the SystemParametersInfo() call with the SPI_GETWORKAREA flag provides screen dimensions not obstructed by the taskbar.

In many applications, it can be useful to know the location of both the Windows and System directories. Sometimes it is also useful to store data or files in a temporary file location such as the Windows Temp directory. The location of these directories, however, can vary on each computer. Fortunately, the Win32 API provides the functionality to obtain this information through the GetWindowsDirectory(), GetSystemDirectory(), and GetTempPath(), respectively.

The last three activities performed by the ButtonSystemInfoClick() event handler retrieves and displays the Windows, Windows System and temporary paths for the OS and uses these API functions. Each of these calls requires two parameters: the size and a string.

CAUTION

You might notice that the order of the parameters among these similar calls is not the same. For some reason the implementer of GetTempPath() unintentionally selected a parameter order that was reverse from the way GetWindowsDirectory(), GetSystemDirectory(), and other routines such as GetUserName() and GetComputerName() were prototyped. Often the assumption is that because these calls all have the first parameter as the address to a string, and the second parameter identifying the string size, the same follows suite for GetTempPath() or any other similar Win32 API function. This proves, once again, that it's good practice to double-check the Help file before going to code.

We have one more feature in this sample code manifested in the `ButtonChangeComputerClick()` event handler. This handler gets kicked off when the user has decided to change the computer name for the system. The `SetComputerName()` Win32 API routine provides the capability to make this change happen. For it to take effect, however, the computer needs to be restarted. The `ExitWindowsEx()` Win32 API provides the capability to do this reboot. Yet, under Windows NT, the user might be restricted in performing automated shutdown and reboots.

`ExitWindowsEx()` is an easy way to shut down or restart Windows, but you can do a lot more than just shut down Windows. The `ExitWindowEx()` function has more flags with which to work. The format is as follows:

```
BOOL ExitWindowsEx(
    UINT uFlags,      // shutdown operation
    DWORD dwReserved      // reserved
  );
```

`uFlags` are flags to specify which shutdown type you wish to perform. Table 14.5 shows the values.

TABLE 14.5   System Shutdown Function Flags

Flags	Value
EWX_FORCE	Forces processes to terminate. When this flag is set, Windows does not send the messages WM_QUERYENDSESSION and WM_ENDSESSION to the applications currently running in the system. This can cause the applications to lose data, so you should use this flag only in an emergency.
EWX_LOGOFF	Shuts down all processes running in the security context of the process that called the ExitWindowsEx() function. Then, it logs the user off.
EWX_POWEROFF	Shuts down the system and turns off the power. The system must support the power-off feature. Windows NT: The calling process must have the SE_SHUTDOWN_NAME privilege. Windows 95: Security privileges are not supported or required.
EWX_REBOOT	Shuts down and restarts the system. Windows NT: The calling process must have the SE_SHUTDOWN_NAME privilege.
EWX_SHUTDOWN	Shuts down the system to a point at which it is safe to turn off the power. All file buffers have been flushed to disk, and all running processes have stopped. Windows NT: The calling process must have the SE_SHUTDOWN_NAME privilege.

The `dwReserved` parameter is currently not used.

Memory Information

Let's now take a look at a shorter example from this sample that uses the Win32 System Service calls to gather and display the memory information (see Listing 14.5).

LISTING 14.5   Windows System Service Utility—Memory Example

```
void __fastcall TFormSystemService::ButtonGetMemInfoClick(TObject *Sender)
{
  MEMORYSTATUS memory ;
  memory.dwLength = sizeof (memory) ;
  GlobalMemoryStatus (&memory) ;

  LabelPTotal->Caption  = FormatSize((memory.dwTotalPhys/1024));
  LabelPFree->Caption   = FormatSize((memory.dwAvailPhys/1024));
  LabelPgTotal->Caption = FormatSize((memory.dwTotalPageFile/1024));
  LabelPgFree->Caption  = FormatSize((memory.dwAvailPageFile/1024));
  LabelVTotal->Caption  = FormatSize((memory.dwTotalVirtual/1024));
  LabelVFree->Caption   = FormatSize((memory.dwAvailVirtual/1024));

  double value1 = double(double(memory.dwAvailPhys*100.0)/memory.dwTotalPhys);
  double value = 100.0-memory.dwMemoryLoad;

  if (value1 > value)
     value = long(value1);

  LabelFree->Caption  = AnsiString(value) + " % free";;
}
```

The ButtonGetMemInfoClick() event handler uses a special Win32 API function called GlobalMemoryStatus(), which enables us to determine memory statistics such as available memory and page size. The MEMORYSTATUS structure used for the memory variable provides the properties that are filled by the GlobalMemoryStatus() call. Let's take a quick look at the MEMORYSTATUS structure.

```
typedef struct _MEMORYSTATUS { // mst
    DWORD dwLength;          // sizeof(MEMORYSTATUS)
    DWORD dwMemoryLoad;      // percent of memory in use
    DWORD dwTotalPhys;       // bytes of physical memory
    DWORD dwAvailPhys;       // free physical memory bytes
    DWORD dwTotalPageFile;   // bytes of paging file
    DWORD dwAvailPageFile;   // free bytes of paging file
    DWORD dwTotalVirtual;    // user bytes of address space
    DWORD dwAvailVirtual;    // free user bytes
} MEMORYSTATUS, *LPMEMORYSTATUS;
```

In our example, each of the memory property values calculated by
GlobalMemoryStatus() are displayed to the user. Also, the percentage of physical
memory available to the system is calculated and displayed. These values and calculations can be extremely useful for your applications in determining performance
capabilities and resource restrictions. In fact, the performance between a Windows
9x box and a Windows NT-based box, such as 2000 or XP, can be very revealing
when using GlobalMemoryStatus().

Drive Information

Let's now take a look at some other code from this sample that uses the Win32
System Service calls to provide drive information such as volume name, serial
number, and available diskspace (see Listing 14.6).

LISTING 14.6   Windows System Service Utility—Drive Information Example

```
void __fastcall TFormSystemService::ButtonGetDriveInfoClick(TObject *Sender)
{
  AnsiString temp;
  AnsiString Drive = AnsiString(DriveComboBox1->Drive) + ":\\"; //EditDrive->Text;

  unsigned int drivetype = GetDriveType(Drive.c_str ());

  switch (drivetype)
  {
    case 1    : temp = "No root directory";   return;
    case DRIVE_REMOVABLE : temp = "Removable";  break;
    case DRIVE_FIXED     : temp = "Fixed";        break;
    case DRIVE_REMOTE    : temp = "Remote (network) drive";  break;
    case DRIVE_CDROM     : temp = "CD-ROM";       break;
    case DRIVE_RAMDISK   : temp = "RAM disk";     break;
    default:  temp = "Unknown"; return;
  }

  LabelDriveType->Caption = temp;
  temp = "";
  DWORD VolumeSerialNumber = 0;
  DWORD MaximumComponentLength = 0;
  DWORD FileSystemFlags = 0;
  char * volumeinfo = new char[255];
  volumeinfo[0] = 0;
  char* FileSystemNameBuffer = new char[255];
  FileSystemNameBuffer[0] = 0;
  GetVolumeInformation (Drive.c_str (), volumeinfo,
```

LISTING 14.6   Continued

```
                            255, &VolumeSerialNumber,
                            &MaximumComponentLength, &FileSystemFlags,
                            ➥FileSystemNameBuffer,255);
    if (strlen(volumeinfo) != 0)
        EditVolumeInfo->Text = volumeinfo ;
    else
        EditVolumeInfo->Text = "- no label -";


    //Translate integer to chars for serial number
    char string1[35];
    char string2[35];
    if (VolumeSerialNumber > 0)
    {
      unsigned int bottom = (LOWORD(VolumeSerialNumber));
      unsigned int top = (HIWORD(VolumeSerialNumber));
      sprintf(string1,"%04X",top);
      sprintf(string2,"%04X",bottom);
      LabelSerialNum->Caption = AnsiString(string1) + "-" + AnsiString(string2);
    }
    else
      LabelSerialNum->Caption = "- unknown -";
    if (MaximumComponentLength > 0)
      LabelMaxComponentLength->Caption = AnsiString(MaximumComponentLength) + "
      ➥characters";
    else
      LabelMaxComponentLength->Caption = "- unknown -";
    if (strlen(FileSystemNameBuffer) != 0)
        LabelFileSystemNameBuffer->Caption = FileSystemNameBuffer;
    else
        LabelFileSystemNameBuffer->Caption = "- unknown -";


    LabelFileSystemFlags->Caption = ""; //AnsiString(FileSystemFlags);
    if (FileSystemFlags & FS_CASE_IS_PRESERVED)
        temp += AnsiString("Filename case is preserved.\n");
    if (FileSystemFlags & FS_CASE_SENSITIVE)
        temp += AnsiString("Lookup is case-sensitive.\n");
    if (FileSystemFlags & FS_UNICODE_STORED_ON_DISK)
        temp += AnsiString("Supports Unicode in filenames.\n");
    if (FileSystemFlags & FS_PERSISTENT_ACLS)
        temp += AnsiString("Preserves and enforces ACLs.\n");
    if (FileSystemFlags & FS_FILE_COMPRESSION)
```

LISTING 14.6   Continued

```
        temp += AnsiString("Supports file-based compression.\n");
    if (FileSystemFlags & FS_VOL_IS_COMPRESSED)
        temp += AnsiString("Volume is compressed. (i.e., DoubleSpace).\n");
    LabelFileSystemFlags->Caption = temp;

    DWORD spc = 0;      //Sectors per cluster
    DWORD bps = 0;      //Bytes per cluster
    DWORD cluster = 0;   //clusters
    DWORD freeclust = 0;    //freeclusters

    GetDiskFreeSpace (Drive.c_str (),&spc,&bps,&freeclust,&cluster) ;
    unsigned long v1 = (unsigned long)cluster;
    unsigned long v2 = (unsigned long) spc;
    unsigned long v3 = (unsigned long) bps;
    unsigned long volsize = (v1 * v2)/1024 * v3;
    LabelVolumeSize->Caption = AnsiString(FormatSize(volsize));

    unsigned long free_bytes = (freeclust * spc)/1024 * bps;
    LabelFreeSpace->Caption = AnsiString(FormatSize(free_bytes));

    if (volsize > 0)
        LabelUsed->Caption = AnsiString(((volsize - free_bytes) * 100) / volsize) +
        ➥" %";
    else
        LabelUsed->Caption = "n/a";
}

//---------------------------------------------------------------------------

void __fastcall TFormSystemService::DriveComboBox1Change(TObject *Sender)
{
  ButtonGetDriveInfoClick(Sender);
}

//---------------------------------------------------------------------------

void __fastcall TFormSystemService::ButtonChangeVolumeLabelClick(TObject *Sender)
{
  AnsiString Drive = AnsiString(DriveComboBox1->Drive) + ":\\"; //EditDrive->Text;

  bool success = SetVolumeLabel(
```

LISTING 14.6 Continued

```
                    Drive.c_str(),
                    EditVolumeInfo->Text.c_str());

if  (!success)
    MessageBox(Handle,
        "Unable to change volume label due to a system restriction.",
        "System Restriction",MB_OK);
else
    ButtonGetDriveInfoClick(Sender);
}
```

In this example, the `ButtonGetDriveInfoClick()` event handler uses three primary Win32 API calls to gather disk information: `GetDriveType()`, `GetVolumeInformation()`, and `GetDiskFreeSpace()`.

`GetDriveType()` is simply used to determine the type of drive the user wants to examine. Options include removable, fixed, and remote drives as well as CD-ROM, which includes DVD drives, and RAM disks.

The `GetVolumeInformation()` provides even more revealing information including the volume label, serial number, maximum allowable filename length (called component length by Microsoft), and associated file system flags. The `GetVolumeInformation()` function has the following parameters:

```
BOOL GetVolumeInformation(
    LPCTSTR lpRootPathName,         // address of root directory of the file system
    LPTSTR lpVolumeNameBuffer,      // address of name of the volume
    DWORD nVolumeNameSize,          // length of lpVolumeNameBuffer
    LPDWORD lpVolumeSerialNumber,   // address of volume serial number
    LPDWORD lpMaximumComponentLength,// address of system's maximum filename length
    LPDWORD lpFileSystemFlags,      // address of file system flags
    LPTSTR lpFileSystemNameBuffer,  // address of name of file system
    DWORD nFileSystemNameSize       // length of lpFileSystemNameBuffer
    );
```

Each of these parameters that are returned by the `GetVolumeInformation()` function provide something of interest that we can display to the user. For developers, a value such as the `lpVolumeSerialNumber` could be found useful in supporting the licensing and registration of software.

Finally, `GetDiskFreeSpace()` is used to determine the size and available space on a drive. The `GetDiskFreeSpace()` function has the following parameters:

```
BOOL GetDiskFreeSpace(
    LPCTSTR lpRootPathName,      // address of root path
    LPDWORD lpSectorsPerCluster,     // address of sectors per cluster
    LPDWORD lpBytesPerSector,     // address of bytes per sector
    LPDWORD lpNumberOfFreeClusters,     // address of number of free clusters
    LPDWORD lpTotalNumberOfClusters      // address of total number of clusters
    );
```

By using a little math, we can determine the volume size and the available free space in terms of bytes, which is a much more universally understood quantity than clusters. Multiplying the lpBytesPerSector and pSectorsPerCluster with the lpTotalNumberOfClusters for the volume size and the lpNumberOfFreeClusters for the available free space does this.

In this example, we also have code in ButtonChangeVolumeLabelClick() that can change the Volume label. This is accomplished using the SetVolumeLabel() API call.

File Information
Finally let's take a look at some code from this sample that uses the Win32 System Service calls to provide file information (see Listing 14.7). This information includes file type, attributes, size, and the date and time the file was last modified.

LISTING 14.7   Windows System Service Utility—Final Information Example

```
void __fastcall TFormSystemService::ButtonGetFileInfoClick(TObject *Sender)
{
  if(OpenDialog1->Execute())
  {
      EditFilename->Text = ExtractFileName(OpenDialog1->FileName);
      LabelLocation->Caption = ExtractFilePath(OpenDialog1->FileName);

      // clear out everything
      LabelAttrib->Caption = "";
      LabelFileID->Caption = "";
      LabelDateTime->Caption = "";

      // let's open the file
      HANDLE FileHandle = CreateFile(OpenDialog1->FileName.c_str(),
              GENERIC_READ, 0, NULL, OPEN_EXISTING, 0, NULL);

      if (FileHandle == INVALID_HANDLE_VALUE)
      {
```

LISTING 14.7   Continued

```
            MessageBox(Handle, OpenDialog1->FileName.c_str(),
                        "Unable to open file", MB_ICONSTOP | IDOK);
        return;
    }
    else // // get file type
    {
        DWORD FileType = GetFileType(FileHandle);
        switch (FileType)
        {
            case FILE_TYPE_DISK:
                LabelFileType->Caption = "Disk File";
                break;
            case FILE_TYPE_CHAR:
                LabelFileType->Caption = "Character";
                return;  // can't do much else
            case FILE_TYPE_PIPE:
                LabelFileType->Caption = "Anonymous Pipe";
                return;  // can't do much else
            default : LabelFileType->Caption = "Unknown";
        }
    }


    // get more information
    BY_HANDLE_FILE_INFORMATION FileInfo;
    GetFileInformationByHandle(FileHandle, &FileInfo);
    AnsiString temp;
    if (FileInfo.dwFileAttributes & FILE_ATTRIBUTE_ARCHIVE)
            temp += "Archive ";
    if (FileInfo.dwFileAttributes & FILE_ATTRIBUTE_COMPRESSED)
            temp += "Compressed ";
    if (FileInfo.dwFileAttributes & FILE_ATTRIBUTE_DIRECTORY)
            temp += "Directory ";
    if (FileInfo.dwFileAttributes & FILE_ATTRIBUTE_HIDDEN)
            temp += "Hidden ";
    if (FileInfo.dwFileAttributes & FILE_ATTRIBUTE_NORMAL)
            temp += "Normal ";
    if (FileInfo.dwFileAttributes & FILE_ATTRIBUTE_OFFLINE)
            temp += "Offline ";
    if (FileInfo.dwFileAttributes & FILE_ATTRIBUTE_READONLY)
            temp += "Readonly ";
    if (FileInfo.dwFileAttributes & FILE_ATTRIBUTE_SYSTEM)
```

LISTING 14.7   Continued

```
                temp += "System ";
        if (FileInfo.dwFileAttributes & FILE_ATTRIBUTE_TEMPORARY)
                temp += "Temporary Storage ";
        LabelAttrib->Caption = temp;

        char string1[35];
        char string2[35];
        sprintf(string1,"%08X",FileInfo.nFileIndexHigh);
        sprintf(string2,"%08X",FileInfo.nFileIndexLow);
        LabelFileID->Caption = "0x" + AnsiString(string1) + AnsiString(string2);
        ➥//hex

        LabelFileSize->Caption =  FormatSize(double(FileInfo.nFileSizeLow / 1024.0));

        SYSTEMTIME SysTime;  // system time and date
        FileTimeToSystemTime(&FileInfo.ftLastWriteTime, &SysTime);
        char date[255];
        char time[255];
        sprintf(date,"%u/%u/%4u",
            SysTime.wMonth, SysTime.wDay, SysTime.wYear);
        sprintf(time,"%2u:%02u.%02u",
            SysTime.wHour, SysTime.wMinute, SysTime.wSecond);
        LabelDateTime->Caption = AnsiString(date) + " " + AnsiString(time);

        CloseHandle(FileHandle);
    }
}
```

The first Win32 API call made in the `ButtonGetFileInfoClick()` event handler routine
is `CreateFile()`. `CreateFile()` can be used for creating or opening the following types
of objects:

- files

- pipes

- mailslots

- communications resources

- disk devices (Windows NT only)

- consoles

- directories (open only)

In this example, CreateFile() is used to obtain a handle to a common file, which will be examined using other API calls within the event handler. The parameters of interest passed into CreateFile() include the filename, which was obtained through Borland's TOpenDialog, a desired access of read-only established through the GENERIC_READ flag, and an action to open an existing file through the OPEN_EXISTING flag.

After the file handle is obtained, a call is made to the Win32 API routine GetFileType() with the handle, which subsequently returns the type of file to be examined. File types include disk file, character, or an anonymous pipe. We're interested in the disk files in this example.

GetFileInformationByHandle() is then used to retrieve the bulk of the file information desired. The GetFileInformationByHandle() function has the following parameters:

```
BOOL GetFileInformationByHandle(
    HANDLE hFile,        // handle of file
    LPBY_HANDLE_FILE_INFORMATION lpFileInformation      // address of structure
    );
```

The second parameter, which points to a variable defined by the LPBY_HANDLE_FILE_INFORMATION, is key for capturing the file information.

Let's take a look at the LPBY_HANDLE_FILE_INFORMATION structure.

```
typedef struct _BY_HANDLE_FILE_INFORMATION { // bhfi
    DWORD    dwFileAttributes;
    FILETIME ftCreationTime;
    FILETIME ftLastAccessTime;
    FILETIME ftLastWriteTime;
    DWORD    dwVolumeSerialNumber;
    DWORD    nFileSizeHigh;
    DWORD    nFileSizeLow;
    DWORD    nNumberOfLinks;
    DWORD    nFileIndexHigh;
    DWORD    nFileIndexLow;
} BY_HANDLE_FILE_INFORMATION;
```

For this example, the properties of interest provided include dwFileAttributes for obtaining the attributes, nFileIndexHigh and nFileIndexLow for determining the file ID, nFileSizeLow for determining the file size, and ftLastWriteTime for determining the file modification date and time.

Finally, it's important to clean up properly by closing the file handle that we've examined. This is accomplished through the CloseHandle() Win32 API routine.

NOTE

We can also obtain the file size using the Win32 API routine `GetFileSize()`, which returns the file size as an integer. `GetFileSize()` is declared as follows:

```
DWORD GetFileSize(
  HANDLE hFile,           // handle to file
  LPDWORD lpFileSizeHigh  // high-order word of file size
);
```

You might be asking, "If `GetFileSize()` returns the file size, what is the second parameter `lpFileSizeHigh` for?" Well, back in the early days of Windows development Microsoft apparently had the foresight to recognize that a single file could eventually get really, really big. In this case, bigger than four gigabytes (GB), since the largest value an unsigned 32-bit integer could represent is 4,294,967,296 (2^{32} bytes). So, for those really big files that are greater than four (GB), the Windows API provides another 32-bit word (called the high-order word) that catches the overflow. If you do the math, you'll realize that Windows is designed to support files up to 17,179,869,184GB (2^{64} bytes) in size. Of course, make sure your hard drive is big enough, before creating a file of that magnitude. Seriously though, you can normally leave the second parameter as `null` because most files today are well less than four GB low-order value. But in the future, who knows, we might be requiring that high-order word support for obtaining the file size.

Spawning Applications and Discovering Window Handles

Microsoft's recommended way to launch an application within Windows is to use the `CreateProcess()` method. Although it might be recommended, you should be forewarned that it's the most difficult. It does, however, provide some distinct advantages over other methods.

Suppose that within an application it's necessary to not only launch (spawn) other applications, but also manage them (as we demonstrated in the Windows Management example earlier). For example, suppose when the main application is minimized, all other applications might need to be minimized as well. Or, when the main application is closed, any other applications that were spawned need to be closed as well. To support these specialized window management responsibilities, it is important to determine (or discover) a handle of another application. The knowledge of a target's application handle enables either standard Windows messages or custom Windows messages to be passed between applications. The `CreateProcess()` function can be used to facilitate the retrieval of an application's handle. The following code snippet shows one way of executing an application and retrieving its application handle:

```
void __fastcall TFormWinMan::ButtonLaunchAppClick(TObject *Sender)
{
  if (ListBoxApps->ItemIndex >= 0) {
```

```cpp
        char * data = (char*)ListBoxApps->Items->Objects[ListBoxApps->ItemIndex];
        AnsiString fullfilename  = AnsiString(data);

        EditFullFileName->Text = fullfilename;
        EditWHandle->Text = "0";
        winhandle = 0;
        processid =  0;

        STARTUPINFO  StartupInfo;
        ZeroMemory( &StartupInfo, sizeof(STARTUPINFO));
        PROCESS_INFORMATION ProcessInfo;
        StartupInfo.cb = sizeof(STARTUPINFO);
        if(CreateProcess(file,         // Windows System Service Call
            parameters,
            NULL,
            NULL,
            TRUE,
            NORMAL_PRIORITY_CLASS,
            NULL,
            NULL,
            &StartupInfo,
            &ProcessInfo))
        {
            // We must close the handles returned in ProcessInfo. We can
            // close the handle at any time, might as well close it now
            CloseHandle(ProcessInfo.hProcess);      // Windows System Service Call
            CloseHandle(ProcessInfo.hThread);        // Windows System Service Call
            processid =  (unsigned long)ProcessInfo.dwProcessId;
        }

    if (processid != 0)
        TimerGetHandle->Enabled = true; // use timer to get handle
    SetForegroundWindow(Handle);
  }
}

//--------------------------------------------------------------------------

void __fastcall TFormWinMan::TimerGetHandleTimer(TObject *Sender)
{
  if (processid != 0)
  {
```

```
          winhandle = LookForWindowHandle(processid);
          if (winhandle != NULL)
          {
              TimerGetHandle->Enabled = false;
              UpdateAppInfo(winhandle);
          }
      }
  }
}

//---------------------------------------------------------------------------
HWND TFormWinMan::LookForWindowHandle(unsigned long processid)
{
    if (!EnumWindows((WNDENUMPROC)GetWinHandle_Specific,processid))
        return swProcess;
    else
        return 0;
}

//---------------------------------------------------------------------------

BOOL CALLBACK TFormWinMan::GetWinHandle_Specific(HWND hwnd, unsigned long hproc)
{
    unsigned long dwProcessId;          // address of variable for process
    ↪identifier
    GetWindowThreadProcessId(
        hwnd,
        &dwProcessId);          // address of variable for process identifier
    if (dwProcessId != hproc)  return true;     // keep enumerating

    char windowtitle[80];
    char classname[80];

    GetWindowText( hwnd, windowtitle, 80);
    if (windowtitle[0] == NULL) return true;

    GetClassName(hwnd, classname, 80);
    int ptr = strcmp(classname, "TApplication");
    if (ptr == 0) return true;

    FormWinMan->swProcess=hwnd;
    return false; //stop enumeration
}
```

In `ButtonLaunchAppClick()` event handler, we use the `CreateProcess()` call to launch an external application and obtain the process ID for that application. After we clean up some unneeded information through the `CloseHandle()` Win32 API call, we immediately start a timer, which calls a custom-function created for this example called `LookForWindowHandle()`. `LookForWindowHandle()` iterates through the list of active applications and performs a process ID match. When a match is found, the application's handle can then be obtained. Both of these functions encapsulate several Win32 API calls from various functional areas and are described in detail in the following paragraphs.

Let's step back for a moment and look at the `CreateProcess()` call used in the `ButtonLaunchAppClick()` event handler. Appropriately named, the `CreateProcess()` function creates a new application process and its execution thread by launching the specified executable file. `StartUpInfo` is a variable passed into the `CreateProcess()` function that specifies how the main window for the new application will appear. `StartUpInfo` is initialized using the `ZeroMemory()` Win32 function, which simply fills the structure with zeros. `StartUpInfo` is defined by the `STARTUPINFO` structure, as described in the Win32 API Help reference.

`CreateProcess()` fills in the `ProcessInfo` variable with information about the newly created process, and its primary thread. `ProcessInfo` is defined by the `PROCESS_INFORMATION` structure shown in the following:

```
typedef struct _PROCESS_INFORMATION
{
    HANDLE hProcess;
    HANDLE hThread;
    DWORD dwProcessId;
    DWORD dwThreadId;
} PROCESS_INFORMATION;
```

The process ID returned by the `CreateProcess()` function is actually extracted from the `dwProcessId` field of the structure. In the example we keep track of the process ID, and kickoff the `TimerGetHandle` timer. The `TimerGetHandleTimer()` event handler will then call `LookForWindowHandle()` each interval and pass the process ID as a parameter.

The process ID aides in determining the Windows handle of the spawned application through the `LookForWindowHandle()` function.

`LookForWindowHandle()` is a custom function that uses the Win32 `EnumWindows()` function. As discussed in the Windows Management section, `EnumWindows()` enumerates through all the top-level windows by utilizing a custom callback function. In this example the callback faction is called `GetWinHandle_Specific()`.

GetWinHandle_Specific() stakes in each enumerated handle and the processed ID that we're trying to find a match. It gathers other information regarding the window handle using various Win32 Windows Management API calls. When a match is found the callback returns false, and the enumeration process halts returning the handle of the application that we spawned. The timer then populates the display with information regarding the spawned application and is disabled.

Graphical Device Interface

The graphical device interface (GDI), supported by the gdi32.dll dynamic link library, provides the capability for a window to draw and to print. This includes drawing lines, text, font service, and color management.

One of the key elements to the GDI is the device context. A device context (DC) represents a data structure defining a set of graphic objects, attributes, and output modes. DCs are created using the CreateDC() and GetDC() functions. There is a myriad of other DC functions that are commonly used as well. In all, seven types of GDI objects can be selected into a device context (see Table 14.6).

TABLE 14.6   The Seven Types of GDI Object

Feature	Description
Bitmap	Used for copying or scrolling parts of the screen.
Brush	Used for painting and filling the interior of polygons, ellipses, and paths.
Font	Used for identifying type, size, and style of a type font.
Palette	Used for defining the set of available colors.
Path	Used for painting and drawing operations.
Pen	Used for line drawing.
Region	Used for clipping and other operations.

There are more than 330 GDI routines available in current versions of Windows. Use Borland's impdef command-line tool or DLL LIB Util, described in the Tip earlier, to determine the full list of the available Windows GDI functions supported by the gdi32.dll.

The Windows GDI can be extremely useful for providing 2D graphic rendering and visualization for business applications. Borland's VCL wraps much of the GDI functionality within the TImage and TCanvas classes. Because the VCL provides a solid encapsulation of the GDI, the benefit of using the raw Win32 GDI is not all that substantial for the C++Builder developer.

The biggest debilitating factor with the GDI, whether used directly or through the VCL, is that its performance is marginal at best. Using the GDI to display real-time, high-speed graphic images often provides a lesson in frustration for both developers and users. In regards to frames per second, it's slow, even with the best hardware. Fortunately, the DirectDraw API, which is part of Microsoft's DirectX Game SDK, provides a much-improved library alternative for 2D graphics display. For those requiring high-performance 2D rendering, DirectDraw is the answer. Although DirectX is considered an extension of the Win32 API because it is supported by Windows 9x, 2000, and XP, it is not within the scope of this chapter.

Discussion and examples specific to the Windows GDI are provided in the Graphics and Multimedia section, see Chapter 15. However, there are some other elements of the GDI that we can explore, which can be used to affect the look of a windows form.

Shaping Your Applications

Manipulating forms and making them do cool and interesting things like we did earlier with animation can help applications be less boring. In this section, we will explore the concept of regions and cover a handful of related functions such as CombinRgn(), CreateEllipticRgn(), and GetClientRect(). These functions can control how windows look. Instead of the same old rectangle window look, regions can change the look of a window, which are part of the GDI. C++Builder makes combining the Win32 API functions to create regions on your system very easy. These and other APIs are located in the WINGDI.H header file.

At this point you might be asking, "What's a region?" A *region* is an area that bounds the window. Anything outside the region is not considered part of the window. The window clips anything else outside the region, giving the window a different look.

Let's now look at some of these special GDI region Win32 API calls.

CreateRoundRectRgn()
This function will create a rectangular window with rounded edges.

The CreateRoundRectRgn() function has the following parameters:

HRGN CreateRoundRectRgn(

```
    int nLeftRect, // x-coordinate of the region's upper-left corner
    int nTopRect, // y-coordinate of the region's upper-left corner
    int nRightRect, // x-coordinate of the region's lower-right corner
    int nBottomRect, // y-coordinate of the region's lower-right corner
    int nWidthEllipse, // height of ellipse for rounded corners
    int nHeightEllipse // width of ellipse for rounded corners
    );
```

- nLeftRect specifies the x coordinate of the upper-left corner of the region.

- nTopRect specifies the y coordinate of the upper-left corner of the region.

- nRightRect specifies the x coordinate of the lower-right corner of the region.

- nBottomRect specifies the y coordinate of the lower-right corner of the region.

- nWidthEllipse specifies the width of the ellipse used to create the rounded corners.

- nHeightEllipse specifies the height of the ellipse used to create the rounded corners.

The following example illustrates how to create a round-edged window:

```
RECT R  = GetClientRect();
HRGN MyRegion = CreateRoundRectRgn(0,0,150,110,15,10);
SetWindowRgn(Handle , MyRegion , true);
```

This is a relatively easy thing to do; The only difficult part is determining the coordinates. It's often necessary to play with them a bit to make the windows look the way you want, but that is the only drawback.

CreateEllipticRgn()

If you want an even more different look, there's another function called CreateEllipticRgn() that gives your window an oval-shaped appearance. It will actually make a window round or oval, depending on the parameters to the function. CreateEllipticRgn() has the following parameters:

```
HRGN CreateEllipticRgn(

    int nLeftRect,
// x-coordinate of the upper-left corner of the bounding rectangle
    int nTopRect,
// y-coordinate of the upper-left corner of the bounding rectangle
    int nRightRect,
// x-coordinate of the lower-right corner of the bounding rectangle
    int nBottomRect
// y-coordinate of the lower-right corner of the bounding rectangle
    );
```

- nLeftRect specifies the x coordinate of the upper-left corner of the bounding rectangle of the ellipse.

- nTopRect specifies the y coordinate of the upper-left corner of the bounding rectangle of the ellipse.

- nRightRect specifies the x coordinate of the lower-right corner of the bounding rectangle of the ellipse.

- nBottomRect specifies the y coordinate of the lower-right corner of the bounding rectangle of the ellipse.

The parameters are somewhat similar to the CreateRoundRectRgn() function, except that you only specify the whole width of the circle. The following example illustrates the use of the CreateEllipticRgn() function:

```
HRGN HRegion
HRegion = CreateEllipticRgn(0,0,Form1->Width, Form1->Height);
SetWindowRgn(Handle , hRgn1 , true);
```

This example code changes your form to a semiround circle (an oval). We started at Left(0) Top(0) and worked our way to the form's width and height, yielding a result that looks like an oval.

CombineRgn()

CombineRgn() function is a powerful function. CombinRgn() can actually take the regions that you specify and merge them together. A number of the programs these days that have the irregular window shapes usually use the CombineRgn() function. Along with the CreateEllipticRgn(), CreateRoundRect(), and CreatePolygonRgn() functions, you can specify regions to make your windows look even more glamorous.

CombineRgn() has the following parameters:

```
int CombineRgn(
    HRGN hrgnDest,      // handle to destination region
    HRGN hrgn1,       // handle to source region
    HRGN hrgn2,       // handle to source region
    int fnCombineMode      // region combining mode
    );
```

- hrgnDest identifies a new region with dimensions defined by combining two other regions. (This region must exist before CombineRgn() is called.)

- hrgn1 identifies the first of two regions to be combined.

- hHrgn2 identifies the second of two regions to be combined.

- fnCombineMode specifies a mode indicating how the two regions will be combined. This parameter can be one of the values in Table 14.7.

TABLE 14.7   CombineRgn() Flags

Flags	Values
RGN_AND	Creates the intersection of the two combined regions.
RGN_COPY	Creates a copy of the region identified by hrgnSrc1.
RGN_DIFF	Combines the parts of hrgnSrc1 that are not part of hrgnSrc2.
RGN_OR	Creates the union of two combined regions.
RGN_XOR	Creates the union of two combined regions except for any overlapping areas.

The return value specifies the type of the resulting region. It can be one of the values shown in Table 14.8.

TABLE 14.8   CombineRgn() Return Values

Return Value	Description
NULLREGION	The region is empty.
SIMPLEREGION	The region is a single rectangle.
COMPLEXREGION	The region is more than a single rectangle.
ERROR	No region is created.

Interestingly enough, the regions do not need to be distinct. For example, if you pass three regions (Region1, Region1, and Region2) as the parameters, you can see that Region1, the original region already passed, will be destined to hold the final region, which is completely okay. However, if you do pass another region separate from the other declared regions, you must pass an already declared region before calling this API.

The following is an example of using CombineRgn() function. Hopefully, the example will clarify any issues you might have and give you a better understanding of how to use the function.

```
HRGN Region1, Region2;
Region1 = CreateRectRgn(0, 0, 100, 100);
Region2 = CreateRectRgn(50, 50, 150, 150);
CombineRgn(Region1, Region1, Region2, RGN_XOR);
SetWindowRgn(Handle , hRgn1 , true);
```

Using this example, you will see your form turn into two boxes with a box hole in the middle of it. The hole is there because the RGN_XOR flag was used. The two regions overlap, but do not combine with the intersecting regions. If we use the RGN_OR flag, you will see they now intersect and combine.

Also, we used Region1 as the destination and a created region. Why did we do this? Well, remember that we need a destination region, and Region1 and Region2 combined will overwrite Region1. Because we passed the parameter, the function knows the coordinates and sends them to the Region1 destination.

But let's not stop here. Earlier, we mentioned something about the CreatePolygonRgn() function. Let's go over that because it's another region function that's quite interesting.

CreatePolygonRgn() function has the following parameters:

```
HRGN CreatePolygonRgn(

    CONST POINT *lppt,    // pointer to array of points
    int cPoints,     // number of points in array
    int fnPolyFillMode     // polygon-filling mode
);
```

- lppt points to an array of POINT structures that define the vertices of the polygon. The polygon is presumed closed. Each vertex can be specified only once.

- CPoints specifies the number of points in the array.

- fnPolyFillMode specifies the fill mode used to determine which pixels are in the region. This parameter can be one of the values shown in Table 14.9.

TABLE 14.9   Possible fnPolyFillMode Modes

Parameter	Value
ALTERNATE	Selects alternate mode (fills area between odd-numbered and even-numbered polygon sides on each scan line)
WINDING	Selects winding mode (fills any region with a nonzero winding value)

To pass the proper parameters to the CreatePolygonRgn() function, we can both use the Win32 API and C++Builder's POINT structure. This function relies on point pixel locations to create a region. This is similar to connect the dots, where the function will create the region based on these dots.

The POINT structure is a structure that defines the x and y coordinates of an object. You simply fill it in. To create a multiple-point coordinate, simply declare a POINT structure variable with an array.

We've only covered the basics of regions here to give you a better understanding of how regions work with C++Builder. If you want to learn more about creating windows with regions, visit Microsoft's MSDN Web site at http://www.microsoft.com/ msdn. Perform a search for window regions or irregular windows.

Multimedia Services

A growing number of applications today incorporate multimedia elements, such as sound and video, to enrich the experience of the user. Some of the extension libraries Microsoft has provided for Windows include the Multimedia System Library (mmsystem.dll), the Microsoft Video for Windows Library (msvfw32.dll), and the Microsoft Audio Compression Manager Library (msacm32.dll). Originally, multimedia features were not part of the Windows API. However, the Windows operating system has evolved to support and promote multimedia. In fact, the modern Windows platform is, for all practical purposes, a multimedia appliance similar to a TV or stereo. Multimedia devices and data formats, such as MIDI, waveform audio, and video, are supported by Windows. The MMYSTEM.DLL, MSVFW32.DLL, and MSACM32.DLL provide a majority of the basic multimedia capabilities. Microsoft has also introduced a multimedia API known as DirectX to better support games, music, and video. However, this section primarily focuses on the capabilities provided by MMYSTEM.DLL, MSVFW32.DLL, and MSACM32.DLL. The multimedia headers files for these DLLs are DIGITALV.H, MCIAVI.H, MMSYSTEM.H, MSACM.H, VCR.H, and VFW.H.

Table 14.10 describes the various multimedia services provided by these libraries.

TABLE 14.10   Multimedia Services

Feature	Description
Audio Compression Manager (ACM)	Provides system-level support for audio compression, decompression, filtering, and conversion (uses MSACM32.DLL).
Audio Mixers	Provides services to control the routing of audio lines to a destination device for playing or recording. Also provides support for manipulating volume and other effects (uses MMYSTEM.DLL).
AVICap	Provides video capture capabilities including interface support for acquiring video and waveform-audio hardware and support for controlling streaming video capturing to disk (uses MSVFW32.DLL).
AVIFile	Provides functions and macros for accessing audio-video interleaved (AVI) files (uses MSVFW32.DLL).
DrawDib	Provide GDI-independent functions used to transfer device-independent bitmaps (DIBs) to video memory (uses MSVFW32.DLL).
Joysticks	Provides support for managing joysticks and other ancillary input devices that track positions within an absolute coordinate system (touch screen, digitizing tablet, and light pen) (uses MMYSTEM.DLL).
MCIWnd Window Class	Provides a window class for controlling multimedia devices. Provides support for easily adding multimedia playback or recording capabilities to an application (uses MSVFW32.DLL).
Media Control Interface (MCI)	Provides device-independent support for playing multimedia devices (waveform audio devices, CD player, MIDI sequencers, and digital-video devices) and recording multimedia resource files (uses MMYSTEM.DLL).

TABLE 14.10   Continued

Feature	Description
Multimedia File	Provides buffered and unbuffered file I/O service and support for Resource Interchange File Format (RIFF) files, such as wave files and video files (uses `MMSYSTEM.DLL`).
Multimedia Timers	Provides support for scheduling periodic, high-resolution timer events (uses `MMSYSTEM.DLL`).
Music Instrument Digital Interface (MIDI)	Provides the MIDI Mapper to translate and redirect the incoming MIDI messages and other various MIDI services, such as querying for devices and managing, streaming, and recording MIDI message data. (Note: MCI services, which provide a MIDI sequencer, can be used in conjunction with the MIDI services.) (Uses `MMSYSTEM.DLL`.)
Video Compression Manager (VCM)	Provides video data compression and decompression support (uses `MSVFW32.DLL`).
Waveform-Audio	Provides utilities for adding (playing and recording) waveform-audio sounds (uses `MMSYSTEM.DLL`).

Among the three DLLs mentioned in Table 14.10, there are more than 240 functions that support the multimedia services in current versions of Windows. Use Borland's `impdef` command-line tool or `DLL LIB Util`, described in the tip earlier, to determine the full list of the available multimedia functions (contained in `MMSYSTEM.DLL`, `MSVFW32.DLL`, and `MSACM32.DLL`). The import libraries for these DLLs are `WINMM.LIB`, `VFW32.LIB`, and `MSACM32.LIB`, respectively.

Let's now create some simple examples in C++Builder that use several of the Multimedia Services. Later, we'll dive into some deeper, more advanced examples in the Graphics and Multimedia chapter (Chapter 15). Playback of media data and multimedia timers are two useful capabilities that we'll look at now.

Multimedia File Playback

Borland provides a VCL component known as `TMediaPlayer` that can be used to manipulate and play multimedia clips. `TMediaPlayer` provides a wrapper to the `MCIWnd` routines supported by the `VFW32.DLL`. Although `TMediaPlayer` is extremely useful, leveraging the `MCIWnd` routines directly can provide a bit more flexibility and is really not that difficult to use. For example, `MCIWndCreate()` provides a fairly simple routine that can be used to play CD music, waveform-audio (wave) files, MIDI files, or video clips (see Figure 14.6). The complete source-code example described in this section is provided in the `MMedia` folder on the CD-ROM that accompanies this book.

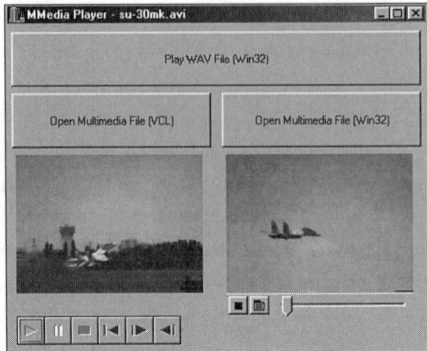

FIGURE 14.6   The multimedia player example using both TMediaPlayer and the Windows MCI.

The following code snippet shows how the multimedia features provided by the Win32 API can be used to play back a video clip:

```
void __fastcall TForm1::SpeedButtonPlayMMFileUsingWin32Click(TObject *Sender)
{
  OpenDialog1->DefaultExt = "AVI";
  OpenDialog1->FileName = "*.avi";
  if (OpenDialog1->Execute())
    MCIWndCreate(PanelMCI->Handle,                // window handle to our panel
        NULL,                                     // instance handle
        WS_VISIBLE | WS_CHILD | MCIWNDF_SHOWALL,  // window styles
        OpenDialog1->FileName.c_str());           // filename
}
```

In this example, `MCIWndCreate()` actually creates a VCR-like window (using the `MCIWND_WINDOW_CLASS`) containing a play/stop control button, a trackbar, and uses a panel we've placed on the form. If we didn't use the `WS_CHILD` flag and we identified a `NULL` window handle, the MCI would have created a brand-new panel for displaying the video if it is a video clip.

Although the MCI can be used to play sound files, a less expensive way to play wave files is to use the `PlaySound()` function as follows:

```
void __fastcall TForm1::SpeedButtonPlayWaveUsingWin32Click(TObject *Sender)
{
  OpenDialog1->DefaultExt = "WAV";
  OpenDialog1->FileName = "*.wav";
  if (OpenDialog1->Execute())
    PlaySound(OpenDialog->FileName.c_str(), NULL, SND_ASYNC);
}
```

PlaySound() is an extremely useful routine provided by the mmsystem.dll. Often, sound files need to be played in the background of an application, to produce a sound effect, for example. PlaySound does not provide the VCR-like controls or a trackbar as MCIWndCreate() does. Furthermore, sounds are played instantaneously when the PlaySound() function is called.

The DirectSound features supported by DirectX provide additional capabilities for sound manipulation and management enabling multiple sounds to be played simultaneously. Also, DirectShow provides a mechanism to playback compressed sound files such as MP3 and Windows Media Audio (WMA) files, and a wide range of video files including MPEG and Windows Media Video (WMV) files. Discussion of DirectSound and DirectShow, however, are not within the scope of this chapter.

Improved Accuracy with the Multimedia Timer

Borland provides a very simple and easy-to-use VCL timer component known as TTimer. TTimer encapsulates the Win32 API Timer functions. It uses the SetTimer() function to enable timer events, provides an event handler, OnTimer, to respond to WM_TIMER message notifications, and uses the KillTimer() function to disable timer events. When the SetTimer() routine is called, an application requests the Windows System to notify the process (the application) of continual updates until the timer is disabled via the KillTimer() routine. The frequency of these updates is based on the interval provided within the SetTimer() interval timeout parameter (also known as the Interval property value within TTimer). Although the interval frequency can be identified in milliseconds, timers are not always that accurate. WM_TIMER message notifications might occur more frequently than expected or, if other processes are tying up the system, less frequently than expected. It's never a sure bet. However, there is one way to receive more accurate updates by using the multimedia timers. The multimedia timer is an extension of the original Win32 API and provides better resolution than the standard Windows timer.

Examination of the mmsystem.h file provided by Microsoft and Borland reveals the functions that are available.

```
/* timer function prototypes */
WINMMAPI MMRESULT WINAPI timeGetSystemTime(LPMMTIME pmmt, UINT cbmmt);
WINMMAPI DWORD WINAPI timeGetTime(void);
WINMMAPI MMRESULT WINAPI timeSetEvent(UINT uDelay, UINT uResolution,
    LPTIMECALLBACK fptc, DWORD dwUser, UINT fuEvent);
WINMMAPI MMRESULT WINAPI timeKillEvent(UINT uTimerID);
WINMMAPI MMRESULT WINAPI timeGetDevCaps(LPTIMECAPS ptc, UINT cbtc);
WINMMAPI MMRESULT WINAPI timeBeginPeriod(UINT uPeriod);
WINMMAPI MMRESULT WINAPI timeEndPeriod(UINT uPeriod);
```

In most cases, timeSetEvent() and timeKillEvent() are all that is required to use the multimedia timer. A callback message needs to be defined within your program to handle the multimedia timer event notifications. An example application that compares the standard VCL timer with the multimedia timer is provided both in Listing 14.8 and in the MMTimer folder on the CD-ROM that accompanies this book. Figure 14.7 shows the application running and demonstrates the differences in elapsed time between the two timers.

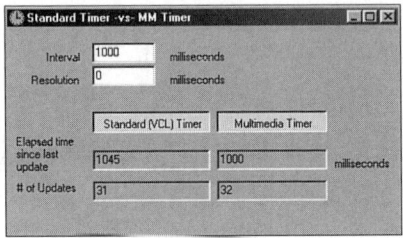

FIGURE 14.7   Difference in accuracy between the VCL timer and the multimedia timer.

LISTING 14.8   Timer Code

```cpp
#include <vcl.h>
#pragma hdrstop

#include "mmtimer.h"
#include <mmsystem.h>
#include <time.h>

//---------------------------------------------------------------------------
#pragma package(smart_init)
#pragma resource "*.dfm"
TFormSystemService *Form1;
//---------------------------------------------------------------------------
__fastcall TForm1::TFormSystemService(TComponent* Owner)
        : TForm(Owner)
{
        MMTimerID = 0;
        MMlasttime = 0;
        STANlasttime = 0;
}
//---------------------------------------------------------------------------
```

LISTING 14.8   Continued

```
void __fastcall TForm1::Timer1Timer(TObject *Sender)
{

        unsigned int clocktime = clock();
        EditStandardTimer->Text = AnsiString(clocktime - STANlasttime);
        STANlasttime = clocktime;
}
//-----------------------------------------------------------------------

void __fastcall TForm1::HandleMMTimerEvent()
{
        unsigned int clocktime = clock();
        EditMMTimer->Text = AnsiString(clocktime - MMlasttime);
        MMlasttime = clocktime;
        //Refresh();
}
//-----------------------------------------------------------------------

void CALLBACK TForm1::TimerProc(unsigned int uID, unsigned int uMsg, DWORD dwUser,
    DWORD dw1, DWORD dw2)
{
        Form1->HandleMMTimerEvent();
}

//-----------------------------------------------------------------------
void __fastcall TForm1::SpeedButtonMMTimerClick(TObject *Sender)
{
 if (SpeedButtonMMTimer->Down)
 {
    int Interval = EditInterval->Text.ToIntDef(0);
    int Resolution = EditResolution->Text.ToIntDef(0);  // 0 = greatest
    ➥possible accuracy
    if (Timer1->Interval > 0)
    {
            MMlasttime = clock();
            MMTimerID = timeSetEvent(Interval, Resolution, TimerProc,NULL,
            ➥TIME_PERIODIC);
    }
 }
 else
 {
```

LISTING 14.8   **Continued**

```
      timeKillEvent(MMTimerID);
      MMTimerID = 0;
  }
}
//----------------------------------------------------------------
void __fastcall TForm1::SpeedButtonStandardTimerClick(TObject *Sender)
{
    if (SpeedButtonStandardTimer->Down)
    {
        Timer1->Interval = EditInterval->Text.ToIntDef(0);
        STANlasttime = clock();
        if (Timer1->Interval > 0)
                Timer1->Enabled = true;
    }
    else
    {
        Timer1->Enabled = false;
    }

}
//----------------------------------------------------------------
void __fastcall TForm1::FormClose(TObject *Sender, TCloseAction &Action)
{
    if (MMTimerID) timeKillEvent(MMTimerID);
}
```

In this example, we kick off each timer with the push of a button; the VCL TTimer and the Win32 API multimedia timer. To get the multimedia timer to work, we provide a user-defined callback called TimerProc(), which is used to handle the timer event as a parameter in the timeSetEvent() API call. Also included with the timeSetEvent() call is the interval and resolution values, both in milliseconds. The resolution is used to indicate the level of accuracy—the smaller the value, the greater the accuracy. However, a larger value reduces system overhead.

The TimerProc() function behaves just like the Timer1 event handler. The difference is that the multimedia timer will trigger the TimerProc() function closer to the expected mark than the TTimer, expecially under Windows 9X and Windows Me. Finally, when we're done with the timer, a call to timeKillEvent() is made.

Common Controls and Dialogs

A collection of predefined, common window controls is provided within Windows through the common control library (COMCTL32.DLL). In addition to controls, a collection of common window dialogs are provided through the common dialog library (COMDLG32.DLL). The idea behind providing common controls and dialogs is to allow developers to quickly utilize common interface elements within a program rather than spending lengthy time and effort writing custom window interfaces. For the most part, Borland C++Builder provides a palette full of common controls and dialogs through the Visual Component Library (VCL). However, it's useful for developers to be aware of the Win32 API common controls and dialogs that are available.

Common Controls

There are at least 22 common controls for Windows in COMCTL32.DLL. Examination of the commctrl.h file provided with C++Builder reveals the Win32 elements available with the common control library. These controls are described in Table 14.11.

TABLE 14.11 Common Controls

Common Control	Description	Borland VCL Equivalent
Animation Control	Plays simple AVI (video) clips without sound.Use ANIMATE_CLASS flag.	TAnimate
ComboBoxEx*	Provides support for item images within a combo box.Use WC_COMBOBOXEX flag.	None
Date and Time Picker	Provides an interface for exchanging date and time information with the user. Use DATETIMEPICK_CLASS flag.	TDateTimePicker
Drag List Box	Provides a list box that allows items to be dragged from one position to another. Use MakeDragList() routine.	None
Flat Scroll Bar*	Provides a unique three-dimensional scrollbar, created using the InitializeFlatSB() routine.	None
Header Controls	Used to place resizable headers above columns of text or numbers. Use WC_HEADER flag.	THeaderControl
Hot-Key Controls	Allows entry of hotkey keystroke combinations. Use HOTKEY_CLASS flag.	THotKey

TABLE 14.11   Continued

Common Control	Description	Borland VCL Equivalent
Image List	Provides a collection of equal size images referenced by an index. Created using the `ImageListCreate()` routine.	TImageList
IP Address*	Allows an IP address to be entered in an easily understood format. Use `WC_IPADDRESS` flag.	None
List View	Displays a collection of items as large icons, small icons, detailed list, or report view within a window control. Use `WC_LISTVIEW` flag.	TListView
Monthly Calendar	Provides a graphical calendar interface for viewing and selecting dates.Use `MONTHCAL_CLASS` flag.	TMonthCalendar
Page Scroller*	Provides a scrollable window containing a child window (such as a control) that is too large to be seen entirely. Use `WC_PAGESCROLLER` flag.	TPageScroller
Progress Bars	Used to provide graphical status feedback for lengthy operations. Use `PROGRESS_CLASS` flag.	TProgressBar
Property Sheets	Presents viewable and editable properties of an item in a tabbed page form.	TPageControl
Rebar (Coolbar)	Used to contain one or more bands composed of any combination of a gripper bar, bitmap, text label, and a child window. Use `REBARCLASSNAME` flag.	TCoolBar
Status Bar	Provides a panel control used to display text and graphical information.Use `STATUSCLASSNAME` flag.	TStatusBar
Tab Controls	Defines multiple pages within the area of a window (similar to dividers in a notebook). Use `WC_TABCONTROL` flag.	TTabControl
Toolbars	Contains one or more selectable buttons within a panel bar. Use `TOOLBARCLASSNAME` flag.	TToolBar

TABLE 14.11 Continued

Common Control	Description	Borland VCL Equivalent
Tooltip Controls	Used to display a small pop-up window displaying a text description. Use TOOLTIPS_CLASS flag.	THintWindow
Trackbars	Provides a slide indicator with optional tick marks used for adjusting an integer value within a specified range. Use TRACKBAR_CLASS flag.	TTrackBar
Tree View Controls	Displays a hierarchical list of items and subitems within a window frame consisting of a label and an optional bitmapped image. Use WC_TREEVIEW flag.	TTreeView
Up-Down Controls	Provides an edit control consisting of a pair of arrow buttons used to increase or decrease a value. Use UPDOWN_CLASS flag.	TUpDown

* Introduced in Internet Explorer 4.0.

Unless otherwise noted, these controls are created by using the CreateWindowEx()
routine and by selecting the proper flags associated with each feature. Let's take a
quick look at the example shown in Listing 14.9.

LISTING 14.9 Common Control Example

```
__fastcall TFormCommCtrl_Dlg::TFormCommCtrl_Dlg(TComponent* Owner)
        : TForm(Owner)
{
   InitCommonControls();    // make sure the the common control DLL is loaded.
   ControlHandle = NULL;
}


//-------------------------------------------------------------------------

void __fastcall TFormCommCtrl_Dlg::ButtonMakeListViewClick(TObject *Sender)
{
 HWND ListBox;
 RECT Rect;

 DWORD dwExStyle = 0;
```

LISTING 14.9   Continued

```
Rect = GetClientRect();
HINSTANCE  hInstance = (HINSTANCE )GetWindowThreadProcessId(
   Handle,    // handle of window
   NULL    // address of variable for process identifier
   );

ControlHandle = CreateWindowEx(0L,
    WC_LISTVIEW,
    NULL,
    WS_VISIBLE | WS_CHILD | WS_BORDER | TVS_HASLINES | TVS_HASBUTTONS |
    ➥TVS_LINESATROOT,
    0, 180,
    Rect.right - Rect.left, Rect.bottom-180,
    Handle,
    0,
    hInstance,
    NULL);
}
```

Before using a common control, be sure to call the `InitCommonControlsEx()` routine to ensure that the common control dynamic-link library (DLL) is properly loaded. In this example, this was done in the constructor for this form. The `ButtonMakeListViewClick()` event handler provides the code for creating a common control widget that is placed on our form. This is accomplished using the `CreateWindowEx()` call with a `WC_LISTVIEW` flag.

In scanning through the table, you'll notice a majority of the common control features are supported by Borland's VCL. There are more than 80 routines available within the common control library (`comctl32.dll`) supporting these and possibly other common controls. Use Borland's `impdef` command-line tool or DLL LIB Util, which was described earlier in a Tip, to determine the full list of the available common control functions supported by the Win32 API. Also examine the latest `commctrl.h` file for identifying the common control macro definitions.

Common Dialogs

In addition to common controls, Microsoft provides common dialogs for applications. There are currently eight common dialogs contained in recent versions of `COMDLG32.DLL`. C++Builder, however, provides VCL wrappers for each of these dialogs, as shown in Table 14.12.

TABLE 14.12   VCL Equivalents for Microsoft API Common Dialog Functions

Common Dialog	Microsoft API Call	VCL Equivalent
Choose Color	ChooseColor()	TColorDialog
Choose Font	ChooseFont()	TFontDialog
Find Text	FindText()	TFindDialog
Open File	GetOpenNameFile()	TOpenDialog
Save File	GetSaveFileName()	TSaveDialog
Print Setup	PageSetupDlg()	TPrinterSetupDialog
Print	PrintDlg()	TPrintDialog
Replace Text	ReplaceText()	TReplaceDialog

Examination of the commdlg.h file provided with C++Builder reveals the Win32 elements available with the common dialog library. Creating the .def file for the commdlg.dll will further reveal the available API routines.

To understand how to use one of these common dialogs, let's look at an example that demonstrates the use of the Choose Color dialog as shown in Figure 14.8.

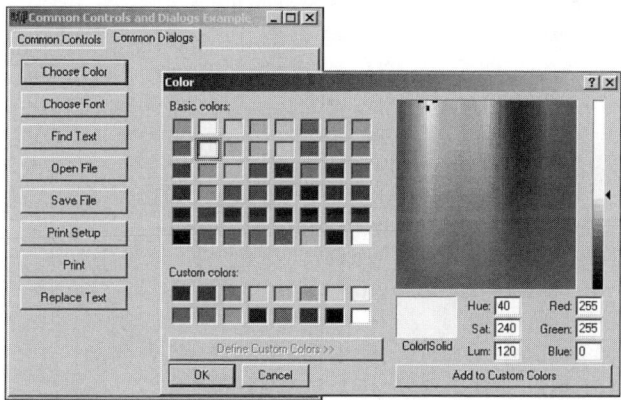

FIGURE 14.8   Example application that uses the Color Common Dialog.

The code used to generate the Color Common Dialog is provided in Listing 14.10.

LISTING 14.10   Common Dialog Example

```
void __fastcall TFormCommCtrl_Dlg::ButtonChooseColorClick(TObject *Sender)
{
    LPCHOOSECOLOR cc;
    COLORREF      initrgb, rgb;
    BOOL          res;
```

LISTING 14.10　Continued

```
DWORD          err;

initrgb= 0x0000FFFF; //yellow

char result[MAX_PATH];

HINSTANCE  hInstance = (HINSTANCE )GetWindowThreadProcessId(
        Handle,    // handle of window
        NULL);     // address of variable for process identifier

DWORD mcolors[15];
mcolors[0]  =  0x00FF0000; // blue
mcolors[1]  =  0x00FF4040; // med blue
mcolors[2]  =  0x00FF8080; // light med blue
mcolors[3]  =  0x00FFFF00; // aqua
mcolors[4]  =  0x0000FF00; // green
mcolors[5]  =  0x0040FF40; // med green
mcolors[6]  = 0x0080FF80; // light med green
mcolors[7]  =  0x0000FFFF; // yellow
mcolors[8]  =  0x000000FF; // red
mcolors[9]  = 0x004040FF; // more pink
mcolors[10] = 0x008080FF; // pink
mcolors[11] = 0x00400040; // purple
mcolors[12] = 0x00808080; // gray
mcolors[13] = 0x00404040; // dk gray
mcolors[14] =  0x00000000; // white
mcolors[15] =  0x00FFFFFF; // black

cc = (LPCHOOSECOLOR)malloc(sizeof(CHOOSECOLOR));
cc->lStructSize = (DWORD) sizeof(CHOOSECOLOR);
cc->hwndOwner = Handle;
cc->hInstance = hInstance;
cc->rgbResult = initrgb;
cc->lpCustColors = mcolors;
cc->Flags = CC_ANYCOLOR | CC_FULLOPEN | CC_RGBINIT;
cc->lCustData = NULL;
cc->lpfnHook = NULL;
cc->lpTemplateName = NULL;

if (!(res = ChooseColor(cc)))
{
```

LISTING 14.10 Continued

```
        err = CommDlgExtendedError();
        sprintf(result,"Error: %d\n",err);
    }
    else{
        rgb=cc->rgbResult;
        sprintf(result,"r g b: %d %d %d\n", ((BYTE) (rgb)) ,((BYTE)
            (((WORD) (rgb)) >> 8)),((BYTE) ((rgb) >> 16))  );
    }
    MessageBox(Handle,result,"Result",MB_OK);
}
```

In this example, we're using the `ChooseColor()` API call to display the Color selection dialog. Within the `ButtonChooseClorClick()` event handler, we set up an array identifying the custom colors we want to load, and a pointer to the `CHOOSECOLOR` structure, which is defined as follows:

```
typedef struct {    // cc
    DWORD         lStructSize;
    HWND          hwndOwner;
    HWND          hInstance;
    COLORREF      rgbResult;
    COLORREF*     lpCustColors;
    DWORD         Flags;
    LPARAM        lCustData;
    LPCCHOOKPROC  lpfnHook;
    LPCTSTR       lpTemplateName;
} CHOOSECOLOR;
```

The `mcolors` array that we've defined and initialized is assigned to the `lpCustColors` flag of the structure. We also identify the windows `handle` and `instance` of our application, plus any `flags` we want associated to the dialog. The `ChooseColor()` call returns the color value selected by the user. If the return is 0, we know that the user opted out of selecting a color.

In addition to dialogs, the `ComDlg32.dll` also provides a couple of trivial functions including `GetFileTitle()` and `LoadAlterBitmap()`. Plus, a useful function to help isolate errors called `CommDlgExtendedError()`.

`GetFileTitle()` is used to retrieve the display name for a specified file. For instance, what is displayed to the user in Windows Explorer is considered the display name. According to the Win32 API, "the display name includes an extension only if that is the user's preference for displaying filenames."

`LoadAlterBitmap()` function is a bit of a mystery. There is no known documentation on this call, but it's presumably made to load an alternate bitmap, such as an icon, associated to the file within its resource file.

`CommDlgExtendedError()` is used to retrieve an error code for a failed dialog call. The Win32 API help file provides more details on each of the error codes, which begin with a prefix of `CDERR_`.

Shell Features

The term *Shell* is used within Windows to describe an application that enables a user to group, start, and control other applications or files. Shell features include drag-and-drop file support, file association support for starting and finding other applications, and the capability to extract icons from other files. The Shell aspect of the Win32 API is a very powerful feature set and is contained within the `Shell32.dll`. The principal header file included within the source code of an application that provides the Shell features is the `SHELLAPI.H`. The basic features of the Shell API are described in Table 14.13.

TABLE 14.13   Basic Features of the Shell API

Shell Feature	Description
Drag-and-Drop	Enables a user to select one or more files in Windows Explorer (or even the old File Explorer provided with Win 3.x) that can be dragged and dropped into an open application that has previously used the `DragAcceptFiles()` Shell function. A `WM_DROPFILES` message is received by the open application, which is used to retrieve the filenames and display the position at which the files were dropped. This is accomplished using the `DragQueryFile()` and `DragQueryPoint()` Shell functions.
File Association Support for Starting and/or Finding Other Applications	Back in the Win 3.x days, Microsoft provided the Associate dialog box within File Explorer. This allowed a user to associate a filename extension with a particular application. Since Windows 95, a more detailed Associate dialog box is provided within Windows Explorer called the `Open With` dialog. The Registry provides an automated association of filename extensions and applications. Within Windows Explorer, a file that is double-clicked and has an association with a specific application will cause the application to load and open the selected file. The `FindExecutable()` and `ShellExecute()` routines contained within the Shell API make use of this file association. The `FindExecutable()` function is used to retrieve

TABLE 14.13   Continued

Shell Feature	Description
	the name and handle to the application associated with a specified file. `ShellExecute()` and `ShellExecuteEx()` are used to open or print a specified file. The application required to open a file is launched based on the file association.
Extracting Icons	Applications, dynamic link libraries, and icon files are typically represented by one or more icons. The handle of an icon can be retrieved easily by using the `ExtractIcon()` Shell routine.

There are more than 120 Shell routines available in current versions of Windows, many of which are undocumented. Use Borland's impdef command-line tool or the DLL LIB Util application, which was described in the previous Tip, to view the full list of the available Shell library functions.

Shell functions are a big thing in Windows 98/2000/XP programming. Newer Shell functions are best known as SH*x* functions because many of them have the SH prefix. A few common ones and new ones supported in Windows 2000 and XP are described later in this section. Several newer Shell functions have replaced the older Win32 API routines because they are more versatile. Although the older API routines can still be used for simple transfers or manipulation, the new API routines provide more flexibility, yet sometimes are very hard to use. We will identify the newer ones from the older ones within our examples.

Using `ShellExecute()` to Open a Browser

With much of today's data available via the World Wide Web, it is often practical for an application to interface with the platform's default Web browser. The Win32 API Shell extensions make it possible to provide this type of interface.

The following code example in Listing 14.11 demonstrates how to use the `ShellExecute()` function to open a browser with a specified address (URL).

LISTING 14.11   Opening the Browser with `ShellExecute()`

```
void __fastcall TForm1::ButtonBrowserClick(TObject *Sender)
{
  if (EditURL->Text.Length() > 0)
  {
    if (! ShellExecute(Handle, "open", EditURL->Text.c_str(),
                       NULL, NULL, SW_SHOW))
    {
        char data[100];
```

LISTING 14.11   Continued

```
        sprintf(data,"Could not run browser with URL '%s'",EditURL->Text);
        MessageBox(NULL,data,"Operation Error!",MB_OK);
    }
  }
  else
    MessageBeep(MB_OK);
}
```

Let's look at the parameters used for ShellExecute() in this example. The first para-meter identifies a handle to the parent. We can actually leave this NULL if we want. The second parameter used for ShellExecute() indicates a desire to "open" a file. Other choices include "print" a file, and "explore" a folder. The third parameter provides information about where that file or folder is located. In this example, our "file" is actually a Universal Resource Locator (URL) address commonly used for Web browsing. The Shell library deciphers URL descriptors and will use the registered browser that supports URLs.

Using ShellExecuteEx() to Spawn an Application

An easy way to launch an external application is by using the slightly more powerful ShellExecuteEx() function, which is illustrated by example in Figure 14.9. ShellExecuteEx() is considered easier to use than the CreateProcess() API routine that we discussed earlier. Unfortunately, it doesn't provide a way to retrieve the handle of the application being spawned like CreateProcess() does.

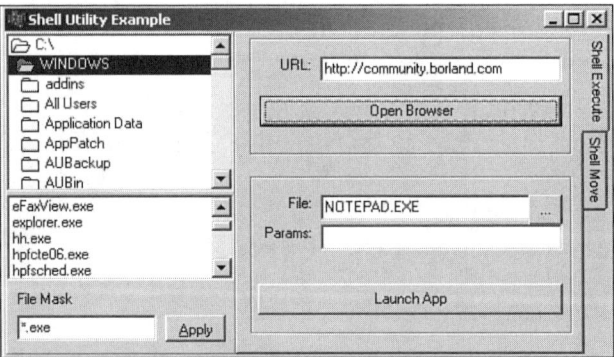

FIGURE 14.9   Shell example for launching an application.

Listing 14.12 demonstrates how ShellExecuteEx() can be used to launch an applica-tion within C++Builder.

LISTING 14.12   Launching an Application with `ShellExecuteEx()`

```
void __fastcall TForm1::ButtonLaunchAppClick(TObject *Sender)
{
  char temp[MAX_PATH];
  char params[MAX_PATH];
  sprintf(temp,"%s\0",EditFile->Text.c_str());
  sprintf(params,"%s\0",EditParams->Text.c_str());

  // Select the program and how it will be run.
  SHELLEXECUTEINFO execinfo ;
  memset (&execinfo, 0, sizeof (execinfo)) ;
  execinfo.cbSize = sizeof (execinfo) ;
  execinfo.lpVerb = "open" ;
  execinfo.lpFile = temp;
  execinfo.lpParameters = params;
  execinfo.fMask = SEE_MASK_NOCLOSEPROCESS ;
  execinfo.nShow = SW_SHOWDEFAULT ;

  // Run the program.
  if (! ShellExecuteEx (&execinfo))
  {
    char data[100];
    sprintf(data,"Could not run program '%s'",EditFile->Text.c_str());
    MessageBox(NULL,data,"Operation Error!",MB_OK);
  }
}
```

In this example, the `execinfo` structure, defined by `SHELLEXECUTEINFO`, is filled and passed as a parameter to the `ShellExecuteEx()` function. The two key attributes of `execinfo` structure are the `open` flag and the file. Command-line arguments can also be passed as parameters. Based on these values, `ShellExecuteEx()` will open the application. In general, the `ShellExecute()` and `ShellExecuteEx()` functions use file association (examine the file extension) to determine how files are opened. If it is an `exe` file representing a standalone application, it will launch, but if it's a file such as a `txt` file, a registered application such as Notepad will launch and open the `txt` file.

Backing-Up Directories and Files

`SHFileOperation()` is a versatile file operation that supports multiple directory transfers. The `SHFileOperation()` is significantly more powerful than the system service `MoveFile()` API call because it can transfer files and directories over to a new volume. It can also transfer children files within a directory. The `SHFileOperation()` is widely used in Windows 95 and later and can be seen in Figure 14.10.

The example code, shown in Listing 14.13, demonstrates how to copy files and subdirectories all at once from one location to another.

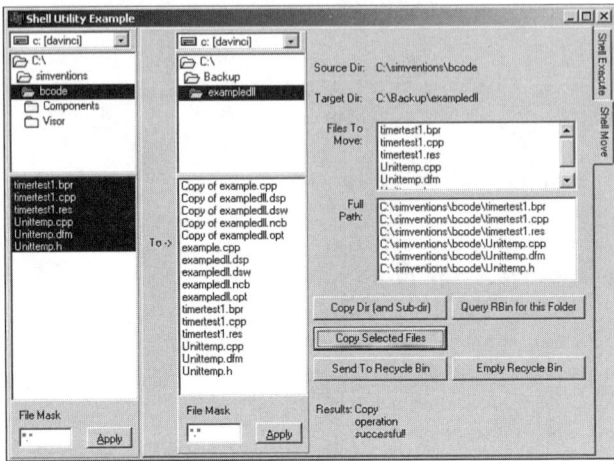

FIGURE 14.10   Shell example for backing-up directories and files.

LISTING 14.13   Using the SHFileOperation() to Copy a Folder

```
void __fastcall TForm1::ButtonCopyDirClick(TObject *Sender)
{
    LabelMoveResults->Caption = "";

    //Declare the SHFILEOPSTRUCT structure to fill in information for use
    //of SHFileOperation function.
    SHFILEOPSTRUCT op;

    //Clear out any thing within the structure
    ZeroMemory(&op, sizeof(op));

    char source[MAX_PATH];
    memset(source, 0, MAX_PATH);
    char dest[MAX_PATH];
    memset(dest, 0, MAX_PATH);

    op.hwnd = Handle;    //This is a handle to the main window, used 0 for ours
    op.wFunc= FO_COPY;   //Tell SHFileOperation to COPY files
    sprintf(source,"%s\0",LabelSourceDir->Caption.c_str());  //Source directory
```

LISTING 14.13 Continued

```
op.pFrom = source;
sprintf(dest,"%s\0",LabelTargetDir->Caption.c_str());    //Destination directory
op.pTo = dest;
op.fFlags= FOF_NOCONFIRMATION + FOF_ALLOWUNDO;

TCursor Save_Cursor = Screen->Cursor;
Screen->Cursor = crHourGlass;    // Show hourglass cursor

try
{
    if (SHFileOperation(&op) == 0)   // so far looks good
    {
        if (op.fAnyOperationsAborted)
            LabelMoveResults->Caption = "Copy process halted!";
        else
            LabelMoveResults->Caption = "Copy operation successful!";
    }
    else   // had a problem
        LabelMoveResults->Caption = "Copy process unsuccessful.";
}
__finally
{
  Screen->Cursor = Save_Cursor; // always restore the cursor
}
DirectoryListBoxTarget->Update();
}
```

When this example is executed, all files and subdirectories within the directory identified by LabelSourceDir->Caption will be copied over to the directory identified by LabelTargetDir->Caption.

You'll notice that one of the first things done in the ButtonCopyDir() event handler is the declaration of a variable, op, based on the SHFILEOPSTRUCT structure and that its values are initialized. The variable op is used by the SHFileOperation() function to carry out the file move operation. The structure SHFILEOPSTRUCT has the following format:

```
typedef struct _SHFILEOPSTRUCT { // shfos
    HWND        hwnd;
    UINT        wFunc;
    LPCSTR      pFrom;
    LPCSTR      pTo;
```

```
    FILEOP_FLAGS fFlags;
    BOOL         fAnyOperationsAborted;
    LPVOID       hNameMappings;
    LPCSTR       lpszProgressTitle;
} SHFILEOPSTRUCT, FAR *LPSHFILEOPSTRUCT;
```

At first glance, there seems to be many items to fill out, however, not all fields are necessary. For instance, the only properties used in our example include wFunc, pFrom, pTo, and fFlags. Let's examine each of these properties.

wFunc indicates the operation to perform. The operation selections are shown in Table 14.14.

TABLE 14.14   Possible Operations

Member	Value
FO_COPY	Copies the files specified by pFrom to the location specified by pTo. You can copy files from one location to another location even across volumes.
FO_DELETE	Deletes the files specified by pFrom. The pTo is ignored because we are just deleting the files. See flags under this parameter for Recycle Bin operations.
FO_MOVE	Moves the files specified by pFrom to the location specified by pTo. This will physically move the source files to another location. It does support over-the-volume transfers.
FO_RENAME	Renames the files specified by pFrom.

In our example, we are copying one directory to another (making a backup), using FO_COPY. Use caution when using FO_MOVE or FO_DELETE.

pFrom represents a pointer to a buffer specifying one or more source filenames or a folder. Multiple names must be null-separated. The list of names must be double–null-terminated. If you have many files in a list, you could use a regular \0, which is the separator for those files. At the end of the list, use double-null termination. In our example, we're identifying a complete directory and any subfolders.

pTo represents a pointer to a buffer that contains the name of the destination file or folder. The buffer can contain multiple destination filenames if the fFlags member specifies FOF_MULTIDESTFILES (see Table 14.14). Multiple names must be null-separated, and the list of names must be double–null-terminated.

In our example, we use the C function sprintf() to set up our null-terminated strings used for pFrom and pTo. This is where we transfer the value from our TEdit controls representing the folders and tack on an additional null terminator.

CAUTION

Not tacking an additional `null` terminator at the end of the string used for `pFrom` or `pTo` is a common miss. Forgetting to do so, will likely cause an error in the `SHFileOperation()` operation.

Next, `fFlags` identifies the flags that control the file operation. This member can be any combination of the values shown in Table 14.15.

TABLE 14.15   File Operation Flags

Flag	Value
FOF_ALLOWUNDO	Preserves undo information, if possible.
FOF_FILESONLY	Performs the operation only on files if a wildcard filename (*.*) is specified.
FOF_MULTIDESTFILES	Indicates that the pTo member specifies multiple destination files (one for each source file) rather than one directory where all source files are to be deposited.
FOF_NOCONFIRMATION	Responds with Yes to All for any dialog box that is displayed.
FOF_NOCONFIRMMKDIR	Does not confirm the creation of a new directory if the operation requires one to be created.
FOF_RENAMEONCOLLISION	Gives a new name to the file being operated on (such as Copy #1 of...) in a move, copy, or rename operation, if a file of the target name already exists.
FOF_SILENT	Does not display a progress dialog box. Nothing will appear while this function is in operation.
FOF_SIMPLEPROGRESS	Displays a progress dialog box, but does not show the file-names.
FOF_WANTMAPPINGHANDLE	Fills in the hNameMappings member. The handle must be freed by using the SHFreeNameMappings() function.

In our example, we are using the FOF_NOCONFIRMATION and FOF_ALLOWUNDO to support our folder copy. To enable a list of files (rather than the contents and subdirectories of a folder), you would use the FOF_MULTIDESTFILES flag. An example is provided in the sample program contained on the CD-ROM.

These are the only properties we're interested in within our example because they relate to SHFILEOPSTRUCT. Be sure to check out the other structure properties, which are explained in the Win32 API Help file.

> **NOTE**
>
> You might have noticed the function ZeroMemory() used in the example. After declaring the SHFILEOPSTRUCT record variable op, we want to NULL out the structure information so that we can start with a blank canvas. The reason is that we don't want any dirty values at the memory location associated to op because there are a wide number of properties that are examined by the SHFileOperation() function and could affect its operation.

Sending Files to the Recycle Bin

One novel way of using the SHFileOperation() function is to delete files and place them in the Recycle Bin. The code example in Listing 14.14 illustrates how to perform a directory deletion.

LISTING 14.14   Deleting All Files in a Directory

```
void __fastcall TForm1::ButtonSendToRecycleBinClick(TObject *Sender)
{
    // initialize
    MemoFilesToMove->Clear();
    ListBoxFilesToMove->Clear();
    LabelMoveResults->Caption = "";

    AnsiString DelDir;     //Our directory handle
    int index = DirectoryListBoxSource->ItemIndex; //keep track of index

    //Get the CURRENTLY selected item in the list...
    DelDir = DirectoryListBoxSource->Directory;

    AnsiString alert;
    alert =  "Are you sure you wish to remove the folder \"" + DelDir + "\" "
            "and all its contents?";

    int response =
        Application->MessageBox(alert.c_str(), "Remove Folder", MB_YESNO);

    if (response == ID_NO)
        return; // get out

    DelDir.SetLength(DelDir.Length() + 1);
        DelDir[DelDir.Length()] = '\0';
    DelDir.SetLength(DelDir.Length() + 1);
        DelDir[DelDir.Length()] = '\0';
```

LISTING 14.14   Continued

```
// before we send the folder and it's contents to the recycle
// bin, lets drop back one folder. This keeps from having a sharing
// violation
DirectoryListBoxSource->Directory = DirectoryListBoxSource->Items
➥->Strings[index-1];
DirectoryListBoxSource->Update();

SHFILEOPSTRUCT op;   //Declare structure variable

//Clear out memory
ZeroMemory(&op, sizeof(op));
//Set up structure for SHFIleOperation for source and destination...
op.hwnd = 0;
op.wFunc= FO_DELETE;     //Delete files flag
op.pFrom = DelDir.c_str();
op.fFlags=FOF_ALLOWUNDO;
int copy_done = SHFileOperation(&op);

if (copy_done == 0)
{
  if (op.fAnyOperationsAborted)
    LabelMoveResults->Caption = "You have halted the removal of the folder."
                "Some files may have been moved to the Recycle Bin. "
                "Go to Recycle Bin to restore those files.";
  else
    LabelMoveResults->Caption  = "Folder removal successful!";
}
else
    LabelMoveResults->Caption  = "Folder removal failed.";

//Update DirectoryListbox
DirectoryListBoxSource->Update();
}
```

When this code runs, it will go through the directory selected by the user and delete all files and children files within that directory. All the files are transferred to the Recycle Bin. To set up SHFileOperation(), it's important to use the FOF_ALLOWUNDO flag for the fFlags attribute in combination with FO_DELETE flag for the wFunc attribute.

The last two examples provided thus far have demonstrated how powerful and flexible the SH*x* functions can be. You might find other SH*x* functions useful, such as SHEmptyRecycleBin(), SHQueryRecycleBin(), and SHBrowseForFolder().

It would take a whole book to cover Shell programming. It's recommended that you refer to C++Builder's Win32 API Reference Guide for more information and experiment with some of the undocumented Shell features contained in the SHELL32.DLL, but, of course, use extreme caution. If not used properly, the Shell API can cause some serious problems such as deleted or misplaced files.

International Features

The Win32 API provides support for non-English development and deployment to international markets. For example, languages other than English and technical symbols are best represented using the 16-bit Unicode character set that is supported by Windows. National Language Support (NLS) functions help target an application for specific international markets. The various internal features are described in Table 14.16.

TABLE 14.16   National Language Support Functions

International Feature	Description
End-User-Defined Characters (EUDC)	Provides support for customized characters that are not available in standard screen or printer fonts. EUDC includes Far Eastern language syntax, such as Japanese and Chinese.
Input Method Editor (IME)	Provides a collection of functions, messages, and structures used to support Unicode and double-byte character sets. IME functionality is provided by imm32.dll.
National Language Support	Provides support for adapting and transitioning applications to various language-specific and location-specific environments.
Unicode and Character Sets	Provides support for character encoding, including the Unicode standard. Character encoding, such as Unicode, enables applications to support multilingual text processing.

Some of these capabilities such as the EUDC and IME require foreign versions of the Windows operating system. Asian versions, for example, use a totally different character set than the English version does. Software being developed for these cultures would benefit from the specific functionality provided by this API functional area. However, providing an example is not within the scope of this book.

Network Services

Network services allow communication between applications on different computers on a network. The network functions are used to create and manage connections to shared resources, such as directories and network printers, on computers in the network. The Win32 network interfaces include Windows Networking, Windows Sockets, NetBIOS, RAS, SNMP, and Network DDE and are described in Table 14.17.

TABLE 14.17   The Win32 Network Interfaces

Network Interface	Description
Windows Networking (WNet)	Provides a set of network-independent functions for implementing networking capabilities within an application. Functionality is provided by the Win32 Network Interface DLL (`mpr.dll`). `WNet` prefixes all network functions.
Ported LAN Manager Functions	Provides functionality for a network operating system and was originally designed for OS/2-based servers. Now it is no longer considered to be part of the Win32 API. However, much of the functionality is still provided by Windows through the `netapi32.dll`.
NetBIOS Interface	Used to communicate via a network with applications on other computers. The Network Basic Input/Output System (NetBIOS) functionality is provided by the `netapi32.dll`.
Network Dynamic Data Exchange	Enables DDE to work over a network. Functionality is provided by the `WFW` DDE Share Interface (`nddeapi.dll`). All network DDE functions are prefixed by `NDde`.
Remote Access Service (RAS)	Allows users at remote locations to connect directly to a computer network, accessing one or more RAS servers. Supports dial-up networking. RAS functionality is provided by the `rasapi32.dll`. All RAS functions are prefixed by `RAS`.
Simple Network Management Protocol (SNMP)	Used for exchanging network management information through the SNMP Internet standard protocol. See Windows Help for more information.
Windows Sockets (WinSock)	Used for TCP and UDP network data exchange. WinSock is based on the Berkeley Software Distribution (BSD) Unix sockets paradigm. Windows Socket functionality is provided by `wsock32.dll` (WinSock version 1.1) or by `ws2_32.dll` (WinSock version 2.0).

By far, the most utilized network component of the Win32 API is Window Sockets (WinSock). WinSock provides the basis for all Internet activity and applications: email, Web browsers, udp broadcasting, ftp, and so on. Let's look at a useful example pertaining to the WinSock library.

Getting Network Info

One of the things that can be really helpful is to know the IP address of the local computer (see Figure 14.11).

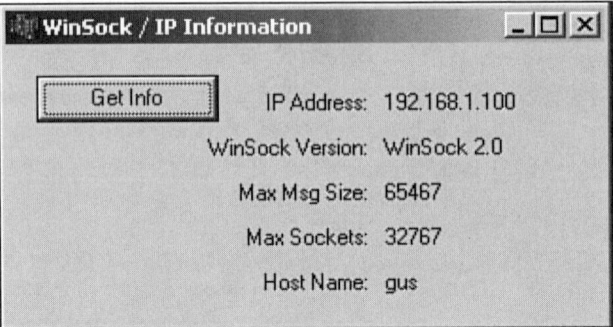

FIGURE 14.11   Network Info Example Using WinSock.

One of the easiest ways to determine the IP address for your primary network card or modem is to use the WinSock library. Other useful information might include the WinSock version, maximum size, and host name. The code example in Listing 14.15 illustrates how we can obtain this information.

LISTING 14.15   Getting Network Info

```
void __fastcall TFormWinSockIPInfo::ButtonGetInfoClick(TObject *Sender)
{
    WSADATA           localWSA;
    if (WSAStartup ((MAKEWORD(1,1)), &localWSA) != 0)
    {
        MessageBox (NULL, "Sorry - Unable to load Windows Sockets - "
                          "Please close other applications and try again.",
                          "UDP Network Interface", MB_OK | MB_ICONASTERISK);
        WSACleanup ();
        return;
    }
    LabelMaxSize->Caption = localWSA.iMaxUdpDg;
    LabelVersion->Caption = AnsiString(localWSA.szDescription);

    char szHost[MAX_PATH];  // should be big enough.
    memset(szHost, 0, MAX_PATH);  // clear it
    gethostname(szHost, MAX_PATH);

    struct hostent *hp;
    hp = gethostbyname(szHost);
    if( ! hp )
          return;
    LabelName->Caption = hp->h_name;
```

LISTING 14.15 Continued

```
char szIpAddress[96];
sprintf(szIpAddress, "%d.%d.%d.%d",
                    UC(hp->h_addr[0]), UC(hp->h_addr[1]),
                    UC(hp->h_addr[2]), UC(hp->h_addr[3]));
LabelIPAddress->Caption = AnsiString(szIpAddress);


// clean-up
WSACleanup ();
}
```

The first WinSock call made in this example is WSAStartup(). This call initiates the use of the Windows Sockets DLL by our program. The first parameter passed into the WSAStarup() call indicates the version of WinSock we need to perform our query of information. In this case, version 1.1 is enough to get the information we need. That is to say that no calls or features require anything newer than WinSock version 1.1. The second item passed into the WSAStartup() call is a pointer to the WSADATA structure defined by the variable localWSA. This is the first nugget of information that we receive. Let's take a look at the WSADATA structure definition.

```
typedef struct WSAData {
        WORD                    wVersion;
        WORD                    wHighVersion;
        char                    szDescription[WSADESCRIPTION_LEN+1];
        char                    szSystemStatus[WSASYS_STATUS_LEN+1];
        unsigned short          iMaxSockets;
        unsigned short          iMaxUdpDg;
        char FAR *              lpVendorInfo;
} WSADATA, FAR * LPWSADATA;
```

The information displayed on the form within our example includes the descriptive version using the character array szDescription, the maximum size of a UDP packet using iMaxUdpDg, and the maximum number of sockets that can be established using iMaxSockets.

After we gather this information using WSAStartup(), we use the gethost() call to determine the host name for the local machine. This information is displayed to the user. Finally, we retrieve the IP address using this host name through a call to gethostbyname(), which returns a pointer to the hostent structure. The hostent structure is defined as follows:

```
struct hostent {
    char FAR *      h_name;
```

```
    char FAR * FAR * h_aliases;
    short           h_addrtype;
    short           h_length;
    char FAR * FAR * h_addr_list;
};
```

Each IP byte is contained in the list for h_addr, which we can access by index. However, this data is contained in an integer. Again, all we care about for each index is the first byte. So, as demonstrated in our example, we apply the following macro, which clears all the values greater than 255 to give us one byte.

```
#  define  UC(b)  (((int)b)&0xff)
```

Using sprintf(), we format the IP address value in its normal notation so that it can be displayed to the user.

Adding System Support

It's sometimes useful to add system-support capabilities to an application, such as the capability to quickly lock an NT workstation, disable Ctrl+Alt+Delete, or shut down (and reboot) a machine. The Win32 API provides many useful routines to help perform these types of tasks. However, it's important to note the danger of providing these types of capabilities. If you're going to implement these types of functionality (and debugging in the process), be sure to save early and often, or you might just wish you had selected another hobby or profession.

Locking an NT Workstation

It's time to introduce you to another new Win32 API named LockWorkStation(), which is used to automatically lock an NT system. LockWorkStation() takes no parameters, and it's automatic. Locking workstations or servers couldn't be easier. The function mimics the well-known Ctrl+Alt+Delete keys and selects Lock Workstation. The system is then locked until later use. This function is in the WINUSER.H header file.

With the following one line of code, you can automate what used to be a manual operation under NT. Unfortunately, Windows 9x does not support this function:

```
LockWorkStation();
```

System Shutdown

A lot of beginners often ask how to automate the shutdown of a Windows PC. By using the ExitWindowsEx() or ExitWindows() function, you can properly shut down the system. The following code demonstrates how to use the ExitWindowsEx() API function:

```
ExitWindowsEx(EWX_SHUTDOWN,0);
```

This routine is not new like the `LockWorkStation()` function, but it sure has a lot of power in manipulating your system—by turning it off. If your PC has power conservation methods in the BIOS, `ExitWindowEx()` will automatically shut down your PC's power, too.

`ExitWindowsEx()` is an easy way to shut down Windows, but you can do a lot more than just shut down Windows. The `ExitWindowEx()` function has more flags with which to work. The format is as follows:

```
BOOL ExitWindowsEx(
    UINT uFlags,      // shutdown operation
    DWORD dwReserved    // reserved
    );
```

`uFlags` are flags to specify which shutdown type you wish to perform. Table 14.18 shows the values.

TABLE 14.18 System Shutdown Function Flags

Flags	Value
EWX_FORCE	Forces processes to terminate. When this flag is set, Windows does not send the messages WM_QUERYENDSESSION and WM_ENDSESSION to the applications currently running in the system. This can cause the applications to lose data, so you should use this flag only in an emergency.
EWX_LOGOFF	Shuts down all processes running in the security context of the process that called the ExitWindowsEx() function. Then it logs the user off.
EWX_POWEROFF	Shuts down the system and turns off the power. The system must support the power-off feature. Windows NT: The calling process must have the SE_SHUTDOWN_NAME privilege. Windows 95: Security privileges are not supported or required.
EWX_REBOOT	Shuts down and then restarts the system. Windows NT: The calling process must have the SE_SHUTDOWN_NAME privilege.
EWX_SHUTDOWN	Shuts down the system to a point at which it is safe to turn off the power. All file buffers have been flushed to disk, and all running processes have stopped. Windows NT: The calling process must have the SE_SHUTDOWN_NAME privilege.

The `dwReserved` parameter is currently not used.

Summary

The functional areas of the Win32 API described in this chapter provide an initial foundation for understanding the composition and capabilities of the API. This chapter has provided a hand full of examples associated within these functional areas illustrating how to use Win32 API calls, callbacks, and structures. It has armed you with the essentials, but it has only scratched the surface of what the API can provide.

You are encouraged to explore, experiment, and use the Win32 API to create better applications and components, resulting in greater choice and satisfaction for Windows users. When either a desired capability is not provided by a VCL, or when performance can be vastly improved by using the Win32 API, look to see what the API offers. Keep in mind that each Windows release and Internet Explorer update potentially introduces even more capabilities and features that you can easily take advantage of with C++Builder.

Graphics and Multimedia Techniques

by Paul Gustavson

Many applications require some type of graphics or multimedia support to reflect visual or audio information to the user. In fact, a growing number of applications are designed specifically for creating, managing, displaying, or playing multimedia files. Contrary to popular belief, applications developed with C++Builder can easily incorporate these types of features and capabilities.

In the last chapter we examined the functional areas of the Win32 API. Two of the things we touched on were the graphics and multimedia capabilities provided by the Win32 API. In this chapter, we will discuss several techniques for supporting graphics and multimedia in an application. On the graphics end, we'll take a deeper look at the Windows GDI, the image support provided by the VCL, and techniques for image processing. Then, we'll take a hard look at the multimedia capabilities and techniques supported by C++Builder for playing audio files, video files, and CD music.

> **NOTE**
>
> Even though this chapter focuses on Windows graphics and multimedia concepts, Linux can support many of the techniques described here through Borland's CLX components. In particular, discussion regarding the VCL elements such as TCanvas, TBrush, TPen, TFont, TBitmap, and TImage can be matched through the equivalent CLX elements.

The Graphical Device Interface (GDI)

The visible aspect of a C++Builder application is built using forms and controls. Some aspects of the application's GUI may consist of graphics and pictures. The display of these graphics and pictures is where the GDI subsection of Windows API comes into play. The GDI is one of the core parts of the Windows operating system and is housed in GDI.DLL and GDI32.DLL. It encompasses hundreds of functions (in recent versions of Windows there are more than 400 exports in GDI32.DLL). Everything that draws in Windows uses the GDI, including Windows itself.

The GDI exists for one main reason: device independence. When you draw using GDI functions, you do not need to know the specifics of programming every video card and printer on the market today and tomorrow. The GDI provides a layer of abstraction between your application code and the hardware, so you don't have to worry about hardware issues.

Borland provides another layer of abstraction between the application code and the GDI, with the TCanvas, TBrush, TPen, and TFont classes. We will examine these shortly, but first it's important to understand some GDI essentials.

> **NOTE**
>
> Unfortunately, there is not enough space to cover all the features available within the GDI. For more information, see the Win32 API help on GDI, or the VCL help starting at TCanvas.

The Windows API and the Device Context

As with just about every other part of Windows programming, a handle is needed to interface with the GDI. This handle is known as the *Device Context* (DC). In the standard Windows API, we can retrieve a DC using the GetDC() routine. After we get the DC, we can use a number of GDI functions to draw within the client area of that window. Let's take a look at an example:

```
void __fastcall TForm1::ButtonDrawGDIClick(TObject *Sender)
{
  HDC hDC = GetDC(Handle);
  Rectangle(hDC,10,10,100,100);
  ReleaseDC(Handle, hDC);
}
```

In this example, we pass the window handle of our application's form as a parameter into the GetDC() function. In return, we receive a DC for the client area associated to that window. The Rectangle() function is a GDI routine that will draw a rectangle using the current pen and brush at the specified location. After we have finished drawing, we release the DC using ReleaseDC().

TIP

To draw anywhere on the desktop, pass NULL as the hWindow argument to GetDC() or
GetWindowDC().

Using TCanvas

When programming using C++Builder, it is preferable to use object-oriented classes
and components over C structured API code to improve efficiency and reuse. This is
the advantage VCL provides over the Windows API. Support for drawing lines and
filled areas is provided by the TCanvas component.

TCanvas is a wrapper around the GDI functionality and is available as a property on
the TForm, TPrinter, TImage, TBitmap, and TToolbar components as well as on a number
of custom control components. You access Canvas as a property of these components. With TCanvas, we can draw the same rectangle we demonstrated earlier as
follows:

```
void __fastcall TForm1::ButtonDrawCanvasClick(TObject *Sender)
{
   Canvas->Rectangle(10, 10, 100, 100);
}
```

In this example, we have used only one line of code to draw a rectangle within the
form, whereas previously it took three lines of code when using the Win32 GDI
functions directly.

TCanvas provides an object-oriented interface to the Windows API. The biggest advantage is that it handles resources for you. There are some fairly complex rules concerning how to manage GDI resources when using the raw API, whereas TCanvas handles
these rules for you seamlessly. Also, TCanvas provides the standard VCL property
system for getting and setting many of the attributes of the underlying Device
Context, which simplifies your code and makes it much easier to read and understand.

Key Properties

TCanvas has several key properties you should know about:

- TPen Pen—The currently selected pen for drawing

- TBrush Brush—The currently selected brush

- TFont Font—The currently selected font

- TPoint PenPos—Positions the pen for drawing

It is important to mention that the canvas will use the current pen, brush, font, and position as appropriate when drawing. Properties to these elements should be changed before any canvas drawing function is called. We'll look at the classes behind some of these properties in a short bit, but first let's take a look at how we can effectively use TCanvas.

Mixing TCanvas with the GDI

TCanvas and its associated classes are coded in the file graphics.pas, but they do not wrap all the GDI functions. Borland has implemented only the most commonly used functions. Although the VCL could be even more helpful, keep in mind that with C++Builder the Windows API is just a function call away.

Because TCanvas provides a Handle property to a device context, we can interweave GDI function calls with our VCL-based code. Going back to our original rectangle example, this could be coded using both the Canvas interface and the GDI as follows:

```
void __fastcall TForm1::ButtonDrawCanvasGDIClick(TObject *Sender)
{
    Rectangle(Canvas->Handle, 10, 10, 100, 100);
}
```

In this example, we are using the standard Win32 GDI function Rectangle() and passing the handle to the Form's Canvas, which is a Device Context. You'll find that this example code achieves exactly the same results as the previous examples.

Drawing Lines, Curves, and Other Shapes

Drawing lines and curves is easy with a TCanvas: Just set up the relevant pen, and then call the appropriate function. There are many functions in TCanvas for line drawing, which are readily available in the C++Builder documentation. A simple line, for example, is drawn using two commands:

```
Canvas->MoveTo(1, 1);
Canvas->LineTo(9, 1);
```

In this example, MoveTo() sets the pen location, and LineTo() draws a straight line from that initial location up to, but not including, the last point specified, which is the position (9,1). This is illustrated in Figure 15.1.

To draw a series of connected curves, such as a sine wave, you can use the PolyBezier() function as shown in Listing 15.1:

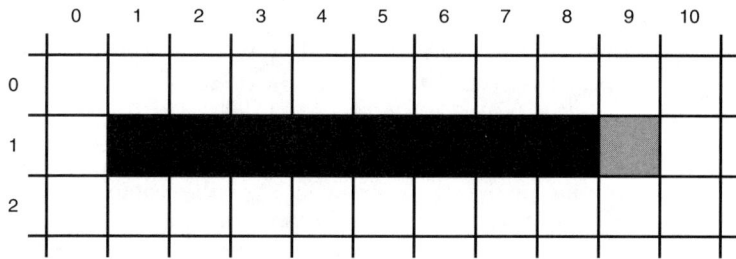

FIGURE 15.1   LineTo(9,1) does not fill in the last pixel.

LISTING 15.1   Drawing a Sequence of Curved Lines (a Sine Wave)

```
void __fastcall TForm1::ButtonDrawSineWaveClick(TObject *Sender)
{
    Canvas->Pen->Color = TColor(EditColor->Text.ToIntDef(0)); //clBlue;
    Canvas->Pen->Style = psSolid; // solid line
    Canvas->Pen->Width = EditPenWidth->Text.ToIntDef(1);

    const int maxpts = 19;
    TPoint pts[maxpts];
    double pi_3 = 3.1415926535897932384626433832795 / 3.0;

    for (int i = 0; i<maxpts; i++)
    {
       pts[i].x = (i+1)*10;
       pts[i].y = (sin(i*pi_3)*200) + 300; // axis (pi) every 3rd one
    }

    Canvas->PolyBezier(EXISTINGARRAY(pts));

    /* Show the points as well as the curve */
    for (int i = 0; i<maxpts; i++)
    {
            Canvas->Rectangle(pts[i].x-3,pts[i].y-3,pts[i].x+3,pts[i].y+3);
    }
}
```

When using PolyBezier(), you need to identify at least four points, which identifies a single curve. The first and fourth points identify the start and end location of the initial curve; the second and third points identify control points for manipulating the curve. Any subsequent curves in the sequence, if they are to be included, require exactly three points per curve. The first two points after the first curve identify control points for the new curve, and the third point identifies the end location for the existing curve and the start location for the next curve if there is to be one.

NOTE

Many of the examples listed in this chapter are designed to point out the API call that's needed to perform the necessary task. There are other elements not shown, such as variables and the identification of header files within the include section. These elements are needed for the code to properly compile. However, all the source described in this chapter can be found on the accompanying CD-ROM.

To draw various polygon shapes, use the Polygon() function. A hexagon, for example, can be drawn as shown in Listing 15.2:

LISTING 15.2   Drawing a Polygon Shape (a Hexagon)

```
void __fastcall TForm1::ButtonDrawHexagonClick(TObject *Sender)
{
  TPoint points[5];
  points[0] = Point(80,140);
  points[1] = Point(140,196);
  points[2] = Point(116,260);
  points[3] = Point(44,260);
  points[4] = Point(20,196);

  Canvas->Brush->Color = clTeal;  // fills hexagon with teal
  Canvas->Polygon(points, 4);
}
```

A hexagon contains five points. In this example, we identify each of those points within a Point array, which is passed in as parameter to the Polygon() function.

Drawing Filled Areas

Filled images use both a *pen* and a *brush*. The pen is used for the outline of a shape, and the brush is used to fill in the interior of a shape. For example, a yellow-filled rectangle with a blue outline could be drawn as shown in Listing 15.3.

LISTING 15.3   Drawing a Filled Rectangle

```
void __fastcall TForm1::ButtonDrawRectClick(TObject *Sender)
{
  TRect MyRect(50,50,100,100);
  Canvas->Pen->Color = clBlue;
```

LISTING 15.3   Continued

```
Canvas->Pen->Style = psSolid; // solid line
Canvas->Pen->Width = 2;
Canvas->Brush->Color = clYellow;
Canvas->Brush->Style = bsSolid;
Canvas->Rectangle(MyRect);
}
```

Notice how we adjust the Pen and Brush attributes before drawing the rectangle. Also, identifying a boundary rectangle is required for other functions such as the Ellipse() function.

```
Canvas->Ellipse(MyRect);
```

In this example, the system draws the ellipse so that it just touches the boundaries of the rectangle.

Drawing Text

There are several ways to draw text using TCanvas. The easiest is to use TextOut(), which starts at a specified (x,y) position. On return, this function positions the PenPos to the end of the drawn text (top right), allowing for easy continuation. Listing 15.4 provides an example.

LISTING 15.4   Writing Out Text Using TextOut()

```
void __fastcall TForm1::ButtonTextOutClick(TObject *Sender)
{
    Canvas->Font->Color = clNavy;
    Canvas->TextOut(20,20,"Here's how you write text ");
    Canvas->TextOut(Canvas->PenPos.x,Canvas->PenPos.y,
                "and how you continue to write text.");
}
```

Another way to write out text is to use TextRect(). TextRect() will draw the text within a rectangle and clip any text that does not fit. A simple example is provided in Listing 15.5.

LISTING 15.5   Writing Out Text Using TextRect()

```
void __fastcall TForm1::ButtonTextRectClick(TObject *Sender)
{
    Canvas->Font->Color = clNavy;
    TRect MyRect(10,10,250,100);
```

LISTING 15.5   Continued

```
Canvas->TextRect(MyRect,10,10,
    "Here's how you write text within a rectangle.");
}
```

The size of the text for either of these functions depends on the font. For a fixed-pitch font, such as Courier, each letter takes up the same amount of space, whether it is an *i* or a *w*. With a variable-pitch font, each letter is a different width, so the *i* takes up less space than the *w*. To calculate the width and height a given string will take up, TCanvas provides the function TextExtent(), which returns a TSize that can be used for positioning the text as appropriate.

As an example, in the analog clock example code, the text is drawn using the following:

```
AnsiString text = "Right Click for Menu...";
TSize textSize = Canvas->TextExtent(text);
int x = (Width - textSize.cx) / 2;
int y = Height - textSize.cy - 2;
Canvas->TextOut(x, y, text);
```

The math performed to calculate x and y in this example ensures that the text is centered at the bottom of the canvas object.

Using TPen

When you draw a line or a lined object, such as an empty circle, on a TCanvas object, the current pen is used to define the color, style, and thickness mode. The Color property identifies the color used to draw lines on the canvas. The Style property determines how the line is drawn: solid, dotted, dashed, and so on. The thickness of line is controlled by the Width property. If the Width is greater than 1, the line will automatically be solid. Therefore, if you need a thick dotted line, one approach is to draw multiple lines next to each other (each line being one pixel apart).

TPen also has a property called Mode, which defines how the pen's color is affected by the underlying color already on the canvas. Of particular interest is the pmNotXor mode, which will perform a "not xor" of the pen's color with the underlying canvas color. This is particularly useful for drawing temporary lines over an image when the line will be erased shortly afterward. The line can then be erased by redrawing the line over the first line because the pmNotXor mode will cancel out the two lines, leaving the original image displayed. This can be used, for example, to paint a zooming region or a crop region within a graphics program. This is shown in Figure 15.2.

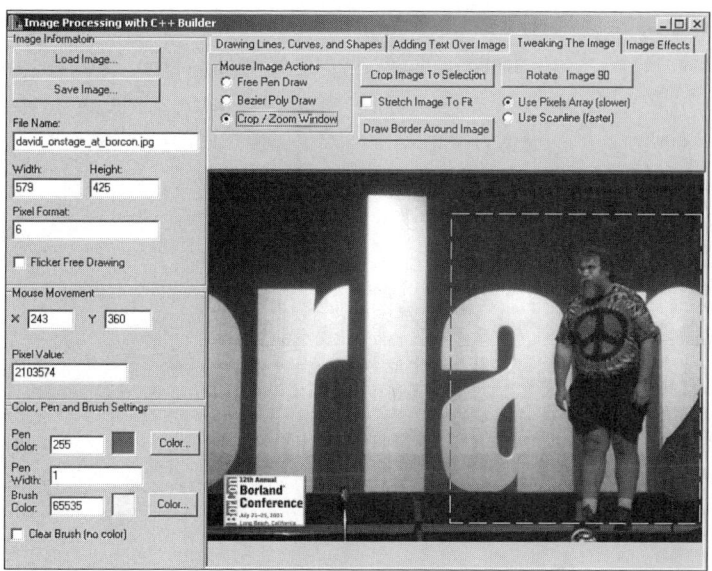

FIGURE 15.2   Painting a crop region over an image.

Let's take a look at the example in Listing 15.6 that shows how to display a crop region in C++Builder.

LISTING 15.6   Displaying a crop region

```
void __fastcall TForm1::FormMouseDown(TObject *Sender, TMouseButton Button,
     TShiftState Shift, int X, int Y)
{
  if (Button == mbLeft)
  {
    oX = X;   // anchor point
    oY = Y;
    lX = X;
    lY = Y;
    Canvas->Pen->Color = clBlack;
    Canvas->Pen->Style = psDash; // dashed line
    Canvas->Pen->Width = 1;
    Canvas->Pen->Mode  = pmNotXor;
    Canvas->Brush->Style = bsClear;
    DrawSelectRegion = true;
  }
}
//  — — — — — — — — — — — — — — — — — — — — — — — — — — — — — —  —  —  —  —  — —  — -.
```

LISTING 15.6   Continued

```
void __fastcall TForm1::FormMouseMove(TObject *Sender, TShiftState Shift,
     int X, int Y)
{
  TRect MyRect;
  if (DrawSelectRegion)
  {
     MyRect = TRect(oX,oY,lX,lY);
     Canvas->Rectangle(MyRect);
     lX = X;
     lY = Y;
     MyRect = TRect(oX,oY,lX,lY);
     Canvas->Rectangle(MyRect);
  }
}
//-------------------------------------------------


void __fastcall TForm1::FormMouseUp(TObject *Sender, TMouseButton Button,
     TShiftState Shift, int X, int Y)
{
  TRect MyRect;
  if (DrawSelectRegion)
  {
     MyRect = TRect(oX,oY,lX,lY);
     Canvas->Rectangle(MyRect);
     DrawSelectRegion = false;
  }
}
```

In this example, when the left mouse button is clicked, an anchor is made at the X, Y point, and the canvas properties are set up for displaying a dashed rectangle. When the mouse moves with the left button still down, the rectangle making up the zoom area changes appropriately in size, and the original picture and objects are still displayed. When the mouse button is released, one last rectangle is drawn to erase the previous crop region. The key to making this work is having the pen Mode property set for pmNotXor, which we set when the mouse button was pressed. Additionally, the brush style set for bsClear, ensures that the existing objects on the Canvas are not masked by the drawn rectangle. Let's take a look at the aspects of TBrush.

Using TBrush

A brush is used to determine how to fill-in the selected region of the canvas. TBrush has the properties Color, Style, and Bitmap. Color is a TColor property used to identify the color to be used by the brush. Style determines whether to fill in the object or use a pattern of lines to shade the area. The Style property takes the values bsSolid, bsCross, bsClear, bsDiagCross, bsBDiagonal, bsHorizontal, bsFDiagonal, and bsVertical. These should be self-explanatory. In the last example we used bsClear to keep the background information visible. The effect of these styles can also be seen in the analog clock program example provided on the CD-ROM and described later. The Bitmap property can also be used to identify an external bitmap image that, like Style, defines a pattern for the brush. This is illustrated in Figure 15.3.

FIGURE 15.3 Placing an image on the canvas of a C++Builder application.

Let's take a look at Listing 15.7, which provides an example on assigning a bitmap brush to the Form Canvas.

LISTING 15.7 Tiling and Stretching a Bitmap onto a Form

```
void __fastcall TForm1::ButtonAssignBitmapToCanvasClick(TObject *Sender)
{
    OpenDialog1->Filter = "Bmp files (*.bmp)|*.BMP";
    if (OpenDialog1->Execute())
    {
        Graphics::TBitmap *BrushBmp = new Graphics::TBitmap;

        try
        {
          BrushBmp->LoadFromFile(OpenDialog1->FileName);
          Canvas->Brush->Bitmap = BrushBmp;
          TRect rect;
          rect.Left = 0;
          rect.Top  = 0;
```

LISTING 15.7 Continued

```
        rect.Right = ClientWidth;
        rect.Bottom = ClientHeight;
        if (CheckBoxStretch->Checked)
                Canvas->StretchDraw(rect, BrushBmp);
        else
                Canvas->FillRect(rect);
    }
    __finally
    {
      Canvas->Brush->Bitmap = NULL;
      delete BrushBmp;
    }
  }
}
```

In this example, a bitmap is loaded that is either *tiled* to the form, or *stretched* to fit across the whole form depending on the value of the CheckBoxStretch control. This capability might be useful for providing skin support in an application. In a short while, we'll look more in depth at working with TBitmap objects.

Using TFont

The current font is used in text functions such as TextOut(). A TFont object has all the attributes that you would expect, such as Color, Name, Style, Height, and Size. The Color property, of course, is used to identify the color of the text to be displayed. The Name property is used to set the type of font, such as Arial, or Courier. The Style property is used to identify whether the text should be bold, underlined, and/or italicized. Let's take a look at the example code in Listing 15.8:

LISTING 15.8 Adjusting the Font of a Canvas

```
void __fastcall TForm1::ButtonFontClick(TObject *Sender)
{
  if (FontDialog1->Execute())
  {
    EditFont->Text = FontDialog1->Font->Name;
    Canvas->Font->Name = FontDialog1->Font->Name;
    Canvas->Font->Style = FontDialog1->Font->Style;
    Canvas->Font->Size = FontDialog1->Font->Size;
    Canvas->Font->Color = FontDialog1->Font->Color;
  }
```

LISTING 15.8   Continued

```
}

//--------------------------------------------------.

void __fastcall TForm1::ButtonApplyTextClick(TObject *Sender)
{
        Canvas->TextOut(100,100,EditText->Text);
}
```

In the `ButtonFontClick()` event hander, we use a `TFontDialog` object to obtain the desired font attributes of the user. These attributes are assigned to the property values of the Font property for the Canvas. Next, the `ButtonApplyTextClick()` event hander is used to write out the text contained within `EditText` using the Font properties that were previously assigned.

The size of the font can be set in two ways: `Height` in pixels or `Size` in points. In general, most users will want to set the font size in points, not in pixels. The `TFontDialog`, for example, requests a font height from the user, not a pixel size. However, programmatically, it's useful to know the pixel height when placing text on a canvas or image. Fortunately, if you set one, the other is automatically calculated and can be used accordingly.

Using `TColor`

One of the commonly modified properties of the Brush, Pen, and Font elements associated to a `TCanvas` object is the `Color`. The color of a graphics object in the VCL is set using the `TColor` property. `TColor` is a VCL mapping of the Windows API `COLORREF` value, which uses a 32-bit number to specify the color. The color is divided into the constituent components Red, Green, and Blue, so Red is (255,0,0), and White is (255,255,255). The following code snippet provides an example of how to set the color:

```
void __fastcall TForm1::ButtonFontColorClick(TObject *Sender)
{
  if (ColorDialog1->Execute())
  {
    Canvas->Font->Color = ColorDialog1->Color;
  }
}
```

In this example, we use a `TColorDialog` object to provide the user with a dialog to select the color. After the color is selected it is assigned to the Canvas Font color.

Not all displays attached to a Windows computer are capable of displaying the full spectrum of colors. The number of colors that can be displayed might be 16, 256, 65536, or 16 million. The number of colors available is also known as the *color depth*. Table 15.1 lists the possible colors and a description.

TABLE 15.1   Representation of Colors at Different Color Depths

Number of Colors	Description
16 colors	With a 16-color VGA display, the colors are fixed and are listed in the help for TColor.
256 colors	A 256-color display is palette-based. This means that only 256 colors can be displayed at one time, but the choice of which colors can be set from the full range of colors.
65,536 colors	The Red, Green, Blue (RGB) values are stored in a 16-bit value. When you choose a color, Windows applies the value closest to the one selected.
16 million colors	All colors are available for display.

> **NOTE**
>
> There is not enough space in this section for us to cover palette management for 256-color displays. For more information, look at a good Windows API reference text such as Petzold's *Programming Windows*, Microsoft Press, ISBN: 157231995X.

To determine the number of colors available on your machine, use the Win32 GDI function GetDeviceCaps().This will identify the number of color planes and the number of bits per pixel. The following code snippet will calculate the number of colors that can be supported:

```
int BitsPerPixel = GetDeviceCaps(Canvas->Handle, BITSPIXEL);
int NumberOfPlanes = GetDeviceCaps(Canvas->Handle, PLANES);
int NumberofColors = 1 << (NumberOfPlanes * BitsPerPixel);
```

An Analog Clock Example

To demonstrate these ideas, an analog clock project, clock.bpr, is provided in the GDIClock folder on the CD-ROM that accompanies this book. This clock is based on an old Borland C++ OWL example, aclock, and shows a simple clock with hour, minute, and second hands. This is shown in Figure 15.4.

This example program is intended to show the use of the Canvas for drawing. The important functions in this example are the form's InitializeImage(), DrawClockToHiddenImage(), and FormPaint().

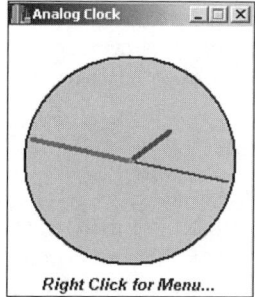

FIGURE 15.4 The analog clock example program.

All drawing is done to the canvas of a hidden TImage that is copied onto the form's Canvas in the OnPaint() event handler. We draw to a hidden image that's the same size of the form to speed up the display update. On each OnPaint() event call for the form, hidden canvas is simply copied to the form canvas.

```
void __fastcall TForm1::FormPaint(TObject *Sender)
{
    // copy the information on the hidden canvas onto the form's canvas.
    Canvas->CopyRect(ClientRect, HiddenImage->Canvas, HiddenImage->ClientRect);
}
```

The result of this processing has the advantage of speeding up the display over the common approach, which is to draw directly on to the canvas during a TForm's OnPaint event. CopyRect() improves performance.

The example program also demonstrates the use of the Font, Brush, and Pen properties of the canvas, along with the drawing of lines for the hands and an ellipse for the clock face. Using a pop-up menu, the brush style of the clock face can be changed to show the different effects, along with the style of the hands.

Working with Images

The Windows GDI provides native support for the *bitmap* file format and presents many GDI functions that are specifically designed for use with bitmap objects. However, if you are interested in displaying other image formats, you will need to use other mechanisms. Specifically, you'll have to provide a conversion routine so that you can construct a bitmap object from the information contained from the nonbitmap image (that is, a JPEG, GIF, or PNG file).

Before diving into nonbitmap image formats, we'll first concentrate on the bitmap object and discuss some of the techniques that can be used. After a few bitmap examples, we'll look at how other image file formats can be supported. Our intention here is not to get into the specifics of each image file format, but to provide a general overview of the most common file formats and how to use them.

The Windows Bitmap Object

The GDI presents two types of bitmaps: device-dependent bitmaps (DDBs) and device-independent bitmaps (DIBs). The former is a type of GDI graphic object, defined by the Win32 API `BITMAP` structure, which can be used in much the same way as most other graphic objects. Namely, you can select a DDB into a memory-device context and use any of the applicable GDI functions to perform rendering. Unfortunately, the GDI does not provide a direct means by which the bits of a DDB can be accessed. In contrast, a DIB is defined by the information contained in a `BITMAPINFO` structure and an array of pixels. In this way, you always have direct access to the bits of a DIB. There is a catch, however: DIBs cannot be selected into a memory device context, so rendering a DIB is generally slower than rendering a DDB.

To overcome the limitations imposed by DDBs and DIBs, Microsoft engineers developed the hybrid *DIB section bitmap*. This is simply a composite of the former two types, defined by the `DIBSECTION` structure.

```
typedef struct tagDIBSECTION {
    BITMAP              dsBm;
    BITMAPINFOHEADER    dsBmih;
    DWORD               dsBitfields[3];
    HANDLE              dshSection;
    DWORD               dsOffset;
} DIBSECTION;
```

Unlike a true DDB, the bits of a DIB section bitmap are readily accessible. Unlike a true DIB, DIB section bitmaps can be selected into a memory-device context. These two complementary aspects are particularly important when both efficient pixel manipulation and efficient rendering are required. In fact, the VCL `TBitmap` class is based on the DIB section bitmap.

Understanding and Using `TBitmap`

The `TBitmap` class is the VCL's encapsulation of the Windows bitmap object. The class descends from the abstract `TGraphic` base class, and it dynamically adapts to use either a DDB or a DIB section bitmap. This functionality is presented by the internal VCL `CopyBitmap()` function. It is from within this function that either a DDB is created via the GDI functions `CreateBitmap()` (for monochrome bitmaps) and `CreateCompatibleBitmap()`, or else a DIB section bitmap is created via the `CreateDIB Section()` GDI function. While it is beyond the scope of this text to discuss the specifics of the CopyBitmap() VCL function, let's examine those properties and member functions of the TBitmap VCL class that provide support for other image types.

The TBitmap class relies heavily on the TBitmapCanvas and TBitmapImage classes. The former, a descendant of the TCanvas class, expands its parent class to encapsulate the GDI memory device context. The latter, a descendant of the TSharedImage class, handles the resource counting and destruction of the DDB or DIB section bitmap. This latter task is accomplished via the DeleteObject() GDI function.

For image rendering support, the TBitmapCanvas class inherits the Draw(), StretchDraw(), and CopyRect() member functions from its parent class. The TBitmapCanvas::CreateHandle() function performs the task of selecting the bitmap (and palette, when appropriate) into the underlying memory device context. Thus, when the Draw(), StretchDraw(), or CopyRect() member function is used, the TCanvas class can rely solely on the StretchBlt() or TransparentStretchBlt() GDI function.

Aside from the rendering member functions presented by the TCanvas class, the TBitmap class provides the ScanLine property. This property uses the internal TBitmap::GetScanLine() member function, which simply returns an offset pointer to the bits of the DIB section bitmap. When you convert from other formats, you'll need access to these bits so that you can directly manipulate the pixels of the image. In this way, the ScanLine property significantly eases the task of pixel manipulation.

Let's now look at some code examples that demonstrate some TBitmap techniques. Much of the image-processing code to be demonstrated in this section is built into the IPro.bpr sample image-processing application project, available in the ImageProcessing folder on the CD-ROM that accompanies this book.

Essential TBitmap Operations

Let's take a look at the example shown in Listing 15.9, which demonstrates how to load a bitmap image. We'll use a TImage component dropped on our form to perform the activities with its AutoSize property set to true. We set it to true so that the TImage object can automatically adjust to different image sizes that could be loaded.

LISTING 15.9   Loading a Bitmap Image

```
void __fastcall TForm1::ButtonLoadClick(TObject *Sender)
{
    OpenDialog1->Filter = "Bmp files (*.bmp)|*.BMP";
    if (OpenDialog1->Execute())
    {
        Image1->Picture->Bitmap->LoadFromFile(OpenDialog1->FileName);
    }
}
```

In this example, we use a TOpenDialog object, called OpenDialog1, to browse for and select a BMP file. Then, we use the LoadFromFile() method provided by the TBitmap class of the Image1 object to load the selected bitmap.

After we have the bitmap displayed within Image1, we can begin to manipulate this image using its canvas. Let's take a look at a simple example (Listing 15.10) that paints a border around the image.

LISTING 15.10   Placing a Border Around an Image

```
void __fastcall TForm1::ButtonBorderClick(TObject *Sender)
{
    // let's draw a border around the image
    TRect MyRect(0,0,Image1->Width,Image1->Height);
    Image1->Canvas->Pen->Color = TColor(EditColor->Text.ToIntDef(0)); //clBlue;
    Image1->Canvas->Pen->Style = psSolid; // solid line
    Image1->Canvas->Pen->Width = EditPenWidth->Text.ToIntDef(1);
    Image1->Canvas->Brush->Style = bsClear;
    Image1->Canvas->Rectangle(MyRect);
}
```

Let's now take a look at Listing 15.11, which demonstrates how to save this bitmap, including the border around the original image.

LISTING 15.11   Saving a Bitmap

```
void __fastcall TForm1::ButtonSaveClick(TObject *Sender)
{
    SaveDialog1->Filter = "Bmp files (*.bmp)|*.BMP";
    if (SaveDialog1->Execute())
    {
        Image1->Picture->Bitmap->SaveToFile(SaveDialog1->FileName);
    }
}
```

In this example, we allow the user to select a filename to save the image, and use the SaveToFile() method provided by the TBitmap class to physically save the file to disk. If a border, text, or anything else was painted on the image, that information will now be saved with the image.

Flicker-Free Bitmap Manipulation

To perform image-processing operations, it's important to know how to access the individual pixel values of the image. The easiest way to obtain individual pixel value is to use the `Pixels` property of `TCanvas`. The following code shows how the mouse position and pixel value can be accessed and displayed to the user when the mouse is moved across the image.

```
void __fastcall TForm1::Image1MouseMove(TObject *Sender, TShiftState Shift,
                                        int X, int Y)
{
    EditX->Text = X;
    EditY->Text = Y;
    Edit PixelValue->Text = Image1->Canvas->Pixels[X][Y];
}
```

The current coordinate of the mouse is passed into the `Image1MouseMove()` event handler as `X` and `Y`. The pixel value is a `TColor`, and its interpretation depends on the `PixelFormat`. For grayscale images, the gray level is given by the lowest-order byte of the pixel value. For 24-bit color images, the lower three bytes represent RGB color intensities for blue, green, and red, respectively. The value `$00FF0000` represents pure blue, `$0000FF00` is pure green, and `$000000FF` is pure red.

You can also change a pixel value using `TCanvas->Pixels[][]`. For example, adding the following line to the `Image1MouseMove()` event handler will mark the movement of the mouse over the image with the color white:

```
Image1->Canvas->Pixels[X][Y] = clWhite;
```

Using `Canvas->Pixels[X][Y]` is straightforward, but extremely slow. Therefore, it should be used only for infrequent or causal access to pixel values. A more efficient method to track and display the movement of the mouse is as shown in Listing 15.12:

LISTING 15.12   Tracking and Displaying a Moving Mouse

```
void __fastcall TForm1::Image1MouseDown(TObject *Sender,
    TMouseButton Button, TShiftState Shift, int X, int Y)
{
    if (Button == mbLeft)
    {
        DoubleBuffered = true;
        Image1->Canvas->MoveTo(X,Y);
        MouseDown = true;
    }
}

// — — — — — — — — — — — — — — — — — — — — — — — — — — — — — — — — ·
```

LISTING 15.12   Continued

```
void __fastcall TForm1::Image1MouseMove(TObject *Sender, TShiftState Shift,
     int X, int Y)
{
        EditX->Text = X;
        EditY->Text = Y;
        EditPixelValue->Text = Image1->Picture->Bitmap->Canvas->Pixels[X][Y];
        if (MouseDown)     // follow movement of the mouse
        {
           Image1->Canvas->Pen->Color = clWhite;
           Image1->Canvas->LineTo(X,Y);
        }
}

//----------------------------------------------.

void __fastcall TForm1::Image1MouseUp(TObject *Sender, TMouseButton Button,
     TShiftState Shift, int X, int Y)
{
        MouseDown = false;
        DoubleBuffered = false;
}
```

In this example, we are using the MoveTo() method to initialize the pen position
when the mouse is pressed, and the LineTo() method is used to reflect the mouse
movement.

To reduce the flicker that's often associated with bitmap manipulation, the form's
DoubleBuffered property is set to true when the mouse-dragging begins. When the
mouse is released, the DoubleBuffered property returns to false. When it's false the
control's image is rendered directly to the window, when it's true the control's image
is first painted to an in-memory bitmap. Keep in mind that although DoubleBuffered
reduces the amount of flicker it is still more memory intensive. That is why we set it
back to false on the release of the mouse button.

Rotating a Bitmap

The ability to rotate an image is one of the common requests when working with
Bitmap images. Digital cameras, for example, are often used in a vertical position to
take a portrait picture. When this portrait picture is pulled off the camera, it will be
brought into an application, such as a paint program, sideways. The user often needs
the capability to rotate the image 90 degrees. Let's take a look at how that can be
done in Listing 15.13.

LISTING 15.13   Rotating an Image

```cpp
void __fastcall TForm1::ButtonRotate90Click(TObject *Sender)
{
    //create and setup a temporary source bitmap
    Graphics::TBitmap *source   = new Graphics::TBitmap;
    source->Assign(Image1->Picture->Bitmap);
    source->PixelFormat  = Image1->Picture->Bitmap->PixelFormat;

    // create and setup a temporary destination bitmap
    Graphics::TBitmap *dest     = new Graphics::TBitmap;
    dest->Width                 = source->Height;
    dest->Height                = source->Width;
    dest->PixelFormat           = source->PixelFormat;

    if (RadioButtonPixelsArray->Checked) //Rotate one pixel at a time
    {
        for (int x=0;x<source->Width;x++)
          for(int y=0;y<source->Height;y++)
            dest->Canvas->Pixels[y][source->Width-1-x] =
                    source->Canvas->Pixels[x][y];
    }
    else  // uses the faster scanline method
    {
      RGBTRIPLE* pixels;
      TColor color;
      for(int y=0;y<source->Height;y++)
      {
        pixels = (RGBTRIPLE*)source->ScanLine[y];
        for (int x=0;x<source->Width;x++)
          dest->Canvas->Pixels[y][source->Width-1-x] =
              TColor(RGB(pixels[x].rgbtRed,
                    pixels[x].rgbtGreen,
                    pixels[x].rgbtBlue));
      }
    }

    //now assign destination bitmap back to Image1 & cleanup
    Image1->Picture->Bitmap = dest;
    delete dest;
    delete source;
}
```

In this example we use two methods to rotate a color image 90 degrees. The first method, based on the value of RadioButtonPixelsArray, walks through all the pixels in the source image row by row and transfers those pixels to the destination image column by column. It's fairly simple, but it is not the most effective way to accomplish the rotation. A better way is provided through the ScanLine() function, which is used for the second method. With ScanLine() we can grab a whole row at one time and transfer the color pixels to each column of the destination image.

WARNING

The scanline example, as provided in Listing 15.13, works only for color images. We used the RGBTRIPLE data type for each pixel anticipating it would contain a red, green, and blue value. The Pixel format for a black and white image is much different. If you try to rotate a black and white image without adding the code to black and white, an access violation will occur.

One of the things that needs to be done before either rotation method is applied, is to properly assign the Height, Width, and PixelFormat of both the destination and source bitmap. When the rotation processing is complete, we need to assign the Canvas with the new rotated image, and then delete the temporary bitmaps that we used.

Cropping a Bitmap

Suppose your application is capable of bringing in an image, but the user is interested in displaying a smaller region of the image in view. In this situation, we need code to be able to crop the image to a selected region. Let's take a look at the example in Listing 15.14.

LISTING 15.14   Crop to Selection

```
void __fastcall TForm1::ButtonCropToSelectionClick(TObject *Sender)
{
    if (lX == -1) return; // no zoom window to work with

    // create and setup a temporary destination bitmap
    Graphics::TBitmap *dest    = new Graphics::TBitmap;
    dest->Width                = abs(lX - oX);
    dest->Height               = abs(lY - oY);

    TRect  OldOne = Rect(oX,oY,lX,lY);
    TRect  NewOne = Rect(0,0,dest->Width, dest->Height);

    FreeZoomWindow();  // frees crop region
```

LISTING 15.14   Continued

```
//create and setup a temporary source bitmap
Graphics::TBitmap *source   = new Graphics::TBitmap;
source->Assign(Image1->Picture->Bitmap);
source->PixelFormat  =  Image1->Picture->Bitmap->PixelFormat;

dest->PixelFormat          = source->PixelFormat;
dest->Canvas->CopyRect(NewOne,source->Canvas,OldOne);

//now assign destination bitmap back to Image1 & cleanup
Image1->Picture->Bitmap->FreeImage();
Image1->Picture->Bitmap->Assign(dest);
delete dest;
delete source;
}
```

In this example, we take the coordinates from our crop region and use the CopyRect()
function to transfer the area of interest into a new bitmap. The new bitmap is then
assigned to the Canvas of the TImage object.

NOTE

All the examples provided on working with bitmaps are applicable to support similar effects
for other images such as JPEG, GIF, and PNG. The key thing to remember is that within the
confines of the VCL and Windows GDI, nonbitmap images should be internally transformed to
a bitmap image during the execution of a program. When managed as a bitmap image
within memory, the techniques described for manipulating a bitmap can be applied.

JPEG Images

A majority of images used by consumers are not Bitmap images, they are mostly
JPEG images (pronounced "jaypeg"). JPEG is an image compression protocol developed by the Joint Photographic Experts Group. Digital cameras, picture CDs, Web
images, scanners all often produce or provide JPEG images. So, more than likely, if
you're interested in supporting image viewing or manipulation in your applications,
you want to be able to support JPEG images.

Unlike bitmap images, JPEG images are compressed in a lossy fashion, meaning that
some information is discarded during compression. Although the decompressed
image is not identical to the original, for most natural images there is little or no
degradation in visual quality. Moreover, the degree of compression can be adjusted,
allowing for decompressed images of varying quality.

NOTE

The JPEG compression process consists of three stages: reduction of pixel redundancy via a Discrete Cosine Transform (DCT), quantization of transform data (DCT coefficients), and reduction of data redundancy. It is in the second stage (quantization) that information is discarded. Typically, this is where human visual system (HVS) characteristics are taken into account, although there is no strict specification for the type of quantization that should be performed. For more information on the JPEG image format specifics, refer to http://www.jpeg.org/.

The VCL provides support for JPEG images through the TJPEGImage class. The main compression and decompression routines are handled via the JPEG image compression library of the Independent JPEG Group (IJG). Like the TBitmap class, TJPEGImage is a descendant of the TGraphic class.

The TJPEGImage class implements the TPersistent::Assign() and AssignTo() member functions so that you can easily convert between instances of TJPEGImage and TBitmap. Moreover, because the TJPEGImage class is designed for use with the Windows GDI and the rest of the VCL, the class maintains an internal bitmap representation of the underlying image such that rendering via the GDI is possible. The JPEG data itself is maintained via the TJPEGData class.

Loading a JPEG

Let's take a look at how to load a JPEG image onto a TImage control, as demonstrated in Listing 15.15.

LISTING 15.15   Loading a JPEG Image onto a TImage Control

```
void __fastcall TForm1::ButtonLoadClick(TObject *Sender)
{
    //This code requires "jpeg.hpp" to be included in the source file
    OpenDialog1->Filter =
       "Bmp files (*.bmp)|*.BMP| JPEG images (*.jpg) | *.jpg; " ;
    if (OpenDialog1->Execute())
    {
        if (!FileExists(OpenDialog1->FileName))
            return; // make sure it exists, else get out.
        AnsiString temp2 = ExtractFileName(OpenDialog1->FileName);
        AnsiString temp = ExtractFileExt(OpenDialog1->FileName);
        AnsiString Ext = temp.LowerCase();

        if (Ext.AnsiPos("jpg") > 0)  // it's a jpg
        {   //— Decompress the jpeg image into a bitmap.
            TJPEGImage *myjpeg = new TJPEGImage();
```

LISTING 15.15 Continued

```
        myjpeg->LoadFromFile(OpenDialog1->FileName);
        myjpeg->DIBNeeded();  // used when jpeg image needs bitmap rep
        Image1->Picture->Bitmap->Assign(myjpeg);
        delete myjpeg;
    }
    else if (Ext.AnsiPos("bmp") > 0)
    {
        Image1->Picture->Bitmap->LoadFromFile(OpenDialog1->FileName);
    }
    EditFile->Text        = OpenDialog1->FileName;
    EditWidth->Text       = Image1->Width;
    EditHeight->Text      = Image1->Height;
    EditPixelFormat->Text = Image1->Picture->Bitmap->PixelFormat;
    }
}
```

In this example we examine the file extension after a file has been selected from the Open dialog. If it is a JPEG image, a `TJPEGImage` object is created, which loads the file using the `LoadFromFile()` method. We use `DIBNeeded()` to reassign the JPEG image internally into a bitmap representation. We can actually leave this call off, however, as soon as we assign a JPEG image to a bitmap. This processing will be performed automatically by the `Assign()` routine if a DIB had not yet been created. After we assign the JPEG image to our `TImage` object, the JPEG image is deleted to free up memory.

Saving an Image as a JPEG

We can also save bitmap images as JPEG images. An example is provided in Listing 15.16.

LISTING 15.16 Saving an Image as a JPEG

```
void __fastcall TForm1::ButtonSaveClick(TObject *Sender)
{
    //This code requires "jpeg.hpp" to be included in the source file
    SaveDialog1->Title = "Save Image";
    SaveDialog1->DefaultExt = "jpg";
    SaveDialog1->Filter =
        "JPEG images (*.jpg) | *.jpg; | Bmp files (*.bmp)|*.BMP" ;
    SaveDialog1->FilterIndex = 1;
    if (SaveDialog1->Execute())
    {
```

LISTING 15.16   Continued

```
        AnsiString temp2 = ExtractFileName(SaveDialog1->FileName);
        AnsiString temp = ExtractFileExt(SaveDialog1->FileName);
        AnsiString Ext = temp.LowerCase();

        if (Ext.AnsiPos("jpg") > 0)  // it's a jpg
        {  //— Decompress the jpeg image into a bitmap.
            TJPEGImage *jp = new TJPEGImage();
            try
            {
              jp->Assign(Image1->Picture->Bitmap);
              jp->SaveToFile(SaveDialog1->FileName);
            }
            __finally
            {
              delete jp;
            }
        }
        else  if (Ext.AnsiPos("bmp") > 0)
        {
            Image1->Picture->Bitmap->SaveToFile(SaveDialog1->FileName);
        }
    }
}
```

In this example, if the user chooses to save the image as a JPEG, we simply `Assign()` the bitmap contained within the `TImage` object to `TJPEGImage` object. The `SaveToFile()` method for the `TJPEGImage` object is then called to save the image to disk. Finally, we delete the `TJPEGImage` object to free up memory.

JPEG Performance Properties

The `TJPEGImage` class provides several properties designed to manage the quality and performance of JPEG data. These properties include `CompresionQuality`, `Performance`, `Scale`, `ProgressiveDisplay`, `ProgressiveEncoding`, and `Smoothing`.

The `CompressionQuality` property can be used to adjust the amount of degradation incurred during compression for an image being saved. Values range from 1 to 100. A lower value will result in a smaller file size, but poorer picture quality. Conversely, a higher value will result in better image quality, but a larger file size.

The `Performance` property is used for decompressing the JPEG data on load, which affects the display of the internal bitmap image. There are two choices: `jpBestQuality` and jpBestSpeed. Setting Performance to jpBestSpeed can lead to some dithering in the internal bitmap image, but it will be faster. The Scale property determines the resolution (size) of the image to be displayed during decompression. Choices include full-size down to an eighth-size image.

The ProgressiveDisplay and ProgressiveEncoding properties allow for support of progressive decompression, where the currently decompressed portion of the image can be viewed before the entire image is decompressed. These properties, along with the Smoothing property, are ideal for situations in which a progressive transmission scheme is employed.

JPEG I/O Operations

Support for file, stream, and Clipboard operations is provided via the LoadFromClipboardFormat(), LoadFromStream(), LoadFromFile(), SaveToClipboardFormat(), SaveToStream(), and SaveToFile() member functions. These are inherited from the TGraphic class, and their use is entirely straightforward. Note that for Clipboard operations, the TJPEGImage class uses internal bitmap representation.

GIF Images

Another popular image format is the Graphics Interchange Format (GIF, pronounced "jiff"), which was created in 1987 by CompuServe Corporation. Unlike JPEG images, GIF images are compressed in a lossless fashion, meaning no information is lost during compression. That is, the decompressed image is identical to the original. GIF images also support progressive display (interlacing), multiple images (animated GIF), and transparency as of the latest format revision (GIF89a). More information on GIF can be found at http://www.geocities.co.jp/SiliconValley/3453/gif_info/.

Many developers are reluctant to support the GIF format, the use of which has been shrouded by licensing issues. In fact, it is not the format itself that is in question; rather it is the specification for the use of the LZW (Lempel-Ziv-Welch) compression algorithm. Unisys Corporation holds the patent for this modification of the Lempel-Ziv 78 (LZ78) compression algorithm. CompuServe has publicly granted a royalty-free license to use the GIF format, but Unisys requires that developers purchase a license.

The VCL does not provide native support for the GIF format. To display GIF images, you'll need to convert the (decompressed) data to the bitmap format. Although this can be done manually through the ScanLine property, there is still the issue of decompressing the data and reading or writing the data to or from a file. There are several third-party libraries available to handle this task. Of particular interest is the TGIFImage VCL component effort from Project JEDI, which can be found at http://www.delphi-jedi.org/ and also http://www.torry.net/gif.htm.

PNG Images

An image format that seems to be growing in popularity is the Portable Network Graphics (PNG, pronounced "ping") format. PNG was designed to expand upon and relieve the patent hassle of the GIF format. Like its predecessor, a PNG image is compressed in a lossless manner. Unlike the GIF format, PNG does not rely on the LZW algorithm. Instead, a variation of the Lempel-Ziv 77 (LZ77) compression algorithm is employed. This is the same compression algorithm used by the major file compression applications such as WinZIP.

Like the GIF format, the PNG format allows for transparent pixels. However, through the use of an Alpha channel, PNG images may also contain pixels of variable transparency (alpha blending). Moreover, in contrast to the GIF format, PNG images are not limited to 256 colors. To compensate for display monitor variations, the PNG specification allows for encoded gamma information. There is also support for progressive display, accomplished via a two-dimensional interlacing scheme. Unfortunately, the PNG format does not allow for multiple images (animation).

To provide support for display of PNG images, you'll need a means by which to convert the PNG format to a DIB. As always, you can perform this conversion manually; in that case, the latest PNG format specifications are needed. You can find them at `http://www.libpng.org/pub/png/spec/PNG-Contents.html`.

As with many image formats, there are several third-party libraries that can perform this conversion for you. For example, the freePNGDIB conversion library by Jason Summers, found at `http://home.mieweb.com/jason/imaging/pngdib/`, provides the `read_png_to_dib()` function that can read a PNG image file and yield a DIB (BITMAPINFO, color table, and bits). It also presents the `write_dib_to_png()` function for writing a PNG file from a DIB.

Using this library, to initialize a TBitmap object with information contained in a PNG file, you first call the `read_png_to_dib()` function to create a DIB from the PNG, and then use the `SetDIBits()` GDI function (or the `ScanLine` property) to fill the TBitmap object. This is demonstrated in Listing 15.17.

LISTING 15.17   Converting a PNG Format Image to a TBitmap

```
if (OpenDialog1->Execute())
{
    TCHAR filename[MAX_PATH];
    lstrcpyn(filename, OpenDialog1->FileName.c_str(), MAX_PATH);

    // declare and clear the PNGD_P2DINFO structure
    PNGD_P2DINFO png2dib;
    memset(&png2dib, 0, sizeof(PNGD_P2DINFO));
```

LISTING 15.17   Continued

```cpp
// initialize the structure size and filename
png2dib.structsize = sizeof(PNGD_P2DINFO);
png2dib.pngfn = filename;

// convert from PNG to DIB
if (read_png_to_dib(&png2dib) == PNGD_E_SUCCESS)
{
    Graphics::TBitmap* Bitmap = Image1->Picture->Bitmap;
    Bitmap->Width = png2dib.lpdib->biWidth;
    Bitmap->Height = png2dib.lpdib->biHeight;

    HBITMAP hBmp = Bitmap->ReleaseHandle();
    HDC hDC = Canvas->Handle;
    try
    {
        //
        // TODO: add palette support...
        //

        // convert from DIB to TBitmap
        SetDIBits(
            hDC, hBmp, 0,
            png2dib.lpdib->biHeight, png2dib.bits,
            reinterpret_cast<LPBITMAPINFO>(png2dib.lpdib),
            DIB_RGB_COLORS
            );
    }
    catch (...)
    {
        Bitmap->Handle = hBmp;
        GlobalFree(png2dib.lpdib);
    }
    Bitmap->Handle = hBmp;
    GlobalFree(png2dib.lpdib);
}
}
```

Similarly, to create a PNG file from information contained in a TBitmap object, you first construct a DIB from the TBitmap via the GetDIBSizes() and GetDIB() VCL utility functions (from graphics.pas), and then use the write_dib_to_png() function to write the PNG file. This is demonstrated in Listing 15.18.

LISTING 15.18   Converting a TBitmap Image to PNG Format

```
if (SaveDialog1->Execute())
{
   TCHAR filename[MAX_PATH];
   lstrcpyn(filename, SaveDialog1->FileName.c_str(), MAX_PATH);

   BITMAPINFO bmi;
   Graphics::TBitmap* Bitmap = Image1->Picture->Bitmap;

   //
   // determine the size of the DIB info
   // (BITMAPINFOHEADER + color table) and the
   // size of the bits (pixels)
   //
   unsigned int info_size = 0, bits_size = 0;
   GetDIBSizes(Bitmap->Handle, info_size, bits_size);

   // allocate memory for the bits
   unsigned char *bits = new unsigned char[bits_size];
   try
   {
      // get the BITMAPINFOHEADER + color table and the bits
      if (GetDIB(Bitmap->Handle, Bitmap->Palette, &bmi, bits))
      {
         // declare and clear the PNGD_D2PINFO structure
         PNGD_D2PINFO dib2png;
         memset(&dib2png, 0, sizeof(PNGD_D2PINFO));

         // initialize the structure
         dib2png.structsize = sizeof(PNGD_D2PINFO);
         dib2png.flags = PNGD_INTERLACED;
         dib2png.pngfn = filename;
         dib2png.lpdib = &bmi.bmiHeader;
         dib2png.lpbits = bits;

         // convert the DIB to PNG, then save to file
         if (write_dib_to_png(&dib2png) != PNGD_E_SUCCESS)
         {
            throw EInvalidGraphic("Error Saving PNG!");
         }
      }
   }
```

LISTING 15.18   Continued

```
   catch (...)
   {
      delete [] bits;
   }
   delete [] bits;
}
```

Included on the companion CD-ROM is a project (PROJ_PNGDIB_DEMO.CPP in the PNGDemo folder) that demonstrates the use of the PNGDIB library.

Working with Multimedia

The Windows multimedia system provides a standard means by which multimedia devices can be controlled. This system simply delegates the communication between an application and a particular device driver. The Media Control Interface (MCI) adds even more flexibility by providing a common means by which applications can communicate with all supported audio and video devices. From the developer's point of view, the specifics of the device are irrelevant; oftentimes, even the type of device is of no concern.

In this section, we'll first discuss the use of the MCI for creating general-purpose audio and video applications. In Chapter 14, we touched on the MCI capabilities provided by the Win32 API. Now, we will dig a little deeper. As you will soon discover, the MCI is perhaps the easiest multimedia interface to work with. Next, we'll examine the use of the waveform-audio interface and how it can be used for increased audio-based functionality. Finally, we'll tackle the issue of audio streams, and examine how to read and write waveform-audio files.

The Media Control Interface (MCI)

In the same way that the GDI offers a generic means by which you can communicate with graphics-based devices, the Windows MCI enables you to program multimedia devices in a device-independent manner. Before the advent of the MCI, developers were required to write code that targeted specific devices. Often this process involved using procedures specific to a particular device driver. It's not hard to imagine the hassle that such a scheme would present, where the consumer base would be limited to a specific range of legacy device types. For example, many of the early DOS-based games required that the sound card be compatible with the original Sound Blaster standard. Otherwise, the game would not generate any audible sound or music from the sound card.

Using Command Messages and Strings

Applications communicate with the MCI via a set of predefined messages and string constants. In much the same way that window messages are used with the user interface services, the MCI provides a set of command messages and strings that can be used to manipulate MCI devices. Many of these messages offer corresponding command strings that can be used for a more intuitive (and readable) approach. Here, we will limit our discussion to the MCI command messages; the message constants are defined in the mmsystem.h header file available with C++Builder.

Similar to the SendMessage() API function that is used to send messages to Windows, the mciSendCommand() function is used to send command messages to MCI devices.

```
MCIERROR mciSendCommand(
    MCIDEVICEID IDDevice,
    UINT uMsg,
    DWORD fdwCommand,
    DWORD dwParam
    );
```

When using the mciSendCommand() function, oftentimes a device identifier is specified as the IDDevice parameter. This serves the same purpose as the hWnd parameter of the SendMessage() function. Namely, the function needs to know to which MCI device to send the message. A device identifier is returned when a device is opened via the MCI_OPEN message.

Decoding Error Constants

The mciSendCommand() function returns a 32-bit value indicating the success or failure of the operation. If successful, this value is set to MMSYSERR_NOERROR, defined in the mmsystem.h header file as identically zero. If an error does occur, the return value is set to one of the predefined error constants. Because these values have little meaning to the user (or the developer), the MCI presents the mciGetErrorString() function, which can be used to translate these error codes into meaningful messages (compared with FormatMessage). Listing 15.19 demonstrates the use of this function.

LISTING 15.19   Decoding MCI-Related Errors Via the mciGetErrorString() Function

```
bool mciCheck(DWORD AErrorNum, bool AReport = true)
{
    if (AErrorNum == MMSYSERR_NOERROR) return true;
    if (AReport)
    {
        char buffer[MAXERRORLENGTH];
        mciGetErrorString(AErrorNum, buffer, MAXERRORLENGTH);
        MessageBox(NULL, buffer,  "MCI Error", MB_OK);
```

LISTING 15.19 Continued

```
    }
    return false;
}
```

Working with MCI Devices

The first step to working with an MCI device is to open or initialize the device; as previously stated, you accomplish this task via the MCI_OPEN message. Because you are interested in retrieving a device identifier, you send this message with a NULL IDDevice parameter. If successful, the identifier of the opened device is returned in the wDeviceID data member of the corresponding MCI_OPEN_PARMS structure; this is the MCI_OPEN_PARMS that was specified as the dwParam argument.

```
typedef struct tagMCI_OPEN_PARMS {
    DWORD        dwCallback;
    MCIDEVICEID  wDeviceID;
    LPCSTR       lpstrDeviceType;
    LPCSTR       lpstrElementName;
    LPCSTR       lpstrAlias;
} MCI_OPEN_PARMS, *PMCI_OPEN_PARMS, *LPMCI_OPEN_PARMS;
```

Typically, the lpstrDeviceType data member is set to NULL, and the lpstrElementName data member is assigned a filename. This is the most robust approach because it enables the MCI to perform automatic type selection. That is, the appropriate device will be selected according to the type of file specified. In cases where the lpstrDeviceType data member is explicitly specified, it is oftentimes assigned a string value corresponding to the type of device requested. For example, to open the CD audio device, you can specify it as cdaudio. Other string identifiers include avivideo, dat, digitalvideo, mmmovie, other, overlay, scanner, sequencer, vcr, videodisc, and waveaudio. However, it should be stressed that unless support for a specific device is intended, it is best to let the MCI perform automatic type selection. This is especially important when a new technology is presented that has no predefined type identifier (for example, the MP3 format). Listing 15.20 demonstrates the use of the MCI_OPEN message via a simple wrapper function.

LISTING 15.20 Using the MCI_OPEN Command Message

```
bool mciOpen(MCIDEVICEID& ADevID, const char* AFileName,
    const char* ADevType = NULL)
{
    MCI_OPEN_PARMS mop;
    memset(&mop, 0, sizeof(MCI_OPEN_PARMS));
```

LISTING 15.20   Continued

```
    mop.lpstrElementName = const_cast<char*>(AFileName);
    mop.lpstrDeviceType = const_cast<char*>(ADevType);

    DWORD flags = 0;
    if (AFileName) flags = flags | MCI_OPEN_ELEMENT;
    if (ADevType) flags = flags | MCI_OPEN_TYPE;
    if (mciCheck(mciSendCommand(NULL, MCI_OPEN, flags,
                            reinterpret_cast<DWORD>(&mop))))
    {
        ADevID = mop.wDeviceID;
        return true;
    }
    return false;
}
```

After the MCI device is open and an identifier is retrieved, your next task is to set the time format of the device. This aspect of the MCI is rather specific to the device type because certain types of devices can support only certain time formats. For example, specifying a track number is valid for CD audio devices, but it is clearly invalid for wave-form audio devices.

You can set the time format for a device via the MCI_SET command message. Whenever applicable, it is best to use the MCI_FORMAT_MILLISECONDS format, which is supported by all devices. An example wrapper function that uses the MCI_SET message is provided in Listing 15.21.

LISTING 15.21   Using the MCI_SET Command Message

```
bool mciSetTimeFormat(MCIDEVICEID ADeviceID, DWORD ATimeFormat)
{
    MCI_SET_PARMS msp;
    memset(&msp, 0, sizeof(MCI_SET_PARMS));
    msp.dwTimeFormat = ATimeFormat;

    return mciCheck(mciSendCommand(ADeviceID, MCI_SET,
                MCI_SET_TIME_FORMAT, reinterpret_cast<DWORD>(&msp)));
}
```

After the time format is set correctly, you're free to work with the device in much the same way as you would its physical counterpart. For example, to play the device, you use the MCI_PLAY message. To rewind or fast-forward the device, you use the MCI_SEEK message. To pause the device, you use the MCI_PAUSE message. Similarly, the MCI_STOP message is used to stop the device, and the MCI_CLOSE message closes the device.

NOTE

For a complete list of messages, refer to http://msdn.microsoft.com.

The wrapper functions presented in Listing 15.22 demonstrate the use of these messages.

LISTING 15.22 Use of the MCI_PLAY, MCI_SEEK, MCI_PAUSE, MCI_STOP, and MCI_CLOSE Command Messages

```
bool mciPlay(MCIDEVICEID ADeviceID, DWORD AStart, DWORD AStop)
{
    MCI_PLAY_PARMS mpp;
    memset(&mpp, 0, sizeof(MCI_PLAY_PARMS));
    mpp.dwFrom = AStart;
    mpp.dwTo = AStop;

    DWORD flags = 0;
    if (static_cast<int>(AStart) >= 0 && static_cast<int>(AStop) >= 0)
        flags = MCI_FROM | MCI_TO;

    return mciCheck(mciSendCommand(ADeviceID, MCI_PLAY | flags,
                    NULL, reinterpret_cast<DWORD>(&mpp)));
}

bool mciSeek(MCIDEVICEID ADeviceID, DWORD APos)
{
    MCI_SEEK_PARMS msp;
    memset(&msp, 0, sizeof(MCI_SEEK_PARMS));
    msp.dwTo = APos;

    return mciCheck(mciSendCommand(ADeviceID, MCI_SEEK, MCI_TO,
                    reinterpret_cast<DWORD>(&msp)));
}

bool mciPause(MCIDEVICEID ADeviceID)
{
    return mciCheck(mciSendCommand(ADeviceID, MCI_PAUSE, 0, 0));
}
```

LISTING 15.22   Continued

```
bool mciStop(MCIDEVICEID ADeviceID)
{
    return mciCheck(mciSendCommand(ADeviceID, MCI_STOP, 0, 0));
}


void mciClose(MCIDEVICEID ADeviceID)
{
    mciCheck(mciSendCommand(ADeviceID, MCI_CLOSE, 0, NULL));
}
```

Illustrated in Figure 15.5, is a sample project included on the companion CD-ROM that demonstrates the use of these MCI messages. See the `Proj_mp3Demo.bpr` project in the `MP3Demo` folder, and specifically the `MCIManip.cpp` source file.

FIGURE 15.5   MP3 player project.

Retrieving the Status of a Device

Often it is necessary to provide feedback to the user about the status of a device. For example, if you want to create a CD player, you'll most likely want to inform the user of the current track, the track length, and the current position within the track. More generally, you need to indicate the operating mode of the device (playing, paused, stopped, and so on) to inform the user as to what functionality is available. This information is retrieved via the `MCI_STATUS` message, as demonstrated in Listing 15.23.

LISTING 15.23   Use of the `MCI_STATUS` Command Message

```
bool mciStatus(MCIDEVICEID ADeviceID, DWORD AQueryGroup, DWORD AQueryItem,
    DWORD AQueryTrack, DWORD& AResult)
{
    MCI_STATUS_PARMS msp;
    memset(&msp, 0, sizeof(MCI_STATUS_PARMS));
    msp.dwItem = AQueryItem;
    msp.dwTrack = AQueryTrack;

    if (mciCheck(mciSendCommand(ADeviceID, MCI_STATUS, AQueryGroup,
                reinterpret_cast<DWORD>(&msp))))
```

LISTING 15.23   Continued

```
    {
        AResult = msp.dwReturn;
        return true;
    }
    return false;
}
```

The project `Proj_CDDemo.bpr` in the `CDDemo` folder on the CD-ROM that accompanies this book is a sample CD player that demonstrates all the techniques shown in these sections. This is illustrated in Figure 15.6.

FIGURE 15.6   CD demo program.

A wide variety of constants can be specified as the `AQueryGroup` parameter, each with a corresponding set of constants that can be assigned to the `AQueryItem` and `AQueryTrack` arguments. For example, to retrieve the total number of tracks present on the media of a CD audio device, you specify `MCI_STATUS_ITEM` as the `AQueryGroup` parameter and `MCI_STATUS_NUMBER_OF_TRACKS` as the `AQueryItem` parameter. To determine the current track number, you set the `AQueryGroup` parameter to `MCI_STATUS_ITEM` and the `AQueryItem` parameter to `MCI_STATUS_CURRENT_TRACK`. Also, note that when retrieving length, position, track, or frame information, the format of the returned data depends on the device's current time format. For a complete listing of status flags, refer to `http://msdn.microsoft.com`.

Polling a Device and MCI Notifications

Although you now have a means of retrieving information about a device, you still need to know when to perform this interrogation. Unfortunately, the MCI presents a limited notification scheme in which only two notification messages, `MM_MCINOTIFY` and `MM_MCISIGNAL`, are defined. The latter is useful only for digital video devices. Although the former message sounds promising, it is posted only after a command operation has completed. For example, if you use the `mciPlay()` wrapper function (of Listing 15.22) to begin the playback of a waveform audio file, the `MM_MCINOTIFY` message will be posted only when the file has finished playing or playback has otherwise been manipulated. Specifically, this message is posted to the window whose handle is specified via the `dwCallback` data member of the structure specified as the `dwParam` argument of the `mciSendCommand()` function. As such, you need to modify the wrapper functions to accept an `hWnd` parameter. The sample project `Proj_mp3Demo.bpr`, in the MP3Demo folder on the CD-ROM that accompanies this book, demonstrates handling the `MM_MCINOTIFY` message.

In most cases, receipt of the `MM_MCINOTIFY` message is a sufficient indication of when to determine the status of the operating mode. For example, you can provide a handler for the `MM_MCINOTIFY` message in which you update the enabled state of your play, pause, and stop buttons. Yet, when retrieving information about a frequently updated attribute such as current position, the `MM_MCINOTIFY` message is not suitable. Instead, you need to poll the device at a regular interval. This task is typically performed in response to timer messages. In some cases, it is sufficient to use system timer messages; in others it is recommended to use the multimedia timer services. See Chapter 14 or visit `http://msdn.microsoft.com` for more information on multimedia timer services.

Concluding Remarks About the MCI

Just what types of files does the MCI support? This depends on the audio/video codecs that are installed on the target platform. Many of these codecs are installed when a newer version of Microsoft Media Player is installed. A good rule of thumb is that if Media Player can support a specific file format, so can the MCI. In fact, Media Player itself relies heavily on the MCI.

Included on the companion CD-ROM are two MCI-related demonstration projects: `Proj_MP3Demo.bpr` in the MP3Demo folder and `Proj_VideoDemo.bpr` in the VideoDemo folder. The former is a simple MP3 audio player, illustrated previously in Figure 15.5, which can actually support waveform audio (RIFF-based) files as well. The latter, illustrated in Figure 15.7, demonstrates the use of the MCI for displaying video files (AVI, MPEG). Again, the actual supported file formats of both of these demonstration projects are limited by the currently installed codecs. Refer to the comments included at the beginning of the source code for more information.

FIGURE 15.7   Video player project.

Although the MCI is perhaps the easiest of all multimedia interfaces to work with, it is quite limited in its functionality. For example, when playing a media file through the MCI, you are never given access to the file's associated data stream. This is especially detrimental if your application is to perform any type of signal processing or format conversion. In this case, you need to go beyond the MCI and work with other multimedia interfaces. For extended audio functionality, this is typically accomplished via the Waveform Audio Interface.

The Waveform Audio Interface

The Windows multimedia service provides the Waveform Audio Interface (waveform API) to allow applications to control the input and output of waveform audio. This interface gives an application direct access to the sound buffer, so in cases where other audio formats must be supported, a simple conversion is all that is necessary. For example, many of the commercial applications that provide support for the MP3 format do so through the waveform API. Moreover, in situations where signal processing is due, direct access to the sound buffer is crucial. For example, if you're interested in creating an audio player with graphic equalization capabilities, you'll need to process the sound buffer before sending it to the output device.

Recall that the `lpstrElementName` data member of the `MCI_OPEN_PARMS` structure is typically assigned the name of a media file that is to be played. In this case, the MCI automatically handles the task of opening and loading the file. However, the waveform API does not present such a structure, and thus you're forced to use other measures for file I/O. For example, one potential solution is to open the file manually using the `TFileStream` VCL class. In this case, you'd need to be sufficiently versed with the waveform audio file format specification (RIFF). An alternative approach is to use the multimedia file I/O services, which is indeed completely valid for many situations. However, because these services are so generalized, working with waveform audio files proves nearly as difficult as the manual solution. Fortunately, Windows provides the AVIFile services, a set of functions and macros specifically designed for use with waveform audio and AVI files. As such, let's now digress from the waveform API and examine the AVIFile services.

Opening and Closing Waveform Audio Files

A waveform audio file is a type of RIFF (Resource Interchange File Format) file that contains time-based audio content. In fact, that's really all you need to know. As mentioned, you do not need to concern yourself with the specifics of the file format itself; instead, you can use the `AVIFile` functions and macros. These functions and macros, presented in the `VFW.H` header file and the `AVIFIL32.DLL` dynamic link library, provide a convenient means of working with waveform audio files and streams.

Before you can use the AVIFile services, you need to initialize the `AVIFIL32.DLL` library via the `AVIFileInit()` function. Similarly, when you're finished with the library, you release it via the `AVIFileExit()` function.

The AVIFile functions rely on OLE for handling file and stream-based operations, so you need to provide a means of error checking. For those functions that return the standard STDAPI type, you can use the SUCCEEDED macro as in the following wrapper function:

```
bool wavCheck(HRESULT AErrorCode)
{
    return SUCCEEDED(AerrorCode);
}
```

Let's begin our examination of the AVIFile services by performing the simplest of tasks, opening a waveform audio file. This is accomplished via the AVIFileOpen() function:

```
bool wavOpenFile(PAVIFILE& ApFile, const char* AFileName,
    unsigned int AMode)
{
    return wavCheck(AVIFileOpen(&ApFile, AFileName, AMode, NULL));
}
```

The AMode parameter specifies the access mode and can be assigned the same access-related constants that are used with the OpenFile() API function (OF_READ, for example). The ApFile argument receives a pointer to an AVIFILE structure that simply holds the address of the filehandler interface. Because this filehandler interface is released only when its reference count drops to zero, it is important that you decrement its reference count when the interface is no longer needed. This is accomplished via the AVIFileClose() function:

```
void wavCloseFile(PAVIFILE& ApFile)
{
    AVIFileClose(ApFile);
    ApFile = NULL;
}
```

Working with Audio Streams

Although opening and closing a waveform audio file is rather trivial, you'll need to work with the stream handler interface to obtain any useful information. This task proves slightly more complicated. Recall that the PAVIFILE type holds a pointer to the filehandler interface. Similarly, a pointer to the stream handler interface is stored in a variable of type PAVISTREAM. You can retrieve a pointer to this latter interface via the AVIFileGetStream() function. You release the interface via the AVIStreamRelease() function. The wrapper functions presented in Listing 15.24 demonstrate the use of these AVIFile functions.

LISTING 15.24   Using the AVIFileGetStream and AVIStreamRelease Functions

```
bool wavOpenStream(PAVISTREAM& ApStream, PAVIFILE ApFile)
{
    return wavCheck(AVIFileGetStream(ApFile, &ApStream, streamtypeAUDIO, 0));
}

void wavCloseStream(PAVISTREAM& ApStream)
{
    AVIStreamRelease(ApStream);
    ApStream = NULL;
}
```

Working with the stream handler interface is not unlike working with the
TMemoryStream class or one of the basic_streambuf descendant classes. However, you
have at your disposal several functions specifically designed for use with waveform
audio and AVI files. For example, the AVIStreamInfo() function can be used to
retrieve information about the content of the stream. This function fills an
AVISTREAMINFO structure with information specific to its media content:

```
bool wavGetStreamInfo(PAVISTREAM ApStream, AVISTREAMINFO& AStreamInfo)
{
    return wavCheck(AVIStreamInfo(ApStream, &AStreamInfo,
                    sizeof(AVISTREAMINFO)));
}
```

When working with an audio stream, you'll need to know the format of the data
itself. For waveform audio files, this information is conveyed via the data members
of a WAVEFORMATEX structure. This structure is simply used to describe how audio
samples are stored in the corresponding waveform audio data. As such, a particularly
useful function when working with waveform audio streams is the
AVIStreamReadFormat() function. It is the role of this function to fill the data members
of the WAVEFORMATEX structure based on information in the stream. The
AVIStreamFormatSize() macro complements this function by reporting the size of the
contained structure. Listing 15.25 demonstrates the use of the AVIStreamReadFormat()
function and the AVIStreamFormatSize() macro.

LISTING 15.25   Using the AVIStreamReadFormat() Function and the
AVIStreamFormatSize() Macro

```
long wavCalcFormatStructSize(PAVISTREAM ApStream)
{
    long required_bytes = 0;
```

LISTING 15.25   Continued

```
    AVIStreamFormatSize(ApStream, 0, &required_bytes);
    return required_bytes;
}


bool wavReadFormatStruct(PAVISTREAM ApStream, WAVEFORMATEX& ApFormatStruct)
{
    memset(&ApFormatStruct, 0, sizeof(WAVEFORMATEX));
    long size = wavCalcFormatStructSize(ApStream);
    return wavCheck(
        AVIStreamReadFormat(ApStream, 0, &ApFormatStruct,  &size)
        );
}
```

Like the TMemoryStream::Read() or the basic_ifstream::read() member function, the
AVIFile services provide a means by which an application can read media content
from a stream. This is the audio data buffer that you're interested in and, as you will
see later, access to this buffer is essential to producing audio output via the waveform API. The AVIStreamRead() function is used to read media content from a stream
into an application-defined buffer. Similarly, the AVIStreamWrite() function is used to
write data from a buffer into a stream. Listing 15.26 demonstrates the use of these
functions.

LISTING 15.26   Reading and Writing Audio Data to and from a Stream

```
long wavCalcBufferSize(PAVISTREAM ApStream)
{
    long required_bytes = 0;

    AVISTREAMINFO StreamInfo;
    if (wavGetStreamInfo(ApStream, StreamInfo))
    {
        required_bytes = StreamInfo.dwLength * StreamInfo.dwScale;
    }
    return required_bytes;
}


long wavReadStream(PAVISTREAM ApStream, long AStart, long ANumBytes,
    char* ABuffer)
{
    long bytes_read = 0;
```

LISTING 15.26 Continued

```
    AVISTREAMINFO StreamInfo;
    if (wavGetStreamInfo(ApStream,  StreamInfo))
    {
        long num_samples = static_cast<float>(ANumBytes) /
                            static_cast<float>(StreamInfo.dwScale);
        AVIStreamRead(ApStream, AStart, num_samples, ABuffer, ANumBytes,
                    &bytes_read, NULL);
    }
    return bytes_read;
}


long wavWriteStream(PAVISTREAM ApStream, long AStart, long ANumBytes,
    char* ABuffer)
{
    long bytes_written = 0;

    AVISTREAMINFO StreamInfo;
    if (wavGetStreamInfo(ApStream, StreamInfo))
    {
        long num_samples = static_cast<float>(ANumBytes) /
                            static_cast<float>(StreamInfo.dwScale);
        AVIStreamWrite(ApStream, AStart, num_samples, ABuffer, ANumBytes,
                    AVIIF_KEYFRAME, NULL, &bytes_written);
    }
    return bytes_written;
}
```

The wavCalculateBufferSize() wrapper function is comparable to the
TMemoryStream::Size property. It uses the wavGetStreamInfo() wrapper function to
calculate the size of the audio buffer. Also note that, as the stream handler interface
is intrinsically linked to the filehandler interface, any data that you write to the
stream will automatically be written to the file once the stream is closed. As such, if
you're interested in manipulating only the content of the stream, you'll need to
create a secondary stream that is not associated with a particular file. For more information on this task, see http://msdn.microsoft.com.

Now that you have a framework by which you can manipulate waveform audio files,
let's return to our examination of the waveform API and investigate the means by
which you can output waveform audio sound. As with the MCI, the functions and
structures of the waveform API are declared and defined, respectively, in the
MMSYSTEM.H header file.

Opening and Closing Waveform Audio Devices

The waveform API provides the waveOutOpen() function for use in opening a waveform audio output device. This function requires an initialized WAVEFORMATEX structure and, if successful, assigns an HWAVEOUT variable the handle to the open device. Similarly, the waveOutClose() function is used to close the waveform audio device. The wrapper functions of Listing 15.27 demonstrates the use of these functions.

LISTING 15.27   Opening and Closing a Waveform Audio Device

```
bool wavPlayOpen(HWAVEOUT& AHWavOut, long ACallback, DWORD ANotifyInstance,
    DWORD AOpenFlags, WAVEFORMATEX& AFormatStruct)
{
    return wavCheck(
        waveOutOpen(&AHWavOut, WAVE_MAPPER, &AFormatStruct, ACallback,
                ANotifyInstance, AOpenFlags)
        );
}

void wavPlayClose(HWAVEOUT AHWavOut)
{
    waveOutReset(AHWavOut);
    waveOutClose (AHWavOut);
}
```

The ACallback, ANotifyInstance, and AOpenFlags parameters can be used to specify a means of notification; we will return to this issue shortly. For the AFormatStruct parameter, you can use the wavReadFormatStruct() wrapper function of Listing 15.25.

After an output device is open, you use the waveOutWrite() function to initiate playback. Specifically, you pass this function a pointer to a buffer of audio data that the function will send to the opened output device driver. However, the audio output device must know the size of the audio block that it's going to receive. For this reason, the waveOutWrite() function cannot accept a plain data buffer; instead, the function requires the address of a WAVEHDR structure.

Among other things, a WAVEHDR structure stores a pointer to the audio data buffer in its lpData data member and the length of this buffer in its dwBufferLength data member. To ensure compatibility with the output device, you must allow the driver to prepare your WAVEHDR structure before you can pass it to the waveOutWrite() function. This task is accomplished via the waveOutPrepareHeader() function. Similarly, after the device driver has finished playing the audio block, you must unprepare the header using the wavOutUnprepareHeader() function before you can free the associated memory. Listing 15.28 demonstrates the use of these functions.

LISTING 15.28   Initiating and Ending Waveform Audio Playback

```
bool wavPlayBegin(HWAVEOUT AHWavOut, WAVEHDR& AWavHdr)
{
    if (wavCheck(waveOutPrepareHeader(AHWavOut, &AWavHdr, sizeof(WAVEHDR))))
    {
        return wavCheck(
            waveOutWrite(AHWavOut, &AWavHdr, sizeof(WAVEHDR))
            );
    }
    return false;
}

void wavPlayEnd(HWAVEOUT AHWavOut, WAVEHDR& AWavHdr)
{
    waveOutReset(AHWavOut);
    waveOutUnprepareHeader(AHWavOut, &AWavHdr, sizeof(WAVEHDR));
}
```

Let's solidify these concepts with a simple example that demonstrates how to play a waveform audio file. An example project called `Proj_DSPDemo.bpr`, can be found on the companion CD-ROM in the `DSPDemo` folder, which is illustrated in Figure 15.8.

FIGURE 15.8   DSP demonstration.

Recall that, because the waveform API presents no native means of loading the audio data from disk, we will first need to use our `AVIFile` wrapper functions. After we read the audio data block from the stream into our buffer, we can then use our waveform API wrapper functions to control playback. The code for this example is presented in Listing 15.29.

LISTING 15.29   Playing a Quantized Waveform Audio File

```
const long MAX_BLOCK_SIZE = 6000 * 1024;

if (!OpenDialog1->Execute()) return;
const char* filename = OpenDialog1->FileName.c_str();
```

LISTING 15.29   Continued

```
PAVIFILE pFile = NULL;
if (wavOpenFile(pFile, filename, OF_READ))
{
    PAVISTREAM pStream = NULL;
    if (wavOpenStream(pStream, pFile))
    {
        long block_size = wavCalcBufferSize(pStream);
        if (block_size < MAX_BLOCK_SIZE)
        {
            char* buffer = new char[block_size];
            if (wavReadStream(pStream, 0, block_size, buffer)
                == block_size)
            {
                QuantizeBuffer(buffer, block_size);

                WAVEFORMATEX FormatStruct;
                if (wavReadFormatStruct(pStream, FormatStruct))
                {
                    HWAVEOUT HWavOut;
                    if (wavPlayOpen(HWavOut, NULL, NULL, NULL,
                                    FormatStruct))
                    {
                        WAVEHDR WavHdr;
                        memset(&WavHdr, 0, sizeof(WAVEHDR));
                        WavHdr.lpData = buffer;
                        WavHdr.dwBufferLength = block_size;

                        if (wavPlayBegin(HWavOut, WavHdr))
                        {
                            ShowMessage("Playing: " +
                                        AnsiString(filename));
                            wavPlayEnd(HWavOut, WavHdr);
                        }
                        wavPlayClose(HWavOut);
                    }
                }
            }
            delete [] buffer;
        }
        wavCloseStream(pStream);
    }
```

LISTING 15.29 Continued

```c
    wavCloseFile(pFile);
}


void QuantizeBuffer(char* ABuffer, long ABufferLength)
{
    short int min_val = 0, max_val = 0;
    for (int index = 0; index < ABufferLength; ++index)
    {
        if (ABuffer[index] < min_val) min_val = ABuffer[index];
        if (ABuffer[index] > max_val) max_val = ABuffer[index];
    }

    for (int index = 0; index < ABufferLength; ++index)
    {
        if (ABuffer[index] < 0) ABuffer[index] = min_val;
        if (ABuffer[index] > 0) ABuffer[index] = max_val;
    }
}
```

Notice in Listing 15.29 that we placed a limit on the size of the audio data block. Indeed, we would not want to load too large of a file so that we deplete system resources. When working with large audio data blocks, small segments of the media content are read from the stream, then sent to the driver in an iterative fashion. That is, after the driver has finished with the current buffer, we continually supply it with new information. However, for such a method to be successful, we will need a means by which we can determine when the driver has finished with the buffer. That is, the waveOutWrite() function returns immediately, so we have no way of knowing when the driver has completed playback. This is where the ACallback parameter of our wavPlayOpen() wrapper function comes in. Specifically, we can assign this argument the handle of a window or an event, an identifier of a thread, or even the address of a specific callback function. In this way, we can establish a crucial means of notification. See http://msdn.microsoft.com for information on the MM_MON_DONE message.

Concluding Remarks on the Waveform Audio Interface

We have covered a wide variety of multimedia functions, structures, messages, and macros, but there are still more to explore. For example, the Windows multimedia system also provides specific interfaces for controlling MIDI and AVI playback. Moreover, each of these interfaces, including the Waveform Audio Interface and the MCI, provides services for sound input as well as output. There is even an interface for working with audio mixer devices. See `http://msdn.microsoft.com` for more information. This latter area is particularly opportune when the volume of specific audio channels needs to be controlled.

Summary

In this chapter, we have examined several methods by which an application can provide graphics or multimedia support. First, we took a closer look at the Windows GDI and how many aspects of this interface are abstracted by the VCL. We looked at the `TCanvas`, `TBrush`, `TPen`, `TFont`, and `TColor` classes and their use in rendering graphical output. We also examined several image file formats and discussed techniques for using `TBitmap` and `TJPEGImage` objects.

Finally, we investigated how multimedia files are supported through use of the MCI. We examined the various MCI-related command messages and discussed their generic use in controlling multimedia devices. We also looked at the `AVIFile` services and Waveform Audio Interface and how these interfaces are used to manage and affect playback of waveform audio files.

Although we covered a lot of ground for supporting graphics and multimedia, there are additional components and libraries available for Windows that you should be made aware. This includes DirectX, which contains DirectShow, DirectSound, and DirectDraw for providing high-performance graphics and multimedia. Unfortunately, a discussion of DirectX is not in the scope of this chapter; however, a lot of material is available on the Web and within the newsgroups that you might find useful. Despite the lack of DirectX discussion, the information provided to you in this chapter is quite extensive and should help you develop interesting and innovative multimedia applications.

16

DLLs

by Paul Gustavson

Windows provides a powerful mechanism for supporting application reuse at the binary level through Dynamic Link Libraries (DLLs). A DLL typically represents a collection of common utilized functions, capabilities, and/or resources *packaged* into a linkable module that can be leveraged by other programs. This linkable module typically has the extension .dll.

There are many practical uses for a DLL. For instance, suppose you have a common set of math models and calculations that need to be used within several applications you develop and maintain. Rather than repetitively copying or linking the code for these models and calculations into each program, you can create and compile a single DLL that each program can load and use as if the code was already embedded within each program. This has several advantages identified as follows:

- A DLL minimizes code re-write since it can be shared and used by multiple applications.

- Applications will be smaller in size because the code in the DLL is isolated from the applications that use the code.

- Applications can be updated without recompilation simply through DLL updates.

This chapter focuses on DLLs. We'll discuss how to build them and how to use them. We'll look at some of the things to watch out for when you build and use them, and we'll examine interesting DLL techniques that you can use with both C++Builder applications and Visual C++ applications.

Creating a DLL Using C++Builder

In this first section, we'll look at how to create a DLL using C++Builder. The simplest way to create a DLL is with the C++Builder's DLL Wizard. You can also create a DLL from scratch almost as easily, simply by starting with a blank header and c or cpp source file.

The primary function that needs to be included in the source of a DLL file is a main entry function. Within the world of Microsoft (specifically Visual C++), this function is called DLLMain().

```
BOOL WINAPI DllMain(HINSTANCE hinstDLL, DWORD fwdreason, LPVOID lpvReserved)
{
        return 1;
}
```

Within the world of Borland (specifically C++Builder and its precursor C++), this function is called DLLEntryPoint().

```
int WINAPI DllEntryPoint(HINSTANCE hinst,
                    unsigned long reason,
                    void* lpReserved)
{
        return 1;
}
```

Borland C++Builder Version 6 now also supports the DLLMain() entry function.

At this point, after a main entry function is in place, you can begin to add the functionality you want to share through a DLL. We'll develop an example shortly, but let's first look at the DLL Wizard, which will shed some light on the different types of DLLs that can be created and supported by C++Builder.

Using the DLL Wizard

The DLL Wizard can be brought up within C++Builder by selecting File, New, and Other from the main menu, and then selecting the DLL Wizard from the New tab of the New Items dialog. The DLL Wizard provides several options for you to choose from (see Figure 16.1).

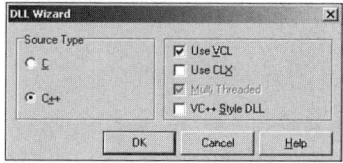

FIGURE 16.1   The following options are presented on the DLL Wizard dialog box.

Source Type:

C   This specifies that the C language will be used as the source type, which allows access to the Multi Threaded, and VC++ Style DLL options. The *Use VCL* and *Use CLX* options are disabled because VCL and CLX are object-oriented classes and can only be included in a C++ project.

C++   This specifies that the C++ language will be used as the source type, which enables access to the *Use VCL, Use CLX, Multi Threaded, VC++ Style* DLL options, as well as the use of object-oriented classes. If this option is chosen, the compiler will use C++ to compile the code in the main module of the DLL, thus enabling you to use C++ code in your DLL.

Options:

Use VCL   This option creates a DLL that can contain VCL components and classes. This causes C++Builder to include the VCL.h file in your main module, and changes the startup code and linker options for compatibility with VCL objects. You will also notice that the Multi Threaded option becomes checked and disabled. The reason for this is because the VCL needs to have multithreading capabilities.

Use CLX   This option creates a DLL that can contain CLX components and classes. This causes C++Builder to include the clx.h file in your main module and changes the startup code and linker options for compatibility with CLX objects. You will also notice that the Multi Threaded option becomes checked and disabled. The reason for this is because the CLX needs to have multithreading capabilities.

Multi Threaded   This option specifies that the DLL will have more than one thread of execution, so if you plan to have multiple threads in your DLL, it would be a good idea to choose this option. Remember that the VCL and CLX need to have this capability, so if you manually try to add components into the DLL later and didn't check this, you may run into a problem. To avoid this, always make sure that this option is checked.

VC++ Style DLL   This option specifies what type of entry point the DLL is going to have. If you want the DLL entry point to be DLLMain(), the Visual C++ style, check the VC++ style option; otherwise, DLLEntryPoint() is used for the entry point function. The choice is up to you.

After you have made your selections and clicked OK, C++Builder will automatically generate a skeleton DLL application. The only function that it creates in the source file, however, is an empty entry point function, DLLMain() or DLLEntryPoint(), which depends on the selection of VC++ Style DLL.

When you use the Wizard, it will create several files for you. A source file that ends in either *.c or *.cpp, a Resource file that ends in *.res, and a Borland Project File called a *.bpf. This is illustrated in Figure 16.2. In most cases, the only file that really matters is the source file. In fact, when you build a DLL from scratch, not using the Wizard, you'll often create a source file and an associated header file. Because the Wizard doesn't create the header file, you might need to create it as well. Typically, we use a header file to expose the functionality of the DLL to other applications.

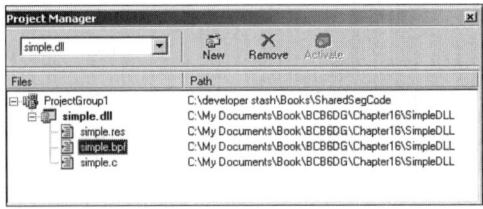

FIGURE 16.2   A project generated from the DLL Wizard.

Filling in DLL Code

Let's go ahead and fill in some code for our entry point function so that we can begin to fully understand how a DLL works, as shown Listing 16.1.

LISTING 16.1   The DLL Entry Point Function

```
bool WINAPI DllMain(HINSTANCE hinstDLL, DWORD fwdReason, LPVOID lpvReserved)
{
    switch(fwdreason)
    {
    case DLL_PROCESS_ATTACH:
            if (lpvReserved)
                    MessageBox(NULL,"Process has attached to DLL (Static Load)",
                        "DLLMain",MB_OK);
            else
```

LISTING 16.1   Continued

```
                    MessageBox(NULL,"Process has attached to DLL (Dynamic Load)",
                        "DLLMain",MB_OK);
                break;
        case DLL_THREAD_ATTACH:
                MessageBox(NULL,"Thread has attached to DLL","DLLMain",MB_OK);
                break;
        case DLL_THREAD_DETACH:
                MessageBox(NULL,"Thread has detached to DLL","DLLMain",MB_OK);
                break;
        case DLL_PROCESS_DETACH:
                MessageBox(NULL,"Process has detached to DLL","DLLMain",MB_OK);
                break;
        }
        return 1; // always return true;
}
```

In this example, our DLL examines the activity associated to the application loading (or unloading) the DLL. Three parameters can be examined within the main entry function. The first parameter, hinstDLL, identifies the handle of the DLL. The second parameter, fwdReason, identifies the type of activity associated to the process or thread loading or unloading. The third parameter, lpvReserved, is NULL if the DLL was dynamically loaded or non-NULL if the DLL was statically loaded (we will discuss DLL loading in a moment). The value we're most interested in is fwdReason. By knowing the action, whether a process or thread is coming or going, we can have the DLL initialize its variables on entry, and destroy existing pointers and threads on exit.

We need to add some functionality to our DLL so that the DLL is useful to outside applications. For starters, let's add a function to the simple.c file that identifies the version of the DLL, and provides some metric conversion, as shown in Listing 16.2.

LISTING 16.2   Examples of DLL Functions

```
const double version = 1.1;

double simpleGetLibVersion()  //the current library version of the DLL.
{
    return version;
}


//- - - - - - - - - - - - - - - - - - - - - - - - - - - - - - - - - - - -.


double feet_to_meters(double feet)
```

LISTING 16.2 Continued

```
{
    return (feet * 0.3048);
}

// — — — — — — — — — — — — — — — — — — — — — — — — — — — — — — — — — —·

double meters_to_feet(double meters)
{
    return (meters * 3.2808);
}
```

Notice a constant identifying the version is included, which is used by the simpleGetLibVersion() function. When an application calls this DLL function, the DLL version as identified by the version variable will be returned. When an application calls the feet_to_meters() function, the value identified by the feet parameter will be converted and returned as meters. Inversely, when an application calls meters_to_feet() function, the value identified by the meters parameter will be converted and returned as feet.

Adding a DLL Header File

To make the function available to an application that loads the DLL, we need to create a header file that exposes the function. This is shown in Listing 16.3.

LISTING 16.3 The DLL Header File

```
#ifndef __SIMPLE_H
#define __SIMPLE_H

#if defined(__cplusplus)
extern "C"
{
#endif
__declspec( dllexport ) double simpleGetLibVersion();
__declspec( dllexport ) double feet_to_meters(double feet);
__declspec( dllexport ) double meters_to_feet(double meters);
#if defined(__cplusplus)
}
#endif

#endif // __SIMPLE_H
```

This header file provides the basis for the DLL interface. The _cplusplus constant is defined if C++Builder is compiling C++ code. In this example, we are compiling C source code because our source file has a c extension, therefore the extern "C" clause will be ignored on compilation. Otherwise, if we were compiling C++ code, the extern keyword tells C++Builder to use the C calling convention. Any compiler that supports C-type exports will be able to import this function.

In this example, we also use the declspec(dllexport) storage class specifier preceding each function. This clause enables you to export functions, data, and objects from a DLL. In our example, we export a function that we want to be able to call from any application that loads the DLL. Furthermore, this clause provides compatibility of our DLL with Microsoft C/C++ applications and eliminates the need for a module-definition (.DEF) file.

Building a DLL

A DLL is built much the same way an EXE application is built within the C++Builder IDE. For example, the simple.dll example, provided on the CD-ROM that accompanies this book, is built by selecting Project, Build simple, as illustrated in Figure 16.3.

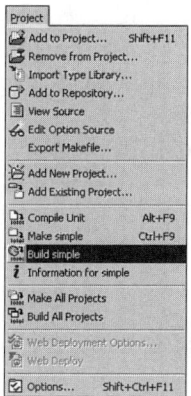

FIGURE 16.3   Building the simple.dll project using C++Builder.

When the DLL is compiled and linked, C++Builder will generate not only a DLL file, but also a LIB file. The LIB file makes it convenient for a C++Builder application to utilize a DLL by simply identifying the LIB file as part of the application's project. This is discussed further in the "Loading a DLL" section.

Loading a DLL

It was mentioned earlier that a DLL can be loaded statically or dynamically; it's important to understand the difference. A statically linked DLL is linked to the executable when the executable is built if the LIB is identified as part of the application's project. The DLL will then be loaded into memory when the executable is run (on start up). A dynamically linked DLL can be loaded and unloaded as needed by the application after start up, which can lessen the amount of resources the program needs to run. Another difference is that with static linking, a program will not run without the DLL, whereas a dynamically linked DLL doesn't have to be present. However, if the application makes a call to a function or attempts to utilize a resource contained within the DLL, but the DLL is not present, an error will occur. Now that we have an example DLL titled simple.dll, let's look at how we can load the DLL both statically and dynamically.

Linking DLLs Statically

To understand how to statically link a DLL, let's create a project that links the LIB file generated when simple.dll was built. The project that we will use as an example can be found on the CD-ROM in the SimpleDLL folder titled AppStatic.bpr. In this example, a Button and Edit control are placed on the main form. The Button, when triggered will call the simpleGetVersion() function of the DLL and fill in the Edit control with the version. The example for this code is provided in Listing 16.4.

LISTING 16.4   Application Example That Uses the DLL Functions

```
#include <vcl.h>
#pragma hdrstop

#include "AppStaticForm.h"
#include "simple.h"
//----------------------------------------------
#pragma package(smart_init)
#pragma resource "*.dfm"
TForm1 *Form1;
//----------------------------------------------
__fastcall TForm1::TForm1(TComponent* Owner)
        : TForm(Owner)
{
}
//----------------------------------------------

void __fastcall TForm1::ButtonGetVersionClick(TObject *Sender)
{
```

LISTING 16.4   Continued

```
    EditVersion->Text = AnsiString(simpleGetLibVersion());
}
//  —  —  —  —  —  —  —  —  —  —  —  —  —  —  —  —  —  —  —  —  —  —  —  —  —  —  —  —  —  —  .


void __fastcall TForm1::ButtonConvertToMetersClick(TObject *Sender)
{
    double meters =  feet_to_meters(EditFeet->Text.ToDouble());
    EditMeters->Text = AnsiString(meters);
}
//  —  —  —  —  —  —  —  —  —  —  —  —  —  —  —  —  —  —  —  —  —  —  —  —  —  —  —  —  —  —  .


void __fastcall TForm1::ButtonConvertToFeetClick(TObject *Sender)
{
    double feet =  meters_to_feet(EditMeters->Text.ToDouble());
    EditFeet->Text = AnsiString(feet);
}
```

In this example, we need to include the header file of the DLL.

```
#include "simple.h"
```

This header file identifies the functions that we want to access from the DLL. The
`ButtonGetVersionClick()` event-handler within our application code will call the DLL
function `simpleGetLibVersion()`. Whereas, the `ButtonCovertToMetersClick()` event-
handler calls `feet_to_meters()`, and `ButtonConvertToFeetClick()` calls `meters_to_feet()`.

If we compile and build the application without identifying the DLL library (LIB file)
in the project we will receive the following error:

```
[Linker Error] Unresolved external '_simpleGetLibVersion'
            referenced from APPSTATICFORM.OBJ
```

Therefore, in this example, we need to include the `.lib` file, as shown in Figure 16.4.

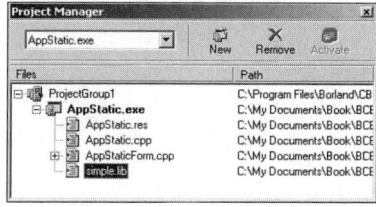

FIGURE 16.4   AppStatic project listing.

After we include the .lib file, we can then build and run our application. In this example, when the application launches, a message appears that is generated by the DLL, as illustrated in Figure 16.5.

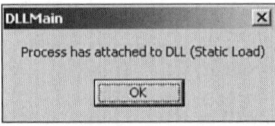

FIGURE 16.5   DLL entry point Message Box displayed by simple.dll.

Following this message, the application GUI appears, and the user can press the buttons labeled Get DLL Version, Convert To Meters, and Convert To Feet, as illustrated in Figure 16.6. The event-handler for these buttons calls the exported DLL functions.

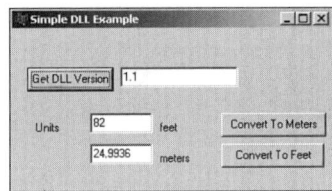

FIGURE 16.6   Screen shot of the AppStatic application.

That's all it takes to link and statically load a DLL. As long as you include the proper header file that identifies the DLL functions or classes to be used and include the .lib file in the project, everything else is the same as calling any other function. Be aware, however, that if the DLL is not physically present when the application launches an error occurs, as illustrated in Figure 16.7.

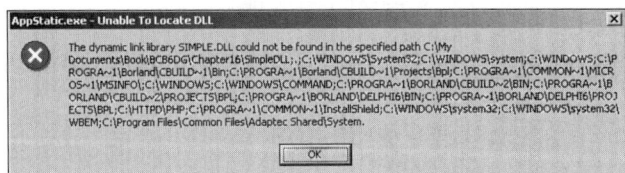

FIGURE 16.7   Unable to locate DLL error.

Loading DLLs Dynamically

The other way to use a DLL is to dynamically load it during execution. There are a few basic steps to dynamically link and use the functionality provided by a DLL:

- Load the DLL and obtain a pointer to it.

- Get a pointer to the function you want to call.

- Call the function.

- Free the DLL.

To load a DLL dynamically, we can use either the LoadLibrary() or LoadLibraryEx() provided by the Win32 API. To understand how to dynamically link a DLL, let's create a project that loads simple.dll using the LoadLibrary() call. The project that we will use as an example can be found on the CD-ROM in the SimpleDLL folder titled AppDynamic.bpr. A screen shot of the application is provided in Figure 16.8.

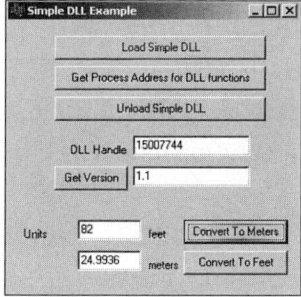

FIGURE 16.8 Screen shot of the AppDynamic application during execution.

First, to make this application work, we need to declare a variable within our program to receive an instance *handle* to the DLL. Within C++Builder, we can place the declaration of the DLL handle as a property within the class of our main form as follows:

```
private:    // User declarations
      HINSTANCE dllhandle;
```

The following code in Listing 16.5 demonstrates how the LoadLibrary() call is made for loading simple.dll.

LISTING 16.5 Using LoadLibrary()

```
void __fastcall TForm1::ButtonLoadLibraryClick(TObject *Sender)
{
    dllhandle = LoadLibrary("simplex.dll"); // keep track of the handle
    EditDLLHandle->Text = AnsiString((int)dllhandle);
    if (dllhandle)
```

LISTING 16.5   Continued

```
    {
        ButtonUnloadLibrary->Enabled = true;
        ButtonProcAddress->Enabled = true;
    }
    else
    {
        ShowMessage("Unable to load the DLL");
    }
}
```

LoadLibrary() attempts to load the DLL identified by its filename. In this example, we used "simple.dll". You can also include a full path here. If just the name is provided, Windows will use the search paths to try and load it. If the DLL cannot be loaded, LoadLibrary() will return NULL.

After we load the DLL, the next step is to get a pointer to the function we want to call. There are two steps for importing functions from DLLs that are dynamically linked:

- Create a new typedef using the exported functions prototype.
- Cast each call to GetProcAddress() to the exported functions prototype.

We need to declare a variable to retrieve the process address of the desired function. However, preceding this variable declaration we need to identify its anticipated function format using a typedef such as this:

```
typedef float (*SIMPLEGETLIBVERSION)();
SIMPLEGETLIBVERSION simpleGetLibVersion;

typedef double (*METERS_TO_FEET)(double);
METERS_TO_FEET meters_to_feet;

typedef double (*FEET_TO_METERS)(double);
FEET_TO_METERS feet_to_meters;
```

Typically, this code is placed in the header file defined for our application, the top of the source file, or within an independent header file that we can include (link) in our code. The use of typedef identifies the format structure for the DLL function. The actual pointer to the DLL Function is then defined based on this type of definition.

In our code we want to cast the result from the GetProcAddress() call to the simpleGetLibVersion, meters_to_feet, and feet_to_meters function pointers. The code in Listing 16.6 demonstrates how the GetProcAddress() call can be used.

LISTING 16.6 Using GetProcAddress()

```
void __fastcall TForm1::ButtonProcAddressClick(TObject *Sender)
{
  if (dllhandle)
  {
    simpleGetLibVersion  =
        (SIMPLEGETLIBVERSION)GetProcAddress(dllhandle,
                                "_simpleGetLibVersion");
    if (simpleGetLibVersion)  ButtonGetVersion->Enabled = true;
    meters_to_feet  =
        (METERS_TO_FEET)GetProcAddress(dllhandle, "_meters_to_feet");
    if (meters_to_feet)  ButtonConvertToMeters->Enabled = true;
    feet_to_meters  =
        (FEET_TO_METERS)GetProcAddress(dllhandle, "_feet_to_meters");
    if (feet_to_meters)  ButtonConvertToFeet->Enabled = true;
  }
}
```

As shown in this example, the Windows API function GetProcAddress()returns a
pointer to the exported functions provided by the DLL. In the first instance, the
resultant is cast into the format identified by SIMPLEGETLIBVERSION type definition and
assigned to the simpleGetVersion pointer. This is repeated for each of the other two
functions provided by the DLL. For all these cases, an instance handle of a DLL and
the title of the exported function we desire is required by the GetProcessAddress()
call.

> **TIP**
>
> The preceding underscores for simpleGetLibVersion, meters_to_feet, and feet_to_meters
> in the GetProcAddress() functions are required because C++Builder adds them to the begin-
> ning of the functions exported in the DLL.

> **TIP**
>
> C++Builder by default adds an underscore to the beginning of the functions it exports. There
> is an option under Project, Options on the Advanced Compiler tab called Generate
> Underscores. If you uncheck this option within the project for your DLL, the function will
> export without the underscore, as shown in Figure 16.9.

> **CAUTION**
>
> Always be sure to check to make sure that the GetProcAddress() function succeeded before
> using the pointer. If the pointer is NULL, the GetProcAddress() call failed. Trying to use an
> invalid pointer will result in an access violation.

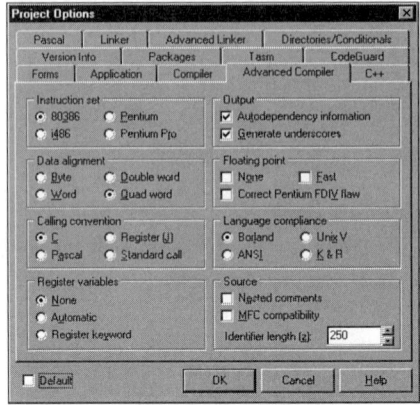

FIGURE 16.9   The Project Options, Advanced Compiler tab.

After you have a valid pointer, you can use it just like you would any other function. This is shown in Listing 16.7.

LISTING 16.7   Making a Call to a DLL Function Based on a Pointer Retrieved Using `GetProcAddress()`

```
void __fastcall TForm1::ButtonGetVersionClick(TObject *Sender)
{

  if (dllhandle)
  {
    EditVersion->Text = AnsiString(simpleGetLibVersion());
  }
}
//———————————————————————————————————————————-·


void __fastcall TForm1::ButtonConvertToMetersClick(TObject *Sender)
{
    double meters =  feet_to_meters(EditFeet->Text.ToDouble());
    EditMeters->Text = AnsiString(meters);
}
//———————————————————————————————————————————-·


void __fastcall TForm1::ButtonConvertToFeetClick(TObject *Sender)
{
    double feet =  meters_to_feet(EditMeters->Text.ToDouble());
    EditFeet->Text = AnsiString(feet);
}
```

You might notice that this piece of code is exactly the same as the previous application that statically loaded `simple.dll`. The `ButtonGetVersionClick()` event-handler makes a call to the function `simpleGetLibVersion()` contained in `simple.dll` to retrieve and display the DLL version.

After we're done using this DLL, we want to free it. DLLs can be freed using the Win32 API function `FreeLibrary()`, which requires the parameter, the `HINSTANCE Dll` that we obtained earlier from the `LoadLibrary()` call. This is shown in Listing 16.8.

LISTING 16.8   Using `FreeLibrary()`

```
void __fastcall TForm1::ButtonUnloadLibraryClick(TObject *Sender)
{
    if (dllhandle)
    {
        FreeLibrary(dllhandle);
        ButtonUnloadLibrary->Enabled = false;
        ButtonProcAddress->Enabled = false;
        ButtonGetVersion->Enabled = false;
        ButtonConvertToMeters->Enabled = false;
        ButtonConvertToFeet->Enabled = false;
        EditDLLHandle->Text = "";
    }
}
```

Those are the basic steps for loading a dynamic DLL.

Perhaps you might be thinking that the static DLL is much easier to use, which is true, but remember that the static DLL loads when your program starts and stays around until your program closes. Keep in mind if the static DLL is missing for some reason, your program won't run at all.

Exporting and Using DLL Classes

Now that you know how to export a simple function from a DLL and use it in an application, let's look into how to export an entire class.

By modifying the `SimpleDll` project slightly, we'll use a class to provide equivalent functionality to external applications. This example can be found in the `SimpleClassDLL` folder within the `simple.bpr` project on the accompanying CD-ROM. The code declarations associated to the header file for our new `simple.dll` is provided in Listing 16.9.

LISTING 16.9   The Header File for a DLL Class

```
#ifndef __SIMPLE_H
#define __SIMPLE_H

enum Tlast_set { meters=0, feet };

__declspec( dllexport ) class TDistance
{
  private:
     double FVersion;
     double FMeters;
     double FFeet;
     void __fastcall SetMeters(double value);
     void __fastcall SetFeet(double value);
     double __fastcall feet_to_meters();
     double __fastcall meters_to_feet();
     Tlast_set last_set;
  public :
     __fastcall TDistance();
     __fastcall ~TDistance();
       double GetLibVersion();
     __property double Version = {read = FVersion};
     __property double Meters = {read = feet_to_meters, write = SetMeters};
     __property double Feet = {read = meters_to_feet, write = SetFeet};
};

#endif // __SIMPLE_H
```

Notice that we're using the same export technique used to export the functions earlier, except we're not using the extern C clause. Also notice how our class within our DLL looks much like a class used in a standard executable.

The code to our source file, which now has a .cpp extension, that is associated to this class is provided in Listing 16.10.

LISTING 16.10   DLL Class Methods

```
__fastcall TDistance::TDistance()
{
   FVersion = 1.1;
   FFeet = 0.0;
   FMeters = 0.0;
```

LISTING 16.10   Continued

```
}
//——————————————————————————————————————.


__fastcall TDistance::~TDistance()
{

}
//——————————————————————————————————————.


double TDistance::GetLibVersion()   //current library version of the DLL.
{
    return FVersion;
}
//——————————————————————————————————————.


void __fastcall TDistance::SetMeters(double value)
{
   FMeters = value;
   last_set = meters;
}
//——————————————————————————————————————.


void __fastcall TDistance::SetFeet(double value)
{
   FFeet = value;
   last_set = feet;
}
//——————————————————————————————————————.


double __fastcall  TDistance::feet_to_meters()
{
   if (last_set == meters)
       return FMeters;
   else
     return (FFeet * 0.3048);
}
//——————————————————————————————————————.


double __fastcall  TDistance::meters_to_feet()
{
   if (last_set == feet)
```

LISTING 16.10 Continued

```
        return FFeet;
    else
      return (FMeters * 3.2808);
}
```

Note that although it's not provided in the listing, we still use the same DLL Entry Point function as the previous example.

This is all we need to save and build the DLL. Let's now test it out with a new application that statically loads the DLL. The header file for this application is provided in Listing 16.11 and can be found under the SimpleClass folder and AppStatic.bpr project on the accompanying CD-ROM.

LISTING 16.11 The Header File for a Sample Application That Uses the DLL Class

```
#ifndef AppStaticFormH
#define AppStaticFormH
//---------------------------------------------
#include <Classes.hpp>
#include <Controls.hpp>
#include <StdCtrls.hpp>
#include <Forms.hpp>
#include "simple.h"
//---------------------------------------------
class TForm1 : public TForm
{
__published:    // IDE-managed Components
        TButton *ButtonGetVersion;
        TEdit *EditVersion;
        TButton *ButtonGetVersion2;
        void __fastcall ButtonGetVersionClick(TObject *Sender);
        void __fastcall ButtonGetVersion2Click(TObject *Sender);
private:    // User declarations
        TDistance *distance;
public:        // User declarations
        __fastcall TForm1(TComponent* Owner);
};
//---------------------------------------------
extern PACKAGE TForm1 *Form1;
//---------------------------------------------
#endif
```

Because our header file now has a property that is defined by the class contained within the DLL, we need to be sure to include the DLL header file inside the application header file.

```
#include "simple.h"
```

The property we declare can be found in the private section of our form's class.

```
TDistance *distance;
```

The application source file is provided in Listing 16.12.

LISTING 16.12 The Source File for a Sample Application That Uses the DLL Class

```
#include <vcl.h>
#pragma hdrstop

#include "AppStaticForm.h"

//---------------------------------.
#pragma package(smart_init)
#pragma resource "*.dfm"
TForm1 *Form1;
//---------------------------------.
__fastcall TForm1::TForm1(TComponent* Owner)
        : TForm(Owner)
{
  distance = new TDistance();
}
//---------------------------------.

void __fastcall TForm1::ButtonGetVersionClick(TObject *Sender)
{
  EditVersion->Text = AnsiString(distance->GetLibVersion());
}
//---------------------------------.

void __fastcall TForm1::ButtonGetVersion2Click(TObject *Sender)
{
  EditVersion->Text = AnsiString(distance->Version);
}
//---------------------------------.

void __fastcall TForm1::EditMetersChange(TObject *Sender)
```

LISTING 16.12   Continued

```
{
  double meters = EditMeters->Text.ToDouble();
  distance->Meters = meters;
}

//--------------------------------------------------------

void __fastcall TForm1::EditFeetChange(TObject *Sender)
{
  double feet = EditFeet->Text.ToDouble();
  distance->Feet = feet;
}
//--------------------------------------------------------

void __fastcall TForm1::ButtonConvertToMetersClick(TObject *Sender)
{
  EditMeters->Text = AnsiString(distance->Meters);
}
//--------------------------------------------------------

void __fastcall TForm1::ButtonConvertToFeetClick(TObject *Sender)
{
  EditFeet->Text = AnsiString(distance->Feet);
}
```

In this example, the form constructor class initializes the simple property to the
TDistance class declared within the DLL header file. This class provides two mechanisms to retrieve the version number: the function GetLibVersion() and the class
property Version. To retrieve the distance in meters or feet, we simply examine the
Meters or Feet property within the TDistance class. The class will perform the appropriate conversion if required. Within the application, we use button event-handlers
to demonstrate the capability to access the class members (function and properties),
as illustrated in Figure 16.10.

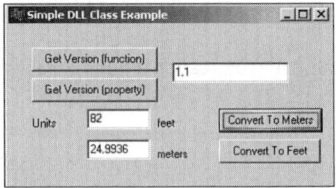

FIGURE 16.10   Screen shot of the AppStatic application using the Distance class
contained within Simple.dll.

The example illustrated in Figure 16.10 demonstrates how to use properties and methods contained within a DLL class. You may notice the coding style is very similar to how we would use a VCL class contained within a VCL Package. In fact, Packages used by C++Builder and Delphi are actually DLLs; there are just a few subtle differences.

Packages Versus DLLs

A Package guarantees that extensions, such as __published and protected property members and the __property keyword for a property, can be supported by the class. These specific extensions are what turn classes into components and, through registration, allow components to be leveraged by the C++Builder IDE at design time; allowing property values to be tweaked using the Object Inspector. The bottom line is that within C++Builder and Delphi (and Kylix), a Package can be more desirable than a DLL due largely to the flexibility a VCL provides.

> **NOTE**
>
> To dynamically load a Package at runtime, you would use LoadPackage() instead of LoadLibrary() and FreePackage() instead of FreeLibrary().

Although there are many advantages to using a Package within C++Builder and Delphi, a disadvantage is that other development tools cannot use a VCL Package because its constructs are specific to C++Builder or Delphi. A Visual C++ application, for instance, will not be able to load and use a Package because it doesn't understand published and protected members of a class. Packages are good for making custom components that are available through the IDE as well as at runtime. Standard DLLs are good for providing reusable functionality that can be used by almost any application, no matter what development tool was used to build it.

Therefore, if you're thinking of supporting applications that might be developed under Visual C++ as well as C++Builder, you should choose to develop a DLL with an interface (header file) that doesn't use and require the VCL. Note that this doesn't preclude developing a DLL that uses a VCL component, such as TForm, within the source code. It's just that the VCL elements cannot be exposed or required by the header file, which is the interface often used by the calling application.

Steps for Creating a Package

Assuming you're developing a component to be used only by C++Builder applications, let's quickly examine how to build a Package. The easiest way to create a Package is to select File, New. Then, choose Package from the New Items dialog, and then press OK (see Figure 16.11).

FIGURE 16.11   The New Items dialog box.

Following these steps, a Package project dialog will be displayed showing the files that were generated associated to the project as illustrated in Figure 16.12.

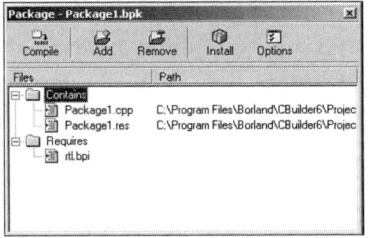

FIGURE 16.12   Package project dialog box.

If you open the Package1.cpp file identified in the dialog box, you'll see a familiar code skeleton for the package. This is shown in Listing 16.13.

LISTING 16.13   The DLL Entry Point Function for a Package

```
#include <basepch.h>
#pragma hdrstop
#pragma package(smart_init)
//————————————————————————————————.
```

LISTING 16.13 Continued

```
//   Package source.
//— — — — — — — — — — — — — — — — — — — — — — — — — — — — — — — — — — —.


#pragma argsused
int WINAPI DllEntryPoint(HINSTANCE hinst, unsigned long reason, void*lpReserved)
{
        return 1;
}
```

Notice the DLL entry point function within this code? It looks exactly like a DLL! The only difference is that instead of windows.h or vcl.h included at the top of the source, the basepch.h header file is included instead. This header file points to the core header file that includes VCL and CLX headers, which is what's needed to construct a Package. Also, when we compile and build the package, a .bpl file will be generated instead of a .dll file. This is as far as we really need to go regarding Packages. Any further discussion would center on VCL-component development, which is not in the scope of this chapter. For more information on how to build and use Packages featuring VCL components see Chapter 4, "Creating Custom Components."

Using Forms in a DLL

One of the unique things you can do with C++Builder is to put forms and other visual controls into your DLLs. These controls can be used so that they appear to be a part of the application that loads the DLL, even though they are not. This can help make a project more modular and also provides the basis for plug-in support allowing an application to be enhanced and extended independently.

Let's look at the sample project titled MDIChild_DLL.bpr, which can be found in the MDIDLL folder on the CD-ROM that accompanies this book. Listing 16.14 provides the header for the example, and Listing 16.15 provides the source code.

LISTING 16.14 The MDIChild_DLL Header File

```
#ifndef MDIChild_DLL
#define MDIChild_DLL

extern "C" void __declspec(dllexport)ShowMDIChildForm(HWND CallingApp);
extern "C" void __declspec(dllexport)ShowSDIFormModal(void);

#endif
```

LISTING 16.15   The `MDIChild_DLL` Source File

```
#include <vcl.h>
#include <windows.h>
#pragma hdrstop
#include "MDIChild_DLL.h"
#include "MDIChildForm.h"
#include "SDIForm.h"

#pragma argsused
TApplication *ThisApp = NULL;
HWND  Handle;

BOOL WINAPI DllMain(HINSTANCE hinstDLL, DWORD fwdreason, LPVOID lpvReserved)
{
    // If the DLL is being unloaded then we need to reset its
    // Application instance to what it originally was.
    if (fwdreason == DLL_PROCESS_DETACH)
    {
      if (ThisApp) // any MDIs
          Application = ThisApp;
    }
    return 1;
}

//— — — — — — — — — — — — — — — — — — — — — — — — — — — — — — —·
void ShowMDIChildForm(HWND CallingApp)
{
    if (!ThisApp)
    {
        ThisApp = Application;
        Application->Handle = CallingApp;
    }
    FormMDIChild = new TFormMDIChild(Application);
    FormMDIChild->Show();
}

//— — — — — — — — — — — — — — — — — — — — — — — — — — — — — — —·

void ShowSDIFormModal(void)
{
    FormSDI = new TFormSDI(NULL);
```

LISTING 16.15 Continued

```
    FormSDI->ShowModal();
    delete FormSDI;
}
```

Basically, this DLL provides the capability for an application to create a child window or a modal form. It's very simple in nature, but provides an example of some of the effects a DLL can provide for an application. The two principle functions provided by this DLL are ShowMDIChildForm() and ShowSDIFormModal(). In a moment we'll look at an example application that utilizes these functions, but first let's look at what is required to embed a form into a DLL.

You'll notice that in the ShowMDIChildForm() function created for this DLL the TFormMDIChild class that is used. Likewise, in ShowSDIFormmmodal(), the TFormSDI class is used. These two classes are identified in the header files listed at the top of our source code.

```
#include "MDIChildForm.h"
#include "SDIForm.h"
```

Using C++Builder, two forms were created; one to represent an MDI child window, and the other to represent an SDI window. These forms are created just like any other C++Builder form. Our project file for the DLL links these forms so that they are contained within the DLL, as illustrated in Figure 16.13. These forms can only be activated when an application calls either ShowMDIChildForm() or ShowSDIFormModal().

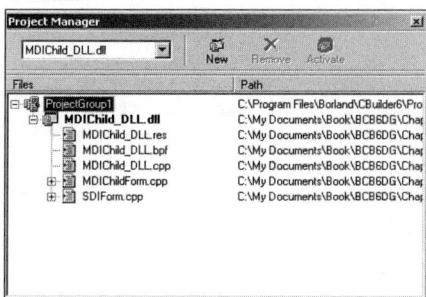

FIGURE 16.13 Project Manager dialog for MDIChild_DLL.

Let's now take a look at some example code that makes use of this DLL functionality.

Modal SDI Windows

It's often useful to provide a Single Document Inferface (SDI) form that can appear to the user to display information or provide a mechanism for input. In our DLL example, `ShowSDIChild()` requires no parameter. We simply call the DLL function within our application, as shown in Listing 16.16.

LISTING 16.16   Code Example Using `ShowSDIForm`, Which Is Contained Within `MDIChild_DLL`

```
void __fastcall TParent::ShowSDIFormModalClick(TObject *Sender)
{
    typedef void __declspec(dllimport)SHOWSDIFORM(void);
    SHOWSDIFORM *ShowSDIForm;

    // See if the DLL is loaded already.
    if (!Dll)
        Dll = LoadLibrary("MDIChild_DLL.dll");

    // Check and make sure the Dll loaded
    if (Dll)
    {
        // Get the address of the function.
        ShowSDIForm = (SHOWSDIFORM *)GetProcAddress(Dll, "_ShowSDIFormModal");
        // Make sure we have the address then call the function.
        if (ShowSDIForm)
            ShowSDIForm();
        else
        {
            ShowMessage(SysErrorMessage(GetLastError()));
            // If we couldn't get the address of the function
            // we want to free the Dll.
            FreeLibrary(Dll);
        }

    }
    else
    {
        ShowMessage(SysErrorMessage(GetLastError()));
        ShowMessage("Unable to load the DLL");
    }
}
```

When ShowSDIForm() is called, the DLL will then use the ShowModal() method to display a single instance of the form embedded within the DLL, which will be placed on top of the calling application. This is illustrated in Figure 16.14.

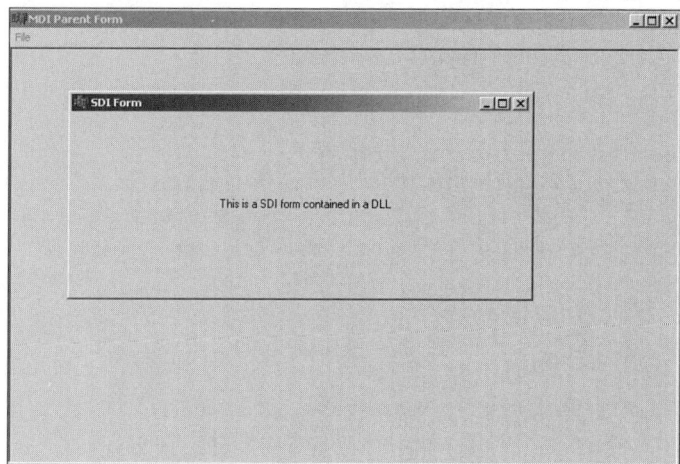

FIGURE 16.14   The MDI parent form displaying a modal SDI form.

A more practical example might be a DLL that generates an About box for an application. We could simply create an About form with generic fields and text, and provide a function with enough parameters to alter the form so that it works for a wide variety of applications. This way, we wouldn't have to re-create a new About form for every application. We can just use the DLL that contains the generic about box. This specific example is demonstrated later in the *Using C++Builder DLLs with Microsoft Visual C++* section.

MDI Child Windows

Let's now look at how we can support a multiple document interface (MDI) for an application through our DLL. We might want to us an MDI feature when displaying multiple windows of similar information to the user. The code used to utilize this functionality within our example DLL is provided in Listing 16.17.

LISTING 16.17   Code Example Using ShowMDIChild, Which Is Contained Within MDIChild_DLL

```
void __fastcall TParent::New1Click(TObject *Sender)
{
    typedef void __declspec(dllimport)SHOWMDICHILD(HWND);
    SHOWMDICHILD *ShowMDIChild;
```

LISTING 16.17   Continued

```
    // See if the DLL is loaded already.
    if (!Dll)
        Dll = LoadLibrary("MDIChild_DLL.dll");

    // Check and make sure the Dll is loaded
    if (Dll)
    {
        // Get the address of the function.
        ShowMDIChild = (SHOWMDICHILD *)GetProcAddress(Dll,
                                        "_ShowMDIChildForm");
        // Make sure we have the address then call the function.
        if (ShowMDIChild)
            ShowMDIChild(Handle);
        else
        {
            ShowMessage(SysErrorMessage(GetLastError()));
            // If we couldn't get the address of the function
            // we want to free the Dll.
            FreeLibrary(Dll);
        }
    }
    else
    {
        ShowMessage(SysErrorMessage(GetLastError()));
        ShowMessage("Unable to load the DLL");
    }
}
//---------------------------------------------
```

For ShowMDIChild(), we simply provide the Handle to our application as the lone parameter. The DLL uses this window handle to associate the application with the MDI
window that will be created. Basically, we trick the DLL into thinking the child form
is part of the application that contains the parent. This is accomplished by switching
the Application instance for the DLL to the Application instance of the calling application (but, we keep track of the DLL Application instance for clean up). The end
result is that the MDI child is fully aware of its parent form. The affect of this capability is illustrated in Figure 16.15.

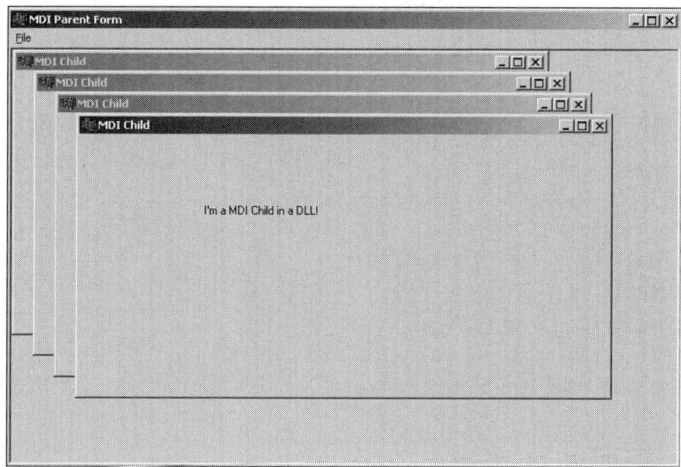

FIGURE 16.15   The MDI parent form with three MDI child forms open within it.

That's all there is to it. We call these functions containing visual controls, such as forms, much the same way we would call any other functions within a DLL. What's appealing about this approach is that the functionally is totally contained within the DLL, and our application can hijack and use this functionality at runtime.

Shared Memory Support in a DLL

Another unique capability that we can provide through a DLL built using C++Builder is support for shared memory between multiple applications.

When a DLL is loaded by an application within Windows, it's designed to be protected within the memory space allocated for the application. If two different applications load and use the same DLL they will not impact each other. In other words, a separate instance of the DLL would exist for both applications. This is part of the protection provided by the Windows 32-bit operating system.

There's a trick, however, that can be applied to create a DLL that can share the same memory segmentation between multiple applications. This can be really useful if you have an application that requires data from other applications during its execution (and you don't want to use COM, pipes, or mail slots). This capability is a form of Interprocess Communications (IPC). The specific IPC technique that we'll look at in this section is often referred to as shared segmentation.

Over the course of the past several years, a handful of books and magazine articles focused on the Win32 API have provided examples of DLL shared segmentation that appear to be exclusive for Visual C++ developers. Within Visual C++, the `pragma data_seg()` clause is used to isolate code to be shared across multiple applications that load the same DLL. A Visual C++ code snippet is provided in Listing 16.18 that demonstrates how to use these pragmas.

LISTING 16.18   Shared Segmentation Area of a Visual C++ DLL Source File

```
#pragma data_seg(".sdata")    // start of section — must initialize!

    int numAutoDealers    = 0;
    SAuto AllDealers      = {0,0,0,0};'
    SAuto Factory         = {100, 100, 100, 100};
    int NextDealerID      = 0;
    SDealer Dealer[MaxDealers] = {false, NULL};
    Bool    DealerLock        = false;

#pragma data_seg()

// these will NOT be global/shared to all modules
// (important only to attached component).

    SAuto LocalDealer = {0, 0, 0, 0};
    int DealerID;
```

The code block that follows the .sdata segment identifies shared data variables. These must be initialized in this section to be effective. The code block that follows the empty data_seg() reverts back to local data, which is not shared across processes.

Also required within Visual C++ is a .def file identifying the shared segmentation area, which is included as part of the project and used by the linker. An example DEF file is shown in Listing 16.19.

LISTING 16.19   Shared Segmentation Declaration in a Visual C++ DLL Definition (DEF) File

```
LIBRARY  SharedSeg ; name of DLL module (output file name)

SECTIONS
    .sdata READ WRITE SHARED    ; shared data
```

Unfortunately, C++Builder does not support these techniques that apply for Visual C++. Fear not though, there is a way.

To fully understand how shared segmentation works, we need a simple example that illustrates the effectiveness of multiple applications that are able to share data. A project called Inventory.bpr has been provided in the SharedSegCode folder on the

CD-ROM. This project provides the basic constructs for a DLL that maintains inventory information among applications that either represent an automobile factory or an automobile dealer. The files included for this DLL project are illustrated in Figure 16.16.

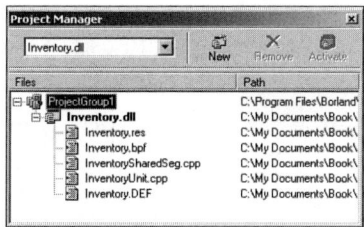

FIGURE 16.16   The Inventory DLL project.

The principal source file in the project is InventoryUnit.cpp. This file is quite lengthy and it's best if we don't get bogged down with the details of each function, therefore, you are encouraged to examine the file on your own to fully understand the functionality provided by the DLL. However, some interesting code elements are unique to supporting shared segmentation under C++Builder. They are provided in Listing 16.20.

LISTING 16.20   Source File of a C++Builder DLL, Which Identifies Variables That Will Be Shared Among Multiple Instances of the DLL

```
#include <windows.h>
#pragma hdrstop
#include <stdio.h>
#include <time.h>

#include "InventoryUnit.h"
#include "InventoryDataTypes.h"

    SAuto LocalDealer = {10, 10, 10, 10};
    int DealerID;

    extern int numAutoDealers;
    extern SAuto AllDealers;
    extern SAuto TotalSold;
    extern int NextDealerID;
    extern SDealerFactory DealerFactory[MaxDealers];
    extern SAuto Factory;
    extern bool InventoryLock;
```

This is just the top few lines of the DLL code (right before the DLLMain()). You'll notice several header files included in the code such as InventoryUnit.h and InventoryDataTypes.h followed by two variables local only to the DLL, and finally a number of extern variables. These extern variables are the variables within our shared segmentation area. The data types associated to all the variables are found in the InventoryDataTypes.h file. Whereas, the InventoryUnit.h file exposes the functions provided by the DLL so that outside applications can interface with the DLL and, through these functions, get at the shared data.

Another important file identified in the project is InventorySharedSeg.cpp, which is provided in Listing 16.21.

LISTING 16.21   The Declaration and Initialization of the Shared Segmentation Variables for the C++Builder DLL

```
#pragma option -zRSHSEG  // change default data segment name
#pragma option -zTSHCLS  // change default data class name

#include "InventoryDataTypes.h"

// Here is the initialized data that will be shared.
    int numAutoDealers   = 0;
    SAuto AllDealers     = {0,0,0, 0}; //false};
    SAuto TotalSold      = {0,0,0,0};
    SAuto Factory        = {100, 100, 100, 100}; // start off with 100 cars
    int NextDealerID     = 0;
    SDealerFactory DealerFactory[MaxDealers] = {false, NULL};
    Bool    InventoryLock   = false;
```

This is probably the most unique and important file of this particular DLL. Notice the two opening pragma clauses.

```
#pragma option -zRSHSEG  // change default data segment name
#pragma option -zTSHCLS  // change default data class name
```

They tell the compiler that the code to follow is to be included in the same shared segmentation and class. Next, we see the InventoryDataTypes.h file, again, which is followed by the variables to be used for containing the data that will be shared through the DLL. What's also vital is the initialization of these variables upon declaration. This is similar to what's required with Visual C++.

The third element of the Inventory DLL is the Inventory.DEF file, which is provided in Listing 16.22.

LISTING 16.22   The DEF File Identifying the Shared Segmentation Class for the
C++Builder DLL

```
LIBRARY Inventory

SEGMENTS
  SHSEG CLASS 'SHCLS' SHARED
```

This piece is also vital. The pragma calls that were used in `InventorySharedSeg.cpp`
identified both `SHSEG` and `SHCLS`. These labels are declared in this definition file and
can be named something else if desired.

To share information contained in a shared segmentation variable, the DLL needs to
provide a function for an application to read or set the shared data. Let's look at just
one function provided in Listing 16.23 that demonstrates this capability.

LISTING 16.23   A C++Builder DLL Function Available to External Applications, Which
Makes Use of the Shared Segmentation Variables

```cpp
int BuySellCar(int model,int quantity)
{
    unsigned int StartTime = clock();
    while (InventoryLock)
    {
        if (StartTime - clock() > MaxWaitTime)
                break;
    }
    InventoryLock = true;

    // dealer can't sell if no cars are available from dealer or factory
    if (quantity > 0)  // dealer can't sell back to factory
    {
      int value = Factory[model];
      if (value >= quantity)   // can't deplete the factory below zero
      {
          LocalDealer[model] += quantity;
          AllDealers[model] += quantity;
          Factory[model] -= quantity;
      }
      else     // the factory has enough cars for order
      {
          LocalDealer[model] += value;
          AllDealers[model] += value;
          Factory[model] -= value;
          MessageBeep(MB_OK); // factory doesn't have enough cars to ship
```

LISTING 16.23   Continued

```
      }
    }
    else // dealer is selling a car
    {
      int value = LocalDealer[model];
      if (value >= abs(quantity)) // can't deplete all the vehicles
      {
          LocalDealer[model] += quantity;
          AllDealers[model] += quantity;
          TotalSold[model] -= quantity;
      }
      else
      {
          LocalDealer[model] -= value;
          AllDealers[model] -= value;
          TotalSold[model] -= value;
          MessageBeep(MB_OK);    // dealer doesn't have enough cars to sell
      }
    }

    // notify other Dealers of local dealer's change Status
    for (int i= 0; i< MaxDealers; i++)
    {
        if (DealerFactory[i].Open) // tell all dealers...
                PostMessage(DealerFactory[i].hwnd,
                      WM_CAR_CHANGE,
                      (WPARAM) i,     // what dealer id changed
                      (LPARAM) model);// what car changed
    }
    InventoryLock = false;
    return DealerID; // no error, return store id
}
```

We do a few things here such as performing a lock to ensure that another application's call to this function won't step on the same data. When locked, we examine the parameter values and assign the data to the appropriate variable whether it is local or shared. We also use a custom windows message to notify other applications, which represent dealers and/or a factory, that new data is available.

Figure 16.17 provides an illustration of our DLL supporting multiple, simultaneous applications that represent either a factory or car dealerships. All these systems are able to share and reflect information, even though they are separate processes.

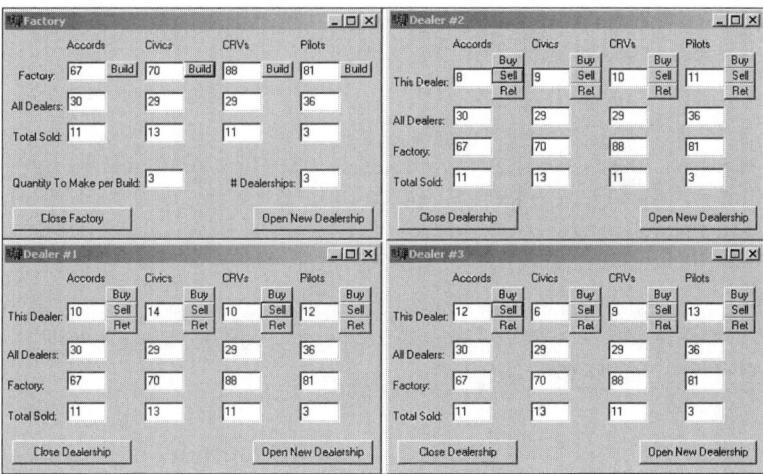

FIGURE 16.17 The automobile inventory simulation featuring one Factory application and three Dealership applications.

This complete project group, including the Factory and Dealership applications as well as the Inventory DLL, is provided on the CD-ROM in the SharedSegCode folder. Also, the Visual C++ code that we started with earlier in this discussion could be used to develop an equivalent Inventory DLL under VisualC++—this is also included on the CD-ROM. Although the myth had been that shared segmentation could only be supported by Visual C++, we've shown that it can indeed be supported by C++Builder.

Using Microsoft Visual C++ DLLs with C++Builder

As powerful as C++Builder is, the majority of DLLs developed and used within the software community are built using Visual C++. Therefore, chances are you will need to interface your C++Builder code with a Visual C++ DLL. Again, there are two ways for a DLL to attach to an application. Either it can be loaded in dynamically, or it can be loaded in statically if the LIB file associated to the DLL is linked at compile time. If that LIB file is a Microsoft LIB file, the DLL won't be able to load. The reason is because of the compatibility issues between the LIB file format for Visual C++ and C++Builder. Both vendors use different exporting conventions. Microsoft supports the Common Object Format File (COFF), whereas Borland uses the Object Model Format (OMF). Fortunately, there is a way to create a Borland OMF import library file that represents a Microsoft built DLL.

To create a Borland compatible .lib file for a Visual C++ DLL, you can use the COFF2OMF command-line tool from Borland, which resides in the Bin folder under

C++Builder. COFF2OMF takes two arguments: the first is the source library's filename; and the second is the destination's filename.

```
Coff2Omf MyDll.lib MyDll_bor.lib
```

In this example, COFF2OMF will generate a new OMF library file called MyDll_bor.lib. Within your C++Builder project, be sure to link using this MyDll_bor.lib file as part of the project file listing.

> **NOTE**
>
> The COFF2OMF utility only works on lib files with simple exported C functions. If C++ classes are exported, it will not work.

If this doesn't work, you need to find out how the functions are being exported and give them an alias that C++Builder will like. To do this, first you should use Impdef.exe to create a definition file (or .def file), which enables you to view all the exported functions' names and ordinal numbers. Next, modify the exported functions in the .def file, so the function looks like this:

```
Old export section
EXPORTS
    _Add@8                          =_Add                  @1


New export section
EXPORTS
    Add=_Add@8
```

After you've made the changes to the library, save the .def file. Now you can use Implib.exe on this file to create a new library file that C++Builder should like. Implib.exe also takes two parameters: the destination and the source. For example

```
Implib MyDll.lib MyDll.def
```

Because you now have a library in C++Builder style, you should be able to include it in your project and use the DLL and .lib.

See the VCppProject folder on the CD-ROM that accompanies this book for the complete C++Builder project CallVCppDll.bpr. This uses the Visual C++ DLL mentioned previously.

Using C++Builder DLLs with Microsoft Visual C++

Sometimes it's important to be sure that programs created by other compilers such as Visual C++ or Visual Basic can access a DLL created by C++Builder. This ensures other vendors can write applications that can access the DLL. There shouldn't be much difficulty for a Visual C++ application to dynamically link a C++Builder DLL by using `LoadLibrary()`, `GetProcessAddress()`, and `FreeMemory()` during execution. But for static linking, which requires a LIB file, compatibility between Visual C++ and C++Builder can be a much different matter. This is because of the different exporting conventions used by the two different companies. As stated earlier, Microsoft supports the Common Object Format File (COFF), whereas Borland uses the Object Model Format (OMF). Fortunately, there is a way to create a Microsoft's COFF import library file that represents a Borland-built DLL.

To create an MS COFF import library file from a Borland OMF DLL a definition (DEF) file must first be created. This is accomplished using the Borland IMPDEF command-line tool at the DOS prompt.

```
impdef mybcbdll_coff.def mybcbdll.dll
```

This creates a definition file called `mybcbdll_coff.def` using the Borland IMPDEF utility, which extracts the function calls from `mybcbdll.dll`. Now, to keep the names consistent so the Microsoft linker knows exactly what to look for in the library representing the DLL, it's important to modify the newly created .def file and remove the additional underscore in front of the function names. For example, suppose the definition file created previously looks like the following:

```
LIBRARY      MYBCBDLL.DLL

EXPORTS
     @@Aboutform@Finalize        @4   ; __linkproc__  Aboutform::Finalize
     @@Aboutform@Initialize      @3   ; __linkproc__  Aboutform::Initialize
     _AboutBox                   @2   ; _AboutBox
     _FormAbout                  @6   ; _FormAbout
     _MsgQuery                   @1   ; _MsgQuery
     ___CPPdebugHook             @5   ; _
```

Notice the underscores; they need to be removed. The .def file should be modified as follows:

```
LIBRARY      MYBCBDLL.DLL

EXPORTS
     @@Aboutform@Finalize        @4   ; __linkproc__  Aboutform::Finalize
     @@Aboutform@Initialize      @3   ; __linkproc__  Aboutform::Initialize
     AboutBox                    @2   ; _AboutBox
     FormAbout                   @6   ; _FormAbout
     MsgQuery                    @1   ; _MsgQuery
     ___CPPdebugHook             @5   ; ___CPPdebugHook
```

Next, the Microsoft Library Manager (LIB)c utility, which ships with Microsoft Visual C++, should be used to create the COFF import library file as follows:

```
lib /DEF:mybcbdll_coff.def
```

NOTE

Make sure to have access to the `lib` command-line program located in the Visual C++ bin directory by including this folder as part of the system Path.

The `mybcbdll_coff.lib`, which is generated by issuing the preceding command line, can now be added and linked by a Microsoft Visual C++ project.

Figure 16.18 provides an illustration of a Visual C++ application using a form contained with a C++Builder DLL. The code for both the C++Builder DLL and the Visual C++ example application is provided on the CD-ROM under the `MyVCProg` folder. (Library Manager)

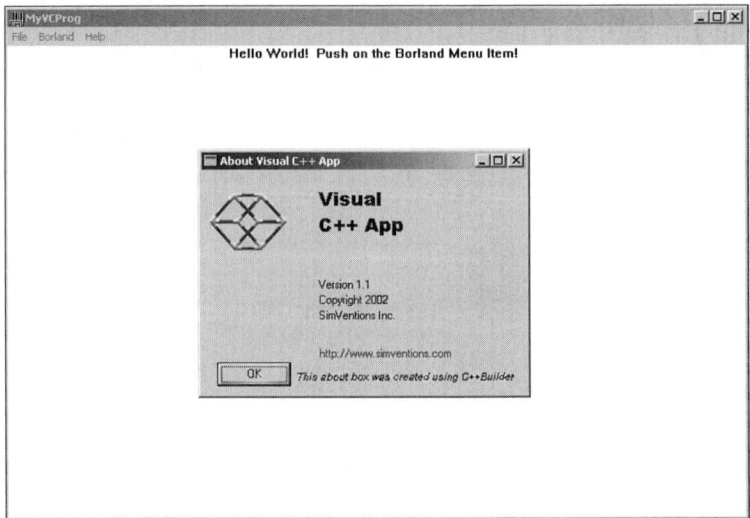

FIGURE 16.18   A Visual C++ Application using a C++Builder DLL.

Summary

In this chapter, we've examined how to build and use DLLs, which includes static and dynamic loading. We've looked at how we can export functions, classes, and visual controls such as forms within a DLL. We looked at how a DLL can be used to share data among multiple applications through shared segmentation. Finally, we looked at how both Visual C++ and Borland C++Builder applications and DLLs can coexist and leverage off of one another.

DLLs are extremely useful for moving code from inside an application and into a more modular and reusable structure. We can also use DLLs to store resources such as strings and icons, or contain COM objects as an out-of-process server (see Chapter 17 for details on COM). Much like application development, the sky is virtually the limit as to what you can do with a DLL. You're encouraged to find ways to reuse code within a DLL or Package so that other applications you develop can benefit from the functionality. DLLs can also be used to provide updates and enhancements to your applications. With a little innovative thinking, you can also discover ways to use DLLs as a plug-in technology for your applications. To find out more about DLLs and packages, see the C++Builder online help and the Win32 Programmer's Reference for DLLs.

17

COM Programming

by Paul Gustavson

IN THIS CHAPTER

- COM Fundamentals
- Creating and Using COM Interfaces
- Adding Automation
- Adding Event Sinks
- Writing the COM Server
- ActiveX Controls
- Recommended Resources

The Component Object Model (COM) is an object-oriented framework for integrating binary software components. The COM supports reuse and the interoperability of objects regardless of the language in which the software was developed. COM-based technologies include COM servers and clients, ActiveX controls, object linking and embedding (OLE), and Automation. The primary platform for COM is Windows, but it also can be supported with other platforms such as Unix—although not as easily.

In this chapter, we'll examine the capabilities provided by COM and COM-based technologies, and how it is used with C++Builder. The breadth and depth that COM provides is extremely vast, therefore, we will only be able to scratch the surface on COM programming with C++Builder. However, COM is a powerful mechanism that is often under utilized. The goal of this chapter is to equip you with the essentials so that your C++Builder applications can benefit from COM.

COM Fundamentals

Before we dig into the COM support provided by C++Builder and examine related code examples, it's helpful to understand the fundamental elements of COM. For those familiar with COM, consider this a review.

COM is designed to enable modular elements of a program to be built so that they can be used by and within other programs. The benefits of COM and related COM-based technologies are two-fold:

- COM specifies a standard at the binary level for developing and using components in any language or development tool.

- COM provides transparency. The user of a component does not have to know where the component actually resides. Even if the component is in a remote server (using DCOM), the client uses it as a local component.

Essentially, COM provides a basis for building on your applications as a cooperative set of independent binary units. This produces an aspect of reusability sometimes referred to as *componentware*.

NOTE

COM has become a big part of Windows and provides a viable mechanism for object-oriented software developers. We can use COM to develop modular elements of a program that can be used by and within other programs. A current example includes the editor for Microsoft Paint, a COM-based program, which can be seamlessly integrated into Word. To see this example, open Word and choose Insert, Object, and Bitmap Image. A copy of the Paint editor should integrate into Word. This COM activity is called *in-place activation* and is touted as one of the Plug-and-Play features of Windows.

The applications you develop can also leverage capabilities available in other COM-based applications, such a Powerpoint and Word. One of the more recent COM-based applications provided by Microsoft that many application developers are taking advantage of is the Microsoft XML (MSXML) parser. Access to the MSXML parser is accomplished using COM. In fact, the TXMLDocument, which is a VCL class provided with Delphi and C++Builder, leverages COM to provide a VCL wrapper for the MSXML parser.

COM Architectural Elements

Five basic architecture elements of COM enable the development and distribution of *componentware*. These elements are described in Table 17.1. It's important to understand each one of these.

TABLE 17.1   COM Architecture Elements

Element	Description
COM Interface	Serves as a contract identifying the public methods used to access a COM object. Equivalent to an abstract class containing pure virtual functions in C++. Interfaces are used by a COM Client and recognized by a COM Server. Note that a COM interface defines usage not implementation.
COM Class	Represents the implementation of one or more COM interfaces, often referred to as a CoClass. Encapsulates the behavior associated to the methods and access to the properties identified in the COM interface declaration. Classes are implemented within a COM Server.

TABLE 17.1   Continued

Element	Description
COM Object	The instantiation of a COM Class within a COM Server is a COM Object. A COM Object is accessed by a COM Client through the COM Interface.
COM Server	Provides the interface implementations that a client can use. A COM Class is instantiated as a COM Object within a COM Server. The two types of servers are *out-of-process* and *in-process*. A server that is its own application (EXE) operates as an out-of-process server. A server that is represented as DLL or ActiveX Control Library operates as an in-process server.
COM Client	Code or program that utilizes a COM interface to communicate with an object contained within a COM Server.

These five architectural elements are the basic tenants required for all things COM, including COM+ and Distributed COM (DCOM). For COM to work effectively each of these elements need to be in place. Figure 17.1 illustrates how these elements interoperate.

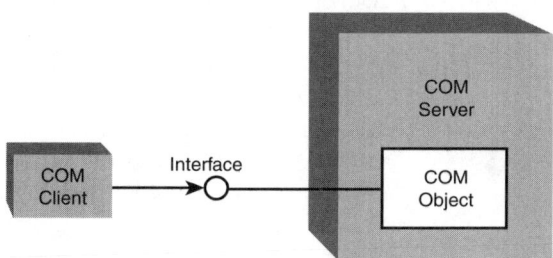

FIGURE 17.1   COM Client/Server communication via a COM Interface.

This illustrates how COM uses a client-server model. The server contains the COM Object accessed by a client via a COM Interface. Later in the chapter, we will look at how these architectural elements are developed and used with C++Builder.

COM Technologies

The other aspect of understanding COM fundamentals is to recognize the various COM technologies and extensions that exist. Table 17.2 provides a listing of the COM technologies supported by C++Builder.

TABLE 17.2   C++Builder COM Support

Item	Description
ActiveX Controls	A compiled software component representing a COM object whose properties can be altered at design time and can integrate and extend the functionality of an application at runtime.
ActiveX Library	An in-process server DLL that hosts one or more ActiveX controls or COM objects.
Property Page	A dialog that enables modification of ActiveX control properties at design time.
Active Form	A simple ActiveX control preconfigured to run on a Web browser. Descends from TActiveForm within C++Builder.
Active Server Object	A COM Object used to transform an existing application to an Active Server Page, which is a script that generates HTML pages and can act as an Automation controller.
Automation Controller	A client application that leverages and reflects capabilities exposed by Automation Objects that are contained within an external application.
Automation Objects	COM objects contained with an application called an Automation Server that can be controlled by other applications programmatically at runtime.
COM+ Event Object	A COM+ Object used for dispatching server events to registered clients. Facilitates publish/subscribe paradigm.
COM+ Subscription Object	A COM+ Object used for registering a client to receive notification of events fired by COM+ publisher applications.
Transactional Object	An element of COM+ allowing support for handling a large number of clients. Features include just-in-time activation, transactions, resource pooling, and security systems.
Type Library	Used to define custom interfaces, dispinterfaces, coclasses, enumerations, aliases, records, unions, and modules. Type libraries can be identified within the system registry for access by other applications.

As you can see, most of the COM technologies center on ActiveX, Automation and COM+. Also identified in this table is the concept of Type Libraries, which we will utilize in the next section by developing COM interfaces and classes.

NOTE

COM+ is an extension of COM that integrates Microsoft Transaction Server (MTS) and Microsoft Message Queue (MSMQ), which makes it more suitable for large-scale distributed development than standard COM. COM+ provides support for transaction control, security, administration, queued components, and publish-and-subscribe event services. COM+

provides a more scalable technology than standard COM, which includes Just-In-Time Activation and lifetime management. Although our discussion is largely focused on COM, keep in mind that the techniques and capabilities of COM discussed here are fully supported by COM+.

Creating and Using COM Interfaces

As identified in Table 17.2, COM takes on many different forms, including ActiveX controls, Automation, ActiveForms, COM+, and DCOM just to name a few. The one common capability provided by these various COM technologies is that COM facilitates *communication* between components, applications, clients, and servers through clearly defined *interfaces*. These interfaces enable the reuse of software components and services provided by COM objects.

Therefore, the most important thing about developing and using COM-based software is to understand interfaces. As stated earlier, an interface defines a set of public methods for accessing a COM object, which is contained within a COM server. From a C++ perspective, an interface is comparable to an abstract class containing pure virtual functions.

IUnknown

All COM interfaces descend from a base class called IUnknown. The primary purpose of IUnknown is to expose an interface so that it can be utilized by other applications. IUnknown is comprised of three virtual methods.

- QueryInterface()

- AddRef()

- Release()

QueryInterface() is used to query and retrieve a reference to a specified interface. The C++ declaration for QueryInterface() is defined as follows:

```
virtual HRESULT QueryInterface(REFIID riid, void ** ppvObject);
```

Notice that there are two parameters associated to QueryInterface(): riid and ppvObject. The riid parameter is used to identify the interface being requested. If the interface exists, QueryInterface() will assign a pointer representing the interface to the ppvObject parameter. If the object doesn't support the interface, QueryInterface() sets ppvObject to NULL and returns a nonzero error code.

AddRef() is used to increment the reference count for the interface and returns the reference count value. When the caller is finished with the interface, it should call the Release() method. Release() will decrement the reference count. If the reference count drops to zero, the object is automatically freed.

CAUTION

Each of the IUnknown methods are virtual and are redefined by the class that inherits IUnknown. Therefore, it's quite possible that a COM object has redefined AddRef() and Release() so that they do not perform the anticipated reference counting. In this case, the reference count might never drop to zero. If this occurs, the object will not be automatically freed, and it will be the responsibility of the application to then free the object.

NOTE

In addition to IUnknown, a custom interface can inherit several other interfaces, which are identified in Table 17.3

TABLE 17.3   COM Common Interfaces

Interface	Description
IDataBroker	Design time interface for remote data modules.
IDispatch	Interface used for providing Automation. (This is used in some of the following examples.)
IEnumVARIANT	Interface used for enumerating a collection of variant objects.
IFont	Interface to a COM font object, which is actually a wrapper around a Windows font object.
IPicture	Interface to a picture object, which is a language-neutral abstraction for bitmaps, icons, and metafiles, and its properties.
IProvider	Provider interface for TClientDataSet.
IStrings	Collection Interface for TStrings.
IUnknown	The base interface for all other interfaces. Introduces the QueryInterface() method, which is useful for discovering and using other interfaces implemented by the same object.

The two most popular interfaces are IUnknown and IDispatch. We will use IDispatch later in discussing Automation.

The first step when defining a custom interface is to establish a physical name for the interface. Let's take a look at a simple C++ example that declares a new COM interface.

```
interface DECLSPEC_UUID("{62648A4D-E9B4-4D92-A3AF-56AB782E233A}")
        IMetricConversion:
```

```
      public IUnknown
{

      virtual HRESULT feet_to_meters(
            double feet/*[in]*/,
            double* meters/*[out]*/) = 0;
      virtual HRESULT meters_to_feet(
            double meters/*[in]*/,
            double* feet/*[out]*/) = 0;
}
```

Notice how our interface inherits IUnknown. Also, an I prefix is used in our physical name to identify the type as an interface. This particular example includes five virtual methods that will need to be implemented as a COM class. In this example, each one of them returns an HRESULT return type, which is the common return type for COM methods. It is equivalent to a LongWord type. Possible HRESULT values are listed in the winerror.h file included with C++Builder. A return value of S_OK indicates success.

Interface ID

For our interface to work in COM, IMetricConversion is identified (keyed) by a Globally Unique Identifier (GUID), which is a 128-bit number. It is this GUID, rather than the C++ type name, that a client uses to reference our interface. When a GUID is associated with an interface, it is known as an Interface ID (IID). In the previous example, the IID for the IMetricConversion interface would be IID_IMetricConversion. In the system registry you'll find IIDs keyed by the GUID. The value data for each GUID in the registry identifies the physical name (for example, IMetricConversion), but programmatically you reference the interface using the IID (for example, IID_IMetricConversion).

If you do choose to utilize inline code that identifies a GUID for a custom interface as shown in the previous sample, you can create your own GUIDs as described in the following tip.

TIP

To generate a GUID at design time within the C++Builder use the Ctrl+Shift+G keystroke in the Code Editor. To create a GUID programmatically, you should first initialize COM by calling the Windows API function CoInitialize(), and then call CoCreateGuid() to generate a unique GUID. C++Builder also generates a GUID when using the Type Library Editor to create interfaces, which will be discussed later.

For a client to latch on to an interface, the QueryInterface() method is used with the IID, as shown in the following psuedocode example.

```
extern GUID IID_IMetricConversion;
IUnknown *pServerUnkn;

// some code is left out here
// use OLE to get IUnknown of Server

IMetricConv *pMetricConversion;
pServerUnkn->QueryInterface(IID_MetricConv, (void **)&pMetricConversion);

// use MetricConversion methods

ServerUnkn->Release();  // release server
pMetricConversion->Release();  // release pointer to pMetricConversion object
```

Keep in mind that this is a pseudocode example. The actual process of getting an
IUnknown pointer to a server that supports the IMetricConversion interface is more
complex than has been shown, and in-depth discussion is beyond our scope at this
time. What's being shown here is how an instance of a COM object is created by
passing the GUID-oriented class identifier (often called a CLSID). The CLSID is associated to the COM class we want to create.

In a short bit, we'll see how C++Builder alleviates much of the complexities through
Microsoft's Active Template Library (ATL) with a class factory, specifically the
TCoClassCreatorT template and CoCreateInstance() call. What's important to understand is that the GUID is utilized within IUnknown's QueryInterface() to retrieve a
pointer to pMetricConversion. After we latch onto an pMetricConversion object we can
utilize the methods associated to the interface, such as meters_to_feet() or
feet_to_meters(). Also, it's important for the client to release the object using the
Release() method associated to the IUnknown interface after it's done.

You might be wondering why a C++ client doesn't delete a COM object as we would
normally expect since an object was instantiated through the QueryInterface() call.
In COM, it's not the responsibility of the client to delete an object pointer to a COM
interface implementation. In fact, it should be avoided since other clients might also
access the object within the server. Instead, a client issues a Release() call when it's
done using the object. The reference counting provided by the IUnknown interface
enables the proper lifetime management of an object. After the reference counting
reaches zero when a Release() call is made, the server is free to delete the object.

Type Libraries

In C++, a header file is often created to share data types such as classes and structures
that can be referenced by other C++ files. Unfortunately the use of a C++ header file
is language-dependent and not practical with COM because it can't be used natively

by other languages such as Delphi or Visual Basic. Therefore, when we create a COM interface in C++Builder, or in any other COM supported language, we need a mechanism to allow other languages to reference the interface we've defined. This is the capability that COM Type Libraries provide.

Type libraries provide a language-neutral mechanism for defining types such as interfaces, methods, classes, and other COM elements that are defined and used by a server and called on by a client. Type libraries are saved as binary files with a `*.tlb` extension or can be contained within the binary file representing the server (`*.dll`, `*.ocx`, `*.exe`, `*.olb`). C++Builder provides support for creating and viewing type libraries through the Type Library Editor. To view a type library, simply select File, Open from the main menu and select type library from the list of file types. Figure 17.2 provides an illustration of C++Builder's Type Library Editor.

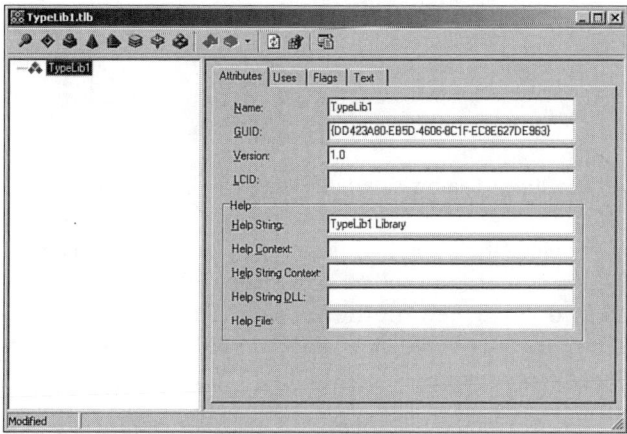

FIGURE 17.2   Borland's Type Library Editor.

We will use a Type Library to define and contain the interfaces we need for our examples. Later we'll also use a type library to create the interface implementation (`CoClass`) for a server.

NOTE

All COM interfaces conform to a Virtual Method Table (VMT), or *vtable,* which maps how an object's functions are laid out in memory. A `vtable` is COM's way of standardizing the organization and order of declared interfaces so that multiple languages can utilize it. A standardized layout of these interfaces, which contains virtual methods, is important in allowing language independence and binary compatibility.

Creating an Interface in C++Builder

The easiest way to create an interface in C++Builder is through Borland's Type Library Editor. This is accomplished by selecting File, New, Other from the IDE's main menu. When the New items dialog appears, select on the ActiveX tab. This view is shown in Figure 17.3.

FIGURE 17.3   New Items Dialog—ActiveX View.

Within this view, select the Type Library icon to activate the Type Library Editor. The Type Library Editor contains a toolbar across the top allowing you to create various COM elements, and a tree view on the left side identifying the elements of your type library. The root node of the tree view always represents the type library itself. To create an interface, you need to select the first red glyph in the top toolbar.

You'll notice in the Attributes tab sheet a GUID is automatically generated for the interface. You can rename your interface, and identify the type of interface you're inheriting, such as IUnknown, in the Parent Interface selection. To add methods to your interface, select the glyph from the toolbar that looks like a green downward right arrow. Again, you can rename the method within the Attributes tab sheet. An example of an interface created using the Type Library Editor is shown in Figure 17.4.

To generate the implementation for the Type Library, select the Refresh Implementation glyph on the toolbar. C++Builder generates/updates a source and header file for your server project that accompanies the TLB. Select F12 to view the source code for the TLB file. The areas of interest within the header file for the TLB we created is shown in Listing 17.1.

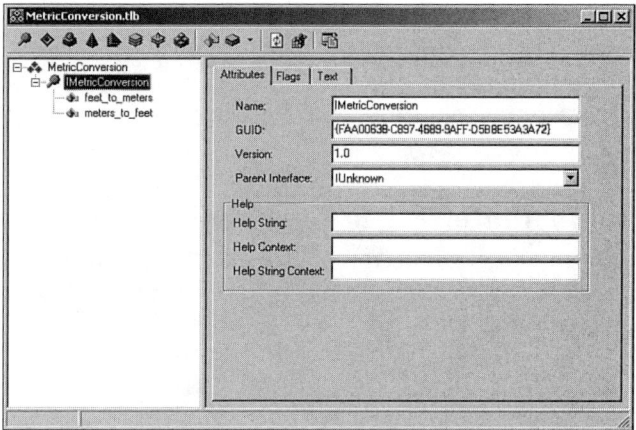

FIGURE 17.4   Using Borland's Type Library Editor to create an interface.

LISTING 17.1   Type Library Header File Declarations

```
// ************************************************************************ //
// Forward declaration of types defined in TypeLibrary
// ************************************************************************ //
interface DECLSPEC_UUID("{FAA00638-C897-4689-9AFF-D5B8E53A3A72}")
        IMetricConversion;
typedef TComInterface<IMetricConversion, &IID_IMetricConversion>
        IMetricConversionPtr;


// ************************************************************************ //
// Interface: IMetricConversion
// Flags:     (320) Dual OleAutomation
// GUID:      {FAA00638-C897-4689-9AFF-D5B8E53A3A72}
// ************************************************************************ //
interface IMetricConversion  : public IUnknown
{
public:
  virtual HRESULT STDMETHODCALLTYPE feet_to_meters(double feet/*[in]*/,
        double* meters/*[out]*/) = 0; // [3]
  virtual HRESULT STDMETHODCALLTYPE meters_to_feet(double meters/*[in]*/,
        double* feet/*[out]*/) = 0; // [4]

};
```

The Type Library Editor enables you to register the Type Library Binary (TLB) for this interface by selecting the Register Type Library glyph. By registering the TLB, we can use the interface for supporting development of other applications in the future (that is, COM servers that implement the interface). This is demonstrated in the following section.

Implementing an Interface in C++Builder

To implement an interface, we need to create a COM class (called a CoClass) within a COM server. A Server can include an out-of-process server such as an EXE application or an in-process server such as DLL.

COM SERVER TYPES

COM servers are binaries that contain the implementation of at least one COM object. Depending on where the server resides, it can be classified as in-process (inproc), out-of-process (outproc), or remote. It's important to select the type of COM Server you wish to implement.

An inproc server is always a DLL (OCX files, where ActiveX controls usually reside, are actually DLLs). This kind of server makes its components reside in the client's address space. The main advantage is speed. The main disadvantage is that if the server crashes, the client will probably crash, too, because they share the same memory segment.

An outproc server is an executable. The main advantage with an EXE is that if the server crashes, the client can potentially recover without much of an incident. The disadvantage is that these servers typically respond slower.

A remote server resides in a different machine than the client. It can be implemented as a DLL (using a surrogate process that wraps the DLL) or an EXE file.

COM+/MTS–compatible objects must be developed in DLLs to take full advantage of these technologies. Therefore, they tend to be the choice when there is no reason to prefer an EXE file.

Start by creating either an ActiveX Library (DLL) or a standard EXE application, which will represent the COM server. To create an ActiveX Library, select the ActiveX library icon in the ActiveX tab of the New items dialog (see Figure 17.3 for reference). After you have you started the DLL or EXE project, you need to select the COM Object icon in the ActiveX tab of the New items dialog (again, see Figure 17.3 for reference). This will open the New COM Object dialog as illustrated in Figure 17.5.

In this illustration, we entered a name for our class. Again, the type that identifies a COM object is often referred to as a component class or CoClass.

Next, we use the type library containing the IMetricConversion interface we created earlier through the Interface Selection Wizard. This is shown in Figure 17.6.

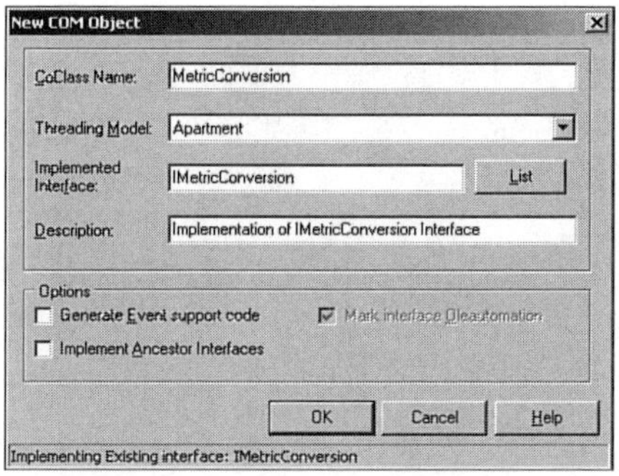

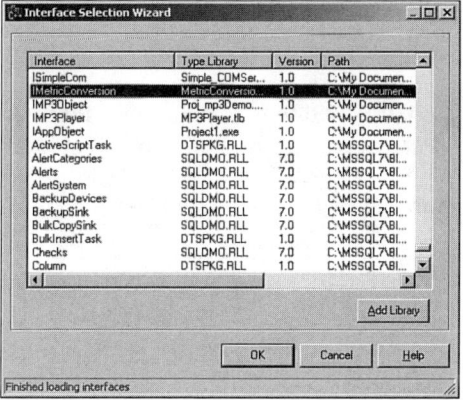

FIGURE 17.5   New COM Object dialog.

FIGURE 17.6   Interface Selection Wizard.

After a class has been created using the Type Library Editor, an icon will appear in the tree view representing our `CoClass`. This is shown in Figure 17.7.

NOTE

The node in the tree view illustrated in Figure 17.7 represents a new `CoClass`, which we expected. If we had checked the Generate Event support code check box in the New COM Object dialog (see Figure 17.5) the Type Library Editor would have generated what's called a dispatch interface (or dispinterface). This combination of a `CoClass` and a dispinterface is sometimes referred to as a dual interface, which allows binding on an object to occur two different ways: late binding and early binding. The *dispinterface* is an interface used to support binding at runtime (called late binding), whereas early binding occurs at compile time, by directly linking to a member function of a *vtable* representing the object (the custom interface). Basically, the *dispinterface* provides runtime access for an object so that it can issue event callbacks to the client. This is part of a two-way automation, which we'll discuss in more detail later in the chapter.

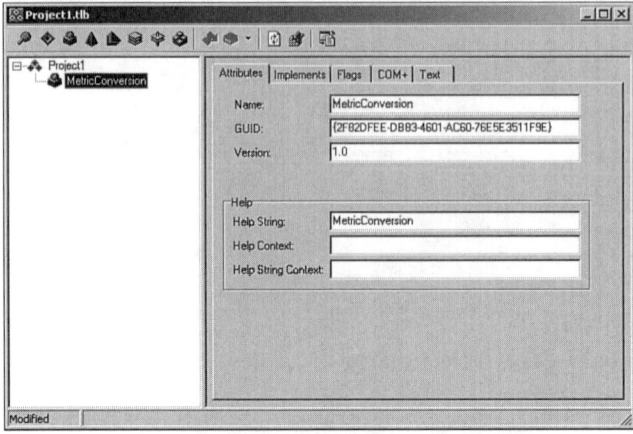

FIGURE 17.7   New CoClass created represented within the Type Library Editor.

When Refresh is selected, C++Builder's Type Library Editor will autogenerate the code needed for our class. Actually several file pairs are created as identified in Table 17.4.

TABLE 17.4   Type Library Editor Autogenerated Files When Creating a New Object

File Pair	Description
Type Library	The C++ TLB code for the COM class. Represented by *_TLB.*.
Active Template Library	The C++ ATL code for the COM class. Represented by *_ATL.*.
Implementation	The C++ implementation boilerplate. Represented by *Impl.*.

The most useful header/source file pair generated from a developer's standpoint, is the implementation boilerplate. Here's where we can fill in the code needed to process a method defined by the original interface, as shown in Listing 17.2.

LISTING 17.2   TMetricConversion CoClass C++ Source Code

```
// TMETRICCONVERSIONIMPL : Implementation of TTMetricConversionImpl
// (CoClass: TMetricConversion, Interface: IMetricConversion)

#include <vcl.h>
#pragma hdrstop

#include "TMETRICCONVERSIONIMPL.H"
#pragma link "MetricConversion_OCX"


///////////////////////////////////////////////////////////////////////////
// TTMetricConversionImpl
```

LISTING 17.2   Continued

```
STDMETHODIMP TTMetricConversionImpl::feet_to_meters(double feet,
  double* meters)
{
    *meters =  feet * 0.3048;
    return S_OK;
}

STDMETHODIMP TTMetricConversionImpl::meters_to_feet(double meters,
  double* feet)
{
    *feet = meters * 3.2808;
    return S_OK;
}
```

As you might except from Borland RAD Tools, the Type Library Editor generates the method calls within the source code, leaving the implementation up to you, the developer. Unfortunately, if any modifications are made to the declarative elements of either the source or header implementation boilerplate, they will not be reflected in the Type Library Editor—it's not quite two-way. In this example, after the boilerplate code was generated, the code representing the behavior for each method was added manually.

NOTE

If you have created an `inproc` ActiveX Library, be sure to register the server after you're satisfied with the implementation. This is accomplished by selecting Run, Register ActiveX Server from the IDE's main menu. When successfully registered, your COM server will be accessible to client applications. Note that you can unregister a COM server by selecting Run, Unregister ActiveX Server.

To register an `outproc` Server, simply run the application after each time it is built.

As you can see, the same basic steps apply to creating a class in C++Builder as they do in creating an interface. It's just that a class must be implemented as part of a server. The accompanying CD-ROM contains an example for both an `inproc` DLL server and an `outproc` EXE server within the `SimpleCOM` folder for this chapter. Just look for the projects titled `MetricConversionServerEXE.bpr` and `MetricConversionServerDLL.bpr`, respectively.

Accessing a COM Object

Now that we have both an inproc and outproc Server, we need to build a simple application known as a COM client that utilizes the MetricConversion object contained within these servers.

The ClientExample program for this chapter, which can be found in the SimpleCom folder for this chapter on the companion CD-ROM, contains two check boxes for selecting the server type at runtime, two edit fields for entering measurement values, and two buttons to access the methods of the object to convert these measurements. Let's take a look at the code for accessing these two different types of servers, as shown in Listing 17.3.

LISTING 17.3   ClientExample C++ Source Code

```cpp
#include <vcl.h>
#pragma hdrstop

#include "ClientForm.h"
#include "MetricConversionServerDLL_TLB.cpp"
#include "MetricConversionServerEXE_TLB.cpp"
//---------------------------------------------------------------------------
#pragma package(smart_init)
#pragma resource "*.dfm"
TForm1 *Form1;
//---------------------------------------------------------------------------
__fastcall TForm1::TForm1(TComponent* Owner)
        : TForm(Owner)
{
//
}
//---------------------------------------------------------------------------


void __fastcall TForm1::ButtonConvertToFeetClick(TObject *Sender)
{
  TCOMIMetricConversion MetricConversion; //
  if (RadioButtonEXE->Checked)
        MetricConversion =
                Metricconversionserverexe_tlb::CoMetricConversion2::Create();
  else
        MetricConversion =
                Metricconversionserverdll_tlb::CoMetricConversion::Create();
```

LISTING 17.3   Continued

```
  double meters = EditMeters->Text.ToDouble();
  double feet;
  MetricConversion->meters_to_feet(meters,&feet);
  EditFeet->Text = AnsiString(feet);
}
//------------------------------------------------------------------

void __fastcall TForm1::ButtonConvertToMetersClick(TObject *Sender)
{
  TCOMIMetricConversion MetricConversion; //
  if (RadioButtonEXE->Checked)
        MetricConversion =
                Metricconversionserverexe_tlb::CoMetricConversion2::Create();
  else
        MetricConversion =
                Metricconversionserverdll_tlb::CoMetricConversion::Create();

  double feet = EditFeet->Text.ToDouble();
  double meters;
  MetricConversion->feet_to_meters(feet,&meters);
  EditMeters->Text = AnsiString(meters);
}
```

For accessing two different servers, there's really not a lot of code required. We only need to include the server's TLB file within our include section. This approach is unlike the approach required for an application that leverages capabilities provided by a standard DLL. With a standard DLL, the application needs to either link with an equivalent LIB at build time or use the Windows LoadLibrary() call at runtime. In COM, C++Builder provides a utility file called utilcls.h, which contains a class template called TcoClassCreatorT, which is used to expose Create() and CreateRemote() routines for clients. This class template is used within our client by CoMetricConversion within the MetricConversionDLL_TLB.h file as shown here.

```
typedef TCoClassCreatorT<TCOMIMetricConversion, IMetricConversion,
             &CLSID_MetricConversion,
             &IID_IMetricConversion> CoMetricConversion;
```

When we make the CoMetricConversion::Create() call as shown in Listing 17.3, the class template actually calls CoCreateInstance(), which is what's used in COM to instantiate an object of the class associated with a specified class identifier (CLSID). In our case the class identifier is CLSID_MetricConversion, which was provided through the typedef declaration that applied the TCoClassCreateorT template.

NOTE

According to the Borland Help:

"CoCreateInstance() first ensures that COM is initialized before attempting to create the specified object. It then connects to the class object specified by [the class identifier], uses its IClassFactory interface to create an instance, releases the class factory, and returns the requested interface."

If the object is successfully created, CoCreateInstance() returns S_OK. Borland's implementation of CoCreateInstance() protects against errors that might occur if the object is not available locally.

Figure 17.8 illustrates this example during execution.

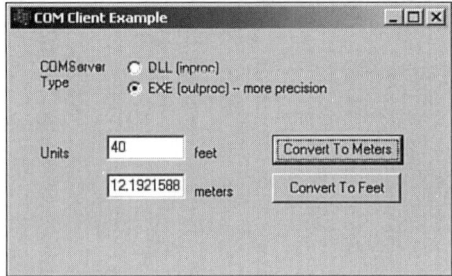

FIGURE 17.8   Snapshot of the COMClient example.

This example also demonstrates how COM servers, which offer varying levels of fidelity while still being based on the very same interface, can be developed and deployed. In this example, the inproc DLL server doesn't provide nearly the same amount of fidelity as the outproc EXE application. However, they both support the same interface.

We can also build clients that utilize a COM server with application development environments such as Delphi, Visual Basic, Visual C++, or even Java. This is one of the benefits over a standard DLL approach because a DLL, to be effective and useful with other languages, needs to be written with C structure function calls and wrappers to any embedded class methods. This isn't uncommon because many of the Win32 API calls, which are contained within DLLs, provide straight C functions. But COM enables us to maintain a more object-oriented design and enforces a guaranteed interface after it's been registered. The same can't be said for a DLL because there's no guarantee it will maintain its interface (and backward compatibility) as it changes and evolves. Additionally, in COM, an interface implementation can be accessed and used as objects externally by clients. Furthermore, with the capabilities of COM such as Distributed COM (DCOM), which will be discussed in the next chapter, clients can leverage and access objects provided by remote servers, not just *inproc* our *outproc* servers on a single platform.

OPERATING AS A COM CLIENT

COM Clients are applications that access COM objects implemented by a server application (EXE) or library (DLL, OCX). Examples of COM Clients include applications that visually reflect an ActiveX control (called an ActiveX container), utilize the services and capabilities provided by an external application (called an Automation controller), or simply access objects and associated data provided through a server application. Although COM Clients vary, the steps in functioning as a COM client are very similar.

COM Clients first must call either the CoInitialize() or CoInitializeEx() function provided by the objbase.h Win32 API file. In our example, this call was made for us within the CoCreateInstance() method, which we described earlier. Initialization needs to be performed before utilizing any other COM function. CoInitializeEx() provides an additional parameter over CoInitializeEx() enabling you to specify the type of threading model. Although there are many types of threading models, the two valid choices for this function are either apartment-threaded or free-threaded. Threading models are discussed later in this chapter and are further defined in Table 17.5. The use of CoInitialize() defaults the threading model to an apartment-threaded.

When initialized, the client can use an interface (or set of interfaces) to a server object and begin to use its properties and methods. However, the client must have access to the interface, which is often provided by a type library.

Importing a Type Library

Because we created the server for our last example, we were fortunate to have the server's TLB header file that we included in our client.

```
#include "MetricConversionServerDLL_TLB.cpp"
```

In many instances, however, the C++ TLB source code for a server will not be provided, only its type library (*.TLB) or within the actual server (*.DLL). Fortunately, there's a mechanism to import a type library within C++Builder.

For a client to digest the COM-type elements a server exposes (including classes and interfaces), follow these steps:

1. Click Project, Import Type Library in the BCB IDE. The Import Type Library dialog appears (see Figure 17.9 later in this chapter).

2. In this example, uncheck the Generate Component Wrapper check box. Having this checked indicates that you want component wrappers to be generated for all CoClasses that are not flagged as Hidden, Restricted, or PreDeclID. An unchecked control will generate the type library definitions, but not the component wrappers.

3. In the Import Type Library list box, select the name of the Type Library of your server. In our example, it is the `MetricConversionServerDLL` Library (Version 1.0). Press the Create Unit button. The file `MetricConversionServerDLL_TLB.cpp` will be added to your project.

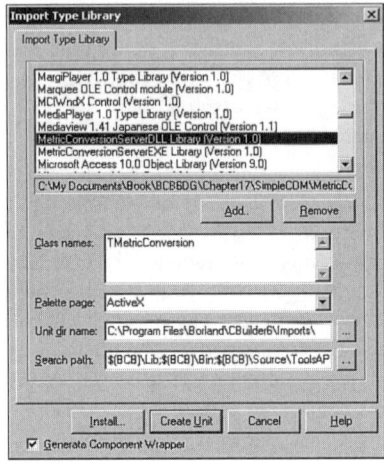

FIGURE 17.9   Importing the `MetricConversionServerDLL` Type Library.

NOTE

If you compare the server sources TLB files `MetricConversionServerDLL_TLB.cpp` and `MetricConversionServerDLL_TLB` with the C++ files generated using the Import Type Library wizard, you will notice that they are equivalent. However, because COM is a binary standard, there is no need to distribute or locate the TLB header file of a server. Also, remember that a server can be written in any COM-supported programming language, not just C++.

The main advantage of distributing the Type Library is that it can be used to generate specific language declarations of all the components and types it describes. That will guarantee that your components (interfaces, dispinterfaces, CoClasses, and other elements) are capable of being used by any development platform.

Adding Automation

In the DLL chapter, we developed a mock simulation environment representing a Honda automobile factory and various dealerships. The collaboration needed to achieve this interoperability between the Inventory keeper (our server) and the factory and dealerships (our clients), was provided through our DLL using shared segmentation and external functions. This DLL provided an example of automation.

Automation is the capability of an application to control, effect and/or access objects within another application.

COM provides an even easier way to support automation. In fact, we can create an *outproc* COM server with the same functionality as our DLL that automated the Honda factory/dealership simulation, which we created in Chapter 16. A COM example of this automation is provided on the companion CD-ROM. You're encouraged to take a look at this example by opening the ProjectGroup1.bpr file within the AutoBusiness folder for this chapter. This project group includes InventoryKeeperServer, Dealership, and Factory projects. The InventoryKeeperServer project is an *outproc* server that mimics the functionality provided in the original shared segmented DLL from Chapter 16. The Dealership and Factory projects represent COM client applications.

We can also take an existing application such as the MP3 player we created originally in Chapter 15, and provide an automation object so that other applications can benefit from the MP3 player's capabilities. Let's take a look at how this is done.

Adding Automation to an Existing Application

To follow along with this example of adding automation to an existing application, copy the MP3Demo folder from Chapter 15 and name it as MP3DemoCOM. Open the project within this folder using C++Builder. We're going to convert the MP3Player into a COM server. This is done by selecting File, New, Other, and then selecting the ActiveX tab within the New Items dialog. Next, select the Automation Object glyph. This will enable us to define both the COM interface and the CoClass within the same Type Library. This is illustrated in Figure 17.10.

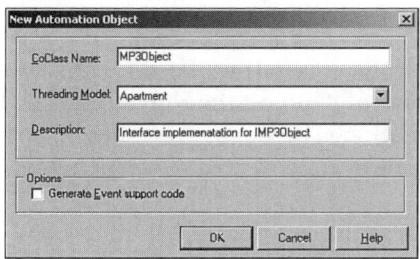

FIGURE 17.10   Adding a COM Automation Object to the MP3Player through the New Automation Object dialog.

If you haven't already, fill in the CoClass Name entry field and Description, then click the OK button. At this time, we don't want to select Generate Event Support Code within this dialog. We'll explain this selection within the Event Sinks section that follows. Also, an Apartment thread will work fine for our example. (For more on threading models see the Threading Model note later in this chapter).

After the OK button is selected, the Type Library Editor will appear, as illustrated in Figure 17.11.

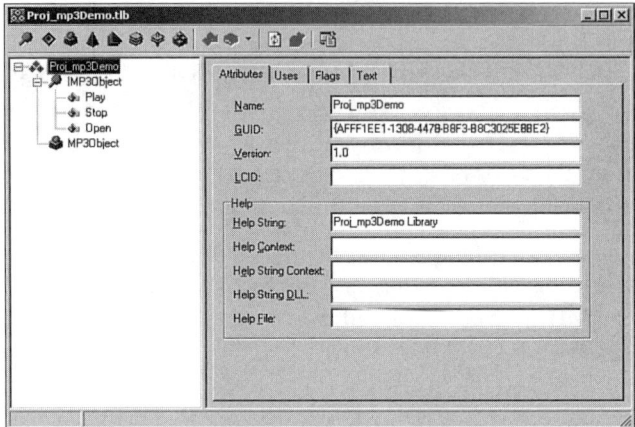

FIGURE 17.11   Type Library Editor for our MP3Player.

You'll notice that within this figure we've added three methods to the IMP3Player interface that was created: Play, Stop, and Open. We could have easily added more methods such as a Pause method. Within the Open method, a File parameter has been added based on the LPSTR type. Our client will use this method to pass in the filename it wants to open. Incidentally, the parent interface for IMP3Player is IDispatch, which is used to support COM automation.

After we're content with the methods we need for our interface, we can then select the Refresh Implementation glyph on the top of the Type Library Editor. This will generate the implementation code discussed earlier in Table 17.4. Listing 17.4 displays the implementation code we need for tapping into our MP3Player.

LISTING 17.4   MP3ObjectImpl.cpp Source File

```
// MP3OBJECTIMPL : Implementation of TAppObjectImpl (CoClass: AppObject,
//                                                  Interface: IAppObject)

#include <vcl.h>
#pragma hdrstop

#include "MP3ObjectImpl.h"
#include "mp3Demo.h"
```

LISTING 17.4 Continued

```
/////////////////////////////////////////////////////////////////////////////
// TAppObjectImpl

STDMETHODIMP TMP3ObjectImpl::Open(LPSTR File)
{
    Form1->OpenMP3File(File);
    return S_OK;
}


STDMETHODIMP TMP3ObjectImpl::Play()
{
    Form1->PlayButtonClick(NULL);
    return S_OK;
}


STDMETHODIMP TMP3ObjectImpl::Stop()
{
    Form1->StopButtonClick(NULL);
    return S_OK;
}
```

One of the few changes that we need to make to the original MP3 player code is the
addition of the `OpenMP3File()` method for assigning a file to the player. This implementation is shown in Listing 17.5.

LISTING 17.5 Code Modification to `MP3Player` Program

```
void __fastcall TForm1::OpenMP3File(char* filename)
{
    bool was_playing = mp3_.playing();
    if (mp3_.open(filename))
    {
        FileText->Caption =
            "  " + ExtractFileName(AnsiString(filename));
        UpdateLengthInfo();
        MP3Timer->Enabled = true;

        if (was_playing) mp3_.play();
    }
}
```

LISTING 17.4   Continued

```
//---------------------------------------------------------------

void __fastcall TForm1::OpenButtonClick(TObject *Sender)
{
    if (OpenDialog1->Execute())
    {
        OpenMP3File(OpenDialog1->FileName.c_str());
    }
}
```

Before our MP3Player program can compile, we need to make a few more minor changes to the MP3Player code. Within the header file called mp3Demo.h, we use a message handler template map to field windows messages. Now that we're linking in with COM, our MESSAGE_HANDLER template has been slightly altered within one of the header files we include. To alleviate this problem, simply change MESSAGE_HANDLER to VCL_MESSAGE_HANDER, as shown here.

```
public:          // User declarations
    void __fastcall OpenMP3File(char* filename);
    __fastcall TFormMP3(TComponent* Owner);


BEGIN_MESSAGE_MAP
    VCL_MESSAGE_HANDLER(MM_MCINOTIFY, TMessage, MMMciNotify)
    VCL_MESSAGE_HANDLER(WM_ENTERSIZEMOVE, TMessage, WMEnterSizeMove)
    VCL_MESSAGE_HANDLER(WM_MOVING, TMessage, WMMoving)
END_MESSAGE_MAP(TForm)
```

Also, we need to include the header file that defines MM_MCINOTIFY at the top of our mp3Demo.h file.

```
#include "MCIDevice.h"
```

And, for this particular example, we need to move the declaration mp3_ from the private section of our form class into the mp3Demo.cpp file so that it's in proper scope for supporting any COM Controllers.

```
#pragma package(smart_init)
#pragma resource "*.dfm"
TForm1 *Form1;
MP3Device mp3;
```

Next, we just need to compile and link our program, and run one time to register it. A view of the application during execution is illustrated in Figure 17.12. Notice that it looks and acts the same as it did before!

FIGURE 17.12   The `MP3Player` during execution.

Creating an Automation Controller

Now, we just need to create a simple automation controller application that can take advantage of the capabilities provided by the `MP3Player` we just modified.

Start by creating a brand-new application. Then, select Project, Import Type Library from the main menu. The Import Type Library dialog will appear. Select `Proj_mp3Demo` Library, as shown in Figure 17.13.

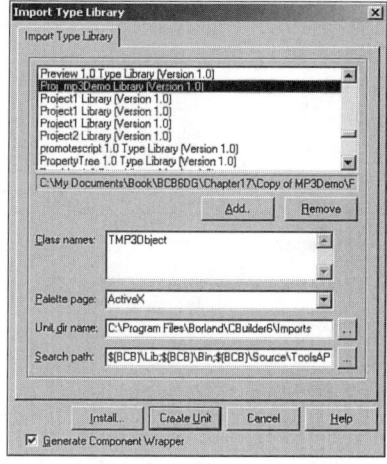

FIGURE 17.13   The Import Type Library.

Select Create Unit for this dialog to create a TLB unit file that will be added to your project. Next, include the header file for the TLB within your Unit's header file as follows:

```
#include "Proj_mp3Demo_TLB.h"
```

Within the private section of your class, add the following declaration.

```
private:      // User declarations
        TCOMIMP3Object  MP3Player;
```

Within the client example provided on the CD-ROM, I've added a Directory List Box and a File List Box that enables the application to operate like a file explorer. In this case, it's only interested in MP3 files. A button has been added that will play a selected MP3 file. The code for this Automation Controller is shown in Listing 17.6.

LISTING 17.6   MP3FileViewerForm.cpp Source Code

```
/*-------------------------------------------------------------------------
  MP3FileViewerForm.cpp
        Chapter 17 - COM Automation Controller Example
        created by Paul Gustavson, 2002
  ------------------------------------------------------------------------*/

#include <vcl.h>
#pragma hdrstop

#include "MP3FileViewerForm.h"

//-------------------------------------------------------------------------
#pragma package(smart_init)
#pragma resource "*.dfm"
TForm1 *Form1;
//-------------------------------------------------------------------------
__fastcall TForm1::TForm1(TComponent* Owner)
        : TForm(Owner)
{
   MP3Player = NULL;
}
//-------------------------------------------------------------------------

void __fastcall TForm1::Button1Click(TObject *Sender)
{
  // let's make sure the file exists
  if (FileListBox1->FileName.Length() == 0)
  {
        MessageBeep(MB_OK);
        return;
  }
```

LISTING 17.6   Continued

```
  // if (!FileExists(EditFileDll->Text))
  if (!FileExists(FileListBox1->FileName))
  {
    ShowMessage(AnsiString("Please select a file, and try again. "));
    MessageBeep(MB_OK);
    return;
  }

  // instantiate COM object
  if (!MP3Player) // if we haven't instantiated MP3 COM object, do it now
      MP3Player = Proj_mp3demo_tlb::CoMP3Object::Create();
  else // stop anything already playing
      MP3Player->Stop();

  MP3Player->Open(FileListBox1->FileName.c_str());
  MP3Player->Play();
}
//-----------------------------------------------------------------
void __fastcall TForm1::FormClose(TObject *Sender, TCloseAction &Action)
{
  if (MP3Player)
    MP3Player->Stop();  // make sure it's stopped.
}

//-----------------------------------------------------------------

void __fastcall TForm1::SpeedButtonApplyMaskClick(TObject *Sender)
{
  FileListBox1->Mask = EditMask->Text;
}
```

The key piece of code to analyze in this listing is the `Button1Click()` event handler. This handler is triggered when the user presses the button to play the selected MP3 file. If the `MP3_object` is `NULL`, it is instantiated using the `CoMP3Player::Create()` method. If it has been previously instantiated, a call is made to ensure that any current files playing have been stopped. It then loads and plays the new file using the methods defined by the `IMP3Player` interface. Figure 17.14 illustrates the Automation activities brought on by the COM Controller during execution.

FIGURE 17.14   The `MP3FileViewer` program utilizing the MCI MP3 Player Demo through COM Automation.

The concepts we used to create an automation controller for the `MP3Player` can be applied for creating automation controllers for other available COM objects. Microsoft Word, for instance, can be leveraged by Automation Controller's that you create. For more information on this topic, see the Microsoft Office Integration chapter in the C++Builder 5 Developer's Guide (Chapter 21), which is provided in PDF format on the book CD-ROM.

THREADING MODELS

When defining a class that will be instantiated as an object for a COM Server, it's important to identify the type of threading model that should be used. The threading model identifies how an object can be accessed in a multithreaded environment. More specifically, it identifies how COM should respond to (or serialize) simultaneous calls to the interface. Within C++Builder, the selection of the threading model in the New COM Object dialog for Automation objects, Active Server objects, ActiveX controls, and COM objects determines how the object will be registered. Table 17.5 identifies the various types of threading models that can be chosen.

TABLE 17.5   Automation Object Threading Models

Threading Model	Description
Single	All client calls to an object are handled by only one common thread within the server. Not well suited for a server that needs to accommodate a large volume of clients simultaneously.

TABLE 17.5 Continued

Threading Model	Description
Apartment	Client calls to an object are handled by separate threads. In this situation, multiple threads can access global memory, which needs to be protected. However, objects can safely access their own instance data (object properties and members). This is also known as single-threaded apartment (STA).
Free	An instantiated object can be accessed by multiple threads within the server at any one time. In this situation, it's important to protect both instance data and global memory. This is also known as multithreaded apartment (MTA).
Both	Each object instance can be called by multiple threads simultaneously, except that all callbacks supplied by clients are executed in the same thread.
Neutral	Allows multiple clients access to an object on different threads simultaneously, but COM arbitrates access ensuring no two method calls conflict. Even though calls are arbitrated, access to global memory and instance data must still be protected. This is not suitable for objects with a user interface. Only available under COM+ within C++Builder, otherwise mapped to the Apartment model.

Adding Event Sinks

If you recall from Chapter 16, for our InventoryKeeper DLL to share information with the various clients (the Honda factory and dealerships), Windows Messaging was used for notification through a PostMessage() call. On reception of a notification from the DLL, a client, such as Dealer or Factory, would than make a function call back into the DLL to retrieve additional information.

With COM, we can do away with PostMessage() calls and client polling by setting up a server to inform clients of new information establishing an outgoing interface specifically called a dispinterface, which is short for dispatch interface. In a moment, we will see how a dispinterface can be implemented using the Type Library Editor.

For this to work, a client, not the server, will need to implement the outgoing interfaces established by the server. Specifically, the client will need an object that implements a dispinterface. Such an object is called an *event sink*.

In short, an event sink is a COM object on the client-side that implements an outgoing interface (dispinterface) associated to a COM object within a server. The client can then connect its event sink to the server through a connection point and start receiving events. The server fires events to the client through the methods of the sink object interface. Figure 17.15 illustrates how it works.

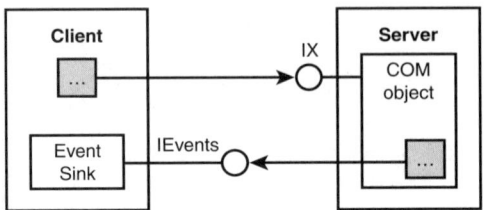

FIGURE 17.15   Event sinks and connection point–based events.

Writing the COM Server

To demonstrate how to fire an event from a server to a client, we'll create an example program that models a restaurant. In this restaurant customers enter, wait to be seated, order their food, wait for their food, eat, pay their bill, and eventually leave. Customers, in our example, will be represented as client applications that will connect to the restaurant using COM interfaces, and will receive service using COM outgoing interfaces. We'll explore building a customer application in a few moments, but first let's look at what it takes to create our Restaurant Automation Server.

For starters, we create a standard GUI application. This will be an `outproc` server. Next, we create a COM Automation Object through the File, New, Other, ActiveX selection, which are the steps we performed earlier. Figure 17.16 illustrates the New Automation Object dialog for the object we'll create.

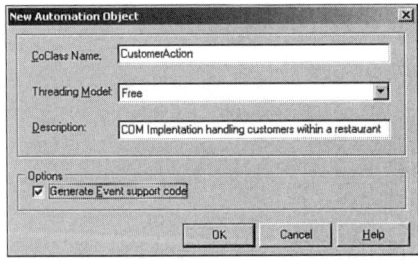

FIGURE 17.16   The New Automation Object dialog for the `CustomerAction` object.

Notice, in this example we are using the Free threading model, and we have checked the Generate Event Code check box. When OK is selected, the Type Library Editor will appear with an interface, a disp interface, and CoClass. We're going to add a few records and enumerate to this type library, as shown in Figure 17.17.

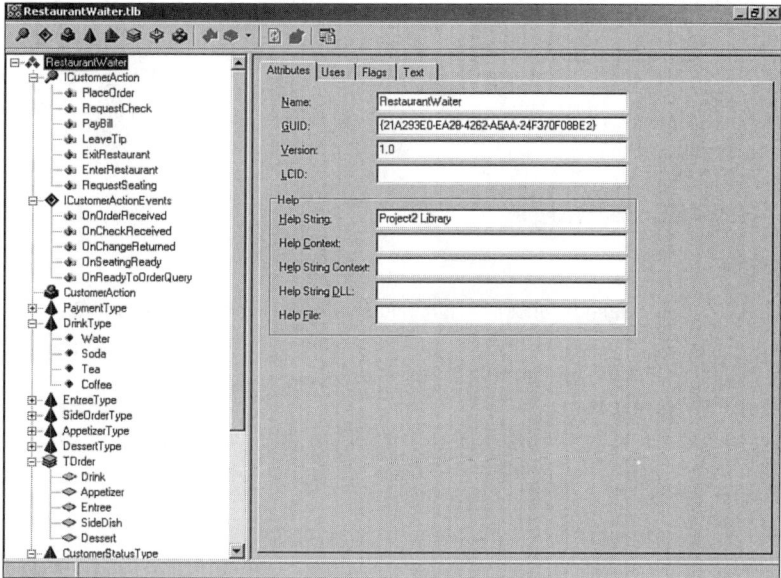

FIGURE 17.17   The Type Library Editor for the CustomerAction object and its related interfaces, enumerations, and records.

Again, when we click Refresh, the TLB code will be generated for our server. Also added to this example is a lot of functionality exposed through the GUI by declaring properties and methods within the public section of our form class. These are accessible by the ConnectionActionImpl code.

You're encouraged to look at the complete Form code within the example source provided on the book CD-ROM, which can be found under the COM_Restaurant folder for this chapter. We'll look at just a couple of methods provided by the form class that illustrate the two-way Automation. First, however, we'll concentrate on the code for the ConnectionActionImpl.cpp file, as shown in Listing 17.7.

LISTING 17.7   ConnectionActionImpl.cpp Source Code

```
// CUSTOMERACTIONIMPL : Implementation of TCustomerActionImpl
// (CoClass: CustomerAction, Interface: ICustomerAction)
// written by Paul Gustavson, 2002.

#include <vcl.h>
#pragma hdrstop

#include "CUSTOMERACTIONIMPL.H"
```

LISTING 17.7   Continued

```cpp
#include "RestaurantForm.h"


///////////////////////////////////////////////////////////////////////////
// TCustomerActionImpl

static TCOMCriticalSection CS;


STDMETHODIMP TCustomerActionImpl::EnterRestaurant(long* customerID)
{
   long result = Form1->AddCustomer(this);
   *customerID = result;
   return S_OK;
}


STDMETHODIMP TCustomerActionImpl::RequestSeating(long customerID)
{
   Form1->RequestSeating(customerID);
   return S_OK;
}


STDMETHODIMP TCustomerActionImpl::PlaceOrder(long customerID, TOrder Order)
{
   Form1->PlaceOrder(customerID,Order);
   return S_OK;
}


STDMETHODIMP TCustomerActionImpl::RequestCheck(long customerID)
{
   Form1->RequestCheck(customerID);
   return S_OK;
}


STDMETHODIMP TCustomerActionImpl::PayBill(long customerID,
   PaymentType Type, double Amount)
{
   Form1->PayBill(customerID,Type, Amount);
   return S_OK;
}


STDMETHODIMP TCustomerActionImpl::LeaveTip(long customerID, double Amount)
{
```

LISTING 17.7 Continued

```
    Form1->LeaveTip(customerID,Amount);
    return S_OK;
}


STDMETHODIMP TCustomerActionImpl::ExitRestaurant(long customerID)
{
    Form1->RemoveCustomer(customerID);
    return S_OK;
}
```

As you can see, there's not a lot of code that we've had to add within this file. For each method, we simply call methods contained in the main application, and immediately return an S_OK response to the client. What's important to understand is that a majority of these Form1 methods are asynchronous; that is, any call we make to Form1 returns immediately. Form1 simply puts items such as a customer waiting for a seat, waiting for food, or waiting for a check into a Timer queue to model the simulation. Let's take a look at some of the important elements of the Form1 code.

Listing 17.8 reflects the code used to identify when a customer has entered the restaurant.

LISTING 17.8 The AddCustomer() Method

```
long __fastcall TForm1::AddCustomer(TCustomerActionImpl* ca)
{
//  MessageBeep(MB_OK);
  long customerID = nextcustomerid;
  nextcustomerid++;
  numcustomers++;

  customer[customerID-1] = TCustomer(lasttimesec); // initialize;

  customer[customerID-1].status = Entered;
  customer[customerID-1].customerID  = customerID;
  customer[customerID-1].customeraction = ca;

  LabelNumCustomers->Caption = AnsiString(numcustomers);
  StringGridCustomers->Cells[0][customerID] = AnsiString(customerID);
  StringGridCustomers->Cells[1][customerID] = "Entered";
  StringGridCustomers->Cells[4][customerID] =
                  SimulationTime(customer[customerID-1].timein);
```

LISTING 17.8   Continued

```
//  if (numseats > 0)
//          StringGridCustomers->Cells[1][customerID] = "Seated";


  return customerID;
}
```

What's important about this code is that a pointer to `TCustomerActinImpl` has been passed in as a parameter. This parameter identifies the interface to the event sink object for the customer. We'll use this later so that the server can fire events back to the customer when seating is ready, when an order is ready, or when the bill is ready, and so on.

Listing 17.9 reflects the code used to capture an order by the customer.

LISTING 17.9   The `PlaceOrder()` Method

```
void __fastcall TForm1::PlaceOrder(long customerID, TOrder order)
{
 if (customerID >= 1)
 {
  StringGridCustomers->Cells[1][customerID] = "Waiting For Meal";
  customer[customerID-1].order  = order;
  customer[customerID-1].status = WaitingForFood;

   if (!customer[customerID-1].timer)
   {
       customer[customerID-1].timer = new TTimer(Form1);
       customer[customerID-1].timer->OnTimer =
           customer[customerID-1].timerevent;
   }
   customer[customerID-1].timer->Interval = (time_ToServeMeal * 60000)
                                                      / multiplier;
   customer[customerID-1].timer->Enabled  = true;
 }

 // click on StringGrid for this customer - show the order
  StringGridCustomers->Row = customerID;
  StringGridCustomersSelectCell(Application,0,customerID,NULL);
}
```

The most important thing to understand in this code is that when a customer order comes through, a unique customer-oriented timer is established, which will be triggered when the simulation time for cooking and serving a meal is reached.

Let's take a look at the timer event handling code in Listing 17.10.

LISTING 17.10   The TCustomer::timerevent() Event Handler

```
void __fastcall  TCustomer::timerevent(TObject *Sender)
{
  // if time up
  timer->Enabled = false;
  if (status == WaitingToBeSeated)
  {
     Form1->StringGridCustomers->Cells[1][customerID] = "Seated with menu";
     status = PreparingToOrder;
     customeraction->Fire_OnSeatingReady(customerID);

     // set up timer for waiter to check to see if customer is ready to order
     timer->Interval = (Form1->time_ReadyToOrder * 60000) / Form1->multiplier;
     timer->Enabled  = true;

  }
  else if (status == PreparingToOrder)
  {
     Form1->StringGridCustomers->Cells[1][customerID] = "Ready To Order Query";
     customeraction->Fire_OnReadyToOrderQuery();
  }
  else if (status == WaitingForFood)
  {
     Form1->StringGridCustomers->Cells[1][customerID] = "Meal Has Arrived";
     status = Eating;
     customeraction->Fire_OnOrderReceived();
  }
  else if (status == Eating)
  {
  }
  else if (status == WaitingForBill)
  {
     Form1->StringGridCustomers->Cells[1][customerID] = "Bill On Table";
     Form1->StringGridCustomers->Cells[2][customerID] =
         FloatToStrF(bill, ffCurrency, 0, 2);
     customeraction->Fire_OnCheckReceived(bill);
```

LISTING 17.10   Continued

```
    }
    else if (status == WaitingForChange_Card)
    {
        Form1->StringGridCustomers->Cells[1][customerID] =
                                "Change / Charge Card Returned";
        status = AfterDinnerChat;
        customeraction->Fire_OnChangeReturned(change);
    }
    else if (status == AfterDinnerChat)
    {
    }
    else if (status == Departed)
    {
    }
}
```

This code is used to handle time-oriented simulation events. When a simulation event of interest occurs, the appropriate event sink method is fired back to the customer client application. This enables the client to not be held up in a synchronous wait for processing to complete. It also frees the client from polling the server for status updates and demonstrates an effective way for a server to notify external applications without resorting to PostMessage() calls.

Implementing Event Sinks within a Client

Now we need to create a client that not only calls the methods of an interface which is handled by our Restaurant server, but can set up the event sink method handlers for the Restaurant server to provide notifications of completed events.

To set up the triggering of events, we need to create a class that implements our event sinks. C++Builder provides a template class TEventDispatcher found in utilcls.h to help us write IDispatch-based event sinks. It implements the IDispatch interface for servers to call when firing events. Its InvokeEvent() method is used to forward the server calls to their corresponding event handlers. InvokeEvent() is defined as follows:

```
// To be overriden in derived class to dispatch events
    virtual HRESULT InvokeEvent(DISPID id, TVariant* params = 0) = 0;
```

TEventDispatcher also exposes some methods for connecting the sink to, and disconnecting it from, a server: ConnectEvents() and DisconnectEvents(), respectively.

We will use the TEventDispatcher template for creating a class that will delegate the processing of the COM event to a C++Builder VCL event handler. Our implementation of the event sinks class to support the ICustomerActionEvents dispinterface is provided in Listing 17.11.

LISTING 17.11   RestaurantSink.h File

```
/*-------------------------------------------------------------------------
   RestaurantSink.h
        Chapter 17 - COM Automation Server Example w/ Event Firing
        created by Paul Gustavson, 2002
   ---------------------------------------------------------------------*/
#if !defined(RESTAURANTSINK_H__)
#define RESTAURANTSINK_H__

#include <atlvcl.h>
#include <atlbase.h>
#include <atlcom.h>
#include <ComObj.HPP>
#include <utilcls.h>
#include "RestaurantWaiter_TLB.h"


typedef void __fastcall (__closure * TOrderReceivedEvent)(void);
typedef void __fastcall (__closure * TCheckReceivedEvent)(double Amount);
typedef void __fastcall (__closure * TChangeReturnedEvent)(double Amount);
typedef void __fastcall (__closure * TSeatingReadyEvent)(long customerID);
typedef void __fastcall (__closure * TReadyToOrderQuery)(void);


//-------------------------------------------------------------------------
// Create a class that handles ICustomerActionEvents
class TRestaurantSink :
    public TEventDispatcher<TRestaurantSink, &DIID_ICustomerActionEvents>
{
protected:
  // Event field  .
  TOrderReceivedEvent   FOnOrderReceived;
  TCheckReceivedEvent   FOnCheckReceived;
  TChangeReturnedEvent  FOnChangeReturned;
  TSeatingReadyEvent    FOnSeatingReady;
  TReadyToOrderQuery    FOnReadyToOrderQuery;

  // Event dispatcher
  HRESULT InvokeEvent(DISPID id, TVariant* params)
```

LISTING 17.11   Continued

```
    {
        if ((id == 1) && (FOnOrderReceived != NULL)) // OnOrderReceived
          FOnOrderReceived();
        else if ((id == 2) && (FOnCheckReceived != NULL)) // OnCheckReceived
          FOnCheckReceived(params[0]);
        else if ((id == 3) && (FOnChangeReturned != NULL)) // OnChangeReturned
          FOnChangeReturned(params[0]);
        else if ((id == 4) && (FOnSeatingReady != NULL)) // OnReadyToOrderQuery
          FOnSeatingReady(params[0]);
        else if ((id == 5) && (FOnReadyToOrderQuery != NULL)) // OnReadyToOrderQuery
          FOnReadyToOrderQuery();
        return S_OK;
    }

    // Reference to the event sender
    CComPtr<IUnknown> m_pSender;

public:
    __property TOrderReceivedEvent OnOrderReceived =
      { read = FOnOrderReceived, write = FOnOrderReceived };

    __property TCheckReceivedEvent OnCheckReceived =
      { read = FOnCheckReceived, write = FOnCheckReceived };

    __property TChangeReturnedEvent OnChangeReturned =
      { read = FOnChangeReturned, write = FOnChangeReturned };

    __property TSeatingReadyEvent OnSeatingReady =
      { read = FOnSeatingReady, write = FOnSeatingReady };

    __property TReadyToOrderQuery OnReadyToOrderQuery =
      { read = FOnReadyToOrderQuery, write = FOnReadyToOrderQuery };

public:
    TRestaurantSink() :
      m_pSender(NULL),
      FOnOrderReceived(NULL),
      FOnCheckReceived(NULL),
      FOnSeatingReady(NULL),
      FOnReadyToOrderQuery(NULL)
    {
```

LISTING 17.11   Continued

```
  }

  virtual ~TRestaurantSink()
  {
     Disconnect();
  }

  // Connect to Server
  void Connect(IUnknown* pSender)
  {
     if (pSender != m_pSender)
        m_pSender = pSender;
     if (NULL != m_pSender)
       ConnectEvents(m_pSender);
  }

  // Disconnect from Server
  void Disconnect()
  {
    if (NULL != m_pSender)
    {
      DisconnectEvents(m_pSender);
      m_pSender = NULL;
    }
  }
};

#endif //RESTAURANTSINK_H__
```

This code exhibits the class needed to handle ICustomerActionEvents. Five methods
are associated to this event sink object: OnOrderReceivedEvent(),
OnCheckReceivedEvent(), OnChangeReturnedEvent(), OnSeatingReadyEvent(), and
OnReadyToOrderQuery(). We also implemented an OnInvokeEvent() method, which is
our dispatcher event method. Within this method, which is invoked by the server,
we examine the id being fired and check to see if an event method has been assigned
to the appropriate dispatch event. Upon a match, the client's event method that was
associated to the dispatch event within the class will be triggered. This header file
needs to be included within the header file for our client application.

```
#include "RestaurantSink.h"
```

Within the private section of our form class we need to identify not only the TCOMICustomerAction interface we desire, but the event sink object created in RestaurantSink.h.

```
private:       // User declarations
    long myid;
    TCOMICustomerAction  Restaurant;
    TRestaurantSink FRestaurantSink;
    double bill;
```

Within the protected section of our form class for the client, we need to declare the event methods.

```
protected:
    void __fastcall OnOrderReceived();
    void __fastcall OnCheckReceived(double amount);
    void __fastcall OnChangeReturned(double amount);
    void __fastcall OnSeatingReady(long customerID);
    void __fastcall OnReadyToOrderQuery();
```

Next, we need to connect these dispatch events within our client, which is depicted in Listing 17.12.

LISTING 17.12   FormCreate() method

```
void __fastcall TForm2::FormCreate(TObject *Sender)
{
  Restaurant = Restaurantwaiter_tlb::CoCustomerAction::Create();

  // Connect dispatch events:
  FRestaurantSink.OnOrderReceived = TForm2::OnOrderReceived;
  FRestaurantSink.OnCheckReceived = TForm2::OnCheckReceived;
  FRestaurantSink.OnChangeReturned = TForm2::OnChangeReturned;
  FRestaurantSink.OnSeatingReady   = TForm2::OnSeatingReady;
  FRestaurantSink.OnReadyToOrderQuery = TForm2::OnReadyToOrderQuery;
  FRestaurantSink.Connect(Restaurant);

  Restaurant->EnterRestaurant(&myid);
  Caption = "Customer #" + AnsiString(myid);
}
```

In this method, we first establish an instance to the interface. Then, we assign event methods defined by our client application to the event sink dispatch methods. Also important is to establish a connection point between the event sink object and the instance to the interface using the event sink's Connect() method, which we defined in the RestaurantSink.h file.

Listing 17.13 shows the code for both a call to a COM object method and an event method handler.

LISTING 17.13   ButtonPlaceorderClick() and OnOrderReceived()

```
void __fastcall TForm2::ButtonPlaceOrderClick(TObject *Sender)
{
    TOrder order;

    order.Drink        = FormMenu->RadioGroupDrink->ItemIndex;
    order.Appetizer    = FormMenu->RadioGroupAppetizer->ItemIndex;
    order.Dessert      = FormMenu->RadioGroupDessert->ItemIndex;
    order.Entree       = FormMenu->RadioGroupEntree->ItemIndex;
    order.SideDish     = FormMenu->RadioGroupSideDish->ItemIndex;

    Restaurant->PlaceOrder(myid,order);
    LabelStatus->Caption = "Placed Order.  Waiting for meal...";
    FormMenu->Close();  // close menu
    ButtonPlaceOrder->Enabled = false;
    ButtonMenu->Enabled = false;
}

//------------------------------------------------------------------
void __fastcall TForm2::OnOrderReceived()
{
    LabelStatus->Caption = "Meal has arrived. You are now eating.";
    ButtonRequestBill->Enabled = true;
}
```

The first method represents the code used when the Customer is ready to order his meal. The actual call made to the object method contained within the server is Restaurant->PlaceOrder(), which returns immediately—it's asynchronous. When the simulation event is complete, the Restaurant server triggers the client's OnOrderReceived() event method.

Figure 17.18 illustrates an active Restaurant serving multiple Customers simultaneously.

You're encouraged to look at the code for the Restaurant and the Customer client to further examine the intricacies of how they both work. Figure 17.19 shows the composition for the projects associated to these two applications.

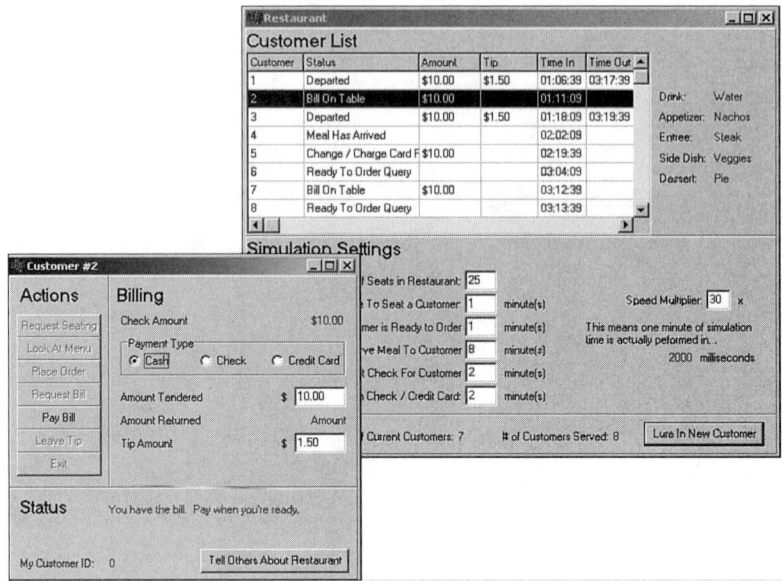

FIGURE 17.18 An execution run of the Restaurant Server Application with multiple Customer Clients.

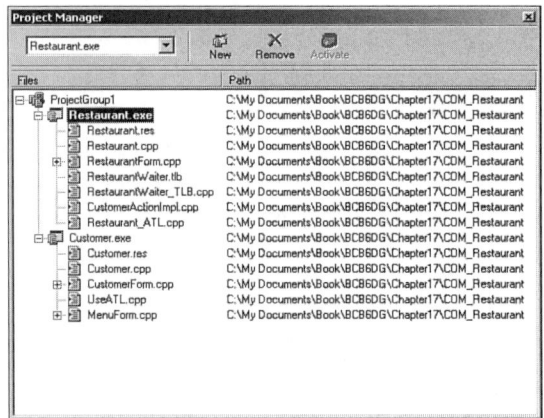

FIGURE 17.19 Project group for the Restaurant Server Application and Customer Client Application.

NOTE

Be sure to add the C++Builder ATL folder to your include path, as shown in Figure 17.20. Otherwise, you'll receive a batch of errors upon compilation indicating the ATL header files cannot be found. The ATL folder and its related files are key elements in C++Builder for supporting COM development.

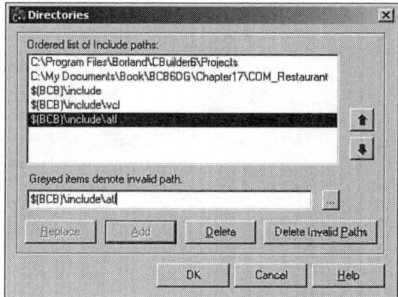

FIGURE 17.20 Adding the ATL path to the Project Options.

ActiveX Controls

Another topic that we could spend a whole chapter discussing is ActiveX controls. Briefly, ActiveX controls are inproc COM servers representing a software component that can be integrated into an existing application to add functionality. In many ways, they are very similar to a VCL control, except it's COM-based and can be used by a number of applications that support ActiveX controls including C++Builder, Delphi, Visual Basic, and Internet Explorer.

Within C++Builder, you can add ActiveX controls to your component palette in the IDE just like a VCL control. The object inspector can be used to modify the properties of an ActiveX control dropped on a form. Property editors can sometimes be provided within an ActiveX control, which enables further property manipulation. To activate a property editor, simply right-click the ActiveX control that has been dropped on your form.

C++Builder provides the ActiveX Control Wizard for creating ActiveX controls based on a VCL. This is illustrated in Figure 17.21.

This wizard enables you to create an ActiveX control that wraps a VCL class. To activate this wizard, start with a clean project by selecting File, New, Other, and select the ActiveX tab within the New Items dialog as illustrated in Figure 17.3. Then, select the ActiveX Control glyph.

Here are the steps associated to creating an ActiveX control within C++Builder.

1. Choose or create a new VCL control that forms the basis of your ActiveX control.

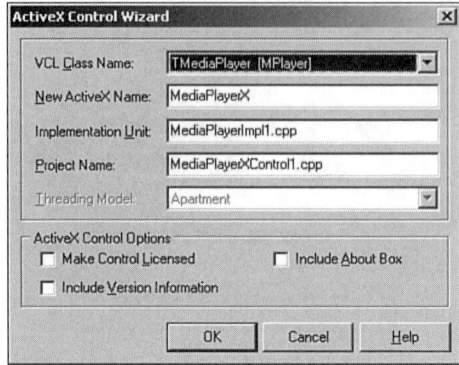

FIGURE 17.21   The ActiveX Control Wizard.

2. Activate the ActiveX control wizard and identify the VCL you've selected or created in Step 1.

3. To create one or more property pages for the ActiveX control, use Borland's ActiveX property page wizard found on the New Items dialog under the ActiveX view.

4. If you created a property page, associate it with the ActiveX control.

5. Build and Register your ActiveX control.

6. Test your ActiveX control by embedding it within potential target applications.

7. If your ActiveX control is Web-capable (through Internet Explorer), deploy it on the Web.

You'll notice when creating ActiveX controls that you start with creating the class to an object before you create the COM interface to our control. This is somewhat in reverse from what we did earlier. After the control is written, the type library can be generated.

Another form of ActiveX control that we can create is an Active Form, which is intended for deployment on the Web. To begin to create an Active Form, start with a clean project by selecting File, New, Other, and select the ActiveX tab within the New Items dialog as illustrated in Figure 17.3. Then, select the Active Form glyph. This will enable you to use the IDE's form designer to create a visual control, such as a dialog, that can be deployed and accessed using the Web.

The Borland Help provides additional information on creating ActiveX controls and Active Forms. You're encouraged to look at this material for further details.

Recommended Resources

We've only scratched the surface on using COM. For more information on C++Builder COM programming, the following books and resources are recommended.

- *C++Builder 4 Unleashed*, Kent Reisdorph, et al.; 1999, Sams Publishing; ISBN 0-672-31510-6

- *C++Builder 5 Developer's Guide*, Hollingworth, Butterfield, Swart, Allsop, et al.; 2001, Sams Publishing; ISBN 0-672-31972-1

To learn more about COM/COM+

- *Essential COM*, Don Box; 1997, Addisson-Wesley Pub; ISBN 0-201-63446-5

- *Inside COM*, Dale Rogerson; 1997, Microsoft Press; ISBN 1-57231-349-8

- *Inside Distributed COM*, Guy Eddon and Henry Eddon; 1998, Microsoft Press; ISBN 1-57231-849-X

- *Understanding COM+*, David S. Platt; 1999, Microsoft Press; ISBN 0-7356-0666-8

- *Mastering COM and COM+*, Ash Rofail and Yasser Shohoud; 1999, Sybex, Inc.; ISBN 0-7821-2384-8

For more information on ATL

- *ATL Internals*, Brent Rector and Chris Sells; 1999, Addison Wesley; ISBN 0-201-69589-8

Delphi related readings

- *Delphi6 Developer's Guide*, Teixeira, Pacheco; 2002, Sams Publishing; ISBN 1-672-32115-7

- *Delphi COM Programming*, Eric Harmon; 2000, Macmillan Technical Publishing; ISBN 1-57870-221-6

Internet resources

- `nntp://newsgroups.borland.com/borland.public.cppbuilder.activex`

- `http://bdn.borland.com/cpp/`

- `http://www.cetus-links.org/oo_ole.html`

- http://www.techvanguards.com/

- http://msdn.microsoft.com/

Summary

In this chapter we've looked at the fundamentals of COM, which included examining how to create and use interfaces, how to add automation to an existing application and create automation controllers, and how to add event sinks so that client applications can be notified of new information by a server object. We also quickly looked at how to create ActiveX controls.

COM has become a foundation for allowing Windows programmers to write and share reusable software modules that can interoperate with other software modules. COM interfaces and objects, and the clients and servers that utilize them, can be implemented by virtually any development language and environment that supports pointers. This includes Visual Basic, C++, and Delphi. In essence, COM enables Windows programmers to achieve essentially three things:

- Writing reusable code and software modules that can be used by a wide variety of programming languages. This includes ActiveX controls.

- Controlling and utilizing elements of other applications. This is accomplished using type libraries and OLE automation.

- Enabling applications and their objects to interoperate with other applications located on remote machines. This is provided through Distributed COM (DCOM).

It is almost certain that COM will continue to have a strong presence within the Windows and .NET programming community in the future. The topics we covered provide the essentials in using COM and its related extensions including COM+ and DCOM. DCOM is discussed in the next chapter.

PART IV

Distributed Computing

IN THIS PART

18

DCOM: Going Distributed

by Mark Cashman

COM objects are an intrinsic part of the Windows operating system today.

More and more of the Windows operating system services are being exposed in the form of COM objects, which are taking the place of traditional Application Programming Interfaces (APIs) from DLLs.

Until recently, COM objects suffered from one big weakness—they could only be used from within the confines of a single computer. It was impossible to move the components to different machines on the network to create a distributed system.

To address this problem, Microsoft created DCOM. DCOM extends COM by providing the capability to activate COM objects remotely. But, DCOM also introduces new security and programming issues.

What Is DCOM?

Distributed COM is Microsoft's solution enabling COM objects to work on different machines across the network. It extends COM by enabling objects to be accessed remotely.

If you take a COM object and put it out somewhere separated from the client across the network, you get a DCOM object. DCOM is just plain COM with distribution and security added to it. Technically speaking, DCOM was made possible by the extension of Remote Procedure Calls (RPCs) to Object RPC, and it first appeared when Microsoft released Windows NT 4.0.

DCOM has been ported to some Unix flavors and can, with some work and platform restriction, be used as a cross-platform solution for distributed systems.

Despite other great competing technologies, DCOM is a mainstream technology. This is becuase of the growing acceptance by the corporate market of the Windows NT and Windows 2000 operating system family.

DCOM uses the concept of location transparency, which means that you can move a COM server to a different machine on the network without requiring code modification. Neither the server nor the client needs to be concerned about where the other is running. They can be on the same machine, on a local area network, or in a wide area network such as the Internet. For the client, the location of the server is a Registry setting that can be easily modified. This is unlike more comprehensive distributed solutions such as CORBA or J2EE that use a name server to identify the location of a remote object and, therefore, offer a truer location transparency.

DCOM clients and servers must abide by the rules of authentication and authorization. This implies that clients must perform some sort of log in to access the machine where the server lives. Servers must authenticate the client, verifying whether he is really who he says he is, and authorize access by checking whether the user has the necessary privileges. DCOM applications can rely on security settings stored in the Registry or can change their security settings through code. These two kinds of security are known as *declarative security* and *programmatic security*, respectively.

Unfortunately, security is often one of the biggest challenges in DCOM—DCOM itself is not that complex. This means a significant amount of this chapter isn't about DCOM per se, but actually is about making security work for DCOM objects.

Windows OS Family and DCOM

DCOM comes standard with Windows 98, Windows NT 4.0, Windows 2000, and Windows XP, but you have to add it to Windows 95. You can download DCOM95 from Microsoft's Web site at http://www.microsoft.com/com or you can do a full install of Internet Explorer 4/5 in Windows 95 to get DCOM95 installed.

> **NOTE**
>
> If your network has a Domain Controller, you should configure your Windows 95 and 98 machines to use user-level security; otherwise, you won't be able to perform authenticated DCOM calls.

Windows 95 and 98 are really only suited for use as DCOM clients because they can't dynamically launch and execute DCOM servers and don't have native security.

The DCOMCnfg **Utility Tool**

The DCOM Configuration Utility (DCOMCnfg.exe) is the tool that you use to modify DCOM settings that are specific to a server or that apply system-wide acting on all registered servers on a given machine.

When you run the DCOMCnfg utility tool, you're presented with a dialog-based screen (see Figure 18.1), which exhibits the following tabs: Applications, Default Properties, Default Security, and Default Protocols.

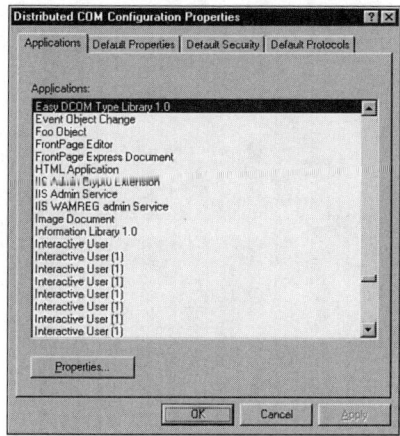

FIGURE 18.1   The DCOMCnfg configuration utility tool.

NOTE

All relevant discussion of DCOMCnfg.exe in this chapter is based on the version that comes with Windows NT 4.0 with Service Pack 4 or later and Windows. Windows 9X presents a slightly modified version of this configuration tool. Windows XP uses the Component Services Administrative Tool, invoked from the Control Panel Administrative Tools, which looks and acts differently. See the Windows XP Help in the Component Services tool for more information on the special features of that tool.

Global Security Settings

The Applications tab shows a list of all the servers containing the AppID Registry key that are registered on the machine. You can select any server and click the Properties button to have access to its settings.

The Default Properties tab (see Figure 18.2) is the place where you can completely enable or disable DCOM on the computer and configure system-wide default levels of authentication and impersonation.

On this tab, you also have the option to enable or disable COM Internet Services (CIS). CIS introduces new features to the DCOM model that enable clients and servers to communicate in the presence of proxy servers and firewalls. You can learn more about CIS on the Microsoft MSDN Web site at `http://msdn.microsoft.com/library/backgrnd/html/cis.htm`.

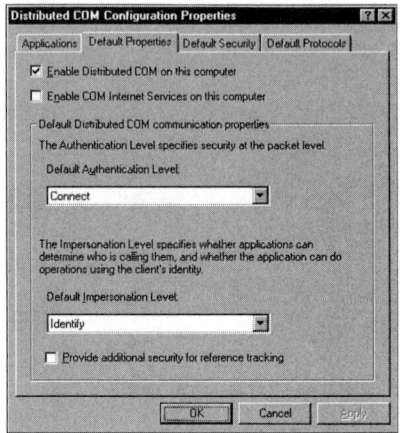

FIGURE 18.2   The Default Properties tab.

Authentication can be configured for when a client first connects, when a method call is made, or on every network packet passed between the client and server.

You can turn off authentication by selecting None at the Default Authentication Level combo box. Although risky, this would allow users without valid security credentials to have access to your server. Users coming from the Internet, for example, could benefit from this option.

The Default Impersonation Level combo box controls whether the server can determine the identity of the connected client and, if it can, use this identity to access system resources acting like the client itself. You can choose from the following:

- Anonymous—The client identity is unavailable.

- Identity—The server can impersonate the client only to obtain its identity.

- Impersonate—The server can impersonate the client to access local system resources on the client's behalf.

- Delegate—The server can impersonate the client to access local and remote resources on the client's behalf. Requires Windows 2000 running Kerberos as the Security Service Provider (SSP).

In the Default Security tab (see Figure 18.3), you can configure system-wide defaults for access, launch, and configuration permissions.

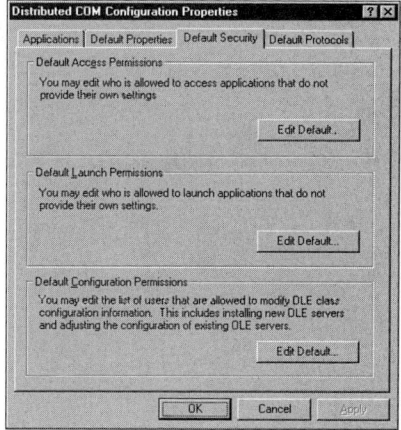

FIGURE 18.3   The Default Security tab.

Default Access Permissions relates to who is allowed or denied access to servers registered on the machine. If you want to let any user access your server, you can allow access permission to the built-in account Everyone.

Default Launch Permissions relates to who is authorized to load and run a server process. If you want to let any user execute your server, you can allow launch permission to the built-in Everyone account. Note that this option cannot be set programmatically.

Default Configuration Permissions states the precise type of access (Read, Full Control, or Special Access) you can set under HKEY_CLASSES_ROOT Registry key. This effectively controls user access rights to Registry entries related to DCOM setting.

The Default Protocols tab (see Figure 18.4) is used to arrange the ordering and availability of network protocols used by DCOM. You can configure DCOM for access over firewalls by selecting the desired network protocol and clicking the Properties button. Unless you have a good understanding of network protocols and operating system administration, you should leave these options unchanged.

Bear in mind that all options in the Default Properties tab and Default Security tab operate system wide. Modifying those options are likely to break some server installed on the system. The best course of action is to only change the settings for an explicit server component.

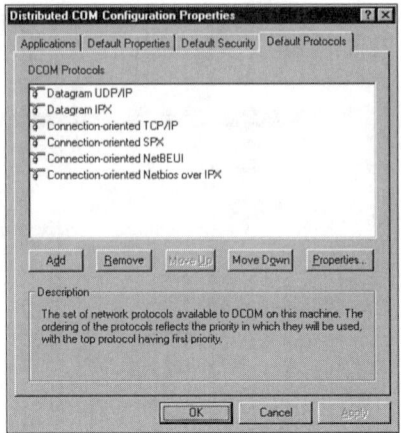

FIGURE 18.4   The Default Protocols tab.

Per-Server Security Settings

Selecting a server from the Applications tab and clicking the Properties button gives you access to the security options related to that specific server.

The General tab (see Figure 18.5) on the Easy DCOM Type Library 1.0 Properties dialog shows the server's registered name, its type, local path, and authentication level. You can use the Authentication Level combo box to modify the authentication level of the server.

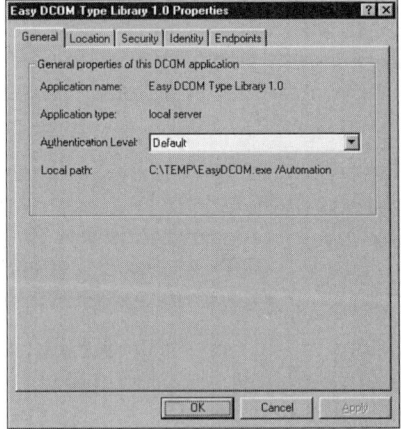

FIGURE 18.5   The General tab.

From the Location tab (see Figure 18.6), you can select from where the server will be executed. For example, by checking the Run application on the following computer option and entering the name of the computer, you can change the location from where the server will be activated.

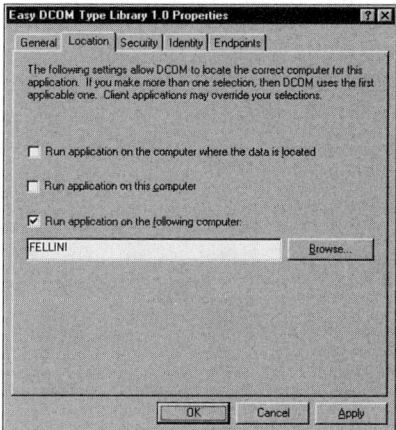

FIGURE 18.6   The Location tab.

The Security tab (see Figure 18.7) enables you to choose between using the system-wide default security settings or using custom security settings. All custom options work the same as the options showed for the Default Security tab (refer to Figure 18.3).

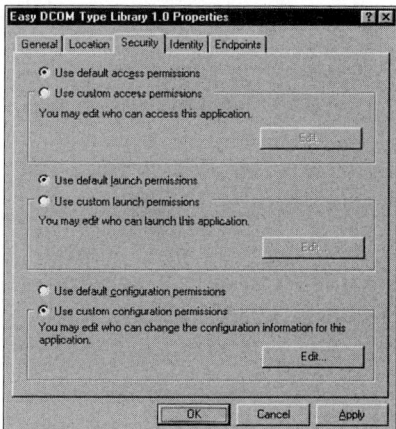

FIGURE 18.7   The Security tab.

The Identity tab (see Figure 18.8) is where you configure the account under which the server will run. The options are

- The interactive user—Uses the account of the user who happens to be logged on at the server's machine. When there is no one logged on the system, the activation request will fail. This option is useful for debugging purposes because the server might have access to the desktop of the logged user.

- The launching user—Uses the account of the user that requested the server object. A new copy of the server process will be created for every distinct client. This is the default option and must be avoided because it is not good for distributed applications.

- This user—Uses a specific account that can be a local or domain account. You can elect to use an already defined account or create a new one to suit your needs. Most of the time, this is the preferred option to choose from because you know beforehand the privileges your server will have when it's running.

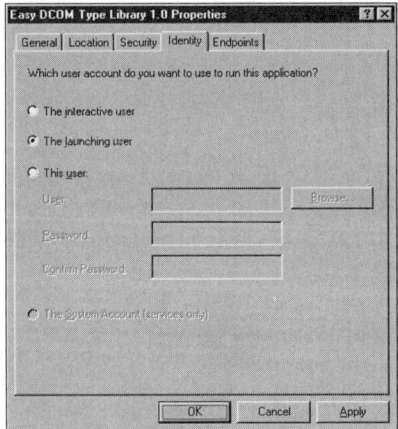

FIGURE 18.8   The Identity tab.

DCOM will use the default global settings stored in the Registry on behalf of every server that has not been customized through the use of the DCOMCnfg utility tool. If you do customize the settings of a server, those settings will take precedence over the global ones. Nevertheless, programmatic security will always take precedence over declarative security.

You should always remember to configure Launch Permissions setting the users or group of users authorized to launch your server. Forgetting to do so might make your server unavailable for remote-client access.

You are not going to cover the Endpoints tab in this chapter. Please refer to the DCOMCnfg documentation for further information.

Field Testing DCOM

You're going to create a very simple COM server and client to experiment with DCOM. This server will be able to return the name of the remote host computer and its current date/time.

The server will be packaged as an EXE binary. You won't use a DLL packaged server because it requires a surrogate program running on the server computer to work out-of-process. The example will use type library marshaling to avoid the registration of a proxy/stub marshaling DLL. You can refer to `http://msdn.microsoft.com` for a variety of articles that can help you get a better understanding of COM marshaling. For the purposes of this chapter, just think of it as packaging function parameters for transmission over the network.

Creating the Server Application

You're free to create whatever directory structure you want, but it is a good idea to use a main folder with two subfolders named `Server` and `Client` for this project.

You can find the code for the example server application in the `EasyDCOM\Server` folder on the CD-ROM that accompanies this book.

To create the server application, do the following:

1. Launch C++Builder.

2. Select File, New, Application from the main IDE menu.

3. Save the project in the `Server` folder as `EasyDCOM.bpr` renaming `Unit1.cpp` to `MainUnit.cpp`.

4. Switch to the main project's form.

5. Press F11 to activate the Object Inspector.

6. Type `frmMain` at the Name Property.

7. Design your project's main form to look like the screen in Figure 18.9.

FIGURE 18.9   The EasyDCOM main form.

8. Select File, New from the main menu.

9. Switch to the ActiveX tab.

10. Double-click Automation Object. The New Automation Object dialog will appear.

11. Type `HostInfo` in the CoClass Name field.

12. Enter `Easy DCOM Type Library 1.0` in the Description field and click OK.

13. Select View, Type Library to bring the Type Library Editor (TLE) to the front.

14. On the left pane, select the `IHostInfo` interface.

15. From the TLE toolbar, click the New, Property button down arrow, and select Read Only from its pop-up menu.

16. Rename `Property1` to `Info`.

17. On the right pane, select the Parameters tab and change Parameters type to `BSTR*` (see Figure 18.10).

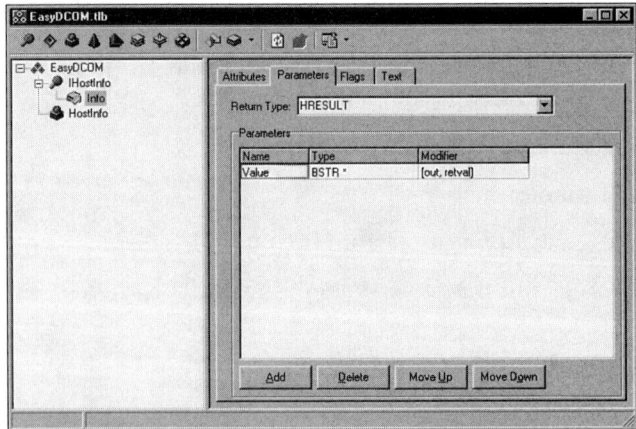

FIGURE 18.10   The TLE editor showing the read-only property info.

18. Press the Refresh button in the TLE editor to update the source files.

19. Switch to the `HostImpl.cpp` file and add the following code to the `get_Info()` method:

```
STDMETHODIMP THostInfoImpl::get_Info(BSTR* Value)
{
    try {
        char lpBuffer[MAX_COMPUTERNAME_LENGTH + 1];
        unsigned long nSize = sizeof(lpBuffer);
```

```
        if (GetComputerName(lpBuffer, &nSize) == 0)
            return HRESULT_FROM_WIN32(GetLastError());

        WideString strVal = AnsiString().
            sprintf("Date and time at %s is: %s",
            lpBuffer, DateTimeToStr(Now()));

        *Value = strVal.Detach();
    }
    catch(Exception &e) {
        return Error(e.Message.c_str(), IID_IHostInfo);
    }
    return S_OK;
};
```

20. Press F9 to compile and run the server.

Have a look at the code for the Info property of your EasyDCOM server.

You start by calling the Win32 API function GetComputerName() to store the computer name in the lpBuffer variable returning the appropriate HRESULT on error.

Then, you instantiate a WideString object based on the computer name and its current date and time.

You invoke the Detach() method of the WideString object to release ownership from the underlying BSTR because COM states that an out parameter has to be released by the client, not the server. Detach() relinquishes ownership over the returned string.

Creating the Client Application

You can find the code for the example client application in the EasyDCOM\Client folder on the CD-ROM that accompanies this book.

To create the client application, do the following:

1. Start a new application and save the project in the Client folder as EasyDCOMClient.bpr, renaming Unit1.cpp to MainUnit.cpp.

2. Design your project's main form, adding the necessary components to look like the screen in Figure 18.11. When done, rename your components as follows:

Original Name	New Name
Form1	frmMain
GroupBox1	gbxLocal

Original Name	New Name
GroupBox2	gbxRemote
Edit1	txtLocal
Edit2	txtRemote
Button1	cmdInfo
Button2	cmdFinish

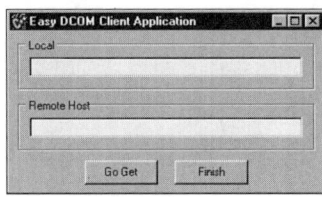

FIGURE 18.11   The `EasyDCOMClient` main form and its components.

3. Open `EasyDCOMClient.cpp` and add the following:

```
USEUNIT("..\Server\EasyDCOM_TLB.cpp");
```

4. Open `MainUnit.h` and add the following:

```
#include "..\Server\EasyDCOM_TLB.h"
```

5. Take advantage of C++Builder technology by declaring a smart interface variable to your EasyDCOM server.

Add the following code under `TfrmMain` class private section:

```
TCOMIHostInfo m_objHost;
```

6. Edit the project's main form source code and add the following code to its constructor:

```
char lpBuffer[MAX_COMPUTERNAME_LENGTH + 1];
unsigned long nSize = sizeof(lpBuffer);

GetComputerName(lpBuffer, &nSize);

txtLocal->Text = AnsiString().sprintf("Date and time at %s is: %s",
                                      lpBuffer, DateTimeToStr(Now()));
```

7. C++Builder also provides us a creator class that has static methods for creating local and remote instances of your object.

Double-click the `cmdInfo` button and add the following code to its `OnClick` event:

```
if (!m_objHost.IsBound()) {
    AnsiString strHost;

    if (InputQuery("Create Server", "Enter computer name:",
        strHost)) {

        if (strHost.IsEmpty())
            OleCheck(CoHostInfo::Create(m_objHost));
        else
            OleCheck(CoHostInfo::CreateRemote(WideString(strHost),
                                              m_objHost));

        WideString strValue;
        OleCheck(m_objHost.get_Info(&strValue));

        txtRemote->Text = strValue;
    }
}
```

8. Double-click the `cmdFinish` button and add the following code to its `OnClick` event:

```
Close();
```

9. Click the project's main form, press F11 to activate the Object Inspector, and switch to its Events tab. Double-click the `OnClose` event and write the following code:

```
m_objHost.Unbind();
```

10. Press F9 to compile and run the client. Click the Go Get button to display the Create Server dialog. When asked for the machine name, leave it blank and click OK to create the server locally.

Let's review the code for the client application.

The constructor code for the main form retrieves and shows the name of the local computer and its date and time.

The handler code for the `cmdInfo` button calls the `IsBound()` method on the smart interface object verifying whether the server object is already instantiated and proceeds accordingly.

The InputQuery() function receives the NETBIOS name, DNS name, or IP address of the remote machine and stores it in the strHost variable.

If strHost is then empty, the server is locally instantiated using the Create method; otherwise, the CreateRemote() method accepts the machine name or IP address stored in strHost and tries to instantiate the server at the specified machine. OleCheck() is used to verify the returned HRESULT, throwing an exception on fail.

The get_Info() method is invoked passing the address of a WideString variable. This variable is then filled with information returned from the hosting machine, and its value is shown in the txtRemote edit control.

Before closing the form, the Unbind() method of the smart interface object is invoked to release the server.

Now it's time to move your EasyDCOM sample to another machine on the network. Copy EasyDCOM.exe to a local drive on the remote machine and run it once to perform self-registration.

NOTE

If you choose a Windows 9X machine to host your server, it won't be able to automatically launch the server; you'll have to launch it manually.

Configuring Launch and Access Permissions

Let's assume, for the sake of your discussion, that the remote and client machines participate in a Microsoft network domain.

You're going to grant launch permission to anyone participating on the network, so proceed as follows:

1. Run DCOMCnfg.exe and double-click Easy DCOM Type Library 1.0 from the Applications tab list box. On XP, use the Component Services Administrative Tool from the Control Panel, and pick Component Services, Computers, My Computer, DCOM Config. Using this tool is outside the scope of this chapter, but information can be found in the help file.

2. For Windows 2000 and NT, go to the Security tab and select Use Custom Launch Permissions. Click the Edit button, and then the Add button. Double-click the built-in account Everyone, and then click OK (see Figure 18.12). This states that anyone on the network can now load and run the server, but you still need to grant access to its services.

3. From the Security tab, select Use custom access permissions. Click the Edit button, and then the Add button. Select the local or domain account to which you want to grant access permission, and then click OK (see Figure 18.13).

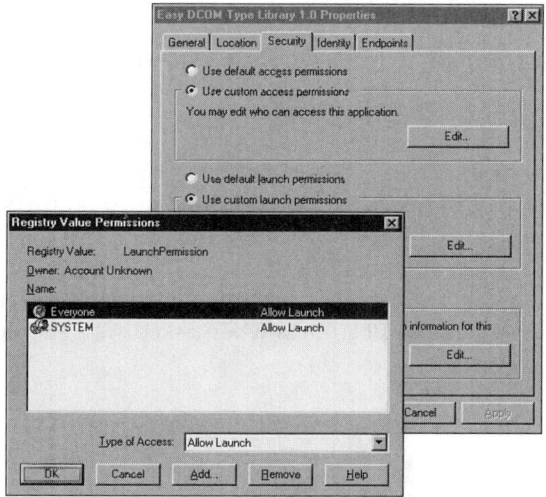

FIGURE 18.12   Granting Launch Permission to the Everyone account.

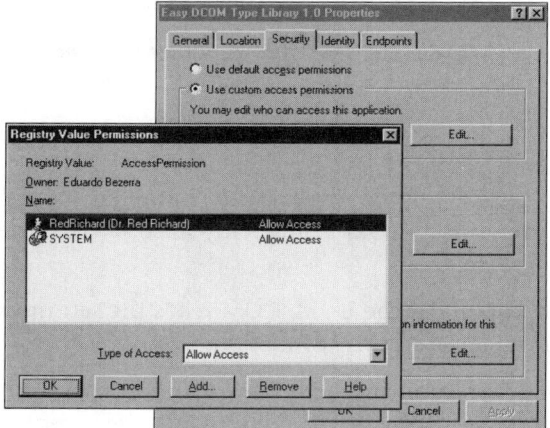

FIGURE 18.13   Granting access permission to a selected account.

Configuring Identity

You're going to choose which account the server will use when running. The best option, as mentioned previously, is to select This User and enter an account that gives the server all the necessary privileges it needs when running.

Go to the Identity tab (refer to Figure 18.8). Select This user and enter or browse for the username. Enter the password, confirm it, and click OK.

Running the Example

What have you accomplished in terms of DCOM security for your sample application?

First, you allowed anyone to launch your server. Then, you selected the user or group of users that have clearance to access your server. Finally, you solved the identity problem of your server by specifying the account it would use when running.

Now you're now ready to go.

Start `EasyDCOMClient.exe` on the client machine, click the Go Get button, and enter the remote machine name or IP address when asked. You should see something like the screen in Figure 18.14.

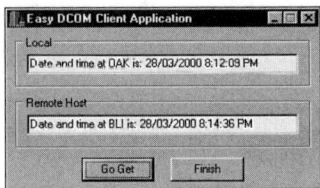

FIGURE 18.14   `EasyDCOMClient` talking to its server on a remote machine.

Programming Security

So far, you have looked at declarative security, but what about programmatic security? Well, as matter of fact, COM is implicitly making calls into its security API for us.

What happens is that under the hood, COM reads the settings stored in the registry and calls the `CoInitializeSecurity()` function.

`CoInitializeSecurity()` is called exactly once for each process that uses COM, establishing process-wide security settings. It configures the security packages that will be used by COM, the authentication level for each process, and which users will be allowed access to the object.

`CoInitializeSecurity` Function Parameters

`CoInitializeSecurity()` is, by far, the most important COM security API function and has the following parameters:

```
PSECURITY_DESCRIPTOR pVoid,    //Points to security descriptor
LONG cAuthSvc,                 //Count of entries in asAuthSvc
SOLE_AUTHENTICATION_SERVICE * asAuthSvc,
                    //Array of names to register
```

```
void * pReserved1,    //Reserved for future use
DWORD dwAuthnLevel,   //Default authentication level
DWORD dwImpLevel,     //Default impersonation level
SOLE_AUTHENTICATION_LIST * pAuthList,
                      //Authentication information for
                      // each authentication service
DWORD dwCapabilities, //Additional client and/or
                      // server-side capabilities
void * pReserved3     //Reserved for future use
```

Some parameters apply to both servers and clients, whereas others apply solely to clients or to servers exclusively.

The first parameter, pVoid, applies only when the process acts like a server. It's used to control access permissions, and its value can be a pointer to an AppID GUID, a SECURITY_DESCRIPTOR, or an IAccessControl interface.

If a NULL pointer value is passed on pVoid, COM will grant access to anyone. This achieves the same functionality as using DCOMCnfg to grant access permission to the built-in Everyone account. If a valid pointer is passed on pVoid, the dwAuthnLevel (fifth parameter) cannot be set to RPC_C_AUTH_LEVEL_NONE.

The second and third parameters, cAuthSvc and asAuthSvc, are also used for servers. They are used for registering the authentication packages with COM and refer to an array of SOLE_AUTHENTICATION_SERVICE structures.

The SOLE_AUTHENTICATION_SERVICE structure has the following members:

```
typedef struct tagSOLE_AUTHENTICATION_SERVICE {
        DWORD       dwAuthnSvc;
        DWORD       dwAuthzSvc;
        OLECHAR*    pPrincipalName;
        HRESULT     hr;
} SOLE_AUTHENTICATION_SERVICE;
```

You can pass -1 (cAuthSvc) and NULL (asAuthSvc) to use the default security packages available on the system. NTLM (NT Lan Manager) is the only authentication service available on Windows NT 4.0, but you can use Kerberos with Windows 2000.

The fifth parameter, dwAuthnLevel, is used for setting the authentication level and applies to both clients and servers. It is equivalent as setting per-server authentication level (refer to Figure 18.5) through the use of DCOMCnfg. For this parameter, the value specified by the server is the minimum allowed. The actual value used will be the higher of the client and server values. If the client calls in with a lower value, the call fails.

The sixth parameter, dwImpLevel, applies only to clients. It sets the impersonation level the client has toward the server. It is equivalent to setting the global impersonation level (refer to Figure 18.2) through the use of DCOMCnfg. The clear advantage here is that you're no longer dependent on system-wide settings; you're now in control of the impersonation level, and this per-client setting cannot be achieved by the use of DCOMCnfg.

You can choose from one of the following impersonation levels:

```
RPC_C_IMP_LEVEL_DEFAULT
RPC_C_IMP_LEVEL_ANONYMOUS
RPC_C_IMP_LEVEL_IDENTIFY
RPC_C_IMP_LEVEL_IMPERSONATE
RPC_C_IMP_LEVEL_DELEGATE
```

As you might have guessed, they're equivalent to their DCOMCnfg counterparts (refer to Figure 18.2).

The eighth parameter, dwCapabilities is used for both clients and servers to describe additional capabilities they might have. The value for this parameter can be one or more of the following bitmasks:

- EOAC_NONE—Indicates that no capability flags are set.

- EOAC_MUTUAL_AUTH—Not used. Mutual authentication is automatically provided by some authentication services.

- EOAC_SECURE_REFS—Determines that reference-counting calls must be authenticated to avoid malicious releases. Refer to Figure 18.2 for the equivalent option using DCOMCnfg.

- EOAC_ACCESS_CONTROL—Must be used when passing an IAccessControl interface pointer as an argument to the parameter pVoid of CoInitializeSecurity().

- EOAC_APPID—Indicates that the pVoid parameter to CoInitializeSecurity() is a pointer to an AppID GUID. CoInitializeSecurity() searches the AppID in the Registry and reads the security settings from there.

Using CoInitializeSecurity

You're going to modify your sample application to completely turn off DCOM security by using CoInitializeSecurity(). This modification will make your sample application suitable for Internet access.

To accomplish this, you must allow access to anonymous users, disable authentication, and disable impersonation. It turns out that this is very simple to implement using CoInitializeSecurity().

As stated earlier, `CoInitializeSecurity()` must be called only once per process just before any significant COM calls. You must make the call on both the client and server sides just after calling `CoInitialize()`.

To turn off security in your `EasyDCOM` sample, do the following:

1. Open `EasyDCOM.cpp`.

2. Add the following code just below the line containing the `try` block inside `WinMain`:

```
CoInitialize(NULL);

CoInitializeSecurity(NULL,
    -1,
    NULL,
    NULL,
    RPC_C_AUTHN_LEVEL_NONE,
    RPC_C_IMP_LEVEL_ANONYMOUS,
    NULL,
    EOAC_NONE,
    NULL);
```

3. Add the following code above the line containing the `return` statement at the end of `WinMain`:

```
CoUninitialize();
```

4. Open `EasyDCOMClient.cpp`, repeat steps 2 and 3 and add the following line below the `include` for `vcl.h`:

```
#include <objbase.h>
```

Let's see what you have done.

You started by calling `CoInitialize()` saying that you wanted to join the main STA. Next, `CoInitializeSecurity()` is called with the appropriate parameters to solve your problem.

For the `pVoid` parameter of `CoInitializeSecurity()`, you passed `NULL`, telling COM that anyone is welcome to access your server.

For the `cAuthSvc` and `asAuthSvc` parameters, you stuck with the defaults of `-1` and `NULL`, respectively, letting COM use the available security packages on the system.

Because you're not interested in authenticating any user calling into your object, you used `RPC_C_AUTH_LEVEL_NONE` for the `dwAuthnLevel` parameter.

For the `dwImpLevel` parameter, you use `RPC_C_IMP_LEVEL_ANONYMOUS` because you're not going to impersonate the client to discover its credentials or act on its behalf. Remember, you actually don't know who the client is.

For the `dwCapabilities` parameter, you just pass `EOAC_NONE`.

That's all; you completely turned off security for your sample application. From now on, any anonymous user will be able to make calls into your server.

NOTE

Servers using connection points over DCOM could also make use of this technique to turn off DCOM security because they will want to access the sink implemented at the client side.

If you try to use an event sink over a DCOM connection, it will fail with an Access Denied error. This is because the client, now acting as a server, will verify if the caller has the necessary credentials to access its sink object. The client will try to ensure that the server account is allowed access to its sink object.

You can work around this problem by making the server account the same as the client account. In other words, the client on the client machine and the identity of the server on the server machine must use a login account with the same name and password.

The problem with this approach is that you must know beforehand what account the client will be using.

Understanding DLL Clients and Security

What if you need to implement the client for your remote server as an ActiveX control to be used inside some container such as Internet Explorer or IIS and Active Server Pages? Well, that's trouble.

An in-proc-server (DLL) is loaded into the address space of a container process and, when this happens, COM has already called `CoInitializeSecurity()`, explicitly or implicitly.

It doesn't matter if the container application issued the call or if COM did it based on Registry settings. Even if you call `CoInitializeSecurity()` in your code, it will be too late; by that time, all COM security settings are already in place.

One possible solution for this case could be the creation of an intermediary out-of-proc server (EXE) that would take care of security issues and make calls into the remote server on behalf of the ActiveX client. To the ActiveX client, this intermediary server would look like the remote server.

The bottom line is that you can't control security through the use of `CoInitializeSecurity()` from inside a DLL. You should keep that in mind when writing DLL clients for your remote servers.

Implementing Programmatic Access Control

You can indicate which individual users or group of users are allowed or denied access to your server by using the pVoid parameter of CoInitializeSecurity(). When providing a valid argument for this parameter, the authentication level must be at least RPC_C_AUTH_LEVEL_CONNECT; otherwise, CoInitializeSecurity() will fail.

Now, you'll learn how to use a SECURITY_DESCRIPTOR, instead of an AppID GUID or IAccessControl interface, to supply security information using the pVoid parameter in a call to CoInitializeSecurity().

The SECURITY_DESCRIPTOR structure has the following members:

```
typedef struct _SECURITY_DESCRIPTOR {
    BYTE  Revision;
    BYTE  Sbz1;
    SECURITY_DESCRIPTOR_CONTROL Control;
    PSID Owner;
    PSID Group;
    PACL Sacl;
    PACL Dacl;
} SECURITY_DESCRIPTOR;
```

Creating a security descriptor with the outdated Win32 Security API is, to say the least, arcane. C++Builder and its ATL support greatly simplify this job with a class called CSecurityDescriptor.

> **NOTE**
>
> Programmatic modification of access control lists (ACLs) via the Win32 Security API is a very complex procedure that requires careful coding and testing.
>
> Beginning in Windows NT 4.0 with Service Pack 2, COM provides the IAccessControl interface. This interface, which is implemented in CLSID_DCOMAccessControl system object, is also considered an easy alternative to programming ACLs other than using the raw security API.

CSecurityDescriptor can be used anywhere a SECURITY_DESCRIPTOR structure is required, thanks to its conversion operators. You can use its methods to initialize a new security descriptor to allow or deny access to particular accounts.

The built-in account SYSTEM must always be included in the access control list because the system's Service Control Manager (SCM) needs this account to manage COM servers.

For demonstration purposes, you're going to change your server to only accept requests from clients using the Guest account. This account is disabled by default when the operating system is first installed.

Let's keep modifying your EasyDCOM sample application by doing the following:

1. Open EasyDCOM.cpp and add the following code below the line containing the include for atlmod.h:

   ```
   #include <atl\atlcom.h>
   ```

2. Add the following code above the line containing the call to CoInitialize():

   ```
   CSecurityDescriptor sd;
   sd.InitializeFromProcessToken();
   sd.Allow("Guest", COM_RIGHTS_EXECUTE);
   sd.Allow("NT_AUTHORITY\\SYSTEM", COM_RIGHTS_EXECUTE);
   ```

3. Replace the call to CoInitializeSecurity() with the following:

   ```
   CoInitializeSecurity(sd, -1, NULL, NULL, RPC_C_AUTHN_LEVEL_CONNECT,
       RPC_C_IMP_LEVEL_IDENTIFY, NULL, EOAC_NONE, NULL);
   ```

4. Open EasyDCOMClient.cpp and delete the lines containing CoInitialize(), CoInitializeSecurity(), and CoUninitialize().

To experiment with the sample, you will need to enable the Guest account and give it the same password on both the client and server machines. As an alternative you can log on as Guest on the machine hosting the server and run the client application from there.

You can replace the Guest account with the name of a valid local or domain account. You must use the format DOMAIN\UserOrGroup or MACHINE\UserOrGroup when passing the account name to the Allow method of CSecurityDescriptor. If you suppress the DOMAIN or MACHINE from the account name, the current machine name is assumed.

If you try to run the sample without being logged as Guest, you will receive an Access Denied error coming from the server. This is because only the Guest account is granted access to the server now.

TIP

Windows 2000 comes with a new command-line utility called RunAs. This utility allows an application to be run under the credentials of a supplied account. RunAs is an excellent tool for testing COM servers under the credentials of different client principals.

Let's examine the code.

A CSecurityDescriptor object, represented by the variable sd, is instantiated and, encapsulated inside it, a new security descriptor is created.

Next, you called the `InitializeFromProcessToken()` method to take care of all subtle details regarding the internals of the security descriptor.

The call to `Allow` passed `Guest` as the account name, and the value `COM_RIGHTS_EXECUTE` to grant access rights to the `Guest` account. You did the same to grant access to built-in `System` account, this time using `NT_AUTHORITY\SYSTEM` as the account name.

Last, `CoInitializeSecurity()` is called passing the `sd` object as an argument for its first parameter. You use `RPC_C_AUTHN_LEVEL_CONNECT` as the authentication value, `RPC_C_IMP_LEVEL_IDENTIFY` as the identity value, and the default values for all other parameters.

Implementing Interface-Wide Security

Up to this point, you have centered your focus on process-wide security settings that can be configured using `CoInitializeSecurity()`. But, what if you need to control security only during method calls; for example, to make a specific call encrypted instead of encrypting the entire process?

`IClientSecurity` Interface

COM helps us with this scenario by providing a finer control of security at the interface level for both clients and servers. At client-side, the underlying remoting layer, represented by the Proxy Manager, implements the `IClientSecurity` interface. At server-side, the Stub Manager implements the `IServerSecurity` interface.

The methods of the `IClientSecurity` interface are `QueryBlanket()`, `SetBlanket()`, and `CopyProxy()`.

`QueryBlanket()` retrieves the authentication information used by the interface proxy. This information is the security information passed to `CoInitializeSecurity()` during process initialization. You call `QueryBlanket()` using `NULL` on all parameters that you don't want to retrieve information.

`SetBlanket()` sets the authentication information to be used by a particular interface proxy. Its use affects all clients of the proxy.

`CopyProxy()` makes a private copy of the interface proxy that you can use later with `SetBlanket()`. This method enables multiple clients to independently change their interface security settings.

The parameters for `QueryBlanket()` and `SetBlanket()` correspond to the parameters of `CoInitializeSecurity()` with one notable exception, the seventh parameter—`pAuthInfo`. This parameter is dependent on the security package in use. It points to a `COAUTHIDENTITY` structure when the NTLM security package is being used.

The `COAUTHIDENTITY` structure has the following members:

```
typedef struct _COAUTHIDENTITY
{
    USHORT *User;
    ULONG UserLength;
    USHORT *Domain;
    ULONG DomainLength;
    USHORT *Password;
    ULONG PasswordLength;
    ULONG Flags;
} COAUTHIDENTITY;
```

You can make calls using the credentials of an arbitrary user if you pass the `pAuthInfo` parameter a `COAUTHIDENTITY` structure pointer filled with username, password, and domain information. When you pass `NULL` to this parameter, each COM method call is made using the credentials of the client process.

To use `IClientSecurity`, you must use `QueryInterface()` on the Proxy Manager for `IID_IClientSecurity`, call one of its methods, and then release the interface. COM makes your life easier by providing wrappers that encapsulate this sequence.

The COM wrapper functions for the methods of the `IClientSecurity` interface are `CoQueryProxyBlanket()`, `CoSetProxyBlanket()`, and `CoCopyProxy()`.

`IServerSecurity` Interface

At the server-side, the `IServerSecurity` interface can be used to identify and impersonate the client. You can call `CoGetCallContext()` from within a method call to obtain an interface pointer to this interface. `IServerSecurity` has the methods `QueryBlanket()`, `ImpersonateClient()`, `RevertToSelf()`, and `IsImpersonating()`.

`QueryBlanket()` is analogous to its sibling in `IClientSecurity` interface; it returns the security settings in use. For example, you could use `QueryBlanket()` to determine whether the client is using encryption or to discover the client identity.

During a method call, you can use `ImpersonateClient()` to enable the server to use the security credentials of the client. The impersonation level used by the client determines if the server can actually access system objects acting as the client itself, or if the server can only use the client's credentials to perform access checks.

`RevertToSelf()` restores the security credentials of the server and stops the server from impersonating the client. COM will automatically restore the server's security credentials prior to leaving a method call, even if you forget to call `RevertToSelf()` explicitly.

`IsImpersonating()` is used to check whether the server is currently impersonating the client.

COM offers the following functions as wrappers for the methods of the
IServerSecurity interface: CoQueryClientBlanket(), CoImpersonateClient(), and
CoRevertToSelf().

Using the Blanket

To demonstrate the use of the IServerSecurity and IClientSecurity interfaces, you're
going to create a brand-new example. This example will enable the client to change
its identity and interrogate the server to discover the current identity in use. It will
also let the server create a local file using the credentials of the client. Later, through
the use of Windows Explorer, you will be able to access the properties of the file
object and see its owner to confirm whether the file was created using the identity
you supplied.

To conduct this experiment, create two local accounts named CommonUser and
ExtraUser, members of the User group, on both the client and server machines, and
log on the client machine using the ExtraUser account.

Use DCOMCnfg to configure the server to allow access and launch permissions to everyone, and set the identity of the server (refer to Figure 18.8) to use the Administrator
account.

The example server application that you will create in the following section is
provided in the Blanket\Server folder on the CD-ROM that accompanies this book.

> **NOTE**
>
> In the absence of an NT Server domain, the workstation machine is, in effect, the only
> member of its own domain.

Create your new sample server as follows:

1. Start by creating an EXE server called Blanket with an Automation Object that
   has a CoClass name of ObjBlanket. Next, use the TLE editor to add the following two methods:

   ```
   [id(1)] HRESULT _stdcall BlanketInfo([out, retval] BSTR * Value);
   [id(2)] HRESULT _stdcall CreateFile([in] BSTR Value);
   ```

2. Now you need to implement the methods. Open ObjBlanketImpl.cpp and add
   the following code to the BlanketInfo method:

   ```
   try {
       *Value = NULL;
       LPWSTR pPrivs;
   ```

```
    OleCheck(CoQueryClientBlanket(NULL, NULL, NULL, NULL, NULL,
                            (LPVOID*)&pPrivs, NULL));

    WideString strInfo = pPrivs;
    *Value = strInfo.Detach();
}
catch(Exception &e) {
    return Error(e.Message.c_str(), IID_IObjBlanket);
}
return S_OK;
```

This method makes use of the `CoQueryClientBlanket()` to retrieve the name of the client principal and return it to the caller. It performs this operation by passing `NULL` to all parameters except the sixth, `pPrivs`. This tells `CoQueryClientBlanket()` that you're only interested in information regarding the identity of the client.

3. Add the following code to the `CreateFile()` method:

```
try {
    OleCheck(CoImpersonateClient());

    HANDLE hFile = ::CreateFile(AnsiString(Value).c_str(),
                            GENERIC_WRITE,
                            FILE_SHARE_WRITE,
                            NULL,
                            CREATE_ALWAYS,
                            FILE_ATTRIBUTE_NORMAL,
                            NULL);

    if (INVALID_HANDLE_VALUE == hFile)
        return HRESULT_FROM_WIN32(GetLastError());

    CloseHandle(hFile);
    OleCheck(CoRevertToSelf());
}
catch(Exception &e) {
    return Error(e.Message.c_str(),IID_IObjBlanket);
}
return S_OK;
```

Here, you started by calling `CoImpersonateClient()` to begin impersonating the client.

You made this call because you wanted to create a local file using the identity supplied by the client instead of the identity currently in use by the server process.

Remember that you manually set the server's identity to use the credentials of the Administrator account. So, if the call to CoImpersonateClient() succeeds, you will be able to see a different owner for the created file.

Before leaving the method, you closed the file handle and called CoRevertToSelf() to tell the server to stop impersonating the client and revert to its own identity.

You can now build the project. When done, copy the server to the remote machine and run it once to perform self-registration.

You can find the code for the example client application in the Blanket\Client folder on the CD-ROM that accompanies this book.

The client will also be an EXE application. To create the client application do the following:

1. Start a new project and save it as BlanketClient renaming Unit1 to MainUnit.

2. Design its main form to look like Figure 18.15, and rename its components as follows:

Original Name	New Name
Form1	frmMain
RadioButton1	rdoLoged
RadioButton2	rdoIdnty
GroupBox1	gbxIdn
GroupBox1	gbxInfo
Label1	lblUser
Label2	lblDomain
Label3	lblPwrd
Edit1	txtUser
Edit2	txtDomain
Edit3	txtPwrd
Edit4	txtInfo
Button1	cmdCallServer
Button2	cmdSetIdentity
Button3	cmdGetInfo
Button4	cmdCreateFile
Button5	cmdFinish

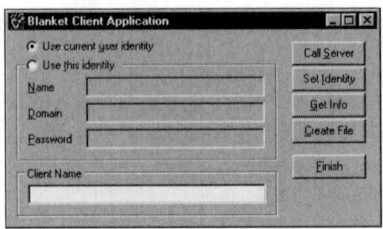

FIGURE 18.15 The BlanketClient main form and its components.

3. Open MainUnit.h and add the following header file to its list of header files:

```
#include "..\Server\Blanket_TLB.h"
```

4. Declare two private data members in the TfrmMain derived class as the following:

```
TCOMIObjBlanket m_objBlanket;
SEC_WINNT_AUTH_IDENTITY m_pAuthInfo;
```

5. Add the following two private member functions to the TfrmMain class:

```
void GetAuthInfo();
void SetAuthInfo();
```

You will find the code for MainUnit.cpp in Listing 18.1.

LISTING 18.1 The Code for MainUnit.cpp, Main Form of the BlanketClient Project

```
#include <vcl.h>
#pragma hdrstop
#include "MainUnit.h"

#pragma package(smart_init)
#pragma resource "*.dfm"

TfrmMain *frmMain;

__fastcall TfrmMain::TfrmMain(TComponent* Owner) : TForm(Owner)
{
    m_AuthInfo.Flags    = SEC_WINNT_AUTH_IDENTITY_ANSI;
    m_AuthInfo.User     = NULL;
    m_AuthInfo.Domain   = NULL;
    m_AuthInfo.Password = NULL;
```

LISTING 18.1   Continued

```
}

void __fastcall TfrmMain::FrmMain_Close(TObject *Sender, TCloseAction &Action)
{
    m_objBlanket.Unbind();

    delete[] m_AuthInfo.User;
    delete[] m_AuthInfo.Domain;
    delete[] m_AuthInfo.Password;
}

void __fastcall TfrmMain::CmdCallServer_Click(TObject *Sender)
{
    if (!m_objBlanket.IsBound()) {
        AnsiString strHost;

        if (InputQuery("Create Server", "Enter computer name:", strHost)) {
            if (strHost.IsEmpty())
                OleCheck(CoObjBlanket::Create(m_objBlanket));
            else
                OleCheck(CoObjBlanket::CreateRemote(WideString(strHost),
                                                    m_objBlanket));
            ShowMessage("Server created");
        }
    }
}

void __fastcall TfrmMain::CmdCreateFile_Click(TObject *Sender)
{
    if (m_objBlanket.IsBound()) {
        AnsiString strFile;

        if (InputQuery("Create File", "Enter path and file name:", strFile)) {
            OleCheck(m_objBlanket.CreateFile(WideString(strFile)));
            ShowMessage("File created");
        }
    }
}

void __fastcall TfrmMain::CmdFinish_Click(TObject *Sender)
{
```

LISTING 18.1   Continued

```
    Close();
}

void __fastcall TfrmMain::CmdGetInfo_Click(TObject *Sender)
{
    if (m_objBlanket.IsBound())
        GetAuthInfo();
}

void __fastcall TfrmMain::CmdIdentity_Click(TObject *Sender)
{
    gbxIdn->Enabled = rdoIdnty->Checked ? true : false;

    txtDomain->Color = rdoIdnty->Checked ? clWindow : clBtnFace;
    txtPwrd  ->Color = rdoIdnty->Checked ? clWindow : clBtnFace;
    txtUser  ->Color = rdoIdnty->Checked ? clWindow : clBtnFace;
}

void __fastcall TfrmMain::CmdSetIdentity_Click(TObject *Sender)
{
    if (m_objBlanket.IsBound()) {
        if (rdoIdnty->Checked)
            SetAuthInfo();

        OleCheck(CoSetProxyBlanket(m_objBlanket,
                                   RPC_C_AUTHN_WINNT,
                                   RPC_C_AUTHZ_NONE,
                                   NULL,
                                   RPC_C_AUTHN_LEVEL_CONNECT,
                                   RPC_C_IMP_LEVEL_IMPERSONATE,
                                   rdoIdnty->Checked ? &m_AuthInfo : NULL,
                                   EOAC_NONE));
    }
}

void TfrmMain::GetAuthInfo()
{
    WideString strInfo;
    OleCheck(m_objBlanket.BlanketInfo (&strInfo));
    txtInfo->Text = strInfo;
}
```

LISTING 18.1   Continued

```
void TfrmMain::SetAuthInfo()
{
    delete[] m_AuthInfo.User;
    delete[] m_AuthInfo.Domain;
    delete[] m_AuthInfo.Password;

    m_AuthInfo.UserLength     = txtUser  ->Text.Length();
    m_AuthInfo.DomainLength   = txtDomain->Text.Length();
    m_AuthInfo.PasswordLength = txtPwrd  ->Text.Length();

    m_AuthInfo.User     = (PUCHAR)new TCHAR[txtUser  ->Text.Length()+1];
    m_AuthInfo.Domain   = (PUCHAR)new TCHAR[txtDomain->Text.Length()+1];
    m_AuthInfo.Password = (PUCHAR)new TCHAR[txtPwrd  ->Text.Length()+1];

    lstrcpy((LPTSTR)m_AuthInfo.User    , (LPCTSTR)txtUser  ->Text.c_str());
    lstrcpy((LPTSTR)m_AuthInfo.Domain  , (LPCTSTR)txtDomain->Text.c_str());
    lstrcpy((LPTSTR)m_AuthInfo.Password, (LPCTSTR)txtPwrd  ->Text.c_str());
}
```

You can see from Listing 18.1 that you initialized some of the members of m_AuthInfo in the constructor of TfrmMain. Microsoft documentation suggests DCOM will keep a pointer to the identity information contained in this structure until a new value is used, or until COM itself is uninitialized.

The SetAuthInfo() private member function acts like a helper method for dealing with the SEC_WINNT_AUTH_IDENTITY structure. It avoids memory leaks and correctly assigns identity information to its members.

The Set Identity button handles client identity change. It performs its action by calling CoSetProxyBlanket() to adjust the interface security settings telling the Proxy Manager to use identity information contained in the m_AuthInfo member variable.

Identity information is toggled between the current logged user identity (process token credentials), and the supplied identity through the use of a NULL argument in the pAuthInfo parameter of the CoSetProxyBlanket() function.

CoSetProxyBlanket() is called with a RPC_C_IMP_LEVEL_IMPERSONATE level of impersonation to let the server effectively behave as the client using the credentials supplied in the pAuthInfo parameter.

The event handler for the Get Info button calls the server's BlanketInfo() method to retrieve the current user identity name and place the result in the txtInfo edit box.

The Create File button handles file creation at the remote machine, asking for a path and a filename and executing the server's CreateFile() method. The remote file is then created using the identity currently in use.

Let's try your sample and proceed as follows:

1. Start BlanketClient.exe and click the Call Server button. Enter the name of the host machine to instantiate the Blanket server.

2. Click the Get Info button, and you should see something similar to the screen in Figure 18.16. This is the result of pressing the Get Info button while BlanketClient is using the credentials of the current logged user, ExtraUser.

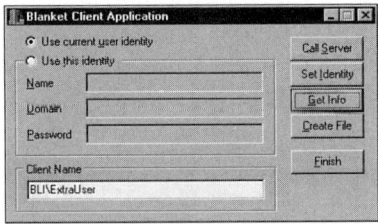

FIGURE 18.16   BlanketClient running under the current logged user account.

3. Click the Create File button and enter C:\RemFile1.Txt to create a remote file named RemFile1.Txt on the root of the host's drive C.

   Figure 18.17 shows the file properties. You can confirm that the remote file was created under credentials of the ExtraUser account.

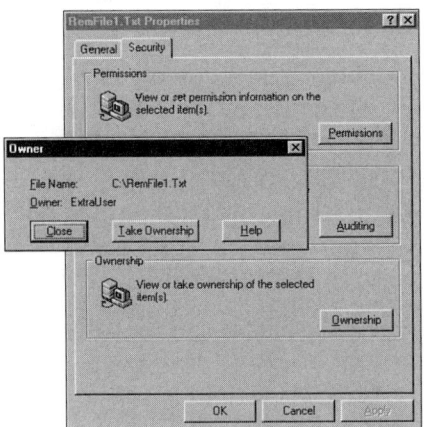

FIGURE 18.17   RemFile1.Txt properties shows ExtraUser as its owner.

4. Fill the identity fields with information from the CommonUser account, and click the Set Identity button to change the client identity. Figure 18.18 shows the result of clicking the Get Info button after performing this operation.

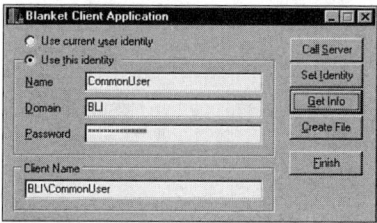

FIGURE 18.18   BlanketClient using the credentials of the CommonUser account.

5. Click the Create File button again. This time, give the remote file the name RemFile2.Txt.

   Figure 18.19 now shows that the remote file was created under credentials of the CommonUser account.

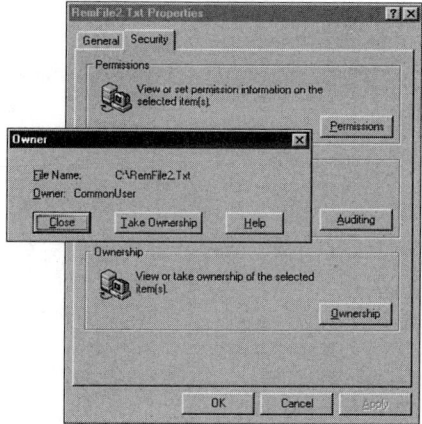

FIGURE 18.19   RemFile2.Txt properties shows CommonUser as its owner.

Summary

DCOM is a very big subject that deserves an entire book by itself. It's a huge technology that has many subtle aspects. In this chapter, it's most important features were addressed.

You were introduced to DCOM and learned that it brings remote capabilities to COM objects, and that it introduces important issues like security as well.

You learned how to use the DCOMCnfg configuration tool to control DCOM settings stored in the Registry for specific components and for all components in the system.

You also saw how to use `CoInitializeSecurity()` to programmatically control security at server- and client-sides, and you learned how to control security at the interface level through the use of `IClientSecurity` and `IServerSecurity` interfaces implemented by the Proxy and Stub managers.

DCOM is not the only distributed systems technology available to you in C++Builder. The following chapters will take you on a tour of what's left.

SOAP and Web Services with BizSnap

by Bob Swart (a.k.a. Dr. Bob)

BizSnap is the name given by Borland to describe the featureset of C++Builder that covers XML-document programming (see Chapter 13, "XML Document Programming and XML Mapper,") as well as Web Services (using SOAP). In this chapter, we'll cover Web Services, then after a short introduction to SOAP, we'll implement our first Web Service in C++Builder 6. Import and usage (consuming) of Web Services written in C++Builder 6 and other development environments will follow.

Note that we can use C++Builder 6 Professional to import and use Web services, but we have to use the Enterprise edition to build our own Web services.

Apart from this chapter, we can also find information on special Web Services that contain SOAP data modules—a combination of BizSnap and DataSnap technology—in Chapter 21 (about "DataSnap Multitier Connections").

Building Web Services

In Chapter 13 we saw the XML document capabilities of C++Builder 6 Enterprise. Now we're ready to examine another XML capability of C++Builder in the shape of SOAP and Web Services. It probably sounds more difficult than it needs to be, but will turn out to be easy, just wait.

SOAP stands for Simple Object Access Protocol, and is a cross-platform and cross-language protocol, which is not only supported in C++Builder 6, but also in Kylix 3 (for Linux), and lots of other tools.

SOAP Server Application

To build Web Services in C++Builder 6 we have to start with a SOAP Server Application. So, start C++Builder 6 Enterprise, File, New, Other, and go to the WebServices tab of the Object Repository. In this tab of the Object Repository, which can be seen in Figure 19.1, we see four icons: the SOAP Server Application, the SOAP Server Data Module, the SOAP Server Interface, and the WSDL Importer.

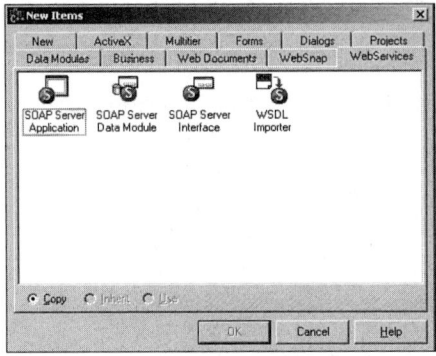

FIGURE 19.1   WebServices tab of Object Repository.

We'll use them all in this chapter, but at this time we need the first one, so select the SOAP Server Application icon and click OK. The New SOAP Server Application Wizard starts and asks about the type of Web server application that we want to use for our Web Service. In this chapter I want to use the simple CGI (common gateway interface) target, which can be seen in Figure 19.2. A CGI target is the easiest to deploy and use. See Chapter 22, "Web Server Programming with WebSnap," for more details about the different Web server application targets.

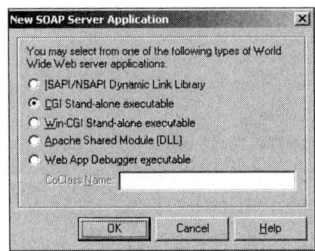

FIGURE 19.2   New SOAP server application.

After you click on the OK button, a new SOAP Server project is created that includes a Web Module. We are also presented with a Confirm dialog, asking if we want to create an interface for the SOAP module (see Figure 19.3). If we answer Yes to this question, the SOAP Server Interface wizard is started (the third icon on Figure 19.1).

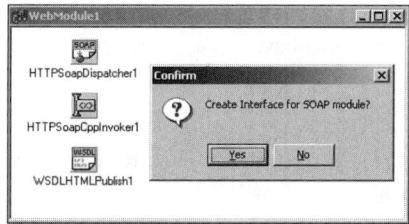

FIGURE 19.3   SOAP server Web module.

However, please just say no to this question at this time because I want to explain a few things that have been generated so far. Specifically, I want to explain the capabilities of the three components on the SOAP Web module, visible in the background of Figure 19.3. Don't worry about closing the Confirm dialog and not creating an interface for the SOAP module right away; we can always start the SOAP Server Interface wizard manually.

SOAP Server Web Module

Before we continue, save all files, placing the SOAP Web module in file SWebMod.cpp and the new SOAP project itself in BCB6WebService.bpr (this will result in a Web service Web server application called BCB6WebService.exe).

The SOAP Web module already contains three components (that can also be found on the WebServices tab of the C++Builder 6 component palette), namely a THTTPSoapDispatcher, a THTTPSoapCppInvoker, and a TWSDLHTMLPublish component.

The THTTPSoapDispatcher component is used to receive incoming SOAP requests and dispatch them to another component (defined by its Dispatcher property) that can interpret the request and execute it. The latter will be done in this case by the THTTPSoapCppInvoker component, which receives the incoming SOAP request, executes (invokes) a C++ method, and produces the response back to the THTTPSoapDispatcher. Before the THTTPSoapCppInvoker can actually invoke the requested C++ method, it first checks to see if the method's interface and implementation class have been registered in the invocation registry (we'll get back to this in a moment).

Where the first two components are used when the Web service is actually consumed, the third component—TWSDLHTMLPublish—is used to produce the WSDL (Web Service Description Language) that defines the interface of the Web service itself.

We don't have to configure the properties or events of these three components; they are already fully prepared to be used. We only have to focus on the task at hand: Build some kind of Web service engine, and define its interface, so it can be published and used. In other words, we can now manually start the SOAP Server

Interface wizard. Open File, New, Other, go to the WebServices tab of the Object Repository, and double-click the SOAP Server Interface icon. This will present us with the Add New WebService dialog, where we can specify the name of the service as well as other options.

To get an idea what kind of functionality is suited to be packaged as a Web Service application, take a look at the list of Web services at http://www.xmethods.org. As a main example for this first section, I want to produce a Web Service that can convert inches to centimeters and back. It's only a small example, but will illustrate the Web Services functionality quite nicely (and it's actually even quite useful if you live in Europe and are used to centimeters, but want to estimate whether or not a 19-inch LCD screen will fit between the table desktop and the bookshelf).

We should specify CmInch as Service Name (see Figure 19.4), which is automatically copied to the Filename identifier. That results in the files CmInch.cpp and CmInch.h, which will be generated and added to the project.

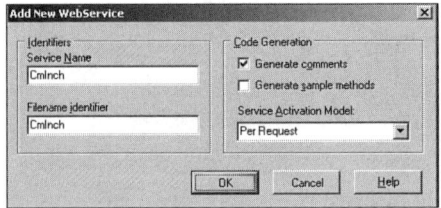

FIGURE 19.4   Generated SOAP server Web module.

In the Code Generation group we can select the option to generate comments (selected by default), or generate sample methods. You can select the latter option if you want, although in this section we will also write our own sample methods (which should be clear enough, so I generally do not need sample methods to be generated). The final option controls the service activation model, which I want to cover in a bit more detail now.

Server Activation Model
The choices for the service activation model are either "per request" (default) or "global." In the latter case, there will be one global Web Service instance to handle all incoming requests from clients. The default choice "per request" means that an instance of the implementation class is created for every incoming request (and destroyed after the request is handled). The code that is generated for the two choices differs in only one place—a special Factory method is generated in case of the global choice. This Factory method checks if an instance already exists and

returns it if this is the case, or creates the single instance if not. For our `CmInch` interface, the `CmInchFactory()` method would be implemented as follows inside `CmInch.cpp`:

```
static void __fastcall CmInchFactory(System::TObject* &obj)
{
  static _di_ICmInch iInstance;
  static TCmInchImpl *instance = 0;
  if (!instance)
  {
    instance = new TCmInchImpl();
    instance->GetInterface(iInstance);
  }
  obj = instance;
}
```

To make sure that this `CmInchFactory()` method is indeed used, it has to be passed as the second argument to the `InvRegistry()->RegisterInvokableClass()` method call, which is shown in this snippet from `CmInch.cpp`):

```
static void RegTypes()
{
  InvRegistry()->RegisterInterface(__interfaceTypeinfo(ICmInch));
  InvRegistry()->RegisterInvokableClass(__classid(TCmInchImpl), CmInchFactory);
}
```

You might wonder why I showed these code snippets in such detail? The reason is to offer you the ability to switch between a "global" and a "per request" server instance by adding the `CmInchFactory()` method implementation and only adding the second argument to the `InvRegistry()->RegisterInvokableClass()` call when planning to use a global server instance. Otherwise, you can omit `CmInchFactory` as second argument and have a "per request" server instance.

So, my advice is to select the Global option for the Service Activation Model, and remove the second argument from `InvRegistry()->RegisterInvokableClass()` if you decide not to use a global instance after all (the code for the `CmInchFactory` won't be used in that case). Save the generated code in files `CmInch.cpp` and `CmInch.h` as indicated previously.

Invokable Registry

Let's backtrack for a moment here, and consider this `InvRegistry` object. This is the aforementioned Invokable Registry, used to register both the Web service interface (definition) as well as the implementation class. At the server side (which we are building at this time), both the interface and implementation have to be registered, of course, but at the client side (the topic of next section), only the Web service interface has to be registered to use it.

Web Service Interface

Now that we have an empty `CmInch` Web service skeleton, we should add some methods. Starting with the interface in `CmInch.h`, where we need to add two new methods, `Cm2Inch()` and `Inch2Cm()`, to the `ICmInch` interface definition as follows:

```
// ********************************************************************** //
//  Invokable interfaces must derive from IInvokable
//  The methods of the interface will be exposed via SOAP
// ********************************************************************** //
__interface INTERFACE_UUID("{F446E03A-0BAE-437A-98A7-FF503836AE02}")
  ICmInch : public IInvokable
{
public:
  virtual float STDMETHODCALLTYPE Cm2Inch(float Cm) = 0;
  virtual float STDMETHODCALLTYPE Inch2Cm(float Inch) = 0;
};
typedef DelphiInterface<ICmInch> _di_ICmInch;
```

Now, before you hit F9 to compile—this won't work, yet, because we've only defined the `ICmInch` interface (inside `CmInch.h`). The `TCmInchImpl` class inside `CmInch.cpp` is the one to actually implement the `ICmInch` interface—or at least the one that should implement it (which is why the code currently doesn't compile). So, switch back to the `CmInch.cpp` file and add the `Cm2Inch()` and `Inch2Cm()` methods to the class definition of `TCmInchImpl` (just copy them from the `ICmInch` definition and remove the `"= 0"` parts at the end). This leads to the following code for the class definition:

```
// ********************************************************************** //
//  TCmInchImpl implements interface ICmInch
// ********************************************************************** //
class TCmInchImpl : public TInvokableClass, public ICmInch
{
public:

  /* IUnknown */
  HRESULT STDMETHODCALLTYPE QueryInterface(const GUID& IID, void **Obj)
                    { return GetInterface(IID, Obj) ? S_OK : E_NOINTERFACE; }
  ULONG STDMETHODCALLTYPE AddRef() { return TInterfacedObject::_AddRef();  }
  ULONG STDMETHODCALLTYPE Release(){ return TInterfacedObject::_Release(); }

  /* ICmInch */
  virtual float STDMETHODCALLTYPE Cm2Inch(float Cm);
  virtual float STDMETHODCALLTYPE Inch2Cm(float Inch);
```

```
  /* Ensures that the class is not abstract */
  void checkValid() { delete new TCmInchImpl(); }
};
```

Now the final step, the actual implementation of the `Cm2Inch()` and `Inch2Cm()` methods. For this we might want to look up the actual conversion rate between centimeters and inches, which is generally defined as 2.54 centimeters per inch. This means that the implementation of the two methods from our Web service class `TCmInchImpl` is as follows:

```
const CmPerInch = 2.54;

float STDMETHODCALLTYPE TCmInchImpl::Cm2Inch(float Cm)
{
  return Cm / CmPerInch;
};

float STDMETHODCALLTYPE TCmInchImpl::Inch2Cm(float Inch)
{
  return Inch * CmPerInch;
};
```

At this time we can save all files, compile the project (and perhaps fix any typos that were made), and get ready to deploy the `CmInch` Web service on the Web.

Deploying the SOAP Server

Before we can deploy the Web service, however, we should first make sure that it can actually be executed on the target machine. By default, C++Builder 6 generates projects that use the dynamic RTL and runtime packages. Resulting in really small executables (the `BCB6WebServices.exe` is only 52,736 bytes), but requiring the dynamic RTL as well as a number of runtime packages. To turn it into a standalone executable (which is easy to install), we must perform a few additional steps.

First of all, we should open the Project, Options dialog, go to the Compiler tab and click on the Release button (just in case). Second, go to the Linker tab, and uncheck the Use dynamic RTL option. Third and last, go to the Packages tab and uncheck the Build with runtime packages option. Now close the Project Options dialog again, and recompile the application. This time, the `BCB6WebService.exe` will be 704,512 bytes big. A significant difference, but at least it can be deployed and used as a standalone CGI Web Service now, by placing it in a cgi-bin or scripts directory of a Web server similar to IIS (Internet Information Service). See Chapter 22, "Web Server Programming with WebSnap," for more deployment details.

Just for your convenience, I've deployed BCB6WebService.exe on my own Web server (hosted by TDMWeb), so it's now available to use as example and demonstration on the Web at http://www.eBob42.com/cgi-bin/BCB6WebService.exe (see also Figure 19.5.)

FIGURE 19.5   CmInch Web service on the Web.

Note that this direct URL shows the two SOAP interfaces ICmInch and IWSDLPublish that are exposed by the BCB6WebService application. ICmInch is the one that we made, and IWSDLPublish is the one that every C++Builder Web service gets for free by using the TWSDLHTMLPublish component (see Figure 19.3).

We can click the link for each of these interfaces, click on their WSDL link, or pass the additional PathInfo/wsdl to the URL to get the WSDL (Web Service Description Language) description, automatically produced by the TWSDLHTMLPublish component, which is shown in Figure 19.6.

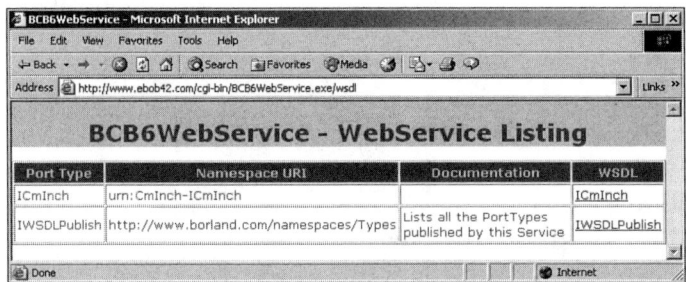

FIGURE 19.6   WebService Listing of BCB6WebService/wsdl.

If you click the link for the WSDL for ICmInch (or directly go to the URL http://www.eBob42.com/cgi-bin/BCB6WebService.exe/wsdl/ICmInch), you get the full WSDL for the ICmInch interface—see Figure 19.7 for details.

As can be seen, the WSDL is an XML document that consists of a number of sections such as the message, portType, binding, or service. We'll see some of these again shortly when we actually use the CmInch Web service.

In the next section of this chapter, we will use this WSDL, so we either need to save the WSDL as shown in Figure 19.7, or the URL itself to let C++Builder 6 itself retrieve the WSDL.

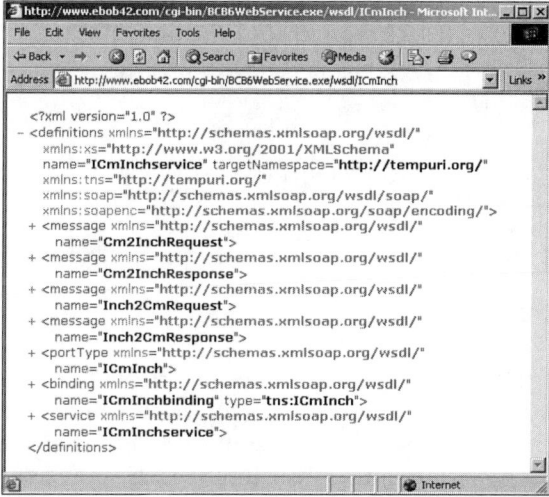

FIGURE 19.7 WebService Listing of BCB6WebService/wsdl/IcmInch.

Consuming Web Services

It's time to import and use—also called consume—Web services. To get an idea what kinds of functionality are suited as Web Service applications, I always recommend taking a look at the list of Web services http://www.xmethods.org, as mentioned previously. In the next section, we will consume a Web service written in a foreign language, but right now we should start by consuming the CmInch Web services we wrote in the previous section using C++Builder 6 itself.

A Web Service consumer can be any kind of application. But to keep things simple, let's just start a new default visual application in C++Builder. Save the form in file MainForm.cpp and the project in BCB6WSClient.bpr. Now we have to add an import unit that represents the CmInch Web service interface—a job for the WSDL Importer.

WSDL Importer

We need to use the WSDL Importer (from the WebServices tab of the Object Repository), because we must import the WSDL that defines the Web service (interface) and generate an C++ import unit that defines the C++ interface of this particular Web service. So, activate File, New, Other, go to the WebServices tab of the Object Repository, and double-click the WSDL Importer icon, which will result in the WSDL Import wizard (see Figure 19.8).

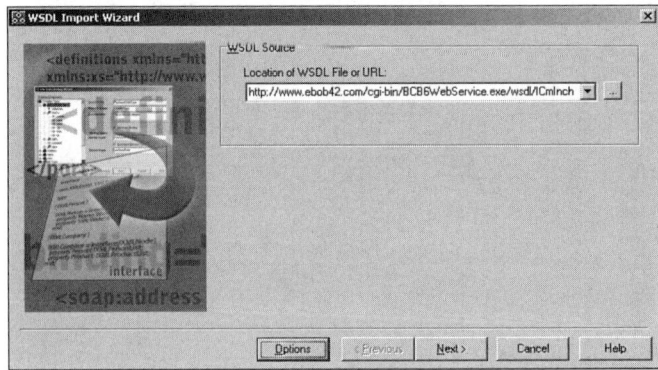

FIGURE 19.8   WSDL importer.

Enter the URL of the Web Service that we've just created. This can be http://localhost/cgi-bin/BCB6WebService.exe/wsdl/ICmInch (on your own localhost machine) or the "real" http://www.eBob42.com/cgi-bin/BCB6WebService.exe/wsdl/ICmInch (for the version deployed on my Web site on the Internet). If you've saved the WSDL in a local file, you can also click on the button with the ellipsis and specify the location of the local file with the WSDL for ICmInch. The benefit of using a local WSDL file is that you don't need an active Internet connection to develop the Web service client application, and you can edit the file and make some changes to it if you want (and know what you're doing).

After we've specified the URL to retrieve the WSDL information for our Web Service, we can take a look at the options by clicking the Option button (see Figure 19.9).

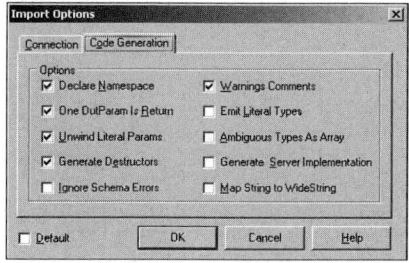

FIGURE 19.9   WSDL Importer (Options).

We can also click the Next button to extract structure information from the WSDL and display this information in a treeview as well as show the code that will be generated, which is shown in Figure 19.10.

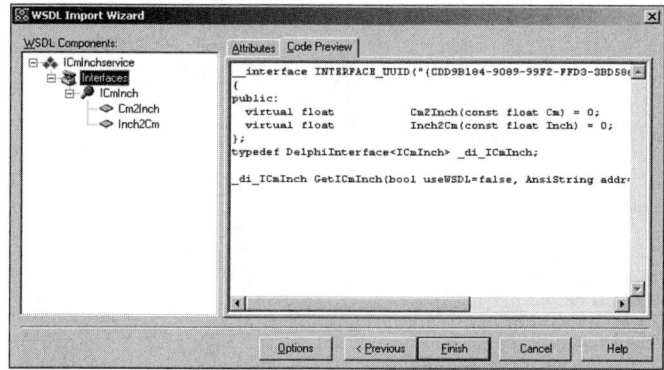

FIGURE 19.10   WSDL Importer (Final Page).

As you can see, the ICmInchservice (Web service) root consists of one interface, called ICmInch, which has two methods: Cm2Inch() and Inch2Cm(). This information was extracted from the retrieved WSDL and not from anything else (the WSDL Importer has no knowledge about what we did in the previous section of this chapter). Note that the WSDL Importer will also work with Web Services that are written in an entirely other development environment (as we will see in the next section), although some interoperability issues between SOAP implementations in other environments may remain to be worked on.

Anyway, we can now click the Finish button to create the Web Service import unit. Save the generated import unit in file ICmInch.cpp, and make sure to #include the

ICmInch.h header file in the MainForm.h header file (after the other #include statements in MainForm.h) as follows:

```
#include "ICmInch.h"
```

The generated unit ICmInch.h has the following contents for the definition of the ICmInch Web service interface:

```
// ********************************************************************* //
// The types declared in this file were generated from data read from the
// WSDL File described below:
// WSDL    : http://www.ebob42.com/cgi-bin/BCB6WebService.exe/wsdl/ICmInch
// Version : 1.0
// (2002-08-15 12:23:22 - $Revision:   1.0.1.0.1.82  $)
// ********************************************************************* //


#ifndef    ICmInchH
#define    ICmInchH

#include <System.hpp>
#include <InvokeRegistry.hpp>
#include <XSBuiltIns.hpp>
#include <SoapHTTPClient.hpp>



namespace NS_ICmInch {

// ********************************************************************* //
// The following types, referred to in the WSDL document are not being
// representedin this file. They are either aliases[@] of other types
// represented or were referredto but never[!] declared in the document.
// The types from the latter categorytypically map to predefined/known
// XML or Borland types; however, they could also
// indicate incorrect WSDL documents that failed to declare or import a schema
// type.
// ********************************************************************* //
// !:float          - "http://www.w3.org/2001/XMLSchema"


// ********************************************************************* //
// Namespace : urn:CmInch-ICmInch
// soapAction: urn:CmInch-ICmInch#%operationName%
// transport : http://schemas.xmlsoap.org/soap/http
// style     : rpc
```

```
// binding   : ICmInchbinding
// service   : ICmInchservice
// port      : ICmInchPort
// URL       : http://www.ebob42.com/cgi-bin/BCB6WebService.exe/soap/ICmInch
// ********************************************************************** //
__interface INTERFACE_UUID("{CDD9B184-9089-99F2-FFD3-3BD586315394}")
   ICmInch : public IInvokable
{
public:
  virtual float          Cm2Inch(const float Cm) = 0;
  virtual float          Inch2Cm(const float Inch) = 0;
};
typedef DelphiInterface<ICmInch> _di_ICmInch;

_di_ICmInch GetICmInch(bool useWSDL=false, AnsiString addr="");



#endif // __ICmInch_h__

};      // NS_ICmInch

#if !defined(NO_IMPLICIT_NAMESPACE_USE)
using  namespace NS_ICmInch;
#endif
```

Note that the definition of the ICmInch interface looks very much like the definition we wrote in the CmInch.cpp unit of the previous section (for the BCB6WebService project). That isn't too strange, of course, if you consider that the entire purpose of the WSDL Importer Wizard is to indeed regenerate the interface (in C++ code).

Even more interesting to look at is the file ICmInch.cpp, which contains the code to get an instance of the ICmInch Web service interface by calling the GetICmInch() method. See Listing 19.1.

LISTING 19.1   Generated Import Unit for ICmInch Web Service

```
// ********************************************************************** //
// The types declared in this file were generated from data read from the
// WSDL File described below:
// WSDL      : http://www.ebob42.com/cgi-bin/BCB6WebService.exe/wsdl/ICmInch
// Version   : 1.0
// (2002-08-15 12:23:22 - $Revision:   1.0.1.0.1.82  $)
```

LISTING 19.1   Continued

```cpp
// ************************************************************************* //

#include <vcl.h>
#pragma hdrstop

#if !defined(ICmInchH)
#include "ICmInch.h"
#endif



namespace NS_ICmInch {

_di_ICmInch GetICmInch(bool useWSDL, AnsiString addr)
{
  static const char* defWSDL= "http://www.ebob42.com/cgi-bin/BCB6WebService.exe
  ➥/wsdl/ICmInch";
  static const char* defURL = "http://www.ebob42.com/cgi-bin/BCB6WebService.exe
  ➥/soap/ICmInch";
  static const char* defSvc = "ICmInchservice";
  static const char* defPrt = "ICmInchPort";
  if (addr=="")
    addr = useWSDL ? defWSDL : defURL;
  THTTPRIO* rio = new THTTPRIO(0);
  if (useWSDL) {
    rio->WSDLLocation = addr;
    rio->Service = defSvc;
    rio->Port = defPrt;
  } else {
    rio->URL = addr;
  }
  _di_ICmInch service;
  rio->QueryInterface(service);
  if (!service)
    delete rio;
  return service;
}



// ************************************************************************* //
// This routine registers the interfaces and types used by invoke the SOAP
// Service.
```

LISTING 19.1 Continued

```
// ********************************************************************* //
static void RegTypes()
{
  /* ICmInch */
  InvRegistry()->RegisterInterface(__interfaceTypeinfo(ICmInch),
    L"urn:CmInch-ICmInch", L"");
  InvRegistry()->RegisterDefaultSOAPAction(__interfaceTypeinfo(ICmInch),
    L"urn:CmInch-ICmInch#%operationName%");
}
#pragma startup RegTypes 32

};    // NS_ICmInch
```

Using ICmInch

Now, move back to the (empty) main form, and drop two TLabeledEdit components (call them edCm and edInch), and two TButton components (call them btnCm2Inch and btnInch2Cm). Set the EditLabel->Caption property of edCm to centimeters, and the EditLabel->Caption property of edInch to inches. Set the Caption properties of btnCm2Inch and btnInch2Cm to Cm to Inches and Inches to Cm, respectively.

Now that the GUI part is done, we need to drop a THTTPRIO component—the left-most component from the Web Services tab of the Component Palette. The THTTPRIO component is a Remote Invokable Object that communicates using HTTP (hence the name HTTPRIO). It will be used by a client application to connect to a Web Service and pretend to implement the Web Services at the client location. To the client, it's as if the THTTPRIO component is behaving as if its a local implementation, whereas, in fact, the THTTPRIO is connecting to the remote Web Service, sending SOAP requests and receiving SOAP answers over HTTP.

This might sound complex, but working with the THTTPRIO component is really easy. Set the WSDLLocation property of the THTTPRIO component to the location of the WSDL, which can be found at either http://localhost/cgi-bin/BCB6WebService.exe/wsdl/ICmInch or http://www.eBob42.com/cgi-bin/BCB6WebService.exe/wsdl/ICmInch (note that the later will be much slower than using the localhost because it requires your THTTPRIO to connect to the Internet for every SOAP request).

> **TIP**
>
> When I started to enter a URL for the WSDLLocation property, I experienced a form of Code Completion because after the first h I immediately got the entire URL for ICmInch for the WSDLProperty. Quite handy, although I'm not sure if this is an official feature.

Now, set the Service property of the THTTPRIO component to ICMInchservice (the only choice if you click the arrow for the drop-down combo box). Finally, set the Port property to ICMInchPort, which is again the only possible choice. This should enable the design of the Web Service client form, which can be seen in Figure 19.11.

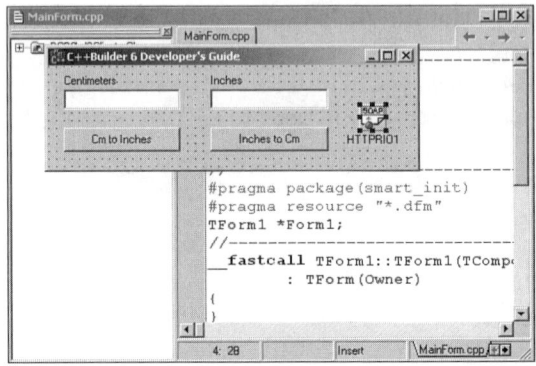

FIGURE 19.11   Centimeters to inch converter Web Service client.

We now need to write the code for the BtnCm2Inch and BtnInch2Cm buttons. We start with BtnCm2Inch first, using the THTTPRIO component and use QueryInterface to extract the _di_ICmInch interface from it. After that, we can use the method Cm2Inch() from this interface, as if it was a simple local method. See the following code snippet:

```
void __fastcall TForm1::btnCm2InchClick(TObject *Sender)
{
  _di_ICmInch service;
  HTTPRIO1->QueryInterface(service);
  if (service) {
    edInch->Text =
      FloatToStr(service->Cm2Inch(
        StrToFloatDef(edCm->Text,0)));
  }
}
```

You can now save, compile, and run the BCB6WSClient application and confirm that you can convert centimeters to inches (but not back, yet).

Apart from using the three WSDLLocation, Service, and Port properties, we can also use just one property: the URL property. This property can be set to the same value as we specified for the WSDLLocation property, with the difference that we have to specify /soap instead of /wsdl. So, in our example, that becomes http://www.eBob42.com/cgi-bin/BCB6WebService.exe/soap/ICmInch. Placing this value in the URL property will clear the WSDLLocation, Service, and Port properties. Recompile the BCB6WSClient application, and you can confirm that you can still convert centimeters to inches.

You might wonder what the difference is between using the single URL property or the WSDLLocation, Service, and Port properties. According the online help, the WSDLLocation, Service, and Port properties are used when you need to dynamically look up connection information from the WSDL document at runtime. If you don't need that, you can use the URL property instead, which can result in clients that execute a bit faster.

Without HTTPRIO

If you think this was easy, watch this: We can even do it without the THTTPRIO component. As you might have noticed, the ICmInch.cpp file contains a function called GetICmInch(), which creates a THTTPRIO component behind the scenes. We can even pass arguments to the GetICmInch() function, which is the first one to specify the use of the WSDLLocation, Service, and Port properties versus the URL property (by default set to use of the URL property). It is the second to specify the address where the Web service can be found. For the conversion of inches to centimeters we can use the GetICmInch() function and obtain the Inch2Cm() method from the resulting _di_ICmInch interface, as in the following code:

```
void __fastcall TForm1::btnInch2CmClick(TObject *Sender)
{
  edCm->Text =
    FloatToStr(GetICmInch()->Inch2Cm(
      StrToFloatDef(edInch->Text,0)));
}
```

After you compile and run the client application, you can enter inches and convert them to centimeters (or vice versa). You can also use C++Builder to consume one of the numerous other available Web Services, or think and produce another Web Service yourself. The sky and your imagination are the limits.

In the next section, we will use an existing Web service available today on the Internet, which provides a bit more functionality than simply converting centimeters to inches (something that we could do a lot faster without Web services in the first place).

Using Other Web Services

We will now examine and use a Web service made available by Google (not implemented in C++Builder 6 Enterprise, but in another development environment), with the obvious functionality to search Google.

Google Web APIs

Information about the official Google Web APIs (Beta 2 at the time of writing this book)—as they call them—can be obtained from the Google Web site at http://www. google.com/apis/. I don't know why they call them simple APIs when, in fact, they are APIs made available as a Web service. Anyway, at the aforementioned URL, you can see that it takes only three steps to start to use the Google APIs:

1. Download the developer's kit

2. Create a Google Account

3. Write your program using your license key

The first step is easy and consists of downloading a 658,031 Byte ZIP file with the complete Google API (currently at Beta 2, released April 11, 2002). Samples for Java as well as .NET, an API reference, and—most importantly for us—the GoogleSearch. wsdl file, which contains the WSDL definition for the GoogleSearch Web service. We'll use this file as a starting point in step 3, when we're building our Web service client with C++Builder 6.

Google Search Key

The second step involves creating a Google account. This sounds more dangerous than it really is. The use of the Google API is free (at least at the time of writing), but you need to pass a personal key that will allow you up to 1,000 search queries per day for noncommercial use only. To get this key, you need to register yourself with an existing email address and a password (although you can forget that password). An email message will be sent to the specified account in order to verify the email address. After you've received the email message and clicked the link inside, you will receive a second message with your special Google Search Key. In my case, that key is 1Wpilaxr+k+hbyYbRLZOJfg7X9NgI837. The key is included in the source code, so the project on the CD-ROM with this book will work right from the start, although it will only work 1,000 times each day (for all combined users of the executable). Therefore, you might want to register yourself and get your own personal Google Search key, which entitles you to 1,000 daily search queries for yourself.

Google Search

Armed with the GoogleSearch.wsdl file and the Google Search Key, we can start C++Builder 6 (Professional or Enterprise) and build our Web service client. Start a new C++Builder project and save the (empty) main form in GoogleForm.cpp and the project itself in Google42.bpr. The first thing we need to do now is to generate a C++ import unit for the WSDL definition found in the GoogleSearch.wsdl file, so activate File, New, Other, and select the WSDL Importer Wizard from the Object Repository.

Instead of specifying a URL for the Google Search, you can use the local
GoogleSearch.wsdl file—this is especially handy in case you do not have a live
Internet connection available at all times because all information is in the local
WSDL file.

Click on the Next button, which will show a preview of the generated import unit as
well as a treeview with the GoogleSearch specific types, interfaces, and methods (as
can be seen in Figure 19.12).

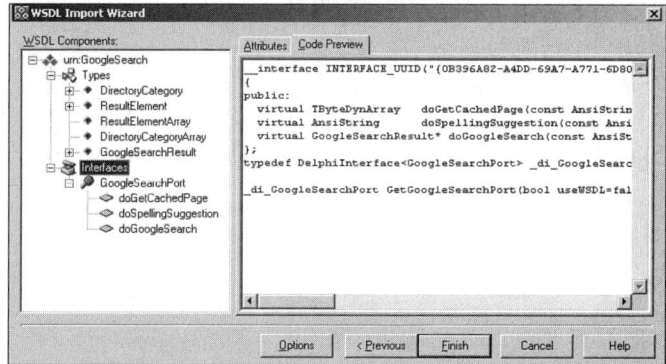

FIGURE 19.12   GoogleSearch types and interfaces.

As we can see in the treeview, there are three structure types: DirectoryCategory,
ResultElement, and GoogleSearchResult; two array types: ResultElementArray and
DirectoryCategoryArray; and one interface called GoogleSearchPort with three member
functions: doGetCachedPage, doSpellingSuggestion, and doGoogleSearch. After we click
the Finish button, the C++ import unit is generated in file GoogleSearch.cpp with the
type definitions in GoogleSearch.h.

To illustrate the things we can do with the result, here are the GoogleSearchResult,
ResultElementArray, and ResultElement type summaries with only their __published
property names (and not their private fields) taken from the generated
GoodleSearch.h file:

```
class ResultElement : public TRemotable {
__published:
  __property AnsiString     summary;
  __property AnsiString          URL;
  __property AnsiString     snippet;
  __property AnsiString       title;
  __property AnsiString cachedSize;
  __property bool         relatedInformationPresent;
```

```
  __property AnsiString    hostName;
  __property DirectoryCategory* directoryCategory;
  __property AnsiString directoryTitle;
};

typedef DynamicArray<ResultElement*> ResultElementArray;
  /* "urn:GoogleSearch" */

class GoogleSearchResult : public TRemotable {
__published:
  __property bool        documentFiltering
  __property AnsiString searchComments
  __property int         estimatedTotalResultsCount
  __property bool        estimateIsExact
  __property ResultElementArray resultElements
  __property AnsiString searchQuery
  __property int        startIndex
  __property int         endIndex
  __property AnsiString searchTips
  __property DirectoryCategoryArray directoryCategories
  __property double      searchTime
};
```

The GoogleSearchPort interface with its three methods and their arguments is defined as follows:

```
__interface INTERFACE_UUID("{0B396A82-A4DD-69A7-A771-6D80F8831A71}")
  GoogleSearchPort : public IInvokable
{
public:
  virtual TByteDynArray   doGetCachedPage(const AnsiString key,
    const AnsiString url) = 0;
  virtual AnsiString      doSpellingSuggestion(const AnsiString key,
    const AnsiString phrase) = 0;
  virtual GoogleSearchResult* doGoogleSearch(const AnsiString key,
    const AnsiString q, const int start, const int maxResults,
    const bool filter, const AnsiString restrict, const bool safeSearch,
    const AnsiString lr, const AnsiString ie, const AnsiString oe) = 0;
};
typedef DelphiInterface<GoogleSearchPort> _di_GoogleSearchPort;
```

And, of course, we also have the helpful GetGoogleSearchPort() function that will return the _di_GoogleSearchPort interface for instant use.

As you might have realized by now, the DirectoryCategory is not a type that we will use at this time, but the ResultItem and GoogleSearchResult are the two result classes that will be used in this section. The GoogleSearchResult contains the resultElements property that points to an array of ResultItems. Finally, the method goGoogleSearch() of the GoogleSearchPort interface is the most interesting, so let's examine that one in more detail.

doGoogleSearch

The definition of the doGoogleSearch() method of the GoogleSearchPort interface is as follows (this time with some meaningful comments for each argument):

```
virtual GoogleSearchResult* doGoogleSearch(
const AnsiString key,        // your own Google Search Key
const AnsiString q,;         // query string
const int start,             // start URLs
const int maxResults,        // maximum results
const bool filter,           // filter alike results?
const AnsiString restrict,   // restrictions
const bool safeSearch,       // adult filter?
const AnsiString lr,         // language?
const AnsiString ie,         // input encoding
const AnsiString oe) = 0;    // output encoding
```

Ouch! A lot of arguments, that's for sure. Fortunately, the Google Search API ZIP-file that we downloaded earlier also contains a file APIs_Reference.html (of 100,417 bytes) containing more information about the search request formats and search results formats; including the meaning of the arguments to doGoogleSearch().

The key argument is the Google Search Key that you have to obtain (we can use the key 1WpiIaxr+k+hbyYbRLZOJfg7X9NgI837). The q argument is the actual query (there's a subsection on the complete query syntax, which includes the site: option to specify that you want to search within a specific Web site). The start argument specifies where you want to start the results, and maxResults specifies how many results you want to receive (with a maximum of 10). Because you can only get a maximum of 10 results at a given time, start can be used to specify where to start. If start is 0, you get the first 10 results. To get the next 10 results, you must pass a value of 10 in start, and so on. This will quickly consume your 1,000 available daily queries, so be aware not to use this to obtain all 142,000 results for "Dr. Bob" on the Web. Personally, I think the first 10 results are just fine, so I use 0 for start and 10 for maxResults. The filter argument can be used to filter results that are very similar, something that I also often use at Google myself, so I pass true as value for filter. The restrict argument can be used to restrict the search query to a specific country or topic within Google. The safeSearch argument can be set to true to make sure you don't get any "adult" search results. Handy if you want to build your own custom search engine for your kids at home (although I haven't tested this fully to make sure it really works as advertised). The lr argument is a bit similar to the restrict argument, and can be used to select results in a specific language (lr), such as Dutch or English (there seem to be no distinction between English, American English, or any of the other English dialects). Finally, the ie and oe arguments specify the Input and Output Encoding, which can be set to latin1 for Dutch and English (see the reference document for more information).

In short, my call to doGoogleSearch(), for a given query string inside an TEdit called edtQuery, would look as follows:

```
GetGoogleSearchPort()->doGoogleSearch("1WpiIaxr+k+hbyYbRLZOJfg7X9NgI837",
edtQuery->Text, 0, 10, True, "", True, "lang_en", "latin1", "latin1");
```

This would give us a result of type GoogleSearchResult, which is derived from TRemoteable. GoogleSearchResult is covered next.

GoogleSearchResult
The GoogleSearchResult has a number of useful properties such as estimatedTotal ResultsCount, searchTime, and resultElements. The last one is an array of which the elements are of type ResultElement, having a number of interesting subproperties such as title, URL, and cachedSize. We can use a TStringGrid to display the results. In fact, let's now build the GUI and actually write some code. The steps are as follows:

1. Drop a TPanel component on the GoogleForm. Set its Align property to alTop, and clear the Caption property.

2. Drop a TButton component on the right of the TPanel, set its Name property to btnSearch, its Caption property to Search, the Anchor->Right subproperty to true, and the Anchor->Left subproperty to false. These last two changes will ensure the button stays glued to the right of the panel, even if you resize the GoogleForm.

3. Drop a TEdit component on the left side of the TPanel, and resize, so it almost reaches the TButton (see Figure 19.13). Set its Name to edtQuery, clear the Text property, and set the Anchor->Right subproperty to true.

4. Drop a TStringGrid component on the GoogleForm, right under the TPanel, set its Align property to alClient, so the TStringGrid occupies the remainder of the GoogleForm. Set its ColCount property to 4, its RowCount property to 11 (that's 10 plus the header), set the DefaultRowHeight property to 21, and finally set the Options->goRowSelect subproperty to true.

5. Now, resize the Form to make the StringGrid fit without scrolling. To initialize the columns of the StringGrid, write the follow code in the OnCreate event handler of the Form:

```
void __fastcall TForm1::FormCreate(TObject *Sender)
{
  StringGrid1->ColWidths[0] = 20;
  StringGrid1->ColWidths[1] = (StringGrid1->ClientWidth - 55) / 2;
  StringGrid1->ColWidths[2] = StringGrid1->ColWidths[1];
  StringGrid1->ColWidths[3] = 32;
  StringGrid1->Cells[0][0] = (AnsiString)" #";
  StringGrid1->Cells[3][0] = (AnsiString)" KB";
}
```

The OnClick event handler of the TButton component can be used to make the call to doGoogleSearch and show the results inside the TStringGrid component. This code is as follows:

```
void __fastcall TForm1::btnSearchClick(TObject *Sender)
{
  for (int row=1; row<=10; row++)
    for (int col=0; col<=3; col++)
      StringGrid1->Cells[col][row] = ""; // clear StringGrid
  GoogleSearchResult* Results =
    GetGoogleSearchPort()->doGoogleSearch("1WpiIaxr+k+hbyYbRLZOJfg7X9NgI837",
    edtQuery->Text, 0, 10, True, "", True, "lang_en", "latin1", "latin1");
  Caption = IntToStr(Results->estimatedTotalResultsCount) +
    " results in " + FloatToStr(Results->searchTime) + " seconds.";
  for (int i=Results->resultElements.Low;
           i <= Results->resultElements.High; i++)
  {
    StringGrid1->Cells[0][i+1] = IntToStr(i+1);
    StringGrid1->Cells[1][i+1] = Results->resultElements[i]->title;
    StringGrid1->Cells[2][i+1] = Results->resultElements[i]->URL;
    StringGrid1->Cells[3][i+1] = Results->resultElements[i]->cachedSize;
  }
}
```

The result is a Windows application that can be used to enter a number of search words and return the top 10 URLs. To jump directly to one of the resulting URLs, we only have to implement the OnDlbClick event handler of the TStringGrid, as follows:

```
void __fastcall TForm1::StringGrid1DblClick(TObject *Sender)
{
  TStringGrid* SG = dynamic_cast<TStringGrid*>(Sender);
  ShellExecute(Handle,"open",SG->Cells[2][SG->Row].c_str(),NULL,0,SW_NORMAL);
}
```

The best thing is that you can integrate this feature in your own (noncommercial) applications as well, of course. As long as an Internet connection is available to talk to Google's official Search Web service.

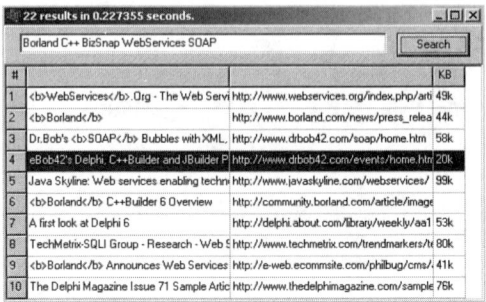

FIGURE 19.13   GoogleSearch Output.

Apart from searching for keywords in a Windows GUI application (or added as a dialog to your own application), another good use of this functionality could be to add it to a Web site, transformed as Web server application. In that case, you can prefix the Query text with the `site:` keyword, including the name of the Web site you're looking at. For example, `"site:www.drbob42.com"` to look for the keyword in pages on my own Web site. As an example of the output, take a look at Figure 19.14 which shows a search for the BizSnap WebServices SOAP combination in the `site:www.drbob42.com`.

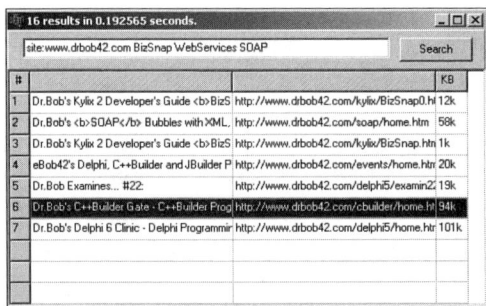

FIGURE 19.14   GoogleSearch Web site–specific results.

Summary

In this chapter we have seen how to use C++Builder 6 to build Web services and how to import and use them—both Web services written in C++Builder and Web services written in other languages. In the last section, we've even seen how to consume foreign Web Services with C++Builder 6. We've seen how to generate the import files based on a WSDL definition of the Web Service, and how to actually call the methods from the Web Service.

For more information about SOAP and Web Services in C++Builder, Delphi, Kylix, or JBuilder check out my SOAP Bubbles Web site at http://www.drbob42.com/SOAP. There you can download full source code for this Google42 Web service client, including any enhancements that I have added since the time of writing.

This ends the coverage of Web Services in C++Builder 6 Enterprise. Note that Chapter 21, "DataSnap Multitier Connections," will cover the combination of Web Services and DataSnap, with the SOAP Data Module and SOAPConnection components.

20

Distributed Applications with DataSnap

by Bob Swart

In this chapter you will learn about DataSnap, the multi-tier database technology previously called Multitier Database Architecture Services (MIDAS).

Using a multitier database architecture, you can partition applications so that you can access data on a second machine (a database server) without having a full set of database tools on your local machine. It also enables you to centralize business rules and processes and distribute the processing load throughout the network.

The examples in this chapter use DataSnap, which means that you must have a copy of the Enterprise Edition of C++Builder to run the programs in this chapter. Note that you can also use the trial version of C++Builder 6 Enterprise to run the examples in this chapter.

Introduction to DataSnap

DataSnap supports a three-tier technology, which in its classic form consists of the following:

- A database server on one (server) machine
- An application server on a second (middle-tier) machine
- A thin client on a third (client) machine

The server should be a tool such as InterBase, Oracle, MS SQL server, and so on. The application server and the thin client should be built in C++Builder. The application server will contain the business rules and the tools for manipulating the data. The client will do nothing more than present the data to the user for viewing and editing.

In some situations, more than one tier can exist on the same machine (similar to the database server and the application server). However, as long as they are separate executables, they can still be considered separate tiers. *N-tier computing* refers to the fact that all these tiers can be spread out across multiple machines. For instance, you might have the employee server on one machine and the payroll server on another machine. One of these application servers might access Oracle data from a third machine, and the other server might access InterBase data from a fourth. Hence, you don't have three tiers, but *n* tiers.

> **NOTE**
> _____
>
> The term n-*tier* can be a bit misleading, at least from some perspectives. No matter how you break up your database servers, application servers, and clients, you still end up with a maximum of three tiers of computing. Just because you have the middle tier spread out over 10 machines doesn't really change the fact that all 10 machines are involved in middle-tier computing.
> _____

DataSnap is based on technology that enables you to package datasets and send them across the network as parameters to remote method calls. It includes technology for converting a dataset into a `Variant` or `XML` package on the server side, and then unbundling the dataset on the client and displaying it to the user in a grid. The latter is done with the aid of the `TClientDataSet` or `TINetxPageProducer` (previously called the `TMidasPageProducer`) component.

Seen from a slightly different angle, DataSnap is a technology for moving a dataset from a `TTable` or `TQuery` object on a server to a `TClientDataSet` object on a client. `TClientDataSet` looks, acts, and feels exactly like a `TTable` or `TQuery` component, except it doesn't have to be attached to the BDE (Borland Database Engine) or any other database driver for that matter—apart from the DataSnap middleware DLL itself. In this particular case, `TClientDataSet` gets its data from unpacking the variant that it retrieves from the server.

DataSnap enables you to use all the standard C++Builder components, including database tools, in your client-side applications. However, the client side is a true thin client: It does not have to include or link any database drivers apart from the `MIDAS.DLL` itself (but at least you're relieved from BDE or ODBC installation scenarios). Installing `MIDAS.DLL` on the client is sometimes referred to as a zero-configuration thin client. And, although it's not exactly zero-configuration, it's indeed very simple to set up a DataSnap client, as this chapter will show.

The two different layers of the DataSnap technology are as follows:

- The components found on the Component Palette and built in the VCL (TDataSetProvider, TClientDataSet, and TXMLBroker). The first two are found on the Data Access tab, and the last one on the InternetExpress tab of the Component Palette.

- The protocol used to send messages over the Internet. This layer might be DCOM, HTTP, or just plain-old TCP/IP (sockets). With C++Builder 6 we can even use SOAP over HTTP. Different connection components can be found on the DataSnap tab of the Component Palette, and will be covered in more detail in the next chapter.

The built-in C++Builder components enable you to easily connect two machines and pass datasets back and forth between them. In the simplest scenarios, they make it possible for you to build middle-tier and client applications with just a few clicks of the mouse.

DataSnap Clients and Servers

The best way to understand what DataSnap is and how it works is to actually build an application, consisting of a client and a server. Usually, I start with the DataSnap server to encapsulate and export the datasets. Then, the next step is to build a DataSnap client that connects to this server and displays the data in some way.

Creating a Simple DataSnap Server

To build your first DataSnap server, select File, New—Application to open a new empty application. The fact that the main form of this application is shown ensures that the DataSnap server will remain loaded (the message loop of the main form keeps the DataSnap server alive). The Caption property of the main form is set to C++Builder 6 Developer's Guide. However, to be able to easily identify the DataSnap server, I always drop a TLabel on the main form, set its Font property to something that's big and readable (like Comic Sans MS 24pt.), its Transparent property to true, and set the Caption property of the TLabel component to the name of the DataSnap server (C++Builder 6 DataSnap Server in this case). Resizing the main form and giving it a noticeable background color in the Color property helps to identify it among your other applications, as shown in Figure 20.1.

To turn a regular application into a middleware database server, you have to add a remote data module to it. This special data module can be found on the Multitier tab of the Object Repository (see Figure 20.2), so select File, New—Other and go to the Multitier tab.

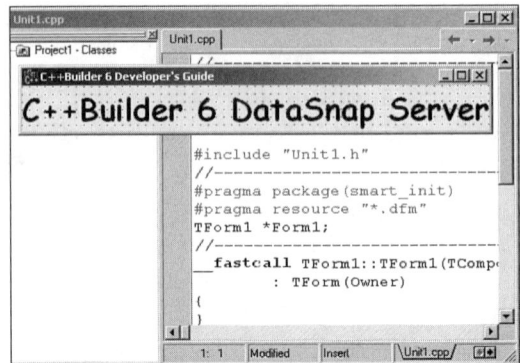

FIGURE 20.1   The C++Builder 6 DataSnap Server main form.

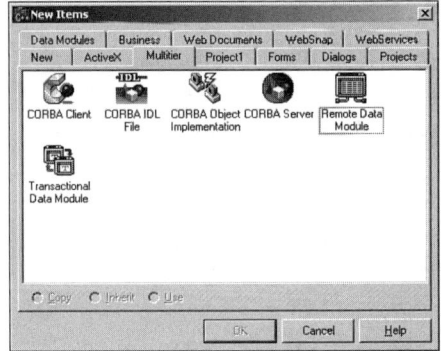

FIGURE 20.2   The Remote Data Module icon inside the Object Repository.

The Multitier tab shows several CORBA wizards, a remote data module, and a Transactional Data Module. The Transactional Data Module can be used with Microsoft Transaction Server (MTS) prior to Windows 2000 or COM+ in Windows 2000 and later; it won't be covered here. It's the normal remote data module that you need to select to create your first simple DataSnap server.

When you select the Remote Data Module icon and click the OK button, the New Remote Data Module Object dialog, which is shown in Figure 20.3, opens.

There are a few options you must specify. CoClass Name is the name of the internal class. This must be a name that you can remember, so use SimpleDataSnapServer at this time (one word, because no spaces are allowed). Threading Model is the second option you can set. By default, it is set to Apartment, which is almost always the correct choice. Alternative choices are Single, Free, Both, and Neutral. Although you almost never need to change this option, it's important to know what they all mean.

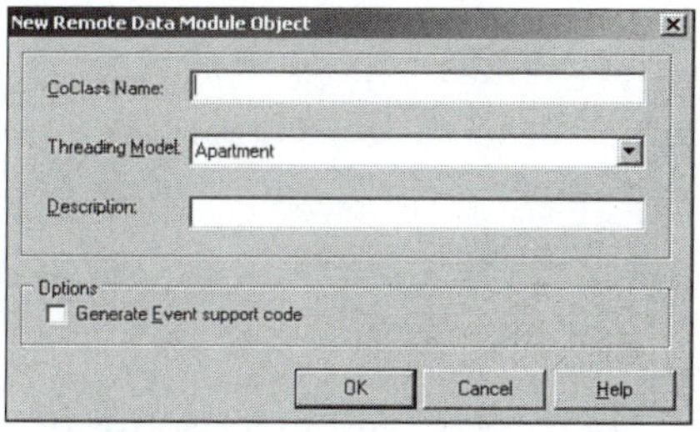

FIGURE 20.3   The New Remote Data Module Object dialog.

The Single threading model setting supports only one client request at a time. If more than one client wants to make a request, they must all wait in line. Only one client request is executed and in a single thread. This avoids all possible multithreading issues, but it can kill your performance (unless you never expect more than one client to make a request at the same time).

The Apartment threading model setting assumes that more than one client can make a request at roughly the same time, meaning that more than one request might need to be handled simultaneously. Using the Apartment threading model means that each instance of the remote data module handles one client request at a time. To handle more client requests, a separate thread is created for each request. As a consequence, each request runs in its own separate little apartment (hence the name) and, although instance data is safe, you must be aware of threading issues with global variables. This model can be used with regular BDE datasets, in which you need a TSession component with AutoSessionName set to true to make sure each thread (that is, each request) gets its own unique BDE session.

The Free threading model means that each thread can handle more than one client request at the same time. This approach gets harder because you must guard against not only global variable threading issues, but also against instance data. This threading model can be selected when you're using ADO datasets.

The Both threading model is a variation on the Free threading model, with serialized callbacks to client interfaces. This will not be covered in this chapter.

The final model is the Neutral threading model. This is a new model that's available only under COM+ (in Windows 2000 or XP) and will otherwise map to the Apartment threading model. On Windows 2000 and later, Neutral means that callbacks will always be serialized.

See the "Choosing a Threading Model" section of Chapter 17, "COM Programming," of this book for more information about the different threading models and their consequences.

After the Threading Model option, you can enter a description. What you enter here will end up in the Registry for the `ProgID` of the application server interface. It is also the help string for the interface in the type library. You can enter anything you want, but I've entered `C++Builder 6 Developer's Guide Simple DataSnap Server`, as you can see in Figure 20.4.

Finally, you might want to let the wizard generate a separate interface for managing events with the Generate Event Support Code option. Managing events in automation objects is not a topic of this chapter, so leave this option unchecked.

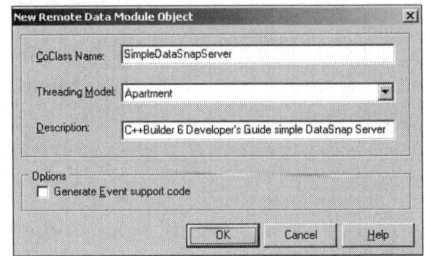

FIGURE 20.4   Completed New Remote Data Module Object dialog.

After you've completed all options inside the New Remote Data Module Object dialog (see Figure 20.4 for my options), press OK to generate the remote data module. The result is a remote data module that looks very much like a regular data module. Visually, there's no difference, and you can treat it like a regular data module by dropping a `TSession` component (from the BDE tab) on it and setting the `AutoSessionName` property of the `TSession` component to `true`. (Remember that you need to do this when using BDE and the Apartment threading model, as discussed earlier.)

After you have a `TSession` component, you can add other components from the Data Access tab of the Component Palette. For example, you can drop a `TTable` component and set its `Name` to `tblCustomer`. Set its `DatabaseName` property to `BCDEMOS` and open the drop-down combo box for the `TableName` property to select the `customer.db` table.

Now it's time to work on the so-called remote aspects of this data module. Go to the Data Access tab of the Component Palette. Here you'll find a `TDataSetProvider` component. This component is the key to exporting datasets from a remote data module to the outside world (more specifically to DataSnap client applications). Drop the `TDataSetProvider` component on the remote data module, set its `Name` to `dspCustomer`, and assign its `DataSet` property to `tblCustomer`. This means that the `TDataSetProvider` will provide or export `tblCustomer` to a DataSnap client application that connects to it (one that you will build in the following section). The `RemoteDataModule` of `SimpleDataSnapServer` should now look similar to Figure 20.5.

NOTE

Later in this chapter, we'll examine the `TDataSetProvider` component in more detail. For now, the most important property is the `Exported` property, which is set to `true` to indicate that `tblCustomer` is exported (by default). You can set this property to `false` to hide the fact that `tblCustomer` is exported from the remote data module, so clients cannot connect to it. This can be useful for example in a 24×7–running middleware data base server where you need to make a backup of certain tables and must ensure that nobody is working on them during the backup. With the `Exported` property set to `false`, no one can make a connection to them (until you set it to `true` again, of course).

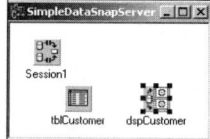

FIGURE 20.5 The `SimpleDataSnapServer` remote data module.

Basically, this is all it takes to create a simple DataSnap server. The only thing that's left for you is to save the project (for example using a Save All). I've put the main form in file `SimpleDataSnapServerMainForm.cpp`, the remote data module will be placed in file `SimpleDataSnapServerImpl.cpp`, and I've put the project itself in `SimpleData SnapServer.bpr`. You can save the type library in SimpleDataSnapServer.tlb. After the project is saved, you need to compile and run it. Running the DataSnap server—which shows only the main form, of course—will register it (inside the Windows Registry), so any DataSnap client can find and connect to it. If you ever want to move the DataSnap server to another directory (on the same machine), you only need to move it and immediately run it again, so it re-registers itself for that new location. This is a very convenient way of managing DataSnap server applications.

Later in this chapter, we'll see how to deploy a DataSnap server on another machine (in case you're wondering at this time).

DataSnap Server Registration

Let's examine this DataSnap server application registration process in a little more detail. Open the header file for the source unit `SimpleDataSnapServerImpl`. Inside `SimpleDataSnapServerImpl.h`, you'll see a function definition for `UpdateRegistry()`, which is repeated in Listing 20.1 for your convenience.

LISTING 20.1 Function `UpdateRegistry`

```
// Function invoked to (un)register object
//
static HRESULT WINAPI UpdateRegistry(BOOL bRegister)
```

LISTING 20.1   Continued

```
{
  TRemoteDataModuleRegistrar regObj(GetObjectCLSID(), GetProgID(),
        GetDescription());
  // Disable these flags in order to disable use by socket or Web connections.
  // Also set other flags to configure the behavior of your application server.
  // For more information, see atlmod.h and atlvcl.cpp.
  regObj.Singleton = false;
  regObj.EnableWeb = true;
  regObj.EnableSocket = true;
  return regObj.UpdateRegistry(bRegister);
}
```

The UpdateRegistry() function ensures that the DataSnap remote data module is registered (or unregistered) automatically when you want to use the middleware application server as an automation server. Note that the UpdateRegistry() method enables both socket and Web connections (using HTTP). If for some reason you want to disable one of these protocols, you simply have to assign false to the EnableWeb or EnableSocket field of the regObj variable.

Borland's C++Builder documentation even treats this as a security feature: If your DataSnap server is not registered to support the socket or Web connection, it won't be visible to a socket or Web connection component at all. C++Builder 4 MIDAS 2 servers never had any of this and, as a result, you could basically run any automation object on the server using the socket connection component. To prevent that, the C++Builder Socket (and Web) connection components will now show only DataSnap servers that are registered properly.

So far, you haven't written a single line of C++ code for the simple DataSnap server. Let's see what it takes to write a DataSnap client to connect to the simple DataSnap Server.

Creating a DataSnap Client

There are a number of different DataSnap clients that you can develop. These include regular Windows (GUI) applications, ActiveForms, and even Web server applications (using Web Broker or InternetExpress). In fact, just about everything can act as a DataSnap client, as you'll see in a moment. For now, you'll create a simple regular Windows application that will act as the first simple DataSnap client to connect to the simple DataSnap server of the previous section. At this stage, you should not be trying to run the client and the server on separate machines. Instead, get everything up and running on one machine, and then later you can distribute the application on the network.

Select File, New—Application to start a new C++Builder application.

NOTE

At this time, you might decide to add a data module to it (using File, New—Other, and selecting a data module from the New tab of the Object Repository). To avoid unnecessary screenshots in this book, I skip the data module and use the main form to drop my nonvisual (DataSnap) components as well as my normal visual components in one place.

Before anything else, your DataSnap client must make a connection with the DataSnap server application. This connection can be made using a number of different protocols, such as (D)COM, TCP/IP (sockets), HTTP, and SOAP. The components that implement these connection protocols are TDCOMConnection, TSocketConnection, TWebConnection, and TSOAPConnection, respectively, and will be covered in more detail in the next chapter. For the first SimpleDataSnapClient, you'll use the TDCOMConnection component, so drop one from the DataSnap tab onto the main form of your DataSnap client.

The TDCOMConnection component has a property called ServerName, which holds the name of the DataSnap server you want to connect to. In fact, if you open the drop-down combo box for the ServerName property in the Object Inspector, you'll see a list of all registered DataSnap servers on your local machine. In your case, this list might include only one item (SimpleDataSnapServer.SimpleDataSnapServer), but all DataSnap servers that are registered will end up in this list eventually. The names consist of two parts: The part before the dot denotes the application name, and the part after the dot denotes the remote data module name. In the current case, select the SimpleDataSnapServer remote data module of the SimpleDataSnapServer application. After you've selected this ServerName, you'll notice that the ServerGUID property of the TDCOMConnection component also gets a value, as found in the Registry. Developers with a good memory are free to type the ServerGUID property here to automatically get the corresponding ServerName name.

The fun really starts when you double-click the Connected property of the TDCOMConnection component, which will toggle this property value from false to true. To actually make the connection, the DataSnap server will be executed (automatically). This results in the automatic execution and opening of the main form of the SimpleDataSnapServer that you created in the previous section. See Figure 20.6 for the resulting SimpleDataSnapServer at runtime.

FIGURE 20.6　The SimpleDataSnapServer at runtime.

NOTE

It might appear now that there are two ways to close the DataSnap server—either by assigning `false` to the `Connected` property of the `TDCOMConnection` component or by simply closing down the `SimpleDataSnapServer` (by clicking the close button of its main form). The former will work, but the latter is not a good idea because a COM Server Warning will try to tell you (see Figure 20.7).

If you still decide to close the DataSnap server this way, the `TDCOMConnection` component on the DataSnap client main form will still think it's connected. In a real-world situation where a DataSnap server (or a connection to it) is terminated, the same thing will happen: The DataSnap client still thinks it has a connection, but in fact the connection is gone. In the "Implementing Error Handling" section of this chapter, we'll cover the error checking that you must include to be able to survive such circumstances without too many problems.

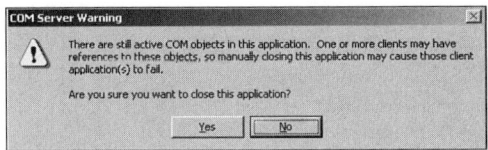

FIGURE 20.7   COM Server Warning when closing `SimpleDataSnapServer` the wrong way.

Double-click the `Connected` property of the `TDCOMConnection` component again to close down the DataSnap server. Now that you've seen you can connect to it, it's time to import some of the datasets that are exported by the remote data module, or rather by the `TDataSetProvider` component on the remote data module. Drop a `TClientDataSet` component on the main form, and connect its `RemoteServer` property to the `TDCOMConnection` component. The `TClientDataSet` component will obtain its data from the DataSnap server. You now need to specify which provider to use—in other words, from which `TDataSetProvider` you want to import the dataset into the `TClientDataSet` component. This can be done with the `ProviderName` property of the `TClientDataSet` component. Just open the drop-down combo box and you'll see a list of all available provider names; those that have their `Exported` property set to `true`. In this case, there is only one—the only `TDataSetProvider` component that you used on the `SimpleDataSnapServer` in the previous section—so select that one (dspCustomer).

NOTE

Before you picked a value for the `ProviderName` property, you closed down the `SimpleDataSnapServer`. However, when you opened up the drop-down combo box to list all available `TDataSetProvider` components on the remote data module that currently have their `Exported` property set to `true`, there is only one way (for C++Builder and the Object Inspector) to know exactly which of these providers are available—by asking the `SimpleDataSnapServer` (more specifically, by actively looking at the remote data module and finding out which of the available TDataSetProvider components have their Exported property set to true. And because the SimpleDataSnapServer was down, it has to be started again to present this list to you in the Object Inspector. As a result, the moment you drop-down the combo box of the ProviderName property, the SimpleDataSnapServer will be started again.

After you've selected the RemoteServer and ProviderName, it's time to open (or activate) the TClientDataSet. You can do this by setting the Active property of the TClientDataSet component to true. At that time, the SimpleDataSnapServer is feeding data from the tblCustomer table via the TDataSetProvider component and a (D)COM connection to the TDCOMConnection component, which routes it to the TClientDataSet component on your simple DataSnap client.

Now you can drop a TDataSource component and move to the Data Controls tab of the Component Palette and drop one or more data-aware controls. To keep the example simple, just drop a TDBGrid component. Connect the DataSet property of the TDataSource component to the TClientDataSet, and connect the DataSource property of the TDBGrid component to the TDataSource. Because the TClientDataSet component was just activated, you should immediately see live data at design time, provided by the SimpleDataSnapServer.

In Figure 20.8 you'll see the SimpleDataSnapClient main form so far. Note that I've enabled Component Captions, an option found in the Preferences tab of the Tools, Environment Options dialog.

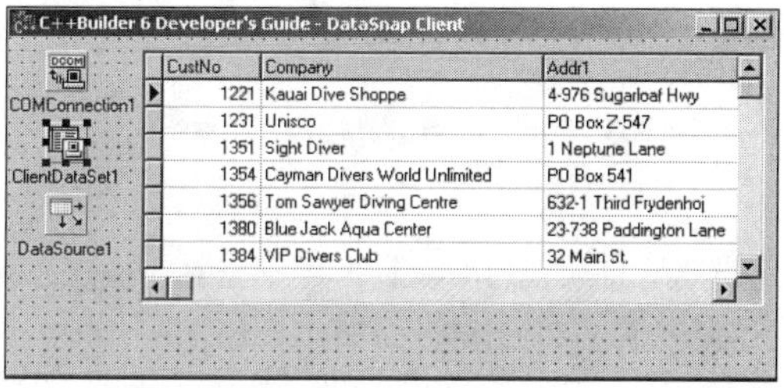

FIGURE 20.8 SimpleDataSnapClient at design time.

Now save your work. Put the main form in the ClientMainForm.cpp file and call the project SimpleDataSnapClient. Now you're ready to compile and run the DataSnap client. Again, you haven't written a single line of C++ code, but rest assured—that will change soon enough in the upcoming sections.

Using the Briefcase Model

When you run the SimpleDataSnapClient, you see the entire CustomerTable data inside the grid. You can browse through it, change field values, even enter new records or delete records. However, after you close the application, all changes are gone, and you're back at the original dataset inside the C++Builder IDE again. No matter how hard you try; the changes that you make to the visual data seem to affect the data inside the (local) TClientDataSet only, and not the (remote) actual tblCustomer.

What you experience here is actually a feature of the so-called *briefcase model*. Using this model, you can disconnect the client from the network and still access the data. To do so, save a remote dataset to disk, shut down your machine, and disconnect from the network. You can then boot up again and edit your (local) data without connecting to the network.

When you get back to the network, you can reconnect and update the database. A special mechanism notifies you of database errors and any conflicts that need to be resolved. For instance, if two people edited the same record, you will be notified and given options to resolve any problem.

You don't actually have to be able to reach the server at all times to be able to work with your data. This capability is ideal for laptop users, or for sites that want to keep database traffic to a minimum.

You've already experienced that (apparently) your SimpleDataSnapClient works on the local data inside your TClientDataSet component only. It appears you can even save the data to a local file and load it again. To save the current content of a TClientDataSet, you need to drop a TButton on the main form, set the Name property to btnSave, set Caption to Save, and write the following C++ code for the OnClick event handler:

```
void __fastcall TForm1::btnSaveClick(TObject *Sender)
{
  ClientDataSet1->SaveToFile("customer.cds",dfBinary);
}
```

This saves all records from the TClientDataSet in a file called customer.cds in the current directory. cds stands for ClientDataSet, but you can use your own file and extension names, of course. Note the dfBinary flag that is passed as the second argument to the SaveToFile method of TClientDataSet. This value indicates that I want to save the data in binary—Inprise/Borland propriety—format. Alternately, I could specify to save the data in XML format, passing the dfXML value. An XML file will be much larger (14,108 versus 7,493 bytes for the entire tblCustomer data), but it has the advantage that it can be used by other applications as well. You won't be doing so in this chapter, so I'll stick to the smaller (and more efficient) binary format.

Similarly, to implement the functionality that you can load the customer.cds file again into your TClientDataSet component, you need to drop another TButton component, set its Name property to btnLoad, set Caption to Load, and write the following C++ code for the OnClick event handler:

```
void __fastcall TForm1::btnLoadClick(TObject *Sender)
{
  ClientDataSet1->LoadFromFile("customer.cds");
}
```

Note that the LoadFromFile method of the TClientDataSet component does not need a second argument; it's obviously smart enough to determine whether it's reading a binary or an XML file. And, although the binary file can probably be generated only by another TClientDataSet component, the XML file could actually have been produced by a different application.

Armed with these two buttons, you can now (locally) save the changes to your data and even reload those changes—even if you stop and start the simple DataSnap client application again.

To control whether the TClientDataSet component is connected to the DataSnap server live, you can drop a third TButton component on the form that toggles the Active property of the TClientDataSet component. Set the Name property of this TButton to btnConnect and give the Caption property the value Connect. Now, write the following code for the OnClick event handler, as can be seen in Listing 20.2.

LISTING 20.2   btnConnect OnClick Event Handler

```
void __fastcall TForm1::btnConnectClick(TObject *Sender)
{
  if (ClientDataSet1->Active) // close and disconnect
  {
    ClientDataSet1->Close();
    DCOMConnection1->Close();
  }
  else // open (will automatically connect)
  {
//  DCOMConnection1->Open();
    ClientDataSet1->Open();
  }
}
```

NOTE

Note that to close the connection, you actually have to close the TClientDataSet component and close the TDCOMConnection as well. To open the connection, you need only to open the TClientDataSet component, which will implicitly open the TDCOMConnection as well.

Finally, there's one more thing you really need to do: make sure the TDCOMConnection and TClientDataSet components are *not* connected to the SimpleDataSnapServer at design time. Otherwise, whenever you open your SimpleDataSnapClient project in the C++Builder IDE again, it will need to make a connection to the SimpleDataSnapServer—loading that DataSnap server. And when—for one reason or another—SimpleDataSnapServer is not found on your machine, you will have a hard time loading the SimpleDataSnapClient project. So, I always make sure they are not connected at design time. To do so, you have to assign false to the Connected property of the TDCOMConnection component (which will unload the main form of the SimpleDataSnapServer) and false to the Active property of the TClientDataSet component (which means you won't see any data at design time anymore).

> **NOTE**
>
> If you try to talk to a DCOM server, but can't reach it, the system will not immediately give up the search. Instead, it can keep trying for a set period of time that rarely exceeds two minutes. During those two minutes, however, the application will be busy and will appear to be locked up. If the application is loaded into the IDE, all C++Builder will appear to be locked up. You can have this problem when you do nothing more than attempt to set the Connected property of the TDCOMConnection component to true.
>
> Note that there is no solution to this problem. This is simply a warning *not* to leave the Connected property of a TDOMConnection set to true because it can cause your IDE (and machine) to appear hung when you next open the project.

Now, when you recompile and run your SimpleDataSnapClient, it will show up with no data inside the TDBGrid component (see Figure 20.9). This is the time to click the Connect button to connect to the SimpleDataSnapServer and obtain all records (from the database server). However, there are times (for example, when you are on the road or not connected to the machine that runs the SimpleDataSnapServer), when you cannot connect to the SimpleDataSnapServer. In those cases, you can click the Load button instead and work on the local copy of the records. Note that this local copy is the one that you last saved, and it is updated only when you click the Save button to write the entire contents of the TClientDataSet component to disk.

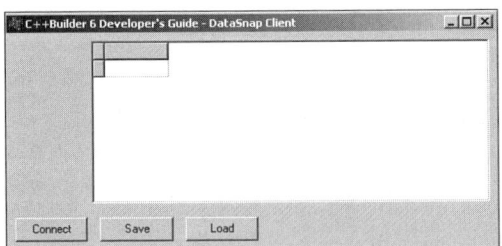

FIGURE 20.9   SimpleDataSnapClient at runtime (without SimpleDataSnapServer running).

At this time you might want to write some additional code that disables the Save button until some data is present inside the `TClientDataSet` component. Otherwise, clicking the Save button has no effect (including not removing or overwriting the current `customer.cds` file—if you have one).

Another useful enhancement consists of changing the `Caption` property of the `btnConnect` buttton from Connect to Disconnect (and back) when connecting. This can be done with the code as shown in Listing 20.3.

LISTING 20.3   `btnConnect OnClick` Event Handler

```
void __fastcall TForm1::btnConnectClick(TObject *Sender)
{
  if (ClientDataSet1->Active) // close and disconnect
  {
    ClientDataSet1->Close();
    DCOMConnection1->Close();
    dynamic_cast<TButton*>(Sender)->Caption = "Connect";
  }
  else // open (will automatically connect)
  {
//  DCOMConnection1->Open();
    ClientDataSet1->Open();
    dynamic_cast<TButton*>(Sender)->Caption = "Disconnect";
  }
}
```

Using `ApplyUpdates`

It's nice to be able to connect or load a local dataset and save it to disk again. But how do you ever apply your updates to the actual (remote) database again? This can be done using the `ApplyUpdates` method of the `TClientDataSet` component.

Drop a fourth button on the `SimpleDataSnapClient` main form, set its `Name` property to `btnApplyUpdates` and the `Caption` property to `Apply Updates`. The `OnClick` event handler of the Apply button should get the following code:

```
void __fastcall TForm1::btnApplyUpdatesClick(TObject *Sender)
{
  ClientDataSet1->ApplyUpdates(0);
}
```

The `ApplyUpdates` method of the `TClientDataSet` component has one argument: the maximum number of errors that it will allow before it stops applying updates. With a single `SimpleDataSnapClient` connected to the `SimpleDataSnapServer`, you will never encounter any problems, so feel free to run your `SimpleDataSnapClient` now. Click the Connect button to connect to (and load) the `SimpleDataSnapServer`, and use the Save and Load buttons to store and read the contents of the `TClientDataSet` component to and from disk. You can even remove your machine from the network and work on your local data for a significant amount of time, which is exactly the idea behind the briefcase model (your laptop being the briefcase). Any changes you make to your local copy will remain visible, and you can apply the changes to the remote database with a click of the Apply Updates button—when you've reconnected to the network with the `SimpleDataSnapServer`.

Implementing Error Handling

What if two clients, both using the briefcase model, connect to the `SimpleDataSnapServer`, obtain the entire `tblCustomer`, and make changes to the first record? According to what you've built so far, both clients could then send the updated record back to the DataSnap server using the `ApplyUpdates` method of the `TClientDataSet` component. If both pass zero as value for the `MaxErrors` argument of `ApplyUpdates`, the second one to attempt the update will be stopped. The second client could pass a numerical value bigger than zero to indicate a fixed number of errors or conflicts allowed before the update is stopped. However, even if the second client passed `-1` as its argument (to indicate that it should continue updating no matter how many errors occur), it will never update the records that have been changed by the previous client. You need reconcile actions to handle updates on already-updated records and fields.

Fortunately, C++Builder contains a very useful dialog especially written for this purpose. Whenever you need to do error reconciliation, you should consider adding this dialog to your DataSnap client application (or write one yourself, but at least do something about it). To use the one available in C++Builder, just select File, New—Other, go to the Dialogs tab of the Object Repository and select the Reconcile Error Dialog icon, which can be seen in Figure 20.10.

After you select this icon and click OK, a new unit is added to your `SimpleDataSnapClient` project. This unit contains the definition and implementation of the Update Error dialog that can be used to resolve database update errors (see Figure 20.11).

After this unit is added to your `SimpleDataSnapProject`, there is something very important you have to check. First save your work (put the new unit in file `ErrorDialog.cpp`).

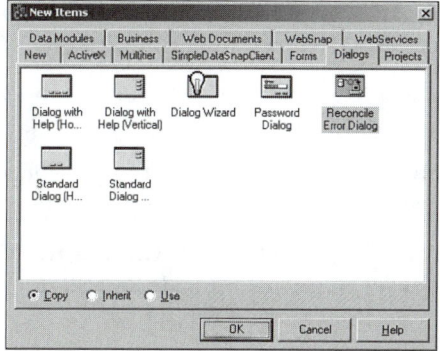

FIGURE 20.10   The Reconcile Error Dialog icon inside the Object Repository.

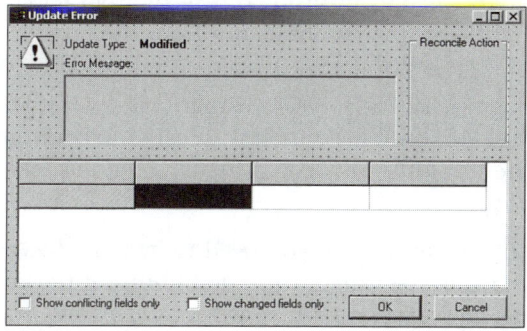

FIGURE 20.11   Update (Reconcile) Error dialog at design time.

When or how do you use this special ReconcileErrorForm? It's actually very simple. For every record for which the update did not succeed (for whatever reason), the OnReconcileError event handler of the TClientDataSet component is called. This event handler of TClientDataSet is defined as follows:

```
void __fastcall TForm1::ClientDataSet1ReconcileError(
    TClientDataSet *DataSet, EReconcileError *E, TUpdateKind UpdateKind,
    TReconcileAction &Action)
{

}
```

This event handler has four arguments: the TClientDataSet component that raised the error, a specific ReconcileError that contains a message about the cause of the error condition, the UpdateKind that generated the error (insert, delete, or modify), and the Action that should be taken. Action can return the following enum values (the order is based on their actual enum values):

- raSkip—Do not update this record, but leave the unapplied changes in the change log. Be ready to try again next time.

- raAbort—Abort the entire reconcile handling; no more records will be passed to the OnReconcileError event handler.

- raMerge—Merge the updated record with the current record in the (remote) database, only changing (remote) field values if they changed on your side.

- raCorrect—Replace the updated record with a corrected value of the record that you made in the event handler (or inside ReconcileErrorDialog). This is the option in which user intervention is required.

- raCancel—Undo all changes inside this record, turning it back into the original (local) record.

- raRefresh—Undo all changes inside this record, but reload the record values from the current (remote) database, not from the original local record you had.

The good thing about ReconcileErrorForm is that you don't really need to concern yourself with all this. You only need to pass the arguments from the OnReconcileError event handler in the TClientDataSet component to the HandleReconcileError function from the ErrorDialog.

This can be done in two steps. First, you need to include the ErrorDialog unit header inside the SimpleDataSnapClient main form definition (or the data module, if you decided to use one). Click the ClientMainForm and select File, Include Unit Hdr... to get the Use Unit dialog (see Figure 20.12).

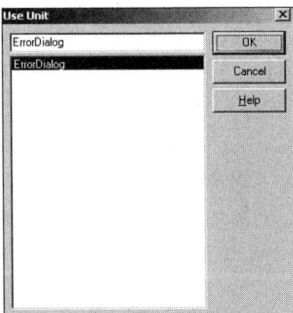

FIGURE 20.12   Add the ErrorDialog unit header to the ClientMainForm unit.

With the ClientMainForm as your current unit, the Use Unit dialog will list the only other available unit, which is the ErrorDialog. Just select it and click OK.

The second thing you need to do is to write one line of code in the OnReconcileError event handler of the TClientDataSet component to call the HandleReconcileError() function from the ErrorDialog unit (that you just added to your ClientMainForm import list). The HandleReconcileError() function has the same four arguments as the OnReconcileError event handler (not a real coincidence, of course), so it's a matter of passing arguments from one to another—nothing more, nothing less. The OnReconcileError event handler of the TClientDataSet component can be coded similar to Listing 20.4.

LISTING 20.4   Completed OnReconcileError Event Handler

```
void __fastcall TForm1::ClientDataSet1ReconcileError(
    TClientDataSet *DataSet, EReconcileError *E, TUpdateKind UpdateKind,
    TReconcileAction &Action)
{
  Action = HandleReconcileError(this, DataSet, UpdateKind, E);
}
```

Demonstrating Reconcile Errors

How does all this work in practice? To test it, you obviously need two (or more) SimpleDataSnapClient applications running simultaneously. For a complete test using the current SimpleDataSnapClient and SimpleDataSnapServer applications, you need to perform the following steps:

1. Start the first SimpleDataSnapClient and click the Connect button (the SimpleDataSnapServer will now be loaded as well).

2. Start the second SimpleDataSnapClient and click the Connect button. Data will be obtained from the SimpleDataSnapServer that's already running.

3. Using the first SimpleDataSnapClient, change the Company field for the first record (for example, change it to "Bob Swart Training Consultancy").

4. Using the second SimpleDataSnapClient, also change the Company field for the first record (make sure you don't change it to the same value as in the previous step—for example, change it to eBob42).

5. Click the Apply Updates button of the first SimpleDataSnapClient. All updates will be applied without any problems.

6. Click the Apply Updates button of the second SimpleDataSnapClient. This time, one or more errors will occur because the first record had its Company field value changed (by the first SimpleDataSnapClient). The OnReconcileError event handler is called.

7. Inside the Update Error dialog (see Figure 20.13), you can now experiment with the Reconcile Actions (Abort, Skip, Cancel, Correct, Refresh, and Merge) to get a feel for what they do. Pay special attention to the differences between Skip and Cancel and those between Correct, Refresh, and Merge.

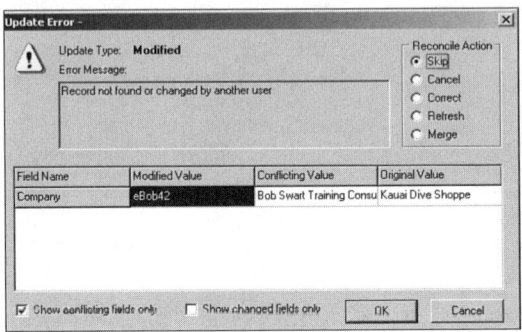

FIGURE 20.13   The Reconcile Error dialog in action.

Skip moves on to the next record, skipping the requested update (for the time being). The unapplied change will remain in the change log. Cancel also skips the requested update, but it cancels all further updates (in the same update packet). The current update request is skipped in both cases, but Skip continues with other update requests, and Cancel cancels the entire ApplyUpdate request.

Refresh just forgets all updates you made to the record and refreshes the record with the current value from the server database. Merge tries to merge the update record with the record on the server, placing your changes inside the server record. Refresh and Merge will not process the change request any further, so the records are synchronized after Refresh and Merge (whereas the change request can still be redone after a Skip or Cancel).

Correct, the most powerful option actually gives you the option of customizing the update record *inside* the event handler. For this you need to write some code or enter the values in the dialog yourself.

Creating a DataSnap Master-Detail Server

Time to start a second, more complex example of a DataSnap server. Because we are using different filenames, you can put it in the same directory as the SimpleDataSnapServer. However, feel free to put each DataSnap Server and Client in its own directory (which is easier to maintain if these applications grow in size and complexity). I've listed the steps you need to perform, to make it a bit easier.

- First, start a new project using File, New—Application. Save the main form in DataSnapServerMainForm.cpp and the project in DataSnapServer.bpr.

- Like the first SimpleDataSnapServer example, make sure the main form can be identified as your (second) DataSnap server application (see Figure 20.14). This means just adding a label, an image, or anything that will help identify this main form, so you'll know immediately when it (and hence your second DataSnap server) is running.

FIGURE 20.14 Master-detail DataSnap server main form.

- Next, start the Remote Data Module Wizard from the Multitier tab of the Object Repository, as you've done before. This time, specify CustomerOrders as CoClass Name, and use the default values for all other options. This will result in a middleware database server with the name DataSnapServer.CustomerOrders, as you'll see when you start to build the DataSnapClient for this server.

- After you have a new remote data module, drop two TTable components. Set the Name property of one to tblCustomer and the other to tblOrders.

- For each of these TTable components, set the DatabaseName property to BCDEMOS.

- Click tblCustomer and select customer.db as the value for the TableName property. Click tblOrders and select orders.db as the value for the TableName property.

You're now ready to define the master-detail relationship between tblCustomer and tblOrders.

- Drop a TDataSource component on the remote data module. Set its Name to dsCustomer, and its DataSet property to tblCustomers. Select the tblOrders, and set its MasterSource property to the DataSource.

- Click the elipsis for the MasterFields property of tblOrders. This will show the Field Link Designer. Select CustNo as Available Index, and select CustNo as both the Detail Field and the Master Field. Next, click the Add button to add the Joined Fields (as shown in Figure 20.15).

- If you click OK again, the Field Link Designer will close and the master-detail relationship between tblCustomer and tblOrders has been created.

Now that you have created the master-detail relationship, it's time to export the tables to the outside world.

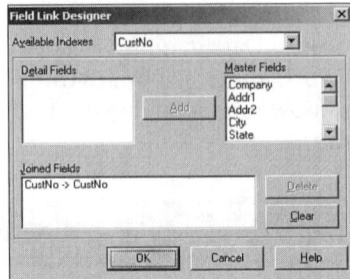

FIGURE 20.15   The Field Link Designer for tblCustomer and tblOrders.

Exporting Master-Detail DataSets

In the SimpleDataSnapServer example, you used a single TDataSetProvider component to export tblCustomer from the remote data module. This time, you might feel the urge to use two TDataSetProvider components: one to export tblCustomer and one to export tblOrders from the remote data module. That would export the two tables all right, but not their master-detail relationship. In fact, you would have to redefine the master-detail relationship at the client side again. This might work for a normal application (defining the master-detail relationship at the client side). However, for a multitier application in which a database server provides the data for the tables, this situation has at least two real problems.

First of all, the detail TClientDataSet component on the DataSnapClient will have to fetch and store all detail records from the database server, even if only a few of the detail records are actually needed at the client side (after the master-detail relationship has been established). A potentially large number of records are sent over for nothing, wasting precious bandwidth. Of course, this problem can be overcome by using parameters, sent from the client to the server, but this involves more work and could introduce bugs that are hard to trace.

The second problem in defining the master-detail relationship on the client side has to do with the fact that it's more difficult to apply updates using two separate client datasets. This is caused by the fact that the TClientData component doesn't apply updates for multiple tables in a single transaction, but on a dataset-by-dataset basis (that is, you must make a separate call to ApplyUpdates for each table).

As a result, you should try not to export master-detail datasets as separate entities. Fortunately, TDataSetProvider is able to export two (or more) tables having a master-detail relationship as a single entity—provided you connect the TDataSetProvider component to the master TTable, being the tblCustomer of your DataSnap server. The trick is that the master table will automatically include a DataSetField for the detail records, and only for those detail records that are relevant to the current master record, sending only those records over the wire that are needed.

- You need only to drop a single TDataSetProvider component (which can be found on the Data Access tab) on the remote data module, set its Name to dspCustomerOrders, and connect its DataSet property to tblCustomer. This will export both tblCustomer and tblOrders (as a nested field) from the remote data module.

- Save your work again (the assigned name is CustomerOrdersImpl.cpp). The Remote Data Module should resemble the one of Figure 20.16.

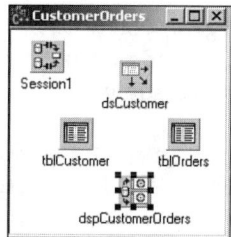

FIGURE 20.16   The Remote Data Module with tblCustomer and tblOrders.

Note again that you didn't have to write a single line of C++ code for the DataSnap server application. Compile the DataSnapServer project and run it to register it on your machine. Now it's time to start working on the DataSnap client application that retrieves this master-detail data.

Creating a DataSnap Master-Detail Client

The new DataSnap server needs a new DataSnap client as well. Start another new application (using File, New—Application). Save the main form as MainForm.cpp and save the project as DataSnapClient.bpr. Drop a TDCOMConnection component (from the DataSnap tab) on the main form. After you open up the drop-down combo box for the ServerName property of the TDCOMConnection component, you should see both SimpleDataSnapServer.SimpleDataSnapServer (the first example) and DataSnapServer.CustomerOrders (the second example). Obviously, you want to select the DataSnapServer.CustomerOrders as the value for the ServerName property. You can set the Connected property of the TDCOMConnection component to true to test if the DataSnapServer actually gets loaded correctly.

Now, drop a TClientDataSet component (which can be found on the Data Access tab) to retrieve the data via the TDCOMConnection component from the remote data module. Connect the RemoteServer property of the TClientDataSet component to the TDCOMConnection component, which is named DCOMConnection1 by default. Next, you need to select the right provider that's exported from the remote data module. In this case, there is still only one provider (you exported only the tblCustomer using dspCustomerOrders), so select the only choice you have as the value for the ProviderName property of the TClientDataSet component, which should be dspCustomerOrders.

Now, drop a TDataSource component under the TClientDataSet component (so you know that they'll belong together). Connect the DataSet property of the TDataSource component to the TClientDataSet component. Move over to the Data Controls tab of the Component Palette to drop a TDBGrid component on the form. Connect the DataSource property of the TDBGrid component to the TDataSource component.

To see live data at design time again, you only have to set the Active property of the TClientDataSet component to true and presto! See Figure 20.17 for remote customer data in the C++Builder IDE at design time.

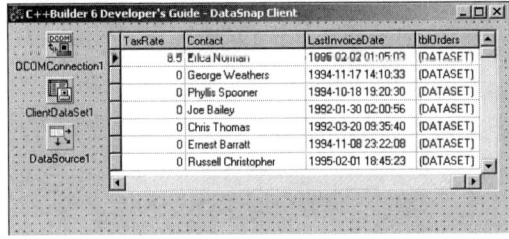

FIGURE 20.17   The DataSnap client main form showing customer data at design time.

Using Nested Tables

You might have noticed (from Figure 20.17 for example) that the TDBGrid appears to show data only from TableCustomers. If you scroll all the way to the right of the TDBGrid component, you'll notice one last field called tblOrders. The TDBGrid component apparently cannot show the actual contents of this field because it only displays (DATASET). Actually, that particular last field named tblOrders is a TDataSetField.

It gets even better when you run the DataSnapClient application and click the tblOrders field inside the DBGrid. This will show an ellipsis, and when you click that ellipsis (or double-click the DATASET field itself), a new pop-up window will appear (see Figure 20.18), showing the detail records belonging to the master record that you just clicked.

I have to admit that—at first—it looks nice to have a new pop-up window show the detail records of the particular master record (that you used to double-click the DATASET column). However, after a few minutes the excitement disappears, and I wonder about my clients. Would they like this interface? Wouldn't it be better to display the detail records in another TDBGrid component right under the first one? Your taste may differ, but at least it's possible, like almost anything in C++Builder.

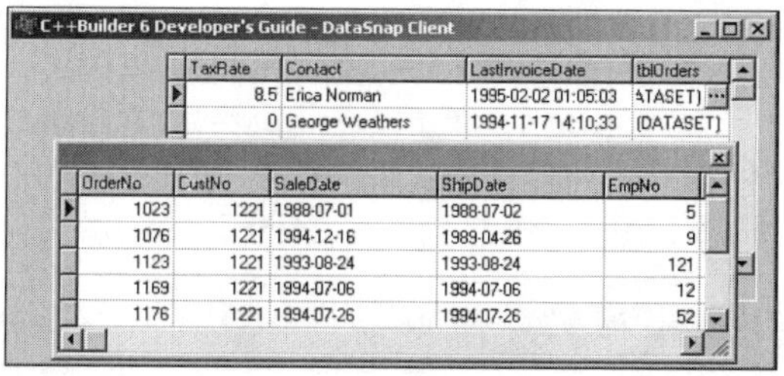

FIGURE 20.18   DataSnap client showing customer data and client detail.

Close the DataSnapClient application if it's still running and return to the
C++Builder IDE. Drop another TClientDataSet component on the main form (which
will be called ClientDataSet2 by default). This time, you need to look at the
DataSetField property of ClientDataSet2; the second TClientDataSet component.
Somehow, you have to connect this property with the persistent tblOrders field of
type TDataSetField. The only problem—which becomes apparent after you drop
down the list of available DataSetFields—is that there are no persistent fields, yet.

To use the nested dataset (the detail records), you must create a persistent DataSet
field for the nested data. This sounds more difficult than it is because the easy way is
just to double-click the first TClientDataSet component (ClientDataSet1) to start the
Fields Editor (at design time), right-click in the Fields Editor, and select Add All
Fields. This will create persistent fields for every field, including a DataSetField for
the nested detail table tblOrders, as can be seen in Figure 20.19.

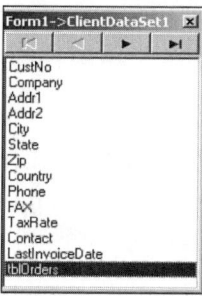

FIGURE 20.19   The Fields Editor showing tblCustomer fields.

After tblOrders has been turned into a persistent field, you can drop down the
combo box for the DataSetField property of the second TClientDataSet component.
The combo box will show the ClientDataSet1.tblOrders as the only possible dataset
field to select, so pick it. Note that this ClientDataSet is not connected directly to a
remote server, but indirectly because it gets its data from the nested dataset that the
first TClientDataSet component received from the remote data server.

You can now drop a second TDataSource component (from the Data Access tab) and a second TDBGrid component (from the Data Controls tab). Connect the second TDataSource (DataSource2) to the second TClientDataSet (ClientDataSet2), and the second TDBGrid (DBGrid) to this second TDataSource (DataSource2). This will show live detail data at design time (see Figure 20.20).

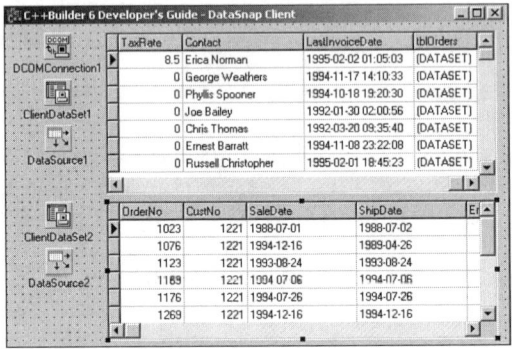

FIGURE 20.20   The DataSnap client main form showing customer and orders data at design time.

This is a good solution for both displaying and updating master-detail relationships. Sometimes displaying the detail in a pop-up window might be what you need, and sometimes my solution using a second TClientDataSet component is more suited.

The problem of updating the master-detail relationship is solved by the fact that you now have only one call to ApplyUpdates to make (from the first TClientDataSet component—the one directly connected to the remote server). This automatically updates the entire nested table.

Understanding DataSnap Bandwidth Bottlenecks

Although even the SimpleDataSnapServer example has some potential (bandwidth) bottlenecks, they will become more noticeable when looking at the master-detail DataSnapServer and DataSnapClient pair.

When a TClientDataSet is set to Active, it makes a request to the TDataSetProvider component on the remote data module to send data over the wire. How much data depends on both the size of the individual records and, of course, the number of records. The latter is determined by the value of the PacketRecords property of the TClientDataSet component. By default, this property is set to -1, meaning TClientDataSet just says "send me all available records."

This is hardly a problem for a relatively small BCDEMOS example using customers.db (only 55 records) and orders.db (only 205 records). But imagine a real-world customer's table. Surely it would hold more than 55 customers. Even a small table of customers could easily hold a thousand or more records. And what about the orders? A few thousand perhaps? At a hundred bytes or more for each table, that could lead to a few hundred kilobytes to send over the wire as soon as the DataSnapClient connects to the DataSnapServer (and requests all data to be sent). And that's in a small shop, not an airline reservation desk or an online bookstore. I'm sure you understand why this has the potential of being a serious performance bottleneck if not a show stopper, especially with multiple DataSnapClients all talking to the same DataSnapServer over the same wire.

Minimizing Bottlenecks Using `PacketRecords`

There are a few ways to minimize the impact of this bottleneck. First and most obvious is to change the `PacketRecords` property to a value other than -1. Depending on the number of records you want to display at the same time, you might want to set `PacketRecords` of the first `TClientDataSet` to 10 or so. This will ensure that only the first 10 records are transferred when the first connection is made. As soon as you start to browse through the `TDBGrid` component and reach for the 21st record, the `TClientDataSet` will perform another request to the `TDataSetProvider` component on the remote data module, to obtain the next set of 10 records. Thus, after two requests, the client shows 20 records inside the `TDBGrid`. This continues until all records have been moved from the remote data module to the `TClientDataSet` component inside the DataSnapClient application.

> **NOTE**
>
> You don't need to modify `PacketRecords` of the second detail `TClientDataSet`. The nested dataset is already at the client side, contained as `DataSetField` within the master record itself.

When you looked closely, you might have noted that the scrollbar thumb of the `TDBGrid` component seems to shrink in size. That's because the first time, the `TClientDataSet` obtained only 10 records, which are shown in the `TDBGrid` component—unlike 55 that are shown when all data is obtained (compare Figures 20.20 and 20.21).

So far so good, however, there are a few things you must be aware of when using this solution. If you run the new DataSnapClient, click the grid, and hit Ctrl+End, you expect to scroll down to the last record. And, sure enough, you do. The bad news is that to show you the last record (the 55th, in this case), the `TClientDataSet` has to make five new requests to the `TDataSetProvider` component on the remote data module. The first request gets records 11–20, and so on, until the fifth request gets records 51–55. In other words, to show you the last record, it has to retrieve all records. And again, in this 55-record scenario, that's not a big deal. But imagine thousands of records, where pressing Ctrl+End could lead to a sudden and significant delay in response time.

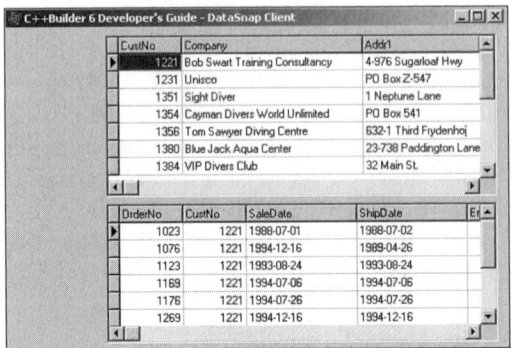

FIGURE 20.21   DataSnapClient showing the first 10 customers with orders in DBGrids.

Minimizing Bottlenecks Using Server Optimization

Apart from the PacketRecords property, which is a client-side optimization technique, it's often far more useful to look at the server side. Remember that the amount of data that is being sent over the wire is the result of multiplying the record size by the number of records. If you did your best by minimizing the number of records, then it's time to look at the record size. Of course, you cannot just hack the tables and try to shrink down the record size, but you *can* look at the available fields and make a well-planned decision about which fields are exported (provided) from the remote data module and which fields aren't. In all previous examples, you've simply exported the entire dataset using the TDataSetProvider component. In fact, with DataSnapServer you've even explicitly added all fields to both tblCustomer and tblOrders. All this information is sent from the DataSnapServer to the DataSnapClient. If you need all these fields, there's nothing you can do about it. However, more often than not, only some of the available fields are used at the client side. That means you send maybe 10 fields over the wire when you only need 3. Although you can specify at the client-side which fields you want to see (at both the TDBGrid and TClientDataSet levels), this doesn't matter anymore at that time because the fields have already been transferred. You need to make a conscious decision at the server side. It will make a difference, even with a table that contains a large number of records. If you pass only one or two fields (out of perhaps a dozen), you're sending only a fraction of the table.

Using the PacketRecords property of the TClientDataSet component for client-side optimizations and reducing the number of fields to include at the server side are just two bandwidth optimization techniques that have proven to be very effective in real-world applications. The remaining part of this chapter focuses on some of the specific DataSnap enhancements that are part of C++Builder 6. The first one is a big issue: the stateless nature of the DataSnap server!

Stateless DataSnap

One of the biggest changes in DataSnap (introduced with MIDAS 3) is that DataSnap applications now support stateless remote data modules (made possible by the DataSnap IAppServer interface). This means you can now share remote data modules without having to write your own custom interfaces (extending the MIDAS 2 IProvider interface) because no state information is maintained. It also means that each client will have to maintain its own state and send it to the server with every request for data. The DataSnap documentation even states that, although each call from the client to the server carries more (state) information, fewer calls are needed, so message traffic is in fact reduced.

To make this change clear, I've compared the events of the TClientDataSet component in C++Builder 4 (MIDAS 2) and C++Builder 6 (DataSnap). New events introduced for the TClientDataSet component in C++Builder 6 are AfterApplyUpdates, AfterExecute, AfterGetParams, AfterGetRecords, AfterPost, AfterRefresh, AfterRowRequest, and AfterScroll, and of course their counterparts BeforeApplyUpdates, BeforeExecute, BeforeGetParams, BeforeGetRecords, BeforePost, BeforeRefresh, BeforeRowRequest, and BeforeScroll. These eight sets of methods are used to send the necessary state information from the client to the server.

A similar list of differences can be seen on the server side, where I've compared the events for the TDataSetProvider component of C++Builder 4 (MIDAS 2) with C++Builder 6 (DataSnap). The new event handlers of TDataSetProvider are AfterApply Updates, AfterExecute, AfterGetParams, AfterGetRecords, and AfterRowRequest. Their counterparts are BeforeApplyUpdates, BeforeExecute, BeforeGetParams, BeforeGetRecords, and BeforeRowRequest. There is also a new OnGetTableName event handler.

The Before events of TDataSetProvider allow necessary state information to be obtained from the client (sent by a corresponding Before event of the TClientDataSet component). The After events of TDataSetProvider enable state information to be passed back to the client (received by the corresponding After events of the TClientDataSet).

Stateful Versus Stateless DataSnap Servers

As an example, let's take the case where we used a value of 10 for PacketRecords again. The use of PacketRecords can have a significant side effect: to allow the DataSnap server to send you the next set of records, it has to somehow remember the state of the client. And, because the client didn't tell the server anything (yet), this means that the DataSnap server is actually stateful. As we'll see in the next chapter, not all connection protocols can support a stateful connection. MTS, HTTP, and SOAP will not support this, and hence if you use a value of 10 for the PacketRecords, you will get the same (first) 10 records every time to request new data. Which might even lead to key violations (because the first 10 records are already present in the local ClientDataSet).

So, let's actually build a Stateless DataSnap Server and implement the way in which TClientDataSet and TDataSetProvider components communicate when asking for the next batch of records. First of all, set the FetchOnDemand property of ClientDataSet1 (the master TClientDataSet component) to false. This is very important; otherwise, you'll get a stack error later, as I'll explain in a moment.

With FetchOnDemand set to false, there will be no automatic mechanism to send (fetch) packets of records from the DataSnap server to the client, so we have to implement it ourselves. An example of a situation in which you want to implement (and control) the fetching of packets of records is when you want (or must) make sure the dataset on the server side is positioned correctly before sending the records over. In this section, we'll see exactly how to do that. This technique can also be important when you're working with stateless environments such as MTS, HTTP, or SOAP.

Now, to get the next batch of records from the TDataSetProvider component on a DataSnap server, the TClientDataSet component (with FetchOnDemand set to false) on the DataSnapClient application should use the BeforeGetRecords event to specify a certain record or position. This is set using the OwnerData parameter of this event handler (given a dataset with a single key field named CustNo, as in your examples), which can be seen in Listing 20.5.

LISTING 20.5   ClientDataSet OnBeforeGetRecords Event Handler

```
void __fastcall TForm1::ClientDataSet1BeforeGetRecords(TObject *Sender,
    OleVariant &OwnerData)
{
  TClientDataSet* Master = (TClientDataSet*) Sender;
  if (Master->Active)
  {
    void* Current = Master->GetBookmark();
    try
    {
      Master->Last();
      OwnerData = Master->FieldByName("CustNo")->AsString;
      Master->GotoBookmark(Current);
    }
    __finally
    {
      Master->FreeBookmark(Current);
    }
  }
}
```

The `Master->Last()` statement is the one that will generate a stack overflow if the `FetchOnDemand` property of the `TClientDataSet` component is set to true. In that case, moving to the last record will actually trigger the `TClientDataSet` component to fetch (on demand) all records, which will fire this `OnBeforeGetRecords` event handler again, and so on until you finally get a stack error.

Anyway, just before the `TDataSetProvider` component on the remote data module from the DataSnapServer sends the requested records, the `BeforeGetRecords` event handler is called, including the `OwnerData` value as you passed on the `ClientDataSet` side (see Listing 20.6).

LISTING 20.6   Server DataSetProvider OnBeforeGetRecords Event Handler

```
void __fastcall TCustomerOrders::dspCustomerOrdersBeforeGetRecords(
      TObject *Sender, OleVariant &OwnerData)
{
  TVariant Variant = OwnerData;
  if (!VarIsEmpty(Variant))
  {
    TLocateOptions LocateOptions;
    TDataSet* DataSet = ((TDataSetProvider*) Sender)->DataSet;
    if (DataSet->Locate("CustNo", Variant, LocateOptions))
      DataSet->Next();
  }
}
```

Now that both `BeforeGetRecords` event handlers have fired, it's time to actually send the records from the DataSnapServer remote data module to the DataSnapClient.

After the records are sent, the `TDataSetProvider` component is able to send some information back to the `TClientDataSet` (like the number of actual records in the entire dataset on the server side). This could be started using the `AfterGetRecords` event handler of the `TDataSetProvider` component as can be seen in Listing 20.7.

LISTING 20.7   Server DataSetProvider OnAftereGetRecords Event Handler

```
void __fastcall TCustomerOrders::dspCustomerOrdersAfterGetRecords(
      TObject *Sender, OleVariant &OwnerData)
{
  TDataSet* DataSet = ((TDataSetProvider*) Sender)->DataSet;
  if (DataSet->Active)
    OwnerData = IntToStr(DataSet->RecordCount);
  else
    OwnerData = AnsiString("n/a");
}
```

Note that you again pass an AnsiString value in the OwnerData parameter (which is of type OleVariant). Passing AnsiString values always seems to work for me, whereas a direct assignment of DataSet->RecordCount to OwnerData doesn't compile.

Now, the value of OwnerData as passed by the OnAfterGetRecords event handler of the TDataSetProvider component will be picked up at the client side by the OnAfterGetRecords event handler of the TClientDataSet component. Storing the value somewhere is a different matter, so I've just used a ShowMessage dialog to display the number of records at the server side, as you can see in Listing 20.8.

LISTING 20.8   ClientDataSet OnAftereGetRecords Event Handler

```
void __fastcall TForm1::ClientDataSet1AfterGetRecords(TObject *Sender,
    OleVariant &OwnerData)
{
  ShowMessage("Number of records at server: " + WideString(OwnerData));
}
```

Using the implementations of the OnBeforeGetRecords and OnAfterGetRecords event handlers for both the TClientDataSet (on the client) and the TDataSetProvider (on the server), you can compile the DataSnapServer and DataSnapClient projects and test them. This is your last chance to set the FetchOnDemand property of the TClientDataSet component to false to prevent a stack error, by the way (as I mentioned at the beginning of this section).

To test them, you need to run the DataSnapClient project, which will load the DataSnapServer when connecting to it. As soon as a connection to the DataSnapServer is made, the TClientDataSet makes its first request for data (calling the GetNextPacket method), which results in a call to the OnBeforeGetRecords() from the TClientDataSet, passing nothing because the Active property is still false at that time. So, the OnBeforeGetRecords method of the TDataSetProvider will be called, but with an empty OwnerData argument, which means no further actions are taken. Then, the first 10 (value of PacketRecords) records are sent by the TDataSetProvider component to the TClientDataSet component. After this, the OnAfterGetRecords event handler of the TDataSetProvider is called, in which it collects the number of records of its DataSet component (the tblCustomer, which has 55 records). The value 55 is passed in OwnerData and is received at the client side when the OnAfterGetRecords event handler of the TClientDataSet is called. This results in a message dialog, seen in Figure 20.22, that shows Number of records at DataSnap server: 55, just as expected.

FIGURE 20.22   Result of manually sending `OwnerData` between client and server.

The DataSnapClient will now show up with only the first 10 records inside the
`DBGrid`. When you browse through these records until number 10, and you want the
next one, you won't get it. Similarly, when you press Ctrl+End, no additional records
are fetched. You see only 10 records at the client (the value of `PacketRecords`), and
you know that 55 exist at the server. Of course, the reason you don't get any more
records at this time is because you've set the `FetchOnDemand` property to `false`. To get
more packets with records, you now have to call the `GetNextPacket` method manually.
This can be done by adding a `TButton` component to the client main form (name it
`btnFetch` and set `Caption` to `Fetch`, as shown in Figure 20.23) with the following code
for the `OnClick` event handler:

```
void __fastcall TForm1::btnFetchClick(TObject *Sender)
{
  ClientDataSet1->GetNextPacket();
}
```

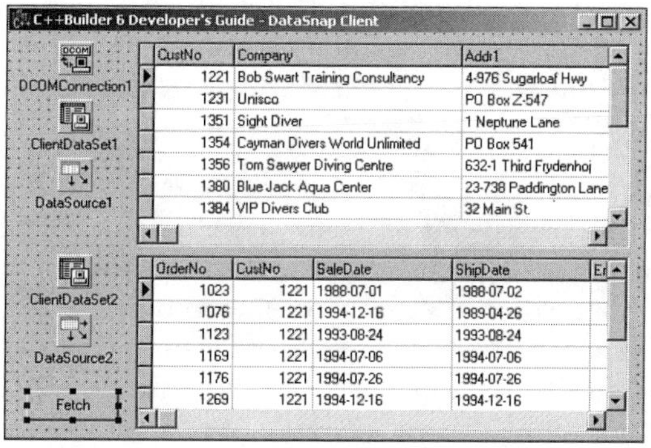

FIGURE 20.23   Manually fetching packets with records from server to client.

If you click the Fetch button, the next packet of 10 records is retrieved, resulting in a
total of 20 records in the client. Clicking Fetch four more times will retrieve the final
35 records. At that time, the `DataSet` at the DataSnapServer will no longer be active,
so you cannot obtain the `RecordCount` anymore (which is why I had to add the `else`
clause in the `OnAfterGetRecords` event for the `TDataSetProvider`).

In short, the DataSnap server doesn't know anything—it is stateless; it has to be told the complete state by the clients, and both clients and server can communicate using the OwnerData parameter of some helpful Before and After event handlers. Note that the OwnerData parameter that is used to pass data is of type OleVariant. You can put just about anything in it, but it helps if you know beforehand what to expect (on the other side), which is why I usually try to pass an AnsiString just to be sure.

Apart from the Before and After events, TClientDataSet has two additional events for Post and Scroll, with no direct counterpart on the TDataSetProvider side. Obviously, these routines have only a DataSet as an argument and no OwnerData.

A final word on this: Assigning true to the FetchOnDemand property of the TClient DataSet will ensure that the relevant state information is automatically sent from the client to the server. However, there are situations in which you might want to be in control, in which case you need to rely on the techniques I showed you in this section. It's also important to be able to manage state by yourself (at the client side) when working with stateless protocols such as MTS, HTTP, or SOAP.

Deployment

Deploying DataSnap is fairly easy. You have to find the correct set of DLLs and packages for your client application and include DataSnap itself (which consists of only MIDAS.DLL for DataSnap). There are no database drivers and no additional setup, only your client and MIDAS.DLL. You might need to register the server on your client machine as well, or at least the type library for the server—see the "Accessing the Server Remotely" section which is covered in the next chapter.

You also need to purchase an official license. A MIDAS 2 license was pretty expensive at U.S. $5,000.00 per hardware server. You are allowed to run as many MIDAS 2 servers on a machine as you want and can. MIDAS 3 and DataSnap have a new lower-than-ever deployment license model, which incidentally has no effect on the MIDAS 2 licensing model (another reason to upgrade your MIDAS 2 applications to MIDAS 3). A MIDAS 3 or DataSnap license for an unlimited server is now only U.S. $299.95. As a result of this much lower price, Borland no longer offers a per-seat client license, making the licensing scheme not only much cheaper, but easier as well.

When do you need to purchase a DataSnap license? That depends on the DataSnap data packet (sent from the provider to the ClientDataSet or XMLBroker and back). In his DataSnap licensing article on the Borland Community site, John Kaster (Borland Developer Relations) has formulated two rules:

1. If the DataSnap data packet goes from one machine to another by any means, a license is required.

2. If the DataSnap data packet always stays on the same machine, you do not need a license.

Note that "by any means" includes copying to a floppy disk, using email, copying from one hard disk to another, backing up from one machine and restoring on another then resolving the data, and so on. Basically, this means any method of transferring the data packet from one machine to another (including retyping or a WAP connection).

This greatly reduced license fee is a tremendous opportunity for C++Builder 6 developers who need to develop *n*-tier solutions. Previously, clients had serious problems with the MIDAS 2 license fees (especially if you had to prove all benefits first), but now I have little reluctance suggesting a multitier DataSnap approach.

And the future might be even better: Delphi 7 Studio (just released at the time of writing) has extended the DataSnap license by including a free deployment of DataSnap applications with Delphi 7 Enterprise or Architect. This means that if you've purchased a copy of Delphi 7 Enterprise (or Architect), you already paid for the DataSnap license of all DataSnap applications that you can build with that. Only for Delphi 7 and Kylix 3, I'm afraid. But C++Builder 7 will most likely contain a similar license schema. Stay tuned...

Summary

In this chapter, you looked at Borland's multitier technology called DataSnap. In particular, you saw how to create servers and clients and how to use DCOM, sockets, and HTTP to connect to a remote server.

This technology is important for several reasons:

- It provides a means of creating thin clients that make few demands on the client system.

- It simplifies—in fact, nearly eliminates—the need to configure the client machine.

- It enables you to partition applications in logical compartments. If you want, each of these compartments can be run on a separate machine, thereby distributing the load of the application.

- It provides a means for distributing a load over several server machines or for routing the load to a specific machine with the power to handle heavy demands.

- It provides a robust architecture for handling and reporting (reconciliation) errors, particularly in a multiuser environment.

- It enables you to use a briefcase technology that stores files locally and allows you to reload them when it is time to update the server. This capability is ideal for laptop users who spend a lot of time on the road.

For many users, this technology is so compelling that it entirely replaces the standard client/server database architectures. These users are attracted to the capability to partition an application into logical pieces, even if the entire application is being run on a single machine. However, the biggest benefits achieved by this architecture become apparent when you bring multiple machines and servers into play.

This chapter should get you started using some of the more sophisticated aspects of this technology. There will come a time when nearly every computer in the world will be continually connected to nearly every other computer. When that occurs, distributed computing will become one of the most essential fields of study in computer programming. DataSnap is a very helpful piece of technology in this respect.

The next chapter will focus on the different connection components and communication protocols. Including the use of Web services as DataSnap servers.

21

DataSnap Multitier Connections

by Bob Swart

The previous chapter introduced DataSnap and mainly focussed on the DataSnap Servers and Clients, and this chapter will focus on the communication protocols and different connection components between the DataSnap Servers and Clients.

The examples in this chapter use DataSnap, which means that you must have a copy of the Enterprise Edition of C++Builder to run the programs in this chapter. Note that you can also use the trial version of C++Builder 6 Enterprise to run the examples in this chapter.

Accessing the Server Remotely Using DCOM

In this chapter, we start with the example projects for the SimpleDataSnapServer and DataSnapServer from the previous chapter. They can be found on the CD-ROM with this book.

The objective in this section is to make the connection not work just locally, but also remotely. In other words, DCOM instead of COM (when both the DataSnap Server and Client are running on the same machine).

When setting up DCOM, it is best to set up the server half of the DCOM program on a machine that's running as a Windows NT/2000/XP domain server. In particular, you don't want to run the DataSnap server on a Windows 95/98/Me machine, and it is best if the server machine is a domain server and the client machines are all part of this domain. If you don't have an NT/2000/XP domain server available, you probably should try to set up your client and server machines to have the same logon and the same password, at least during the initial stages of testing. Windows 98/Me ships with DCOM as part of the system, whereas Windows 95 machines need to have DCOM added to the system. You can download the DLLs necessary to implement DCOM on a Windows 95 machine from the Microsoft Web site (although Microsoft officially doesn't support Windows 95 anymore—nor Windows NT for that matter).

You must have the DataSnap server registered on both the client and the server. The client program could still locate and launch the server if you failed to register it, but COM could not marshal data back and forth if the type library for the server is not registered on the client machine. You can do so by running the DataSnap server once on both machines. However, it's not very convenient to run the DataSnap server on all client machines, so an easier solution is running the DataSnap server once on the server, and then registering the TLB file on the clients using TRegSvr.exe (in the CBuilder6\Bin directory). In this case, the TLB file is called SimpleDataSnapServer.tlb. This file was generated automatically when you created the DataSnap server.

When you access the DataSnap server remotely from a client machine, you need to copy the single C++Builder client executable to the client side only. No database tools are needed, other than the MIDAS.DLL file, which contains the ClientDataSet functionality.

HTTP WebConnection

Apart from using DCOM as a communication protocol, as implemented using the TDCOMConnection component, DataSnap supports two other protocols as well: TCP/IP (sockets) and HTTP. The latter is called TWebConnection and is especially useful in situations where you need to go through a proxy or firewall, which can be quite a problem (or at least quite a task) using the regular TDCOMConnection component.

Before we start using the TWebConnection component in C++Builder 6, I have to warn you that this component does not operate correctly with C++Builder 6, including Update 2. The problem that you'll encounter is an Access Denied message when the DataSnap client tries to connect to the DataSnap server. We have been unable to solve this problem, and can only report that it used to work just fine, and hopefully some forthcoming patch or update from Borland for C++Builder will fix it again in the future.

TWebConnection is found on the DataSnap tab of the Component Palette. It is perfect to use for stateless HTTP communication connecting to a DataSnap server (which is also stateless, as you've seen).

For the remainder of this section, you should probably copy the DataSnapClient project from its original directory (from the previous chapter) to a new directory, where you can experiment on it using the TWebConnection component. Note that this precaution is only necessary with the DataSnapClient project; we won't be modifying the DataSnapServer at all.

Using the DataSnapClient project, you can replace the current TDCOMConnection component with a TWebConnection component. Now the TWebConnection component has to connect to the DataSnapServer you created in this chapter. The TWebConnection component makes this connection by using the HTTP protocol. However, to use a WebConnection, you must make sure that WININET.DLL is installed on the client system (which is available if you have Internet Explorer version 3 or higher installed), the server must have Internet Information Server version 4 or higher or Netscape Enterprise version 3.6 or higher, and finally you must install a special Borland-made ISAPI DLL called HTTPSRVR.DLL (found in the CBuilder6\Bin directory) in a cgi-bin or scripts directory on the Web server that the TWebConnection component uses to connect to. HTTPSRVR is responsible for launching the DataSnapServer on the Web server and will marshal all requests from the client to the application server interface, sending packets of records back.

For more information on Web servers, ISAPI DLLs, and general Web server programming, see Chapter 22, "Web Server Programming with WebSnap."

As a direct consequence, the URL property of the WebConnection component must point to http://localhost/cgi-bin/httpsrvr.dll (which points to the scripts directory on my local machine—I could also have used http://127.0.0.1/scripts /httpsrvr.dll). Next, you can click the ServerName property, open the list of available DataSnap servers, and select the DataSnapServer.CustomerOrders DataSnap server. You can make sure that the connection actually works by double-clicking the Connected property of the TWebConnection component. If the value turns to true, you're okay.

> **NOTE**
>
> Note that you don't actually see the DataSnap Web server running. That's because HTTPSRVR (started by the server) is activated by another user (the default Internet user), and as a result you don't see any visual representation of the middleware server at this time (as you did when using a DCOM or the upcoming Sockets middleware server).

To make sure the server is actually running, you can always take a look at the Task Manager, of course. Inside the Task Manager, you'll see the DataSnapServer running, but (not so) surprisingly, no indication of that is seen at the desktop.

Other than this, the TWebConnection component works exactly the same as the TDCOMConnection component, with one difference—security. The TWebConnection component enables you to take advantage of SSL security and to communicate with a DataSnapServer application that is protected behind a firewall. For all this, the TWebConnection component has a number of helpful properties such as Proxy, ProxyByPass, UserName, and Password. The UserName and Password properties of TWebConnection can be used to go through a proxy or if the Web server requires authorization or authentication.

Unfortunately, as I wrote in the start of this section, the TWebConnection component will produce an "Access Denied" error when trying to connect a DataSnap Client to the DataSnap Server.

Object Pooling

Finally, a Web connection can use object pooling. This feature enables the server to create a pool of multiple server instances for client requests. This way, the DataSnapServer doesn't use the resource for the remote data module and database connection unless it's actually needed.

Object pooling gives you the ability to set a maximum for the number of instances of the remote data module inside the DataSnap server application. Whenever a client request is received, the DataSnap server checks to see if a free remote data module exists in the pool. If not, it creates a remote data module instance (but never more than the specified maximum number of remote data module instances) or raises an exception with the message Server too busy. The remote data module, in its turn, services the client requests and duly waits for the next one. After a certain period of time without client requests, the remote data module is freed automatically (by the object pooling mechanism).

In previous versions of DataSnap, this feature would not have been possible, because we now have instances of a remote data module that services more than one client. As a result, the server cannot rely on state information—this has to be maintained by the client. As indicated previously, DataSnap is indeed stateless.

The big question should now be: How do we enable object pooling for HTTP connections? We must get inside the UpdateRegistry() method again—found in the header file of your remote data module. Inside the UpdateRegistry() method, an object regObj is used to configure the behavior of the application server. With object pooling, we must set three additional property values.

First, regObj.MaxObjects specifies the maximum number of instances. If the DataSnap server receives a client request and no remote data modules are available, an exception with message Server too busy is raised.

Second, regObj.Timeout specifies the number of minutes the remote data module can wait idle in the pool of remote data modules. After spending the specified amount of time without a single client request, the remote data module will be freed automatically by the DataSnap server. According to the documentation, the DataSnap server checks every six minutes to see if any remote data module should be freed. Specifying a timeout value of 0 means that the remote data module will never time out, so in that case the only useful feature you're using is the limit on the amount of remote data module instances.

After these two property settings, the regObj.RegisterPooled must be set to true to indicate that you want to use object pooling.

In practice, there's a fourth property value you can set, regObj.Singleton, which specifies whether the remote data module should be a singleton (but we already set that to false). If you set it to true, the number of instances and timeout arguments will be ignored, and only a single remote data module (which must be free threaded) will be created to handle all client requests.

An example modified UpdateRegistry for a remote data module with up to 10 instances that time out after 42 minutes of inactivity can be seen in Listing 21.1.

LISTING 21.1   UpdateRegistry to enable Connection Pooling

```
// Function invoked to (un)register object
//
static HRESULT WINAPI UpdateRegistry(BOOL bRegister)
{
  TRemoteDataModuleRegistrar regObj(GetObjectCLSID(),
                                    GetProgID(), GetDescription());
  // Disable these flags to disable use by socket or Web connections.
  // Also set other flags to configure the behavior of your application server.
  // For more information, see atlmod.h and atlvcl.cpp.
  regObj.Singleton = false;
  regObj.MaxObjects = 10;
  regObj.Timeout = 42;
  regObj.RegisterPooled = true;  regObj.EnableWeb = true;
  regObj.EnableSocket = true;
  return regObj.UpdateRegistry(bRegister);
}
```

Note that I've used hard-coded magic numbers 10 and 42 here. This is not a good idea in real life, especially because it means that you need to recompile the DataSnap server whenever you want to make some changes (for example, if you add new memory to the server, which can then handle more than 10 instances). That's not even considering that the same DataSnap server could be placed on multiple machines, each of a different configuration (see the section "Object Broker," later in this chapter). I always recommend using an external configuration file where you can specify—for each machine, and for every time you first start the DataSnap server application—the number of instances and timeout minutes. This adds flexibility to the power already present in object pooling.

TCP/IP SocketConnection

So far, you've mainly worked with the TDCOMConnection component and the TWebConnection component. However, DataSnap can also employ a third protocol: TCP/IP (plain sockets). This is done by using the TSocketConnection component (the third of the Connection components available on the DataSnap tab of the Component Palette from C++Builder 6 Enterprise).

If you don't have an NT domain server available on your network, you should probably not try to use DCOM at all and instead should use plain TCP/IP. A socket connection will work even if no NT server is in the equation, and it is usually much easier to set up than a DCOM connection. However, security is much more difficult to enforce on a socket connection (unlike the TWebConnection component, for example).

You can easily convert either SimpleDataSnapClient or DataSnapClient into a TCP/IP application. You don't even need to make any changes to your DataSnap servers to make it work. To get started building your sockets-based DataSnap program, run the ScktSrvr.exe program found in the CBuilder6\Bin directory on the server machine. This program must be running on the server or this system will not work. Note that ScktSrvr.exe can either be run as a normal application or be used as an NT service (using the -install and -uninstall command-line parameters).

Drop a TSocketConnection component from the DataSnap page of the Component Palette on the main form of the DataSnapClient application. Set its Address property to the IP address of the machine where the DataSnapServer application resides. This can be a remote machine or your current machine (such as localhost). Fill in the ServerName property, just as you did in the DCOM example earlier in this chapter, by dropping down the ServerName combo box and selecting the DataSnapServer.CustomerOrders DataSnap Server. You should now be able to test your connection by setting the Connected property of the TSocketConnection component to true. As I explained earlier, you should not leave the Connected property set to true at design time.

Assuming you have dropped down a TSocketConnection component on the form and set its ServerName property correctly, you can drop a new TButton component, set its Name property to ButtonSocket, Caption to Socket, and write the event handler code as seen in Listing 21.2:

LISTING 21.2   SocketConnection to Remote Machine

```
void __fastcall TForm1::ConnectTCPIP1Click(TObject *Sender)
{
  AnsiString S;
  if (InputQuery("Enter Machine Name or IP-Address:",
                 "Machine Name/IP-Address", S))
  {
    SocketConnection1->Address = S;
    ClientDataSet1->RemoteServer = SocketConnection1;
    ClientDataSet1->Active = true;
  }
}
```

When the user clicks on the Socket button, he is prompted for the IP address of the machine where the server resides. Assuming your system is set up correctly, you can also pass in the human-readable equivalent of that IP address, such as localhost or—in my case—www.eBob42.com.

The code sets the Address property of the TSocketConnection component to the address supplied by the user. It then changes the RemoteServer property of the TClientDataSet so that it no longer points at the TDCOMConnection component, but at that TSocketConnection component. Finally, it sets the Active property of the TClientDataSet to true. Setting the Active property to true will automatically cause the TSocketConnection.Connected property to be set to true as well, as you've seen earlier.

At this stage, you should be fully connected to your server and viewing your data. This approach will work equally well whether the server is on the same machine or on a remote machine. Furthermore, you don't need an NT domain server or even an NT server, though I always recommend that you use one when working with DataSnap.

Note that the DataSnap server does not have to be changed to connect to a client using DCOM or sockets (TCP/IP). In fact, after you have a working DataSnap server, you only need to run it to enable it to register itself (so you can locate it and connect to it from a DataSnap client). This COM-specific Registry is done by the inherited UpdateRegistry call, and is performed by all versions of DataSnap. It's actually quite convenient because if you want to move the server application to another location (on the same machine), you only need to rerun it to reregister itself and enable clients to connect to it.

Usually, I write DataSnap applications that communicate using DCOM. However, in some cases you might want to use plain sockets instead. A regular remote data module can communicate using sockets, provided you've left that particular communication protocol enabled in the `UpdateRegistry` method. Clients need to connect to the remote data module using the `SocketConnection` component. However, for a connection to be made to the DataSnap application server, you also need to run the socket server on the server machine. Using C++Builder 4, you had two socket server applications: `ScktSrvr.exe` (the socket server) or `ScktSrvc.exe` (the NT service edition of the socket server). In C++Builder 5 and 6, these two are combined in a single `ScktSrvr.exe` that can either be run as a normal application or be used as an NT service (using the `-install` and `-uninstall` command-line parameters).

Registered Servers

As I mentioned before, the C++Builder 5 and 6 `ScktSrvr` checks the Registry to see if a DataSnap server has enabled the socket communication protocol (that is, whether the `EnableSocket` field of the `regObj` has been assigned to `true` inside the `UpdateRegistry()` function). For C++Builder 4 DataSnap servers, this isn't present, which means that if you upgrade a C++Builder 4 DataSnap server to C++Builder 5 or 6, you must not forget to include a new `UpdateRegistry` method. If, for any reason, the new DataSnap server doesn't register itself as using the socket communication protocol, you can always use the C++Builder 6 socket server (and not the C++Builder 4 socket server). In the Connections menu you can specify that you don't want `Registered Object Only` (you want to see unregistered objects as well, as can be seen in Figure 21.1).

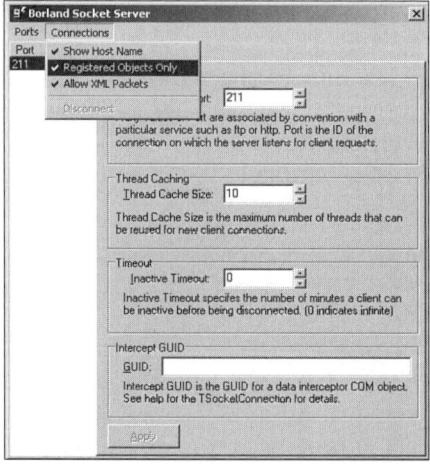

FIGURE 21.1   Borland socket server looking at registered objects only.

This change will not take affect until the socket server is restarted, but then you can see C++Builder 6 DataSnap servers using the `TSocketConnection` component—registered or not.

A final new feature regarding the `TSocketConnection` component has to do with callbacks. `TDCOMConnection` components always support callbacks, and `TWebConnection` components never support callbacks. With a `TSocketConnection` component you can specify using the `SupportCallbacks` property, whether the `TSocketConnection` component will marshal calls from the DataSnapServer to the DataSnapClient over an interface supplied as a callback. If you don't want to do that, you can set `SupportCallbacks` to `false` (it's `true` by default). Setting it to `false` has the advantage that you then need only Winsock 1 support to deploy your DataSnapClient, whereas otherwise (with `SupportCallbacks` set to `true`) you need Winsock 2 or higher. Because Windows 95 doesn't include Winsock 2 by default, this means one less deployment problem (believe it or not there are still clients out there using Windows 95).

Object Broker

You've now seen three possible connection components that exist in C++Builder Enterprise: `TDCOMConnection`, `TWebConnection`, and `TSocketConnection` all connecting to a single DataSnap server application. However, sometimes you don't have a single DataSnap server to connect to, but multiple DataSnap servers. Reasons for having multiple DataSnap servers can be diverse, but most often this is done for load balancing and failover. If one server goes down, others can take over, and having 10 servers all over the world usually results in fewer bottlenecks than having one big server.

Imagine having to determine at the client side which of these DataSnap Servers to connect to. You'd need to know exactly which servers are available (or you might miss one—maybe the last one that's available at the time) and how to connect to them. In an ideal world, you wouldn't want all your clients to know about this. Fortunately, DataSnap offers a helpful hand in this case, by means of the concept called Object Brokering.

With Object Brokering, you make a connection from the client to a server without knowing which server you'll end up with. Each of the three connection components has a property called `ObjectBroker`. This property can be used to connect to a component derived from `TCustomObjectBroker`. It will then be responsible for telling the connection component which server to use (by specifying the `ServerName` or `ServerGUID`). Note that when you actually use an `ObjectBroker`, the local values specified for the `ServerName` and `ServerGUID` properties will be ignored as far as your application is concerned; `ObjectBroker` will supply you with dynamic values at runtime.

As an example of how to implement your own Object Brokering techniques, C++Builder Enterprise comes with a `TSimpleObjectBroker` component (found on the DataSnap tab of the Component Palette).

`TSimpleObjectBroker` itself contains two interesting properties. `Servers` contains a list of available servers, for each of which you can specify the `ComputerName`, the `Port` (211 by default), and `Enabled`. Note that you as a developer must make sure that this list is filled and maintained properly. If you add a new server or a server goes down, you must update the list.

The second property is `LoadBalanced`. As the name indicates, this property tries to ensure that the servers are load balanced, or at least that a request is balanced among the servers. The technique used here is based on a random generator. When `LoadBalanced` is set to `true`, each connection component will be connected to a random server from the list. When `LoadBalanced` is set to `false` (the default), each connection component on the client application will be connected to the first server on the list.

The `TSimpleObjectBroker` component is implemented in unit `ObjBrkr` (found in the `$(BCB)\Source\Vcl` directory) and contains a fairly simple algorithm. Picking a random server isn't such a bad idea, but obviously it's not really intelligent, either. If you ever need to write your own Object Broker algorithm, `TSimpleObjectBroker` might be a good place to start.

One final word on Object Brokering: After a connection component is connected to a DataSnap server, it will remain connected to that particular server until the `Connected` property is set to `false` again. When you reconnect (set `Connected` back to `true`), you might end up with a different server.

New DataSnap Connections

Apart from the new name DataSnap replacing DataSnap, C++Builder 6 introduced some real new enhancements as well, such as local connections and connection brokers. The former was introduced because the role of the `TClientDataSet` component was significantly enlarged in C++Builder 6. We now have the `TClientDataSet` component in the Professional version of C++Builder, instead of only the Enterprise version. And, we can now have local DataSetConnections instead of only remote DataSetConnections, as we'll see in this section.

Specifically, I want to focus on two new components with icons that (almost) look alike: the `TConnectionBroker` and the `TLocalConnection` component (I won't cover the `TSharedConnection`). The final section of this chapter will focus exclusively on DataSnap and SOAP (using SOAP Data Modules and the `TSOAPConnection` component).

TLocalConnection

Let's start with the `TLocalConnection` component. This component can be handy for people who want to start building distributed applications, but are not ready to implement the server, yet. As you might know, it's not really required to put the

`TDataSetProvider` and `TClientDataSet` in different tiers of a multitier application. They can actually reside in the same single-tier application (previously leaving the `RemoteServer` property of the `TDataSetProvider` component a bit useless). However, this single-tier application might be a convenient way to prepare your multitier application. You are limited because you cannot implement actual access to the `IAppServer` interface (the interface that's normally provided by the remote data module to the client application, and through which the `TDataSetProvider` exports its dataset property to the local `TClientDataSet`). To take the single-tier simulation one step further, Borland has now provided us with the `TLocalConnection` component. This is, in fact, almost a dummy component with one great feature: It implements the `IAppServer` interface and can be used to assign any `TDataSetProvider` to (as if the data was retrieved from the `Connection` component by some communication means). The benefit should be obvious: The client part of the application (still single-tier at this time) can now implement and test the use of the `IAppServer` interface as implemented by the `TLocalConnection` component. This means that you can postpone the actual split of your application in two physical tiers until you're really ready, which might help to keep things under control (and maintainable as well as manageable).

I understand if that doesn't really make much sense to you (especially if you've seldom built prior multitier applications using DataSnap). So, let's just build a practical example where I'll show you exactly where and when the `TLocalConnection` component comes into play, and how it changes the rules of the game.

BDE "legacy" Application

We could have used any database access layer in C++Builder 6 for this example, but because dbExpress can already make use of embedded `TClientDataSet` components (in the `TSQLClientDataSet` component—see Chapter 12), it seems more appropriate to use the Borland Database Engine (BDE) as our start point. That way we can also keep the illusion of a legacy application that needs to be upgraded to a multitier architecture.

To build our "legacy" application, start C++Builder 6 and create a new application using File, New—Application. Save the project in `Legacy.bpr` and the main form in `LegacyMainForm.cpp`. Click File, New—Data Module to add a new data module, and save that in `DataMod.cpp`. Note that the main form will only be used to show the contents of the datasets on the data module. I assume you can manage to build that part yourself (so won't cover it in this chapter).

Now, we'll move on to the data module. Because we're building a BDE application, we need to drop a `TDataBase` component from the BDE tab of the Component Palette, set its `DatabaseName` property to BDE, and its `AliasName` property to DBDEMOS. Add a `TSession` component and set its `AutoSessionName` property to true. Now drop two `TTable` components on the data module, assign their `DatabaseName` properties to BDE (the one we've just made), and rename them to `tblCustomer` and `tblOrders`, respectively. Now, set the `TableName` property of `tblCustomer` to `customer.db`, and the `TableName` property of `tblOrders` to the `orders.db` table.

We're now ready to define a master-detail relationship between tblCustomer and tblOrders, using a TDataSource component from the Data Access tab. Set its name property to dsCustomerOrders, and its DataSet property to tblCustomer. Now, click tblOrders, and set its MasterSource property to the dsCustomerOrders DataSource. Click the ellipsis for the MasterFields property to start the Field Link Designer, use the CustNo index, and select the CustNo field for both tables to be the field for the master-detail link. Click OK to create the master-detail relationship. See Figure 21.2 for the data module, so far, that we can use in a normal (legacy) BDE application right away.

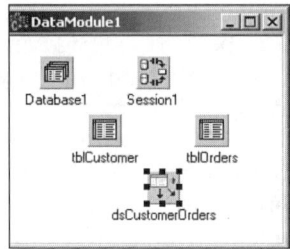

FIGURE 21.2   New Data Module.

Preparing to Upgrade

Now, although the BDE application we've just created works just fine, there might come a day when you need to turn it into a distributed application—or at least make the preparations to do so. For example, because the database must be placed on its own—more secure—machine, or because you will also be required to accept browser-based clients in the near future (apart from Windows GUI clients).

A distributed application is based on a TDataSetProvider component on a Remote Data Module at the server side, and a TxxxConnection and TClientDataSet at the client side (where TxxxConnection can be any of the connection component we've seen). To prepare for that architecture, we should now drop a TDataSetProvider component from the Data Access tab onto the data module. Set its Name to dspCustomerOrders (we will use it to provide both the Customer master and the Orders detail records), and set its DataSet property to tblCustomer. The TDataSetProvider will now export the Customer master table with the Orders detail records embedded as a so-called nested dataset.

However, because the TDataSetProvider is used on a normal data module, and not a regular data module, there is no way it will be actually exported to the outside world. Fortunately, we can still use it (and have used it in the past), as a local TDataSetProvider. The trick is that a local TClientDataSet will be able to connect to a local TDataSetProvider as long as they both share the same owner. In other words, as long as they are both placed on the same data module or form, they can talk to each other!

So, drop a TClientDataSet component on the data module, set its Name to cdsCustomer and assign its ProviderName property to dspCustomerOrders. This method also worked with C++Builder 5. However, there is a better way that also helps if you want the TClientDataSet to use more than just the TDataSetProviders that are available on this single-data module. It's also better if you want to make specific IAppServer method calls to prepare yourself for a move to a real distributed architecture (where the TDataSetProvider will end up in the server tier, and the TClientDataSet component will have to use a TxxxConnection component to talk to the server and get a list of TDataSetProviders). The better way consists of dropping the TLocalConnection component (the topic of this section). Using a TLocalConnection component, a TClientDataSet component can have access to all available (local) TDataSetProvider components in your entire application—not just the ones that exist in the same data module or form.

To show the "better" way, drop a TLocalConnection component (from the DataSnap tab) on the data module. This component only has two properties: Name and Tag, so there's nothing you can customize or configure. Note that it's a global application component, and you only need one of them to service your entire application.

After the TLocalConnection component is in place, you can go back to your cdsCustomer TClientDataSet component, and assign its RemoteServer property to LocalConnection1; the local connection component. This time, when you open the drop-down combo box for the ProviderName property of cdsCustomer, you will get a list of all DataSourceProviders in your entire application (there is still only one, but believe me, you'll get them all at this time). Select dspCustomerOrders to connect to this particular TDataSetProvider. Note that we now connect to the TDataSetProvider through the IAppServer interface (which is implemented by the TLocalConnection component). The difference is that it will be much easier to migrate to a real RemoteServer using a TxxxConnection component later—because we will see in the remainder of this section.

To finish the data module example, you need to drop a TDataSource component, set its Name property to dsCustomer, and connect it to the cdsCustomer ClientDataSet. If you want to explicitly use the Orders detail records as well, you must right-click the cdsCustomer ClientDataSet, start the Fields Editor, right-click in the Fields Editor and select Add All Fields. The list of fields will include a field named tblOrders. This is the nested dataset (of type DataSetField) that we created earlier in this example. We can use this explicit (also called persistent) DataSetField to feed another TClientDataSet component. So, drop a second TClientDataSet on the data module, set its Name property to cdsOrders and this time you only have to open the drop-down combo box for the DataField property and select the (only) value cdsCustomertblOrders. A TDataSource component named dsOrders connected to the cdsOrders finishes the preparation to this point (see Figure 21.3).

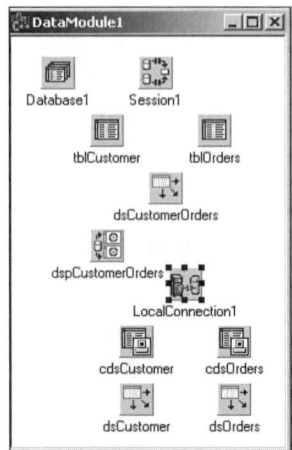

FIGURE 21.3   LocalConnection.

You can now use the dsCustomer and dsOrders DataSources to connect to data-aware controls (on the main form).

ApplyUpdates
Of course, working with ClientDataSets means caching your data, so there's one more change that you have to make to the data module. You must make sure to call the ApplyUpdates method of the cdsCustomer ClientDataSet to apply all changes (edits, inserts, deletes) from the ClientDataSet back (through the TLocalConnection component) to the DataSetProvider and the actual database tables. Note that you don't need to do this for the cdsOrders ClientDataSet because that one isn't even connected to a RemoteServer or ProviderName; it's simply connected to a DataSetField.

For the cdsCustomer, there are a few ways to make sure the ApplyUpdates method is called. First of all, you can put a button on your form and ask your end user to click the button to explicitly call ApplyUpdates. Of course, this means that you must know for sure that the end user will in fact click the button. This is something that you can't debug or fix; you just have to trust it. When you do this, at least make sure to ask the user to save all changes when she tries to close the main form. The ClientDataSet maintains a ChangeCount property, which holds the number of changes. If this property has a value greater than zero, you know for sure that some changes have been made (and have not been applied, yet). I always implement this as follows in the OnClose event of the main form:

```
#include "DataMod.h"

void __fastcall TForm1::FormClose(TObject *Sender, TCloseAction &Action)
{
```

```
  if (DataModule1->cdsCustomer->ChangeCount > 0)
  {
   if (MessageDlg("Save all changes?", mtConfirmation,
       mbYesNoCancel, 0) == mrYes)
     DataModule1->cdsCustomer->ApplyUpdates(-1);
  }
}
```

At least then we know for sure that the user can never forget to save the changes and updates (she can refuse them, but not by accident).

As a final remark, note that the ApplyUpdates might fail when another (concurrent) user has also changed the same record in the remote database. Because we're currently only preparing to upgrade our legacy BDE application to a distributed multitier architecture, I won't discuss that topic. For more information about the Reconcile Error Dialog, see the previous Chapter 20, "Distributed Applications with DataSnap."

At this time, we have a data module that is still a single tier, but has all aspects of a multitier solution inside. The application can now make use of the dsCustomer and dsOrders DataSources, as well as the cdsCustomer and cdsOrders ClientDataSets, and even the IAppServer interface exposed by the RemoteServer that the cdsCustomer ClientDataSet is connected to. The fact that—in this version of the data module—the RemoteServer points to a TLocalConnection component doesn't matter; we can still use the IAppServer interface as if we're already working in a multitier distributed architecture. This way, without actually having multiple physical tiers, you can already prepare and set up the entire presentation layer of your application—the GUI part, for example, or a TXMLBroker component, which also has to connect to a RemoteServer to get to the DataSetProvider.

We'll continue with the example application(s) by continuing our potential upgrade to multitier path with the new TConnectionBroker component.

TConnectionBroker

The TConnectionBroker component is another component that can come in handy when you want to configure or maintain your DataSnap application. Like all actual TxxxConnection components, the TConnectionBroker component is only useful in DataSnap client applications, and can be used as an additional layer between TClientDataSets and the actual TxxxConnection components. As such a layer, it can be used to quickly switch between different TxxxConnection components. In case you wonder why this would be useful for a single or even a few TClientDataSet components (which can easily be moved from one TxxxConnection component to another), just consider the situation where you have one hundred TClientDataSet components.

Believe me, this will turn out to be a nightmare if you want to switch them over from one TxxxConnection component to another. Just imagine for a moment that you accidentally forget to switch one ClientDataSet over! Your application will still compile, and it will even run, but then the problems start (especially if you've deployed it to your clients already). Unless the ClientDataSets are all connected to the TConnectionBroker component, which can then be used to switch from, say a TLocalConnection to a TDCOMConnection or a TSocketConnection component with the ease of a single-mouse click.

To show this particular feature in action, let's continue with the previous example application, taking it one step further by adding an actual TDCOMConnection component, and then using the TConnectionBroker to switch between the TLocalConnection and the TDCOMConnection. Of course, this requires a DataSnap server as well, so let's start with the server now, and then come back to modify our data module (which is already getting pretty crowded for a small example).

DataSnap BDE Server

If we take a look at the data module that we have so far, it should be clear that we can actually split it in two separate parts (also called tiers): a server part and a client part. The separation should take place right between the TLocalConnection and the TDataSetProvider component. The server side consists of the TDataBase, TSession, two TTables, a TdataSource, and the TDataSetProvider, and the client side contains the rest. Because we don't want to break the legacy application, we won't actually remove the server-side components from the remote data module, but simply copy them. But first we need to create the DataSnap Server using File, New—Application. Save the project in DataSnapServer.bpr and the main form in MainForm.cpp. This time we need to add a remote data module. Click File, New—Other, go to Multitier and select the Remote Data Module icon. The Remote Data Module will be the remote object that implements the IAppServer interface on the server side. The Remote Data Module Wizard asks for the CoClass name of the Remote Data Module (the name of your class as well as interface, which will be derived from IAppServer). Let's take RemoteDataMod42 (see Figure 21.4). Leave the Threading Model value at its default—see the previous chapter for more information about this setting.

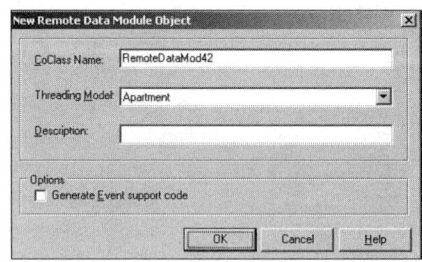

FIGURE 21.4   Remote Data Module Wizard.

When you click OK, the new Remote Data Module has been created. If you start the Type Library Editor from the Views menu, you'll notice that it contains the definition of the IRemoteDataMod42 interface, and that the parent interface of IRemoteDataMod42 is set to IAppServer. If you want, you can now add your custom properties and methods to IRemoteDataMod42.

Close the Type Library Editor (we'll get back to it later), and click File, Open to open the file DataMod.cpp from the Legacy.bpr project—without actually opening the project itself. Select the TDataBase, TSession, tblCustomer, tblOrders, dsCustomerOrders, and dspCustomerOrders. Copy them to the clipboard, move back to your Remote Data Module and paste them. See Figure 21.5 for the remote data module on my machine.

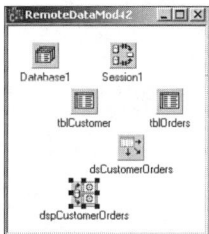

FIGURE 21.5 RemoteDataMod42.

The only thing left to do now is to compile and run the DataSnap server application. This will register it on my local machine, so I can connect to it from the DataSnap client application using one of the many different connection types.

DataSnap Client

Let's return to the DataSnap client application. By this I mean the original Legacy.bpr application that currently uses a TLocalConnection component on the data module. We will now extend this data module with a new way to connect to the actual DataSnap Server that we just built. Because I'm testing on my local machine, the easiest way is to add a TDCOMConnection component. However, because my main point it to show how to use the TConnectionBroker component to easily switch between different TxxxConnection components, you can also pick a TSocketConnection or TWebConnection component at this time—the choice is yours.

After you've dropped the TDCOMConnection component on the data module, you can open the drop-down combo box for the ServerName property (showing three DataSnap servers). In our example, we need to select DataSnapServer.RemoteDataMod42 as ServerName. If you set the Connected property of the TDCOMConnection component to true, the DataSnapServer will be started (it will pop up and also appear in the taskbar). If you set the Connection property to false again, the DataSnapServer should be shut down again.

After you've configured and tested the TDCOMConnection component, you can take the cdsCustomer TClientDataSet component and point it to the TDCOMConnection component instead of the TLocalConnection component. Whenever you now activate (or open) the cdsCustomer, you will use the new connection—resulting in the DataSnapServer to be invoked (if it wasn't running already), and your DataSnap client to retrieve data from the remote data module on the DataSnapServer. Note that you do not have to change the cdsOrders TClientDataSet component because this one is simply connected to the tblOrders DataSetField inside cdsCustomer (which has already been taken care of).

Switching Connections

For a single ClientDataSet, it didn't take long to switch from one TxxxConnection component to another. But a real-world situation often uses more than a single, sometimes even more than a few dozen or hundred TClientDataSets. In those situations, you need a little help from your friend the TConnectionBroker. Drop the TConnectionBroker component from the DataSnap tab onto the data module (see Figure 21.6). The TConnectionBroker has three important properties: Connection, Connected, and LoginPrompt. The most important one is the Connection property, which can be set to either the TLocalConnection or the TDCOMConnection component—or to another TConnectionBroker (but a circular reference to the same TConnectionBroker itself is not allowed, of course). You can now click cdsCustomer again, and set its RemoteServer property to the TConnectionBroker. Whenever you need to switch between TxxxConnection components, you now only have to point a single RemoteServer property of the TConnectionBroker to another server. That's it, and you can even do this at runtime (make sure to close down the connection nicely, by setting Connected to false, before you attempt to switch from one Connection type to another). In fact, your client application can decide at runtime which connection to use, even before making the actual connection and opening the TClientDataSets. You only have to assign the right TxxxConnection component to the RemoteServer property of the ConnectionBroker component.

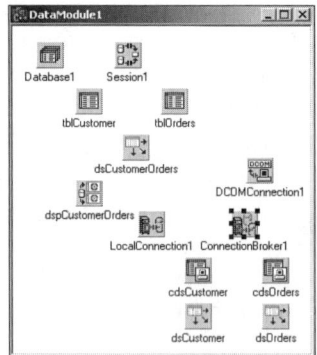

FIGURE 21.6 ConnectionBroker.

Using the combination of the TLocalConnection and the TConnectionBroker component enables you to write standalone applications that have the capability to switch to a multitier architecture when needed. You can even put a specific TxxxConnection component in it already (like we just did in our example) and make sure that the multitier edition of the application is tested thoroughly (on a few machines) before everyone switches over from the standalone version to the multitier version. After that happens, your end users will probably not even be aware of the change. (The actual presentation layer doesn't change—and will not need to change because the interface to it remains connected to the TClientDataSet and TDataSource components on the lower-right corner of the data module—independent of the fact whether we're connected to a remote server or just have a local connection.)

TSOAPConnection

One of the big DataSnap enhancements in Delphi 6 is the TSOAPConnection component from the Web Services tab of the component palette. The TSOAPConnection can be used for DataSnap applications, provided the DataSnap server is set up to act as a Web service (and is using a SOAP Server Data Module instead of a regular remote Data Module).

The SOAP Connection is a bit similar to the Web Connection because both use HTTP as the transport protocol. The difference is that the SOAP Connection component is used to connect to a Web server application (using HTTP) that implements the IAppServer interface as a Web service. Using a specific URL, we must specify the path info of the THTTPSoapDispatcher on the application server.

SOAP is the protocol that underlies Delphi's support for Web Service applications. SOAP marshals method calls using an XML encoding, whereas SOAP connections use HTTP as a transport protocol. SOAP connections have the advantage that they work in cross-platform applications because they are supported on both Windows and Linux. Because SOAP connections use HTTP, they have the same advantages as Web connections: HTTP provides a lowest-common denominator that you know is available on all clients, and clients can communicate with an application server that is protected by a firewall. As with HTTP connections, you can't use callbacks via SOAP. SOAP connections also limit you to a single remote data module in the application server.

When using SOAP as communication protocol, we cannot just use a regular Windows application as DataSnap server. Instead, we must explicitly make sure to use a Web server application (one that exposes the IAppServer interface).

We must use the URL property of the SOAPConnection component to point to the THTTPSoapDispatcher component inside the DataSnap server application. For example, URL could be of the form:

```
http://localhost/cgi-bin/DataSnapServer.exe/SOAP
```

For more information about SOAP and Web Services please read Chapter 19, "SOAP and Web Services with BizSnap."

C++Builder 6 Enterprise Soap Server

For multitier applications in C++Builder 6 (on Windows) to connect to Kylix 3 (on Linux), the communication has to be based on SOAP—the only communication protocol both C++Builder and Kylix have in common. This means we have a SOAP (remote) Data Module and `TDataSetProvider` component on the server side, and a `TSOAPConnection` component on the client side. In the remainder of this chapter, I will show the steps to build a Soap Server and Client using C++Builder 6 Enterprise (the steps are similar for Kylix 3 for C++).

Let's start by building a SOAP DataSnap CGI executable Server in C++Builder 6 Enterprise, which consists of the following steps:

1. Start C++Builder 6 Enterprise and close the default project (if any).

2. Click File, New—Other, and go to the WebServices tab of the Object Repository.

3. Double-click the SOAP Server Application icon, which gives the New Soap Server Application dialog.

4. Select CGI executable and click the OK button. A new Soap Server Application has now been generated for you.

5. Answer No to the question Create Interface for SOAP module.

6. The Soap Web Module contains three automatically generated components: `THTTPSoapDispatcher`, `THTTPSoapCppInvoker`, and `TWSDLHTMLPublish`. See Chapter 19 for more information about these components.

7. Save the Soap Web Module in file `SWebMod.cpp` and the project in file `SoapServer42.bpr`.

8. Now, click File, New—Other, and go back to the WebServices tab of the Object Repository.

9. This time, double-click the SOAP Data Module icon, which results in the Soap Data Module Wizard.

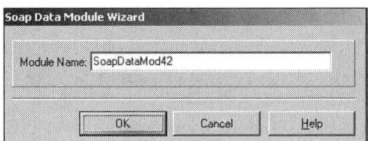

FIGURE 21.7   New Soap Data Module Wizard.

10. Enter `SoapDataMod42` as Class Name (see Figure 21.7), and click the OK button. A new Soap Data Module has now been generated for you.

11. Save this new unit with the Soap Data Module as `SDataMod.cpp`.

12. Drop a `TClientDataSet` component on the Soap Data Module; set its `Name` property to `cdsBiolife`. Set its FileName property to `biolife.xml`. (The `biolife.xml` table can be found in the `C:\Program Files\Common Files\Borland Shared\Data` directory.)

13. Drop a `TDataSetProvider` component on the Soap Data Module, set its `Name` property to `dspBiolife`, and its `DataSet` property to `cdsBiolife` (see Figure 21.8).

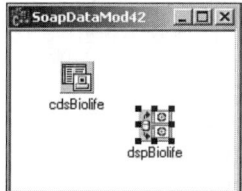

FIGURE 21.8   SOAP Server Data Module.

14. Click the Soap Data Module; go to the Events tab of the Object Inspector, and write the following code in the `OnCreate` event handler of the Soap Data Module:

```
void __fastcall TSoapDataMod42::SoapDataModuleCreate(TObject *Sender)
{
  cdsBiolife->Open();
}
```

This will make sure that the `cdsBiolife TClientDataSet` is opened when the SOAP Data Module is created. As an alternative you can set the `Active` property of the `cdsBiolife TClientDataSet` to `true` at design time, which will load the entire contents of the `biolife.xml` file in `cdsBiolife` (also leading to a bigger `SDataMod.dfm` file).

15. Compile and deploy your `SoapServer42` application in the cgi-bin or scripts directory of your Web server. Make sure to remember the URL. If the Web server is installed on your local machine, this can be something like `http://localhost/cgi-bin/SoapServer42.exe`.

16. You can test the output in a browser using the `/wsdl` switch. You're set if you see the interfaces `IWSDLPublish`, `IAppServer`, and `IAppServerSOAP`, as well as `ISoapDataMod42`, as can be seen in Figure 21.9.

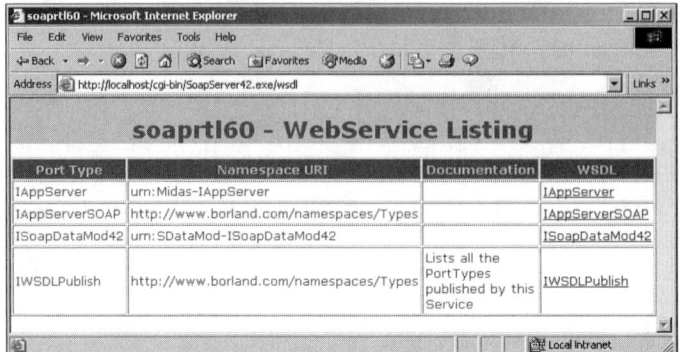

FIGURE 21.9   WebService Listing in Netscape browser.

Note that for real-world deployment you probably want to ensure that you compile the SOAP Server without the dynamic RTL and runtime packages, so you only have to deploy the executable together with the MIDAS.dll and Borlndmm.dll (which is easier than having to deploy all packages too). See Chapter 19 for more information on SOAP and Web Services.

C++Builder 6 Enterprise SOAP Client

Now that we have a SOAP DataSnap CGI executable Server written in C++Builder 6 Enterprise, we can start writing the Soap DataSnap Client written in C++Builder 6 Enterprise, using the following steps:

1. Start C++Builder 6 Enterprise, and start the project type that you want (anything works). I will assume that we use a regular Windows client, so do File, New—Application.

2. Save Unit1.cpp as `ClientForm.cpp`, and the project in file `SoapClient.bpr`.

3. Drop a `TSoapConnection` component from the Web Services tab of the C++Builder 6 Enterprise Component Palette.

4. Set the `URL` property of the `TSoapConnection` component to `http://localhost/cgi-bin/` (where server is the name or IP address of your SOAP server machine). Followed by the name of the SOAP Server application (`SoapServer42.exe`), then followed by `/soap`, and the interface name of your SOAP Data Module (`/ISoapDataMod42`) resulting in `http://localhost/cgi-bin/SoapServer42.exe/soap/ISoapDataMod42`.

5. Drop a `TClientDataSet` component, and set its `RemoteServer` property to the `TSoapConnection` component.

6. Now, open the `ProviderName` property, which will list `dspBiolife` (as exported from the SOAP Data Module). If at this time you do not see the name of the exported `TDataSetProvider`, you have to go two steps back and see if you made a mistake in the value for the `URL` property (you might want to try to replace `ISoapDataMod42` with `IAppServerSoap`).

7. Drop a `TDataSource` component and set its `DataSet` property to the `TClientDataSet` component.

8. Drop a `TDBGrid` component and set its `DataSource` property to the `TDataSource` component.

9. Drop a `TDBNavigator` component and set its `DataSource` property to the `TDataSource` component, too.

10. Drop a `TDBImage` component, set its `DataSource` property to the `TDataSource` component, and its `DataField` property to `'Graphic'`. Note that it might take a few seconds for the combo box of the `DataField` property to drop down because of the fact that the `TClientDataSet` has to request the meta data (to obtain the field names) from the SOAP Server.

11. Now, finally, set the `Active` property of the `TClientDataSet` component to `true` to get live data at design time, as can be seen in Figure 21.10.

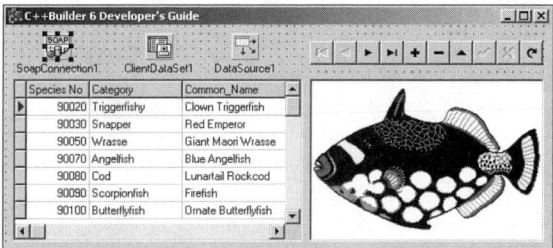

FIGURE 21.10   SOAP Client connecting to SOAP Server WebService.

Again, if you want to make modifications to the client application and send these back to the server, you need to call the `ApplyUpdates` methods (see Chapter 20 regarding the DataSnap for more details on this).

A final word on performance issues: Please note that it might take a while before you get a response when you first click any of the two buttons. The delay is caused by the fact that a SOAP request has to be put in a SOAP envelope and sent over the Internet to the Web service (using HTTP). At the server machine, the Web server CGI executable has to be started. Then, it must unpack the SOAP envelope, dispatch the SOAP request, execute the C++ method, pack the result back in a SOAP envelope again, send it back to the Web service consumer (again over the Internet using

HTTP), and then exit the Web service CGI executable again. A more efficient approach for real-world Web services will certainly be to deploy them as ISAPI/NSAPI DLLs or Apache DSO modules.

Summary

In this chapter, we looked at Borland's multitier technology called DataSnap. Specifically, we've seen the different ways in which DataSnap clients and servers can communicate, using DCOM, TCP/IP sockets, HTTP, and even SOAP.

Web Server Programming with WebSnap

by Bob Swart

This chapter covers Web server programming: CGI/WinCGI, ISAPI/NSAPI, Apache, and the Web App Debugger supported by C++Builder 6 Enterprise with the new WebSnap technology. WebSnap is an extension of the WebBroker technology (covered in Chapter 13 of *Sams C++Builder 5 Developer's Guide*—available on the CD-ROM). WebBroker has been available in C++Builder from the start and is present in the Professional and Enterprise editions of C++Builder 6.

WebAppDebugger

Before we start with C++Builder 6 Enterprise features contained in WebSnap, we want to show you the new general enhancements that have been made in C++Builder 6 Web server application support (in other words, available in C++Builder 6 Professional, too).

In order to start a new Web server application, just click File, New—Other and select the Web Server Application icon on the first tab from the Object Repository. This will show the new New Web Server Application Wizard, which now contains five possible Web server project targets instead of three (in contrast, Kylix only supports standard CGI and Apache DSO dynamic-shared objects on Linux).

The new options include support for Apache-shared modules (DLLs) on Windows as well as a special Web App Debugger executable. When you select the latter, you must also specify the CoClass Name of your Web server debug

application. In the screenshot, as shown in Figure 22.1, we've specified DrBob42 as
CoClass name:

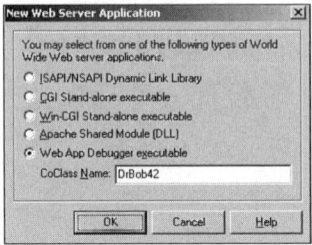

FIGURE 22.1   New Web Server application types.

If you selected a Web App Debugger executable target and clicked OK, you not only
get a new project with a Web module, but with a normal form as well. In fact, the
form is the first unit of your project, so I've saved my project files in WADMainForm.cpp
(for my Web App Debugger main form), WebMod.cpp (for my Web module), and
DebugWebApp.bpr (for my main project file).

Default Web Action Item

Of course, before we can debug or even run a Web server application, we should first
add at least one Web action item. Right-click the Web module, and start the Action
Editor. Press Insert to create a new WebActionItem, set the Default property to true to
make it the default (just in case), and let it return some dynamic HTML:

```
void __fastcall TWebModule2::WebModule2WebActionItem1Action(
     TObject *Sender, TWebRequest *Request, TWebResponse *Response,
     bool &Handled)
{
  Response->Content = "Hello, C++Builder 6 World!";
}
```

Now, we'll show you how to debug this very simple Web server application using the
C++Builder 6 Web Application Debugger (and without the need for an actual Web
server on your machine).

Debugging

If you hit F9, you just run the application with the empty form. Just let it run there
because to debug the Web server application, you need to start the Web Application
Debugger from the Tools menu or from the CBuilder6\bin directory as webappdbg.exe.

Starting the Web Application Debugger will give you the dialog box as shown in Figure 22.2.

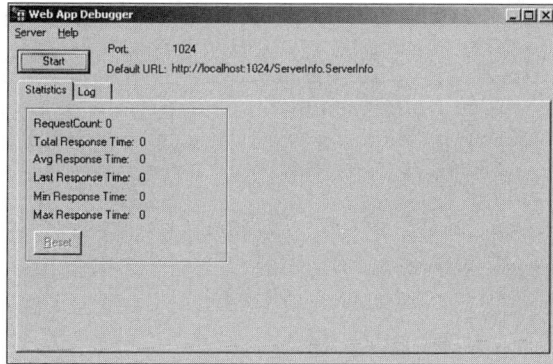

FIGURE 22.2   The C++Builder 6 Web Application Debugger.

We must first click the Start button, which turns the Default URL label into a real "url" that we can click to activate the Internet Explorer browser that we can use to view the Web server application. As soon as we click the Default URL of the Web Application Debugger, we get a list of registered servers, which includes the ServerInfo.ServerInfo as well as DebugWebApp.DrBob42 (and perhaps other Web server debug applications that have already been registered on your machine), as can be seen in Figure 22.3.

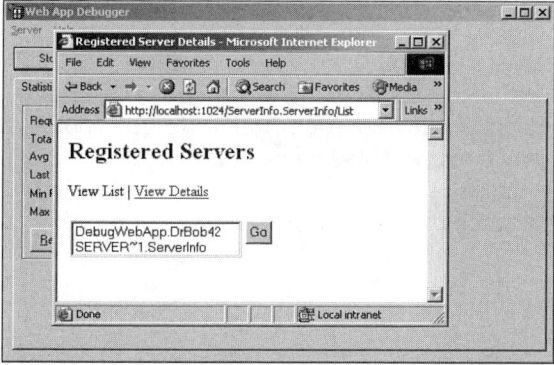

FIGURE 22.3   Registered Servers.

You can select a specific Web server application from the list and click GO to execute its default action. However, you can also first click the View Details link to see some more details of each Web server application. The details include the location of the

Web server application as well as the ability to "Clean" the registry (that is, remove all information about this particular Web server application from the registry). This is very helpful because we still have numerous old MIDAS 3 (and new DataSnap) application servers that we forgot to unregister before we removed them. At least with the Web Application Debugger you can remove registry information from Web server applications even long after the actual applications have been removed. There's just one warning: Do not remove the registry information for the `serverinfo.ServerInfo` application because that's the one that actually provides the Web Application Debugger with the list of registered Web server applications. Without the registry information for `serverinfo.ServerInfo`, the Web Application Debugger won't be able to get that list again. That is, until we re-run `serverinfo.exe` from the `CBuilder6\bin` to register it again.

Debug Web Server Application

As you can see in the details listing, each Web server application has a number of ways by which it can be identified. We have the CISID (or the GUID), the ProgID (like the `serverinfo.ServerInfo` and `DebugWebApp.DrBob42`). The third way specifies the full path to the registered application. Finally, the File Status reflects whether the Web server application was actually found at the specified location. Sometimes, you get Not Found Here, which might indicate that you've cleaned up your project, but forgot to clean the registry (this has happened to me a few times more than I care to admit).

Either of the three underlined links can be used to actually trigger the default action of the Web server application, in our case resulting in a simple "Hello, world!" Alternately, you could go back to the View List option, and just select the Web server application you want to debug and press on the GO button. In both cases, the Web Application Debugger will make a request to your (running) Web server application. And, because the latter was running from within the C++Builder IDE, any breakpoint that was set will be triggered after you reach it (a really cool way to enable debugging of Web server applications without the need for a real Web server). When you're done debugging, you can always move the Web module to a "normal" Web server application (the old trick to use multiple projects, each with a different target, all sharing the same Web module).

After you're done debugging, you should first close the Web server application, and then the browser window. That leaves the Web Application Debugger window, where you can now click the Stop button again. The Web Application Debugger dialog will show some statistics, and even more interesting information on the Log tab, including the event, time, elapsed time, path, content length, and content type.

Let's now start with the main course: WebSnap, the new Web server application framework available in the Enterprise edition of C++Builder 6.

WebSnap Demo

WebSnap is a new extension of the WebBroker Technology, but is not very well documented. It does combine lots and lots of possibilities with a significant learning curve, and is best demonstrated in practice. I have done some experiments with WebSnap and this section starts my (multipart) coverage of this Web server development featureset. This time, I will show you step-by-step how to write a simple WebSnap application that requires us to write very few lines of custom code (if any at all). In the next sections, I will focus on the alternative choices and steps that are possible along the way, including master-detail relationships (which are a bit more tricky than the simple table that we're using this time).

WebSnap can be compared with InternetExpress in that it's an extension of WebBroker, and it clearly uses some of the same ideas (which isn't too strange, if you consider that Jim Tierney, the architect of WebSnap, is also the same person who designed InternetExpress a few years ago).

WebSnap Components

To start a new WebSnap application, we need to click File, New—Other, and go to the WebSnap tab of the Object Repository. Here, we'll see three icons that make up the WebSnap wizards: one for a WebSnap application, one for a WebSnap Data Module, and one for a WebSnap Page Module, as can be seen in Figure 22.4:

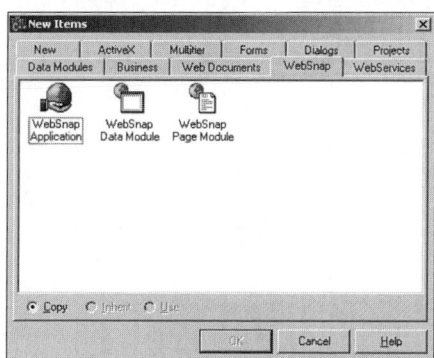

FIGURE 22.4   WebSnap Application, Data Module, and Page Module.

The difference will be made clear in a moment, but let's start with a new WebSnap application first. The New WebSnap Application wizard (of Figure 22.5) is a big dialog compared to the old WebBroker Application dialog (of Figure 22.1). It asks for a lot of information, but right now we should only specify the type of application (a CGI standalone executable), the Application Module Components being used (a Page Module instead of just a Data Module), and the Page Name itself, which can be set to Home.

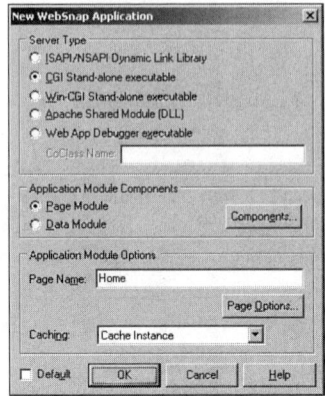

FIGURE 22.5   New WebSnap application.

We can specify some additional different options by clicking the Components button or the Page Options button, but these will be covered in more detail later in this chapter.

WebSnap Web Module

For now, just click the OK button to generate the new CGI project and Web module for our WebSnap application, which can be seen in Figure 22.6.

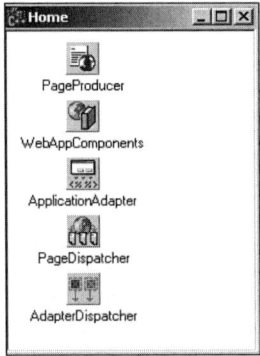

FIGURE 22.6   Home WebModule.

The Web module already contains five components: TPageProducer, TWebAppComponents, TApplicationAdapter, TPageDispatcher, and TAdapterDispatcher.

Now, save the new Web module in file pmHome.cpp and the project in file CGI.bpr, so we don't have to do it later.

WebSnap Data Module

We must now create a WebSnap data module, so we can actually add some datasets to connect to data (like the biolife table). We can do this by doing another File, New—Other, moving to the WebSnap tab of the Object Repository again, but this time selecting the second icon for the WebSnap data module. This will present us with the following dialog for a New WebSnap Data Module, as can be seen in Figure 22.7.

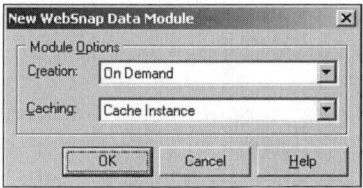

FIGURE 22.7 New WebSnap data module .

If we just leave it at the default settings and click OK, a new WebSnap data module has been added to our WebSnap CGI project. Save it in file wDataMod.cpp. Now, drop any datasets on this data module, such as a regular TClientDataSet component from the Data Access tab of the C++Builder 6 Component Palette. Set the Name property to cdsBiolife, and connect its Filename property to C:\Program Files\Common Files\ Borland Shared\data\biolife.xml for the biolife table with memo field and picture, among others.

Now, right-click the cdsBiolife component and start the Fields Editor. Right-click again and select Add all Fields. To let the WebSnap client application maintain its own state, we must now specify a primary key field (one that the client can use to tell the WebSnap server which record we want to work on). For the cdsBiolife table, we can just select the Species No field as keyfield, although generally any unique field would do. To specify that Species No is the key field, we need to select Species No in the fields editor, go to the Object Inspector, open up the ProviderFlags property, and set the pfInKey subproperty value to true.

DataSetAdapter

Now that we have a cdsBiolife dataset on the WebSnap data module, we can drop a TDataSetAdapter component next to it (third component from the left of the WebSnap tab), and call it dsaBiolife. We should assign the cdsBiolife to the DataSet property of the dsaBiolife TDataSetAdapter component. Next, open the TDataSet Adapter in the Object Treeview (new in C++Builder 6). Right-click the Actions to add all eleven possible actions (DeleteRow, FirstRow, PrevRow, NextRow, LastRow, EditRow, BrowseRow, NewRow, Cancel, Apply, and RefreshRow). Next, right-click the Fields to add all fields. The adapter fields that are generated correspond to the dataset fields from the cdsBiolife. This is an important moment of your design. If you want to hide some fields from your view (from the view that will be represented by this particular TDataSetAdapter), you should remove these fields now. If there are some fields that you don't ever want to use, you should remove them even from the persistent field list of the TClientDataSet—you should not wait until they appear in the TDataSetAdapter field list.

For the list of actions you should also consider carefully which actions you want to allow (that is, make available) for the end users, using this particular TDataSetAdapter. You might have correctly guessed by now that you can actually have more than one TDataSetAdapter connected to a T(Client)DataSet, each of these different TDataSetAdapter components corresponding to a different view (showing potentially a different set of fields, with potentially a different set of actions to apply on these fields). For the example, at this time we want to enable all actions and show all fields (so we don't have to delete anything).

WebSnap Page Module

It's now time to add the actual content-generating page modules to our WebSnap Web module application. We can do this with the third and last icon on the WebSnap tab of the Object Inspector: the WebSnap Page Module wizard (see Figure 22.8).

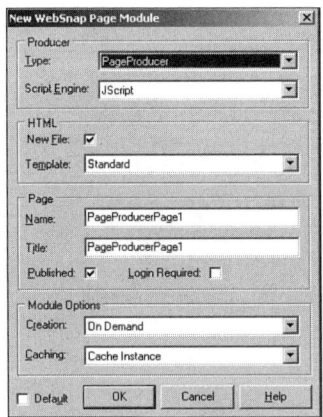

FIGURE 22.8   New WebSnap Page Module Wizard.

To work with our previously constructed TDataSetAdapter, do not leave the default properties set (still shown in the previous figure), but select an AdapterPageProducer instead of the regular PageProducer, give it a nice Name and Title such as Biolife. The Name, however, might not contain any spaces (it must be a valid identifier), but the

Title can, of course. Make sure you keep the Published property enabled, so the page module will be made visible with a link from our Home page that we created earlier. Also, if like me, you selected a CGI application, don't bother with the Login Required feature, since it does not work with CGI applications! This is caused by the fact that the Login feature uses a session component that is kept in the memory of the Web server application, so it has to remain up-and-running between requests (and a CGI application exits after each request). Later in this Clinic, I'll show you some more of the Login Required details (for ISAPI DLLs), but you don't have to select it for now.

After you click the OK button, a new Page Module is created for us, including an AdapterPageProducer component that we selected. Save the file in pmBiolife.cpp. Now, go to the Object TreeView, and open up the AdapterPageProducer. Right-click WebPageItems and select the New Component dialog. The New Component dialog will always only show the new components that are relevant for the particular situation. In this particular situation, we can add either an AdapterForm or a LayoutGroup. A LayoutGroup can be used to specify some layout options, and will be available at other locations as well. For now, add an AdapterForm. Right-click the AdapterForm, and this time add an AdapterFieldGroup (to show fields from cdsBiolife) as well as an AdapterCommandGroup (to operate on cdsBiolife, using the actions that we added to the dsaBiolife TDataSetAdapter component earlier).

We now still need to make a few connections. For the AdapterCommandGroup, we must assign its DisplayComponent property to point to the AdapterFieldGroup. The only thing left now is to make sure that the AdapterFieldGroup connects to the dsaBiolife TDataSetAdapter (from the unit wDataMod). To do so, we must first include the header of the wDataMod unit to the current unit (for example, using Alt+F11 or File, Include Unit Hdr...), and then assign the Adapter property of the AdapterFieldGroup to WebDataModule1->dsaBiolife to make the final connection.

Deployment

Before you can deploy WebSnap applications on a Web server (machine), there are two special files that have to be installed and deployed on that machine first. For more information, you should always read deploy.txt in your CBuilder6 directory. Basically, you must register WebBrokerScript.tlb as well as stdvcl40.dll on the Web server machine using tregsvr.exe—all found in the CBuilder6\bin directory. Also, WebSnap applications require the Microsoft Active Scripting Engine, which is included in IE5 and later, and installed on Windows 2000 and later (but if it's not on your Web server, you can download it from http://msdn.microsoft.com/scripting).

And finally, you must ensure that the XML files that the ClientDataSets are using are also available on the Web server (if you remove the PATH portion in the FileName property, then you can put them in the same directory as your Web server application).

After these preparations, let's turn to the CGI.exe project. By default, all C++Builder projects have their options set to generate small executes, by using the dynamic RTL as well as runtime packages. However, this results in additional files that you have to deploy on the Web server. And, because I do not want to do that (I always want to limit the number of files that I have to deploy), we should start the Project, Options dialog. On the Compiler tab, click the Release button; on the Linker tab, uncheck the Use dynamic RTL option, and finally on the Packages tab, uncheck the Build with runtime packages option. Now, do Project, Build CGI to build the project. This should result in a CGI.exe of 2,096,128 bytes—mainly caused by the fact that the wDataMod.dfm is 2,487,537 bytes big if the ClientDataSet is open at design time (so the data is made persistent inside this .dfm file). But, even without an active ClientDataSet, the WebSnap executable will still be over one megabyte in size. Without having written one line of C++ code!

Anyway, we now need to deploy both the executable CGI.exe as well as all .html files: pmHome.html (for the Home page) and pmBiolife.html (for the biolife Page Module). These two .html files are the ones that can be modified using Dreamweaver or FrontPage. Deploying the files means moving them to the cgi-bin or Scripts directory of your Web server. If you do this on your local machine, the URL to view the CGI.exe can be something like http://localhost/Scripts/CGI.exe or http://localhost/cgi-bin/CGI.exe. You can view the results of the CGI.exe in a browser and get the main home page, which is still empty because we didn't do anything special with the TPageProducer component on the main WebModule, see Figure 22.9.

FIGURE 22.9   CGI.exe.

Next to the home page is a link to the Biolife page, and when you click it, you get the real results of the WebSnap application, as can be seen Figure 22.10.

Remember that we added all fields to the DataSetAdapter, which explicitly included the Graphic field. If we hadn't made sure to add all fields at that place, the Graphic field would not have been part of the displayed fields (even if by default you get all fields when you didn't select any). My best guess is that it's part of some helpful default optimization rule.

FIGURE 22.10   Output of WebSnap application in Internet Explorer.

Tweaking

We haven't yet written a single line of C++ code. But this is about to change because we do need some tweaking at this point. The project source code that has been generated so far contains a little bug that prevents the command buttons from operating. Click the NextRow or LastRow button and you'll see what I mean—we are still at the first record! Believe me when I tell you that the problem is not related to the fact that we have been building CGI standalone executable targets because you will also be unable to move to the next record with an ISAPI Dynamic link library or a Web App Debugger executable.

The problem has to do with multipart requests, and specifically the `ReqMulti.obj` file, which isn't linked with our application. If you take a look at the WebSnap demos in `CBuilder6\Examples\WebSnap`, you'll notice that these projects all work just fine, but their source code differs slightly from the source code generated by C++Builder 6.

To make a long story short—to fix the problem, do Project, View Source, and add one line of code (under the three #pragma lines that are already present in `CGI.bpr`):

```
#pragma link "ReqMulti.obj"
```

Now, save, recompile, and redeploy the CGI project, as can be seen in Figure 22.11. Now you can use the buttons to navigate through the Biolife table (First, Prev, Next, and Last), or even edit the content of these fields and make changes to the bitmap. In case of the bitmap, you need to specify a filename on your local disk, which will be sent to the Web server application after you click the Apply button (which is shown if you click the Edit button first). You then want to continue to the browse state, using the BrowseRow button.

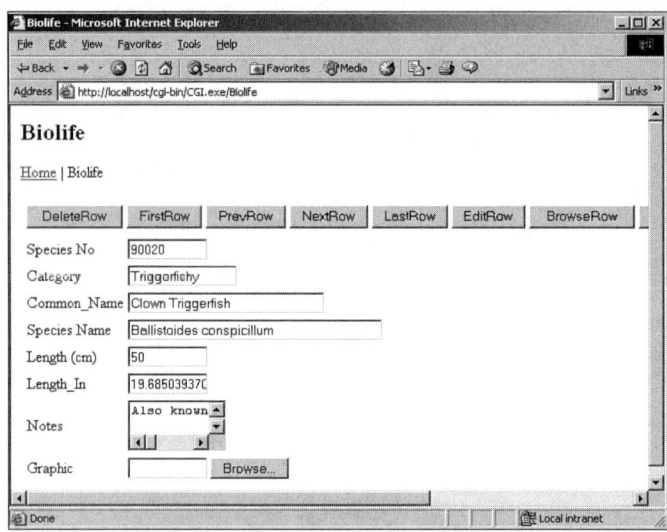

FIGURE 22.11   Edit WebSnap output in Internet Explorer.

If you don't see the correct new picture, you might need to refresh the page before you see it (for some reason, I always have to—probably an Internet Explorer 6 issue).

Let's see how this all works by examining the WebSnap Architecture, Adapters, and Components from the ground up. While we do this, we'll discover some handy properties to make it look even better (the output of Figures 22.10 and 22.11 was much too wide because of the long captions on the buttons, for example).

WebSnap Architecture

So far, we've seen only a number of WebSnap components and wizards in use. We can already compare the general working of WebSnap with that of WebBroker (see Chapter 13 of *Sams C++Builder 5 Developer's Guide* for WebBroker details). In this section we will discuss a number of the differences between WebBroker and WebSnap, explain why you can use WebBroker components in a WebSnap environment, but not (easily) the other way around, and finally start the description of the most important WebSnap building blocks: the adapters.

Actions Versus Pages

Where WebBroker was working with a single Web module, using Web action items (and PathInfo) to distinguish the incoming requests, the new WebSnap architecture uses Page Modules to prepresent individual pages (again dispatched using PathInfo). Using WebBroker you have a choice in using the HTMLDoc (internal) or HTMLFile (external) property to store the HTML template, and the default was using the internal HTMLDoc property (such as the MidasPageProducer).

The WebSnap architecture now uses external HTML templates as default, which makes it easier to connect these external HTML files to Web editors such as Dreamweaver or FrontPage (or even Notepad). So, we see Actions versus Pages as one of the main differences.

WebSnap Web Modules

Where a WebBroker application starts with a Web module, a WebSnap application starts with either a TWebAppDataModule or a TWebAppPageModule. Both are just a container for WebSnap system components that we'll see later, such as dispatchers, global adapters (the TApplicationAdapter), a user list, and session components.

The WebSnap Application Wizard will automatically create the Web Module of choice (either a TWebAppDataModule or a TWebAppPageModule) including the selected components. However, you can always add more components later (or remove existing components), but you cannot change a TWebAppDataModule into a TWebApp PageModule or vice versa. TWebAppComponents is the component in a TWebAppDataModule that references all of the system components in use by the WebSnap application.

TWebAppDataModule **Versus** TWebAppPageModule

The difference between a WebAppPageModule and a TWebAppDataModule is that the former generates a page. The PageProducer property references the producer component responsible for generating content. This property must not be nil or no content will be generated. The WebSnap Application Wizard automatically adds a page producer component when it creates a new TWebAppPageModule.

WebSnap Page Modules

A TWebPageModule holds all the components needed for generating a specific Web page. The WebSnap Page Module Wizard creates a TWebPageModule descendant as well as the selected PageProducer for generating the content of the Web page. It also adds code to the initialization section of the unit it creates that registers the TWebPageModule descendant with a factory object that the WebSnap application can use to create the Web page module.

The page producer that the wizard adds to the Web page module becomes the value of the PageProducer property (and if you replace it with another PageProducer property later, it will automatically be set to the PageProducer property). If the

PageProducer property is nil, the Web page module can't generate the content of a Web page.

WebSnap Data Modules

TWebDataModule is compatible with WebSnap applications. The initialization section of TWebDataModule registers a factory that is used by the WebSnap application to create the data module. Use TWebDataModule as a container for components that can be used by other modules in your WebSnap application.

WebSnap Versus WebBroker

WebBroker is Action-based, whereas WebSnap is Page-based. The support for multiple (optionally cached) data modules and page modules make it easier to maintain bigger Web sites than was previously possible. Server side scripting adds to the flexibility as well. And finally, WebSnap wouldn't be possible without Adapter components to glue the Delphi code to the scripting side (and back).

Server Side Scripting

One of the nice new features of WebSnap is the support for Server Side Scripting. In the previous version of C++Builder, we had Internet Express, which enabled support for Client Side Scripting (the JavaScript that was used to bind XML data packets to HTML input controls), but this was limited to prewritten client-side JavaScript. With WebSnap, we can not only use generated Server Side JavaScript, but can also easily add our own scripting code, or use external Web page editors (such as the aforementioned Dreamweaver or FrontPage) to help write the server-side scripting.

We can use the HTML tab in the C++Builder code editor to modify the generated HTML and even add our own scripting snippets. A very simple example script that displays the Name of the Page as HTML title is programmed as follows (inside the main WebSnap Web Module):

```
<html>
<head>
<title>
<%= Page.Title %>
</title>
</head>
<body>
<h1><%= Application.Title %></h1>
```

In case you wonder, the <%= and %> are just shortcuts for the JavaScript code Response.Write to write the text between them.

As usual a good starting point to playing with server-side scripting is the code that C++Builder generates, such as the login and user information on the main home page, which is coded as follows:

```
<% if (EndUser.Logout != null) { %>
<%   if (EndUser.DisplayName != '') { %>
  <h1>Welcome <%=EndUser.DisplayName %></h1>
<%   } %>
<%   if (EndUser.Logout.Enabled) { %>
  <a href="<%=EndUser.Logout.AsHREF%>">Logout</a>
<%   } %>
<%   if (EndUser.LoginForm.Enabled) { %>
  <a href=<%=EndUser.LoginForm.AsHREF%>>Login</a>
<%   } %>
<% } %>
```

WebSnap Adapters

We've seen that the WebSnap architecture uses adapters as a communication layer between the data layer and the presentation layer. As data layer we can use anything that can store or retrieve data, including the obvious choice: a dataset. As presentation layer, WebSnap produces HTML in different formats (or modes) such as browsing, editing, and so forth.

In this section, we'll explain how an adapter works, and which adapters are available in the C++Builder 6 Enterprise implemenation of WebSnap.

Adapters

There are five available Adapter components on the WebSnap tab of C++Builder 6: the regular TAdapter, the TPagedAdapter (showing adapter output in multiple pages), TDataSetAdapter (a logic connection between an adapter and a dataset), and the TLoginFormAdapter (to provide you with a login form). Finally, we also have the TApplicationAdapter and TendUserAdapter, but these are singleton adapters and usually only added to your main WebSnap Web module.

Adapters consist of fields and actions, and if you right-click any TAdapter (or derived component) you can select the Fields Editor and the Actions Editor; usually the place to add custom fields and/or their actions.

Adapter Fields   The Adapter Fields are storage places for data. Think of them as the properties of WebSnap adapter layer. For the regular TAdapter component, there can be six different kinds of Adapter Fields: AdapterBooleanField, AdapterField (the generic value), AdapterFileField, AdapterImageField, AdapterMemoField, and finally AdapterMulti ValueField.

All Adapter Fields are derived directly or indirectly from the TCustomAdapterField, which has no published properties or events, but does call event handlers to retrieve the Adapter Field value (OnGetValue), validate a value (OnValidateValue), update the value (OnUpdateValue), as well as customize the displayed output (OnGetDisplayText).

Adapter Actions   The Adapter Fields can be seen as placeholders for the data, whereas the Adapter Actions can be seen as methods or routines that can operate on this data. Although it's useful for the user to see or be able to enter data, there is always some kind of action (login, move to the next page, submit the data, delete record, and so forth) that has to be taken, so there's always need for Adapter Action components.

For each Adapter Action, we can define the Name of the action as well as the ActionName and DisplayLabel (to be used on buttons, for example, as we'll see later when we combine Adapter Actions with AdapterCommandGroups inside AdapterPageProducers).

An Adapter Action can also define its ExecuteAccess, which specifies the access rights needed to execute this particular action. The server-side script accesses the CanExecute property and this value is checked against the end user's rights. This is something that we'll see again when we add users to a userlist for the Login functionality.

Adapter Actions also have a number of events, namely the OnExecute (the most important one), OnAfterGetResponse, OnBeforeGetResponse, OnGetEnabled, and OnGetParams.

TAdapter
A regular TAdapter component has regular Adapter Fields and custom Adapter Actions. Adapter components are used in combination with a TAdapterPageProducer component—connecting the Adapter Fields to DisplayComponents (like an AdapterField Group or AdapterGrid) and the Adapter Actions to AdapterActionButtons (from an AdapterCommandGroup).

TPagedAdapter
A TPagedAdapter is a TAdapter component with an additional PageSize property that defines the size of the items on a particular page. If you didn't already add explicit actions to the Adapter, you'll see NextPage, PrevPage, and GotoPage actions automatically (they will disappear as soon as you set the PageSize property back to zero again).

TDataSetAdapter
The TDataSetAdapter is one of the most useful TAdapter components, connecting to a TDataSet, mapping dataset fields and operations to Adapter Fields and Actions. Furthermore, like the TPagedAdapter, a TDataSetAdapter also has a PageSize property that specifies the number of records that are displayed on a single page. Very useful!

TLoginFormAdapter

The TLoginFormAdapter has default adapter fields for user name, password, and next page (which enables the user to select a Web page to open after logging in). TLoginFormAdapter has a single default action for logging in. If the WebSnap application also contains an end user adapter such as TEndUserAdapter or TEndUserSession Adapter, TLoginFormAdapter will call the end user adapter's Login() method to log the user in. This adapter will be covered in more detail in the WebSnap Login section of this chapter.

TApplicationAdapter

The TApplicationAdapter is a global adapter that is used only in the main WebApp Web Module. It contains a single field called Title that gets its value from the ApplicationTitle property. We can add custom adapter fields and actions to the TApplicationAdapter, use server-side script, and use the Application variable to access fields and actions of the ApplicationAdapter. For example, <%= Application.Title %> writes the title of the application.

TEndUserAdapter

The TEndUserAdapter is another global adapter that is used only in the main WebApp Web Module. The TEndUserAdapter has two default Adapter fields: DisplayName and LoggedIn. These fields contain the user's name and login state. We can write code in the OnGetDisplayName and OnIsLoggedIn event handlers to override their values. TEndUserAdapter also has two default actions: LoginForm and LogoutOut. The former displays a login form, whereas the latter logs the user out. We can use the LoginPage property to specify the Page Module name of the login page, and can respond to the OnLogin and OnLogout event handlers.

At the scripting side, we have the EndUser script variable, which can be used to display end user fields and execute end user actions. The following JavaScript snippet displays the name of the end user when logged in:

```
<% if (EndUser.LoggedIn) { %>
<h1>Welcome <%= EndUser.DisplayName %> </h1>
<% } %>
```

The following JavaScript snippet displays a login or logout hyperlink.

```
<%    if (EndUser.Logout.Enabled) { %>
  <a href="<%=EndUser.Logout.AsHREF%>">Logout</a>
<%    } %>
<%    if (EndUser.LoginForm.Enabled) { %>
  <a href=<%=EndUser.LoginForm.AsHREF%>>Login</a>
<%    } %>
```

TEndUserAdapter also specifies the access rights for the end user. If the WebSnap application contains a TWebUserList, TEndUserAdapter uses the TWebUserList to obtain rights for the specific end user. We can also write code for the OnHasRights event handler to perform this task.

TEndUserSessionAdapter

The TEndUserSessionAdapter is a special TEndUserAdapter that we will always use in combination with the TSessionsService component (more about this in the WebSnap Sessions section of this chapter).

Custom Adapter Components

We can derive from TAdapter or TCustomAdapter to create our own custom WebSnap adapter components. See my Web site at http://www.drbob42.com/BobAdapt for a plug-in wizard to create your own custom adapter components for Delphi, Kylix, and C++Builder.

WebSnap Producers

Apart from Adapters, the WebSnap Architecture depends on a special TPageProducer to actually produce the dynamic HTML. The TTableProducer components have a small(er) role in the WebSnap world.

TAdapterPageProducer

A regular TPageProducer uses the HTMLDoc or HTMLFile properties to store a HTML template to be filled in (using the OnHTMLTag event handler), whereas the TAdapterPageProducer uses an external template file, and generated dynamic HTML as well as scripting code to connect AdapterFields to DisplayComponents and AdapterActions to CommandButtons.

Apart from the TAdapterPageProducer, which is the WebSnap-specific PageProducer, we can also select a regular TPageProducer, a TDataSetPageProducer (both inherited from WebBroker), a TInetXPageProducer (from InternetExpress), and finally a TXSLPageProducer, which uses XML and XSL. However, it's the TAdapterPageProducer that can work with TAdapters——the core of WebSnap.

Enough theoretical overview already, let's return to WebSnap and cover Login, Sessions, and the final WebSnap application combining everything together.

WebSnap Login

In the previous demo we used WebSnap to produce a Web server application that could be used to browse, edit, and search (I didn't show that) the biolife table. This time, I want to extend that example in two ways. For one thing, I want to show how to produce a master-detail relationship using the well-known customer and orders tables. But first, I want to use some kind of authentication, using a login form (and as a consequence, managing a list of known users and passwords at the same time).

WebSnap Application

To start the new WebSnap application, click File, New—Other, and go to the WebSnap tab of the Object Repository for the WebSnap application icon. This will result in the WebSnap Application Wizard, which needs some specific options set (compared to last time, when we mainly used the default settings). I want to select the Web App Debugger executable with DrBob42 as CoClass name again.

The second group of options specifies the Application Module Components. We'll leave this set to a Page Module (instead of a regular Data Module). However, this time we need to click the Components button to add some additional components that we need for this example. We need to select the End User Session Adapter (drop down the End User Adapter combobox and select the TEndUserSessionAdapter), Session Service, and User List Service (the only two we don't need are the Dispatch Actions and Locate File Service), resulting in Figure 22.12.

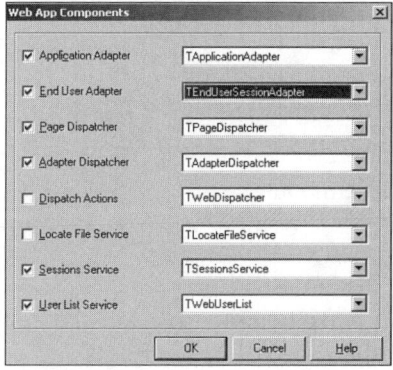

FIGURE 22.12   Specific Web App components.

The third group of options are the Application Module Options. I always use Home as the name for the first page (instead of PageProducerPage1), but I leave all other Page Options set at their default. This is the starting page of the application, so it can be a general welcome to anyone, without the need to login.

After you click OK, a new WebSnap application is generated. Along with a bit more than that, actually. You'll noticed an empty new form as well as your page module. The empty form is generated because we selected the Web App Debugger server type. The best thing to do now is to save your project, renaming Unit1 (the empty form) to MainForm.cpp, Unit2 (the page module) to pmHome.cpp, and the project itself to WAD.bpr (again—you might want to save everything in a new directory).

You can resize the main form, add a nice label to it (to remind you that—when you see it—the new WAD WebSnap application is running).

WebSnap Page Module

The WebSnap Page Module for the first (Home) page contains a few more components than last time. Apart from the `PageProducer`, we now also have `WebAppComponents`, `ApplicationAdapter`, `EndUserSessionAdapter`, `PageDispatcher`, `AdapterDispatcher`, `SessionService`, and a `WebUserList`, as can be seen in Figure 22.13.

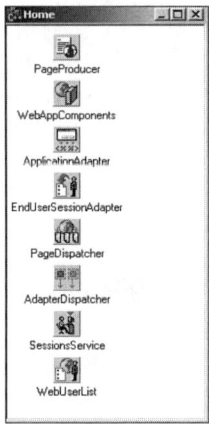

FIGURE 22.13   Home page module.

WebUserList

We actually need to start with the latter to create a list of "known" users, their passwords, and (optionally) their specific access rights and permissions. So, double-click the `WebUserList` to get into the `WebUserList->UserItems` editor. You can add new users, their password, and access rights here. I always leave the latter empty, but in real-world situations, the access rights field can be a convenient way to make a distinction between normal users and administrators (or database managers), for example.

Press Ins or click the left button to add a new `UserItem`. Then, select a `UserItem` and use the Object Inspector to assign values to the `AccessRights` (left empty), `Password`, and `UserName`.

For now, I've just added a few users and their passwords, resulting in the following list of five users and their passwords, as can be seen in Figure 22.14.

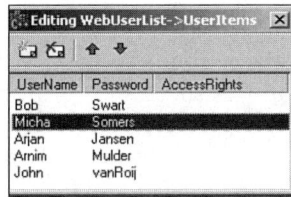

FIGURE 22.14   WebUserList editor.

Login Page Module

After we have a list of users and passwords, we can start to make the official Login page of our WebSnap application. For this, we need to add a new WebSnap Page Module (the usual way).

We need to make a few changes in this dialog (see Figure 22.15). First of all, the Producer Type must change from a regular PageProducer to an AdapterPageProducer. Second, the Name property of the Page options should be set to Login (or something like that). The Title will automatically follow the changes in the Name.

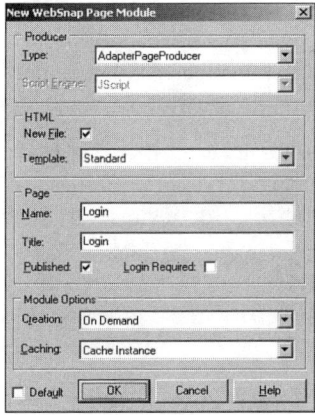

FIGURE 22.15   New WebSnap Page Module.

Note that we should not check the Login Required option at this time because this is the login dialog itself. Or at least, we'll make it the Login dialog in just a second.

When you click OK, a new Page Module is created, with only an AdapterPageProducer inside. Save this file in pmLogin.cpp, and go to the WebSnap tab of the C++Builder 6 component palette to drop a TLoginFormAdapter on the Login Page Module.

LoginFormAdapter

The `LoginFormAdapter` knows about Login names, passwords, and the next page that a user wants to visit (if the login was successful). Remember last time when we connected dataset fields via a `DataSetAdapter` to adapter fields from the `AdapterPage` `Producer`? Well, the `LoginFormAdapter` will show a slightly different way to connect to an `AdapterPageProducer`.

To see the internal fields of the `LoginFormAdapter`, just double-click it so the Field Editor starts. Then, select Fields and right-click it and select Add All Fields. This results in three (explicitly) persistent fields: `AdaptUserName`, `AdaptPassword`, and `AdaptNextPage`. You can select each individual adapter field and change some properties, such as the `DisplayLabel` for the `AdaptUserName` (change it from `UserName` to simply `User`). If you've decided to leave the `Password` field empty for one or more of your users (in the `WebUserList`), this is generally no problem. However, I always want to enforce the use of passwords, and you can do so (at design time), by setting the `PasswordRequired` property of the `LoginFormAdapter` component to true.

Login Form

The three new adapter fields will now need to be connected to the `AdapterPage` `Producer`, resulting in a visual Login form that we can use. To actually build the Login Form, we need to go back to the `AdapterPageProducer` on the Login Page Module (after all, it's the Page Producer that generates the HTML). If you double-click the `AdapterPageProducer` you get the Web Page Editor.

In the Web Page Editor, select the `AdapterPageProducer` (it's the only component anyway), and right-click with the mouse to get the Add New Components dialog. Alternately, you can press the Ins key or press the button in the upper-left corner of the Web Page Editor. In whatever way you do it, make sure you select the `AdapterForm`. Then, for the `AdapterForm`, right-click it and add an `AdapterCommandGroup` as well as an `AdapterFieldGroup` (note that you can do a multiselect in the Add Web Component dialog).

We'll now get two design time warnings that are easy to solve (see Figure 22.16).

Select the `AdapterCommandGroup` component, and assign the `AdapterFieldGroup` to its `DisplayComponent` property. Next, select the `AdapterFieldGroup` component and assign the `LoginFormAdapter` to its Adapter property. This last step will not only remove the last warning, but will also result in a preview of the Login form. Note the `UserName` field, which only displays the label `User` (as we specified earlier).

You might want to move the `AdapterFieldGroup` up in the list of the `AdapterForm` (if only to make sure the `Login` button itself—which is part of the `AdapterCommandGroup`— is shown under the three input fields).

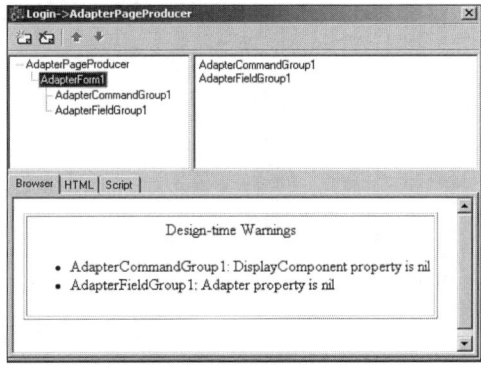

FIGURE 22.16   Web Page surface designer editor.

Incorrect Login

Before we continue to test this, we need to do a few more things. First of all, we need to have some pages to select as Next Page that actually require Login. We'll do that in a moment. What we need to do first is to make sure that the user will get some useful feedback when an attempt to login has failed. For that, or generally any error situation, we need an `AdapterErrorList` (which—as you probably can guess—displays a list of error messages). Select the `AdapterForm` component, click Ins, and select an `AdapterErrorList` to give Login (and general error) feedback. As usual, we get a design time warning that the `Adapter` property of the `AdapterErrorList` is not assigned yet, therefore, we should assign it to the `LoginFormAdapter` (just like we did with the `AdapterFieldGroup`), see Figure 22.17.

The main visual difference (at design time) between the `AdapterErrorList` and the `AdapterFieldGroup` or `AdapterCommandGroup` is that the former isn't displayed in the left pane, but only in the right pane of the Web Page Editor. It's not such a big deal if you think about it because it only means that the `AdapterErrorList` cannot get any child components of its own (whereas the `AdapterFieldGroup` and `AdapterCommandGroup` can).

But what did we just do with the `AdapterErrorList`? Nothing, really, it seems. We only assigned the `Adapter` property back to the `LoginFormAdapter`. Which means that if anything goes wrong, it will be displayed inside the HTML that is produced by the `LoginFormAdapter`. And that means the same Login form where the user tried to login, as we will see later, when we're finally ready to try to Login to our WebSnap application.

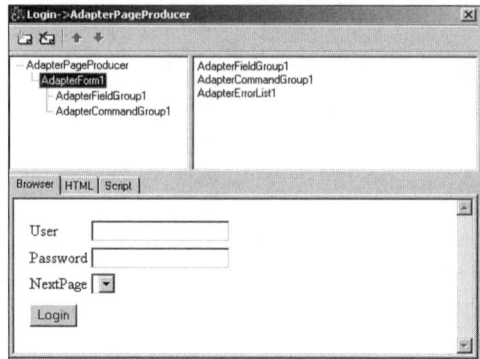

FIGURE 22.17   Final preview of Login form in the Web Page Editor.

EndUserSessionAdapter

And that's not all, because we now have to tell the WebSnap application that the Login page is ready to be used. In other words, should anyone (who is not yet logged in) want to enter a page with the Login Required option set, this person must be sent to the Login page we just made. To specify the Login page, we must go back to the first Page Module (the pmHome unit), select the EndUserSessionAdapter component, and set its LoginPage property to Login (the name of your Login Page Module).

You can now save everything and run the WAD application. Remember that you have to start the Web App Debugger to view and login to the WebSnap application. For a more interesting demo (with more than just the login and home page), we will add session support to our WebSnap application.

WebSnap Sessions

Apart from the ability to login to a Web site, which is very useful of course, we should also be able to maintain state in WebSnap applications; in other words, session management. Using WebBroker, this can be done in three ways: using fat URLs, using hidden fields, or using cookies. Using WebSnap, however, this can be done somewhat easier. In the previous section, we used the TLoginFormAdapter and the TWebUserList components to enable the login functionality in our WebSnap application. You might not have realized it, but this also requires the maintenance of state—logged in or not—in your current session. The thing is that it was done implicitly and behind our back (like many of the WebSnap features). But you can use the same techniques to store any information in the user's session, using the TSessionsService component. The TSessionsService component is able to store name=value pairs for us with little effort.

TSessionsService

To spoil the surprise right from the start, `TSessionsService` is in fact using cookies to store session IDs, but not the session values themselves. (Those are stored in memory in the `TSessionsService` object, which is the reason why they don't work for CGI executables that are shutdown between requests, and why we must keep our WAD Web App Debugger executable up and running to remain logged in). Login and Session support works best in ISAPI applications.

Let's continue with the WebSnap application to show how we can use the `TSessionsService` component to maintain some session information. First, add a new Page Module to obtain some session-related state information such as the date-of-birth of the particular visitor (it might be a nice idea to be able to greet a visitor on his or her birthday).

Click File, New—Other; go to the WebSnap tab and select the WebSnap Page Module Wizard to add a new page. Set its Name/Title to Birthday, and make sure it uses an `TAdapterPageProducer` component because we will be using an Adapter component itself in a moment (see Figure 22.18).

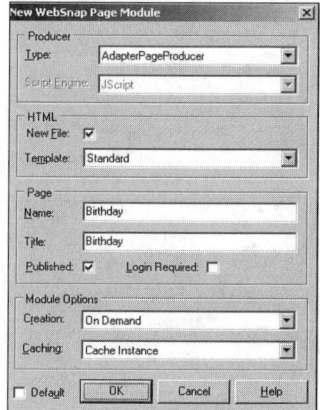

FIGURE 22.18   New WebSnap Page Module Birthday.

Click OK and save the Page Module in `pmBirthday.cpp`.

On the `TWebPageModule`, we now need to drop a regular `TAdapter` component, which will be used to request the date of birth for this particular visitor. While we're at it, we might as well ask for his or her name (it wouldn't be nice to congratulate someone with the message "congratulations visitor on your birthday!"). It would, of course, be so much more personal to use a person's own name.

TAdapter **Fields**

What we need to do first, is to right-click the Adapter component to start the Adapter Fields Editor to define two new adapter fields named Name and Birthday. When you click Insert inside the Adapter Fields Editor, the Add Web Component dialog pops up (see Figure 22.19). Here, you can define what kind of AdapterField you want.

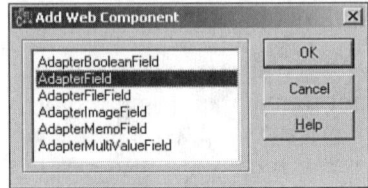

FIGURE 22.19   Add new AdapterField.

Both the Name and Birthday should be a regular (string) AdapterField, so just add two AdapterField components and name them Name and Birthday, see Figure 22.20.

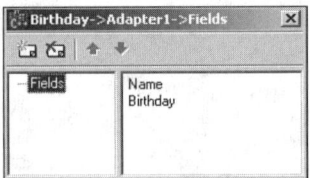

FIGURE 22.20   Birthday.Adapter1.Fields overview.

To make the appearance of the two AdapterFields more user friendly, make sure to change the DisplayLabel property of Name to "What's your name?" and the DisplayLabel property of Birthday to "When were you born?" In a moment, this will give a great and inviting message to the visitor.

TAdapterPageProducer

To make the connection between the Tadapter, its fields, and the generated output, we must now double-click the TAdapterPageProducer to start the Web Page Editor again. Right-click the AdapterPageProducer and add an AdapterForm. Then, right-click the AdapterForm and add an AdapterFieldGroup. This will give you the expected design time warning (the Adapter property is nil), which is solved by assigning the Adapter property of the AdapterFieldGroup to the Adapter component we dropped just a minute ago, see Figure 22.21.

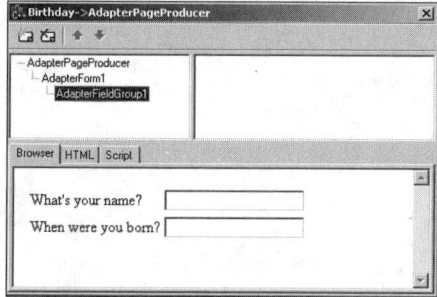

FIGURE 22.21 Birthday input adapter form.

It's nice to be able to fill in your name and birthday, but it would be really useful if we could actually submit these values to the WebSnap Web server application. So, let's add an `AdapterCommandGroup` component to the `AdapterForm`, which, of course, yields another design time warning that is solved by assigning the `DisplayComponent` property of the `AdapterCommandGroup` component to the `AdapterFieldGroup`.

TAdapter **Actions**

Before we can actually add a submit button (and optionally a reset button) to the `AdapterCommandGroup`, we must first make sure there's a corresponding action in the `Adapter` component (`AdapterFields` correspond with `DisplayFields`, and `AdapterActions` correspond with `CommandButtons`, remember?).

Close the Web Page Editor for now, and return to the `TAdapter` component. Right-click it and this time start the Actions Editor. We need just one action—to submit our name and birthday—so add one `AdapterAction` of name `SubmitNameAndBirthday`. We'll get back to the implemenation in a moment, let's return to add the buttons first.

Double-click the `TAdapterPageProducer` again, and in the Web Page Editor select the `AdapterCommandGroup` and right-click to select Add All Commands. This will automatically (explicitly) create a new button with name `CmdSubmitNameAndBirthday` and caption `SubmitNameAndBirthday`, so you might want to add some spaces here and there in the `Caption` property of this button, as can be seen in Figure 22.22.

Now, you can recompile the application, run it (using the WebApp Debugger), go to the `Birthday` page, fill in your Name and Birthday, click the Submit Name And Birthday button, and nothing will happen. Using Netscape the page will even be cleared, and even using Internet Explorer you can click Home and Return to Birthday, empty the page and start all over again. Nothing is saved! Which is not so strange because we still need to implement the `SubmitNameAndBirthday` action event handler, of course.

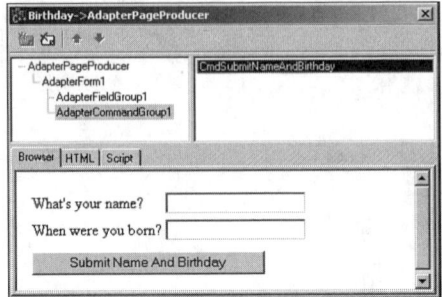

FIGURE 22.22   Final birthday input adapter form.

Go back to the TAdapter component, right-click it to select the Actions Editor, select the (only) action SubmitNameAndBirthday, move to the Events tab of the Object Inspector, and write the following code for the OnExecute event handler:

```
const char* const strName = "Name";
const char* const strBirthday = "Birthday";

void __fastcall TBirthday::SubmitNameAndBirthdayExecute(TObject *Sender,
    TStrings *Params)
{
  _di_IActionFieldValue MyValue;
  MyValue = Name->ActionValue;
  if (MyValue->ValueCount == 1)
    Session->Values[strName] = MyValue->Values[0];
  MyValue = Birthday->ActionValue;
  if (MyValue->ValueCount == 1)
    Session->Values[strBirthday] = MyValue->Values[0];
}
```

Now, you can again recompile the application and run it, but it won't work the way you hoped it would. The information is stored in your session, but other than that nothing will happen—the page is still cleared and you can start all over again. Again not so strange because we only store and never retrieve the session data.

We need to modify the Name and Birthday AdapterFields to make sure that—when we need them—their values are retrieved from the current session. That would ensure these two fields are initialized by the session data, resulting in a nonempty screen when we return.

To implement this, we need to right-click the Adapter component, select the Fields Editor, and for each of the Adapter Fields write a single line of code for the OnGetValue event handler, as follows:

```
void __fastcall TBirthday::NameGetValue(TObject *Sender, Variant &Value)
{
  Value = Session->Values[strName];
}

void __fastcall TBirthday::BirthdayGetValue(TObject *Sender, Variant &Value)
{
  Value = Session->Values[strBirthday];
}
```

This will ensure that the values entered are persistent during the lifetime of the session (i.e. when you close your browser, the data is gone again), but it's a start (see Figure 22.23).

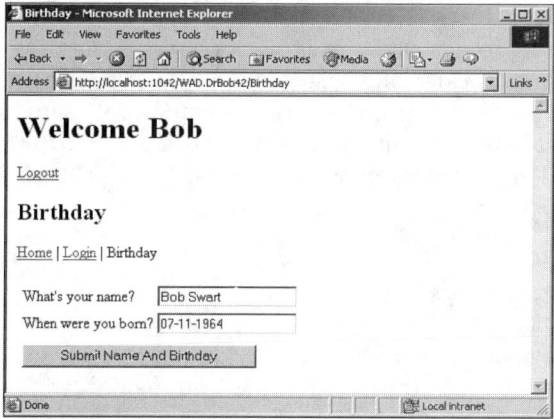

FIGURE 22.23 Final birthday input adapter form.

TSessionsService

Here is a final technique to show how we can access the session ID; we can modify the HTML generated by the Birthday page to include the session ID itself. Just add the following scripting snippet to the HTML tab of the Page Module, and you'll see for yourself:

```
<p>
Session: <%= Session.SessionID.Value %>
</p>
<hr>
```

WebSnap Master-Detail Example

For the master-detail overview, we must create a WebSnap data module, so we can actually add some datasets to connect to real-world data (the customer and orders tables). So, click File, New—Other again, and select the WebSnap Data Module from the WebSnap tab of the Object Repository. This will present us with a dialog for a New WebSnap Data Module. If we just leave it at the default settings and click OK, a new WebSnap data module has been added to our WebSnap project. We should now drop any datasets on this data module, such as two regular TClientDataSet components from the Data Access tab of the C++Builder 6 Component Palette. Rename the ClientDataSet components to cdsCustomer and cdsOrders, and connect their filename property to C:\Program Files\Common Files\Borland Shared\data\customer.xml and orders.xml. Now save the data module in file wDataMod.cpp (make sure it ends up in the project directory, and not in the data directory again).

Right-click both ClientDataSet components and start the fields editor. Right-click again and make sure to Add all fields (you can remove any field from that list, but make sure to leave the CustNo and OrderNo fields because we need them in a moment). Now we need a TDataSource component, pointing to the cdsCustomer dataset, to create a master-detail relationship. Assign the DataSource to the MasterSource property of the cdsOrders dataset, and then click the ellipsis next to the MasterFields property, so we can assign this to the CustNo fields of both datasets.

Primary Key

We already saw that to enable the WebSnap client application to maintain its own state, we must now specify a primary key field (one that the client can use to tell the WebSnap server which record we want to be working on). For the cdsCustomer dataset, we must select the CustNo field, so go to the Object Inspector, open the ProviderFlags property and set the pfInKey subproperty value to true. For the cdsOrders dataset, we must do the same for the OrderNo field.

DataSetAdapter

Now that the cdsCustomer and cdsOrder datasets are ready, it's time to drop two TDataSetAdapter components from the WebSnap tab of the component palette; call them dsaCustomer and dsaOrders—see Figure 22.24. The DataSet property of dsaCustomer should point to the cdsCustomer dataset, and dsaOrders should point to cdsOrders.

Go to the Object Treeview, select the DataSetAdapters and right-click the Actions property to add all possible Actions. Do the same with the Fields property, so we have adapter fields for every field in the two ClientDataSets. Now, although the cdsOrders is already configured to be a detail of the cdsCustomer master table, we still need to specify that the dsaCustomer is a MasterAdapter of the dsaOrders. We can do this by assigning dsaCustomer to the MasterAdapter property of dsaOrders.

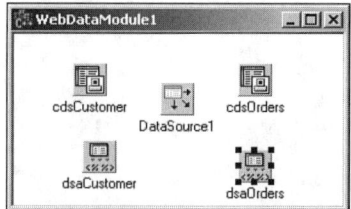

FIGURE 22.24 WebSnap Data Module.

This is again a very important moment in your design. If you want to remove some fields from your view (from the view that will be represented by a particular DataSetAdapter), you should remove these fields from the DataSetAdapter. If there are some fields that you don't ever want to use, you should remove them from the persistent field list of the ClientDataSet—and not wait until they appear in the DataSetAdapter field list.

For the list of actions you should also consider carefully which actions you want to allow (that is, make available) for the end users, using this particular DataSetAdapter. You might have correctly guessed by now that you can actually have more than one DataSetAdapter connected to a (Client)DataSet, each of these different DataSetAdapter components corresponding to a different view (showing potentially a different set of fields, with potentially a different set of actions to apply on these fields).

WebSnap Page Module

Now that we have a master-detail relationship between the ClientDataSets (and even the DataSetAdapters), it's time to create a new WebSnap Page Module to show the actual data. Click File, New—Other, go to the WebSnap tab, and double-click the WebSnap Page Module icon. Because we want to use the DataSetAdapters, we must change the Producer Type from a regular PageProducer to an AdapterPageProducer (as usual). Apart from that, you will probably want to change the name (and, hence, the title as well) to something like Customer, see Figure 22.25.

The final option that you need to check is the Login Required field. This will make sure that we won't be able to get to this page unless we're logged into the system. We'll see this in a moment.

When you click OK, the new Page Module is created, including an AdapterPageProducer component. Save this new unit in file pmCustomer.cpp, and press Alt+F11 to include the header of the wDataMod unit, so we can access the DataSetAdapters on the data module.

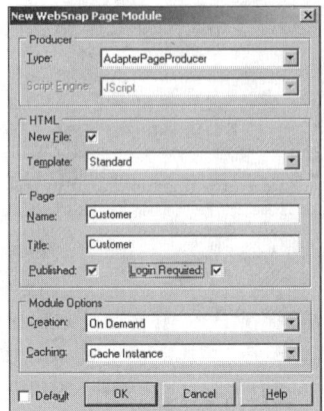

FIGURE 22.25   New WebSnap Page Module.

Next, double-click the AdapterPageProducer to start the Web Page Editor again. This time, we're going to build a master-detail output form. In the Web Page Editor, we can always right-click a component to get the New Component dialog that will produce subcomponents. First, we need to add an AdapterForm under the AdapterPageProducer. Then, an AdapterCommandGroup, AdapterFieldGroup, and AdapterGrid under the AdapterForm. Now we have three design time warnings, that should be easy to fix. The AdapterCommandGroup should have its DisplayComponent property point to the AdapterFieldGroup. The AdapterFieldGroup should have its Adapter property point to the WebDataModule1->dsaCustomer (the master table). The AdapterGrid should have its Adapter property point to WebDataModule1->dsaOrders (note that the DataSetAdapters are coming from WebDataModule1, which is the reason that the header of unit wDataMod must be included, or else you won't be able to find the two DataSetAdapters to use). The final results should be as shown in Figure 22.26.

Note that the buttons are again very wide (just like in the first example shown in Figures 22.10 and 22.11). Fortunately, we can do something about that. Go to the Web Page Editor, right-click the AdapterCommandGroup and Add All Commands. Now, for each command button, go to the Object Inspector and change the Caption property. Remove all Row from the button captions to result in a much nicer view as can be seen in Figure 22.27.

It's time to compile the application and run it. As you will see, the Home page contains four links (to Home, Login, Birthday, and Customer) as well as a link to the Login page in the upper-left corner. This means that the visitor can decide to Login at any time during the session (not only when it's needed). Let's not login right away, but just click the Customer link (which requires Login).

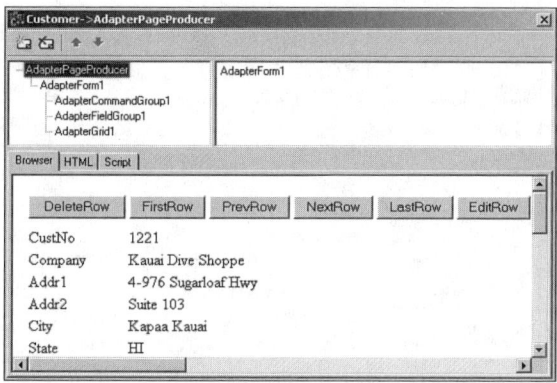

FIGURE 22.26   Customer-Orders data at design time.

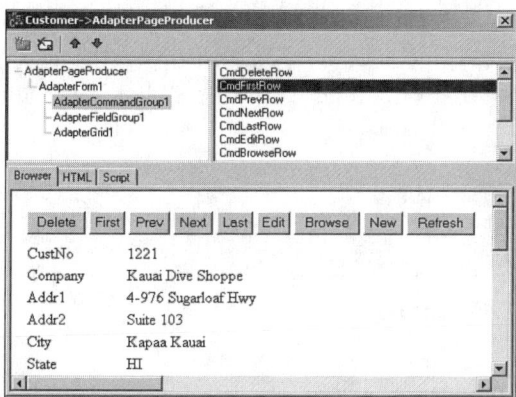

FIGURE 22.27   Final Customer-Orders data at design time.

As can be expected, we do not end up on the Customer page, but rather on the Login page. We have to specify our User (Name) and Password here, and the NextPage is already preselected with the Customer page that we wanted to go to, see Figure 22.28. How nice!

Just enter the correct User and Password, click Login and you'll end up in the Customer page. If you didn't specify the correct Password (or an unknown User), you'll get an error message presented in the same Login page (because we made sure to point the AdapterErrorList back to the LoginFormAdapter). Right now, the error message is presented below the Login button, which can be fixed (if you want) by moving the AdapterErrorList higher in the list of subcomponents from the AdapterForm on the Login Page Module.

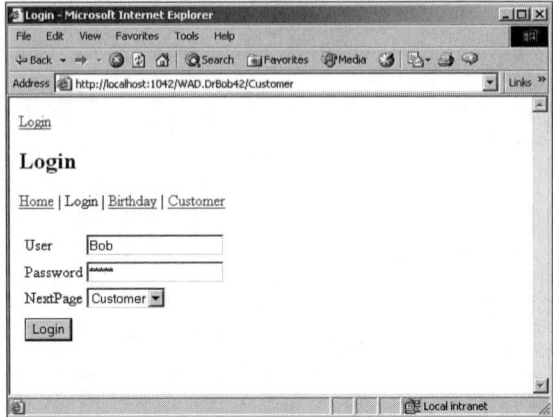

FIGURE 22.28   WebSnap Login page of WAD.

If you've logged in correctly, you get a view of the Customer-Orders overview on the Customer page (note that I'm afraid it isn't possible to see the details in Figure 22.29, but believe me—they're there).

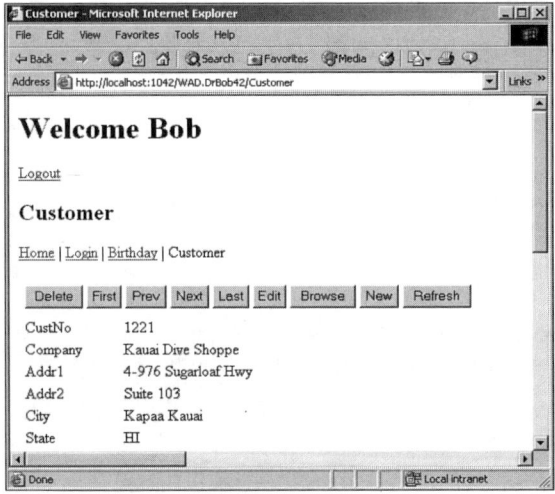

FIGURE 22.29   WebSnap Customer page of WAD.

Linking Pages by Name

So far, we've only seen the main master page, with the details listed on the same page (although the page was a bit long to show all details in the same screen shot).

However, sometimes you want to have a special page for the masters only, and then use buttons to link to pages that show the single master and all details.

For this I want to create two more new TWebPageModules: one for the master (customer) table, displayed in a grid-like output, and one for the master and details (customer-orders) displayed in a field group for the master and grid for the details. We've just made the latter, but let's make the former now (the customers in a grid), including a link from one page to another.

Click File, New—Other and select the WebSnap Page Module Wizard to add yet another Page Module to our project. Make sure to select the AdapterPageProducer again, and call it Customers (instead of the previous one, which was called Customer—showing a single customer at a time, instead of all customers). Also, don't forget to check the Login Required option as well as the Published option.

After you've created the new WebSnap Page Module, save it in pmCustomers.cpp and make sure to press Alt+F11 to include the header of the WebSnap Data Module (in wDataMod), so you can access the dsaCustomers TDataSetAdapter. This is a very convenient way to authorize users and actions with the Customer data.

Next, double-click the AdapterPageProducer to start the Web Page Editor again. This time, we're going to build a master grid-output form. Right-click in the Web Page Editor to add an AdapterForm under the AdapterPageProducer. Then, add an AdapterCommandGroup and AdapterGrid under the AdapterForm. We get two design time warnings, which are easy to fix (as always). The AdapterCommandGroup should have its DisplayComponent property point to the AdapterGrid. The AdapterGrid should have its Adapter property point to WebDataModule1->dsaCustomers (one of the DataSetAdapters from WebDataModule1, and the reason that the header of wDataMod must be included), resulting in Figure 22.30.

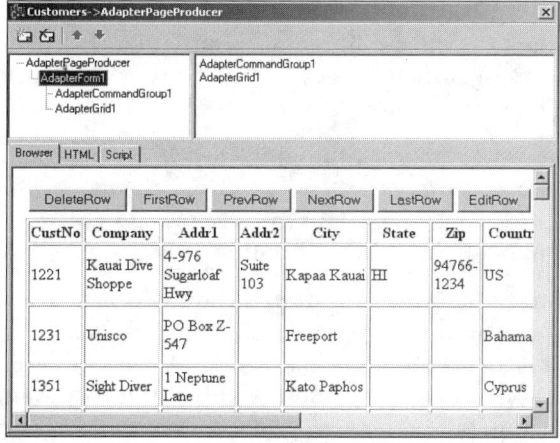

FIGURE 22.30   Customers data at design-time.

Now, as you can see from Figure 22.30, there are far more buttons that I want to see. In fact, I would never want to enable the user to edit anything inside an AdapterGrid display. So, select the AdapterCommandGroup, right-click it, and make sure to select only the Components (buttons) for the Actions you want such as FirstRow, PrevRow, NextRow, LastRow, and BrowseRow.

The new design time output is getting closer to what we want already, see Figure 22.31.

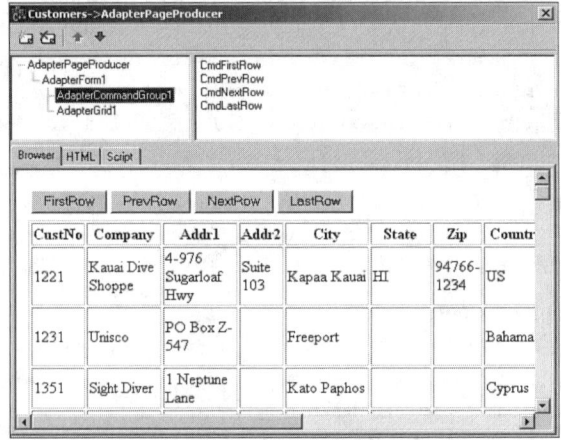

FIGURE 22.31   Customers data at design-time.

Apart from removing some of the buttons, we should also consider removing some of the fields. Especially because I want to add a special command button (to view the details) in the last column—which currently is out of view. To do this we must not only remove some dataset fields, but also add a new column to the AdapterGrid. Right-click the Adapter Grid, do Add All Columns, and then remove the columns you don't need (leaving only the CustNo, Company, City, Country, and Contact fields, for example), see Figure 22.32.

After that, it's time to add a new column to the AdapterGrid, so right-click the AdapterGrid, select New Component, which gives us a dialog with three choices: AdapterCommandColumn (displaying a button), AdapterDisplayColumn (displaying a field value), or AdapterEditColumn (giving the option to edit a value), see Figure 22.33.

Clearly, we need the AdapterCommandColumn, so add that one. Warning: Your display might look ugly once again because by default the new AdapterCommandColumn will show all available AdapterActions. To fix this, just select the AdapterCommandColumn component and right-click on it to add the only action you want (this time don't do an Add All Command, but only do an Add Command) and select the BrowseRow Command which is the easiest to use in this situation.

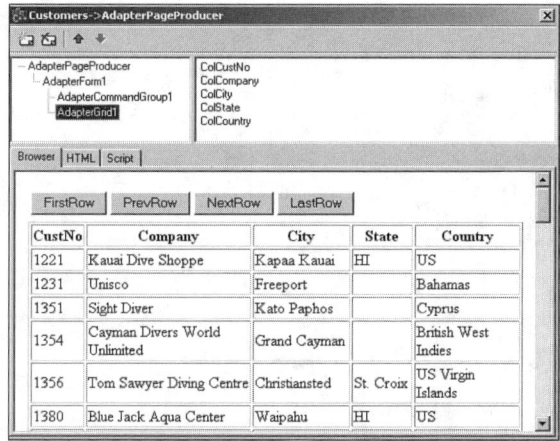

FIGURE 22.32   Add All Columns.

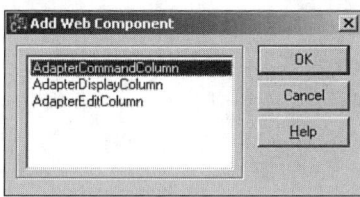

FIGURE 22.33   Add New Column.

Select the BrowseRow button, go to the Object Inspector and specify the name of the Customer (single value) Page Module in the PageName property. This will make sure that whenever we click the BrowseRow button, we will jump to the Customer Page Module, within the context that we were (that is, the current row in which the button was shown).

Finally, make sure the buttons get some nicer captions (such as Details for the BrowseRow button), and the final output at design time can be seen in Figure 22.34.

If you save your work, recompile it, and run it, you can use the Web App Debugger again to view the WebSnap application in action. Whenever you click the Details button, you will jump to the master-detail page with the complete information of the customer and orders database, including the option to click the Edit button at that location to change the data, if you want.

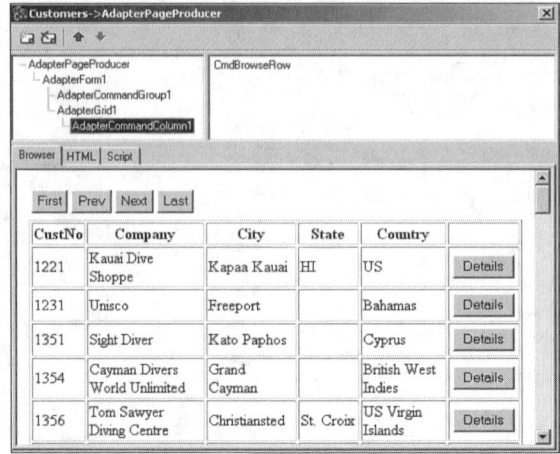

FIGURE 22.34 Final output.

Tweaking and Turning

Now, let's do some final tweaking and turning before it's time to wrap this topic (follow-up articles on WebSnap will be published on my Web site at http://www. drbob42.com/CBuilder). The first thing I want to do is to actually hide the Customer Page Module because we now have a Customers Page Module with a Grid as a new entrance (so no need to show both the Customer and Customers page from the top-level menu). But when we created both Page Modules, we checked the Published option already. So, how can we unpublish a WebSnap Page Module? Fortunately, that's not too difficult. For our example, open the file pmCustomer.cpp and go to the last line. Now, place the << wpPublished option in comments, which will unpublish the page module:

```
static TWebPageInit WebInit(__classid(TCustomer), crOnDemand, caCache,
  PageAccess /* << wpPublished */ << wpLoginRequired, ".html", "", "", "", "");
```

If you recompile and run the WebSnap application again, you will notice that the Customer menu is gone, but you can still get there using the Details button on the Customers page. Exactly the way I want it.

Final Deployment

Although the Web App Debugger application is really nice to debug and test without the need for a real Web server, it is not a result that you can deploy. In fact, you can deploy any target except for the Web App Debugger project. Fortunately, you can just start another WebSnap application, remove the intial Application Module, and move all units (except for the first empty main form) over to this new WebSnap application. If you do this in a project group, you can even work on the WebSnap projects at the same time, sharing the WebSnap data and page modules among the different targets. Take a look at the `CBuilder6\Examples\WebSnap` directory for the example projects that are all available as ISAPI DLLs and as Web App Debugger executables.

Summary

We've covered a lot of WebSnap including Application Modules, Page Modules, Data Modules, Adapters, the `AdapterPageProducer`, server-side Scripting, login, state and session management, database producing, debugging, and deployment. All with very little C++ code that we had to write (mainly for the session support). There's far more to cover, but this chapter should at least give you a good idea of what the possibilities are with WebSnap in C++Builder 6 Enterprise.

PART V

Open Tools API

IN THIS PART

23

The Tools API: Extending the Borland IDE

by Paul Gustavson

Most of the discussion thus far in this book has been centered on adding functionality to the applications you produce using C++Builder, but did you know you can also add new functionality and capabilities to C++Builder itself? It's true! Borland's Tools API allows new wizards, menu items, editor features, debugging support, tool bar buttons, and much more to be added to both the C++Builder and Delphi IDEs. It's quite powerful, and in this chapter we'll look at how to make use of the Tools API for C++Builder.

Tools API Fundamentals

Before we jump into examples, it's important to understand the fundamentals of the Tools API. The Tools API provides a set of *interfaces* to access the IDE. Under C++Builder 6 there are 109 interfaces. If you're up on COM, you know that an interface is akin to an abstract class identifying properties and methods to a block box object. This means we're not privy to the implementation, we just know how to interface to the object containing the implementation. We can only affect the behavior contained within the implementation by what's provided through the interface methods. Like COM, Tools API interfaces are identified by a GUID, accessed using a query with an Interface ID (IID), and provide automatic reference counting for memory management.

The Tools API is really a combination of two basic categories of interfaces and services that are interrelated: the Open Tools API and the Native Tools API. In this chapter, we'll take a look at both of these APIs.

Open Tools API (OTA)

The Open Tools API (OTA) provides a set of abstract interfaces and services that allow extensions that can be applied to multiple versions of an IDE (for example, C++Builder 5, C++Builder 6, Delphi 6, and so on). You can use the OTA to write extensions that can access the source editor, the debugger, the message view, modules to a project, packages, to-do items, provide key bindings for the IDE, and much more.

The OTA is, to the core, very COM-like, which, theoretically, allows a single extension such as a wizard to work for multiple versions of C++Builder or Delphi because it is interface focused and not implementation focused—the interface will not change across multiple versions. This also means that a wizard can be written either in Delphi or C++Builder and work for an environment representing the opposite language. In fact, any language that supports COM interfaces, which can also deal with Borland's __fastcall calling convention and the AnsiString data type, can potentially be used to write an IDE extension.

Native Tools API (NTA)

The Native Tools API (NTA) is a slightly different animal, but not by much. It provides a set of *native* interfaces and services into the IDE, enabling us to get directly at IDE elements (thus, some of the implementation elements). This includes components, the form designer, the menu bar, toolbar buttons, a project's action list(s) and images list(s), as well as the project's to-do list, code insight, and much more. It's pretty powerful, but keep in mind that custom extensions that use an NTA interface are often tied to the specific version of the IDE because the NTA is more implementation focused. Furthermore, because of the IDE dependency, extensions deployed as DLLs require the VCL package.

Although most discussions within newsgroups, on the Web, and in literature center primarily on the Open Tools API, make no mistake, discussion often includes aspects of the Native Tools API. That's because it's hard to focus and use the Open Tools API without also being tempted to use the Native Tools API to create IDE extensions. Basically, they are a matched pair—like bread and butter. And, from this point forward, this chapter treats these two APIs as a combined pair.

Tools API Capabilities

To recap, the Tools API interfaces allow you to interact with, and control elements of, the IDE. These elements include the following:

- main-menu bar
- tool bars
- action lists

- image lists

- source editor

- keyboard macros and bindings

- form editor

- debugger

- code completion

- message view

- modules

- packages

- To-Do list

We could go on. If you browse through the ToolsAPI.hpp file located in the Cbuilder6\source\Toolsapi folder on your system, you'll find a listing of all the available interfaces provided by the Tools API. Typically, we access and control these IDE elements through an extension we develop known as a wizard. In the example that we will build on, we'll be using many of these interfaces.

NAMING CONVENTIONS

You might have noticed, as you browsed through the Tools API header file, a number of acronyms that are used as prefixes for classes, interfaces, and data types. Table 23.1 provides a few of the more common ones used with the Tools API.

Table 23.1 Tools API Naming Convention Prefixes

Acronymn	Description
IOTA	Prefix representing an Open Tools API interface, which is COM-like. Custom extensions that use IOTA interfaces exclusively are not tied to the specific version of the IDE, allowing the extension to be useful for other versions of the Borland IDE.
INTA	Prefix representing a Native Tools API interface, which provides direct (native) access to IDE objects. Custom extensions that use a Native Tools interface are tied to the specific version of the IDE and require the VCL package for DLL implementations.
_di_	Prefix used to represent a Delphi Interface wrapper around an interface. In C++Builder, these data types are used in code for declaring variables to associate to an interface.
IIDG	Used to identify an Interface ID for an interface. (*COM programmers should know this one*).

As stated in the Borland Help, using the Tools API within an extension you might develop (that is, a wizard) is simply a matter of writing classes that implement certain interfaces, and calling on services provided by other interfaces. In fact, writing a Tools API class is similar to writing a property or component editor. The Tools API-based code you develop can be compiled and installed into the IDE as a design time VCL package. It's also possible to provide extensions to the IDE through a DLL, but the DLL has to be identified in the Windows Registry with the IDE for its extensions to take affect. We'll talk more about DLLs a little later in the chapter.

> **NOTE**
>
> If you're not familiar with VCL packages and registering components, you might want to review the material provided in Chapter 4, which focuses on VCL Components and Packages.

Creating a Wizard

Let's get our feet wet and create a simple wizard that integrates into the C++Builder IDE using the Tools API. So that we develop something practical, the wizard we will create will provide a mechanism for users to gauge the memory performance of their applications under development—it is called the MemStat Wizard. We won't get into the specifics of how to attain and measure memory performance (examine the code on the CD-ROM for that insight). Instead, our goal here is to understand how to establish a wizard and extend the IDE using the Tools API.

> **NOTE**
>
> You can follow along with the MemStat Wizard example we develop in this book by locating the following folders for this chapter on the CD-ROM that accompanies this book.
>
> - `wizard_part1_simple`
>
> - `wizard_part2_services`
>
> - `wizard_part3_notifier`
>
> - `wizard_part4_editor`
>
> - `wizard_part5_dll`
>
> Each folder represents progressions of our MemStat Wizard that we build on within this chapter. The label tacked on to the end of each folder identifies the example for the section being discussed. For instance, the example contained in the `wizard_part2_services` folder is discussed in the "Creating and Using Services," section within this chapter. The project name for each of these examples is `wizard.bpk`.

Selecting a Wizard Interface

The first step is determining the type of wizard interface we need for the MemStat Wizard. The ToolsAPI.hpp file reveals four different types of wizard interfaces as listed in Table 23.2.

Table 23.2 Tools API Wizard Interfaces

Wizard Interface	Description
IOTAFormWizard	Used to represent a wizard that generates a new unit or form. This type of wizard resides in the Object Repository, which can be accessed through the New Items dialog box.
IOTAMenuWizard	Used to represent a simple wizard such as a dialog box that is accessed from the IDE's Help menu.
IOTAProjectWizard	Used to represent a wizard that generates a new project or application. This type of wizard resides in the Object Repository, which can be accessed through the New Items dialog box.
IOTAWizard	This is the root interface for the other three wizard interfaces. It's used to represents a simple wizard such as a dialog that can be custom configured to the IDE's menu bar or tool bar.

What differentiates these four interfaces is how each one is invoked. The first three are automatically associated to either the Object Repository or the IDE's Help menu. The last interface, IOTAWizard, must be manually associated to an IDE element.

For simplicity and prototyping the IOTAMenuWizard provides the type of interface we need for building and demonstrating our example. All we want, initially, is a wizard that can be invoked from the Help menu bar.

Next, we need to build a specialized wizard class that inherits the IOTAMenuWizard interface. That sounds fairly simple, but there are other interfaces involved that we need to inherit as well.

Reconstructing TNotifierObject for C++Builder

It might be obvious that IOTAMenuWizard is a descendent of IOTAWizard, but IOTAWizard descends from another interface called IOTANotifier. We need to pay special attention to IOTANotifer because the compiler is expecting our custom class to support its methods. Let's take a look at how this interface is defined to see what methods we need to implement.

```
__interface IOTANotifier;
typedef System::DelphiInterface<IOTANotifier> _di_IOTANotifier;
__interface INTERFACE_UUID("{F17A7BCF-E07D-11D1-AB0B-00C04FB16FB3}")
            IOTANotifier  : public IInterface
```

```
{

public:
    virtual void __fastcall AfterSave(void) = 0 ;
    virtual void __fastcall BeforeSave(void) = 0 ;
    virtual void __fastcall Destroyed(void) = 0 ;
    virtual void __fastcall Modified(void) = 0 ;
};
```

IOTANotifier is a Tools API interface used by the IDE to notify an item (such as a wizard) of important events. We'll talk more about some of the specialized Notifier interfaces provided by the Tools API in the "Creating and Using Notifiers" section, but, for the case of our wizard, we need to understand the underpinnings provided by IOTANotifier. The four methods associated to IOTANotifier are explained in Table 23.3.

Table 23.3   Tools API—IOTANotifier Methods

Method	Description
AfterSave	Call immediately after the associated item is successfully saved. Not called for IOTAWizard.
BeforeSave	Called immediately before the associated item is saved. Not called for IOTAWizard.
Destroyed	The associated item is being destroyed.
Modified	The associated item is being modified. Note: not called for IOTAWizard.

Although we are creating a simple wizard that has no real concern for notifications at this point, the IDE still expects our custom class to be capable of supporting the abstract methods of IOTANotifier. We need something in its place that provides empty implementations for IOTANotifer methods because the compiler is expecting to find these methods. To fill-in for IOTANotifier and support custom wizards, Borland provides a convenient class within Delphi called TNotifierObject, which is designed to be inherited by a custom wizard class in place of IOTANotifer. In Delphi, this class integrates seamlessly for supporting wizards. Unfortunately the ToolsAPI header file provided within C++Builder does not include a TNotifierObject class!

So, what do we do? The easiest thing to do is to build our own TNotifierObject C++ class and stick it in a file that we can use to support our Tools API implementations for C++Builder. We need TNotifierObject so that we can build a Wizard class that supports the methods identified in the interfaces it inherits. A newly created header file called ToolsAPIEX.h contains the declaration for this TNotifierObject class, which is shown in Listing 23.1.

Listing 23.1   ToolsAPIEx Header File—TNotifierObject Class Declaration

```cpp
#ifndef ToolsAPIExH
#define ToolsAPIExH
//— — — — — — — — — — — — — — — — — — — — — — — — — — — — — — — — — — — — —.

#include <ToolsAPI.hpp>
#include <typeinfo>

// macro for implementing interfaces
#define QUERY_INTERFACE(T, iid, obj)       \
  if ((iid) == __uuidof(T))                \
  {                                        \
    *(obj) = static_cast<T*>(this);        \
    static_cast<T*>(*(obj))->AddRef();     \
    return S_OK;                           \
  }

#ifdef DLL   // we'll need this for building a DLL
#define BorlandIDEServices LocalIDEServices
extern _di_IBorlandIDEServices LocalIDEServices;
#endif


class PACKAGE TNotifierObject : public IOTANotifier {
public:
  __fastcall TNotifierObject() : ref_count(0) {}
  virtual __fastcall ~TNotifierObject();
  void __fastcall AfterSave();
  void __fastcall BeforeSave();
  void __fastcall Destroyed();
  void __fastcall Modified();
protected:
  // IInterface
  virtual HRESULT __stdcall QueryInterface(const GUID&, void**);
  virtual ULONG __stdcall AddRef();
  virtual ULONG __stdcall Release();
private:
  long ref_count;
};

#endif
```

Notice one of the first things we do in setting up to use the Tools API is to include the ToolsAPI.hpp file. You'll then notice a macro at the top called QUERY_INTERFACE. This macro was defined and used, as suggested by Borland, to simplify the processing required for querying each of the interfaces that a custom wizard inherits and uses (getting a pointer to an interface object). The effect is identical to what's required with COM using the QueryInterface() method. In a short while, you'll see this macro being utilized.

Following the definition of this macro, you'll see support for handling a DLL implementation, which we will talk about a little later. Finally, we come across the declaration for our TNotiferObject class. In addition to the four methods contained by IOTANotifer, there are three other methods we've defined in our class: QueryInterface(), AddRef(), and Release(). The IOTANotifer interface, which we are modeling, descends from IInterface, which is the base class for all Object Pascal interfaces. In C++Builder, IInterface is a child interface of IUnknown. If you're familiar with COM, you'll recognize that IUnknown is the base class for all COM interfaces. In this case, our TNotiferObject needs to support the methods of IInterface to operate accordingly. The implementation for the entire class, which is contained in our ToolsAPIEx.cpp source file that we've created, is provided in Listing 23.2.

Listing 23.2   ToolsAPIEx Source File—TNotifierObject Class Implementation

```
#pragma hdrstop

#include "ToolsAPIEx.h"
#pragma package(smart_init)

HRESULT __stdcall
TNotifierObject::QueryInterface(const GUID& iid, void** obj)
{
  QUERY_INTERFACE(IInterface, iid, obj);
  QUERY_INTERFACE(IOTANotifier, iid, obj);
  return E_NOINTERFACE;
}


// — — — — — — — — — — — — — — — — — — — — — — — — — — — — — — —·


ULONG __stdcall TNotifierObject::AddRef()
{
  return InterlockedIncrement(&ref_count);
}

// — — — — — — — — — — — — — — — — — — — — — — — — — — — — — — —·
```

LISTING 23.2   Continued

```
ULONG __stdcall TNotifierObject::Release()
{
  ULONG result = InterlockedDecrement(&ref_count);
  if (ref_count == 0)
    delete this;
  return result;
}

//———————————————————————————————————————.

__fastcall TNotifierObject::~TNotifierObject()  {}
void __fastcall TNotifierObject::AfterSave()  {}
void __fastcall TNotifierObject::BeforeSave() {}
void __fastcall TNotifierObject::Destroyed()  {}
void __fastcall TNotifierObject::Modified()   {}
```

The implementation for QueryInterface() method queries each interface that we've inherited or used. In this case it is IInterface and IOTANotifer. AddRef() and Release() handle the interface reference counting (saving and releasing the interface). You'll notice it's very COM-like—as designed.

For the purposes of our demonstration, and for supporting future custom wizards, the TNotifierObject class interface and implementation have been saved to the ToolsAPIEx.h and ToolsAPIEx.cpp files included on the companion CD-ROM for this chapter. You can use this file as part of any C++Builder project used to build custom wizards for the IDE.

NOTE

Although the Tools API supports C++ implementations through C++Builder, its native language is Delphi. Keep in mind that the IDE for C++Builder is written in Delphi as well. Although this chapter is focused on using C++ to extend the IDE, it's quite possible to extend the IDE for C++Builder using Delphi code units. This is something to consider because many of the examples available on the Internet and in print format are written in Delphi. The companion CD-ROM for this book provides an example, which consists of a C++Builder project mixed with a Delphi unit. This project, titled Wizard_using_delphi.bpr, can be found under the HelloWorldWizard folder.

If you're like me and you prefer to use C++, you can still benefit from the Delphi code examples that are out there. Examining code examples that are written in Delphi will shed a little bit of light on what will be needed for implementing it in C++Builder.

Defining a Custom Wizard Class

Now we have a TNotifierObject defined and implemented; let's dive in and begin to create our custom C++ wizard class, as shown in Listing 23.3. This code is contained in the wizard_memstatus.h file found in the wizard_part1_simple folder on the companion CD-ROM.

Listing 23.3   MemStatusWizard Class Definition

```
class PACKAGE MemStatusWizard : public NotifierObject, public IOTAMenuWizard {
  typedef TNotifierObject inherited;
public:
  __fastcall MemStatusWizard();
  __fastcall ~MemStatusWizard();

  // IOTAWizard
  virtual AnsiString __fastcall GetIDString();
  virtual AnsiString __fastcall GetName();
  virtual TWizardState __fastcall GetState();
  virtual void __fastcall Execute();

  // IOTAMenuWizard
  virtual AnsiString __fastcall GetMenuText();

  void __fastcall AfterSave();
  void __fastcall BeforeSave();
  void __fastcall Destroyed();
  void __fastcall Modified();
protected:
  // IInterface
  virtual HRESULT __stdcall QueryInterface(const GUID&, void**);
  virtual ULONG __stdcall AddRef();
  virtual ULONG __stdcall Release();
};
```

This class inherits multiple interfaces, including the TNotifierObject class we just created, and IOTAMenuWizard. The TNotifierObject class needs to be identified as the base class for our wizard. This is done using the following typdef clause.

```
typedef TNotifierObject inherited;
```

If you have ever used the Tools API with Delphi, you might notice that our C++Builder class identifies a few more methods than a comparable Delphi example would. Although Delphi and C++Builder are similar, there are also some peculiarities between the two. In this case, Delphi can handle the creation of abstract classes, whereas C++Builder can't. We need to be able to create an instance of our custom wizard when we register it with the IDE. To elevate the C++Builder class from an abstract class, we need override the member functions of `IOTAMenuWizard`, `IOTAWizard`, and `TNotifierObject`.

The code for our custom wizard class is contained in the `wizard_memstatus.cpp` source file as shown in Listing 23.4.

Listing 23.4   `MemStatusWizard` Class Implementation

```
ULONG __stdcall MemStatusWizard::AddRef()  { return inherited::AddRef(); }
ULONG __stdcall MemStatusWizard::Release() { return inherited::Release(); }
HRESULT __stdcall MemStatusWizard::QueryInterface(const GUID& iid, void** obj)
{
  QUERY_INTERFACE(IOTAMenuWizard, iid, obj);
  QUERY_INTERFACE(IOTAWizard, iid, obj);
  return inherited::QueryInterface(iid, obj);
}

void __fastcall MemStatusWizard::AfterSave()  {}
void __fastcall MemStatusWizard::BeforeSave() {}
void __fastcall MemStatusWizard::Destroyed()  {}
void __fastcall MemStatusWizard::Modified()   {}

AnsiString __fastcall MemStatusWizard::GetIDString()
{
  return "CBuilderDevelopersGuide.MemStat Wizard";
}

AnsiString __fastcall MemStatusWizard::GetName()
{
  return "MemStat Wizard";
}

TWizardState __fastcall MemStatusWizard::GetState()
{
  TWizardState result;
  result << wsEnabled;
  return result;
}

AnsiString __fastcall MemStatusWizard::GetMenuText()
```

LISTING 23.4 Continued

```
{
  return "MemStat Wizard...";
}

void __fastcall MemStatusWizard::Execute()
{
  TFormMemStat* FormMemStat = new TFormMemStat(0);
  FormMemStat->ShowModal();
  delete FormMemStat;
}

__fastcall MemStatusWizard::MemStatusWizard()
{
}

__fastcall MemStatusWizard::~MemStatusWizard()
{
}

namespace Wizard_memstatus
{
  void __fastcall PACKAGE Register()
  {
    RegisterPackageWizard(new MemStatusWizard ());
  }
}
```

You're encouraged to browse through this code to see what's happening; it's fairly self-explanatory. Again, we use QueryInterface() to latch onto the interfaces we inherit and use. GetIDString() is used to uniquely identify our custom wizard. Similarly, GetName() is used to identify a friendly name for the custom wizard, whereas GetMenuText() is used to identify the text for our menu item found under the Help menu. The GetState() method is used to identify the state for the menu item linked to invoke the custom wizard.

Probably the most important method of our class is Execute(). When the wizard is invoked from the IDE, the Execute() method is called. In this example, a form containing the GUI and processing for attaining and measuring system memory is opened using the familiar ShowForm() method. We could have just as easily called any other form created using C++Builder, or placed a call to a simple ShowMessage() window.

Although it's not depicted in this example, we can also add additional methods to our class, which we will demonstrate a little later.

Registering a Wizard Class

You'll notice that last thing included in the previous code listing is the `Register()` function wrapped around the unit's namespace. An instance of `MemStatusWizard` is used with the Tools API `RegisterPackageWindow()` function to register the custom wizard with the IDE. The `Register()` function is called when the source file is included with a package. Figure 23.1 illustrates the package used to register the `MemStatusWizard`. This package, called `wizard.bpk`, can be found on the companion CD-ROM under the `wizard_part1_simple` folder for this chapter. To learn more about creating and registering packages see Chapter 4.

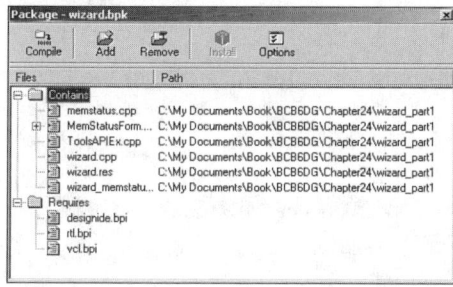

FIGURE 23.1   `MemStatusWizard` Package.

Also, we need to make sure that our package is a design-time package. Look under the Description tab of the Project Options, as illustrated in Figure 23.2, to see the proper usage.

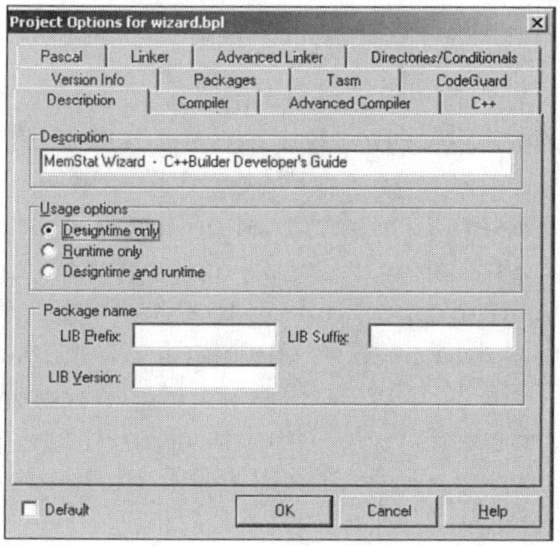

FIGURE 23.2   Setting the Project options for a wizard package.

The End Result

Now that we have our custom wizard class registered, it's time to see if it works. Click the Help menu of the IDE and scroll down and select MemStat Wizard...as illustrated in Figure 23.3.

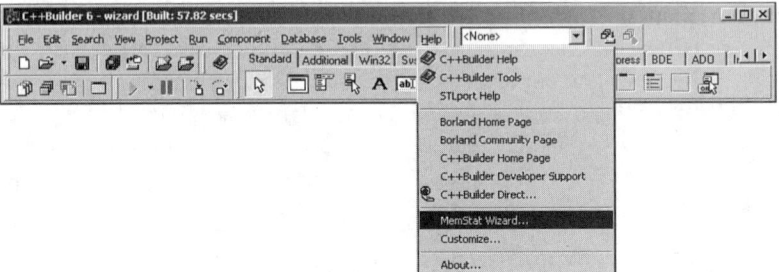

FIGURE 23.3   Launching the MemStat Wizard from the IDE.

The MemStat Wizard should then appear, as seen in Figure 23.4.

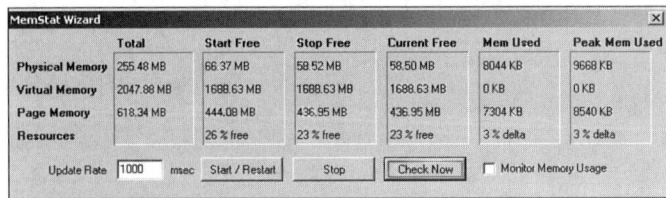

FIGURE 23.4   The MemStat Wizard.

Creating and Using Services

Right now our wizard is pretty limited. In fact, you might be thinking, "It's really not a wizard. It's just an application that gets launched off the help menu." Well, from a user's perspective, you're right. We need to add some more capability to really integrate it with the applications that get built and launched from the C++Builder IDE. Specifically, we want our Wizard to be able to measure the memory degradation of an application from launch to exit. More precisely, we need the Wizard to be able to build and execute the application associated to the active project. Before it executes a project, we need to have it trigger the first memory check. Finally, the wizard needs to be informed when the execution is complete to perform the final memory check. This will result in the display of the memory usage.

This gets us to the heart of what the Tools API can do through the *services* it offers. The service interfaces offered by the Tools API enables our wizard to access, obtain, and even manipulate elements of the IDE at various modes of operation such as edit mode and debug mode.

Selecting a Service Interface

We need to determine the type of service interface for the enhanced version of our MemStat Wizard. The ToolsAPI.hpp file reveals thirteen basic types of service interfaces, as listed in Table 23.4.

Table 23.4   Tools API Service Interfaces

Service Interface	Description
IOTAActionServices	Used to perform file actions, such as opening a file in the IDE, and closing and saving files.
IOTACodeInsightServices	Used to query Code Insight managers, and to add and install a custom Code Insight manager.
IOTADebuggerServices	Used to access the IDE's debugger.
IOTAEditorServices	Used to access the source editor and its internal buffers.
IOTAKeyBindingServices	Used to define individual key bindings for the IDE. An example key binding is Shift-Ctrl-I, which tabs any selected text uniformly to the right.
IOTAKeyboardServices	Used to define and query for individual key bindings, and recording and playing keyboard macros.
IOTAMessageServices	Used to access the IDE's message view window. You can add or clear messages, or add, remove, or show a tab display.
IOTAModuleServices	Used to retrieve a list of modules open in the IDE, creating new files, saving or closing active files, or even registering a virtual file system.
IOTAPackageServices	Used to retrieve a list of installed packages and their associated components.
IOTAToDoServices	Used to query To-Do Items, or register a custom To-Do list manager.
IOTAWizardServices	Used to register or unregister an external wizard. RegisterPackageWizard, on the other hand, does not provide support unregistering a wizard, nor can it be used for a wizard contained within a DLL.
IOTAServices	Used to provide general services not supported by any other service interface.register or unregister an external wizard. RegisterPackageWizard, on the other hand, does not provide support unregistering a wizard nor can it be used for a wizard contained within a DLL.
INTAServices	Used to provide access to the native components of the IDE. Modify, add, or remove items menu bar, tool bars, image list, and/or action list using this native tool service.

For our MemStat Wizard example, we need to be able to detect the active project. A project is a form of module, so we need to iterate through all the modules to find the active project. We will need to use the IOTAModuleServices interface to perform this action. We also should provide some feedback to the user through the IDE's Message View. This is the same window that provides compilation warnings and errors and search results. The service interface we need for this capability is the IOTAMessageServices. Finally, we need a way to launch the active project. The easiest way to perform this operation is to automate the key press of the Run/Run menu item, so we need access to the IDE's main menu. This is achieved using the INTAServices.

In the next section, we will take a look at how we can put it all together. Keep in mind, we'll be making no changes to the original MemStatus Wizard form.

Accessing a Service

The key element to accessing services is the BorlandIDEServices variable, which provides the source for all service interfaces. Actually, to obtain any of the specialized services, we need to use either the QueryInterface() or Supports() method provided by the BorlandIDEServices. For example, the following code grabs the IOTAModuleServices interface by using the BorlandIDEServices variable.

```
_di_IOTAModuleServices ModServices;
BorlandIDEServices->Supports(ModServices);
```

It's really that simple. The _di_IOTAModuleServices identifies the Delphi Interface wrapper to the IOTAModuleServices. ModServices is the interface object. The call to the Supports() method assigns an object instance of the interface to the ModServices object, allowing us to access the interface's properties and methods (just like a class object).

NOTE

The BorlandIDEServices, which provides the source for querying all service interfaces, is a globally available variable within a Package hosting an IDE extension (such as a wizard). For a DLL, however, the access to this service interface is only provided through the first parameter passed by the DLL Entry Point function. Therefore, a BorlandIDEServices variable needs to be defined for DLLs, as shown in the following code excerpt.

```
#ifdef DLL
#define BorlandIDEServices LocalIDEServices
extern _di_IBorlandIDEServices LocalIDEServices;
#endif
```

We'll discuss more on DLLs a little later in the chapter.

Utilizing a Service

Now that we know what service interfaces we need, and we know how to create an instance of an interface, let's see how these services can be utilized within the Execute() method of our revamped MemStat Wizard. This code is shown in Listing 23.5, which can be found in the wizard_memstatus.cpp source file in the wizard_part2_services folder for this chapter on the companion CD-ROM.

Listing 23.5 MemStatusWizard Class—Execute() Method

```cpp
void __fastcall MemStatusWizard::Execute()
{
  Application->ProcessMessages();  // let menu processing complete

  bool launch = true;  // unless instrueted otherwise, run the application
  TFormMemStat* FormMemStat = NULL;

  SetupMessageViewAccess();

  _di_IOTAModuleServices ModServices;
  BorlandIDEServices->Supports(ModServices); // get access to Modules)

  _di_IOTAProject project = FindCurrentProject(ModServices);
  if (project)
  {
      _di_IOTAProjectBuilder projectbuilder = project->ProjectBuilder;
    if (projectbuilder->ShouldBuild)
    {
        MessageServices->AddTitleMessage(
             AnsiString(GetName() + " - Project needs to be built first"),
             MessageGroup);

        AnsiString filename = ExtractFileName(project->FileName);
        AnsiString message = "MemStatus Wizard detected that the " +
                             filename + " project needs to be built first.\n"
                             "Do you wish to continue?";
        int result = MessageBox(NULL,message.c_str(),
                          "MemStat Wizard - Build Project?",
                          MB_YESNO);
        if (result == IDYES)
        {
            projectbuilder->BuildProject(cmOTAMake,true,true);  // build proj
        }
```

LISTING 23.5   Continued

```
        else launch = false; // user doesn't want to run now
    }
}
else  // could not find project
{
    AnsiString message = GetName() + " - Project not loaded. Unable to run.";
    MessageServices->AddTitleMessage(message,MessageGroup);
    MessageBox(NULL,message.c_str(),"MemStat Wizard - Build Project?", MB_OK);
    launch = false;
}

if (launch)  // if launch is still a go
{
  MessageServices->AddTitleMessage(
      AnsiString(GetName() + " - Project is built and ready to run"),Message
      ➥Group);

 _di_INTAServices NativeServices;
BorlandIDEServices->Supports(NativeServices); // get access to IDE (menu bar)

  // let's find the Run top menu item...
  TMenuItem* MenuItem =
      FindMenuItemCaption(NativeServices->MainMenu->Items,"Run");
  if (MenuItem)
  {
      // now let's find the Run (F9) menu item
      TMenuItem* temp = FindMenuItemCaption(MenuItem,"Run");
      MenuItem = temp;
      if (MenuItem)
      {
          if (MenuItem->Enabled)
          {
              int result = MessageBox(NULL,
                      "MemStat Wizard is ready to launch active project and "\
                      "measure memory performance. \n\n" \
                      "It's recommended that you close all other "\
                      "applications with the exception of C++Builder "\
                      "before running the memory test. \n\n" \
                      "Do you wish to continue?",
                      "MemStat Wizard - Ready to Run",MB_YESNO);
              if (result == IDYES)
```

LISTING 23.5   Continued

```
            {
                FormMemStat = new TFormMemStat(0);// instantiate MemStat form
                FormMemStat->Show();  // show the wizard
                Application->ProcessMessages(); //let FormMemStat complete
                FormMemStat->SpeedButtonStartClick(0); // measure memory first
                MessageServices->AddTitleMessage(
                    AnsiString(GetName() + " - " +
                    FormMemStat->GetMemoryStartFree()),MessageGroup);
                MenuItem->OnClick(0);  // run the app
            }
            else
            {
                MessageServices->AddTitleMessage(
                    AnsiString(GetName() +
                    " - User aborted run"),MessageGroup);
            }
        }
      }
    }
  if (!MenuItem)
  {
            MessageServices->AddTitleMessage(
                AnsiString(GetName() + " - Unable to run application. " \
                "Project not loaded."),MessageGroup);
  }
}

// little loop processing here - but don't tie up system (check and get out)
if (FormMemStat)
{
    while (FormMemStat->Visible)  // check
    {
        Application->ProcessMessages(); //get out (process current messages)
    }
    delete FormMemStat;
}
MessageServices->AddTitleMessage(GetName() + " - Completed",MessageGroup);
}
```

In addition to a totally revamped Execute() method, we've also added a few new methods to our custom wizard class to support some of the service processing we need to perform. These methods include `SetupMessageViewAccess()`, `FindMenuItemCaption()`, and `FindCurrentProject()`. In addition to these methods, there are a few properties added to our wizard class within the `wizard_memstatus.h` file as shown in Listing 23.6:

Listing 23.6   Excerpt of the `MemStatusWizard` Class Definition

```
private:
  _di_IOTAMessageServices  MessageServices;
  _di_IOTAMessageGroup     MessageGroup;

  void __fastcall SetupMessageViewAccess();
  TMenuItem* FindMenuItemCaption(TMenuItem* topmenu,  AnsiString Caption);
  _di_IOTAProject FindCurrentProject(_di_IOTAModuleServices ModServices);
```

In the following sections, we will walk through the `Execute()` method code as provided in Listing 23.5, and look at some of these new support methods we've added. This examination will enable us to fully understand how to use these particular Tool API services.

Look Before You Leap with `ProcessMessages()`

Notice the first thing we do in the `Execute()` method is call `Application ->ProcessMessages()`. When we're dealing with a myriad of messages being thrown around the IDE and, as a wizard, we're a part of that IDE, it's a good idea to make sure we've given a chance for other messages to be processed first before we get going. This enables our wizard to utilize the service interfaces properly. For example, because our Wizard is launched from the Help Menu Item, the menu processing is still occurring when our Wizard launches. If we don't allow these messages to be processed, we might not get clean access to the IDE's menu items, which, in our example, we need later to *Run* the active project within C++Builder.

Providing Feedback Through the IDE Message View

The next critical thing we do in the `Execute()` method, is call a custom method that's been added to `wizard_memstatus.cpp` called `SetupMessageViewAccess()`. The implementation for this custom method is provided in Listing 23.7.

Listing 23.7   `MemStatusWizard` Class—`SetupMessageViewAccess()` Method

```
void __fastcall MemStatusWizard::SetupMessageViewAccess()
{
    BorlandIDEServices->Supports(MessageServices); // get access to Message View
    MessageGroup = MessageServices->AddMessageGroup(GetName());
    MessageServices->ClearMessageGroup(MessageGroup); // need a clean canvas
```

LISTING 23.7   Continued

```
    MessageServices->ShowMessageView(MessageGroup);    // make it visible
    MessageServices->AddTitleMessage(GetName() + " - Activated",MessageGroup);
}
```

In this method, we grab the `IOTAMessageServices` interface, which allows access to the IDE's Message View. The `AddMessageGroup()` function sets a new message tab if it does not exist. In this case, the `GetName()` method is passed as a parameter which provides the name of our wizard. `ClearMessageGroup()` is used to clean the message view canvas for our message group. `ShowMessageView()` ensures that the message view is visible. Finally, the one method we use repetitively is `AddTitleMessage()` to write out text to our message group.

Locating and Building the Active Project
In the wizard's `Execute()` method we grab a local copy of the `IOTAModuleServices`, which will enable us to find the active project for which the Wizard will collect memory information.

```
    _di_IOTAModuleServices ModServices;
    BorlandIDEServices->Supports(ModServices); // get access to Modules)
    _di_IOTAProject project = FindCurrentProject(ModServices);
```

`FindCurrentProject()` is another custom method we've provided for our wizard that has been added to the `wizard_memstatus.cpp` source file. This method is shown in Listing 23.8.

Listing 23.8   MemStatusWizard Class—FindCurrentProject Method

```
_di_IOTAProject        MemStatusWizard::FindCurrentProject(_di_IOTAModuleServices
➥ModServices)
{
    //To obtain the active IOTAProjectGroup reference,
    //iterate over all open modules and find the one module that
    //supports the IOTAProjectGroup interface.

    if (!ModServices) return NULL; // get out, no modules to search

    _di_IOTAModule module;
    _di_IOTAProjectGroup projectgroup = NULL;
    _di_IOTAProject project = NULL;

    bool done = false;
    int index = 0;
```

LISTING 23.8   Continued

```
MessageServices->AddTitleMessage(
    AnsiString(GetName() + " - Locating Active Project..."),MessageGroup);
while (!done)
{
    if (index < ModServices->ModuleCount)
    {
        module = ModServices->Modules[index];
        // cast module into project (if you can)
        projectgroup = (_di_IOTAProjectGroup)module;
        if (projectgroup)
        {
            //done = true;
            project = projectgroup->ActiveProject;
            MessageServices->AddTitleMessage(
              AnsiString(GetName() + " - Project Found = " +
                      project->FileName),MessageGroup);
            done = true;
        }
        else
        index++;
    }
    else
    {
      done = true;
      MessageServices->AddTitleMessage(
        AnsiString(GetName() + " -  Unable to locate project"),MessageGroup);
    }
} // while
return project;
}
```

This method iterates through all the active modules, which might include files, forms, resource files, projects, and the project group. What we're looking for is the lone project group (there can only be one project group loaded by the IDE at one time). To hunt down the lone project group, we cast each iterated module into a project group, as follows:

```
projectgroup = (_di_IOTAProjectGroup)module;
```

If projectgroup is not NULL, it has been found! From here, we can locate the active project by using the project group's ActiveProject() method, and return it to the Execute() method.

If a valid active project is returned by FindCurrentProject(), we can examine the project build information by accessing the project's ProjectBuilder() property as shown in the following code snippet.

```
_di_IOTAProjectBuilder projectbuilder = project->ProjectBuilder;
if (projectbuilder->ShouldBuild)
{

    — —

    — —

    if (result == IDYES)
    {
        launch = projectbuilder->BuildProject(cmOTAMake,true,true);
    }
    else launch = false; // user doesn't want to run now
}
```

The ShouldBuild() property provided by the _di_IOTAProjectBuilder interface enables us to determine if the project needs to be built. A true condition means a modification to the code represented in that project has occurred and these changes are not yet reflected in the executable. For our MemStatus Wizard, we want to make sure the project is built before we initiate any memory measurements. If it's not built, the Tools API allows our wizard to create the executable by using the BuildProject() method, which is provided by the _di_IOTAProjectBuilder interface. Notice that there are three parameters for the BuildProject() call. Let's look at its declaration.

```
bool __fastcall BuildProject(TOTACompileMode CompileMode,
                       bool Wait,
                       bool ClearMessages) = 0;
```

The first parameter of BuildProject(), CompileMode, identifies how the IDE (or our Wizard from a user's perspective) should compile the project. We can compile only modified files, all files, check the syntax, or compile the current module only. In this example, cmOTAMake was used to compile only modified files. The second parameter, Wait, identifies whether the dialog box should be appear displaying to the user the compiler progress and completion status, or if control should return immediately to the wizard after compilation is complete. A value of true, as used in our example, will require the user to click the OK button of the dialog box for control to be returned to our wizard. The third parameter, ClearMessages, identifies if the Build message view should be cleared before compiling. A true value, fortunately, will not clear our custom Wizard message view that we created, but will clean the Build message view. Finally, BuildProject() will return true, if the compilation was successful.

Hacking into the IDE Responsibly

After we've located an active project, and we know it's been built, we're ready to launch it and measure memory performance. To execute the project, however, is not entirely straightforward.

One common way is to access the integrated debugger using the `IOTADebuggerServices` interface, and use it's `CreateProcess()` method. This method starts the application representing the project loaded in the IDE. However, the `CreateProcess()` method creates the process initially stopped at the first line of execution code. To use `IOTADebuggerServices` properly, we would need to use a thread notifier to detect when the process stopped and restart the process automatically. There's a lag in this execution that is less than desired for the purpose of our example.

Another way is to hack into the IDE as a virtual user and emulate clicking the Run menu item by using the `INTANativeServices` interface. If the project is built, it will run without the stop/start condition associated to the `CreateProcess()` method. The trick, however, is to locate the Run menu item. We start by grabbing a copy of the `INTANativeServices` interface to the IDE:

```
_di_INTAServices NativeServices;
BorlandIDEServices->Supports(NativeServices); // get access to IDE (menu bar)
```

This will enable us to access the IDE's MainMenu. This interface also allows access to other IDE elements besides the MainMenu, such as ActionList, ImageList, and ToolBar. In our example, we just want access to the MainMenu, so we can find the "Run" menu item.

```
// let's find the Run top menu item...
TMenuItem* MenuItem =
    FindMenuItemCaption(NativeServices->MainMenu->Items,"Run");
```

A custom method called `FindMenuItemCaption()` has been added to the `wizard_memstatus.cpp` source file to iterate through the subitems of a menu item until a text match is found. This method is provided in Listing 23.9.

Listing 23.9   MemStatusWizard Class—`FindMenuItemCaption()` Method

```
TMenuItem * MemStatusWizard::FindMenuItemCaption(TMenuItem* topmenu,
            AnsiString Caption)
{
    TMenuItem *menuitem = NULL;
    bool done = false;
    if (!topmenu) return menuitem; // get out, no menu to search
    int index = 0;
    while (!done)
```

LISTING 23.9 Continued

```
{
    if (index < topmenu->Count)
    {
        menuitem = topmenu->Items[index];
        if (menuitem->Caption.AnsiPos(Caption))
        {
            done = true;
        }
        index ++;
    }
    else
    {
        done = true;
        menuitem = NULL;
    }
}  // while
return menuitem;
}
```

The FindMenuItemCaption() locates the menu item that matches the Caption. If it exists, a new TMenuItem is returned to the caller. In this example, the caller is the wizard's Execute() method. Within the Execute() method, we then look for the next "Run" menu item sub to the menu item that was just returned. This is done by placing another call to FindMenuItemCaption(). After we finally locate the "Run" menu item, we can trigger the OnClick() event for the specific menu item as depicted in the following code snippet from the wizard_memstatus.cpp source file.

```
FormMemStat = new TFormMemStat(0);// instantiate MemStat form
FormMemStat->Show();  // show the wizard
Application->ProcessMessages(); //let FormMemStat complete
FormMemStat->SpeedButtonStartClick(0); // measure memory first
MenuItem->OnClick(0);  // run the app
```

This code also reveals what we do to ready our memory measurement analysis. First, we create an instance of the form that we're going to display. We then Show() it. Previously, we used the ShowModal() call, which forced our program to wait synchronously until it was closed (see Listing 23.4). With the Show() method, control is returned immediately to our Execute() method. Notice the use of the ProcessMessages() method again. We use it in this instance to ensure that the form we just displayed through the Show() method will be properly processed before we activate any memory analysis.

In the previous MemStat Wizard example, the user was required to do things manually. This included initiating the memory analysis by clicking the start button off the MemStat Wizard form, and then launching the application to evaluate after the MemStat Wizard memory analysis had started. Now, we're automating these actions by calling the form's `SpeedButtonStartClick()` method after the form is displayed enabling us to get an accurate read on the memory prior to launching the application under test. We launch that application, again, by triggering the `OnClick()` event for the IDE's Run menu item. It behaves as if the user has made these selections manually.

Additional Processing with Services

In the first example provided in Listing 23.4, we used the `ShowModal()` method to open our form, and when we were done with the form we knew when control was returned. In this example, we have no idea precisely when the form is closed because we are using the `Show()` method. The reason we are using the `Show()` method is because we need to do some additional processing within our `Execute()` code (using Services while the form is up). Specifically, we need to automate the Run using the native services provided by the IDE after our memory form was shown. This example is not unique. You may also find a case for your custom wizards where additional processing needs to occur within your wizard while a form is already active. The key is knowing how to gracefully detect when the form has closed. One way to do this without making any modifications is to use a processing loop as shown in the following code snippet found in the `wizard_memstatus.cpp` source file:

```
// little loop processing here - but don't tie up system (check and get out)
if (FormMemStat)
{
    while (FormMemStat->Visible)  // check
    {
        // if you need to check on anything else, do it now
        Application->HandleMessage(); //get out (process current messages)
    }
    delete FormMemStat;  //form no longer visible, we created it, let's delete it
}
MessageServices->AddTitleMessage(GetName() + " - Completed",MessageGroup);
```

Notice we only do the looping if `FormMemStat` exists and if it is visible. We don't want to tie up the system, so we just check for when the form is visible, and then, within our loop process, we relinquish control to the kernel using the `HandleMessage()` method, thereby allowing other messages in the system queue to be processed. Certainly, other ways to check for form closure exist, including threading and windows messaging, but this approach works very effectively.

You'll notice the last thing we do in our `Execute()` method is call `MessageServices ->AddTitleMessage()` to write out the final text within the Message View. This is depicted in Figure 23.5.

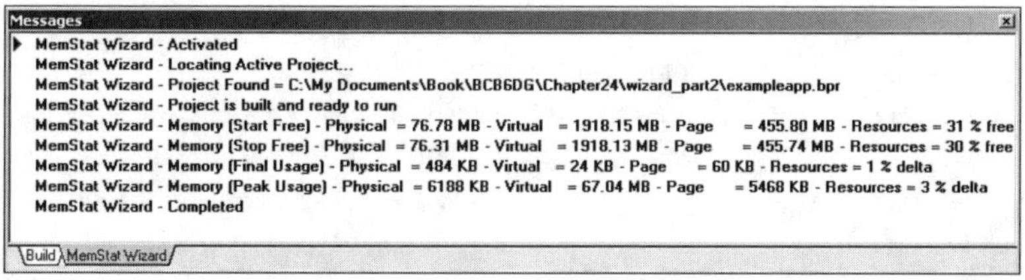

Figure 23.5   Messages for MemStat Wizard.

Creating and Using Notifiers

Services such as displaying text in the Message View, building a project, and automating a menu selection are used by our wizard to affect the IDE. What we need next is a way for the IDE to affect our wizard by notifying when the execution of the application has stopped. This is the job of *notifiers*. The combination of services and notifiers is what allows for the two-way RAD capability provided by Delphi and C++Builder. The Tools API enables us to profit from this RAD capability within the extensions we create. For the MemStat Wizard example that we are enhancing, we need a notifier to signal us through the IDE's debugger when an application process has stopped.

Let's take a look at the various types of notifiers provided by the Tools API as shown in Table 23.5.

Table 23.5   Tools API Service Notifiers

Notifier Interface	Description
IOTABreakpointNotifier	Used to retrieve breakpoint activities such as when the breakpoint is triggered or the user wants to modify the breakpoint.
IOTADebuggerNotifier	Used to retrieve debug notifications such as when the debugger starts debugging a process, finishes debugging a process, or when breakpoints are added or deleted.
IOTAEditLineNotifier	Used to retrieve edit activities such as when the user inserts or deletes lines in a source file.
IOTAEditorNotifier	Used to retrieve activities associated to the source editor such as a modification of text.
IOTAFormNotifier	Used to retrieve activities associated with the form editor such as when a property is altered or when a component on the form is renamed.

Table 23.5   Continued

Notifier Interface	Description
IOTAIDENotifier	This is the base class for all IDE notifiers.
IOTAMessageNotifier	Used to retrieve activities associated to the message view such as when a message is added or removed, or a message view tab is added or selected.
IOTAModuleNotifier	Used to retrieve events associated to a particular module such as when a module's source file has been modified.
IOTAProcessModNotifier	Used to notify when a specified module is loaded.
IOTAProcessNotifier	Used to retrieve events associated to a process being debugged such as when the integrated debugger loads or unloads a module, or when a process is created or destroyed.
IOTAThreadNotifier	Used to retrieve events associated to a thread being debugged such as when the integrated debugger loads or unloads a module, or when a thread is created or destroyed.
IOTAToolsFilterNotifier	Used to retrieve activities associated to a Build Tool such as filtering output generated by the Build Tool.

In our example, we want to know when the process representing the application under test is complete. The notifier best suited for this task is the IOTADebuggerNotifier. This notifier has two methods that are useful: ProcessCreated() and ProcessDestroyed(). The ProcessCreated() method is triggered when our application is executed, and the ProcessDestroyed() method is triggered when our application under test is completed.

Defining a Custom Debugger Notifier Class

Let's take a look at Listing 23.10, which illustrates how we can set up the class to represent this notifier for our MemStat Wizard. This code has been added to the wizard_memstatus.h file located in the wizard_part3_notifier folder for this chapter, which can be found on the companion CD-ROM.

Listing 23.10   DebugNotifier Class Declaration

```
class DebugNotifier: public TNotifierObject, public IOTADebuggerNotifier
{
  typedef TNotifierObject inherited;
public:
  __fastcall DebugNotifier(const _di_IOTADebuggerServices debugger,
                           const MemStatusWizard*   wizard);
  __fastcall ~DebugNotifier();

  // IOTADebuggerNotifer
```

LISTING 23.10   Continued

```
  virtual void __fastcall BreakpointAdded(_di_IOTABreakpoint Breakpoint);
  virtual void __fastcall BreakpointDeleted(_di_IOTABreakpoint Breakpoint);
  virtual void __fastcall ProcessCreated(_di_IOTAProcess Process);
  virtual void __fastcall ProcessDestroyed(_di_IOTAProcess Process);

  // override NotifierObjectObject  methods
  void __fastcall AfterSave();
  void __fastcall BeforeSave();
  void __fastcall Destroyed();  // implement this
  void __fastcall Modified();


protected:
  // override IInterface  methods
  virtual HRESULT __stdcall QueryInterface(const GUID&, void**);
  virtual ULONG   __stdcall AddRef();
  virtual ULONG   __stdcall Release();

private:
  const MemStatusWizard*  wizard; // keep track of the wizard that owns this
  ➥notifier
  _di_IOTADebuggerServices debugger; // keep track of debuggerservice that added me
as a notifier
  AnsiString name; // remember the debugger's old name
  int index; // Notifier index
};
```

We create a notifier by defining a class that implements a specific notifier interface. Note that this is very similar to how we created our custom wizard. In fact, our Wizard class is also a descendent of a notifier (remember all that discussion on IOTANotifier earlier).

In our case the specific notifier interface we need is IOTADebuggerNotifier. Like the wizard, we also inherit TNotifierObject. The constructor method of the DebugNotifier class will provide the processing for assigning a notifier to an interface. That is why the first parameter of the constructor method requires a _di_IOTADebuggerServices service interface. The second parameter will provide a pointer to our wizard class, MemStatusWizard, so we have a way to directly notify the wizard of IDE changes. This, incidentally, requires a few new methods and properties to be added in the public section of our custom wizard class within the wizard_memstatus.h file so that the notifier can provide the anticipated notification. This is shown in Listing 23.11.

Listing 23.11   MemStatWizard Class—Public Declarations

```
class PACKAGE MemStatusWizard : public TNotifierObject, public IOTAMenuWizard
{
  typedef TNotifierObject inherited;
public:
  __fastcall MemStatusWizard();
  __fastcall ~MemStatusWizard();


    — —
    — —


  void __fastcall SetProcessActive(bool value);  // used by debug notifier

  // expose these properties (used mainly for debugmessaging by the debug notifier)
  _di_IOTAMessageServices  MessageServices;
  _di_IOTAMessageGroup     MessageGroup;


    — —
    — —


};
```

The DebugNotifier class will use the properties and methods that are shown in bold.
Let's now look at the methods created for DebugNotifier that have been added to the
wizard_memstatus.cpp file as shown in Listing 23.12.

Listing 23.12   DebugNotifier Class Methods

```
__fastcall DebugNotifier::DebugNotifier(const _di_IOTADebuggerServices debugger,
                        const MemStatusWizard*  wizard)
: index(-1), debugger(debugger), wizard(wizard) {
    // register the notifier
    index =  debugger->AddNotifier(this);

    #ifdef DebugMessages
    char value[MAX_PATH];
    sprintf(value," - [Debug] - DebugNotifer has been created.  Index = %d",index);
    wizard->MessageServices->AddTitleMessage(
       AnsiString(wizard->GetName() + value),wizard->MessageGroup);
    #endif
}


// — — — — — — — — — — — — — — — — — — — — — — — — — — — — — — — — -·
```

LISTING 23.12   Continued

```
__fastcall DebugNotifier::~DebugNotifier()
{
   //unregister the notifier if that hasn't happend yet
   if (index >= 0)
   {

   #ifdef DebugMessages
   char value[MAX_PATH];
   sprintf(value," - [Debug] - About to call RemoveNotifer - inside ~Debug
   ➥Notifier() - Index = %d",index);
   wizard->MessageServices->AddTitleMessage(
      AnsiString(wizard->GetName() + value),wizard->MessageGroup);
   #endif
   debugger->RemoveNotifier(index);
   }
   debugger = 0;
}


// – – – – – – – – – – – – – – – – – – – – – – – – – – – – – – – – – – – –.

ULONG    __stdcall DebugNotifier::AddRef()  { return inherited::AddRef(); }
ULONG    __stdcall DebugNotifier::Release() { return inherited::Release(); }
HRESULT  __stdcall DebugNotifier::QueryInterface(const GUID& iid, void** obj)
{
  QUERY_INTERFACE(IOTADebuggerNotifier, iid, obj);
  return inherited::QueryInterface(iid, obj);
}

void __fastcall DebugNotifier::AfterSave()  {}
void __fastcall DebugNotifier::BeforeSave() {}
void __fastcall DebugNotifier::Destroyed()
{
   //unregister the notifier if that hasn't happend yet
   if (index >= 0)
   {
    #ifdef DebugMessages
    char value[MAX_PATH];
    sprintf(value," - [Debug] - About to call RemoveNotifer "
                  "- inside Destroyed() - Index = %d",index);
    wizard->MessageServices->AddTitleMessage(
       AnsiString(wizard->GetName() + value),wizard->MessageGroup);
```

LISTING 23.12   Continued

```
    #endif

    debugger->RemoveNotifier(index);
    index = -1;
    }
    debugger = 0;
}

void __fastcall DebugNotifier::Modified()    {}

void __fastcall DebugNotifier::BreakpointAdded(_di_IOTABreakpoint Breakpoint)
{
    #ifdef DebugMessages
    wizard->MessageServices->AddTitleMessage(
        AnsiString(wizard->GetName() + " - Breakpoint Added..."),
                        wizard->MessageGroup);
    #endif
}

//----------------------------------.

void __fastcall DebugNotifier::BreakpointDeleted(_di_IOTABreakpoint Breakpoint)
{
    #ifdef DebugMessages
    wizard->MessageServices->AddTitleMessage(
        AnsiString(wizard->GetName() + " - Breakpoint Deleted..."),
                        wizard->MessageGroup);
    #endif
}

//----------------------------------.

void __fastcall DebugNotifier::ProcessCreated(_di_IOTAProcess Process)
{
    wizard->SetProcessActive(true);

    #ifdef DebugMessages
    wizard->MessageServices->AddTitleMessage(
        AnsiString(wizard->GetName() + " - Process Created - Process ID = " +
AnsiString((int)Process->ProcessId)),wizard->MessageGroup);
    #endif
```

LISTING 23.12   Continued

```
}


//----------------------------------------.

void __fastcall DebugNotifier::ProcessDestroyed(_di_IOTAProcess Process)
{
    wizard->SetProcessActive(false);

    #ifdef DebugMessages
    wizard->MessageServices->AddTitleMessage(
        AnsiString(wizard->GetName() + " - Process Destroyed - Process ID = " +
AnsiString((int)Process->ProcessId)),wizard->MessageGroup);
    #endif
}
```

Again, the constructor for the DebugNotifier class self registers as a notifier by using the AddNotifier() method associated to the _di_IOTADebuggerServices object, which is passed in as the parameter. The class's destructor and the Destroyed() method both provide a way to clean up the notifier, which needs to be done or we'll end up having IDE woes.

The two key methods we need to implement from this notifier interface are ProcessCreated() and ProcessDestroyed(). Both of these methods call the SetProcessActive() method, available from the wizard, to indicate if a process is active or not. Let's look at this new wizard method in Listing 23.13, which has been added to the wizard_memstatus.cpp file.

Listing 23.13   MemStatusWizard Class—SetProcessActive() Method

```
void __fastcall MemStatusWizard::SetProcessActive(bool value)
{
  ProcessActive = value;
}
```

There's not a lot of complexity in SetProcessActive(), it just simply resets the ProcessActive property associated to our custom wizard. As we will see shortly, the Execute() method of our wizard checks on this variable to provide the final automation of the memory analysis process.

Utilizing Our Debugger Notifier

Now, let's take a look at how we set up and utilize this debug notifier in the
Execute() method for our MemStat Wizard located within the wizard_memstatus.cpp
file. Depicted in bold within Listing 25.14 are all the new additions to the Execute()
method since our last update.

Listing 23.14   MemStatusWizard Class—Execute() Method

```
void __fastcall MemStatusWizard::Execute()
{
  Application->ProcessMessages();  // let menu processing complete

  bool launch = true;  // unless instrueced otherwise, run the application
  TFormMemStat*  FormMemStat = NULL;

  SetupMessageViewAccess();

  _di_IOTADebuggerServices DebuggerServices;  // we'll use these a little later
  DebugNotifier* debugnotifier;         // keep track of debugnotifier

  _di_IOTAModuleServices ModServices;
  BorlandIDEServices->Supports(ModServices); // get access to Modules
  _di_IOTAProject project = FindCurrentProject(ModServices);
  if (project)
  {
     _di_IOTAProjectBuilder projectbuilder = project->ProjectBuilder;
    if (projectbuilder->ShouldBuild)
    {
        MessageServices->AddTitleMessage(
            AnsiString(GetName() + " - Project needs to be built first"),
            MessageGroup);

        AnsiString filename = ExtractFileName(project->FileName);
        AnsiString message = "MemStatus Wizard detected that the " +
                            filename + " project needs to be built first.\n"
                            "Do you wish to continue?";
        int result = MessageBox(NULL,message.c_str(),
                            "MemStat Wizard - Build Project?",
                            MB_YESNO);
        if (result == IDYES)
        {
            launch = projectbuilder->BuildProject(cmOTAMake,true,true);
```

LISTING 23.14   Continued

```
            }
            else launch = false; // user doesn't want to run now
    }



}
else  // could not find project
{
    AnsiString message = GetName() + " - Project not loaded. Unable to run.";
    MessageServices->AddTitleMessage(message,MessageGroup);
    MessageBox(NULL,message.c_str(),
            "MemStat Wizard - Build Project?", MB_OK);
    launch = false;
}

if (launch)  // if launch is still a go
{
  MessageServices->AddTitleMessage(
      AnsiString(GetName() + " - Project is built and ready to run"),
            MessageGroup);

  _di_INTAServices NativeServices;
  BorlandIDEServices->Supports(NativeServices); // get access to IDE (menu bar)

  // let's find the Run top menu item...
  TMenuItem* MenuItem =
      FindMenuItemCaption(NativeServices->MainMenu->Items,"Run");
  if (MenuItem)
  {
      // now let's find the Run (F9) menu item
      TMenuItem* temp = FindMenuItemCaption(MenuItem,"Run");
      MenuItem = temp;
      if (MenuItem)
      {
          if (MenuItem->Enabled)
          {
              int result = MessageBox(NULL,
                  "MemStat Wizard is ready to launch active project and "\
                  "measure memory performance. \n\n" \
                  "Although not required, it's recommended that you "\
                  "close all other applications with the exception of "\
```

LISTING 23.14   Continued

```
                "C++Builder before running the memory test. This will "\
                "allow the MemStat Wizard to more precisely measure "\
                "memory performance of the application under test.\n\n"\
                "Do you wish to continue?",
                "MemStat Wizard - Ready to Run",MB_YESNO);
        if (result == IDYES)
        {
            FormMemStat = new TFormMemStat(0);//instantiate MemStat
            FormMemStat->Show();  // show the wizard
            MessageServices->AddTitleMessage(
                AnsiString(GetName() + " - " +
                FormMemStat->GetMemoryTotal()),MessageGroup);

            // get interace to debuggerservices and a notifier
            BorlandIDEServices->Supports(DebuggerServices);
            debugnotifier = new DebugNotifier(DebuggerServices,this);

            Application->ProcessMessages(); //let FormMemStat complete

            FormMemStat->SpeedButtonStartClick(0); //measure memory
            MessageServices->AddTitleMessage(
                AnsiString(GetName() + " - " +
                FormMemStat->GetMemoryStartFree()),MessageGroup);

            MenuItem->OnClick(0);  // run the app through the menu item

            // here's how we could run the app from the debugger service
            #ifdef RunFromDebugger
             _di_IOTAProcess Process;
             // figure out exe name
             AnsiString exename = ExtractFileNameNoExt(
                                    project->FileName,true) + ".exe ";
             if (FileExists(exename))
             {
                MessageServices->AddTitleMessage(
                        AnsiString(GetName() + " - " +
                        "Create Process = " + exename),MessageGroup);
                DebuggerServices->CreateProcess(exename, "", "");
                Process = DebuggerServices->CurrentProcess;
                 if (Process)
                 {
```

LISTING 23.14   Continued

```
                              MessageServices->AddTitleMessage(
                                AnsiString(GetName() + " - " +"Process = " +
                                AnsiString(Process->ProcessId)),MessageGroup);
                              //Process->Pause(); // Pause
                              //Process->Run(ormRun);    // Run Normally
                        }
                    }
                    #endif // RunFromDebugger
              }
              else
              {
                  MessageServices->AddTitleMessage(
                      AnsiString(GetName() +
                      " - User aborted run."),MessageGroup);
              }
          }
        }
    }
  if (!MenuItem)
  {
          MessageServices->AddTitleMessage(
              AnsiString(GetName() + " - Unable to run application. " \
              "Project not loaded."),MessageGroup);
  }
}


// little loop processing here - but don't tie up system (check and get out)
if (FormMemStat)
{
    while (FormMemStat->Visible)  // check
    {
        if (!ProcessActive)  // process is no longer active / shut it down
        {
            FormMemStat->SpeedButtonStopClick(0); // final measurement
            FormMemStat->Close();
        }
        Application->ProcessMessages(); //get out (process current messages)
    }

    if (ProcessActive) // wizard has been shut down, but app remains
    {
```

LISTING 23.14   Continued

```
        int result = MessageBox(NULL,
                "MemStat Wizard has been shut down, but the application "\
                "under test is still active. \n\n" \
                "Do you wish to close application under test as well?",
                "MemStat Wizard - Terminated",MB_YESNO);
        if (result == IDYES)
        {
            _di_IOTAProcess Process;
            Process = DebuggerServices->CurrentProcess;
            if (Process)
                Process->Terminate();
        }
    }

    MessageServices->AddTitleMessage(
        AnsiString(GetName() + " - " +
        FormMemStat->GetMemoryStopFree()),MessageGroup);
    MessageServices->AddTitleMessage(
        AnsiString(GetName() + " - " +
        FormMemStat->GetMemoryFinalUsage()),MessageGroup);
    MessageServices->AddTitleMessage(
        AnsiString(GetName() + " - " +
        FormMemStat->GetMemoryPeakUsage()),MessageGroup);
    delete FormMemStat;
  }
  if (debugnotifier)  // little clean-up
  {
    debugnotifier->Destroyed();
    debugnotifier =  NULL;
  }
  MessageServices->AddTitleMessage(GetName() + " - Completed",MessageGroup);
}
```

To get a notifier we need a service interface that can provide it. In this case it is the
_di_IOTADebuggerServices interface. This interface provides a method called
AddNotifier() that we will use in the constructor for our DebugNotifer. Earlier, we
used the RegisterPackageWizard() method for registering a custom wizard. For notifiers, we use the AddNotifier() method. Later, we will use the RemoveNotifer() within
our notifier's destructor and Destroyed() method for proper clean up (release) of the
notifier.

After we instantiate a debug notifier by passing the `DebuggerServices` interface to the `DebugNotifier` constructor, the notifier is ready to receive notification from the IDE of debugger activities.

After the application under test is launched, and the form for MemStatus Wizard is activated, we check within our looping process to see if the `DebugNotifier` object has set our wizard's `ProcessActive` flag to `false`. This flag identifies if the application under test is active or not. If it is not active, we mark the memory, close the MemStatus Wizard form, and report the memory status within our message group window. If the form for the wizard is shutdown while the application under test is still active, we query the user and, based on his response, we terminate the process. This is accomplished by attaining the current process through the `CurrentProcess()` property for the `DebuggerServices` interface. After we have the current process we can call its `Terminate()` method.

Finally, we clean up by calling the `Destroyed()` method of our debug notifier.

With this code in place, our wizard is fully automated. Originally, we started off with just a form that came into view requiring full user intervention. Then, we figured out when to start the memory analysis after the application was launched by using interface services. This time we figured out how to precisely know when to stop the memory analysis, and how to clean up using notifiers. But the capabilities that we can add don't just have to stop there.

Creating and Using Creators

The Tools API also provides a way to create common IDE objects such as a file (unit), a module, or a project by creating a class that's derived from one its Creator interfaces. Suppose, in our example, we want our Wizard to dump out some text, viewable in the IDE, that displays the memory information for each run of the loaded application. We would need to create a file that's included with the project associated to the application we want to test.

Let's take a look at the various types of creator interfaces provided by the Tools API.

Table 23.6   Tools API Creator Interfaces

Creator Interface	Description
IOTACreator	This is the base class for all creators.
IOTAAdditionalFilesModuleCreator	Used to create additional files such as documentation, a Web page, or other text files associated with a unit.
IOTAModuleCreator	Used to create a module such as a new unit, form, or text file for a project, or to supply custom file contents or filenames.

Table 23.6   Continued

Creator Interface	Description
IOTAProjectCreator50	Used to create a default application, library, or package, or to supply custom file contents or filenames.
IOTAProjectGroupCreator	Used to create a project group, or a new module for opening up an existing project group.

In addition to this list, one other Tools API interface that is typically used to support a creator interface is IOTAFile. IOTAFile is used to supply custom file content, such as source code for a new file, for a creator.

Defining a Custom Creator Class

For our wizard, IOTAModuleCreator provides the interface we need to generate a text file. To use it, we need to create a custom class representing this interface to the wizard_memstatus.h file as shown in Listing 23.15.

Listing 23.15   Creator Class Declaration

```
class Creator: public IOTAModuleCreator
{
public:
  __fastcall Creator(const AnsiString creator_type,
                     const MemStatusWizard*  wizard);

  virtual __fastcall ~Creator();

  // IOTAModuleCreator methods
  virtual AnsiString __fastcall GetAncestorName();
  virtual AnsiString __fastcall GetImplFileName();
  virtual AnsiString __fastcall GetIntfFileName();
  virtual AnsiString __fastcall GetFormName();
  virtual bool __fastcall GetMainForm();
  virtual bool __fastcall GetShowForm();
  virtual bool __fastcall GetShowSource();
  virtual _di_IOTAFile __fastcall NewFormFile(
       const AnsiString FormIdent, const AnsiString AncestorIdent);
  virtual _di_IOTAFile __fastcall NewImplSource(
       const AnsiString ModuleIdent, const AnsiString FormIdent,
       const AnsiString AncestorIdent);
  virtual _di_IOTAFile __fastcall NewIntfSource(
       const AnsiString ModuleIdent, const AnsiString FormIdent,
```

LISTING 23.15 Continued

```
        const AnsiString AncestorIdent);
    virtual void __fastcall FormCreated(
        const _di_IOTAFormEditor FormEditor);

    // IOTACreator methods
    virtual AnsiString __fastcall GetCreatorType();
    virtual bool __fastcall GetExisting();
    virtual AnsiString __fastcall GetFileSystem();
    virtual _di_IOTAModule __fastcall GetOwner();
    virtual bool __fastcall GetUnnamed();

protected:
    // override IInterface methods
    virtual HRESULT __stdcall QueryInterface(const GUID&, void**);
    virtual ULONG   __stdcall AddRef();
    virtual ULONG   __stdcall Release();

private:
    long ref_count;
    const AnsiString creator_type;
    const MemStatusWizard*  wizard; // keep track of the wizard
                                    // that owns this notifier
};
```

Although there are a lot of methods, the key methods we are most interested in are the Creator constructor and the NewImplSource() method. For all the other methods we simply return the default values. Now, let's look at the implementation for these methods that have been added to the wizard_memstatus.cpp file as shown in Listing 23.16.

Listing 23.16 Creator Class—Constructor Method

```
__fastcall Creator::Creator(const AnsiString creator_type,
                    const MemStatusWizard*  wizard)
  : ref_count(0), creator_type(creator_type), wizard(wizard)
{
    #ifdef DebugMessages
    char value[MAX_PATH];
    sprintf(value," - [Debug] - Creator has been created.  Index = %d",index);
    wizard->MessageServices->AddTitleMessage(
        AnsiString(wizard->GetName() + value),wizard->MessageGroup);
```

LISTING 23.16   Continued

```
    #endif
}
```

In our constructor, we pass in the type of module we are going to create, and also a pointer to our wizard so that we can access some of the data we want to display. It's important to identify the proper type of module to be created. Table 23.7 identifies the various creator types.

Table 23.7   Tools API Creator Types

Creator Type	Description
sApplication	Used to create a default application. Applies to IOTAProjectCreator interface.
sConsole	Used to create a default console application. Applies to IOTAModuleCreator interface.
sForm	Used to create a default form. Applies to IOTAModuleCreator interface.
sLibrary	Used to create a default library. Applies to IOTAProjectCreator interface.
sPackage	Used to create a default package. Applies to IOTAProjectCreator interface.
sText	Used to create an empty text file. Applies to IOTAModuleCreator interface.
sUnit	Used as a default unit source file. Applies to IOTAModuleCreator interface.

In our example, we will use the sText creator type.

The method that actually generates and fills in the text for the Wizard's result file is the NewImplSource() function, which has been added to the wizard_memstatus.cpp source file and is shown in Listing 23.17.

Listing 23.17   Creator Class—NewImplSource() Method

```
_di_IOTAFile __fastcall Creator::NewImplSource(
    const AnsiString ModuleIdent, const AnsiString FormIdent,
    const AnsiString AncestorIdent)
{
    AnsiString dtstring;
    TDateTime adatetime;
    adatetime = adatetime.CurrentDateTime();

    dtstring = adatetime.FormatString("mm/dd/yyyy hh:nn:ss am/pm");

    // let's grab data from Wizard that we want in the text file.

    AnsiString form_source  = "Memory Analysis Results \n\n";
    form_source += "Project = " + wizard->projectname + "\n";
```

LISTING 23.17   Continued

```
    form_source += "Run Date = " + dtstring + "\n";
    form_source += wizard->memtotal + "\n";;
    form_source += wizard->memstartfree + "\n";;
    form_source += wizard->memstopfree + "\n";;
    form_source += wizard->memfinalusage + "\n";;
    form_source += wizard->mempeakusage + "\n\n\n";;
    form_source += "Enter your notes below...";;

    _di_IOTAFile file = new File(form_source);
    return file; // Expand(form_source, ModuleIdent, FormIdent, AncestorIdent);
}
```

You'll notice in this method that we access some of the public data we are now providing in our wizard class. This method returns a new file to our wizard for the current project. To support our NewImplSource() method we need a way to generate an _di_IOTAFile interface. This requires another custom class as shown in Listing 23.18, which has been added to the wizard_memstatus.h file.

Listing 23.18   File Class Declaration

```
class File : public IOTAFile {
public:
    __fastcall File(const AnsiString source);
    virtual __fastcall ~File();
    AnsiString __fastcall GetSource();
    System::TDateTime __fastcall GetAge();
protected:
    // override IInterface  methods
    virtual HRESULT __stdcall QueryInterface(const GUID&, void**);
    virtual ULONG __stdcall AddRef();
    virtual ULONG __stdcall Release();
private:
    long ref_count;
    System::TDateTime age;
    AnsiString source;
};
```

Utilizing Our Creator

Although that might have seemed like a lot of effort to create a couple of classes, utilizing our creator class is fairly simple. The bolded text in the following code excerpt (as shown in Listing 23.19) has been added to our wizard's Execute() method within the wizard_memstatus.cpp source file.

Listing 23.19   MemStatWizard Class—Execute() Method Custom Creator Utilization

```cpp
// little loop processing here - but don't tie up system (check and get out)
if (FormMemStat)
{
    while (FormMemStat->Visible)  // check
    {
        if (!ProcessActive)  // process is no longer active / shut it down
        {
            FormMemStat->SpeedButtonStopClick(0); // final measurement
            FormMemStat->Close();
        }
        Application->HandleMessage(); //get out (process current messages)
    }

    if (ProcessActive) // wizard has been shut down, but app remains
    {
        int result = MessageBox(NULL,
                "MemStat Wizard has been shut down, but the application "\
                "under test is still active. \n\n" \
                "Do you wish to close application under test as well?",
                "MemStat Wizard - Terminated",MB_YESNO);
        if (result == IDYES)
        {
            _di_IOTAProcess Process;
            Process = DebuggerServices->CurrentProcess;
            if (Process)
                Process->Terminate();
        }
    }
    memstopfree = FormMemStat->GetMemoryStopFree();
    memfinalusage = FormMemStat->GetMemoryFinalUsage();
    mempeakusage = FormMemStat->GetMemoryPeakUsage();

    MessageServices->AddTitleMessage(
        AnsiString(GetName() + " - " +
        memstopfree),MessageGroup);
    MessageServices->AddTitleMessage(
        AnsiString(GetName() + " - " +
        memfinalusage),MessageGroup);
```

LISTING 23.19 Continued

```
    MessageServices->AddTitleMessage(
        AnsiString(GetName() + " - " +
        mempeakusage),MessageGroup);

    // dump out log file with memory performance data
    _di_IOTAModule module = ModServices->CreateModule(new Creator(sText,this));

    delete FormMemStat;
}
if (debugnotifier)  // little clean-up
{
    debugnotifier->Destroyed();
    debugnotifier = NULL;
}



    MessageServices->AddTitleMessage(GetName() + " - Completed",MessageGroup);
}
```

In this newly added code, we call the CreateModule() associated to the project module we found earlier using ModServices, by passing in an instance to our Creator class. To instantiate this Creator object, we pass the type of file we want to create, sText, and the pointer to the wizard, which is represented by the this clause. This triggers a call to the NewImplSource() method for our Creator object, and produces our results text file, as shown in Figure 23.6.

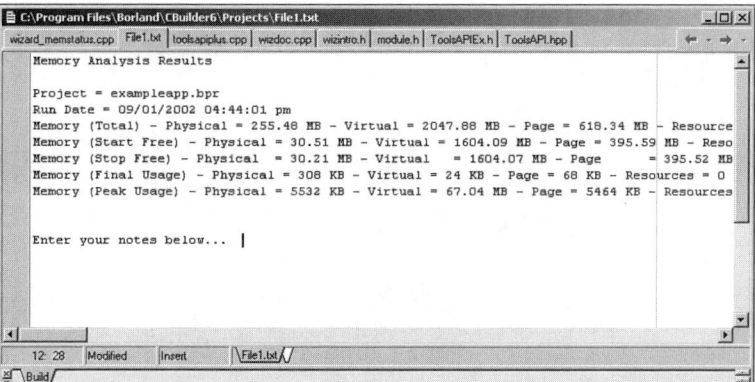

Figure 23.6 New text file associated to project, which contains results of memory performance.

Using Editors

The Tools API also provides a way to gain access to the various IDE Editors. For our Wizard example, we won't be demonstrating any of the interfaces that are available, but let's take a look at the various types of editor interfaces provided by the Tools API, as shown in Table 23.18.

Table 23.8   Tools API Editor Interfaces

Editor Interface	Description
IOTAEditor	This is the base class for all editors.
INTAFormEditor	Used to gain direct access to the form designer.
IOTAFormEditor	Used to gain access to the form editor at design time.
IOTASourceEditor	Used to access a source file within the IDE.
IOTATypeLibEditor	Used to access a type library file.
IOTAProjectResource	Used to access and change a projects resource file.

In addition to this list, one other Tools API interface that is typically used to support editing is IOTAComponent. IOTAComponent is used to examine and modify component properties, select the component in the form editor, delete the component, and do almost anything the user can do in the form editor.

INTAComponent is a native interface for a component. You can cast an IOTAComponent interface to INTAComponent instance using QueryInterface() or Supports() method. This will enable you to access the component instance directly.

Debugging Your IDE Extensions

Before you install your wizard as a package, you may find yourself wanting to debug your code. This can be accomplished by setting the C++Builder executable as the host application for your package as illustrated in Figure 23.7.

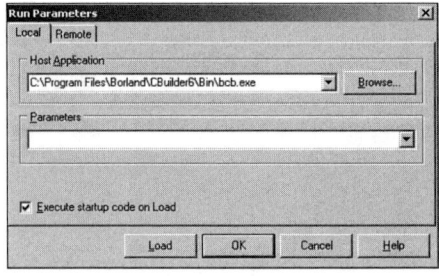

Figure 23.7   Run Parameters Dialog—Setting up to debug a Wizard package.

With this added, when you run your package, another instance of C++Builder will load up. In that new instance, you'll need to install your Wizard package (the bpl file) using the Components\Install Package menu item. Any breakpoints you set in your wizard code will now be accessible in the original instance of C++Builder. Within this instance of C++Builder, you should be able to trace into [F7], step over [F8], and reach breakpoints in your code just as you would with a normal application.

However, there are a few caveats to make sure this works properly. First, make sure that the package is not already installed. If it is, you can remove it by selecting Install Packages from the Component menu. This will open a filtered version of the Project Options dialog, which contains only an enabled Packages view. This is illustrated in Figure 23.8.

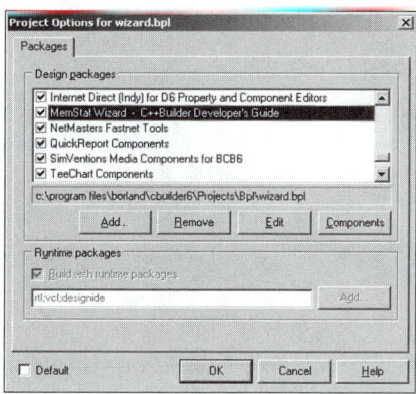

Figure 23.8   Packages view.

To remove a package, simply select the Remove button.

Also make sure you include all the debug libraries by enabling them in your project options. Finally, make sure you have enough memory. Remember that you're loading a second instance of C++Builder, which requires a little bit of memory.

Building and Deploying DLLs

We've focused solely on creating packages for representing IDE extensions such as wizards, but a standard DLL can also be used to host IDE extensions. The DLL that you create must export a function initialization function called INITWIZARD0001. An example implementation for this function is shown here.

```
extern "C" bool __stdcall __declspec(dllexport) INITWIZARD0001(
        const _di_IBorlandIDEServices services,
```

```
        TWizardRegisterProc RegisterProc,
        TWizardTerminateProc&)
{
  LocalIDEServices = services;
  RegisterProc(new MemStatusWizard());
  return true;
}
```

The IDE looks for this function when it loads the DLL. So we can differentiate
between a package and a DLL, the following code, shown in Listing 23.20, has been
added to the wizard_memstatus.cpp source file.

Listing 23.20   *Handling Builds Between Packages and DLLs*

```
#ifndef DLL // it's a package
namespace Wizard_memstatus
{
  void __fastcall PACKAGE Register()
  {
    RegisterPackageWizard(new MemStatusWizard());
  }
}
#endif


#ifdef DLL  // it's a dll
extern "C" bool __stdcall __declspec(dllexport) INITWIZARD0001(
        const _di_IBorlandIDEServices services,
        TWizardRegisterProc RegisterProc,
        TWizardTerminateProc&)
{
  LocalIDEServices = services;  // found in ToolsAPIEx
  RegisterProc(new MemStatusWizard());
  return true;
}
#endif
```

If we build a standard DLL, we no longer need the PACKAGE Register() function. To
identify the type of build to be performed, the ToolsAPIEx.h file contains the following definition.

```
//#define DLL  // enable this if building a DLL


#ifdef DLL   // we'll need this for building a DLL
```

```
#define BorlandIDEServices LocalIDEServices
extern _di_IBorlandIDEServices LocalIDEServices;
#endif
```

Notice the #define DLL line commented out. If we remove the comment qualifier, and recompile and link our program, a DLL with a .bpl file extension will be produced for our wizard.

Next, the key is for the DLL to be identified in the Windows Registry with the IDE for the IDE extension to take affect. This is accomplished by adding an entry to the registry under the following key:

```
HKEY_CURRENT_USER\Software\Borland\C++Builder\6.0\Experts
```

Always use a unique name for the entry such as the ID string that was set using our wizard's GetIDString() method. Also, include the full path to the DLL for the value field. Figure 23.9 illustrates the entry made in the registry.

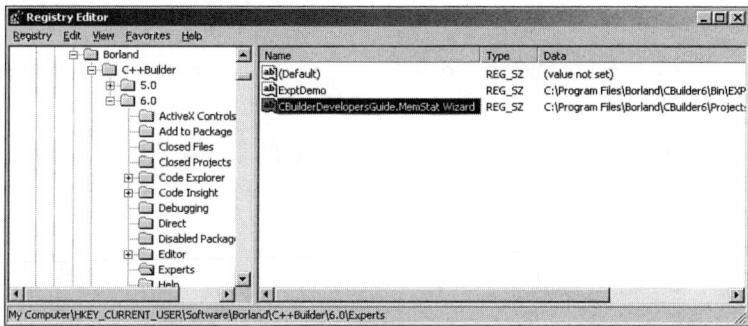

Figure 23.9   The Registry Editor.

The next time C++Builder launches, it will load the library files it encounters in the registry.

WHICH ONE—PACKAGE OR DLL?

Most developers find that it's simpler to incorporate an IDE extension inside a package rather than a DLL. Furthermore, it is easier to reload design-time packages rather than DLLS when you're developing your extension because you can see your results immediately (no need to close and reopen the IDE). However, the one drawback with packages is that unit name and form name clashes are more susceptible than a DLL implementation. Therefore, one recommendation is to port your code into a DLL for final delivery when you're happy with your IDE extension. Keep in mind that the DLL should always be built with the VCL runtime package if it uses any of the Native Tool API interfaces.

Recommended Readings

Although the Tools API is not broadly discussed within the C++Builder community, there are several resources identified in the following listing that you might find useful.

- *C++Builder Developer's Guide Manual*—http://www.bcbdev.com   Don't confuse the book you're reading with the manual that comes with the C++Builder 6 Pro and C++Builder 6 Enterperise. There is an excellent chapter on Extending the IDE that focuses on the Tools API (see Chapter 28).

- *C++Builder Help File*—http://www.bcbdev.com   Much of what can be found in the Developer's Guide manual, is provided in the C++Builder Help. Index on *Tools API*.

- *Tools API Source Code*—You can learn a lot by looking at the source code for the Tools API. Open and look at the ToolsAPI.pas and ToolsAPI.hpp files both found under the CBuilder6\Source\ToolsAPI\ folder to familiarize yourself with the available interfaces.

- *Delphi 6 Developer's Guide*, Xavier Pacheco and Steve Teixeira, (2001), Sams, pp. 1169, ISBN 0672321157—It might be Delphi focused, but this book provides excellent examples on using the Tools API (see Chapter 17).

- *Erik's Open Tools API FAQ and Resources*—http://gexperts.org/opentools/   This is one of the better resources on the Internet for Tools API information. Most of the examples are in Delphi though.

- *Tempest Software—Open Tools API*—http://www.tempest-sw.com/opentools/   Author Ray Lischner, who manages this site, is one of the strongest advocates and experts on the Tools API. His site provides a solid tutorial and a number of Delphi examples. Ray has also written several Delphi books that tackle the Tools API.

- *Hidden Paths of Delphi 3: Experts, Wizards, and the Open Tools API*, Ray Lischner, Danny Thorpe (Editor), Lori Ash (Editor), (1997), Informant Communications Group, pp. 350, ISBN 0965736601—This provides an excellent resource on the Open Tools API supported by Delphi 3, which is still relevant.

- *Borland Newsgroups*—news://newsgroups.borland.com   There are several Borland newsgroup discussion forums on the Tools API. They include Borland.public.delphi.nativeapi, Borland.public.delphi.opentoolsapi, Borland.public.cppbuilder.nativeapi, and Borland.public.cppbuilder. opentoolsapi. The Delphi.opentoolsapi forum has been around the longest, and probably contains the most information. The other forums have only recently been added (September 2002). C++Builder developers should be able to pick up quite a bit of knowledge from the Delphi focused forums.

Summary

In this chapter, we've touched on the various elements of the Tools API such as wizards, notifiers, services, creators, and editors. We have provided some practical examples on how to use the Tools API. The more you play around with the Tools API, the more comfortable you'll become in hacking and extending the IDE. (Note: Always hack responsibly). If you come up with an idea that adds a great new feature to the IDE, you're encouraged to build it, wrap it up in a DLL, and share it with the rest of the Borland community. That way we all benefit, Delphi developers included.

There's no doubt Borland has provided a fairly significant piece of technology in the Tools API. Being able to extend an IDE's capability using COM-like interfaces is a clever approach for Borland allowing their engineers to more easily add improvements to their development environments as well as opening the door for third-party developers to provide new IDE plug-ins. One of the benefits is that a DLL that hosts an IDE extension can be designed to work for future releases, as long as it's not dependent on any Native Tools API interfaces. The bottom line is that the flexibility of the Tools API can be used to further the capabilities of your C++Builder IDE—and that's a good thing!

PART VI

Appendixes

IN THIS PART

A

C++Builder Example Applications

by Paul Gustavson

The set of example applications included with C++Builder 6 is perhaps one of the best available resources for developers. You can find these examples in your installation directory under the example folder. Unfortunately, very little documentation accompanies the product CD that describes these examples. In this appendix we will highlight the capabilities provided by these examples.

Overview of C++Builder Example Applications

The examples provided with C++Builder 6 are identified and briefly described in Table A.1.

TABLE A.1 Borland C++Builder Example Applications

Folder	Description
Ado	Contains two examples related to using ActiveX Data Objects (ADO): Briefcase and Shape.
AppEvents	This example demonstrates the use of the TApplicationEvents component including intercepting application messages, exposing event handlers, and posting text to list boxes.
Apps	There are too many to list in this table. See Table A.2 for more details.
CodeGuard	An application containing a memory leak, which is used to demonstrate the effectiveness of CodeGuard.

TABLE A.1   Continued

Folder	Description
Controls	Contains four folders demonstrating various types of controls. The SingleInst folder provides a control for limiting the number of instances of an application. The Source folder provides a set of packages (and source code) that represent the controls found on the Samples tab of the VCL palette. The Traydemo provides an example application showing various effects that can be made to the system tray. The VersionInfo folder provides a set of packages that represent controls for identifying version info elements for an application such as product version, file description, generic label, copyright label, and comments.
ConvertIt	An application demonstrating the conversion of various units related to area, distance, mass, temperature, time, and volume. (See Figure A.1 for an illustration of this example).

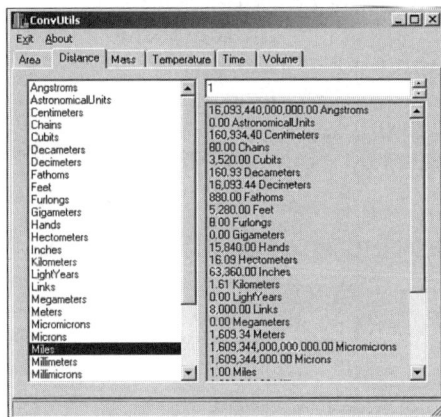

FIGURE A.1   The ConvertIt example application.

Corba	Contains two applications demonstrating the effectiveness of Corba: atm and corbamidas.
CustomDraw	A custom draw TreeView example that demonstrates how to change font and background including assigning a bitmap to the canvas of a TTreeView control.
DBTasks	Contains a number of applications related to database tasks. There are too many to list in this table; see Table A.3 for more details.
DDraw	Contains a number of C++Builder DirectDraw examples.
Doc	Contains a mix of applications related to document elements. There are too many to list in this table; see Table A.4 for more details.
Docking	Application shows how docking works in several scenarios, including conjoined tab hosts.

TABLE A.1   Continued

Folder	Description
Experts	Contains an application illustrating the development of experts, and miscellaneous C++Builder component operations.
FastNet	Contains a number of applications using NetMaster components.
Games	Contains three game examples for C++Builder: a Pong-like game in the EarthPng folder, Coleco-like football game in the Football folder, and a game called Swat! in the Swat folder. (See Figure A.2 for an illustration of the Football example.)

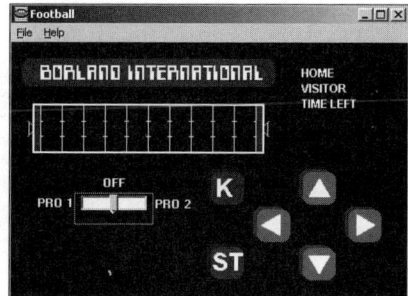

FIGURE A.2   The Football game application.

Indy	Contains a number of examples that demonstrate the Indy network components.
Internet	Contains two Internet-based applications: Chat and a Hello World Dynamic Shared Object (DSO) for Apache.
MFC	Contains five Microsoft Foundation Class (MFC) library usage examples.
Midas	Contains seven useful examples demonstrating Midas technologies.
OpenGL	Contains two OpenGL API examples: Drawing and Rotate.
PWordDemo	Demonstrates automation of Microsoft Word services within a C++Builder app.
ShellControls	Contains package source for Shell controls, and an example that demonstrates the use of these Shell controls.
StdLib	A Standard Template Library (STL) example that runs miscellaneous demos of STL algorithms and types.
Teechart	An example application that demonstrates the Tee Chart Pro component.
Toolsapi	Contains a set of examples demonstrating how to use Borland's Tools API using C++Builder. Examples include extensions to filters, action lists, native tool services, and key bindings.
VirtualListView	This program demonstrates how to create a file explorer application.
WebServ	An example of a Common Gateway Services application for Web servers.

TABLE A.1   Continued

Folder	Description
WebServices	Contains three Web Services examples: EchoService, PostSOAP, and SOAPDataModule. EchoService provides two example ISAPI and CGI servers, and a client application.
WebSnap	Contains a number of useful WebSnap examples. There are too many to list here. See Table A.5 for details.
WinTools	A C++Builder Command Line Tools GUI example. (See Figure A.3 for an illustration of this example.)

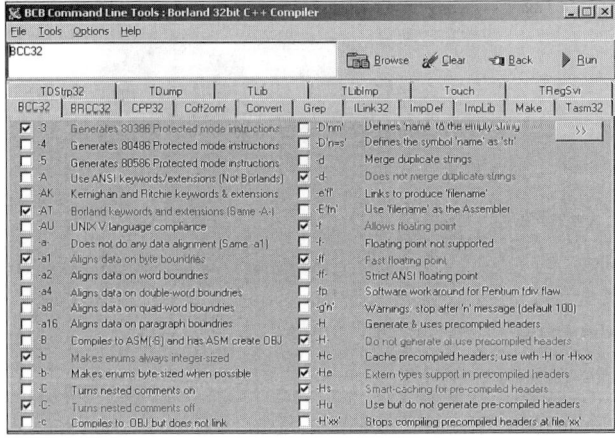

FIGURE A.3   The WinTools command-line GUI application.

Let's drill down further and identify some of the other examples that were too broad to list in Table A.1.

"Apps" Example Applications

A number of examples are found under the Examples/Apps folder where C++Builder is installed. These are identified and briefly described in Table A.2.

TABLE A.2   Apps Example Applications

Folder	Description
Autocon	Example of an OLE Automation Controller, which uses both VTable methods and Dispatch methods to access a COM object. Requires the automation server within the Autosrv folder to be registered (built and run) to execute. (See Figure A.4 for an illustration of this example.)

TABLE A.2   Continued

Folder	Description
Autosrv	A simple COM Automation Server, which is used by the example Automation Controller provided within the `Autocon` folder. (See Figure A.4 for an illustration of this example.)

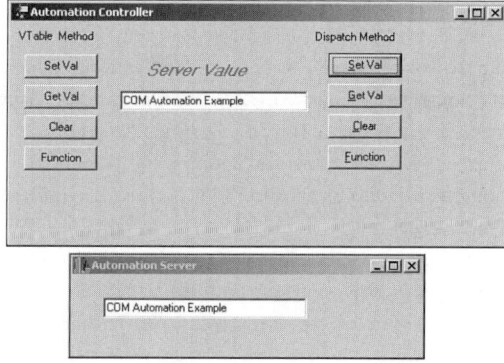

FIGURE A.4   Demonstration of COM automation using the `AutoCon` and `Autosrv` applications.

Canvas	Demonstrates the rotation of lines drawn on a canvas over time.
Colordlg	Demonstrates the use of the Color common dialog to change the color of a form.
Cursors	An example that demonstrates how to toggle the shape of a cursor.
Doodle	A doodle paint program. (See Figure A.5 for an illustration of this example.)

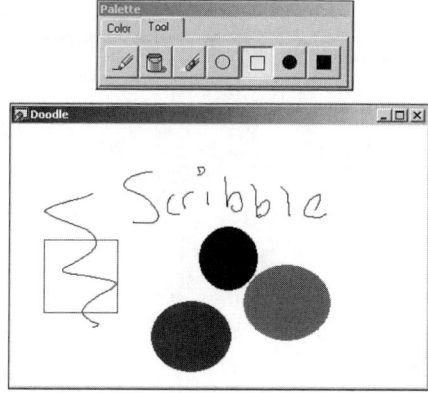

FIGURE A.5   The Doodle program.

TABLE A.2 Continued

Folder	Description
FindRep	Demonstrates how to use the Find and Replace Dialogs within a `RichEdit` application.
Header	An example that uses a `HeaderControl` to resize the objects contained within each column.
ImageView	An example application used to navigate a hard disk to view image files (BMP, ICO, WMF, and EMF).
IpcDemos	Contains two applications, `monitor` and `client`, which demonstrate interprocess communication (IPC) in Win32. Communication is accomplished between these two applications using Threads, Events, Mutexes, and Shared memory.
MiniComp	Example of a small, nonvisual counter component.
MultiPag	A multipage dialog application that demonstrates the capabilities provided by a `TPageControl`.
OwnerList	This example provides a WYSIWG display of the fonts available on a system demonstrating how to create and use an owner drawn list box.
Printing	Demonstrates how to send text within a memo control to a printer. Uses `TPrintDialog`.
ProcView	An example that lists the processes that are running on a machine, and provides the capability to kill them. Uses the Win32 API: `EnumWindows()`, `GetClassName()`, `GetWIndowText()`, and `TerminateProcess()`.
RichEdit	A Rich Text word-processor example very similar to WordPad. Includes an English, French, and Dutch version. (See Figure A.6 for an illustration of this example.)

FIGURE A.6 The `RichEdit` word processor program.

Scrollbar	Demonstrates the use of a ScrollBar control.
Switch	A simple example that demonstrates how to dynamically change event handlers at runtime.

TABLE A.2   Continued

Folder	Description
SysSound	Enumerates the system sounds installed within Windows and demonstrates how to play them using the Win32 API MessageBeep().
Tab	A multipage dialog application that demonstrates the capabilities provided by a TTabControl.
Threads	Demonstrates how to derive a class from TThread to perform three types of sorts: Bubble Sort, Selection Sort, and Quick Sort.
TrayIcon	Demonstrates how to place an active icon for an application in the system tray, and toggle the icon's state.
TwoForms	A simple application demonstrating how to instantiate and activate a second form on a button clicked from the main form.
Wpm	Example test application that measures the number of words per minute you can type.

"DBTask" Example Applications

A few examples are found under the Examples/DBTask folder where C++Builder is installed. These are identified and briefly described in Table A.3.

TABLE A.3   DBTasks Example Applications

Folder	Description
BkQuery	Demonstrates how to perform a background query on an SQL database using threads.
CachedUp	This example demonstrates how cached updates can be used in conjunction with live data using the BDE and nonlive data using the UpdateSQL component. Requires Interbase Server.
Contacts	An example app demonstrating how customer orders are managed using TQuery, TTable, and TDataSource. (See Figure A.7 for an illustration of this example.)
CSDemos	An example Internet Client application. Requires Interbase Server and SQL Links.
CtrlGrid	A simple app, which displays database fields in a grid using TDBGrid, TDBCtrlGrid, TDBNavigator, and TDBEdit.
DBErrors	An example that demonstrates how to use Data Modules to centralize coding. Includes a one-to-many form and illustrates how to trap and control database errors.
Filter	An application that demonstrates how to filter records using a Data Module with a Query linked through a Datasource. Uses TDBGrid and TDBNavigator.
Find	Demonstrates how to find records in a database. Uses TDBNavigator, TDataSource, and TDBGrid.

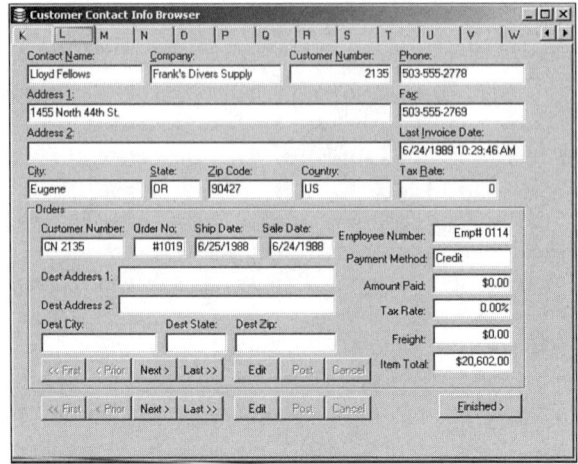

FIGURE A.7   The Contacts database application.

TABLE A.3   Continued

Folder	Description
FishFact	An example application that accesses a database of fish facts. Uses TDBImage, TDataSource, TDBGrid, and TDBText. (See Figure A.8 for an illustration of this example.)

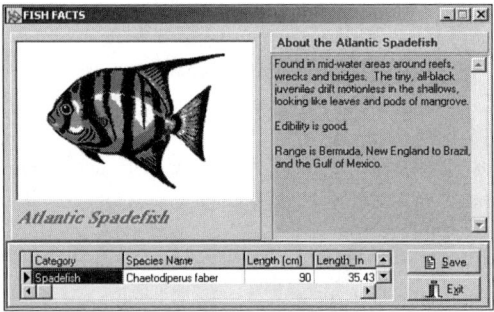

FIGURE A.8   The FishFact database application.

Gds	The Global Dive Supply example that shows two views of data and filter capabilities. Uses TDataModule, TDataSet, and TDBGrid.
GDSDemo	Another Global Dive Supply example that uses TTable, TDatabase, TDataSource, TDBNavigator, and much more. A bit more sophisticated than Gds.
IBDemo	An application that demonstrates how to use InterBase event alerts.

TABLE A.3   Continued

Folder	Description
LookUp	Demonstrates how to use lookup fields and calculated fields using TDBNavigator, TDBGrid, TdataSource, and TCurrencyField.
MastApp	A very sophisticated database example that uses QuickReports with multiple data. Uses TTable, TDataSource, TQuery, TDataBase, TQuickReport, and more.
MstPool	Demonstrates how to pool database objects and measure the amount of time needed to open and close a database connection.
NavMDI	An MDI database example that uses TDBNavigator, TDataSource, TDBGrid, and more.
NavSDI	A multiform SDI database example that uses TDBNavigator, TDataSource, TDBGrid, and more.
NDXBuild	Shows how to build indexes for database tables using TTable, and more.
QBFDemo	Demonstrates how to enable users to define their own queries. Uses TDBGrid, TDBNavigator, and TDataSource.
QJoin	Demonstrates how to join two tables by using an SQL query. Uses TQuery, TDataSource, and TDBGrid.
QuickRpt	Demonstrates how to use QuickReport types for viewing and printing. Uses TQuickRep, TQRGroup, TQRExpr, TQRDetailLink, and much more. (See Figure A.9 for an illustration of this example.)

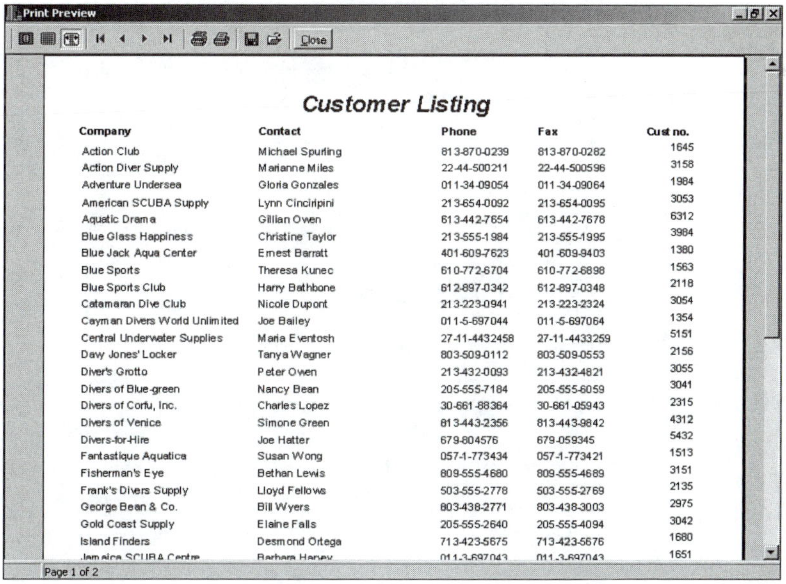

FIGURE A.9   The QuickRpt print preview.

TABLE A.3   Continued

Folder	Description
TextData	Demonstrates how to create and use a DataSet component to work with text files. Uses TDataSet.

"Doc" Example Applications

A few examples are found under the Examples/Doc folder where C++Builder is installed. These are identified and briefly described in Table A.4.

TABLE A.4   Doc Example Applications

Folder	Description
AutoProj	An OLE automation server example that demonstrates how to set a property and call a method of an automation server (SRVR) from an automation client (TESTAP).
CBrowse	Calendar Browser application that uses the TCalendar component.
DirOutIn	An example application that uses TDirectoryOutline and TFileListBox. (See Figure A.10 for an illustration of this example.)

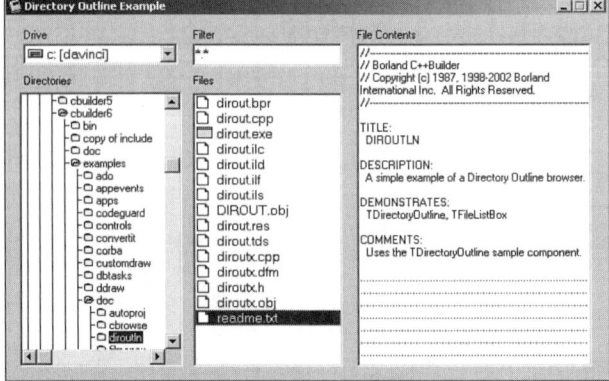

FIGURE A.10   The DirOutIn example application.

Filmanex	A file manager–example application that also uses TDirectoryOutline.
GraphEx	An application that demonstrates how to draw lines on a canvas, which can be saved as a bitmap.
OleCtnrs	Actually, two projects that demonstrate effective ways to use a TOLEContainer. One is an SDI app, and the other an MDI. (See Figure A.11 for an illustration of this example.)

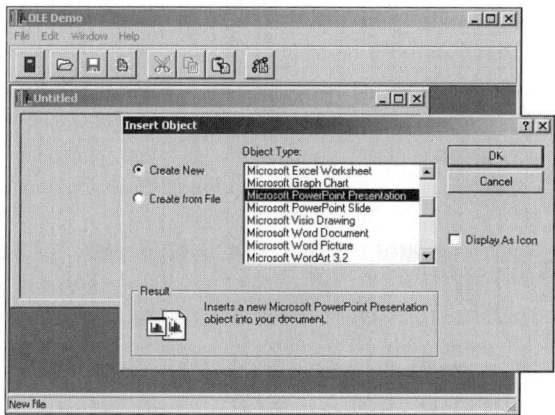

FIGURE A.11   The OLEMDI example application.

TABLE A.4   Continued

Folder	Description
OLEWord1	Demonstrates an OLE automation controller that uses MS Word when it is running.
OLEWord2	Similar to OLEWord1, but with a few more bells and whistles. Word also doesn't need to be running ahead of time for this application to run.
TextEdit	A sample MDI application that uses RichEdit controls. Also demonstrates how to print and change font attributes of text.
VarArray	An application that demonstrates how to use one-dimensional and two-dimensional Variant Arrays.
VarLock	Demonstrates how to create and display contents of a Variant Array.
VarToInt	Demonstrates how to instantiate an Automation object representing MS Word using CreateOleObject(), and then assign Word's IDispatch interface pointer to a variant.

"WebSnap" Example Applications

WebSnap components and wizards, which are provided with C++Builder Enterprise, are used to build advanced Web server applications that interact with a Web browser. Some useful WebSnap examples are found under the Examples/WebSnap folder where C++Builder is installed. These are identified and briefly described in Table A.5. Keep in mind these applications require C++Builder Enterprise to build.

TABLE A.5   WebSnap Example Applications

Folder	Description
Biolife	Biolife Server-side examples, which includes a login prompt for browser access into a database. Uses TApplicationAdapter, TAdapterDispatcher, TPageProducer, TPageDispatcher, TWebAppComponents, and much more. (See Figure A.12 for an illustration of this example.)

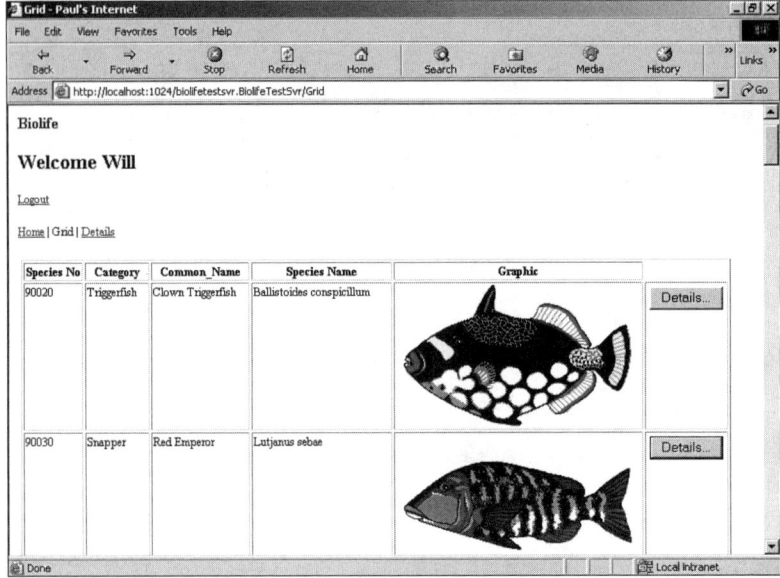

FIGURE A.12   Web page access to the Biolife data base.

CountryEditor	Server-side examples that use the TDataSetAdapter and TAdapterPageProducer to demonstrate how to build a grid page and a form page to edit a country table.
CountryReport	Server-side examples that use TDataSetAdapter and custom JavaScript to display a simple report using a country table.
DumpModules	Server-side examples that demonstrate how to use JavaScript to traverse the modules, adapters, and fields, and actions in a Web application. The JavaScript is contained in the DumpModulesInc.html.
LocateFileService	Server-side examples that demonstrate how HTML templates and server side–include files can be retrieved by a client using the TLocateFileService.OnFindStream event.

TABLE A.5   Continued

Folder	Description
MasterDetail	Server-side examples that demonstrate how to view and edit master-detail relationship using TDataSetAdapter through a Web page. (See Figure A.13 for an illustration of this example.)
PhotoGallery	Code for building a server-side application that provides a Web-based photo gallery. (See Figure A.14 for an illustration of this example.)
StreamImage	Server-side examples that demonstrates how to stream an image from a server to a Web page.

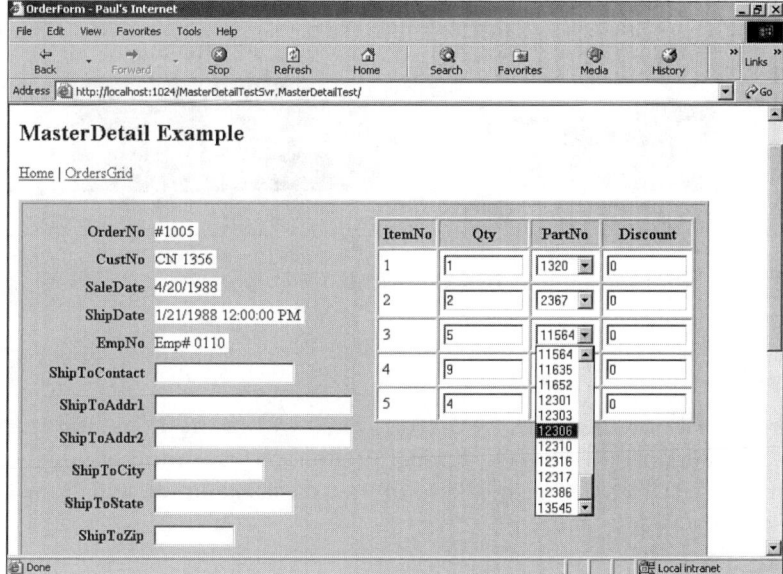

FIGURE A.13   Editing database information via the Web page via the MasterDetail server.

Most of these examples contain one ISAPI server-side project and a Web Debugger server-side project. To run the Web App Debugger version of any of the projects contained within these example folders, compile the project (with the project name ending in Debugger) and run it once to register it.

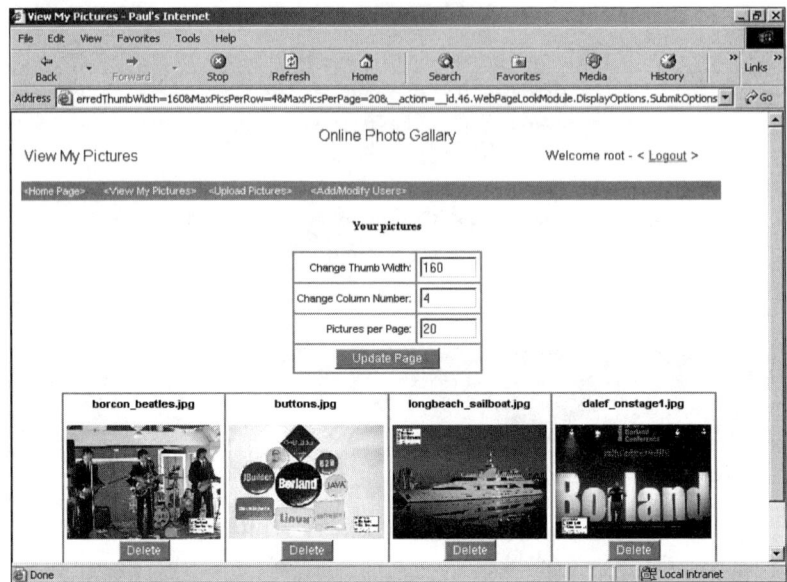

FIGURE A.14   Accessing the `PhotoGallery` via a Web browser.

Summary

In addition to the examples we've demonstrated within this book, the examples provided by Borland with the C++Builder product provide another tangible resource you can leverage. You're encouraged to try out these examples, and "look under the hood" to see how they are put together.

B

C++ Mobile Application Development

by Paul Gustavson

At the time of this writing, Borland is preparing to deliver a new C++ environment for mobile application development called C++ Mobile Edition. The initial release for this environment, formerly known as Edison, will be provided as a plug-in for C++Builder 6. This plug-in will support the development of C++ applications for mobile devices such as Nokia's Series 60 platform, which is run on the Symbian Operating System (OS). Future C++ mobile releases will include a new Borland ARM C++ compiler supporting additional mobile devices such as Microsoft CE devices, Palm and Embedded Linux, along with Mobile CLX components to help rapidly compose mobile applications.

The first public preview of the Edison technology was at the 13th Annual Borland Conference (BorCon) in May 2002 in Anaheim, California. However, Borland first provided development support for mobile applications in Java with the release of Borland JBuilder MobileSet 2.0 in January 2001.

Although Java support is first to market for Borland, C++ is seen as an ideal language for native, phone-specific applications. The C++ Mobile Edition will provide deployment support from within the C++Builder development environment, simplifying the task of deploying C++ applications to 2.5 and 3G phones.

In this appendix, we will take a look at C++ Mobile Edition and what's required to begin developing mobile applications for a wireless market that continues to explode. We'll also look ahead to see what else Borland is planning to put in the hands of mobile application developers.

NOTE

As you peruse through this appendix a caveat should be mentioned. The descriptions and examples provided in this appendix are based on an early development version of the C+ Mobile Edition that was provided by Borland at the time of this writing. It's quite likely that the official release of the C++ Mobile Edition will offer a slightly different look and feel and might provide further extensions. However, the functionality and techniques provided in this text should be very much applicable to the release version of the C++ Mobile Edition.

C++ Mobile Edition Overview

Borland C++ Mobile Edition is a plug-in that works for any edition of C++Builder 6 (Personal, Professional, Enterprise). However, you might find some features that are not available in all editions. Regardless, the C++ Mobile Edition plug-in will enable you to develop mobile applications within the C++Builder 6 development environment, as illustrated in Figure B.1.

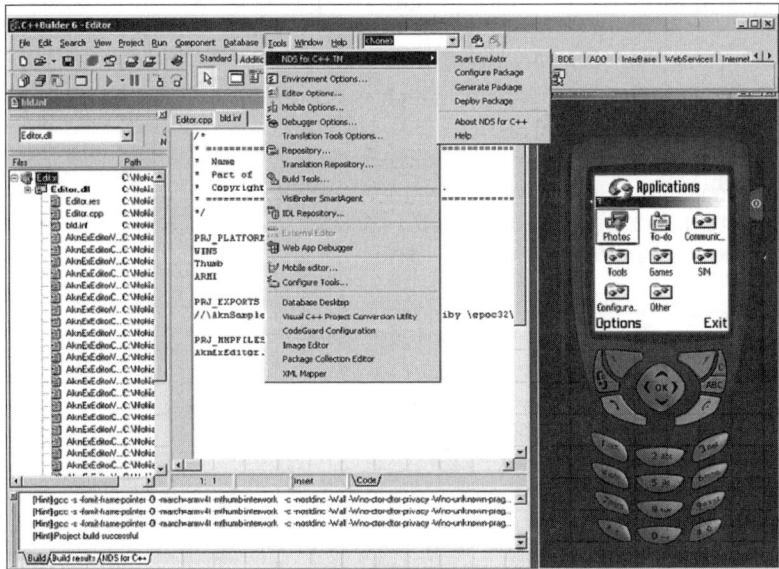

FIGURE B.1   C++Builder IDE with the C++ Mobile Edition plug-in.

Let's briefly look at what's required to begin to develop mobile applications.

- Windows 2000 or Windows XP Professional
- C++Builder 6 Service Update 3 or later

- Symbian SDK (such as the Nokia Series 60 C++ Toolkit or Symbian Quartz 6.1)

- Java Runtime Environment (JRE) 1.31 or later

- Perl 5.6.1 or later

- Borland C++ Mobile Edition (Edison) Plug-In

Hopefully, you already have the first two items in the list. Next, the Symbian SDK, such as the Nokia Series 60 C++ Toolkit, must be installed prior to installing the C++ Mobile Edition plug-in. You might be surprised to see that the Java Runtime Environment (JRE) and Perl are also identified in this list. Both Java and Perl are required to support the Symbian build process. Some of the Symbian SDK utilities are Java applications, and, to use these utilities, the JRE needs to be installed. Furthermore, the Symbian build scripts that are used during compilation are written in Perl.

Fortunately, Borland will release a combined setup that includes the Nokia Series 60 C++ Toolkit, the JRE, Perl, the C++ Mobile Edition plug-in, and a Series 60 emulator, which we'll talk more about in a moment.

Symbian SDK

A Symbian Software Development ToolKit (SDK) provides a development framework for the Symbian OS within Windows, which includes APIs, documentation, development tools and scripts for supporting mobile application development. One of the more popular SDKs is the Nokia Series 60 C++ Toolkit, which is a native C++ development framework for the Symbian OS that is centered on Nokia's Series 60 platform. The Toolkit contains a phone emulator, APIs and documentation, and is used to support development for smart-phone devices such as the Nokia 3650, which is illustrated in Figure B.2.

One of the things that you might come across in the SDK documentation is that the Nokia Series 60 SDK requires Microsoft Visual C++. This can be disregarded, given that Borland provides the necessary wrappers and linkage into the SDK enabling you to not only develop your mobile application, but to test and debug your application within the C++Builder environment using the C++ Mobile Edition plug-in.

Another SDK supported by the C++ Mobile Edition is the Symbian Quartz 6.1 SDK. It is anticipated that other SDKs closely tied with the Symbian OS and specific mobile devices will be offered in the near future.

FIGURE B.2   The Nokia 3650 Symbian OS-based smart phone.

C++ Mobile Edition Plug-In

After a Symbian SDK is installed, the C++ Mobile Edition can then be installed. When you install the C++ Mobile Edition plug-in for C++ Builder, the EPOCROOT and Path environment variables will be set to allow proper access to the Symbian SDK and Emulator, if one is present. This will ensure mobile applications can compile and build properly within C++Builder.

> **NOTE**
>
> EPOC was the original name for the Symbian OS. References to EPOC are really aliases to the Symbian OS components.

> **NOTE**
>
> One of the things that is possible within the C++ Mobile Edition is to use multiple mobile SDKs in your development. However, when building mobile applications, you will need to change your path variables to identify the appropriate SDK that represents the mobile device you are trying to target.

With the first C++ Mobile Edition release, there are no VCL or CLX components that you can drop on to a form representing the mobile application you are developing, as you could for a Windows or Linux application that you are developing. Therefore, you'll need to develop your mobile application the old-fashion way and incorporate the Symbian SDK API routines within your code. Fortunately, you will at least be within the familiar C++Builder environment containing the integrated code editor, compiler, debugger, a project manager, and an emulator, which enables you to debug and test your mobile application. Furthermore, the wizard support provided by the C++ Mobile Edition plug-in provides assistance in establishing new mobile projects and importing existing mobile projects from the examples provided by the Nokia Series 60 SDK and other SDKs.

Even if you don't have a Symbian OS-based mobile device, you can still go through the motions of developing and testing a mobile application. In fact, there are three potential ways to test a mobile application.

- Use a software Emulator

- Use a software-based hardware Simulator

- Deploy to an actual mobile device

The first two items represent ways to test and run your application without the actual hardware, whereas the last bullet should be obvious. In fact, it's possible to even debug a mobile application on a mobile device.

Emulator Versus Simulator

At this point you might be asking, "What's the difference between an emulator and simulator? Aren't they basically the same?"

Actually, no; there is a distinction between the two. Although both are pieces of software that run on the development machine and appear to replicate the appearance and operation of a mobile device, they are fundamentally different. An emulator provides the general operations and capabilities associated to a mobile device, but not at the same fidelity or authenticity as a simulator, which fully mimics the hardware.

In more general terms, an emulator provides a constructive software environment for testing and debugging your mobile applications, whereas a simulator provides a virtual hardware environment for testing your mobile applications. The C++ Mobile Edition can support both emulators and simulators within the IDE. The emulator support is provided out of the box when you install because it is typically provided with SDK. To support a simulator, however, the C++ Mobile Edition needs to detect its presence within the system registry.

NOTE

A hardware simulator is not included with the initial release of the C++ Mobile Edition plug-in. However, the C++ Mobile Edition should be capable of supporting simulators that are currently available on the market such as the Virtio or the ARMulator virtual platforms.

You should notice a difference in the performance of your mobile application between an emulator and a simulator. Because a simulator is fully mimicking the hardware and running on top of an existing operating system, it can be more processor intensive and slower than the real hardware or even an emulator. The benefit of a simulator, however, is that it provides a more authentic environment for validating and verifying your application with the mobile device on which your application will be deployed.

An emulator is useful for testing your mobile application before it's been targeted for the actual mobile device. To test your mobile application when it's been targeted for the actual device, you can use a simulator. In a moment, we'll show you how to select the target for your mobile application when it's being built.

Creating a Mobile Application

Let's now examine the specifics of creating a mobile application. With the C++ Mobile Edition there are two ways to *establish* a project. Either *import* an existing mobile application project, such as one of the projects that can be found in the SDK installation folders, or create a brand-*new* project. For learning, the easiest thing to do is to import an existing SDK example. You can also load the sample Hello World project provided on the companion CD-ROM for this book. This project can found under the MadeInBorland folder for this appendix.

The process of establishing a mobile project within C++Builder is performed by selecting File/New/Other from the main menu, and then by selecting the Mobile Tab on the New Items dialog. This is illustrated in Figure B.3.

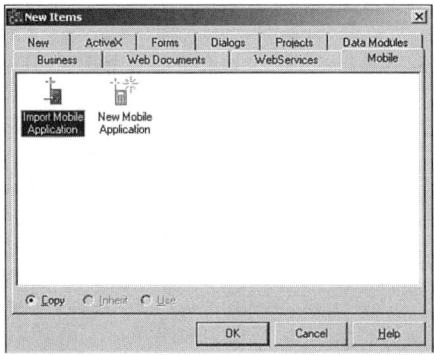

FIGURE B.3　New Items dialog—Mobile Tab.

If you select the New Mobile Application glyph and press OK within this Dialog view, a brand-new mobile application will be generated representing a mobile dll project consisting of a .cpp and .res file. You can then begin to use the Borland text editor to code your application. Be sure to refer to the SDK documentation for details on utilizing the Symbian OS API classes.

If you select the Import Mobile Application glyph and press OK within this Dialog view, an open dialog will appear as illustrated in Figure B.4.

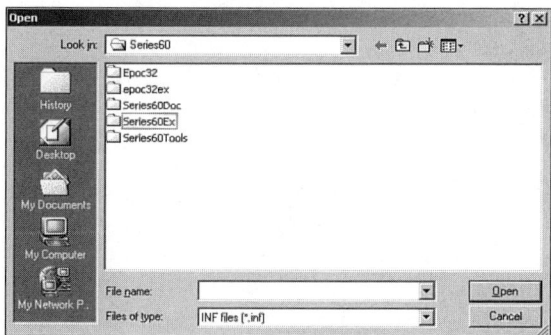

FIGURE B.4   Open dialog.

The folders ending with the Ex tag identify the available mobile examples that can be imported. The epoc32ex folder contains generic Symbian OS examples, whereas the Series60Ex folder contains examples pertinent to not only the Symbian OS but also the Nokia Series 60-based phones. Borland recommends you use the projects found in the Series60Ex folder, unless you are developing for a pen-based mobile device.

NOTE

Many of the examples contained within the epoc32ex folder were written by Symbian for use with the Symbian OS 6.1, Quartz user interface. Quartz is a pen-based UI, with a different form factor from the Series 60. Because the Series 60 Emulator presents a one-handed, buttons only interface it is nearly impossible to interact with most of the pen-based examples.

These two options, New Items dialog and Mobile Tab, illustrate how to establish a new project within C++Builder. For our purposes, we will use the Hello World mobile application provided with the companion CD to highlight the build and test process, and to understand the composition of a mobile application.

NOTE

If you're yearning for more (after we examine the Hello World application), it's recommended that you further explore and learn by importing example applications such as the `Query` example, which can be found with the Nokia Series 60 SDK under the `Series60Ex\Query\group` folder. Select the `BLD.INF` file within this folder. C++Builder, in concert with the Mobile Edition plug-in, will load this project. Build and run as described in the "Building a Mobile Application" section.

Let's now look specifically how to load and build the Hello World project, and test the application using the Nokia emulator.

Loading the Hello World Example

We have already described the step of importing an existing project. The Hello World mobile application provided on the companion CD-ROM can either be loaded using this import method by selection of the `BLD.INF` file associated to the project, or it can be loaded directly by using the `Open Project` menu item and selecting the `MadeInBorland_Project` project group file.

If you choose the import method, you will be prompted for a Project and a Project Group filename when you go to build the project. You're free to choose any name you'd like, but keep in mind that names have already been prescribed for the project as provided on the CD-ROM.

Building a Mobile Application

One of the first steps in building a mobile application is to make sure the project options are set properly. The project options dialog for the C++ Mobile Edition is shown in Figure B.5.

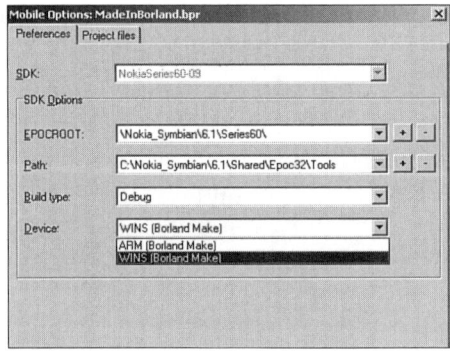

FIGURE B.5   Project Options dialog—Preferences Tab.

You'll notice that the project options dialog is quite a bit different from the project options dialog associated with a typical C++Builder application. At this stage, C++ Mobile Edition is dependent on the Symbian and Nokia tools and scripts and less reliant on its own utilities. Furthermore, the Symbian OS is a different animal than Windows and requires fewer settings.

To test our mobile application locally on a Windows platform, we need to set the target Device type to WINS and the Build Type to Debug.

WINS identifies that a Windows OS will be used to host the mobile application, in other words the application will be compiled to run on the emulator. To test an application on a simulator or deploy to a mobile device, the Target you must select within the build options is the ARM target. ARM identifies the type of processor utilized by the mobile device. A Nokia 3650, for example, uses an ARM-based processor. When you select the ARM target, C++Builder will actually use the GNU ARM C++ compiler provided with the Symbian SDK to compile the source code, and the Symbian OS utilities to link the project.

After the mobile project options are set, we can now build the mobile application. Under the Project menu within the IDE, select the Build menu item pertaining to the loaded project. Then, you will see C++Builder's Compiling dialog identifying the various phases of the build process within the Status field. When it's complete, you should see a "Project Build Successful" status.

WARNING

When creating a new project, consider saving the project beneath the EPOCROOT folder. Otherwise, the mobile project might not compile and load properly within the Nokia emulator.

Testing the Application

You're now ready to test run the Hello World mobile application. This is achieved simply by selecting the Run button on the C++Builder IDE toolbar. The Nokia emulator will begin to load. The load is complete after you see the main menu for the Nokia emulator appear as illustrated in emulator phone display on the left side of Figure B.6.

This figure illustrates how to access the Hello World application that was built within the C++Builder IDE and loaded by the Nokia emulator. From the main menu within the Nokia emulator, select the Other glyph using the O keypad button, and then select the HelloWorld glyph, which represents the Hello World application.

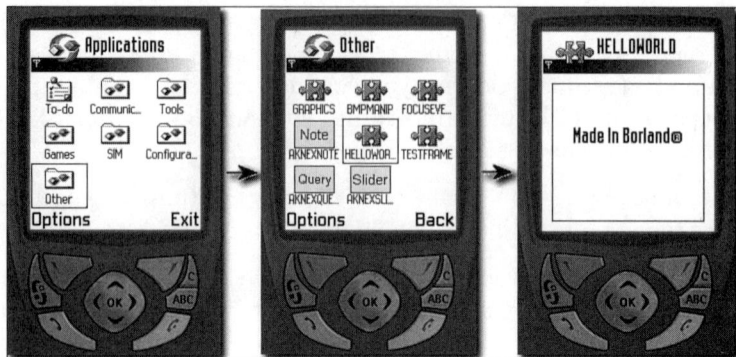

FIGURE B.6   Nokia Emulator—Displays.

TIP

Occasionally, a project that has been built and loaded within the emulator might not reflect future changes if it is modified and rebuilt again within the C++Builder IDE. In these circumstances, you can delete the folder representing the mobile application that was built from the Symbian OS System folder. To locate this folder, go to where the Symbian SDK was installed and trace down the following path:

`Series60\Epoc32\Release\winsb\UDEB\Z\SYSTEM\apps`

You should then see a list of folders, one of which represents your application. Simply delete the specific folder representing your mobile application and rebuild it within C++Builder. The folder will then be regenerated and when you run the Nokia emulator the updated application should appear with the `Other` menu.

WARNING

If you modify a file related to your mobile project, selecting `Run` will not necessarily automatically rebuild the project. Instead, select either `Make` or `Build` prior to selecting `Run`.

Mobile Project Composition

Now, let's examine the project file structure for our "Made in Borland" Hello World application.

The obvious way to view files that are associated to a project in C++Builder is by examining the Project Manager dialog as illustrated in Figure B.7.

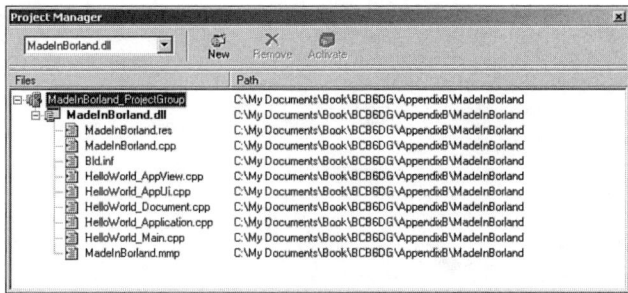

FIGURE B.7   Project Manager Dialog for the "Made in Borland" Hello World Application.

There are a number of different types of files used to represent a project for a mobile application. They include one or more Mobile Management Project (MMP) files, a component description file identified as BLD.INF, and a Package Description (PKG) file. In addition to these three types of files, traditional source (CPP) and header (H) files are created by the developer to represent the aspects of the mobile application. Also, a resource (RSS) file containing UI definitions can be used and created within a mobile application project.

MOBILE EDITOR

The Project Files tab found on the Mobile Options dialog, which we used earlier to modify the project options, displays the principal files associated to our mobile project and is illustrated in Figure B.8.

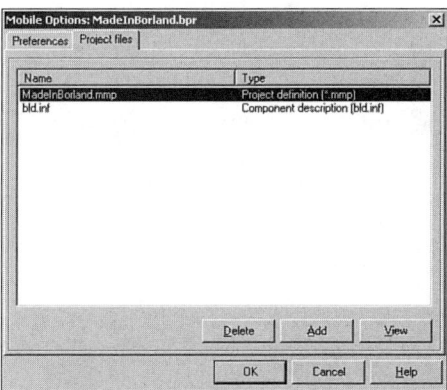

FIGURE B.8   Project Options dialog—Project Files Tab.

In this figure, two files are identified: HelloWorld.mmp and bld.inf. One of the tools Borland has provided with the C++ Mobile Edition is the Mobile Editor dialog. If you select view for either one of the two files listed in the Project Files tab the Mobile Editor dialog will appear, as illustrated in Figure B.9.

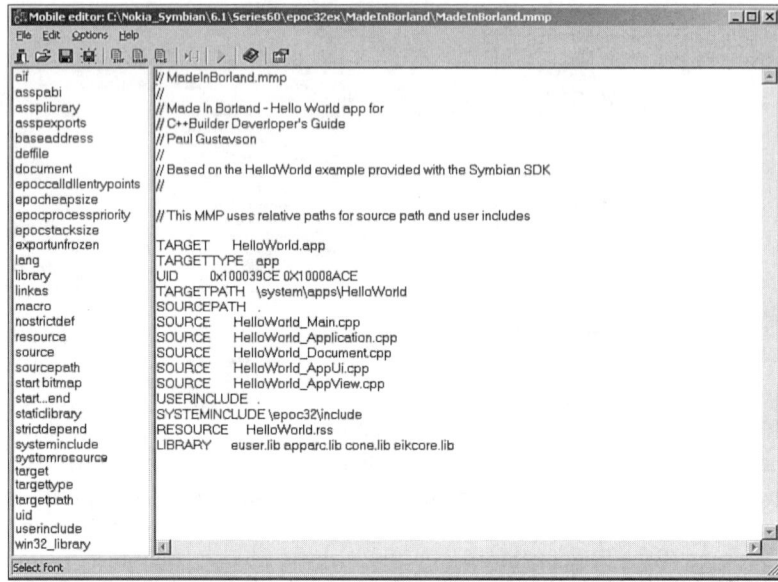

FIGURE B.9   Mobile Editor.

The Mobile Editor is a useful tool for constructing and adding elements to MMP, INF, and PKG files. The left column identifies the key elements that can be added to the file that is displayed on the right panel, which serves as an editor. By double-clicking a key element it will be reflected at the cursor position within the editor on the right side.

MMP Files

An MMP file defines the properties of a mobile application project. An example is provided in Listing B.1.

LISTING B.1   The MadeInBorland.MMP File

```
TARGET MadeInBorland.app
TARGETTYPE app
UID 0x100039CE 0x10004299
TARGETPATH \system\apps\MadeInBorland
SOURCEPATH .
SOURCE MadeInBorland _Main.cpp
SOURCE MadeInBorland _Application.cpp
SOURCE MadeInBorland _Document.cpp
SOURCE MadeInBorland _AppUi.cpp
SOURCE MadeInBorland _AppView.cpp
```

LISTING B.1   Continued

```
USERINCLUDE .
SYSTEMINCLUDE \epoc32\include
RESOURCE MadeInBorland.rss
LIBRARY euser.lib apparc.lib cone.lib eikcore.lib
```

Within this file, there are no dependencies on the intended target platform or the compiler. It typically identifies the target filename, the target type, a Unique ID for the project, the source path indicating the location of the source files, the names of the source files being used, the location of the user and system include files, and any resource or library files that might be required. Comments within the MMP file can be made using C++ style comments.

Multiple MMP files can be included within a mobile application project. If your mobile application contains more than one module or DLL, you should include separate MMP files.

BLD.INF **File**

Every mobile application project has a BLD.INF file, which identifies all the components of the projects. The BLD.INF file enables you to specify the MMP files required for building the components associated to the mobile application. Table B.1 identifies the elements of a BLD.INF file.

TABLE B.1   BLD.INF Elements

Element	Description
PRJ_PLATFORMS	Identifies the type of platform to which you are deploying.
PRJ_EXPORTS	Used to specify the source file.
PRJ_MMPFILES	Used to identify the MMP files.
PRJ_TESTMMPFILES	Used to identify MMP files for test only.

In our example, the BLD.INF file is shown in Listing B.2.

LISTING B.2   The MadeInBorland BLD.INF File

```
// BLD.INF
//
// Made In Borland - Hello World app for
// C++Builder Deverloper's Guide
// Paul Gustavson
//
// Based on the HelloWorld example provided with the Symbian SDK
```

LISTING B.2   Continued

```
//


PRJ_MMPFILES

HelloWorld.mmp
```

You'll notice this BLD.INF file is very simple. We only needed to identify the MMP file using PRJ_MMPFILES tag. As your confidence grows in developing mobile applications, you'll find that your BLD.INF file will become meatier.

Source Code Files

Like standard C++ applications, a mobile project contains one or more header files, source files, resource files and, sometimes, localization files.

Header File

In our example, we have one central header file that identifies the key classes required for our Hello World application. This header file is provided in Listing B.3.

LISTING B.3   The "Made in Borland" HelloWorld.h File

```
// HelloWorld.h
// ——————
//
// Made In Borland - Hello World app for
// C++Builder Deverloper's Guide
// Paul Gustavson
//
// Based on the HelloWorld example provided with the Symbian SDK
//


/////////////////////////////////////////////////////////////////////
// MadeInBorland (HelloWorld app)
// —————
//
//
// The class definitions for the simple example application
// containing a single view with the text "Made In Borland" drawn
// on it.
//
```

LISTING B.3 Continued

```
// The class definitions are:
//
// CExampleApplication
// CExampleAppUi
// CExampleAppView
// CExampleDocument
//
//
////////////////////////////////////////////////////////////////////////
#ifndef __HELLOWORLD_H
#define __HELLOWORLD_H

#include <coeccntx.h>

#include <eikenv.h>
#include <eikappui.h>
#include <eikapp.h>
#include <eikdoc.h>
#include <eikmenup.h>

#include <eikon.hrh>

#include <helloworld.rsg>
#include "helloworld.hrh"




////////////////////////////////////////////////////////////////////////
//
// CExampleApplication
//
////////////////////////////////////////////////////////////////////////

class CExampleApplication : public CEikApplication
    {
private:
                // Inherited from class CApaApplication
    CApaDocument* CreateDocumentL();
    TUid AppDllUid() const;
    };
```

LISTING B.3   Continued

```
//////////////////////////////////////////////////////////////////////
//
// CExampleAppView
//
//////////////////////////////////////////////////////////////////////
class CExampleAppView : public CCoeControl
    {
public:
    static CExampleAppView* NewL(const TRect& aRect);
    CExampleAppView();
    ~CExampleAppView();
    void ConstructL(const TRect& aRect);

private:
                // Inherited from CCoeControl
    void Draw(const TRect& /*aRect*/) const;

private:
    HBufC*   iExampleText;
    };



//////////////////////////////////////////////////////////////////////
//
// CExampleAppUi
//
//////////////////////////////////////////////////////////////////////
class CExampleAppUi : public CEikAppUi
    {
public:
    void ConstructL();
    ~CExampleAppUi();

private:
                // Inherirted from class CEikAppUi
    void HandleCommandL(TInt aCommand);

private:
    CCoeControl* iAppView;
    };
```

LISTING B.3 Continued

```
//////////////////////////////////////////////////////////////////////
//
// CExampleDocument
//
//////////////////////////////////////////////////////////////////////
class CExampleDocument : public CEikDocument
     {
public:
     static CExampleDocument* NewL(CEikApplication& aApp);
     CExampleDocument(CEikApplication& aApp);
     void ConstructL();
private:
               // Inherited from CEikDocument
     CEikAppUi* CreateAppUiL();
     };
#endif
```

This header file identifies the classes that are defined within the multiple source files associated to our mobile project.

Source Files

A mobile application is typically composed of a number of C++ source files. In our example, each source file defines one of the specific classes identified by our HelloWorld.h header file. Rather than examining each source file pertaining to our example, we'll look strictly at the HelloWorld_AppView.cpp source file that defines the CExampleAppView class. This file is shown in Listing B.4.

LISTING B.4 The "Made in Borland" HelloWorld_AppView.cpp File

```
// HelloWorld_CExampleAppView.cpp
// — — — — — — — — — — — — — —
//


//////////////////////////////////////////////////////////////////////
//
// Source file for the implementation of the
// application view class - CExampleAppView
//
//////////////////////////////////////////////////////////////////////


#include "HelloWorld.h"
```

LISTING B.4   Continued

```
//
//              Constructor for the view.
//
CExampleAppView::CExampleAppView()
    {
    }



//              Static NewL() function to start the standard two
//              phase construction.
//
CExampleAppView* CExampleAppView::NewL(const TRect& aRect)
    {
    CExampleAppView* self = new(ELeave) CExampleAppView();
    CleanupStack::PushL(self);
    self->ConstructL(aRect);
    CleanupStack::Pop();
    return self;
    }



//
//              Destructor for the view.
//
CExampleAppView::~CExampleAppView()
    {
    delete iExampleText;
    }



//              Second phase construction.
//
void CExampleAppView::ConstructL(const TRect& aRect)
    {
                        // Fetch the text from the resource file.
        iExampleText = iEikonEnv->AllocReadResourceL(R_EXAMPLE_TEXT_HELLO);
                // Control is a window owning control
        CreateWindowL();
                // Extent of the control. This is
                // the whole rectangle available to application.
                // The rectangle is passed to us from the application UI.
```

LISTING B.4   Continued

```
    SetRect(aRect);
                        // At this stage, the control is ready to draw so
                // we tell the UI framework by activating it.
    ActivateL();
    }


//              Drawing the view - in this example,
//              consists of drawing a simple outline rectangle
//              and then drawing the text in the middle.
//              We use the Normal font supplied by the UI.
//
//              In this example, we don't use the redraw
//              region because it's easier to redraw to
//              the whole client area.
//

void CExampleAppView::Draw(const TRect& /*aRect*/) const
    {
            // Window graphics context
    CWindowGc& gc = SystemGc();
            // Area in which we shall draw
    TRect      drawRect = Rect();
                    // Font used for drawing text
    const CFont*    fontUsed;

            // Start with a clear screen
    gc.Clear();
                    // Draw an outline rectangle (the default pen
            // and brush styles ensure this) slightly
            // smaller than the drawing area.
    drawRect.Shrink(10,10);
    gc.DrawRect(drawRect);
            // Use the title font supplied by the UI
    fontUsed = iEikonEnv->TitleFont();
    gc.UseFont(fontUsed);
                    // Draw the text in the middle of the rectangle.
    TInt   baselineOffset=(drawRect.Height() - fontUsed->HeightInPixels())/2;
    gc.DrawText(*iExampleText,drawRect,baselineOffset,CGraphicsContext::ECenter,
    ➥0);
            // Finished using the font
```

LISTING B.4   Continued

```
    gc.DiscardFont();
    }
```

In the `ConstructL()` method for the `CExampleAppView` class provided in this code listing, text identified by the `R_EXAMPLE_TEXT_HELLO` is fetched from the resource file and contained in the `iExampleText` class property. In a moment we will look at this resource file that contains this string.

In the `Draw()` method, a Symbian windows graphics context is created. A rectangle and the string associated to the `iExampleText` is then drawn to this graphics context. Notice the use of Symbian OS API calls in many of these methods.

Resource File

Let's now take a look at the resource file associated for our "Made in Borland" Hello World project. The `MadeInBorland.RSS` file is provided in Listing B.5.

LISTING B.5   The "Made in Borland" `HelloWorld.RSS` Resource File

```
// HelloWorld.RSS
//
// Made In Borland - Hello World app for
// C++Builder Deverloper's Guide
// Paul Gustavson
//
// Based on the HelloWorld example provided with the Symbian SDK

NAME HEWO

#include <eikon.rh>
#include <eikcore.rsg>

#include "helloworld.hrh"

RESOURCE RSS_SIGNATURE { }

RESOURCE TBUF { buf=""; }

RESOURCE EIK_APP_INFO
    {
    hotkeys=r_example_hotkeys;
    menubar=r_example_menubar;
```

LISTING B.5   Continued

```
    }



RESOURCE HOTKEYS r_example_hotkeys
    {
    control=
        {
        HOTKEY { command=EEikCmdExit; key='e'; }
        };
    }

RESOURCE MENU_BAR r_example_menubar
    {
    titles=
        {
        MENU_TITLE { menu_pane=r_example_first_menu; txt="MBorland"; }
            };
    }

RESOURCE MENU_PANE r_example_first_menu
     {
     items=
            {
            MENU_ITEM { command=EExampleItem0; txt="Item 0"; },
            MENU_ITEM { command=EExampleItem1; txt="Item 1"; },
            MENU_ITEM { command=EExampleItem2; txt="Item 2"; }
        };
     }



RESOURCE TBUF r_example_text_Hello { buf="Made In Borland®"; }
RESOURCE TBUF r_example_text_Item0 { buf="Item 0"; }
RESOURCE TBUF r_example_text_Item1 { buf="Item 1"; }
RESOURCE TBUF r_example_text_Item2 { buf="Item 2"; }
```

Notice the r_example_text_Hello resource string that identifies the tag that we want
displayed when this application is launched.

Additional Files

There are other files associated to a mobile project that you might encounter as well. One, for example, is a multi-bitmap (MBM) file, which represents the Symbian OS icon used for a mobile application. The common tool used to create and modify MBM files is the Icon Designer that is part of AIF Builder utility application provided with the Symbian OS SDK. The AIF builder is a Java application (thus another reason for the JRE). Another file is an Application Information File (AIF), which is used to describe the application features such as icons and captions. This AIF file is generated from an RSS file.

In a moment we'll also talk about the Package Description (PKG) files and Symbian Installation System (SIS) files used for deploying a mobile application.

GUIDELINES FOR MOBILE DEVELOPMENT

Keep in mind that a mobile device does not have as much functionality or screen space as a desktop or laptop. Furthermore, the functionality and screen space varies greatly among mobile devices such as cell phones and Personal Digital Assistants (PDAs). For instance, the standard form factor for a Series 60 device, such as the Nokia 3650, provides a screen size resolution of 176×208 pixels, which is relatively large for a cell phone. A typical PocketPC, however, provides a resolution of 320×240 pixels.

If you're developing for the Series 60 device, the good news is that the same user interface and form factor can be used by *all* series 60 licenses, including Nokia, Siemens, Samsung, and Matsushita (Panasonic). This allows applications targeted for a Series 60 device immediate portability across the major phone manufacturers.

Therefore, the mobile applications you develop need to be practical and easy to use. In addition, the majority of mobile devices have limited keyboards, memory space, and power capacity. The design of a mobile application needs to consider these attributes. Focus on easy navigation and efficient memory management. It's recommended that you refer to the mobile SDK documentation during design and development, which provides an API reference and Style guides for the device you're targeting.

Deploying a Mobile Application

At some point you'll eventually want to deploy your application to a mobile device. After an application has been developed and tested using an emulator (or simulator), it's ready to go through the process of being deployed to a mobile device.

PKG and SIS Files

For an application to be installed and loaded on a mobile device, a Symbian Installation System (SIS) file needs to be generated representing the mobile application. This is accomplished through the creation of a Package Description (PKG) file that identifies the installation information for the mobile application. It contains a unique identifier (UID) for the mobile application that must be included to differentiate one app from another. Again, this PKG file is used to build the SIS file, which calls the deployment tool (for example, `epocinst.exe`, the EPOC install program).

There are several ways to create a PKG file using C++Builder:

- Use the standard editor to create a PKG file by hand.

- Use the Mobile Editor provided by the C++ Mobile Edition.

- Use the Nokia Developer's Suite (NDS) utilities.

The most promising method identified is using the NDS utilities. NDS is geared to automate the process of creating the SIS file. This includes configuring a package, generating a package, and deploying a package to a mobile device. At the time of this writing, Borland is working out the issues for providing the NDS utilities as a wizard that can be accessed from the `Tools` menu in the C++Builder IDE. Borland is hopeful that the NDS wizard will be available for the first release of C++ Mobile Edition, although it might not appear until a later release.

Tools and Methods

An application can be deployed to the target device in two ways. Either the SIS file can be copied to the device, and then installed locally, or the installation can be done remotely using the connection software (for example, PC Suite for Nokia 7650). Two items are required to accomplish either one of these activities:

- Symbian OS-based mobile device

- Connectivity tool such as Nokia 7650 PC Suite

The connectivity tool is a software application that will enable you to download your mobile application to your mobile device, usually via infrared (IrDA), Bluetooth, or even RS-232. The Nokia 7650 PC Suite is a programming interface between your PC and Nokia GSM mobile phones. Specifically, the SDK enables communication with Nokia GSM phones and development of PC applications that utilize the features supported by the phones.

The NDS utilities, described earlier, can be used to leverage this connectivity tool and deploy the SIS file to the host using IrDA, RS232, or Bluetooth.

Symbian OS

Our discussion thus far has centered largely on developing mobile applications for the Symbian OS. It's important to understand the community interest and architecture associated to this OS.

The Symbian OS is the most widely licensed operating system among manufacturers of next-generation mobile phones. The Symbian OS effort is the brainchild of Ericsson, Nokia, Motorola, and Psion, and has been licensed to Samsung, Sony Ericsson, Fujitsu, and Matsushita (Panasonic). It is a full-fledged 32-bit multitasking operating system that provides the following capabilities for mobile devices.

- data management

- communications

- graphics

- multimedia

- security

- application engines

- messaging engine

- Bluetooth support

- browser engines support

- data synchronization and internationalization

Symbian-based phones support GSM, GPRS, and in the future WCMDA, CDMA 2000 (see sidebar on *Mobile Technology Acronyms*). Borland's C++ support for Symbian OS is geared to facilitate the development of 2.5G/3G mobile device applications and take advantage of these aforementioned capabilities and technologies.

MOBILE TECHNOLOGY ACRONYMS

There are lots of confusing acronyms associated to mobile industry. A handful of some of the more common and emerging acronyms is provided in Table B.2.

TABLE B.2   Mobile Technology Acronyms

Acronym	Definition
2G	Second-Generation technology
3G	Third-Generation technology
BSSGP	Base Station Subsystem GPRS Protocol
CDMA	Code Division Multiple Access
CDPD	Cellular Digital Packet Data
DSP	Digital Signal Processor
EDGE	Enhanced Data Rates for GSM
GPRS	General Packet Radio Service
GSM	Global System for Mobile Communications
GTP	GPRS Tunneling Protocol

TABLE B.2   Continued

Acronym	Definition
HDR	High Data Rate
HSCSD	High-Speed, Circuit-Switched Data
IXRTT	One Times Radio Transmission Technology
L2CAP	Logical Link Control and Adaptation Protocol
LLC	Logical Link Control
MMS	Multimedia Message Service
PCS	Personal Communications System Evolution
PDA	Personal Digital Assistant
RLC/MAC	Radio Link Control/Medium Access Control
SMS	Short Message Service
SNDCP	SubNetwork Dependent Convergence Protocol
SoC	Systems-on-a-Chip
TETRA	TErrestrial Trunked RAdio
WAP	Wireless Access Protocol
WCMDA	Wideband CDMA
WML	Wireless Markup Language

Borland's support includes the capability to develop applications for different form factors and for different uses. Figure B.2 provided an illustration of one of the more recent Symbian OS products developed by Nokia. A list of current products is also provided here.

- Nokia 9210/9210i—Nokia 9290

- Sony Ericsson P800

- Nokia 3650/7650

An excellent white paper titled "Getting Started with C++ on the Nokia 9200 Series Communicator," which is available online, will get you started in developing C++ mobile apps even if you don't have the C++ Mobile Edition. You can find this white paper at http://www.symbian.com/developer/techlib/papers/cpp_9200/C++_Nokia_9200. html. To develop the Hello World example that's described in this online paper, you should obtain the Nokia 9200 Series Software Development Kit (SDK) for Symbian OS (see http://www.forum.nokia.com/).

NOTE

The Nokia 9200 Series SDK provides documentation, tools, sample code, and a Microsoft Windows–hosted emulator to facilitate development of mobile apps. In the absence of C++ Mobile Edition, the SDK is essential for developing, testing, and debugging C++ applications.

Future Borland C++ Mobile Products

The C++ Mobile Edition is just the beginning for Borland. Current plans include an IDE project code named Kittyhawk that will include a Borland ARM C++ compiler and Mobile CLX components.

Borland ARM C++ Compiler

The initial release of C++ Mobile Edition uses the GNU C++ Compiler to generate ARM-executable instruction code. This compiler is currently used to target Symbian OS-based devices that use the ARM-based chipset. Borland, however, has bigger plans than strictly supporting application development for Symbian OS-based devices. Their goal is to support a variety of ARM-based chipset devices including WinCE devices such as a PocketPC, Embedded Linux devices, and next-generation Palm Pilots. To achieve this objective, Borland is creating a brand-new C++ compiler that produces applications with ARM executable instruction code that can be targeted and run on various devices.

Borland's recent efforts with the compact .NET framework, and the current development of this ARM C++ compiler satisfies one of the long-time desires of C++Builder developers. The common wish that has been echoed within the newsgroups for the past few years is the capability to develop applications for the PocketPC and Palm using C++Builder. It appeared for a while that this capability would remain only a wish by developers; however, Borland's emphasis over the last several years has been focused on cross-platform development, which now includes the wireless and handheld market. Borland's ARM C++ Complier will enable applications to be developed and deployed for handheld devices that use the ARM-based processor such as the PocketPC. This is only one of the exciting things to expect from Borland.

Mobile CLX Framework

In the near future, Borland plans to develop and release the Mobile RAD environment, which consists of brand-new Mobile RAD IDE and Mobile CLX components. The Mobile CLX components are expected to be a subset of the CLX (and VCL) components provided with C++Builder 6 and Kylix 3. However, in addition to embracing a set of the common CLX components, there will be new components that are exclusive to supporting mobile development, which will consist of wrappers around existing Symbian OS API classes and frequently used Symbian third party libraries. Anticipated examples include components for managing phone calls, text messages, multimedia, calendar, and location-based services. These Mobile CLX components will be designed for portability to other Symbian OS-based platforms. Mobile CLX components for other ARM-based devices are anticipated as well.

Additional Resources

A number of useful resources are available online that contain more information regarding mobile devices. Here are just a few that are relevant to C++ mobile application development.

- www.symbian.com

- www.forum.nokia.com

- portals.devx.com/Nokia/Door/6213

- www.ericsson.com/mobilityworld/

Summary

Borland has made some significant strides in putting together a RAD environment for mobile application development for both Java and C++ developers. The ability to use a familiar environment such as C++Builder to develop C++ applications for Symbian OS-based smart phones, and, in the near future, hand-held computing devices is extremely appealing. The advent of Mobile CLX components should also be well received.

In foresight, Borland's focus on RAD development tools for the mobile market is well timed. It is anticipated that the number of people using wireless devices to stay connected and access the Internet will exceed a half billion by the year 2005. What will draw the interest of these half billion users will be cutting-edge applications that utilize Web-based technologies such as Multimedia Message Service (MMS). A RAD mobile application development environment that enables the creation of these types of applications will be a welcomed capability for developers and those involved in the wireless industry.

C

Information Resources

by Paul Gustavson

IN THIS APPENDIX

- Borland-Sponsored Web Sites
- Useful Developer Web Sites
- Newsgroups
- Books and Magazines
- The Borland Developers Conference (BorCon)

This appendix will point you to many of the useful resources available online or in print regarding C++Builder development. We'll look at resources ranging from Web sites, newsgroups, magazines, and books dedicated exclusively to C++Builder, as well as resources focused on C++, VCL, and CLX development, Windows technologies such as COM and DirectX, and much more. Much of the information available in the resources provided here will help direct you to answers to your C++Builder development-related issues.

Borland-Sponsored Web Sites

Let's start off with Borland-sponsored Web sites. Borland, obviously, provides some of the most focused and current information for C++Builder available on the Internet. They have several sites that we'll examine briefly.

- *Borland Home Page*—http://www.borland.com
- *Borland Developer Network*—http://bdn.borland.com
- *CodeCentral*—http://codecentral.borland.com
- *QualityCentral*—http://qc.borland.com

Borland Home Page

The first site listed is Borland's corporate site (as shown in Figure C.1) where you can find product and company information, press releases, technical support contacts, and the latest C++Builder downloads and patches including Help file updates. Be sure to check this site periodically for product updates.

FIGURE C.1   The Borland corporate home page (`http://www.borland.com`).

Also, vendors who produce shrink-wrapped and downloadable software that support Borland products such as C++Builder can partner with Borland and list their products on the Borland Web site. To get a listing of the Tools and Components provided by these developers, look for the Partners, Partner Directory Link and select the product of interest (which is C++Builder). This will open a Web page with links to a wide range of tool and component areas including ActiveX Controls, Case Tools, Installation, Software Utilities, and Web Tools.

Borland Developer Network

The second Web site listed is the Borland Developer Network (BDN), which was formerly known as the Borland Community Web site. BDN contains many relevant articles from staff and independent writers on development topics specific to Borland products and technologies such as Web services, VCL, .NET, and templates. This, by far, is the must-see site for any Borland developer.

Figure C.2 shows the main BDN page as it looks at the time of this writing. Down the left side you'll find links to general areas of interest including a Search window, Shopping area, Chat area, Editorials, and much more. Across the top you can drill down to a particular product area (AppServer, C++, CORBA, Delphi & Kylix, Interbase, Java, Linux, and TeamSource DSP).

FIGURE C.2   The main page of the Borland Developer Network
(`http://bdn.borland.com`).

NOTE

To fully benefit and access all the areas of BDN, sign up as a Borland Community member, which is free. Membership provides access to the Downloads page, enables you to get involved in the online chats, provides access to CodeCentral (covered later in the "CodeCentral" section), and lets you participate in the surveys. Furthermore, BDN membership is required upon product registration for qualifying and receiving product updates.

TIP

One of the great opportunities to learn about some of the advanced features of C++Builder is to fire questions at the Borland R&D (Research and Development) team through the regular live chats that are held on specific topics. The schedule of upcoming live chats is available from the Chat page. Some previous topics include the C++Builder compiler, libraries, debugger, and ActiveX. Transcripts of past chats are available.

If you drill down into the C++ area, a list of *Neighborhoods* will be listed on the left-hand side that include discussion on the following:

- Components

- Databases

- Distributed Computing

- Higher Education

- Multimedia/Graphics

- Platforms

- Programming

- Tools

- Web Technologies

Access into many of these Neighborhoods will reveal a listing of Streets. For example, if you drill down into the Components Neighborhood, the following Streets will be listed.

- ActiveX

- Linux

- Motif

- OWL

- VCL

No matter which Neighborhood or Street you are on, the Web site will offer access to relevant White Papers, FAQs (Frequently Asked Questions), and TIPs (Technical Information Papers).

TIP

Because of the similarities between C++Builder and Delphi, you should also look at related Delphi articles and information on the Web. Typically, what's applicable to Delphi 6, for example, can be applied and used within C++Builder 6. Even the VCLs, which are written in Object Pascal, can be compiled and used by C++Builder. The same also applies for CLX components, which are now supported by C++Builder 6.

CodeCentral

CodeCentral, as shown in Figure C.3, is a Web-based repository for code samples related to Borland development products. It's an excellent resource for developers. If you're looking for a code sample on how to make something work, CodeCentral is the place to go. More importantly, if you have discovered a solution to a technical/programming problem with a Borland product you're encouraged to share it with the rest of the world by posting your example code and an explanation on CodeCentral.

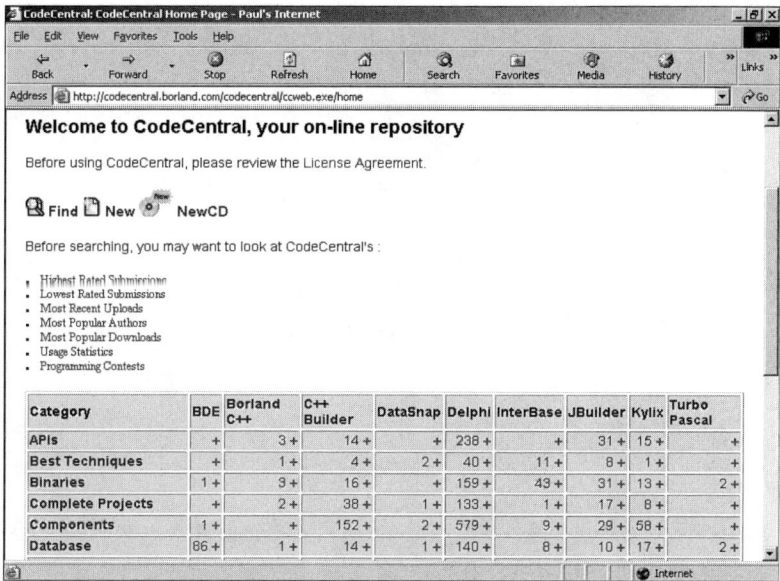

FIGURE C.3   CodeCentral Web site—(http://codecentral.borland.com).

CodeCentral provides a links matrix delineated across the top by Product and down the left side by Categories. It's quite simple, and yet very effective. You can also query for code samples by authors or search for a code sample based on a topic.

NOTE

You must be a member of BDN (membership is free) for full access to the CodeCentral and QualityCentral services.

QualityCentral

The fourth and final Borland site to mention is QualityCentral. QualityCentral provides a community-supported repository to capture issues, suggestions, bugs, feature requests, ideas, and feedback for Borland products. In essence it's a bug-tracking system. If you're an active user of Borland development tools such as C++Builder, and you want to identify issues you've stumbled upon and help shape the next version of C++Builder, download and use the QualityCentral GUI at the QualityCentral site. The GUI, as illustrated in Figure C.4, is a client-side application used to submit and track bugs and suggestions to Borland using Web services.

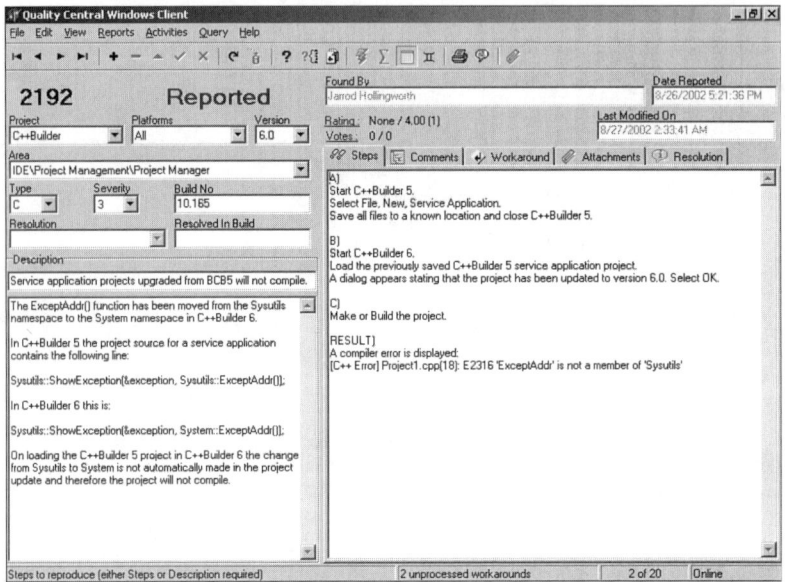

FIGURE C.4   The QualityCentral GUI application, which is available at
`http://qc.borland.com`.

Useful Developer Web Sites

While we are on the subject of Web sites, it's a good time to mention some other Web sites useful for C++Builder developers. There's a mix of the types of Web sites categorized into the following:

- C++Builder

- C++ Resources

- Components and Tools

- Web Services

- Windows Technologies

C++Builder Sites

Let's start off by recognizing some of the Web sites developed and supported by fellow developers who have a passion for Borland and C++Builder. These sites contain how-to's, technical articles, and answers to frequently asked questions. Some of the best Web sites are provided in the following list.

- *BCBDev.COM*—http://www.bcbdev.com   This site, managed by Harold Howe a TeamB member, is a favorite of many C++Builder developers. Harold has assembled an FAQ that provides, arguably, the most concise and useful information available online. He also has many unique articles on effective ways to use C++Builder.

- *BCB–CAQ*—http://bcbcaq.bytamin-c.com/   The BCB CAQ, managed by Damon Chandler and hosted by Bytamin-C, provides answers to Commonly Asked Questions. Damon, an active member of TeamB, has done a phenomenal job on this site. It contains news, tips, and tricks, and lots of example code related to C++Builder.

- *Dr.Bob's C++Builder Gate* —http://www.drbob42.com/cbuilder   Our own Bob Swart, a co-author of this book, and his cohort Ruurd Pels, manage the C++Builder Gate Web site, which is part of the extremely popular Dr. Bob's Programming Clinic. Dr. Bob keeps this site updated regularly with the latest information regarding Borland and C++Builder. It features a number of useful articles on C++Builder and Delphi. Many of the Delphi topics are also applicable to C++Builder.

- *Temporal Doorway*— http://www.temporaldoorway.com/programming/cbuilder This site is managed by our own Mark Cashman, a co-author of this book and a prominent TeamB member. Mark has a number of useful articles and Quick Tips applicable to C++Builder.

- BCB—An Intro to Cultural Simulation and Visualization— http://www.sscnet.ucla.edu/geog/gessler/borland/   This site is managed by Nicholas Gessler, and provides a number of useful C++Builder tips and code examples related to simulations and artificial worlds, which is a focus of several courses in Human Complex Systems offered at UCLA.

- *The BITS C++Builder Information and Tutorials* Site—http://www.thebits.org This site provides a number of tutorials on various C++Builder topics.

This, by no means, is an exhaustive list. Many members of the Borland community, sometimes referred to as the Borland Nation, have devoted Web space to C++Builder. Unfortunately, there is not ample room or time to list them all in this appendix.

C++ Resources

The number of C++–focused sites is vast, but the following provides just a few of the more useful resource sites related to object-oriented C++ development.

- *C++.org*—`http://www.cplusplus.org/`   Certainly these guys lucked out with the domain name. Fortunately, they live up to the name by providing a good starting point—a portal—for C++ development. The site includes well-organized links to a wide variety of FAQs, C++ resources, and articles.

- *cprogramming.com*—`http://www.cprogramming.com/`   This Web site is designed to help individuals learn C or C++ and provide you with C and C++ programming resources. It contains a number of tutorials and source code.

- *Dr. Dobb's Journal C/C++ Programming*—`http://www.ddj.com/topics/cpp`   This site hosted by *Dr. Dobb's* magazine has reasonable activity with a number of relevant articles and C++ links.

Components and Tools

A number of independent and vendor Web sites provide very useful components and tools that you can use with C++Builder. Keep in mind that C++Builder can compile and use Delphi code. Therefore, C++Builder developers have an abundance of third-party components from which to choose. The following Web sites are just a few of the more popular resources that provide components and tools that you can use with C++Builder.

- *ComponentSource*—`http://www.componentsource.com`
  ComponentSource provides an online store featuring thousands of components for multiple development environments, including VCL, CLX, and ActiveX components for Borland C++Builder and Delphi.

- *Delphi Pages*—`http://www.delphipages.com`   The Delphi Pages is a comprehensive component and resource site for C++Builder and Delphi, listing more than 1,500 components in various categories.

- *DelphiSource*—`http://www.delphisource.com`
  DelphiSource provides a large repository of components for C++Builder and Delphi supporting many categories.

- *Delphi Super Page*—`http://delphi.icm.edu.pl/`   One of the more popular component resources for all versions of C++Builder and Delphi. It contains more than 5,500 files to download and attracts more than 30,000 visitors per week.

- *Eagle Software*—`http://eagle-software.com/` Eagle Software offers a number of useful tools and components including CodeRush, a plug-in editor available for Delphi, and the Component Developer's Kit (CDK).

- *Indy (Internet Direct) Components*—`http://www.nevrona.com/Indy` Indy is a set of free Internet VCL components and comes with full source.

- *Raize Software*—`http://www.raize.com` Home of the Raize Components native VCL component suite, containing a slew of VCL and CLX visual components, and the popular CodeSite debugging tool.

- *Torry's Delphi Pages*—`http://www.torry.net/` This is another popular site providing components, apps, source code and tools for all versions of C++Builder and Delphi. There are over 9,000 files to download from this site.

- *TurboPower Software Company*—`http://www.turbopower.com` TurboPower is renowned for its award-winning component suites and tools. Products include Abbrevia, a set of data compression components; AsyncProfessional for serial, FTP, Fax, and paging communications; MemorySleuth for defect tracking; Internet Professional for Internet communications; LockBox for data encryption; Orpheus, a set of visual components; and much more.

- *TMS Software*—`http://www.tmssoftware.com` TMS Software offers some exceptional components including a very popular Advanced StringGrid, and many other visual components (and nonvisual components) that can be easily dropped onto C++Builder and Delphi applications.

- *QaDRAM.Delphi*—`http://delphi.qadram.com/` This is an extremely useful repository site for Borland-related articles and components.

- *Woll2Woll*—`http://www.woll2woll.com` Woll2Woll produces several award-winning component suites for C++Builder and Delphi, including InfoPower, a set of greatly enhanced, data-aware components including grid and combo-lookup controls, and many other components.

The components provided by these repositories and vendors can save you time (and money) by saving you the hassle of reinventing existing functionality. This is the idea of component reuse. Some components are free, whereas others are sold as shareware or commercial products. If you buy a VCL or CLX component, be sure the vendor includes the source code as well the binary packing for debugging and extending a component's capabilities.

Web Services

Clearly one of the hottest technologies emerging in the 21st century is Web Services. The most recent versions of C++Builder and Delphi provide Web service support using XML, the Simple Object Access Protocol (SOAP) and the Web Service Description Language (WSDL). The following sites are focused on Web services.

- *XMethods*—`http://xmethods.net/`　XMethods is a Web services directory used frequently by Delphi and C++Builder developers. This site provides an access point to many of the Web services implemented using Delphi, C++Builder, and a myriad of other development tools. You're encouraged to develop SOAP client examples that interface with services listed at XMethods.

- *World Wide Web Consortium (W3C)*— `http://www.w3.org`　The W3C represents a standards body for interoperable technologies including specifications, guide-lines, software, and tools that are focused to lead the Web to its full potential. It's an invaluable resource for developers who want to stay abreast of the latest Web-based interoperability standards including XML, WSDL, and SOAP.

- *WebServices.org (W3C)*—`http://www.webservices.org`　Stay informed with the latest Web service news at WebServices.org. Includes papers, discussions on architectures, press releases. Furthermore, WebServices.org is host for the annual XML World Conference.

Windows Technologies

Although it's anticipated that a growing number of developers will target the Linux platform with CLX-based applications, the majority of development using C++Builder will likely continue to be targeted for the Windows platform. Access to information on Windows-related technology will be vital for some time to come. The following provides a few of the many Windows Technologies–related Web sites.

- *Microsoft Developer Network (MSDN)*—`http://www.msdn.microsoft.com`　The MSDN Web site provides a wealth of developer-related information on the latest Windows technologies. The site provides links to articles, downloads including SDKs and ActiveX components, and the MSDN Library as illustrated in Figure C.5.

- *Microsoft COM Technologies*— `http://www.microsoft.com/com/`　This site provides information about COM-based technologies including COM+, DCOM, and ActiveX Controls. A personal favorite found at this site is Dr. GUI's Gentle Guide to COM, located at `http://www.microsoft.com/com/news/drgui.asp`.

Numerous sites provide Windows development information, but none that are quite as extensive as what Microsoft provides—the MSDN Library in particular.

FIGURE C.5   Microsoft's MSDN Library, which is available at
`http://msdn.microsoft.com`.

The navigation tree on the left side panel of the MSDN Web site provides access to the various elements of the MSDN Library including COM, DCOM, DirectX, .NET, Windows, and XML. Search queries can also be performed on topics of interest.

In addition to the MSDN Library, Microsoft also offers the MSDN Code Center, which contains example code for various Windows-related technologies. This is illustrated in Figure C.6.

Like the MSDN Library, a navigation tree is provided to access various code examples as they relate to specific technologies. Quite often, Visual C++ examples can be used with C++Builder.

The technology components themselves, such as the DirectX SDK, the .NET Platform, and Microsoft XML Parser can be downloaded from the MSDN Downloads link as illustrated in Figure C.7.

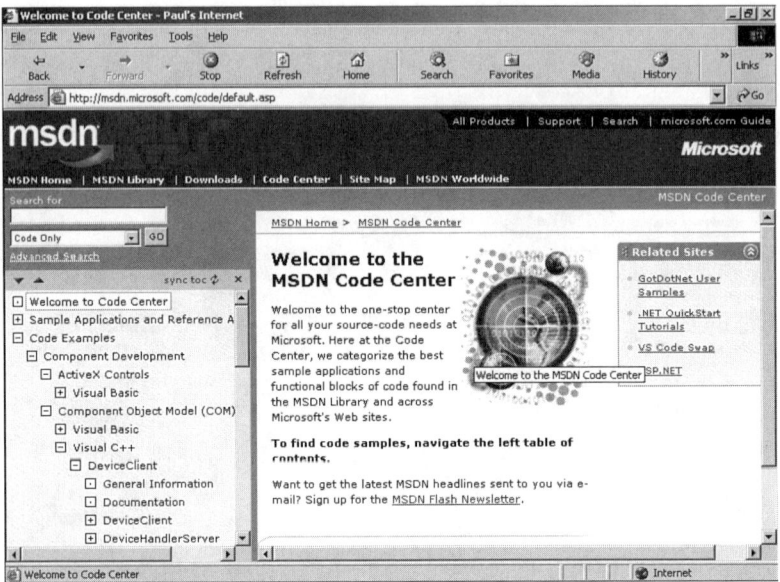

FIGURE C.6   Microsoft's MSDN Code Center, which is available at
`http://msdn.microsoft.com`.

FIGURE C.7   Microsoft's MSDN Downloads, which are available at
`http://msdn.microsoft.com`.

Newsgroups

Borland hosts a large set of newsgroups, covering just about every aspect of their products. These newsgroups can be accessed via newsgroups.borland.com—Borland's own news server. Figure C.8 illustrates the variety of topics covered for C++Builder users through the Borland Newsgroups.

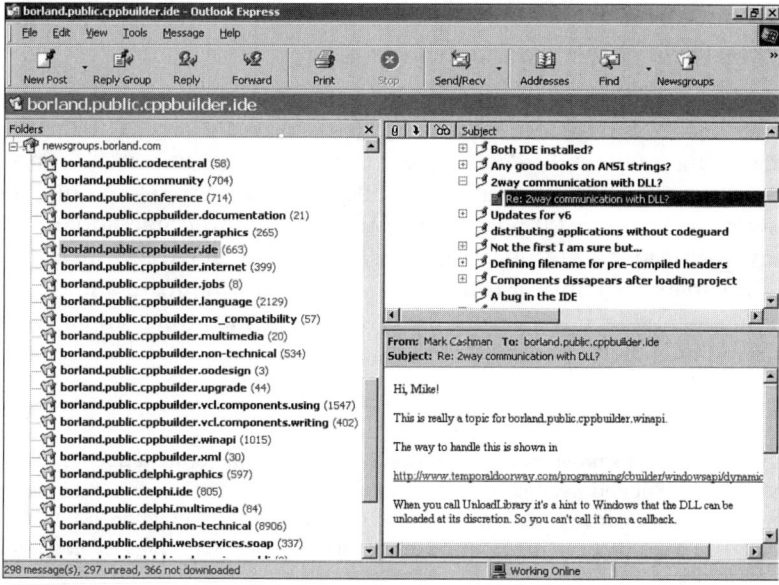

FIGURE C.8   Borland newsgroups accessed through Outlook Express.

NOTE

The Borland newsgroups are probably the most useful collaboration resource for developers. More information on these newsgroups can be found on the Borland Web site at http://www.borland.com/newsgroups, including general newsgroup etiquette and advice.

Many other general newsgroups are supported by most news services, which provide an excellent forum for topics such as C++, Windows, graphics, DirectX, XML, and much more. Some of these include the following:

- comp.lang.c++

- comp.lang.c++.moderated

- comp.std.c++

- comp.os.ms-windows.programmer.graphics

- `comp.os.ms-windows.programmer.win32`

- `microsoft.public.win32.programmer.directx.sdk`

These are just a handful of useful newsgroups. You're encouraged to browse through the available newsgroups provided by Usenet by visiting `http://www.ibiblio.org/usenet-i/`. The Microsoft newsgroup in the previous listing is supported independently through `msnews.microsoft.com news server`, which also provides excellent resource.

By far, one of the most helpful mechanisms for performing newsgroup queries is the Google Groups Web page located at `http://groups.google.com`. When presented with a programming problem, I frequently use Google Groups to search for previous posts that might provide quick answers to my dilemma. I'm very seldom disappointed; if the answers aren't there, I'll post my question to the applicable Borland newsgroup using my newsreader (i.e. Outlook Express) that's configured for the Borland newsgroups. Invariably, an answer is returned within a few hours to a few days. Often times a member of TeamB provides the answer, and sometimes an answer is provided by a Borland engineer.

> **NOTE**
>
> While Google Groups provides an excellent mechanism for performing queries, posting a message to the Borland newsgroups via Google Groups will invariably result in your post never reaching the Borland News Server, which is managed solely by Borland. Instead, use your mail program that can act as a newsreader such as Outlook Express or Euduora, to post your messages.

Special recognition of TeamB, however, is warranted in this text. TeamB members are dedicated to answering technical support questions. They seem to always be checking posts, and providing support answers. They are skilled and yet perform this activity as volunteers. Hats off to you guys! There's no doubt that you are a key part of what makes the Borland community so strong.

Books and Magazines

Perhaps the most popular source of information on software development is found in books and magazines. Books tend to contain a large amount of relevant information, and magazines provide a constant stream of regular articles. Both cover a wide variety of topics.

In this section, we will look at several books and magazines related to C++Builder. Detailed information on books, online purchasing, and book reader reviews can be found at reputable online book stores, such as Amazon.com (`http://www.amazon.com`), FatBrain (`http://www.fatbrain.com`), or Barnes and Noble (`http://www.bn.com/`).

> **TIP**
>
> Excerpts from many books published by Pearson imprints (Sams, Que, and so on) can be found at InformIT. The excerpts include selected chapters and, in some cases, the entire book! Join for free and read at `http:// safari.informit.com`.

C++Builder Books

To date, there have been close to a dozen books written about C++Builder, including this one. Although this book provides a lot of in-depth material and practical examples, it is, by no means, exhaustive. Some of the previously published C++Builder books listed here provide additional insight that might still be relevant under C++Builder 6.

- *Borland C++Builder 4 Unleashed*, Reisdorph, K. (1999), Sams, pp. 1248, ISBN 0672315106—This book covers many topics, from beginner to advanced experience levels, with the focus on the intermediate level. It covers databases and distributed programming quite well, which account for almost 30% of the content. *Borland C++Builder 4 Unleashed* is a perfect companion to *C++Builder 6 Developer's Guide*.

- *C++Builder How-To: The Definitive C++Builder Problem Solver*, Miano, J., Cabanski, T. and Howe, H. (1997), Waite Group, pp. 822, ISBN 157169109X—Somewhat dated, this book still contains many useful how-to's and techniques for C++Builder programmers. When it was first published, it was the C++Builder book to own. Unfortunately, it only covers features of Borland C++Builder 3, many of which have changed in later versions of C++Builder. However, this book is still practical.

- *Sams Teach Yourself Borland C++Builder 4 in 24 Hours*, Reisdorph, K. & Gill, B. (1999), Sams, pp. 451, ISBN 0672316269—Aimed at beginner-intermediate programmers, this book is all about learning how to program with C++Builder. It provides a general overview to the most common programming tasks and techniques.

Because of the similarities between C++Builder and Delphi, books written on Delphi can also be very relevant. Here are a few that you might find as useful resources.

- *Delphi 6 Developer's Guide*, Teixeira, S., Teixeira, J., and Pacheco, X. (2002), Sams, pp. 1169, ISBN 0672321157—This is a fantastic resource for Delphi developers and for C++Builder developers who want to understand the technology behind CLX, BizSnap, DataSnap, and SOAP.

- *Mastering Delphi 6*, Cantu, M. (2002), SYBEX, pp. 1104, ISBN 0782128742—For another perspective on Delphi that covers many of the features also supported by C++Builder 6, Marco Cantu's book can be an extremely helpful resource. Although it's not quite as advanced as *Delphi 6 Developer's Guide*, it still covers a wide range of topics including COM, XML, and SOAP.

We mention these books because C++Builder and Delphi share a lot of common features: similar IDE and Wizards, compatible Delphi components, equivalent SOAP client/server capabilities, and much more. In fact, the primary difference between C++Builder 6 and Delphi 6 is the programming language itself. If you are versed in C++, it is not too difficult to understand Delphi's Object Pascal and apply it to your C++ development. For a list of other relevant books available, try searching the online bookstores for *C++Builder* or *Delphi*. In fact, excerpts from *Delphi 6 Developer's Guide, and Delphi 5 Developer's Guide* are available online at InformIt.

General C++ Books

A vast number of C++ books are available and in print that developers find extremely useful. The most popular (and arguably the best) are listed here with brief comments.

- *Sams Teach Yourself Borland C++ in 21 Days* (Fourth Edition), Liberty, J. (1999), Sams, pp. 912, ISBN 067232072—Aimed at beginner-intermediate programmers, this might be the most practical reference for both C++ neophytes and C++ veterans. It covers the latest ANSI/ISO Standard C++ and provides a solid foundation on object-oriented development techniques with C++.

- *Thinking in C++, Vol. 1* (Second Edition), Eckel, B. (2000), Prentice-Hall, pp. 720, ISBN 0139798099—In this, the second edition of his *Thinking in C++* tutorial, Bruce Eckel explains the ins and outs of the C++ programming language in a clear and concise manner that has proved invaluable to novices and experts alike. It is provided for free on the companion CD-ROM that ships with *C++Builder Professional and Enterprise*, and it is also available online from http://www.mindview.net/Books/TICPP/ThinkingInCPP2e.html.

- *Effective C++ (Second Edition)*, Meyers, S. (1997), Addison-Wesley, pp. 304, ISBN 0201924889—This is also a must-have book for C++ developers. It isn't designed to teach the C++ language but, with great use of examples, it gives tips on improving your C++ programming techniques, particularly class design.

- *The C++ Programming Language* (Third Edition), Stroustrup, B. (1997), Addison-Wesley, pp. 928, ISBN 0201889544—The creator of C++, Bjarne Stroustrup, presents the full specification of the language and standard template library. This is not really a book for the beginner, but it is the ultimate C++ reference and is essential for everyone who is serious about programming with C++.

For details on other C++–related books, search for *C++* on the online bookstores previously mentioned. The full copy of *Sams Teach Yourself C++ in 21 Days,* Third Edition, and various excerpts from other C++ books are available at InformIT.

Magazines

There are several magazines relevant to C++Builder. One devoted entirely to C++Builder, whereas others contain articles on C++ in general. There are also several Delphi magazines. Some of the most relevant magazines are described in the following list.

- *C++Builder Developer's Journal*—Published by Bridges Publishing, provides a monthly periodical containing tips and techniques for C++Builder. This journal contains many high-quality articles from prominent developers each month. It is available in print via subscription. Registered customers can access back issues online. For a list of back issues, and subscription information, visit `http://www.bridgespublishing.com/`.

- *C/C++ Users Journal*—This monthly magazine is available in print, and several articles each month are made available online. For more information visit `http://www.cuj.com`.

- *Delphi Informant*—This monthly magazine focused on Delphi is available in print, and many articles are made available online. We mention it here because many of the concepts associated to Delphi are applicable to C++Builder. For information visit `http://www.delphizine.com/`.

The Borland Developers Conference (BorCon)

Each year Borland puts together an amazing developer's conference called BorCon (as shown in Figure C.9). Arguably, it might be the most definitive resource on the planet for getting information regarding Borland products and technologies. Although multiple BorCon's are held at several locations around the world each year, the BorCon that gets all the attention is held in the United States. The thirteenth annual U.S. conference, which was held in May 2002, attracted more than 2,000 attendees. BorCons have also been held in countries such as Australia, France, Germany, and the UK.

BorCons are feature-packed. Over the course of five days, dozens of tutorials and technical sessions are presented on emerging technologies and Borland products—including C++Builder—by experts including Borland engineers. Often, the hardest part is deciding which of the great sessions to attend! Apart from the tutorials and technical sessions, there are opening and closing keynotes, product addresses, exhibitor sessions, informal "birds of a feather" sessions, special (not to be missed) events, and a computer lab allowing attendees to test drive the latest Borland products.

FIGURE C.9   BorCon 2001—Long Beach, California.

In short, BorCon is one of the best places to get intense training on a variety of topics and provides an excellent opportunity to talk to Borland engineers, fellow C++Builder developers, authors, and speakers face-to-face. For information on the upcoming BorCon in 2003, visit `http://www.borland.com/conf2003/`.

Summary

It's impossible to mention all the practical resources available online or in print for C++Builder. Search engines such as Yahoo! and InfoSeek will certainly reveal more useful sites, and Amazon will reveal many more books. However, the Borland newsgroup is really one of the best places to start if you have questions or concerns. It provides a two-way forum for collaboration. Borland has also done a phenomenal job with the combination of the BDN, CodeCentral, and QualityCentral Web sites.

One thing not mentioned in this Appendix is the applicability of the Borland Help file provided with C++Builder. Additionally, the Microsoft Win32 SDK Help file provides pertinent information as well. Keep in mind the documentation shipped with the C++Builder product, specifically the Developer's Guide (which should not be confused with this book), also provides a lot of meaty information. Finally, throughout this book itself, in many of the chapters on specific topics such as COM and the Tools API, references to various Web sites and literature are made that might have not been reiterated in this Appendix.

If you stumble and you can't find an answer to an issue, you're encouraged to go back to the chapter within this book that deals with the subject of interest, and load up the code provided on the accompanying CD. More often than not, as developers, our questions can be self-answered when time is taken out trying to examine and play with the code. And, if you come up with an answer to a difficult problem or a frequently asked question, you're encouraged to share it with the rest of the world.

D

Enabling TXMLDocument for C++Builder Professional

IN THIS APPENDIX

- TXMLDocument VCL Registration Code

- TXMLDocument VCL Package Assembly

by Paul Gustavson

The eXtensible Markup Language (XML) is a technology standard that literally has exploded within the information technology industry. XML provides a way to describe structured data in a very powerful and simple way. It can be used as a standard text-based format for information exchange among businesses and applications.

Seizing on the capabilities of XML, Borland developed a VCL component called TXMLDocument that allows you, as a developer, to take advantage of XML documents within your applications. TXMLDocument is a component-based wrapper to an external DOM (Document Object Model) parser, such as the Microsoft XML Parser, the Open XML parser, or the IBM Xerces parser. Disappointingly though, Borland chose not to include the TXMLDocument as a registered "VCL" component in either C++Builder 6 Professional or Delphi 6 Professional.

The reason sited as to why the TXMLDocument component was not originally considered for the Professional version is that XML and XML technologies such as SOAP are oriented more toward client/server development, which is targeted exclusively by the Enterprise version. Logically, there's no reason why Borland shouldn't have included it as a component since TXMLDocument's scope is NOT limited to client/server enterprise development. To their credit however, Borland did include the TXMLDocument class with the Professional version, which can be used as a data type within your code. But, having been spoiled by the VCL constructs, users prefer a TXMLDocument component that can be grabbed off the VCL palette and modified using design-time property editors provided through the Object Inspector.

The good news is that there's a way to expose the TXMLDocument on your C++Builder Professional palette. In this appendix, we will look at an "above-board" approach to register the TXMLDocument class as a component and install it on the palette. Note: the solution we'll describe works for both C++Builder 6 Pro and Delphi 6.02 Pro users.

TXMLDocument VCL Registration Support

Really all that's involved in making TXMLDocument available as a component is registering it and providing the property editors. According to one Borland source, Pro users actually have most of the property editor code needed to componentize TXMLDocument.

In order for us to "emulate" the designer code used in the enterprise SKU we need to create a Delphi unit, and, in the end, register the component. Keep in mind C++Builder can compile Delphi code. Let's take a look at this Delphi code in Listing D.1, which can found in the code folder for this appendix on the companion CD-ROM.

LISTING D.1   xmlcomponent.pas Package Source

```
{*******************************************************}
{                                                       }
{ TXMLDocument VCL Registration Support for BCB6/D6 Pro }
{                                                       }
{ Developed by Paul Gustavson                           }
{          - pgustavson@simventions.com                 }
{                                                       }
{ Special Thanks to Mark Edington of Borland for his    }
{ guidance.                                             }
{                                                       }
{ This is open source.                                  }
{                                                       }
{*******************************************************}


unit xmlcomponent;


//{$DEFINE D6BUILD}   // comment this out for BCB6 build


interface
```

LISTING D.1   Continued

```delphi
uses
    Dialogs,
{$IFDEF D6BUILD}
    StrEdit, // use this for Delphi compilation /
             // not fully available under BCB6 compilation
{$ENDIF}
    Classes, DesignEditors, DesignIntf, ToolsAPI, XMLDoc, HTTPProd,
    msxmldom, oxmldom, XMLIntf;


type

{ TXMLDocumentEditor }

  TVerbProc = procedure of object;
  TVerbInfo = record
    Description: string;
    VerbProc: TVerbProc;
  end;
  TVerbInfoArray = array of TVerbInfo;

  TXMLDocumentEditor = class(TComponentEditor)
  private
    FVerbs: TVerbInfoArray;
    FDocument: TXMLDocument;
  protected
    procedure AddVerbInfo(const Description: string; const VerbProc: TVerbProc);
    property Document: TXMLDocument read FDocument;
    property Verbs: TVerbInfoArray read FVerbs;
  public
    procedure AfterConstruction; override;
    procedure Edit; override;
    procedure ExecuteVerb(Index: Integer); override;
    function GetVerb(Index: Integer): string; override;
    function GetVerbCount: Integer; override;
    procedure EditXMLFile;
    procedure OpenXMLFile;
    procedure SaveXMLFile;
  end;

{ TXMLDocumentFileProperty }
```

LISTING D.1   Continued

```
  TXMLDocumentFileProperty = class(TStringProperty)
  public
    function GetAttributes: TPropertyAttributes; override;
    procedure Edit; override;
  end;

{ TXMLDocumentDOMVendorProperty }

  TXMLDocumentDOMVendorProperty = class(TClassProperty)
  public
    function GetAttributes: TPropertyAttributes; override;
    procedure GetValues(Proc: TGetStrProc); override;
    function GetValue: string; override;
    procedure SetValue(const Value: string); override;
  end;

{ TXMLNodeIndentStrProperty }

  TXMLNodeIndentStrProperty = class(TStringProperty)
  protected
    function LiteralToDesc(const Literal: string): string;
  public
    function GetAttributes: TPropertyAttributes; override;
    procedure GetValues(Proc: TGetStrProc); override;
    function GetValue: string; override;
    procedure SetValue(const Value: string); override;
  end;

{ TXMLProperty }    // unable to support this property in BCB6
{$IFDEF D6BUILD}
  TXMLProperty = class(TStringListProperty)
  public
    function GetValue: string; override;
  end;
{$ENDIF}

{ TXMLDocumentSelectionEditor }

  TXMLDocumentSelectionEditor = class(TSelectionEditor)
  public
    procedure RequiresUnits(Proc: TGetStrProc); override;
```

LISTING D.1   Continued

```
  end;

  procedure Register;    { this must appear in the interface section }

//--------------------------------------------------------------------------
//--------------------------------------------------------------------------

implementation

uses ExtActns, SysUtils, xmldom;

const
  Tab = #9;
  STab = 'tab';
  SSpace = ' space';
  SOpenXMLTitle = 'Open XML Document';
  SXMLExtension = '.xml';
  SXMLFilter = 'XML Files (*.xml)|*.xml|XSL Files (*.xsl)|*.xsl|Schema Files
➥(*.xsd,*.xdr,*.biz)|*.xsd;*.xdr;*.biz|XML Skin Files (*.xkn)|*.xkn|HTML Files
➥(*.html)|*.html;*.htm|All files (*.*)|*.*';
  sXMLEditDataFile = 'Edit XML file (code editor)';
  sXMLOpenDataFile = 'Open XML file (external editor)';
  sXMLSaveDataFile = 'Save XML file...';

//--------------------------------------------------------------------------

{ TXMLDocumentEditor }
procedure TXMLDocumentEditor.AfterConstruction;
begin
  inherited;
  FDocument := GetComponent as TXMLDocument;
end;

//--------------------------------------------------------------------------

procedure TXMLDocumentEditor.AddVerbInfo(const Description: string;
  const VerbProc: TVerbProc);
var
  OldLen: Integer;
begin
  OldLen := Length(Verbs);
```

LISTING D.1   Continued

```
  SetLength(FVerbs, OldLen+1);
  Verbs[OldLen].Description := Description;
  Verbs[OldLen].VerbProc := VerbProc;
end;


//----------------------------------------------------------------------------

procedure TXMLDocumentEditor.Edit;
begin
  EditXMLFile;
end;


//----------------------------------------------------------------------------

procedure TXMLDocumentEditor.EditXMLFile;
var
  ActServ: IOTAActionServices;
begin
  ActServ := BorlandIDEServices as IOTAActionServices;
  if DesignerFileManager <> nil then
    ActServ.OpenFile(DesignerFileManager.QualifyFileName(Document.FileName))
  else
    ActServ.OpenFile(Document.FileName)
end;


//----------------------------------------------------------------------------

procedure TXMLDocumentEditor.OpenXMLFile;
begin
  with TFileRun.Create(nil) do
  try
    FileName := Document.FileName;
    if DesignerFileManager <> nil then
      FileName := DesignerFileManager.QualifyFileName(FileName);
    Execute;
  finally
    Free;
  end;
end;


//----------------------------------------------------------------------------
```

LISTING D.1   Continued

```
procedure TXMLDocumentEditor.SaveXMLFile;
var
  InitialDir, FileName: string;
begin
  FileName := Document.FileName;
  InitialDir := ExtractFilePath(FileName);
// if PromptForFileName(FileName, SXMLFilter, SXML, '', InitialDir, True) then
  if PromptForFileName(FileName, SXMLFilter, SXMLExtension, '',
        InitialDir, True) then
    Document.SaveToFile(FileName);
end;

//--------------------------------------------------------------------------


procedure TXMLDocumentEditor.ExecuteVerb(Index: Integer);
begin
  inherited;
  Verbs[Index].VerbProc;
end;

//--------------------------------------------------------------------------


function TXMLDocumentEditor.GetVerb(Index: Integer): string;
begin
  Result := Verbs[Index].Description;
end;

//--------------------------------------------------------------------------


function TXMLDocumentEditor.GetVerbCount: Integer;
begin
  if Document.FileName <> '' then
  begin
    if FileExists(Document.FileName) then
    begin
      AddVerbInfo(sXMLEditDataFile, EditXMLFile);
      AddVerbInfo(sXMLOpenDataFile, OpenXMLFile);
    end;
    if Document.Active then
      AddVerbInfo(sXMLSaveDataFile, SaveXMLFile);
  end;
```

LISTING D.1   Continued

```pascal
  Result := Length(Verbs);
end;


//---------------------------------------------------------------------------


{ TXMLDocumentFileProperty }

function TXMLDocumentFileProperty.GetAttributes: TPropertyAttributes;
begin
  Result := [paDialog, paMultiSelect];
end;


//---------------------------------------------------------------------------


procedure TXMLDocumentFileProperty.Edit;
const
  SXMLExt = 'xml'; { Do not localize }
var
  FileName: string;
begin
  FileName := GetValue;
  if PromptForFileName(FileName, SXMLFilter, SXMLExt, SOpenXMLTitle) then
    SetValue(FileName);
end;


//---------------------------------------------------------------------------


{ TXMLDocumentDOMVendorProperty }

function TXMLDocumentDOMVendorProperty.GetAttributes: TPropertyAttributes;
begin
  Result := [paValueList, paMultiSelect];
end;


//---------------------------------------------------------------------------


procedure TXMLDocumentDOMVendorProperty.GetValues(Proc: TGetStrProc);
var
  I: Integer;
begin
  for I := 0 to DOMVendors.Count - 1 do
```

LISTING D.1   Continued

```pascal
      Proc(DOMVendors[I].Description);
end;

//---------------------------------------------------------------------------

function TXMLDocumentDOMVendorProperty.GetValue: string;
begin
  if Assigned(TXMLDocument(GetComponent(0)).DOMVendor) then
    Result := TXMLDocument(GetComponent(0)).DOMVendor.Description else
    Result := '';
end;

//---------------------------------------------------------------------------

procedure TXMLDocumentDOMVendorProperty.SetValue(const Value: string);
var
  DOMVendor: TDOMVendor;
begin
  if Value = '' then
    DOMVendor := nil else
    DOMVendor := DOMVendors.Find(Value);
  TXMLDocument(GetComponent(0)).DOMVendor := DOMVendor;
  Modified;
end;

//---------------------------------------------------------------------------


{ TXMLNodeIndentStrProperty }
function TXMLNodeIndentStrProperty.LiteralToDesc(const Literal: string):
string;
var
  PropLen: Integer;
  Desc: string;
begin
  { Translate the literal string into a descriptive string (' ' = <1 space>) }
  if Literal = Tab then
    Desc := STab
  else
  begin
    PropLen := Length(Literal);
```

LISTING D.1   Continued

```
    if StringOfChar(' ', PropLen) = Literal then
    begin
      Desc := IntToStr(PropLen)+ SSpace;
      if PropLen > 1 then
        Desc := Desc + 's';
    end;
  end;
  if Desc <> '' then
    Result := '<'+Desc+'>'
  else
    Result := Literal;
end;

//---------------------------------------------------------------------------


function TXMLNodeIndentStrProperty.GetAttributes: TPropertyAttributes;
begin
  Result := [paValueList, paMultiSelect];
end;

//---------------------------------------------------------------------------


function TXMLNodeIndentStrProperty.GetValue: string;
begin
  Result := LiteralToDesc(inherited GetValue);
end;

//---------------------------------------------------------------------------


procedure TXMLNodeIndentStrProperty.GetValues(Proc: TGetStrProc);
var
  I: Integer;
begin
  Proc('<'+STab+'>');
  Proc('<1'+SSpace+'>');
  for I := 2 to 8 do
    Proc('<'+IntToStr(I)+SSpace+'s>');
end;

//---------------------------------------------------------------------------
```

LISTING D.1   Continued

```
procedure TXMLNodeIndentStrProperty.SetValue(const Value: string);
var
  I: Integer;
  literal: string;
begin
  { If it's <1 space> or <tab> then translate it }
  if LiteralToDesc(Tab) = Value then
    inherited SetValue(Tab)
  else
  begin
    for I := 1 to 8 do
    begin
      Literal := StringOfChar(' ', I);
      if LiteralToDesc(Literal) = Value then
      begin
        inherited SetValue(Literal);
        Exit;
      end;
    end;
    { Otherwise, just store what we got }
    inherited SetValue(Value);
  end;
end;


//---------------------------------------------------------------------------


{ TXMLProperty }   // unable to support this property in BCB6

{$IFDEF D6BUILD}
function TXMLProperty.GetValue: string;
begin
  with (GetComponent(0) as TXMLDocument) do
    if (XML.Count > 0) and (FileName = '') then
      Result := '(XML)'
    else
      Result := '(xml)';
end;
{$ENDIF}


//---------------------------------------------------------------------------
```

LISTING D.1   Continued

```
{ TXMLDocumentSelectionEditor }
procedure TXMLDocumentSelectionEditor.RequiresUnits(Proc: TGetStrProc);
begin
  Proc('xmldom');
  Proc('XMLIntf');
end;


//-------------------------------------------------------------------------

// "register" procedure...
procedure Register;
  begin
    RegisterComponents('Internet', [TXMLDocument]);
    RegisterComponentEditor(TXMLDocument, TXMLDocumentEditor);
    RegisterPropertyEditor(TypeInfo(TDOMVendor), TXMLDocument,
        'DOMVendor',    TXMLDocumentDOMVendorProperty);
    RegisterPropertyEditor(TypeInfo(WideString), TXMLDocument,
        'FileName',     TXMLDocumentFileProperty);
    RegisterPropertyEditor(TypeInfo(WideString), TXMLDocument,
        'NodeIndentStr', TXMLNodeIndentStrProperty);
{$IFDEF D6BUILD}
    RegisterPropertyEditor(TypeInfo(TStrings), TXMLDocument,
        'XML', TXMLProperty);    // unable to support this property in BCB6
{$ENDIF}
    RegisterSelectionEditor(TXMLDocument, TXMLDocumentSelectionEditor);
  end;

end.
```

You'll notice in this code, that a compilation flag is used to differentiate between a C++Builder build and Delphi build. One of the issues is that C++Builder won't compile with StrEdit in the Uses clause. You'll receive a Pascal Fatal Error - "File not found: 'StrEdit.DCU'." However, if you compile the code under Delphi, everything is fine. While most of the expected capabilities are supported by C++Builder, not all the property elements are available. For those elements that are not available, we simply choose to ignore them under C++Builder using a compile time constant that we've defined called D6BUILD. Despite missing a few elements for C++Builder, there's still plenty of design-time support that will be provided.

TXMLDocument VCL Package Assembly

There are some other file elements that are needed to represent the package fully under C++Builder. This includes a resource file containing the TXMLDocument icon, the C++ file containing the DLL entry point function for the BPL, and the required compiled packages that need to be linked. Figure D.1 illustrates the package assembly needed for C++Builder.

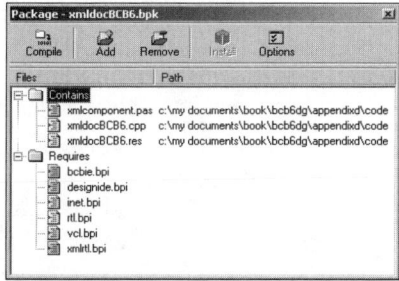

FIGURE D.1   Package assembly for the TXMLDocument Component.

The package dialog provided by the C++Builder IDE will allow you to compile, link, and install the package. Once installed, the TXMLDocument component will be available off the Internet tab on the C++Builder Pro SKU's VCL Palette.

WARNING

Users of C++Builder Professional who have not updated the IDE with the second patch update from Borland might need to remove the `bcbie.bpi` library from the *requires* section of the `xmldocBCB6.bpk` package included on the companion CD-ROM. Otherwise, the package might not properly register and install.

Using TXMLDocument

What was once restricted to only C++Builder Enterprise, can now be accessed as a component under C++Builder 6 Pro. This is illustrated in Figure D.2.

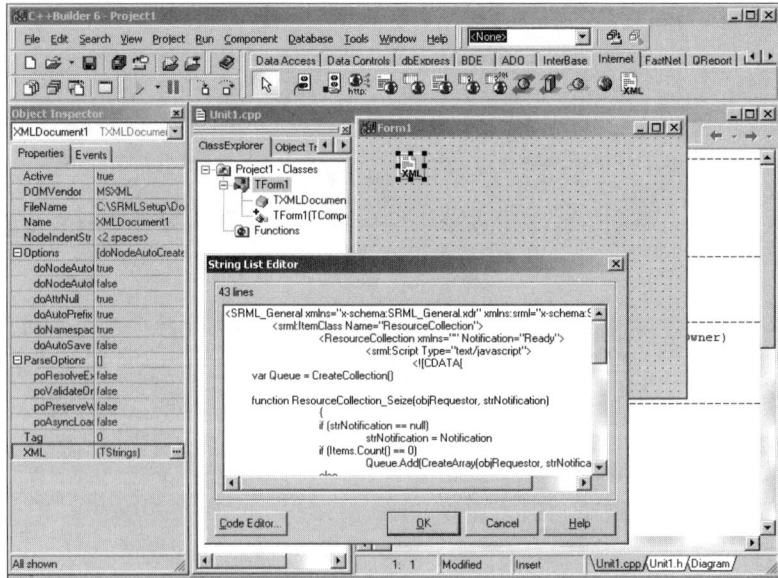

FIGURE D.2 TXMLDocument control on a form and the Object Inspector.

The object inspector allows you to tweak the properties of TXMLDocument such as selecting a filename, or selecting a registered XML DOM parser (i.e. MSXML, Open XML). Dr. Bob provides an excellent overview of how to use TXMLDocument in Chapter 13.

NOTE

Although we were able to take advantage of something available initially in the Enterprise version, there are many other features provided exclusively by the Enterprise version that can't possibly be accessed and used within the Pro version. Enterprise features include the capability to create SOAP servers, which is an XML-based technology, and much more. The Pro version does, however, enable you to create SOAP clients and certainly has a lot of great capabilities in its own right.

Summary

In this appendix, we've shown how to emulate the designer code used in the Enterprise version for TXMLDocument in order to provide the same functionality under C++Builder Professional. This will enable Pro users to utilize TXMLDocument as a drop-in component within the applications they develop.

Index

G

How can we make this index more useful? Email us at indexes@samspublishing.com

nodefault keyword, 203-204

NodeIndentStr property (TXMLDocument component), 469

Nokia 9200 Series SDK, 969

None command (View menu), 37

nonmodal forms, 89-92

nonpersistent data, 111

Non-POD (Non-Plain Old Data) objects, 100

nonVCL types, TTypeInfo structure

  creating manually, 328-330

  obtaining from existing property and class, 319-328

NonVCLTypeInfoPackage package, 292

nonvisual components, 159, 191

  creating, 204-205

  designtime versus runtime, 216-218

  events, 205-208

  events, linking, 221-224

  exceptions, 211-212

  keywords

    default, 203

    namespace, 213-214

    nodefault, 203-204

    stored, 204

  linking, 218-221

  messages, responding to, 214-216

  methods, 208-209

    protected, 209-211

    public, 209

  properties

    arrays, 201-203

    published, 199-201

    types of, 198-199

    unpublished, 195-198

    writing, 195

Notification() function, 219-221

notifications (MCI), 615-616

notifiers

  custom DebugNotifier class

    class declaration, 904-905

    cleaning up, 915

    executing, 910-914

    methods, 906-909

  defined, 903

  interfaces, 903-904

nRightRect parameter

  CreateEllipticRgn() function, 545

  CreateRoundRectRgn() function, 544

NT Workstations, 576

NTA (Native Tools API), 878. See also Tools API

nTopRect parameter

  CreateEllipticRgn() function, 544

  CreateRoundRectRgn() function, 544

NULLREGION return value (CombineRng() function), 546

nWidthEllipse parameter (CreateRoundRectRgn() function), 544

O

Object Broker, 819-820

Object Inspector, 15, 36-37, 219

  access violations, 259

  Object Tree view, 39, 388-389

  opening, 24

property categories

  Action, 38

  Data, 38

  Database, 38

  Drag, Drop, and Docking, 38

  filtering, 37

  Help and Hints, 38

  Input, 38

  Layout, 38

  Legacy, 38

  Linkage, 38

  Locale, 38

  Localizable, 38

  viewing, 37

Object Inspector command (View menu), 24

object pooling, 814-816

Object Tree view, 39, 388-389

objects. See also components

  ADO (ActiveX Database Objects) components, 435-436

    advantages of, 436-437

    cautions, 437

    compared to BDE, 436

    copying, 437

    database applications, 447-448

    database connections, 439-441

    dataset access, 441-445

    error handling, 450

    events, 445-447

    inheritance, 438

    multitier applications, 450-451

    performance optimization, 448-450

How can we make this index more useful? Email us at indexes@samspublishing.com

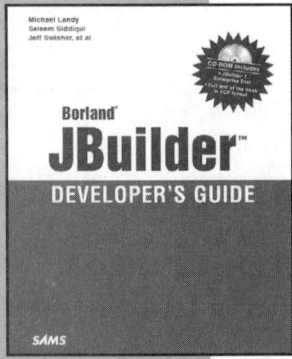

JBuilder™ Developer's Guide

Michael Landy, Saleem Siddiqui, Jeff Swisher, with Erik Nickelson and Todd Story

067232427x
$59.99US/$89.95CAN

JBuilder™ Developer's Guide provides comprehensive coverage of the award-winning JBuilder from the practitioner's viewpoint. The authors develop a consolidated application throughout the chapters, allowing conceptual cohesion and illustrating the use of JBuilder to build 'real world' applications. The examples can be compiled and run under JBuilder Personal edition, a free edition of JBuilder. *JBuilder™ Developer's Guide* is not version specific but explains the latest JBuilder 6 and 7 features such as enterprise J2EE application development, CORBA, SOAP, XML tools, Enterprise JavaBeans™, JavaServer Pages/Servlets, and JavaBeans® technology. JBuilder repeatedly wins "developer's choice" awards as the best visual tool for developing Java applications.

Delphi™ 6 Developer's Guide

Xavier Pacheco and Steve Teixeira

0672321157
$64.99US/$96.95CAN

Xavier Pacheco and Steve Teixeira offer the best techniques and tricks for Delphi 6. Learn to apply real-world applications, solutions, and projects to your own programs to become a more efficient and better Delphi developer. Included in this edition is the latest information on CLX™, DataSnap™, Web Services/BizSnap™, wireless application development, and more!

Kylix™ Developer's Guide

Charlie & Margie Calvert, John Kaster, Bob Swart

0672320606
$59.99US/$89.95CAN

The Kylix™ Developer's Guide introduces programmers to the new Borland® Delphi compiler for Linux. The book provides comprehdsive coverage of CLS, a VCL-like visual programming library that runs on both Windows and Linux. You'll learn the Linux system environment, development of databases with CLX, and Web development with Kylix.